World History
INTERACTIVE

Social Studies Reimagined

 To start, download the free **BouncePages** app on your smartphone or tablet. Simply search for the BouncePages app in your mobile app store. The app is available for Android and IOS (iPhone®/iPad®).

Make your book come alive! Activate your digital interactivities directly from the page.

To launch the myStory video look for this icon.

To activate more interactivities look for this icon. 🅱 BOUNCE to Activate

1. **AIM** the camera over the image so it is easily viewable on your screen.

2. **TAP** the screen to scan the page.

3. **BOUNCE** the page to life by clicking the icon.

Savvas Learning Company LLC, 15 East Midland Avenue, Paramus, NJ 07652

Cover: Kneeling Archer, Terracotta Chinese Army: David Davis Photoproductions RF/Alamy Stock Photo; Sarcophagus of Menrekhmut: Martin Thomas Photography/Alamy Stock Photo; American World War II Red Cross Helmet: Chris Howes/Wild Places Photography/Alamy Stock Photo; Leonardo's Horse, Leonardo da Vinci and Nina Akamu: Roman Belogorodov/Alamy Stock Photo; Young Hispanic Woman: David Tiberio/Alamy Stock Photo; Young Indian Man: Michael Jung/Shutterstock; Moctezuma II Headdress: Alexander Klein/AFP/Getty Images; Young Asian Man: Asier Romero/Shutterstock; Young African American Woman: Radius Images/Design Pics/Alamy Stock Photo; British Suffragette: Smith Archive/Alamy Stock Photo; Nelson Mandela: Oistein Thomassen/Alamy Stock Photo; Circuit Board: Raigvi/Shutterstock

Attributions of third party content appear on page 1256, which constitutes an extension of this copyright page.

Savvas™ and **Savvas Learning Company™** are the exclusive trademarks of Savvas Learning Company LLC in the U.S. and other countries.

Savvas Learning Company publishes through its famous imprints **Prentice Hall®** and **Scott Foresman®** which are exclusive registered trademarks owned by Savvas Learning Company LLC in the U.S. and/or other countries.

enVision® and **Savvas Realize™** are exclusive trademarks of Savvas Learning Company LLC in the U.S. and/or other countries.

NBC LEARN™ is a trademark of NBCUniversal Media, LLC. Used under license.

Unless otherwise indicated herein, any third party trademarks that may appear in this work are the property of their respective owners, and any references to third party trademarks, logos, or other trade dress are for demonstrative or descriptive purposes only. Such references are not intended to imply any sponsorship, endorsement, authorization, or promotion of Savvas Learning Company products by the owners of such marks, or any relationship between the owner and Savvas Learning Company LLC or its authors, licensees, or distributors.

ISBN-13: 978-1-418-33036-1
ISBN-10:   1-418-33036-1

5 21

Authors and Partners

World History Authors

Elisabeth Gaynor Ellis

Elisabeth Gaynor Ellis holds a BS from Smith College and an MA and MS from Columbia University. Before she began writing textbooks, Ms. Ellis taught World Cultures, European History, and Russian Studies in Ardsley, New York. Ms. Ellis co-authored Prentice Hall's *World History: Connections to Today* with Dr. Anthony Esler. Ms. Ellis has also written other social studies materials, including *America's Holidays*, individual state histories, and a variety of Teacher's Edition materials.

Anthony Esler

Anthony Esler is an Emeritus Professor of History at the College of William and Mary in Williamsburg, Virginia. His books include several studies of the conflict of generations in world history, half a dozen historical novels, and two other surveys of world and Western history besides this one. He is a member of the American Historical Association, the World History Association, and the Authors Guild. He has received Fulbright, Social Science Research Council, and other research grants, and is listed in the *Directory of American Scholars*, the *Directory of Poets and Fiction Writers*, and *Who's Who in America*. Books by Dr. Esler include *Bombs, Beards, and Barricades*, *Forbidden City*, and *The Human Venture*.

Program Partners

NBC Learn, the educational arm of NBC News, develops original stories for use in the classroom and makes archival NBC News stories, images, and primary source documents available on demand to teachers, students, and parents. NBC Learn partnered with Savvas to produce the myStory videos that support this program.

Constitutional Rights Foundation is a nonprofit, nonpartisan organization focused on educating students about the importance of civic participation in a democratic society. Constitutional Rights Foundation is the lead contributor to the development of the Civic Discussion Topic Inquiries for this program. Constitutional Rights Foundation is also the provider of the Civic Action Project (CAP) for the *Economics* and *Magruder's American Government* programs. CAP is a project-based learning model for civics, government, and economics courses.

Reviewers & Academic Consultants

Program Academic Consultants

Jeffery D. Long
Professor of Religion and Asian Studies
Elizabethtown College
Elizabethtown, Pennsylvania

Gordon Newby
Professor of Islamic, Jewish and
    Comparative Studies
Department of Middle Eastern and
    South Asian Studies
Emory University
Atlanta, Georgia

Mark Peterson
Associate Professor
Department of Asian and Near
    Eastern Languages
Brigham Young University
Provo, Utah

William Pitts
Professor, Department of Religion
Baylor University
Waco, Texas

Benjamin Ravid
Professor Emeritus of Jewish History
Department of Near Eastern and
    Judaic Studies
Brandeis University
Waltham, Massachusetts

Harpreet Singh
College Fellow
Department of South Asian Studies
Harvard University
Cambridge, Massachusetts

Christopher E. Smith, J.D., Ph.D.
Professor
Michigan State University
MSU School of Criminal Justice
East Lansing, Michigan

John Voll
Professor Emeritus of Islamic History
Georgetown University
Washington, D.C.

Michael R. Wolf
Associate Professor
Department of Political Science
Indiana University-Purdue University
    Fort Wayne
Fort Wayne, Indiana

Project Imagine: World History

Program Hosts

Keith Hughes
Instructional Technology Coach,
Buffalo Public Schools
Adjunct Professor of New Literacies,
Graduate School of Education,
University at Buffalo (SUNY)

Kezia Pearson
Educator, Buffalo Public Schools

Academic Consultants

Timothy Hugh Barrett
Professor Emeritus of East Asian
History
School of Oriental and African Studies
(SOAS), University of London

Jessey J.C. Choo
Associate Professor of Chinese
History and Religion
Rutgers University

Francesca Fiorani
Professor of Art History
University of Virginia

Jeff Horn
Professor of History
Manhattan College

Jennifer Keene
Professor and Chair, Department of
History
Wilkinson College of Arts,
Humanities, and Social Science
Chapman University

Audrey Peterson
Associate Director of News and
Information
Brooklyn College

Eric W. Robinson
Professor of History
Indiana University

Wiliam Worger
Professor Emeritus of History
University of California, Los Angeles
(UCLA)

Program Contributors

iv

Social Studies Today

Social studies is more than the story of the past.

It's how we shape our world today. It's seeing how yesterday's stories change our perspective on today. And in today's fast-paced world, it's essential.

Welcome to the next generation of interactive social studies!

Savvas' new *Interactive Social Studies* program was created in collaboration with educators, social studies experts, and students nationwide. The program uses tested best practices to engage students in social studies content through current events, dynamic technology, active classroom strategies, inquiry-based learning and more, so students are college- and career-ready.

The Program Includes:

- Inquiry-focused projects, civic discussions, and document analysis questions that develop content and skills mastery in preparation for real-world challenges.

- Essential Questions, personal myStory videos, Connections to Today and current events to spark interest and increase long-term understanding for students.

- Higher-level content with differentiation tools to support students' access to complex text, acquire core content knowledge, and tackle rigorous questions.

- Digital activities on Savvas Realize that are dynamic, flexible, and use the power of technology to bring social studies to life.

>> Go online to learn more and see the program overview video.

Connect
Make meaning personal

Investigate
Acquire knowledge and skills

Assess Mastery

Demonstrate
Show understanding

Synthesize
Practice knowledge and skills

SAVVAS
realize™

The digital course on Realize!

The program's digital course on Realize puts rich and engaging content, embedded assessments with instant data, and flexible tools at your fingertips.

Connect: Make Meaning Personal

CONNECT! Students will begin *Interactive Social Studies* by engaging in the topic story and connecting it to their own lives.

>> **Connections to Today** brings the past to the present. Students will be introduced to a topic by seeing how history influenced today. Educators will find more resources on the Savvas Realize course.

>> Instruction begins with an **Essential Question**. These thought-provoking questions engage students and introduce the Topic.

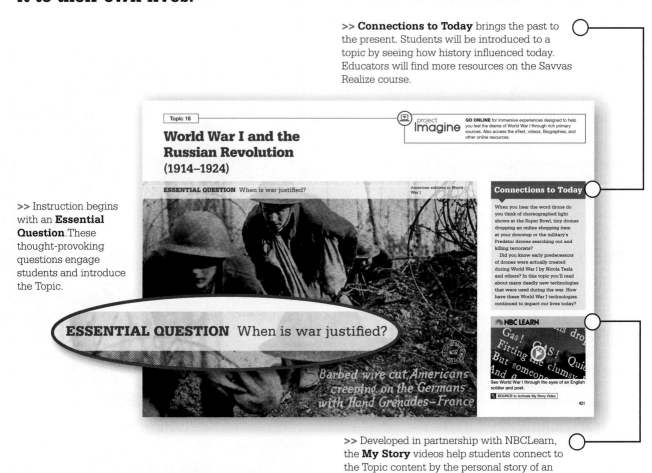

ESSENTIAL QUESTION When is war justified?

>> Developed in partnership with NBCLearn, the **My Story** videos help students connect to the Topic content by the personal story of an individual whose life is related to the content students are about to learn.

QUEST! INQUIRY

>> **Quest Inquiry activities** include projects, civic discussions, and document-based activities. Students will demonstrate their knowledge of the topic and practice real-world skills by creating presentations, videos, conduct discussions, and more.

INVESTIGATE! Step two of *Interactive Social Studies* allows students to investigate the topic story through a number of engaging features as you learn the content.

>> **Active Classroom Strategies** integrated in the daily lesson plans help to increase in-class participation, raise energy levels and attentiveness, all while engaging in the story. These 5–15 minute activities have you use what you have learned to draw, write, speak, and decide.

project Imagine

>> Be Part of History with **Project Imagine** digital immersive experiences. These dynamic activities are found in key topics to reinforce students' understanding of history and increase historical empathy.

 **Listenwise**

>> Connect through Current Events! We've partnered with **Listenwise** to bring you daily news updates to help bring what's happening outside your classroom into your daily instruction.

Investigate

>> Feel like you are a part of the story with **interactive 3-D models, primary sources, maps, and more.**

>> Reinforce content with **leveled lesson summaries** and **lesson video recaps** found on the Savvas Realize course.

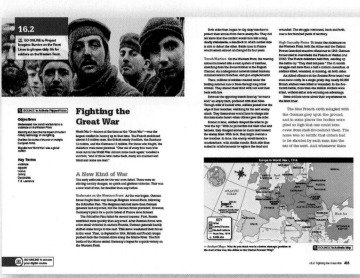

>> Learn content by reading narrative text online or in a printed Student Edition.

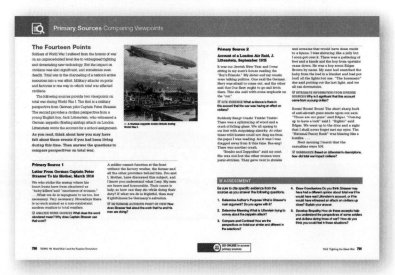

>> See history from a different perspective. **Comparing Viewpoints** provides students with contrasting primary sources to understand all sides of history.

Synthesize: Practice Knowledge and Skills

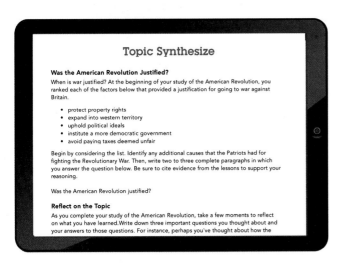

SYNTHESIZE!

In step three of the Mastery System, pause to reflect on what you learn and revisit an essential question.

Demonstrate: Show Understanding

DEMONSTRATE! The final step of *Interactive Social Studies* is to demonstrate understanding of the content.

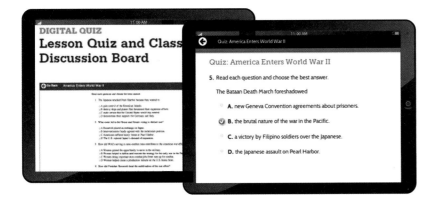

>> **Assessment:** At the end of each lesson and topic, demonstrate understanding through Lesson Quizzes, Topic Tests, and Topic Inquiry performance assessments. Topics Tests are available in three different content levels so educators can reach all students.

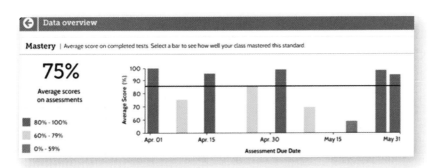

>> **Class and Data** features on Realize make it easy to use students' data to show if time is needed to re-teach or move ahead.

Table of Contents

Table of Contents

Topic 7   Medieval Christian Europe (330–1450)   228

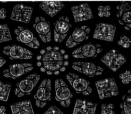

Topic 8   The Muslim World and Africa (730 B.C.–A.D. 1500)   300

Table of Contents

Topic 11 New Global Connections (1415–1796) 456

Table of Contents

Topic 14

Nationalism and the Spread of Democracy (1790–1914)

642

Table of Contents

Topic 17   The World Between the Wars (1910–1939)   804

Topic 18   World War II (1930–1945)   868

Table of Contents

Topic 21

The World Today (1990–Present) **1026**

Print Resources ———————————————————————

Primary Source Excerpts

Print Resources

Timelines

Maps

Print Resources _____

Charts, Graphs, and Tables

Print Resources

Infographics

Digital Resources

project Imagine ⟨⟩ GO ONLINE for immersive experiences and rich primary sources.

Ancient Greece
- Museum Mission: Enter the Art of Gods and Mortals
- Role Play: Experience Life and Death in Ancient Greece
- Opinion Poll: Is Athenian democracy a good model for other Greek cities?
- 360° Exploration: Tour a Greek Temple and the First Olympic Stadium
- Interactive Map and Timeline: Survey Centuries of Greek Culture

Tang and Song China
- Interactive Map and Timeline: Travel Through Time in Tang and Song China
- 360° Exploration: Explore Buddhist and Daoist Religious Sites
- Opinion Poll: Do Foreign Ideas Help or Hurt China?
- Decision Tree: Make Your Way in Song China
- Role Play: Use New Technology in Song China

The Renaissance
- Interactive Map and Timeline: Trace the Birth and Development of the Renaissance
- Role Play: Step Into Life in Renaissance Florence
- Opinion Poll: Should You Exile the Medici Family from Florence?
- Museum Mission: See Life Through an Artist's Eyes
- 360° Exploration: Visit Renaissance Sites in London and Venice

The Early Industrial Revolution
- Interactive Map and Timeline: Trace the Growth of Early Industry
- Decision Tree: Make Your Fortune in Industry
- Opinion Poll: Should Child Labor Be Regulated?
- Museum Mission: Visit the Crystal Palace
- Role Play: Experience Life in Industrial Britain

World War I
- Role Play: Follow the Paths to War
- Interactive Map and Timeline: Experience Total War
- 360° Exploration: Survive on the Front Lines
- Decision Tree: Do Your Bit for Britain
- Opinion Poll: How Should Germany Be Treated After the War?

Africa, 1945–1985
- 360° Exploration: Visit French and British Colonies in Africa
- Decision Tree: Help Build an Independent Senegal
- Role Play: Experience African Independence Movements
- Interactive Map and Timeline: Explore Life After Independence
- Opinion Poll: Should African Nations Follow Tanzania's Example?

Interactivities

Interactive 3-D Models
- Egyptian Pyramids, Topic 2 Lesson 4
- Aztec Temple, Topic 4 Lesson 1
- The Pantheon, Topic 6 Lesson 3
- Medieval Monastery, Topic 7 Lesson 3
- The Dome of the Rock, Topic 8 Lesson 2
- A Ming Vase, Topic 9 Lesson 3
- Duomo in Florence, Topic 10 Lesson 1
- Explorer's Ship, Topic 11 Lesson 1
- Living in a Tenement, Topic, 13 Lesson 3
- Trench Warfare, Topic 16 Lesson 2
- The B-24 Liberator, Topic 18 Lesson 4

Interactive Cartoons
- Characteristics of the Three Estates, Topic 12 Lesson 6
- Metternich Resists Liberal Ideas, Topic 14 Lesson 1
- A Political Game of Chess, Topic 14 Lesson 3
- The Boulanger Scandal, Topic 14 Lesson 6
- Uncle Sam Takes Off - United States Imperialism, Topic 15 Lesson 8
- Nationalist Struggles in the Balkans, Topic 16 Lesson 1
- League of Nations Fails to Stop Aggression, Topic 17 Lesson 5
- Hitler's March to European Domination, Topic 18 Lesson 1

GO ONLINE to access the eText, videos, Interactive Primary Sources, Biographies, and Project Imagine immersives designed to bring key moments in history to life.

Digital Resources

- Reformation Art, Topic 10 Lesson 3
- A Scientific Revolution in Medicine, Topic 10 Lesson 5
- Changing Views of the Universe, Topic 10 Lesson 5
- Navigating the World, Topic 11 Lesson 1
- Art of Spain's Golden Century, Topic 12 Lesson 1
- The Palace of Versailles, Topic 12 Lesson 1
- The Achievements of Peter the Great, Topic 12 Lesson 2
- Protections of the English Bill of Rights, Topic 12 Lesson 3
- Music of the Enlightenment, Topic 12 Lesson 4
- The Reign of Terror, Topic 12 Lesson 7
- The Industrial Revolution and the Textile Industry, Topic 13 Lesson 1
- Life of the Working Class, Topic 13 Lesson 2
- Advances in Medicine During the Industrial Age, Topic 13 Lesson 3
- Artistic Movements During the Industrial Revolution, Topic 13 Lesson 4
- The New Social Order and Changing Roles of Women, Topic 13 Lesson 4
- Latin American Independence Movements, Topic 14 Lesson 2
- Leaders of Italian Unification, Topic 14 Lesson 4
- Famine Changes Ireland, Topic 14 Lesson 5
- The Siege of Paris, Topic 14 Lesson 6
- Tug of War - Reform and Repression by Russian Tsars, Topic 14 Lesson 8
- Technology Advances Imperialism, Topic 15 Lesson 1
- European Powers and the Ottoman Empire, Topic 15 Lesson 3
- The Suez Canal, Topic 15 Lesson 3
- The Sepoy Rebellion, Topic 15 Lesson 4
- The Boxer Rebellion, Topic 15 Lesson 5
- The Meiji Restoration, 1868–1912, Topic 15 Lesson 6
- The Panama Canal, Topic 15 Lesson 8
- Military Technology in World War I, Topic 16 Lesson 2
- World War I Propaganda Posters, Topic 16 Lesson 3
- Revolutionary Art, Topic 17 Lesson 1
- The Mexican Revolution, Topic 17 Lesson 1
- Writers of the Négritude Movement, Topic 17 Lesson 2
- Influences of Gandhi, Topic 17 Lesson 3
- Revival of Japanese Glory, Topic 17 Lesson 4
- Modern Art Develops, Topic 17 Lesson 5
- The Makings of an Italian Totalitarian State, Topic 17 Lesson 6

- Art as Propaganda, Topic 17 Lesson 7
- Growing Up in Nazi Germany, Topic 17 Lesson 8
- Axis Aggression, Topic 18 Lesson 1
- London Blitz, Topic 18 Lesson 2
- Remembering the Holocaust, Topic 18 Lesson 3
- Cold War Technologies, Topic 19 Lesson 1
- The Cuban Missile Crisis, Topic 19 Lesson 1
- Suburbanization in Postwar America, Topic 19 Lesson 2
- Communism in China, Topic 19 Lesson 3
- Fighting a Different War, Topic 19 Lesson 4
- Indian Independence and Partition, Topic 20 Lesson 1
- India on the Rise, Topic 20 Lesson 2
- Protests in Tiananmen Square, Topic 20 Lesson 2
- Independence in Congo, Topic 20 Lesson 3
- Environmental Challenges in Africa, Topic 20 Lesson 4
- Argentina's Long Road to Democracy, Topic 20 Lesson 7
- Children of the Developing World, Topic 21 Lesson 1
- Evolution of the European Union, Topic 21 Lesson 2
- Aspects of Globalization, Topic 21 Lesson 3
- Smart Phones - American Made?, Topic 21 Lesson 3
- Women's Lives in the 21st Century, Topic 21 Lesson 4
- September 11, 2001, Topic 21 Lesson 5

Interactive Images
- The Discovery of Perspective, Topic 10 Lesson 1
- Illuminated Manuscripts to Printed Pages, Topic 10 Lesson 3
- From Words to Action - Ideology in the American Revolution, Topic 12 Lesson 5
- Declaration of the Rights of Man, Topic 12 Lesson 6
- The Imperial Durbar, 1877, Topic 15 Lesson 4
- Commodore Perry's Expedition to Japan, Topic 15 Lesson 6

Interactive Maps
- Migrations of Homo Sapiens, Topic 1 Lesson 1
- River Valley Civilizations, Topic 1 Lesson 3
- Sumer and the Fertile Crescent, Topic 2 Lesson 1
- Mesopotamian Empires, Topic 2 Lesson 2
- Ancient Egyptian Lands, Topic 2 Lesson 4
- Early Civilizations in South Asia, Topic 3 Lesson 1
- The Origins and Spread of Buddhism, Topic 3 Lesson 2
- Maurya and Gupta Empires, Topic 3 Lesson 3
- The Silk Road Connects East and West, Topic 3 Lesson 5
- Settlements of Civilizations in Mesoamerica, Topic 4 Lesson 1

- Civilizations of the Andes, Topic 4 Lesson 2
- Spanish and Portuguese Colonies in the Americas, about 1700, Topic 4 Lesson 3
- Native American Architecture, Topic 4 Lesson 4
- Persian Wars, 490 B.C.-479 B.C., Topic 5 Lesson 2
- Growth of the Roman Republic, 500 B.C. to 44 B.C., Topic 6 Lesson 1
- Invasions of the Roman Empire, A.D. 378–533, Topic 6 Lesson 2
- The Spread of Christianity, Topic 6 Lesson 4
- Invasions of Europe, 700–1000, Topic 7 Lesson 1
- Spread of Christianity in Europe, Topic 7 Lesson 3
- The Crusades, 1096–1204, Topic 7 Lesson 4
- The Growth of France, 987–1328, Topic 7 Lesson 5
- The Black Death, 1347–1351, Topic 7 Lesson 7
- The Hundred Years' War, 1337–1453, Topic 7 Lesson 7
- Growth of Russia, 1300–1584, Topic 7 Lesson 8
- Jewish Migrations and Expulsions, 500–1650, Topic 7 Lesson 8
- Spread of Islam, Topic 8 Lesson 2
- Growth of the Ottoman and Safavid Empires, Topic 8 Lesson 4
- Africa's Vegetation Regions, Topic 8 Lesson 5
- Trans-Saharan Trade, 750 B.C.-A.D. 1600, Topic 8 Lesson 6
- Journeys of Ibn Battuta, Topic 8 Lesson 7
- The Delhi Sultanate and the Mughal Empire, Topic 9 Lesson 1
- The Mongol Empire, Topic 9 Lesson 3
- Korea's Three Kingdoms, Topic 9 Lesson 4
- Topography of Southeast Asia, Topic 9 Lesson 6
- Renaissance Italy's City-States, Topic 10 Lesson 1
- Major European Religions, About 1600, Topic 10 Lesson 4
- Early Voyages of European Exploration, 1487–1522, Topic 11 Lesson 1
- Trade Among Europe, Africa, and Asia, Topic 11 Lesson 2
- Spanish and Portuguese Colonies in the Americas, about 1700, Topic 11 Lesson 3
- European Colonization of North America, about 1700, Topic 11 Lesson 4
- Triangular Trade Routes, Topic 11 Lesson 5
- The Columbian Exchange, Topic 11 Lesson 6
- Maps of Europe, 1648 and 1700, Topic 12 Lesson 2
- Napoleon's Europe (1804–1815), Topic 12 Lesson 8
- Advances in Transportation in England, 1800s, Topic 13 Lesson 1
- Revolutionary Uprisings, 1830–1848, Topic 14 Lesson 1
- Latin American Independence, Topic 14 Lesson 2
- Italian Regions Before Unification, Topic 14 Lesson 4
- Expansion of the United States, 1783–1898, Topic 14 Lesson 7
- The Balkan Powder Keg, Topic 14 Lesson 8
- The New Imperialism, Topic 15 Lesson 1
- Effects of Imperialism on African Regions, Topic 15 Lesson 2
- European Imperialism in Africa, Topic 15 Lesson 2
- Imperialist Spheres of Influence in China, Topic 15 Lesson 5
- Imperialism in Southeast Asia, 1900, Topic 15 Lesson 7
- Europe in World War I, 1914–1918, Topic 16 Lesson 2
- Effects of World War I on European Boundaries, Topic 16 Lesson 3
- From Russian Empire to Soviet Union, 1914–1923, Topic 16 Lesson 4
- African Resistance to Colonial Rule, Topic 17 Lesson 2
- Axis Aggression, Topic 18 Lesson 2
- Life in the Concentration Camps, Topic 18 Lesson 3
- World War II in Europe, 1942–1945, Topic 18 Lesson 4
- World War II in the Pacific, 1942–1945, Topic 18 Lesson 5
- The Korean War, Topic 19 Lesson 3
- The Fall of the Soviet Union, Topic 19 Lesson 5
- South Asian Borders, Topic 20 Lesson 1
- Imperialism and Independence in Africa, Topic 20 Lesson 3
- Religious Diversity in the Middle East, Topic 20 Lesson 5
- Changing Boundaries of the State of Israel, Topic 20 Lesson 6
- Economic Activities in Latin America, Topic 20 Lesson 7
- Global Population Growth, Topic 21 Lesson 1
- Global Environmental Challenges, Topic 21 Lesson 4
- Terrorist Movements Around the World, Topic 21 Lesson 5

Interactive Timelines
- Roman Rulers Who Made History, Topic 6 Lesson 2
- The Origins of Islam, Topic 8 Lesson 1
- Rise and Decline of an Arab Empire, Topic 8 Lesson 2
- Timeline of the English Reformation, Topic 10 Lesson 4
- England Divided - The Monarchy and Parliament Fight for Power, Topic 12 Lesson 3
- The French Revolution Enters a More Radical Phase, Topic 12 Lesson 7

Digital Resources

- The Rise and Fall of Napoleon, Topic 12 Lesson 8
- Transportation Milestones, Topic 13 Lesson 3
- German Unification, Topic 14 Lesson 3
- Britain Reformed, Topic 14 Lesson 5
- The Women's Rights Movement, Topic 14 Lesson 7
- The Rise and Fall of the Weimar Republic, Topic 17 Lesson 8
- Key Events of World War II in Europe and the Pacific, Topic 18 Lesson 5

- Vietnam, 1945–1965 - From Independence Struggle to Cold War Battleground, Topic 19 Lesson 4
- Fall of Communism in Eastern Europe, Topic 19 Lesson 5
- The Struggle Against Apartheid, Topic 20 Lesson 4
- Conflicts in the Middle East, Topic 20 Lesson 6
- War in Bosnia, Topic 21 Lesson 2
- The Age of Space Exploration, Topic 21 Lesson 6
- Medical Milestones, Topic 21 Lesson 6

Core Concepts

Culture
- What Is Culture?
- Families and Societies
- Language
- Religion
- The Arts
- Cultural Diffusion and Change
- Science and Technology

Economics
- Economics Basics
- Economic Process
- Economic Systems
- Economic Development
- Trade
- Money Management

Geography
- The Study of Earth
- Geography's Five Themes
- Ways to Show Earth's Surface
- Understanding Maps

- Earth in Space
- Time and Earth's Rotation
- Forces on Earth's Surface
- Forces Inside Earth
- Climate and Weather
- Temperature
- Water and Climate
- Air Circulation and Precipitation
- Types of Climate
- Ecosystems
- Environment and Resources
- Land Use
- People's Impact on the Environment
- Population
- Migration
- Urbanization

Government and Civics
- Foundations of Government
- Political Systems
- Political Structures

- Conflict and Cooperation
- Citizenship

History
- How Do Historians Study History?
- Measuring Time
- Historical Sources
- Archaeology and Other Sources
- Historical Maps

Personal Finance
- Your Fiscal Fitness: An Introduction
- Budgeting
- Checking
- Investments
- Savings and Retirement
- Credit and Debt
- Risk Management
- Consumer Smarts
- After High School
- Taxes and Income

Landmark Supreme Court Cases

- *Korematsu* v. *United States*
- *Marbury* v. *Madison*
- *McCulloch* v. *Maryland*
- *Gibbons* v. *Ogden*
- *Worcester* v. *Georgia*
- *Dred Scott* v. *Sandford*

- *Plessy* v. *Ferguson*
- *Schenck* v. *United States*
- *Brown* v. *Board of Education*
- *Engel* v. *Vitale*
- *Sweatt* v. *Painter*
- *Mapp* v. *Ohio*

- *Hernandez* v. *Texas*
- *Gideon* v. *Wainwright*
- *Wisconsin* v. *Yoder*
- *Miranda* v. *Arizona*
- *White* v. *Regester*

- *Tinker* v. *Des Moines School District*
- *Roe* v. *Wade*
- *Baker* v. *Carr*
- *Grutter* v. *Bollinger*

- *Edgewood* v. *Kirby*
- *Texas* v. *Johnson*
- *National Federation of Independent Businesses et al.* v. *Sebelius et al.*

- *Mendez* v. *Westminster* and *Delgado* v. *Bastrop*

Selected Interactive Primary Sources

See the course for a full list of Interactive Primary Sources.

- Hymn to the Nile
- Code of Hammurabi
- Psalm 23
- Analects, Confucius
- Two Poems from the Book of Songs
- Medea, Euripides
- The Persian Wars, Herodotus
- Bhagavad-Gita, Vyasa
- Tao Te Ching, Laozi
- The Republic, Plato
- Politics, Aristotle
- Edicts, Asoka
- De re publica
- First Letter to the Corinthians, Paul
- The Quran
- Rustem and Sohrab, Firdawsi
- The Tale of Genji, Murasaki Shikibu
- The Magna Carta
- Sundiata: An Epic of Old Mali, D.T. Niane
- The Inferno, Dante Alighieri
- Travels, Ibn Battuta
- The Prince, Niccolò Machiavelli
- The Destruction of the Indies, Bartolomé de Las Casas
- John Calvin, Institutes of the Christian Religion
- Mayflower Compact
- The New Organon [The New Method], Francis Bacon
- English Petition of Right
- English Bill of Rights
- Guru Granth Sahib, Guru Nanak
- Two Treatises of Government, John Locke
- The Spirit of Laws, Baron de Montesquieu
- The Social Contract, Jean-Jacques Rousseau

- The Interesting Narrative of the Life of Olaudah Equiano
- "Give Me Liberty or Give Me Death," Patrick Henry
- "Remember the Ladies," Abigail Adams
- Common Sense, Thomas Paine
- The Wealth of Nations, Adam Smith
- Declaration of Independence
- "To His Excellency, General Washington," Phillis Wheatley
- Articles of Confederation
- Iroquois Constitution
- Declaration of the Rights of Man and the Citizen
- Democracy in America, Alexis de Tocqueville
- Declaration of Sentiments and Resolutions
- The Communist Manifesto: Karl Marx and Friedrich Engels
- "Ain't I a Woman?," Sojourner Truth
- Uncle Tom's Cabin, Harriet Beecher Stowe
- Emancipation Proclamation, Abraham Lincoln
- Gettysburg Address, Abraham Lincoln
- Red Cloud's Speech at Cooper Union, 1870
- "I Will Fight No More Forever," Chief Joseph
- How the Other Half Lives, Jacob Riis
- Atlanta Exposition Address, Booker T. Washington
- "The White Man's Burden," Rudyard Kipling
- The Jungle, Upton Sinclair
- Hind Swaraj, Mohandas Gandhi
- The Fourteen Points, Woodrow Wilson
- Two Poems, Langston Hughes
-
- All Quiet on the Western Front, Erich Maria
- The Revolution Betrayed, Leon Trotsky
- Four Freedoms, Franklin D. Roosevelt
- Anne Frank: The Diary of a Young Girl, Anne Frank
- Charter of the United Nations
- "The Sinews of Peace," Winston Churchill

Digital Resources

- Universal Declaration of Human Rights
- Autobiography, Kwame Nkrumah
- Inaugural Address, John F. Kennedy
- Silent Spring, Rachel Carson
- "I Have a Dream," Martin Luther King, Jr.
- "Letter From Birmingham Jail," Martin Luther King, Jr.
- "Tear Down This Wall," Ronald Reagan
- "Freedom From Fear," Aung San Suu Kyi

- A Thousand Points of Light, George H. W. Bush
- "Glory and Hope," Nelson Mandela
- Sixth State of the Union Address: Bill Clinton, 1998
- State of the Union address, George W. Bush, 2002
- 16th Birthday Speech at the United Nations, Malala Yousafzai
- COVID-19 Briefing, Dr. Tedros Adhanom Ghebreyesus
- Speech at the United Nations Climate Action Summit, Greta Thunberg

Selected Biographies

See the course for a full list of Interactive Primary Sources.

- Abigail Adams
- John Adams
- John Quincy Adams
- Samuel Adams
- Alexander the Great
- James Armistead
- Ashoka
- Crispus Attucks
- James A. Baker III
- Emily Greene Balch
- William Blackstone
- Simón Bolívar
- Napoleon Bonaparte
- Chief Bowles
- Omar Bradley
- Michelangelo di Buonarroti Simoni
- Augustus Caesar
- Julius Caesar
- Charlemagne
- César Chávez
- Wentworth Cheswell
- Winston Churchill
- Henry Clay
- Bill Clinton
- Confucius
- Constantine
- Nicolaus Copernicus
- David
- Jefferson Davis
- Martin De León

- Rene Descartes
- *Desidarius Erasmus*
- Dwight Eisenhower
- James Fannin
- James L. Farmer, Jr.
- Benjamin Franklin
- Milton Friedman
- Betty Friedan
- Galileo Galilei
- Bernardo de Gálvez
- Hector P. Garcia
- King George III
- William Gladstone
- Mikhail Gorbachev
- Ulysses S. Grant
- José Gutiérrez de Lara
- Alexander Hamilton
- Hammurabi
- Warren Harding
- Vaclav Havel
- Friedrich Hayek
- Jack Coffee Hays
- Patrick Henry
- Adolf Hitler
- Oveta Culp Hobby
- James Hogg
- Shi Huangdi
- Kay Bailey Hutchison
- Hypatia
- St. Ignatius of Loyola
- Andrew Jackson
- John Jay
- Thomas Jefferson
- Lyndon B. Johnson
- Anson Jones

- Barbara Jordan
- Justinian
- John F. Kennedy
- John Maynard Keynes
- Martin Luther King, Jr.
- *Kublai Khan*
- Marquis de Lafayette
- Mirabeau B. Lamar
- Robert E. Lee
- Abraham Lincoln
- John Locke
- Martin Luther
- Niccolò Machiavelli
- James Madison
- John Marshall
- George Marshall
- Karl Marx
- George Mason
- Joseph McCarthy
- James Monroe
- Charles de Montesquieu
- Moses
- Wolfgang Amadeus Mozart
- Benito Mussolini
- José Antonio Navarro
- Isaac Newton
- Chester A. Nimitz
- Richard M. Nixon
- Barack Obama
- Sandra Day O'Connor
- Thomas Paine
- Quanah Parker
- Rosa Parks
- George Patton

- John J. Pershing
- John Paul II
- Ronald Reagan
- Hiram Rhodes Revels
- Franklin D. Roosevelt
- Theodore Roosevelt
- Antonio Lopez de Santa Anna
- Juan N. Seguín
- William Shakespeare
- Roger Sherman
- Prince Shotoku
- Adam Smith
- Alexander Solzhenitsyn
- Joseph Stalin
- William Graham Sumner
- Raymond L. Telles
- Alexis de Tocqueville
- Hideki Tojo
- William B. Travis
- Harry Truman
- Lech Walesa
- Mercy Otis Warren
- George Washington
- Daniel Webster
- Lulu Belle Madison White
- William Wilberforce
- James Wilson
- Woodrow Wilson
- Yohanan ben Zaccai
- Lorenzo de Zavala
- Mao Zedong

GO ONLINE to access the eText, videos, Interactive Primary Sources, Biographies, and Project Imagine immersives designed to bring key moments in history to life.

21st Century Skills

- Identify Main Ideas and Details
- Set a Purpose for Reading
- Use Context Clues
- Analyze Cause and Effect
- Categorize
- Compare and Contrast
- Draw Conclusions
- Draw Inferences
- Generalize
- Make Decisions
- Make Predictions
- Sequence
- Solve Problems
- Summarize
- Analyze Media Content
- Analyze Primary and Secondary Sources
- Compare Viewpoints
- Distinguish Between Fact and Opinion
- Identify Bias
- Analyze Data and Models

- Analyze Images
- Analyze Political Cartoons
- Create Charts and Maps
- Create Databases
- Read Charts, Graphs, and Tables
- Read Physical Maps
- Read Political Maps
- Read Special-Purpose Maps
- Use Parts of a Map
- Ask Questions
- Avoid Plagiarism
- Create a Research Hypothesis
- Evaluate Web Sites
- Identify Evidence
- Identify Trends
- Interpret Sources
- Search for Information on the Internet
- Synthesize
- Take Effective Notes
- Develop a Clear Thesis
- Organize Your Ideas

- Support Ideas With Evidence
- Evaluate Existing Arguments
- Consider & Counter Opposing Arguments
- Give an Effective Presentation
- Participate in a Discussion or Debate
- Publish Your Work
- Write a Journal Entry
- Write an Essay
- Share Responsibility
- Compromise
- Develop Cultural Awareness
- Generate New Ideas
- Innovate
- Make a Difference
- Work in Teams
- Being an Informed Citizen
- Paying Taxes
- Political Participation
- Serving on a Jury
- Voting

Atlas

- United States: Political
- United States: Physical
- Oklahoma: Political
- Oklahoma: Physical
- World Political
- World Physical
- World Climate
- World Ecosystems
- World Population Density
- World Land Use
- North Africa and Southwest Asia: Political
- North Africa and Southwest Asia: Physical

- Sub-Saharan Africa: Political
- Sub-Saharan Africa: Physical
- South Asia: Political
- South Asia: Physical
- East Asia: Political
- East Asia: Physical
- Southeast Asia: Political
- Southeast Asia: Physical
- Europe: Political
- Europe: Physical
- Russia, Central Asia, and the Caucasus: Political
- Russia, Central Asia, and the Caucasus: Physical

- North America: Political
- North America: Physical
- Central America and the Caribbean: Political
- Central America and the Caribbean: Physical
- South America: Political
- South America: Physical
- Australia and the Pacific: Political
- Australia and the Pacific: Physical

DECLARATION OF INDEPENDENCE

When it issued the Declaration of Independence in 1776, the Continental Congress did more than announce the separation of the 13 American colonies from Great Britain. It also summed up the most basic principles that came to underlie the American government. The section known as the preamble states:

> *"We hold these Truths to be self-evident, that all Men are created equal, that they are endowed by their Creator with certain unalienable Rights, that among these are Life, Liberty and the Pursuit of Happiness. That to secure these Rights, Governments are instituted among Men, deriving their just Powers from the Consent of the Governed."*

The Declaration, largely written by Thomas Jefferson, is one of the most important documents in the history of the world. It not only declared the independence of a colony from its mother country, it also established the first government of, by, and for the people.

Both the Declaration of Independence and the American Revolution inspired people around the world. In 1789, the French Revolution began. French revolutionaries issued the Declaration of the Rights of Man and the Citizen.

Toussaint L'Ouverture, leader of the rebellion that led to Haiti's independence.

After an armed uprising of enslaved people the French colony of Haiti became the second independent nation in the Americas. Other Latin American nations soon followed. Haitian leaders issued their own Declaration of Independence in 1804.

Liberia, on the west coast of Africa, was founded as a colony for freed African Americans in 1847, Liberia also issued a Declaration of Independence.

> *"We recognize in all men certain inalienable rights, among these are life, liberty, and the right to acquire, possess, enjoy, and defend property."*

☑ ASSESSMENT

1. **Identify Central Idea** Discuss the similarities between the document from Liberia and the Declaration of Independence.

2. **Draw Conclusions** Why do you think the American Revolution and the Declaration of Independence had an impact around the world?

CONSTITUTION DAY ASSEMBLY

September 17 is Constitution Day, and your school may hold an assembly or other celebration in honor of the day. As part of this celebration, your teacher may ask you to participate in planning and holding a Constitution Day assembly.

Organize As a class, create the basic plan for your assembly. Discuss the following:

1. When and where should the assembly take place?

2. How long should it take? Should you plan on a short program taking a single class period or a longer program?

3. Who should be involved? Will other classes or other grades take part? Will you invite outsiders, such as parents or people from the community?

4. What activities might be included?

Plan After your discussion, divide the class into committees to complete jobs such as getting permission from the school administration, preparing a program, inviting any guests, advertising the plan beforehand, and blogging about it afterward.

Give thought to the types of activities that might be included in the assembly. You might invite a guest speaker from your community. You might run an essay contest among students and have the winners read their essays during the assembly. Some students might prepare a video presentation about the Bill of Rights. Others might write and perform a skit or song about what the Declaration of Independence or U.S. Constitution means to them.

Consider asking those who present speeches, essays, videos, or skits to address this question: What are the key tenets or principles of American democracy?

For additional support, go to the Social Studies Resource Center on Realize and refer to the Constitution Day Resources, including the Celebrate Freedom documents and the Declaration of Independence.

Communicate Present your Constitution Day assembly. After the assembly is over, discuss the event with the class. Ask yourselves questions such as these:

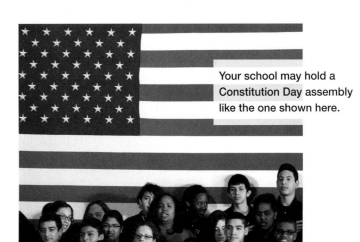

Your school may hold a Constitution Day assembly like the one shown here.

1. How well was the assembly planned and organized? What improvements could we have made?

2. How would you rate each of the presentations or other activities of the assembly?

3. Was the audience engaged?

4. How effectively did the class work together?

Origins of Civilization
(Prehistory–300 B.C.)

ESSENTIAL QUESTION Why is culture important?

GO ONLINE to access the eText, videos, Interactive Primary Sources, Biographies, and other online resources.

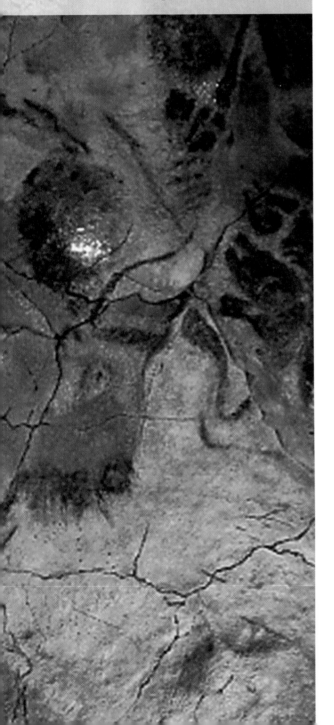

A prehistoric cave painting in northern Spain

Connections to Today

Where does your food come from? Have you ever stopped to think of the complicated journeys food takes from farm fields to your table? In the modern world, machines often collect crops from fields, then trucks take them to factories to be processed into packaged foods. More trucks bring these to warehouses and your local supermarket before you buy them.

In this topic, you'll read about how food production changed in Neolithic times. How has food production changed since then?

NBC LEARN

Learn about an archaeological dig at an ancient Mayan site in Mexico.

 BOUNCE to Activate My Story Video

Topic 1 Overview

In this Topic, you will learn about early humans and the development of civilization, including human migration, early toolmaking, farming, and settlement in river valleys. Look at the lesson outline and explore the timeline. As you study this Topic, you will complete the Quest inquiry.

LESSON OUTLINE

1.1 Learning About Our Past

1.2 The Neolithic Revolution

1.3 Civilization Begins

Early Civilizations

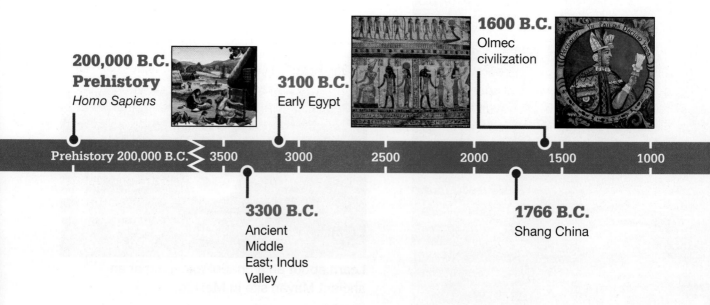

200,000 B.C.
Prehistory
Homo Sapiens

3100 B.C.
Early Egypt

1600 B.C.
Olmec civilization

Prehistory 200,000 B.C. ⌇ 3500   3000   2500   2000   1500   1000

3300 B.C.
Ancient Middle East; Indus Valley

1766 B.C.
Shang China

QUEST!

Create an Early Cultures Video Game

How did culture develop and why is it important? In this Quest you will research, plan, and create a video game that will explore the development of early cultures and civilizations.

STEP 1

Discuss the early cultures and civilizations you will study (Stone Age, hunter-gatherer, and river valley). With your team, brainstorm the features of these cultures.

STEP 2

Each team will choose a specific culture to investigate. Begin your research using reliable sources.

STEP 3

Once your team has gathered information, start writing a narrative for your video game. Choose images. Remember, make your video game interactive.

STEP 4

Work with your team to build your video game. Reflect on how cultures develop and the impact of culture on the development. Are there any factors that have continued to shape today's civilizations?

Studying ancient footprints is one way scientists can learn about the past. These footprints, preserved in volcanic ash, were made in Tanzania some 3.5 million years ago.

BOUNCE to Activate Flipped Video

Objectives

Learn how scholars study the historical past.

Find out how anthropologists investigate the period of prehistory.

Understand how discoveries in Africa and beyond have influenced anthropologists' views about early humans and their ancestors.

Key Terms

prehistory
historian
artifact
anthropology
culture
archaeology
Mary Leakey
Louis Leakey
Olduvai Gorge
technology
Donald Johanson

Learning About Our Past

More than 5,000 years ago, groups of people in different parts of the world began to keep written records. The development and use of writing marked the beginning of recorded history. Humans and their ancestors, however, had lived on Earth for many tens of thousands of years before recorded history. The long period of time before people invented writing is called **prehistory.**

Studying Prehistory

Understanding Our Past Most of the events you will read about here comes from the work of historians. **Historians** are experts in the study of how people lived in the historical past. Historians study **artifacts,** or objects made by humans. Clothing, coins, artwork, and grave sites are all types of artifacts.

However, historians rely even more on written evidence, such as letters or tax records. Historians of the recent past also study such evidence as photographs or films.

Sometimes historians have a wealth of written records. They can study diaries, official histories, birth and death records, and eyewitness accounts. At other times, they have relatively few records, or records that merely list a name or date.

Like a detective, a historian must evaluate all evidence to determine if it is reliable. Do records of an official meeting tell us exactly what was said? Who took notes? Was a letter writer really giving an eyewitness account or just passing on rumors? Is the letter a forgery? Historians try to find the answers to questions like these.

GO ONLINE to access your digital course

Historians must then interpret the evidence and explain what it means. Often, the historian's goal is to determine the causes of a certain event, such as a war or an economic collapse. By explaining why things occurred in the past, historians can help us understand current events and, possibly, what might happen in the future.

Generally, historians try to give a straightforward account of events. However, personal experiences, cultural backgrounds, or political opinions sometimes affect their interpretations. Other times, historians disagree with one another about what the evidence proves. Such differences can lead to lively debates.

The first historians began writing thousands of years ago. Early historians wrote mostly about the deeds of well-known people, such as kings and queens, or about great battles. Their histories were generally about political events.

Today, historians still write about political events. Yet other historians study the lives of ordinary people, They study social or economic history at the local level. How did workers earn a living? What was family life like? How were women or children treated? The answers to these and other questions increase our understanding of the past.

☑ **SUMMARIZE** What kinds of evidence do historians use to study the past?

Investigating Prehistory

The study of prehistory began in the 1800s, when scholars and scientists started to investigate the age of the Earth and the life it supported. They developed fascinating new fields of study that shed light on people and their lives, from prehistoric times to the present.

The Field of Anthropology Since ancient times, people have been interested in the study of their own and other societies. By the mid-1800s, thinkers had begun the organized study of **anthropology,** or the study of humans, past and present. Anthropologists wanted to learn about the origins and development of people and their societies.

Anthropology includes all aspects of human life in all parts of the world. This field of study is so huge that modern anthropologists specialize. For example, some anthropologists study the bones of our ancestors to understand how physical traits changed over time. Others focus on the characteristics of human culture.

In anthropology, **culture** refers to the way of life of a society,which includes its beliefs, values,

and practices. Culture is handed down from one generation to the next through learning and experience.

The Field of Archaeology Another branch of anthropology is archaeology (ahr kee AHL uh jee). **Archaeology** is the study of past people and cultures through their material remains. These remains include artifacts such as tools, weapons, pottery, clothing, and jewelry. Buildings and tombs are other remains that reveal much to archaeologists. Some archaeologists specialize in the study of prehistoric people, while others look at artifacts from historical times.

By analyzing artifacts, archaeologists learn about the beliefs, values, and activities of our ancestors. Archaeologists recognize that the story of the past is never fully known. Often, they uncover new evidence that causes them to revise their ideas about a culture they are studying.

Archaeologists at Work Finding and analyzing artifacts can be difficult, but archaeologists have devised useful techniques to help in their work. In the 1800s and early 1900s, archaeologists picked a likely place, called a site, to dig for artifacts. The deeper they dug, the older the artifacts they found.

Sometimes, the long-buried objects they found crumbled as soon as they were exposed to light and

>> **Analyze Information** On archaeological sites, scientists have to pay attention to details. Why do you think archaeologists have to be so precise?

🔊 BOUNCE to Activate Gallery

air. Today, archaeologists and other scientists have ways of preserving such fragile artifacts.

Archaeologists now make detailed maps that identify the location of every artifact they find at an archaeological site. By analyzing this evidence, they can usually tell what activities took place at different locations within the site. Chips of flint stone might suggest the workplace of a toolmaker. Piles of shells or gnawed bones may show a prehistoric garbage pit.

Scientists Help Archaeologists Archaeologists work with experts in many fields of science. Archaeologists studying very ancient sites need to find out how old an artifact is. For help determining the age of objects, they turn to geologists, or experts on earth science. Geologists can date the age of rocks found in and around an archaeological site.

Other scientists, such as botanists and zoologists—experts on plants and on animals—examine seeds and animal bones to learn about the diets of our ancestors. Experts on climate can help archaeologists determine what conditions our ancestors faced on the plains of Africa or in ice-covered parts of Europe.

Biologists analyze fragments of human bone to determine the person's gender or age. In recent decades, advances in genetics, or the study of heredity and inherited characteristics, have provided

new evidence about early people, such as their migration, or movement, across the world.

Today, archaeologists use many modern technologies to study and interpret their findings. Computers are used to store and sort data or to develop accurate site maps. Aerial photography can reveal patterns of how people used the land. Chemists and physicists have developed techniques that measure radioactivity, which allows them to determine the age of objects.

☑ **DESCRIBE** Why is it that the farther down an archaeologist digs, the more he or she can find out about the past?

Discoveries in Africa and Beyond

Since the 1870s, scholars have worked to learn about the ancestors of modern humans. They have examined fossils, or remains of ancient life preserved in ancient rock. Fossils might include footprints, impressions of leaves, bones, or even skeletons.

Prehistoric groups did not have cities, countries, organized central governments, or complex inventions, so clues about them were hard to find. Before the 1950s, anthropologists knew little about early humans and their ancestors. However, archaeologists in East Africa started uncovering ancient footprints, bones, and tools. With these first key discoveries, scholars began to form a picture of life during prehistory.

East Africa In the 1930s, anthropologists **Mary Leakey** and **Louis Leakey** started searching for clues to the human past in a deep canyon in Tanzania called **Olduvai Gorge** (OHL duh vy). Geologists have dated the bottom layers of Olduvai Gorge to an age of 1.7 to 2.1 million years.

As the Leakeys searched the sides of the gorge, they found very ancient tools chipped from stone. Although these tools looked simple, with jagged edges and rough surfaces, they showed that whoever had made them had learned to develop technologies to help them survive.

Technology refers to the skills and tools people use to meet their basic needs and wants. More recent stone tools proved more sophisticated—both smooth and polished—but the older ones were exciting to the Leakeys. They felt there must be evidence of the makers of those tools in Olduvai Gorge as well.

In 1959, after more than two decades of searching, Mary Leakey found pieces of bone embedded in

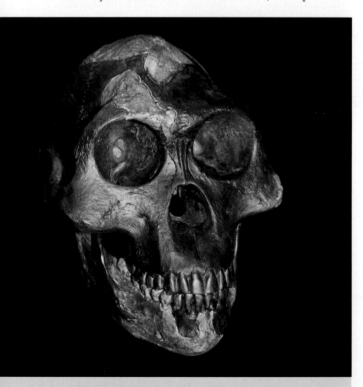

>> "Lucy" was discovered in Ethiopia in 1974. Scientists date the skeleton to at least 3 million years ago. It was the first time archaeologists had enough of one skeleton to reconstruct and view an actual hominid.

Attributes of Early Hominids

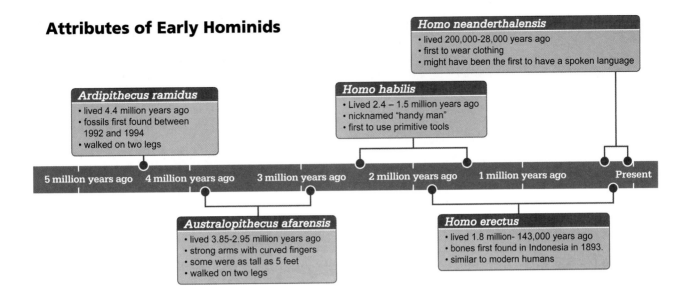

Source: Smithsonian Institution

>> As the centuries passed, hominid groups developed physically and gained new skills.

ancient rock at Olduvai Gorge. After careful testing, the Leakeys concluded that the bone belonged to an early hominid who lived almost 2 million years ago. Hominids, a group that includes humans and their closest relatives, all walk upright on two feet. Humans are the only hominids that live today.

Additional evidence of early hominids was found in 1974 by anthropologist **Donald Johanson.** In Ethiopia, Johanson found a complete skeleton, which was dated to at least 3 million years ago. For the first time, archaeologists had enough of one skeleton to piece together and really look at an early hominid. Johanson named his historic find "Lucy" after a Beatles' song. Studying Lucy's skeleton, Johanson could see that she was an upright walker who was about 4 feet (1.2 meters) tall.

Early Hominid Groups As of today, scientists and anthropologists have discovered and studied numerous remains and artifacts of hominids. From this work, they have established that a number of different groups of hominids lived over the course of several million years. They call the earliest group of hominids australopithecines (aw stray loh PITH uh synz).

Lucy and the hominids who left their footprints in Laetoli were australopithecines. All the australopithecines lived in Africa. Anthropologists think that they may have lived there as early as 7 million years ago.

About 2 million years ago, a group of hominids called *Homo habilis* emerged. Scholars gave the group this name, which means "handy man," because they thought they were the first hominids to make stone tools. Since the discovery of *Homo habilis*, anthropologists have uncovered even older stone tools—2.6 million years in age—but they have not determined which hominids created them.

By studying many stone tools, anthropologists have concluded that *Homo habilis* used their tools for purposes such as cutting, scraping, chopping, or sawing plants, animals, and wood.

Another group of hominids, called *Homo erectus,* also appeared around 2 million years ago. They were given their name, which means "upright man," because their skeletons show that they were fully upright walkers. *Homo erectus* were notable for having larger brains and bones and smaller teeth than other hominids.

They also showed a greater range of capabilities. For example, *Homo erectus* are thought to be the first hominids to learn how to use fire. They also pioneered a new form of stone tool, called a hand ax, that could be used as the earlier tools were but also worked for digging, shattering stone or bone, and boring holes into hard surfaces. *Homo erectus* remains have been found in Asia and Europe, making scholars think they were the first hominids to migrate out of Africa.

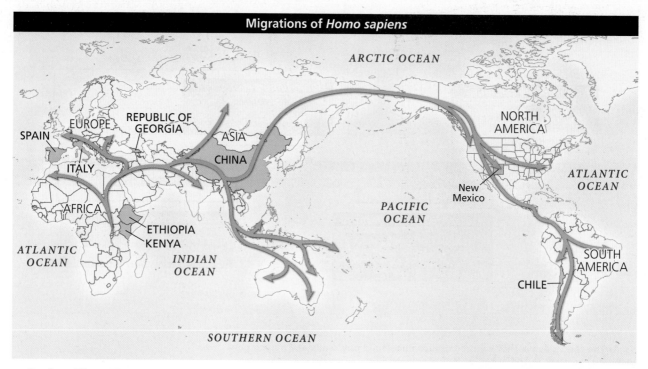

Migrations of *Homo sapiens*

>> **Analyze Maps** *Homo sapiens* migrated along the routes shown on the map. Why would early *Homo sapiens* follow large herds of animals?

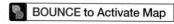
BOUNCE to Activate Map

Evidence of *Homo Sapiens* Scientists think that between 250,000 and 100,000 years ago, *Homo erectus* disappeared and a new group of hominids emerged. This new group, called *Homo sapiens*, is the group to which modern humans belong. There is some dispute over where *Homo sapiens* first lived. Many scholars think the archaeological and scientific evidence supports the "Out of Africa" theory, which says that *Homo sapiens* first lived in Africa and then migrated into other areas of the world. Other scientists think that *Homo erectus* developed into *Homo sapiens* around the same time in different parts of the world.

Either way, scholars think that two groups of *Homo sapiens* soon arose—Neanderthals and the earliest modern humans. Early modern humans eventually spread all over the world, while Neanderthals lived mostly in Europe and western Asia. Sometime between 50,000 and 30,000 years ago, the Neanderthals disappeared, leaving early modern humans as the only hominids on Earth.

☑ **CONNECT** How did *Homo habilis* use the tools they fashioned?

☑ ASSESSMENT

1. **Apply Concepts** What types of obstacles do historians have to overcome to give a straight-forward account of past events?

2. **Describe** Describe the "Out of Africa" theory.

3. **Connect** How have anthropologists learned about the ancestors of modern humans?

4. **Explain** Why did scholars give *Homo habilis* the nickname "handy man?"

5. **Connections to Today** Citing evidence from the text on early hominids' use of tools, what can you infer about how they obtained food? How does that differ from how we obtain food today?

1.2

Scholars believe that Stone Age hunters followed animal herds across a land bridge that once connected Asia and North America.

The Neolithic Revolution

Historians have divided the long period of human prehistory into two main periods. They call the earliest period of human history the **Old Stone Age,** or **Paleolithic Period.** This long period dates from the time that the ancestors of early humans began to make tools—about 2 million years ago—up to about 12,000 years ago. Historians have identified a second period as the **New Stone Age,** or **Neolithic Period.** This age began about 12,000 years ago and ended with the development of metalworking about 5,000 years ago.

Old Stone Age Skills and Beliefs

During both periods, people made and used stone tools. During the New Stone Age, however, people in some parts of the world developed new skills and technologies that led to dramatic changes in their ways of life.

Over tens of thousands of years, people developed various skills that affected daily life. Recent discoveries offer evidence that the ancestors of modern humans may have used fire as early as one million years ago. Learning to control fire was a huge advance, allowing early humans to cook food, keep animals away at night, and stay warm.

Slowly, scholars and scientists have pieced together evidence to suggest how early people lived. Paleolithic people were **nomads,** or people who move from place to place in search of food. The evidence shows that early people lived in small hunter-gatherer societies, numbering about 20 or 30 people.

In general, men hunted or fished. Women and children gathered food such as berries, fruits, nuts, wild grains, roots, or even shellfish. This food kept the band alive when game animals were scarce.

BOUNCE to Activate Flipped Video

Objectives

Describe the skills and beliefs that early modern humans developed during the Old Stone Age.

Analyze why the development of agriculture is considered the start of the New Stone Age and the Neolithic Revolution.

Explain how the Neolithic Revolution dramatically changed the way people lived.

Key Terms

Old Stone Age
Paleolithic Period
New Stone Age
Neolithic Period
nomad
animism
Neolithic Revolution
domesticate
Jericho
Çatalhöyük
surplus

Strategies for Survival Early people depended heavily on their environment for survival. They found ways to adapt to their surroundings and meet their basic needs for food and shelter. People made simple tools and weapons, such as digging sticks, spears, and axes, out of the materials at hand—stone, bone, or wood. These tools were modified depending on people's needs. For example, preparing a foot-long fish to be cooked requires different tools than skinning and cutting up a buffalo. At some point, Stone Age people developed spoken language, which let them cooperate during the hunt and perhaps discuss plans for the future.

During the Old Stone Age, people developed many different technologies. Many of these technologies were developed in response to the environment. By about 40,000 years ago, people living near rivers or along coastlines had learned to make rafts or canoes. They could then cross large bodies of water. Scientists have found evidence that people used water craft to travel from Southeast Asia to Australia. Although these migrating people may have island-hopped slowly over centuries, they had to cross up to 40 miles (64 kilometers) of open ocean.

Hunter-gatherer societies adapted to the environment in other ways. People who lived near water learned to fish. Those who lived in climates with harsh winters used animal skins and fur to make clothing and blankets to stay warm. They also stored food to prepare for hard times.

Early Religious Beliefs Toward the end of the Old Stone Age, people began to leave evidence of their belief in a spiritual world and developed religious rituals. Early humans—like some of their descendants—most likely believed the world was full of spirits, such as the spirits of the animals they hunted. Other forces might reside in natural objects, or dreams. The belief that spirits inhabit plants, animals, or other natural objects, is known as **animism.**

In Europe, Australia, and Africa, cave or rock paintings vividly portray deer, horses, and buffalo. Some cave paintings show stick figures of people, too. The paintings often lie deep in caves, far from a hunting band's living quarters. Such cave paintings may have been part of religious rituals in which hunters sought help from the spirit world for an upcoming hunt.

About 100,000 years ago, some people began burying their dead with great care. This practice suggests a belief in life after death. Old Stone Age people may have believed the afterlife would be similar to life in this world so they provided the dead with tools, weapons, and other needed goods. Burial customs like these survived in many places into modern times.

☑ **DESCRIBE** Describe the tools used by hunter-gatherer societies.

Farming Begins a New Stone Age

About 12,000 years ago, bands of nomadic people made a breakthrough that had far-reaching effects. They learned to farm. By producing their own food crops, people could remain in one place instead of hunting and gathering. Slowly, these early farmers settled into permanent villages and developed a whole new range of skills and tools. This change, from nomadic life to settled farming, ushered in the New Stone Age.

The Neolithic Revolution No one knows exactly how or when people began to plant seeds for food or raise certain animals for their own use. Some of the earliest evidence of farming has been found in the Middle East. Farming, however, probably developed independently throughout the world.

No matter which way it occurred, the change had such dramatic effects that historians call it the Neolithic Revolution. The **Neolithic Revolution**

>> **Draw Conclusions** Based on this illustration, what evidence would archaeologists use to learn about the interior of Neolithic houses?

📓 BOUNCE to Activate Gallery

refers to the change in human societies from hunting and gathering to a more settled way of life based on agriculture and the domestication of animals.

The Domestication of Plants and Animals Early food gatherers may have been the first humans to **domesticate** plants and animals—that is, to raise them in a controlled way that makes them best suited to human use. The domestication of plants may have begun with food gatherers who noticed that if seeds were scattered on the ground they produced new plants the next year. Perhaps a band of hunter-gatherers camped at a place where plants grew and began cultivating them season after season.

All these changes occurred slowly. Eventually, people began to select and plant seeds from the best producers, which led to larger fruits or better grains. Among the earliest domesticated plants were figs, wheat, barley, and rice from different parts of Asia. Potatoes and beans were domesticated in South America while squash and maize were grown in Central America.

By the new Stone Age, people had learned to domesticate some of the animals they had once hunted. Domesticating wild animals would have taken time. Perhaps hunters rounded up and enclosed some wild animals rather than wait for them to return each year as they migrated. People either kept the animals in rough enclosures or herded them to good grasslands.

Only some wild animals could be domesticated. People then used these animals as they always had— for food or skins—as well as for other benefits, such as milk or eggs. A few animals were even used for pulling.

Dogs were probably the first animals people domesticated, perhaps as early as 20,000 years ago. They became guard dogs and companions to humans. About 10,000 years ago people in parts of Asia and Africa domesticated goats, sheep, pigs, and cattle. Later, llamas and alpacas were domesticated in South America.

☑ **IDENTIFY MAIN IDEAS** How did farming change the lives of Neolithic people?

Dramatic Change with the Neolithic Revolution

The Neolithic Revolution enabled people to become food producers for the first time. It led to a growth in population, which in turn led to more interaction among human communities. No greater change in the way people lived took place until the Industrial Revolution that began in the late 1700s.

>> The ruins of the Neolithic village of Çatalhöyük

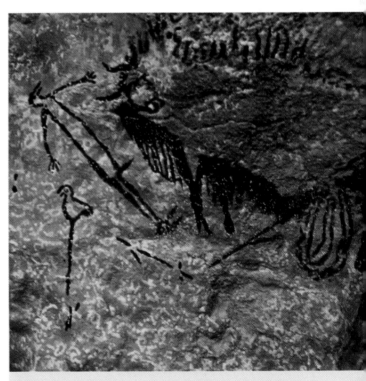

>> Scientists study cave art to understand early religious beliefs known as animism.

🅱 BOUNCE to Activate Gallery

During the Neolithic Revolution, people slowly relied more on the food they grew than on their hunting and gathering efforts. As they developed better seeds and produced better harvests, their numbers grew, and they settled into the first farming villages.

Establishing the Earliest Villages Archaeologists have unearthed the remains of Neolithic villages that reveal much about early farming people. The oldest Neolithic settlements consisted of a handful of huts. A Neolithic village that grew over time was **Jericho** (JEHR ih koh), located in the Jordan River valley in the Middle East. The village was tiny—about the size of a few soccer fields. Only a few thousand people lived in it.

About 10,000 years ago, a huge stone wall was built around the village with a deep ditch beyond the wall. Archaeologists do not know whether the wall was built to protect the village from attack or from floods. The size of the wall suggests that Jericho had a strong leader or government able to organize a large building project.

A larger Neolithic site is **Çatalhöyük** (chah TAHL huh YOOK) in modern-day Turkey. It dates back to about 7,200 B.C. and may have had a population of 6,500 people. The village included hundreds of rectangular mud-brick houses, all connected and all about the same size.

Settled People Change Their Ways of Life Like their Paleolithic ancestors, early farmers probably divided up the work by gender and age. Still, important differences began to emerge. In settled farming communities, men came to dominate family, economic, and political life, and the status of women declined. These changes did not mean that women lost their influence. Rather, they show that village life was reshaping the roles of both men and women.

In Neolithic villages, heads of families, probably older men, formed a council of elders. They were responsible for important decisions such as when to plant and harvest. In time, a village chief may have emerged. When food was scarce, warfare increased and some men gained prestige as warriors. These elite warriors asserted power over others in the community.

Settled people accumulated more personal property than their nomadic ancestors. As Neolithic families began to have more possessions than their neighbors, differences in wealth began to appear.

New Technologies To farm successfully, people had to develop new technologies. Like farmers today, they had to find ways to protect their crops and measure out enough seed for the next year's harvest. They also needed to measure time accurately to know when to plant and harvest. Gradually, people developed systems of measurement and created the

Before and After the Neolithic Revolution

Thousand of years after it began, the Neolithic Revolution still affects our lives.

BEFORE	AFTER
STRATEGIES FOR SURVIVAL	**STRATEGIES FOR SURVIVAL**
• Nomadic hunters and gatherers • Depended on environment for food and shelter	• Domesticated plants and animals • Settled in farming villages • Surpluses of food
GOVERNMENT	**GOVERNMENT**
• People organized into families	• Village government with chief and council • Cities had organized government • Built public works construction projects
ECONOMY	
• People provide for their family's needs • Limited exchange through barter	**ECONOMY**
	• New economy—merchants, trade
TECHNOLOGY	**TECHNOLOGIES**
• Stone tools • Hunting and gathering skills	• Plowing • Weaving • Pottery • Calendars

>> **Analyze Charts** Based on this chart, which statement would be correct? Paleolithic people were more advanced than Neolithic people; or Neolithic people were more advanced than Paleolithic people.

first calendars. In some places, farmers learned to use animals such as oxen or water buffalo to plow the fields.

Artifacts found in Jericho and Çatalhöyük reveal that Neolithic people learned to weave cloth from animal hair or plant fibers. They also mastered the skill of making clay into pots for cooking and storage. In village workshops, people made much better tools and weapons than their ancestors. Archaeologists have learned about life during this period from finds such as "the Iceman"—the body of a Neolithic man found preserved in snow in the European Alps alongside various tools and belongings.

Inventions and new technologies did not take place everywhere at the same time. Technologies might travel slowly from one area to another, taking thousands of years to spread across continents. Other technologies were invented separately in different parts of the world.

The Neolithic Impact The Neolithic Revolution marked a major turning point and is sometimes called the greatest revolution in human history. The development of agriculture and the domestication of animals created a reliable food supply that allowed people to settle in permanent villages.

During the Neolithic Revolution, people developed many new technologies that changed their way of life. Villages organized governments. People acquired new skills. Neolithic farmers began to irrigate, or water, their crops by digging ditches to carry water from rivers or springs.

As farming improved, people produced food surpluses. A **surplus** refers to the goods left over after all needs have been met. These surpluses fed growing populations and allowed food to be stored for future use.

The Neolithic Revolution took thousands of years. Scholars are still piecing together how it unfolded. More than 14,000 years later, the Neolithic Revolution still shapes our lives. None of the recorded events we study in world history would have taken place without the Neolithic Revolution.

☑ **IDENTIFY** What role did gender play in early Neolithic villages?

☑ **ASSESSMENT**

1. **Analyze** Why was being able to control fire important to people in the Old Stone Age?

2. **Explain** When did humans develop language, and how did language benefit them?

3. **Determine Relevance** Why is farming considered the beginning of the Neolithic Revolution?

4. **Draw Conclusions** How did the social status of males change in villages during the Neolithic Revolution?

5. **Hypothesize** What technological development led to the growth of cities?

6. **Connections to Today** How did people's ways of obtaining food change during the Neolithic Revolution? How do those changes affect the ways we obtain food today?

1.3

Farming, shown in this ancient Egyptian painting, was crucial to the development of the first civilizations.

BOUNCE to Activate Flipped Video

Objectives

Analyze the conditions under which the first cities and civilizations arose.

Outline the basic features that define civilization.

Understand the ways in which civilizations have changed over time.

Key Terms

civilization
steppe
polytheistic
artisan
traditional economy
pictograph
scribe
cultural diffusion
city-state
empire

Civilization Begins

The Neolithic Revolution led to the rise of **civilization.** A civilization is an advanced stage of human society marked by a well-organized government and high levels of culture, science, and industry. At different times in different parts of the world, food surpluses allowed some Neolithic villages to grow into cities, the central feature of civilization.

The First Cities and Civilizations

River Valley Civilizations The world's earliest civilizations developed independently in four river valleys. The civilization of Sumer rose along the Tigris and Euphrates rivers in the Middle East. A second river valley civilization developed along the Nile River in Egypt. The Indus and other rivers in present-day Pakistan and India were home to the Indus Valley civilization. A fourth river valley civilization, the Shang, emerged along the Huang, or Yellow River in China.

These four river valleys offered benefits to Neolithic farmers. The soil was fertile, and the rivers provided a regular water supply as well as a means of transportation.

The animals that gathered to drink at the rivers offered a source of food. These favorable conditions helped farmers produce the food surpluses needed to support the growing populations in cities.

Other conditions in the river valleys affected farming. Floodwaters from the rivers spread silt—fine sand, soil, or other material—across the valleys. The silt renewed the soil in the river valleys, keeping it fertile. Flooding posed problems, however, to early farmers, just as it does today.

Floodwaters could destroy crops and even whole villages. People had to learn to control floodwaters and redraw boundaries

GO ONLINE to access your digital course

washed away by the water. They also needed to take water from the rivers to irrigate crops. Work on dikes and irrigation ditches had to be organized and managed. Historians think that the need for complex flood control and irrigation projects led to the rise of strong, well-organized governments, another foundation of civilization.

Civilizations in the Americas Unlike the first civilizations in Asia and Africa, early civilizations in the Americas did not develop in river valleys. The earliest civilizations in the Western Hemisphere developed in two regions. In Mesoamerica, today part of Mexico and Central America, the Olmec, Maya, and Aztec civilizations developed. In Peru, a series of early civilizations led to the Inca civilization.

In the Americas, Neolithic farmers cultivated corn, beans, squash, and potatoes in fertile lowlands and mountain valleys. In Mesoamerica, they reclaimed land from swamps to grow more crops. In Peru, they built terraces into steep mountainsides for new cropland.

Life Away From Cities Away from the first cities, many people continued to hunt, gather food, or live in farming villages. On some less fertile lands or on sparse, dry grasslands called **steppes,** nomadic herders tended cattle, sheep, goats, or other animals. Because the lands did not have abundant water or

grass, these nomads had to keep moving to find new pastures.

☑ **DESCRIBE** Describe how river valleys were ideal locations for the development of civilization.

Features That Define Civilization

What did the early civilizations that rose in different parts of the world have in common? While cities are the central feature of civilization, historians distinguish seven other features found in most early civilizations: (1) well-organized governments, (2) complex religions, (3) job specialization, (4) social classes, (5) arts and architecture, (6) public works, and (7) sometimes writing.

Organized Governments As cities grew, they needed to maintain a steady food supply. To produce large amounts of food and oversee irrigation projects, new forms of government rose. City governments were far more powerful than the councils of elders and local chiefs in farming villages.

At first, priests probably had the greatest power. In time, warrior kings emerged as the chief political leaders. They replaced the old councils of elders and set themselves up as hereditary rulers who passed power from father to son.

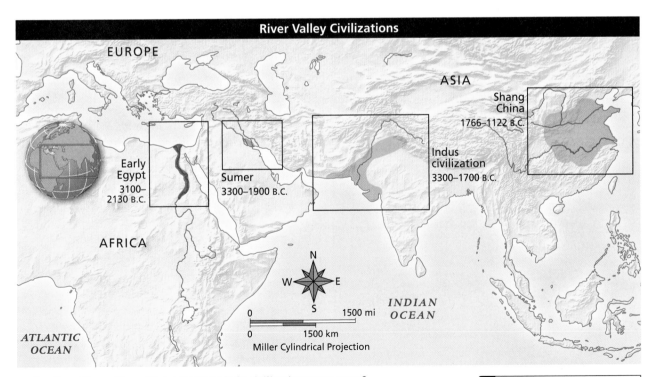

River Valley Civilizations

EUROPE

ASIA

Shang China
1766–1122 B.C.

Early Egypt
3100–2130 B.C.

Sumer
3300–1900 B.C.

Indus civilization
3300–1700 B.C.

AFRICA

N
W E
S

0   1500 mi
0   1500 km
Miller Cylindrical Projection

INDIAN OCEAN

ATLANTIC OCEAN

>> **Analyze Maps** How did river valleys help civilizations to prosper?

BOUNCE to Activate Map

Almost always, rulers claimed that their right to rule came from the gods. They thus gained and held religious, as well as political power.

Governments became more complex as rulers issued laws, collected taxes, and organized systems of defense. To enforce order, rulers relied on royal officials. Over time, separate departments evolved to oversee different functions of government. These separate departments oversaw tax collection, irrigation projects, or the military.

Complex Religions Like their Stone Age ancestors, most ancient people were **polytheistic,** which means they believed in many gods. People appealed to sun gods, river goddesses, and other spirits that they believed controlled natural forces. Other gods were thought to control human activities such as birth, trade, or war.

In ancient religions, priests and worshipers sought to gain the favor of the gods through complex rituals such as ceremonies, dances, prayers, and hymns.

To ensure divine help, people built temples and sacrificed animals, crops, or sometimes other humans to the gods. Sacrifices and other ceremonies required the full-time attention of priests, who had special training and knowledge.

>> These daggers are from the tomb of an Egyptian pharaoh, or ruler. The dagger on top has a blade of gold. The bottom dagger has a blade of iron.

Job Specialization The lives of city dwellers differed from those of their nomadic Stone Age ancestors. Urban people developed so many new crafts that a single individual could not master all the skills needed to make tools, weapons, or other goods.

For the first time, individuals began to specialize in certain jobs. Some became **artisans,** or skilled craftspeople, who made pottery, finely carved statues, or woven goods. Among the crafts that developed in cities, metalworking was particularly important. People learned to make tools and weapons, first out of copper and later out of bronze, a more durable mixture of copper and tin.

Cities had other specialists, too. Bricklayers built city walls. Soldiers defended the walls. Merchants sold goods in the marketplace. Singers, dancers, and storytellers entertained on public occasions. Specialization made people dependent on others for their various needs.

As some villages swelled into the world's first cities, people could work at jobs other than farming. This was a radical departure from the traditional economies of the Stone Age. A **traditional economy** relies on custom or tradition and tends not to change over time.

Social Classes In cities, social organization became more complex. People were ranked according to their jobs, which led to the growth of social classes. Priests and nobles usually occupied the top level of an ancient society. Next came a small class of wealthy merchants, followed by artisans. Below them stood the vast majority of people— peasant farmers who lived in the surrounding villages and produced food for the city.

In many civilizations, slaves occupied the lowest social level. Poor families sometimes sold family members into slavery to pay their debts. Others were prisoners captured in war. Because male captives were often killed, women and children made up the largest number of slaves in some societies.

Arts and Architecture The arts and architecture of ancient civilizations expressed the talents, beliefs, and values of the people who created them. Temples and palaces often dominated the city landscape, reassuring people of the strength and power of their government and religion.

Skilled workers decorated these massive buildings. In museums today, you can see the temple wall paintings and statues of gods and goddesses.

Furniture and jewelry found in ancient tombs around the world are also on display. These artifacts give ample evidence of the artistic genius of the first civilizations.

Basic Features of Civilizations

FEATURE	DESCRIPTION
Cities	• Larger and more complex than villages • Support the other features of civilization
Governments	• Coordinate public-works projects such as bridge and dam construction • Establish laws and organize defense
Complex Religions	• Belief in one or more Gods or Goddesses • Institution of rituals
Job Specialization	• Different types of jobs that lead workers to specialize on one task
Social Classes	• Ranked groups are based on job or status
Arts and Architecture	• Artwork that expresses a society's talents, beliefs, and values
Public Works	• Large-scale projects for the benefit of a city and its people
Writing	• Structured writing system initially used by governments and merchants to record important information

>> **Analyze Charts** Which features do you think most affected the daily lives of average people?

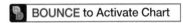 BOUNCE to Activate Chart

Public Works Closely linked to the temples and palaces in the cities were vast public works that strong rulers ordered to be built. Such projects included irrigation systems, roads, bridges, and defensive walls.

These projects were costly, requiring masses of human labor and sometimes even the lives of workers. Still, they were meant to benefit the city, protect it from attack, ensure its food supply, and, of course, enhance the reputation of its ruler.

Writing Almost all early civilizations developed a critical skill—writing. Writing may have begun in temples, where priests needed to record precise rituals and prayers, accurate information about the seasons, and amounts of grain collected. Other writing systems may have developed around rulers who proclaimed their great achievements on stone monuments.

Writing systems emerged in different places at different times. They varied greatly. Yet all represented organized efforts to record information. Archaeologists have found masses of ancient writings, ranging from treaties and tax rolls to business and marriage contracts.

Early writing was often made up of **pictographs** (or pictograms), simple drawings that look like the objects they represent. In time, symbols were added.

They might stand for sounds of words or for ideas that could not be expressed easily in pictures.

As writing grew more complex, only specially trained people called **scribes** could read and write. Scribes were educated in temple schools and kept records for priests, rulers, and merchants. Only a few societies permitted women to attend temple schools. As a result, women were generally excluded from becoming scribes, an occupation that could lead to political power.

Nomads and City Dwellers Many people remained nomads, following traditional routes as they grazed herds. Nomadic cultures did not build cities. Their governments were simple. Nomadic peoples, however, had their own leaders, religious beliefs, and technologies. They often excelled in the arts. Many nomads had rich oral traditions in poetry. They composed fine music, developed beautiful weavings, and produced exquisite jewelry.

Nomads and city dwellers came into contact through trade and warfare. Nomads needed goods produced by settled peoples. So they traded goods such as meat, furs, and livestock for the grains, cloth, and weapons of city dwellers.

The relationship between nomads and settled people was a driving force throughout history. At times, conflict replaced trade when new nomadic people moved into an area. Nomads might attack settlements or even organize a large enough force to topple great civilizations. Once they conquered a civilization, however, they in turn became settled peoples, giving up the nomadic way of life.

☑ **IDENTIFY CENTRAL IDEAS** What role did religion play in early civilizations?

Civilizations Change

All societies and civilizations change. In fact, history itself might be defined as the story of these changes. Ancient civilization changed in many ways over time. Among the chief causes of change were shifts in the physical environment and interactions among people.

The Effect of the Environment Like their Stone Age ancestors, people in early civilizations depended heavily on the physical environment. They needed ample rain and fertile soil to produce crops. Significant changes in the environment could have an immediate impact on people's lives.

At times, sudden, drastic events such as an earthquake, flood, or volcano could devastate a community. Survivors had to rebuild on the ruins. Farming the same land year after year could reduce soil fertility. Silt could clog rivers, making waters too salty. Environmental catastrophes—whether sudden or slow—could force people to abandon cities and migrate to new areas.

Cities needed resources such as stone, timber, and metals, along with land. If people used up all the local timber or ran out of other building resources, they would have to adapt to this scarcity. They might, for example, trade with areas where such resources were available. Or they might use alternate building materials such as reeds.

Cultural Diffusion Change often came as a result of **cultural diffusion,** the spread of ideas, customs, and technologies from one people to another. Cultural diffusion occurred through migration, trade, and warfare.

As famine, drought, or other disasters led people to migrate, they interacted with other people whose cultures differed from their own. As a result of such interactions, people often shared and adapted skills, customs, and ideas. In prehistoric times, migrating people could have shared technologies that led to farming.

As people settled in cities, trade increased. Trade is one of the greatest forces for cultural diffusion because it introduces people to new goods, ideas, and technologies. In ancient times, skills such as bronze-making and writing passed from one society to another through trade. Traders spread religious beliefs, artistic styles, and oral histories.

Warfare brought change too. Often, victorious armies imposed their rule and culture on the people they defeated. Sometimes, though, the process worked in reverse. Nomadic conquerors were often absorbed into city life.

In China, for example, conquering people were often absorbed by China's more advanced civilization. To avoid this, some nomadic rulers lived in camps outside the city, keeping their own customs.

Cities Become City-States Some Neolithic cities expanded to become city-states. A **city-state** is a political unit that includes a city and its surrounding lands and villages. Peasants in these surrounding lands had to give a significant portion of each harvest to support the government and temples. Sumerian civilization in the Tigris-Euphrates Valley consisted of a number of rival city-states.

The First Empires During ancient times, ambitious rulers conquered a wide swath of land that included many cities and villages. They created the first empires. An **empire** is a group of states or territories

>> This store room in Pompeii shows various bowls and the remains of one person who was buried alive after a volcano rained hot ash down on the ancient city.

controlled by one ruler. For the conquered people, defeat was often painful and cruel. As you will read, the rulers of these empires imposed their government on many peoples.

☑ **CONNECT** How did warfare influence cultural diffusion?

☑ ASSESSMENT

1. **Compare** How did the development of early Asian and African civilizations compare to the development of early American civilizations?

2. **Explain** How was the need for a food supply related to the development of government in the first cities?

3. **Summarize** How did the establishment of a writing system change civilization?

4. **Draw Conclusions** How did trade enable cultural diffusion?

5. **Quest Connections** How did cultures change with the development of early civilizations?

>> The ancient Egyptians built grand palaces, tombs, and other buildings that showed the wealth of their civilization.

The Legend of Yu the Great, from the *Shujing*

China's first dynasty, the Xia Dynasty, emerged around 2000 B.C. in the Huang River valley at the dawn of Chinese civilization. For hundreds of years, people memorized and retold accounts of the Xia Dynasty. The *Shujing* did not collect these accounts in writing until around 400 B.C. This ancient source includes the legend of Yu the Great, the founder of the Xia Dynasty.

According to this legend, Yu tamed the flooding waters of the Huang. Evidence shows that the Huang valley flooded during the 1900s B.C. much as this legend describes. The legend of Yu may be one of the earliest historical accounts of Chinese civilization.

>> A later portrait of the legendary emperor Yu the Great

Primary Source

In ancient times, Emperor Yao was . . . able to make the capable and virtuous distinguished . . . He also regulated and polished the people of his domain, who all became brightly intelligent. Finally, he united and harmonized the myriad states of the empire. . . .

The Emperor said, "Who will search out for me a man for these times, whom I may promote and put to work?"

Fangqi said, "There is your son and heir Zhu, who is highly intelligent."

The Emperor said, "Alas! He is insincere and quarrelsome. Is he really capable?" . . . "Who will search out for me a man worthy for me to choose?"

Huandou said, "Oh! There is the Minister of Works, who just completed some modest work."

The Emperor said, "Alas! He can talk when he's idle, but his actions turn out differently. He only appears to be reliable.

See! The floods attack the heavens." The Emperor said, "Oh! Minister of the Four Mountains, destructive in their overflow are the waters of the flood. In their vast extent they embrace the mountains and overtop the hills, threatening the heavens . . . so that the common people groan and murmur. Is there a capable man who can manage this?"

☑ **DETERMINE CENTRAL IDEAS** What urgent problem does the Emperor want a capable manager to solve?

Everyone there said, "Ah! What about Kuan?"

. . .

The Emperor said [to Kuan], "Go and do your duty!" For nine years he worked, but he accomplished nothing.

. . .

The Emperor said, "Show me someone among the nobility, or even from among the poor and wretched."

Everyone there said, "There is a . . . man among the common people called Yu Shun."

The Emperor said, "Yes? I've heard of him. What do you have to say about him?"

The Minister said, "He is the son of a blind man. His father is stubborn and combative. His stepmother is insincere. His half brother Xiang is arrogant. He has been able to live among them in harmony thanks to his respect for his family. He has managed to bring them under control, so that they no longer engage in wickedness."

☑ **DRAW INFERENCES** What qualities of Yu Shun might make him appealing to the Emperor?

The Emperor said, "I will try him!"

. . .

The Emperor said, "Come, Yu. The floodwaters filled me with dread, when you accomplished truly [what you had promised], and completed your service—thus showing your superiority to other men. Full of hardworking seriousness in the service of the country, and sparing in your spending on your family, and this without being full of yourself and elated, you [again] show your superiority to other men. You are without any prideful assumption, but no one under heaven can compete with you in ability; you make no boasting, but no one under heaven can compete with you in merit. I see how great is your virtue, how admirable your vast achievements. The appointment of Heaven rests on your person; you must eventually ascend [the throne] of the emperor.

☑ **IDENTIFY SUPPORTING DETAILS** What qualities or achievements of Yu make the Emperor think that Yu should follow him as emperor?

[These are the accomplishments of Yu:]

Yu divided the land. Following the course of the hills, he cut down the trees. He determined the highest hills and largest rivers. . . .

The nine branches of the He [River] were made to keep their proper channels. . . . and the Wei and Zi were made to keep their [old] channels. . . . The Huai and the Yi [rivers] were regulated. . . .

[Thus], throughout the nine provinces a similar order was put in place:—the grounds along the waters were everywhere made livable; the hills were cleared of their superfluous wood . . . ; the sources of the rivers were cleared; the marshes were well contained; and access to the capital was secured for all within the four seas.

☑ **IDENTIFY CAUSE AND EFFECT** What were the main effects of Yu's actions?

☑ ASSESSMENT

1. **Cite Evidence** What does this source suggest about the ways in which China's emperors governed?

2. **Draw Inferences** Why might the emperor's advisers hesitate to suggest that he appoint a man from "among the common people"?

3. **Hypothesize** Why might Yu's origin "among the common people" make him a popular figure for later generations of Chinese?

4. **Draw Conclusions** Why might a man who had tamed floods be seen as a heroic founding figure in a river valley civilization?

Connections to Today

Food-processing workers producing sweets on an assembly line

Take Action to Understand Our Food Supply

During the Neolithic Revolution, people first began growing crops and raising livestock for their own families. Today, food goes through a complex process on its way from the farm to the consumer's table.

1. **Choose** Select one of the following topics related to food in today's world:

   - **Where supermarkets get their food:** Research how food gets to grocery stores. What are all the steps from farms to store shelves? What are the benefits and drawbacks of this system?

   - **Food deserts:** What happens when there are no grocery stores nearby? Research food deserts, their impact on health, and efforts to fix the problem.

   - **Eating local:** Because transporting food uses energy, many people seek to eat locally grown food. Research the benefits and drawbacks of the Community Sustained Agriculture (CSA) model.

2. **Ask Questions** Make a list of questions you have about your topic.

3. **Learn** about the topic. Find both sides of the main issues and disagreements about this topic. Collect specific statistics relating to your topic.

4. **Write a Letter** Write a letter to the editor of a local newspaper or local official with your findings. Raise issues you have found and suggest possible solutions.

Use the texts, quizzes, interactivities, Quest Inquiries, Flipped Videos, and other resources from this Topic to prepare for the Topic Test.

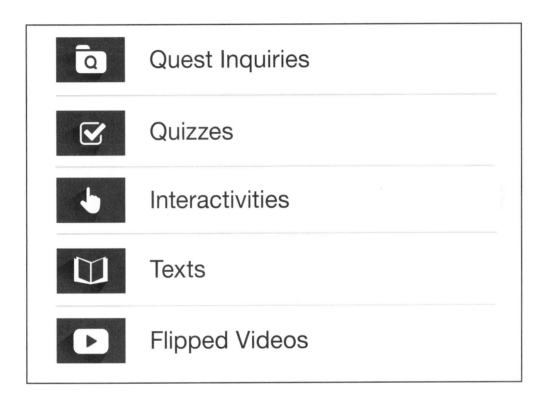

Quest Inquiries

Quizzes

Interactivities

Texts

Flipped Videos

While online you can also check the progress you've made learning the topic and course content by viewing your grades, test scores, and assignment status.

LESSON SUMMARIES

Use these Lesson Summaries, and the longer versions available online, to review the key ideas for each lesson in this Topic.

Lesson 1: Learning About Our Past

Historians, archaeologists, and anthropologists use careful research and observation to learn about the human past. Many scientists think that modern humans first arose in Africa.

Lesson 2: The Neolithic Revolution

During the Old Stone Age, people hunted and gathered plants. During the Neolithic Period or New Stone Age, people learned to farm. This greatly changed the way they lived. They began to live in settled villages and develop new technologies.

Lesson 3: Civilization Begins

Cities first developed in Africa and Asia in river valleys where conditions favored farming. The first civilizations, involving organized governments and complex ways of life, developed in these river valleys and in fertile regions in the Americas.

QUEST! FINDINGS

Create Your Early Cultures Video Game Refer to your responses to the Quest Connections to help you create your video game to present to the class. Use the rubric and other Quest resources online to guide your work.

GO ONLINE to access lesson summaries

VISUAL REVIEW

Use these graphics to review some of the key terms, people, and ideas from this Topic.

Scholars Who Study the Past

HISTORIANS	ANTHROPOLOGISTS/ARCHAEOLOGISTS
Study and write about the people and events of history	Study the origins and developments of people and their societies during prehistory and history; study physical and cultural traits of people
Primarily analyze written records; also analyze artifacts	Primarily analyze artifacts and material remains; also analyze written records
Evaluate the evidence using reasonable judgments and the work of other scholars	Evaluate the evidence using reasonable judgments, modern innovations, and the work of other types of scholars
Interpret and explain the evidence	Interpret and explain the evidence
Sort out disagreements over the evidence and change theories in light of new evidence	Sort out disagreements over the evidence and change theories in light of new evidence

Key Stages of Human Development

OLD STONE AGE	NEW STONE AGE	RISE OF CIVILIZATIONS
• creation of stone, bone, and wood tools and weapons • use of fire • spoken language • ability to travel across water in boats • belief in a spiritual world • creation of cave paintings • burial of the dead	• farming and domestication of plants and animals • settling of permanent villages • gaining of prestige by warriors • appearance of difference in wealth • creation of first calendars • more elaborate tools and new technologies	• production of surpluses of food • expansion of populations • development of civilizations, with cities and governments • government oversight of large-scale projects • belief in polytheistic religions • job specialization • development of social classes • development of art and architecture • invention of writing systems • expansion of some cities into city-states and empires

KEY TERMS, PEOPLE, AND IDEAS

1. How are **artifacts** used by historians?

2. Describe the significance of the work done by **Louis** and **Mary Leakey.**

3. Why were Old Stone Age people **nomads**?

4. Why is the **Neolithic Revolution** considered a turning point for humanity?

5. What do burial customs suggest about the beliefs of early peoples?

6. How did **surplus** food production affect life for Neolithic people?

7. Describe the characteristics of river valley civilizations.

8. How did the rise of cities contribute to the emergence of **artisans**?

9. How did **cultural diffusion** affect ancient civilizations?

CRITICAL THINKING

10. **Summarize** What were the basic features of early civilizations?

11. **Explain** Why was it important for farming societies to create calendars?

12. **Summarize** How were government and religion closely linked in early civilizations?

13. **Analyze Information** What factors do you think contributed to the migration of early peoples?

14. **Draw Conclusions** How did job specialization lead to the emergence of social classes in early civilizations?

15. **Make Comparisons** Compare the ways Old Stone Age hominids adapted the environment to the ways that Neolithic farmers adapted the environment to their needs.

16. **Analyze Images** What kinds of information might this archaeologist be hoping to find?

17. **Writing Activity: Write an Explanatory Essay** After the discovery of Lucy's skeleton in 1974, Donald Johanson said:

> "Normally, we are happy to find a fragment of jaw, a few isolated teeth, a bit of an arm, a bit of a skull. But to find associated body parts is extremely rare. I realized that . . . it was going to be important because so few discoveries had arms associated with legs, bits of skull associated with a pelvis."

What do you think this find might have revealed to Johanson's research team about early hominids? Using what you read and the information from this Topic, write a brief essay noting conclusions that might have been reached.

18. **Connections to Today** Consider the energy required to grow, process, and transport the foods that we eat. What changes could we make in our food supply today if we wanted to reduce energy consumed by food production and transport in order to reduce the impact of food production on the environment?

DOCUMENT-BASED QUESTIONS

When archaeologists make new finds, they are not always sure exactly what they have discovered. Read the documents below describing the finds of researchers, then answer the questions that follow.

DOCUMENT A

"Scientists have discovered a new species of ancient human that lived 18,000 years ago on an island east of the Java Sea—a prehistoric hunter.... These "little people" stood about three feet tall and had heads the size of a grapefruit...The research team...described the remains—a fairly complete skull, the jawbone and much of the skeleton—as those of a 30-year-old woman...The team also found...the remains of between five and seven people in all."

—*Guy Gugliotta,* Washington Post, *October 28, 2004*

DOCUMENT B

"So what was this strange creature, and what was it doing on [the island of] Flores? The [researchers] have had to make difficult choices in deciding how to classify the creature, although it is clear that this person was definitely not a modern human. The small brain size and hip-bone shape might favour classification as an australopithecine, whereas the size and shape of the skull might suggest a primitive form of *H. erectus*. Given the unique combination of features, the [researchers] have decided to give the specimen a new name: *"Homo floresiensis."*

—*Chris Stringer,* Nature, *October 27, 2004*

DOCUMENT C

"The researchers estimate that the tiny people lived on [the island of] Flores from about 95,000 years ago until at least 13,000 years ago. The scientists base their theory on charred bones and stone tools found on the island. The [tools] were apparently used to hunt big game....The Flores people used fire in hearths for cooking and hunted stegodon, a primitive dwarf elephant found on the island... Almost all of the stegodon bones, associated with the human artifacts are of juveniles [youths], suggesting the tiny humans selectively hunted the smallest stegodons."

—*Hillary Mayell, nationalgeographic.com, October 27, 2004*

DOCUMENT D

An adult *Homo floresiensis* skull (left) beside an adult modern human skull

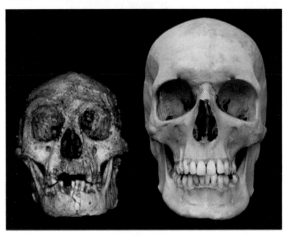

19. Documents A and C describe the discovery of
    A. modern human remains.
    B. australopithecine remains.
    C. *Homo erectus* remains.
    D. *Homo floresiensis* remains.

20. Which is NOT a theory that researchers have expressed about the tiny hominids whose remains were found in Flores?
    A. The tiny hominids lived at least 13,000 years ago.
    B. The tiny hominids were juveniles.
    C. The tiny hominids had small heads and brains.
    D. The tiny hominids hunted dwarf elephants.

21. Which is the most accurate conclusion that can be drawn from Document D about the relative sizes of *Homo floresiensis* and modern human adults?
    A. Modern human adults have larger bodies than *Homo floresiensis* adults.
    B. Modern human adults have larger skulls than *Homo floresiensis* adults.
    C. The modern human skull pictured is larger than the *Homo floresiensis* skull pictured.
    D. The *Homo floresiensis* skull pictured is older than the modern human skull pictured.

22. **Writing Tasks** Which information given in Documents A, B, C, and D seems the most reliable to you? Use information from the Topic along with specific information from these documents to support your answer.

The Ancient Middle East and Egypt
(3200 B.C.–500 B.C.)

ESSENTIAL QUESTION How much does geography affect people's lives?

Gold burial mask of King Tutankhamen

Connections to Today

What should government do? While there are many possible answers to that question, governments are often responsible for the construction and maintenance of roads, bridges, and other public works projects.

Thousands of years ago, early governments used their resources for similar projects. In this topic, you'll read about the construction of large monuments and other public works, such as temples, pyramids, and roads. How do governments today make decisions about how to use public resources?

Learn about the story of Hatshepsut, a ruler of ancient Egypt.

 BOUNCE to Activate My Story Video

Topic 2 Overview

In this Topic, you will learn about the civilizations that developed thousands of years ago in the Middle East and Egypt. These civilizations were a powerful influence on those that came later, affecting the development of science, culture, religion, and government. Look at the lesson outline and explore the timeline. As you study this Topic, you will complete the Quest Inquiry.

LESSON OUTLINE

2.1 A Civilization Emerges in Sumer

2.2 Empires in Mesopotamia

2.3 The Hebrews and the Origins of Judaism

2.4 Egyptian Civilization

Key Events in the Ancient Middle East and Egypt

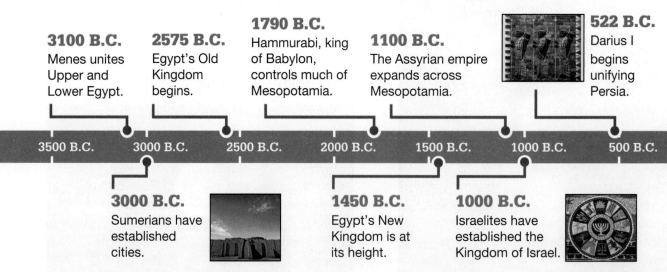

3100 B.C.
Menes unites Upper and Lower Egypt.

2575 B.C.
Egypt's Old Kingdom begins.

1790 B.C.
Hammurabi, king of Babylon, controls much of Mesopotamia.

1100 B.C.
The Assyrian empire expands across Mesopotamia.

522 B.C.
Darius I begins unifying Persia.

3500 B.C.   3000 B.C.   2500 B.C.   2000 B.C.   1500 B.C.   1000 B.C.   500 B.C.

3000 B.C.
Sumerians have established cities.

1450 B.C.
Egypt's New Kingdom is at its height.

1000 B.C.
Israelites have established the Kingdom of Israel.

QUEST!

INQUIRY

What Is the Function of the Law?

Ancient Mesopotamians, Egyptians, and Israelites were the first to formulate law codes that reflected the values and beliefs of their societies. In this Quest, you will research examples of law codes as well as investigate the writings of people in the legal profession to answer this question: What is the function of the law?

STEP

With a partner, write a definition for a law and share it with the class. Compare and contrast the definitions.

STEP

Examine the documents relating to what the function of law is. Determine the central idea of each and evaluate the authors' differing points of view.

STEP

Write a clear, coherent essay supporting the conclusions you have drawn. Address the strengths and limitations of your position and respond to at least one opposing position.

STEP 4

Revise your writing. Is your paper logically organized? Did you use specific evidence from the documents to support your viewpoint? Share your finished work with the class.

GO ONLINE to access complete Quest materials

Gilgamesh, king of Uruk, sought eternal life and obtained the plant of youth. However, a snake ate it, which, according to the legend, is why people do not live forever.

BOUNCE to Activate Flipped Video

Objectives

Understand how geography influenced the development of civilization in the Fertile Crescent.

Outline the main features of Sumerian civilization.

Explain how the advances in learning made by the Sumerians left a lasting legacy for later peoples to build on.

Key Terms

Fertile Crescent
Mesopotamia
Sumer
The Epic of
  Gilgamesh
ziggurat
hierarchy
cuneiform

A Civilization Emerges in Sumer

The Middle East was home to Sumerian civilization, one of the world's first civilizations. In part because of its location and other environmental features, the ancient Middle East posed unique challenges to this early civilization. The Sumerians were the first of many peoples to contribute to the civilization of the region. They made distinctive contributions that influenced a long line of later people both in the Middle East and in other parts of the world.

Civilizations Arise in the Fertile Crescent

Geography of the Fertile Crescent Sumerian civilization rose more than 5,000 years ago along the Tigris and Euphrates rivers in what is today Iraq. The Tigris-Euphrates Valley lies in the eastern **Fertile Crescent,** an area that stretches in an arc from the Persian Gulf to the Mediterranean Sea.

Early on, the fertile soil of the Tigris-Euphrates Valley attracted Stone Age farmers, who began to raise crops on the land. In time, their descendants produced the surplus food needed to support growing populations. Much later, the ancient Greeks called the Tigris-Euphrates Valley **Mesopotamia,** which means "between the rivers." Around 3300 B.C., the world's first civilization developed in southeastern Mesopotamia, in a region called **Sumer.** Over the centuries, a wide variety of civilizations would emerge in Mesopotamia.

The Tigris and Euphrates rivers flow from the highlands of modern-day Turkey through Iraq into the Persian Gulf. In the spring or early summer, melting snows from the mountains can cause the rivers to overflow. In some years, savage floods cause huge damage. Despite the danger of flooding, farmers planted a variety of crops. Silt left by floodwaters made the soil fertile. Good soil meant that the people of Mesopotamia could rely on a stable food supply in most years.

A World Crossroads The Fertile Crescent has often been called the crossroads of the world in part because it commands access to three continents: Asia, Africa, and Europe. The region has few natural barriers. Nomadic herders, ambitious invaders, and traders moved through the deserts and crossed the mountains leading into the Fertile Crescent. As a result, the region also became a crossroads where people and ideas met and mingled. Each new group that arrived made its own contributions to the turbulent history of the region. In time, the civilizations that emerged in this region passed on their achievements, which spread both eastward toward India and westward into Europe.

Sumerians Overcome Environmental Challenges Control of the Tigris and Euphrates was key to the rise of civilization in Mesopotamia. From time to time, the rivers rose in terrifying floods that washed away topsoil and destroyed mud-brick villages. In ancient times, people told stories about the wanderings of a hero named Gilgamesh.

Eventually, these stories were collected into a long narrative poem, **_The Epic of Gilgamesh._** It describes a great flood that destroys the world. Archaeologists have found clear evidence that catastrophic floods occurred regularly in ancient times. In addition to floods, lower Mesopotamia suffered summer droughts and hot winds, which could turn fertile soil to dust, shrivel crops, and cause famine.

To survive, early farming communities along the rivers had to work together to build dikes, dams, and irrigation systems. Over time, the construction and upkeep of increasingly complex irrigation systems led to the rise of an elaborate, well-run government. Temple priests and, later, royal officials provided the leadership needed to ensure cooperation and a large work force. They organized villagers to build dikes to hold back floodwaters and irrigation ditches to carry water to fields.

Successful farming communities in Mesopotamia grew into cities, which gave rise to Sumerian civilization. Like river valley civilizations that emerged in other parts of the world, Sumerian civilization thrived thanks to fertile soil, water, and the complex organization of government, religion, and specialized classes.

Sumerian City-States By 3000 B.C., Sumerians built a number of cities. Each city and the land surrounding formed a city-state. The Sumerians had

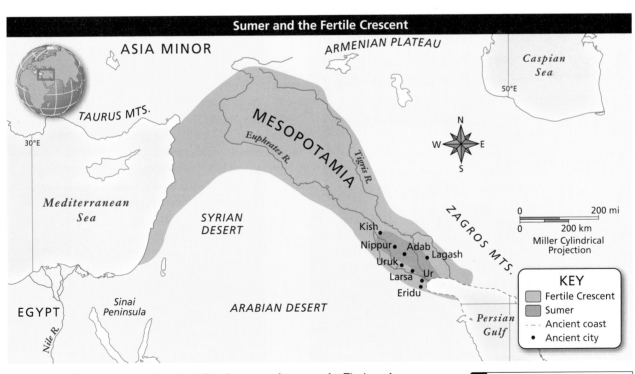

Sumer and the Fertile Crescent

>> **Analyze Maps** A series of early civilizations arose between the Tigris and Euphrates rivers, called Mesopotamia. What natural features may have limited the expansion of these civilizations?

BOUNCE to Activate Map

few natural resources to build these cities, but they made the most of what they did have. They lacked building materials such as timber or stone, so they built with clay and water. They used the clay to make bricks, which they shaped in wooden molds and dried in the sun. These bricks were the building blocks for some of the world's first great cities, such as Ur and Uruk.

☑ **IDENTIFY MAIN IDEAS** How did geography influence the development of civilizations in the Fertile Crescent?

Sumerian Civilization Develops

Beginning around 3500 B.C., a number of cities had emerged in Mesopotamia, each numbering in the tens of thousands. Each city and the land surrounding formed a city-state. The Sumerians had few natural resources, but they made the most of what they had. They lacked building materials such as timber or stone, so they made bricks of clay. These bricks were the building blocks for some of the world's first great cities, such as Ur and Uruk.

>> The Ziggurat of Ur is an ancient temple built by Sumerians to honor their moon god, Nanna. Ziggurats were part of a temple complex that usually served as the administrative center of the city.

The First Cities Sumerian cities had broad avenues used for religious processions or victory parades. The largest buildings were **ziggurats** (ZIG oo rats), pyramid-temples that soared toward the heavens. On top of each ziggurat stood a shrine to a particular god or goddess. Each city had its own chief god or goddess, but it might have several ziggurats honoring other gods.

Rulers lived in magnificent palaces with spacious courtyards. Most people, though, lived in tiny houses packed in a web of narrow alleys and lanes. Artisans who practiced the same trade, such as weavers or carpenters, lived and worked in the same street. These workshop-lined streets formed a bazaar, the ancestor of today's shopping mall.

Economic Life Trade brought riches to the Sumerian cities. Traders sailed along the rivers or risked the dangers of desert travel to exchange goods with distant regions. Archaeologists have found goods from as far away as Egypt and India in the rubble of Sumerian cities. Although it is unclear where and when the wheel was invented, the Sumerians may have made the first wheeled vehicles. Using wheeled carts, Sumerian traders were able to carry larger loads on longer journeys.

Government Rival city-states often battled for control of land and water. For protection, people turned to war leaders. Over time, these war leaders became hereditary rulers, leading to the rise of monarchies. A monarchy is a form of government led by a king or queen born into a ruling family.

In each city-state, the ruler was responsible for maintaining the city walls and irrigation systems. He led its armies in war and enforced the laws. As government grew more complex, the ruler employed scribes to carry out functions such as collecting taxes and keeping records. The ruler also had religious duties. In the early city-states, rulers probably were priest-kings; that is, the rulers were seen as the chief servants of the gods and led ceremonies meant to please them.

Social Classes Each Sumerian city-state had a distinct social **hierarchy** (HY ur ahr kee), or system of ranking groups. The highest class included the ruling family, leading officials, and high priests. A small middle class was made up of scribes, merchants, and artisans.

At the base of society were the majority of people, who were mostly peasant farmers. Some had their own land, but most worked land belonging to the king or to temples. Some were enslaved.

Sumerian Social Hierarchy

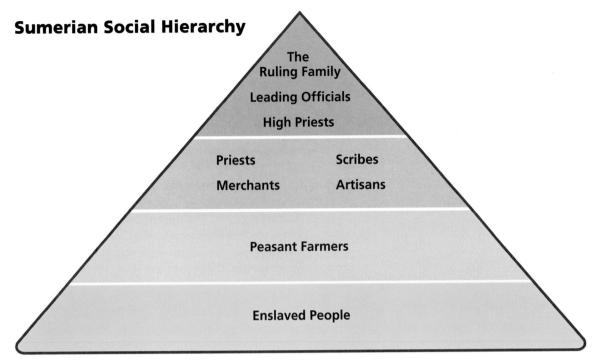

The
Ruling Family
Leading Officials
High Priests

Priests   Scribes
Merchants   Artisans

Peasant Farmers

Enslaved People

>> **Analyze Information** What does the information on the chart indicate about how Sumerian society supported itself?

Most enslaved people had been captured in war. Some, though, had sold themselves into slavery to pay their debts.

The role of women in Mesopotamian society changed over time. In Sumer, goddesses were highly honored in religious practice. Perhaps because of the importance of female deities, women held a higher social standing in Sumer than in later civilizations of the region. However, Sumerian women never held legal rights equal to those of men. But some rulers' wives had supervisory powers, and a number wrote songs about their husbands, revealing to later scholars that they had learned writing and music. On rare occasion, a woman may have inherited property.

Religious Beliefs Like most ancient peoples, the Sumerians were polytheistic, worshiping many gods. These gods were thought to control every aspect of life, especially the forces of nature. Sumerians believed that gods and goddesses behaved like ordinary people—they ate, drank, married, and raised families. Although the gods favored truth and justice, they were also responsible for causing violence and suffering.

Sumerians believed their highest duty was to keep their gods and goddesses happy and, by doing so, ensure the safety of their city-state. Each city-state had its own special god or goddess to whom people prayed and offered sacrifices of animals,

grain, or wine. Sumerian rulers served as the high priest for their city-state's chief deity, or god.

People celebrated many holy days with ceremonies and processions. The most important ceremony occurred at the new year when the king sought and won the favor of Inanna, the life-giving goddess of love. The king then took part in a symbolic wedding to Inanna. This ritual, Sumerians believed, would make the new year fruitful and prosperous.

The Sumerians believed in an afterlife. At death, they thought, a person descended into a grim underworld from which there was no release. In *The Epic of Gilgamesh*, a character describes the underworld as "the place where they [the dead] live on dust, their food is mud, / . . . and they see no light, living in blackness. . ."

Sumerian Writing By 3200 B.C., Sumerians had invented the earliest known writing. It was later called **cuneiform** (kyoo NEE uh fawrm), from the Latin word *cuneus* for "wedge," because scribes wrote by making wedge-shaped marks on clay tablets. Cuneiform grew out of a system of pictographs used to record goods brought to temple storehouses. Later, the Sumerians developed symbols to represent more complicated thoughts. As their writing evolved, the Sumerians used it to record not only economic exchanges but also myths, prayers, laws, and business contracts.

Sumerian scribes had to go through years of difficult schooling to acquire their skills. Discipline was strict. Untidy copying or talking in class could be punished by caning. Students who did well often learned about religion, mathematics, and literature as well.

☑ **SUMMARIZE** Describe the three levels of Sumerian society.

Sumer's Legacy

Beginning around 2500 B.C., conquering armies swept across Mesopotamia and gradually overwhelmed the Sumerian city-states. The newcomers built on Sumerian learning and advances in many fields. They then helped spread the Sumerian legacy across the Middle East.

Language and Culture Newcomers to the region adopted many ideas and innovations from the Sumerians. The myths and gods of the newcomers became mingled with those of Sumer. In the process, names changed. The Sumerian goddess Inanna, for example, became Ishtar.

The Akkadians, Babylonians, and Assyrians adapted cuneiform so it could be used with their own languages. These peoples then helped spread Sumerian learning across the Middle East.

The river-valley civilization that began in Sumer featured a number of elements, beyond a written language, that reappeared in other, later civilizations. Sumer's patriarchal family structure, agricultural-based economies, government structures, and the beginning of a trade base influenced later empires and the rise of classical civilizations, such as Greece and Rome. Later peoples also elaborated on Sumerian oral narratives, such as *The Epic of Gilgamesh*, which was written down in cuneiform by both the Akkadians and the Babylonians.

Astronomy and Mathematics Over the centuries, inventive Sumerians made advances in astronomy and mathematics. To measure and solve problems of calculation, they developed basic algebra and geometry. They based their number system on 60, dividing the hour into 60 minutes and the circle into 360 degrees, as we still do today.

Priests studied the skies, recording the movements of planets, stars, and the moon. This knowledge enabled them to make accurate calendars, which are essential to a farming society. Building on the learning of the Sumerians, later Mesopotamian astronomers developed ever more accurate calendars and learned to predict eclipses of the sun and moon.

Technology The Sumerians built the earliest known wheeled carts and wagons. They then developed the

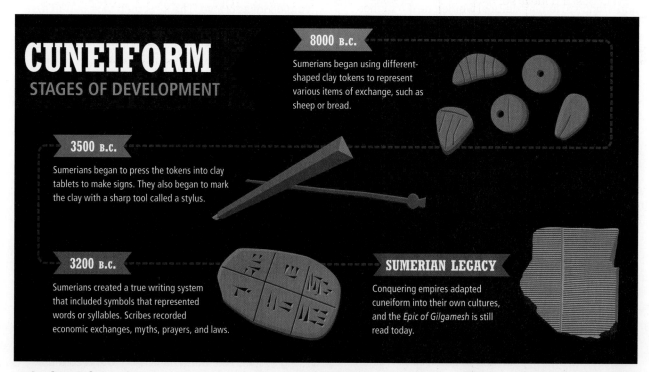

CUNEIFORM
STAGES OF DEVELOPMENT

8000 B.C.
Sumerians began using different-shaped clay tokens to represent various items of exchange, such as sheep or bread.

3500 B.C.
Sumerians began to press the tokens into clay tablets to make signs. They also began to mark the clay with a sharp tool called a stylus.

3200 B.C.
Sumerians created a true writing system that included symbols that represented words or syllables. Scribes recorded economic exchanges, myths, prayers, and laws.

SUMERIAN LEGACY
Conquering empires adapted cuneiform into their own cultures, and the *Epic of Gilgamesh* is still read today.

>> **Analyze Information** How did cuneiform writing allow Sumerians to communicate more effectively?

BOUNCE to Activate Gallery

potter's wheel, which is used to shape wet clay into bowls and other kinds of pottery. They used bronze to make tools and weapons and developed looms to weave cloth. Equally important was the technology and engineering skills they invented to build irrigation systems and flood control projects.

Achievements in the Arts Sumerians produced fine gold, wood, and stone carvings. They invented a stringed musical instrument, called the lyre, and performed on other instruments such as pipes and drums. Archaeologists have uncovered intricate jewelry in ivory and precious stones as well as small statues of gods and goddesses. Sumerians also produced cylinder seals, or small round stones bearing a carved design. These seals were rolled onto wet clay as a way of "signing" documents with the carved design representing the "name" of an individual or temple.

Sumerian Literature The early Sumerians had a rich oral literature, reaching far back in time. Oral poems told of the heroic deeds of warrior leaders. Eventually, Sumerian oral literature was written. Much of it was preserved by later peoples who conquered Mesopotamia.

An Ancient Heritage is Passed Along Even though the Sumerian city-states were conquered and the Sumerian language disappeared, Sumerian inventions and ideas survived. As you will read, many peoples conquered the Middle East, including the Akkadians, Babylonians, Assyrians, and Persians.

These people preserved and furthered Sumerian knowledge and achievements. The rich heritage of Mesopotamian civilizations was later passed on to the Greeks and Romans. From them, this ancient legacy was carried to the Western world. In this way, developments and innovations made more than 5,000 years ago came to shape Western civilization today.

☑ **SYNTHESIZE** What advances did the Sumerians make in mathematics and astronomy?

>> The Standard of Ur is a small wooden panel covered on both sides with mosaics composed of stones and jewels. This image shows a banquet scene with the king and his servants.

☑ ASSESSMENT

1. **Describe** What are some Sumerian inventions and advances in learning that influenced the development of later civilizations?

2. **Determine Relevance** How might the invention of cuneiform writing have strengthened Sumerian government and religious practices?

3. **Compare** In what way was Sumer both a monarchy and theocracy?

4. **Explain** What were two ways people typically became enslaved in Sumerian society?

5. **Synthesize** How did the geography of the Fertile Crescent affect the development of Sumer's economy?

6. **Connections to Today** Sumerian rulers were responsible for maintaining city walls and irrigation systems. What similar responsibilities do government leaders today have?

King Sargon created the first known empire, Akkad. He conquered Sumerian city-states one by one and expanded his empire from present-day Lebanon to the Taurus Mountains of Turkey.

🅑 BOUNCE to Activate Flipped Video

Objectives

Outline the achievements of the first empires that arose in Mesopotamia

Understand how conquests brought new empires and ideas into the Middle East.

Describe the major political, religious, and cultural influences of Persia.

Summarize the contributions the Phoenicians made to the ancient Middle East.

Key Terms

Sargon
Hammurabi
codify
criminal law
civil law
Nebuchadnezzar
bureaucracy
barter economy
money economy
Zoroaster
colony
alphabet

Empires in Mesopotamia

Invasion and conquest were prominent features in the history of the ancient Middle East. Again and again, nomadic peoples or ambitious warriors descended on the rich cities of the Fertile Crescent. While many invaders simply looted and burned, some stayed to rule. Powerful leaders created large, well-organized empires, bringing peace and prosperity for a time to the region. Over several thousand years, these empires made advances in government, technology, and learning that influenced later civilizations from Greece and Rome to India and beyond.

Empires Emerge in Mesopotamia

The First Empire About 2300 B.C., **Sargon,** the ruler of neighboring Akkad, invaded and conquered the city-states of Sumer. He built the first empire known to history. An empire is a group of regions or countries that are controlled by one ruler or government. By uniting many groups of people, Sargon ruled over the first multicultural empire in Mesopotamia. Sargon's remarkable achievement did not last long. After his death, other invaders swept into the land between the rivers, tumbling his empire into ruin.

Scholars link the decline of the Akkadian empire to changes in rainfall. Its downfall came at a time when severe drought led people from the dry north to migrate into the irrigated lands of southern Mesopotamia ruled by Sargon's heirs. Archaeologists have uncovered evidence of a 100-mile long wall built to hold back the invaders, but without success. The newcomers disrupted the social and political structure of the empire, which collapsed.

In time, the Sumerian city-states revived, and resumed their endless power struggles. Eventually, new conquerors followed in Sargon's footsteps and imposed unity over the Fertile Crescent.

🖥 GO ONLINE to access your digital course

The Babylonian Empire About 1790 B.C., **Hammurabi** (hah muh RAH bee), king of Babylon, brought much of Mesopotamia under the control of his empire. He took steps to unite the large Babylonian empire, which included a variety of peoples with their own traditions. Perhaps his most lasting achievement was in the area of law. To ensure unity, he published a remarkable set of laws, known as the Code of Hammurabi.

Hammurabi's Code Hammurabi was not the author of the code that bears his name. Most of the laws had been around since Sumerian times. Hammurabi, however, wanted people to know the legal principles his government would follow. So he had artisans carve some 282 laws on a stone pillar for all to see. Hammurabi's Code was the first important attempt by a ruler to **codify,** or arrange and set down in writing, all the laws that would govern a state.

Hammurabi's Code was the first major collection of laws in history and was set out for all to see, even though few people could read. The code listed both **criminal laws,** dealing with murder, assault, and theft, and **civil laws,** dealing with private rights and matters, such as business contracts, property inheritance, taxes, marriage, and divorce. Most important, Hammurabi's Code embodied the idea that a ruler had a responsibility to ensure justice and order.

Hammurabi's Code was designed to ensure peace and project his power across his vast empire. Atop the pillar with his code, Hammurabi is shown receiving the laws directly from the Babylonian god Marduk. Over time, Hammurabi's Code influenced ideas about the responsibility of government to set up a uniform system of law for all people and to enforce the law. Although modern law codes are much changed from Hammurabi's time, they have their roots in this code.

Civil Law and Woman Many laws in the civil code aimed to protect the powerless, including women and enslaved people. Some laws allowed a woman to own property and pass it on to her children. One spelled out the rights of a married woman. If a woman was blameless for problems in her marriage, she could leave her husband and return to her father's home. If she were found to be at fault, however, she could be thrown into the river.

In general, Babylonian civil law strictly regulated the behavior of women. It expected a woman to remain in her husband's home and be dependent on him. A husband, however, had a legal duty to support her. The code also gave a father nearly unlimited authority over his children. The Babylonians believed that an orderly household, headed by a strong male authority, was necessary for a stable empire.

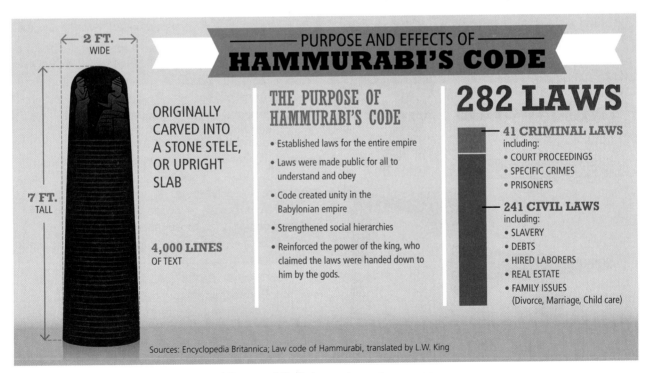

← 2 FT. → WIDE

7 FT. TALL

PURPOSE AND EFFECTS OF
HAMMURABI'S CODE

ORIGINALLY CARVED INTO A STONE STELE, OR UPRIGHT SLAB

4,000 LINES OF TEXT

THE PURPOSE OF HAMMURABI'S CODE

- Established laws for the entire empire
- Laws were made public for all to understand and obey
- Code created unity in the Babylonian empire
- Strengthened social hierarchies
- Reinforced the power of the king, who claimed the laws were handed down to him by the gods.

282 LAWS

41 CRIMINAL LAWS
including:
- COURT PROCEEDINGS
- SPECIFIC CRIMES
- PRISONERS

241 CIVIL LAWS
including:
- SLAVERY
- DEBTS
- HIRED LABORERS
- REAL ESTATE
- FAMILY ISSUES
  (Divorce, Marriage, Child care)

Sources: Encyclopedia Britannica; Law code of Hammurabi, translated by L.W. King

>> **Analyze Information** The purpose of Hammurabi's Code was to create common bonds among the diverse people of the society. Why was it important that Hammurabi's Code was a written legal code?

Criminal Law The laws in Hammurabi's Code also addressed criminal law. This branch of law deals with offenses against others, such as robbery, assault, or murder. The penalties varied according to the status of the victim or the offender. By today's standards, the punishments in Hammurabi's Code often seem cruel, following the principle of "an eye for an eye and a life for a life." For example, if a house collapsed because of poor construction and the owner died as a result, the builder of the house could be put to death. Still, Hammurabi's Code brought more order than older traditions, which allowed individuals or families to pursue unrestricted personal vengeance.

Hammurabi's Other Accomplishments Although most famous for his code of laws, Hammurabi took other steps to bring order and prosperity to his empire. He improved irrigation systems, organized a well-trained army, and ordered the repair of many temples. To encourage religious unity, he promoted Marduk, the patron god of Babylon, over older Sumerian gods. In time, Marduk became the chief god of Babylonian worship.

☑ **DRAW CONCLUSIONS** What was the most important and lasting legacy of Hammurabi's Code?

New Empires and Ideas

Later empires shaped the Middle East in different ways. Some conquerors, such as the Hittites, brought new skills to the region. Others uprooted the peoples they defeated. By forcing people to move elsewhere, these upheavals led to the spread of ideas. Even as warfare disrupted lives, trade continued, further helping the exchange of products and ideas.

Hittites and the Secret of Ironworking The Hittites pushed out of Asia Minor into Mesopotamia in about 1400 B.C. They had learned to extract iron from ore—an important new technology. Tools and weapons made with iron were harder and had sharper edges than those made out of bronze or copper. Because iron was plentiful, the Hittites were able to arm more people at less expense.

The Hittites tried to keep this valuable technology secret. But as their empire collapsed around 1200 B.C., Hittite ironsmiths migrated to serve customers elsewhere.

Migration, trade, and conquest slowly spread ironworking technology across Mesopotamia. In time, the use of iron weapons and tools was carried even farther across Asia, Africa, and Europe, ushering in the Iron Age.

>> The Babylonian empire is known for the flourishing of art, science, music, mathematics, astronomy, and literature. This Babylonian roller seal was used on official documents.

>> The Hittites, known for their ironwork, adapted and improved the horse-drawn chariot. Hittite charioteers used lances, bows and arrows, and axes like the ones shown in the photo.

🖐 BOUNCE to Activate Gallery

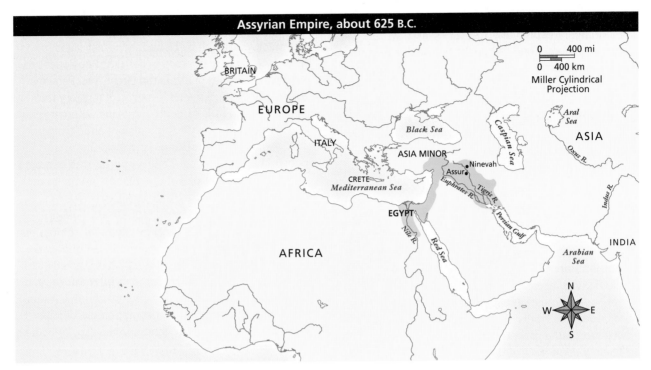

0 400 mi
0 400 km
Miller Cylindrical Projection

>> Analyze Maps The Assyrian empire controlled much of the land in the ancient Middle East. What earlier empires did the Assyrians conquer in order to build their large empire?

Assyrian Warriors Build a Warrior Empire

Among the many peoples who invaded the Fertile Crescent were the Assyrians. They were hardy nomads who had settled on the upper Tigris as early as 2000 B.C. There, they built a city-state named after their chief god, Assur, and acquired iron technology. Beginning about 1100 B.C., the Assyrians began expanding their empire across Mesopotamia. For 500 years, they spread terror among the peoples they conquered, earning a reputation as one of the most warlike people in history.

To frighten their enemies and ensure their power, Assyrian rulers boasted of their brutal treatment of the peoples they conquered. One told of capturing Babylon. He proclaimed, "The city and its houses, from top to bottom, I destroyed and burned with fire." The Assyrians collected tribute, or payments from conquered people, amassing great riches in this way.

Assyrian Society

Despite their fierce reputation, Assyrian rulers encouraged a well-ordered society. Riches from trade, tribute, and loot from war paid for splendid palaces in the well-planned cities. Assyrians were also the first rulers to develop extensive laws regulating life within the royal household. Under these rules, women of the palace were confined to secluded quarters and had to be veiled when they appeared in public.

At Nineveh (NIN uh vuh), King Assurbanipal (ahs ur BAH nee pahl) founded one of the world's first libraries. There, he kept cuneiform tablets that he ordered scribes to collect from all over the Fertile Crescent. Those tablets have provided modern scholars with a wealth of information about the ancient Middle East. The Assyrians did more than simply amass information from other people; they are often credited with developing glassmaking technology and making the first lock and key device.

The New Babylonian Empire In 612 B.C., shortly after Assurbanipal's death, neighboring peoples joined forces to crush the once-dreaded Assyrian armies. Before long, an aggressive and ruthless king, **Nebuchadnezzar** (neb yuh kud NEZ ur), revived the power of Babylon. His new Babylonian empire stretched from the Persian Gulf to the Mediterranean Sea.

Nebuchadnezzar oversaw the rebuilding of the canals, temples, walls, and palaces of Babylon. Near his main palace, Nebuchadnezzar is said to have built the famous Hanging Gardens—known as one of the "seven wonders of the ancient world." Although no remains have yet been found, the gardens were probably made by planting trees and flowering plants on the steps of a huge ziggurat. According to legend, Nebuchadnezzar had the gardens built to please his wife, who was homesick for the hills where she had grown up.

Nebuchadnezzar turned Babylon into a magnificent capital city. Centuries later, writers in the ancient world still spoke of it with awe and wonder. Surrounding the city was a moat and an 85-foot thick wall. Streams of people passed through nine great gateways dedicated to different gods. The famous Ishtar Gate, uncovered by modern archaeologists, was made of bright blue glazed bricks and decorated with lions symbolizing the goddess Ishtar, mythical dragons symbolizing the god Marduk, and bulls symbolizing the god Hadad. In the center of Babylon, Nebuchadnezzar enlarged and beautified ziggurats to the gods and restored the temple honoring Marduk, the city's chief god.

Babylonian Astronomy Under Nebuchadnezzar, the Babylonians pushed the frontiers of learning into new areas. Priest-astrologers were especially eager to understand the stars and planets, which they believed had a great influence on all events on Earth. Their observations of the heavens contributed to the growing knowledge of astronomy.

☑ **IDENTIFY** Name a significant contribution made by the Hittites, Assyrians, and Babylonians after each group's conquest in the Middle East.

Rise of the Persian Empire

The thick walls built by Nebuchadnezzar failed to hold back new conquerors. In 539 B.C., Babylon fell to the Persian armies of Cyrus the Great. The Persians eventually controlled a wide sweep of territory that stretched from Asia Minor to India, including present-day Turkey, Iran, Egypt, Afghanistan, and Pakistan.

In general, Persian kings were tolerant of the people they conquered. They respected the customs and religious traditions of the diverse groups in their vast empire.

Darius Unites Many Peoples The real unification of the Persian empire was accomplished under the emperor Darius I, who ruled from 522 B.C. to 486 B.C. A skilled organizer, Darius set up a **bureaucracy,** or a system of managing government through various bureaus or departments run by appointed officials. The efficient, well-run Persian bureaucracy became a model for later rulers.

To rule his vast empire, Darius divided the empire into provinces, each headed by a governor called a satrap. Each satrapy, or province, had to pay taxes based on its resources and wealth. Special officials, known as "the Eyes and Ears of the King," visited each province to check on the satraps.

A system of royal roads united the far-flung empire. To improve communication even further, the

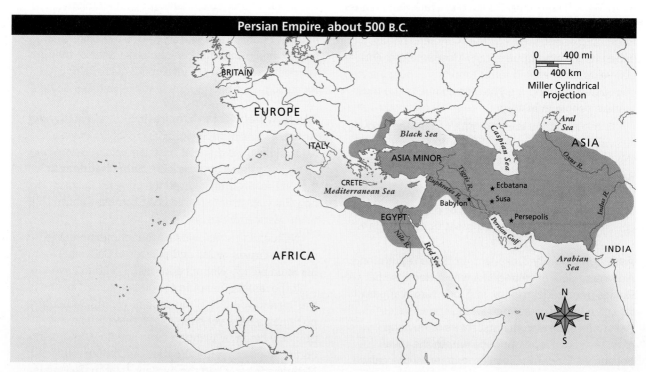

Persian Empire, about 500 B.C.

>> **Analyze Maps** Study the locations of the Persian capitals. Were they well placed for rule over the entire empire?

Persians set up a mail system to carry government documents. Government mail carriers sped along royal roads, dotted with rest stops supplied with fresh horses and new messengers.

Like Hammurabi, Darius adapted laws from the people he conquered and drew up a single code of laws for the empire. To encourage unity, he had hundreds of miles of roads built or repaired. Roads made it easier to communicate with different parts of the empire. Darius himself kept moving from one capital to another. In each, he celebrated important festivals and was seen by the people.

Persia's Economy To improve trade, Darius set up a common set of weights and measures to be used throughout the empire. He encouraged the use of coins, which the Lydians of Asia Minor had first introduced. Most people continued to be part of the **barter economy,** or the exchange of one set of goods or services for another. Coins, however, brought merchants and traders into an early form of a **money economy.** In a money economy, people pay for goods and services by exchanging tokens of an agreed value, such as coins. By minting his own gold coins, Darius hoped not only to project his power but also expand commerce and trade across his empire.

Birth of a New Religion Religious beliefs put forward by the Persian thinker **Zoroaster** (ZOH ruh as tur) also helped to unite the empire. Zoroaster lived about 600 B.C. He rejected the old Persian gods and taught that a single wise god, Ahura Mazda (AH hoo ruh MAHZ duh), ruled the world. Ahura Mazda, however, was in constant battle against Ahriman (AH rih mun), the prince of lies and evil. Each individual, said Zoroaster, had to choose which side to support.

Zoroastrian teachings were collected in a sacred book, the *Zend-Avesta.* According to Zoroaster, Ahura Mazda would triumph over the forces of evil. On a final judgment day, all individuals would be judged for their actions. Those who had done good would enter paradise. Evildoers would be condemned to eternal suffering.

Three other religions that emerged in the Middle East, Judaism, Christianity, and Islam, also stressed ideas of an individual's freedom to choose good or evil, and the latter two religions also included the concepts of heaven and hell, and a final judgment day.

Persia's Legacy The Persian empire is often seen as one of the most important civilizations of the ancient world in part because of its influence on later people. The empire stretched across a huge area and brought diverse people under its control. Its rulers

>> Nebuchadnezzar rebuilt Babylon. The Ishtar Gate to the city, a reconstruction of which is shown here, is famous for its blue bricks and depictions of various Babylonian gods.

>> These archers decorated the palace of Darius I, whose military campaigns expanded the Persian empire. Darius also encouraged cultural and artistic growth and developed judicial systems.

practiced tolerance for the cultural diversity of its many people. Even though Persian rulers followed Zoroastrian beliefs, they respected the gods of the Babylonians, Sumerians, Akkadians, and others. They developed efficient forms of government to rule their empires. Royal roads and the world's first mail system were models for later empires in the region.

Under Persian rule, scholars drew on 3,000 years of Mesopotamian learning and added their own advances to this rich heritage. In time, achievements of this Mesopotamian civilization filtered eastward into India and westward into Europe. Other conquerors would overwhelm the Persian empire. As you will read, the Greeks, under Alexander the Great, and later the Romans conquered much of the Persian empire. Both the Greeks and Romans picked up learning, technology, and many other ideas from Persian civilization.

☑ **DESCRIBE** Describe the steps Darius took to unite the Persian empire.

Phoenician Contributions

While powerful rulers subdued large empires, many small states of the ancient Middle East made their own contributions to the civilizations of the ancient Middle East. The Phoenicians (fuh NISH unz), for example, gained fame as sailors and traders.

They occupied a string of cities along the eastern Mediterranean coast, in the area that today is Lebanon and Syria.

Manufacturing and Trade Expands The coastal land was too narrow to support a large farming population. Instead, the resourceful Phoenicians turned to manufacturing and trade. They made glass from coastal sand. From a tiny sea snail, they produced a widely admired purple dye, called "Tyrian purple" after the city of Tyre.

Phoenicians traded with people all around the Mediterranean Sea. To promote trade, they set up colonies from North Africa to Sicily and Spain.

A **colony** is a territory settled and ruled by people from another land. A few Phoenician traders braved the stormy Atlantic and sailed as far as Britain. There, they exchanged goods from the Mediterranean for tin. Some scholars have suggested that a Phoenician expedition may have sailed down the Red Sea and followed the East African coast to its southern tip.

Phoenicians also used papyrus, a plant that they brought from Egypt, to make scrolls, or rolls of paper for books. The words *Bible* and *bibliography* come from the Phoenician city of Byblos.

The Phoenician Alphabet Historians have called the Phoenicians "carriers of civilization" because

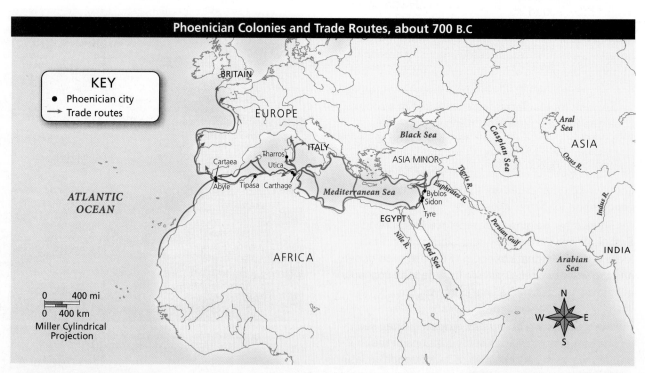

Phoenician Colonies and Trade Routes, about 700 B.C

KEY
• Phoenician city
→ Trade routes

>> **Analyze Maps** What information on the map supports the claim that the Phoenicians were skilled sailors?

BOUNCE to Activate Map

COMPARISON OF WRITING SYSTEMS

Phoenician	Early Greek	Early Latin	Modern English Capitals
✗	◁	⋏	A
৭	8	B	B
⦣	˥	‹	C
৭	Δ	D	D

>> **Analyze Information** How was the alphabet used today in English influenced by the Phoenicians?

they spread Middle Eastern civilization around the Mediterranean. Yet the Phoenicians made their own contribution to our world, creating the basis for our alphabet.

At first, the Phoenicians used cuneiform, but the uniform wedges in which symbols represent syllables or whole words may have proved too awkward. Phoenician traders needed a quick, flexible form of writing to record business deals. So they adapted the idea of using symbols to represent spoken sounds. Their system of 22 symbols for consonant sounds became the first real alphabet. An **alphabet** is a system of writing that uses symbols to represent a single basic sound, such as a consonant or vowel.

Later, the Greeks adapted the Phoenician alphabet and added symbols for the vowel sounds. From this Greek alphabet came the letters in which this sentence is written—that is, the alphabet we use today.

☑ **INTEGRATE INFORMATION** How has the Phoenician development of an alphabet been a lasting contribution to civilization?

☑ ASSESSMENT

1. **Synthesize** How did the Hittites contribute to cultural diffusion of early Mesopotamian culture and ideas, and what was one of their important technological advancements?

2. **Synthesize** Describe the location of Persia and some of its major influences.

3. **Compare** How was the culture of the Akkadian empire different from the culture of the civilizations that had come before it, such as the Sumerian city-states?

4. **Synthesize** Explain how the Phoenicians spread ideas among different peoples in the ancient Middle East.

5. **Quest Connections** Based on Babylon's civil code, what conclusion can be drawn regarding the relative power of a wife compared to that of her husband?

GO ONLINE to access this biography: Hammurabi

2.3

Torah in Hebrew means "teaching" or "guidance" and the Torah scroll, stored in a special decorated container called an ark, consists of the first five books of the Tanakh, the complete Hebrew Bible.

 BOUNCE to Activate Flipped Video

Objectives

Understand what made the ancient Israelites' belief system unique from others at the time.

Outline the main events in the early history of the Israelites.

Analyze the central moral and ethical ideas of Judaism.

Key Terms

monotheistic
Torah
Abraham
covenant
Moses
David
Solomon
patriarchal
Sabbath
prophet
ethics
Diaspora

The Hebrews and the Origins of Judaism

The ancient land of Israel was located at the far western end of the Fertile Crescent, the site of the modern State of Israel, on the eastern coast of the Mediterranean Sea. The first ancient Israelites inhabited small villages in the hill country of central Israel, called at that time Canaan, sharing land and many cultural attributes with other Canaanites. Although archaeology teaches us that they shared a common physical culture, the ancient Israelites' worship of a single God was unique. More than 3,000 years ago, the ancient Israelites developed the religion of Judaism, which became a defining feature of their culture. Today, Judaism is one of the world's major faiths.

The Ancient Israelites' Unique Belief System

The beliefs of the ancient Israelites, also called the Hebrews for the first three generations, differed in basic ways from those of nearby peoples. The Israelites were **monotheistic,** believing that there was only one god. At the time, all other peoples worshiped many gods.

A few religious leaders, such as the Egyptian pharaoh Akhenaton, spoke of a single powerful god. However, such ideas did not have the lasting impact that Israelite beliefs did.

The Israelites believed in an all-knowing, all-powerful God who was present everywhere. In their views, history and faith were interconnected. Each event reflected God's plan for the people of Israel, and the Israelites' choices and actions made the plan unfold. The **Torah** (TOH ruh), their most sacred text, is the story of the

GO ONLINE to access your digital course

ancient Israelites and their continuing relationship with God. The Torah includes the first five books of the Hebrew Bible—that is, the books of Genesis, Exodus, Leviticus, Numbers, and Deuteronomy. The Hebrew Bible includes a total of 24 books. Additional laws, customs, legends, and ethics written down much later make up another important lengthy text, the Talmud, containing over 12,000 pages.

☑ **SUMMARIZE** How did the beliefs of ancient Israelites differ from those of other nearby peoples?

The Ancient Israelites

Abraham is considered the father of the Israelites and their religion, Judaism. According to the Torah, Abraham was born near Ur in Mesopotamia, in present-day Iraq, and moved to Haran in present-day Syria about 2000 B.C. According to Jewish belief, God called to Abraham in Haran. God made an offer to Abraham, telling him that if he left his home and his family, then God would make him the founder of a great nation and bless him. So he and his extended family migrated, herding their sheep and goats into a region called Canaan (KAY nun). Abraham believed that everything was created by a single God, and he began to teach this belief to others.

God's Covenant With the Israelites The Israelites believed that God had made the following **covenant,** or promise and agreement, with Abraham:

You shall be the father of a multitude of nations. . . . I will make nations of you, and kings shall come forth from you. And I will establish my covenant between me and you and your descendants after you throughout their generations for an everlasting covenant, to be God to you and to your descendants after you. And I will give to you, and to your descendants after you, the land of your sojournings [short stay], all the land of Canaan. . . .

—Genesis 17:4–8

The covenant described in the Torah included two declarations that became the basis of two key beliefs of Judaism. First, God declared that He would have a special relationship with Abraham and his descendants. The Israelites believed that God had chosen them to fulfill certain obligations and duties in the world. Second, God declared that Canaan would one day belong to the Israelites. As a result, the Israelites viewed Canaan as their "promised land."

As described in the Book of Genesis, Abraham and his descendants left their home in Ur and adopted a nomadic lifestyle, traveling for many years.

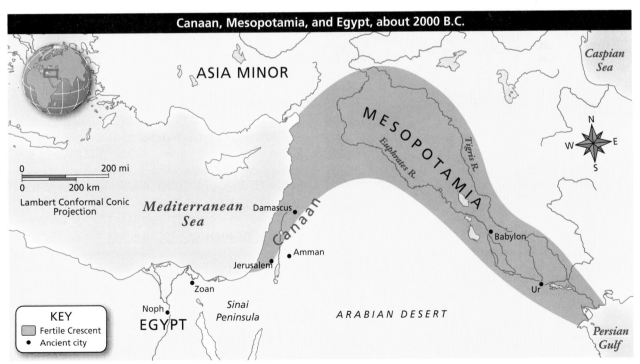

Canaan, Mesopotamia, and Egypt, about 2000 B.C.

>> **Analyze Maps** What factors may have led to Canaan's becoming a crossroads in the ancient Middle East?

>> In this 17th-century painting, Moses is depicted holding out his staff as the Red Sea is parted by God. According to the Bible, the Israelites were able to cross the sea and escape from Egypt.

BOUNCE to Activate Gallery

>> This mosaic from a synagogue wall in Jerusalem shows the symbols of the 12 tribes of Israel. Each tribe represents one of the twelve sons of Jacob.

Late in life, Abraham and his wife Sarah had a son named Isaac. Isaac had two sons, one named Jacob. Jews believe that Jacob was blessed by God and given the name Israel. Jacob fathered 12 sons, and his many descendants are known as the children of Israel.

Jacob's son Joseph was placed in charge of Egypt's food supplies after he interpreted the pharaoh's dream as predicting a famine. When a famine did strike, Jacob moved his entire family into Egypt, where the pharaoh welcomed them and they lived peacefully. After many years, a new pharaoh came to power. He feared the growing power and numbers of the children of Israel and made them slaves.

Years later, according to the Torah, an Israelite named **Moses** renewed God's covenant with the Israelites. In the book of Exodus, Moses tells the Israelites that in return for faithful obedience to God, God will lead them out of bondage in Egypt and into the promised land.

Moses led the Israelites in their exodus, or departure, from Egypt, from slavery to freedom. After 40 years, they reached Canaan, although Moses died just before they arrived.

The Kingdom of Israel By 1000 B.C., the Israelites had set up the Kingdom of Israel. The Torah tells of twelve separate tribes of Israel that were not united before this time. Saul, the first king of Israel, united these tribes into a single nation. The strong and wise second king of Israel, **David,** established Jerusalem as its national capital and led successful military campaigns creating secure borders for Israel.

According to the Torah, David's son **Solomon** followed him as king. Solomon undertook the task of turning the city of Jerusalem into an impressive capital. Jerusalem was praised for its splendid Temple dedicated to God, which David had planned and Solomon constructed. Solomon also won fame for his wisdom and understanding. Additionally, he tried to increase Israel's influence around the region by negotiating with powerful empires in Egypt and Mesopotamia.

Israel Is Divided and Conquered Solomon's building projects required such high taxes and so much forced labor that revolts erupted after he died about 922 B.C. The kingdom then split into Israel in the north and Judah in the south.

The Israelites remained independent for 200 years but eventually fell to more powerful peoples. In 722 B.C., the Assyrians conquered the northern Kingdom of Israel. From this time, since most of the remaining Israelites came from the tribe of Judah and were now part of the Kingdom of Judah, they became known

The Ten Commandments

COMMANDMENT	EXPLANATION
1st I the Lord am your God, who brought you out of the land of Egypt, the house of bondage.	to recognize God as the one and only God and to understand the relationship between people and God
2nd You shall have no other gods besides Me. You shall not make for yourself a sculptured image, or any likeness of what is in the heavens above, or on the earth below, or in the waters under the earth.	to not worship any other God or false idols
3rd You shall not swear falsely by the name of the Lord your God.	to speak the truth, seen today in legal oaths
4th Remember the sabbath day and keep it holy.	to dedicate one day to rest and worship
5th Honor your father and your mother.	to respect and love one's parents
6th You shall not murder.	to not murder others
7th You shall not commit adultery.	to ensure faithfulness to one's spouse; seen today in divorce laws
8th You shall not steal.	to prevent taking another person's belongings
9th You shall not bear false witness against your neighbor.	to prevent lying; seen today by laws against testifying falsely in a court of law
10th You shall not covet your neighbor's house, nor his wife… nor anything that is your neighbor's.	to prevent wanting other people's possessions, life, or spouse.

SOURCE: Book of Exodus 20:2-18, *JPS Hebrew-English Tanakh*, Jewish Publication Society (JPS) 1985.

>> Over time, the ideas in the Ten Commandments have influenced aspects of some modern legal and political systems.

 BOUNCE to Activate Chart

as *yehudi,* or Jews. In 586 B.C., Babylonian armies captured Judah. Nebuchadnezzar destroyed the great temple and forced many of those he defeated into exile in Babylon. This period of exile, called the Babylonian Captivity, lasted about 50 years.

In 539 B.C., the Persian ruler Cyrus the Great conquered Babylon and soon freed the Jews. Many Jews returned to Judah, where they rebuilt a smaller version of Solomon's Temple. However, like other groups in the region, they lived under Persian rule.

☑ **IDENTIFY MAIN IDEAS** According to the Torah, where did the Israelites go once they left Egypt? What was special to them about their destination?

Judaism's Legacy

From early times, the concept of law was central to the Israelites. The Torah includes many laws and is thus often referred to as the Books of the Law. Some of the laws deal with everyday matters such as cleanliness and food preparation. Others define criminal acts. The Torah also establishes moral principles.

Like other early civilizations, Israelite society was **patriarchal,** which means that men held the greatest legal and moral authority. A family's oldest male relative was the head of the household, but women were respected and had more rights than women in many other ancient societies. A few outstanding women, such as the judge and military leader Deborah and the prophetess Miriam won great honor.

The Ten Commandments as a Guide At the heart of Judaism are the Ten Commandments, a set of laws that Jews believe God gave to them through Moses. The first four commandments stress religious duties toward God, such as keeping the **Sabbath,** a holy day for rest and worship. The rest address conduct toward others. They include "Honor your father and mother," "You shall not murder," and "You shall not steal." In addition to establishing a moral law, the Ten Commandments also helped develop the "rule of law," the idea that laws should apply to everyone equally. Finally, the Ten Commandments guided the ancient Jews in setting up their society and government, an influence that endures into our own time.

A Strong Code of Ethics Often in Jewish history, spiritual leaders emerged to interpret God's will. These **prophets,** such as Isaiah and Jeremiah, reminded the Jewish people of their duties.

The prophets also taught a strong code of **ethics,** or moral standards of behavior. They urged both personal morality and social justice, calling on the rich and powerful to protect the poor and weak. All people, they said, were equal before God. Unlike many ancient societies in which the ruler was seen as a god, Jews saw their leaders as fully human and bound to obey God's law.

Scholars have been able to learn more about ancient Israelite culture and ethics as a result of the discovery of the Dead Sea Scrolls. The Scrolls are fragments of early Jewish religious documents. These documents have shed light on the way the Bible and Torah were transmitted to us and have illuminated the religious backgrounds of both Judaism and Christianity.

The spiritual ideas of the ancient Israelites later influenced Western culture, morality, ethics, and conduct. Judaism influenced both Christianity and Islam, two other monotheistic faiths that also arose in the Middle East. Jews, Christians, and Muslims alike honor Abraham, Moses, and the prophets. The interaction between Judaism and Christianity and Islam resulted in all three teaching the ethical worldview developed by the Israelites. Today, in the West, this shared heritage of Jews and Christians is known as the Judeo-Christian tradition.

Judaism Spreads For a 500-year period that began with the Babylonian Captivity, many Jews left Judah and moved to different parts of the world. This spreading out of the Jewish people was called the **Diaspora** (dy AS pur uh). Some Jews were exiled, others moved to farther reaches of the empires that controlled their land, and yet others moved because of discontent with political rulers. Wherever Jews settled, many maintained their identity as a people by living in close-knit communities and obeying their religious laws and traditions. These traditions helped them survive centuries of persecution, or unfair treatment inflicted on a particular group of people, which you will read about in later Topics.

Today, Judaism is numbered among the world's major religions for its contributions to religious thought as well as its strong influence on two later religions, Christianity and Islam. All three of these monotheistic faiths emerged in the Middle East and spread to other parts of the world. Although their beliefs differ in many ways, Jews, Christians, and Muslims all honor Abraham, Moses, and the Hebrew prophets. All three teach the ethical worldview developed by the Israelites.

Judeo-Christian Influences Some people have suggested that Judeo-Christian traditions had an even more far-reaching impact on world history.

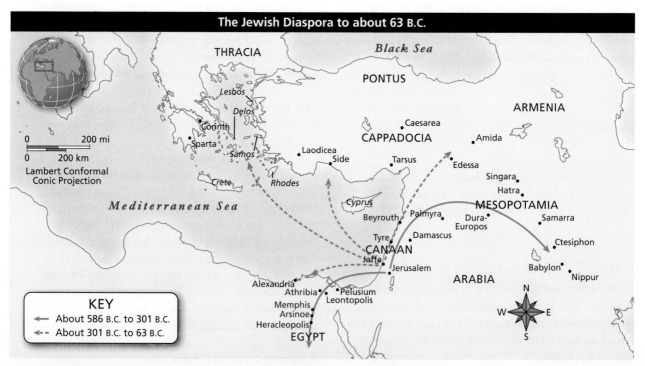

>> **Analyze Maps** The Jewish Diaspora began with the Babylonian Captivity in 6th century B.C. and has continued throughout history. How did the Diaspora contribute to the spread of Judaism?

They trace today's democratic-republican forms of government to the teachings of these religions, such as ideas about the worth of the individual, the importance of social responsibility, and the concept that all believers were equal before God. They look to Judeo-Christian legal traditions for the origins of such rights and concepts as trial by jury and innocent until proven guilty. Indeed, the Ten Commandments, the teachings of the Hebrew prophets, and the historical traditions of the ancient Israelites helped shape Western culture, morality, ethics, and conduct over many centuries.

☑ **EXPLAIN** How did the prophets help Jews uphold the law?

☑ ASSESSMENT

1. **Identify Main Ideas** How did the religion of the ancient Israelites differ from those of its neighbors?

2. **Support Ideas with Examples** Name two events from Jewish history that reflect the Israelites' belief that God had a plan for the people of Israel.

3. **Identify Cause and Effect** Explain what happened to the Israelites after the death of Solomon.

4. **Summarize** Identify the points in Israel's early history when it was unified, divided, or ruled by outsiders.

5. **Quest Connections** How did Judeo-Christian ideas and religious traditions influence legal traditions in Western countries?

Ancient Laws

Some ancient Middle East civilizations developed legal codes, or collections of the laws that governed society. One of the first was Hammurabi's Code. The Code established laws for the Babylonian empire and reinforced the power of Hammurabi, who said they were handed down by the gods.

The first five books of the Hebrew Bible, called the Torah, contain hundreds of different laws and commandments that guided the ancient Israelites and were, according to Jewish tradition, given to the Israelites by God. The most famous of these are the Ten Commandments, which are in the Book of Exodus. The Torah also includes other ethical and ritual laws.

Hammurabi's Code and the Book of Exodus are excerpted below. **As you read, compare their viewpoints on laws.**

>> This stone stele is carved with Hammurabi's Code.

Primary Source 1

Hammurabi's Code

If anyone bring an accusation . . . and does not prove what he has charged, he shall, if it be a capital offense charged, be put to death. . . .

If anyone steal the property of a temple or of the court, he shall be put to death. . . .

If anyone is committing a robbery and is caught, then he shall be put to death. . . .

If a son strike his father, his hands shall be hewn off.

If a man put out the eye of another man, his eye shall be put out.

If he break another man's bone, his bone shall be broken.

☑ **ANALYZE RHETORIC** How does the wording of these laws make them easy for people to understand?

If he put out the eye of a freed man, or break the bone of a freed man, he shall pay one gold mina.

If anyone strike the body of a man higher in rank than he, he shall receive sixty blows with an ox-whip in public. . . .

If the slave of a freed man strike the body of a freed man, his ear shall be cut off. . . .

☑ **DRAW CONCLUSIONS** What do these laws tell you about the relative importance of different people in Babylonian society?

If a physician make a large incision with an operating knife and cure it. . . . he shall receive ten shekels in money. . . .

If a physician make a large incision with the operating knife, and kill him. . . . his hands shall be cut off. . . .

If a builder build a house for someone, and does not construct it properly, and the house which he built fall in and kill its owner, then that builder shall be put to death.

Primary Source 2

The Book of Exodus

Exodus 21: 12-37
He who fatally strikes a man shall be put to death. If he did not do it by design, but it came about by an act of God, I will assign you a place to which he can flee. When a man schemes against another and kills him treacherously, you shall take him from My very altar to be put to death.

He who strikes his father or his mother shall be put to death.

He who kidnaps a man—whether he has sold him or is still holding him—shall be put to death.

When men fight, and one of them pushes a pregnant woman and a miscarriage results, but no other damage ensues, the one responsible shall be fined according as the woman's husband may exact from him . . . But if other damage ensues, the penalty shall be life for life, eye for eye, tooth for tooth, hand for hand, foot for foot, burn for burn, wound for wound, bruise for bruise.

☑ **COMPARE AND CONTRAST** How do these punishments compare to modern punishments for similar crimes of manslaughter and murder?

When a man strikes the eye of his slave, male or female, and destroys it, he shall let him go free on account of his eye. . . .

When a man steals an ox or a sheep, and slaughters it or sells it, he shall pay five oxen for the ox, and four sheep for the sheep.

Exodus 22: 8-21
In all charges of misappropriation—pertaining to an ox, [a donkey], a sheep, a garment, or any other loss, whereof one party alleges, "This is it"—the case of both parties shall come before God: he whom God declares guilty shall pay double to the other.

You shall not wrong a stranger or oppress him, for you were strangers in the land of Egypt.

☑ **MAKE CONNECTIONS** How does this reference to the history of the Israelites inform Jewish values on how to treat those from outside the community?

You shall not ill-treat any widow or orphan. If you do mistreat them, I will heed their outcry as soon as they cry out to Me. . . .

If you take your neighbor's garment in pledge, you must return it to him before the sun sets; it is his only clothing, the sole covering for his skin. In what else shall he sleep? Therefore, if he cries out to Me, I will pay heed, for I am compassionate.

☑ ASSESSMENT

Be sure to cite specific evidence from the sources as you answer the following questions.

1. **Describe** What details about life in ancient Babylon can you learn from Hammurabi's Code?

2. **Analyze Information** Do you think the punishments described in the Book of Exodus are fair? Why or why not?

3. **Compare and Contrast** How are the sources similar? How do they differ?

4. **Predict** How do you think these and other early laws and commandments might have paved the way for later law codes?

5. **Develop Empathy** In what ways do the sources demonstrate empathy?

6. **Summarize** Why do you think these laws were written down and codified?

2.4

These statues at Thebes stood in front of a temple destroyed by the Nile's flooding. Egyptians learned to control the flooding and use the Nile for agriculture as well as transportation.

 BOUNCE to Activate Flipped Video

Objectives

Understand the ways in which geography helped shape ancient Egypt.

Explain how Egypt grew strong during the New Kingdom.

Describe the ways in which religious beliefs shaped the lives of ancient Egyptians.

Explain how the Egyptians organized their society.

Outline the advances that the Egyptians made in learning, the arts, science, and literature.

Key Terms

cataract	Osiris
delta	Isis
dynasty	mummification
pharaoh	Akhenaton
vizier	hieroglyphics
Hatshepsut	papyrus
Thutmose III	decipher
Ramses II	Rosetta Stone
Amon-Re	

Egyptian Civilization

The fertile lands of the Nile River Valley attracted Stone Age farmers. In prehistoric times, migrating people reached Egypt from the Mediterranean area, from the hills and deserts near the Nile, and from other parts of Africa. In time, the Nile Valley became the birthplace of a powerful civilization that depended heavily on the control of river waters.

Geography Shapes Egypt

The Rich Nile Valley "Egypt," said the ancient Greek historian Herodotus, "is wholly the gift of the Nile." Without the Nile, Egypt would be just the barren desert that surrounds the river. But while the desert protected Egypt from invasion, it also limited where people could settle.

In ancient times, as today, farming villages dotted the narrow band of land watered by the Nile. Beyond the rich, irrigated "Black Land," generally no more than 10 miles wide, lay the "Red Land," a sun-baked desert that stretches across North Africa. Farmers took advantage of the fertile soil of the Nile Valley to grow wheat and flax, a plant whose fibers were used for clothing.

Benefits of Nile Flooding The Nile rises in the highlands of Ethiopia and the lakes of central Africa. Every spring, the rains in this interior region send water racing down streams that feed the Nile River. In ancient times, Egyptians eagerly awaited the annual flood. It soaked the land with life-giving water and deposited a layer of rich silt, or soil.

People had to cooperate to control the Nile floods. They built dikes, reservoirs, and irrigation ditches to channel the rising river and store water for the dry season.

GO ONLINE to access your digital course

Two Regions United Ancient Egypt had two distinct regions, Upper Egypt in the south and Lower Egypt in the north. Upper Egypt stretched from the Nile's first **cataract,** or waterfall, of the Nile northward to within 100 miles of the Mediterranean Sea. Lower Egypt covered the delta region where the Nile empties into the Mediterranean. A **delta** is a triangular area of marshland formed by deposits of silt at the mouth of some rivers.

About 3100 B.C., Menes, the king of Upper Egypt, united the two regions and set up his capital at Memphis near the Nile delta. Menes and his successors used the Nile as a highway linking north and south. They could send officials or armies to towns along the river. The Nile thus helped make Egypt one of the world's first unified states.

The river also served as a trade route. Egyptian merchants traveled up and down the Nile in sailboats and barges, exchanging the products of Africa, the Middle East, and the Mediterranean world.

☑ **IDENTIFY MAIN IDEAS** How did the yearly floods of the Nile influence life in ancient Egypt?

The Old Kingdom

Scholars divide the history of ancient Egypt into three main periods: the Old Kingdom (about 2575 B.C.–2130 B.C.), the Middle Kingdom (about 1938 B.C.–1630 B.C.), and the New Kingdom (about 1539 B.C.–1075 B.C.). During these periods, power passed from one **dynasty,** or ruling family, to another, but Egypt generally remained united.

A Structured Government During the Old Kingdom, Egyptian rulers, later called **pharaohs** (FEHR ohz), organized a strong, centralized state. Pharaohs claimed divine support for their rule. Egyptians believed the pharaoh was a god. The pharaoh thus had absolute power, owning and ruling all the land. Still, the pharaoh was also seen as human and was expected to behave morally.

Pharaohs of the Old Kingdom took pride in maintaining justice and order. A pharaoh depended on a **vizier** (vih ZEER), or chief minister, to supervise the government. The vizier headed the bureaucracy, or government departments, that looked after matters such as tax collection, farming, and the all-important irrigation system. Thousands of scribes carried out the vizier's instructions.

About 2450 B.C., a wise vizier, Ptah-hotep (ptah HOH tep), took an interest in training young officials. Based on his vast experience of government, he

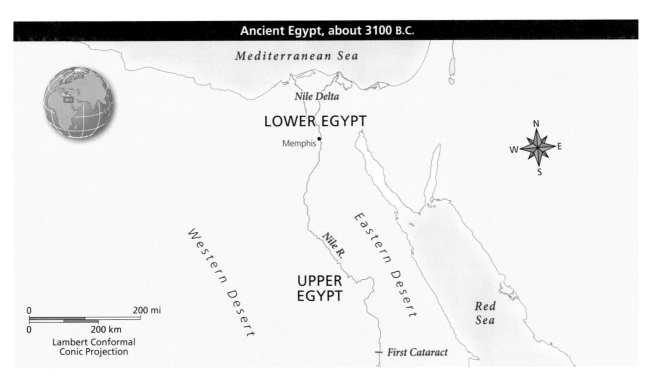

Ancient Egypt, about 3100 B.C.

Mediterranean Sea

Nile Delta

LOWER EGYPT

Memphis

Western Desert

Nile R.

Eastern Desert

UPPER EGYPT

Red Sea

First Cataract

0 ⎯ 200 mi
0 ⎯ 200 km
Lambert Conformal
Conic Projection

N E S W

>> **Analyze Maps** The Nile extends another 3,600 miles south of its first cataract. What geographic features might have limited the expansion of civilization beyond the Nile Valley?

wrote a book, *Instructions of the Vizier Ptah-hotep*. In it, he advised ambitious young people to be humble and honest, obedient to one's father and superiors, and fair in dealing with other officials of all ranks.

Building the Great Pyramids The Old Kingdom is sometimes called the Pyramid Age because during this time, the Egyptians built the majestic pyramids that still stand at Giza, near present-day Cairo.

Tombs within the pyramids were considered homes in which the deceased would live for eternity. Because Egyptians believed in an afterlife, they preserved the bodies of their dead rulers and provided them with everything they would need in their new lives.

To complete the pyramids, workers hauled and lifted millions of limestone blocks, some weighing as much as 15 tons each. Workers quarried each stone by hand, pulled them on sleds to the site, and hoisted them up earthen ramps to be placed on the slowly rising structure. Building a pyramid took so many years that often a pharaoh would begin construction on his tomb as soon as he inherited the throne.

The pyramids suggest the strength of ancient Egyptian civilization. These costly projects took years to complete and required enormous planning and organization. Thousands of farmers, who had to be fed each day, worked on the pyramids when not planting or harvesting crops.

☑ **CHECK UNDERSTANDING** How was the Egyptian government structured during the Old Kingdom?

Middle and New Kingdom Egypt

Power struggles, crop failures, and the cost of building the pyramids all contributed to the collapse of the Old Kingdom. After more than a century of disunity, new pharaohs eventually reunited the land, ushering in a new era, the Middle Kingdom.

The Middle Kingdom The Middle Kingdom was a turbulent period. The Nile did not rise as regularly as it had in the past. Corruption and rebellions were common. Still, strong rulers did organize a large drainage project, creating vast new stretches of arable, or farmable, land. Egyptian armies occupied part of Nubia (also known as Kush), the gold-rich land to the south. Traders also had greater contacts with the peoples of the Middle East and the Mediterranean island of Crete.

Catastrophe struck about 1700 B.C., when foreign invaders, the Hyksos (HIK sohs), occupied the Nile delta region. The Hyksos awed the Egyptians with their horse-drawn war chariots. In time, the

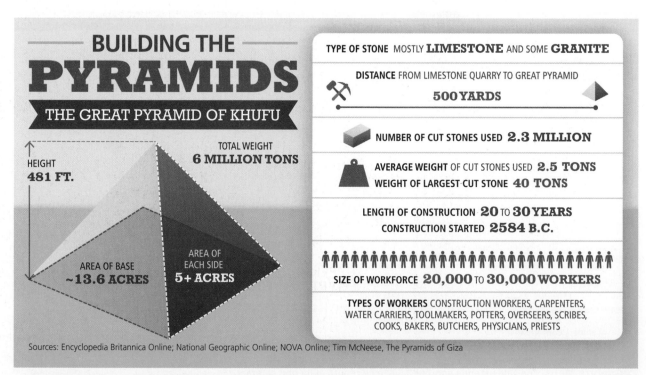

BUILDING THE PYRAMIDS
THE GREAT PYRAMID OF KHUFU

HEIGHT
481 FT.

TOTAL WEIGHT
6 MILLION TONS

AREA OF BASE
~13.6 ACRES

AREA OF EACH SIDE
5+ ACRES

TYPE OF STONE MOSTLY **LIMESTONE** AND SOME **GRANITE**

DISTANCE FROM LIMESTONE QUARRY TO GREAT PYRAMID
500 YARDS

NUMBER OF CUT STONES USED **2.3 MILLION**

AVERAGE WEIGHT OF CUT STONES USED **2.5 TONS**
WEIGHT OF LARGEST CUT STONE **40 TONS**

LENGTH OF CONSTRUCTION **20 TO 30 YEARS**
CONSTRUCTION STARTED **2584 B.C.**

SIZE OF WORKFORCE **20,000 TO 30,000 WORKERS**

TYPES OF WORKERS CONSTRUCTION WORKERS, CARPENTERS, WATER CARRIERS, TOOLMAKERS, POTTERS, OVERSEERS, SCRIBES, COOKS, BAKERS, BUTCHERS, PHYSICIANS, PRIESTS

Sources: Encyclopedia Britannica Online; National Geographic Online; NOVA Online; Tim McNeese, The Pyramids of Giza

>> **Analyze Data** Pharaohs spent a great deal of resources and time building pyramids. Based on the information here, why do you think Giza pyramids built after Khufu's were not as large as his?

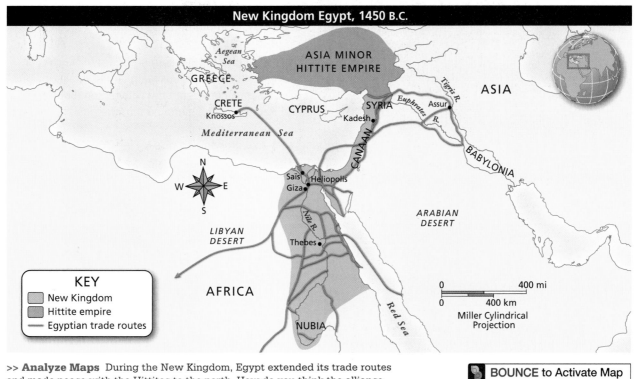

KEY
New Kingdom
Hittite empire
Egyptian trade routes

>> **Analyze Maps** During the New Kingdom, Egypt extended its trade routes and made peace with the Hittites to the north. How do you think the alliance with the Hittites helped Egypt reach its greatest extent?

BOUNCE to Activate Map

Egyptians mastered this new military technology. The Hyksos, in turn, were so impressed by Egyptian civilization that they soon adopted Egyptian customs, beliefs, and even names. Finally, after more than 100 years of Hyksos rule, new Egyptian leaders arose, drove out the foreigners, and set up the New Kingdom.

The New Kingdom During the New Kingdom, powerful and ambitious pharaohs created a large empire, and Egyptian civilization flourished. At its height around 1450 B.C., the Egyptian empire reached as far north as Syria near the Euphrates River. This age of conquest brought Egyptians into greater contact with the people of the Middle East as well as other parts of Africa.

Under the strong leadership of New Kingdom pharaohs, Egypt prospered. Rulers undertook huge building projects while Egyptians made advances in medicine, hygiene, dentistry, and the arts.

Queen Hatshepsut Among the outstanding rulers of the New Kingdom was **Hatshepsut** (haht SHEP soot), who reigned from about 1472 B.C. to about 1457 B.C. Like some earlier Egyptian queens, Hatshepsut began by ruling in the name of a male heir too young to take the throne. However, she then took the bold step of declaring herself pharaoh and won the support of key officials. Because Egyptians saw kingship as a male privilege, she donned a false beard as a sign of authority. She encouraged trade with eastern Mediterranean lands and along the Red Sea coast of Africa. Her stepson, **Thutmose III** (thoot MOH suh), took over as pharaoh once he reached adulthood. A great military general, Thutmose III stretched Egypt's borders to their greatest extent ever.

Ramses II The later pharaoh **Ramses II** (RAM seez) won fame for his military victories. For much of his long reign from 1279 B.C. to 1213 B.C., he pushed Egyptian control northward, again bringing Syria under Egyptian rule. On temples and monuments, he boasted of his conquests, although his greatest reported victory may not actually have taken place. In a battle against the Hittites of Asia Minor, only the desperate bravery of Ramses himself prevented a crushing defeat. Back home, however, Ramses had inscriptions carved on a monument that made the near defeat sound like a stunning victory.

After years of fighting, the Egyptians and the Hittites signed a peace treaty, the first such document in history known to have survived. The

>> Ramses II is known for the wars he waged with the Hittites and Libyans and for numerous building projects. He solidified the peace treaty with the Hittites by marrying a Hittite princess.

>> The ancient Egyptians believed in many gods and goddesses, each of whom had a role in maintaining peace and prosperity across Egypt.

treaty declared that Egypt and the Hittites "shall be at peace and in brotherhood forever."

Egypt Declines After Ramses II, Egyptian power slowly declined. Invaders, such as the Assyrians and the Persians, conquered the Nile region. Later Greek and Roman armies marched into the rich Nile Valley. Each new conqueror was eager to add the fertile Nile Valley to a growing empire.

Egypt and Nubia To the south of Egypt, the kingdom of Nubia had developed along the Nile. For centuries, Egyptians traded or fought with their southern neighbor. From Nubia, they acquired ivory, cattle, and enslaved people. During the New Kingdom, Egypt armies conquered Nubia. The pharaoh Ramses II used gold from Nubia to pay charioteers in his army. Nubians served in Egyptian armies and left their mark on Egyptian culture. Much Egyptian art of this period shows Nubian soldiers, musicians, or prisoners.

As Egypt declined, Nubia regained its independence. Then about 750 B.C., Nubian kings marched north, adding Egypt to their own lands. For 100 years, Nubian kings ruled an empire that stretched from what is today Sudan to the Mediterranean.

The Nubians saw themselves not as foreign conquerors but as restorers of Egyptian glory. They ruled Egypt like the pharaohs of earlier centuries. About 650 B.C., Assyrians, armed with iron weapons, descended on Egypt. They pushed the Nubians back into their original homeland, where Nubian monarchs ruled for 1,000 years more.

☑ **CHECK UNDERSTANDING** In what ways was the Middle Kingdom turbulent?

Religion Shapes Ancient Egyptian Life

Egyptians inherited from their earliest ancestors a variety of religious beliefs and practices. Inscriptions on monuments and wall paintings in tombs reveal how Egyptians appealed to the divine forces that they believed ruled this world and the afterlife.

Important Gods and Goddesses In the sun-drenched land of Egypt, the chief god was the sun god **Amon-Re** (AH mun ray). The pharaoh, whom Egyptians viewed as god as well as king, was closely linked to Amon-Re. Only the pharaoh could conduct certain ceremonies for the sun god. Like many ancient civilizations, Egypt was a type of theocracy, or a system of government in which the ruler is a religious figure, such as a priest, or rules in the name of God or a god. For Egyptians, the pharaoh had religious authority to rule.

Most Egyptians related more easily to the god **Osiris** (oh SY ris) and the goddess **Isis** (EYE sis), whose story touched human emotions such as love, jealousy, and fear of death. An Egyptian myth tells how Osiris ruled Egypt until he was killed and carved up by his jealous brother, Set. Isis, the wife of Osiris, finds the scattered parts of her husband's body and brings him back to life. Because Osiris could no longer rule over the living, he became god of the dead and judge of souls seeking admission to the afterlife.

To Egyptians, Osiris was especially important. Not only did he rule over the underworld, but he was also god of the Nile. In that role, he controlled the annual flood that made the land fertile. Isis had special appeal for women, who believed that she had first taught women to grind grain, spin flax, weave cloth, and care for children. Like Osiris, Isis promised the faithful that they would have life after death.

Egyptian Views of the Afterlife As you have read, Egyptians believed that Osiris and Isis had promised them eternal life after death. Belief in the afterlife affected all Egyptians, from the highest noble to the lowest peasant.

To win eternal life, Egyptians believed that each soul had to pass a test. After the dead was ferried across a lake of fire to the hall of Osiris, the god weighed each soul's heart against the feather of truth. Those he judged to be sinners were fed to the crocodile-shaped Eater of the Dead. Worthy souls entered the Happy Field of Food. To survive the dangerous journey through the underworld, Egyptians relied on the *Book of the Dead*. It contained spells, charms, and magic formulas meant to help the dead in the afterlife.

Mummification Egyptians believed that the afterlife would be much like life on Earth. As a result, they buried their dead with everything they would need for eternity.

To give a soul use of its body in the afterlife, Egyptians perfected scientific skills in **mummification** (mum uh fih KAY shun), the preservation of dead bodies by embalming them and wrapping them in cloth. At first, mummification was a privilege reserved for rulers and nobles. Eventually, ordinary Egyptians also won the right to mummify their dead, including beloved pets.

King Tutankhamen's Tomb Many pharaohs of the New Kingdom were buried in the desolate Valley of

>> To complete a pyramid, workers quarried millions of huge limestone blocks. They transported the cut stones on barges along the Nile then pulled them up a ramp to build the pyramid.

BOUNCE to Activate 3D Model

>> According to Egyptian myth, Osiris became the god of the dead and his wife Isis became the goddess of magic and motherhood.

the Kings. Their tombs, filled with fantastic riches, were a temptation to robbers in ancient times. As a result, most royal tombs were stripped of their treasures long ago.

In 1922, however, British archaeologist Howard Carter unearthed the tomb of the pharaoh Tutankhamen (toot ahng KAH mun), which had remained almost untouched for more than 3,000 years. The tomb and its treasures have provided scholars a wealth of evidence about Egyptian civilization.

The mummified body of the 18-year-old "King Tut" had been placed in a solid-gold coffin, nested within richly decorated outer coffins. Today, the dazzling array of objects found in the tomb fills several rooms in the Egyptian Museum in Cairo. The objects include chariots, weapons, furniture, jewelry, toys, and games. Tutankhamen was a minor king. Imagine the treasures that must have filled the tombs of great pharaohs like Ramses II.

An Attempt to Reshape Religion About 1380 B.C., a young pharaoh challenged the powerful priests of Amon-Re. He devoted his life to the worship of Aton, a minor god whose symbol was the sun's disk. The pharaoh took the name **Akhenaton** (ah keh NAH tun), meaning "he who serves Aton." With the support of his wife Nefertiti, Akhenaton tried

to sweep away all other gods in favor of Aton. He ordered priests to worship only Aton and to remove the names of other gods from their temples.

Scholars disagree about whether or not Akhenaton was trying to introduce a new religion based on worship of a single god. Akhenaton's radical ideas had little success, however. Priests of Amon-Re resisted the revolutionary changes. Nobles also deserted the pharaoh because he neglected his duty of defending the empire. After Akhenaton's death, priests of the old gods reasserted their power.

☑ **DRAW CONCLUSIONS** How did mummification reflect Egyptian beliefs about the afterlife?

Organization of Egyptian Society

Like other early civilizations, Egypt had its own class system. As both a god and an earthly leader, the pharaoh stood at the top of society, along with the royal family. Directly under the pharaoh were government officials and the high priests and priestesses, who served the gods and goddesses. Next came the nobles, who fought the pharaoh's wars. A tiny class of merchants, scribes, and artisans developed slowly. They provided for the needs of the rich and powerful. At the base of society were the majority of Egyptians, the peasants who worked the land.

Peasant Farmers Most Numerous Most Egyptians were peasant farmers. Many were enslaved. Men and women spent their days working the soil and repairing the dikes. In the off-season, peasant men were expected to serve the pharaoh, laboring to build palaces, temples, and tombs. Besides working in the fields, women also spent much time raising children, collecting water, and preparing food.

One ancient record describes the life of a typical Egyptian peasant. "When the water is full he irrigates [the fields] and repairs his equipment. He spends the day cutting tools for cultivating barley, and the night twisting ropes."

Changes to Social Structure During the New Kingdom, society became more fluid as trade and warfare increased. Trade offered new opportunities to the growing merchant class. Foreign conquests brought riches to Egypt, which in turn meant more business for artisans. These skilled craftworkers made fine jewelry, furniture, and fabrics for the palaces and tombs of pharaohs and nobles.

>> Tutankhamen, or "King Tut," reigned for only eight or nine years. However, his tomb has unraveled many mysteries about his life and death. His solid gold funeral mask is shown here.

Higher Status for Egyptian Women Egyptian women generally enjoyed a higher status and greater independence than women elsewhere in the ancient world. Ramses II declared, "The foot of an Egyptian woman may walk where it pleases her and no one may deny her." Under Egyptian law, women could inherit property, enter business deals, buy and sell goods, go to court, and obtain a divorce.

Although there were often clear distinctions between the occupations of women and men, women's work was not confined to the home. Women manufactured perfume and textiles, managed farming estates, and served as doctors. Women could also enter the priesthood, especially in the service of goddesses. Despite their many rights and employment opportunities, few women learned to read and write. Even if they did, they were excluded from becoming scribes or holding government jobs.

☑ **IDENTIFY** Which social class grew in size as a result of trade and warfare?

Egyptian Learning Advances

Ancient Egyptians left a vast record of their achievements. Stone temples and monuments along with all paintings and written records reveal much about Egyptian life and religious beliefs. They also show Egyptian knowledge and advances in many fields such as medicine, astronomy, and mathematics. The Egyptians were a practical people. When they had a problem, they used trial and error to find a solution.

Written Records Like people in other early civilizations, the ancient Egyptians developed a form of picture writing called **hieroglyphics** (hy ur oh GLIF iks). In this system of writing, hieroglyphs, or symbols and pictures, represent objects, concepts, or sounds. The Egyptians used hieroglyphs to keep important records. Early on, priests and scribes carved hieroglyphs onto stone. Inscriptions on temples and other monuments preserved records of Egyptian culture for thousands of years.

Egyptian scribes also developed hieratic (hy ur AT ik) writing, a simpler script for everyday use. Much later, a third system of writing, demotic, replaced hieratic script.

Scribes In ancient Egypt, scribes played a central role keeping the records that reveal so much about Egyptian society. Records describe religious

>> Since hieroglyphs, seen here, took a lot of time and care to write, Egyptian scribes also developed the cursive hieratic and demotic scripts for quicker use.

🅑 BOUNCE to Activate Gallery

ceremonies and give information about taxes or gifts made to the pharaoh or temples. Scribes served as government and temple officials. Some acquired skills in mathematics, medicine, and engineering. With skill and luck, a scribe from a poor family might become rich and powerful.

Most likely, scribes were behind the Egyptian invention of a paper-like writing material made from **papyrus** (puh PY rus), a plant that grows along the Nile. (Paper would not be invented until about A.D. 100, in China.) Writing cursive scripts with reed pens and ink on the smooth surface of papyrus strips was much easier than chiseling words onto stone. Scribes used demotic script for many records, but when writing official histories, they continued to carve hieroglyphs.

The Rosetta Stone Unlocks Egyptian Writing
After the New Kingdom declined, Egyptians lost the skills of reading ancient hieroglyphs. Not until the early 1800s did a French scholar, Jean Champollion (zhahn shahm poh LYOHN), unravel the then mysterious writings on Egypt's great monuments.

Champollion managed to **decipher,** or figure out the meaning of, texts written on the **Rosetta Stone.** This flat, black stone has the same text carved in hieroglyphics, demotic script, and Greek. By comparing the three versions, Champollion worked out the meanings of many hieroglyphic symbols. That breakthrough allowed scholars to begin reading the thousands of surviving records from ancient Egypt.

Medicine Like most doctors until recent times, Egyptian physicians believed in various kinds of magic. Yet through their knowledge of mummification, they learned a great deal about the human body. They became skilled at observing symptoms, diagnosing illnesses, and finding cures. Doctors also performed complex surgical operations, which are described on papyrus scrolls. Many medicines prescribed by Egyptian doctors are still used, including anise, castor beans, and saffron.

Mathematics Egyptians developed mathematics partly in response to problems that they faced. Nile floods forced Egyptians to redraw the boundaries of their fields each year. To do this, they developed practical geometry to survey the land. Egyptian engineers also used geometry to calculate the exact size and location of each block of stone to be placed in a pyramid or temple. Huge projects such as building pyramids or irrigation systems required considerable skills in design and engineering.

Astronomy Egyptian priest-astronomers studied the heavens, mapping constellations and charting the movement of planets. With this knowledge, they developed a calendar that had 12 months of 30 days each and 5 days added at the end of each year. With a few changes, this ancient Egyptian calendar became the basis for our modern calendar.

Egyptian Arts The arts of ancient Egypt included statues, wall paintings in tombs, and carvings on temples. Some show everyday scenes of trade, farming, family life, or religious ceremonies. Others boast of victories in battle.

Painting styles remained almost unchanged for thousands of years. The pharaohs and gods always appeared much larger than other human figures, symbolizing their importance in the hierarchy. Artists usually showed people with their heads and limbs in profile but their shoulders facing the viewer.

Statues often displayed people in stiff, standard poses. Some human figures have animal heads that represent special qualities. The Sphinx that crouches near the Great Pyramids at Giza portrays an early pharaoh as a powerful lion-human.

Besides the pyramids, Egyptian constructed many other great stone buildings and monuments. The magnificent temple of Ramses II at Karnak

Spread of Egyptian Mathematical and Scientific Advancements

FEATURE	DIFFUSION OF IDEAS
Plant-based medicines	According to papyrus records, ancient Egyptians used herbal treatments to cure themselves. Many of the herbs were carried from Canaan, Persia, and eastern Africa by traders and conquerors.
Anatomy	Greek and Roman conquerors adapted Egyptian knowledge of the human body; their studies of anatomy were definitive for over a thousand years.
Astronomy	Greek astronomers combined Egyptian knowledge with their own, helping them determine how to calculate the size of the Earth and make other astronomical advances.
Egyptian Calendar	The Ancient Egyptian civil calendar had 365 days in a year; after Romans conquered Egypt, Julius Caesar added a leap year to the Egyptian calendar.
Geometry	Egyptians used geometry to survey land and construct pyramids. Greek mathematician Pythagoras traveled to Egypt in 535 B.C. to learn mathematics, geometry, and astronomy.

>> **Analyze Information** In 332 B.C., the Greek ruler Alexander the Great conquered Egypt. According to the information on the chart, how was Egyptian knowledge passed along to other cultures?

contains a vast hall with towering 80-foot columns. Much later, the Romans would adopt building techniques like those used a Karnak.

Egyptian Literature Through their literature, ancient Egyptians reveal much about their values, attitudes, and even their sense of humor. The oldest Egyptian literature includes hymns and prayers to gods, proverbs, and love poems. Other writings tell of royal victories in battle or, like *Instructions of the Vizier Ptah-hotep*, give practical advice.

In Egypt, as in other early societies, folk tales were popular, especially *The Tale of Sinuhe*. It relates the wanderings of Sinuhe (SIN oo hay), an Egyptian official forced to flee into what is today Syria. He fights his way to fame among the nomadic desert people, whom the Egyptians considered uncivilized. As he gets older, Sinuhe longs to return home. The story ends happily when the pharaoh welcomes him back to court. The story of Sinuhe helps us see how Egyptians viewed both themselves and the people of the surrounding desert.

The Legacy of Ancient Egypt Long after its power declined, Egypt remained a center of learning and culture in the African and Mediterranean worlds. It also retained its economic importance as a source of grain and other riches.

Invaders, traders, and scholars spread the legacy of ancient Egypt. The Phoenicians, for example, learned to use papyrus for writing. People from distant lands respected Egyptian advances in medicine, mathematics, and astronomy and helped to preserve this ancient knowledge. Egyptian stories like *The Tale of Sinuhe* were retold in different forms by other people. As you will read in later lessons, the Greeks under Alexander the Great set up a great center of learning in Alexandria, Egypt, where they built on the extensive knowledge of ancient Egyptian civilization. Eventually, this rich legacy would find its way into the Western world

☑ **IDENTIFY** What art forms were common in ancient Egypt?

>> The sphinx, shown here, is a mythical creature with the body of a lion and a human head. The Egyptians thought of sphinxes as guardians at the entrances of temples or pyramids.

☑ **ASSESSMENT**

1. **Summarize** How did the Nile play an important role in uniting Egypt and allowing Egypt to expand during the New Kingdom?

2. **Draw Conclusions** Which details about the Egyptian gods show the importance of agriculture to Egyptian society?

3. **Determine Relevance** What does mummification reveal about ancient Egyptian religious views?

4. **Describe** Describe some of the main achievements of the ancient Egyptians.

5. **Describe** Describe the organization of Egyptian society.

6. **Connections to Today** Egyptian pharaohs placed great importance on building pyramids, which took many years and thousands of workers. How do government leaders today use public resources on large scale projects?

Hymn to the Nile, translated by Paul Guieysse

The Nile River's annual flood brought rich silt and life-giving water to the Nile River Valley, making farming possible and leading to the birth of Egyptian civilization. The Greek historian Herodotus called Egypt "the gift of the Nile," and ancient Egyptians were well aware of the river's importance to their lives.

The source below is an ancient hymn, or song, written about the Nile. Historians do not know exactly when the hymn was written, but it may have been during the Middle Kingdom years, perhaps to have been read or sung at festivals honoring the river. The excerpts below make clear how important the Nile and its floods were to ancient Egypt.

>> The Nile was vitally important to ancient Egyptians.

Primary Source

Adoration to the Nile!
Hail to thee, O Nile!
Who manifesteth thyself over this land
And comest to give life to Egypt!
Mysterious is thy issuing forth from the
    darkness,
On this day whereon it is celebrated!
Watering the orchards created by Ra
To cause all the cattle to live,
Thou givest the earth to drink,
    inexhaustible one!. . .

☑ **ANALYZE STYLE AND RHETORIC** What does the author mean by "mysterious is thy issuing forth from the darkness"?

Lord of the fish, during the inundation,
No bird alights on the crops.
Thou createst the corn, thou bringest forth
    the barley,
Assuring perpetuity to the temples.
If thou ceasest thy toil and thy work,
Then all that exists is in anguish.
If the gods suffer in heaven
Then the faces of men waste away.

Then he torments the flocks of Egypt,
And great and small are in agony.
But all is changed for mankind when he
    comes. . .

He brings the offerings, as chief of
    provisioning;
He is the creator of all good things,
As master of energy, full of sweetness in
    his choice.
If offerings are made it is thanks to him.
He brings forth the herbage for the flocks,
And sees that each god receives his
    sacrifices.
All that depends on him is a precious
    incense.
He spreads himself over Egypt,
Filling the granaries, renewing the marts,
Watching over the goods of the unhappy. . . .

Where misery existed, joy manifests itself;
All beasts rejoice. . . .
He shines when he issues forth from the
    darkness,
To cause his flocks to prosper.

It is his force that gives existence to all
    things;
Nothing remains hidden for him.
Let men clothe themselves to fill his
    gardens.
He watches over his works,
Producing the inundation during the
    night. . . .
The night remains silent,
But all is changed by the inundation;
It is a healing-balm for all mankind. . . .

☑ **PARAPHRASE** What does the author mean by "all
is changed by the inundation/It is a healing-balm for
all mankind"?

A festal song is raised for thee on the harp,
With the accompaniment of the hand.
Thy young men and thy children acclaim
    thee
And prepare their (long) exercises.
Thou art the august ornament of the earth,
Letting thy bark advance before men,
Lifting up the heart of women in labour,
And loving the multitude of the flocks.

When thou shinest in the royal city,
The rich man is sated with good things,
The poor man even disdains the lotus;
All that is produced is of the choicest;
All the plants exist for thy children.
If thou hast refused [to grant] nourishment,
The dwelling is silent, devoid of all that is
    good
The country falls exhausted.

O inundation of the Nile,
Offerings are made unto thee,
Oxen are immolated to thee,
Great festivals are instituted for thee.
Birds are sacrificed to thee,
Gazelles are taken for thee in the mountain,
Pure flames are prepared for thee.
Sacrifice is made to every god as it is made
    to the Nile. . . .

☑ **DRAW CONCLUSIONS** Why might people make
offerings to the Nile?

Men exalt him like the cycle of the gods,
They dread him who creates the heat,
Even him who has made his son the
    universal master
In order to give prosperity to Egypt.
Come (and) prosper! come (and) prosper!
O Nile, come (and) prosper!

☑ **DETERMINE CENTRAL IDEAS** Why does the
author invite the Nile to come?

☑ ASSESSMENT

1. **Determine Central Ideas** What is the main
   point of this hymn?

2. **Analyze Word Choices** Why do you think the
   author refers to the Nile as if it were a living
   being?

3. **Compare and Contrast** How does this source
   contrast Egypt with and without the benefits of
   the Nile?

4. **Analyze Word Choices** Why does the source
   call the Nile "the creator of all good things"?

Connections to Today

Take Action About the Use of Public Resources

Since governments first arose thousands of years ago, leaders had to make decisions about how to spend resources on specific projects. How do governments today take responsibility for large scale projects? Who decides how to spend public resources on these projects, and are these decisions always wise?

1. **Choose** one of the following types of public projects:

   - Transportation (such as roads or trains)

   - Government buildings (such as town halls, libraries, or schools)

   - Private-public partnerships (such as sports stadiums)

2. **Ask Questions** Generate a list of questions you have about the topic.

3. **Learn** about the topic and the major issues related to the topic. Are there any major debates related to the topic or issues? What are the strongest arguments on each side of the debate? Take notes as you conduct your research and continue to generate questions as you learn more.

4. **Take Action** Write a short summary of the topic or issue and create a poster advocating your position on the issue. Use the poster to educate your classmates and community about the topic. Create a written or oral presentation about the ways in which governments use public resources on large projects. Be prepared to present your findings and perspective as directed by your teacher.

Use the texts, quizzes, interactivities, Quest Inquiries, Flipped Videos, and other resources from this Topic to prepare for the Topic Test.

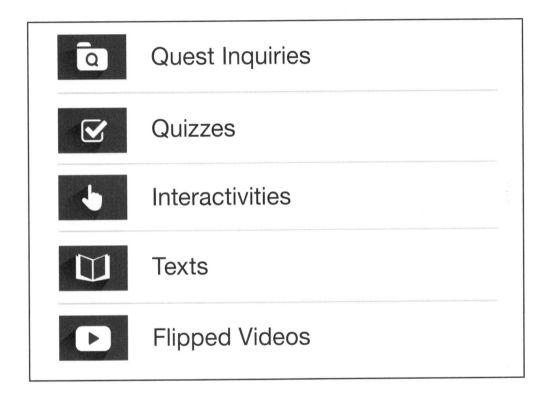

Quest Inquiries

Quizzes

Interactivities

Texts

Flipped Videos

While online you can also check the progress you've made learning the topic and course content by viewing your grades, test scores, and assignment status.

LESSON SUMMARIES

Use these Lesson Summaries, and the longer versions available online, to review the key ideas for each lesson in this Topic.

Lesson 1: A Civilization Emerges in Sumer

The world's first civilization developed in the Fertile Crescent of Mesopotamia. The Sumerians invented a writing system, established a government, made advancements in mathematics and science, and developed arts and culture. Conquering armies spread Sumerian ideas, influencing later civilizations.

Lesson 2: Empires in Mesopotamia

Powerful leaders created empires in the region. Hammurabi codified a system of civil and criminal laws. Nebuchadnezzar grew and restored Babylon to greatness. Under Persian rule, the development of a bureaucracy and new religious beliefs helped unify the region. The Phoenicians created an alphabet. They were skilled sea traders and spread their culture in their travels.

Lesson 3: The Hebrews and the Origins of Judaism

The ancient Israelites developed Judaism, a monotheistic religion, which was unique at that time. The sacred text is the Torah. It tells the story of the Israelite people and their relationship with God. The Torah also contains laws, including the Ten Commandments, which stress moral standards of behavior and religious duty for all people equally. The spiritual ideas of Judaism influenced both Christianity and Islam and helped shape Western culture and ethics.

Lesson 4: Egyptian Civilization

Egyptian civilization developed around the Nile River. Pharaohs ruled the kingdoms, organizing a central government and extending Egypt's borders. Religion was an important feature of Egyptian life. People worshipped many gods and believed in life after death. Egyptians created a writing system using symbols called hieroglyphics. They also made advances in medicine, astronomy and mathematics.

QUEST! FINDINGS

Write Your Essay Refer to your responses to the Quest Connections to help you create your essay to present to the class. Use the rubric and other Quest sources online to guide your work.

GO ONLINE to access lesson summaries

VISUAL REVIEW

Use these graphics to review some of the key terms, people, and ideas from this Topic.

The Rise of Civilization

- **3000 B.C.** City-states flourish in Sumer.
- **2575 B.C.** Egypt's Old Kingdom begins.
- **2300 B.C.** Sargon, the ruler of Akkad, conquers Sumer.
- **1790s B.C.** Hammurabi, the king of Babylon, issues the first written law code.
- **1100 B.C.** The Assyrians expand across Mesopotamia.
- **1000 B.C.** The kingdom of Israel is established, and Israelite beliefs develop into a major religion, Judaism.
- **522 B.C.** Darius begins to unify the Persian empire.

Key Innovations

- **Sumer:** social hierarchy; cuneiform writing; advances in astronomy and mathematics
- **Egypt:** bureaucracy; pyramids; peace treaty; mummification; social hierarchy; hieroglyphic, hieratic, and demotic writing; papyrus; advances in medicine, astronomy, and mathematics; 365-day calendar
- **Babylon:** legal code; advances in astronomy and mathematics
- **Hittites:** ironworking
- **Assyrians:** legal regulation of royal household; libraries
- **Israel:** monotheistic religion of Judaism
- **Persians:** government organized into provinces with governors; roads; common set of weights and measures; use of coins and money economy; new Zoroastrian religion
- **Phoenicians:** Tyrian purple dye; alphabet

Key Civilizations

CIVILIZATION	TIME PERIOD	NOTABLE RULERS
Sumer	3300 B.C.–1900 B.C.	
Egypt	Old Kingdom 2575 B.C.–2130 B.C. Middle Kingdom 1938 B.C.–1630 B.C. New Kingdom 1539 B.C.–1075 B.C.	Hatshepsut, Thumose III, Ramses II
Akkad	2300 B.C.–2150 B.C.	Sargon
Babylon	Old 1790 B.C.–1595 B.C. New 626 B.C.–539 B.C.	Hammurabi Nebuchadnezzar
Hittite	1650 B.C.–1200 B.C.	
Assyria	1350 B.C.–609 B.C.	Assurbanipal
Israel	1000 B.C.–586 B.C.	David, Solomon
Persia	539 B.C.–323 B.C.	Cyrus the Great, Darius I

KEY TERMS, PEOPLE, AND IDEAS

1. How did the Egyptian religious practice of **mummification** affect the field of medicine?

2. What are **ethics**?

3. Describe Sumer's social **hierarchy**.

4. What did Israelites believe God's **covenant** required of them?

5. Explain the significance of **Hammurabi's** Code.

6. Why was **Hatshepsut** significant in the history of Egypt?

7. What role did **prophets** have in ancient religions?

8. What are the geographic characteristics of the Nile **Delta**?

9. Why was the **Rosetta Stone** significant?

CRITICAL THINKING

10. **Draw Conclusions** How did improvements in technology influence the development of early civilizations?

11. **Determine Central Ideas** What achievements did the Egyptians make in each of the following fields: medicine, astronomy, and mathematics?

12. **Identify Cause and Effect** How was the development of writing in Sumer influenced by economic needs?

13. **Use Visual Information** Look at the map below. Based on the map, and on your knowledge of the Topic, how did geography influence the development of civilizations in Mesopotamia?

14. **Summarize** What distinct characteristics did the early civilizations and empires of the Middle East and Egypt develop?

15. **Compare and Contrast** Compare the views about the afterlife of the ancient Egyptians, Zoroaster, and the Sumerians. How were they similar and different?

16. **Analyze Interactions** Conquest by different leaders and peoples was a constant theme of life in the ancient Middle East and Egypt. In what ways did leaders attempt to unite the often distant and culturally different lands they ruled?

17. **Explain An Argument** Many ancient peoples, including the Babylonians, Assyrians, and Israelites, lived in societies guided by well-established laws. Do you think that having a code of laws was an essential aspect of early civilizations? Why or why not?

18. **Writing Activity: Write an Explanatory Essay** Write a two-paragraph essay based on the excerpt below. Use your knowledge of this Topic and the quote to explain how the story of God's covenant with Abraham, as described in the Book of Genesis, became the basis of two key beliefs of Judaism.

> You shall be the father of a multitude of nations. . . . I will make nations of you, and kings shall come forth from you. And I will establish by covenant between me and you and your descendants after you throughout their generations for an everlasting covenant, to be God to you and to your descendants after you. And I will give to you, and to your descendants after you, the land of your sojournings [short stay], all the land of Canaan. . . .
> —Genesis 17:4–8

19. **Connections to Today** Consider how ancient leaders and governments used public resources on projects. How does this compare to modern government projects and practices? What does the way in which modern governments use public resources say about their priorities? Do they always use these resources wisely? Give examples supporting your perspective.

DOCUMENT-BASED QUESTIONS

Invasion and conquest were common in the ancient Middle East and Egypt. Examine the documents below, then answer the questions that follow.

DOCUMENT A

"Luli, king of Sidon, whom the terror-inspiring glamor of my lordship had overwhelmed, fled far overseas and perished. . . . As to Hezekiah [the king of Judah], . . . I laid siege to his strong cities, walled forts, and countless small villages, and conquered them. . . . I drove out 200,150 people, young and old, male and female, horses, mules, donkeys, camels, big and small cattle beyond counting, and considered them slaves. Himself I made a prisoner in Jerusalem, his royal residence, like a bird in a cage. . . . Thus I reduced his country, but I still increased the tribute and the presents to me as overlord. . . . Hezekiah himself, did send me, later, to Nineveh, my lordly city, together with 30 talents of gold, 800 talents of silver, precious stones, . . . and all kinds of valuable treasures."

— From King Sennacherib of Assyria

DOCUMENT B

"In the eighteenth year of my rule I crossed the Euphrates for the sixteenth time. [King] Hazael of Damascus put his trust upon his numerous army and called up his troops in great number. . . . I fought with him and inflicted a defeat upon him, killing with the sword 16,000 of his experienced soldiers. I took away from him 1,121 chariots, 470 riding horses as well as his camp. . . . I followed him and besieged him in Damascus, his royal residence. I cut down his gardens. . . . I marched as far as the mountains of Hauran, destroying, tearing down and burning innumerable towns, carrying booty away from them which was beyond counting. I marched as far as the mountains of Ba'li-ra'si . . . and erected there a stela [stone pillar] with my image as king."

— From King Shalmaneser III of Assyria

DOCUMENT C

"[My troops] were like lions roaring upon the mountaintops. The chariotry consisted of runners, of picked men, of every good and capable chariot-warrior. The horses were quivering in every part of their bodies, prepared to crush the foreign countries under their hoofs. . . . Those who reached my frontier, . . . their heart and their soul are finished forever and ever. Those who came forward together on the sea, the full flame was in front of them at the river-mouths, while a stockade of lances surrounded them on the shore. . . . I have made the lands turn back from (even) mentioning Egypt; for when they pronounce my name in their land, then they are burned up."

— From Pharaoh Ramses III of Egypt

DOCUMENT D

This relief carving shows Assyrian archers in a battle from Sennacherib's campaign in Judah.

20. Documents A, B, and C are told from the perspective of
    A. a victim of an ambush.
    B. the ally of a conquering ruler.
    C. the enemy of a conquering ruler.
    D. the leader of a successful campaign.

21. What can you learn from Document D?
    A. who won the battle shown
    B. how many soldiers fought in each battle
    C. where each battle took place
    D. what weapons the soldiers used in battle

22. What did the narrator of Document B do in the mountains of Ba'li-ra'si after he conquered the king of Damascus?
    A. conquer a great city
    B. set up a monument showing his image
    C. chase the enemies' leader
    D. receive tribute from the conquered people

23. **Writing Task** Why would ancient rulers have had inscriptions, artwork, and other such documents created to record their triumphs and conquests? Do you think documents such as these are reliable records of historical events? Why or why not? Use your knowledge of the Topic and specific information from these documents to support your opinion.

GO ONLINE to access more practice

Ancient India and China
(3300 B.C.–A.D. 550)

ESSENTIAL QUESTION How are religion and culture connected?

A terracotta army guards the tomb of China's first emperor.

Connections to Today

Today, government agencies work to protect Americans from flooding and other emergencies. The U.S. Army Corps of Engineers, for example, designs and constructs flood-control structures. Suppose a flood threatened your safety. The work of the Corps could protect you.

In this topic you'll read how the Chinese government in ancient times justified their rule partly through their efforts to protect their people from the devastating floods of the river known as the Huang He.

NBC LEARN

Learn about Shi Huangdi, China's first emperor.

BOUNCE to Activate My Story Video

In this Topic, you will learn about the complex civilizations and powerful dynasties that developed in ancient India and China. As you will see, the developing beliefs of Hinduism, Buddhism, Confucianism, and Daoism significantly affected ancient Indian and Chinese cultures and governments. Look at the lesson outline and explore the timeline. As you study this Topic, you will complete the Quest inquiry.

LESSON OUTLINE

3.1 Early Civilization in South Asia

3.2 The Origins of Hinduism and Buddhism

3.3 Powerful Empires Emerge in India

3.4 Ancient Civilization in China

3.5 Strong Rulers Unite China

Key Events in India and China

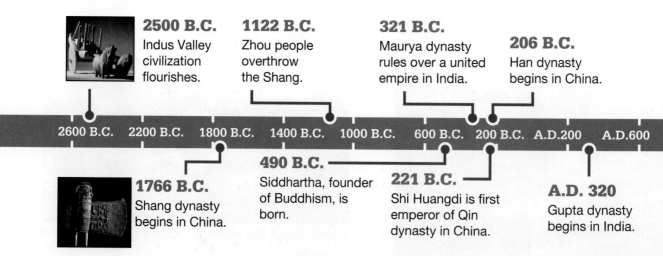

2500 B.C. Indus Valley civilization flourishes.

1122 B.C. Zhou people overthrow the Shang.

321 B.C. Maurya dynasty rules over a united empire in India.

206 B.C. Han dynasty begins in China.

| 2600 B.C. | 2200 B.C. | 1800 B.C. | 1400 B.C. | 1000 B.C. | 600 B.C. | 200 B.C. | A.D.200 | A.D.600 |

1766 B.C. Shang dynasty begins in China.

490 B.C. Siddhartha, founder of Buddhism, is born.

221 B.C. Shi Huangdi is first emperor of Qin dynasty in China.

A.D. 320 Gupta dynasty begins in India.

QUEST! INQUIRY

Write an Essay on Order in Society

Religions, or belief systems, were important contributions to the cultures of the early civilizations of India and China. Each religion imparted certain values and behavioral guidelines that shaped family structure, society, and government. In this project, you will examine primary and secondary sources to arrive at your own conclusion about the following question: What makes an ordered society?

STEP ❶
With a partner, discuss what helps unify a society. Consider how a society governs itself and creates a common purpose.

STEP ❷
Examine the documents relating to how religion is related to the structure of a society. Determine the central idea of each document and its major points.

STEP ❸
Write a clear, coherent essay supporting the conclusions you have drawn. Address the strengths and limitations of your position and respond to at least one opposing position.

STEP ❹
Revise your writing. Is the paper logically organized? Is specific evidence from the documents used to support your viewpoint? Share the finished essay with the class.

 GO ONLINE to access complete Quest materials

3.1

The Indus civilization produced sophisticated arts and crafts, including these small oxen and cart figures made around 2000 B.C. in Mohenjo-Daro.

 BOUNCE to Activate Flipped Video

Objectives

Describe the Indian subcontinent's geography.

Understand the clues archaeology has provided about the rise and fall of the Indus civilization.

Analyze the main characteristics of the Vedic civilization.

Explain what ancient Indian epics reveal about life in the Vedic age.

Key Terms

subcontinent
plateau
monsoon
Harappa
Mohenjo-Daro
acculturation
Vedas
rajah
varna
Brahman
mystic

Early Civilization in South Asia

In 1922, archaeologists made some startling discoveries in northwestern India. While digging in the Indus River valley, they unearthed bricks, small statues, clay seals, and other artifacts unlike any they had seen before. They soon realized they had uncovered a "lost civilization"—forgotten for some 3,500 years. Though later discoveries have added to our knowledge of the cities of the region, many mysteries remain about this civilization that flourished almost 5,000 years ago.

Geography of the Indian Subcontinent

The Indus Valley is located in the region known as South Asia, which includes the Indian subcontinent. A **subcontinent** is a large landmass that juts out from a continent. The Indian subcontinent is a huge, wedge-shaped peninsula extending into the Indian Ocean.

Today, it includes three of the world's ten most populous countries—India, Pakistan, and Bangladesh—as well as the island nation of Sri Lanka (sree LAHNG kuh) and the mountain nations of Nepal and Bhutan.

Towering, snow-covered mountain ranges mark the northern border of the subcontinent, including the Himalayas and the Hindu Kush. These mountains limited contacts between India and other lands and helped its people develop a distinct culture. The mountains, however, were not a complete barrier. Steep passes through the Hindu Kush served as gateways to migrating and invading peoples for thousands of years.

Mountains, Plateaus, and Plains of India The Indian subcontinent is divided into three major zones: the northern plain, the dry Deccan plateau, and the coastal plains on either side of the Deccan.

The northern plain lies just south of the Himalayas. This fertile region is watered by mighty rivers: the Indus, which gives India its name, the Ganges (GAN jeez), and the Brahmaputra (brah muh POO truh). These rivers and their tributaries carry melted snow from the mountains to the plains, making agriculture possible. To many people of the Indian subcontinent, rivers are sacred, especially the Ganges. An Indian name for river is *lokmata,* or "mother of the people."

The Deccan **plateau,** or raised area of level land, occupies the southern interior. The Deccan lacks the melting snows that feed the rivers of the north and provide water for irrigation. As a result, much of the plateau is hot and dry. The region is harder to farm, so it is less densely populated than India's fertile plains.

India's third region, the coastal plains, are separated from the Deccan plateau by low-lying mountain ranges, the Eastern and Western Ghats. Rivers and heavy seasonal rains provide water for farmers. From very early times, coastal people used the seas for fishing and as highways for trade.

Life-Giving Monsoons Today, as in the past, a defining feature of life in the Indian subcontinent is the **monsoon,** a seasonal wind that is part of global wind patterns. In October, the winter monsoon blows from the northeast, bringing dry air that withers crops. During May and June of each year, the wet summer monsoon begins to blow from the southwest. These winds pick up moisture over the Indian Ocean and drench the land with downpours.

The monsoon shaped Indian life. Each year, people welcomed the rains that were desperately needed to water the crops. If the rains were late, famine and starvation might occur. However, if the rains were too heavy, rushing rivers would unleash deadly floods.

Cultural Diversity India's great size and varied landscape fostered linguistic and cultural diversity, as did acceptance of different religions. Still, there was an underlying cultural unity around sacred texts and religious teachings. At the same time, unique languages and traditions developed in different parts of India and influenced a larger shared culture.

☑ **CHECK UNDERSTANDING** What geographical feature limited the Indian subcontinent's contact with other peoples?

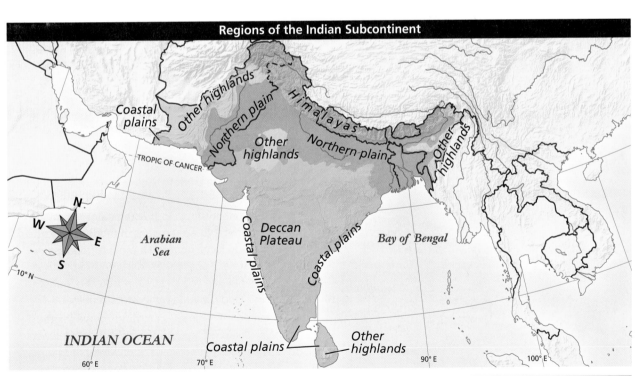

Regions of the Indian Subcontinent

>> **Analyze Maps** The Indian subcontinent includes the countries of South Asia except for Afghanistan. What makes this region a subcontinent?

🅑 BOUNCE to Activate Map

The Forgotten Indus Civilization

The first civilization in the Indian subcontinent emerged in the valleys of the Indus River and the Ghaggar-Hakra River (identified by some scholars as the Saraswati River) in present-day Pakistan and India. The Indus Valley civilization flourished from about 3300 B.C. to about 1700 B.C. Its once-prosperous cities were only rediscovered in the 1920s, unearthed by archaeologists' picks and shovels.

Archaeologists have not fully uncovered many Indus Valley sites. Still, we do know that the Indus Valley or Harappan civilization covered the largest area of any civilization until the rise of Persia more than 1,000 years later. We know, too, that its great cities were as impressive as those of Sumer.

Well-Planned Cities Reveal Organized Government In recent years, archaeologists have discovered more than 1,000 settlements along the Indus and Ghaggar-Hakra rivers. At least eight of the settlements are larger cities that archaeologists believe may have been prominent during the course of the civilization's history.

Since their discovery in the 1920s, the Indus cities of **Harappa** and **Mohenjo-Daro** (moh HEN joh DAH roh) have been considered possible twin capitals of the civilization, or cities that ruled the area one after the other. Both were large, some three miles in circumference. Each was dominated by a massive hilltop structure whose exact purpose is unknown. Both cities had huge warehouses to store grain. Clearly, farmers produced enough surplus food to support thousands of city dwellers.

The most striking feature of the Indus cities is that they were carefully planned. They were laid out in a grid pattern, with long, wide main streets and large rectangular blocks. Houses were mostly built with baked clay bricks of a standard size.

Indus houses had complex plumbing systems, with baths, drains, and water chutes that led into sewers beneath the streets. Merchants in the marketplace used a uniform system of weights and measures—additional evidence of careful planning.

From this evidence, archaeologists have concluded that Indus Valley cities were planned by a well-organized government. The rigid pattern of building and uniform brick sizes suggest government planners at work. These experts must have been skilled in mathematics and surveying to lay out the cities so precisely.

Farming and Trade As in other early civilizations, most Indus Valley people were farmers. They grew a wide variety of crops, including wheat, barley, melons, and dates. They also may have been the first people to cultivate cotton and weave its fibers into cloth.

Some people were merchants and traders. Their ships carried cargoes of cotton cloth, grain, copper, pearls, and ivory combs to distant lands. By hugging the coast of the Arabian Sea and sailing up the Persian Gulf, Indus vessels reached the cities of Sumer.

Scholars have not yet learned how to read the Indus Valley writing system and still have many questions about this ancient civilization.

Indus Religious Beliefs Like other ancient peoples, Indus people seem to have worshiped more than one form of God. Some religious images show features that are present in modern Hinduism. They seem to have honored a mother goddess, representing the source of creation, along with a male form of God, whom some scholars connect to the Hindu God Shiva in a meditating posture.

Indus people also seem to have viewed some animals as sacred, including cattle. Some scholars think these early practices resemble modern Hindu beliefs. Hindus honor cattle as generous, life-sustaining beings that provide milk and plow the earth.

>> Archaeologists discovered cities of the ancient Indus civilization in the 1920s. This excavated drainage system is in the city of Lothal, discovered in 1945.

BOUNCE to Activate Chart

A Mysterious Decline By about 1750 B.C., the quality of life in the Indus Valley was declining. The once orderly cities no longer kept up the old standards. Crude pottery replaced the finer works of earlier days.

Mohenjo-Daro was abandoned. The populations of the other Indus cities and towns also dwindled. While people continued to live in the Indus Valley, Indus civilization fell apart and eventually disappeared.

Scholars do not know exactly why Indus civilization collapsed. They once thought that invaders destroyed the cities, but this explanation now seems unlikely.

> The Indus Civilization remains an historical enigma [puzzle]. A remarkably uniform [culture] distributed over a vast geographical area utterly disappears without an apparent successor. Cities, writing, the high achievement of their crafts, the use of standardized weights, long distance trade with the Gulf, and their exceptional system of urban sanitation simply disappear from the South Asian social landscape.
>
> —Carl Lamberg-Karlovsky, archaeologist

Today, scholars think that environmental factors undermined Indus civilization. The lower Indus became subject to severe flooding, which destroyed towns and cities. Over time, rainfall in the area decreased, slowly turning it into the desert or semiarid land it is today. Without adequate rainfall, a civilization that relied on farming could not survive.

Scholars think that these events contributed to the end of Indus civilization. As the ruined cities disappeared, all memory of them faded. Some scholars, though, argue that features of Indus culture survived the end of this civilization to become part of the Vedic civilization that followed.

☑ **CITE EVIDENCE** What evidence shows that the Indus civilization included a well-organized government?

Vedic Civilization

During the centuries between 1700 B.C. and 1500 B.C., a new civilization developed after the decline of the Indus civilization. Although there is debate about

>> The Vedas were recited for many years before they were written down. This page is from the *Rig Veda,* or "Knowledge of the Hymns of Praise," the largest Veda, containing over 1,000 hymns.

how this civilization formed, it would shape the subcontinent for centuries to come.

Society in the Vedic Period Some of the people who shaped this era spoke an Indo-European language. They intermarried with other groups. Through **acculturation,** or the blending of two or more cultures, these groups formed what would later be known as Vedic civilization in South Asia.

Indians in the Vedic period built no cities and left no statues or stone seals. Most of what we know about them comes from the **Vedas,** a collection of hymns, chants, ritual instructions, and other religious teachings.

Vedic priests memorized and recited the Vedas for a thousand years before they ever wrote down these sacred teachings. As a result, the period from 1500 B.C. to 500 B.C. is often called the Vedic period.

In the earliest Vedas, Vedic people appear as warriors who fought in chariots with bows and arrows. Vedic people valued cattle, which provided them with food and clothing. Later, when they became settled farmers, families continued to measure their wealth in cows and bulls, since these animals provided milk, plowed the fields, and were crucial to farming.

From Nomads to Farmers Gradually, Vedic people gave up nomadic ways and settled into villages to cultivate crops and breed cattle. From local survivors of the Indus civilization, they learned to raise crops. They also took up other skilled crafts.

In time, Vedic people spread eastward to settle in the heavily forested Ganges basin. By about 800 B.C., they had learned to make tools out of iron. Equipped with iron axes and weapons, restless pioneers carved farms and villages out of the rain forests of the northeast.

Vedic people had a tribal political system that later formed the basis for the small independent kingdoms that formed in northwestern India. Vedic tribes were led by chiefs called **rajahs.** A rajah, who was often the most skilled war leader, had been elected to his position by an assembly of warriors.

As he ruled, he considered the advice of a council of elders made up of the heads of families. Rajahs often fought with one another over trade and territory. Some rajahs became powerful hereditary rulers, extending their influence over many villages.

Vedic Society The Vedas describe four personality types, or **varna.** In all societies, different people are drawn to different roles. At first, people were not born into varna roles. Instead, they were assigned to varna through their abilities and actions.

Those who pursued knowledge were the Brahmin (BRAH min). Those who were leaders or exercised power were the Kshatriya (KSHAHT ree yuh). Those who sought to own land or engage in business were the Vaishya (VYSH yuh). Those who worked with their hands were the Shudra (SHOO druh). These are the four traditional varna described in the Vedas.

Later, the society was divided by occupational groups. During the medieval period, these ancient divisions would evolve into a more rigid, hierarchical system known as the caste system. People were rigidly fixed in the class or caste into which they were born.

The *Rig Veda* describes how the universe was created from the body of a divine Universal Being referred to as Purusha. From Purusha, everything, including the planets, air, animals, and plants came into being. The people of the four classes in society are also said to have been created from Purusha.

The Vedic Religion Vedic people worshiped Gods and Goddesses who embodied natural forces such as sky, sun, storm, and fire. They viewed these deities as manifestations of a single, divine absolute, or God.

The chief Vedic deity was fierce Indra, the God of war. Indra's weapon was the thunderbolt, which he used not only to destroy demons but also to

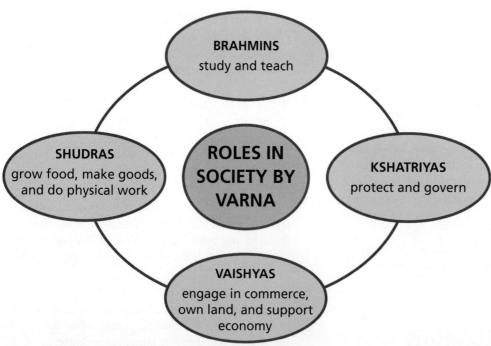

SOURCE: Hindu American Foundation

>> Vedic society was divided into groups, based on people's abilities and interests.
Infer How is each role needed for a society to function well?

announce the arrival of rain, so vital to Indian life. Other major Gods included Varuna, the God of order and creation, and Agni, the God of fire and the messenger who communicated human wishes to the Gods. Vedic people also honored animal deities, such as monkey and snake Gods.

Brahmins offered sacrifices of food and drink to Gods, seeing divinity in all of nature. Chanting prayers and hymns in the sacred Sanskrit language, these priests asked the Gods to help their communities.

As the lives of Vedic people changed, so, too, did their beliefs. Some religious thinkers were moving toward the notion of **Brahman,** a universal divine spirit that expressed itself through the universe and that resided in all things. There was also a move toward mysticism. **Mystics** are people who seek direct communion with the divine.

Vedic mystics practiced meditation and yoga, spiritual and bodily disciplines designed to enhance the attempt to achieve direct contact with the divine. The religions that emerged in India after the Vedic period were influenced by both mysticism and the notion of Brahman.

☑ **INFER** How might the idea of Brahman be connected to mysticism?

>> Artworks depicting scenes from the *Mahabharata* have been created since ancient times. This modern folk-art painting on cloth shows the God Krishna in a chariot pulled by horses.

The Great Vedic Epics

By 500 B.C., a new Indian civilization had emerged. Although it consisted of many rival kingdoms, the people shared a common culture rooted in Vedic traditions. By this time, too, the Indian people had begun writing in Sanskrit. Priests then began writing down their sacred texts.

Vedic people maintained a strong oral tradition as well. They continued to memorize and recite ancient hymns, as well as two long epic poems, the *Mahabharata* (muh hah BAH rah tuh) and the *Ramayana* (rah MAH yuh nuh). Like the Sumerian *Epic of Gilgamesh*, the Indian epics mix history, mythology, adventure, and religion.

Mahabharata Describes Warfare and Religion

The *Mahabharata* is India's greatest epic. Through its nearly 100,000 verses, we hear echoes of the battles that rival Vedic tribes fought to gain control of the Ganges region.

Five royal brothers, the Pandavas, lose their kingdom to their cousins. After a great battle that lasts 18 days, the Pandavas regain their kingdom and restore peace to India. One episode, known as the

Bhagavad-Gita (BUG uh vud GEE tuh), or *Sacred Song,* reflects important Hindu religious beliefs about the immortality of the soul and the value of performing one's duty. In its verses, the god Krishna instructs Prince Arjuna on the importance of duty over personal desires and ambitions.

Ramayana **Teaches Values** The *Ramayana* is much shorter but equally memorable. It recounts the fantastic deeds of the daring hero Rama and his beautiful bride Sita. Early on, Sita is kidnapped by the demon-king Ravana. The rest of the story tells how Rama finally rescues Sita with the aid of the monkey general Hanuman.

Like Hinduism, these epics evolved over thousands of years. Priest-poets added new morals to the tales to teach different lessons. For example, they pointed to Rama as a model of virtue or as an ideal king. Likewise, Sita came to be honored as an ideal woman who remained loyal and supportive to her husband through many hardships.

☑ **DRAW CONCLUSIONS** How do the Vedas relate to history in India during the Vedic period?

1. **Identify Cause and Effect** How has geography affected where people live on the subcontinent?

2. **Describe** How did people in the Indus civilization make a living?

3. **Summarize** How was Vedic society structured?

4. **Connect** How do the Indian epics reveal the values of Vedic people, and what are some of those values?

5. **Connections to Today** How do cattle link the Indus civilization, Vedic people, and modern India?

3.2

Visvamitra visits Vasishtha in ancient India. Both men wrote parts of the Vedas, the sacred scriptures of Hinduism. How does the artist convey respect between the authors?

The Origins of Hinduism and Buddhism

Thousands of years ago, two major religions—Hinduism and Buddhism—emerged in ancient India. The ethical and spiritual messages of these religions profoundly shaped Indian civilization.

Hindu Beliefs Develop

Unlike most major religions, Hinduism has no single founder and no single sacred text. It evolved over at least 3,500 years and grew out of the overlapping beliefs of the diverse groups who settled India. Over those thousands of years, Hinduism developed in richness and complexity, with many different branches.

As a result, Hinduism became one of the world's most complex religions, with countless Gods and Goddesses and many forms of worship existing side by side. Despite this diversity, all Hindus share certain basic beliefs.

One Force Unites Everything "God is one, but wise people know it by many names." This ancient proverb from the Vedas reflects the Hindu belief that everything in the universe is part of the unchanging, all-powerful spiritual force called Brahman. In Hinduism, Brahman is too complex an idea for most people to understand. So Hindus worship a variety of Gods who give concrete form to Brahman.

The most widely worshipped Hindu Gods are Vishnu, the Preserver; Shiva, the Transformer; and Shakti, the Great Goddess, who is believed to be the protective mother of the universe and who

BOUNCE to Activate Flipped Video

Objectives

Describe the origins and central beliefs of Hinduism.

Understand India's caste system.

Describe the origins and central beliefs of Buddhism.

Explore how Buddhism grew and changed as it spread beyond India.

Key Terms

atman
moksha
reincarnation
karma
dharma
ahimsa
caste
jati
Siddhartha Gautama
Four Noble Truths
Eightfold Path
nirvana
sect

GO ONLINE to access your digital course

battles the forces of evil. Each can take many forms, human or animal, to represent the various aspects of Brahman with which he or she is associated.

Sacred Texts Show Hindu Beliefs

Over many hundreds of years, Hindu teachings were recorded in the sacred texts of the Vedas. The Upanishads (oo PAN ih shadz) are a section of the Vedas that present Hindu mystical teachings. These sacred texts use vivid images to examine complex ideas about the human soul and the connectedness of all life. In addition, literary works such as the *Bhagavad-Gita* were also revered for their teachings and beauty.

The Ultimate Goal of Moksha

To Hindus, every person has an essential self, or **atman** (AHT mun). Some believe atman is the same as Brahman. Others believe it has the same nature as Brahman but is still different from Brahman. The ultimate goal of existence, Hindus believe, is achieving **moksha** (MOHK shuh), or union with Brahman.

To do that, many Hindus believe they must love and serve God unconditionally, while others believe they must free themselves from selfish thoughts that separate them from Brahman. Most people cannot achieve moksha in one lifetime, but Hindus believe in **reincarnation,** or rebirth in another bodily form.

>> A statue of the wheel of dharma, a Hindu symbol of life, death, and rebirth. In Hinduism, how does one escape the wheel of fate?

BOUNCE to Activate Gallery

Reincarnation allows people to continue working toward moksha through many lifetimes.

Karma and Dharma

In each existence, Hindus believe, a person can come closer to achieving moksha by obeying the law of karma. **Karma** refers to both action and result. Thus, someone's good and moral actions lead to good results either in this lifetime or the next. A life filled with misdeeds will lead to hardship and suffering in either this life or the next.

Hindus believe that all existence is an expression of Brahman. Thus animals, plants, and objects like rocks or water are treated with great respect and even venerated.

To Hindus, all of existence is ranked by levels of consciousness—the higher one's consciousness, the greater the chance of achieving union with Brahman and the ultimate goal in life, moksha. People who live virtuously earn good karma and are reborn with a higher level of consciousness. Those who do evil acquire bad karma and are reborn into a lower level of consciousness and a life of suffering. In Indian art, this cycle of death and rebirth is symbolized by the image of the wheel.

To escape the cycle of birth and rebirth, Hinduism stresses the importance of **dharma** (DAHR muh), the religious and moral duties of an individual. These duties include concepts such as truthfulness, and living in moderation. Dharma may also vary according to one's role in society, gender, and age.

Another key moral principle of Hinduism is **ahimsa** (uh HIM sah), or nonviolence. To Hindus, all people and things are aspects of Brahman and therefore deserve respect. Many Hindus try to practice ahimsa.

Jainism Develops

About 500 B.C., the teacher Mahavira (mah hah VEE ruh) founded the Jain community. Jainism (JY niz um), a religion that began in eastern India, is still practiced today.

Mahavira stressed the importance of acting ethically and unselfishly. Jain teachings emphasize meditation, self-denial, and an extreme form of ahimsa. To avoid accidentally killing a living thing, even an insect, Jain monks carry brooms to sweep the ground in front of their feet. Jains often put the value of ahimsa into practice in different ways, including through vegetarianism—as many Hindus do.

☑ **SUMMARIZE** How do the Hindu Gods relate to the concept of Brahman?

India's Caste System

Vedic people divided society into the four varna, sometimes known as **castes.** This system later coexisted with another system based on occupation. People in each occupation belonged to groups called **jati,** sometimes known in English as subcastes.

Complex Rules of the Caste System Varna and jati evolved over time into a birth-based system supported by many religious leaders. At first, individuals were not born into varna. Those in jati for priests and teachers, though, came to be seen as Brahmin; warriors and kings were seen as Kshatriya; traders and merchants became Vaishya; and laborers became Shudra.

Over time, thousands of birth-based jati developed in India, each with its own religious practices and social customs. Jati were not based on Hindu religious teachings. Instead, they were social and cultural institutions. In fact, members of religions other than Hinduism also belonged to jati. While the Indian caste system had religious support, it is not an essential feature of Hinduism.

People with jobs such as digging graves, cleaning streets, or turning animal hides into leather were considered so impure that they were called "untouchables." These people, now known as Dalits, faced harsh and restricted lives. Other castes feared "pollution"" from contact with an untouchable. Untouchables had to live apart and sound a wooden clapper to warn of their approach. Today, untouchability is outlawed, as is discrimination based on caste.

Caste Affects Social Structure Despite its inequalities, caste ensured a stable social order. In time, people came to believe that the law of karma determined their caste. While they could not change their status in this life, they could reach a higher state in a future life by faithfully fulfilling the duties of their present caste. Many modern Hindus, however, reject any connection between religion and caste.

The caste system, though, gave many people a sense of identity and interdependence. Each jati had its own occupation and its own leaders. Jati members cooperated to help one another. In addition, each jati had its own special role in Indian society.

Although strictly separated, different jati depended on one another for their basic needs. A lower-caste carpenter, for example, built the home of a higher-caste scholar.

As people migrated into the subcontinent, they formed new jati. Other jati grew out of new

Hochzeitsprocession zu Madras.

>> **Infer** Chair-bearers, or "dolavahi," were part of the caste of untouchables in ancient India and in later times, as shown in this 19th century image. Who in this image would be a higher-caste person?

occupations and religions. This flexibility allowed people with diverse customs to live side by side in relative harmony. By modern times, there were thousands of major castes and subcastes.

☑ **ANALYZE INFORMATION** How did the caste system provide a sense of order in Indian society?

The Buddha's Key Teachings

More than 2,500 years ago, warring princes battled across the northern plain of India. During this troubled time, people in India sought new answers to spiritual questions.

In the foothills of the Himalayas, a reformer named **Siddhartha Gautama** (sih DAHR tuh GOW tuh muh), also known as the Buddha, founded a new religion. That religion is Buddhism. The Buddha's teachings built upon earlier concepts found in the Vedas and the Upanishads. The Buddha's teachings eventually spread across Asia to become the core beliefs of one of the world's most influential religions.

From Boy to Buddha The facts of Gautama's early life are known mostly through traditional stories. He was born into a Kshatriya family about 490 B.C. According to tradition, his mother dreamed that a radiant white elephant descended to her from heaven. Signs such as this led a sage to predict that the boy would someday become a wandering holy man. To prevent that from happening, Gautama's father kept him in the family's palaces, surrounded by comfort and luxury. Gautama married a beautiful woman, had a son, and enjoyed a happy life.

Over several days, as Gautama defied his father to ride beyond the palace gardens, he saw for the first time an old person, a sick person, and a dead body. Suddenly, Gautama became aware of human suffering. Deeply disturbed, he bade farewell to his family and left the palace, never to return. He set out to discover "the realm of life where there is neither suffering nor death."

Gautama Gains Enlightenment Gautama wandered for six years, seeking answers from scholars and holy men whose ideas failed to satisfy him. He fasted and meditated. Eventually, he sat down to meditate under a giant fig tree, determined to stay there until he understood the mystery of life. This tree is now known as the bodhi tree: the tree of awakening.

For weeks, according to legend, evil spirits tempted Gautama to give up his meditations. Then, Buddhists believe, he suddenly gained insight into the cause of and cure for suffering and sorrow. When he rose, he was no longer Gautama. He had become the Buddha, or "Enlightened One."

>> **Describe** This ancient statue of the Buddha in a meditating pose is in Sri Lanka. What does the Buddha's facial expression show?

The Four Noble Truths The Buddha spent the rest of his life teaching others what he had learned. In his first sermon, he explained the **Four Noble Truths** that stand at the heart of Buddhism:

- All life is full of suffering, pain, and sorrow.
- The cause of suffering is rooted in evils such as greed, desire, and hatred.
- The only cure for suffering is to overcome desire and other evils.
- The way to overcome desire and other evils is to follow the Eightfold Path.

The Buddha described the **Eightfold Path** as "right views, right aspirations, right speech, right conduct, right livelihood, right effort, right mindfulness, and right contemplation." The first two steps involved understanding the Four Noble Truths and committing oneself to the Eightfold Path. Next, a person had to live a moral life, avoiding evil words and actions. The Buddha stressed moral principles such as honesty, charity, and kindness to all living creatures. Through meditation, a person might at last achieve enlightenment.

For the Buddhist, the final goal is **nirvana**, or absorption in a state of consciousness free from all clinging and desire. This leads to release from the cycle of rebirth.

Buddhism and Hinduism Buddhism had its roots in the Vedas and built on Hindu scriptures that explored the methods of understanding the self, God, and the nature of the world. It also included Hindu concepts of including karma, dharma, and reincarnation. Ahimsa, or nonviolence, was central to both religions.

Yet Buddhism differed from Hinduism in several ways. The Buddha said that the Gods of Hinduism were not truly divine. The Buddha rejected the priests and formal rituals of the Vedas. Instead, the Buddha urged each person to seek enlightenment through meditation. Buddhism offered the hope of nirvana to all who earnestly sought it.

☑ **SEQUENCE EVENTS** How did Siddhartha Gautama become the Buddha?

Buddhism Spreads

The Buddha attracted many disciples, or followers, who accompanied him as he preached across northern India. Many men and women who accepted the Buddha's teachings set up monasteries and

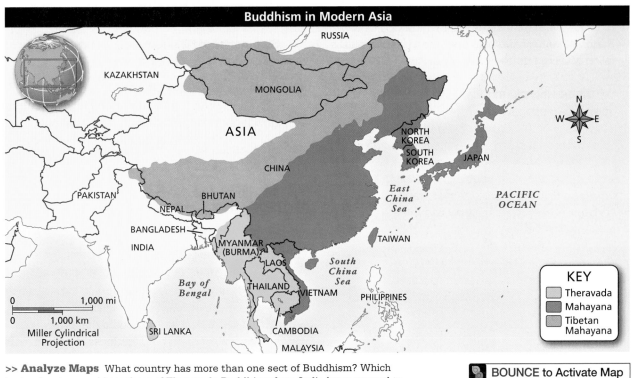

Buddhism in Modern Asia

KEY
- Theravada
- Mahayana
- Tibetan Mahayana

>> **Analyze Maps** What country has more than one sect of Buddhism? Which body of water would teachers of Theravada Buddhism from India have crossed to reach the countries where it is practiced today?

BOUNCE to Activate Map

convents for meditation and study. Some Buddhist monasteries grew into major centers of learning.

The Buddha's death, like his birth, is clouded in legend. At age 80, according to tradition, he is said to have eaten spoiled food. As he lay dying, he told his disciples, "Decay is inherent [exists in] in all things. Work out your own salvation with persistent effort."

Collecting the Teachings of the Buddha After the Buddha's death, his followers collected his teachings into a sacred text called the *Tripitaka*, or "Three Baskets of Wisdom." One of the "baskets" includes sayings like this one, which echoes the Hindu emphasis on duty: "Let a man, after he has discerned his own duty, be always attentive to his duty." Other sayings give the Buddha's version of the golden rule: "Overcome anger by not growing angry. Overcome evil with good. Overcome the liar by truth."

Two Branches of Buddhism Missionaries and traders spread Buddhism across India and to many parts of Asia. Gradually, Buddhism split into two major schools: Theravada (thehr uh VAH duh) Buddhism and Mahayana (mah huh YAH nuh)

Buddhism. These schools in turn became subdivided into **sects,** or subgroups.

Theravada Buddhism closely followed the Buddha's original teachings. It required a life devoted to hard spiritual work. Only the most dedicated seekers, such as monks and nuns, could hope to reach nirvana. The Theravada school spread to Sri Lanka and Southeast Asia.

The Mahayana school made Buddhism easier for ordinary people to follow. Even though the Buddha had forbidden followers to worship him, Mahayana Buddhists pictured him and other holy beings as compassionate godlike beings. People turned to these beings for help in solving daily problems as well as in achieving salvation.

Mahayana Buddhists believed in a variety of divine or cosmic beings, including Boddhisattvas, or those who had achieved nirvana but remained available to human beings out of compassion, to help others achieve nirvana. Mahayana Buddhism spread to China, Tibet, Korea, and Japan.

Buddhism Declines in India Although Buddhism took firm root across Asia, it slowly declined in India. With its great tolerance of diversity, Hinduism eventually absorbed some Buddhist ideas and made room for the Buddha as another Hindu God. A few Buddhist centers survived until the 1100s, when they fell to Muslim armies from Central Asia.

☑ **INFER** How did the *Tripitaka* help Buddhism spread beyond India?

1. **Summarize** In Hinduism, what is the role of reincarnation in achieving moksha?

2. **Identify Cause and Effect** How did Hinduism become a diverse religion with many Gods and Goddesses and many forms of worship?

3. **Summarize** What is the final goal of Buddhists in their practice of the religion?

4. **Sequence Events** What sequence of events after Buddha's death caused Buddhism to spread beyond India?

5. **Quest Connection** How did the caste system contribute to the development of an ordered society in India?

3.3

These are the remains of a Buddhist stupa in Bihar, India, built during the Maurya period.

Powerful Empires Emerge in India

Northern India was often a battleground where rival princes fought for control of the rich Ganges valley. But in 321 B.C., a young adventurer, Chandragupta Maurya (chun druh GUP tuh MOWR yuh), forged the first Indian empire.

The Maurya Empire Builds a Strong Government

We know about **Chandragupta Maurya** largely from reports written by Megasthenes (muh GAS thuh neez), a Greek ambassador to the Mauryan court. He described the great Mauryan capital at Pataliputra. It boasted schools and a library as well as splendid palaces and temples. An awed Megasthenes reported that the wall around the city "was crowned with 530 towers and had 64 gates."

Chandragupta Unites India Chandragupta first gained power in the Ganges valley, then conquered northern India. His son and grandson later pushed south, adding much of the Deccan to their empire. From 321 B.C. to 185 B.C., the Maurya dynasty ruled over a vast, united empire.

 BOUNCE to Activate Flipped Video

Objectives

Analyze how Mauryan rulers created a strong central government for their empire.

Explore the kingdoms that arose across the Deccan.

Explain why the period of Gupta rule in India is considered a golden age.

Understand how family and village life shaped Indian society.

Key Terms

Chandragupta
   Maurya
dissent
Ashoka
missionaries
golden age
decimal system
joint family
dowry

>> The Maurya emperor Ashoka gave up the ruthless ways of a warrior, and then ruled by moral example instead of excessive force.

>> Ashoka had stone pillars erected throughout India. Writing on the pillars provides moral advice and Ashoka's promise of a just government for all.

Chandragupta maintained order through a well-organized bureaucracy. Royal officials supervised the building of roads and harbors to benefit trade. Other officials collected taxes and managed state-owned factories and shipyards. People sought justice in royal courts and from the emperor himself.

Chandragupta's rule was effective but harsh. A brutal secret police force reported on corruption, crime, and **dissent**—ideas that opposed those of the government. Fearful of his many enemies, Chandragupta had specially trained women warriors guard his palace. Servants tasted his food to protect him from poisoning. Secret passages in the palace let him move about, unseen.

Ashoka Governs by Example The most honored Maurya emperor was Chandragupta's grandson, **Ashoka** (uh SHOH kuh). A few years after becoming emperor in 268 B.C., he converted to Buddhism. Some years later, Ashoka fought a long, bloody war to conquer the Deccan region of Kalinga.

Then, horrified at the slaughter—more than 100,000 people are said to have died—Ashoka turned his back on further conquests. He embraced Buddhism, rejected violence, and resolved to rule by moral example.

Showing respect for all life, Ashoka stopped eating most meats and limited animal sacrifices. He sent **missionaries,** or people sent on a religious mission, to spread Buddhism across India and to Sri Lanka. By doing so, he paved the way for the spread of Buddhism throughout Asia. Although Ashoka promoted Buddhism, he also preached tolerance for other religions.

Ashoka had stone pillars set up across India, announcing laws and promising a just government. He then took steps to improve life across his empire. He built hospitals, roads, and rest houses for travelers. "I have had banyan trees planted on the roads to give shade to people and animals," he noted. "I have planted mango groves, and I have had [wells] dug and shelters erected along the roads."

Division and Unity Ashoka's rule brought peace and prosperity and helped unite the diverse peoples within his empire. After his death, however, Maurya power declined. By 185 B.C., rival princes again battled for power across the northern plain.

During its history, India seldom remained politically united for long. In ancient times, as today, the subcontinent was home to many peoples who shared an underlying cultural unity. Although Indians shared a common civilization, regional kingdoms in the north and south began to grow, adding to the political divisions.

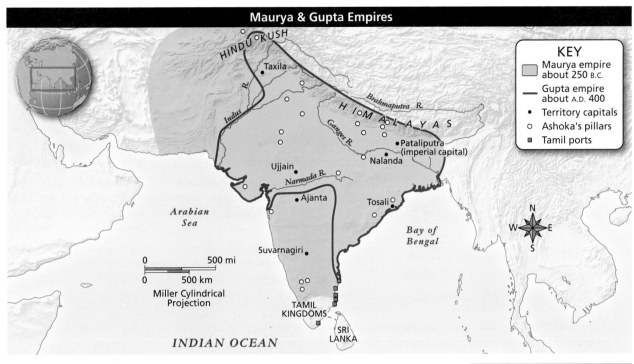

Maurya & Gupta Empires

KEY
- Maurya empire about 250 B.C.
- Gupta empire about A.D. 400
- • Territory capitals
- ○ Ashoka's pillars
- ■ Tamil ports

>> **Analyze Maps** Maurya and Gupta emperors united much of India under their rule. How did geography limit the northward expansion of both empires? What region of the Indian subcontinent remained separate from both empires?

BOUNCE to Activate Map

Contributing to the turmoil, foreign invaders frequently pushed through mountain passes into northern India. Some came to plunder rich Indian cities, but stayed to rule. The divided northern kingdoms were often unable to resist these conquerors. Still, the Maurya rulers had shown that a well-organized government could unite a vast empire.

☑ **ANALYZE INFORMATION** What was the basic structure of Chandragupta Maurya's government?

Deccan Kingdoms Arise

Most Indian goods shipped overseas were shipped from cities in the Deccan. Like the northern plain, the Deccan was divided into many kingdoms. Each kingdom had its own capital with magnificent temples and bustling workshops.

Although India shared a common cultural legacy, the peoples of the Deccan South had distinct languages and traditions. Women, for example, seemed to have attained a high status and economic power. The Tamil kingdoms were sometimes ruled by queens.

Over the centuries, Hindu and Buddhist traditions and Sanskrit writings drifted south and blended with local cultures. Deccan rulers, like their North Indian counterparts, generally tolerated all religions as well as the many foreigners who settled in their busy ports.

In the Tamil kingdoms, which occupied much of the southernmost part of India, trade was important. Tamil rulers improved harbors to support overseas trade. The various Tamil kingdoms traded with one another, as well as with China and Southeast Asia. Tamil merchants sent spices, fine textiles, and other luxuries westward to eager buyers in the Roman empire.

The Tamil kingdoms left a rich and diverse literature. Tamil poets described fierce wars, heroic deeds, and festive occasions, along with the ordinary routines of peasant and city life.

☑ **DETERMINE RELEVANCE** How did trade help link the separate kingdoms of the Deccan?

A Golden Age Under Gupta Rulers

Although many kingdoms flourished in the Deccan, the most powerful Indian states rose in the north. About 500 years after the Mauryas, the Gupta dynasty again united much of India. Under the Guptas, who ruled from A.D. 320 to about 540, India enjoyed a **golden age,** or period of great cultural achievement.

A Time of Peace and Prosperity Gupta emperors organized a strong central government that promoted peace and prosperity. Gupta rule was probably looser than that of the Mauryas. Much power was left in the hands of individual villages and city governments elected by merchants and artisans. Faxian (fah shen), a Chinese Buddhist monk who visited India in the 400s, reported on the mild nature of Gupta rule:

> The people are numerous and happy . . . Only those who cultivate the royal land have to pay [a portion of] the grain from it. . . . The king governs without corporal punishment. Criminals are simply fined, lightly or heavily, according to the circumstances [of each case].
>
> —Faxian, A Record of Buddhistic Kingdoms

Trade and farming flourished across the Gupta empire. Farmers harvested crops of wheat, rice, and sugar cane. In cities, artisans produced cotton cloth and pottery, and made advances in metal-ware. Their goods were sold in local markets and exported to East Africa, the Middle East, and Southeast Asia. The prosperity of Gupta India contributed to a flowering in the arts and learning.

>> Indian physicians often used Ayurveda, an approach that treats illness by addressing every part of the patient's life, including diet and exercise. Ayurveda is still used in India, alongside modern medicine.

🅱 BOUNCE to Activate Gallery

Gupta Rule Encourages Learning In India, as elsewhere during this period, students were educated in religious schools. In Hindu and Buddhist centers, learning was not limited to religion and philosophy. The large Buddhist monastery-university at Nalanda, which attracted students from many parts of Asia, taught mathematics, medicine, physics, languages, literature, and other subjects.

Indian advances in mathematics had a wide impact on the rest of the world. Gupta mathematicians devised the simple system of writing numbers that we use today. These numerals are often called "Arabic" numerals because Arabs carried them from India to the Middle East and Europe. Indian mathematicians originated the concept of zero and developed the **decimal system** of numbers based on the number 10, which we still use today.

Advances in mathematics spurred progress in astronomy. Books by Indian mathematicians and scientists were translated into Arabic, which influenced learning in the Middle East. From there, advances in astronomy and mathematics eventually reached Europe.

By Gupta times, Indian physicians were using herbs and other remedies to treat illness. Surgeons were skilled in setting bones and in simple surgery to repair facial injuries. Doctors may also have begun vaccinating people against smallpox about 1,000 years before this practice was used in Europe.

Expanding India's Literature During Gupta times, many fine writers added to the rich heritage of Indian literature. They collected and recorded fables and folk tales in the Sanskrit language. In time, Indian fables were carried west to Persia, Egypt, and Greece.

The greatest Gupta poet and playwright was Kalidasa. His most famous play, *Shakuntala* (shahk oon TAH luh), tells the story of a king who marries the lovely orphan Shakuntala. Under an evil spell, the king forgets his bride. After many plot twists, he finally recovers his memory and is reunited with her.

The Decline of the Gupta Empire Eventually, Gupta India declined under the pressure of civil war, weak rulers, and foreign invaders. From central Asia came the White Huns, a nomadic people who overran the weakened Gupta empire, destroying its cities and trade. Once again, India split into many kingdoms. It would see no other great empire like those of the Mauryas or Guptas for almost 1,000 years.

☑ **DRAW CONCLUSIONS** What role did religion play in influencing learning and the arts in Gupta India?

Family and Village Life Shape Indian Society

Most Indians were probably not aware of the dazzling courts of the Mauryas or Guptas. The vast majority were peasants who lived in the villages that dotted the Indian landscape. In Indian society, everyday life revolved around the rules and duties associated with caste, family, and village.

Joint Family Structure Within the village, the basic unit was the **joint family,** in which several generations of parents and children shared a common dwelling. The joint family was usually achieved only by the wealthy, since people in poor families often died young. Still, even when they did not share the same house, close ties linked brothers, uncles, cousins, and nephews. Adult sons lived with their parents even after they married and had children.

The Indian family was patriarchal—the father or oldest male headed the household. Because he was thought to have wisdom and experience, the head of the family enjoyed great authority.

Still, his power was limited by sacred laws and tradition. Usually, he made decisions after consulting his wife and other family members. Property belonged to the whole family.

Family Duties The family performed the essential function of training children in the traditions and duties of their castes. Thus family interests came before individual wishes. Children worked with older relatives in the fields or at a family trade.

While still young, a daughter learned that as a wife she would be expected to serve and obey her husband and his family. A son learned the rituals to honor the family's ancestors. Such rites linked the living and the dead, deepening family bonds across the generations.

For parents, an important duty was arranging good marriages for their children based on caste and family interests. Marriage customs varied.

In northern India, for example, a bride's family commonly provided a **dowry,** or payment to the bridegroom, and financed the costly wedding festivities. After marriage, the daughter left her home and became part of her husband's family. A daughter's duty was to serve her husband and produce children.

Role of Women Changes Over Time Attitudes and customs affecting women changed over time and varied greatly across India. In early Vedic society, women seem to have enjoyed a higher status

>> The ancient Indian ideal of a joint family—several generations of family members living under one roof—emphasizes the cultural importance of obligations within families.

than in later times. Women even composed a few Vedic hymns.

Women were thought to have shakti, a creative energy that men lacked. In marriage, a woman's shakti helped to make the husband complete. Still, shakti might also be a destructive force. A husband's duty was to channel his wife's energy in the proper direction.

By late Gupta times, upper-class women were increasingly restricted to the home. In some communities, women were expected to cover themselves when outside the home. Other women, particularly in the lower classes, labored in the fields or worked at spinning and weaving.

Village Life The size of villages varied, from a handful of people to hundreds of families. A typical village included a cluster of homes made of earth or stone. Beyond these dwellings stretched the fields, where farmers grew wheat, rice, cotton, sugar cane, or other crops according to region.

In most of India, farming depended on the rains brought by the summer monsoons. Too much or too little rain meant famine. Most farmers worked the land of wealthy landowners. They had to give the landowner part of each harvest.

Like other farming-based societies, India had a traditional economy, an economic system in which

>> Both in ancient India and today, village members worked together on projects that benefited the community. Projects might include digging a well, working on a road, or building irrigation systems.

Village Government Each village ran its own affairs based on caste rules and traditions. It faced little outside interference as long as it paid its share of taxes. A village headman and council made decisions and dealt with outside authorities when necessary.

Members of the council included the most respected people of the village. In early times, women served on the council. As Indian law began to place greater restrictions on women, they were later excluded.

The headman and council organized villagers to cooperate on vital local projects such as building irrigation systems and larger regional projects like building roads and temples. The village was also home to people of different castes, each performing their caste roles.

☑ **SYNTHESIZE** Why was the joint family so important to everyday Indian life?

custom and tradition shape the goods and products a society makes. Villages generally produced almost all the food and goods that they needed. Still, they relied on trade for some essentials, such as salt and spices, and later for manufactured goods.

Villagers met and mingled with people from nearby villages while attending weddings, visiting relatives, or exchanging goods at local markets. These contacts helped spread ideas across a region and beyond.

☑ ASSESSMENT

1. **Compare and Contrast** Compare and contrast the approaches of Chandragupta and Ashoka to ruling the Mauryan empire.

2. **Analyze Information** Choose three achievements of the Gupta period and explain why they made the Gupta period a golden age.

3. **Explain** How did geography influence trade in the Tamil kingdoms?

4. **Draw Conclusions** What characteristics of family and village life shaped Indian society?

5. **Quest Connection** How did religion influence Ashoka's effort to create an ordered society in India?

GO ONLINE to access this biography: Ashoka

Arthashastra, Chanakya

Chanakya was a learned man who lived in India around 300 B.C. He became the teacher and advisor of the young Chandragupta Maurya. Chanakya helped his student raise an army and conquer northern India to found the Maurya empire. After Chandragupta's death, Chanakya advised his son, Bindusara. As advisor to these emperors, Chanakya helped shape the Maurya empire.

Chanakya was the author and editor of the *Arthashastra*, whose title means "the science of material gain." This book offers advice to rulers, including principles for governing an empire. This excerpt from the *Arthashastra* advises the emperor—or king—on how he should live and rule.

>> A modern artist's image of Chanakya

Primary Source

If a king is energetic, his subjects will be equally energetic. If he is reckless, they will not only be reckless likewise, but also [undermine] his works. Besides, a reckless king will easily fall into the hands of his enemies. Hence the king shall ever be wakeful.

He shall divide both the day and the night into eight nālikas [1½ hours] . . .

[D]uring the first one-eighth part of the day, he shall post watchmen and attend to the accounts of receipts and expenditure; during the second part, he shall look to the affairs of both citizens and country people; during the third, he shall not only bathe and dine, but also study; during the fourth, he shall not only receive revenue in gold, but also attend to the appointments of superintendents; during the fifth, he shall correspond in writing with the assembly of his ministers and receive the secret information gathered by his spies; during the sixth, he may engage himself in his favorite amusements or in contemplation; during the seventh, he shall superintend elephants, horses, chariots, and [foot soldiers]; and during the eighth part, he shall consider various plans of military operations with his commander-in-chief. At the close of the day, he shall observe the evening prayer.

☑ **DETERMINE AUTHOR'S PURPOSE** Why might Chanakya specify what the king should be doing at each time of day?

During the first one-eighth part of the night, he shall receive secret emissaries; during the second, he shall attend to bathing and supper and study; during the third, he shall enter the bedchamber amid the sound of trumpets and enjoy sleep during the fourth and fifth parts; having been awakened by the sound of trumpets during the sixth part, he shall recall to his mind the [knowledge he has gained from study] as well as the day's duties; during the seventh, he shall sit considering [policies] and send out spies; and during the eighth division of the night, he shall receive blessings from sacrificial priests, teachers, and the high priest, and having seen his physician, chief cook, and astrologer, and having saluted both a cow with its calf and a bull by [walking in a circle] round them, he shall get into his court.

Or in conformity to his capacity, he may change the schedule and attend to his duties.

☑ **HYPOTHESIZE** Why might a king have to change the detailed schedule laid out by Chanakya?

When in the court, he shall never cause his petitioners to wait at the door, for when a king makes himself inaccessible to his people and entrusts his work to his immediate officers, he may be sure to engender confusion in business, and to cause thereby public displeasure and [make] himself a prey to his enemies.

He shall, therefore, personally attend to the business of gods, of heretics, of Brahmins learned in the Vedas, of cattle, of sacred places, of minors, the aged, the afflicted, and the helpless, and of women—all this . . . according to the urgency or pressure of those works.

All urgent calls he shall hear at once, but never put off; for when postponed, they will prove too hard or impossible to accomplish. . . .

☑ **DETERMINE CENTRAL IDEAS** Why does Chanakya say that it is important for the king to respond to the needs of his subjects personally?

In the happiness of his subjects lies his happiness; in their welfare his welfare; whatever pleases himself he shall not consider as good, but whatever pleases his subjects he shall consider as good.

Hence the king shall ever be active and discharge his duties; the root of wealth is activity, and of evil its reverse.

In the absence of activity acquisitions present and to come will perish; by activity he can achieve both his desired ends and abundance of wealth.

☑ **EXPLAIN AN ARGUMENT** Why does Chanakya say that the king needs to be active?

☑ ASSESSMENT

1. **Determine Central Ideas** What is the main point of this passage from the *Arthashastra*?

2. **Cite Evidence** What can you learn about the values of Maurya India from the daily schedule that Chanakya suggests for the emperor?

3. **Draw Inferences** Based on the evidence from this excerpt, how was the Maurya government structured?

4. **Draw Conclusions** How might the advice in this excerpt have helped the Mauryas to maintain power?

GO ONLINE to access primary sources

The Huang River is also called the Yellow River. Its color comes from the loess, or soil, that settles in the water. To control the river's frequent floods, ancient Chinese rulers built flood-control structures like this dam.

Ancient Civilization in China

China was the most isolated of the river valley civilizations. Long distances and physical barriers separated China from Egypt, the Middle East, and India. This isolation contributed to the Chinese belief that China was the center of Earth and the sole source of civilization. These beliefs in turn led the ancient Chinese to call their land Zhongguo (joong gwoh), or the Middle Kingdom.

Geography Influences Chinese Civilization

Geographic Barriers Set China Apart To the west and southwest of China, brutal deserts and high mountain ranges—the Tian Shan (tyen shahn) and the Himalayas—blocked the easy movement of people. To the southeast, thick rainforests divided China from Southeast Asia. To the north lay a forbidding desert, the Gobi. To the east lay the vast Pacific Ocean.

Despite these formidable barriers, the Chinese did have contact with the outside world. They traded with neighboring people and, in time, Chinese goods reached the Middle East, Africa, and Europe.

More often, the outsiders whom the Chinese encountered were nomadic invaders. To the Chinese, these nomads were barbarians who did not speak Chinese and lacked the skills and achievements of a settled society. Nomads conquered China from time to time, but they were usually absorbed into the advanced Chinese civilization.

The Varied Regions of China As the Chinese expanded over an enormous area, their empire came to include many regions. The

 BOUNCE to Activate Flipped Video

Objectives

Understand how geography influenced early Chinese civilization.

Analyze how Chinese culture took shape under the Shang and Zhou dynasties.

Describe the origins, central ideas, and spread of Confucianism and Daoism.

List some achievements made in early China.

Key Terms

loess
clan
dynastic cycle
feudalism
Confucius
philosophy
filial piety
Laozi
oracle bone
characters
calligraphy

GO ONLINE to access your digital course

Chinese heartland lay along the east coast and the valleys of the Huang, or Yellow, River and the Chang River. In ancient times, as today, these fertile farming regions supported the largest populations. Then, as now, the rivers provided water for irrigation and served as transportation routes.

Beyond the heartland are the outlying regions of Xinjiang (shin jyang), Mongolia, and Manchuria. These large regions have harsh climates and rugged terrains. Until recent times, they were mostly occupied by nomads and subsistence farmers. Yet these outlying regions played a key role in China's history.

Nomads repeatedly attacked and plundered Chinese cities. At times, powerful Chinese rulers conquered or made alliances with the people of these regions. China also extended its influence over the Himalayan region of Tibet, which the Chinese called Xizang (shee dzahng).

The "River of Sorrows" Chinese history began in the Huang River valley, where Neolithic people learned to farm. As in other places, the need to control the flow of the river through large water projects probably led to the rise of a strong central government. In time, the small farming villages gave rise to ancient Chinese civilization, sometimes called the Yellow River civilization.

The Huang River got its name from the **loess,** or fine windblown yellow soil, that it carries eastward from Siberia and Mongolia. Long ago, the Huang River earned a bitter nickname, "River of Sorrows." As loess settles to the river bottom, it raises the water level. Chinese peasants labored constantly to build and repair dikes to prevent the river from overflowing.

When heavy rains and winter snowmelt swelled the river, it ran high above the surrounding plains. If the dikes broke, floodwaters burst over the land, destroying crops, and leading to mass starvation. In Chinese writing, the character for misfortune is a river with a blockage that causes flooding.

☑ **EXPLAIN** What are some ways that geographical features shaped how people lived in ancient China?

The Shang Dynasty Begins to Form China

The earliest Chinese civilization may date back 4,000 or more years, but these origins are shrouded in legend. By about 1766 B.C., China's first historical dynasty, the Shang, dominated a part of the Yellow River valley. The Shang ruled the region until about 1122 B.C.

Early Government Archaeologists have uncovered some of the large palaces and rich tombs of Shang rulers. The evidence shows that the Shang capital at Anyang was a walled city. From there, the Shang controlled the North China plain and fought off nomads from the northern steppes and deserts.

Shang kings probably controlled only a small area. Princes and nobles loyal to the Shang dynasty governed most of the land. They were likely the heads of important **clans,** or groups of families who claim a common ancestor.

Thus, Shang China probably more closely resembled the small kingdoms of Vedic India than the centralized governments ruled by the Egyptian pharaohs. Still, the most powerful Shang kings could muster armies of several thousand to battle threats to their land.

The richly furnished tombs of the kings showed that they were at the top of the social hierarchy. In one Shang tomb, archaeologists discovered the burial place of Fu Hao (foo how), wife of the Shang king Wu Ding. Artifacts show that she owned land and helped to lead a large army against invaders. This evidence suggests that noblewomen may have had considerable status during the Shang period.

>> Shang dynasty artisans were skilled in creating detailed objects in a variety of materials, including bronze and jade. This is a ceremonial bronze axe head.

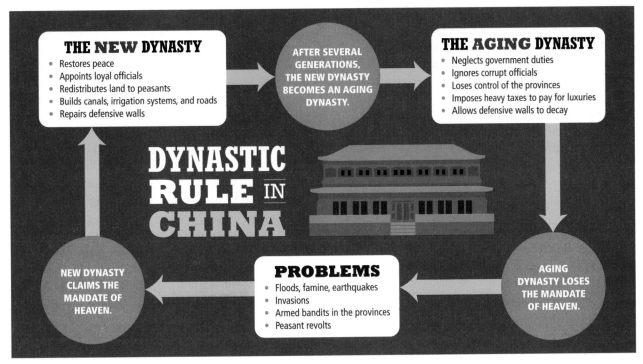

DYNASTIC RULE IN CHINA

THE NEW DYNASTY
- Restores peace
- Appoints loyal officials
- Redistributes land to peasants
- Builds canals, irrigation systems, and roads
- Repairs defensive walls

AFTER SEVERAL GENERATIONS, THE NEW DYNASTY BECOMES AN AGING DYNASTY.

THE AGING DYNASTY
- Neglects government duties
- Ignores corrupt officials
- Loses control of the provinces
- Imposes heavy taxes to pay for luxuries
- Allows defensive walls to decay

NEW DYNASTY CLAIMS THE MANDATE OF HEAVEN.

PROBLEMS
- Floods, famine, earthquakes
- Invasions
- Armed bandits in the provinces
- Peasant revolts

AGING DYNASTY LOSES THE MANDATE OF HEAVEN.

>> **Analyze Information** What causes a dynasty to lose the Mandate of Heaven?

Social Classes Develop Shang society mirrored that in other early civilizations. Along with the royal family at the top of society was a class of noble warriors who owned land. Shang warriors used leather armor, bronze weapons, and horse-drawn chariots. The chariots may have come through contact with people of western Asia. Noble families lived in large timber or stone houses.

Early Chinese cities supported a class of artisans and merchants. Artisans produced goods for nobles, including bronze weapons, silk robes, and jade jewelry. Merchants organized trade, exchanging local food and crafts for salt, certain types of shells, and other goods not found in northeastern China.

The majority of people in Shang China were peasants. They clustered together in farming villages. Many lived in thatch-roofed pit houses whose earthen floors were dug several feet below the surrounding ground. Such homes preserved the heat in winter and remained cool in summer.

Peasants led grueling lives. All family members worked in the fields, using stone tools to prepare the ground for planting or to harvest grain. When they were not in the fields, peasants had to repair the dikes. If war broke out between noble families, peasant men had to fight alongside their lords.

☑ **SUMMARIZE** How did the Shang kings govern China?

The Zhou Dynasty

About 1122 B.C., the battle-hardened Zhou (joh) people marched out of their kingdom on the western frontier to overthrow the Shang. They set up the Zhou dynasty, which ruled what had been Shang civilization. The Zhou dynasty held power until 256 B.C.

The Zhou Claim the Mandate of Heaven To justify their rebellion against the Shang, the Zhou promoted the idea of the Mandate of Heaven, or the divine right to rule. The cruelty of the last Shang king, they declared, had so outraged the gods that they had sent ruin on him. The gods then passed the Mandate of Heaven to the Zhou, who "treated the multitudes of the people well."

The Chinese later expanded the idea of the Mandate of Heaven to explain the **dynastic cycle,** or the rise and fall of dynasties. As long as a dynasty provided good government, it enjoyed the Mandate of Heaven. If the rulers became weak or corrupt, the Chinese believed that heaven would withdraw its support.

Floods, famine, or other catastrophes were signs that a dynasty had lost the favor of heaven. In the resulting chaos, an ambitious leader might seize power and set up a new dynasty. His success and strong government showed the people that the new dynasty had won the Mandate of Heaven. The dynastic cycle would then begin again.

A Feudal State Is Established The Zhou rewarded their supporters by granting them control over different regions. Thus, under the Zhou, China developed into a feudal state. **Feudalism** (FYOOD ul iz um) was a system of government in which local lords governed their own lands but owed military service and other forms of support to the ruler.

Zhou kings ruled China for some 850 years—in name at least. For the first two centuries, they did enjoy great power and prestige. After about 771 B.C., though, feudal lords exercised the real power and profited from the lands worked by peasants within their domains.

Economic Growth During the Zhou period, China's economy grew. Knowledge of iron working had reached China by about 600 B.C. As iron axes and ox-drawn iron plows replaced stone, wood, and bronze tools, farmers produced more food. Peasants also began to grow new crops, such as soybeans. Some feudal lords organized large-scale irrigation works, making farming even more productive.

Commerce expanded too. The Chinese began to use money for the first time. Chinese copper coins were made with holes in the center so that they could be strung on cords.

>> The holes punched at the top of these bronze coins from the Zhou dynasty allowed the coins to be strung on cords, making it easier to carry money securely.

This early form of a cash, or money, economy made trade easier. Merchants also benefited from new roads and canals organized by feudal lords.

Economic expansion led to an increase in China's population. People from the Huang River heartland moved into central China and soon began to farm the immense Chang River basin. Feudal nobles also expanded their territories and encouraged peasants to settle in the conquered territories.

Zhou Rule Ends By 256 B.C. China was a large, wealthy, and highly developed center of civilization. Yet the Zhou rulers were too weak to control feudal lords who ignored the emperor and battled one another in savage wars. Out of these wars rose a ruthless leader who toppled the Zhou and set out to impose political unity on China. His triumphs ushered in a new dynasty called the Qin (chin) dynasty.

☑ **EXPLAIN** What are three ways that China expanded during the Zhou dynasty?

Religious Beliefs in Early China

By Shang times, the Chinese had developed complex religious beliefs, many of which would influence later practices. They prayed to many gods and nature spirits. Chief among them was the supreme being, Shang Di (shahng dee). The king was seen as the link between the people and Shang Di.

By making the correct prayers to Shang Di, the king ensured the god's favor, which was essential for good harvests. The Shang king—and later Chinese emperors—were called the Son of Heaven. In this way, Chinese rulers served as both priests and kings.

Veneration of Ancestors Gods as great as Shang Di, the Chinese believed, would not respond to the pleas of mere mortals. Only the spirits of the greatest people, such as the ancestors of the king, could possibly get the ear of the gods. Thus, the prayers of rulers and nobles to their ancestors were thought to serve the community as a whole, ensuring such benefits as good harvests or victory in war.

The ruler's power came in part from this veneration of ancestors. At first, only the royal family and other nobles were believed to have ancestors important enough to influence the gods. Gradually, other classes shared in these rituals.

The Chinese called on the spirits of their ancestors to bring good fortune to the family. To honor their ancestors' spirits, they offered them sacrifices of food and other necessities. When westerners reached China, they mistakenly called this practice "ancestor worship."

☑ **SUMMARIZE** What steps did early Chinese communities take to ensure good harvests?

Two Major Belief Systems Take Root

During late Zhou times, wars raged across China. Economic and social changes were disrupting old ways of life. Two belief systems, Confucianism and Daoism, emerged at this time, Both put forward ideas on how to restore social order and maintain harmony with nature. They also shaped Chinese civilization for more than 2,500 years.

Confucius Spreads His Wisdom The philosopher-teacher Confucius was born in 551 B.C. The name **Confucius** is the Western form of the name Kong Fuzi, or Master Kong. According to tradition, he belonged to a noble but poor family. A brilliant scholar, he hoped to become an adviser to a local ruler.

For years, he wandered from court to court talking to rulers about how to govern. Unable to find a permanent government position, he turned to teaching. As his reputation for wisdom grew, he attracted many students.

The Analects Like two other influential thinkers who lived about the same time—Siddhartha Gautama in India and Socrates in Greece—Confucius never wrote down his ideas. After his death, his students collected his sayings in the *Analects*. The sayings offered advice for living a good and honorable life.

> The Master said, if out of the three hundred *Songs* I had to take one phrase to cover all my teaching, I would say 'Let there be no evil in your thoughts.'

> The Master said, Yu, shall I teach you what knowledge is? When you know a thing, to recognize that you know it, and when you do not know a thing, to recognize that you do not know it. That is knowledge.

—*Analects*

>> A scholar and teacher, Confucius had an enormous cultural influence on early Chinese civilization.

▶ **BOUNCE to Interactive Chart**

Unlike the Buddha, Confucius took little interest in spiritual matters such as salvation. Instead, he developed a **philosophy,** or system of ideas, that was concerned with worldly goals, especially those of ensuring social order and good government. Confucius studied ancient texts to learn the rules of conduct that had guided the ancestors.

Five Relationships Shape Behavior Confucius taught that harmony resulted when people accepted their place in society. He stressed five key relationships: ruler to subject, parent to child, husband to wife, elder brother to younger brother, and friend to friend. Confucius believed that, except for friendship, none of these relationships were equal. In traditional China, older people were superior to younger ones and men were superior to women.

According to Confucius, everyone had duties and responsibilities, depending on his or her position. Superiors should care for their inferiors and set a good example, while inferiors owed loyalty and obedience to their superiors. Correct behavior, Confucius believed, would bring order and stability.

Confucius put **filial piety,** or respect for parents, above all other duties, even loyalty to the state. Other Confucian values included honesty, hard work, and concern for others. "Do not do to others," he declared, "what you do not wish yourself."

Government Confucius also taught that it was a ruler's responsibility to provide good government. In return, the people would be respectful and loyal subjects. Confucius believed that people were naturally good. The best ruler, he taught, was a virtuous man who led by example: "If a ruler is upright, all will go well without orders. But if he himself is not upright, even though he gives orders, they will not be obeyed."

Confucius put great emphasis on education for men. "By nature, men are pretty much alike," he said. "It is learning and practice that set them apart." He urged rulers to take the advice of wise, educated men. In time, education would become the road to advancement in Chinese society.

Confucianism Has Great Influence In the centuries after Confucius died, his ideas influenced many aspects of Chinese life. Confucianism never became a religion, as Buddhism did. But over many centuries, Chinese rulers would base their governments on Confucian ideas. Only scholars educated in Confucian thought could become government officials.

The Confucian emphasis on filial piety bolstered traditions such as reverence for ancestors and the importance of family. Confucianism reinforced the social hierarchy of inferior and superior while stressing the mutual duties of each.

Confucianism also adopted an enduring Chinese belief that the universe reflected a delicate balance between two forces, yin and yang. Yin was linked to Earth, darkness, and female forces, while yang stood for heaven, light, and male forces. To the Chinese, these forces were not in opposition.

Rather, the well-being of the universe depended on harmony between yin and yang. People could play a role in maintaining this harmony. For example, the king had to make the proper sacrifices to heaven, while at the same time taking practical steps to rule well.

Confucianism Spreads After Confucius's death, dedicated students of his teachings kept his ideas alive. For some future dynasties, Confucianism became the official state philosophy. As Chinese civilization spread, hundreds of millions of people in Korea, Japan, and Vietnam accepted Confucian beliefs. Nearly one third of the world's population came under the influence of these ideas.

Daoism Teaches Harmony With Nature The second school of thought or belief system that influenced China was a philosophy called Daoism (DOW iz um). Unlike Confucianism, Daoism was not concerned with bringing order to human affairs. Instead, Daoists sought to live in harmony with nature.

The founder of Daoism was a mysterious figure known as **Laozi** (LOW dzih), or "Old Master." He is said to have "lived without leaving any traces" at the time of Confucius. Although little is known about Laozi, he is credited with writing the *The Way of Virtue*, a book that had enormous influence on Chinese life.

Seeking "the Way" Laozi looked beyond everyday worries to focus on the Dao, or "the way" of the universe. How does one find the Dao? The Dao, he explained, was hard to understand fully or put into words. "Those who know the Dao do not speak of it," said Laozi. "Those who speak of it do not know it." Daoists often gave such seemingly puzzling answers to show the conflict between human desires and the simple ways of nature.

Daoists rejected the world of conflict and strife. Instead, they emphasized the virtue of yielding. Water, they pointed out, does not resist, but rather yields to outside pressure—yet it is an unstoppable force. In the same way, Daoists might give way in a conflict, only to return again, like water, to their natural course.

>> The yin and yang symbol represents the Chinese belief that the universe reflects a delicate balance between yin, linked to earth, darkness, and female forces, and yang, which stands for heaven, light, and male forces.

Many Daoists turned from the "unnatural" ways of society. Some became hermits, artists, or poets. Daoists viewed government as unnatural and, therefore, the cause of many problems. "If the people are difficult to govern," Laozi declared, "it is because those in authority are too fond of action." To Daoists, the best government was one that governed the least.

Confucianism and Daoism Evolve Although Chinese scholars followed Laozi's original teachings, Daoism evolved into a popular religion with Gods, Goddesses, and magical practices. Chinese peasants turned to Daoist priests for charms to protect them from unseen forces.

Instead of accepting nature as it was, Daoist priests searched for a substance to bring immortality, or everlasting life. They experimented with alchemy (AHL kuh mee), trying to transform ordinary metals into gold.

To achieve this goal, alchemists mixed chemistry and magic. Sometimes, their experiments led to advances in science. Their experiments may have contributed to discoveries in medicine. Daoists are thought to have invented gunpowder, which they first used in firecrackers to frighten ghosts.

Confucian and Daoist ideas influenced everyone from nobles and scholars to the poorest peasants. Although the philosophies differed, people took beliefs and practices from each. Confucianism showed them how to behave. Daoism influenced their view of the natural world.

☑ **CONTRAST** Compare the basic ideas of Confucianism and Daoism in their approach to how people should live their lives.

A Time of Achievements in Early China

The Chinese made progress in many areas during the Shang and Zhou periods. Astronomers observed Halley's Comet, studied the movements of planets, and recorded eclipses of the sun. Their findings helped them develop an accurate calendar with 365 and ¼ days. In addition, the Chinese also made remarkable achievements in the art and technology of bronze-making. They produced stunning bronze weapons and ritual vessels covered with intricate decorations.

Discovering the Secret of Making Silk By about 1000 B.C., the Chinese learned how to make a silk thread from the cocoons of silkworms. Soon, the Chinese were cultivating both silkworms and the mulberry trees on which the worms fed. Women did

>> Living in harmony with nature is one of the central ideas of Daoism. Daoist paintings reflect that philosophy with a focus on trees, mountains, rivers, and other objects found in nature.

>> Silk thread or silk woven into magnificent fabrics were key trading items for the Chinese. Because of this, the process of converting raw silk to smooth cloth was a closely guarded secret.

BOUNCE to Activate Gallery

>> Poems and odes from the *Book of Songs* were put on strips of bamboo as part of a painting, or on wooden screens such as this one.

the laborious work of tending the silkworms and processing the cocoons into thread. They then wove silk threads into a smooth cloth that was colored with brilliant dyes.

Only royalty and nobles could afford luxurious silk robes. In time, silk became China's most valuable export. To protect their control of this profitable trade item, the Chinese kept the process of silk making a secret for hundreds of years.

The Chinese Develop a System of Writing The ancient Chinese developed a system of writing. It used both pictographs and ideographs, signs that expressed thoughts or ideas. The oldest examples of Chinese writing appear on **oracle bones,** used by priests to predict the future. Shang priests wrote questions addressed to the gods or to the spirit of an ancestor on animal bones or tortoise shells. These questions generally required a yes or no answer. Priests then heated the bone or shell until it cracked. By interpreting the pattern of cracks, they could provide answers or advice from the ancestors.

Written Chinese took shape almost 4,000 years ago. Over time it evolved to include tens of thousands of **characters,** or written symbols. Each character represented a word or idea and was made up of a number of different strokes. By contrast, alphabet-based languages such as English or Arabic contain only two dozen or so symbols that represent basic sounds. In recent years, the Chinese have simplified their characters, but Chinese remains one of the most difficult languages to learn.

Despite its complexity, the written language supported unity. Isolated by geographic barriers, people in different parts of China often could not understand one another's spoken language, but they all used the same system of writing. Not surprisingly, in earlier times, only the well-to-do could afford the years of study needed to master the skills of reading and writing. Working with brush and ink, Chinese scholars later turned writing into an elegant art form called **calligraphy.**

Creating the First Books Under the Zhou, the Chinese made the first books. They bound thin strips of wood or bamboo together and then carefully drew characters on the flat surface with a brush and ink. The earliest Chinese books included histories and religious works. *I Ching,* a handbook for diviners, is still used by people who want to foretell the future.

Among the greatest Zhou works is the *Book of Songs*, a collection of poems that address the lives of farming people, praise kings, or describe court ceremonies. The book also includes tender or sad love songs.

☑ **ANALYZE INFORMATION** How did a uniform system of writing benefit the Chinese?

☑ ASSESSMENT

1. **Analyze Information** How did China's geography both help and hinder China's development as a country?

2. **Synthesize** What characteristics did the Shang and Zhou governments and social structures have in common?

3. **Describe** What aspects of Confucianism and Daoism do you think contributed to their long-lasting impact on Chinese society?

4. **Synthesize** Why do you think that many Daoist painters featured water in paintings that represented Daoist beliefs?

5. **Connections to Today** Citing evidence from this lesson about China's geography, explain whether you think China's government today is still concerned with flood control.

GO ONLINE to access this biography: Confucius

Analects, Confucius

The *Analects* of Confucius (551–479 B.C.) is a collection of teachings by the great Chinese philosopher published in China around the year 1190. Divided into 20 "books," the *Analects* features Confucius dialoguing with his students about numerous moral and ethical matters. Among the topics are how to respect one's elders, how to comport oneself in society, and how to maintain a government that is honest and principled.

>> A later artist's image of Confucius

Primary Source

BOOK I

. . . CHAP. III. The Master said, "Fine words and an insinuating [subtle, crafty] appearance are seldom associated with true virtue." CHAP. IV. The philosopher Tsang said, "I daily examine myself on three points:— whether, in transacting business for others, I may have been not faithful;— whether, in intercourse [conversation] with friends, I may have been not sincere;— whether I may have not mastered and practiced the instructions of my teacher." . . . CHAP. VI. The Master said, "A youth, when at home, should be filial [respectful of one's parents], and, abroad, respectful to his elders. He should be earnest and truthful. He should overflow in love to all, and cultivate the friendship of the good. When he has time and opportunity, after the performance of these things, he should employ them in polite studies." CHAP. VII. Tsze-hsia said, "If a man withdraws his mind from the love of beauty, and applies it as sincerely to the love of the virtuous; if, in serving his parents, he can exert his utmost strength; if, in serving his prince, he can devote his life; if, in his intercourse with his friends, his words are sincere:— although men say that he has not learned, I will certainly say that he has."

☑ **DETERMINE CENTRAL IDEAS** What does Confucius teach about relationships in this excerpt?

BOOK II

CHAP. I. The Master said, "He who exercises government by means of his virtue may be compared to the north polar star, which keeps its place and all the stars turn towards it."

☑ **ANALYZE STYLE AND RHETORIC** How does Confucius make use of comparison to illustrate his point?

CHAP. II. The Master said, "In the *Book of Poetry* [a very old collection of Chinese poetry, collected by Confucius] are three hundred pieces, but the design of them all may be embraced in one sentence— 'Having no depraved [very evil] thoughts.'" CHAP. III. 1. The Master said, "If the people be led by laws, and uniformity sought to be given them by punishments, they will try to avoid the punishment, but have no sense of shame." 2. "If they be led by virtue, and uniformity sought to be given them by the rules of propriety [morally correct behavior], they will have the sense of shame, and moreover will become good."

☑ **IDENTIFY AUTHOR'S POINT OF VIEW** How do the pieces in the Book of Poetry exemplify virtue, as Confucius describes it?

BOOK XV

CHAP. XVII. The Master said, "The superior man in everything considers righteousness to be essential. He performs it according to the rules of propriety. He brings it forth in humility. He completes it with sincerity. This is indeed a superior man." CHAP. XVIII. The Master said, "The superior man is distressed by his want [lack] of ability. He is not distressed by men's not knowing him." . . . CHAP. XX. The Master said, "What the superior man seeks, is in himself. What the mean man seeks, is in others." CHAP. XXI. The Master said, "The superior man is dignified, but does not wrangle [quarrel, bicker]. He is sociable, but not a partisan [a very strong supporter of a particular idea or person]." CHAP. XXII. The Master said, "The superior man does not promote a man simply on account of his words, nor does he put aside good words because of the man." CHAP. XXIII. Tsze-kung asked, saying, "Is there one word which may serve as a rule of practice for all one's life?" The Master said, "Is not RECIPROCITY such a word?"

☑ **DRAW CONCLUSIONS** Is Confucius' "superior man" likely to be motivated by fame or power? Explain.

☑ ASSESSMENT

1. **Summarize** What does Confucius say will happen if people are led by virtue rather than laws?

2. **Determine Central Ideas** What are the qualities of a "superior man," in Confucius' view? Cite examples from the text.

3. **Analyze Style and Rhetoric** The *Analects* is structured as a dialogue. Is the structure effective for Confucius' teachings? Cite examples from the text.

4. **Draw Inferences** How might Confucius' teachings about the "superior man" relate to his teachings about honest government? Cite details from the text to support your answer.

GO ONLINE to access primary sources

3.5

China's first strong emperor had a massive tomb built for himself and filled with sculptures such as this model of an imperial chariot.

Strong Rulers Unite China

From his base in western China, the powerful ruler of the state of Qin (chin) set out to unify all of China. An ancient Chinese poet and historian described how the ruler crushed all his rivals: "Cracking his long whip, he drove the universe before him, swallowing up the eastern and the western Zhou and overthrowing the feudal lords."

Shi Huangdi Unifies China

In 221 B.C., the ruler of Qin proclaimed himself **Shi Huangdi** (shur hwahng dee), or "First Emperor." Although his methods were brutal, he set up patterns in government and other areas that shaped future Chinese civilization.

The Emperor Centralizes Power Shi Huangdi was determined to end the divisions that had splintered Zhou China. He spent nearly 20 years conquering most of the warring states. Using rewards for merit and punishments for failure, he built a strong, authoritarian government.

The emperor abolished the old feudal states and divided China into 36 military districts, each ruled by appointed officials. Inspectors, who were actually more like spies, checked on local officials and tax collectors.

Shi Huangdi forced noble families to live in his capital at Xianyang (shen yahng), where he could keep an eye on them, and divided their lands among the peasants. Still, peasants had to pay high taxes to support Shi Huangdi's armies and building projects.

BOUNCE to Activate Flipped Video

Objectives

Understand how Shi Huangdi unified China and established a Legalist government.

Outline why the Han period is considered a Golden Age of Chinese civilization.

Analyze how the Silk Road facilitated the spread of ideas and trade in China.

Analyze why Buddhism spread through China.

Key Terms

Shi Huangdi
Wudi
monopoly
expansionism
civil servants
warlords
acupuncture

GO ONLINE to access your digital course

>> Standardized weights and coins, such as this one, were part of the Qin dynasty's efforts to promote unity among various Chinese states.

>> Building the Great Wall required intense labor. Each stone was cut to a specific size and carried or dragged to the wall before being set in place.

To promote unity, the First Emperor standardized weights and measures and replaced the diverse coins of the Zhou states with Qin coins. He also had scholars create uniformity in Chinese writing. Workers repaired and extended roads and canals to strengthen the transportation system. A new law even required cart axles to be the same width so that wheels could run in the same ruts on all Chinese roads.

Legalism Establishes Harsh Rule Shi Huangdi centralized power with the help of Legalist advisers. Legalism was a very different school of thought from Confucianism or Daoism. Legalism was based on the teachings of Hanfeizi (hahn fay dzuh), who died in 233 B.C.

According to Hanfeizi, "The nature of man is evil. His goodness is acquired." Greed, he declared, was the motive for most actions and the cause of most conflicts. Hanfeizi rejected the Confucian idea that people would follow the example of a good ruler. Instead, he insisted that the only way to achieve order was to pass strict laws and impose harsh punishments.

To Legalists, strength, not goodness, was a ruler's greatest virtue. "The ruler alone possesses power," declared Hanfeizi, "wielding it like lightning or like thunder." During the Zhou period, many feudal rulers chose Legalism as the most effective way to keep order. Shi Huangdi made it the official policy of the Qin government.

His laws were so cruel that later generations despised Legalism. Yet Legalist ideas survived in laws that forced people to work on government projects and punished those who shirked their duties.

Shi Huangdi moved harshly against his critics. He jailed, tortured, killed, or enslaved many who opposed his rule. Hardest hit were the feudal nobles and Confucian scholars who loathed his laws. To end dissent, Shi Huangdi approved a ruthless campaign of book burning, ordering the destruction of all works of literature and philosophy. Only books on medicine and agriculture were spared.

Building the Great Wall Shi Huangdi's most remarkable and costly achievement was the Great Wall. In the past, individual feudal states had built walls to defend their lands against raiders. Shi Huangdi ordered the walls to be joined.

Hundreds of thousands of laborers worked on the wall for years, through bitter cold and burning heat. They pounded earth and stone into a mountainous wall almost 25 feet high and topped with a wide brick road. Many workers died in the harsh conditions.

Over the centuries, the wall was extended and rebuilt many times. Eventually, it snaked for thousands of miles across northern China. While the wall did not keep invaders out of China, it did demonstrate the emperors' ability to mobilize China's vast resources. In the long run, the Great Wall became an important symbol to the Chinese people, dividing and protecting their civilized world from the nomadic bands north of the wall.

Qin Dynasty Collapses Shi Huangdi thought his empire would last forever. But when he died in 210 B.C., anger over heavy taxes, forced labor, and cruel policies exploded into revolts. As Qin power collapsed, Liu Bang (lyoh bahng), an illiterate peasant leader, defeated rival armies and founded the new Han dynasty. Like earlier Chinese rulers, Liu Bang claimed the Mandate of Heaven.

☑ **COMPARE** How does Legalism differ from Confucianism?

The Han Dynasty Creates a Strong China

As emperor, Liu Bang took the title Gao Zu (gow dzoo) and set about restoring order and justice to his empire. Although he continued earlier efforts to unify China, he lowered taxes and eased the Qin emperor's harsh Legalist policies. In a key move, he appointed Confucian scholars as advisers. His policies created strong foundations for the Han dynasty, which is dated from 206 B.C. until A.D. 220.

Emperor Wudi Brings Great Changes The most famous Han emperor, **Wudi** (woo dee), took China to new heights. During his long reign from about 141 B.C. to 87 B.C., he strengthened the government and economy. Like Gao Zu, he chose Confucian men of "wisdom and virtue" as officials. To train scholars, he set up an imperial university at Xi'an (shee ahn).

Wudi boosted economic growth by improving canals and roads. He had granaries set up across the empire so the government could buy grain when it was abundant and sell it at stable prices when it was scarce.

He reorganized finances and imposed a government monopoly on iron and salt. A **monopoly** is the complete control of a product or business by one person or group. The sale of iron and salt gave the government a source of income other than taxes on peasants.

Wudi followed a policy of **expansionism,** or expanding a country's territory. His endless campaign to secure and expand China's borders earned him the title "Warrior Emperor." Wudi fought many battles to drive nomadic peoples beyond the Great Wall.

>> Shi Huangdi had a 20-square-mile compound built for his tomb. The emperor had himself buried with an army of about 8,000 life-size clay soldiers to guard him after his death. They carried actual weapons and were grouped in military formation.

▶ BOUNCE to Activate Gallery

>> The Han emperor, Wudi, receives a letter from a messenger.

Chinese armies added outposts in Manchuria, Korea, northern Vietnam, Tibet, and Central Asia. Soldiers, traders, and settlers slowly spread Chinese influence across these regions. To cement alliances with nomads on the western frontier, Wudi and later emperors arranged marriages between nomad chiefs and noble Chinese women.

The Silk Road Links China to the West The emperor Wudi opened up trade routes, later called the Silk Road, that would link China and the West for centuries. During Han times, new foods such as grapes, figs, cucumbers, and walnuts flowed into China from western Asia. Traders brought horses from Central Asia and muslin cloth from India to China. At the same time, the Chinese sent large quantities of silk westward to fill a growing demand for the prized fabric.

In time, the Silk Road stretched for more than 4,000 miles, and linked China to the Middle East. The Silk Road was not a single route, but a network of intersecting trade routes. Goods were relayed in stages, from one set of traders to another. At the western end, trade was controlled by various peoples, including the Persians. From the Middle East, some trade goods were sent across the Mediterranean to Rome.

Importance of the Silk Road Growing trade along the Silk Road contributed to the economic prosperity of the Han empire. Important cultural exchanges also took place because ideas as well as goods traveled along the Silk Road. Missionaries and traders carried Buddhism from India into China. Daoism traveled west out of China into Central Asia and beyond. Much later, the religion of Islam was carried eastward from the Middle East.

Cultural influences spread along the trade route. Turkish folk tales inspired Chinese poetry. Central Asian harpists and dancers introduced their art to the Chinese people. Many Chinese inventions, such as the stirrup, traveled westward.

Scholar-Officials Run the Government Han emperors made Confucianism the official belief system of the state. Confucian scholars ran the many departments in the huge government bureaucracy. A scholar-official was expected to match the Confucian ideal of a gentleman. He would be courteous and dignified and possess a thorough knowledge of history, music, poetry, and Confucian teachings.

The Han Civil Service System Han emperors adopted the idea that **civil servants,** or government officials, should gain their positions by merit,

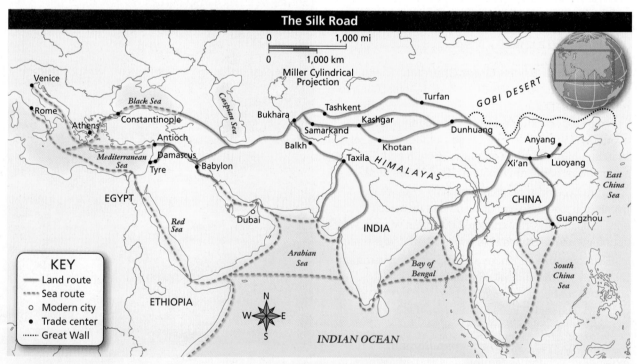

>> **Analyze maps** The Silk Road stretched from China to the Mediterranean. New ideas, as well as goods, were exchanged along the Silk Road. Describe two possible travel routes for a shipment of silk traveling from Taxila to Babylon.

BOUNCE to Activate Map

rather than through family background. To find the most qualified officials, they set up a system of exams. In time, these civil service exams were given at the local, provincial, and national levels. To pass, candidates studied the Confucian classics, a collection of histories, poems, and handbooks on customs that Confucius was said to have compiled.

In theory, any man could take the exams. In practice, only those who could afford years of study, such as the sons of wealthy landowners or officials, could hope to succeed.

Occasionally, a village or wealthy family might pay for the education of a brilliant peasant boy. If he passed the exams and obtained a government job, he, his family, and his clan all enjoyed immense prestige and moved up in society. Confucian teachings about filial piety and the superiority of men prevented women from taking the civil service exam. As a result, women were excluded from government jobs.

The civil service system had enormous impact on China for almost 2,000 years. It remained in use until 1912. It put men trained in Confucian thought at every level of government and created an enduring system of values. Dynasties rose and fell, but Confucian influence survived.

The Han Empire Falls As the Han dynasty aged, signs of decay appeared. Court intrigues undermined emperors who could no longer control powerful **warlords,** or local military rulers. Canals and roads fell into disrepair.

A series of natural disasters were seen as evidence of the anger of heaven. Burdened by heavy taxes and crushing debt, many peasants revolted.

In A.D. 220, ambitious warlords toppled the last Han emperor. After 400 years of unity, China broke up into separate kingdoms. Adding to the disorder, invaders poured over the Great Wall and set up their own states. In time, many of these newcomers were absorbed into Chinese civilization.

Impact of Han China Han rulers forged a vast and varied land into a united China. They created an empire roughly the size of the continental United States and set up patterns of government, based on Confucian ideas, that would survive for 2,000 years. Han China deeply influenced East Asia, just as Greek and Roman civilizations shaped the Western world. Confucian ethics spread across most of East Asia and dominated Chinese government and culture.

Again and again, China would break up and be painfully reassembled. Still, on the whole, Chinese civilization flourished in a united land. After periods

>> During the Han dynasty, Confucianism became the official belief system of the state. Children attended classes at a young age under the watchful eye of a Confucian scholar.

>> Zhang Liang helped the first Han emperor win power in the late 200s B.C. Later Han emperors failed to maintain that power. The empire disintegrated in the early 200s A.D. into a country of separate kingdoms.

of disunity, a new dynasty would turn to Confucian scholars to revive the days of Han greatness.

☑ **ANALYZE INFORMATION** Why do you think the Silk Road is sometimes called the Road of Civilization?

The Han Golden Age

Han rulers left their stamp on all areas of Chinese life. Han China made such tremendous advances in so many fields that the Chinese later called themselves "the people of Han." Han China lasted for over 400 years. Its rulers presided over a golden age in government, technology, and the arts.

Advances in Science and Medicine Han scientists wrote texts on chemistry, zoology, botany, and other subjects. Han astronomers improved earlier calendars and invented better timekeeping devices. A Chinese scientist invented a simple seismograph to detect and measure earthquakes.

The scientist Wang Chong disagreed with the widely held belief that comets and eclipses showed heaven's anger. "On the average, there is one moon eclipse about every 180 days," he wrote, "and a solar eclipse about every 41 or 42 months. Eclipses . . . are not caused by political action." Wang Chong argued that theories should only be accepted if they could be proved by scientific evidence.

Chinese physicians diagnosed diseases, developed anesthetics, and experimented with herbal remedies and other drugs. Many promoted the use of **acupuncture.** In this medical treatment, developed thousands of years ago, the doctor inserts needles into the skin at specific points to relieve pain or treat various illnesses.

Advances in Technology At the time, Han China was the most technologically advanced civilization in the world. Cai Lun (tsy loon), an official in the Han court, invented a method for making paper out of wood pulp. His basic method is still used to manufacture paper today. The Chinese made advances in methods of shipbuilding and invented the rudder to steer.

Other practical inventions included fishing reels, wheelbarrows, and suspension bridges. The Chinese invented the water-powered trip-hammer, a huge, heavy device used to pound ores and grains. Some of these ideas moved westward slowly, reaching Europe hundreds of years later.

The Arts Flourish The walled cities of Han China boasted splendid temples and palaces set in elegant parks. Although these wooden buildings have not survived, Han poets and historians have described their grandeur. Artisans produced delicate jade and ivory carvings and fine ceramic figures. Bronze-workers and silk makers improved on earlier techniques and set high standards for future generations.

Much of our knowledge about Han China comes from a massive history, *Records of the Grand Historian,* written about 100 B.C. Its author, Sima Qian, is sometimes called the father of Chinese history. Sima Qian's work covers more than 2,000 years, from China's legendary origins through the reign of emperor Wudi.

Around A.D. 100, Ban Zhao (bahn jow) wrote *Lessons for Women*, an influential handbook of behavior. In it, she carefully spells out the proper behavior for women and men. While Ban Zhao did argue in favor of equal education for boys and girls, she stressed that women should be obedient, respectful, and submissive. "Let a woman modestly yield to others," she advised. "Let her respect others."

☑ **CONNECT** What are some examples of Han inventions or technologies still used today?

>> Zhang Heng developed the earliest known seismograph to detect and measure earthquakes. Tremors move a pendulum that opens the jaw of the dragon. The event is recorded when the ball drops from the dragon's mouth into the mouth of the toad below.

Buddhism Spreads to China

By A.D. 100, missionaries and merchants had spread Mahayana Buddhism from India into China. At first, the Chinese had trouble with the new faith. For example, Chinese tradition valued family loyalty, while Buddhism honored monks and nuns who gave up the benefits of family life for a life of solitary meditation. In addition, the Chinese language had no word for an unfamiliar concept like nirvana.

Despite such obstacles, Buddhism became increasingly popular, especially in times of crisis. Its great appeal was the promise of escape from suffering. Mahayana Buddhism offered the hope of eternal happiness and presented the Buddha as a compassionate, merciful god. Through prayer, good works, and devotion, anyone could hope to gain salvation. Neither Daoism nor Confucianism emphasized this idea of personal salvation.

In China, Buddhism absorbed Confucian and Daoist traditions. Some Chinese even believed that Laozi had gone to India, where he taught the Buddha. Chinese Buddhist monks stressed filial piety and honored Confucius as a person who had achieved enlightenment.

By A.D. 400, Buddhism had spread throughout China. From time to time, Chinese rulers persecuted Buddhists, but the new religion was generally tolerated. Large Buddhist monasteries became important centers of learning and the arts.

☑ **ANALYZE INFORMATION** Why did so many people in China find Buddhism appealing?

☑ ASSESSMENT

1. **Explain** How did Shi Huangdi secure allegiance to a central government?

2. **Summarize** Why was the Han period considered a Golden Age of Chinese civilization?

3. **Analyze Information** How did the Silk Road bring ideas to and from China?

4. **Explain** What factors helped Buddhism spread through China?

5. **Quest Connection** How did Confucianism help promote an ordered society under the Han dynasty?

>> Han dynasty artists created items of great beauty. This mythical beast, called a "Bixie," is made of bronze and was used to ward off evil spirits.

>> This giant statue of Buddha was carved directly into a sheer cliff that leads to a Buddhist temple in China.

🛜 **GO ONLINE** to access this biography: Shi Huangdi

Connections to Today

Flooding in New Orleans after Hurricane Katrina in 2005

Take Action on Disaster Preparedness

In ancient China, emperors won support by building dikes to prevent floods. Today, government agencies aim to limit damage from disasters in the United States and face sharp criticism when they fail.

1. **Choose** Select one of these topics related to disaster prevention in the United States:

   • **Earthquake preparedness:** How have state and federal agencies met citizens' wishes to be better prepared for earthquakes?

   • **Flood protection:** How have state and federal agencies responded to citizens' demands for flood protection?

2. **Ask Questions** What are some of the things you want to learn about disaster preparedness today? Write a list of questions.

3. **Learn** Research the topic you have chosen. Sources of information might include the websites of the U.S. Army Corps of Engineers or the National Earthquake Hazards Reduction Program. Collect specific examples related to your topic. Look for recent news articles with criticism or praise for government agencies' actions.

4. **Raise Awareness** Create a written report or oral presentation on your findings about disaster preparedness in the United States today. Be prepared to present your findings.

Use the texts, quizzes, interactivities, Quest Inquiries, Flipped Videos, and other resources from this Topic to prepare for the Topic Test.

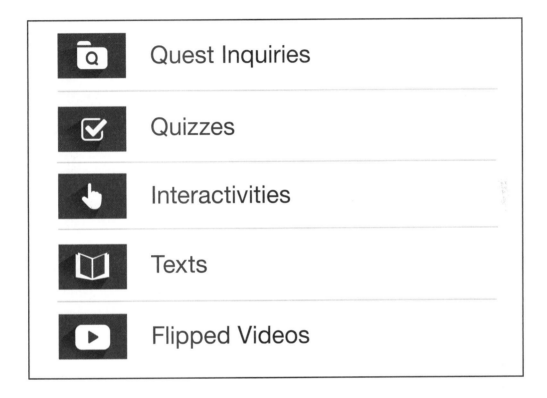

Quest Inquiries

Quizzes

Interactivities

Texts

Flipped Videos

While online you can also check the progress you've made learning the topic and course content by viewing your grades, test scores, and assignment status.

Topic 3 Quick Study Guide

LESSON SUMMARIES

Use these Lesson Summaries, and the longer versions available online, to review the key ideas for each lesson in this Topic.

Lesson 1: Early Civilization in South Asia

The ancient Indus civilization of the Indian subcontinent built an organized society. The Indus civilization declined, but the Vedic civilization followed it. The ancient texts of the Vedic people provide insight into the religious and moral values of their society.

Lesson 2: The Origins of Hinduism and Buddhism

Hinduism originated with the Vedic civilization. Through right behavior, Hindus aim for union with Brahman, the spiritual force behind the universe. In India's caste system, people are born into their social and economic group. Buddhism came from the teachings of the Buddha. Buddhists seek nirvana, or liberation from the cycle of rebirth.

Lesson 3: Powerful Empires Emerge in India

The Maurya empire unified most of ancient India under an organized system of government. The regional kingdoms that followed promoted trade. Then the Gupta empire brought advances in mathematics, medicine, and the arts. Ancient Indian society was based on family and village life.

Lesson 4: Ancient Civilization in China

In geographic isolation, a complex Chinese society emerged during the Shang dynasty. Later, the Zhou dynasty established a feudal system. China had traditional religious beliefs but also gave rise to Confucianism, calling for social order, and Daoism, calling for harmony with nature. China developed silk production and a complex writing system.

Lesson 5: Strong Rulers Unite China

Founding the Qin dynasty, China's first emperor united China and ruled harshly. After his death, the Han dynasty ruled for centuries. It created a civil service, and a new trade network—the Silk Road—opened.

QUEST! FINDINGS

Write Your Essay on Order in Society Refer to your responses to the Quest Connections to help you create your essay for presentation to your class. Use the rubric and other Quest resources online to guide your work.

GO ONLINE to access lesson summaries

VISUAL REVIEW

Use these graphics to review some of the key terms, people, and ideas from this Topic.

Eras of Civilization

INDIA		CHINA	
Indus civilization	3300 B.C. to 1700 B.C.	Shang dynasty	1766 B.C. to 1122 B.C.
Vedic civilization	1500 B.C. to 500 B.C.	Zhou dynasty	1122 B.C. to 256 B.C.
Maurya empire	321 B.C. to 185 B.C.	Qin dynasty	221 B.C. to 206 B.C.
Gupta empire	A.D. 320 to A.D. 540	Han dynasty	202 B.C. to A.D. 220

RELIGIONS FOUNDED IN INDIA

Hinduism

- Originated with the Vedic people
- Ultimate goal: moksha
- Moksha: union with universe
- Way to moksha:
  1. Obey dharma
  2. Build good karma

Buddhism

- Founded by the Buddha
- Ultimate goal: nirvana
- Nirvana: liberation from reincarnation
- Way to nirvana:
  1. Accept the Four Noble Truths
  2. Follow the Eightfold Path

Unification of China

CAUSE AND EFFECT

IMMEDIATE CAUSES

- The ruler of Qin conquers the warring states of Zhou and overthrows the feudal lords.
- The ruler of Qin proclaims himself Shi Huangdi ("First Emperor").

LONG-TERM CAUSES

- Confucian ideas dominate education.
- China's isolation permits development without much outside interference.
- A common system of writing evolves.

IMMEDIATE EFFECTS

- Shi Huangdi abolishes feudalism.
- Shi Huangdi standardizes weights and measures and money.
- The government cracks down on dissenters.
- Shi Huangdi supervises work on the Great Wall.

LONG-TERM EFFECTS

- China advances in government and trade.
- Confucian-educated officials hold most government jobs.
- Its common culture helps China survive upheavals.

KEY TERMS, PEOPLE, AND IDEAS

1. What two major religions arose in ancient India, and what beliefs did they share?

2. Toward the end of the Vedic period, how did the idea of **Brahman** relate to the Gods mentioned in the **Vedas**?

3. In Buddhism, how is the **Eightfold Path** connected to **nirvana**?

4. How did the actions of **Ashoka** as emperor reflect Buddhist beliefs?

5. Why is the development of the **decimal system** a sign that India enjoyed a **golden age** under the Guptas?

6. What was the view of **Confucius** on **filial piety**?

7. How did ancient China's belief systems shape Chinese people's relations with one another and the natural world?

8. Why did the empire of **Shi Huangdi** collapse after he died?

9. How might **civil servants** have contributed to the **expansionism** of **Wudi**?

CRITICAL THINKING

10. **Analyze Interactions** Describe two ways in which geography and climate have influenced the people of the Indian subcontinent.

11. **Identify Key Steps in a Process** Explain the roles of karma, dharma, and reincarnation in the process of achieving moksha, according to Hindu beliefs.

12. **Cite Evidence** Use evidence from the text to identify three achievements of the Gupta period that made it a golden age.

13. **Draw Conclusions** Consider two major achievements made in ancient China—Shi Huangdi's expansion of the Great Wall and Wudi's opening up of the Silk Road. How did each affect China's relationship with the outside world?

14. **Draw Inferences** Compare the initial intention of feudalism with its resulting effect on the Zhou dynasty. Under what circumstances might feudalism have been more successful?

15. **Identify Cause and Effect** Confucianism lay at the foundations of the Chinese civil service system, which lasted for 2,000 years. What about Confucianism do you think led to such a stable administrative structure?

16. **Analyze Visuals**

Look at this painting of the Buddha from the Jokhang Temple in Tibet, which today is part of China. (a) How does the painting show the Buddha as greater in spiritual power or importance than ordinary people? (b) If you look at the ordinary Buddhists shown in the painting, what does the painting suggest about the relationship between the Buddha and his followers?

17. **Writing Activity: Write an Explanatory Essay** The passage below is from one of Ashoka's rock edicts—edicts or announcements that Emperor Ashoka had carved on rocks mounted at various places around his empire.

> "Beloved-of-the-Gods, King Piyadasi [a name used by Ashoka], conquered the Kalingas eight years after his coronation. One hundred and fifty thousand were deported, one hundred thousand were killed and many more died (from other causes). After the Kalingas had been conquered, Beloved-of-the-Gods came to feel a strong inclination towards the Dhamma [Buddhist teachings], a love for the Dhamma and for instruction in Dhamma. Now Beloved-of-the-Gods feels deep remorse for having conquered the Kalingas. . . . Now it is conquest by Dhamma that Beloved-of-the-Gods considers to be the best conquest. . . . "

Use evidence from the passage to answer the questions in a brief explanatory essay. (a) What does the edict say about the effect of the conquest of the Kalingas on Ashoka? (b) What new priority did Ashoka adopt after that conquest? Explain how Ashoka's new priority might have affected the policies of his government.

18. **Connections to Today** Consider the importance of flood control to governments from ancient China to today. How might Americans respond today if flooding caused a loss of life and property due to inadequate government funding for flood protection?

DOCUMENT-BASED QUESTIONS

China's belief systems helped shape many aspects of China's culture, including Chinese attitudes toward government. Read the documents below, then answer the questions that follow.

DOCUMENT A

"[Confucius] said: 'Guide them with policies and align them with punishments and the people will evade them and have no shame. Guide them with virtue and align them with *li* [ritual] and the people will have a sense of shame and fulfill their roles' . . .Ji Kangzi asked Confucius about governance, saying, 'How would it be if I were to kill those who are without the *dao* [Way] in order to hasten others towards the *dao*?' Confucius replied, 'Of what use is killing in your governance? If you desire goodness, the people will be good. The virtue of the junzi [nobleman] is like the wind and the virtue of common people is like the grasses: when the wind blows over the grasses, they will surely bend.'"

—From R. Eno, translator, Confucius, *The Analects of Confucius*

DOCUMENT B

"Run the country by doing what's expected.
Win the war by doing the unexpected.
Control the world by doing nothing.
How do I know that?
By this.
The more restrictions and prohibitions in the world, the
    poorer people get.
The more experts the country has, the more of a mess it's in.
The more ingenious the skillful are, the more monstrous
    their inventions.
The louder the call for law and order, the more the thieves
    and con men multiply."

—Laozi, *Daodejing* (from *Tao te Ching, A New English Version* by Ursula K. LeGuin)

DOCUMENT C

"It is aptly said that the Chinese scholar was a Confucian when in office and a Daoist when out of office. Daoism, which flourished among the common people, was the school most opposite to the elitist prescriptions of Confucianism. Dao means 'the path,' 'the way.' It expressed the common people's naturalistic cosmology and belief in the unseen spirits of nature, much of which was shared by the scholar-elite. Daoism was an enormous reservoir of popular lore. It also provided an escape from Confucianism . . . It was a refuge from the world of affairs."

—John King Fairbank and Merle Goldman, *China: A New History*

19. Which principle of government appears in both Document A and Document B?

    A. respect for elders

    B. avoiding harsh punishments

    C. interfering as little as possible in people's lives

    D. offering a virtuous example

20. Which principle of government in Document A might the author of Document B criticize?

    A. trying to mold people's behavior by example

    B. avoiding killing people as a punishment

    C. the use of examples from nature

    D. limiting interference in people's lives

21. What aspect of Confucianism, as identified in Documents A and B, might explain why Chinese scholars preferred Confucianism when they held office, as Document C states?

    A. the call for rulers to be virtuous

    B. the focus on relations between parents and children

    C. the focus on relations between rulers and the ruled

    D. the call to avoid harsh punishments

22. **Writing Task** How did the belief systems of Daoism and Confucianism affect Chinese attitudes toward government? Use specific evidence from the documents above, along with information from this Topic, to support your answer.

The Americas
(Prehistory–A.D. 1570)

ESSENTIAL QUESTION How much does geography affect people's lives?

GO ONLINE to access the eText, videos, Interactive Primary Sources, Biographies, and other online resources.

Machu Picchu

Connections to Today

Astronomers and other scientists use many tools to explore the far reaches of the universe, planets, and stars. Their studies teach us much about our universe and our own planet, Earth.

In this topic, you'll read about how the Maya, Aztecs, and other people of the ancient Americas studied the skies, developing calendars linked closely to the movement of the stars. How—and why—do people today continue to learn about the stars and planets?

NBC LEARN

Learn about the story of Emperor Pachacuti.

BOUNCE to Activate My Story Video

In this Topic, you will learn about the early civilizations in the Americas. The Olmec, Maya, and Aztec arose in Mesoamerica. Other American civilizations included the Inca in present-day Peru and the Mississippians of North America. Look at the lesson outline and explore the timeline. As you study this Topic, you will complete the Quest team project.

LESSON OUTLINE

4.1 Civilizations of Middle America

4.2 The World of the Incas

4.3 The Peoples of North America

Key Events in The Americas

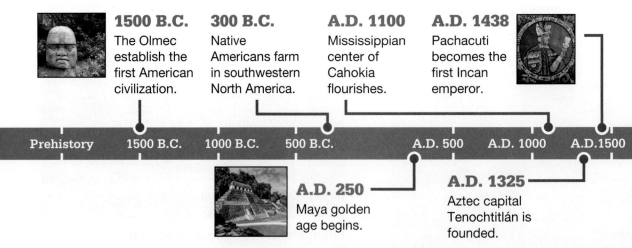

1500 B.C. The Olmec establish the first American civilization.

300 B.C. Native Americans farm in southwestern North America.

A.D. 1100 Mississippian center of Cahokia flourishes.

A.D. 1438 Pachacuti becomes the first Incan emperor.

Prehistory | 1500 B.C. | 1000 B.C. | 500 B.C. | A.D. 500 | A.D. 1000 | A.D.1500

A.D. 250 Maya golden age begins.

A.D. 1325 Aztec capital Tenochtitlán is founded.

QUEST! INQUIRY

Create an Online Historical Atlas

It is hard to overemphasize the impact of geography on the civilizations that arose in the Americas. In this Quest, you will gain a better understanding of this impact and how it changed the way in which these civilizations emerged and thrived. As you work, keep in mind this Topic's Essential Question: How much does geography affect people's lives?

STEP
Read the fictional letter from the Geographic Society of the Americas. Underline the key point in the letter and think about how you will address these points in your online atlas.

STEP
With your team, conduct research on your assigned civilization and the geography of its location. Take care to use only reliable sources.

STEP
As a group, synthesize your research. Create and edit content, maps, charts, and graphs for your portion of the online atlas. Then build your website and write a conclusion.

STEP
Present your online atlas to your audience. Then with your group, reflect on how geography and the environment have affected people's lives in the past.

GO ONLINE to access complete Quest materials

4.1

Maize was an important staple for early Native Americans, who ate it, made it into flour, and used it for ceremonial purposes.

 BOUNCE to Activate Flipped Video

Objectives

Explain when and where people first settled the Americas.

Analyze the rise of the Olmec civilization.

Describe the major developments of the Maya and Aztec civilizations.

Explain how prior civilizations influenced the Maya and Aztec.

Key Terms

Mesoamerica
maize
Olmec
stela
Valley of Mexico
Tenochtitlán
chinampa
tribute
Teotihuacán

Civilizations of Middle America

The Americas refers to two continents, North America and South America. Within these two regions is a cultural region that historians call Middle America or Mesoamerica, which is made up of Mexico and Central America. Some of the earliest civilizations in the Americas developed in Mesoamerica.

Civilizations Develop in the Americas

Scholars disagree about exactly when and how the first people reached the Americas. A common theory held that between 12,000 and 10,000 years ago, Paleolithic people reached North America from Asia. This migration took place during the last Ice Age, which lasted from about 100,000 years ago to about 10,000 years ago. At the time, so much water froze into thick ice sheets that the sea levels dropped, exposing a land bridge between Siberia and Alaska in the area that is now the Bering Strait.

Early evidence supported the theory that bands of hunters and food gatherers followed herds of bison and mammoths across the land bridge between Siberia and Alaska. They slowly moved south through North America, Central America, and South America. Recent evidence suggests that people may have reached the Americas much earlier. They may have paddled small boats and fished along the coasts. As archaeologists have discovered new evidence, they have modified their theories. Researchers now base the dates of migration into the Americas mostly on evidence found at prehistoric sites.

Adapting to New Environments The first Americans faced a variety of environments in which they could settle. For example, great mountain chains—the Rockies, the eastern and western Sierra Madre, and the Andes—dominate the western Americas. In addition, through the continents flow three of the world's five longest rivers, the Amazon of South America and the Missouri and Mississippi rivers of North America.

Far to the north and south of the continents, people learned to survive in icy, treeless lands. Closer to the Equator, people settled in the hot, wet climate and dense vegetation of the Amazon rain forest. Elsewhere, hunters adapted to deserts like the Atacama of Chile, woodlands like those in eastern North America, and the fertile plains of both continents.

Farming Begins In the Americas, as elsewhere, the greatest adaptation occurred when people learned to domesticate plants and animals. These changes took place slowly between about 8500 B.C. and 2000 B.C. In **Mesoamerica,** or Middle America, Neolithic people cultivated a range of crops, including beans, sweet potatoes, peppers, tomatoes, squash, and **maize**— the Native American name for corn. People in South America cultivated crops such as maize and cassava and domesticated llamas and other animals valued for their wool. By 3000 B.C. in parts of South America and 1500 B.C. in parts of Mesoamerica, farmers had settled in villages. Populations then expanded, and some villages eventually grew into the great early cities of the Americas.

Olmec Civilization Emerges Many scholars consider the **Olmec** the first American civilization; it emerged in the fertile coastal areas along the Gulf of Mexico and lasted from about 1200 to 400 B.C. Compared to other civilizations such as the Maya, Aztec and Inca, archaeologists know little about the Olmec. We do not even know what they called themselves. In fact, Olmec is the name the Aztecs later used for these people. But rich tombs and temples suggest that they had a powerful class of priests. The Olmec did not build true cities, but rather priests and other leaders may have lived in ceremonial centers, while the common people lived in surrounding farming villages.

Olmec Culture and Trade Ceremonial centers had large pyramid-shaped temples and other important buildings. Much of Olmec art is carved stone. The smallest examples include jade figurines of people and gods. The most dramatic remains are 14 giant stone heads found at the major ceremonial centers of San Lorenzo and La Venta.

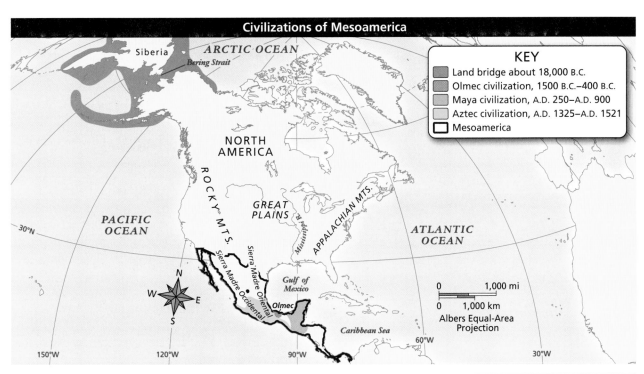

Civilizations of Mesoamerica

KEY
- Land bridge about 18,000 B.C.
- Olmec civilization, 1500 B.C.–400 B.C.
- Maya civilization, A.D. 250–A.D. 900
- Aztec civilization, A.D. 1325–A.D. 1521
- Mesoamerica

>> **Analyze Maps** Early people are thought to have crossed the Bering Strait from Asia to the Americas either on foot or in small boats. What might have been one of the biggest geographic influences on Mesoamerican civilizations?

B BOUNCE to Activate Map

>> Archaeologists discovered the giant Olmec stone heads, made of volcanic rock and weighing up to five tons each, during excavations. The Olmec moved them to ceremonial sites from distant quarries.

>> The ruins of San Bartolo have murals deep within the pyramidal complex of Las Pinturas.

Scholars think that these colossal heads, which the Olmec carved from 40-ton stones, are portraits of actual rulers. No one knows exactly how the Olmec moved these stones from distant quarries without wheeled vehicles or draft animals. Still, the evidence shows that the Olmec could mobilize a large labor force.

The Olmec also engaged in trading jade, obsidian, serpentine, mica, rubber, feathers, and pottery; through such trade, they influenced a wide area. The grinning jaguars and serpents that decorate many Olmec carvings appear in the arts of later Mesoamerican peoples. The Olmec also invented a calendar, and they carved hieroglyphic writing into stone. Recent archaeological excavations in Mexico indicate they may have developed a writing system, which would make them the first Mesoamerican civilization to do so.

Influence of the Olmec Through trade, Olmec influence spread over a wide area. Archaeologists have identified Olmec religious and artistic influences on two later Mesoamerican civilizations—the Maya and Aztec.

Both these civilizations built pyramid-shaped temples similar to those of the Olmec. Olmec ceremonial centers had the remains of ball courts linked to religious rituals. Similar ball courts have been found at Maya and later Aztec sites.

The ball game was fast paced and involved great skill on the part of the players. They had to keep a rubber ball in motion and send it through hoops high on a stone wall. The ball was not allowed to touch the ground. Archaeologists do not know the exact meaning of the game, but it had religious and political importance. It also was a source of entertainment for crowds of spectators.

The grinning jaguars, serpents, and other images that decorate Olmec carvings appear in the arts of later people. A figure similar to the Maya god of maize is found in Olmec paintings on the walls at San Bartolo, and the Olmec snake god is seen in the Maya gods Kukulcan and the Aztec Quetzalcoatl. The Olmec calendar and its number system were passed on to later people. Their most important legacy, however, may have been the tradition of priestly leadership and the religious rituals that were central to later Middle American civilizations.

☑ **INFER** Why don't archaeologists know where the Olmec came from?

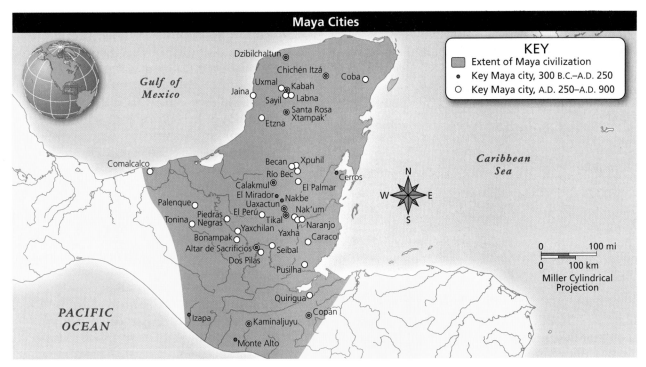

Maya Cities

KEY
- Extent of Maya civilization
- • Key Maya city, 300 B.C.–A.D. 250
- ○ Key Maya city, A.D. 250–A.D. 900

Gulf of Mexico

Dzibilchaltun
Chichén Itzá
Coba
Uxmal Kabah
Jaina Labna
Sayil
Santa Rosa
Etzna Xtampak'

Comalcalco
Becan Xpuhil
Río Bec
Calakmul Cerros
El Mirador El Palmar
Palenque Uaxactun Nakbe
Piedras El Perú Nak'um
Tonina Negras Tikal
Yaxchilan Naranjo
Bonampak Yaxha
Altar de Sacrificios Caracol
Dos Pilas Seibal
Pusilha

Quirigua
Izapa Copán
Kaminaljuyu
Monte Alto

Caribbean Sea

PACIFIC OCEAN

0   100 mi
0   100 km
Miller Cylindrical Projection

>> **Analyze Maps** Maya cities were centered around temples used for ceremonial purposes and for observations of the stars, from which the Maya calculated mathematics and astronomy. Where were most of the later cities established?

The Maya

Scholars have long thought that among the peoples the Olmec influenced were the Maya. New evidence suggests that the Maya may have developed ceremonial centers about the same time as the Olmec. By 300 B.C., the Maya were building large cities, such as El Mirador in Guatemala. By about A.D. 250, the Maya golden age—known as the Classic Period—began, with city-states flourishing from the Yucatán Peninsula in southern Mexico through much of Central America.

Farming Methods Before the Maya developed large population centers, like those later constructed by the Inca and Aztecs, they lived scattered across the land. They developed two farming methods that allowed them to thrive in the tropical environment. In many areas, farmers burned down forests and then cleared the land in order to plant on it. After a few years, the fields were no longer fertile. The Maya would then abandon these lands until they could be used once again.

In the meantime, farmers would burn and clear new lands for farming. In addition, along the banks of rivers, Maya farmers built raised fields to lift crops up above the annual floodwaters. These methods allowed the Maya to produce enough maize and other crops to support rapidly growing cities.

City-States Ruled Over the People The Maya cities that developed before and during the Classic Period never formed an empire. Instead, individual and powerful city-states evolved. The smaller city-states ruled over the people living directly within and near their borders. The largest ones reigned over neighboring areas as well—often requiring nearby cities to show allegiance to their kings and to participate in their ritual activities. Over the course of hundreds of years, many different city-states held power, with warfare and trade a constant theme of life among them. Cities such as Palenque, Copán, and Piedras Negras all carried great influence in their time, but the largest and most supreme power resided in the rulers of Tikal and Calakmul.

While the Maya were not united politically as later Aztec and Inca civilizations came to be, city-states maintained regular contact through a system of economic exchange, which generated much wealth. Traders carried valuable cargoes long distances by sea and along roads made of packed earth. Trade goods included items of daily use—such as honey, salt, and cotton—and nonessential but prized items such as feathers, jade, and jaguar pelts. These goods might have been used in ceremonies or to show status.

>> Maya temples were built in the shape of pyramids using hand-cut limestone blocks. The interior usually consisted of a few narrow rooms, indicating that they were intended for ceremonial purposes rather than for the public.

🅑 BOUNCE to Activate Gallery

>> Maya artifacts reflect their lifestyle and culture. Maya rulers and other nobles commissioned art such as this carved ceremonial mask.

Social Hierarchy Each Maya city had its own ruler, who was usually male. Maya records and carvings show that women occasionally governed on their own or in the name of young sons. Nobles served many functions in support of the ruler. Some were military leaders, while some collected taxes and enforced laws. Others managed public works, similar to the way the Olmec used collective labor for monument and temple building. Scribes, painters, and sculptors were also very highly respected. Merchants may have formed a middle class in society, though the wealthiest and most powerful merchants were certainly nobles, as they had been in the Olmec civilization.

The majority of the Maya were farmers. They grew maize, beans, and squash—the basic food crops of Mesomerica—as well as fruit trees, cotton, and brilliant tropical flowers. To support the cities, farmers paid taxes on food and worked on construction projects. Some cities also included a population of slaves, who generally were commoners who had been captured in war.

☑ **EXPLAIN** How did the Maya operate politically without a centralized government?

Maya Cultural Life

The cultural life of the Maya included impressive advances in learning and the arts. In addition, the Maya developed a complex polytheistic religion, perhaps inherited from the Olmec, that influenced their cultural life as well as their spiritual beliefs. Many Maya today maintain elements of the traditional religion established by the ancient Maya, such as the belief that each person's spirit is associated with a particular animal.

A Legacy in Stone The cities of the Maya are known today for their towering temples and palaces built from stone. Temples rested on pyramid-shaped platforms, reflective of the Olmecs' first pyramid, that were often quite large. Atop the temples, priests performed rites and sacrifices, while the people watched from the plazas below. Some temples also served as burial places for rulers, nobles, and priests. Palaces may have been used as royal residences as well as locations for meetings, courts, and other governmental activities. The multi-use aspect of royal residences is reminiscent of the Olmec ceremonial centers.

The Maya placed elaborately carved sculpture on many of their buildings. They also sculpted tall stone monuments, as did the Olmec, each of which is called a **stela** (STEE luh). These carvings

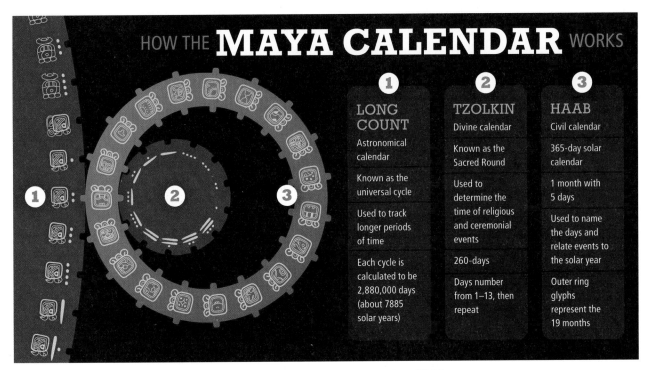

HOW THE MAYA CALENDAR WORKS

① LONG COUNT

Astronomical calendar

Known as the universal cycle

Used to track longer periods of time

Each cycle is calculated to be 2,880,000 days (about 7885 solar years)

② TZOLKIN

Divine calendar

Known as the Sacred Round

Used to determine the time of religious and ceremonial events

260-days

Days number from 1–13, then repeat

③ HAAB

Civil calendar

365-day solar calendar

1 month with 5 days

Used to name the days and relate events to the solar year

Outer ring glyphs represent the 19 months

>> **Analyze Information** The Maya calendar consists of three linked calendars. Which calendar is closest to the one we use today?

preserve striking images of nobles, warriors in plumed headdresses, and powerful rulers. They also represent the Maya gods, including the creator god Itzamna (et SAHM nah), the rain god Chac (chakh), and the sun god K'inich Ajaw (keen EECH ah HOW).

Scribes Record History The Maya also developed a hieroglyphic writing system, which scholars did not decipher until recent decades. Maya scribes carved inscriptions on stelae that include names of rulers, mentions of neighboring city-states, and dates and descriptions of events. They also wrote about astronomy, rituals, and other religious matters in books made of bark paper. Spanish conquerors later burned most of these books, considering any works that were written by non-Christians to be unacceptable. Three books, however, were taken to Europe and have survived into the present.

Astronomy and Mathematics Maya texts reveal that priests were dedicated students of astronomy and astrology, the study of the stars and planets that assumes heavenly bodies influence human affairs. Advances in astronomy were closely linked to mathematics. Maya priests needed to measure time accurately in order to produce an accurate calendar. They developed a 365-day solar calendar as well as a 260-day religious calendar, recording the correct timing for important ceremonies.

Maya priests also invented a counting system based on three symbols: a dot to represent one, a bar for five, and a shell for zero. With these three symbols, they could keep track of events. Even peasants could use this simple form of arithmetic for trade. The Maya were one of the only early civilizations to understand the concept of zero. Along with counting, the Maya developed other, more sophisticated concepts in mathematics.

Maya Civilization Declines About A.D. 900, the Maya abandoned many of their cities. In the Yucatán Peninsula, cities flourished for a few more centuries, but there, too, the Maya eventually stopped building them. By the time the Spanish arrived in the 1500s, the Maya mostly lived in farming villages. Archaeologists do not know for sure why Maya civilization declined, although theories abound. For example, frequent warfare may have taken its toll on society, or overpopulation could have led to over-farming and exhaustion of the soil.

Throughout the region, however, the remoteness of their jungle and mountain locations allowed many Maya to survive the encounter with the Spanish. Today, more than two million Maya people live in Guatemala and southern Mexico.

☑ **EXPLAIN** What made it important for Maya mathematicians and astronomers to work in unison?

The Aztec

Sometime shortly after about A.D. 1200, bands of nomadic people from the north migrated into the **Valley of Mexico,** which lies in the high plateau of central Mexico. These people identified themselves as separate tribes, such as the Mexica (may SHEE kah), from whom Mexico gets its name. All the tribes spoke one language—Nahuatl (NAH hwaht el)—and believed their origins began in the same legendary birthplace, Aztlan. Together, these tribes are known as the Aztecs.

Empire Building In A.D. 1325, the Aztecs founded their capital city, **Tenochtitlán** (teh nawch tee TLAHN). According to Aztec legend, the gods had told the Aztecs to search for an eagle holding a snake in its beak and perching atop a cactus. When they saw this sign, they would know where to build their capital.

Indeed, they finally saw the sign on a swampy island in Lake Texcoco (tesh KOH koh), and there they built their city. Today, Mexico City sits atop this same site.

As their population grew, the Aztecs found ingenious ways to create more farmland in their lake environment, just as the Maya had modified their environment by farming raised beds in the river valley.

The Aztec built **chinampas,** artificial islands made of mud piled atop reed mats that were anchored to the shallow lake-bed with willow trees. On these "floating gardens," the Aztecs raised maize, squash, and beans, the same crops grown by their predecessors the Maya. They gradually filled in parts of the lake and created canals for transportation. Wide stone causeways linked Tenochtitlán to the mainland.

The Empire Expands In the 1400s, the Aztecs greatly expanded their territory. Through a combination of fierce conquests and shrewd alliances, they spread their rule across most of Mexico, from the Gulf of Mexico in the east to the Pacific Ocean in the west. By 1517, the Aztec empire numbered an estimated 5 to 6 million people.

Government and Society War brought immense wealth as well as power to the Aztec empire. **Tribute,** or payment from conquered peoples, helped the Aztecs turn their capital into a magnificent city. From its temples and royal palaces to its zoos and floating gardens, Tenochtitlán seemed a city of wonders. It was also the center of a complex, well-ordered empire.

Like the Maya, the Aztecs had a clear social hierarchy. A council of nobles, priests, and military leaders elected the emperor, whose primary function

Aztec Hierarchy

ELITE		
EMPEROR	**COUNCIL OF NOBLES**	**PRIESTS/PRIESTESSES**
elected by council of nobles, priests and military leaders; function was to lead war	officials, judges, governors of conquered provinces; owned/received land	peformed rituals to please the gods and prevent droughts and other disasters
COMMONER		
WARRIORS	**MERCHANTS**	
military; could become nobles depending on victories in battle	long-distance, not local, traveling traders; could become nobles depending on trades artisans	
PEASANT FARMERS	**SERFS/ENSLAVED PEOPLE**	
could not own land	prisoners of war/debtors; enslaved people could own land and buy their freedom	

>> **Analyze Information** In Aztec society, birth determined social status. Rank was visible in Aztec clothing. Nobles dressed in fine textiles, often cotton, and sandals. Where could a woman have influence in Aztec society?

was to lead in war. Below him, nobles served as officials, judges, and governors of conquered provinces. Next came the warriors, who could rise to noble status by performing well on the battlefield. The priests were a class apart. They performed rituals to please the gods and prevent droughts or other disasters.

The Aztec had a powerful middle class, which included long-distance traders, who ferried goods across the empire and beyond. With goods from the highlands such as weapons, tools, and rope, they bartered for tropical products such as jaguar skins and cocoa beans.

The majority of people were commoners who farmed the land. At the bottom of society were serfs and enslaved people, who were mostly prisoners of war or debtors. Despite their low status, enslaved people's rights were clearly established by law. For example, enslaved people could own land and buy their freedom.

Religion and Mythology Like the Olmec and the Maya before them, the Aztecs believed in many gods. They revered Huitzilopochtli (weets ee loh POHCH tlee) as the patron god of their people. His temple towered above central Tenochtitlán.

The Aztecs also worshipped Quetzalcoatl (ket sahl koh AHT el), which was akin to the Olmec snake god and the Maya god Kukulcan, the feathered serpent who reigned over earth and water. The Aztecs also worshiped the other powerful gods of an earlier culture that had been centered at the city of Teotihuacán (tay oh tee wah KAHN.)

Teotihuacán had dominated life in the Valley of Mexico from about A.D. 200 to A.D. 750. The city was well planned, with wide roads, massive temples, and large apartment buildings to house its population of perhaps 200,000. Along the main avenue, the enormous Pyramid of the Sun and the Pyramid of the Moon rose majestically toward the sky.

Citizens of Teotihuacán worshiped gods such as Quetzalcoatl and Tlaloc (TLAH lohk), the rain god. After Teotihuacán fell, possibly to invaders, its culture survived and greatly influenced later peoples of Mesoamerica. The Aztecs, for example, believed that the gods had created the world multiple times. In their mythology, it was in Teotihuacán that the gods created the world in which the Aztecs lived.

In Aztec mythology, the gods frequently sacrificed themselves for the good of the people. They believed a god named Nanahuatzin (nah nah WAHTS een) had sacrificed himself to become the sun. To give the sun strength to rise each day, the Aztecs offered human sacrifices. Most of the victims were prisoners of war, who were plentiful because the Aztecs carried on almost continuous warfare.

>> Tenochtitlán was one of the largest cities in the world at the height of the Aztec empire, with some 200,000 inhabitants in the early 1500s. The Spanish later constructed Mexico City, shown here in the 1600s, on the same site.

>> An Aztec temple, like the one shown in this illustration, was the place priests went to pray and make ritualistic sacrifice. Unlike Maya temples, Aztec temples have stairs on only one side.

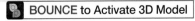

BOUNCE to Activate 3D Model

>> Spanish explorers and invaders found the Aztec empire at the height of its size and power in the early 1500s. This painting shows how a European artist imagined a meeting between the Aztec emperor Moctezuma and the Spanish conqueror Hernán Cortés.

Keepers of Knowledge Priests were the keepers of Aztec knowledge. They recorded laws and historical events in the Aztec hieroglyphic writing system. Some priests ran schools. Others used their knowledge of astronomy and mathematics to foretell the future.

Ideas developed in Aztec civilization in astronomy enabled the Aztecs to develop two calendars. One major idea was the development of a 260-day ritual calendar based on the movements of the sun. Aztec astronomers observed that it was 260 days for the sun to cross a certain point in the sky. This calendar was a ritual calendar used to schedule the best days to build houses and conduct ceremonies.

A second major idea was the development of a second 365-day calendar that was based on the movements of the constellation Pleiades. The Aztec astronomers watched the course of Pleiades across the night sky. When the constellation disappeared, and the sun was at its highest point, the Aztecs knew the rainy season was beginning. When Pleiades began to appear, it marked the dry season. These ideas in astronomy developed in Aztec civilization allowed the Aztecs to plant and harvest crops.

The Aztec civilization developed important ideas in mathematics, too. One major idea was the development of a numbering system based on 20. They used their numbering system to do precise measurements of land holdings and to calculate the area of fields for taxation. A second major idea was the use of symbols to write numbers and other symbols, such as the arrow, heart, and hands, to stand for fractions. The Aztec civilization developed ideas about multiplication and division, as well as some principles of geometry.

Like many other ancient peoples, the Aztecs believed that illness was a punishment from the gods. Still, Aztec priests used herbs and other medicines to treat fevers and wounds. Aztec physicians could set broken bones and treat dental cavities. They also prescribed steam baths as cures for various ills, a therapy still in use today.

Discontent Grows The Aztecs developed a sophisticated and complex culture. But among many of the peoples they conquered, discontent festered and rebellion often flared up. At the height of Aztec power, word reached Tenochtitlán that pale-skinned, bearded men had landed on the east coast. When these armies from Spain arrived, the Spanish found ready allies among peoples who were ruled by the Aztec empire.

☑ **SUMMARIZE** Describe the religion and mythology developed by the Aztecs.

☑ ASSESSMENT

1. **Compare Points of View** What are two possible theories about how people first settled the Americas?

2. **Summarize** What methods of recording of history were used by the Maya and the Aztec?

3. **Contrast** What is the main difference between the Aztec and Maya regarding the governing of their societies?

4. **Identify Patterns** How did the Olmec influence the Maya and the Aztecs?

5. **Connections to Today** How did the Aztecs use their studies of the sun and stars? How is this similar to or different from modern uses of astronomy?

Bernardino de Sahagún, *General History of the Things of New Spain,* translated by Arthur J.O. Anderson and Charles E. Dibble

Introduction

Bernardino de Sahagún was a Spanish Franciscan friar who worked as a missionary among the Aztecs during the 1500s. With the help of native students, Sahagún compiled the *General History of the Things of New Spain,* a 12-volume work on Aztec culture recorded in the Aztec language of Nahuatl (nah HWAHT el) and translated into Spanish. The work documented Aztec religious beliefs, social life, history, and customs as described by native peoples and illustrated by native artists. In the excerpts below, the History describes two important Aztec gods, Tlaloc (TLAH lohk) and Quetzalcoatl (ket sahl koh AHT el), and also describes some of the ways in which people made offerings to the gods.

>> This image from the *General History* shows four Aztec gods, including Quetzalcoatl (at top left).

Primary Source

BOOK 1—The Gods

Tlaloc the priest. To him was attributed the rain; for he made it, he caused it to come down, he scattered the rain like seed, and also the hail. He caused to sprout, to blossom, to leaf out, to bloom, to ripen, the trees, the plants, our food. And also by him were made floods of water and thunder-bolts. . . .

Quetzalcoatl—he was the wind, the guide and road-sweeper of the rain gods, of the masters of the water, of those who brought rain. And when the wind rose, when the dust rumbled, and it crackled and there was a great din, and it became dark and the wind blew in many directions, and it thundered; then it was said: "[Quetzalcoatl] is wrathful.". . .

☑ **SUMMARIZE** According to Aztec belief, how were Tlaloc and Quetzalcoatl connected to natural phenomenon?

BOOK 2—The Ceremonies

Offerings

Thus were offerings made: with food . . . were offerings made, and with all kinds of living things—perchance turkeys, perchance birds. . . Or else whatever was newly formed—perchance maize, or chia, or flowers, or whatever [was newly grown].

And thus did the young [unmarried] women make offerings: Before dawn their mothers and fathers awoke them. So they went about making offerings of gifts carried in the palms of their hands—little tortillas, [which were] very small,—and thus they quickly proceeded to lay gifts before the devil; in bowls they carried them thus to present them [to the gods]. . . .

ANALYZE INFORMATION Why might Aztec people have emphasized the use of living things in their offerings?

And thus was the offering of incense performed, with an incense ladle. It was made of clay, with [stones in its hollows making] a rattle. Then they laid live coals in the incense ladle. When these blazed up, then they filled it with *copal* incense, and then came forth. . . in the middle of the courtyard, where arose the brazier. [This] was made of clay.

And when they came up . . . then they dedicated the incense burner to the four directions, thus offering incense. . . .

USE CONTEXT CLUES Why do you think the Aztecs offered incense to the four directions?

The eating [kissing] of the earth was thus done, when men came into any place: everyone kissed the earth, with one finger [touched to the ground and then to the mouth]. . .

. . . When one put not much faith in [another's] word, thus he said unto him:

"If what thou sayest is true, do thou kiss the earth."

Whosoever it was then thus kissed the earth, and thus he bore witness to [the truth of] his words. . . .

When anything was to be eaten, and was not yet eaten, perchance of the food first a very small morsel was cut and cast in front of the hearth. When they had cast it, then they began to eat. No one first ate [before], indeed, libations [offerings of food or liquid] had been cast in front of the hearth.

DRAW CONCLUSIONS Why do you think the Aztecs offered food to the gods?

ASSESSMENT

1. **Summarize** In your opinion, what is the main point of this excerpt?

2. **Draw Conclusions** What does this source suggest about how the Aztecs understood the weather and other natural events?

3. **Determine Author's Purpose** Sahagún was a Christian missionary. Why do you think he compiled the *General History*?

4. **Draw Conclusions** How did the Aztec ritual offerings reflect the belief that the gods regularly intervened in human life?

The interior of the temple complex at Chavín de Huántar included relief carvings of human, serpent, crocodile, feline, and bird images. Scholars believe that Chavín religious beliefs unified the surrounding region.

The World of the Incas

The first cultures of South America developed in the Andean region along the western edge of the continent. This region includes a variety of climates and terrains. The narrow coastal plain is a dry, lifeless desert crossed by occasional rivers. Further inland, the snow-capped Andes Mountains rise steeply, leveling off into high plateaus that bake by day and freeze at night. East of the Andes, dense jungles stretch from Peru into Brazil.

Cultures of the Andes

Thousands of years ago, people settled in fishing villages along the desert coast of Peru and Chile. Gradually they expanded inland, farming the river valleys that run up into the highland plateaus. Using careful irrigation, they grew maize, cotton, squash, and beans. On mountain slopes, they cultivated potatoes, eventually producing 700 varieties. On high plateaus, they domesticated the llama and the alpaca. Eventually, they built large ceremonial centers and developed skills in pottery and weaving.

The Chavín Archaeologists have pieced together a chronology of various cultures that left their mark on the Andean region over the course of 2,000 years. The earliest of these was the **Chavín** (chah VEEN) culture, named for ruins at Chavín de Huantar (chah VEEN day WAHN tahr). There, in about 900 B.C., people built a huge temple complex. Archaeologists are not sure of the Chavín political structure, but they think the culture's religion unified people throughout northern and central Peru. Chavín arts and religion continued to influence later peoples of Peru as well.

 BOUNCE to Activate Flipped Video

Objectives

Examine the early cultures of the Andes.

Understand how Inca emperors extended and maintained their empire.

Describe the major developments of Inca civilization.

Key Terms

Chavín
Moche
adobe
Nazca
Huari
Tiahuanaco
Pachacuti Inca
  Yupanqui
Sapa Inca
Cuzco
quipu
ayllu
Inti

GO ONLINE to access your digital course

The Moche Between A.D. 100 and A.D. 700, the **Moche** (MOH chay) people—named after their most famous city—forged a culture along the arid north coast of Peru. Skilled Moche farmers developed methods for fertilizing the soil and used canals to irrigate the land. Their leaders built roads and organized networks of relay runners to carry messages, ideas that a later Andean civilization, the Inca, would adopt.

At the city of Moche, builders constructed the largest adobe structure in the ancient Americas. **Adobe** is a mixture of clay and plant fibers that becomes hard as it dries in the sun. Moche artisans perfected skills in textile production, goldworking, and woodcarving and produced ceramic vessels in lifelike imitation of people and animals.

Nazca, Huari, and Tiahuanaco Many other Andean cultures emerged, and some left behind intriguing clues about their lives and beliefs. Between about 200 B.C. and A.D. 600 along the southern coast of Peru, the **Nazca** (NAHS kah) people etched geoglyphs in the desert. A geoglyph is a figure or line made on Earth's surface by clearing away rocks and soil.

The Nazca geoglyphs include straight lines that run for miles as well as giant birds, whales, and other animals. Most researchers think that the geoglyphs carried some sort of spiritual meaning.

The city of **Huari** (WAH ree) developed east of the Nazca culture. It controlled much of Peru's mountain and coastal areas. At the same time, a powerful city, **Tiahuanaco** (tee ah wah NAH koh), developed on the southern shores of Lake Titicaca, in modern-day Bolivia. It reigned over parts of modern-day Argentina, Chile, and Peru. Many of the same artistic styles appear at Huari and Tiahuanaco, leading scholars to think that these two southern powers shared religious or trade affiliations.

☑ **IDENTIFY PATTERNS** In what ways did the Chavín and the Moche influence later Andean cultures?

The Powerful Inca Empire

The most powerful of the Andean civilizations—the Inca civilization—came into being in the 1100s with the founding of its first dynasty. For the next three centuries, the Inca civilization stood out no more than any other. But in 1438, a historic change occurred. **Pachacuti Inca Yupanqui** (pahch ah KOO tee ING kuh yoo PANG kee), a skilled warrior and leader, proclaimed himself **Sapa Inca,** or emperor.

From his small kingdom at Cuzco in a high mountain valley, Pachacuti set out on a campaign of conquest. Once he subdued neighboring peoples, he enlisted them in his armies. His son, emperor Topa Inca Yupanqui, continued the expansion. With **Cuzco** as its capital, the resulting empire stretched more than 2,500 miles along the Andes, from Ecuador in the north to Chile in the south.

Inca Government The Sapa Inca held absolute power. Claiming to be divine, the son of the sun itself, he was also the empire's religious leader. Gold, considered the "sweat of the sun," served as his symbol. His queen, the Coya, carried out important religious duties and sometimes governed in his absence.

The Sapa Inca laid claim over all the land, herds, mines, and people of his empire. As the Inca people had no personal property, there was little demand for items for barter or sale, and trade played a much smaller role in the Inca economy than it had in the earlier Maya economy. Periodically, the Sapa Inca would call upon men of a certain age to serve as laborers for short periods, perhaps a few months. By so doing, he could access millions of laborers at once.

Inca rulers ran an efficient government. Nobles ruled the provinces along with local chieftains whom

>> Pachacuti Sapa Inca was a master strategist who expanded the Inca empire by taking over enemy territory both by force and through peaceful negotiation.

🅱 BOUNCE to Activate Map

the Inca armies had conquered. Below them, officials carried out the day-to-day business of enforcing laws and organizing labor.

Specially trained officials kept records on a **quipu,** a collection of colored strings that were knotted in different ways to represent various numbers. Scholars think that the Inca, who never invented a writing system, may have used quipus to record economic, bureaucratic, religious, and other information. The Inca then took the quipu and used it with the yupanas, a system of stone grids representing various mathematical values, to make complex calculations.

Uniting the Empire with Language and Roads

To unite their empire, the Inca imposed their language, Quechua (KECH wuh) and their religion on the people they conquered. The Inca also created one of history's great road networks. At its greatest extent, it wound about 14,000 miles through mountains and deserts, passing through an area inhabited by almost 10 million people. Hundreds of bridges spanned rivers and deep gorges. Steps were cut into steep slopes and tunnels dug through hillsides. The expanse of the Inca road system was unmatched in the early Americas.

The roads allowed armies and news to move rapidly throughout the empire. At stations set regular distances apart, runners waited to carry messages.

Relays of runners could carry news of a revolt swiftly from a distant province to the capital. Inca soldiers stood guard at outposts throughout the empire. Within days of an uprising, they would be on the move to crush the rebels. Ordinary people were restricted from using the roads at all.

Cuzco as Capital All roads led through Cuzco. People from all the culture groups ruled by the empire lived in the city. Members of a given group lived in a particular part of the city and wore the traditional clothing and practiced the traditional crafts of their region of origin. In the heart of the city stood the great Temple of the Sun, its interior walls lined with gold. Like Inca palaces and forts—and like the temples and other buildings of the Maya and the Aztec—the temple was made of enormous stone blocks, each polished and carved to fit exactly in place without mortar used to secure it. Inca engineers were so precise that many of their buildings have survived severe earthquakes.

☑ **SYNTHESIZE** How did the Sapa Inca consolidate his power and keep control of his large empire?

>> Machu Picchu, built at the height of the Inca empire, is a complex located almost 8,000 feet above sea level. It is composed of some 220 structures that were used for agricultural, ceremonial, and astronomical purposes.

🅑 BOUNCE to Activate Gallery

Inca Life

The Inca strictly regulated the lives of millions of people within their empire. The leaders of each Inca village, called an **ayllu** (EYE loo), carried out government orders. They assigned jobs to each family and organized the community to work the land. Government officials arranged marriages to ensure that men and women were settled at a certain age.

Terraced Farming Inca farmers expanded step terraces built by earlier Andean peoples. They carved out flat strips of land on steep hillsides and built stone walls to hold the land in place. The terraces the Inca created kept rains from washing away the soil and made farming possible in places where naturally flat land was scarce.

Farmers spent part of each year working land for their community, and part working land for the emperor and the temples. The government allotted part of each harvest to specific groups of people or for particular purposes. It stored the rest in case of disasters such as famine.

Masters of Metalwork and Weaving The Inca were some of the most skilled metalworkers in the

Americas. They learned to work and alloy, or blend, copper, tin, bronze, silver, and gold. While they employed copper and bronze for useful objects, they reserved precious metals for statues of gods and goddesses, eating utensils for the nobles, and decoration.

The Inca also mastered the art of weaving, a practice passed down to them from earlier Andean peoples. They raised cotton and sheared the wool from llamas and alpacas to create colorful textiles to be worn as clothing or as adornments, such as belts and bags.

Medical Practices The Inca developed important medical practices, including surgery on the human skull. In such operations, they cleaned the area to be operated on and then gave the patient a drug to make him or her unconscious—procedures similar to the modern use of antiseptics and anesthesia.

This is not dissimilar from the Aztec, whose doctors set bones and prepared prescriptions to cure illnesses. The Inca also used medical procedures to mummify the dead.

Religion and Ritual The Inca worshipped many gods linked to the forces of nature. People offered food, clothing, and drink to the guardian spirits of the home and the village. Each month had its own festival, from the great ripening and the dance of the young maize to the festival of the water. Festivals were celebrated with ceremonies, sports, and games.

A powerful class of priests served the gods. Chief among the gods was **Inti,** the sun god. His special attendants, the "Chosen Women," were selected from each region of the empire. During years of training, they studied the mysteries of the religion, learned to prepare ritual food and drink, and made the elaborate wool garments worn by the Sapa Inca and the Coya. After their training, most Chosen Women continued to serve Inti. Others joined the Inca's court or married nobles.

Comparing Three Civilizations The three major civilizations of the Americas differed in location, origins, and early history. Their customs, languages, and traditions differed, too. Still, like civilizations elsewhere, the Maya, Aztecs, and Inca shared key features: well-organized governments, complex religions, job specialization, social classes, architecture and arts, and public works. Of the three, only the Inca did not have a system of writing, although their quipu are thought to have preserved records. All built on the achievements of earlier peoples in their regions, but each created its own style in the arts, legends, and view of the world.

Characteristics of Inca Life

CHARACTERISTIC	DESCRIPTION
Farming	• Built terraced fields • Grew corn, potatoes, beans, squash, peanuts, avocados, cotton, coca (fought hunger, thirst, pain), rare orchids (for medicine)
Domesticated Animals	• Alpaca (for wool) • Llamas (carried goods)
Crafts	• Metal work (gold, silver, bronze): eating utensils for nobles, decoration • Weaving: colorful wool, cotton textiles with gold and feathers woven in • Goldwork: ornaments such as jewelry and objects for religious ceremonies • Pottery: coiled technique and used for everyday use and decoration
Recordkeeping	• Quipu: a system of strings and tied knots
Medical practices	• Surgery • Early antiseptics/anesthesia • Mummification
Religion	• Worshipped many gods, most importantly sun god; • Inca girls and women were attendants to gods
Clothing	• Two-piece loose tunics without sleeves slipped over the head • Cloaks as outer garments fastened at neck with pin • Caps for men; women pulled cloaks over head

>> **Analyze Information** Inca society was sophisticated, and much of daily life was structured and strictly regulated by government officials. How was their religion similar to many other cultures?

Inca Hierarchy

SAPA INCA
Emperor:
absolute power;
descendant of sun god

WIFE OF SAPA INCA
acted in emperor's stead

FIRST MINISTER AND HIGH PRIEST

APÚ- CURACAS (INCA NOBLES)
4 provincial governors, Supreme Council to emperor

TOCRICOQ (PROVINCIAL GOVERNOR)
ethnic Inca, broad judicial and administrative powers

YANACONA (PERSONAL SERVANTS TO NOBILITY)
did not pay tribute or farm

HATUN RUNA (COMMONERS)
worked state lands

>> **Analyze Information** The highly structured Inca society allowed the government to regulate the lives of the millions of people who lived within the empire. Who had a higher position in Inca society, Tocricoq or Hatun Runa?

Within these broad features of civilizations, the Maya, Aztec, and Inca developed different political and economic patterns. While the Maya ruled city-states, the Aztecs and Inca built large empires. Although all three were polytheistic, each had its own gods, goddesses, and religious rituals. The Maya and Aztec developed their own form of the popular ball game that originated with the Olmec.

Each of these three civilizations adapted to its particular environment—like civilizations in Africa and Asia. The Maya built raised beds along flood-prone rivers. The Aztecs created chinampas in their swampy lake bed, and the Inca constructed terraced fields on steep mountainsides. All three depended on farming, but the Inca developed some different crops and were less involved in trade than the two Mesoamerican civilizations.

A Breakdown of Power At its height, the Inca civilization was a center of learning and political power. But in 1525, the emperor Huayna Capac (WY nuh kah PAHK) died suddenly of illness. Civil war broke out over which of his sons would reign next, weakening the empire at a crucial moment—the eve of the arrival of Spanish invaders.

☑ **CONNECT** How did the Inca use and improve upon skills they learned from earlier peoples?

☑ ASSESSMENT

1. **Cite Evidence** Why do scholars think that the cities of Huari and Tiahuanaco were affiliated by either trade or religion?

2. **Explain** What features and policies of the Inca government helped the emperor control his empire?

3. **Draw Conclusions** How was the development of the quipu helpful to the government and economy of the Inca?

4. **Identify** In what crafts and technical achievements did the Inca excel?

5. **Quest Connections** How were the Moche able to farm along the arid north coast of Peru?

4.3

Like the Maya, the Hohokam built ball courts. Hohokam games were thought to put players in touch with the spiritual world, and attendance at the games was both ceremonial and a means to socialize.

 BOUNCE to Activate Flipped Video

Objectives

Understand how groups of people adapted to the desert environment of the Southwest.

Analyze the evidence from which we have learned about the emergence of culture in eastern North America.

Examine the cultures that developed in three very different geographic regions.

Key Terms

Mesa Verde
pueblo
Pueblo Bonito
kiva
earthwork
Cahokia
potlatch
Iroquois League

The Peoples of North America

Hundreds of Native American cultural groups lived in North America before A.D. 1500 and the arrival of Europeans. Based on the environments in which people lived, scholars have categorized them into ten culture areas: Arctic, Subarctic, Northwest Coast, California, Great Basin, Plateau, Southwest, Plains, Southeast, and Northeast. In each area, people adapted to geographic conditions that influenced their ways of life.

Cultures Develop in the Desert Southwest

For millennia, Native American groups lived by hunting, fishing, and gathering wild plants. After farming spread north from Mesoamerica, many people raised corn and other food crops. Some people farmed so successfully that they built large permanent settlements. Some of the earliest farming cultures arose in what is today the southwestern United States.

The Hohokam, Pima, and Papago Perhaps as long ago as 300 B.C., fields of corn, beans, and squash bloomed in the desert of present-day Arizona, near the Salt and Gila rivers. These fields were planted by a people later called the Hohokam, or "Vanished Ones," by their descendants, the Pima and the Papago. To farm in the desert, the Hohokam built a complex irrigation system that included numerous canals. The canals carried river water to fields as far as several miles away. The Hohokam also built temple mounds and ball courts similar in appearance to those of Mesoamerica. Evidence indicates that, for unknown reasons, the Hohokam left their settlements sometime during the A.D. 1400s.

GO ONLINE to access your digital course

The Ancestral Puebloans About A.D. 100, Ancestral Puebloans lived in what is today the Four Corners region of Arizona, New Mexico, Colorado, and Utah. Within a few hundred years, they were building villages, some inside caves and some outside.

Between A.D. 1150 and A.D. 1300, the Ancestral Puebloans (also known as Anasazi) built their famous cliff residences. Using hand-cut stone blocks, they constructed housing complexes on cliffs along canyon walls. Such cliffs offered protection from raiders. The largest of these cliff dwellings, at **Mesa Verde** (MAY suh VEHR dee) in present-day Colorado, included more than 200 rooms. People climbed ladders to reach their fields on the flatlands above or the canyon floor below.

The Ancestral Puebloans also built freestanding villages, which were similar in structure to the cliff dwellings. These communities, which the Spanish later called **pueblos** (PWEB lohs), were made of multi-floor houses that were connected to one another by doorways and ladders.

Remains of **Pueblo Bonito,** the largest such pueblo, still stands in New Mexico. The huge complex consisted of 800 rooms that could have housed about 3,000 people. Builders used stone and adobe bricks to erect a crescent-shaped compound rising five stories high. In the center of the great complex lay a plaza. There, the Ancestral Puebloans dug their **kiva** (KEE vuh), a large underground chamber used for religious ceremonies and political meetings. In the kiva, they carved out a small hole in the floor, which represented the birthplace of the tribe. They also painted the walls with geometric designs and scenes of ritual or daily life.

In the late 1200s, a long drought forced the Ancestral Puebloans to abandon their dwellings. Attacks by Navajos and Apaches—peoples from the north—may have contributed further to their decline. However, Ancestral Puebloan traditions survived among several groups of descendants. Known collectively as Pueblo Indians, many of these groups continue to live in the southwestern United States today.

☑ **INFER** What does the nature of the Ancestral Puebloans' buildings tell you about the people who built them?

Cultures Develop in the East

Far to the east of the Ancestral Puebloans, in the Mississippi and Ohio river valleys, other farming cultures emerged after about 1000 B.C. They, too, left behind impressive constructions from which we can learn a great deal about their lives.

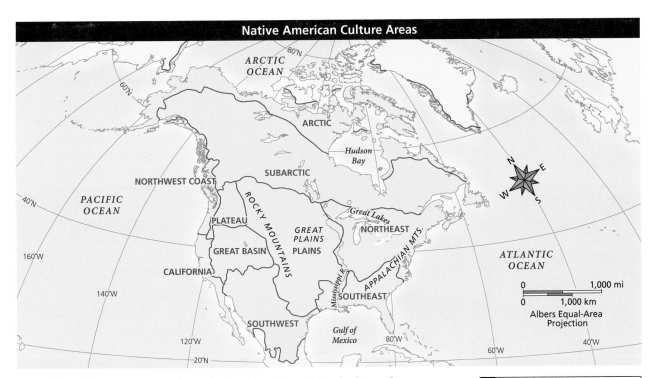

Native American Culture Areas

>> **Analyze Maps** Native Americans developed a wide variety of cultures. In each culture area, people shared fairly similar environments and ways of life. Which culture area was the farthest south?

🅑 BOUNCE to Activate Map

>> Cahokia was a large city with buildings constructed in rows, with a central plaza in the middle and agricultural land surrounding it. The reasons for Cahokia's decline are unknown, but theories have ranged from climate change to war or disease.

>> The Great Serpent Mound, built by the Adena people, is some 1300 feet long and ranges in width from three to twenty feet. Inside the mound, which is made of yellow clay, are hollow cave-like openings.

The Adena and Hopewell Both the Adena and the later Hopewell people of the Northeast are known for giant **earthworks** that they built for various purposes by heaping earth in piles and shaping them. Some of the earthworks were large burial mounds, others served as platforms for structures such as temples, and still others served as defensive walls. Mounds were usually cone-shaped, oval, or formed into the shape of an animal. The Adena's Great Serpent Mound in Ohio wriggles and twists in the shape of a snake for almost a quarter of a mile.

Some of the objects found in the Hopewell mounds show that traders extended their influence over a wide area. They acquired goods such as conch shells from the Gulf of Mexico, grizzly bear teeth and obsidian from the Rocky Mountains, and copper from the Great Lakes region. Skilled artisans then hammered and shaped the copper into fine ornaments.

The Mississippians By A.D. 800, these early eastern cultures had disappeared. A new people, whom today we refer to as the Mississippians, gained influence in the Southeast and Mississippi River valley regions. As their culture spread, the Mississippians built clusters of earthen mounds and ever larger towns and ceremonial centers.

The greatest Mississippian center, **Cahokia** in present-day Illinois housed as many as 20,000 people by about A.D. 1100. Cahokia boasted 120 mounds, atop some of which sat the homes of rulers and nobles. The largest mound probably had a temple on its summit, where priests and rulers offered prayers and sacrifices to the sun.

The Natchez The Mississippians left no written records. Artifacts from the remains of settlements such as Cahokia provide clues into their culture. Their traditions have survived among the Natchez people, who are known for their worship of the sun. They called their ruler, who held absolute power, the Great Sun. He and his family lived on the top of pyramid mounds. Society was divided into castes; the highest group was called the suns.

☑ **IDENTIFY** How do we know that the Mississipians existed if they left no written record?

>> The Inuit had to overcome the challenges of living in the harsh Arctic climate. They built kayaks with wood or whale bone, over which they stretched animal skins, and used harpoons and other weapons to hunt seals.

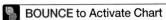
BOUNCE to Activate Chart

Distinct Cultures Develop in Different Geographic Regions

Distinct ways of life developed in each Native American culture area. Here, we examine three culture areas—the Arctic, the Northwest Coast, and the Eastern Woodlands—in which varied climates and natural environments helped unique cultures develop.

The Inuit In the far northern stretches of Canada, the Inuit (IN oo it; often called the Eskimo) adapted to the harsh climate of the Arctic. By about 2000 B.C., they had settled there, using the resources of the frozen land to survive. Small bands lived by hunting and fishing. Seals and other sea mammals provided them with food, skins for clothing, bones for needles and tools, and oil for cooking.

The Inuit paddled kayaks in open waters or used dog sleds to transport goods across the ice. In some areas, the Inuit constructed igloos, or dome-shaped homes made from snow and ice. In others, they built sod dwellings that were partly underground.

Cultures of the Northwest Coast The peoples of the Northwest Coast lived in an environment far richer in natural resources than the Inuit did. Rivers teemed with salmon, and the Pacific Ocean offered

a supply of other fish and sea mammals. Hunters tracked deer, wolves, and bears in the forests. In this land of plenty, people built large permanent villages with homes made of wood. They traded their surplus goods, gaining wealth that was then shared in a ceremony called **potlatch.** At this ceremony, which is still practiced in Canada and the Northwest coast of the United States today, a person of high rank and wealth distributes lavish gifts to a large number of guests. By accepting the gifts, the guests acknowledge the host's high status.

The Iroquois On the other side of the continent, the Northeast was home to numerous Native American groups. Many of these spoke the Iroquois (IHR uh kwoy) language, shared similar traditions, and were known collectively as the Iroquois. Typically, the Iroquois cleared land and built villages in the forests. While women farmed, men hunted and frequently fought wars against rival groups.

According to Iroquois tradition, the prophet Dekanawidah (deh kan ah WEE dah) urged these rivals to stop their constant wars. In the late 1500s, he became one of the founders of the unique political system known as the **Iroquois League.** This was an alliance of five Iroquois groups—the Mohawk, Oneida, Onondaga, Cayuga, and Seneca—who were known as the Five Nations. The Iroquois League did not always succeed in keeping the peace. Still, it was the best-organized political group north of Mexico.

Member nations governed their own villages, but met jointly in a council when they needed to address larger issues. Only men sat on the council, but each clan had a "clan mother" who could name or remove members of the council.

The Iroquois League emerged at the same time that Europeans arrived in the Americas. Just as encounters with Europeans would topple the Aztec and Inca empires, so too would they take a fearful toll on the peoples of North America.

☑ **SUMMARIZE** How did the Inuit protect themselves from the harsh Arctic cold?

☑ ASSESSMENT

1. **Draw Conclusions** How did the Ancestral Puebloans adapt their housing to the building materials that were available in the arid Southwest?

2. **Infer** What purposes did the earthwork mounds of the Adena and Hopewell serve? How can archaeologists know that?

3. **Summarize** How did the potlatch help the societies of the Northwest?

4. **Identify** What was the initial purpose of the Iroquois League in the Northeast?

5. **Quest Connections** How did climate and specific natural environments help the Native American peoples of the Arctic, the Northwest, and the Northeast develop distinct cultures?

Connections to Today

This composite image, taken by NASA's Hubble and Spitzer telescopes, shows the Messier 81 (M81) galaxy, a spiral galaxy nearly 12 million light years away from Earth.

Take Action to Understand Space Exploration

In recent decades, space exploration—including both human spaceflights and robotic spacecraft—have brought new knowledge about our solar system to astronomers and other scientists. How have recent astronomical studies contributed to our understanding of the universe?

1. **Choose** one of the following missions, studies, or other forms of space exploration:

   - International Space Station, Hubble Telescope, Mars Curiosity rover, Mars Odyssey and Mars Reconnaissance Orbiter, Voyager 1 and 2, Parker Solar Probe

2. **Ask Questions** What are some of the things you want to know about the topic you chose? Write a list of questions you want to answer or ideas you want to learn more about.

3. **Learn** Research the topic you have chosen. In addition to online sources, find at least one or two print sources.

4. **Develop a Presentation** Create an engaging presentation about the topic you chose, explaining what scientists have learned from the mission or study and how these studies have affected our understanding of the universe. Be sure to include any practical impacts on people on Earth. Include images and videos in your presentation.

LESSON SUMMARIES

Use these Lesson Summaries, and the longer versions available online, to review the key ideas for each lesson in this Topic.

Lesson 1: Civilizations of Middle America

The first Americans arrived from Asia more than 10,000 years ago and began to spread across the Americas, adapting to a variety of climates and environments. In about 1500 B.C., the first civilizations began to develop in Mesoamerica, including the Olmec, Maya, and Aztec. Each of these civilizations engaged in trade, built large pyramids and monuments, had polytheistic religions with priests who performed rituals, and developed complex hieroglyphics and calendars. The Maya built large cities in present-day Guatemala from about A.D. 300 to A.D. 900. In the Valley of Mexico, the Aztec began to build a vast and powerful empire around A.D. 1325.

Lesson 2: The World of the Incas

From small fishing villages along the coast of present-day Peru and Chile, early South American people eventually expanded inland and began farming the arid regions along river valleys. Beginning in about 900 B.C., a number of cultures rose in the Andes, including the Chavín, Moche, and Tiahuanaco. They built temples, adobe homes, roads, and created beautiful artwork that influenced the Inca, the region's most powerful civilization. Through conquest and trade, the Inca created a vast and wealthy empire that stretched more than 2,500 miles along the Andes.

Lesson 3: The Peoples of North America

Hundreds of culture groups emerged across North America, adapting to its varied environments and geography. Early cultures in the arid Southwest created irrigation systems allowing them to grow crops. In the Mississippi and Ohio river valleys, scholars have found evidence of complex cultures that worshiped the sun and traded far and wide. Cultures from diverse regions such as the Arctic, Northwest Coast, and Eastern Woodlands learned to survive and thrive in their environments.

QUEST! FINDINGS

Write Your Essay Refer to your responses to the Quest Connections to help you create your essay to present to the class. Use the rubric and other Quest sources online to guide your work.

GO ONLINE to access lesson summaries

VISUAL REVIEW

Use these graphics to review some of the key terms, people, and ideas from this Topic.

Maya and Aztec Civilizations

MAYA	BOTH
• 250–900 • Yucatán Peninsula • Large independent city-states	• Large pyramids • Crops on raised fields • Trade • Polytheism • Calendars • Hieroglyphic writing system • Astronomy
AZTEC	
• 1325–1521 • Valley of Mexico • Empire with capital city	

The Inca Empire

- 1438–1533
- Large empire of about 10 million people
- Covered much of the west coast of South America
- Sapa Inca held absolute power
- Had 14,000 miles of roads
- Language and religion helped unite the empire

North American Culture Groups

CULTURE AREA	CULTURE GROUPS	ACCOMPLISHMENTS
Southwest	Hohokum, Pima, Papago, Ancestral Puebloans	• Built irrigation canals and farmed • Constructed housing complexes
Northeast: Ohio and Mississippi Valley	Adena, Hopewell, Mississippians, Natchez	• Created giant earthworks that served various functions • Conducted extensive trade • Mississippians built center at Cahokia that may have housed 20,000 people
Northeast: Eastern Woodlands	Iroquois (including Mohawk, Oneida, Onondaga, Cayuga, and Seneca)	• Cleared land to farm • Built villages • Hunted • Shared language in the region (Iroquois) • Five Nations created the Iroquois League
Arctic	Inuit	• Hunted and fished • Used kayaks and dog sleds for transportation • Constructed igloos of snow and ice
Northwest Coast	Haida, Bella, Coola, Nootka, Tlingit	• Hunted and fished • Built homes made of wood • Traded • Some groups built totem poles.

KEY TERMS, PEOPLE, AND IDEAS

1. Describe what you might see on a Maya **stela**.

2. How did the Aztecs build **chinampas**? For what purpose?

3. From whom did the Aztecs collect **tribute**?

4. What is **adobe**? What did Moche people build with it?

5. Describe a **quipu**. What do scholars think the Inca may have used quipus for?

6. What was an Inca **alyllu**?

7. How were Ancestral Puebloan **kivas** constructed? What did each one represent?

8. What is a **potlatch**? In what culture area of North America was it originally practiced?

9. What was the **Iroquois League**? What was its main goal?

CRITICAL THINKING

10. **Draw Inferences** How do the land-bridge and coastal theories of how people migrated in the Americas differ? How does the time frame of the migration change depending on the theory?

11. **Compare and Contrast** How were the farming methods developed by the Maya, the Aztecs, and the Inca different?

12. **Predict Consequences** As Europeans began to arrive in greater numbers in the 1500s, the peoples of the Americas would face the threat of conquest by outsiders. Which peoples might you expect to fare best against attack? Consider location in relation to other groups of people as well as natural features, language, and social or political organization.

13. **Cite Evidence** How was the role of trade in Inca society unique as compared to trade in the Maya and Aztec societies?

14. **Summarize** How were the Ancestral Puebloans innovative in the building of dwellings?

15. **Draw Conclusions** What circumstances helped the civilizations and diverse cultures of the Americas to develop in ways both common and unique?

16. **Analyze Maps** Study the map on this page. Which civilization might best be able to defend against enemies? Which one would have the hardest time? Explain your answers.

Civilizations of Mesoamerica and South America

SOUTH AMERICA

N
W — E
S

KEY
- Olmec civilization
- Maya civilization
- Aztec empire
- Inca empire

17. **Writing Activity: Write a Narrative** Write a two- to three-paragraph narrative that uses dialogue and points of view to describe what brought the leaders of the five American Indian nations together to create the Iroquois League and agree to a constitution.

> I am Dekanawidah and with the Five Nations' Confederate Lords I plant the Tree of Great Peace. . . . and all the affairs of the Five Nations shall be transacted at this place. . . .
> The Lords of the Confederacy of the Five Nations shall be mentors of the people for all time. The thickness of their skin shall be seven spans—which is to say that they shall be proof against anger, offensive actions and criticism. Their hearts shall be full of peace and good will and their minds filled with a yearning for the welfare of the people of the Confederacy. With endless patience they shall carry out their duty and their firmness shall be tempered with a tenderness for their people. Neither anger nor fury shall find lodgement in their minds and all their words and actions shall be marked by calm deliberation.
> —The Constitution of the Iroquois League

18. **Connections to Today** During the period you read about in this topic, the Maya, Aztecs, and other peoples of the ancient Americas used their observations of the skies to develop calendars, plan religious ceremonies, and otherwise shape their lives. How do discoveries made through astronomy and space exploration in recent decades affect your life today? How might future space exploration affect you in the years to come?

DOCUMENT-BASED QUESTIONS

In Aztec society, a person's place in society was based on rank and family as well as ability. The roles of men, women, and children were well defined. The education of Aztec youth was considered especially important. Read or view the documents below, then answer the questions that follow.

DOCUMENT A

This excerpt is from a nobleman's advice to his son.

> First: thou art to be one who riseth from sleep. One who holdeth vigil thought the night. Thou art not to five thyself excessively to sleep, lest...thou wilt be named a heavy sleeper... a dreamer...
>
> And second, thou art to be prudent in thy travels; peacefully, quietly, tranquilly, deliberately art though to go...
>
> Third: though art to speak very slowly, very deliberately...
>
> Fourth: thou art to pretend not to dwell upon that which is done, that which is performed. Especially art thou to... forsake evil...
>
> —*General History of the Things* of New Spain by Fray Bernardino de Sahagún

Documents B and C are excerpts from books by historians.

DOCUMENT B

[A]t fifteen...youths might enter either the *calmecac*, temple or monastery in which they were entrusted to priests, or the school called the *telpochcalli*, "the house of the young men", which was run by masters chosen from among the experienced warriors...In theory the *calmecac* was kept for the sons and daughters of the dignitaries, but the children of the trading class were also admitted.

> —From *Daily Life of the Aztecs* by Jacques Soustelle

DOCUMENT C

But even those who inherited high rank had to prove themselves and validate their status. Diplomatic skills or prowess on the battlefield could promote upward mobility. But the close ties of family and lineage—the reality of birthright—were the fundamental cement of Mexica society.

> —From *The Aztecs* by Brian M. Fagan

DOCUMENT D

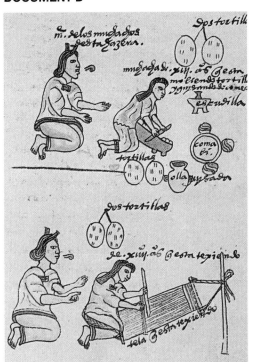

This illustration from the 1553 Codex Mendoza shows Aztec girls making tortillas and weaving cloth.

19. Document A advises against
    - **A.** speaking freely.
    - **B.** traveling too often.
    - **C.** sleeping too much.
    - **D.** doing good.

20. What is the main point of Document B?
    - **A.** The Aztecs only educated youths from trading families.
    - **B.** Aztec higher education involved training by priests or warriors.
    - **C.** *Calmecacs* were temples or monasteries where children of noble and trade families could receive higher education.
    - **D.** The Aztecs provided higher education to only the talented youths.

21. Based on Document C, how might youths who were not of noble birth advance themselves?
    - **A.** A. by marrying into a noble family
    - **B.** by training in the best schools
    - **C.** by a stroke of good fortune
    - **D.** by pursuing a career in trade

22. **Writing Activity** Consider the advice of a nobleman in Document A. How might an aspiring Aztec tradesman advise his son or daughter?

Ancient Greece
(1750 B.C.–133 B.C.)

ESSENTIAL QUESTION How much power should the government have?

The Parthenon

Connections to Today

In June 2016, the citizens of the United Kingdom voted on whether the United Kingdom should leave or remain with the European Union. These citizens were participating in a referendum, a vote which allows policy questions to be decided by citizens. A referendum is a form of direct democracy. In this topic, you will learn about the ancient city-state of Athens, Greece which developed the world's first democracy, or rule by the people. How is democracy today different from democracy in ancient times?

Learn about Pericles and the golden age of Athens.

 BOUNCE to Activate My Story Video

Topic 5 Overview

In this Topic, you will learn about the ancient Greeks, who created one of the most influential civilizations in world history. Democracy was born in the city-state of Athens, where citizens participated in lawmaking and in the courts. Look at the lesson outline and explore the timeline. As you study the Topic, you will complete the Quest inquiry.

LESSON OUTLINE

5.1 Early Greece

5.2 The Greek City-States

5.3 Greek Thinkers, Artists, and Writers

5.4 Alexander the Great and the Legacy of Greece

Key Events in Ancient Greece

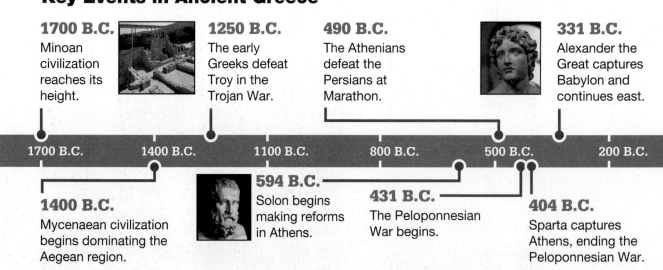

1700 B.C.
Minoan civilization reaches its height.

1250 B.C.
The early Greeks defeat Troy in the Trojan War.

490 B.C.
The Athenians defeat the Persians at Marathon.

331 B.C.
Alexander the Great captures Babylon and continues east.

1700 B.C. 1400 B.C. 1100 B.C. 800 B.C. 500 B.C. 200 B.C.

1400 B.C.
Mycenaean civilization begins dominating the Aegean region.

594 B.C.
Solon begins making reforms in Athens.

431 B.C.
The Peloponnesian War begins.

404 B.C.
Sparta captures Athens, ending the Peloponnesian War.

QUEST! INQUIRY

Athens or Sparta?

The lives of the people of Athens and Sparta were considerably different. Do you think it would have been better to live in Athens instead of Sparta? In this Quest, you will research and prepare a discussion panel to determine the answer to this question.

STEP 1

Begin your research. Review what you have learned about Athens and Sparta. Discuss important points with your team.

STEP 2

Divide the team to take a YES or NO position. Evaluate the evidence. Use evidence to support your team's position.

STEP 3

Begin to draw conclusions. Listen carefully to arguments for and against living in each city-state. Determine the best arguments for each side.

STEP 4

Consider a different point of view. Are you willing to change your earlier position? Reflect on what you have learned about the importance of careful research and discussions in shaping opinions.

GO ONLINE to access complete Quest materials

📶 **GO ONLINE to Project Imagine: Enter the Art of Gods and Mortals** to explore Homer's epics and other aspects of Greek culture.

 BOUNCE to Activate Flipped Video

Objectives

Identify the influences on Minoan culture and how the civilization prospered.

Summarize how the Mycenaeans ruled the sea trade and describe the Trojan War story set in Mycenaean times.

Describe the works of Homer and their influence on Greek culture.

Key Terms

Knossos
shrine
fresco
Trojan War
strait
Homer

Early Greece

The island of Crete (kreet) was the cradle of an early civilization that later influenced Greeks living on the European mainland. The people of Crete, however, had absorbed many ideas from the older civilizations of Egypt and Mesopotamia.

Minoans Prosper From Trade

Washed by the warm waters of the Aegean (ee JEE un) Sea, Crete was home to a brilliant early civilization—and the first European civilization. We do not actually know what the people who built this civilization called themselves. However, the British archaeologist Arthur Evans, who unearthed its ruins in the early 1900s, called them Minoans after Minos, a legendary king of Crete. Minoan civilization lay buried for more than 2,500 years. Excavations by Evans and later archaeologists revealed much about this early civilization. Today, the Minoans are recognized not only for their unique civilization but also for their contribution to the rise of civilization in Greece, on the nearby mainland of Europe.

A Crossroads Location Location affected the early people of Crete. They lived at the crossroads of three continents: Africa, Asia, and Europe. Early on, they engaged in seaborne trade. From their island home in the eastern Mediterranean, they crossed the seas to the Nile Valley and the Middle East. Through contact with the older civilizations of Egypt and Mesopotamia, they acquired artistic ideas and technologies such as metalworking that they adapted to their own culture.

Minoans developed several systems of writing during their long history. They first used hieroglyphs, although they do not seem related to Egyptian hieroglyphs and have not yet been deciphered. Later, Minoans used two other scripts, each somewhat different. Most writing appeared on seals or disks.

📶 **GO ONLINE to access** your digital course

An Economy Based on Trade Abundant resources and trade helped Minoans build a prosperous economy. Unlike the early civilizations of Egypt and Mesopotamia, the success of the Minoans was based on trade, not conquest.

Minoan traders set up outposts across the Aegean and beyond. From Crete, they exported timber, food, wine, wool, and many other goods. From Egypt and the Middle East, they brought back cargoes of precious stones, copper, ivory, gold, and silver as well as tin. The nearest tin mines were located in Spain, Britain or Persia, suggesting that Minoan traders acquired goods that had traveled great distances.

The Palace at Knossos Minoan civilization reached its height, or greatest success, between about 1700 B.C. and 1400 B.C. During this time, Minoan kings built a vast palace at **Knossos** (NAHS us).

The palace housed rooms for the royal family, banquet halls, and working areas for artisans. It also included religious **shrines,** areas dedicated to the honor of gods and goddesses. There, ceremonies and rituals were held to please the gods.

Like most people in the ancient world, the Minoans were polytheistic, worshipping gods who were thought to control the forces of nature. Archaeological evidence shows the importance of a snake goddess. Figures show this goddess holding a snake in either hand. Much later, the Greeks associated the snake with the god of healing. Along with other ancient civilizations, the bull held a place of honor in Minoan religious beliefs.

Minoan Frescoes Show Palace Life The walls of the palace at Knossos were covered with colorful **frescoes,** paintings in watercolor done on wet plaster. These frescoes provide evidence of Minoan life. Leaping dolphins suggest the importance of the sea. Some frescoes show young nobles, both men and women, strolling through gardens outside the palace. These images suggest that women appeared freely in public and may have enjoyed more rights than women in most other ancient civilizations.

A startling fresco depicts men and women in a dangerous athletic contest, jumping through the horns of a charging bull. Minoan sculptors also created works showing bull leapers. Scholars think that bull leaping was part of a religious activity

Minoan Civilization Disappears Archaeologists have found that Minoan palaces were destroyed and rebuilt more than once. But some time around 1400 B.C., palaces were destroyed and not rebuilt again. Evidence shows fire and sudden destruction.

Scholars do not know why Minoan civilization fell. A volcanic eruption on a nearby island may have rained flaming death or clouds of ash on Knossos. Or perhaps an earthquake destroyed the palace, followed by an immense tidal wave that drowned many inhabitants. However, it is certain that invaders played a role in the destruction of Minoan civilization. These intruders were the Mycenaeans (my suh NEE unz), the first Greek-speaking people of whom we have a written record.

With the destruction of its palaces, Minoan civilization slowly disappeared, surviving only in legend for thousands of years. In the last century, its legacy was recovered as archaeologists revealed its influence on later Western civilization.

☑ **IDENTIFY** How does the art at Knossos reflect Minoan culture?

Mycenaean Civilization

During prehistoric times, groups of peoples speaking related Indo-European languages moved across Europe and Asia. Among them were the Myceneaens who moved into southeastern Europe.

>> Archaeologists rebuilt these room walls and stairway at the Minoan palace of Knossos on Crete.

Trade by Sea Brings Wealth Mycenaean civilization dominated the Aegean world from about 1400 B.C. to 1200 B.C. Like the Minoans, the Mycenaeans were sea traders. They reached out beyond the Aegean to Sicily, Italy, Egypt, and Mesopotamia. The Mycenaeans learned many skills from the Minoans, including the art of writing. They, too, absorbed Egyptian and Mesopotamian customs, many of which they passed on to later Greeks.

The Mycenaeans lived in separate city-states on the mainland. In each, a warrior-king built a thick-walled fortress from which he ruled the surrounding villages. Wealthy rulers amassed treasure, including fine gold ornaments that archaeologists have unearthed from their tombs.

The Trojan War The Mycenaeans are best remembered for their part in the **Trojan War,** which may have taken place around 1250 B.C. The conflict may have had its origins in economic rivalry between Mycenae and Troy, a rich trading city in present-day Turkey, that controlled the vital **straits,** or narrow water passages, connecting the Mediterranean and Black seas.

In Greek legend, however, the war had a more romantic cause. When the Trojan prince, Paris, kidnaps Helen, the beautiful wife of a Greek king, the Mycenaeans sail to Troy to rescue her. For the next 10 years, the two sides battle until the Greeks finally seize Troy and burn the city to the ground.

For centuries, most people regarded the Trojan War as pure legend. Then, in the 1870s, a wealthy German businessman, Heinrich Schliemann (HYN rik SCHLEE mahn), set out to prove that the legend was rooted in fact.

As Schliemann excavated the site of ancient Troy, he discovered that the city had been rebuilt many times and included at least nine layers. At the layer dating to about 1250 B.C., he found evidence of fire and war. Though any exact details remain lost in legend, most modern scholars now agree there is a kernel of truth in the ancient legends.

☑ **DESCRIBE** How did trade shape Mycenaean society?

Homer and the Great Greek Legends

Not long after the likely date of the Trojan War, the Mycenaeans themselves came under attack from sea raiders and also from another Greek-speaking people, the Dorians, migrating from the north. As Mycenaean power faded, their people abandoned the cities and trade declined. People forgot many skills, including the art of writing. From the end of the Mycenaean civilization in about 1100 B.C. until about

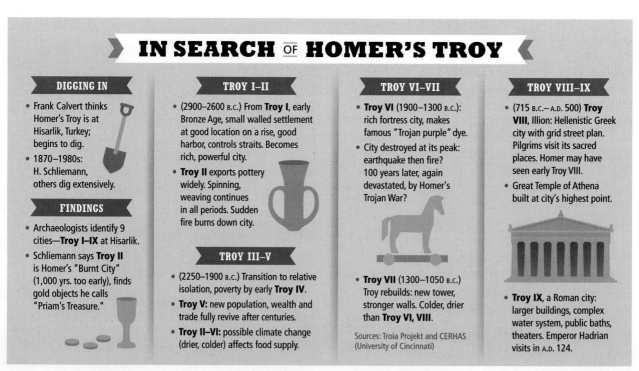

IN SEARCH OF HOMER'S TROY

DIGGING IN
- Frank Calvert thinks Homer's Troy is at Hisarlik, Turkey; begins to dig.
- 1870–1980s: H. Schliemann, others dig extensively.

FINDINGS
- Archaeologists identify 9 cities—**Troy I–IX** at Hisarlik.
- Schliemann says **Troy II** is Homer's "Burnt City" (1,000 yrs. too early), finds gold objects he calls "Priam's Treasure."

TROY I–II
- (2900–2600 B.C.) From **Troy I**, early Bronze Age, small walled settlement at good location on a rise, good harbor, controls straits. Becomes rich, powerful city.
- **Troy II** exports pottery widely. Spinning, weaving continues in all periods. Sudden fire burns down city.

TROY III–V
- (2250–1900 B.C.) Transition to relative isolation, poverty by early **Troy IV**.
- **Troy V:** new population, wealth and trade fully revive after centuries.
- **Troy II–VI:** possible climate change (drier, colder) affects food supply.

TROY VI–VII
- **Troy VI** (1900–1300 B.C.): rich fortress city, makes famous "Trojan purple" dye.
- City destroyed at its peak: earthquake then fire? 100 years later, again devastated, by Homer's Trojan War?
- **Troy VII** (1300–1050 B.C.) Troy rebuilds: new tower, stronger walls. Colder, drier than **Troy VI, VIII**.

Sources: Troia Projekt and CERHAS (University of Cincinnati)

TROY VIII–IX
- (715 B.C.–A.D. 500) **Troy VIII**, Illion: Hellenistic Greek city with grid street plan. Pilgrims visit its sacred places. Homer may have seen early Troy VIII.
- Great Temple of Athena built at city's highest point.
- **Troy IX**, a Roman city: larger buildings, complex water system, public baths, theaters. Emperor Hadrian visits in A.D. 124.

>> Since the late 1800s, archaeologists have excavated cities buried beneath a hill in western Turkey thought to be the site of ancient Troy.

800 B.C., Greek civilization seemed to step backward. Over time, the newcomers absorbed stories and traditions from the Mycenaeans into their own heritage. In this way, they built on the legacy of earlier civilizations to forge a new, Greek civilization.

Two Epic Poems Historians know little about this period when the Dorians arrived in Greece, but we get hints about life at the time from two great epic poems, the *Iliad* and the *Odyssey.* These epics may have been the work of many people, but they are credited to the poet **Homer,** who probably lived about 750 B.C. According to tradition, Homer was a blind poet who wandered from village to village, singing of heroic deeds. Like the great Indian epics, Homer's tales were passed on orally for generations before they were finally written down.

The *Iliad* The epic tale told in the *Iliad* is our chief source of information about the Trojan War. It describes the deeds of gods and goddesses, and brave heroes. At the start of the poem, Achilles (uh KIL eez), the mightiest Greek warrior, has withdrawn from battle because he has been unfairly treated and insulted by his commander. The war soon turns against the Greeks, but Achilles stubbornly refuses to listen to pleas that he rejoin the fighting. Only after his best friend is killed does Achilles return to battle to strike down many Trojans.

The *Iliad*'s first word and major theme is anger, especially the anger of Achilles. The singer-storyteller calls on the goddess of memory to tell the story of how anger caused great losses and misery for Greeks and Trojans alike.

The *Odyssey* The *Odyssey* tells of the many struggles of the Greek hero Odysseus (oh DIS ee us) on his return home to his faithful wife, Penelope, after the fall of Troy. On his long voyage, Odysseus encounters a sea monster, a race of one-eyed giants, and a beautiful sorceress who turns men into swine.

In the *Odyssey*, the first word is man, and the story shows the many sides of the man Odysseus. He is a determined, resourceful hero who must overcome great odds to make it home. The *Odyssey* features the story of the Trojan Horse, which allowed the Greeks to win their victory over Troy.

The *Iliad* and *Odyssey* reveal much about the values and culture of the ancient Greeks. The heroes display honor, courage, and eloquence, as when Achilles rallies his troops:

"Let not the Trojans," he cried,
"keep you at arm's length, Achaeans,

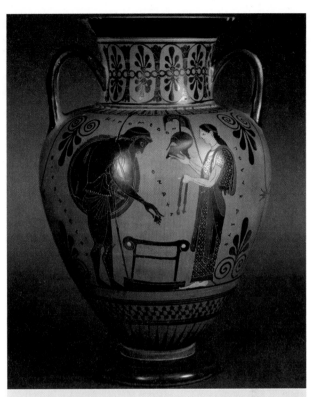

>> In this scene from the *Illiad,* the water goddess Thetis, mother of Achilles, brings her son new divinely forged armor after his best friend Patroclus dies wearing Achilles's armor.

 BOUNCE to Activate Gallery

but go for them and fight them man for man. However valiant I may be, I cannot give chase to so many and fight all of them . . . nevertheless, so far as in me lies I will show no slackness of hand or foot nor want of endurance, not even for a moment . . ."

—Homer, *Iliad* (translated by Samuel Butler)

Legacy of Homer's Epics Tales from the *Iliad* and *Odyssey* have been told and retold for almost 3,000 years. The Greeks thought of Homer as their greatest poet, a cultural hero. His epics have been admired throughout later Western civilization, and their stories have inspired Western writers and artists to the present.

The epics portray a wide range of characters, some brave and courageous, others cowardly and weak. Almost every kind of character written about since then was first captured in Homer's epics, including the faithful dog Argus, who waited patiently for the return of his master, Odysseus.

Homer's epics reflected the Greek world view, which later had much influence on the Western

Early Aegean Civilizations, c. 1600 B.C.–1000 B.C.

CIVILIZATION	CHARACTERISTICS	ACCOMPLISHMENTS
Minoan 1600 B.C.–1500 B.C. (Vanished by 1400 B.C.)	• Sea traders based on Crete • Absorbed ideas from Egypt, Mesopotamia • Worshiped bull and mother goddess	• Later influenced Greeks living on European mainland • Colorful, graceful frescos at Knossos palace; women perhaps enjoyed more rights than in most other ancient civilizations
Mycenaean 1400 B.C.–1200 B.C. (Ended around 1100 B.C.)	• Sea traders • Absorbed ideas from Egypt, Mesopotamia; also reached Italy, Sicily; learned from Minoans (including writing) • Lived in separate city-states on mainland; warrior kings rule surrounding villages from thick-walled fortresses	• First Greek-speaking culture which left written records, spoke Indo-European language • Fine gold ornaments found in their tombs • Conquered Greek mainland, then Crete; may have taken part in Trojan War, around 1250 B.C.
Dorian 1100 B.C.–1000 B.C. Swept away Minoans and Mycenaeans, initiated cultural dark age	• Originated in northern and northwestern Greece, attacked Mycenaeans from the north • Conquered and settled cities of Sparta, Corinth, and Argos, as well as in today's Sicily, Italy, North Africa, and along the Black Sea coast	• Greek-speaking people, relatively low cultural level, inventors of iron slashing sword • Their restrained, powerful, monumental art an important influence on later Greek art

>> **Analyze Charts** A series of Greek civilizations grew, flourished, and fell on the mainland and islands of the eastern Mediterranean. Which civilizations absorbed ideas from Egypt and Mesopotamia? How did they learn about these ideas?

world. The poems were not sacred religious texts. The gods played a role, but they had the same weaknesses as humans. The key figures were individual humans who displayed reason, intelligence, courage, honor and restraint.

A Legacy for the Future After the Dorian invasions, the land of Greece passed several centuries in obscurity. The people lived in small isolated villages and had few contacts with the outside world. Over time they made the stories about Crete and Mycenae a part of their heritage, and they built upon the legacy of those and other civilizations to forge a new Greek civilization. When it emerged, this Greek civilization would not only dominate the region; it would ultimately extend the influence of Greek culture over most of the Western world.

☑ **DESCRIBE** What do Homer's epics reveal about Greek culture?

☑ **ASSESSMENT**

1. **Identify Cause and Effect** How did the Minoans create a brilliant early civilization?

2. **Draw Conclusions** How do frescoes on the walls of the palace of Knossos reflect the history of the Minoan culture in which they were produced?

3. **Infer** Why do you think the Minoans and Mycenaeans absorbed ideas, customs, and skills from other cultures?

4. **Hypothesize** Why do you think that for centuries most people thought the Trojan War was just a legend?

5. **Summarize** What is known about the causes of the Trojan War?

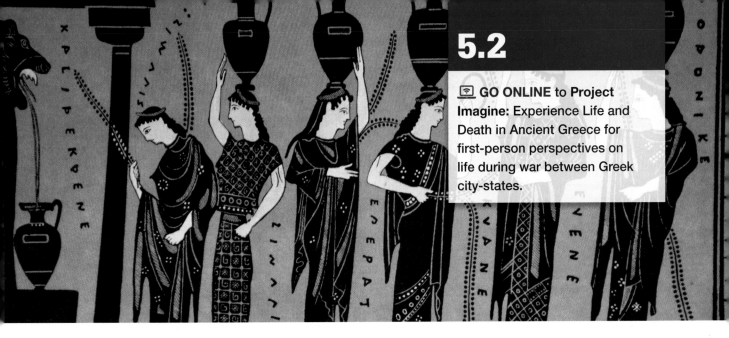

5.2

🖥 **GO ONLINE to Project Imagine:** Experience Life and Death in Ancient Greece for first-person perspectives on life during war between Greek city-states.

The Greek City-States

The ancient Greeks absorbed many ideas and beliefs from the older civilizations of Mesopotamia and Egypt. At the same time, they developed their own ways that differed greatly from those of the river valley empires. In particular, the Greeks developed new ideas about how best to govern a society.

Geography Shapes Greek City-States

As you have read, geography helped to shape the early river valley civilizations. There, strong rulers organized irrigation works that helped farmers produce food surpluses needed to support large cities. A very different set of geographic conditions influenced the rise of Ancient Greek civilization.

Landscape Forms Political Borders Greece is part of the Balkan peninsula, which extends southward into the eastern Mediterranean Sea. Mountains divide the peninsula into isolated valleys. Beyond the rugged coast, hundreds of rocky islands spread toward the horizon.

The Greeks who farmed the valleys or settled on the scattered islands did not create a large empire such as that of the Egyptians or Persians. Instead, they built many small city-states, cut off from one another by mountains or water. Each included a city and its surrounding countryside. Greeks felt strong loyalty to their city-states and fiercely defended their independence. Endless rivalry led to frequent wars between the city-states—and in time, to the conquest of Greece by outsiders.

 BOUNCE to Activate Flipped Video

Objectives

Understand how geography influenced the Greek city-states.

Explain how democracy and other forms of government developed in Ancient Greece.

Describe the influence of Ancient Greek concepts related to the rights and responsibilities of citizenship.

Identify the culture and values shared by Ancient Greeks.

Summarize how the Persian and Peloponnesian Wars affected Greece.

Key Terms

polis	legislature
acropolis	alliance
citizen	Pericles
monarchy	stipend
aristocracy	direct democracy
oligarchy	jury
phalanx	ostracism
Sparta	
Athens	
democracy	
tyrant	

Living by the Sea The Mediterranean and Aegean seas were as central to the Greek world as the Nile was to Egypt. The mainland of Greece is largely rocky and mountainous. As a result, farming was more difficult than in the river valley civilizations. This meant that the economies of some Greek city-states depended on trade to obtain adequate food, such as grain, to support growing populations.

The seas provided a vital link to the world outside. With its hundreds of bays, the Greek coastline offered safe harbors for ships. Like the Phoenicians, the Greeks became skilled sailors. Carrying cargoes of olive oil, wine, and marble, Greek traders sailed to Eygpt, the Middle East, and Asia Minor.

They returned not only with grains and metals but also with ideas, which they adapted to their own needs. For example, the Greeks expanded the Phoenician alphabet. The resulting alphabet in turn became the basis for all later Western alphabets.

By 750 B.C., rapid population growth was forcing many Greeks to leave their own overcrowded valleys. With fertile land limited, the Greeks expanded overseas. Gradually, a scattering of Greek colonies took root all around the Mediterranean from Spain to Egypt. Wherever they traveled, Greek settlers and traders carried their ideas and culture.

Rise of Greek City-States As their world expanded after 750 B.C., the Greeks evolved a unique version of the city-state, which they called the *polis* (POH lis). Typically, the polis was built on two levels.

On a hilltop stood the **acropolis** (uh KRAH puh lis), or high city, with its great marble temples dedicated to different gods and goddesses. On flatter ground below lay the walled main city with its marketplace, theater, public buildings, and homes.

The population of each city-state was fairly small, which helped the **citizens,** or free residents, share a sense of responsibility for its triumphs and defeats. In the warm climate of Greece, free men spent much time outdoors in the marketplace, debating issues that affected their lives. The whole community joined in festivals honoring the city's special god or goddess. The rights of citizens, however, varied from city to city, and everywhere men held all political power.

Types of Government Evolve Between 750 B.C. and 500 B.C. Greeks developed different forms of government. At first, the ruler of the polis, like those in the river valley empires, was a king.

A government in which a hereditary ruler, such as a king or queen, exercises central power is a **monarchy.** Slowly, however, power shifted to a class of noble landowners. Because only they could afford bronze weapons and chariots, these nobles were also the military defenders of the city-states. At first these nobles defended the king. In time, however, they won power for themselves. The result was an **aristocracy,** or rule by a landholding elite.

As trade expanded, a new middle class of wealthy merchants, farmers, and artisans emerged in some cities. They challenged the landowning nobles for power and dominated some city-states. The result was a form of government called an **oligarchy.** In an oligarchy, power is in the hands of a small, wealthy elite.

New Ways of War Shape Greece Changes in military technology increased the power of the middle class. By about 650 B.C., iron weapons replaced bronze ones. Since iron was cheaper, ordinary citizens could afford iron helmets, shields, and swords. Meanwhile, a new method of fighting emerged—the **phalanx,** a massive tactical

FORMS OF GOVERNMENT		
MONARCHY	**ARISTOCRACY**	**OLIGARCHY**
Hereditary ruler (king, queen) holds central power.	Hereditary landholding upper class rules.	Small wealthy elite exercises power.
Examples: England (1558–1603), France (1643–1715), Russia (1762–1796), Oman, Saudi Arabia	Examples: England (1688–1832), France (1700s before French Revolution)	Examples: Renaissance Florence, South Africa under apartheid, former Soviet Union

>> **Analyze Charts** Athenian democracy evolved from these basic forms of government, which have been used over time in many other places. Describe how an aristocracy and an oligarchy are similar and different.

formation of heavily armed foot soldiers. It required long hours of drill to master. Shared training created a strong sense of unity among the citizen-soldiers.

By putting the defense of the city-state in the hands of ordinary citizens, the phalanx reduced class differences. The new type of warfare, however, led the two most influential city-states—Athens and Sparta—to develop very different ways of life. While Sparta stressed military virtues and stern discipline, Athens glorified the individual and extended political rights to more citizens.

☑ **IDENTIFY** How did the sea coast contribute to Greek commerce?

Discipline and Warfare in Sparta

The Spartans were Dorian invaders from the north who conquered Laconia, in the southern part of Greece, and built the city-state of **Sparta.** They enslaved the people they had conquered, turning them into *helots* who were owned by the state and made to work the land. Because the helots greatly outnumbered their rulers, the Spartans set up a brutal system of strict control.

The Spartan government included two kings and a council of elders who advised the monarchs. An assembly made up of all citizens approved major decisions. Citizens were male, native-born Spartans over the age of 30. The assembly also elected five ephors, or officials, who ran day-to-day affairs.

Discipline Rules Daily Life From childhood, a Spartan prepared to be part of a military state. Officials examined every newborn, and sickly children were abandoned to die. Spartans wanted future soldiers and the future mothers of soldiers to be healthy.

At the age of seven, boys began training for a lifetime in the military. They moved into barracks, where they were toughened by a coarse diet, hard exercise, and rigid discipline. This strict and harsh discipline made Spartan youths excellent soldiers. To develop cunning and supplement their diet, boys were even encouraged to steal food. If caught, though, they were beaten severely.

At the age of 20, a man could marry, but he continued to live in the barracks for another 10 years and to eat there for another 40 years. At the age of 30, after further training, he took his place in the assembly.

Spartan Women Girls, too, had a rigorous upbringing. As part of a warrior society, they were

>> The Spartans put great emphasis on the strength and agility of the human body. This sculpture from 530 B.C. shows a Spartan woman exercising, a task rarely expected of other Greek women.

expected to produce healthy sons for the army. They therefore were required to exercise and strengthen their bodies—something no other Greek women did.

Like other Greek women, Spartan women had to obey their fathers or husbands. Yet under Spartan law, they had the right to inherit property. Because men were occupied with war, some women took on responsibilities such as running the family's estate.

Citizens and Noncitizens To be a citizen of Sparta, a person had to be descended from the Dorians who invaded the land. Spartan citizens owned land, but did not farm it since that was the job of the helots. Although foreigners lived in Sparta, they were unwelcome guests and could be expelled. In Sparta, noncitizens outnumbered citizens, but they had few rights and were strictly controlled by the government.

Sparta Stands Alone The Spartans isolated themselves from other Greeks. They looked down on trade and wealth, forbade their own citizens to travel, and had little use for new ideas or the arts. While other Greeks admired the Spartans' military skills, no other city-state imitated their rigorous way of life. "Spartans are willing to die for their city," some suggested, "because they have no reason to live."

>> The Parthenon holds center stage on the ancient Athenian Acropolis. Originally a temple honoring the city's patron goddess, Athena, the Parthenon is one of the world's most famous and influential buildings.

>> Solon (630 B.C.–560 B.C.) became so famous for his wise political and economic reforms that today in English we call a wise and skillful lawgiver a *solon*.

In the long run, Sparta suffered from its rigid ways and inability to change. Over time, its warrior class shrank, and its power declined.

☑ **EXPLAIN** Why was discipline important in Sparta?

Democracy Evolves in Athens

Athens was located in Attica, just north of the Peloponnesus. As in many Greek city-states, Athenian government evolved from a monarchy into an aristocracy. By 700 B.C. noble landowners held power and chose the chief officials. Nobles judged major court cases and dominated the assembly.

Discontent Drives Change Under the aristocracy, Athenian wealth and power grew. Yet discontent spread among ordinary people. Merchants and soldiers resented the power of the nobles. They argued that their service to Athens entitled them to more rights. Foreign artisans, who produced many of the goods that Athens traded abroad, were resentful that Athenian law barred them from becoming citizens. Farmers, too, demanded change. During hard times, many farmers were forced to sell their land to nobles. A growing number even sold themselves and their families into slavery to pay their debts.

As discontent spread, Athens moved slowly toward **democracy,** or government by the people. As you will see, the term had a different meaning for the ancient Greeks than it has for us today.

Solon Makes Reforms Solon, a wise and trusted leader, was appointed archon (AHR kahn), or chief official, in 594 B.C. Athenians gave Solon a free hand to make needed reforms. He outlawed debt slavery and freed those who had already been sold into slavery for debt. He opened high offices to more citizens, granted citizenship to some foreigners, and gave the Athenian assembly more say in important decisions.

Solon introduced economic reforms as well. He encouraged the export of wine and olive oil. This policy helped merchants and farmers by increasing demand for their products.

Despite Solon's reforms, citizenship remained limited, and many positions were open only to the wealthy landowners. Continued and widespread unrest led to the rise of **tyrants,** or people who gained power by force. Tyrants often won support from the merchant class and the poor by imposing reforms to help these groups. Although Greek tyrants

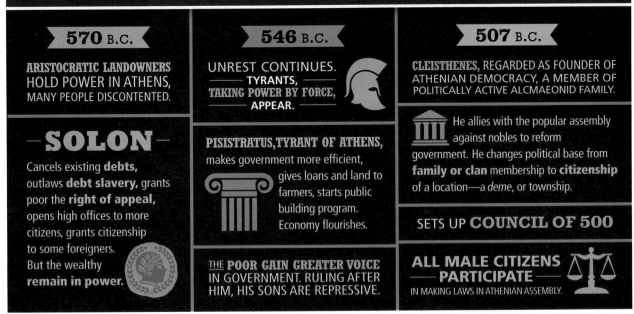

STEPS TO DEMOCRACY — REFORMERS AND TYRANTS

570 B.C.

ARISTOCRATIC LANDOWNERS HOLD POWER IN ATHENS, MANY PEOPLE DISCONTENTED.

— SOLON —

Cancels existing **debts,** outlaws **debt slavery,** grants poor the **right of appeal,** opens high offices to more citizens, grants citizenship to some foreigners. But the wealthy **remain in power.**

546 B.C.

UNREST CONTINUES. **TYRANTS, TAKING POWER BY FORCE,** APPEAR.

PISISTRATUS, TYRANT OF ATHENS, makes government more efficient, gives loans and land to farmers, starts public building program. Economy flourishes.

THE **POOR GAIN GREATER VOICE** IN GOVERNMENT. RULING AFTER HIM, HIS SONS ARE REPRESSIVE.

507 B.C.

CLEISTHENES, REGARDED AS FOUNDER OF ATHENIAN DEMOCRACY, A MEMBER OF POLITICALLY ACTIVE ALCMAEONID FAMILY.

He allies with the popular assembly against nobles to reform government. He changes political base from **family or clan** membership to **citizenship** of a location—a *deme*, or township.

SETS UP **COUNCIL OF 500**

ALL MALE CITIZENS — **PARTICIPATE** — IN MAKING LAWS IN ATHENIAN ASSEMBLY.

>> Motivated by widespread discontent with the aristocracy ruling Athens, political reforms by Solon, Pisistratus, and Cleisthenes were steps in Athenian democracy's evolution.

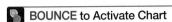 BOUNCE to Activate Chart

often governed well, the word *tyrant* has come to mean a vicious and brutal ruler.

Citizens Share Power and Wealth The Athenian tyrant Pisistratus (py SIS truh tus) seized power in 546 B.C. He helped farmers by giving them loans and land taken from nobles. New building projects gave jobs to the poor. By giving poor citizens a greater voice, he further weakened the aristocracy.

In 507 B.C. another reformer, Cleisthenes (KLYS thuh neez), broadened the role of ordinary citizens in government. He set up the Council of 500, whose members were chosen by lot from among all citizens over the age of 30. The council prepared laws considered by the assembly and supervised the day-to-day work of government.

Cleisthenes made the assembly a genuine **legislature,** or lawmaking body, that debated laws before deciding to approve or reject them. All male citizens were members of the assembly and were expected to participate.

Cleisthenes's reforms advanced some of the basic principles of Athenian democracy. He supported the idea of equal participation. Up until then, equal participation had applied to the aristocracy. Cleisthenes expanded it to include all citizens who met certain qualifications. This was very different from a modern representative democracy, but it was the beginning of a new system for Athens.

Democracy Within Limits By modern standards, Athenian democracy was quite limited. Only citizens could participate in government—voting to choose officials and pass laws or holding office—and citizenship was eventually restricted to men with two Athenian parents. Citizenship meant a responsibility to serve in government and fight for their polis as soldiers when needed.

Women were excluded from political activities even if their families were Athenian citizens. Foreign merchants and children of non-citizens also had no political rights. Neither did tens of thousands of enslaved people, who also lacked any personal freedom. In fact, citizens depended on the forced labor of the enslaved to give them the free time to participate in government. Despite the limits on democracy, Athens gave more people a say in decision making than any other ancient civilization.

Athenian Women In Athens, as in other Greek city-states, women had no share in political life. The respected Athenian thinker Aristotle reflected the general view that women were imperfect beings who lacked the ability to reason as well as men. He wrote: "The man is by nature fitter for command than the female just as an older person is superior to a younger, more immature person."

Although some men disagreed, most Greeks accepted the view that women must be guided

>> **Compare** This drinking cup from 480 B.C. illustrates subjects Athenian boys studied: speech and playing the lyre. How does this image show the differences between Athenian and Spartan systems of education?

🅑 BOUNCE to Activate Gallery

>> An entire Greek family brings a bull for sacrifice to Asclepius, the god of health, and Hygieia, his daughter (the large figures at left), in this marble relief from the 400s B.C.

by men. In court, fathers or guardians represented women, as they did for children. In well-to-do Athenian homes, women lived a secluded existence, shut off and "protected" from the outside world.

Greek playwrights such as Sophocles, and Aristophanes prominently featured women or families in their tragedies and comedies. Social, political, and religious issues often were played out within family dramas, as in Sophocles's *Antigone*, where a heroine's disobedience of a ruler's command puts her into conflict with her uncle and guardian. In Aristophanes's comedy, *The Clouds*, a father tries to take control of his spendthrift son.

Women played their most significant public role in religion. Their participation in sacred processions and ceremonies was considered essential for the city's well-being. In well-to-do Athenian homes, women managed the entire household. They spun and wove, cared for their children, and prepared food, but lived a secluded existence and were rarely seen in public. Their children or enslaved servants were sent to buy food and to collect water from the well. Only poor women went shopping alone in Athens.

They worked outside the home, often beside their husbands. They obtained water, did the family wash in a stream, and tended sheep or worked as spinners, weavers, or potters.

Educating the Young Unlike girls, who received little or no formal education, boys attended school if their families could afford it. Besides learning to read and write, they studied music, and memorized poetry. Equally important, they learned the skill of public speaking because, as citizens in a democracy, they would have to voice their views.

Young men received military training and, to keep their bodies healthy, participated in athletic contests. Unlike Sparta, which put military training above all else, Athens encouraged young men to explore many areas of knowledge.

☑ **DEFINE** How was democracy limited in Athens?

Forces for Unity

Strong local identification, an independent spirit, and economic rivalry led to fighting among the Greek city-states. Despite these divisions, Greeks shared a common culture. They spoke the same language, honored the same ancient heroes, participated in common festivals, and prayed to the same gods.

164 **TOPIC 5** Ancient Greece

Myths and Beliefs Like most other ancient people, the Greeks were polytheistic, believing in more than one deity. According to their myths, or traditional stories that explain the ways of nature or the gods, the gods lived on Mount Olympus in northern Greece. In Greek myths, the most powerful Olympian was Zeus (zoos), who presided over the affairs of gods and humans. His children included Ares (EHR eez), god of war, and Aphrodite (af ruh DY tee), goddess of love. His daughter Athena (uh THEE nuh), goddess of wisdom, gave her name to Athens.

Greeks honored their gods with temples and festivals, which included processions, sacrifices, feasts, plays, choral singing, and athletic competitions. Greeks consulted oracles, who were priests or priestesses through whom the gods were thought to speak. However, some Greek thinkers came to believe that the universe was regulated not by the gods but by natural laws.

Legacy of Greek Myths All Greeks shared a common heritage through their myths and legends. The stories were told and retold in different forms. Early on, Homer's epic poems, the *Iliad* and *Odyssey*, captured the tales of great heroes like Achilles and the gods whose jealousies and clashes affected the Trojan War. Later, Greek playwrights and artists created works portraying legendary heroes, gods, and goddesses.

As Greek power faded, the rising new power, Rome, adopted many Greek gods as their own and adapted the Greek myths for their own uses. As you will read, the legacies of both Greek and Roman cultures helped shape Western civilization.

The Olympic Games A unifying force among the Greek states was the celebration of the Olympic games. Every four years in the sacred valley of Olympia, the Greeks held athletic contests to honor Zeus, their chief god. The competitive spirit of the games mirrored the rivalries that kept the dozens of small Greek city-states in a state of near-constant war. The games reflected the value Greeks placed on physical fitness. From their earliest days, Greek city-states wanted citizens to build strong bodies needed to fight in their frequent wars.

As the time for the games drew near, the Greeks called a truce, or temporary suspension of hostilities, so that athletes and spectators could reach Olympia safely. At first, the games were a one-day festival with just one event, a short foot race. Later the games expanded into a five-day festival with sports such as running, jumping, shot put, discus throwing, javelin, boxing, and chariot races. The games were

>> At this Tholos Temple in Delphi, Greeks offered sacrifices to Athena, guardian of the famous oracle, before asking their questions. This *tholos,* or circular structure, was built about 400 B.C.

open only to free born men and boys. Married women were forbidden even to watch the games although unmarried women could attend.

The Olympic games lasted for more than 11 centuries, long after the Greek city-states were conquered by Rome. In A.D. 393, however, the games were abolished. By then, Roman emperors had become Christian, and the ancient games were seen as a pagan, or non-Christian religious tradition that had no place in the empire.

Greek View of Foreigners As trade expanded and colonies multiplied, the Greeks came in contact with people who spoke different languages and had different customs. Greeks felt superior to non-Greeks and called them *barbaroi,* people who did not speak Greek. The English word *barbarian* comes from this Greek root.

These "barbarians" included people such as the Phoenicians and Egyptians, from whom the Greeks borrowed important ideas and inventions. This sense of uniqueness and superiority would help the Greeks face a threat from the mightiest power in the Mediterranean world—the Persian empire.

☑ **IDENTIFY** What factors united the city-states of Greece?

Greek Wars with Persia

In 500 B.C., the Greek world was small. It included hundreds of rival city-states in a small area at the tip of the Balkan peninsula and a growing number of Greek colonies scattered around the Mediterranean. The Greeks, as you have read, were often bitterly divided. Athens, the wealthiest Greek city-state, had rivals that bitterly resented their rich neighbor. But far more powerful than any Greek city-state was the huge Persian empire, that lay to the east, just across the Aegean Sea. When the Persians threatened them, the Greeks briefly put aside their differences to defend their freedom.

The Persians had conquered a huge empire stretching from Asia Minor to the border of India. Their subjects included the Greek city-states of Ionia in Asia Minor. Though under Persian rule, these Ionian city-states were largely self-governing. Still, they resented their situation.

In 499 B.C., Ionian Greeks rebelled against Persian rule. Athens sent ships to help them. As the historian Herodotus wrote some years later, "These ships were the beginning of mischief both to the Greeks and to the barbarians." They triggered the Persian Wars, a series of wars that lasted on and off for half a century.

Athens Wins at Marathon The Persians soon crushed the rebel cities in Ionia, but Persian emperor Darius I was furious at the role Athens had played in the uprising. In time, Darius sent a huge force across the Aegean to punish Athens for its interference. The mighty Persian army landed near Marathon, a plain north of Athens, in 490 B.C.

The Persians greatly outnumbered Athenian forces. Yet the invaders were amazed to see "a mere handful of men coming on at a run without either horsemen or archers." The Persians responded with a rain of arrows, but the Greeks rushed onward. They broke through the Persian line and engaged in fierce hand-to-hand combat. Overwhelmed by the fury of the Athenian assault, the Persians hastily retreated to their ships.

The Athenians celebrated their triumph. Still, the Athenian leader, Themistocles (thuh MIS tuh kleez), knew the victory at Marathon had bought only a temporary lull in the fighting. He urged Athenians to build a fleet of warships and prepare other defenses.

Greek City-States Join Together In 480 B.C. Darius's son Xerxes (ZURK seez) sent a much larger force to conquer Greece. By this time, Athens had persuaded Sparta and other city-states to join in the fight against Persia.

Once again, the Persians landed in northern Greece. A small Spartan force guarded the narrow mountain pass at Thermopylae (thur MAHP uh lee). Led by their great warrior-king Leonidas (lee AHN ih dus), the Spartans held out heroically against the enormous Persian force but were defeated in the end. The Persians marched south and burned Athens. The city was empty, however. The Athenians had already withdrawn to safety, putting their faith in the fleet of ships that Themistocles had urged them to build.

The Athenians lured the Persian fleet into the narrow strait of Salamis (SAHL uh mis), near Athens. There, Athenian warships rammed, burned, and sank the Persian fleet. From the shore, Xerxes watched helplessly.

The next year, the Greeks defeated the Persians on land in Asia Minor. This victory marked the end of the Persian invasions. In a brief moment of unity, the Greek city-states had saved themselves from the Persian threat.

>> The Persian king Darius I is portrayed receiving tribute on this wall relief at the great palace in Persepolis, in present-day Iran.

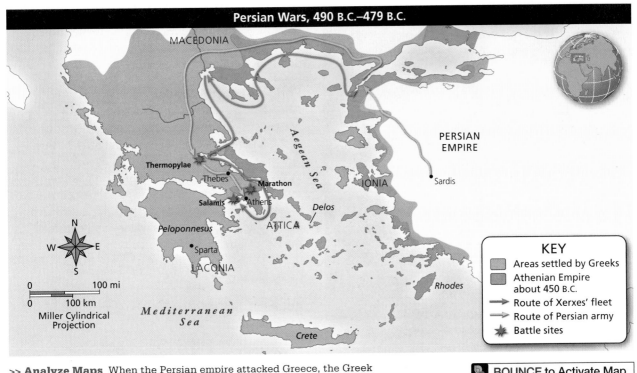

KEY
Areas settled by Greeks
Athenian Empire about 450 B.C.
Route of Xerxes' fleet
Route of Persian army
Battle sites

>> **Analyze Maps** When the Persian empire attacked Greece, the Greek city-states briefly joined forces for defense. Describe the routes of the Persian army and navy toward Athens.

BOUNCE to Activate Map

Athens Leads the Delian League Victory in the Persian Wars increased the Greek sense of their own uniqueness. The gods, they felt, had protected their superior form of government—the city-state—against invaders from Asia.

Athens emerged from the war as the most powerful city-state in Greece. To meet continued threats from Persia, it organized with other Greek city-states an **alliance,** or a formal agreement between two or more nations or powers to cooperate and come to one another's defense. Modern scholars call this alliance the Delian League after Delos, the location where the league held meetings.

From the start, Athens dominated the Delian League and slowly used its position of leadership to create an Athenian empire. It moved the league treasury from the island of Delos to Athens and forced reluctant allies to remain in the league against their will. It even used money contributed by other city-states to rebuild its own city. Yet, while Athens was enforcing its will abroad, Athenian leaders were championing political freedom at home

☑ **DESCRIBE** What factors led to the Persian defeat?

Pericles, Democracy, and War

The years after the Persian Wars were a golden age for Athens. Under the able statesman **Pericles** (PEHR uh kleez), the economy thrived and the government became more democratic. Because of his wise and skillful leadership, the period from 460 B.C. to 429 B.C. is often called the Age of Pericles.

Democracy in Athens By the time of Pericles, the Athenian assembly met several times a month. A Council of 500, selected by lot, conducted daily government business. Pericles believed that all male citizens, regardless of wealth or social class, should take part in government. Athens therefore began to pay a **stipend,** or fixed salary, to men who participated in the Assembly and its governing Council. This reform enabled poor men to serve in government.

Under Pericles, Athens was a **direct democracy,** or a system of government in which citizens take part directly in the day-to-day affairs of government. By contrast, in most democratic countries today, citizens participate in government indirectly through elected representatives. In both the assembly and the Council of 500, Athenians discussed issues of importance to them. They debated questions such

>> Athena, patroness of Athens and goddess of wisdom, observes citizens fulfilling one of their most important responsibilities in a democracy—voting.

>> *Ostraka*, pieces of pottery with names written on them as shown, were used in Greek city-states to banish dangerous citizens without bringing charges against them.

as what is the best form of government or what constitutes the good life. A central theme of their debates, though, was war, because Athens, like the other Greek city-states, was frequently at war.

Pericles' Funeral Oration Thucydides (thoo SIHD uh deez), a historian who lived in the Age of Pericles, recorded a speech given by Pericles at the funeral of Athenians slain in battle. In this famous Funeral Oration, or speech, Pericles praised the Athenian form of government. He pointed out that Athenian citizens bore a special responsibility to take an interest in public affairs. In this speech, Pericles described essential values and beliefs of the Athenians, including equality of citizens before the law, the responsibility of citizens, and service to the state.

Athenian Justice Among the responsibilities of Athenian citizens was serving on juries. A **jury** is a group of people who have the authority to make a decision in a legal case. Unlike a modern American trial jury, which usually has 12 members, an Athenian jury might include as many as 500 or more jurors.

Citizens over 30 years of age were chosen by lot to serve on the jury for a year. Effectively, Athenian citizens were tried by a jury of their peers, a basic legal principle echoed in England's Magna Carta, the U.S. Sixth Amendment, and in American jury trials today. Also, the fundamental legal concepts of the "rule of law" (all must obey the laws) and "innocent until proven guilty" were substantially embodied in the laws of Athens and Sparta.

Athenian citizens could also vote to banish, or send away, a public figure whom they saw as a threat to their democracy. This process was called **ostracism** (AHS truh siz um). The person with the largest number of votes cast against him was ostracized, meaning that that individual would have to live outside the city, usually for a period of 10 years.

Athenian Culture Thrives Athens prospered during the Age of Pericles. With the empire's riches, Pericles directed the rebuilding of the Acropolis, which the Persians had destroyed. With the help of an educated foreign-born woman named Aspasia (as PAY shuh), Pericles turned Athens into the cultural center of Greece. They encouraged the arts through public festivals, dramatic competitions, and building programs. Such building projects increased Athenians' prosperity by creating jobs for artisans and workers.

The Peloponnesian War Many Greeks outside Athens resented Athenian domination. Before long, the Greek world was split into rival camps.

To counter the Delian League, Sparta and other enemies of Athens formed the Peloponnesian League. In 431 B.C. warfare broke out between Athens and Sparta. This 27-year Peloponnesian War not only pitted these two rivals against one another, but soon engulfed all of Greece.

Athens Defeated by Sparta Despite its riches and powerful navy, Athens faced a serious geographic disadvantage. Because Sparta was located inland, it could not be attacked from the sea. Sparta, however, with its powerful army, only had to march north to attack Athens. When Sparta invaded the lands surrounding Athens, Pericles allowed people from the countryside to move inside the city walls. The overcrowded conditions led to disaster. A terrible plague broke out, killing at least a third of the population, including Pericles himself. His successors were much less able leaders, and their power struggles undermined the city's democratic government.

As the war dragged on, both sides committed savage acts against each other. Sparta even allied itself with Persia, the longtime enemy of the Greeks. Finally, in 404 B.C., with the help of the Persian navy, the Spartans captured Athens. The victors stripped the Athenians of their fleet and empire. However, Sparta rejected calls from its allies to destroy Athens.

The Decline of Greek Dominion The Peloponnesian War ended the greatness of the Athenian golden age. Although the Athenian economy eventually revived and Athens remained the cultural center of Greece, its spirit and vitality declined. In Athens, as elsewhere in the Greek world, democratic government suffered.

Fighting continued to disrupt the Greek world. Sparta itself soon suffered defeat at the hands of Thebes, another Greek city-state. As Greeks battled among themselves, a new power rose in Macedonia (mas uh DOH nee uh), a kingdom to the north of Greece. By 359 B.C. its ambitious ruler stood poised to conquer the quarrelsome Greek city-states.

☑ **DESCRIBE** Describe Pericles' influence on Athens.

>> The Greek hoplite was named after his unique shield, the *hoplon.* These heavily armored soldiers were usually men from the middle class who could afford to purchase the armor and weapons.

☑ ASSESSMENT

1. **Contrast** the earliest civilizations, which rose in fertile river valleys, with the geographical conditions that influenced the rise of ancient Greek civilization. How did these conditions affect the economic development of Greece?

2. **Draw Conclusions** How do you think Greek concepts related to the rights and responsibilities of citizenship influence modern societies?

3. **Infer** How do you think the culture and values shared by Greeks both united and divided them?

4. **Summarize** how the Persian and Peloponnesian Wars affected Greece.

5. **Connections to Today** Explain how democracy evolved in ancient Greece from earlier forms of government. What elements of Athenian democracy are part of democracies today?

The Governments of Athens and Sparta

Athens and Sparta were two of the most powerful city-states in ancient Greece. Athens was a center for learning, philosophy, and the arts, and it was also where the roots of democracy flourished. Sparta, a military state and the undisputed land power of the time period, had a mixed form of government. These differences are addressed in the following excerpts. The first is from Pericles, a commander-in-chief of the Athenian forces during the Peloponnesian War. It is a funeral oration that honors the soldiers who fell in battle and also praises democracy in Athens. The second source is from Aristotle, a Greek philosopher whose works became the foundation for Western thinking. In this section from *Politics*, Aristotle discusses the Spartan constitution.

As you read, look for differences in their viewpoints about government. Then answer the questions comparing the governments of Athens and Sparta.

>> This relief sculpture shows Democracy crowning Demos (the People of Athens).

Primary Source 1

The Funeral Oration of Pericles (431 B.C.)

Our constitution does not copy the laws of neighboring states; we are rather a pattern to others than imitators ourselves. Its administration favors the many instead of the few; this is why it is called a democracy. If we look to the laws, they afford equal justice to all in their private differences.

☑ **SUMMARIZE** According to Pericles, why is Athens a democracy?

As for social standing, advancement in public life falls to reputation for capacity. Class considerations are not allowed to interfere with merit; nor again does poverty bar the way. If a man is able to serve the state, he is not hindered by the obscurity of his condition [low social status].

☑ **PARAPHRASE** What does the following phrase mean: "Class considerations are not allowed to interfere with merit; nor does poverty bar the way"?

The freedom which we enjoy in our government extends also to our ordinary life. . . .

But all this ease in our private relations does not make us lawless as citizens. Against this, fear is our chief safeguard, teaching us to obey the magistrates [government officials] and the laws, particularly such as regard the protection of the injured, whether they are actually on the statute book, or belong to that code which, although unwritten, yet cannot be broken without acknowledged disgrace.

And here is another point. When our work is over, we are in a position to enjoy all kinds of recreation for our spirits. There are various kinds of contests and sacrifices regularly throughout the year; in our own homes we find a beauty and a good taste which delight us every day and which drive away our cares.

☑ **EXPLAIN** How was the democracy protected?

Primary Source 2

Aristotle: On the Lacedaemonian Constitution (340 B.C.)

At Sparta everyone is eligible, and the body of the people, having a share in the highest office, want the constitution to be permanent. Some, indeed, say that the best constitution is a combination of all existing forms, and they praise the Lacedaemonian [Spartan] because it is made up of oligarchy, monarchy, and democracy, the king forming the monarchy, and the council of elders the oligarchy while the democratic element is represented by the Ephors; for the Ephors are selected from the people. Others, however, declare the Ephoralty to be a tyranny, and find the element of democracy in the common meals and in the habits of daily life. At Lacedaemon, for instance, the Ephors determine suits about contracts, which they distribute among themselves, while the elders are judges of homicide, and other causes are decided by other magistrates.

☑ **EXPLAIN** What were the basic elements of Spartan government?

There is a tradition that, in the days of their ancient kings, they were in the habit of giving the rights of citizenship to strangers, and therefore, in spite of their long wars, no lack of population was experienced by them; indeed, at one time Sparta is said to have numbered not less than 10,000 citizens. Whether this statement is true or not, it would certainly have been better to have maintained their numbers by the equalization of property.

☑ **DESCRIBE** How was the population of Sparta maintained?

. . . the Ephors are chosen from the whole people, and so the office is apt to fall into the hands of very poor men, who, being badly off, are open to bribes. The Ephoralty certainly does keep the state together; for the people are contented when they have a share in the highest office, and the result, whether due to the legislator or to chance, has been advantageous.

☑ **DETERMINE AUTHOR'S POINT OF VIEW** Why does Aristotle criticize the Ephors?

☑ ASSESSMENT

Be sure to cite specific evidence from the sources as you answer the following questions.

1. **Describe** How does Pericles express pride in Athens?

2. **Explain** Aristotle criticized the Ephors. What argument might Pericles have given to defend their importance in the Spartan government?

3. **Compare and Contrast** Discuss the treatment of Athenian and Spartan citizens under their respective governments.

4. **Drawing Conclusions** Why was citizenship important in Athenian democracy?

5. **Develop Empathy** How do you think a Spartan citizen would have reacted to living in Athens? How do you think an Athenian citizen would have reacted to living in Sparta?

5.3

💻 **GO ONLINE** to Project Imagine: Tour a Greek Temple and the First Olympic Stadium to view Greek achievements in architecture and art, including carvings of lifelike figures.

 BOUNCE to Activate Flipped Video

Objectives

Analyze the political and ethical ideas developed by ancient Greek philosophers.

Understand how balance and order governed ancient Greek art and architecture.

Identify the themes explored by ancient Greek writers and historians.

Key Terms

philosopher
logic
rhetoric
Socrates
Plato
Aristotle
Parthenon
tragedy
comedy
Herodotus

Greek Thinkers, Artists, and Writers

Even in the midst of wars and political turmoil, Greeks had confidence in the power of the human mind. Driven by curiosity and a belief in reason, Greek thinkers, artists, and writers explored the nature of the universe and the place of people in it. To later admirers, Greek achievements in the arts represented the height of human development in the Western world. They looked back with deep respect on what one poet called "the glory that was Greece."

Philosophers and the Pursuit of Wisdom

As you have read, some ancient Greek thinkers challenged the belief that events were caused by the whims of gods. Instead, they used observation and reason to find causes for events. The Greeks called these thinkers **philosophers,** meaning "lovers of wisdom."

Greek philosophers explored many subjects, from mathematics and music to **logic,** or rational thinking. Through reason and observation, they believed, they could discover laws that governed the universe. Much modern science traces its roots to the Greek search for such principles.

Debating Morality and Ethics Some Greek philosophers were interested in ethics and morality. They debated such questions as what was the best kind of government and what standards should rule human behavior.

In Athens, the Sophists questioned accepted ideas. To them, success was more important than moral truth. They developed skills in **rhetoric,** the art of skillful speaking. Ambitious men could use clever and persuasive rhetoric to advance their careers. The turmoil of the Peloponnesian War led many young Athenians to follow the Sophists. Older citizens, however, accused the Sophists of undermining traditional Greek values.

Socrates Challenges Tradition One outspoken critic of the Sophists was **Socrates,** an Athenian stonemason and philosopher. Most of what we know about Socrates comes from his student **Plato.** Socrates himself wrote no books. Instead he passed his days in the town square asking people about their beliefs.

Using a process we now call the Socratic method, he would pose a series of questions to a student or passing citizen, and challenge them to examine the implications of their answers. To Socrates, this patient examination was a way to help others seek truth and self-knowledge. To many Athenians, however, such questioning was a threat to accepted values and traditions.

When he was about 70 years old, Socrates was put on trial. His enemies accused him of corrupting the city's youth and failing to respect the gods. Standing before a jury of 501 citizens, Socrates offered a calm and reasoned defense. But the jurors condemned him to death.

Loyal to the laws of Athens, Socrates accepted the death penalty. He drank a cup of hemlock, a deadly poison.

Plato Describes a Perfect Society The execution of Socrates left Plato with a lifelong distrust of democracy. He fled Athens for 10 years. When he returned, he set up a school called the Academy. There, he taught and wrote about his own ideas. Like Socrates, Plato emphasized the importance of reason. Through rational thought, he argued, people could discover unchanging ethical values, recognize perfect beauty, and learn how best to organize society.

In his book *The Republic*, Plato described his vision of an ideal state. He rejected Athenian democracy because it had condemned Socrates just as it tended to other excesses. Instead, Plato argued that the state should regulate every aspect of its citizens' lives in order to provide for their best interests. He divided his ideal society into three classes: workers to produce the necessities of life, soldiers to defend the state, and philosophers to rule. This elite class of leaders would be specially trained to ensure order and justice. The wisest of them, a philosopher-king, would have the ultimate authority.

Plato thought that, in general, men surpassed women in mental and physical tasks, but that some women were superior to some men. Talented women, he said, should be educated to serve the state. The ruling elite, both men and women, would take

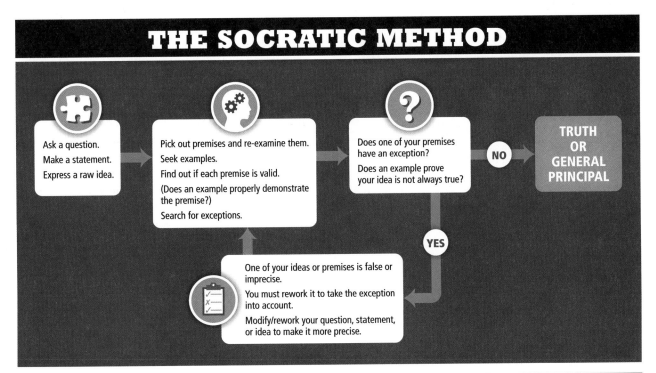

>> The Socratic method uses questions and answers as steps in a reasoning process that aims to arrive at truths by logically examining the underlying assumptions and implications of statements.

BOUNCE to Activate Chart

>> Aristotle (384 B.C.–322 B.C.) is counted among the greatest philosophers and scientists of Western history. His system of thought provided a framework for later Christian and Islamic philosophy.

>> The builders of the Parthenon (shown here), seeking to reflect a harmonious universe, used geometric proportions to convey a dignified sense of order that feels balanced.

▶ BOUNCE to Activate Gallery

military training together and raise their children in communal centers for the good of the republic.

Aristotle Seeks the Golden Mean Plato's most famous student, **Aristotle,** developed his own ideas about government. He analyzed all forms of government, from monarchy to democracy, and found good and bad examples of each. Like Plato, he was suspicious of democracy, which he thought could lead to mob rule. In the end, he favored rule by a single strong and virtuous leader.

Aristotle also addressed the question of how people ought to live. In his view, good conduct meant pursuing the "golden mean," a moderate course between the extremes.

He promoted reason as the guiding force for learning. He set up a school, the Lyceum, for the study of all branches of knowledge. He left writings on politics, ethics, logic, biology, literature, and many other subjects. When the first European universities evolved some 1,500 years later, their courses were based largely on the works and ideas of Aristotle.

☑ **DESCRIBE** What contributions did Aristotle make to education?

Conveying Ideals in Architecture and Art

Plato argued that every object on Earth had an ideal form. The work of ancient Greek artists and architects reflected a similar concern with balance, order, and beauty.

Monumental Architecture Greek architects sought to convey a sense of perfect balance to reflect the harmony and order of the universe. The most famous example of Greek architecture is the **Parthenon,** a temple dedicated to the goddess Athena. The basic plan of the Parthenon is a simple rectangle, with tall columns supporting a gently sloping roof. The delicate curves and placement of the columns add dignity and grace.

Greek architecture has been widely admired for centuries. Today, many public buildings throughout the world have incorporated Greek architectural elements, such as columns, in their designs.

Crafting Lifelike Human Forms Early Greek sculptors carved figures in stiff, standard poses, similar in style to the art of ancient Egypt. By 450 B.C., however, Greek sculptors had developed a new style that emphasized more natural forms. While their work was lifelike, it was also idealistic. That is, sculptors carved gods, goddesses, athletes, and famous men in a way that showed human beings in their most perfect, graceful form.

The only Greek paintings to survive are on pottery. They offer intriguing views of everyday Greek life. Women carry water from wells, warriors race into battle, and athletes compete in javelin contests. Each scene is designed to fit the shape of the pottery.

☑ **DESCRIBE** How did Greek art reflect the idea of an ideal form?

Greek Literature

In literature, as in art, the ancient Greeks developed their own style. To later Europeans, Greek styles were a model of perfection. They admired what they called the "classical style," referring to the elegant and balanced forms of traditional Greek works of art.

Early Greek literature began with the epic poems of Homer, whose stirring tales inspired later writers. In later times, the poet Sappho sang of love and of the beauty of her island home, while the poetry of Pindar celebrated the victors in athletic contests.

Greek Tragedy Perhaps the most important ancient Greek contribution to literature was in the field of drama. The first Greek plays evolved out of religious festivals, especially those held in Athens to honor the god of fertility and wine, Dionysus (dy uh NY sus).

Plays were performed in large outdoor theaters with little or no set. Actors wore elaborate costumes and stylized masks. A chorus sang or chanted comments on the action taking place on stage. Greek dramas were often based on popular myths and legends. Through these familiar stories, playwrights discussed moral and social issues or explored the relationship between people and the gods.

The greatest Athenian playwrights were Aeschylus (ES kih lus), Sophocles (SAH fuh kleez), and Euripides (yoo RIP ih deez). All three wrote **tragedies,** plays that told stories of human suffering that usually ended in disaster. The purpose of tragedy, the Greeks felt, was to stir up and then relieve the emotions of pity and fear. For example, in his play *Oresteia* (aw res TEE uh), Aeschylus showed a powerful family torn apart by betrayal, murder, and revenge. Audiences saw how even the powerful could be subject to horrifying misfortune and how the wrath of the gods could bring down even the greatest heroes.

>> Thousands of surviving painted vases provide us with much of what we know about daily life in ancient Greece. This vase from the 300s B.C., for example, shows women in conversations at home.

>> A Roman fresco from Pompeii believed to be of the Greek poet Sappho (610 B.C.–570 B.C.). Over the ages, readers have been impressed with her writing style and lively personality.

In *Antigone* (an TIG uh nee), Sophocles explored what happens when an individual's moral duty conflicts with the laws of the state. Antigone is a young woman whose brother has been killed leading a rebellion. King Creon forbids anyone to bury the traitor's body. When Antigone buries her brother anyway, she is sentenced to death. She defiantly tells Creon that duty to the gods is greater than human law.

> . . . it was not Zeus that had published me that edict [law]; not such are the laws set among men by the Justice who dwells with the gods below; nor deemed [judged] I that thy decrees were of such force, that a mortal could override the unwritten and unfailing statutes of heaven.

—Sophocles, *Antigone* (translated by Richard C. Jebb)

Like Sophocles, Euripides survived the horrors of the Peloponnesian War. That experience probably led him to question many accepted ideas of his day.

His plays suggested that people, not the gods, were the cause of human misfortune and suffering. In *The Trojan Women,* he stripped war of its glamour by showing the suffering of women who were victims of the war.

Greek Comedy Some Greek playwrights wrote **comedies,** humorous plays that mocked people or customs. Almost all the surviving ancient Greek comedies were written by Aristophanes (a rih STAHF uh neez). In *Lysistrata,* he shows the women of Athens banding together to force their husbands to end a war against Sparta. Unlike tragedy, which focused on events of the past, comedies ridiculed individuals of the day, including political figures, philosophers, and prominent members of society. Through ridicule, comic playwrights sharply criticized society, much as political cartoonists do today.

☑ **IDENTIFY** How was drama used to influence Greek society?

Studying History

The Greeks also applied observation, reason, and logic to the study of history. **Herodotus** is often called the "Father of History" in the Western world because he went beyond listing names of rulers or the retelling of ancient legends. Before writing *The Persian Wars,* Herodotus visited many lands, collecting information from people who remembered the actual events he chronicled. In fact, Herodotus used the Greek term *historie*, which means inquiry, to define his work. Our *history* comes from this word, but its definition has evolved today to simply mean the recording and study of past events.

Herodotus cast a critical eye on his sources, noting bias and conflicting accounts. However, despite this special care for detail and accuracy, his writings reflected his own view that the war was a clear moral victory of Greek love of freedom over Persian tyranny. He even invented conversations and speeches for historical figures.

Another historian, Thucydides, who was a few years younger than Herodotus, wrote about the Peloponnesian War, a much less happy subject for the Greeks. He had lived through the war and vividly described the war's savagery and corrupting influence on all those involved. Although he was an Athenian, he tried to be fair to both sides.

Both writers set standards for future historians. Herodotus stressed the importance of research. Thucydides showed the need to avoid bias.

☑ **IDENTIFY MAIN IDEAS** Why is Herodotus considered the "Father of History"?

>> Herodotus (*c.* 484 B.C.–*c.* 425 B.C.) was born under Persian rule at Halicarnassus, a Greek city in Asia Minor. His *The Persian Wars* is famous as the ancient world's first great narrative history.

1. **Identify Cause and Effect** Why did Socrates question Athenians about their beliefs?

2. **Cite Evidence** How did balance and order govern Greek architecture?

3. **Explain** What was the main contribution that Herodotus made to the study of history?

4. **Contrast** the subject matters of Greek tragedy and Greek comedy.

5. **Determine Point of View** How do you think the points of view of Herodotus and Thucydides influenced their approaches to writing history?

6. **Quest Connections** Create a discussion between an historian writing about the values of Sparta and an historian writing about the values of Athens.

The Archaeology from The *History of the Peloponnesian War*

Thucydides, an Athenian general, wrote the *History of the Peloponnesian War*. It recounts 21 of the 28 years of war between Athens and Sparta. Even though it is unfinished and there are most likely inconsistencies, it is regarded as an important scholarly work. What we know about Thucydides' life comes from the *History*. He was born in Athens. He was a general in the war, and he lived through the brutal plague that struck Athens a year before the war began. He was exiled for 20 years by the Athenian government when he failed to save the city of Amphipolis from the Spartans. During those 20 years of exile, he visited all parts of the Greek world and wrote his history. He states that because of his exile, "being present with both parties [Athens and Sparta] and more especially with the Peloponnesians by reason of my exile, I had leisure to observe affairs more closely."

>> A modern artist's depiction of the Battle of Coronea during the First Peloponnesian War

The following excerpt is from the opening chapters of the *History*. It is known as the "Archaeology" which, in the case of this work, means the "account of ancient things." In it, Thucydides gives a history of ancient Greece.

Primary Source

Thucydides, an Athenian, wrote the history of the war between the Peloponnesians and the Athenians, beginning at the moment that it broke out, and believing that it would be a great war and more worthy of relation [telling] than any that had preceded it. This belief was not without its grounds. The preparations of both the combatants were in every department in the last state of perfection; and he could see the rest of the Hellenic [Greek] race taking sides in the quarrel; those who delayed doing so at once having it in contemplation [were deciding when to side with one of the combatants]. Indeed, this was the greatest movement yet known in history, not only of the Hellenes [Greeks], but of a large part of the barbarian world—I had almost said of mankind. For though the events of remote antiquity, and even those that more immediately preceded the war, could not from lapse of time be clearly ascertained [known], yet the evidences which an inquiry carried as far back as was practicable leads me to trust, all point to the conclusion that there was nothing on a great scale, either in war or in other matters.

☑ **SUMMARIZE** According to Thucydides, why was it difficult for him to write about the distant past?

For instance, it is evident that the country now called Hellas [Greece] had in ancient times no settled population; on the contrary, migrations were of frequent occurrence, the several tribes readily abandoning their homes under the pressure of superior numbers. Without commerce, without freedom of communication either by land or sea, cultivating no more of their territory than the exigencies [necessities] of life required, destitute of [having little] capital, never planting their land (for they could not tell when an invader might not come and take it all away, and when he did come they had no walls to stop him), thinking that the necessities of daily sustenance could be supplied at one place as well as another, they cared little for shifting their habitation, and consequently neither built large cities nor attained to any other form of greatness.

☑ **EXPLAIN** According to Thucydides, why were there no settled peoples in ancient Greece?

The richest soils were always most subject to this change of masters; such as the district now called Thessaly, Boeotia, most of the Peloponnese, Arcadia excepted, and the most fertile parts of the rest of Hellas. The goodness of the land favoured the aggrandizement [benefit] of particular individuals, and thus created faction [war] which proved a fertile source of ruin. It also invited invasion.

☑ **DETERMINE CENTRAL IDEAS** Why did Thessaly and Boeotia face frequent invasion?

Accordingly, Attica [the region around Athens], from the poverty of its soil enjoying from a very remote period freedom from faction [for a long time having no wars], never changed its inhabitants. And here is no inconsiderable exemplification [proof] of my assertion [statement] that the migrations were the cause of there being no correspondent growth in other parts. The most powerful victims of war or faction from the rest of Hellas took refuge with the Athenians as a safe retreat; and at an early period, becoming naturalized, swelled the already large population of the city to such a height that Attica became at last too small to hold them, and they had to send out colonies to Ionia.

☑ **SUMMARIZE** Why did population increase in Attica?

☑ **ASSESSMENT**

1. **Draw Conclusions** How reliable is Thucydides' *History* to historians?

2. **Determine Author's Purpose** Why did Thucydides choose to write about the Peloponnesian War?

3. **Determine Central Ideas** What is Thucydides' main point about Attica?

4. **Cite Evidence** Citing evidence from the text, how might geography have affected the economy of ancient Greece?

5. **Determine Author's Purpose** How might readers react to the early history of Athens in light of how powerful it became? Why do you think Thucydides added this story to his narrative?

5.4

📡 **GO ONLINE** to **Project Imagine: Survey Centuries of Greek Culture** to review Greek history from its earliest days through Alexander's reign to its continuing legacy.

🅑 BOUNCE to Activate Flipped Video

Objectives

Explain how Alexander the Great built an extensive empire.

Describe the empire's cultural impact.

Identify major Hellenistic Greek scientists and their discoveries and innovations.

Key Terms

Alexander the Great
Philip II
assassination
assimilate
Alexandria
Pythagoras
heliocentric
Archimedes
Hippocrates

Alexander the Great and the Legacy of Greece

In 338 B.C., Athens fell to the Macedonian army. Athens and the other Greek city-states lost their independence. Yet the disaster ushered in a new age in which Greek culture spread from the Mediterranean to the borders of India. The architect of this new era was the man who would eventually become known to history as Alexander the Great.

The New Era of Alexander the Great

To the Greeks, the rugged, mountainous kingdom of Macedonia was a backward, half-civilized land. The rulers of this frontier land, in fact, were of Greek origin and kept ties to their Greek neighbors. As a youth, **Philip II** had lived in Thebes and had come to admire Greek culture. Later, he hired Aristotle as a tutor to his young son Alexander.

Philip II Takes Control of Greece When Philip II gained the throne in 359 B.C. he dreamed of conquering the prosperous city-states to the south. He built a superb and powerful army. Through threats, bribery, and diplomacy, he formed alliances with many Greek city-states. Others he conquered. In 338 B.C., when Athens and Thebes joined forces against him, Philip II defeated them at the battle of Chaeronea (kehr uh NEE uh). He then brought all of Greece under his control.

Philip had a still grander dream—to conquer the Persian empire. Before he could achieve that plan, though, he was assassinated at his daughter's wedding. **Assassination** is the murder of a public figure, usually for political reasons. Philip's queen, Olympias, then outmaneuvered his other wives and children to put her own son, Alexander, on the throne.

Alexander Conquers Persia Alexander was only 20 years old. Yet he was already an experienced soldier who shared his father's ambitions. With Greece subdued, he began organizing the forces needed to conquer Persia. By 334 B.C. he had enough ships to cross the Dardanelles, the strait separating Europe from Asia Minor.

Persia was no longer the great power it had once been. The emperor Darius III was weak, and the provinces were often in rebellion against him. Still, the Persian empire stretched more than 2,000 miles from Egypt to India.

Alexander won his first victory against the Persians at the Granicus River. He then moved from victory to victory, marching through Asia Minor into Palestine and south to Egypt before turning east again to take Babylon in 331 B.C. Other cities followed. But before Alexander could capture Darius, the Persian emperor was murdered.

The March into India With much of the Persian empire under his control, the restless Alexander headed farther east. He crossed the Hindu Kush into northern India. There, in 326 B.C., his troops for the first time faced soldiers mounted on war elephants. Although Alexander never lost a battle, his soldiers were tired of the long campaign and refused to go farther east.

Reluctantly, Alexander agreed to turn back. After a long and difficult march, they reached Babylon, where Alexander began planning a new campaign.

The Early Death of Alexander Before he could set out again, the thirty-two-year-old fell victim to a sudden fever. As Alexander lay dying, his commanders asked to whom he left his immense empire. "To the strongest," he is said to have whispered.

No one leader proved strong enough to succeed Alexander. Instead, after years of disorder, three generals divided up the empire. Macedonia and Greece went to one general, Egypt to another, and most of Persia to a third. For the next 300 years, their descendants competed for power over the lands Alexander had conquered.

☑ **EXPLAIN** Why was Alexander the Great able to conquer the Persian empire?

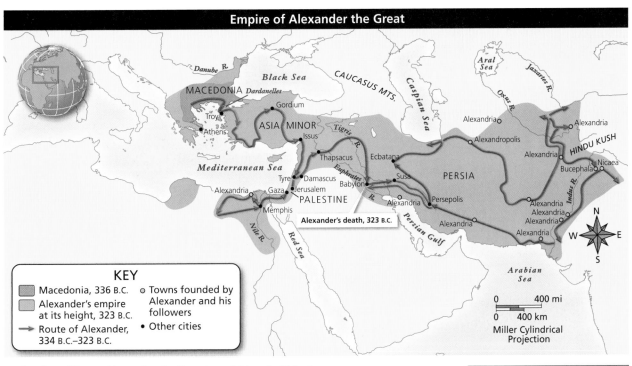

Empire of Alexander the Great

KEY
- ▢ Macedonia, 336 B.C.
- ▢ Alexander's empire at its height, 323 B.C.
- → Route of Alexander, 334 B.C.–323 B.C.
- ⊙ Towns founded by Alexander and his followers
- • Other cities

Alexander's death, 323 B.C.

0 — 400 mi
0 — 400 km
Miller Cylindrical Projection

>> **Analyze Maps** Alexander the Great's ambitions led him to conquer lands across a vast area. Judging from this map, do you think his empire would be difficult to keep united? Explain your reasoning.

▶ BOUNCE to Activate Map

Alexander's Legacy

Although Alexander's empire soon crumbled following his premature death, he had unleashed changes that would ripple across the Mediterranean world and the Middle East for centuries. His most lasting achievement was the spread of Greek culture.

Cultures Blend Across his far-flung empire, Alexander founded many new cities, most of them named after him. The generals who succeeded him founded still more. Greek soldiers, traders, and artisans settled these new cities. From Egypt to the borders of India, they built Greek temples, filled them with Greek statues, and held athletic contests as they had in Greece. Local people **assimilated,** or absorbed, Greek ideas. In turn, Greek settlers adopted local customs.

Alexander had encouraged a blending of eastern and western cultures when he had married a Persian woman and urged his soldiers to follow his example. He had also adopted many Persian customs, including Persian dress. Gradually, after his death, a vital new culture emerged that blended Greek, Persian, Egyptian, and Indian influences. This Hellenistic civilization would flourish for several centuries.

>> The famous Pharos lighthouse in Alexandria was one of the Seven Wonders of the World. Built in 280 B.C., it stood more than 350 feet high until an earthquake destroyed it in the 1300s.

Alexandria: The Cultural Capital At the very heart of the Hellenistic world stood the city of **Alexandria,** Egypt. Located on the sea lanes between Europe and Asia, its markets boasted a wide range of goods, from Greek marble to Arabian spices to East African ivory. A Greek architect had drawn up plans for the city, which would become home to almost a million people. Among the city's marvelous sights was the Pharos, an enormous lighthouse that soared more than 350 feet into the air.

Alexander and his successors encouraged the work of scholars. The rulers of Alexandria built the great Museum as a center of learning. The Museum boasted laboratories, lecture halls, and a zoo. Its library had thousands of scrolls representing the accumulated knowledge of the ancient world. Unfortunately, the library was later destroyed in a fire.

Women Take New Roles Paintings, statues, and legal codes show that women were no longer restricted to their homes during the Hellenistic period. More women learned to read and write. Some became philosophers or poets. Royal women held considerable power, working alongside husbands and sons who were the actual rulers. In Egypt, the able and clever queen Cleopatra VII came to rule in her own right.

☑ **MAKE JUDGMENTS** Why was the formation and spread of Hellenistic culture by Alexander the Great and his successors significant?

Hellenistic Arts and Sciences

The cities of the Hellenistic world employed armies of architects and artists. Temples, palaces, and other public buildings were much larger and grander than the buildings of classical Greece. The elaborate new style reflected the desire of Hellenistic rulers to glorify themselves as godlike.

New Philosophies Emerge Political turmoil during the Hellenistic age contributed to the rise of new schools of philosophy. The most influential was Stoicism. Its founder, Zeno, urged people to avoid desires and disappointments by accepting calmly whatever life brought. Stoics preached high moral standards, such as the idea of protecting the rights of fellow humans. They taught that all people, including women and the enslaved, though unequal in society, were morally equal because all had the power of reason. Stoicism later influenced many Roman and Christian thinkers.

Math and Astronomy Advance During the Hellenistic age, scholars built on earlier Greek, Babylonian, and Egyptian knowledge. They expanded on the work of **Pythagoras** (pih THAG uh rus), an earlier Greek thinker who had derived a formula to calculate the relationship between the sides of a right triangle. His interest in the principles of mathematics, the relations between numbers, and the idea of a proof influenced Plato, Aristotle, and later western thought.

Euclid, (YOO klid) wrote *The Elements,* a textbook that brilliantly compiled earlier works and became the basis for modern geometry. From stated axioms, or assumptions, Euclid built a logical and rigorous geometry. *The Elements* had a powerful impact on Islamic mathematics, and Latin translations of Arabic versions first made it known in Europe. Since it was first printed in 1482, more than a thousand editions have been published.

Using mathematics and careful observation, the astronomer Aristarchus (a ris TAHR kus) argued that Earth rotated on its axis and orbited the sun. This theory of a **heliocentric,** or sun-centered, solar system was not accepted by most scientists until almost 2,000 years later. His ideas about Earth's motion inspired the Polish astronomer Copernicus in the early 1500s. Aristarchus also used geometry to calculate the sizes and distances of the sun and the moon. Another Hellenistic astronomer, Eratosthenes (eh ruh TAHS thuh neez) showed that Earth was round and accurately calculated its circumference. His *On the measurement of the Earth* was lost, but other ancient authors preserved some details of his calculations.

The most famous Hellenistic scientist, **Archimedes** (ahr kuh MEE deez) of Syracuse, applied principles of physics to make practical inventions. He mastered the use of the lever and pulley and boasted, "Give me a lever long enough and a place to stand on, and I will move the world."

Then, to demonstrate the power of his invention, Archimedes used it to draw a ship over the land before a crowd of awed spectators. In 212 B.C., at the request of the King of Syracuse, Archimedes devised machines of war to defend his hometown against Roman attack. He also invented the Archimedes screw, a mechanical pump still used in many parts of the world to lift water to higher levels for irrigation.

Medical Practice Improves About 400 B.C. the Greek physician **Hippocrates** (hih PAH kruh teez) studied the causes of illnesses and looked for cures. The Hippocratic oath attributed to him set ethical standards for doctors. Greek physicians swore to

>> Pythagoras and his followers speculated about using numbers to measure and compare things. They had intuitive feelings of the *harmonia* ("fitting together") of the *kosmos* ("order of things").

BOUNCE to Activate Gallery

>> Archimedes's screw is shown in a French illustration from the early 1700s. In this image, it uses a rotating spiral tube wound around an axis to raise water from *A* to *B*. Pulling the rope turns the tube.

THE GREEK LEGACY

GOVERNMENT	CULTURE	ARTS	MATHEMATICS, SCIENCE, AND TECHNOLOGY
• Written code of laws • Citizens bring charges of wrongdoing • Trial by jury • Citizenship expands to all free adult men, except foreigners • Athenian assembly makes laws • Direct democracy: male citizens rule by majority vote	• Greek language: many roots, prefixes, suffixes used in English • Mythology about gods and goddesses • Olympic games • Philosophers searching for truth, apply reason, question tradition	• Drama and poetry • History: encouraging research, unbiased accounts • Sculpture portraying lifelike human forms and ideal beauty • Painted pottery with scenes of everyday Greek life and legendary tales • Classical architecture embodies balance, grace	• Properties of numbers and proportion studied • Disagreement whether sun or Earth at center of universe • Accurate estimate of circumference of Earth • Development of lever, pulley, pump • Natural not divine causes and cures of illness sought, code of ethics for physicians

>> Ancient Greece's legacy has been as broad as it is deep, including major concepts, institutions, and inventions in government, culture, the arts, mathematics, the sciences, and technology.

"help the sick according to my ability and judgment but never with a view to injury and wrong." Doctors today still take a similar oath.

A Remarkable Legacy With its conquest of Asia Minor in 133 B.C. Rome replaced Greece as the dominant power in the Mediterranean world. However, the Greek legacy remains. Greek works in the arts and sciences set a standard for later people of Europe. Greek ideas about law, freedom, justice, and government continue to influence political thinking to the present day.

Socrates, Plato, Aristotle, and other Greek philosophers developed an ideal of critical thought and self-examination that allowed people to question ideas and institutions. Citizens could participate and judge governments. Later, the founders of Western political systems, including of the United States, studied these ancient Greek ideas as part of their classical educations. The Athenian experiment in direct democracy by citizen participation thus had a deep and far-reaching impact on modern politics and governments.

These achievements and their impact were especially remarkable because they were produced by a scattering of tiny city-states whose rivalries left them too weak to defend themselves from conquest.

Later, you will learn how the Greek legacy influenced the civilizations of Rome and of Western Europe.

☑ **IDENTIFY** In what fields did Hellenistic civilization make advancements?

☑ ASSESSMENT

1. **Evaluate** Why was Macedonia's conquest of Greece of such great significance?

2. **Infer** Why do you think Alexander the Great and his generals founded so many new cities?

3. **Cite Evidence** How did Alexander and his successors spread Greek culture through the Hellenistic world?

4. **Identify** Which Greek scientist invented a pump that continues to be used for irrigation in many parts of the world today? What does his invention do?

5. **Connections to Today** Why do you think trial by jury was significant in the Athenian democracy? What kind of court system exists in the United States today?

Connections to Today

Citizens in India show their identity cards as they prepare to vote.

Take Action To Learn About Democracy

There are two types of democracies—direct and representative. In a direct democracy, citizens can participate in policy decisions. In a representative democracy, citizens elect officials to make political decisions and laws. Still, the characteristics of democracy vary from one country to another.

1. **Choose** two countries below. Research the democracies of each. Consider the following: What kind of democracy? How long has the country been governed this way? What are the features? How do citizens feel about their government?

    *   Norway
    *   India
    *   Australia
    *   Canada
    *   Japan

2. **Ask Questions** Generate a list of questions you have about the topic.

3. **Learn** about the topic and the major issues related to the topic. How many countries have a democratic form of government? How successful are these democracies? Which countries are moving toward democracy? Take notes as you conduct your research and continue to generate questions as you learn more.

4. **Raise Awareness** Citizen participation is critical in making a democracy work. Create a poster encouraging citizens to participate and stay informed. List ways in which this can be accomplished.

LESSON SUMMARIES

Use these Lesson Summaries, and the longer versions available online, to review the key ideas for each lesson in this Topic.

Lesson 1: Early Greece

The earliest civilization in Greece evolved on the island of Crete, where people we call the Minoans were influenced by, and traded with, older civilizations in Egypt and the Middle East. In turn, the Minoans influenced the development of Mycenaean civilization on mainland Greece. Mycenaean cities and trade declined after the Dorian invasions, but memories of the Minoans and the Mycenaeans survived, especially in Homer's poems called the *Iliad* and the *Odyssey*, which describe events during and following the Trojan War.

Lesson 2: The Greek City-States

The mountainous land of Greece divided communities, which eventually evolved into independent city states that were dependent on the sea and resources from the wider world. Greek city-states were competitive and frequently at war with one another. They developed different forms of government, including democracy, and sent out settlers who spread Greek civilization around the Mediterranean Sea. In Athens, democracy was limited to free adult male citizens, and women had little freedom. Despite their differences, the Greeks shared a common language and religion and united to defeat two invasions by the Persian Empire. However, rivalry developed between Athens, where democracy emerged and Sparta, a militaristic state. In 431, the 27-year-long Peloponnesian War broke out between Athens and Sparta, ending with the defeat of Athens.

Lesson 3: Greek Thinkers, Artists, and Writers

The Greeks created inspiring works of art, architecture, philosophy, and literature that continue to influence the modern world. Greek confidence in the ability of human reason to solve problems led to advances in mathematics and the sciences and helped launch the study of history. During the Classical period, Greek art and architecture reflected the pursuit of ideal forms, balance, and harmony of parts.

Lesson 4: Alexander the Great and the Legacy of Greece

In the late 300s B.C., King Philip of Macedonia brought all of Greece under his control. His son Alexander conquered Persia, spreading Greek culture east as far as India. After Alexander's death, his generals carved their own kingdoms out of his empire, and their descendants ruled these kingdoms for the next 300 years. During this time, Greek culture merged with local traditions to create a Greek-dominated Hellenistic civilization. Women gained more freedom, and Hellenistic cities such as Alexandria became rich centers of culture and science, creating a cultural legacy that would help shape the development of civilization.

QUEST! FINDINGS

Prepare a discussion panel Refer to your responses to the Quest Connections to help you create your discussion panel. Use the rubric and other Quest resources online to guide your work.

GO ONLINE to access lesson summaries

VISUAL REVIEW

Use these graphics to review some of the key terms, people, and ideas from this Topic.

Foundations of Greek Civilization

1700–1400 B.C. Height of Minoan Civilization

1400–1200 B.C. Mycenaeans dominate Greece

1200 B.C. Attacks on Mycenaeans from sea raiders and others

1100–800 B.C. Greek cities are abandoned, trade declines, writing forgotten

c. 750 B.C. Greek civilization revives Homer's epic poems take shape

Rival City-States

ATHENS	SPARTA
• Democracy develops • Few rights for women • Valued philosophy and the arts, trade and wealth	• Two kings, advisory council, citizen assembly • Women could inherit property • Scorned trade, wealth and the arts • Valued discipline and military training

Greek Achievements

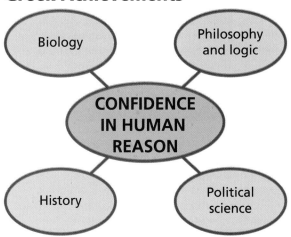

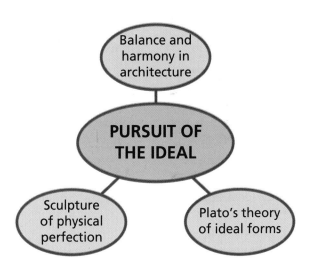

KEY TERMS, PEOPLE, AND IDEAS

1. What does the palace of **Knossos** reveal about the status of women in Minoan society?

2. What may have caused the conflict known as the **Trojan War**?

3. Where in an ancient Greek city would the **acropolis** be found, and what kind of buildings stood there?

4. Who controlled power in a Greek **oligarchy**?

5. How was **ostracism** used in ancient Athens?

6. Why did many Athenians consider **Socrates** a threat?

7. What moral lesson did **Herodotus** want to teach in his history of the Persian Wars?

8. What were the achievements of **Alexander the Great**?

9. Why was **Alexandria** such a rich and cultured city?

CRITICAL THINKING

10. **Draw Conclusions** Why would early Greek civilization have collapsed under the force of invasion or attack?

11. **Compare and Contrast** Make an argument that Athenian-style direct democracy would be an impractical system in the modern United States.

12. **Draw Inferences** What problems do you think might arise in Plato's ideal state?

13. **Summarize** In what ways did Hellenistic culture differ from Greek culture of the earlier, classical period?

14. **Compare and Contrast** What was Athens' great disadvantage and Sparta's advantage during the Peloponnesian War?

15. **Evaluate Explanations** Why was the study of rhetoric important in Athens?

16. **Use Visual Information** Study the map. What problems might the huge Persian army have faced in its invasion of Greece?

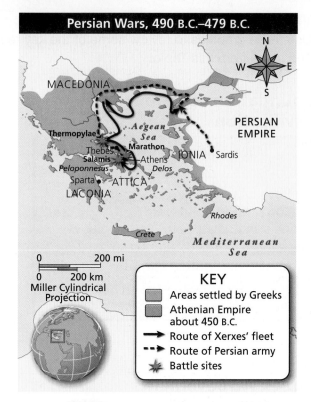

Persian Wars, 490 B.C.–479 B.C.

KEY
- Areas settled by Greeks
- Athenian Empire about 450 B.C.
- Route of Xerxes' fleet
- Route of Persian army
- Battle sites

17. **Writing Activity: Write a Narrative** In Athens, dramatists explored social issues, such as the relationship between the individual and the state. In the following excerpt from a tragedy, Antigone, a young woman, responds to Creon, the king of Thebes, who wants to know why she has defied the law by burying her brother, a rebel against the state.

> ". . . it was not Zeus that had published me that edict [law], not such are the laws set among men by the Justice who dwells with the gods below; nor deemed [judged] I that thy decrees were of such force, that a mortal could override the unwritten and unfailing statutes of heaven."
> —Sophocles, *Antigone* (translated by Richard C. Jebb)

Continue writing a few paragraphs that show how the king might have responded to Antigone's defiance, and how she, in turn might have, answered him.

18. **Connections to Today** Rule of the people or democracy in Athens did not include all the people. However, it did pave the way to a new governing process. How has the rule of the people and the governing process of a democracy expanded to the democracy we have today?

DOCUMENT-BASED QUESTIONS

Throughout ancient times, the Greeks debated the strengths and dangers of different forms of government. Read the documents below, then answer the questions that follow.

DOCUMENT A

In this excerpt from *Politics*, Aristotle warns of dangers that may emerge as the three social classes struggle for power.

"The legislator should always include the middle class in his government; if he makes laws oligarchical, to the middle class let him look; if he makes them democratical, he should equally by his laws try to attach this class to the state. There only can the government ever be stable where the middle class exceeds one or both of the others; and in that case there will be no fear that the rich will unite with the poor against the rulers. . . ."
        —***Politics,*** Aristotle

DOCUMENT B

In this excerpt from the *Republic*, Plato explains why politicians continually threaten society in their greed for power.

"[F]or the truth is that you can have a well-governed society only if you can discover for your future rulers a better way of life than being in office; then only will power be in the hands of men who are rich, not in gold, but in the wealth that brings happiness, a good and wise life. All goes wrong when, starved for lack of anything good in their own lives, men turn to public affairs hoping to snatch from thence the happiness they hunger for. The set about fighting for power and this internecine conflict ruins them and their country."
        —***Republic,*** Plato

DOCUMENT C

DOCUMENT D

In this excerpt from *The Histories*, the Greek writer Polybius uses a metaphor to describe Athenian democracy.

"For the Athenian populace always more or less resembles a ship without a commander. In such a ship when fear of a storm induces the sailors to be sensible and attend to the orders of the skipper, they do their duty admirably. But when they grow over-confident and begin to entertain contempt for their superiors and to quarrel with each other, not only does the spectacle strike anyone who watches it as disgraceful, but the position of affairs is a source of actual danger to the rest of those on board; so that often after escaping from the perils of the widest seas and fiercest storms they are shipwrecked in harbor and when close to the shore. This is what has more than once befallen the Athenian state."
        —*The Histories*, Polybius

19. In Document A, Aristotle suggests that governments can only be stable if
  A. the rich stop fighting with the poor.
  B. the middle class is strong enough.
  C. the rich take control.
  D. the poor unite with the middle class.

20. In Document B, Plato says that corrupt politicians struggle to gain wealth and power because
  A. they think this is the only way to gain happiness.
  B. they are not philosophers.
  C. they are devoted to public service.
  D. the people want a well-governed society.

21. In Document C, ostraca, or the pieces of pottery shown here, were used as part of a system
  A. to elect a leader.
  B. to banish an Athenian.
  C. to select jury members.
  D. to sentence a criminal to death.

22. In Document D, Polybius uses the metaphor of the ship
  A. to promote democracy.
  B. to support oligarchy.
  C. to warn of the dangers of democracy.
  D. to promote an aristocratic government.

23. Writing Task Write a paragraph describing how the Greeks viewed the strengths and weaknesses of different forms of government. Use the sources on this page and what you have learned in this topic to formulate your response.

GO ONLINE to access more practice

Ancient Rome and the Origins of Christianity (509 B.C.-A.D. 476)

ESSENTIAL QUESTION What Makes a Government Successful?

GO ONLINE to access the eText, videos, Interactive Primary Sources, Biographies, and other online resources.

The Colosseum in Rome

Connections to Today

In large stadiums, sports fans cheer on their favorite baseball, basketball, football, soccer, and hockey teams. There are fans who enjoy boxing, wrestling, skiing, figure skating, and many more sports. Athletes risk injury often in return for high payouts.

As you will read in this topic, the ancient Romans enjoyed sporting events and built large stadiums like the Colosseum to hold tens of thousands of spectators. Romans enjoyed wrestling, chariot racing, and gladiator events. Why do you think people enjoy watching sports?

NBC LEARN

Learn about Augustus and the Pax Romana.

BOUNCE to Activate My Story Video

191

In this Topic, you will learn how the Roman civilization started as a single city on the Tiber River and grew to cover Europe and the area around the Mediterranean. You also will learn how a new religion, Christianity, began during the Roman empire. Look at the lesson outline and explore the timeline. As you study the Topic, you will complete the Quest Inquiry.

LESSON OUTLINE

6.1 The Roman Republic

6.2 The Roman Empire: Rise and Decline

6.3 The Legacy of Rome

6.4 The Origins of Christianity

Key Events in Ancient Rome and the Origins of Christianity

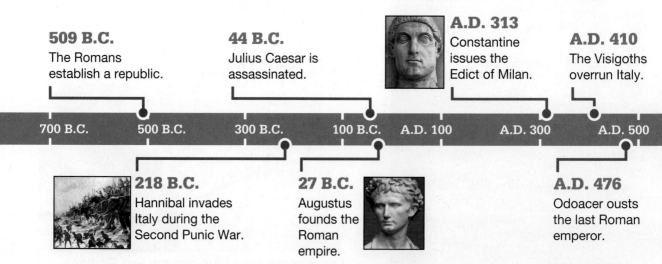

509 B.C.
The Romans establish a republic.

44 B.C.
Julius Caesar is assassinated.

A.D. 313
Constantine issues the Edict of Milan.

A.D. 410
The Visigoths overrun Italy.

700 B.C.   500 B.C.   300 B.C.   100 B.C.   A.D. 100   A.D. 300   A.D. 500

218 B.C.
Hannibal invades Italy during the Second Punic War.

27 B.C.
Augustus founds the Roman empire.

A.D. 476
Odoacer ousts the last Roman emperor.

 INQUIRY

The Collapse of Empires

What causes empires to collapse? In this Quest, you will research and create a presentation about the rise and collapse of the Roman empire, the Han dynasty, or the Inca empire. Then you will determine whether there are common factors that led to the collapse of these empires.

STEP 1
With your team, conduct research on the rise and collapse of your assigned empire. Take care to use only reliable sources.

STEP 2
As a group, synthesize your research. Then brainstorm ideas on how to present your information and create an outline for your presentation.

STEP 3
Use your outline to write the presentation and any elements, such as timelines and maps, that it will include. Then write a conclusion stating what you have learned about your assigned empire.

STEP 4
Give your presentation to your audience. Then compare your conclusion with conclusions of the other teams. Explore how the rise and fall of these empires is relevant to government today.

GO ONLINE to access complete Quest materials

6.1

The Romans learned Etruscan engineering techniques, including how to build the arch, a foundation of structural design.

 BOUNCE to Activate Flipped Video

Objectives

Describe the development of the classical civilization of Rome.

Outline how the Roman republic was structured and governed.

Understand the rights and religious practices that characterized Roman society.

Explain how the Roman republic grew and used its political influence.

Key Terms

Etruscans
republic
patrician
plebeian
consul
dictator
tribune
veto
legion

The Roman Republic

Rome rose from a small city-state on the Italian peninsula to become the dominant power in the Mediterranean world. Romans ruled over a vast, ethnically diverse empire. Rome's 1000-year history had many lasting effects, including the spread of important aspects of the civilizations of Greece, Egypt, and the Fertile Crescent into Europe.

The Rise of the Roman Civilization

Italy is a peninsula that looks like a boot jutting into the Mediterranean Sea and kicking the island of Sicily toward Africa. The city of Rome sits toward the center of Italy. This location would benefit the Romans as they expanded—first within Italy and then into the lands bordering the Mediterranean.

The Italian Peninsula Because of its geography, Italy proved much easier to unify than Greece. Unlike Greece, Italy is not broken up into small, isolated valleys. In addition, the Apennine Mountains, which run down the length of the Italian peninsula, are less rugged than the mountains of Greece. Finally, Italy has broad, fertile plains in the north and the west. These plains supported the growing population.

Early Settlements in Italy By about 800 B.C., the ancestors of the Romans, called the Latins, had migrated into Italy. The Latins settled along the Tiber River in small villages scattered over seven low-lying hills. There, they herded and farmed. Their villages would in time grow together into Rome, the city on seven hills.

GO ONLINE to access your digital course

Legend held that twin brothers, Romulus and Remus, had founded the city. Romans regarded this tale highly because the twins were said to be sons of a Latin woman and the war god Mars, lending Rome a divine origin.

The Romans shared the Italian peninsula with other peoples. Among them were Greek colonists whose city-states dotted southern Italy and the **Etruscans** (ih TRUHS kuhnz), who lived mostly north of Rome. The origins of the Etruscan civilization are uncertain. One theory says they migrated from Asia Minor, while another suggests they came from the Alps. What is certain is that, for a time, the Etruscans ruled much of central Italy, including Rome.

The Romans learned much from Etruscan civilization. They adapted the alphabet that the Etruscans had earlier acquired from the Greeks. The Romans also learned from the Etruscans to use the arch in construction, and they adapted Etruscan engineering techniques to drain the marshy lands along the Tiber.

Many of the early Roman religious beliefs came from the Etruscans. Over time, the Romans adopted some Etruscan gods and goddesses who became merged with Roman deities. For example, the Roman god Jupiter and the Etruscan god Tinia are similar. The Romans also borrowed some of their ideas concerning how temples should be designed from the Etruscans.

☑ **IDENTIFY MAIN IDEAS** How did geography influence the origins and expansion of Rome?

The Early Roman Republic

In 509 B.C., the Romans drove out their Etruscan king. This date is traditionally considered to mark the founding of the Roman state. Determined never again to be ruled by a monarch, the Romans set up a new government in which officials were chosen by male citizens. They called it *res publica*, or "that which belongs to the people." This form of government, in which people choose their officials, is today called a **republic.** In a republic, Romans thought, no single individual would be able to gain too much power.

Structure of Roman Society Early Roman society consisted of three main groups. **Patricians,** or members of the landholding upper class, made up the first group. Only patricians were eligible to hold office in Rome's early government.

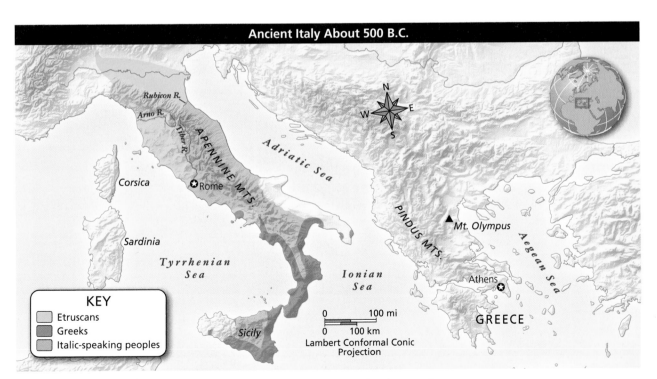

>> **Analyze Maps** Various ancient civilizations lived on the Italian peninsula around 500 B.C. What was one of Rome's geographical advantages?

Plebeians (plih BEE uhnz) belonged to the next group of Roman society. They were the farmers, merchants, and artisans who made up most of the population. Plebeians held less wealth than patricians. Although they were citizens of Rome, they were ineligible to hold political office.

Enslaved people made up the third group of Roman society. Slaves were captured as prisoners of war or were born into enslavement. People also could become enslaved for failing to repay their debts. Slaves held no political power in ancient Rome.

Structure of Rome's Republic In the early republic, the most powerful government body was the senate. It made the laws and controlled the government. At first, its 300 members were all patricians.

Each year, the senators nominated two **consuls** from the patrician class. Their job was to supervise the business of government and command the armies. Consuls, however, could serve only one term and were expected to approve each other's decisions.

They were also expected to consult with the senate. By limiting their time in office and making them responsible to each other, Rome had a system of checks on the power of government.

In a serious military emergency, the senate might choose a **dictator,** a ruler who has complete control over a government. A Roman dictator was granted power to rule for six months. After that time, he had to give up power. One famous dictator was Cincinnatus (SIHN suh NA tuhs). Within fifteen days he left his farm, organized an army, led it to victory, and went back to work in his fields.

Plebeians Demand Equality At first, all government officials were patricians. Plebeians were citizens but had little influence. Plebeian demands for power shaped politics in the early republic.

The plebeians' first breakthrough came in 450 B.C., when the government had the laws of Rome inscribed on 12 tablets, which were set up in the Forum, Rome's marketplace. For the first time, the Laws of the Twelve Tables made it possible for plebeians to appeal a judgment handed down by a patrician judge.

In time, the plebeians gained the right to elect their own officials, called **tribunes,** to protect their interests. The tribunes could **veto,** or block, laws that they felt were harmful to plebeians. Little by little, plebeians forced the senate to choose plebeians as consuls, appoint them to high offices, and finally to admit them to the senate. These changes made Rome's government more representative.

A Lasting Legacy Although the senate still dominated the government, the common people had gained access to power and won safeguards for their rights without having to resort to war or revolution.

LAWS OF THE TWELVE TABLES			
TABLE I	Procedure: for courts and trials	**TABLE VII**	Land rights
TABLE II	Trial continuance and evidence	**TABLE VIII**	Torts and delicts (Laws of injury)
TABLE III	Debt	**TABLE IX**	Public law
TABLE IV	Rights of fathers (paterfamilias) over the family; infanticide	**TABLE X**	Sacred law
TABLE V	Legal guardianship and inheritance laws	**TABLE XI**	Marriage between a patrician and a plebeian forbidden
TABLE VI	Acquisition and possession; marriage	**TABLE XII**	Binding law: power of the people

>> **Analyze Charts** Posting the Laws of the Twelve Tables in the Forum made Rome's laws accessible to all of its citizens. Which of the Twelve Tables laws dealt with family law?

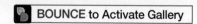 BOUNCE to Activate Gallery

More than 2,000 years later, the framers of the United States Constitution would adapt such Roman ideas as the senate, the veto, and a system of checks and balances on political power.

☑ **DESCRIBE** Describe the basic social structure of ancient Rome.

Roman Society

The family was the basic unit of Roman society. Under Roman law, the male head of the household—usually the father—had absolute power in the family. He enforced strict discipline and demanded total respect for his authority. His wife was subject to his authority and was not allowed to administer her own affairs. The ideal Roman woman was loving, dutiful, dignified, and strong.

The Role of Women During the early Roman Republic, women had few rights. Later, they gained more freedom, and played a larger role in society than did Greek women. They could own property, and, in later Roman times, women from all classes ran a variety of businesses, from small shops to major shipyards. Aristocratic women earned respect by supporting the arts or paying for public festivals. However, most women worked at home, raising their families, spinning, and weaving.

Over the centuries, Roman women gained even greater freedom and influence. Patrician women went to the public baths, dined out, and attended the theater or other forms of public entertainment with their husbands. Some women, such as Livia (LIHV ee uh) and Aggripina the Younger (ag ruh PY nuh), had highly visible public roles and exercised significant political influence.

Roman Education Girls and boys from the upper and lower classes learned to read and write. By the later years of the republic, many wealthy Romans hired private tutors, often Greeks, to educate their children. Children memorized major events in Roman history. Boys who wanted to pursue political careers studied rhetoric.

Roman Mythology and Religion The Romans believed in many gods and goddesses, who resembled those of the Etruscans and Greeks. Like the Greek god, Zeus, the Roman god Jupiter ruled over the sky and the other gods. According to Roman myths, his wife Juno, like the Greek goddess Hera, protected marriage. Romans also prayed to Neptune, god of the sea, whose powers were the same as

>> In battle, Rome's legions of citizen-soldiers were fierce, well-armed, and disciplined. The spoils of war was payment for their services.

those of the Greek god Poseidon. On the battlefield, they turned to Mars, the god of war.

The Roman calendar was full of feasts and other celebrations to honor the gods and goddesses and to ensure divine favor for the city. As loyal citizens, most Romans joined in these festivals, which inspired a sense of community. Throughout Rome, dozens of temples housed statues of the gods. In front of these temples, Romans took part in ritual activities such as worshipping the gods and asking for divine assistance.

☑ **IDENTIFY** What social rights did women have in the republic?

The Roman Republic Expands

The Roman Republic lasted almost 500 years, During that time, its armies expanded Roman power across Italy. First, they conquered their neighbors in central Italy, including the Etruscans. Then they overpowered the Greek city-states in the south. By about 270 B.C., Rome controlled most of the Italian peninsula.

Citizen-Soldiers Rome's success was due to skillful diplomacy and to its loyal, well-trained army. The basic military unit was the **legion,** each of which included about 5,000 men. As in Greece, Roman armies consisted of citizen-soldiers who supplied their own weapons and fought without pay. Eventually, they received a small stipend, or payment, but their main compensation was always a share of the spoils of victory. Well-trained in military skills and raised to value loyalty and courage, Roman soldiers chalked up a series of brilliant victories.

To ensure success, Roman commanders mixed rewards with harsh punishment. Young soldiers who showed courage in action won praise and gifts. If a unit fled from battle, however, one out of every ten men from the disgraced unit was put to death.

Rome's Treatment of Conquered People Rome's armies could be ruthless, killing or enslaving those who resisted. However, if surrender was negotiated, terms could be more favorable. Conquered peoples had to acknowledge Roman leadership, pay taxes, and supply soldiers for the Roman army. In return, Rome let them keep their own customs, money, and local government. Once its rule was established, Rome generally treated its conquered peoples with justice, provided they did not rebel.

To a few privileged groups among the conquered people, Rome gave the highly prized right of full citizenship. Others became partial citizens, who were allowed to marry Romans and carry on trade in Rome. As a result of such generous policies, most conquered lands remained loyal to Rome even in troubled times.

Building Unity To protect its conquests, Rome posted soldiers throughout the land. It also built a network of all-weather military roads to link distant territories to Rome. As trade and travel increased, local peoples incorporated Latin into their languages and adopted many Roman customs and beliefs. Slowly, Italy began to unite under Roman rule.

☑ **DESCRIBE** What rights and responsibilities did Rome extend to conquered peoples?

☑ ASSESSMENT

1. **Describe** What were some of the major geographic features of the Italian peninsula, where Roman civilizations would eventually appear?

2. **Identify** How did the classical civilization of Rome develop? Describe some aspects of its culture.

3. **Explain** How did the republic's structure of government change and develop over time?

4. **Interpret** What was Cincinnatus's contribution to Roman history? How does he reflect some of the ideals of Roman civilization?

5. **Paraphrase** What attributes of Rome's citizen-soldiers made them so important to the republic's growth?

6. **Quest Connections** How might Rome's treatment of conquered peoples have contributed to its decline?

Roman Women Protest: Livy

Women had few rights in the Roman republic. Yet in 195 B.C., Roman women gathered in public in great numbers to protest the Oppian Law. The law had been passed after a major Roman defeat in 216 B.C. Widows and orphan daughters inherited wealth from their husbands and fathers. To pay for wars, the Roman government passed the Oppian Law which required the women to deposit their fortunes with the state and restricted them from displays of wealth in and around Rome.

After Rome won the Second Punic War, the law was lifted for women who lived outside of Rome. But Roman women were still under the law. As the tribunal debated the repealing law, Roman women flooded the streets staging a rare public protest demanding the repeal of the law. In the following primary sources, the Roman historian Livy describes the protest and a subsequent debate about it in the tribunal between Cato and Lucius Valerius.

>> A woman from Pompeii, a part of the Roman empire.

Primary Source 1

Livy's account of the women protesting

The matrons [married women] whom neither counsel [advice] nor shame nor their husbands' orders could keep at home, blockaded every street in the city and every entrance to the Forum. As the men came down to the Forum, the matrons besought [begged] them to let them, too, have back the luxuries they had enjoyed before, giving as their reason that the republic was thriving and that everyone's private wealth was increasing with every day. This crowd of women was growing daily, for now they were even gathering from the towns and villages. Before long they dared go up and solicit [speak to] consuls, praetors [type of representative], and other magistrates.

☑ **ANALYZE WORD CHOICES** Why do you think Livy used the words "shame" and "dared" in his description of the women?

When the speeches for and against the law had been made, a considerably larger crowd of women poured forth in public the next day; as a single body they besieged the doors of the tribunes, who were vetoing their colleagues' motion, and they did not stop until the tribunes took back their veto. After that there was no doubt that all the tribes would repeal the law.

☑ **IDENTIFY CAUSE AND EFFECT** What cause brought women into the streets? What effect did the women have on the tribunes' vote on the Oppian Law?

Primary Source 2

Livy's account of the debate in the tribunal

Cato: If each man of us, fellow citizens, had established that the rights and authority of the husband should be held over the mother of his own family, we should have less difficulty with women in general; now, at home our freedom is conquered by female fury, here in the Forum it is bruised and trampled upon, and because we have not contained the individuals, we fear the lot. . . . .

Our ancestors did not want women to conduct any - not even private - business without a guardian; they wanted them to be under the authority of parents, brothers, or husbands; we. . . even now let them snatch at the government and meddle in the Forum and our assemblies. What are they doing now on the streets and crossroads, if they are not persuading the tribunes to vote for repeal? . . .

☑ **IDENTIFY AUTHOR'S POINT OF VIEW** What is Cato's opinion of the women protesting?

If they are victorious now, what will they not attempt? As soon as they begin to be your equals, they will have become your superiors. . . What honest excuse is offered, pray, for this womanish rebellion? . . .

I vote that the Oppian Law should not, in the smallest measure, be repealed.

☑ **DESCRIBE** What warning does Cato give the members of the tribunal?

Lucius Valerius: I shall defend the motion, not ourselves, against whom the consul has hurled this charge. He has called this assemblage 'succession' and sometimes 'womanish rebellion,' because the matrons have publicly asked you, in peacetime when the state is happy and prosperous, to repeal a law passed against them during the straits of war. Not too far back in history, in the most recent war, when we needed funds, did not the widows' money assist the treasury? . . .

☑ **IDENTIFY AUTHOR'S POINT OF VIEW** What is Lucius Valerius's opinion of the women protesting?

Since our matrons lived for so long by the highest standards of behavior without any law, what risk is there that, once it is repealed, they will yield to luxury? . . .

All are unhappy and indignant when they see the finery denied them permitted to the wives of the Latin allies, when they see them adorned with gold and purple, when those other women ride through the city and they follow on foot, as though the power belonged to the other women's cities, not to their own. . . .

Of course, if you repeal the Oppian Law, you will not have the power to prohibit that which the law now forbids; . . . daughters, wives, even some men's sisters will be less under your authority . . . The more power you possess, all the more moderately should you exercise your authority.

☑ **CITE EVIDENCE** For what reasons does Lucius Valerius believe in the repeal of the Oppian Law?

☑ ASSESSMENT

1. **Compare and Contrast** How do the points of view of Cato and Lucius Valerius differ? How are their points of view similar?

2. **Analyze Information** Do you think that the historian Livy was objective in his account of the women's protest? Why or why not?

3. **Analyze Interactions** If the protestors had been men, how might the debate be different? Would there have been a debate?

4. **Determine Meaning** What do you think Lucius Valerius meant when he said, "The more power you possess, all the more moderately should you exercise your authority."?

GO ONLINE to access primary sources

6.2

Praetorian Guards were skilled and loyal bodyguards who protected generals during the time of the late republic. Later, they became an elite guard for Roman emperors.

The Roman Empire: Rise and Decline

After conquering the Italian peninsula, Rome began to build an empire around the Mediterranean Sea. This expansion brought great riches but created conflicts that divided Roman society and weakened and finally crushed the republic. Out of the rubble, however, rose the Roman empire and a new chapter in Rome's long history.

Empire Building Through Conquest

Rome's conquest of the Italian peninsula brought it into contact with Carthage, a city-state on the coast of North Africa. Settled by Phoenician traders and people from North Africa, Carthage ruled over a vast trading empire that stretched across North Africa and the western Mediterranean, including parts of Spain. As Rome spread into the Mediterranean, conflict between these two powers became inevitable.

The Punic Wars Between 264 B.C. and 146 B.C., Rome fought three wars against Carthage. They are called the Punic Wars, from *Punicus*, the Latin word for Phoenician. In the First Punic War, Rome defeated Carthage and won the islands of Sicily, Corsica, and Sardinia.

The Carthaginians sought revenge in the Second Punic War. In 218 B.C., the Carthaginian general Hannibal (HA nuh buhl) led his army, including dozens of war elephants, on an epic march across the Pyrenees, through France, and over the Alps into Italy. The trek cost Hannibal one-third of his army. But Hannibal still managed to surprise the Romans, who had expected an invasion

---

BOUNCE to Activate Flipped Video

Objectives

Identify the events leading to the decline of the Roman republic.

Summarize the fundamental ideas and institutions of Western civilizations that originated in Rome.

Explain how and why the Roman empire divided.

Identify the factors that led to the decline and fall of Rome.

Key Terms

imperialism
latifundia
Tiberius Gracchus
Gaius Gracchus
Julius Caesar
Augustus
census
Hadrian
Diocletian
inflation
Constantine
Constantinople
Huns
mercenaries

GO ONLINE to access your digital course

from the south. For 15 years, Hannibal and his army moved across Italy, winning battle after battle.

However, the Carthaginians failed to capture Rome itself. In the end, the Romans outflanked Hannibal by sending an army to attack Carthage. Hannibal returned to defend his homeland, where the Romans defeated him at last. Under the peace terms ending the war, Carthage had to give up all its lands outside of Africa and pay a huge tribute, or tax, to Rome. Victory gave Rome mastery of the Mediterranean.

Carthage Is Destroyed Despite Hannibal's defeat, many Romans still feared their old rival. They wanted revenge for the terrible destruction that Hannibal's army had brought to Italy. For years, the Roman senator Cato ended his every speech declaring, "Carthage must be destroyed."

Finally, in the Third Punic War, Rome completely destroyed the 700-year-old city of Carthage. Survivors were killed or sold into slavery. Carthage and the region surrounding it became the new Roman province of Africa. For the Romans, "Africa" meant this area and not the whole continent.

Ruler of the Mediterranean World "The Carthaginians fought for their own preservation and the sovereignty of Africa," observed a Greek witness

to the fall of Carthage; "the Romans, for supremacy and world domination." Like other ancient powers, the Romans followed a policy of **imperialism,** or establishing control over foreign lands and peoples. While Rome fought Carthage in the west, it was also expanding into the eastern Mediterranean. There, Romans confronted the Hellenistic rulers who had divided up the empire of Alexander the Great.

Sometimes to defend Roman interests, sometimes simply for plunder, Rome launched a series of wars in the area. One by one, Macedonia, Greece, and parts of Asia Minor surrendered and became Roman provinces. Other regions, such as Egypt, allied with Rome. By 133 B.C., Roman power extended from Spain to Egypt. Truly, the Romans were justified in calling the Mediterranean *Mare Nostrum*, or "Our Sea."

Conquests Impact Rome Conquests and greatly expanded trade brought incredible riches into Rome. Generals, officials, and traders amassed fortunes from loot, taxes, and commerce. A new class of wealthy Romans emerged. They built lavish mansions and filled them with luxuries imported from the east. Wealthy families bought up huge farming estates, called **latifundia** (LA tuh FUHN dee uh).

With every new conquest, Rome acquired more enslaved people. Some were well-educated Greeks or other highly skilled people. Romans brought enslaved Greeks into their homes as teachers for their children. Unskilled slaves, however, faced brutally harsh lives.

The growth of slavery greatly changed Rome. The widespread use of enslaved labor hurt small farmers, who were unable to produce food as cheaply as the latifundia could. The farmers' problems grew when huge quantities of grain pouring in from the conquered lands drove down grain prices. Many farmers fell into debt and had to sell their land.

In despair, landless farmers flocked to Rome and other cities looking for jobs. There, they joined an already restless class of unemployed people. As the gap between rich and poor widened, angry mobs began to riot. In addition, the new wealth led to increased corruption.

Attempts at Reform Bring Violence Two young plebeians, brothers named **Tiberius** (ty BIHR ee uhs) and **Gaius Gracchus** (GAY us GRAK us), were among the first to attempt reform. Tiberius, elected a tribune in 133 B.C., called on the state to distribute land to poor farmers. Gaius, elected a tribune ten years later, sought a wider range of reforms, including the

>> In the second Punic War, Hannibal's army used elephants to battle the Romans.

use of public funds to buy grain to feed the poor. The reforms of the Gracchus brothers angered the senate, which saw them as a threat to its power. The brothers and thousands of their followers were killed in waves of street violence set off by senators and their hired thugs.

☑ **IDENTIFY** What economic challenges did Rome face while building an empire around the Mediterranean Sea?

The Roman Republic Declines

A century of turmoil and civil wars engulfed Rome after the murders of the Gracchus brothers, whose attempts to bring reforms had failed. At issue was who should hold power—the senate, which wanted to govern as it had in the past, or popular political leaders, who wanted to weaken the senate and enact reforms.

The turmoil sparked uprisings of enslaved people at home and revolts among Rome's allies. Meanwhile, the old legions of Roman citizen-soldiers became professional armies whose first loyalty was to their commanders. Once rival commanders had their own armies, they could march into Rome to advance their ambitions. Power struggles among ambitious generals would help weaken the republic and lead to its overthrow.

Caesar's Bid for Power Out of this chaos emerged **Julius Caesar,** an ambitious military commander. For a time, Caesar and another brilliant general, Pompey, dominated Roman politics.

Caesar and Pompey joined with Marcus Licinius Crassus, one of Rome's wealthiest citizens, to form the First Triumvirate. Caesar used this unofficial alliance to win a consulship in 59 B.C. The First Triumvirate influenced Roman politics until Crassus's death in 53 B.C. Soon after, Caesar and Pompey became political rivals.

In 58 B.C., Caesar set out with his army to make new conquests. After nine years of fighting, he completed the conquest of Gaul—the area that is now France and Belgium. Jealous and fearful of Caesar's success, Pompey persuaded the senate to order Caesar to disband his army and return to Rome. Caesar defied the order. Acting swiftly and secretly, he led his army across the Rubicon River into northern Italy and headed toward Rome. Once again, Rome was plunged into civil war.

>> The brothers Tiberius and Gaius Gracchus tried to reform Rome's government.

>> Caesar dictated his commentaries on war to scribes who recorded his words.

Caesar crushed Pompey and his supporters. He then swept around the Mediterranean, suppressing rebellions. "Veni, vidi, vici"—"I came, I saw, I conquered"—he announced after one victory. Later, returning to Rome, he forced the senate to make him dictator. Although he maintained the senate and other features of the republic, he was in fact the absolute ruler of Rome.

Caesar's Reforms Between 48 B.C. and 44 B.C., Caesar pushed through a number of reforms intended to deal with Rome's many problems. He launched a program of public works to employ the jobless and gave public land to the poor. He also reorganized the government of the provinces and granted Roman citizenship to more people.

Caesar's most lasting reform was the introduction of a new calendar based on that of the Egyptians. The Roman calendar, later named the Julian calendar, was used in Western Europe for more than 1,600 years. With minor changes, it is still our calendar today.

The Death of Caesar Caesar's enemies worried that he planned to make himself king of Rome. To save the republic, they plotted against him. In March of 44 B.C., as Caesar arrived in the senate, his enemies stabbed him to death.

The death of Julius Caesar plunged Rome into a new round of civil wars. Mark Antony, Caesar's chief general, and Octavian (ahk TAH vee uhn), Caesar's grandnephew, joined forces to hunt down the murderers. The two men soon quarreled, setting off another bitter struggle for power. In 31 B.C., Octavian finally defeated Antony and his powerful ally, Queen Cleopatra of Egypt.

☑ **DRAW CONCLUSIONS** How did the military structure of the late Roman republic contribute to the rise of Julius Caesar?

The Roman Empire

The senate gave the triumphant Octavian the title of **Augustus** (aw GUHS tuhs), or Exalted One, and declared him princeps, or first citizen. Although he was careful not to call himself king, a title that Romans had hated since Etruscan times, Augustus exercised absolute power and named his successor, just as a king would do.

Under Augustus, who ruled until A.D. 14, the 500-year-old republic came to an end. Romans did not know it at the time, but a new age had dawned—the age of the Roman empire. Augustus was its first emperor.

Augustus Reforms Government Through firm but moderate policies, Augustus laid the foundation for a stable government, helping Rome to recover from its endless civil wars. He left the senate in place and created an efficient, well-trained civil

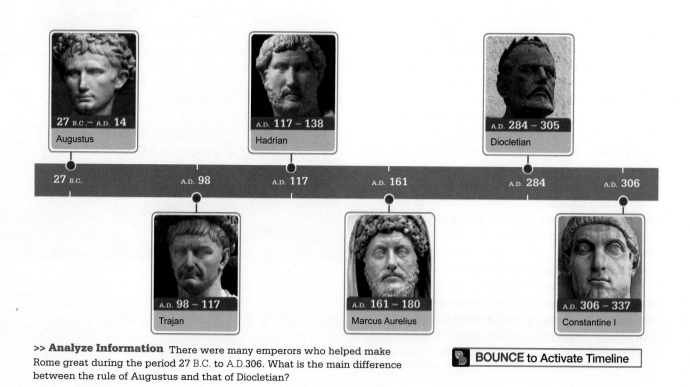

>> **Analyze Information** There were many emperors who helped make Rome great during the period 27 B.C. to A.D.306. What is the main difference between the rule of Augustus and that of Diocletian?

🅑 BOUNCE to Activate Timeline

Comparing Structures of Government

ROMAN REPUBLIC		ROMAN EMPIRE
HIGHEST OFFICIALS		**HIGHEST OFFICIALS**
Two Consuls • annually elected • held equal power	**Dictator** • appointed in times of emergency • held office for 6 months only	**Emperor** • inherited power • served for life • if served well, was worshipped as a god after death
GOVERNING BODIES		**GOVERNING BODIES**
Senate • issued advisory decrees to magistrates and people • in practice, held enormous power • had about 300 members	**Popular Assemblies** • two assemblies: centuriate (miltary), tribal (nonmilitary) • elected magistrates, held legislative power, made key decisions	**Senate** • issued binding decrees, acted as a high court, elected magistrates • in practice, held little power as compared to the emperor • had about 600 members

>> **Analyze Charts** There were significant differences between the governments of the Roman republic and the Roman empire. For a plebeian, which of the two structures of government would be preferable?

service to enforce the laws. High-level jobs were open to men of talent, regardless of their class. In addition, he cemented the allegiance of cities and provinces to Rome by allowing them a large amount of self-government.

Augustus also undertook economic reforms. To make the tax system more fair, he ordered a **census,** or population count, of the empire so there would be records of all who should be taxed. He set up a postal service and issued new coins to make trade easier. He put the jobless to work building roads and temples and sent others to farm the land.

During the Roman republic, Rome's territorial claims were rather vague. Augustus sought to define these claims and expand the empire. To do this, he planned to extend Rome's territorial borders to natural boundaries, such as rivers, deserts, and ocean shores, that were easier to defend. Under Augustus, Rome conquered Egypt to the southeast, northern Spain to the west, and parts of central Europe to the north. Roman soldiers also invaded Germany.

The government that Augustus organized functioned well for 200 years. Still, a serious problem kept arising: Who would rule after an emperor died? Romans did not accept the idea of power passing automatically from father to son. As a result, the death of an emperor often led to intrigue and violence.

Emperors after Augustus Not all Augustus' successors were great rulers. Some were weak and incompetent. Two early emperors, Caligula (kuh LIH gyuh luh) and Nero, were considered evil and perhaps insane. Caligula, for example, appointed his favorite horse as consul. Nero viciously persecuted Christians and was even blamed for setting a great fire that destroyed much of Rome.

Between A.D. 96 and A.D. 180, the empire benefited from the rule of a series of "good emperors." **Hadrian** (HAY dree uhn), for example, codified Roman law, making it the same for all provinces. He also had soldiers build a wall across Britain to hold back attackers from the non-Roman north.

Marcus Aurelius (MAHR kuhs uh REE le uhs), who read philosophy while on military campaigns, was close to being Plato's ideal of a philosopher king. His *Meditations* show his commitment to duty: "Hour by hour resolve firmly . . . to do what comes to hand with correct and natural dignity."

The Pax Romana The 200-year span that began with Augustus and ended with Marcus Aurelius is known as the period of the *Pax Romana*, or "Roman Peace." During that time, Roman rule brought peace, order, unity, and prosperity to lands stretching from the Euphrates River in the east to Britain in the west, an area roughly equal in size to the continental United States.

During the Pax Romana, Roman legions maintained and protected the roads, and Roman fleets chased pirates from the seas. Trade flowed freely to and from distant lands. Egyptian farmers supplied Romans with grain. From other parts of Africa came ivory and gold, as well as lions and other wild animals used for public entertainment. From India came spices, cotton, and precious stones. Trade caravans traveled along the great Silk Road, bringing silk and other goods from China. People, too, moved easily within the Roman empire, spreading ideas and knowledge, especially the advances of the Hellenistic east.

Bread and Circuses Throughout the empire, rich and poor alike loved spectacular forms of entertainment. At the Circus Maximus, Rome's largest racecourse, chariots thundered around an oval course, making dangerously tight turns at either end. Fans bet feverishly on their favorite teams—the Reds, Greens, Blues, or Whites—and successful charioteers were hailed as heroes.

Gladiator contests were even more popular. Many gladiators were enslaved people who had been trained to fight. In the arena, they battled one another, either singly or in groups. Crowds cheered a skilled gladiator, and a good fighter might even win his freedom. But if a gladiator made a poor showing, sometimes the crowd turned thumbs down, a signal that he should be killed.

Staging games was part of an emperor's job, as was making sure the city of Rome had enough to eat. But some ancient writers criticized both the lavish games put on to entertain the Roman people and the free grain supplied to the city. Famously, the writer Juvenal complained that in olden days Roman citizens used to run their own government, but in his day they only wanted "bread and circuses," meaning free food and public entertainment.

☑ **EXPLAIN** How did Augustus lay the foundation for stable government in the Roman empire?

The Roman Empire Splits

After ruling the Mediterranean for hundreds of years, the Roman empire faced threats from inside and outside. Political and economic problems, along with foreign invasions, shook the empire. In fact, these problems had existed since the late republic. Roman greatness did not end overnight. As decay set in, some emperors tried to halt the decline. But no ruler was able to reverse the long, slow collapse.

Political Violence Political turmoil rocked the Roman empire. The long Roman Peace ended when

THE ROMAN EMPIRE DECLINES

	CAUSE	EFFECT
POLITICAL TURBULENCE	Government oppression; corrupt officials	Government loses popular support
	Political violence leads to 26 emperors in 50 years	Empire becomes unstable
	Power shifts to eastern half of Roman empire	Roman empire is divided into eastern and western halves
ECONOMIC TURBULENCE	Over-cultivated farmland; slave labor	Abandonment of land, reduced agricultural productivity; unemployment
	High taxes; epidemic diseases	Civil unrest; decline in population
SOCIAL TURBULENCE	Decline in patriotism, discipline and devotion to duty	Citizen-soldiers replaced with less loyal mercenaries; upper-class no longer provides leaders
	"Bread and circuses"	Self-reliance of masses is undermined
MILITARY ATTACKS	Invading Huns attack Germanic peoples on Rome's borders	Germanic peoples seek safety in Roman empire
	Weakened Roman legions cannot stop invaders	Roman empire surrenders territories to German invaders
	German invaders conquer Italy and attack Rome	German leader Odoacer ousts Roman emperor; Eastern Byzantine empire lasts for another 1,000 years

>> **Analyze Information** There were many factors that led to the decline of the Roman empire. What were some of the effects of over-cultivated farmland and slave labor?

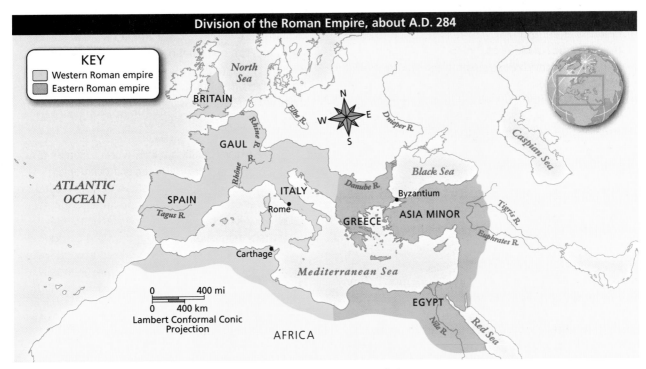

KEY
- Western Roman empire
- Eastern Roman empire

>> **Analyze Maps** Diocletian divided the empire into eastern and western halves to make governing more manageable. Why might the eastern Roman empire be considered more desirable?

power struggles led to a new pattern in politics. Violence replaced the orderly succession to power. One after another, ambitious generals seized power with the support of their legions. The successful general ruled for a few months or years and then was overthrown or assassinated by a rival, who then made himself emperor. In one 50-year period, at least 26 emperors reigned. Political violence and instability had become the rule.

Economic and Social Issues At the same time, the empire was shaken by disturbing economic and social trends. High taxes to support the army and the bureaucracy placed heavy burdens on business people and small farmers. Some farmlands had been over-cultivated and lost their productivity.

As a result, many poor farmers left their land and sought protection from wealthy landowners. Living on large estates, they worked for the landowners and farmed small plots for themselves. Although technically free, they were not allowed to leave the land.

The Empire Is Divided In 284, the emperor **Diocletian** (DY uh KLEE shuhn) set out to restore order. To better handle the challenge of governing the huge empire, he divided it into two parts. He kept control of the wealthier eastern part for himself and appointed a co-emperor, Maximian (mak SIH mee uhn), to rule the weaker western provinces.

Diocletian also took steps to end the empire's economic decay. To slow **inflation,** or the rapid rise of prices, he fixed the prices of many goods and services. Other laws forced farmers to remain on the land. In cities, sons were required to follow their fathers' occupations. These rules were meant to ensure steady production of food and other goods.

Constantinople Becomes the Center of Power In A.D 312, the talented general **Constantine** gained the throne. As emperor, Constantine continued Diocletian's reforms. More important, he took two steps that changed the course of European history. First, he granted toleration to Christians. Second, he set up a new capital at the centuries-old city of Byzantium, located near the Black Sea in what is now Turkey. He renamed it **Constantinople** (KAHNSTAN tuhn OH puhl). With this "New Rome," he made the already wealthier and more populated eastern half of the empire the center of power.

Reforms Fail The reforms of Diocletian and Constantine had mixed results. They revived the economy, and by increasing the power of government, they helped hold the empire together for another century. Still, the reforms failed to stop the long-term decline. In the end, internal problems, along with attacks from the outside, brought the empire down.

☑ **ANALYZE** How did Rome's unstable government affect the economy?

Rome Faces Invasions

For centuries, Rome had faced attacks from the Germanic peoples who lived along its borders. When Rome was powerful, its legions on the frontiers held back the invaders. Some of the Germanic tribes along the borders of the empire had learned Roman ways and become allies.

Migrating Nomads Attack As early as A.D 200, wars in East Asia set off a chain of events that would eventually overwhelm Rome, thousands of miles to the west. Those wars sent a nomadic people, the **Huns,** migrating from central Asia toward eastern Europe, which they reached by A.D 370. These skilled riders fought fierce battles to dislodge the Germanic peoples in their path. The Visigoths, Ostrogoths, and other Germanic peoples sought safety by crossing into Roman territory.

As the empire declined, Rome was hard pressed to halt the invaders. Slowly, Roman legions pulled back from the borderlands. Under pressure from attacks, Rome had to withdraw its legions, first from Britain, then from France and Spain. In time, invaders pushed into Italy and threatened Rome itself.

Rome Is Attacked In A.D 378, when a Roman army tried to turn back the Visigoths at Adrianople, it suffered a stunning defeat. Roman power was fading. New waves of invaders were soon hammering at Rome's borders, especially in the west. In A.D 410, the Visigoth general Alaric overran Italy and plundered Rome. Other invaders, the Vandals, took over Spain and North Africa before sacking Rome. Gradually, other Germanic peoples occupied large parts of the western Roman empire.

For Rome, the worst was yet to come. Starting in A.D 434, Hun leader Attila (uh TIHL luh) embarked on a savage campaign of conquest across much of Europe. Christians called Attila the "scourge of God" because they believed his attacks were a punishment for the sins of humankind. The Hun invasions sent still more Germanic peoples fleeing into the lands of the Roman empire.

Finally, in A.D 476, Odoacer (OH duh WAY suhr), a Germanic leader, ousted the emperor in Rome. Later,

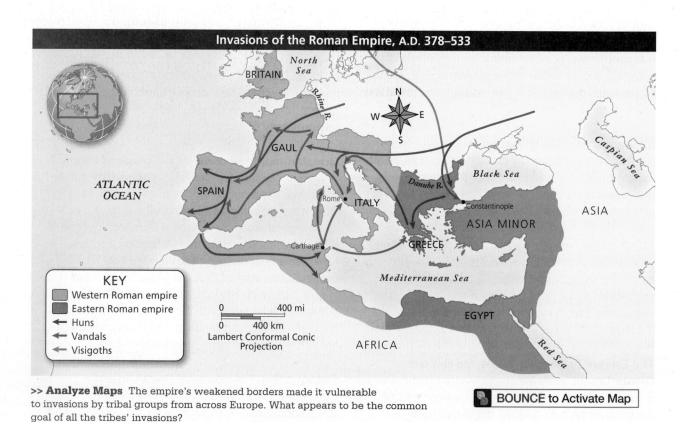

Invasions of the Roman Empire, A.D. 378–533

KEY
- ▨ Western Roman empire
- ▨ Eastern Roman empire
- ← Huns
- ← Vandals
- ← Visigoths

0 ____ 400 mi
0 ____ 400 km
Lambert Conformal Conic Projection

>> **Analyze Maps** The empire's weakened borders made it vulnerable to invasions by tribal groups from across Europe. What appears to be the common goal of all the tribes' invasions?

🅱 **BOUNCE to Activate Map**

historians referred to that event as the "fall" of Rome. By then, however, the Roman empire had already lost many of its territories, and Roman power in the west had ended. By contrast, the Roman empire in the east would continue to flourish for centuries to come.

☑ **IDENTIFY MAIN IDEAS** How did the Hun invasion weaken the Roman empire?

Why Did Rome Fall?

The "fall" of Rome is often seen as an important event in the history of Western civilization. Why did Rome "fall"? Modern historians identify a number of interrelated causes.

Military Causes Perhaps the most obvious cause of Rome's fall was the invasions. Still, these attacks were successful partly because Roman legions of the late empire lacked the discipline and training from which earlier Roman armies had benefited. To meet its need for soldiers, Rome hired **mercenaries,** or foreign soldiers serving for pay, to defend its borders. Many were Germanic warriors who, according to some historians, felt little loyalty to Rome.

Political Turmoil Political problems also contributed to Rome's decline. First, as the government became more oppressive and authoritarian, it lost the support of the people. Growing numbers of corrupt officials undermined loyalty, too. So did the frequent civil wars over succession. Rival armies battling to put their commanders on the throne weakened Roman power.

Perhaps most important, dividing the empire when it was under attack may have weakened it beyond repair. Faced with its own invasions, the richer and stronger eastern Roman empire did little to help the west.

Economic Causes Rome faced widespread economic problems, including an ever greater tax burden on its people. To support the huge government bureaucracy and military that ruled the empire, Rome imposed heavy taxes. As the wealth of the empire declined, over-taxed farmers abandoned their land and the middle class sank into poverty. At the same time, reliance on the labor of enslaved people discouraged Romans from exploring new technology. Rome, rich from its conquests, also lost a vital source of income as it lost territories. Finally, the population itself declined as war and epidemic diseases swept the empire.

>> Romans line up to pay their taxes. The government, desperate for funds to support its massive army, imposed oppressive taxes on Rome's citizens.

>> Wealthy Romans depended on enslaved people to support their lavish lifestyle, as shown in this modern illustration.

Social Causes For centuries, worried Romans pointed to the decline in values such as patriotism, discipline, and devotion to duty on which the empire was built. The upper class, which had once provided leaders, devoted itself to luxury and prestige. Besides being costly, providing "bread and circuses" may have undermined the self-reliance of the masses.

Did Rome Fall? Although we talk of the "fall" of Rome, the Roman empire did not disappear from the map in A.D 476. An emperor still ruled the eastern Roman empire, which later became known as the Byzantine Empire and lasted for another 1,000 years.

The phrase "the fall of Rome" is, in fact, shorthand for a long, slow change from one way of life to another. In Italy, people continued to live much as they had before, though under new rulers. Many still spoke Latin and obeyed Roman laws.

Over the next centuries, however, Germanic customs and languages replaced much of Roman culture. Old Roman cities crumbled, and Roman roads disappeared. Still, the Christian Church, which had become the official religion of Rome, preserved many elements of Roman civilization. Far from disappearing with the "fall" of Rome, Roman civilization and Christian traditions eventually gave rise to medieval civilization in Western Europe.

☑ **SUMMARIZE** What social problems contributed to the decline of the Roman empire?

☑ ASSESSMENT

1. **Identify Main Ideas** Why did Diocletian decide to split the empire?

2. **Identify Cause and Effect** What led to the Punic Wars, and how did they affect Rome?

3. **Draw Conclusions** What factors caused Rome to plunge into civil wars and how did they weaken the republic?

4. **Analyze Information** Why did a new class of wealthy Romans emerge after the conquests?

5. **Summarize** What political and social reforms did Caesar make to address the Roman republic's many problems?

6. **Connection to Today** Review the text under the heading "Bread and Circuses." How do American sports fans compare to Roman sports fans?

GO ONLINE to access these biographies: Julius Caesar, Constantine

This fresco of daily life from a villa near Pompeii shows the realism often depicted in Roman art.

The Legacy of Rome

Through war and conquest, Romans spread their Latin language and Roman civilization to distant lands. Yet the civilization that developed was not simply Roman. Rather, it blended Greek, Hellenistic, and Roman achievements.

Roman Literature, History, and Philosophy

Greco-Roman Civilization In its early days, Rome absorbed ideas from Greek colonists in southern Italy, and it continued to borrow heavily from Greek culture after it conquered Greece. To the Romans, Greek art, literature, philosophy, mathematical, and scientific genius represented the height of cultural achievement. Their admiration never wavered, leading the Roman poet Horace to note, "Greece has conquered her rude conqueror."

Over time, Romans adapted Greek and Hellenistic achievements, just as the Greeks had once absorbed ideas from Egypt and the Fertile Crescent. The blending of Greek, Hellenistic, and Roman traditions produced what is known as Greco-Roman civilization. During the Pax Romana, trade and travel helped spread this vital new civilization.

Roman Writers In literature, the Romans greatly admired, and owed a debt to the Greeks. Many Romans spoke Greek and imitated Greek styles in prose and poetry. Still, the greatest Roman writers used Latin to create their own literature.

In his epic poem the *Aeneid*, **Virgil** tried to show that Rome's past was as heroic as that of Greece. He linked his epic to Homer's work by telling how Aeneas escaped from Troy to found Rome.

BOUNCE to Activate Flipped Video

Objectives

Summarize the works of Roman literary figures, historians, and philosophers.

Describe the art and architecture developed by the Romans.

Understand how the Romans applied science and mathematics for practical use.

Explain how Rome's rule of law influenced modern legal systems.

Summarize the Roman ideas and institutions that have influenced Western civilization.

Key Terms

Virgil
satirize
mosaic
engineering
aqueduct
Ptolemy

GO ONLINE to access your digital course

>> The fight between Aeneas and King Turnus, from Virgil's epic poem, the *Aeneid*.

>> Livy's writings featured Roman heroes such as Horatius. Horatius defended Rome's Sublician bridge against the entire Etruscan army.

Virgil wrote the *Aeneid* soon after Augustus came to power. He hoped it would arouse patriotism and help unite Rome after years of civil wars.

Other poets used verse to **satirize,** or make fun of, Roman society. Horace's satires were gentle, using playful wit to attack human folly. Those of Juvenal and Martial were more biting. Martial's poems, for example, were so harsh that he had to use fictitious names to protect himself from retribution.

Roman Historians Roman historians pursued their own theme—the rise and fall of Roman power. Like the poet Virgil, the historian Livy sought to arouse patriotic feeling and restore traditional Roman virtues by recalling images of Rome's heroic past. In his history of Rome, Livy recounted tales of great heroes, such as Horatius and Cincinnatus. In this passage, Livy comments on the importance of studying history:

> . . . in history you have a record of the infinite variety of human experience plainly set out for all to see; and in that record you can find for yourself and your country both examples and warnings: fine things to take as models, base things, rotten through and through, to avoid.
>
> —Livy, *The History of Rome*

Another historian, Tacitus, wrote bitterly about Augustus and his successors, who, he felt, had destroyed Roman liberty. He admired the simple culture of the Germans who lived on Rome's northern frontier and would later invade the empire.

Roman Philosophers Romans borrowed much of their philosophy from the Greeks. The Hellenistic philosophy of Stoicism impressed Roman thinkers such as the emperor Marcus Aurelius. Stoics stressed the importance of duty and acceptance of one's fate. They also showed concern for the well-being of all people, an idea that would later be reflected in Christian teachings.

☑ **IDENTIFY MAIN IDEAS** How did Roman writers promote patriotism?

Roman Art, Architecture, and Drama

Rome left a vast legacy of art and architecture across its empire. To a large degree, Roman art and architecture were based on Greek and Etruscan models. However, as with their literature, Romans adapted these influences to develop their own style.

Roman Art Expresses Realism The Romans imported Greek statues to decorate their homes, gardens, and public monuments. Roman sculptors adapted the realistic style of Hellenistic works, showing subjects with warts or veins in place. The Romans also broke new ground, creating portraits in stone or on coins that revealed a person's character. A statue might capture an expression of smugness or haughty pride.

Some Roman sculpture was more idealistic, in the tradition of the classic Greek statues of gods and athletes. Sculptors transformed Augustus, who was neither handsome nor imposing, into a symbol of power and leadership.

Wealthy Romans displayed fine works of art, such as colorful frescoes, or murals, in their homes. They also hired artists to depict scenes from daily life or Roman myths in **mosaics,** or pictures made from chips of colored stone. Examples of Roman murals, mosaics, and other decorative items were preserved in Pompeii, a city buried by volcanic ash after Mount Vesuvius erupted in A.D. 79.

Roman Theater The Romans loved to attend theater. Some playwrights, like the Roman philosopher and dramatist Seneca, based their plays, such as *Hercules Furens*, on myths and legends. Roman audiences enjoyed comedies, including those by Plautus. His comedies were based on Roman life and featured songs and dances, along with slapstick and mistaken identity.

Roman Architecture From England to Spain, to North Africa and the Middle East, Roman buildings still stand today. Roman architecture combined both Greek and Roman elements. Roman builders used Greek columns, but where the Greeks aimed for simple elegance, the Romans emphasized grandeur. Immense palaces, temples, stadiums, and victory arches stood as monuments to Roman power.

The Romans improved on building devices such as columns and arches. They invented concrete, which was used as a building material, and developed the rounded dome to roof large spaces. The most famous domed structure is the Pantheon,

>> Attending the theater was a popular pastime in Rome. Here, actors don costumes and masks before a performance.

a temple that honored all the Roman gods. It still stands in Rome today.

Another famous Roman building, the Colosseum, was a public arena that stood 12 to 15 stories high (159 feet) and could hold as many as 50,000 spectators. A system of tunnels and stairs allowed crowds to exit the building quickly. Many of today's sports stadiums have similar features.

Roman advances in architecture, such as the use of concrete, arches, and domes, were passed to other cultures. First in Europe and later in North America, builders looked to Roman models. In Washington, D.C., public buildings such as the Jefferson Memorial and the Capitol use elements of Roman architecture.

☑ **CONTRAST** How did Roman architecture differ from Greek architecture?

Roman Achievements in Science and Engineering

The Romans generally left scientific research to the Greeks, who were citizens of the Roman empire. While Greek scientists and mathematicians sought to learn more about the world, the Romans put

>> The Pont du Gard in France was a Roman aqueduct built in 19 B.C. The three tiers of arches rise about 155 feet (47 m).

🅱 BOUNCE to Activate 3D Model

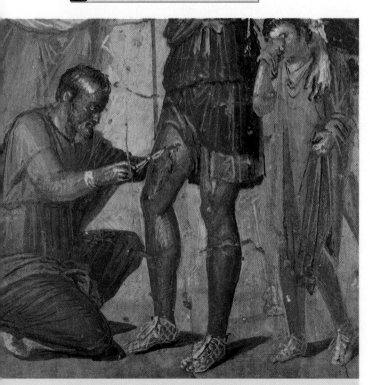

>> Romans valued medical knowledge. The army had medical officers, physicians provided healthcare for the poor, and hospitals were built.

🅱 BOUNCE to Activate Gallery

science to practical uses. They used Greek principles to construct roads and bridges and to make advances in medical care.

Science and Engineering The Romans excelled in **engineering,** or the application of science and mathematics to develop structures and machines. They perfected engineering skills as they built roads, bridges, and harbors across the empire. Roman roads were so solidly built that many remained in use long after Rome fell.

Roman engineers built immense **aqueducts,** or bridge-like stone structures that carried water from the hills into Roman cities. The availability of fresh water was important to the Romans. Wealthy homes piped in water. Almost every city had public baths for men and women. Here, people gathered not only to bathe, but to hear the latest news and exchange gossip.

New Ideas in Science In Roman times, Alexandria, Egypt, remained a center of learning, where Hellenistic scientists exchanged ideas freely. It was there that astronomer-mathematician **Ptolemy** proposed his theory that the Earth was the center of the universe, a mistaken idea that was accepted in the Western world for nearly 1,500 years.

The Greek doctor Galen advanced the frontiers of medical science by insisting on experiments to prove a conclusion. Galen compiled a medical encyclopedia summarizing what was known in the field at the time. It remained a standard text for more than 1,000 years.

While the Romans rarely did original scientific investigations, they did put science to practical use. They applied geography to make maps and medical knowledge to help doctors improve public health. Like Galen, they collected knowledge into encyclopedias.

Pliny the Elder, a Roman scientist, compiled volumes on geography, zoology, botany, and other topics, all based on other people's works. In his 37-volume *Natural History*, he explained that his goal was to "set forth in detail all the contents of the entire world." Even into the Middle Ages, copies of his work could be found in the larger libraries of Europe.

In A.D. 79, Pliny's eagerness for knowledge led to his death. He ventured too close to Mount Vesuvius as the volcano near Pompeii was erupting. He was smothered to death in hot ashes.

☑ **IDENTIFY MAIN IDEAS** How did Romans put science to practical use?

Roman Law Unites the Empire

"Let justice be done," proclaimed a Roman saying, "though the heavens fall!" Probably the greatest legacy of Rome was its commitment to the rule of law and to justice—ideas that later shaped Western civilization. Many centuries later, key principles of Roman law became the basis for legal systems throughout the world, including that of the United States.

Rome's System of Law Emerges During the republic, Rome developed a system of law, known as the civil law, that applied to its citizens. As Rome expanded, however, it ruled many foreigners who were not covered under the civil law. Gradually, a second system of law, known as the law of nations, emerged. It applied to all people under Roman rule, both citizens and non-citizens. Later, when Rome extended citizenship across the empire, the two systems merged.

Principles of Roman Law As Roman law developed, certain basic principles evolved. Many of these principles are familiar to Americans today. Among the most important was that an accused person is presumed innocent until proven guilty. A second principle ensured that the accused was allowed to face the accuser and mount a defense against the charge. A third idea was that guilt must be established "clearer than daylight," using solid evidence. Still another idea was that judges interpret the laws and make fair decisions.

Many other principles of Roman law were later adapted by the Western world. The idea of a trial by jury is sometimes traced to Roman law practices. Cases where the accused faced the death penalty might be tried in front of hundreds of people from the community.

Some Roman principles differed from today's laws. Penalties varied according to social class, and lower-class defendants could be treated more harshly. The idea of equality before the law for all would take centuries to be accepted.

☑ **SUMMARIZE** What basic principles of Roman law were a foundation for laws in the United States?

>> The tablets are inscribed with a Roman law that protects citizens from extortion.

🅑 BOUNCE to Activate Chart

☑ ASSESSMENT

1. **Identify Central Ideas** Identify examples of how literature reflects the history of Rome.

2. **Support Ideas with Examples** Describe the architectural elements developed or adapted by the Romans. Provide examples of their influence on Western architecture.

3. **Identify** What were the sources of Roman ideas in mathematics, science, and technology, and what was their enduring impact?

4. **Summarize** Explain the concept of "trial by jury" that is sometimes traced back to Rome.

5. **Connections to Today** Give two examples of American legal principles that had their foundation in Roman law.

Christians believe that the Church of the Holy Sepulchre in Jerusalem is the burial site of Jesus. They continue to make pilgrimages to the church.

 BOUNCE to Activate Flipped Video

Objectives

Understand the diverse religions included in the early Roman empire.

Describe the development and central ideas of Christianity.

Summarize the spread of Christianity.

Outline the development of the early Christian Church.

Key Terms

messiah
Christian Bible
apostle
Paul
martyr
clergy
bishop
patriarch
pope
heresy
Augustine

The Origins of Christianity

Early in the Pax Romana, a new religion, Christianity, arose in a distant corner of the Roman empire. At first, Christianity was one of many religions practiced in the empire. But the new faith grew rapidly, and by A.D. 395 it had been declared the official religion of the Roman empire.

Romans Accept Many Religions

As it gained strength and spread through the empire, Christianity reshaped Roman beliefs. When the Roman empire fell, the Christian Church took over much of its role, becoming the central institution of Western civilization for nearly 1,000 years.

Rome Tolerates Diversity Within the vast Roman empire, numerous religious beliefs thrived. Generally, Rome tolerated these varied religious traditions. As long as citizens showed loyalty by honoring Roman gods such as Jupiter and Mars and by accepting the divinity of the emperor, they were allowed to worship as they pleased. Since most people were polytheistic, they were content to worship the Roman gods alongside their own.

As Rome expanded, people came into contact with different religious traditions, including those in Egypt and the Fertile Crescent. During turbulent times, a growing number of people turned to the so-called mystery religions, which emphasized secret rituals and promised special rewards to believers. Among the most popular of these was the cult of Isis, which originated in Egypt and offered women equal status with men. Roman soldiers favored the cult of the Persian god Mithras, who championed good over evil and offered life after death.

Divisions in Judea Among the many peoples within the Roman empire were the Jews. By 63 B.C., the Romans had conquered Judea. The Romans tolerated the religion of the Jews and even excused Jews, who were monotheistic, from worshiping Roman gods.

Among the Jews themselves, however, religious ferment was creating deep divisions. During the Hellenistic age, many Jews absorbed Greek customs and ideas. Concerned about the weakening of their religion, Jewish conservatives rejected these influences and called for strict obedience to Jewish laws and traditions.

The turmoil also had a political side. While most Jews were reluctantly willing to live under Roman rule, others, called zealots, were not. They called on Jews to revolt against Rome and reestablish an independent state. Some Jews believed that a **messiah,** or anointed king sent by God, would lead the Jewish people to freedom.

Rome Crushes the Jewish Revolt In A.D. 66, discontent flared into rebellion. Four years later, Roman forces crushed the rebels, captured Jerusalem,and destroyed the Jewish Temple. When revolts broke out again in the next century, Roman armies leveled Jerusalem. Thousands of Jews were killed in the fighting, and many others were enslaved and transported to various parts of the empire.

Faced with a devastated land and defeated in their efforts to regain political independence, many other Jews decided to leave Judea. They joined Jewish communities around the Mediterranean, or in other parts of the Roman empire. Some Jews remained in the northern part of Judea, near the Galilee.

Over the centuries, Jewish religious teachers called rabbis extended and preserved the Jewish law and began to record their discussions in the Talmud. They developed the form of Judaism still practiced today, focusing on the study of the Torah, prayer, and acts of kindness. Despite the loss of the Temple in Jerusalem, Judaism survived.

☑ **CHECK UNDERSTANDING** What were citizens expected to do in exchange for toleration of their religious beliefs and practices?

The Teachings of Jesus

As turmoil engulfed the Jews in Judea, a new religion, Christianity, arose among them. It began among the followers of a Jew named Jesus. Almost all the information we have about the life of Jesus comes from the Gospels, the first four books of the New Testament of the **Christian Bible.** Early Christians attributed the writing of these accounts to four followers of Jesus—Matthew, Mark, Luke, and John.

Early Life and Teachings Jesus was born about 4 B.C. in Bethlehem, near Jerusalem. According to the Gospels, he was a descendant of King David of Israel. The Gospels say an angel told Jesus' mother, Mary, that she would give birth to the messiah. "He will be great," said the angel, "and will be called the Son of the Most High God."

Growing up in the small town of Nazareth, Jesus worshiped God and followed Jewish law. As a young man, he may have worked as a carpenter. At the age of 30, the Gospels relate, he began preaching to villagers near the Sea of Galilee. Large crowds gathered to hear his teachings, especially when word spread that he had performed miracles of healing. Jesus often used parables, or short stories with simple moral lessons, to communicate his ideas.

>> The Roman destruction of Jerusalem's temple in A.D.70 was one of the devastating consequences of the Jewish rebellion.

According to the Gospels, Jesus recruited 12 disciples, or close followers, to help him in his mission. They were called **apostles,** a name that in Greek means "a person sent forth." After three years, Jesus and his disciples went to Jerusalem to spread his message there.

The Message of Jesus Jesus' teachings were firmly rooted in Jewish tradition. Jesus believed in one God and accepted the Ten Commandments. He preached obedience to the laws of Moses and defended the teachings of the Jewish prophets.

However, Jesus also preached new beliefs. According to his followers, he called himself the Son of God. Many people believed Jesus was the long-anticipated messiah. Jesus proclaimed that his mission was to bring spiritual salvation and eternal life to anyone who believed in him.

In the Sermon on the Mount, Jesus summarized his ethical message, which echoed Jewish ideas of mercy and sympathy for the poor and helpless:

"Blessed are the meek, for they shall inherit the earth.

Blessed are those who hunger and thirst for righteousness, for they shall be satisfied.

Blessed are the merciful, for they shall obtain mercy.

Blessed are the pure of heart, for they shall see God.

Blessed are the peacemakers, for they will be called sons of God."

—Matthew 5:5-9

Jesus emphasized God's love and taught the need for justice, morality, and service to others. According to Jesus, a person's major duties were to observe the Jewish command to "love the Lord your God with all your heart" and to "love your neighbor as yourself." Jesus also emphasized the importance of forgiveness. Shared Judeo-Christian beliefs about the just treatment of individuals and equality before the law would later influence Western legal systems as well as the governments of many Western democracies.

Condemned and Crucified According to the Gospels, Jesus traveled to Jerusalem near the time of the Jewish festival of Passover, a celebration of the exodus from Egypt. To the Roman authorities, Jesus was a threat because his speeches could inflame those eager to end Roman rule.

The Gospels state that Jesus was betrayed by one of his disciples. He was arrested by the Romans, tried, and condemned to death by crucifixion. In this method of execution, which the Romans often used, a person was nailed or bound to a cross and left to die. Jesus' crucifixion threw his disciples into confusion.

But then rumors spread through Jerusalem that Jesus was not dead at all. The Gospels report that his disciples saw and talked with Jesus, who was resurrected, or raised from the dead. The Gospels go on to say that Jesus, after commanding his disciples to spread his teachings to all people, ascended into heaven.

According to the Gospels, before his crucifixion and resurrection, Jesus prophesied, or predicted, that he would return. In this return to Earth, Jesus said he would bring salvation to his followers and that they would always be with him.

☑ **SUMMARIZE** Summarize the main ideas of Jesus' teachings.

>> The apostles accompanied Jesus and later spread his teachings.

▶ BOUNCE to Activate Gallery

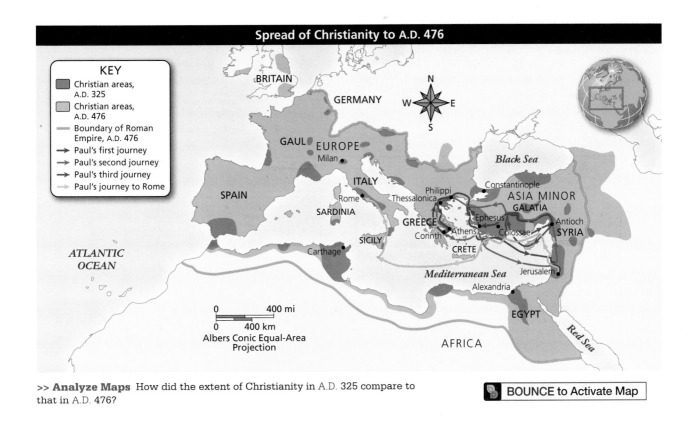

KEY
- ◼ Christian areas, A.D. 325
- ◼ Christian areas, A.D. 476
- — Boundary of Roman Empire, A.D. 476
- → Paul's first journey
- → Paul's second journey
- → Paul's third journey
- → Paul's journey to Rome

BRITAIN
GERMANY
GAUL EUROPE
Milan
ITALY
SPAIN
Rome
SARDINIA
ATLANTIC OCEAN
Carthage
SICILY
Black Sea
Constantinople
Philippi
Thessalonica
ASIA MINOR
GALATIA
GREECE
Ephesus
Athens
Corinth
Colossae
Antioch
SYRIA
CRETE
Mediterranean Sea
Jerusalem
Alexandria
EGYPT
AFRICA
Red Sea

0   400 mi
0   400 km
Albers Conic Equal-Area Projection

>> **Analyze Maps** How did the extent of Christianity in A.D. 325 compare to that in A.D. 476?

ⓑ BOUNCE to Activate Map

Christianity Spreads

After Jesus' death, the apostles and other disciples spread his message. At first, they preached only among the Jews of Judea. Others traveled to the communities of the Jewish diaspora, including Rome. According to tradition, the apostle Peter traveled to Rome to spread the word of Jesus.

At first, a few Jews accepted the teaching that Jesus was the messiah, or the Christ, from the Greek word for "anointed one." They were the first Christians. These early Christians remained a small group within Judaism. Then **Paul,** a Jew from Asia Minor, began the wider spread of the new faith, and Christianity took root across the Roman world.

The Work of Paul Paul had never met Jesus. In fact, he had been among those who persecuted Jesus' followers. According to his own writings, Paul had a vision in which Jesus spoke to him. He immediately converted to the new faith and made an important decision. He would spread Jesus' teachings beyond Jewish communities to gentiles, or non-Jews.

Paul's missionary work set Christianity on the road to becoming a world religion. A tireless traveler, Paul journeyed around the Mediterranean and set up churches in Asia Minor and Greece. In long letters to these Christian communities, Paul explained

Christian teachings. He answered questions from believers and judged disputes.

Paul emphasized that Jesus had sacrificed his life to atone, or make amends, for the sins of humankind. Paul taught that those who believed Jesus was the son of God and complied with his teachings would achieve salvation, or eternal life. His letters became part of the New Testament.

Persecution of Christians Rome's tolerant attitude toward religion did not extend to Christians. Roman officials suspected Christians of disloyalty to Rome because they refused to honor the emperor with sacrifices or honor the Roman gods. When Christians met in secret to avoid persecution, rumors spread that they were engaged in evil practices.

In times of trouble, persecution increased. Roman rulers, like Nero, used Christians as scapegoats, blaming them for social or economic ills. Over the centuries, thousands of Christians became **martyrs,** or people who suffer or die for their beliefs. According to tradition, both Peter and Paul were martyred in Rome during the reign of Nero.

The Message Wins Converts Despite the attacks, Christianity continued to spread throughout the Roman world. The reasons were many. Jesus had welcomed all people, especially the lowly, the poor,

>> Renaissance painter Raphael depicts the cross in the sky that Constantine saw before a battle. After his victory, Constantine ended the persecution of Christians.

>> This baptismal font survives among the ruins of the Church of St. Mary in Ephesus, Turkey.

and the oppressed. These people found comfort in his message of love, as well as in Christian teachings about equality and a better life beyond the grave.

As they did their work, Christian missionaries like Paul added ideas from Plato, the Stoics, and other Greek thinkers to explain Jesus' message. Educated Romans, in particular, were attracted to a religion that incorporated the discipline and moderation of Greek philosophy.

The unity of the Roman empire also eased the work of missionaries. Christians traveled along Roman roads and across the Mediterranean Sea, which was protected by Roman fleets. Early Christian documents were usually written in Greek or Latin, languages that many people across the empire understood.

Even persecution brought new converts. People who witnessed the willingness of Christians to die for their religion were impressed by the strength of their beliefs. "The blood of the martyrs is the seed of the [Christian] Church," noted one Christian.

Rome Embraces Christianity The persecution of Christians finally ended in A.D. 313, when the emperor Constantine issued the Edict of Milan. It granted freedom of worship to all citizens of the Roman empire. By the end of the century, the emperor Theodosius (thee uh DOH shus) had made Christianity the official religion of the Roman empire and repressed the practice of other faiths. Gradually, the Christian Church emerged as a well-organized, powerful force in the Roman world, sending missionaries to distant lands to win more converts to the faith.

☑ **IDENTIFY SUPPORTING DETAILS** What factors enabled Christianity to spread throughout the Roman empire?

The Growth of the Christian Church

Early Christian communities shared a common faith in the teachings of Jesus and a common way of worship. Only gradually did these scattered communities come together under the authority of a well-organized Christian Church.

Early Christian Communities To join the Christian community, a person had to be baptized, or blessed with holy water. Baptism at first signified acceptance of Christian teachings along with purification, or the forgiveness of sins. Members of the community were considered equals, and they addressed each other

The Christian Clergy

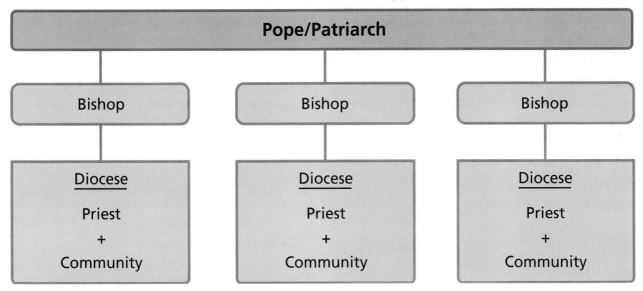

```
                        Pope/Patriarch

    Bishop                 Bishop                 Bishop

   Diocese                Diocese                Diocese
   Priest                 Priest                 Priest
     +                      +                      +
   Community              Community              Community
```

>> **Analyze Charts** Over time, the clergy of the Christian church developed into a hierarchy. What are some positive and negative elements that may arise from this type of organizational structure?

as "brother" or "sister." Early Christians gathered on Sunday for a ceremony of thanksgiving that included elements of Jewish traditions and Christian beliefs. They celebrated the sacred rite of the Eucharist, in which they consumed bread and wine, taken in memory of Jesus, whose last supper is described in the Gospels.

The Role of Women Many women welcomed Christianity's promise that in the Christian faith, "there is neither Jew nor Greek . . . neither slave nor free . . . neither male nor female." In early Christian communities, women served as teachers and administrators. Even when they were later barred from any official role in the Christian Church, they still worked to win converts and supported Christian communities across the Roman world.

The Structure of the Christian Church During the first centuries A.D., Christian communities developed a formal church structure with its own **clergy,** or people who conduct worship services. At first, the Christian clergy included priests and **bishops,** the highest-ranking Church officials. A bishop presided over a diocese, which included a number of Christian communities and their priests.

As the church expanded, archbishops were appointed to oversee the bishops. An archbishop's territory was called a province. This type of

organization in which officials are arranged according to rank is called a hierarchy.

As the Christian Church grew more organized, women lost their influence. They could not become priests or conduct Mass, the Christian worship service. Still, they continued to work as missionaries and even suffered martyrdom for their faith.

In time, the bishops of the most important cities in the Roman empire—Rome, Antioch, Alexandria, Jerusalem, and Constantinople— gained greater authority and were called **patriarchs.** Like all bishops, they traced their spiritual authority to the apostles and Jesus.

Eventually, in the Latin-speaking western empire, the bishop of Rome assumed a dominant position, claiming that the apostle Peter had made Rome the center of the Christian Church. He took the title **pope,** or father of the Church. Patriarchs in the eastern Roman empire rejected the pope's claim to be supreme ruler of the Church.

Rivalries Within the Church Together, the clergy, including archbishops, bishops, and priests, helped keep Christianity alive in the early years of persecution. They also maintained order and discipline in the Church.

Despite its strong structure, the Church faced constant battles against **heresies,** or beliefs said to be contrary to official Church teachings. To end

>> Augustine was the bishop of Hippo in North Africa. A noted Church scholar, he combined Christian doctrine with the philosophy of Plato.

disputes over questions of faith, councils of Church leaders met to decide which ideas or practices the Church would accept. Among the most important was the Council of Nicaea in Asia Minor, where they drew up the Nicene Creed, a statement of basic Christian beliefs.

Scholars Further Define Christian Teachings For centuries, Christian scholars debated issues of theology, or the study of religious faith and practice. Two leading scholars of the early Church were Clement and Origen. Both worked as teachers in Alexandria, Egypt, a major center of learning in the Roman world.

Perhaps the best known Christian theologian was **Augustine,** bishop of Hippo in North Africa. His writings have greatly influenced Christian thought and philosophy up to the present. In *City of God*, Augustine defended Christianity against critics who claimed the sack of Rome in A.D.410 was a punishment for abandoning their traditional gods.

☑ **DESCRIBE** How was the early Christian clergy organized?

☑ ASSESSMENT

1. **Summarize** What were the historical origins of Christianity, and how did that reflect the development of monotheism in the Roman empire?

2. **Describe** How was the work of missionaries vital in the spread of Christianity through the Roman empire?

3. **Identify Main Ideas** What were the central beliefs in Christianity?

4. **Identify** What was the role of women in early Christian communities?

5. **Describe** What were some of the traditions and customs of early Christian communities?

Connections to Today

Football is a popular sport in many high schools, but requires safety equipment.

Take Action by Learning About the Impact of Sports

1. **Choose** one of the following topics about sports today:

   - **Safety in Sports:** Conduct research to find out what safety measures are in place for professional sports or high school sports.

   - **Economics:** Conduct research to find out how much professional athletes are paid as well as other income streams they have access to.

   - **College Sports:** Conduct research to find out how athletes are recruited to play at universities and colleges.

2. **Ask Questions** Generate a list of questions about the topic you have selected. What are the major issues or controversies surrounding your topic? What are the main arguments on both sides? What might you want to know about your topic?

3. **Learn** about your topic by using a variety of sources. Use the Internet and your library to find newspaper or magazine articles, and data. Consider interviewing people who feel strongly about the issue.

4. **Raise Awareness** Create a survey on the topic you have selected to find out how students in your school feel about the issue. Publish the results of your survey in the school or local newspaper.

LESSON SUMMARIES

Use these Lesson Summaries, and the longer versions available online, to review the key ideas for each lesson in this Topic.

Lesson 1: The Roman Republic

Rome began as a small village in central Italy ruled by kings. In 509 B.C, according to tradition, the Romans overthrew their king and established a republic. Over time, this republic developed a sophisticated system of government that was a model to the American framers. The Roman republic slowly came to dominate Italy, absorbing conquered people and their cultures.

Lesson 2: The Roman Empire: Rise and Decline

In the 200s B.C., the Roman republic began to expand outside Italy. It defeated its rival Carthage and eventually conquered the entire Mediterranean world. Conquests led to political crises, civil wars, and the establishment of one-man rule by Augustus, the first Roman emperor. The Roman empire lasted for centuries, but eventually civil wars, foreign invasions, other factors led to its collapse in the west in the 400s A.D. The empire's eastern half survived.

Lesson 3: The Legacy of Rome

Roman culture spread across the empire and blended with Greek elements to create what historians call Greco-Roman civilization. Roman culture left an enormous legacy for the modern world. Roman literature and art continue to inspire. Roman architects and engineers invented new techniques and built buildings and aqueducts that still stand. Roman law continues to influence legal codes.

Lesson 4: The Origins of Christianity

Christianity arose in the Roman province of Judea among the followers of Jesus. According to the Christian Bible, Jesus performed miracles and spread his teachings. He was killed by the Roman authorities but, Christians believe, came back from the dead. Belief in Jesus and his teachings spread beyond his early followers and developed into the religion of Christianity. It survived persecution by the Roman government and became the official religion of the Roman empire.

QUEST! FINDINGS

Create Your Presentation Refer to your responses to the Quest Connections to help you create your group presentation on the collapse of one or more empires. Use the rubric and other Quest resources to guide your work.

VISUAL REVIEW

Use these graphics to review some of the key terms, people, and ideas from this Topic.

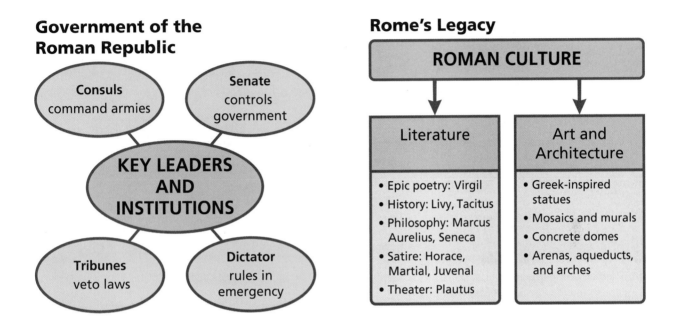

Government of the Roman Republic

- **Consuls** command armies
- **Senate** controls government
- **KEY LEADERS AND INSTITUTIONS**
- **Tribunes** veto laws
- **Dictator** rules in emergency

Rome's Legacy

ROMAN CULTURE

Literature
- Epic poetry: Virgil
- History: Livy, Tacitus
- Philosophy: Marcus Aurelius, Seneca
- Satire: Horace, Martial, Juvenal
- Theater: Plautus

Art and Architecture
- Greek-inspired statues
- Mosaics and murals
- Concrete domes
- Arenas, aqueducts, and arches

Key People and Roles in Early Christianity

INDIVIDUALS/ GROUPS	ROLE
Jesus	Jesus taught a new faith which came to be called Christianity. He recruited followers and spread his message widely.
Apostles	These 12 men were close followers of Jesus. They spread Christianity after his death.
Paul	Through his teachings and writings, Paul spread Christianity throughout the Roman empire.
Priests	These leaders of Christian communities formed the majority of the church clergy.
Bishops	These church officials ranked over the priests. Each served in an area called a diocese. They were considered successors of the apostles.
Patriarchs	These men were bishops of major cities and exercised authority other bishops in their area.

Topic 6 Assessment

KEY TERMS, PEOPLE, AND IDEAS

1. How did the **Etruscans** Influence early Rome?

2. Why did the Romans elect two **consuls** instead of a single leader?

3. How did **Augustus** permanently change Roman government?

4. What do **mercenaries** do and why might hiring them have been dangerous for Rome?

5. Why did **Constantine** found **Constantinople**?

6. What was **Virgil's** main contribution, and how was he influenced by Greek culture?

7. What is the purpose of an **aqueduct** and how did aqueducts affect life in Roman cities?

8. Who were the **apostles** and how did they help spread Christianity?

9. What was the job of a **bishop** in the early Church?

CRITICAL THINKING

10. **Predict Consequences** How do you think allowing ten elected tribunes to veto any law would affect Roman government?

11. **Identify Cause and Effect** Why did the creation of professional armies help lead to the collapse of the Roman republic?

12. **Make Generalizations** How did civil wars help cause the collapse of the Roman republic?

13. **Explain** Which advance in Roman architecture or engineering most benefited everyday Romans? Explain your answer.

14. **Summarize** What did the philosophy of Stoicism teach? Why might it have appealed to an emperor like Marcus Aurelius?

15. **Draw Conclusions** Some Roman emperors persecuted Christians because they refused to worship the Roman gods and emperors. Why do you think they considered this threatening or dangerous?

16. **Analyze Maps** Look at the map. What areas did Carthage control before its wars with Rome? Why do you think Rome defeated Carthage before it started expanding to the east?

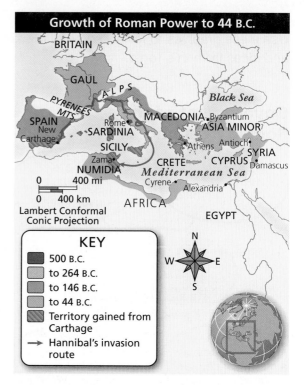

Growth of Roman Power to 44 B.C.

KEY
- 500 B.C.
- to 264 B.C.
- to 146 B.C.
- to 44 B.C.
- Territory gained from Carthage
- → Hannibal's invasion route

17. **Writing Activity: Write an Argument** The Roman republic had its critics, even among politicians like the Gracchi brothers. The Greek historian Plutarch quoted the following speech, supposedly given by Tiberius Gracchus:

> "The wild beasts that roam over Italy . . . have every one of them a cave or lair to lurk in; but the men who fight and die for Italy enjoy the common air and light, indeed, but nothing else; houseless and homeless they wander about with their wives and children . . . they fight and die to support others in wealth and luxury, and though they are styled [referred to as] masters of the world, they have not a single clod of earth that is their own."
> —Plutarch, Life of Tiberius Gracchus

The Roman republic benefited the Roman people in some ways, but, as Tiberius Gracchus argues, it was not perfect. On balance, was the Roman republic better for common Romans than the rule of the emperors? Choose a side, then use your knowledge of this Topic and the quote to write a short argument essay. Be sure to support your claim with evidence.

18. **Connections to Today** What role do you think sports plays in your high school?

DOCUMENT-BASED QUESTIONS

Historians debate all sorts of questions about the fall of the Roman empire. As you read, there is even a debate about whether it fell at all. Did the Roman world transform gently into the medieval world, or was the empire's end a disaster that harmed everyday people?

DOCUMENT A

"The Roman empire lasted a lot longer than its supposed date of collapse . . . Things don't change overnight in a big, lazy empire. The life of the cities remained much more vigorous than was thought . . . Even after the official end of the empire, as late as 476 A.D., many of the social structures we associate with the empire endured..."

—*Historian Peter Brown*

DOCUMENT B

"It is deeply unfashionable to state that anything like a 'crisis' or a 'decline' occurred at the end of the Roman empire, let alone that a 'civilization' collapsed and a 'dark age' ensued. The new orthodoxy is that the Roman world, in both East and West, was slowly, and essentially painlessly, 'transformed' into a medieval form. However, there is an [unsolvable] problem with this new view: it does not fit the mass of archaeological evidence now available, which shows a startling decline in western standards of living during the [A.D. 400s to 600s.] This was a change that affected everyone, from peasants to kings, even the bodies of saints resting in their churches. It was no mere transformation—it was decline on a scale that can reasonably be described as 'the end of a civilization'.

—*Historian Bryan Ward-Perkins*

DOCUMENT C

This photograph shows mosaics from a church built in Italy in the 500s, decades after the collapse of the Western Roman empire. This mosaic depicts the Eastern Roman emperor Justinian, his soldiers, and members of his royal court.

DOCUMENT D

The forum was once the heart of the ancient city of Rome. Like much of the rest of the city, it fell into ruins in the years after the fall of the Western Roman empire. In recent years much of the forum has been excavated. This image shows it as it looked in the 1700s, before its excavation and restoration.

19. What do documents A and C have in common?
  A. Both stress the total collapse of Roman civilization.
  B. Both show that Roman culture survived past A.D. 476
  C. Both show how common people experience the fall of Rome.
  D. Both show that historians continue to argue about this topic.

20. What is the main idea of Document B?
  A. The fall of Rome was barely noticeable to common people.
  B. The fall of Rome led to sharp decline in standards of living.
  C. Rome did not really fall but transitioned gently into the medieval world.
  D. The fall of Rome led to an economic boom that benefitted peasants.

21. Which statement best explains Documents C and D?
  A. Some parts of the Roman empire continued to thrive after A.D. 476.
  B. Roman culture disappeared everywhere after A.D. 476.
  C. The collapse of cities caused the decline and fall of the Roman empire.
  D. The techniques of Roman art were adapted by people from outside the empire.

22. **Writing Task** Take a stand on this debate. Was the fall of the Roman empire a gentle transition or a dramatic catastrophe? Use evidence from these documents and elsewhere in the topic to support your answer.

Medieval Christian Europe (330–1450)

ESSENTIAL QUESTION What should governments do?

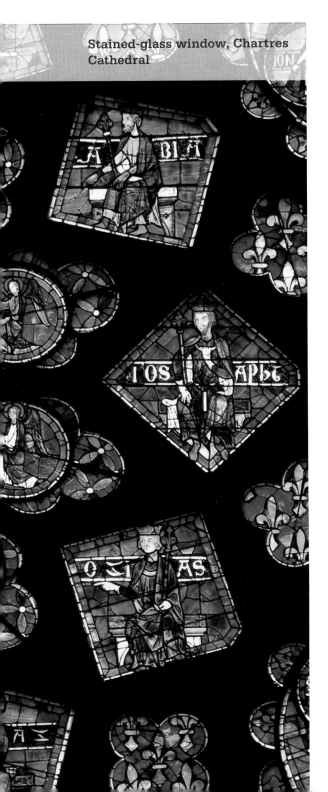

Stained-glass window, Chartres Cathedral

Connections to Today

The 21st century has seen several global outbreaks of highly contagious diseases— swine flu, bird flu, Ebola, and COVID-19, among others. Our interconnected world poses a high risk that these diseases will spread rapidly. In this topic, you will read about the growth of trade during the medieval period and the outbreak of plague that killed millions. How do governments and international institutions today protect against the negative consequences of global interconnectedness while promoting its benefits?

NBC LEARN

Learn how modern craftspeople build a castle using medieval tools and techniques.

BOUNCE to Activate My Story Video

229

Topic 7 Overview

In this Topic, you will learn about the political, social, and economic factors that shaped medieval Europe. Look at the lesson outline and explore the timeline. As you study this Topic, you will complete the Quest team project.

LESSON OUTLINE

7.1 The Early Middle Ages

7.2 Feudalism and the Manor Economy

7.3 The Medieval Christian Church

7.4 Economic Expansion and Change: The Crusades and After

7.5 The Feudal Monarchs and the Church

7.6 Learning, Literature, and the Arts of the Middle Ages

7.7 The Later Middle Ages: A Time of Upheaval

7.8 Russia and Eastern Europe

Key Events of Medieval Christian Europe

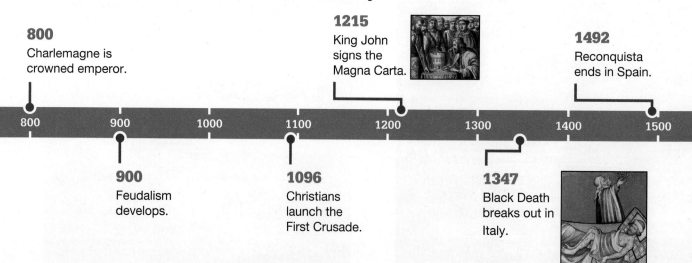

800
Charlemagne is crowned emperor.

1215
King John signs the Magna Carta.

1492
Reconquista ends in Spain.

900
Feudalism develops.

1096
Christians launch the First Crusade.

1347
Black Death breaks out in Italy.

800 | 900 | 1000 | 1100 | 1200 | 1300 | 1400 | 1500

QUEST!

Publish a Graphic Novel about Medieval Europe

If you were able to travel back in time and you landed in Europe during the middle ages what would you see? In this Quest, your team will research life in Europe at that time and use it to create an eight-panel spread (two-facing pages) for a graphic novel.

STEP 1
Learn about graphic novels. How can your team present an impressive spread?

STEP 2
Choose your topic. Start your research. Synthesize what you learn to answer the following question: What was life like in the Middle Ages for people at different economic and social levels?

STEP 3
Write, edit, and choose images for your pages. Examine software you may need to present your novel.

STEP 4
Present your completed novel. Reflect on what you have learned about differences then and now in society, government, religion, and the economy.

King Clovis of the Franks rallies his warriors during one of many battles he fought to build his kingdom. His conversion to Christianity set an example for other Germanic rulers.

 BOUNCE to Activate Flipped Video

Objectives

Summarize ways in which the Byzantine empire flourished after the decline of Rome.

Explain the impact of the fall of Rome on Western Europe.

Describe how Germanic tribes carved Europe into small kingoms.

Explain how Charlemagne briefly reunited much of Western Europe and what happened to his empire after his death.

Key Terms

Constantinople
Justinian
Justinian's Code
autocrat
Theodora
medieval
Franks
Clovis

Charles Martel
battle of Tours
Charlemagne
Magyars
Vikings

The Early Middle Ages

In European history, the thousand-year span between the fall of the Roman empire and the beginning of the Renaissance period is known as the Middle Ages. Perhaps best remembered today for knights on horseback and towering Gothic cathedrals, this medieval period began with the collapse of the western Roman empire.

The Byzantine Empire Thrives

You have read that as German invaders pounded the Roman empire in the west, the Roman emperor Constantine and his successors shifted their base to the eastern Mediterranean. Constantine rebuilt the Greek city of Byzantium and then renamed it after himself—**Constantinople.** By 330, he made Constantinople the new capital of the empire. From this "New Rome," roads fanned out to the Balkans, to the Middle East, and to North Africa. In time, the eastern Roman empire became known as the Byzantine empire.

Constantinople Grows The vital center of the empire was Constantinople. The city was located on the shores of the Bosporus, a strait that links the Mediterranean and Black seas. Constantinople had an excellent harbor and was guarded on three sides by water. Emperors after Constantine built an elaborate system of land and sea walls to bolster its defenses.

Equally important, Constantinople commanded key trade routes linking Europe and Asia. For centuries, the city's favorable location made it Europe's busiest marketplace. There, merchants sold silks from China, wheat from Egypt, gems from India, spices

GO ONLINE to access your digital course

from Southeast Asia, and furs from Viking lands in the north.

At the center of the city, Byzantine emperors and empresses lived in glittering splendor. Dressed in luxurious silk, they attended chariot races at the Hippodrome arena. Crowds cheered wildly as rival charioteers careened around and around in their vehicles. The spectacle was another reminder of the city's glorious Roman heritage.

A Blending of Cultures After rising to spectacular heights, the Byzantine empire eventually declined to a small area around Constantinople itself. Yet it was still in existence nearly 1,000 years after the fall of the western Roman empire. As the heir to Rome, it promoted a brilliant civilization that blended ancient Greek, Roman, and Christian influences with other traditions of the Mediterranean world.

☑ **IDENTIFY** Why did Constantinople become a rich and powerful city?

The Age of Justinian

The Byzantine empire reached its greatest size under the emperor **Justinian,** who ruled from 527 to 565. Justinian was determined to revive ancient Rome by retaking lands that had been overrun by invaders.

Led by the brilliant general Belisarius, Byzantine armies reconquered North Africa, Italy, and the southern Iberian peninsula. However, the fighting exhausted Justinian's treasury and weakened his defenses in the east. Moreover, the victories were only temporary. Justinian's successors would lose the bitterly contested lands, one after the other.

Hagia Sophia Justinian left a more lasting monument in the structures of his capital. In 532, riots and a devastating fire swept Constantinople. Many buildings were destroyed and many lives were lost.

To restore Roman glory, Justinian launched a program to make Constantinople grander than ever. His great triumph was rebuilding the church of Hagia Sophia (AH yee uh suh FEE uh), which means "Holy Wisdom."

Hagia Sophia's immense, arching dome improved on earlier Roman buildings. The interior glowed with colored marble and embroidered silk curtains. Seeing this church, the emperor recalled King Solomon's temple in Jerusalem. "Glory to God who

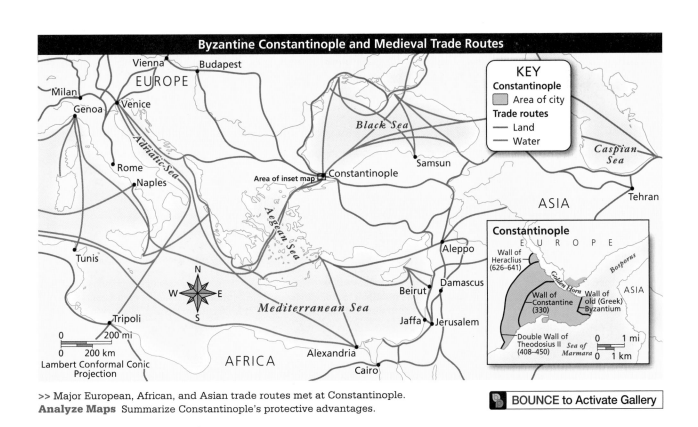

>> Major European, African, and Asian trade routes met at Constantinople.
Analyze Maps Summarize Constantinople's protective advantages.

🔵 BOUNCE to Activate Gallery

has judged me worthy of accomplishing such a work as this!" Justinian exclaimed. "O Solomon, I have surpassed you!"

Justinian's Code and Its Impact Even more important than expanding the empire and rebuilding its capital was Justinian's reform of the law. Early in his reign, he set up a commission to collect, revise, and organize all the laws of ancient Rome.

The result was the Corpus Juris Civilis, or "Body of Civil Law," popularly known as **Justinian's Code.** This massive collection included laws passed by Roman assemblies or decreed by Roman emperors, as well as the legal writings of Roman judges and a handbook for students.

Justinian's Code had a legal and political impact far beyond the Byzantine empire. By the 1100s, it had reached Western Europe. There, monarchs modeled their laws on its principles, which would slowly, over many centuries, help them to centralize their power. Later, the code also guided legal thinkers who began to put together the international law in use today.

Justinian Rules With Absolute Power To Justinian, the law was a means to unite the empire. Yet he himself was an **autocrat,** or sole ruler with complete authority. Like earlier Roman emperors, he had a large bureaucracy to carry out his orders.

The emperor also had power over the Church. He was deemed Christ's deputy on Earth.

As a Byzantine official wrote, "The emperor is equal to all men in the nature of his body, but in the authority of his rank he is similar to God, who rules all." His control was aided by his wife, **Theodora.** A shrewd politician, she served as advisor and co-ruler to Justinian. At times, she even challenged the emperor's orders and pursued her own policies.

Economic and Military Power The Byzantine empire flourished under a strong central government, which exercised strict control over a prosperous economy. Peasants formed the backbone of the empire, working the land, paying taxes, and providing soldiers for the military. In the cities of the empire, trade and industry flourished. As coined money disappeared from areas once ruled by the Roman empire in the west, the Byzantine empire preserved a healthy money economy. The bezant, the Byzantine gold coin stamped with the emperor's image, circulated from England to China.

A prosperous economy allowed the Byzantines to build one of the strongest military forces in the world. Soldiers, ships, and sailors protected the empire, and fortifications protected its capital. The Byzantines also relied on a secret weapon called Greek fire, a liquid that probably contained petroleum. Thrown

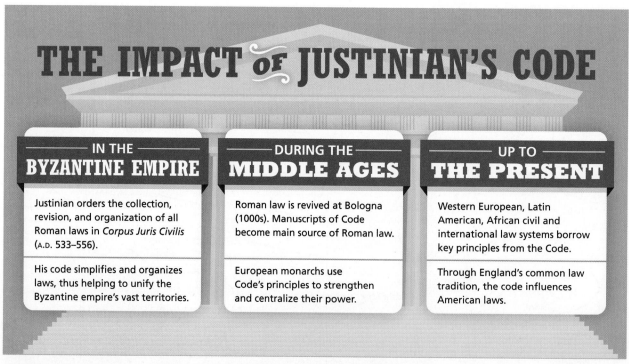

THE IMPACT OF JUSTINIAN'S CODE

IN THE BYZANTINE EMPIRE	DURING THE MIDDLE AGES	UP TO THE PRESENT
Justinian orders the collection, revision, and organization of all Roman laws in *Corpus Juris Civilis* (A.D. 533–556).	Roman law is revived at Bologna (1000s). Manuscripts of Code become main source of Roman law.	Western European, Latin American, African civil and international law systems borrow key principles from the Code.
His code simplifies and organizes laws, thus helping to unify the Byzantine empire's vast territories.	European monarchs use Code's principles to strengthen and centralize their power.	Through England's common law tradition, the code influences American laws.

>> Justinian commissioned an important reform of ancient Rome's laws. **Analyze Charts** How did Justinian's Code help rule the Byzantine empire? Why did the Code become so valuable later?

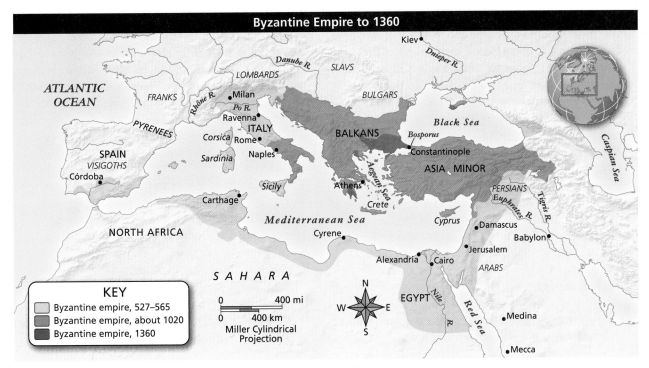

KEY
Byzantine empire, 527–565
Byzantine empire, about 1020
Byzantine empire, 1360

0   400 mi
0   400 km
Miller Cylindrical
Projection

>> The Byzantine empire reached its greatest size by 565. **Analyze Maps** Describe the Byzantine empire's extent in 1020. **Infer** What does the empire's size in 565 suggest about Justinian's rule?

toward an enemy, it would ignite on contact, and its fire could not be put out with water. For centuries, Greek fire was an effective and terrifying weapon of the Byzantine navy.

The Empire Declines The fortunes of the Byzantine empire rose and fell in the centuries after Justinian. Time and again, its skilled forces held off attacks by invaders. The empire withstood successive attacks by Persians, Slavs, Vikings, Huns, Arabs, and Turks. The empire thus served as a buffer for Western Europe by absorbing the brunt of invasions from the east. Among the fiercest attacks came from the Arab armies that were carrying a new religion, Islam, into the Mediterranean world and beyond.

In the 600s and 700s, Arab armies overran the wealthy Byzantine provinces of Egypt and Syria before advancing on Constantinople. The city held out, eventually turning back the attacks. By resisting the Arab advance, the Byzantine empire gave a measure of security to the small, weak Germanic kingdoms that had divided up Western Europe after the fall of Rome.

☑ **DESCRIBE** What were Justinian's accomplishments?

Changes in Western Europe

In Europe, the centuries after the fall of Rome are called the Middle Ages, which lasted from about 500 to 1350. The Middle Ages refers to the time between the ancient and modern worlds. During this long stretch of time, Western Europe passed through two distinct phases: the early Middle Ages, lasting from about 500 to 1050, and the late Middle Ages, lasting from about 1050 to 1350.

A Shift to the North At its height, the Roman empire included much of Western Europe. Rome unified the region and spread classical ideas, the Latin language, and Christianity to the tribal peoples of Western Europe. But Rome was a Mediterranean power. The Germanic peoples who ended Roman rule in the west shifted the focus to the north. There, the peoples of Europe would begin to create a new civilization, building on the legacy of Rome.

Despite the disorder and decay that came with the fall of Rome, Western Europe was a place of great potential. It had fertile land and other resources, such as timber, furs, and tin. In the early Middle Ages, gradual changes took place that would eventually bring a measure of order.

A Time of Decline As Rome declined and withdrew from its provinces in Western Europe, these lands suffered severe blows. Waves of invaders swept in, and Roman civilization slowly disappeared. Wars raged constantly. Trade slowed to a trickle, towns emptied, and learning virtually ceased.

The early Middle Ages was a harsh and difficult time for the peoples of Europe. Much later, some people looked back on this time and called it the "dark ages" because of the disorder and loss of Roman civilization. Today, historians recognize that the Middle Ages were, in fact, a time of new beginnings. During this long period, Greek, Roman, Germanic, and Christian traditions were slowly blended and gave rise to a new **medieval** civilization. *Medieval* comes from the Latin term for "middle age."

☑ **DESCRIBE** What was Western Europe like after the collapse of the western Roman empire?

Germanic Kingdoms

The Germanic tribes that conquered parts of the Roman empire included the Goths, Vandals, Saxons, and **Franks.** Their culture was very different from

>> In this illustration from the 1800s, Charles Martel swings his hammer (or "martel") against Muslim invaders in the battle of Tours, stopping their further advance into Europe.

that of the Romans. They were mostly farmers and herders, so they had no cities or written laws. Instead, they lived in small communities governed by unwritten customs. Their kings were elected leaders, chosen by tribal counsels. Warriors swore loyalty to the king in exchange for weapons and a share in the plunder taken from defeated enemies. Between 400 and 700, these Germanic tribes carved Western Europe into small kingdoms.

The Kingdom of the Franks The strongest and most successful kingdom was that of the Franks. In 486, **Clovis,** king of the Franks, conquered the former Roman province of Gaul. Later, this area would be known as France.

Clovis ruled his new lands according to Frankish custom. At the same time, however, he managed to preserve much of the Roman legacy in Gaul.

Clovis took an important step when he converted to Christianity, the religion of his subjects in Gaul. In doing so, he not only earned their support, but he also gained a powerful ally in the pope, leader of the Christian Church of Rome.

Muslim Armies Advance Into Europe As the Franks and other Germanic peoples carved up Europe, a powerful new force, Islam, swept out of the Middle East across the Mediterranean world. Islam is a religion that began in Arabia around 622. Over the next 200 years, Muslims, or believers in Islam, built a huge empire and created a major new civilization.

The pope and the Christian kingdoms in Europe watched with alarm as Muslim armies overran Christian lands from Palestine to North Africa and Spain. When a Muslim army crossed into France, **Charles Martel** rallied Frankish warriors.

At the **battle of Tours** in 732, Christian warriors triumphed. To them, the victory was a sign that God was on their side.

Muslims advanced no farther into Western Europe, although they continued to rule most of what is now Spain. To European Christians, the Muslim presence in Spain and around the Mediterranean was a source of anxiety and anger. Even when the Muslim armies were no longer a threat, Christians continued to have a hostile view of the Muslim world. Still, medieval Europeans did learn from the Arabs, whose knowledge in many areas, especially science and mathematics, was extensive and exceeded their own.

☑ **IDENTIFY** How did the Germanic tribes govern their kingdoms?

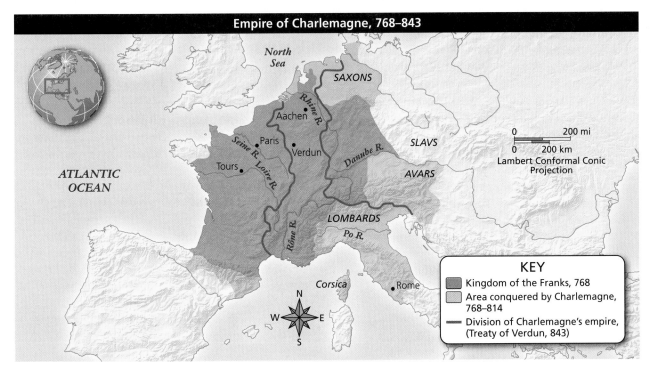

Empire of Charlemagne, 768–843

North Sea

SAXONS

Aachen

Rhine R.

Seine R. Paris
Verdun
Loire R.

Tours

Danube R.

SLAVS

AVARS

ATLANTIC OCEAN

Rhône R. *Po R.*

LOMBARDS

Corsica

● Rome

0   200 mi
0   200 km
Lambert Conformal Conic Projection

KEY
◼ Kingdom of the Franks, 768
◻ Area conquered by Charlemagne, 768–814
— Division of Charlemagne's empire, (Treaty of Verdun, 843)

>> Charlemagne built an empire his descendants could not hold together. **Locate** Charlemagne's empire in 814. **Predict Consequences** What might be one result of the division of his empire? Explain.

Charlemagne Builds an Empire

In 768, the grandson of Charles Martel became king of the Franks. He built an empire reaching across what is now France, Germany, and parts of Italy and Spain. The founder of this empire became known as **Charlemagne** (SHAHR luh mayn), or Charles the Great.

Charlemagne spent much of his 46-year reign fighting Muslims in Spain, Saxons in the north, Avars and Slavs in the east, and Lombards in Italy. Charlemagne loved battle and was a successful conqueror who reunited much of the old Roman empire in Europe.

Emperor of the Romans In 799, Pope Leo III asked Charlemagne for help against rebellious nobles in Rome. Charlemagne aided the pope against his attackers. On Christmas Day in the year 800, the pope showed his gratitude by placing a crown on Charlemagne's head and proclaiming him Emperor of the Romans.

This ceremony would have enormous significance. A Christian pope had crowned a Germanic king successor to the Roman emperors. In doing so, Pope Leo III revived the ideal of a united Christian community, which came to be called Christendom.

The pope's action also outraged the eastern Roman emperor in Constantinople. The Byzantine emperor saw himself as the sole Roman ruler. In the long run, the crowning of Charlemagne would deepen an already growing split between the eastern and western Christian worlds. Perhaps even more important, the crowning sowed the seeds for a long and desperate power struggle between later popes and Germanic emperors.

Creating a Unified Christian Empire Charlemagne set out to exercise control over his lands and create a united Christian Europe. Many of his subjects were pagans, as non-Christians were called. Charlemagne worked closely with the Church to spread Christianity to the conquered peoples on the fringes of his empire. During his reign, missionaries won converts among the Saxons and Slavs.

Like other Germanic kings, Charlemagne appointed powerful nobles to rule local regions. He gave them land so they could offer support and supply soldiers for his armies. To keep control of these provincial rulers, he sent out officials called *missi dominici* (MIH see daw mih NEE chee) to check on roads, listen to grievances, and see that justice was done. Charlemagne instructed the *missi* to "administer the law fully and justly in the case of the holy churches of God and of the poor, of wards and of widows, and of the whole people."

Charlemagne Revives Latin Learning

Learning Charlemagne hoped to make his capital at Aachen (AH kun) a "second Rome." To achieve this goal, he made a determined effort to revive Latin learning.

Charlemagne could read but not write. He is said to have kept a slate by his bed so that he could practice making letters. For him, education also served to strengthen his empire as he saw the need for records and clear reports.

To ensure a supply of educated officials, Charlemagne set up a palace school and brought scholars there from all over. He asked a famous scholar, Alcuin of York, to run his palace school. There, scholars were set to work copying ancient manuscripts including the Bible and Latin works of history and science.

Charlemagne's Legacy Although Charlemagne's empire crumbled, the great Frankish ruler left a lasting legacy. He extended Christian civilization into northern Europe and furthered the blending of Germanic, Roman, and Christian traditions. He also set up a system for strong, efficient government. Later medieval rulers looked to his example when they tried to strengthen their own kingdoms.

☑ **DESCRIBE** How did Charlemagne unify Europe after the collapse of Rome?

New Invasions Pound Europe

After Charlemagne died in 814, his son Louis I took the throne. Later, Louis's sons battled for power. Finally, in 843, Charlemagne's grandsons drew up the Treaty of Verdun, which split the empire into three regions. The empire was divided just at a time when these lands were faced with new waves of invasions.

Three Sources of Attack Between about 700 to about 1000, Western Europe was battered by invaders from other lands. Muslims, Magyars, and Vikings conquered lands across the region. Even after their defeat at Tours in 732, Muslim forces kept up their pressure on Europe. In the late 800s, they conquered the island of Sicily, which became a thriving center of Muslim culture. Not until the 900s, when power struggles erupted in the Middle East, did Muslim attacks finally subside.

The Magyars About 900, a new wave of nomadic people, the **Magyars,** overran Eastern Europe and attacked the Byzantine empire. They moved on to plunder Germany, parts of France, and Italy. Finally, after about 50 years, they were turned back and settled in what is today Hungary.

Early Magyars lived in clans, or small groups of related people that governed themselves. These

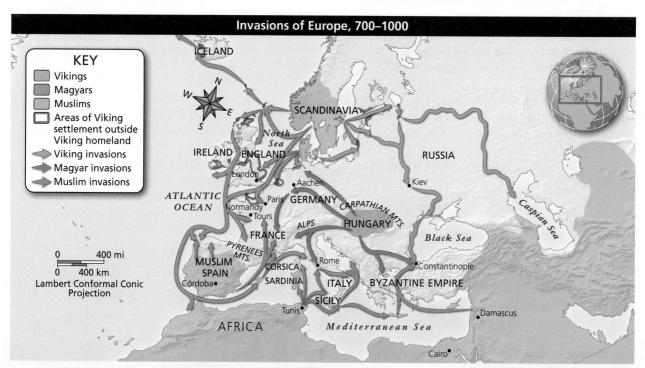

Invasions of Europe, 700–1000

KEY
- Vikings
- Magyars
- Muslims
- Areas of Viking settlement outside Viking homeland
- Viking invasions
- Magyar invasions
- Muslim invasions

0   400 mi
0   400 km
Lambert Conformal Conic Projection

>> **Analyze Maps** Use the map to find total distances the invaders traveled and number of routes taken. Rank the invaders from longest to shortest total distances traveled and most to least routes taken.

BOUNCE to Activate Map

groups were primarily nomadic and spent their time herding animals. In the late 800s, the Árpád dynasty was founded and the government began to unify around the dynasty's leader. By about 1000, most Magyars had become farmers and were no longer nomadic. The Magyars were pagans. However, Christianity was spreading rapidly during this time, and many Magyars gradually converted to the new religion.

Viking Raids from the North The most destructive raiders, however, were the **Vikings.** At home, they were independent farmers ruled by land-owning chieftains. When they took to the seas, they snapped the last threads of unity in Charlemagne's empire. These expert sailors and ferocious fighters burst out of Scandinavia, a northern region that now includes Norway, Sweden, and Denmark. They looted and burned communities along the coasts and rivers of Europe from Ireland to Russia.

There are a number of reasons that the Vikings left their homeland to raid others. Their land was becoming overpopulated. Many Vikings sought excitement and adventure. They also wanted to gain wealth and realized they could easily steal valuable goods and land from helpless victims.

The Vikings were pagans who worshipped many gods. As they learned about Christianity through their travels and settled in places populated by Christians, many Vikings converted to Christianity.

The Vikings were not just fierce warriors. They were traders and explorers as well. In their far-ranging voyages, they sailed around the Mediterranean Sea and crossed the Atlantic Ocean.

Leif Erikson set up a short-lived Viking colony on the continent of North America in about the year 1000. Other Vikings opened trade routes that linked northern Europe to Mediterranean lands. Vikings also settled in England, northern France (Normandy), Ireland, and parts of Russia.

☑ **DESCRIBE** What European invasions took place after Charlemagne's death?

>> An illustration from the 1800s shows Charlemagne sitting back to listen as scholars and lords at his court read aloud to him, engage in lively discussion, and write in their manuscripts.

☑ ASSESSMENT

1. **Summarize** In what ways did Justinian contribute to the flourishing of the Byzantine empire after the decline of Rome?

2. **Identify** What was the impact of political and legal ideas contained in Justinian's Code?

3. **Explain** What impact did the fall of Rome have on Western Europe?

4. **Describe** How did Germanic tribes carve Europe into small kingdoms?

5. **Describe** Describe the social, religious, and cultural development of the Franks.

6. **Quest Connection** What would the growth and then break up of Charlemagne's empire have meant for the lives of people living in the empire?

🖥 **GO ONLINE** to access these biographies: Justinian I and Charlemagne

A monarch dubs a kneeling young man a knight. Two knights sponsor and stand by him in this French illustration from the late 1200s.

 BOUNCE to Activate Flipped Video

Objectives

Describe the development of the political and social system of feudalism.

Summarize the life of knights and nobles.

Analyze how the economic system of manorialism worked and how it affected peasants and nobles.

Key Terms

feudalism
vassal
feudal contract
fief
knight
tournament
Eleanor of Acquitaine
chivalry
troubadour
manor
manor system
serf

Feudalism and the Manor Economy

In the face of invasions by Vikings, Muslims, and Magyars, kings and emperors were too weak to maintain law and order. People needed protection for themselves, their homes, and their lands. In response to this basic need for protection, a decentralized political and economic structure evolved, known as **feudalism.** Feudalism was a loosely organized system of rule in which powerful local lords divided their landholdings among lesser lords. In exchange, these lesser lords, or **vassals,** pledged service and loyalty to the greater lord.

Feudalism Develops

In practice, feudalism varied greatly from place to place, and its traditions changed over time. Overall, however, feudalism became the basis for the political and economic system that governed life during the Middle Ages and beyond.

Mutual Obligations Medieval society involved a network of mutual obligations between the ruler and the ruled. The relationship between lords and vassals was both political and economic. It was based on the exchange of land for loyalty and military service. These vows were conducted publicly in front of witnesses.

The relationship between lord and vassal grew out of custom and tradition and involved an exchange of pledges known as the **feudal contract.** Under this system, a powerful lord granted his vassal a **fief** (feef), or estate. Fiefs ranged from a few acres to hundreds of square miles. In addition to the land itself, the fief included peasants to work the land, as well as any towns or buildings on it.

As part of this agreement, the lord promised to protect his vassal. In return, the vassal pledged loyalty to his lord. He also agreed to provide the lord with 40 days of military service each year, certain money payments, and advice.

A Complex System Everyone had a place in medieval feudal society. At the top of the power structure stood the monarch. Below the monarch were the most powerful lords, who might have had titles such as duke or count. They held the largest fiefs. Each of these lords had vassals, and these vassals in turn had their own vassals. In many cases, the same man was both vassal and lord—vassal to a more powerful lord above him and lord to a less powerful vassal below him.

Because vassals often held fiefs from more than one lord, relationships between them grew very complex. A vassal who had pledged loyalty to several lords could have serious problems if his overlords quarreled with each other. What was he to do if both demanded his aid? To solve this problem, a vassal usually had a liege lord to whom he owed his first loyalty.

☑ **IDENTIFY** What was the relationship between lords and vassals?

Nobles, Knights, and Warfare

During the Middle Ages, warfare was constant. For medieval lords and vassals, it was a way of life. Rival lords battled constantly for power. Both greater and lesser nobles trained from boyhood for a future occupation as a **knight,** or mounted warrior.

The Life of a Knight At the age of seven, a boy slated to become a knight was sent away to the castle of his father's lord. There, he learned to ride and fight. He also learned to keep his armor and weapons in good condition. Training was difficult and discipline was strict. Any laziness was punished with an angry blow or even a severe beating.

With his training finished, the youth was named a knight, often in a public ceremony. An older knight or the boy's future lord said words like these: "In the name of God, Saint Michael, and Saint George, I dub thee knight; be brave and loyal." Then the young knight took his place beside other warriors.

Knights usually fought on horseback using swords, axes, and lances, which were long poles. They wore armor and carried shields for protection. Other soldiers fought on foot using daggers, spears, crossbows, and longbows.

As the fierce fighting of the early Middle Ages lessened in the 1100s, **tournaments,** or mock battles, came into fashion. A powerful lord would invite knights from the area to a tournament to enter contests of fighting skill. At first, tournaments were as dangerous as real battles. In time, they acquired more ceremonies and ritual.

Castles and War During the early Middle Ages, powerful lords fortified their homes to withstand attack. The strongholds gradually became larger and grander. By the 1100s, monarchs and nobles owned sprawling stone castles with high walls, towers, and drawbridges over wide moats.

Castles were fortresses. Wars often centered on seizing castles that commanded strategic river crossings, harbors, or mountain passes. Castle dwellers stored up food and water so they could withstand a long siege. In time of war, peasants from nearby villages might take refuge within the castle walls.

The Lives of Noblewomen Noblewomen played active roles in this warrior society. While her husband or father was off fighting, the "lady of the manor" took over his duties. She supervised vassals, managed the household, and performed necessary agricultural and medical tasks. Sometimes she might even have to go to war to defend her estate.

>> The Frankish knight Godfrey of Bouillon led his men in crucial battles against the Muslims. In victory, he refused the title of "king of Jerusalem" but accepted the crown.

🅱 BOUNCE to Activate Gallery

Some medieval noblewomen, like **Eleanor of Aquitaine,** took an active hand in politics. Eleanor inherited vast lands in southwestern France.

Through two marriages, she became queen of France and, later, queen of England. For more than 50 years, Eleanor was a leading force in European affairs.

A woman's right to inheritance was severely restricted under the feudal system, although women did sometimes inherit fiefs. Land usually passed to the eldest son in a family. A woman frequently received land as part of her dowry, and fierce marriage negotiations swirled around an unmarried or widowed heiress. If her husband died before her, a woman gained her rights to her land.

Like their brothers, the daughters of nobles were sent to friends or relatives for training. Before her parents arranged her marriage, a young woman was expected to know how to spin and weave and how to supervise servants. A few learned to read and write. In her role as wife, a noblewoman was expected to bear many children and be dutiful to her husband.

The Code of Chivalry In the later Middle Ages, knights adopted a code of conduct called **chivalry.** Chivalry required knights to be brave, loyal, and true to their word. In warfare, they had to fight fairly.

>> This diagram of the lands of a manor during the Middle Ages shows where the lord's family and peasants' families live. **Contrast** How does this compare with the bird's-eye view shown later in the lesson?

For example, a knight agreed not to attack another knight before the opponent had a chance to put on his armor. Warriors also had to treat a captured knight well or even release him if he promised to pay his ransom. Chivalry had limits, though. Its elaborate rules applied to nobles only, not to commoners.

But chivalry also dictated that knights protect the weak, and that included both peasants and noblewomen. Few real knights could live up to the ideals of chivalry, but they did provide a standard against which a knight's behavior could be measured.

Chivalry raised women to a new status. In theory, if not always in practice, chivalry placed women on a pedestal. **Troubadours,** or wandering musician-poets, composed their love songs, praising the beauty and wit of women throughout the ages.

In epic stories and poems, they told stories of brave knights and their devotion to a beloved woman. Much later, ideas of chivalry would shape our modern ideas of romantic love.

☑ **DESCRIBE** How was warfare central to life in the Middle Ages?

Manorialism

The heart of the medieval economy was the **manor,** or lord's estate. Most manors included one or more villages and the surrounding lands. Peasants, who made up the majority of the population in medieval society, lived and worked on the manor.

An Economic System Under the **manor system,** also called the manorial system, the lord of the manor exercised legal and economic power over the peasants who lived on the estate. The lord administered justice and provided land and protection. In return, peasants owed their lord labor and goods.

Historians have described several factors that contributed to the development of the economic system of manorialism. These were largely the same as those that led to the development of feudalism. Kings and emperors in Western Europe had become too weak to provide security. Trade declined sharply. Local communities had to become self-sufficient economic systems capable of meeting their own needs. These communities were manors.

Most peasants on a manor were **serfs,** bound to the land. Serfdom was not slavery; serfs could not be bought or sold. Still, they were not free. They could not leave the manor without the lord's permission. If the manor was granted to a new lord, the serfs went along with it.

>> A bird's-eye view of a typical medieval manor, which might include a manor house, a village church, a grain mill, storage barns, a blacksmith's shop, clustered peasant huts, and fields for crops and grazing.

BOUNCE to Activate Chart

The Mutual Obligations of Lords and Peasants
Peasants and their lords were tied together by mutual rights and obligations. Peasants had to work several days a week farming the lord's lands. They also repaired his roads, bridges, and fences. Peasants had to ask the lord's permission to marry. Peasants paid the lord a fee when they inherited their father's acres or when they used the local mill to grind grain. Other payments fell due at Christmas and Easter. Because money had largely disappeared in late Roman times, peasants had to pay fees with products such as grain, honey, eggs, or chickens.

In return for a lifetime of labor, peasants had the right to farm a certain amount of land for themselves. Under the system of mutual obligations, they were entitled to their lord's protection from raids or warfare. Although they could not leave the manor without permission, they also could not be forced off it. In theory, at least, they were guaranteed food, housing, and land.

The manor system supported feudalism. Lords and knights relied on their estates to provide them with food, lodging, horses, armor, weapons, money, and time to train for warfare.

A Self-Sufficient World During the early Middle Ages, the manor was generally self-sufficient. That is, the peasants who lived there produced almost everything they needed, from food and clothing to simple furniture and tools. Most peasants never ventured more than a few miles from their village. They had no schooling and no knowledge of a larger world outside.

A typical manor included cottages and huts clustered close together in a village. Nearby stood a water mill to grind grain, a church, and the lord's manor house. The fields surrounding the village were divided into narrow strips. Each family had strips of land in different fields so that good land and bad land were shared evenly.

Beyond the fields for growing crops, there were pastures for animals and meadows that provided hay. Only the lord had the right to chop wood or hunt animals in the forests that lay beyond the cleared land.

The Life of a Peasant For most peasants, life was harsh. Men, women, and children worked long hours, from sunup to sundown. During planting season, a man might guide an ox-drawn plow through the fields while his wife walked alongside, urging the ox on with a pointed stick. Children helped in the fields, planting seeds, weeding, and taking care of pigs or sheep.

The peasant family ate a simple diet of black bread with vegetables such as cabbage, turnips, or onions. They seldom had meat—that was reserved for the lord. Peasants who poached, or illegally killed wild game on their lord's manor, risked harsh punishment. If they lived near a river, peasants might add fish to their diet. At night, the family and their livestock—cows, chickens, pigs, or sheep—slept together in their hut.

Seasons and Celebrations Like farmers everywhere, peasants in Europe plowed in spring and autumn. In summer, they harvested and hayed. At other times, they weeded and repaired. Hunger was common, especially in late winter when the harvest was exhausted. Disease took a heavy toll, and few peasants lived beyond the age of 35.

Still, peasants found occasions to celebrate, such as marriages and births. Welcome breaks came on holidays, such as Christmas and Easter. At these times, the lord might allow his people to butcher an animal for a feast. There would also be dancing and rough sports, from wrestling to ball games.

☑ **DESCRIBE** How did the manor system operate?

☑ ASSESSMENT

1. **Describe** Why did feudalism develop as a political and social system?

2. **Summarize** How did the lives of knights and nobles demonstrate the importance of warfare in the Middle Ages?

3. **Describe** What did noblewomen contribute to medieval warrior society?

4. **Identify Cause and Effect** What do you think caused peasants working on medieval manors to die so young?

5. **Quest Connections** How did the economic system of manorialism work, and how did it affect peasants and nobles?

Pilgrims, like these characters in an illustration from Chaucer's *Canterbury Tales,* were a common sight on the roads of medieval Europe.

The Medieval Christian Church

Religion was woven into the fabric of the medieval world. Indeed, the Middle Ages has often been called Europe's "age of faith." The commanding force behind that faith was the Christian Church.

The Church Shapes Everyday Life

The Spread of Christianity During the early Middle Ages, the Church sent missionaries to spread Christianity to the diverse peoples of Europe. In 597, Pope Gregory I sent Augustine to convert the Anglo-Saxons in England. Other missionaries carried Christianity to Germanic tribes elsewhere in Europe.

By the late Middle Ages, Western Europe had built a civilization based on Christianity. Differences in language, culture, and government divided the peoples of Europe, but they shared a common faith and viewed non-Christians with suspicion and hostility.

The Parish Priest Christian rituals and faith were part of the fabric of everyday life. In villages, the priest of the parish, or local region, was often the only contact people had with the Church. The priest celebrated the mass and administered the other **sacraments**, the sacred rites of the Church. Medieval Christians, like many Christians today, believed that they needed the sacraments to achieve salvation, or the deliverance from sin into everlasting life. Priests passed on Church teachings and helped the sick and needy. If he could read or write, the local priest served as the only teacher in the village.

BOUNCE to Activate Flipped Video

Objectives

Explain how the Christian Church shaped medieval life.

Understand monastic life and the influence of medieval monks and nuns.

Analyze how the power of the Church grew during the Middle Ages and how reformers worked for change in the Church.

Describe the situation of Jews in medieval Europe.

Analyze how Christianity in the Byzantine empire differed from Christianity in the West.

Key Terms

sacrament	St. Francis of Assisi
Benedictine Rule	anti-Semitism
secular	usury
papal supremacy	schism
canon law	icon
excommunication	Great Schism
interdict	
friar	

GO ONLINE to access your digital course

Priests also collected the tithe, or tax that must be paid each year to the Church. The tithe was equal to a tenth of a person's income. In the early Middle Ages, the tithe supported the local parish. Later, increasing amounts of money were sent to Rome.

The Village Church By the later Middle Ages, the church had grown into a social center as well as a place of worship, in part because it was the largest building in a village. Life revolved around the church calendar, which included holidays such as Easter and other holy days dedicated to important saints, or deceased people recognized for their holiness or virtue by the Church. The main events of a person's life took place at the church. The sacrament of baptism is a ceremony that admits a person to the Christian community. Marriage, another sacrament, was performed at the entrance to a church. The dying also received a sacrament, and when dead, were buried in the churchyard.

At first the village church was a simple building. Later, prosperous communities built larger churches of stone, rather than wood. Some churches housed relics, or the possessions or remains of saints and other holy figures. During the Middle Ages, many people made pilgrimages, or journeys to a sacred place, to pray or touch the relics.

The medieval writer Geoffrey Chaucer noted that, when spring comes,

> Then people long to go on pilgrimages . . .
>
> To seek the stranger strands
>
> Of far-off saints, hallowed in sundry lands
>
> —Geoffrey Chaucer, *The Canterbury Tales*

The Rise of Cathedrals Bishops, who supervised parish priests, managed larger churches called cathedrals. These magnificent buildings were a source of pride to the communities that built them. Cities all over Europe competed to build grander, taller cathedrals. Members of the Church contributed money, labor, and skills to help build these monuments glorifying their God.

Women and the Church The Church taught that men and women were equal before God. But on Earth, women were viewed as weak and easily led into sin. Thus, they needed the guidance of men.

At the same time, the Church offered the ideal woman, modest and pure in spirit, as reflected in Mary, whom Christians believe was the mother of Jesus. Many churches were dedicated to Mary, called the "mother of God" and the "queen of heaven." During the Middle Ages, Mary was revered by many Christians who saw her as a sympathetic figure who could intercede for them with Jesus.

The Church took some steps to protect women. It set a minimum age for marriage. Church courts sometimes fined men who seriously injured their wives. Yet the medieval Church upheld a double standard, punishing women more harshly than men for similar offenses.

☑ **EXPLAIN** How did the Church play a unifying role in Europe during the Middle Ages?

>> This mosaic from the 800s shows Saint Mary, the infant Jesus, and two other saints.

🅱 BOUNCE to Activate Map

>> Monasteries were centers of religious, educational, and community life in medieval Europe.

BOUNCE to Activate 3D Model

Life in Monasteries and Convents

During the Middle Ages, some men and women withdrew from worldly life to become monks and nuns. Behind the walls of monasteries and convents, they devoted their lives to spiritual goals.

The Benedictine Rule About 530, a monk named Benedict organized the monastery of Monte Cassino in central Italy. He created rules to regulate monastic life. In time, the **Benedictine Rule** was used by monasteries and convents across Europe.

Under the Benedictine Rule, monks and nuns took three vows. The first was obedience to the abbot or abbess who headed the monastery or convent. The second was poverty, or giving up worldly goods, and the third was chastity, or purity. Each day was divided into periods for worship, work, and study.

Benedict believed in the spiritual value of manual labor and required monks to work in the fields or at other physical tasks. Like peasants all over Europe at the time, monks and nuns cleared and drained land. They also experimented with crops. By helping to develop new farming methods, they contributed to the gradual improvement in the farm economy, which supported medieval life.

A Life of Service In a world without hospitals, public schools, or social programs, monasteries and convents often provided basic social services. Monks and nuns looked after the poor and sick and set up schools for children. Travelers, especially Christian pilgrims traveling to holy shrines, could find food and a night's lodging at many monasteries and convents.

Some monks and nuns worked in the outside world as missionaries. During the Middle Ages, men and women risked their lives to spread Christian teachings across Europe. Patrick was a monk who set up the Church in Ireland. Augustine was a missionary to the Angles and Saxons in England. Later, the Church honored some of its missionaries by declaring them saints.

Centers of Learning Monasteries and convents performed a vital cultural function by preserving the writings of the ancient world. Their libraries contained Greek and Roman works, which monks and nuns copied as a form of labor. Most monks and nuns had little education, but some were well educated. They wrote and taught Latin or Greek, the languages of the ancient world. In England, the Venerable Bede wrote the most important history of England in the early Middle Ages.

Convents Offer Opportunities for Women During the Middle Ages, many women entered convents.

For some capable and inquiring women, convents offered an escape from the restrictions of medieval society. In the 1100s, Hildegard of Bingen served as abbess, heading her own convent. She composed religious music and wrote scholarly books. Hildegard also had visions of the future. As reports of her prophecies spread, popes and rulers sought her advice.

By the late Middle Ages, the Church had begun to restrict the activities of nuns. The Church withdrew rights nuns had once had, such as to hear confessions. It frowned on too much learning for women, preferring them to accept Church authority.

☑ **DRAW CONCLUSIONS** How did monks and nuns contribute to their surrounding communities?

The Growth of Church Power

During the Middle Ages, the Church became the most powerful institution in Western Europe. The Church not only controlled the spiritual life of Christians but also exercised enormous influence over **secular,** or nonreligious, affairs.

A Spiritual and Worldly Empire During the Middle Ages, the Christian Church split into eastern and western churches. The western church, headed by the pope in Rome, became known as the Roman Catholic Church. The Roman Catholic Church grew stronger and wealthier during the Middle Ages.

The pope was the spiritual leader of Roman Catholic Christians but also ruled vast lands in central Italy, later called the Papal States. As the spiritual heir and representative of Christ on Earth, according to Church teachings, the medieval pope eventually claimed **papal supremacy,** or authority over all secular rulers.

The pope headed an army of clergy who not only supervised church activities but also influenced political affairs. The high clergy, such as bishops and archbishops, were usually nobles. Like other feudal lords, they had their own territories and armies. Since they were often well educated, feudal rulers appointed them to administer their own governments. Because of this, church officials were closely linked to secular rulers. In addition, Church officials were often related to secular rulers.

Church Law and Authority The Church had complete power over spiritual matters and determined who could receive the sacraments. Without the sacraments, Christians believed that they faced everlasting suffering after death. The Church also developed its own body of laws, known as **canon law,** and had its own courts. Canon law was based on religious teachings and governed many aspects of life, from the behavior of the clergy to morals, marriages, and wills.

Anyone who disobeyed Church law faced a range of penalties. The most severe and terrifying penalty was **excommunication.** People who were excommunicated were cut off from the Church and its sacraments.

A powerful noble who opposed the Church could face the **interdict,** an order excluding an entire town, region, or kingdom from receiving most sacraments and Christian burial. Even the strongest ruler was likely to give in rather than face the interdict, which might cause revolts by the people under his rule.

Working for Peace By about 1000, the Church had begun to use its authority to limit feudal warfare. It tried to enforce periods of peace known as the Truce of God. It demanded that fighting stop between Fridays and Sundays and on religious holidays. Such efforts may have contributed to the gradual decline in private feudal wars that had raged in Europe for centuries.

>> This illustration of Pope Sylvester II, who reigned from 999 to 1003, shows the splendor and pomp of medieval European popes.

CRITICISMS OF THE CHURCH

Church Political Power Grows	The Church accumulated vast amounts of wealth and even controlled its own armies.
Simony	Simony involved the selling of Church land, spiritual offices, holy relics, or sacred property. The practice gave spiritual authority to people interested in monetary or political gain.
Selling of Indulgences	A complex system calculated earthly penance for sins and the time a person must spend in purgatory, which the Church taught was a physical place where the soul was punished for sins, after death. Priests promised to reduce a person's penance or time in purgatory in exchange for contributions to the Church.
Growth of Church Wealth	Everyone was required to pay a tithe, or one-tenth, of his or her income to the Church. Peasants lacking money were required to provide goods, food, or livestock and regularly work on the Church's land without pay.

>> **Analyze Charts** Which criticism do you think common people felt most strongly? Why?

The Legacy of Judeo-Christian Teachings By the late Middle Ages, traditions that had grown out of Christianity and Judaism had helped shape many aspects of life in Western Europe. The blending of Jewish and Christian teachings much later were called Judeo-Christian ideas. The teachings of these religions, along with ancient Greek and Roman ideas about law and government, would lead to new ways of thought. In time, these ideas became the basis for republican forms of government in the modern world that emphasized democracy and human rights and rejected the power of hereditary rulers.

Judeo-Christian teachings emphasized the value of the individual and the importance of social responsibility, or the idea of people helping one another, especially those in need. These teachings also included the idea of free will, or the freedom of humans to make choices for themselves. Christianity emerged in the Greco-Roman world, where it absorbed ideas of equality before the law, consent of the governed, and individual liberty.

☑ **IDENTIFY CENTRAL IDEAS** How did the Church gain secular power?

The Church Faces Calls to Reform

The very success of the medieval Church brought problems. As its wealth and power grew, discipline weakened. Powerful clergy grew more worldly, and many lived in luxury. Monks and nuns often ignored their vows. Priests, who were allowed to marry during this time, sometimes devoted more time to the interests of their families than to Church duties. The growing corruption and decay led to calls for reform.

Reform Movements In the early 900s, Abbot Berno set out to reform his monastery of Cluny in eastern France. First, he revived the Benedictine Rule, which required vows of obedience, poverty, and chastity. He then encouraged monks to follow solely religious pursuits and refused to allow nobles or bishops to interfere in monastery affairs. Instead, Cluny was placed under the direct protection of the pope. Over the next 200 years, many monasteries and convents copied these reforms.

In 1073, Gregory VII, a former monk, became pope and extended the Cluniac reforms throughout the entire Church. He prohibited simony (SY muh nee), or the selling of Church offices, and outlawed marriage for priests. Gregory then called on Christians to renew their faith. To end outside influence, he insisted that the Church, and not kings and nobles, choose Church officials. That policy would lead to a bitter battle of wills with the German emperor.

Preaching Orders A different approach to reform was taken by **friars**, or monks who traveled widely preaching to the poor, especially in Europe's growing towns. The first order of friars, the Franciscans, was founded by a wealthy Italian later known as **St. Francis of Assisi.** Giving up a comfortable life, he devoted himself to preaching the Gospels and teaching by his own example of good works.

The Spanish reformer St. Dominic also set up a preaching order of friars to work in the larger world. He called on friars to live in poverty, as the early Christians had. Dominic was particularly concerned about the spread of heresies, or religious beliefs that differed from accepted Church teachings. The Dominicans worked to teach people about official Christian doctrines so they would not be tempted into heresies.

Some women responded to the call for reform. They became Dominican nuns or joined orders like the Poor Clares, which was linked to the Franciscans. Often these orders welcomed only well-born women whose families gave a dowry, or gift, to the church. Another group, the Beguines (BEHG eenz), welcomed poor women who could not be accepted by other religious orders.

☑ **SUPPORT IDEAS WITH EXAMPLES** How did monks contribute to reforming the Church?

>> A Jewish religious procession winds its way through a medieval European street in the 1400s.

Jewish Communities in Medieval Europe

Medieval Europe was home to numerous Jewish communities. During Roman times, Jewish communities had sprung up all around the Mediterranean. After Rome put down the Jewish uprising in A.D. 70, Jews scattered farther afield. In their new homes, Jews preserved the oral and written laws that were central to their faith.

Communities in Spain and Northern Europe

Many Jewish communities thrived in Spain. The Arab Muslims who gained control of Spain in the 700s were generally tolerant of both Christians and Jews. Jewish culture flowered in Muslim Spain, which became a major center of Hebrew scholarship. Jews also served as officials in Muslim royal courts.

Jews also lived in northern Europe. During the early Middle Ages, Christians and Jews often lived side by side in relative peace. Many Christian rulers valued and protected Jewish communities, although they taxed them heavily. Early German kings had given educated Jews positions in their royal courts.

Persecution Often, however, medieval Christians persecuted Jews. During the Middle Ages, the Church and local rulers barred Jews from many occupations such as trade and handicrafts. More damaging, the Church forbade Jews from owning land. Popes and rulers still turned to Jews as financial advisers and physicians, but in much of Europe, Jews lived in increasingly isolated communities.

By the late 1000s, as the Church's power had increased, **anti-Semitism,** or prejudice against Jews, grew. Christians blamed Jews for disasters such as epidemic diseases, famine, or economic hardship. Christians saw Jews as unfamiliar people and were suspicious of their culture and beliefs.

In some areas, Jews were required to wear identifying clothing, or to live in a specific crowded and forcibly segregated part of a city called a ghetto.

The Church forbade Christians from **usury,** or the practice of lending money at interest. Because Jews were barred from so many other professions, some Jews became moneylenders. Moneylenders played a key role as the medieval economy grew, but nobles and others who borrowed heavily resented their debts, which further added to anti-Semitism.

Between 1096 and 1450, Jews were persecuted and expelled from major European cities and states, including England, France, and parts of what is today Germany, Italy, Austria, and Hungary. In response to growing persecution, and after these

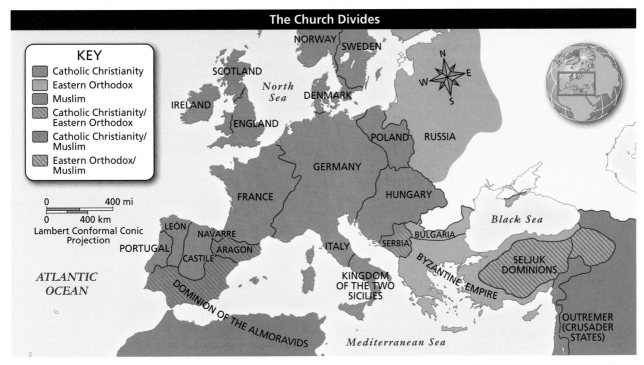

The Church Divides

KEY
- Catholic Christianity
- Eastern Orthodox
- Muslim
- Catholic Christianity/ Eastern Orthodox
- Catholic Christianity/ Muslim
- Eastern Orthodox/ Muslim

0 — 400 mi
0 — 400 km
Lambert Conformal Conic Projection

>> **Analyze Maps** What part of Europe was influenced by both the Roman Catholic and Eastern Orthodox Churches?

BOUNCE to Activate Chart

expulsions, many thousands of Jews migrated into Eastern Europe. Some local rulers there welcomed their skills and knowledge. Jewish communities grew, experiencing times of relative tolerance and prosperity, as well as periods of persecution.

☑ **DRAW CONCLUSIONS** Why did prejudice against Jews increase as Christianity spread in the later Middle Ages?

The Christian Church Is Divided

During the Middle Ages, a growing divide split Christendom, as the Christian world was sometimes called. The divide opened up differences between Byzantine Christians in the east and Roman Catholics in lands to the west.

In general, Christians in both regions originally shared a common theology, or set of beliefs, and the same holy days in the Christian calendar, such as Christmas and Easter. Over time, however, the practices of Christians in the east and west grew apart. Long simmering controversies broke into open conflict, leading to a **schism,** or great divide, within the Christian world.

Differences East and West Since early Christian times, differences had emerged over Church leadership. Although the Byzantine emperor was not a priest, he controlled Church affairs and appointed the patriarch, or highest Church official, in Constantinople. Byzantine Christians rejected the pope's claim to authority over all Christians.

Other differences emerged during the Middle Ages. While reform movements in the West ended up forbidding the clergy to marry, Byzantine priests were allowed to marry. Greek, not Latin, was the language of the Byzantine Church. As in the Roman Church, the most significant Byzantine holy day was Easter, celebrated as the day Jesus rose from the dead. However, Byzantine Christians placed somewhat less emphasis on Christmas—the celebration of the birth of Jesus—compared to Christians in the West.

Dispute Over Icons Differences in customs and celebrations were a growing sign of the divide. A huge controversy erupted in the 700s over the issue of **icons,** or holy images. This dispute contributed further to the divide.

Many Byzantine Christians prayed using images of Jesus, Mary, and the saints. In 730, however, a Byzantine emperor outlawed the veneration, or honoring, of icons, saying it violated God's commandment against worshiping "graven images." The ban set off violent battles within the Byzantine empire. The pope took a hand in the dispute, excommunicating the Byzantine emperor. Although a later Byzantine ruler restored the use of icons, the conflict left great resentment against the pope.

The Great Schism By 1054, other controversies had worsened the divide, leading to the **Great Schism,** or the permanent split between eastern and western Christianity. The Byzantine Christian Church became known as the Eastern Orthodox Church. In the west, the Church became known as the Roman Catholic Church.

After the Great Schism, other differences grew between the two branches of Christianity. Popes in Rome had long asserted their claim to papal supremacy. The patriarchs in the eastern Christian Church continued to reject this claim. The Roman Catholic Church had a single leader, the pope, while the Eastern Orthodox Church recognized a number of patriarchs, or high-ranking clergy.

During the many controversies that erupted between the Roman Catholic and Eastern Orthodox churches, popes and patriarchs excommunicated each other. Although both churches still followed the same faith, the centers of power saw each other as rivals. During the Middle Ages and after, their contacts remained guarded and distant.

Orthodox Christianity as a Unifying Force
Within the Byzantine empire, Christianity was a strong unifying social and political factor, just as it had been in the western Roman empire. The people followed the same traditions, such as the use of icons, and celebrated holy days according to the Orthodox religious calendar. The use of Greek, the official language of the Byzantine church, was also a unifying factor, just as Latin unified the Roman Catholic Church in Western Europe. The patriarch of Constantinople traditionally blessed the Byzantine emperor and the emperor took a strong hand in Church affairs, affirming the unity between political and religious authority.

☑ **COMPARE AND CONTRAST** Prior to the Great Schism, how did the practice of Christianity in the Byzantine empire differ from that in Western Europe?

☑ ASSESSMENT

1. **Support Ideas with Examples** In what ways did the Church gain economic power during the Middle Ages?

2. **Synthesize** What were some of the effects of the Great Schism?

3. **Explain** How were Jews treated in Muslim Spain during the Middle Ages?

4. **Support Ideas with Examples** What were Church attitudes towards women in medieval Europe?

5. **Quest Connections** What role did the Church play in daily life during the Middle Ages?

7.4

New farming technologies changed medieval Europe. In the fields, a new type of harness distributed pressure along the shoulders of the horse, which allowed the plowing of heavier soils.

Economic Expansion and Change: The Crusades and After

By about 1000, Europe was undergoing an economic revival. Over the next few centuries, remarkable changes greatly strengthened Western Europe. These changes began in the countryside, where peasants adopted new farming technologies that made their fields more productive. The result was an agricultural revolution that transformed Europe.

Changes in Agriculture Transform Europe

Farming Technology Improves By about 800, peasants were using iron plows that carved deep into the heavy soil of northern Europe. These plows were an improvement over wooden plows, which were designed for light Mediterranean soils rather than heavier northern soils.

Also, a new kind of harness allowed peasants to use horses rather than oxen to pull the plows. Faster moving horses could plow more land in a day than oxen could, so peasants could enlarge their fields and plant more crops.

Food Output and Population Grow Other changes brought still more land into use. Peasants adopted a new way of rotating crops: the three-field system. They planted one field with grain; a second

 BOUNCE to Activate Flipped Video

Objectives

Summarize how new technologies sparked an agricultural revolution, and the revival of trade led to the growth of towns and cities.

Explain how a commercial revolution changed society and how guilds led to the rise of the middle class.

Explain the causes and effects of the Crusades.

Summarize how Christians in Spain carried out the Reconquista.

Key Terms

charter
capital
partnership
tenant farmer
middle class
guild
apprentice
journeyman
Crusades

Holy Land
Pope Urban II
Reconquista
Ferdinand and
Isabella
Inquisition

with legumes, such as peas and beans; and the third they left unplanted. The legumes restored fertility to the soil and added protein to the peasants' diet. The new method allowed peasants to plant two thirds of their land, rather than half. In addition, lords who wanted to boost the incomes of their manors had peasants clear forests, drain swamps, and reclaim wasteland for farming and grazing.

All these improvements allowed farmers to produce more food. With more food available, the population began to grow. Between about 1000 and 1300, the population of Europe almost tripled.

☑ **CHECK UNDERSTANDING** Why did agricultural production improve?

Trade Expands and Towns Grow

Europe's growing population needed goods that were not available on the manor. Peasants needed iron for farm tools. Wealthy nobles wanted fine wool, furs, and spices from distant lands. As foreign invasions and feudal warfare declined, traders reappeared, crisscrossing Europe to meet the growing demand for goods.

New Trade Routes Enterprising traders formed merchant companies that traveled in armed caravans for safety. They followed regular trade routes, many of which had hardly been used for centuries. Along these routes, merchants exchanged local goods for those from remote markets in the Middle East and from still farther east in Asia.

In Constantinople, merchants bought Chinese silks, Byzantine gold jewelry, and Asian spices. They shipped these goods by sea to Venice, where traders loaded their wares onto pack mules and headed north to Flanders. There, other traders bought the goods at trade fairs and sent them to England and lands along the Baltic Sea. Northern Europeans paid for these goods with products such as honey, furs, cloth, tin, and lead.

Trade Fairs and the Hanseatic League Annual trade fairs were an early sign of economic revival. Traders from all over Europe met at fairs near navigable rivers or where trade routes met. Trading lasted for weeks. The fairs became elaborate events with entertainments as well as goods.

The trade fairs gradually declined, in part because of competition from the Hanseatic League, an association of towns in northern Germany that banded together to protect their trading interests. The league used its shipping fleets to clear the northern seas of pirates and boost trade in furs, timber, and fish.

TRADE IN MEDIEVAL EUROPE

By the 1300s, established trade networks crisscrossed Europe. Goods came into Europe from China, Byzantium, the Middle East, and Africa. Europe also sent goods out into the world, shipping through major trading centers in England, France, Italy, and Spain.

GOODS COMING → INTO EUROPE

GOODS GOING ← OUT FROM EUROPE

WOOL · SWORDS · TIMBER · GOLD, SILVER, COPPER · SPICES · GRAIN · PAPER · EXOTIC JEWELRY · SILKS · FUR

>> Active trade routes brought in new ideas as well as new goods.

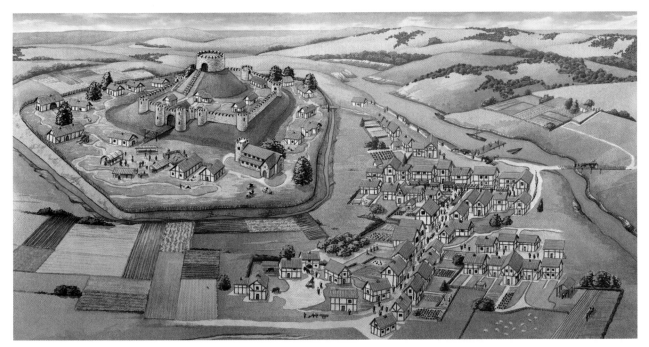

>> **Analyze Visuals** Population growth in medieval towns led to growth and changes in many other areas as well. What evidence do you see of change that supports population growth?

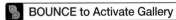
BOUNCE to Activate Gallery

Towns and Cities Expand Many trade fairs closed in the autumn, when the weather made roads impassable. Merchants might wait out the winter near a castle or in a town. These settlements attracted artisans who made goods that merchants could sell.

Slowly, these small centers of trade and handicraft became the first medieval cities. Some boasted populations of 10,000, and by the fourteenth century, a few topped 100,000. Europe had not seen towns of this size since Roman times. The richest cities emerged in northern Italy and Flanders—the two ends of the profitable north-south trade route. Both areas were centers of the wool trade and had prosperous textile industries.

To protect their interests, the merchants who set up a new town asked the local lord, or the king himself, for a **charter.** This written document set out the rights and privileges of the town. In return, merchants paid the lord or the king a large sum of money, a yearly fee, or both.

Although charters varied from place to place, they almost always granted townspeople the right to choose their own leaders and control their own affairs. A common saying of the late Middle Ages was "Town air makes free."

Town and City Life Medieval towns and cities were surrounded by high, protective walls. As a city grew, space within the walls filled to overflowing, and newcomers had to settle in the fields outside the walls. Because of overcrowding, city dwellers added second and third stories to their houses and shops. Therefore, a typical medieval city was a jumble of narrow streets lined with tall houses.

Most towns were filthy, smelly, noisy, and crowded—a perfect breeding ground for disease. Even a rich town had no garbage collection or sewer system, so residents simply flung their wastes into the street. Fire was a constant danger with wooden houses so closely packed together. Despite the drawbacks of town and city life, people were attracted to the opportunities available there.

☑ **CHECK UNDERSTANDING** How and why did medieval towns and cities grow?

Economic Changes

During the turmoil of the early Middle Ages, coined money largely disappeared. As trade revived after 1000, money again appeared in circulation, coined by rulers. In time, the need for **capital,** or money for investment, grew. Merchants, for example, needed capital to buy goods, so they borrowed from moneylenders. Over time, the need for capital led to the growth of banking houses.

>> This image shows banking operations in the 1400s. The man at the right is depositing a bag of gold.

>> Letters of credit worked like medieval credit cards. Purchases or cash withdrawals could be made without money actually changing hands.

New Ways of Doing Business To meet the needs of the changing economy, Europeans developed new ways of doing business. Groups of merchants joined together in **partnerships.** They pooled their funds to finance a large-scale venture that would have been too costly for any individual trader. This practice made capital more easily available. It also reduced the risk for any one partner because no one had to invest all his or her capital in the company.

Later, merchants developed a system of insurance to help reduce business risks. For a small fee, an underwriter insured the merchant's shipment. If the shipment was lost or destroyed, the underwriter paid the merchant most of its value. If the goods arrived safely, the merchant lost only the insurance payment.

Europeans adopted some practices from the Arab and Muslim merchants with whom they traded. Among the most important were bills of exchange and letters of credit. With a bill of exchange, a merchant would deposit money with a banker in his home city. The banker would issue a bill of exchange, which the merchant could exchange for cash in a distant city. The merchant could thus travel without carrying gold coins, which were easily stolen. A letter of credit guaranteed payment of a set sum of money after the seller met certain conditions.

Changes Affect Medieval Society These new business practices were part of a commercial revolution that transformed the medieval economy. Slowly, they also reshaped medieval society.

For example, the use of money undermined serfdom. Feudal lords needed money to buy fine goods. As a result, many peasants began selling farm products to townspeople and paying rent to their lord in cash rather than in labor. By 1300, most peasants in Western Europe were either **tenant farmers,** who paid rent for their land, or hired farm laborers.

In growing towns, the old social order of nobles, clergy, and peasants also changed. By 1000, a new class appeared that included merchants, traders, and artisans. They formed a **middle class,** standing between nobles and peasants.

☑ **DESCRIBE** Describe three economic changes in medieval Europe.

A New Middle Class

The new middle class ranked between nobles and peasants. The status of the merchants, artisans, and tradespeople who made up this new class was not tied to the farming economy, but to business and commerce.

Nobles and the clergy often despised the new middle class. To nobles, towns were a disruptive influence beyond their control. To the clergy, the profits that merchants and bankers made from usury, or lending money at interest, were immoral.

Guilds Shape Town Life In medieval towns, the middle class gained economic and political power. First, merchants and artisans formed associations known as **guilds.** Merchant guilds appeared first. They dominated town life, passing laws and levying taxes. They also decided whether to spend funds to pave the streets with cobblestones or make other town improvements.

In time, artisans came to resent the powerful merchants. They organized craft guilds. Each guild represented workers in one occupation, such as weavers, bakers, or goldsmiths. In some towns, struggles between craft guilds and the wealthier merchant guilds led to riots.

Guild members cooperated to protect their economic interests. To prevent competition, they limited guild membership and also made membership a requirement to work in any trade in the city. Guilds made rules to protect the quality of their goods, regulate hours of labor, and set prices. Guilds also provided social services. They operated schools and hospitals, looked after the needs of their members, and provided support for the widows and orphans of their members.

Becoming a Guild Member Becoming a guild member took many years of hard work. At the age of seven or eight, a child might become an **apprentice,** or trainee, to a guild master. The apprentice usually spent seven years learning the trade. The guild master paid no wages, but was required to give the apprentice food and housing. These arrangements were usually part of a formal legal document that bound both the apprentice and the guild master. For example:

I, Peter Borre, in good faith and without guile, place with you, Peter Feissac, weaver, my son Stephen, for the purpose of learning the trade or craft of weaving, to live at your house, and to do work for you . . . for four continuous years, promising you by this agreement to take care that my son does the said work, . . .

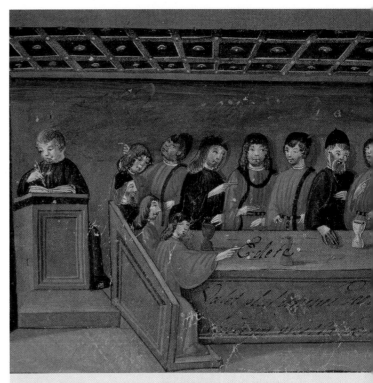

>> This Italian painting from the 1300s shows guild members meeting to discuss issues important to the guild and the town.

>> A guild master oversees apprentices in the making of coins. The scale is used to ensure that the coins have the proper amount of gold in them.

will neither steal nor take anything away from you, or flee or depart from you for any reason, until he has completed his apprenticeship.

—French apprenticeship agreement, 1248

Few apprentices ever became guild masters unless they were related to one. Most worked for guild members as **journeymen,** or salaried workers. Journeymen often accused masters of keeping their wages low so that they could not save enough to open a competing shop.

Women in the Guilds Women worked in dozens of crafts. A woman often engaged in the same trade as her father or husband and might inherit his workshop if he died. Because she knew the craft well, she kept the shop going and sometimes became a guild master herself. Young girls became apprentices in trades such as ribbon-making and paper-making. Women dominated some trades and even had their own guilds.

In Paris, they far outnumbered men in the profitable silk and wool guilds. A third of the guilds in Frankfurt were composed entirely of women.

Middle Class Family Life Family life in the towns and cities differed in some ways from the lives of

>> This woman and young girl are working at a loom weaving wool.

peasants on farms. Unlike peasants, middle class families did not grow their own food. Instead, they bought food and other goods in the town's market. Although the calendar still determined everyday life from harvests to holidays, artisans, merchants, and other townspeople saw the seasons differently. They had to make or sell goods during all seasons.

In towns, children were apprenticed out or worked in the business of their parents, rather than in the fields. Some middle class families sent their boys to schools, which were more common in towns than on the manor. Boys might attend a local church school, learning the basics of reading and writing. A few privileged boys might even get the chance for a higher education. In a world where most people were illiterate, or unable to read and write, a basic education was a valuable skill.

☑ **CHECK UNDERSTANDING** Why were guilds important in town life?

The Crusades

By 1050, Western Europe was just emerging from centuries of isolation. For the first time since the fall of Rome, Western Europeans were strong enough to break out of their narrow world and take the offensive against other lands.

Starting in 1096, thousands of Europeans took part in the **Crusades,** a series of wars in which Christians battled Muslims for control of land in the Middle East. During these wars, both sides committed bloody acts. The First Crusade freed Jerusalem from Muslim rule and established a string of European-ruled Crusader states. They were surrounded by Muslim-ruled lands, however, and Arab counterattacks reconquered the last European outpost in 1291.

Conflict in the Holy Land By the 1050s, the once prosperous Byzantine empire was facing a serious threat from the Seljuk Turks.

The Turks had migrated from Central Asia into the Middle East, where they converted to Islam. Before long, the Seljuks had overrun most Byzantine lands in Asia Minor (present-day Turkey) and extended their power over the **Holy Land.** This area included Jerusalem and other places where Christians believe Jesus had lived and preached. For centuries, Christians had made pilgrimages to the Holy Land.

The conflict between the Seljuk Turks and the Byzantines disrupted travel to the Holy Land and was threatening the very survival of the Byzantine

>> **Analyze Maps** Urged on by Pope Urban II, thousands of Europeans joined the Crusades to expel Muslims from the Holy Land. What route did English crusaders take? Why do you think they took that route?

BOUNCE to Activate Map

empire. In 1095, the Byzantine emperor Alexius I urgently asked **Pope Urban II** for Christian knights to help him fight the Muslim Turks. Although Roman popes and Byzantine emperors were longtime rivals, Urban agreed.

The Pope Calls for War At the Council of Clermont in 1095, Urban incited bishops and nobles to action. "From Jerusalem and the city of Constantinople comes a grievous report," he began. "An accursed race . . . has violently invaded the lands of those Christians and has depopulated them by pillage and fire." Urban then called for a crusade to free the Holy Land:

> Both knights and footmen, both rich and poor . . . [must] strive to help expel [the Seljuk] from our Christian lands before it is too late. . . . Christ commands it. Remission of sins will be granted for those going thither.

—Fulcher of Chartres, *Chronicle of the First Crusade*

"God wills it!" roared the assembly. By 1096, thousands of knights were on their way to the Holy Land. As the crusading spirit swept through Western Europe, armies of ordinary men and women inspired by fiery preachers also left for the Holy Land. Few returned.

Why did so many people embark on the Crusades? Religious reasons played a large role. Yet many knights hoped to win wealth and land. Some crusaders sought to escape troubles at home. Others yearned for adventure.

The pope, too, had mixed motives. In addition to his religious motivations, Urban hoped to increase his power in Europe and perhaps heal the schism, or split, between the Roman and Byzantine churches. He also saw lands in the Middle East as an outlet for Europe's growing population of knights. Sending Christian knights to fight Muslims instead of one another would help ease warfare at home.

Waves of Crusaders Head Eastward Only the First Crusade came close to achieving its goals. After a long and bloody campaign, Christian knights captured Jerusalem in 1099 and killed the Muslim and Jewish residents of the city.

The crusaders divided their captured lands into four small states, called crusader states. The Muslims repeatedly sought to destroy these Christian states, prompting Europeans to launch new crusades.

By 1187, Jerusalem had fallen to the able Muslim leader Salah al-Din, known to Europeans as Saladin. On the Third Crusade, Europeans failed to retake

Jerusalem. After negotiations, though, Saladin did reopen the holy city to Christian pilgrims.

Europeans also mounted crusades against other Muslim lands, especially in North Africa. All ended in defeat. During the Fourth Crusade, the crusaders were diverted from fighting Muslims to fighting other Christians. After helping merchants from the northern Italian city of Venice defeat their Byzantine trade rivals in 1204, crusaders captured and looted Constantinople, the Byzantine capital.

Meanwhile, Muslim armies overran the crusader states. By 1291, they had captured the last Christian outpost, the port city of Acre, and killed its Christian residents.

☑ **ANALYZE INFORMATION** Did the Christian kings of Europe achieve their goals during the Crusades?

The Effects of the Crusades

The Crusades failed in their chief goal—the conquest of the Holy Land. They also left a bitter legacy of religious hatred. In the Middle East, both Christians and Muslims committed atrocities in the name of religion. In Europe, crusaders sometimes turned their religious fury against Jews, killing entire communities.

>> Crusaders returned to Europe with spices, perfumes, and other trade goods from the Middle East, and trade began to grow.

The Crusades did have positive effects on Europe, however. They began just as Europe was undergoing major economic and political changes, and the Crusades helped quicken the pace of those changes, contributing to the end of the medieval period in Europe.

A Growing Demand for Goods Even before the Crusades, Europeans had developed a taste for luxuries that merchants brought from the Byzantine empire. The Crusades increased the level of trade. Returning crusaders brought even more fabrics, spices, and perfumes from the Middle East to a larger market. Trade increased and expanded.

Merchants in Venice and other northern Italian cities built large fleets to carry crusaders to the Holy Land. They later used those fleets to open new markets in the crusader states. Even after the Muslims recaptured Acre, Italian merchants kept these trade routes open. Our words *sugar*, *cotton*, and *rice*, which were borrowed from Arabic, show the range of trade goods brought back to Europe.

The Crusades further encouraged the growth of a money economy. To finance a journey to the Holy Land, nobles needed money. They therefore allowed peasants to pay rents in money rather than in grain or labor. Peasants began to sell their goods in towns to earn money, a practice that helped to undermine serfdom.

Changes for Monarchs and the Church The Crusades helped to increase the power of monarchs. They managed to gain the power to levy, or collect, taxes in order to support the Crusades.

Some rulers, such as the French king Louis IX and the English king Richard I, called the Lionheart, led crusades, which added greatly to their prestige.

Enthusiasm for the Crusades brought papal power to its greatest height. The growing power of the Church, however, soon brought popes into a bitter struggle with feudal rulers in Europe. Also, the Crusades did not end the split between the Roman and Byzantine churches as Pope Urban had hoped. In fact, Byzantine resentment against the West hardened as a result of the Fourth Crusade, which ended in the sack of Constantinople.

Europe Gains a Wider View of the World Contacts with the Muslim world led Christians to realize that millions of people lived in regions they had never even known existed. Soon, a few curious Europeans left to explore far-off places such as India and China.

In 1271, a young Venetian, Marco Polo, set out for China with his merchant father and uncle. After many years in China, he returned to Venice

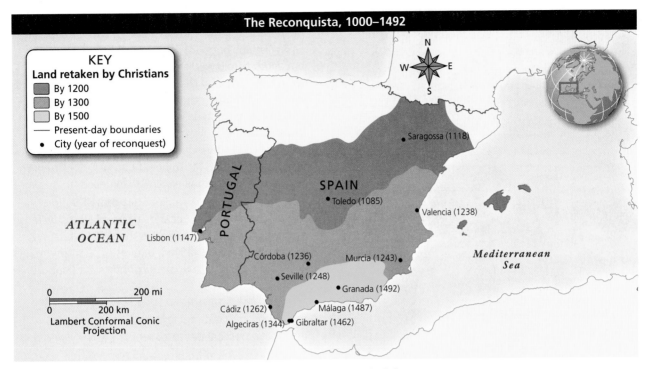

KEY
Land retaken by Christians
By 1200
By 1300
By 1500
— Present-day boundaries
• City (year of reconquest)

Saragossa (1118)

SPAIN

PORTUGAL

Toledo (1085)

Valencia (1238)

ATLANTIC OCEAN

Lisbon (1147)

Córdoba (1236)

Murcia (1243)

Mediterranean Sea

Seville (1248)

Granada (1492)

0   200 mi
0   200 km
Lambert Conformal Conic Projection

Cádiz (1262)

Málaga (1487)

Algeciras (1344)   Gibraltar (1462)

>> **Analyze Maps** The Reconquista took many years and reflected political changes in Spain. The union of Ferdinand and Isabella and their countries gave their forces the power to take back most of Spain. How did the union of the countries of Castile and Aragon help the Reconquista?

and wrote a book about the wonders of Chinese civilization. Europeans who heard his stories dubbed him a liar, rejecting his incredible tales of government mail service and black stones (coal) that were burned to heat homes.

The experiences of crusaders and of travelers like Marco Polo expanded European horizons and contributed to the end of medieval Europe by bringing Europe into a wider world from which it had been cut off since the fall of Rome. By the 1400s, a desire to trade directly with India and China would lead Europeans to a new age of exploration.

Impact on the Middle East and the Byzantine Empire The Crusades occurred during a time when Muslims in the Middle East were locked in frequent local power struggles. On occasion, rival Muslim rulers joined forces to fight the European invaders. Saladin briefly united lands from Egypt to Syria, but divisions soon reappeared.

The Fourth Crusade further weakened the Byzantine empire, which had already lost most of its lands. As the empire continued to decline, it faced a new threat, this time from the Ottoman Turks. In 1453, it finally fell to the invaders led by Mehmet II.

☑ **SUMMARIZE** Summarize the effects of the Crusades.

The Reconquista

The crusading spirit continued long after the European defeat at Acre. It flourished especially in Spain, where Christian warriors had been battling Muslims since the time of Charlemagne.

Spain is part of the Iberian peninsula, which also includes present-day Portugal. During the 700s, Muslims from North Africa had conquered most of the peninsula. These Muslims, called Moors by Christian Europeans, carried Islamic civilization to Spain. In the north, several tiny Christian kingdoms survived the Muslim conquest. They slowly expanded their borders, taking over Muslim lands. Their campaign to drive Muslims from Spain became known as the **Reconquista,** or "reconquest."

Christian Forces Advance Efforts by Christian warriors to expel Muslims began in the 700s. Their first real success did not come, however, until 1085, when they captured the city of Toledo.

During the next 200 years, Christian forces pushed slowly and steadily southward. By 1300, Christians controlled the entire Iberian Peninsula except for Granada. Muslim influences remained strong, though, and helped shape the arts and literature of Christian Spain.

>> A later illustration shows prisoners being led to the stake during the Inquisition.

Conditions for Muslims and Jews worsened. Both Muslims and Jews were ordered to accept baptism as Christians or go into exile. Many were baptized but secretly followed their former faith. Converts were often tried by the Inquisition. If they were found guilty of practicing their old religion, they faced punishments such as torture or burning at the stake. In 1492, Queen Isabella expelled all Jews who did not convert to Christianity. Hundreds of thousands of Jews fled Spain. Over the next century, hundreds of thousands of Muslims were also expelled from Spain.

Spain achieved religious unity, but at a high price. Hundreds of thousands of people, mostly Jews and Muslims, fled into exile in the years after 1492. Many of them were skilled, educated people who had contributed much to Spain's economy and culture.

☑ **CHECK UNDERSTANDING** How did the monarchy in Spain emerge, and what were its distinctive political developments?

1. **Draw Conclusions** Why was the invasion of the Byzantine empire by the Seljuk Turks in the 1050s significant?

2. **Determine Relevance** How did the Crusades accelerate change in Europe?

3. **Draw Inferences** What were the advantages of living in a medieval city? Would you rather have lived in the country or a city in medieval Europe? Why?

4. **Draw Conclusions** Why was the revival of trade so important?

5. **Quest Connections** How did improvements in agriculture in the countryside likely affect the lives of townspeople?

In 1469, the marriage of Ferdinand of Aragon and Isabella of Castile created the unified state called Spain. Using their combined forces, **Ferdinand and Isabella** made a final push against the Muslim stronghold of Granada. In 1492, Granada fell. The Reconquista was complete. Ferdinand and Isabella then set out to impose unity on their diverse peoples. Isabella was determined to bring religious as well as political unity to the kingdom.

Spain Forces Non-Christians to Leave Under Muslim rule, Spanish Christians, Jews, and Muslims lived in relative peace, worshipping as they chose. Isabella ended that tolerance. With the support of the **Inquisition,** a Church court set up to try people accused of heresy, Isabella launched a new crusade.

7.5

This image from an 11th-century Bible shows a king receiving fealty from his nobles.

The Feudal Monarchs and the Church

During the early Middle Ages, hundreds of feudal nobles ruled over territories of varying size. Feudal nobles had their own courts and armies and collected their own taxes. Most feudal lords acknowledged a king or other overlord, but royal rulers had little power. The Church, too, was a center of power with its own laws, system of justice, and methods of raising money. Both nobles and the Church could at times have as much power as a monarch.

Feudal Monarchs Begin to Centralize Power

From about 1000 to 1300, sometimes called the High Middle Ages, the balance of power slowly shifted. Feudal monarchs began to exert royal authority over their nobles and the Church. Some feudal monarchs succeeded in centralizing power and built the framework for nation-states such as Britain and France. (A nation-state refers to an independent political unit that has a single government and usually shares a common culture and history.)

Monarchs used various means to centralize power. First, they sought to extend royal law and justice over their kingdoms. To do so, they had to crush the power of rival courts of justice run by feudal nobles and the Church. To provide efficient government and a steady source of income, feudal monarchs set up government bureaucracies that administered justice and taxation. With a larger income, monarchs could afford to support a standing army, rather than rely on the military service of their nobles.

 BOUNCE to Activate Flipped Video

Objectives

Learn how monarchs gained power over nobles and the Christian Church, and how English kings strengthened their power.

Describe how traditions of government evolved under King John and later English monarchs.

Explain how strong monarchs unified France.

Describe the formation of the Holy Roman Empire and how some emperors struggled with the papacy to control specific religious and secular issues.

Analyze how the Church reached the height of its power under Pope Innocent III.

Key Terms

William the
  Conqueror
common law
King John
Magna Carta
due process of law
habeas corpus
Parliament

Louis IX
Holy Roman Empire
Gregory VII
Henry IV
lay investiture
Frederick Barbarossa
Pope Innocent III

The growth of towns and the money economy also strengthened royal rulers. Townspeople in the middle class often turned to monarchs, rather than nobles, who could ensure the peace necessary for successful commerce.

☑ **CHECK UNDERSTANDING** During the High Middle Ages, how did the balance of power shift between kings, noblemen, and the Church?

English Kings Expand Their Power

During the early Middle Ages, Angles, Saxons, and Vikings invaded and settled in England. Although feudalism emerged in England, as it did elsewhere in Europe, English monarchs generally kept their kingdoms united.

The Anglo-Saxons The term "Anglo-Saxon" is used to describe the Germanic people that migrated to England in the 400s, including the Angles and the Saxons. The different dialects the people spoke eventually evolved into Old English. At first, the Anglo-Saxons kept to their small tribal groups. However, by the 800s, the country was divided into four larger kingdoms. The Anglo-Saxons were pagans and had superstitious beliefs. Starting in the late 500s, they began converting to Christianity.

>> William of Normandy, called the Conqueror, ended Anglo-Saxon rule in England.

 BOUNCE to Activate Gallery

To pass on their history, they told stories, such as *Beowulf,* which is about a heroic prince. Eventually these stories were written down.

The Norman Conquest of England In 1066, however, the Anglo-Saxon king, Edward, died without an heir. His death triggered a power struggle that changed the course of English history. A council of nobles chose Edward's brother-in-law Harold to rule. But William, Duke of Normandy, in what is present-day France, also claimed the throne. The answer to the rival claims lay on the battlefield.

In France, William raised an army and won the support of the pope. He then sailed across the English Channel to England.

At the Battle of Hastings, William and his Norman knights triumphed over Harold. **William the Conqueror,** as he was now called, became king of England on Christmas Day 1066.

William Exerts Firm Control Once in power, William exerted firm control over his new lands. Like other feudal monarchs, he granted fiefs to the Church and to his Norman lords, or barons, but he also kept a large amount of land for himself. He monitored who built castles and where. He required every vassal to swear first allegiance to him rather than to any other feudal lord.

To learn about his kingdom, William had a complete census of its land and livestock taken in 1086. The result was the Domesday (pronounced "doomsday"), which listed every castle, field, and pigpen in England.

As the title suggests, the survey was as thorough and inevitable as doomsday, believed to be God's final day of judgment that no one could escape. Information in the Domesday Book helped William and later English monarchs build an efficient system of tax collection.

Although William's French-speaking Norman nobles dominated England, the country's Anglo-Saxon population survived. Over the next 300 years, there was a gradual blending of Norman French and Anglo-Saxon customs, languages, and traditions.

Extending Royal Power William's successors strengthened two key areas of government: finance and law. They created the royal exchequer, or treasury, to collect taxes, fees, fines, and other dues. In 1154, an energetic, well-educated king, Henry II, inherited the English throne. He broadened the system of royal justice. As a ruler, he could not simply write new laws but had to follow accepted customs. Henry, however, found ways to expand old customs into laws. He then sent out traveling justices to enforce these royal laws.

The decisions of the royal courts became the basis for **common law,** or a legal system based on custom and court rulings. Unlike local feudal laws, it was "common," meaning that it was the same for all the people. In time, people brought their disputes to royal courts rather than to those of nobles or the Church. Since the royal courts charged fees, the exchequer benefited from the growth of royal justice.

The Early Jury System Under Henry II, England also developed an early jury system. When traveling justices visited an area, local officials collected a jury, or group of men sworn to speak the truth. These early juries determined which cases should be brought to trial and were the ancestors of today's grand jury. Later, another jury developed that was composed of 12 neighbors of an accused person. It was the ancestor of today's trial jury.

A Tragic Conflict with the Church Henry's efforts to extend royal power over the clergy led to a bitter dispute with the Church. Henry claimed the right to try clergy in royal courts. Thomas Becket, the archbishop of Canterbury and once a close friend of Henry, fiercely opposed the king on this issue.

The conflict simmered for years. At last, Henry's fury exploded. "What cowards I have brought up in my court," he cried. "Who will rid me of this meddlesome priest?" Four hot-headed knights took Henry at his word. In 1170, they murdered Archbishop Thomas Becket in his own cathedral. Henry denied any part in the attack. Still, to make peace with the Church, he eased his attempts to regulate the clergy. Meanwhile, Becket was honored as a martyr and declared a saint. Pilgrims flocked to his tomb at Canterbury, where miracles were said to occur.

☑ **DESCRIBE** What was Henry II's argument with the Church?

Developing New Traditions of Government

Later English rulers repeatedly clashed with nobles and the Church as they tried to raise taxes or to impose royal authority over traditional feudal rights. Out of those struggles evolved traditions of government that would have great influence on the modern world.

King John Battles Powerful Enemies A son of Henry II, **King John** was a clever, cruel, and

>> This image shows prisoners brought before judges and a jury. The men sitting at the table writing on scrolls are recording the court activities, much like today's court reporters.

>> In this illustration from the 1800s, King John lays a token of his submission before the feet of Pope Innocent III's representative, conceding defeat.

untrustworthy ruler. During his reign, he faced three powerful enemies: King Philip II of France, Pope Innocent III, and his own English nobles. He lost each struggle.

Ever since William the Conqueror, Norman rulers of England had held vast lands in France. In 1205, John suffered his first setback when he lost a war with Philip II and had to give up lands in Anjou and Normandy.

Next, John battled with Innocent III over selecting a new archbishop of Canterbury. When John rejected the pope's nominee, the pope excommunicated him, or prevented him from participating in the sacraments and services of the Church.

Innocent also placed England under the interdict, which forbade Church services to the entire kingdom. Even the strongest ruler was likely to give in to that pressure. To save himself and his crown, John had to accept England as a fief of the papacy and pay a yearly fee to Rome.

The Magna Carta Finally, John angered his own nobles with oppressive taxes and other abuses of power. In 1215, a group of rebellious barons cornered John and forced him to sign the **Magna Carta,** or great charter. In this document, the king affirmed a long list of feudal rights. Besides protecting their own privileges, the barons included a few clauses recognizing the rights of townspeople and the Church.

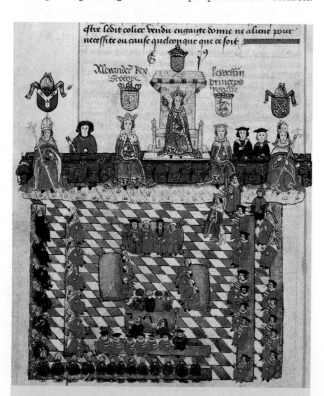

>> This image from the 1200s shows Edward I attending an English parliamentary meeting.

The Magna Carta contained two very important ideas that in the long run would shape political and legal traditions in England. First, it asserted that the nobles had certain rights. Over time, these rights that had been granted to nobles were extended to all English citizens. Second, the Magna Carta made it clear that the monarch must obey the law.

Among other clauses in the Magna Carta that would have lasting impact were those that protected freemen from arbitrary arrest, imprisonment, and other legal actions, except "by legal judgment of his peers or by the law of the land." This clause would much later become the basis of the right we know today as **due process of law,** which safeguards the legal rights of the individual.

Over the centuries, the English would rely on the Magna Carta to develop other political and legal ideas and traditions. In the 1600s, the idea of protecting people from arbitrary arrest and imprisonment would evolve into the right of **habeas corpus,** the principle that no person can be held in prison without first being charged with a specific crime.

In the Magna Carta, King John also had to agree not to raise new taxes without first consulting his Great Council of lords and clergy. Many centuries later, American colonists would claim that those words meant that any taxation without representation was unjust. In 1215, though, neither the king nor his lords could have imagined such an idea.

Parliament Develops During the 1200s, English rulers often called on the Great Council for advice. Eventually, this council evolved into **Parliament,** which later became England's legislature. As Parliament acquired a larger role in government, it helped unify England.

In 1295, King Edward I summoned Parliament to approve money for his wars in France. "What touches all," he declared, "should be approved by all." He had representatives of the "common people" join with the lords and clergy. The "commons" included two knights from each county and representatives of the towns.

Much later, this assembly became known as the Model Parliament because it set up the framework for England's legislature. In time, Parliament developed into a two-house body: the House of Lords with nobles and high clergy and the House of Commons with knights and middle-class citizens.

Over the centuries, Parliament gained the crucial "power of the purse": the right to approve any new taxes. With that power, Parliament could insist that the monarch meet its demands before voting for taxes. In this way, it could check, or limit, the power of the monarch.

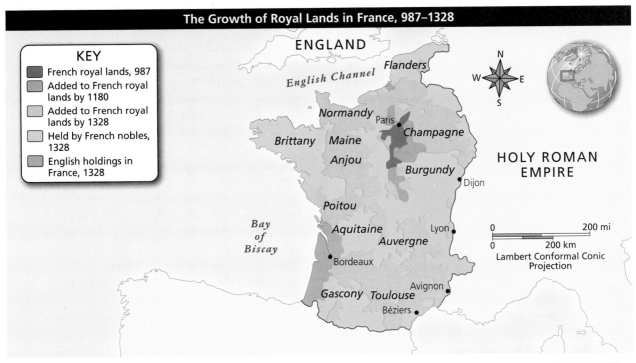

The Growth of Royal Lands in France, 987–1328

KEY
- French royal lands, 987
- Added to French royal lands by 1180
- Added to French royal lands by 1328
- Held by French nobles, 1328
- English holdings in France, 1328

ENGLAND

Flanders

English Channel

Normandy · Paris
Champagne
Brittany · Maine
Anjou
Burgundy
· Dijon

HOLY ROMAN EMPIRE

Poitou
Bay of Biscay
Aquitaine · Lyon
Auvergne
· Bordeaux

0   200 mi
0   200 km
Lambert Conformal Conic Projection

Gascony · Toulouse · Avignon
· Béziers

>> Capetian kings gradually extended royal control over more than half of France. **Analyze Maps** What overall trend in French royal power does the map show? Where and by whom might that power be challenged after 1328? Explain your answer.

BOUNCE to Activate Map

☑ **DESCRIBE** What was the political, legal, and economic impact of the ideas contained in the Magna Carta?

Growth of the French Monarchy

Unlike William the Conqueror in England, monarchs in France did not rule over a unified kingdom. The successors to Charlemagne had little power over a patchwork of French territories ruled by powerful feudal lords.

France Under the Capetians In 987, these feudal nobles elected Hugh Capet, the count of Paris, to fill the vacant French throne. They may have chosen him because they thought he was too weak to pose a threat to them. Hugh's own lands around Paris were smaller than those of many of his vassals.

Nevertheless, Hugh and his heirs slowly increased royal power. First, they made the throne hereditary, passing it from father to son. The Capetian dynasty lasted for 300 years, making the kingdom more stable. Next, they added to their lands by playing rival nobles against each other. They also won the support of the Church.

Perhaps most important, the Capetians built an effective bureaucracy. Government officials collected taxes and imposed royal law over the king's lands. By establishing order, they increased their prestige and gained the backing of the new middle class.

Philip Augustus Increases Power and Prosperity In 1179, Philip II became king of France. Called Philip Augustus, he was a shrewd and able ruler. He strengthened royal government in many ways. Instead of appointing nobles to government jobs, he used paid middle-class officials who owed their loyalty to him. He granted charters to many new towns and introduced a new national tax.

Philip also quadrupled royal land holdings. Through trickery, diplomacy, and war, he gained control of English-ruled lands in Normandy, Anjou, and elsewhere. He then began to take over southern France. At the pope's request, he sent knights to suppress a heresy among the Albigensians (al buh JEN see unz) in the south and then added this vast area to his domain. Before his death in 1223, Philip had become the most powerful ruler in Europe.

Louis IX Rules France Perhaps the most admired French ruler of this time was **Louis IX,** grandson of Philip Augustus. Louis embodied the ideal of the medieval monarch—he was generous, noble, and devoted to justice and the rules of chivalry.

A deeply religious man, Louis pursued religious goals that Christians admired at the time. He persecuted heretics and Jews and led thousands of French knights in two wars against Muslims. Within 30 years of his death, the Church declared him a saint.

Louis did much to improve royal government. Like Charlemagne, he sent out traveling officials to check on local administrators. He expanded the royal courts, outlawed private wars, and ended serfdom in his personal domain. To ensure justice, he even heard cases himself. His enormous personal prestige helped create a strong national feeling among his subjects. By the time of his death in 1270, France was emerging as an efficient centralized monarchy.

Conflicts with the Pope Louis's grandson, Philip IV, ruthlessly extended royal power. Always pressed for money, he tried to collect new taxes from the clergy. These efforts led to a clash with Pope Boniface VIII.

Declaring that "God has set popes over kings and kingdoms," the pope forbade Philip to tax the clergy without papal consent. Philip threatened to arrest any clergy who did not pay. As their quarrel escalated, Philip sent troops to capture Boniface. The pope escaped, but he died soon afterward.

>> The Estates General did not limit the power of the French king. However, it did give townspeople (at right) a voice equal to nobles (center) and clergy (left).

Shortly after, in 1305, a Frenchman was elected pope. Four years later, the pope moved the papal court to Avignon (ah vee NYOHN), just outside the southern border of France. There, French rulers could exercise more control over the Church. The move to Avignon later sparked a crisis in the Church when a rival pope was elected in Rome. The rival popes each claimed to be the true leader of the Church.

The King Sets Up the Estates General During this struggle with the pope, Philip rallied French support by setting up the Estates General in 1302. This body had representatives from all three estates, or classes of French society: clergy, nobles, and townspeople. Although later French kings consulted the Estates General, it never gained the power of the purse or otherwise served as a balance to royal power.

☑ **DESCRIBE** How did French kings increase royal power?

The Holy Roman Empire

In the early Middle Ages, Charlemagne had brought much of what is today the nation of Germany under his rule. After his death, these German lands dissolved into a patchwork of separate states ruled by counts and dukes. In time, the dukes of Saxony began to extend their power over neighboring German lands.

In 936, Duke Otto I of Saxony took the title King of Germany. Like other feudal monarchs, he and his successors set out to increase royal power. In doing so, they came into fierce conflict with the Church. The longest and most destructive of these power struggles pitted Otto's successors, who ruled over lands called the **Holy Roman Empire,** against the pope in Rome.

Otto I Becomes Emperor Like Charlemagne, Otto I worked closely with the Church. He appointed bishops to top government jobs. He also took an army into Italy to help the pope defeat rebellious Roman nobles. In 962, a grateful pope crowned Otto emperor of the German states of Central Europe. Later, Otto's successors took the title Holy Roman emperor—"holy" because they were crowned by the pope, and "Roman" because they saw themselves as heirs to the emperors of ancient Rome.

German Emperors Face a Challenge The Holy Roman Emperor had the potential to be the strongest monarchy in Europe. German emperors claimed

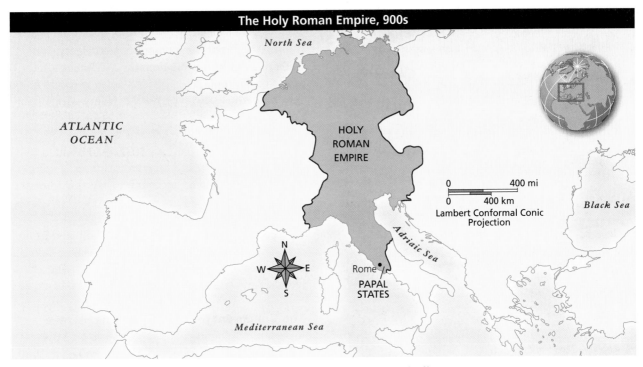

>> The Holy Roman Empire was a vast kingdom that bordered several important bodies of water. This aided in trade as well as defense. **Analyze Maps** Locate: (a) the North Sea, (b) the Adriatic Sea, (c) the Mediterranean Sea

authority over much of central and eastern Europe as well as parts of France and Italy. In fact, the real rulers of these lands were the emperor's vassals—hundreds of nobles and Church officials. For German emperors, the challenge was to control their vassals. It was a challenge they never met.

The Conflict with the Church Begins The close ties between Otto and the Church held the seeds of conflict. Holy Roman emperors saw themselves as protectors of Italy and the pope. They repeatedly intervened in Italian affairs and were tempted by the growing rich cities of northern Italy.

A key conflict between emperors and popes involved who would control appointments to high Church office. Like rulers in England and France, the Holy Roman emperor often appointed bishops and abbots. As popes sought to reform the Church, they tried to end such outside interference by secular rulers.

☑ **DESCRIBE** Describe the Holy Roman Empire.

A Pope and an Emperor Feud

Under the reforming pope **Gregory VII,** the conflict between emperors burst into flames. Gregory was one of the greatest medieval popes. He was also one of the most controversial. Pope Gregory ruled at the same time as the German emperor **Henry IV.** These two strong-willed rulers clashed over competing claims to power.

Gregory Undertakes Reforms Gregory was determined to make the Church independent of secular rulers. To achieve this goal, he banned the practice of **lay investiture.** Under this practice, the emperor or another lay person (a person who is not a member of the clergy) "invested," or presented, bishops with the ring and staff that symbolized their office. Only the pope, said Gregory, had the right to appoint and install bishops in office.

The Emperor Responds Pope Gregory's ban brought an angry response from the Holy Roman emperor, Henry IV. He argued that bishops held their lands as royal fiefs. Since he was their overlord, Henry felt entitled to give them the symbols of office. The feud heated up as the two men exchanged

>> Pope Gregory VII stands above Henry IV, who is wearing the clothing of a penitent and humbling himself in the snow before the pope.

>> Frederick Barbarossa, or Frederick Red-Beard, leads soldiers in battle against the Seljuk Turks.

insulting letters. Meanwhile, rebellious German princes undermined Henry by supporting the pope.

In 1076, Gregory excommunicated Henry, freeing Henry's subjects from their allegiance to the emperor. The pope then headed north to crown a new emperor. Faced with revolts, Henry was forced to make peace.

Henry Repents In January 1077, he presented himself to the pope as a repentant sinner. Gregory knew that Henry was just trying to save his throne. But according to tradition and Church law, the pope, as a priest, had to forgive a confessed sinner. Gregory then lifted the order of excommunication, and Henry returned to Germany to subdue his rebellious nobles. In later years, he took revenge on Gregory when he led an army to Rome and forced the pope into exile.

The Concordat of Worms The struggle over investiture dragged on for almost 50 years. Finally, in 1122, both sides accepted a treaty known as the Concordat of Worms (vawrmz). This treaty declared that the Church had the sole power to elect and invest bishops with spiritual authority. The emperor, however, still invested them with fiefs. Although this compromise ended the investiture struggle, new battles were soon raging between popes and emperors.

☑ **DESCRIBE** Describe the feud between the pope and the emperor.

The Battle for Italy

The struggle between popes and emperors moved from the battle over investiture to a battle for Italy. During the 1100s and 1200s, ambitious German emperors sought to control Italy. As they headed south across the Alps, they came into conflict not only with the pope but also with the wealthy cities of northern Italy.

German Emperors In Italy The Holy Roman emperor Frederick I, called **Frederick Barbarossa,** or "Red Beard," dreamed of building an empire from the Baltic to the Adriatic. For years, he fought to bring the wealthy cities of northern Italy under his control. With equal energy, they resisted. By joining forces with the pope in the Lombard League, they finally managed to defeat Barbarossa's armies.

Barbarossa did succeed, however, in arranging a marriage between his son Henry and Constance, the heiress to Sicily and southern Italy. That move entangled German emperors even more deeply in Italian affairs.

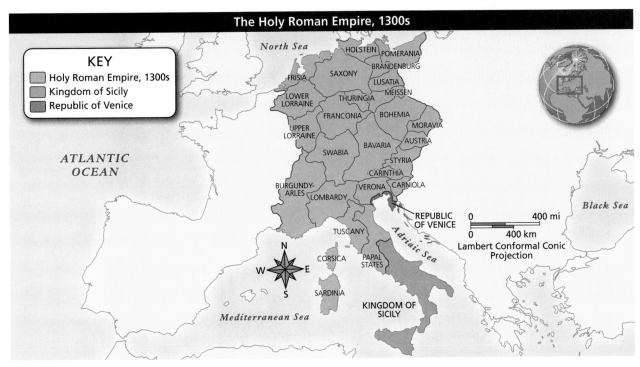

The Holy Roman Empire, 1300s

KEY
- Holy Roman Empire, 1300s
- Kingdom of Sicily
- Republic of Venice

>> Frederick II spent much of his rule fighting for territory around the Kingdom of Sicily.
Analyze Maps Why do you think that the barons and nobility of areas such as Saxony and Bavaria were successful in breaking into independent states?

Frederick II Barbarossa's grandson, Frederick II, was raised in Sicily, a rich island kingdom in the Mediterranean. Frederick was bright and well educated. An able but arrogant leader, he was willing to use any means to achieve his ends.

As Holy Roman emperor, Frederick spent little time in Germany. Instead, he pursued his ambitions in Italy, clashing repeatedly and unsuccessfully with several popes. Like his grandfather, Frederick also tried but failed to subdue the cities of northern Italy.

Effects of the Struggle While Frederick II was occupied in Italy, German nobles grew more independent. The Holy Roman Empire survived, but remained a patchwork of feudal states. Unlike France and England, Germany would not become a nation-state for another 600 years.

Southern Italy and Sicily also faced centuries of upheaval. There, popes turned to the French to overthrow Frederick's heirs.

A local uprising against French rule in Sicily led to 200 years of chaos as French and Spanish rivals battled for power. The region that had once been a thriving center of culture was left in ruins.

☑ **DESCRIBE** What obstacles did German emperors face in Italy?

Church Power Reaches Its Peak

In the 1200s, the Roman Catholic Church reached the height of its political power. Reforming popes like Gregory VII claimed the right to depose kings and emperors. Gregory's successors greatly expanded papal power. In addition, a more powerful Church was able to spread its influence to new areas, increasing religious unity in Europe.

Popes Assert Their Power Pope Innocent III, who took office in 1198, embodied the triumph of the Church. As head of the Church, Innocent III claimed supremacy over all other rulers. The pope, he said, stands "between God and man, lower than God but higher than men, who judges all and is judged by no one."

Innocent III clashed with all the powerful rulers of his day, and he usually won. As you have read, when King John of England dared to appoint an archbishop of Canterbury without the pope's approval, Innocent excommunicated the king and placed his kingdom under interdict. Innocent ordered the same punishment for France when Philip II tried unlawfully to annul, or invalidate, his marriage. The Holy Roman emperor Frederick II also felt the wrath of the powerful pope.

In 1209, Innocent, aided by Philip II, launched a brutal crusade against the Albigensians in southern France. The Albigensians wanted to purify the Church and return to the simpler ways of early Christianity. The Church saw them as heretics because they rejected Catholic beliefs and rituals. Knights from all over western Europe took part in the fighting. Tens of thousands of people were slaughtered in the Albigensian Crusade.

Innocent strengthened papal power within the Church as well. He extended the Papal States, reformed the Church courts, and changed the way that Church officials were chosen. Finally, he called a council that issued decrees that justified the pope's new power.

Papal Power Begins to Decline For almost a century after Innocent's death, popes pressed their claim to supremacy. During this period, though, the French and English monarchies grew stronger. In 1296, Philip IV of France successfully challenged Pope Boniface VIII on the issue of taxing the clergy. After Philip engineered the election of a French pope, the papacy entered a period of decline.

☑ **DESCRIBE** How did Innocent III embody the Church's political power?

☑ ASSESSMENT

1. **Analyze Information** How were nobles and the Church obstacles for monarchs who wanted more power?

2. **Summarize** How did William increase royal power in England?

3. **Summarize** Explain the social, religious, and cultural development of the Anglo-Saxons from the time they immigrated to Britain to the Norman Conquest.

4. **Compare** In what ways was the religious development of the Viking, Magyar, and Anglo-Saxon societies the same?

5. **Analyze Information** How did increasing Church power help create political unity in Europe?

The Magna Carta

King John ruled England from 1199 to 1216. During his troubled reign, he found himself in conflict with England's feudal barons. The nobles especially resented John's attempts to tax them heavily. In 1215, the barons forced John to sign the Magna Carta, or Great Charter. Most of this document was intended to protect the rights of the barons. However, over time, the document came to guarantee some basic rights of English citizens. When English colonists came to North America, they brought these ideas with them. Eight of the 63 clauses of the Magna Carta are printed here.

The second primary source describes events leading to the meeting between King John and the barons.

>> King John signs the Magna Carta.

Primary Source 1

12. No [tax] nor aid shall be imposed on our kingdom, unless by common counsel [consent] of our kingdom, except for ransoming our person, for making our eldest son a knight, and for once marrying our eldest daughter; and for these there shall not be levied more than a reasonable aid. . . .

30. No sheriff or bailiff [tax collector] of ours, or other person, shall take the horses or carts of any freeman for transport duty, against the will of the said freeman.

31. Neither we nor our bailiffs shall take, for our castles or for any other work of ours, wood which is not ours, against the will of the owner of that wood. . . .

☑ **SUMMARIZE** What promise is made in Clause 12?

38. No bailiff for the future shall, upon his own unsupported complaint, put any one to his "law," without credible [believable] witnesses brought for this purpose.

39. No freeman shall be taken or imprisoned . . . or exiled or in any way destroyed, nor will we go upon him nor send upon him, except by the lawful judgment of his peers [people of equal rank] or by the law of the land.

40. To no one will we sell, to no one will we refuse or delay, right or justice. . . . 45. We will appoint as justices, constables, sheriffs, or bailiffs only such as know the law of the realm [kingdom] and mean to observe it well. . . .

63. Wherefore it is our will, and we firmly enjoin [order], that the English Church be free, and that the men in our kingdom have and hold all the aforesaid liberties, rights, and concessions, well and peaceably, freely and quietly, fully and wholly, for themselves and their heirs, of us and our heirs, in all respects and in all places for ever, as is aforesaid.

☑ **COMPARE AND CONTRAST** How do the principles expressed in Clauses 38–40 apply to the U.S. justice system?

Primary Source 2

King John, when he saw that he was deserted by almost all, so that out of his regal superabundance of followers he scarcely retained seven knights, was much alarmed lest the barons would attack his castles. . . . Accordingly, at the time and place pre-agreed on, the king and nobles came to the appointed conference, and when each party had stationed themselves apart from the other, they began a long discussion about terms of peace and the aforesaid liberties. . . . At length, after various points on both sides had been discussed, king John, seeing that he was inferior in strength to the barons, without raising any difficulty, granted the underwritten laws and liberties, and confirmed them by his charter. . . .

☑ **DRAW CONCLUSIONS** What change had occurred in feudalism that allowed the barons to force King John to meet their demands?

☑ ASSESSMENT

1. **Compare Perspectives** How was King John's view of his reign different from the barons' view?

2. **Determine Central Ideas** What do you think is the most important right that this excerpt from the Magna Carta protects? Explain your answer.

3. **Identify Steps in a Process** How was the Magna Carta an important first step in the development of constitutional democracy?

GO ONLINE to access primary sources

7.6

This Italian illustration from about the 1300s shows a lawyer lecturing his students in a medieval school.

Learning, Literature, and the Arts of the Middle Ages

By the 1100s, Europe was experiencing dynamic changes. No longer was everyone preoccupied with the daily struggle to survive. A more reliable food supply and the revival of trade and growth of towns were signs of increased prosperity.

The Rise of Medieval Universities

As economic and political conditions improved in the High Middle Ages, the need for education expanded. The Church wanted better-educated clergy. Royal rulers also needed literate men for their growing bureaucracies. By acquiring an education, the sons of wealthy townspeople might hope to qualify for high positions in the Church or with royal governments.

Early Universities By the 1000s, schools had sprung up around the great cathedrals to train the clergy. Some of these schools evolved into the first European universities. They were organized like guilds, with charters to protect the rights of members and set standards for training.

As early as the 900s, Salerno in Italy had a respected medical school. Bologna's university, set up in 1158, became famous for legal studies. Paris and Oxford founded universities in the later 1100s. In the next century, other cities rushed to organize universities. Students often traveled from one university to another to study different subjects.

Medieval universities brought prestige and profit to the cities in which they were located. Local merchants provided students

 BOUNCE to Activate Flipped Video

Objectives

Explain the emergence of universities and their importance to medieval life.

Understand how newly translated writings from the past and from other regions influenced medieval thought.

Describe the literature, architecture, and art of the High and Late Middle Ages.

Examine the lasting heritage of the Byzantine Empire.

Key Terms

Christine de Pisan
scholasticism
Thomas Aquinas
vernacular
Dante Alighieri
Geoffrey Chaucer
Gothic style
flying buttresses
illumination
icon

with housing, food, clothing, and entertainment. But students could also create problems for university communities. The priest Jacques de Vitry complained, "They were always fighting and engaging in scuffles."

Student Life University life offered few comforts. A bell wakened students at about 5 A.M. for prayers. Students then attended classes until 10 A.M., when they had their first meal of the day.

Afternoon classes continued until 5 P.M. Students usually ate a light supper and then studied until bedtime. Since the first medieval universities did not have permanent buildings, classes were held in rented rooms or in the choir loft of a church. Students sat for hours on hard benches as the teacher dictated and then explained Latin texts. Students were expected to memorize what they heard.

A program of study covered the seven liberal arts: arithmetic, geometry, astronomy, music, grammar, rhetoric, and logic. There were separate programs for the further study of law, medicine, and theology. To show mastery of a subject, students took an oral exam. Earning a degree as a bachelor of arts took between three and six years. Only after several more years of study could a man qualify to become a master of arts and a teacher. Theology was the longest course of study. One Italian scholar and teacher wrote:

They tell me that, unlike everyone else, you get out of bed before the first bell sounds in order to study, that you are the first into the classroom and the last to leave it. And when you get back home you spend the whole day going over what you were taught in your lessons . . . Many people make themselves permanently ill through excessive study; some of them die and others . . . waste away day after day.

—Boncomagno da Sigma

Women and Education During the Middle Ages, women were expected to pursue their "natural" gifts at home—raising children, managing the household, and doing needlework. Only men were expected to seek an education or write books. Women were not allowed to attend universities. This exclusion seriously affected their lives. Since most did not even attend school, they were deprived of the mental stimulation that was an important part of an educated person's life. Without a university education, women could not become doctors, lawyers, or church officials.

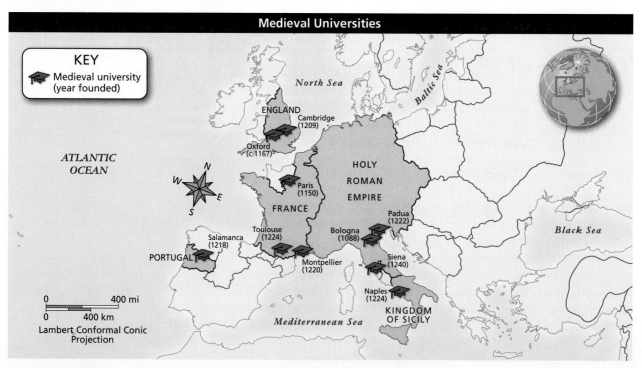

>> Most medieval universities were supported by a church or monastery. **Analyze Maps** Which area had the greatest number of universities? What factors do you think contributed to this?

Despite restrictions, a few women did get an education. Most convents educated girls. Some nuns became scholars and writers. Still, women like **Christine de Pisan** (duh pee ZAHN) were the exceptions. In *The City of Ladies*, she asks whether women are less capable of learning and understanding, as men insist, and a character replies.

> If it were customary to send daughters to school like sons, and if they were then taught the same subjects, they would learn as thoroughly and understand the subtleties of all arts and sciences as well as sons.
>
> —Christine de Pisan

Learning for Children Few children in the Middle Ages received any education. At home, and perhaps in the parish church, they learned basic Christian beliefs.

Overall, education for most children was informal. They learned by doing. Within the family, they were assigned tasks appropriate to their age. Older children looked after younger ones. Children often took on demanding tasks in the fields or towns where they lived. They carried heavy loads, cleared land, or learned skilled trades if they were apprenticed out by their families.

☑ **DESCRIBE** What was university life like in medieval Europe?

New Knowledge Reaches Europe

Universities received a further boost from an explosion of knowledge that reached Europe in the High Middle Ages. Many of the "new" ideas had originated in ancient Greece but had been lost to Western Europeans after the fall of Rome.

Ancient Learning Is Brought to Europe In the Middle East, Muslim scholars had translated the works of Aristotle and other Greek thinkers into Arabic. Their translations and commentaries on these ancient texts spread across the Muslim world. In Muslim Spain, Jewish and Christian scholars translated these works into Latin, the language of Christian European scholars.

Aristotle's Ideas Challenge Christian Thinkers
In the 1100s, these new translations were reaching Western Europe. There, they set off a revolution in the world of learning.

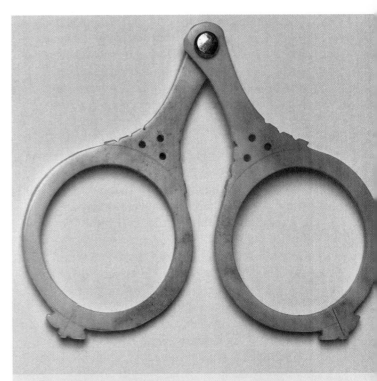

>> During the Middle Ages, metal-framed eyeglasses like these and a variety of other inventions were the result of new knowledge.

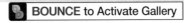 **BOUNCE to Activate Gallery**

The writings of the ancient Greeks posed a challenge to Christian scholars. Aristotle taught that people should use reason to discover basic truths. Christians, however, accepted many ideas on faith. They believed that the Church was the final authority on all questions. How could they use the logic of Aristotle without undermining their Christian faith?

Christian scholars, called scholastics, tried to resolve the conflict between faith and reason. Their method, known as **scholasticism,** used reason to support Christian beliefs. Scholastics studied the works of the Muslim philosopher Averroës (uh VEER uh weez) and the Jewish rabbi Maimonides (my MAHN uh deez). These thinkers, too, used logic to resolve the conflict between faith and reason.

Thomas Aquinas The writings of these philosophers influenced the famous scholastic **Thomas Aquinas** (uh KWY nus). In a monumental work, *Summa theologica*, Aquinas concluded that faith and reason exist in harmony.

Aquinas's work concluded that both lead to the same truth, that God rules over an orderly universe. Aquinas thus brought together Christian faith and classical Greek philosophy.

Aquinas also wrote about government and natural law, or a set of unwritten moral principles based on fairness and reason. Aquinas believed that government should work for the "common good" that benefits all. He also argued that people are not obliged to obey unjust laws or the rulers who enact them.

The ideas Aquinas developed about natural law, unjust laws, and rebellion influenced European philosophers in the 1600s and 1700s. Their ideas, in turn, influenced men like Thomas Jefferson, who wrote the American Declaration of Independence, and others who authored the U.S. Constitution.

Science and Mathematics Scientific works, translated from Arabic and Greek, also reached Europe from Spain and the Byzantine empire. Christian scholars studied Hippocrates on medicine and Euclid on geometry, along with works by Arab scientists. They saw, too, how Aristotle had used observation and experimentation to study the physical world.

Yet science made little real progress in Europe in the Middle Ages because most scholars still believed that all true knowledge must fit with Church teachings. It would take many centuries before Christian thinkers changed the way they viewed the physical world.

>> Rodrigo Díaz de Vivar, known as El Cid, was an epic hero in Spanish medieval literature. Like Roland, his story features bravery in battle and personal honor.

In mathematics, Europeans adopted Hindu-Arabic numerals, commonly called Arabic numerals. In fact, the Arabs had adapted these numerals from India. Hindu-Arabic numerals were much easier to use than the cumbersome system of Roman numerals that Europeans had used for centuries. In time, but long after the Middle Ages, the use of Hindu-Arabic numerals allowed both scientists and mathematicians to make extraordinary advances in their fields.

☑ **DESCRIBE** What were some elements of the new learning of medieval Europe?

Medieval Literature

While Latin remained the written language of scholars and churchmen, new writings began to appear in the **vernacular,** or the everyday languages of ordinary people, such as French, German, and Italian. These writings captured the spirit of the late Middle Ages. Medieval literature included epics, or long narrative poems, about feudal warriors and chivalry as well as tales of the common people.

Heroic Epics Capture the Imagination Across Europe, people began writing down oral traditions in the vernacular. French pilgrims traveling to holy sites loved to hear the chansons de geste, or "songs of heroic deeds." The most popular was the *Song of Roland*, written around 1100, which praises the courage of one of Charlemagne's knights. A true chivalric hero, Roland loyally sacrifices his life out of a sense of honor.

Spain's great epic, *Poem of the Cid*, tells the story of Rodrigo Díaz de Vivar, a bold and fiery Christian lord who fought both with and against Muslim forces. His nickname, El Cid, comes from the Arabic word for "lord."

Heroic epics that told thrilling tales of heroism appealed to Christians across Europe. Nobles in the late Middle Ages adopted ideas about honor and chivalry in theory, if not in practice. Epic tales found a ready audience among all classes of medieval society. The tales varied from region to region, but people took pride in their great heroes.

Dante's Journey "In the middle of the journey of life, I found myself in a dark wood, where the straight way was lost." So begins the *Divine Comedy*, written in the early 1300s by the Italian poet **Dante Alighieri** (DAHN tay ah leeg YEH ree). The poem takes the reader on an imaginary journey into hell and purgatory, where souls await forgiveness. Finally, Dante describes a vision of heaven.

"Abandon all hope, ye that enter here" is the warning Dante receives as he approaches hell. There, he talks with people from history who tell how they earned a place in hell.

Dante's *The Divine Comedy* contains both humor and tragedy rooted in the familiar medieval quest for spiritual understanding. As he journeys through heaven and hell, he reflects on moral and ethical questions that Christians faced and shows how people's actions in life determine their fate in the afterlife.

Chaucer's *Canterbury Tales* In the *Canterbury Tales*, the English writer **Geoffrey Chaucer** follows a band of English pilgrims traveling to Thomas Becket's tomb. In brilliant word portraits, he sketches a range of characters, including a knight, a plowman, a merchant, a miller, a monk, and a nun. Each character tells a story to entertain the group. Whether funny, romantic, or bawdy, each tale adds to our picture of medieval life.

☑ **DESCRIBE** What were three works of medieval literature? What were their subjects?

>> This scene from Chaucer's *Canterbury Tales* shows the merchant, nun, and priest, who are among several who tell stories during the pilgrimage.

Architecture and Art

"In the Middle Ages," wrote French author Victor Hugo, "men had no great thought that they did not write down in stone." Those "writings" were the great buildings of the Middle Ages. With riches from trade and commerce, townspeople, nobles, and monarchs indulged in a flurry of building. Their greatest achievements were the towering stone cathedrals that served as symbols of their wealth and religious devotion.

Romanesque Buildings In the year 1000, monasteries and towns were building solid stone churches that reflected Roman influences. These Romanesque churches looked like fortresses with thick walls and towers. The roofs were so heavy that they had to be supported with massive stone walls with no windows or only tiny slits of windows. Larger windows, builders feared, would weaken the support for the roof. As a result, the interiors of Romanesque churches were dark and dimly lit.

Graceful Gothic Cathedrals About 1140, Abbot Suger (SooZHAY) wanted to build a new abbey church at St. Denis near Paris. He hoped that it "would shine with wonderful and uninterrupted light." There, builders developed what became known as the **Gothic style** of architecture.

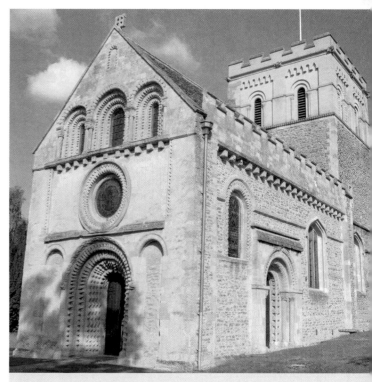

>> Romanesque churches like this one reflect the most common form of church architecture throughout Europe.

>> The multicolored and multipaned Rose window in Notre Dame Cathedral in Paris thrilled medieval church-goers.

BOUNCE to Activate Gallery

>> This panel of the Bayeaux Tapestry shows a scene from the Battle of Hastings in 1066.

A key feature of the new Gothic style was the **flying buttresses,** or stone supports that stood outside the church. These supports allowed builders to construct higher, thinner walls and leave space for large stained-glass windows. Gothic churches soared to incredible heights. Their graceful spires and tall windows carried the eye upward to the heavens. "Since their brilliance lets the splendor of the True Light pass into the church," declared a medieval visitor, "they enlighten those inside."

Splendid Art in Stone and Glass As churches rose, stonemasons carved sculptures to decorate them inside and out. Sculptures included portraits and scenes from the lives of saints and illustrated stories from the Bible. Sculptors also carved plants and animals, both real and imaginary. Some stone pieces were gargoyles, grotesque figures with a spout that carried water off the roof and away from the walls of the building. They also carved whimsical or frightening images of mythical creatures such as dragons and unicorns.

Other skilled craft workers created the colorful stained-glass windows that added to the splendor of Gothic churches. Stained-glass windows illustrated dramatic scenes from the Bible and other Christian beliefs. Stained-glass windows and carvings in stone served an essential purpose. They helped educate the masses of people who could not read about the Christian faith.

Paintings and Tapestries Medieval artists created other works, including splendid altarpieces that decorated the space behind the church altar. Altarpieces could be paintings, relief sculptures, or both.

Like stained-glass windows, they illustrated Christian subjects and were designed to inspire devotion among the faithful. Most altarpieces hung in churches, although wealthy families might have a chapel and altarpiece in their homes.

Both churches and the houses of the rich were decorated with "paintings" in thread. Stone churches and castles were cold, drafty places. Tapestries, or woven wall hangings, added color and warmth. The famous Bayeux Tapestry is an embroidery piece that illustrates in detail the story of William the Conqueror and the Battle of Hastings in 1066. Although no one knows who wove it or exactly when, it has been used to learn details of the event.

Illuminated Manuscripts Throughout the Middle Ages, monks, nuns, and other skilled artisans decorated the handwritten books of the time with elaborate designs and illustrations, known as

illumination. The most spectacular decorations in these books were made of gold and silver.

Some illuminations depicted biblical scenes. Others, such as prayer books called Books of Hours, showed scenes of daily life in towns and castles with peasants in the field along with nobles on horseback.

☑ **DESCRIBE** What types of artistic works were found in medieval churches?

The Byzantine Heritage

The Byzantine empire contributed to the civilizations of the eastern Mediterranean and of Western Europe. Byzantine civilization rose out of many traditions, blending Christian beliefs with Greek philosophy, science, and the arts. It also extended Roman achievements in engineering and law.

As the medieval world expanded, so did its contacts with Byzantine civilization, and Byzantine influence radiated across Europe. Even though the Byzantine empire fell to the Ottomans in 1453, the conquerors adapted features of Byzantine government, arts, and culture.

Contributions in the Arts Byzantine artists made unique contributions, especially in religious art and architecture, that influenced Western styles. **Icons,** images designed to evoke the presence of God, gave viewers a sense of personal contact with the sacred.

Mosaics brought scenes from the Bible to life. In architecture, Byzantine palaces and churches blended Greek, Roman, Persian, and other Middle Eastern styles.

Preserving and Spreading Knowledge
Byzantine scholars preserved the classic works of ancient Greece and Rome. In addition, they produced their own great books, especially in the field of history.

Like the Greek historians Herodotus and Thucydides, Byzantine historians were mostly concerned with writing about their own times. Procopius, an advisor to the general Belisarius, chronicled the Byzantine campaign against Persia. In his *Secret History*, Procopius savagely criticizes the Emperor Justinian and the Empress Theodora. He calls the emperor "both an evil-doer and easily led into evil . . . never of his own accord speaking the truth."

Anna Comnena is considered by many scholars to be the Western world's first important female historian. In the *Alexiad*, she analyzes the reign of her father, Emperor Alexius I. Comnena's book portrays Latin Crusaders as greedy barbarians.

>> This religious icon showing Mary and the baby Jesus showcases the Byzantine style.

As the Byzantine empire tottered in the 1400s, many Greek scholars left Constantinople to teach at Italian universities. They took valuable Greek manuscripts to the West, along with their knowledge of Greek and Byzantine culture. The work of these scholars contributed to the cultural flowering in Europe that became known as the Renaissance.

☑ **DESCRIBE** What were some Byzantine contributions to art and learning?

☑ ASSESSMENT

1. **Analyze Information** How did new knowledge, based on Aristotle and other Greek thinkers, pose a challenge to Christian scholars?

2. **Identify Central Issues** How was religion central to the art and architecture of the Middle Ages?

3. **Predict Consequences** How might universities that drew students from many places affect European life in the future?

4. **Demonstrate Reasoned Judgment** Why was the Byzantine empire so important to Western Europe?

5. **Quest Connections** Why were heroic epics in the vernacular popular with medieval Europeans?

This medieval illustration shows a man dying of the plague. The disease was characterized by boils erupting all over the body and it claimed many victims, partly because it spread through contact.

 BOUNCE to Activate Flipped Video

Objectives

Understand how the Black Death caused social and economic decline.

Describe the problems facing the Church in the late Middle Ages and how the Church reacted.

Summarize the causes, turning points, and effects of the Hundred Years' War.

Key Terms

Black Death
epidemic
longbow

The Late Middle Ages: A Time of Upheaval

To Europeans in the mid-1300s, the end of the world seemed to have come. First, widespread crop failures brought famine and starvation. Then plague and war ravaged populations. Europe eventually recovered from these disasters. Still, the upheavals of the 1300s and 1400s marked the end of the Middle Ages and the beginning of the early modern age.

The Black Death Spreads Across Europe

The Arrival In the autumn of 1347, a fleet of Genoese trading ships loaded with grain left the Black Sea port of Caffa and set sail for Messina, Sicily. By midvoyage, sailors were falling sick and dying. Soon after the ships tied up at Messina, townspeople, too, began to fall sick and die.

Within months, the disease that Europeans called the **Black Death** was raging through Italy. By 1348, it had reached Spain and France. From there, it ravaged the rest of Europe. One in three people died—a death rate worse than in any war in history.

A Global Epidemic The deadly illness was bubonic plague, a disease spread by fleas carried on rats. In the pre-modern world, rats infested ships, towns, and even the homes of the rich and powerful. Bubonic plague had broken out before in Europe, Asia, and North Africa but had subsided. One strain of the disease, though, had survived in Mongolia.

GO ONLINE to access your digital course

In the 1200s, Mongol armies conquered much of Asia, probably setting off the new **epidemic,** or outbreak of rapid-spreading disease. In the early 1300s, rats spread the plague in crowded Chinese cities, killing about 35 million people there. Fleas jumped from those rats to infest the clothes and packs of traders traveling west. As a result, the disease spread from Asia to the Middle East and then to Europe.

Social Upheaval In Europe, the plague brought terror and bewilderment, as people had no way to stop the disease. Some people turned to magic and witchcraft for cures. Others plunged into wild pleasures, believing they would soon die anyway. Still others saw the plague as God's punishment. They beat themselves with whips to show that they repented their sins. Normal life broke down as people fled cities or hid in their homes to avoid contracting the plague from neighbors and relatives.

Some Christians blamed Jews for the plague, charging unjustly that they had poisoned the wells to cause the disease. In the resulting hysteria, thousands of Jews were murdered.

Economic Impact As the plague kept recurring in the late 1300s, the European economy plunged to a low ebb. When workers and employers died, production declined. Survivors demanded higher wages, but as the cost of labor soared, prices rose, too.

Landowners and merchants pushed for laws to limit wages. To limit rising costs, landowners converted croplands to land for sheep raising, which required less labor. Villagers forced off the land looked for work in towns. There, guilds limited opportunities for advancement.

Coupled with the fear of the plague, these restrictions sparked explosive revolts. Angry peasants rampaged in England, France, Germany, and elsewhere. In the cities, artisans fought for more power, usually without success. Revolts erupted on and off through the 1300s and 1400s. The plague had spread death and social unrest. It would take Western Europe more than 100 years to fully recover from its effects.

The plague returned repeatedly during the later Middle Ages and into early modern times. Daniel Defoe's *Journal of the Plague Year* vividly chronicles the impact of mass deaths in England in the 1600s.

The Black Death contributed to the end of medieval Europe by transforming Europe's economy and society. Although rulers were able to put down peasant revolts, in the long run, they did not succeed in limiting wages. With a shortage of labor after the

Black Death, market forces gave peasants in western Europe more bargaining power. They were able to demand higher wages. In addition, peasants were able to substitute the payment of cash rents for the legal obligations of serfdom that had been the basis of manorialism. The shift to a market economy in western Europe brought the end of the medieval order and ushered in the Renaissance and the modern age.

At the same time, landed nobles suffered from the loss of bargaining power to peasants. Because their incomes were reduced, they were less able to support knights and other fighting men. At the same time, the growth of a market economy supported a growing middle class of artisans and merchants in Europe's towns and cities. In thriving cities in kingdoms such as England, France, and Castile, kings were able to raise taxes from the middle classes. They used these funds to protect both themselves and their trade from bandits and extortionate nobles. In this way, the Black Death led to a growth in the power of kings, more centralized states, and the gradual breakdown of the key feature of medieval Europe—feudalism.

☑ **CHECK UNDERSTANDING** How did the Black Death affect Europe?

>> This image is of an angry mob storming a nobleman's fortress. Because of the plague, crops often rotted in the field. Peasants often blamed the lord of the manor for leaving fields fallow.

▶ BOUNCE to Activate Map

>> Pope Clement V receives a noblewoman at the papal court in Avignon. Papal wealth would bring later trouble to the Church.

>> English reformer John Wycliffe's ideas would help launch the Protestant Reformation years later.

Crisis in the Church

The late Middle Ages brought spiritual crisis, scandal, and division to the Roman Catholic Church. Many priests and monks died during the plague. Their replacements faced challenging questions. Survivors asked, "Why did God spare some and kill others?"

Divisions in the Church The Church was unable to provide the strong leadership needed in this desperate time. In 1309, Pope Clement V had moved the papal court to Avignon outside the border of southern France. It remained there for about 70 years under French domination. This period is often called the Babylonian Captivity of the Church, referring to the time when the ancient Hebrews were held captive in Babylon.

In Avignon, popes reigned over a lavish court. Critics lashed out against the worldly, pleasure-loving papacy, and anticlerical sentiment grew. Within the Church itself, reformers tried to end the "captivity."

In 1378, reformers within the Church elected their own pope to rule from Rome. French cardinals responded by choosing a rival pope. The election of two and sometimes even three rival popes created a schism, or divide, in the Church. This second Great Schism, like the earlier split into eastern and western branches of Christianity, hurt the Church and weakened its moral authority, contributing to the gradual end of medieval Europe. Not until 1417 did a Church council at Constance finally end the crisis.

New Heresies Threaten the Church With its moral standing and leadership in decline, the Church faced still more problems. Popular preachers challenged its power. In England, John Wycliffe, an Oxford professor, attacked corruption in the Church.

Wycliffe insisted that the Bible, not the Church, was the source of all Christian truth. He supported the idea of translating the Bible into English so that people could read it themselves rather than rely on the clergy to read and interpret it for them. Czech students at Oxford carried Wycliffe's ideas to Bohemia—today's Czech Republic. There, Jan Hus led the call for reforms, supported by his followers, known as Hussites.

The Church responded to these calls for reform by persecuting Wycliffe and his followers and suppressing the Hussites. Hus was tried for preaching heresy—ideas contrary to Church teachings. Found guilty, he was burned at the stake in 1415.

The ideas of Wycliffe and Hus survived. Their calls for reform had taken root in response to the worldliness of the Church and feuds among its leaders. These reformers looked on the Bible, rather

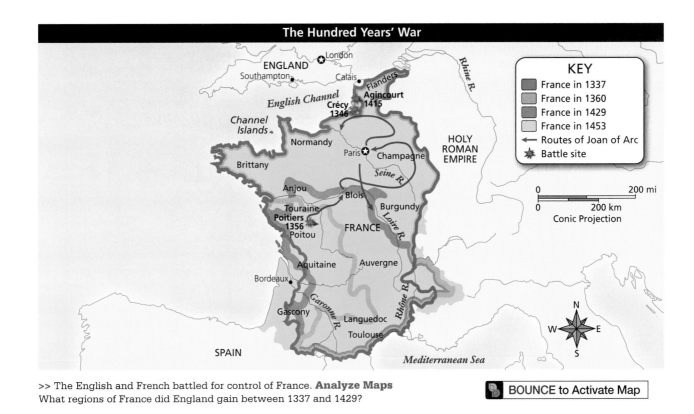

KEY
France in 1337
France in 1360
France in 1429
France in 1453
→ Routes of Joan of Arc
★ Battle site

0   200 mi
0   200 km
Conic Projection

>> The English and French battled for control of France. **Analyze Maps**
What regions of France did England gain between 1337 and 1429?

🅑 BOUNCE to Activate Map

than the pope or bishops, as the source of Christian faith. In the next century, other reformers echoed similar demands, calling for the faithful to rely on the Bible and for limiting the role of the clergy. This new reform movement would split the Roman Catholic Church forever and transform Western Europe.

☑ **DESCRIBE** Describe two threats to Church power.

The Hundred Years' War

On top of the disasters of famine, plague, and economic decline came a long, destructive war. Between 1337 and 1453, England and France engaged in a series of conflicts, known as the Hundred Years' War. The fighting devastated France and drained England.

Rival Powers: England and France English rulers had battled for centuries to hold on to the French lands of their Norman ancestors. But French kings were intent on extending their own power in France. When Edward III of England claimed the French crown in 1337, war erupted anew between these rival powers. Once fighting started, economic rivalry and a growing sense of national pride made it hard for either side to give up the struggle.

Early Victories for England At first, the English won a string of victories—at Crécy in 1346, Poitiers

in 1356, and Agincourt in 1415. They owed much of their success not to braver or more skillful knights but to the **longbow,** a powerful new weapon wielded by English archers. The longbow was six feet long and took years to master. But it could discharge three arrows in the time a French archer with his crossbow fired just one. Its arrows pierced all but the heaviest armor.

The English victories took a heavy toll on French morale, or spirit. England, it seemed, was likely to bring all of France under its control. Then, in what seemed like a miracle to the French, their fortunes were reversed.

Joan of Arc In 1429, a 17-year-old peasant woman, Joan of Arc, appeared at the court of Charles VII, the uncrowned king of France. She told him that God had sent her to save France. She convinced the desperate French king to let her lead his army against the English.

To Charles's amazement, Joan inspired the battered and despairing French troops to fight anew. In one astonishing year, she led the French to several victories and planted the seeds for future triumphs.

Joan paid for success with her life. She was taken captive by allies of the English and turned over to her enemies for trial. To discredit her, the English had Joan tried for witchcraft. She was convicted and burned at the stake. That action, however, only strengthened her value to the French, who saw

Causes and Effects of the Hundred Years' War

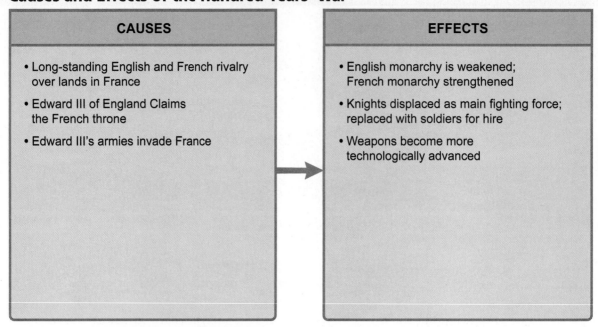

CAUSES	EFFECTS
• Long-standing English and French rivalry over lands in France • Edward III of England Claims the French throne • Edward III's armies invade France	• English monarchy is weakened; French monarchy strengthened • Knights displaced as main fighting force; replaced with soldiers for hire • Weapons become more technologically advanced

>> This shows the causes and effects of the Hundred Years' War. **Analyze Charts** What event began the Hundred Years' War?

her as a martyr. Much later, the Church declared her a saint.

Results of the Long War After Joan's death, the French took the offensive. With a powerful new weapon, the cannon, they attacked English-held castles. By 1453, the English held only the port of Calais in northwestern France.

In the end, the Hundred Years' War set France and England on different paths. The war created a growing sense of national feeling in France and allowed French kings to expand their power.

On the other hand, during the war, English rulers turned repeatedly to Parliament for funds, which helped that body win the "power of the purse." England ended up losing its French lands, but that setback was not disastrous for them. With their dreams of a continental empire shattered, English rulers turned to new trading ventures overseas.

Change and Recovery The Hundred Years' War brought many changes to the late medieval world. The longbow and cannon gave common soldiers a new importance on the battlefield and undermined the value of armored knights on horseback. Although neither nobles nor commoners knew it then, feudal society was changing and medieval Europe was coming to an end. Knights and castles were doomed to disappear. Strong monarchs needed large armies, not feudal vassals, to fight their wars.

As Europe recovered from the Black Death, the population expanded, and manufacturing grew. These changes led to increased trade. Italian cities flourished as centers of trade and shipping. Europeans borrowed and developed new technologies. This recovery set the stage for further changes during the Renaissance, the Reformation, and the Age of Exploration.

☑ **IDENTIFY** What effect did the Hundred Years' War have on medieval warfare?

☑ ASSESSMENT

1. **Recognize Cause and Effect** What were three effects of the Black Death on late medieval Europe?

2. **Draw Inference** How did the second Great Schism affect Church authority and power and contribute to the end of medieval Europe?

3. **Cause and Effect** How did Joan of Arc's execution affect the French forces?

4. **Compare** Compare the effects of the Hundred Years' War on France and England.

5. **Connections to Today** What were some factors that allowed the Black Death to spread so quickly in medieval Europe? Did COVID-19 spread as quickly? Why or why not?

7.8

Stefan Dusan was called the Emperor of the Serbs, Greeks, and Albanians and was considered the greatest ruler of medieval Serbia.

Russia and Eastern Europe

While feudalism and the Roman Catholic Church were shaping Western Europe in the Middle Ages, another culture was emerging in Russia to the east. Russia lies on the vast Eurasian plain that stretches from Europe to the borders of China. Although mapmakers use the Ural Mountains to mark the boundary between Europe and Asia, these ancient mountains were long ago worn away to wooded hills. They posed no great obstacle to the movement of peoples who were constantly migrating from other parts of Asia into Russia.

The Geography of Russia

During the Middle Ages, Russia—like Western Europe—was battered by invasions. Russia, however, had never been part of the Roman empire, and its early rulers looked to the Byzantine world, adapting much of its advanced civilization.

Three Regions Three broad regions with different climates and resources helped shape early Russian life. The first included the northern forests, which supplied lumber for building and fuel. Fur-bearing animals attracted hunters, but poor soil and a cold, snowy climate hindered farming. Farther south lay a second zone of fertile land, where farmers settled and grew crops. This region, which includes what is today Ukraine, was home to Russia's first civilization. The fertile soil and relatively mild climate of this region would eventually make it the "breadbasket" of Russia because of the vast fields of wheat grown there.

A third region, the southern **steppe,** is an open, treeless grassland. It offered splendid pasture for the herds and horses of nomadic peoples. With no natural barriers, the steppe was a great highway along which streams of nomads migrated.

 BOUNCE to Activate Flipped Video

Objectives

Describe how geography influenced the rise of Russia, and how Kiev grew to be the center of the first Russian state.

Explain how Mongol rule affected Russia.

Describe how Moscow took the lead in Russia and how its rulers developed authoritarian control.

Describe how geography influenced the development of Eastern Europe.

Understand how migration contributed to cultural diversity in Eastern Europe, and learn about three early Eastern European kingdoms.

Key Terms

steppe
Kiev
Cyrillic
Ivan the Great
Ivan the Terrible
Balkan Peninsula
ethnic group
diet
Golden Bull of 1222

 **GO ONLINE to access** your digital course

>> This reconstruction of a Viking ship unearthed in Russia is an example of the swift Viking trading ships that traveled Russia's many rivers.

>> Letters were added to the medieval Greek alphabet, with some based on Hebrew, to reflect the rich sounds of the Slavic language.

Rivers Russia's network of rivers provided transportation for both people and goods. The Dneiper (NEE puhr) and Volga rivers became productive trade routes. Major rivers ran from north to south, linking Russia early on to the advanced Byzantine world to the south.

☑ **ANALYZE CONTEXT** How did geography affect Russian settlement and growth?

Early Russia

Russia's early history was similar to that of much of Western Europe. Migrating peoples settled on the land, which was fragmented into many small kingdoms. Early Russia included a collection of small cities that were in time united into an empire.

Slavs and Vikings During Roman times, migrating Slavic peoples expanded into southern Russia. Like the Germanic people who pushed into Western Europe, the Slavs had no political organization more complex than the clan. They lived in small villages, farmed, and traded along the rivers connecting the Baltic in the north to the Black Sea in the south.

In the 700s and 800s, while some Viking leaders pushed into Western Europe, others steered their long ships out of Scandinavia into Russia. These Vikings, whom the Russians later called Varangians, traveled south along the rivers, trading with and collecting tribute, or forced payment, from the Slavs.

The Vikings also conducted a thriving trade with Constantinople. Located at the heart of this trade was the city of **Kiev,** which would later become the center of the first Russian state. Within a few generations, the Varangians who had settled among the Slavs were absorbed into the local culture. Viking names like Helga and Waldemar became the Slavic names Olga and Vladimir.

Byzantine Influences Trade had already brought Kiev into the Byzantine orbit. In the 800s, Constantinople sent Christian missionaries to convert the Slavs. About 863, two Greek brothers, Cyril and Methodius, adapted the Greek alphabet so they could translate the Bible into the Slavic tongue. This **Cyrillic** (suh RIL ik) alphabet became the written script that is still used today in Russia, Ukraine, Serbia, Bulgaria, and other countries of Eastern Europe.

In 957, Olga, the reigning princess of Kiev, converted to Byzantine Christianity. But it was not until the reign of Olga's grandson Vladimir that the religion spread widely. After his conversion, Vladimir married the sister of a Byzantine emperor. Soon, Greek priests arrived in Kiev to preside over the mass baptisms organized by Vladimir.

With Byzantine Christianity came many changes. As Russians adopted their new written language, a class of educated Russian priests emerged. Russians adapted Byzantine religious art, music, and architecture. Byzantine domes, capped with colorful, carved "helmets," became the onion-shaped domes of Russian churches.

Byzantine Christianity set the pattern for close ties between Church and state. Kievan princes, like the Byzantine emperor, controlled the Church and made it dependent on them. As the Russian Orthodox Church evolved, it remained a pillar of state power, not a rival as in Western Europe.

Kiev's Golden Age Under Yaroslav Kiev enjoyed a golden age under Yaroslav the Wise, who ruled from 1019 to 1054. To improve justice, he issued a written law code.

A scholar, he translated Greek works into his language. He arranged marriages between his children and the families of royal rulers in Western Europe.

Kiev declined in the 1100s, as rival families battled for the throne. Also, Russian trading cities like Kiev declined because Byzantine prosperity was fading. As Russian princes continued to feud among themselves, Mongol invaders from central Asia struck the final blow.

☑ **CHECK UNDERSTANDING** Why did Kiev become an important city?

The Mongols Conquer Russia

In the early 1200s, a young leader united the nomadic Mongols of central Asia. As his mounted bowmen overran lands from China to eastern Europe, he took the title Genghis Khan (GENG is kahn), or "World Emperor."

Between 1236 and 1241, Batu, the grandson of Genghis, led Mongol armies into Russia. Known as the Golden Horde because of the color of their tents, these invaders looted and burned Kiev and other Russian towns. So many inhabitants were killed, declared a Russian historian, that "no eye remained to weep for the dead."

Mongol Rule From their capital on the Volga, the Golden Horde ruled Russia for more than 150 years.

>> Skilled warriors, Mongol armies swept through southwest Russia. They were called the Golden Horde because of the color of their tents that presented a sea of golden cloth that stretched for miles.

Areas that were not directly controlled by the Mongols were raided by Mongol armies.

The Mongols, while fierce conquerors, were generally tolerant rulers. Russian princes had to acknowledge the Mongols as their overlords and pay heavy tribute. But as long as the tribute was paid, the Mongols left the Russian princes to rule without much other interference.

Effects of Mongol Conquest Historians have long debated how Mongol rule affected Russia. Peasants felt the burden of heavy taxes to pay tribute to the Mongols. Some fled to remote regions, while others sought protection from Mongol raids by becoming serfs of Russian nobles. Even though the Mongols had converted to Islam, they tolerated the Russian Orthodox Church, which grew more powerful during this period. The Mongol conquest also brought peace to the huge swath of land between China and Eastern Europe, and Russian merchants benefited from new trade routes across this region.

The absolute power of the Mongols served as a model for later Russian rulers. Russian princes developed a strong desire to centralize their own power without interference from nobles, the clergy, or wealthy merchants. Perhaps most important,

Mongol rule cut Russia off from contacts with Western Europe at a time when Europeans were making rapid advances in the arts and sciences.

☑ **DESCRIBE** What are some aspects of Mongol rule of Russia?

Moscow Surpasses Kiev

During the Mongol period, the princes of Moscow steadily increased their power. Their success was due in part to the city's location near important river trade routes. They also used their positions as tribute collectors for the Mongols to subdue neighboring towns. When the head of the Russian Orthodox Church made Moscow his capital, the city became Russia's religious center as well as its political center.

As Mongol power declined, the princes of Moscow took on a new role as defenders of Russia against foreign rule. In 1380, they rallied other Russians and defeated the Golden Horde at the battle of Kulikovo (koo lih KOH vuh). Although the Mongols continued their terrifying raids, their strength was much reduced.

Ivan the Great A driving force behind Moscow's successes was Ivan III, known as **Ivan the Great.**

Between 1462 and 1505, he brought much of northern Russia under his rule.

Ivan built the framework for absolute rule. He tried to limit the power of the *boyars*, or great landowning nobles. After he married a niece of the last Byzantine emperor, Ivan adopted Byzantine court rituals to emphasize Russia's role as the heir to Byzantine power.

Like the Byzantine emperors, he used a double-headed eagle as his symbol and sometimes referred to himself as tsar, the Russian word for Caesar. In 1504, a Russian church council echoed Byzantine statements, declaring, "By nature, the tsar is like any other man, but in power and office he is like the highest God."

Ivan the Terrible In 1547, Ivan IV, grandson of Ivan the Great, became the first Russian ruler officially crowned tsar. He further centralized royal power by limiting the privileges of the old boyar families and granting land to nobles in exchange for military or other service. At a time when the manor system was fading in Western Europe, Ivan IV introduced new laws that tied Russian serfs to the land.

About 1560, Ivan IV became increasingly unstable. He trusted no one and became subject to violent fits of rage. In a moment of madness, he even killed his own son.

Growth of Russia, 1300–1584

KEY

- Moscow, about 1300
- Land added, 1300–1462
- Land added, 1462–1533
- Land added, 1533–1584
- Empire of the Golden Horde, 1300
- ✳ Battle site

ARCTIC OCEAN

SWEDEN
Novgorod
LITHUANIA   Moscow
POLAND
Warsaw
Kulikovo
Kiev
KAZAN
Constantinople
Bukhara   Samarkand

0   500 mi
0   500 km
Lambert Conformal Conic Projection

>> **Analyze Maps** Between 1300 and 1584, Russian lands expanded from a small area around Moscow to a large territory. In which period did Novgorod come under Moscow's rule?

▶ **BOUNCE to Activate Map**

Eastern Europe, Russia, and the Byzantine Empire in 1300

>> **Analyze Maps** Locate on the map regions where Eastern Europe meets Asia. What might happen in these regions?

He organized the *oprichniki* (ah PREECH nee kee), agents of terror who enforced the tsar's will. Dressed in black robes and mounted on black horses, they slaughtered rebellious boyars and sacked towns where people were suspected of disloyalty. Their saddles were decorated with a dog's head and a broom, symbols of their constant watchfulness to sweep away their master's enemies.

The tsar's awesome power, and the ways he used it, earned him the title **Ivan the Terrible.** When he died in 1584, he left a land seething with rebellion. But he had introduced Russia to a tradition of extreme absolute power that would shape Russia into modern times.

☑ **DESCRIBE** How did Ivan III and Ivan IV establish authoritarian power?

The Geography of Eastern Europe

Many peoples and nations flourished in Eastern Europe over the centuries. In part because of its location, the region was often shaped by migration and foreign conquest.

Location The region called Eastern Europe refers to a wide swath of territory between German-speaking Central Europe to the west and Russia to the east. It reaches from the chilly Baltic Sea down through the plains of Poland and Hungary into the mountainous **Balkan Peninsula.** Often called the Balkans, this roughly triangular area juts southward into the warm Mediterranean.

Diverse Cultural Influences In the early Middle Ages, Slavs migrated into Eastern Europe. Like the Germanic peoples who settled Western Europe, the Slavs were a diverse group of tribes. Other peoples also migrated into Eastern Europe, enriching its culture. In the 900s, Ibrahim-ibn-Yaqub, a Spanish-Jewish traveler, left this account of the region:

The lands of the Slavs stretch from the Syrian Sea to the Ocean in the north . . . They comprise numerous tribes, each different from the other . . . if not for the disharmony amongst them, caused by the multiplication of factions and by their fragmentation into clans, no people could match them for strength.

—Ibrahim-Ibn-Yaqub

Geographic Features Shape Eastern Europe

Much of the region lies on the great European Plain that links up with the steppes of southern Russia. Its main rivers, such as the Danube and the Vistula (VISH chuh luh), flow either south into the Black Sea or north into the Baltic Sea.

Goods and cultural influences traveled along these river routes. As a result, the Balkans in the south felt the influence of Byzantine civilization and Eastern Orthodox Christianity, which also shaped Russia. Later, the Muslim Ottoman empire brought other cultural influences. In contrast, the northern regions of Eastern Europe that bordered Germany and the Baltic Sea forged closer links to Western Europe.

☑ **CHECK UNDERSTANDING** How did Eastern Europe's rivers affect the region?

Migrations Increase Diversity

Eastern Europe has long been a crossroads and buffer. Many peoples migrated into the region, which had no difficult geographic barriers such as high mountains or wide deserts. As a result, Eastern Europe today includes a wealth of languages and cultures.

Often, migrating peoples and even invaders stopped their advances in Eastern Europe. By absorbing waves of newcomers, Eastern Europe served as a barrier protecting Western Europe.

A Mix of Peoples During the early Middle Ages, various groups of Slavs migrated into Eastern Europe. The West Slavs filtered into present-day Poland and the Czech and Slovak republics. The South Slavs occupied the Balkans, where they became some of the ancestors of the Serbs, Croats, and Slovenes.

Other ethnic groups settled in the Balkans. (An **ethnic group** is a group of people who share the same language and cultural heritage.) Waves of Asian peoples migrated into Eastern Europe, among them the Huns, Avars, Bulgars, Khazars, and Magyars. Vikings and other Germanic peoples added to the mix.

Diverse Religious Influences Powerful neighboring states brought different religions to the region. Byzantine missionaries spread Eastern Orthodox Christianity throughout the Balkans. German knights and missionaries from the West brought Roman Catholic Christianity to Poland, Hungary, the Czech area, and the western Balkans. In the 1300s, the Ottomans invaded the Balkans and brought Islam to the region.

Jews Settle in Eastern Europe By about 1100, Jews had begun to settle in Eastern Europe.

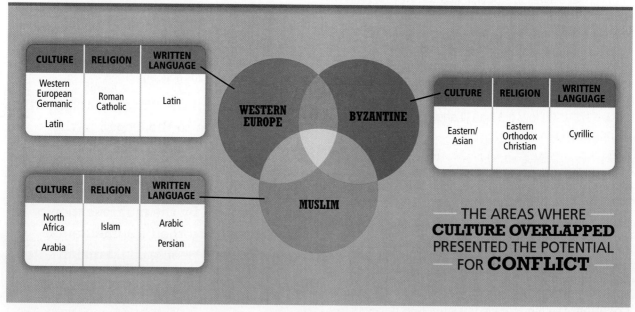

BALKANS DIFFERENT LANGUAGES, RELIGIONS, AND CULTURES

CULTURE	RELIGION	WRITTEN LANGUAGE
Western European Germanic Latin	Roman Catholic	Latin

CULTURE	RELIGION	WRITTEN LANGUAGE
Eastern/ Asian	Eastern Orthodox Christian	Cyrillic

CULTURE	RELIGION	WRITTEN LANGUAGE
North Africa Arabia	Islam	Arabic Persian

WESTERN EUROPE

BYZANTINE

MUSLIM

THE AREAS WHERE **CULTURE OVERLAPPED** PRESENTED THE POTENTIAL FOR **CONFLICT**

>> **Analyze Charts** Which cultural influences are present in the Balkans?

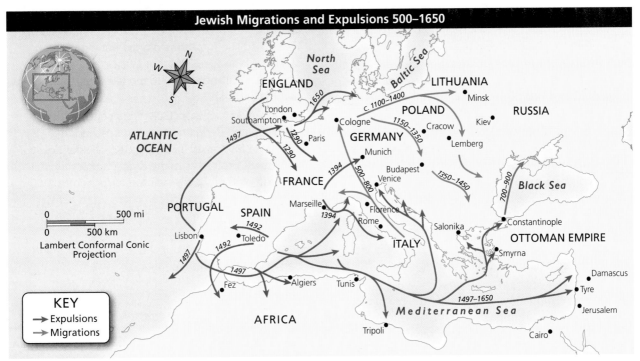

KEY
→ Expulsions
→ Migrations

>> **Analyze Maps** The constantly changing treatment of Jews throughout medieval Europe led to periods of migration and expulsion for the Jewish people. Was the movement of Jews into Eastern Europe a result of migration or expulsion?

BOUNCE to Activate Map

Settlements were probably organized by merchants. Jews carried on trade along routes that connected what is today Poland, Hungary, and the Balkans.

In the late Middle Ages, Eastern Europe had become a refuge for Jews. Christians in Western Europe launched attacks on Jewish communities during the Crusades and the Black Death. To escape persecution, Jews fled east. As monarchs centralized power in England, France, and Spain, they expelled Jews from their lands. These groups, too, migrated eastward.

A growing number of Jews settled in Poland. By 1264, Jews had gained a charter, or official document, from Prince Boleslaw of Krakov. The charter protected the rights of Jews in his territory. Over the next 500 years, other Polish towns gave shelter to Jews. By about 1650, about 500,000 Jews lived in Poland and Lithuania, the largest population of Jews in Europe. During this period, Poland became a cultural and spiritual center for Jews. Although some Polish leaders encouraged Jews to settle in their lands, Jews still faced persecution throughout Eastern Europe.

Jewish merchants and scholars contributed to the economic and cultural development of Poland and other parts of Eastern Europe where they settled. Owing to their ties with Jewish communities abroad, Jewish merchants were very successful in European

and overseas trade. Merchants often mastered many languages, including Arabic. Educated Jews had studied Greek and Latin as well as Hebrew. Jews expelled from Spain in 1492 brought a large range of skills to their new homes.

☑ **DESCRIBE** How did three major religions spread to Eastern Europe?

Early Kingdoms of Eastern Europe

During the Middle Ages, wars constantly shifted boundaries in Eastern Europe. Sometimes strong empires absorbed national groups. Alliances or royal marriages might bind others together. The histories of three kingdoms—Poland, Hungary, and Serbia—illustrate the shifting fortunes that the peoples of Eastern Europe faced.

Poland Missionaries brought Roman Catholicism to the West Slavs of Poland in the 900s. Within a century, the first Polish king was crowned. To survive, Poland often had to battle Germans, Russians, and Mongols.

Poland's greatest age came after a royal marriage united Poland and Lithuania in 1386. Under the

Jagiello (yahg YEH loh) dynasty, Poland-Lithuania was the largest state in Europe. Its empire stretched from the Baltic to the Black Sea.

Unlike in Russia or Western Europe, where royal rulers limited the power of nobles, Polish nobles gradually gained power at the expense of the monarch. They met in a **diet,** or assembly, where the vote of a single noble could block the passage of a law. This *liberum veto*, or "free veto," made it hard for the government to take decisive action.

Without a strong central government, Poland-Lithuania declined. It enjoyed a final moment of glory in 1683 when the Polish king Jan Sobieski (yahn soh BYEH skee) broke the Ottoman siege of Vienna. In the next century, however, Poland and Lithuania were gobbled up by ambitious neighbors.

Hungary Hungary was settled by the Magyars, who had raided Europe from the Asian steppes. About 970, the Magyar adopted Roman Catholic Christianity.

In the Middle Ages, Hungary was larger than it is today. Its rulers controlled present-day Slovakia, Croatia, and parts of Romania.

Like King John of England, the Hungarian king was forced to sign a charter recognizing nobles' rights. Known as the **Golden Bull of 1222,** it strictly limited royal power.

The Mongols overran Hungary in 1241, killing as much as half its population. These invaders soon withdrew, so the Mongol invasion did not have the lasting impact on Hungary that it had on Russia. The expansion of the Ottoman Turks, though, did end Hungarian independence in 1526. Later, the Austrian Hapsburgs replaced the Ottomans as rulers of Hungary.

Serbia During the 600s, South Slavs settled in the mountainous Balkans. Serbs, Croats, Slovenes, and other Slavic peoples in the Balkans had different histories during the Middle Ages. The Serbs accepted Orthodox Christianity. By the late 1100s,

they set up their own state, which reached its height under Stefan Dusan (STEH vahn DOO shahn). He battled the Byzantine empire and conquered Macedonia in the 1300s. Yet Dusan encouraged Byzantine culture and even modeled his law code on that of Justinian.

Dusan's successors lacked his political gifts, however, and Serbia could not withstand the advance of Ottoman Turks. At the battle of Kosovo in 1389, Serbs fought to the death, a memory still honored by their descendants. During almost 500 years of Ottoman rule, Serbs preserved a sense of their own identity.

☑ **SYNTHESIZE** How did Poland, Hungary, and Serbia lose their independence?

☑ ASSESSMENT

1. **Cause and Effect** How did Russia's geography affect its early history?

2. **Determine Relevance** How important was Byzantine influence on Russia and other countries in Eastern Europe?

3. **Synthesize Information** What were major causes and effects of Mongol rule on Russia's economy and political structure?

4. **Analyze Information** How did a tradition of absolute rule develop in Russia?

5. **Quest Connections** How did Eastern Europe become home to so many ethnic groups?

Connections to Today

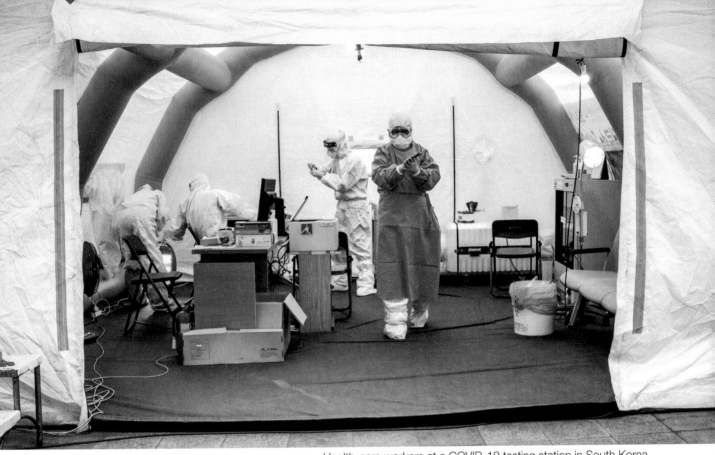

Health-care workers at a COVID-19 testing station in South Korea.

Take Action to Learn About Global Epidemics

Our world is more connected today than it ever has been. That interconnectedness can quickly turn a disease outbreak into an epidemic.

1. **Choose** one of the following topics:

   - **Groups:** Learn about the many groups that respond to outbreaks of diseases around the world and any challenges they face while doing their work.

   - **Our Connected World:** Find data on annual international travel for both commercial and recreational purposes and the resulting positive and negative outcomes.

   - **Outbreaks:** Research specific recent cases of contagious disease outbreaks around the world, including as many details as possible.

2. **Ask Questions** What are some of the things you want to know about the connections between global health and the interconnectedness of the world today? Write a list of questions.

3. **Learn** Research the topic you have chosen. Find both online and print sources.

4. **Create an Infographic** Create a colorful and engaging infographic showing the information you found during your research into one of the topics listed above.

LESSON SUMMARIES

Use these Lesson Summaries, and the longer versions available online, to review the key ideas for each lesson in this Topic.

Lesson 1: The Early Middle Ages

The collapse of the Roman Empire ushered in the thousand year span known as the Middle Ages. Charlemagne became king of the Franks. In 800, the pope crowned him as Emperor of the Romans. He ruled as emperor just over thirteen years.

Lesson 2: Feudalism and the Manor Economy

Medieval society was shaped by a political and economic system called feudalism.

Lesson 3: The Medieval Christian Church

The Church was the most dominant institution in medieval life. However, in spite of its power, there were calls for reform. Jewish communities often faced discrimination. Thousands migrated to Eastern Europe where they were welcomed.

Lesson 4: Economic Expansion and Change: The Crusades and After

Despite the violence of the Crusades, it did spark a demand for spices, silks, perfumes, and new foods such as coffee. The demand resulted in a trade revival and a long period of economic expansion known as the commercial revolution.

ⓠ QUEST! FINDINGS

Create Your Graphic Novel Refer to your responses to the Quest Connections to help you create your graphic novel to share with the class. Use the rubric and other Quest resources online to guide your work.

Lesson 5: The Feudal Monarchs and the Church

As medieval monarchs gradually increased royal authority over the Church, new traditions of government evolved.

Lesson 6: Learning, Literature and Art of the Middle Ages

Improved economic and political conditions in Europe by the 1100s opened opportunity for cultural achievements.

Lesson 7: The Later Middle Ages: A Time of Upheaval

The Black Death epidemic ravaged the land and caused social and economic upheaval. Reformers challenged the authority of the Church.

Lesson 8: Russia and Eastern Europe

In Eastern Europe, Byzantine culture influenced Russia's early history. The Mongols, united by Genghis Khan, invaded Eastern Europe between 1237 and 1241.

📶 **GO ONLINE** to access lesson summaries

VISUAL REVIEW

Use these graphics to review some of the key terms, people, and ideas from this Topic.

Feudalism and the Manor System

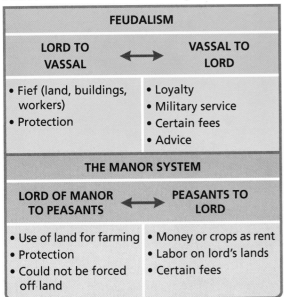

FEUDALISM	
LORD TO VASSAL	**VASSAL TO LORD**
• Fief (land, buildings, workers) • Protection	• Loyalty • Military service • Certain fees • Advice
THE MANOR SYSTEM	
LORD OF MANOR TO PEASANTS	**PEASANTS TO LORD**
• Use of land for farming • Protection • Could not be forced off land	• Money or crops as rent • Labor on lord's lands • Certain fees

Role of the Church

DAILY LIFE	ECONOMIC POWER	POLITICAL POWER
• Mass • Sacraments • Religious calendars • Aid to needy • Moral guidance	• Owned large tracts of land • People willed riches to Church • Agricultural and commercial activity in monasteries	• Papal supremacy • Threat of excommuni-cation, interdict • Raised own armies • Clergy served in governments • Moral authority

Why Did Europe Decline?

- The western Roman empire collapsed.
- Invaders swept across the region.
- Trade, travel, towns, and learning all decreased.
- Germanic kingdoms carved up a once-unified empire.

Topic 7 Assessment

KEY TERMS, PEOPLE, AND IDEAS

1. How did **Constantinople** become the center of the Byzantine Empire?

2. How did **Justinian's Code** change laws?

3. Why did **feudalism** develop?

4. How did the Crusades affect feudalism?

5. How did the Magna Carta gradually change legal ideas in England?

6. What new ideas were introduced with **scholasticism**?

7. How did the **Black Death epidemic** cause an upheaval in Medieval Europe?

8. What is the significance of the **steppe** in the geography of Russia?

9. What impact did Mongol rule have on Russia?

CRITICAL THINKING

10. **Summarize** In what way was the Byzantine Empire a departure from the old Roman Empire?

11. **Draw Conclusions** How did the manor serve the needs of the early Middle Ages?

12. **Analyze Information** (a) How did the Church increase its secular power? (b) How did riches and power lead to Church abuses and then to reforms?

13. **Understanding Main Ideas** How did changes in agriculture and trade lead to the growth of towns and commerce?

14. **Analyze Information** What effect did the collapse of the Western Roman Empire have on Europe?

15. **Identify Central Issues** How was religion central to the art and architecture of the Middle Ages?

16. **Use Visual Information** Look at the image of the manor village in the next column. What evidence is there that the manor system was able to provide for an entire village?

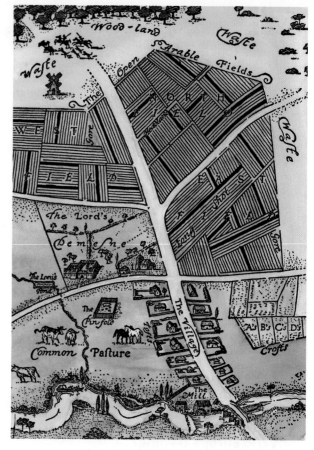

17. **Writing Activity: Write an Informative Essay**
An informative essay explains a particular topic or idea. Read the primary source below. In it, Giovanni Boccaccio writes about the Black Death. Use the excerpt and your knowledge of the spread of the plague to write an informative essay about how it affected Italian society and its immediate effect on the population.

> . . . this scourge had implanted so great a terror in the hearts of men and women that brothers abandoned brothers, uncles their nephews, sisters their brothers, and in many cases wives deserted their husbands. But even worse, and almost incredible was the fact that fathers and mothers refused to nurse and assist their own children, as though they did not belong to them.

18. **Connections to Today** Consider how connected the world is today. In a single 18-hour flight you can be on the other side of the planet. How much greater is the risk of spreading infectious diseases now as compared to the Middle Ages? What modern advances help limit that risk? What more could be done to reduce that risk?

DOCUMENT-BASED QUESTIONS

Richard I, king of England from 1189 to 1199, spent only six months in England during his reign. The rest of the time he was at war abroad, most famously as one of the leaders of the Third Crusade. On his way home from the Holy Land, Richard was held for ransom by Emperor Henry IV of the Holy Roman Empire. It took his mother, Eleanor of Aquitaine, a year to raise the money to free him. Read the documents below, then answer the questions that follow.

DOCUMENT A

"Some . . . advised the king against engaging such a large army, as he then only had around fifty knights with him. Yet their trepidation [fear] only made him more courageous. Putting spur to horse, he charged into the enemy, broke through and scattered their battleline, destroying them. . . . When this was over the king put out an edict by public crier. All the locals who wanted peace could freely come and go, unhindered by his people, and enjoy guaranteed liberty"

> —*Itineerarium Peregrinorum et Gesta Regis Ricardi, eyewitness account of the Third Crusade*

DOCUMENT B

"Yet to the sad 'tis comfort to complain
Friends I have many, and promises abound;
Shame will be theirs; if, for winters twain,
Unramsom'd, I still bear a tyrant's chain.
Full well they know, my lords and nobles all. . .
Ne'er did I slight my poorest vassal's call. . .
They know this well who now are rich and strong. . .
That far from them, in hostile bonds I strain."

> —*poem by King Richard I, written while imprisoned by Holy Roman Emperor Henry IV*

DOCUMENT C

"The "[King Richard I] of England is one of the most romantic figures of all English history. . . Richard has become the very epitome [symbol] of chivalry, the knight fighting bravely for his kingdom, his church, and his lady with ax, shield, and horse. . . . That in actual history, [he] does not quite measure up to the standards of his own legend does not dull his allure [appea]. He was a brilliant military mind and a fearsome general. . . in single combat he was unrivaled in bravery and recklessness. . . . Richard is remembered for his bravado [daring] and cunning—and his extravagance. He is not remembered for his compassion, his tact, or his restraint.

> —*Warriors of God, by James Reston, Jr. 2001*

DOCUMENT D

19. According to Document A, Richard I
    A. was brave, but foolishly rushed at the enemy when he was outnumbered.
    B. was a good commander who stayed in the background.
    C. was a brave conqueror and a town crier
    D. was an impressive warrior and compassionate conqueror.

20. Which of the following statements BEST summarizes Reston's view of Richard the Lion-heart?
    A. Although he was a brave warrior, he does not measure up to his own legend.
    B. He was compassionate and tactful.
    C. He is a truly heroic figure worthy of his reputation.
    D. His legend leaves out his good qualities.

21. What do the creators of Documents A and D want to convey about Richard I?
    A. his bravery and compassion
    B. his bravery and skill as a poet
    C. his bravery and skill as a warrior
    D. his greatness as a Christian ruler

22. **Writing Tasks** Which of the documents above are most reliable, and why? How does each one help you understand Richard's character? Write your own description of Richard's character, using at least three of the documents to support your thesis.

GO ONLINE to access more practice

The Muslim World and Africa
(730 B.C.–A.D. 1500)

ESSENTIAL QUESTION How are religion and culture connected?

Decorative carving at the Alhambra palace complex, Spain

Connections to Today

Today, many Africans from different countries communicate across borders in Arabic or Swahili. People in many countries enjoy Arabic movies from Egypt or Swahili movies from Tanzania. African business people are able to communicate with business partners in other countries in Arabic or Swahili.

In this topic you'll read how Arabic and Swahili first spread across Africa through trade. How do those trade connections from long ago continue to affect life in Africa today?

NBC LEARN

Learn about the travels of Ibn Battuta.

BOUNCE to Activate My Story Video

Topic 8 Overview

In this Topic you will learn about the rise of the Muslim empire and the early kingdoms and city-states of Africa. Look at the lesson outline and explore the timeline. As you study this Topic, you will complete the Quest team project.

LESSON OUTLINE

8.1 The Origins of Islam

8.2 A Muslim Empire

8.3 Achievements of Muslim Civilization

8.4 The Ottoman and Safavid Empires

8.5 Early Civilizations of Africa

8.6 Kingdoms of West Africa

8.7 Trading States of East Africa

8.8 Diverse People and Traditions in Africa

Key Events of the Muslim World and Africa

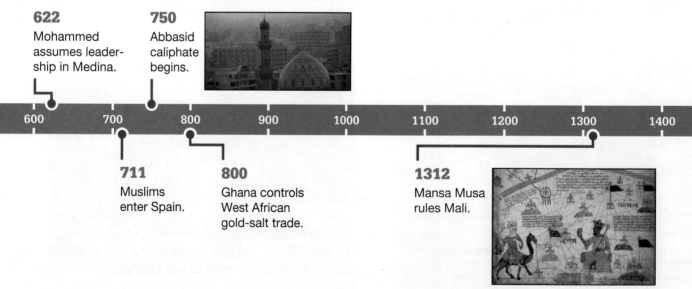

622 Mohammed assumes leadership in Medina.

750 Abbasid caliphate begins.

600 | 700 | 800 | 900 | 1000 | 1100 | 1200 | 1300 | 1400

711 Muslims enter Spain.

800 Ghana controls West African gold-salt trade.

1312 Mansa Musa rules Mali.

QUEST! INQUIRY

Participate in a Civic Discussion

Was the Battle of Tours the decisive event that stopped the spread of Islam in Europe? In this Quest you will research and prepare a discussion panel to determine the answer to this question.

STEP 1

Begin your research. Review what you have learned about the rise of the Umayyad caliphs and the expansion of the Muslim empire. Discuss important points with your team.

STEP 2

Divide the team to take a YES or NO position. Evaluate the evidence. Use evidence to support your team's position.

STEP 3

Begin to draw conclusions. Listen carefully to arguments for and against the issue. Determine the best arguments for each side.

STEP 4

Now switch sides. Consider a different point of view. Are you willing to change your earlier position? Reflect on what you have learned about the importance of careful research and discussion in shaping opinions.

GO ONLINE to access complete Quest materials

8.1

The oasis town of Mecca was a thriving center of religion and trade before the time of Muhammad. This illustration shows Muhammad's grandfather arriving in Mecca as a young boy.

 BOUNCE to Activate Flipped Video

Objectives

Understand how Muhammad spread Islam.

Describe the central ideas of Islam.

Explain how Islam helped shape the way of life of its believers.

Key Terms

Bedouin
Muhammad
Mecca
Kaaba
Yathrib
hijra
Medina
Quran
mosque
hajj
Sharia

The Origins of Islam

The religion of Islam, whose followers are called Muslims, emerged in the Arabian Peninsula. This region of southwestern Asia is mostly desert, yet it was home to many Arab tribes in the A.D. 500s. Nomadic herders called **Bedouins** (BED oo inz) moved through the desert to reach seasonal pasturelands for their camels, goats, and sheep. Competition for water and grazing land often led to warfare. Bedouins also traded with settled Arab tribes in oasis towns and protected the caravan trading routes.

Muhammad and Early Islam

Muhammad, an Arab man whom Muslims honor as the prophet of Islam, was born in the oasis town of Mecca around A.D. 570. **Mecca** was a bustling market town at the crossroads of several caravan routes. It was also a thriving pilgrimage center. Many Arabs came to pray at the **Kaaba,** an ancient temple that housed statues of pagan gods and goddesses. The pilgrims helped make Mecca's merchants wealthy. All weapons had to be laid down near the temple, making Mecca a safe and peaceful place to do business.

Muhammad's Early Life Arabia's deserts and trade centers shaped Muhammad's early life. In his youth, he worked as a shepherd among the Bedouins. Later, he led caravans across the desert and became a successful merchant. When he was about 25, Muhammad married Khadija (ka DEE jah), a wealthy widow who ran a prosperous caravan business. According to tradition, Muhammad became known for his honesty in business and was a devoted husband and father.

Muhammad the Messenger Muhammad was troubled by the moral ills of Meccan society, especially greed. He often went to a cave in the hills near Mecca to meditate. According to Muslim belief, when he was about 40 years old he heard the voice of the angel Gabriel calling him to be the messenger of God. Muhammad was terrified and puzzled. How could he, an illiterate merchant, become the messenger of God?

Khadija encouraged him to accept the call. She became the first convert to the faith called Islam, from the Arabic word that means "to submit to God." Muhammad devoted his life to spreading Islam. He urged Arabs to give up their worship of pagan gods and to instead worship God. In Arabic, the word for God is *Allah.*

The Hijra: From Mecca to Medina At first, few people listened to Muhammad's teachings. His rejection of traditional Arab gods angered Mecca's merchants, who feared that neglect of their gods would disrupt the pilgrim trade. Facing persecution, in 615 some of Muhammad's followers left Mecca for Axum, located across the Red Sea, where they received protection from Axum's Christian king.

In 622, faced with the threat of murder, Muhammad and his followers left Mecca for **Yathrib,** a journey known as the **hijra** (HIJ ruh). Later, Yathrib was renamed **Medina,** or "city of the Prophet," and 622 became the first year of the Muslim calendar.

The hijra was a turning point for Islam. In Medina, local people welcomed Muhammad and agreed to follow his teachings. They became a community of Muslims, or *umma.* Loyalty to the umma was based on Islam instead of old family rivalries. Muhammad created rules that governed and united Muslims and brought peace among many but not all of the clans of Medina. As his reputation grew, thousands of Arabs adopted Islam. Meanwhile, Meccan leaders grew more hostile toward the Muslims, seizing Muslim property. After Muslims attacked several Meccan caravans, the Meccans prepared for war.

Return to Mecca After winning battles with the Meccans, Muhammad triumphantly returned to Mecca in 630. He destroyed the Arab icons in the Kaaba, the temple that he believed Abraham had built to worship the one true God. He rededicated the Kaaba to Allah, and it became the most holy place in Islam. For the next two years, Muhammad worked to unite the Arabs under Islam. Muhammad died in 632, but the faith that he proclaimed continued to spread. Today, Islam is one of the world's major religions.

☑ **SEQUENCE EVENTS** What sequence of events led to Muhammad devoting his life to the spread of Islam?

>> When Muhammad came to Medina, he not only drew thousands to the new religion of Islam but also showed how Islam could be a unifying force for Arabs in the region. This would be a key strength in the growth of the Muslim empire.

>> This modern photograph shows Muslim pilgrims at the Kaaba, located in the center of the Haram Sharif Great Mosque in Mecca. More than two million Muslims make a pilgrimage to Mecca each year.

B BOUNCE to Activate Timeline

>> The Quran contains 114 *suras,* or chapters. This page shows a portion of the Cave Sura, named after its story about God protecting persecuted people by causing them to sleep safely in a cave.

>> The Muslim declaration of faith—written here—expresses the importance of monotheism in the religion.

BOUNCE to Activate Gallery

Teachings of Islam

Like Judaism and Christianity, Islam is monotheistic, based on belief in one God. The **Quran** (koo RAHN), the sacred text of Islam, teaches that God is all-powerful and compassionate. It also states that people are responsible for their own actions. Islam does not require priests to mediate between the people and God. Muslims believe that God had sent other prophets, including Abraham, Moses, and Jesus, but that Muhammad was the last and greatest prophet.

The Quran To Muslims, the Quran contains the sacred word of God as revealed to Muhammad. It is the final authority on all matters discussed in the text. The Quran teaches about what Muslims believe to be God's will and provides a guide to life. Its ethical standards emphasize honesty, generosity, and social justice.

It sets penalties for crimes such as stealing or murder. According to the Quran, each individual will stand before God on the final judgment day to face either eternal punishment in hell or eternal bliss in paradise.

Muslims believe that the Quran is the direct, unchangeable word of God and that its meaning and poetic beauty reside in its original language of Arabic. For that reason, all Muslims, including converts to Islam, are expected to learn the Quran and required prayers in Arabic. This shared language has helped unite Muslims from many regions throughout the world.

The Five Pillars of Islam All observant Muslims perform five basic duties, known as the Five Pillars of Islam. The first is to make a declaration of faith. The Muslim profession of faith states, "There is no god but God; Muhammad is the messenger of God." The second is to pray five times daily. After a ritual washing, Muslims face the holy city of Mecca to pray.

Although Muslims may pray anywhere, they often gather in houses of worship called masjids or **mosques.** A mosque official called a muezzin (moo EZ in) calls the faithful to prayer.

The third pillar is to give charity to the poor. The fourth is to fast from sunrise to sunset during the holy month of Ramadan—the month in which Muslims believe Muhammad received his first revelations from God. The fifth pillar is to make the **hajj,** or pilgrimage to Mecca, if a person is able. Pilgrims participate in ceremonies commemorating the actions of Muhammad, Abraham, and Abraham's family. Their simple attire symbolizes the abandonment of the material world for the sake of God.

"People of the Book" According to Muslim belief, Muslims, Jews, and Christians worship the same God. The Quran teaches that Islam is God's final and complete revelation, while Hebrew scriptures and the Christian Bible contain portions of earlier revelations. Muslims consider Jews and Christians to be "People of the Book," spiritually superior to polytheistic idol worshipers. Although Jews and Christians did not have the same rights as Muslims in early Muslim societies, and often faced burdensome taxes and restrictions, they were to a limited degree able to practice their religions.

☑ **INFER** Why do Muslims follow the Five Pillars of Islam?

Islam as a Way of Life

Islam is both a religion and a way of life. Its teachings shape the lives of Muslims around the world. Islamic law governs daily life, and Muslim traditions determine ethical behavior and influence family relations.

Islamic Law Over time, Muslim scholars developed the **Sharia,** a body of law that includes interpretation of the Quran, examples of behavior from Muhammad's life, and Muslim traditions. Similar to Jewish law, the Sharia regulates moral conduct, family life, business practices, government, and other aspects of individual and community life. It does not separate religion from criminal or civil law, but applies religious principles to all legal situations.

Women in Early Muslim Society Before Islam, the position of women in Arab society varied. In some communities, women were active in religion, trade, or politics. As in most societies at that time, however, most women had limited rights. Arab women could not inherit property and had to obey a male guardian. Among a few tribes, unwanted daughters were sometimes killed at birth.

Islam extended rights and protection to women by affirming the spiritual equality of all Muslims. The Quran teaches that "Whoever does right, whether male or female, and is a believer, all such will enter the Garden." The Quran prohibited the killing of daughters, granted women the right to inherit, and allowed women to reject a marriage offer. Islam also encouraged education for men and women so that all Muslims could study the Quran.

>> This illustration shows a beggar asking for alms. Muslims are expected to give charity, or aid, to the poor.

>> Reading the Quran is an important aspect of Muslim beliefs, so many Muslims study the Quran to better understand and practice their religion.

Although spiritually equal under Islam, men and women had different roles and rights. For example, women inherited less than men and had a more difficult time getting a divorce.

Islamic Practices Change As Islam spread throughout Asia, Africa, and Europe, Muslims adopted practices of conquered peoples. For example, the practices of veiling upper-class women and secluding them in a separate part of the home were Persian customs. The Quran says that women should dress modestly, which has been interpreted in multiple ways. Still, women's lives varied according to region and class. In rural areas, peasant women often needed to work and did not wear a veil, but took care to dress modestly.

☑ **CONTRAST** How are the Quran and Sharia different?

☑ ASSESSMENT

1. **Identify Cause and Effect** Why did Mecca become a busy trade center?

2. **Apply Concepts** Why was the hijra a turning point for Islam?

3. **Draw Conclusions** Why is declaring faith the first of the Five Pillars of Islam?

4. **Infer** How do the Quran and Sharia guide Muslims?

5. **Draw Conclusions** Why might women in Arab society have welcomed Islam?

The Quran

The Quran, the holy scriptures of Islam, contains 114 *suras*, or chapters, which are divided into verses. Muslims believe that the Quran is the word of God as revealed to Muhammad. They also believe that God instructed Muhammad to arrange the chapters into the order in which they appear. The following excerpts from the Quran tell Muslims how to be righteous and faithful. They also encourage believers to fast and observe the holy month of Ramadan.

The two excerpts following the Quran are observations about Muhammad from his disciples.

>> A page from the Quran

Primary Source 1

Righteousness is not whether you turn your face towards East or West; but the righteousness is to believe in Allah, the Last Day, the Angels, the Books [Scriptures] and Prophets, and to spend wealth out of love for Him on relatives, orphans, helpless, needy travelers, those who ask for and on the redemption [freedom by payment of ransom] of captives; and to establish Salah (prayers), to pay Zakah (alms) [charity given freely to the poor], to fulfill promises when made, to be steadfast in distress, in adversity [misfortune], and at the time of war. These people are the truthful and these are the pious.

—The Quran 2:177

☑ **DETERMINE MEANING** According to the Quran, what factors determine whether a person is righteous?

O, believers! Fasting is prescribed [ordered] for you as it was prescribed for those before you so that you may learn self-restraint. Fast the prescribed number of days; except if any of you is ill or on a journey, then fast a similar number of days later. For those who can not endure it for *medical reasons,* there is a ransom [act of devotion]: the feeding of one poor person for each missed day. Whoever does more good *than this* voluntarily, it is better for him. However, if you truly understand the *rationale of fasting,* it is better for you to fast.

It is the month of Ramadhān in which the Qur'an was revealed, a guidance for mankind with clear teachings showing the Right Way and a criterion of *truth* and *falsehood.* Therefore, anyone of you who witnesses that month should fast therein, and whoever is ill or upon a journey shall fast a similar number of days later on. Allah intends your well-being and does not want to put you to hardship. He wants you to complete the prescribed period so that you should glorify His Greatness and render [give] thanks to Him for giving you guidance.

—The Quran 2:183–185

☑ **EXPLAIN AN ARGUMENT** Why do Muslims fast during Ramadan?

Primary Source 2

Umm Ma'bad gives her description of Muhammad:

When he spoke, his speech was brilliant. Of all people he was the most handsome and the most pleasant, even when approaching from a distance. In person, he was unique and most admirable. Graced with eloquent logic, his speech was moderate. His logical arguments were well organized as though they were a string of gems. He was not too tall or too short, but exactly in between. . . He had companions who affectionately honored him. When he spoke, they listened to him attentively. When he gave orders, they were quick to execute them. They rallied around him guarding him. He never frowned or spoke frivolously."

—*Hadith,* al Bayhaqi

Anas ibn Malik gives his description:

"I served the Prophet of Allah, upon him be peace, for ten years. During that time, he never once said to me as much as 'Oof' if I did something wrong. He never asked me, if I had failed to do something, 'Why did you not do it?,' and he never said to me, if I had done something wrong, 'Why did you do it?'"

—*Hadith,* al Bukhari

☑ **SUMMARIZE** Based on these descriptions, what kind of man was Muhammad?

☑ ASSESSMENT

1. **Determine Central Ideas** Why do Muslims consider Ramadan an important and holy month?

2. **Identify Supporting Details** Islam has Five Pillars, or primary obligations: profession of faith, prayer, almsgiving, fasting during Ramadan, and pilgrimage to Mecca. How do these excerpts from the Quran support the Five Pillars?

3. **Identify Cause and Effect** How do you think the Quran has affected the lives of Muslims?

4. **Draw Conclusions** Based on the way in which Muhammad's disciples described him, how do you think Muhammad might have drawn followers to Islam?

GO ONLINE to access primary sources

This illustration from the 1100s shows Muslim soldiers setting up their tents by a river. Arab Muslim armies had a remarkable series of military victories under Abu Bakr and his successors.

A Muslim Empire

The death of Muhammad plunged his followers into grief. Muhammad had been a pious man and a powerful leader. No one else had ever been able to unify so many Arab tribes. Could the community of Muslims survive without him?

Islam Faces Challenges

Muslims faced a problem when Muhammad died because he had not named a successor to lead the community. Eventually, they agreed that **Abu Bakr** (uh BOO BAK ur), Muhammad's father-in-law and an early convert to Islam, should be the first **caliph,** or successor to Muhammad. Abu Bakr sternly told the faithful, "If you worship Muhammad, Muhammad is dead. If you worship God, God is alive."

Arabs Join Together Under Islam Abu Bakr faced an immediate crisis. The loyalty of some Arab tribal leaders had been dependent on Muhammad's personal command. They refused to follow Abu Bakr and withdrew their loyalty to Islam. After several battles with the rebellious tribes, Abu Bakr succeeded in reuniting the Muslims, based on their allegiance to Islam.

Once reunited, the Muslims set out on a remarkable series of military campaigns. They began by converting the remaining Arab tribes to Islam, which ended warfare between Arabs and united them under one leader.

Arab Muslims Win Victories Then, under the first four caliphs, the Arab Muslims marched from victory to victory against the neighboring Byzantine and Persian empires, capturing territory in parts of Asia, Europe, and Africa. The Byzantines and Persians had competed with each other over control of lands in the Middle East. Once the Arabs united, they surprised their neighbors, conquering

BOUNCE to Activate Flipped Video

Objectives

Describe the spread of Islam.

Identify the divisions that emerged within Islam.

Describe the rise of Umayyad and Abbasid dynasties.

Explain why the Abbasid empire declined.

Key Terms

Abu Bakr
caliph
Sunni
Shiite
Sufi
Umayyad
Abbasid
Baghdad
minaret
sultan

GO ONLINE to access your digital course

>> The Dome of the Rock in Jerusalem is the oldest surviving Islamic building. Construction began soon after Muslims captured the city. According to Muslim teaching, Muhammad ascended to heaven from the rock inside this building.

BOUNCE to Activate 3D Model

>> Medina is the second holiest site in Islam. Like Mecca, it is an important part of the hijra and Muhammad's journey. Both sites attract many pilgrims.

great portions of the Byzantine empire and defeating the Persians entirely. First, they took the provinces of Syria and Palestine from the Byzantines, including the cities of Damascus and Jerusalem. Then they captured the weakened Persian empire and swept into Byzantine Egypt.

☑ **INFER** Why do you think the Byzantines and Persians were surprised by the strength of the Arab Muslims?

Divisions Split Islam

When Muhammad died, Muslims disagreed about who should be chosen to be the leader of the community. The split between **Sunni** (SOO nee) and **Shiite** (SHEE yt) Muslims had a profound impact on later Islamic history.

Differing Ideas About Leaders One group of Muslims felt that Muhammad had designated his son-in-law, Ali, to be his successor. They were called Shiites, after *shi'at Ali*, or followers of Ali. Shiites believe that the true successors to Muhammad are the descendants of Ali and Muhammad's daughter, Fatima. They believe that these descendants, called Imams, are divinely inspired religious leaders, who are empowered to interpret the Quran and the actions of Muhammad.

Another group felt that any good Muslim could lead the community, since there could be no prophet after Muhammad. This group soon divided and fought among themselves as well as with others over issues of who could be defined as a "good" Muslim.

The majority of Muslims eventually compromised around the view that the successor to Muhammad should be a pious male Muslim from Muhammad's tribe. This successor is called a caliph and is viewed as a political leader of the religious community, without any divine or prophetic functions.

Members of the compromise group, which forms the majority of Muslims in the world today, are known as Sunnis, since they follow the custom of the community, or *sunna*. The Sunni believe that inspiration comes from the example of Muhammad as recorded by his early followers.

Sunni and Shiite Beliefs Like the schism between Roman Catholic and Eastern Orthodox Christians, the division between Sunni and Shiite Muslims has survived to the present day.

Members of both branches of Islam believe in the same God, look to the Quran for guidance, and follow

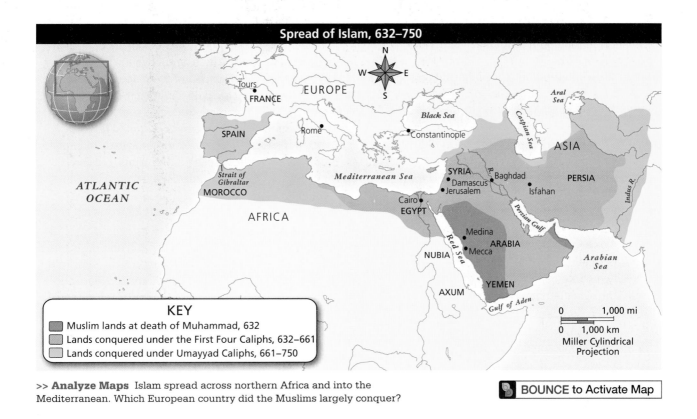

KEY
- Muslim lands at death of Muhammad, 632
- Lands conquered under the First Four Caliphs, 632–661
- Lands conquered under Umayyad Caliphs, 661–750

0   1,000 mi
0   1,000 km
Miller Cylindrical
Projection

>> **Analyze Maps** Islam spread across northern Africa and into the Mediterranean. Which European country did the Muslims largely conquer?

BOUNCE to Activate Map

the Pillars of Islam. However, Sunnis and Shiites differ in such areas as religious practice, law, and daily life. Today, about 90 percent of Muslims are Sunni. Most Shiites live in Iran, Lebanon, Iraq, and Yemen. The Shiite branch itself has further split into several different subgroups.

Over the centuries, the division between Sunnis and Shiites has sometimes been a source of conflict. When Sunni rulers held power, they often favored other Sunnis and deprived Shiites of wealth and power. When Shiites gained power, Sunnis often stood to lose. This sometimes bitter rivalry remains a source of tension in the Middle East today.

Sufis Emerge In both the Sunni and Shiite branches of Islam, a group called the **Sufis** emerged. Sufis are Muslim mystics who sought communion with God through meditation, fasting, and other rituals. Sufis were respected for their piety and some were believed to have miraculous powers.

Like Christian monks and nuns, some Sufis helped spread Islam by traveling, preaching, and being good examples to others. They carried the faith to remote villages, where they blended local traditions and beliefs into Muslim culture.

☑ **CONTRAST** How did ideas about leadership differ between Shiites and Sunnis?

Umayyad Caliphs Create an Arab Empire

Islamic civilization expanded from the Middle East despite great distances and physical barriers, such as mountains and deserts. After the death of Ali, a powerful Meccan clan set up the **Umayyad** (oo MY ad) caliphate, a dynasty of Sunni caliphs that ruled the Muslim empire until 750. From their capital at Damascus in Syria, they directed the conquests that extended Arab rule from Spain and Morocco in the west to the Indus River Valley in the east. Because it stood near the points where Asia met Europe and Africa, Damascus provided a good location from which to expand the empire. In addition, the city's central location helped it become a social, cultural, and economic hub. Although Islam also spread peacefully through trade and cultural exchange— reaching East Africa as early as the mid-700s—these conquests spread Muslim civilization to many parts of Europe, Asia, and Africa.

The Muslim Empire Expands From Egypt, Arab Muslim armies moved west, defeating Byzantine forces across North Africa.

In 711, Muslim forces crossed the Strait of Gibraltar and conquered Spain. In 731, a Muslim army moved north into France to settle new areas.

There, Christian Frankish forces defeated the Muslims at the battle of Tours in 732. Muslims ruled parts of Spain for centuries, but advanced no farther into Europe. Elsewhere, Muslim forces besieged the Byzantine capital of Constantinople, but failed to take the well-defended city.

Why the Muslim Empire Succeeded Several factors help explain the series of Muslim victories. One factor was the weakness of the Byzantine and Persian empires. The longtime rivals had fought each other to exhaustion. Many people also welcomed the Arabs as liberators from harsh Byzantine or Persian rule. Another factor was the Arabs' bold, efficient fighting methods. The Bedouin camel and horse cavalry mounted aggressive and mobile offensives that overwhelmed more traditional armies.

Another key reason for the Arab success was the common faith Muhammad had given his people. Islam united a patchwork of tribes into a determined and unified state. Belief in Islam and certainty of paradise for those who fell in battle spurred Arab armies to victory.

>> A Jewish pharmacist dispenses medicine in a market in Spain, under Muslim rule not long before this illustration was made. Muslim-ruled regions were religiously diverse.

Conquered People Under Islamic Rule The advancing Arabs brought many people under their rule in Asia, North Africa, and beyond. These Arabs imposed certain restrictions and a special tax on non-Muslims, but allowed Christians, Jews, and Zoroastrians to practice their own faiths and follow their own religious customs to a limited degree within those restrictions. Early Umayyads did not attempt to convert these non-Muslims, because the tax supported the Arab troops who settled in conquered areas. As Muslim civilization developed, many Jews and Christians played key roles as officials, doctors, and translators.

Muslim leaders prohibited looting and destruction of conquered lands, ensuring continued wealth and prosperity for the empire in the form of tribute and taxes. However, the rulers also urged Arab settlers to stay separate from the native populations, which created an Arab upper class throughout the empire.

In time, many non-Muslims converted to Islam. Some converted to gain political or economic advantages. Others were drawn to Islam's message. In later centuries, Turkish and Mongol converts helped spread Islam far across Asia.

Impact on North Africa The Islamic presence in North Africa—or the Maghrib, as early Muslims called the region—led to rapid change. Arab Muslims destroyed Carthage and built a new city called Kairouan, which became known as a holy city of Islam.

They built many mosques throughout North Africa. Many of the peoples of North Africa who quickly converted to Islam, including the Berber people, also adopted some Arab customs.

As the Muslim empire expanded into North Africa in the 7th and 8th centuries, trade with West Africa across the Sahara grew. Merchants carried gold, salt, and ivory across the desert. Large West African kingdoms like Ghana, Mali, and Songhai later grew wealthy from this trade.

In addition to trade goods, enslaved people were also taken across the Sahara by merchants. However, at this time most enslaved people in the Islamic world came from Europe and Asia. You will learn more about the status of enslaved people in the Islamic world later in this Topic.

The Umayyad Caliphate Declines As military victories and negotiation expanded the Muslim empire, the Umayyads faced numerous problems. First, Arabs had to adapt from living in the desert to ruling large cities and huge territories. In many ways, the caliphs ruled like powerful tribal leaders, rather than kings with large bureaucracies. To govern their empire, the Umayyads often relied on local officials. Although they helped govern the empire, non-Arabs often did not have the same privileges that Arabs had, even if they converted to Islam.

While conquests continued, vast wealth flowed into Umayyad hands. When conquests slowed in the 700s, economic tensions increased between wealthy Arabs and those who had less. In addition, more and more resources were used to support the caliphs' luxurious lifestyle. By the eighth century, many Muslims criticized the court at Damascus for abandoning the simple ways of the early caliphs. Shiites considered the Umayyad caliphs to be illegitimate rulers of the Islamic community. Unrest also grew among non-Arab converts to Islam, who had fewer rights than Arabs.

☑ **SUMMARIZE** What factors contributed to the success of the Ummayad conquests?

>> This gold dinar, dating from 695–6, shows a Umayyad caliph dressed in traditional Arab head-dress and robes and holding a sword. On the other side of the coin is a design modified from the image of a Byzantine cross on steps.

New Rule Under the Abbasid Dynasty

Discontented Muslims found a leader in Abu al-Abbas, descended from Muhammad's uncle. With strong support from Shiite and non-Arab Muslims, he captured Damascus in 750. Soon after, he had members of the defeated Umayyad family killed. Only one survived, escaping to Spain. Abu al-Abbas then founded the **Abbasid** (uh BAS id) dynasty, which lasted until 1258.

The Abbasids Make Changes The Abbasid dynasty tried to create an empire based on the equality of all Muslims. The new rulers halted the large military conquests, ending the dominance of the Arab military class. The empire of the caliphs reached its greatest wealth and power under the early Abbasids, and Muslim civilization flourished.

Under the Abbasids, the government became more representative of the people because non-Arab Muslims could hold positions of power. Official policy encouraged conversion to Islam and treated all Muslims equally. The Abbasids created a more sophisticated bureaucracy and encouraged learning.

>> The Abbasid dynasty had a lasting impact on the Muslim world with its significant cultural and political accomplishments. In addition, the Abbasid capital of Baghdad remains an important city and is the capital of modern-day Iraq.

The Abbasids also moved the capital from Damascus to Baghdad, a small market town on the banks of the Tigris river. This move closer to Persia allowed Persian officials to hold important offices in the caliph's government. It also allowed Persian traditions to influence the development of the caliphate. Although these traditions strongly influenced Arab culture, Islam remained the religion of the empire and Arabic its language. The most important official was known as the vizier, or the head of the bureaucracy, a position that had existed in Persian government.

The Amazing City of Baghdad The second Abbasid caliph, al-Mansur, chose **Baghdad** as his new capital. The city walls formed a circle, with the caliph's palace in the center. Poets, scholars, philosophers, and entertainers from all over the Muslim world flocked to the Abbasid court. Under the Abbasids, Baghdad exceeded Constantinople in size and wealth. Visitors no doubt felt that Baghdad deserved its title "City of Peace, Gift of God, Paradise on Earth."

The city was beautiful, with many markets, gardens, and mosques. Domes and **minarets** (min uh RETS), slender towers of the mosques, loomed

>> Mesue the Elder, a Christian Persian physician, was received by the Caliph Haroun-al-Rashid, the fifth and most famous ruler of the Abbasid dynasty. Mesue was personal physician to four caliphs.

overhead. Five times each day, muezzins climbed to the tops of the minarets and called the faithful to prayer. Merchants sold goods from Africa, Asia, and Europe. The palace of the caliph bustled with activity.

A Muslim State in Spain The surviving member of the Umayyad family had fled to Spain. There, Muslim rulers presided over brilliant courts, where the arts and learning thrived. In general, they were tolerant of other religions. At centers of learning, such as the city of Córdoba, rulers employed Jewish officials and welcomed Christian scholars to study science and philosophy. Architects built grand buildings, such as the Alhambra, a fortified palace in Granada. Its lovely gardens, reflecting pools, and finely decorated marble columns mark a high point of Muslim civilization in Spain. Muslim rule endured in parts of Spain until 1492.

Causes and Effects of the Development of Islamic Caliphates You have now read about two Islamic caliphates, the Umayyads and Abbasids. The development of these Islamic caliphates was a major turning point in world history.

Historians have identified several major causes of the development of Islamic caliphates. One major cause was the emergence of Islam in Arabia, and the creation of a large empire through conquest by early Arab Muslims. Islamic caliphates developed when new families of leaders took power in the empire. The conquests that led to the creation of this empire, as you read, were helped along by the weakness of the Byzantine and Persian empires. By adopting ways of governing from the Byzantines and Persians, however, the new Muslim rulers were able to build stable states.

In addition to identifying the major causes of the development of Islamic caliphates, historians have also described the effects of this turning point in world history. This includes the impact of Islamic caliphates on Asia, Africa, and Europe.

For example, Islam emerged in Asia, on the Arabian peninsula. Under the rule of Islamic caliphates, Islam and the Arabic language began to spread to other parts of Asia, including areas that are now part of Iraq and Syria. Similarly, Islam and Arabic spread in North Africa. Today they are the majority language and religion in North Africa and in parts of Asia. These are among the lasting legacies of the Islamic caliphates.

Unlike North Africa, Spain is not mostly Islamic or Arabic-speaking today. However, you can see the impact of the Islamic caliphate that ruled there on

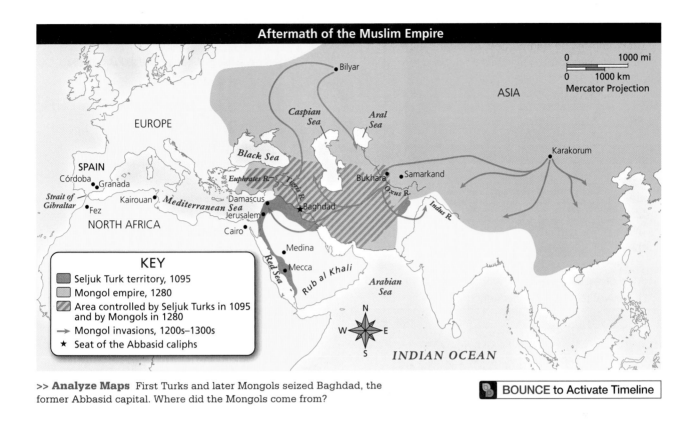

Aftermath of the Muslim Empire

KEY
- Seljuk Turk territory, 1095
- Mongol empire, 1280
- Area controlled by Seljuk Turks in 1095 and by Mongols in 1280
- → Mongol invasions, 1200s–1300s
- ★ Seat of the Abbasid caliphs

>> **Analyze Maps** First Turks and later Mongols seized Baghdad, the former Abbasid capital. Where did the Mongols come from?

BOUNCE to Activate Timeline

this European country's architecture and even in its language. Many Spanish words today come from Arabic. For example, *hasta,* meaning "until," comes from the Arabic word *hatta.*

☑ **DRAW CONCLUSIONS** Why did the Abbasids change the structure of the Arab Muslim empire?

Decline of the Arab Empire

Starting about 850, Abbasid control over the empire fragmented. In Egypt and elsewhere, independent dynasties ruled states that had been part of a unified empire. As the caliph's power faded in some regions, Shiite rulers came to power. Between 900 and 1400, a series of invasions added to the chaos.

Seljuk Turks Gain Control In the 900s, Seljuk Turks migrated into the Middle East from Central Asia. They adopted Islam and built a large empire across the Fertile Crescent. By 1055, a Seljuk **sultan,** or ruler, controlled Baghdad, but he kept the Abbasid caliph as a figurehead. As the Seljuks pushed into Asia Minor, they threatened the Byzantine empire. The conflict prevented Christian pilgrims from traveling to Jerusalem, leading Pope Urban II to call for the First Crusade in 1095.

Mongols Advance Through Central Asia In 1216, Genghis Khan led the Mongols out of Central Asia across Southwest Asia. Mongol armies returned again and again.

In 1258, Hulagu, the grandson of Genghis, burned and looted Baghdad, killing the last Abbasid caliph. Later, the Mongols living in central and southwest Asia adopted Islam as they mingled with local inhabitants.

In the late 1300s, another Mongol leader, Timur the Lame, or Tamerlane, led his armies into the Middle East. Though he was a Muslim, Tamerlane's ambitions led him to conquer Muslim as well as non-Muslim lands. His armies overran Southwest Asia before invading Russia and India.

The Mongols' physical destruction of Baghdad brought an end to the city's glories. But even with the end of the Arab caliphate, Islam continued to expand from West Africa to South and Southeast Asia.

The end of the last Arab caliphate meant the loss of Islamic influence on government. Muslims at times faced persecution while Christians in the region had increased status. The conversion of Mongol rulers to Islam helped restore influence to Muslims. Mosques rose up throughout the empire.

A Divided Muslim World By the late 1200s, the Arab empire had fragmented. Independent Muslim caliphates and states were scattered across North Africa and Spain, including the Mamluk state in Egypt and Syria, while a Mongol khan ruled much of the Muslim Middle East. After five centuries, Dar al-Islam—the world of Islam—was as politically divided as the Christian world.

Even though the Arab empire crumbled, Islam continued to link diverse people across an enormous area. Other Muslim empires emerged to rule the Middle East and India. Muslims also benefited from the advanced civilization that had taken root under the Abbasids.

☑ **CAUSE AND EFFECT** What events led to the decline of the Abbasid dynasty?

☑ ASSESSMENT

1. **Cause and Effect** What effect did Abu Bakr have on the spread of Islam?

2. **Compare and Contrast** In what ways are Sunni and Shiite beliefs alike and different?

3. **Explain** What did Muslim forces hope to accomplish at the Battle of Tours and what actually happened?

4. **Contrast** In what way were the rise of the Umayyads and the rise of the Abbasids different?

5. **Explain** How did the location of Damascus help the caliphs expand their empire?

6. **Quest Connections** What effect did the Battle of Tours have on the spread of Islam into Europe under the Ummayads?

8.3

The interior of the Great Mosque at Córdoba. The original 8th century mosque had 10 arcades. After Christians retook the city, the mosque became a Catholic cathedral.

Achievements of Muslim Civilization

Under the Abbasids, Muslim civilization absorbed traditions from many cultures. In the process, a flourishing new civilization arose in cities from Baghdad to Córdoba. It incorporated all the people who lived under Muslim rule, including Jews and Christians.

Economic and Social Changes

The spread of Muslim civilization changed the cultures, economies, and social structures of lands under Muslim rule. It exposed both Muslims and others to new ideas and practices.

Diffusion of Learning The great works produced by scholars of the Abbasid period shaped Muslim culture and civilization. Through contacts in Spain and Sicily, Christian European scholars began to study Muslim philosophy, art, and science. Muslim scholars also reintroduced knowledge of Greco-Roman civilization to later Europeans.

Muslim rulers united diverse peoples, including Arabs, Persians, Africans, and Europeans. Later, Mongols, Turks, Indians, and Southeast Asians joined the Muslim community. Muslim civilization absorbed and blended many of their traditions.

Trade in the Muslim World Merchants were honored in Muslim culture, in part because Muhammad had been a merchant. A traditional collection of sayings stated:

BOUNCE to Activate Flipped Video

Objectives

Describe the role of trade in Muslim civilization.

Identify the traditions that influenced Muslim art, architecture, and literature.

Describe the major ideas in mathematics, science, and technology that occurred in Muslim civilization.

Key Terms

social mobility
Firdawsi
Omar Khayyám
calligraphy
Ibn Rushd
Ibn Khaldun
al-Khwarizmi
Muhammad al-Razi
Ibn Sina

GO ONLINE to access your digital course

> I commend the merchants to you, for they are the couriers of the horizon and God's trusted servants on Earth.
>
> —Sayings of the Prophet

Between 750 and 1350, merchants built a vast trading network across Muslim lands and beyond. Caravans crossed the Sahara into West Africa, where West Africans traded gold for salt, bronze, cloth, books, and ceramics. West Africans also sold enslaved persons. In turn, North Africans traded gold to Europe in exchange for European goods such as beads and utensils, and provided the gold used in European buildings, art, and coins.

Muslim, Jewish, and Christian traders traveled the Silk Road toward China and were a vital link in the exchange of goods between East Asia and Europe. Monsoon winds carried Arab ships from East Africa to India and southeast Asia. Some traders made great fortunes.

Spreading Products and Ideas Trade spread products, technologies, knowledge, and culture. Muslim merchants introduced an Indian number system to Europe, where they became known as Hindu-Arabic numerals, or Arabic numerals. Merchants introduced Islam to people in many new regions. Traders also carried sugar from India and papermaking from China. As more people converted to Islam and learned Arabic, the common language and religion helped the global exchange grow and thrive.

Extensive trade and a money economy led Muslims to pioneer new business practices. They created partnerships, bought and sold on credit, formed banks to change currency, and invented the ancestors of today's bank checks. In fact, the English word *check* comes from the Arabic word *sakk*. Bankers developed a sophisticated system of accounting. They opened branch banks in all major cities, so that a check written in Baghdad might be cashed in Cairo. These economic ideas eventually spread to Europe, where they influenced the rise of modern economic systems.

High Demand for Manufactured Goods Muslim artisans produced a wealth of fine goods. Steel swords from Damascus, leather goods from Córdoba, cotton textiles from Egypt, and carpets from Persia were highly valued. Workshops also turned out fine glassware, furniture, and tapestries.

As in medieval Europe, handicraft manufacturing in Muslim cities was typically organized by guilds. The heads of the guilds, chosen by their members, often had the authority to regulate prices, weights and measures, methods of production, and the quality of the product. Most labor was done by wage workers.

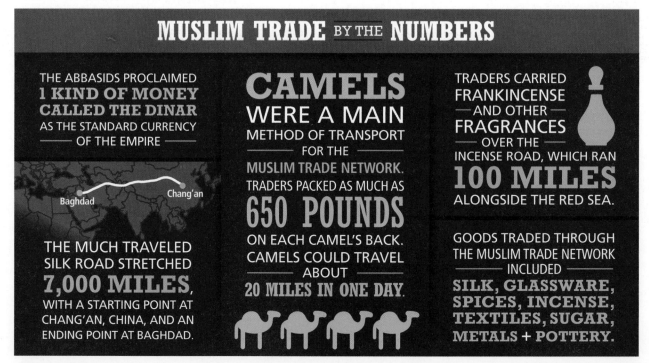

MUSLIM TRADE BY THE NUMBERS

THE ABBASIDS PROCLAIMED **1 KIND OF MONEY CALLED THE DINAR** AS THE STANDARD CURRENCY OF THE EMPIRE

THE MUCH TRAVELED SILK ROAD STRETCHED **7,000 MILES,** WITH A STARTING POINT AT CHANG'AN, CHINA, AND AN ENDING POINT AT BAGHDAD.

Baghdad — Chang'an

CAMELS WERE A MAIN METHOD OF TRANSPORT FOR THE MUSLIM TRADE NETWORK. TRADERS PACKED AS MUCH AS **650 POUNDS** ON EACH CAMEL'S BACK. CAMELS COULD TRAVEL ABOUT **20 MILES IN ONE DAY.**

TRADERS CARRIED FRANKINCENSE AND OTHER FRAGRANCES OVER THE INCENSE ROAD, WHICH RAN **100 MILES** ALONGSIDE THE RED SEA.

GOODS TRADED THROUGH THE MUSLIM TRADE NETWORK INCLUDED **SILK, GLASSWARE, SPICES, INCENSE, TEXTILES, SUGAR, METALS + POTTERY.**

>> **Analyze Data** Trade across the desert brought great wealth to Muslim merchants. How do you think having a standard currency in the Abbasid caliph affected trade?

Agriculture Flourishes Outside the cities, agriculture flourished across a wide variety of climates and landforms. Both Umayyad and Abbasid rulers took steps to preserve and extend agricultural land. Small farming communities in desert areas faced a constant scarcity of water. To improve farm output, the Abbasids organized massive irrigation projects and drained swamplands between the Tigris and Euphrates rivers. In addition to other crops raised for food, farmers cultivated sugar cane, cotton, medicinal herbs, and flowers that were sold in far-off markets. Farmers began to grow crops that came from different regions.

The deserts continued to support nomads who lived by herding. Still, nomads and farmers shared economic ties. Nomads bought dates and grain from settled peoples, while farming populations acquired meat, wool, and hides from the nomads. Pastoral groups also provided pack animals and guides for the caravan trade.

Social Structure and Slavery Muslim society in the 700s and 800s was more open than that of medieval Christian Europe. Muslims enjoyed a certain degree of **social mobility,** or the ability to move up in social class. People could improve their social rank through religious, scholarly, or military achievements.

As in many earlier societies, slavery was a common institution in Muslim lands, though Islamic law encouraged the freeing of enslaved people as an act of charity. In Muslim society, people were not enslaved because of their race. Muslims often enslaved people in conquered lands because they were not supposed to enslave other Muslims.

Some enslaved people bought their freedom, often with the help of charitable donations or even state funds. However, if enslaved non-Muslims converted to Islam, they did not automatically become free. An enslaved woman who bore a child by her Muslim enslaver gained freedom upon his death. Children born of an enslaved mother and free father were also considered free.

Most enslaved people worked as household servants, while some were skilled artisans. To help break down the tribal system, Abbasid caliphs also created a class of Turkish enslaved soldiers who were loyal only to the caliph. Often educated in Islamic law and government, some of these men rose to high positions in the government, such as vizier. This set the stage for the Turks to become powerful later in the Abbasid era.

☑ **DESCRIBE** What new business practices did merchants introduce in Muslim lands?

>> Persians were famous for their Kilim carpets.

>> While cities and farming grew, nomads continued their way of life in deserts.

>> Many copies of the Quran were richly illustrated with elaborate designs and detailed patterns.

>> This illustration from *Shah Namah* shows the marriage of the three daughters of Sero, King of Yemen.

Literature, Art, and Architecture

Muslim art and literature reflected the diverse traditions of the various peoples who lived under Muslim rule, including Greeks, Romans, Persians, Indians, and North Africans. As in Christian Europe and Hindu India, religion shaped the arts and literature of Muslim civilization. The great work of Islamic literature was the Quran itself. Because the Quran strictly banned the worship of idols, Muslim religious leaders forbade artists to portray God or human figures in religious art. This gave Islamic art a distinctive style.

A Rich Tradition of Literature Long before Muhammad, Arabs had a rich tradition of oral poetry. In musical verses, poets chanted the dangers of desert journeys, the joys of battle, or the glories of their clans.

Their most important themes—chivalry and the romance of nomadic life—recurred in Arab poetry throughout the centuries. Later Arab poets developed elaborate formal rules for writing poetry and explored both religious and worldly themes. The poems of Rabiah al-Adawiyya expressed Sufi mysticism and encouraged the faithful to worship God selflessly without hope of reward. "If I worship Thee in hope of Paradise / Exclude me from Paradise," she wrote in one prayer poem.

Persians also had a fine poetic tradition. **Firdawsi** (fur DOW see) wrote in Persian using Arabic script. His masterpiece, the *Shah Namah,* or *Book of Kings,* tells the history of Persia. **Omar Khayyám** (OH mahr ky AHM), famous in the Muslim world as a scholar and an astronomer, is best known for *The Rubáiyát* (roo by AHT). In this collection of four-line stanzas, Khayyám meditates on fate and the fleeting nature of life:

> The Moving Finger writes; and having writ,
>   Moves on; nor all your Piety nor Wit
>   Shall lure it back to cancel half a line,
>   Nor all your Tears wash out a word of it.

—Omar Khayyám, The Rubáiyát

Arab writers also prized the art of storytelling. Along with ancient Arab tales, they gathered and adapted stories from Indian, Persian, Greek, Jewish,

Egyptian, and Turkish sources. The best-known collection is *The Thousand and One Nights,* a group of tales narrated by a fictional princess. They include romances, fables, adventures, and humorous anecdotes, many set in Harun al-Rashid's Baghdad. Later versions filtered into Europe, where children heard about "Aladdin and His Magic Lamp" or "Ali Baba and the Forty Thieves."

Religion Shapes Architecture The main purpose of early mosques was to serve as community centers for the faithful. These simple buildings were hubs for social interaction, Islamic study, and group prayer. Later, domed mosques and high minarets dominated Muslim cities. Adapted from Byzantine buildings, domes and arches became symbolic of Muslim architecture.

Just as Islam is an important part of the daily life of Muslims, so too is it integral to Muslim architecture. While Islamic religious buildings had some elements borrowed from Christian building styles, they were designed to meet the needs of Muslims, with places to call people to worship and large halls for prayer. Each mosque also featured a mihrab, an indented wall that faced toward Mecca. Completed in 715, the Great Mosque of Damascus includes minarets, a large area for prayer, and a mihrab.

Art in the Muslim Empire Early Muslims believed that God should be worshiped directly, not through representations. Early artists avoided picturing God or Muhammad, believed to be God's messenger. Instead, they emphasized the importance of God's word.

They used **calligraphy,** the art of beautiful handwriting, to add physical beauty to the spiritual words of the Quran. Religious artists decorated the handwritten pages with borders containing geometric shapes and arabesques, or flowered patterns.

The Muslim style of religious art could be seen in mosques across the empire. Inside, the walls and ceilings of mosques were decorated with elaborate abstract, geometric patterns. They worked the flowing Arabic script, especially verses from the Quran, into decorations on buildings. The Dome of the Rock in Jerusalem, completed around 692, provides exquisite examples of early Muslim art.

Some Muslim artists painted human and animal figures in nonreligious art. Arabic scientific works, including those of the human body, were often lavishly illustrated. Literary works sometimes showed stylized figures. Later Persian, Turkish, and Indian

>> This courtyard is in the Umayyad Mosque, or Great Mosque of Damascus, which was built in the early 700s.

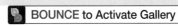
BOUNCE to Activate Gallery

artists excelled at painting miniatures to illustrate books of poems and fables.

☑ **IDENTIFY** Which traditions influenced Muslim literature, art, and architecture?

An Emphasis on Knowledge

Although Muhammad could neither read nor write, his respect for learning inspired Muslims to make great advances in philosophy, history, mathematics, and the sciences. Wealthy families might educate their boys and even allow their girls to learn to read and write in order to study the Quran. Most people, however, were illiterate, and they memorized the Quran. Institutions of higher learning included schools for religious instruction and for the study of Islamic law.

Muslim Centers of Learning The caliph Al-Mamun and his successors established Baghdad as the greatest Muslim center of learning. Its libraries attracted well paid and highly respected scholars. Other cities, like Cairo, Córdoba, and Timbuktu, were also known as centers of learning. In these places, scholars made advances in philosophy, science, mathematics, medicine, and other fields. They also preserved the learning of earlier civilizations by translating ancient Persian, Sanskrit, and Greek texts into Arabic.

Studying Philosophy and History Muslim scholars translated the works of the Greek philosophers, as well as many Hindu and Buddhist texts. Scholars tried to harmonize Greek ideas about reason with religious beliefs based on divine revelation. In Córdoba, the philosopher **Ibn Rushd**—known in Europe as Averroës—put all knowledge except the Quran to the test of reason. His writings on Aristotle were translated into Latin and influenced Christian scholastics in medieval Europe.

Another Arab thinker, **Ibn Khaldun** (IB un kal DOON), set standards for the scientific study of history. He stressed economics and social structure as causes of historical events. He also warned about common causes of error in historical writing, such as bias, exaggeration, and overconfidence in the accuracy of sources. Ibn Khaldun urged historians to trust sources only after a thorough investigation.

Advances in Mathematics and Astronomy One of the greatest Muslim mathematicians was

>> Astronomers like these at a Turkish observatory made significant scientific advances that helped change how people thought about and explored the world. What tools are they using?

BOUNCE to Activate Gallery

al-Khwarizmi (al KWAHR iz mee). He pioneered the study of algebra (from the Arabic word *al-jabr*). In the 800s, he wrote a book that was translated into Latin and became a standard mathematics textbook in Europe. Like many scholars of the time, al-Khwarizmi contributed to other fields too. He developed a set of astronomical tables based on Greek and Indian discoveries.

Muslim scholars studied the works of the ancient Greeks, such as Euclid and Ptolemy. They translated these and other ancient mathematical works into Arabic and used them as a basis for a complete system of mathematics, including an organized method for equations. Soon, Muslim works on mathematics spread to Europe, where they were studied with interest.

Over time, Europeans in all fields of business adopted Hindu-Arabic numerals and used them in their day-to-day lives. They also adopted new tools and technologies developed or improved by Muslim astronomers, including the quadrant and the astrolabe. These two instruments were used to observe the positions of stars and aid in navigation.

Improvements in Medicine Building on the knowledge of the ancient Greeks, Muslims made remarkable advances in medicine and public health. Under the caliphs, physicians and pharmacists had to pass a test before they could practice their professions. The government set up hospitals, where injured people could get quick treatment at a facility similar to today's emergency room. Some physicians traveled to rural areas to provide healthcare to those who could not get to a city, while others regularly visited jails.

One of the most original medical thinkers was **Muhammad al-Razi,** head physician at Baghdad's chief hospital. He wrote many books on medicine, including a pioneering study of measles and smallpox. He also challenged accepted medical practices. Treat the mind as well as the body, he advised young doctors. He theorized that if doctors were hopeful with their patients, recovery would be faster.

The famous Persian physician **Ibn Sina** (IB un SEE nah) was known in Europe as Avicenna. By the age of 16, he was a doctor to the Persian nobility. His great work was the *Canon on Medicine*, a huge encyclopedia of what the Greeks, the Arabs, and he himself had learned about diagnosing and treating diseases. The book includes many prescriptions, made with such ingredients as mercury from Spain, myrrh from East Africa, and camphor from India.

Other Muslim surgeons developed a way to treat cataracts, drawing fluid out of eye lenses with a hollow needle. For centuries, surgeons around the world used this method to save patients' eyesight. Arab pharmacists were the first to mix bitter medicines into sweet-tasting syrups and gums.

Eventually, these and other Muslim medical ideas spread to Europe. European physicians began to attend Muslim universities in Spain. Arabic medical texts were translated into Latin, and the works of Avicenna and al-Razi became the standard medical textbooks at European schools for 500 years. Through this diffusion of ideas, Europeans were introduced to the concepts of training physicians and creating hospitals.

☑ **SUMMARIZE** What ideas about medicine were developed during the time of the Muslim empire?

☑ ASSESSMENT

1. **Draw Conclusions** Why did trade play such an important role in the Muslim empire?

2. **Contrast** What is an important difference between medieval Muslim and Christian art?

3. **Infer** In what ways did Islamic art and literature show diversity, and what important trait do they have in common?

4. **Cite Evidence** What evidence supports the claim that learning was important in the Arab Muslim empire?

5. **Draw Conclusions** Why were Europeans interested in the ideas of mathematician al-Khwarizmi and physicians Muhammad al-Razi and Ibn Sina?

6. **Quest Connections** Did the Battle of Tours keep Islamic culture from influencing Europe? Cite examples from the text in your response.

Until the Ottomans invaded, the high, thick walls and well-positioned defenses of Constantinople had repelled invaders for a thousand years.

 BOUNCE to Activate Flipped Video

Objectives

Explain the impact of the Ottoman empire on Eastern Europe.

Describe the characteristics of Ottoman culture.

Explain how Abbas the Great strengthened the Safavid empire.

Key Terms

Ottoman
Istanbul
Suleiman
janizary
Safavid
shah
Shah Abbas the
   Great
Isfahan
Qajar
Tehran

The Ottoman and Safavid Empires

By the 1400s, two powerful new empires had emerged in the Middle East: the Ottoman and the Safavid empires. Both were Muslim empires, and both ruled diverse peoples. Most important, both owed their success in part to a new military technology, gunpowder. For this reason, the Ottoman and Safavid empires are often called "gunpowder empires." Gunpowder led to the use of new weapons such as cannons that blasted through defensive walls. Later, muskets made a new kind of army possible, giving firepower to ordinary foot soldiers and reducing the importance of mounted warriors.

Growth of the Ottoman Empire

Like the Seljuks, the **Ottomans** were a Turkish-speaking dynasty whose ancestors had migrated from Central Asia into northwestern Asia Minor (present-day Turkey). By the 1300s, they were spreading across Asia Minor and into Eastern Europe's Balkan Peninsula.

The Ottomans Conquer Constantinople Ottoman expansion threatened the crumbling Byzantine empire. After several failed attempts to capture Constantinople, the Ottoman sultan Mehmet II finally succeeded in 1453. In a surprise move, the Ottomans hauled ships overland and launched them into the harbor outside Constantinople. After a nearly two-month siege, Ottoman cannons finally blasted gaps in the great defensive walls of the city, and it became the new capital of the Ottoman empire. From Constantinople, which gradually also became known as **Istanbul,** the Ottoman Turks continued their conquests for the next 200 years.

GO ONLINE to access your digital course

Suleiman the Magnificent The Ottoman empire enjoyed a golden age under the sultan **Suleiman** (soo lay MAHN), who ruled from 1520 to 1566. His people called him "the Lawgiver," while Europeans called him Suleiman the Magnificent.

A brilliant general, Suleiman modernized the army and conquered many new lands. He extended Ottoman rule eastward into the Middle East, and also into Kurdistan and Georgia in the Caucasus Mountain region. In the west, Suleiman advanced deeper into Europe through a combination of diplomacy and warfare. In 1529, his armies besieged the Austrian city of Vienna, sending fear through the kingdoms of Western Europe.

Although they failed to take Vienna, the Ottoman armies threatened the divided kingdoms of Europe, which feared invasion from the east. While European powers formed alliances to keep Suleiman from expanding further into Europe, France tried to weaken its rivals by signing a treaty with the Ottomans.

French leaders hoped to take advantage of Ottoman pressure to weaken the Hapsburg empire, which included the Holy Roman Empire and the Netherlands. The treaty also allowed French merchants to travel and trade throughout the Ottoman empire—unlike traders from other European countries.

Ottomans Control Trade The Ottoman empire controlled major trade routes between Europe, Africa, and Asia. As a result, Istanbul became one of the great trading capitals of the world.

The Ottoman empire strengthened its trading position by bringing merchants into Istanbul, particularly European Jewish traders. European navies had taken control of the Mediterranean Sea from Venice, but in 1533, Suleiman created an enormous fleet that dominated all trade in the eastern Mediterranean. Eventually, the Portuguese and other European navies commanded new trade routes around Africa and ended Ottoman control of both land and sea routes.

Ottoman Government Still, the Ottomans ruled the largest, most powerful empire in both Europe and the Middle East for centuries. At its height, the empire stretched from Hungary to Arabia and Mesopotamia and across North Africa. Suleiman felt justified in claiming to be the rightful heir of the Abbasids and caliph of all Muslims. To the title of "Emperor," he added the symbolic name of "Protector of the Sacred Places" (Mecca and Medina).

Suleiman was a wise and capable ruler. He strengthened the government of the rapidly growing empire and improved its system of justice. As sultan, Suleiman had absolute power, but he ruled with the help of a grand vizier and a council. A huge bureaucracy supervised the business of government, and the powerful military kept the peace. Ottoman law was based on the Sharia, supplemented by royal edicts. Government officials worked closely with religious scholars who interpreted the law.

☑ **ANALYZE CONCEPTS** The Ottoman empire took Constantinople and then threatened Eastern Europe. Which European power did the Ottoman sign a treaty with, and what did that country gain?

Ottoman Society

Ottoman society was divided into classes, each with its appointed role. At the top were "men of the sword"—soldiers who guarded the sultan and defended the state—and "men of the pen"— scientists, lawyers, judges, and poets. Below them were "men of negotiation," such as merchants, tax collectors, and artisans who carried out trade and production. Finally, there were "men of husbandry," or farmers and herders who produced food for the community.

>> The Ottomans attempted to expand their empire west into Hungary and Vienna, but they could not keep a large invading force well supplied so far from Istanbul.

 BOUNCE to Activate Illustration

>> The Selimiye Mosque in Turkey displays the glory of Ottoman culture when the empire was at its height.

>> The janizaries, or the elite military force made up mostly of converted Christians, suppressed any revolt within the Ottoman empire because they controlled the military, even dethroning Sultan Beyezid II.

Religion in Ottoman Society The Ottomans ruled diverse peoples of many religions. The men of the sword and men of the pen were almost all Muslims, but the other classes included non-Muslims. The people were organized into millets, or religious communities. These included Muslims, Greek Christians, Armenian Christians, and Jews.

Each millet had its own leaders who were responsible for education and some legal matters. The Jewish millets included many Jews who had been expelled from Spain in 1492. They brought international banking connections with them, plus a new technology for making cloth that helped the Ottoman empire finance its expansion.

Treatment of Conquered Peoples Like earlier Muslim empires, the Ottomans recruited officers for the army and government from among the huge populations of conquered peoples in their empire. The Ottomans levied a "tax" on Christian families in the Balkans, requiring them to turn over their young sons for government service.

The boys were converted to Islam and put into rigorous military training at the palace school. The best soldiers won a prized place in the **janizaries** (JAN ih sehr eez), the elite force of the Ottoman army. The brightest students received special education to become government officials. They might serve as judges, poets, or even grand vizier.

Non-Muslim girls from eastern Europe were sometimes enslaved as servants in wealthy Muslim households. There, they might be accepted as members of the household. Some of the enslaved girls were freed after the death of their masters.

Literature and the Arts The arts blossomed under Suleiman. Ottoman poets adapted Persian and Arab models to produce works in Turkish. Influenced by Persian artistic styles, Ottoman painters produced detailed miniatures and illuminated manuscripts.

The royal architect Sinan, a janizary military engineer, designed hundreds of mosques and palaces. He compared his most famous building, the Selimiye Mosque at Edirne, to the greatest church of the Byzantine empire. "With God's help and the Sultan's mercy," Sinan wrote, "I have succeeded in building a dome for the mosque which is greater in diameter and higher than that of Hagia Sophia."

Decline of the Ottomans After Suleiman's death in 1566, Ottoman government and society began to change slowly. Suleiman had killed two of his most able sons because he suspected them of treason. His son and successor Selim II left most of the governing

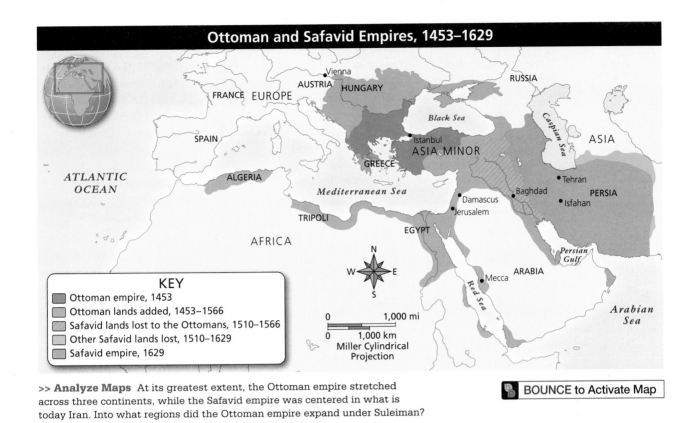

Ottoman and Safavid Empires, 1453–1629

KEY
- Ottoman empire, 1453
- Ottoman lands added, 1453–1566
- Safavid lands lost to the Ottomans, 1510–1566
- Other Safavid lands lost, 1510–1629
- Safavid empire, 1629

0   1,000 mi
0   1,000 km
Miller Cylindrical
Projection

>> **Analyze Maps** At its greatest extent, the Ottoman empire stretched across three continents, while the Safavid empire was centered in what is today Iran. Into what regions did the Ottoman empire expand under Suleiman?

BOUNCE to Activate Map

to his ministers, and government bureaucracy became corrupt.

By the 1700s, European advances in both commerce and military technology were leaving the Ottomans behind. Russia and other European powers captured Ottoman lands, while local rulers in North Africa and elsewhere broke away from Ottoman control. Sultans tried to revive Ottoman power with limited success.

☑ **CATEGORIZE** Who were the men of the sword, the men of the pen, the men of negotiation, and the men of husbandry, and what was their overall purpose?

The Rise of the Safavids

By the early 1500s, the **Safavid** (sah FAH vid) dynasty had united an empire in Persia (present-day Iran). Sandwiched between two expansionist powers—Mughal India and the Ottoman empire—the Safavids often engaged in warfare. Religion played a role in the conflict. The Safavids were Shiite Muslims who enforced their beliefs in their empire. The Ottomans were Sunni Muslims who viewed the Shiites as heretics.

Abbas the Great The most outstanding Safavid ruler, or **shah,** was **Shah Abbas the Great** who revived the glory of ancient Persia. From 1588 to 1629, he centralized the government and created a powerful military force modeled on the Ottoman janizaries. Abbas used a mixture of force and diplomacy against the Ottomans. He also sought alliances with European states that had reason to fear Ottoman power.

To strengthen the economy, Abbas reduced taxes on farmers and herders and encouraged the growth of industry. Unlike earlier Safavids, Abbas tolerated non-Muslims and valued their economic contributions. He built a new capital at **Isfahan** (is fah HAHN), which eventually reached a population of one million, with hundreds of mosques, schools, parks, libraries, and public baths.

A Center of Art and Trade Under Shah Abbas, Isfahan flourished. It became a center for the arts and architecture, and the shah welcomed artists, poets, and scholars to his court. Palace workshops produced magnificent paintings, metalwork, textiles, and rugs.

Isfahan also became a center of the international silk trade. Armenians controlled the trade, so Abbas brought thousands of Armenians to Isfahan. He had a

>> Under Shah Abbas, art, architecture, and learning flourished. Tile mosaics combined with mathematical precision created this masterpiece, the Shah (Imam) Mosque in Isfahan, Iran.

settlement built for these Christians just outside the capital, where they governed themselves.

The Decline of the Safavid Empire Safavid glory slowly faded after the death of Shah Abbas and under continuing pressure from Ottoman armies. Shiite scholars also challenged the authority of the shah by stressing their own authority to interpret law and determine government policy. They encouraged persecution of religious minorities, pushing Sunni Afghans to rebel. The rebels defeated imperial armies, captured Isfahan, and forced the last Safavid ruler to abdicate in 1722.

In the late 1700s, a new dynasty, the **Qajars** (kuh JAHRZ), won control of Iran. They made **Tehran** their capital and ruled until 1925. Still, the Safavids left a lasting legacy. They established Shiism firmly in Iran and gave Persians a strong sense of their own identity.

☑ **DRAW CONCLUSIONS** What was the effect of Shah Abbas centralizing the government and the economy, creating a powerful military, and tolerating non-Muslims?

☑ ASSESSMENT

1. **Identify Central Ideas** How did Shah Abbas strengthen the Safavid empire and leave a lasting legacy in Persia?

2. **Draw Conclusions** Which were the important characteristics of the Ottoman and Safavid empires?

3. **Identify Cause and Effect** After the Ottoman empire conquered the Balkans, how were young Christian people from this region affected?

4. **Infer** Why do you think the Ottoman and Safavid rulers allowed some religious tolerance?

5. **Compare and Contrast** How was France's response to the aggression of the Ottoman empire different from that of other European powers? What did France want to accomplish by its response?

6. **Quest Connections** What effect did the Battle of Tours have on the spread of Islam into Europe under the Ottomans?

8.5

The Nubian capital of Meroë was once a center of trade. Today, its ruins bake in the hot sun.

Early Civilizations of Africa

Africa is the world's second largest continent, larger than Europe, China, and the United States combined. Its size led to the development of a diverse variety of cultures over its history.

The Geography of Africa

Africa's geography is immensely varied. It contains a wide range of climates, vegetation, and terrains.

Climate and Vegetation Zones Africa's vegetation regions create wide bands that stretch across the continent. Along the equator is a band of tropical rain forest. Moving north and south from this band are the continent's largest and most populated regions, the **savannas,** or grassy plains. Beyond the savanna to the north lies the **Sahara,** the largest desert in the world.

Although the Sahara did become a highway for migration and trade, its size and harsh terrain limited movement. The Kalahari and Namib deserts in the south are smaller but equally forbidding.

Along the Mediterranean coast of North Africa and the tip of southern Africa lie areas of fertile farmland. The fertile Nile Valley, for example, offered a favorable environment to early farmers.

Geographic Features In addition to deserts and rain forests, other geographic features have acted as barriers to easy movement of people and goods. Although Africa is surrounded by oceans and seas, it has few good natural harbors. Also, much of the interior is a high plateau. As rivers flow down to the coast, they cascade through a series of rapids and **cataracts,** or waterfalls, that hinder travel between the coast and the interior.

 BOUNCE to Activate Flipped Video

Objectives

Understand how geography affected migration, cultural development, and trade in Africa.

Describe the rise and decline of Nubia.

Explain how outside influences led to change in North Africa.

Key Terms

savanna
Sahara
cataract
desertification
Bantu
Nubia
Piankhi
Meroë
Septimius Severus

GO ONLINE to access your digital course

Within the interior, though the same rivers, including the Zambezi, Congo, and Niger, serve as open highways.

Despite geographic barriers, people did migrate, both within Africa and to neighboring continents. Like the rivers, the Great Rift Valley of East Africa served as an interior corridor. People also traveled across the savanna lands. The Red Sea and Indian Ocean linked East Africa to the Middle East and other Asian lands, while North Africa formed the southern rim of the Mediterranean world.

Resources and Trade Africa sits atop great mineral and other natural resources. Since ancient times, mineral wealth spurred trade among various regions. Salt, gold, iron, and copper were important items in early trade networks. Much later, in the 1800s, desire for gold and diamonds was one cause that led Europeans to seek control of lands in Africa.

Trade between Africa and Asia increased with the introduction of the camel. By A.D. 200, camels had been brought to North Africa from Asia. These hardy "ships of the desert" revolutionized trade across the Sahara. Although daring traders had earlier made the difficult desert crossing in horse-drawn chariots, camel caravans created new trade networks.

>> At first, trade in the Sahara Desert was hindered by inhospitable conditions, but new forms of transportation, including the use of the camel, revolutionized commerce in the region.

BOUNCE to Activate Map

Camels could carry loads of up to 500 pounds and could plod 20 or 30 miles a day, often without water. The caravan brought great profits to merchants on both sides of the Sahara.

☑ **CHECK UNDERSTANDING** How did geographic features affect movement in Africa?

Migration of People and Ideas

Archaeologists have uncovered evidence that points to the Great Rift Valley as home to some of the earliest ancestors of modern people. Gradually, their descendants migrated out of Africa and beyond to populate every corner of the Earth.

Stone Age Cultures In Africa, as elsewhere, Paleolithic people developed skills as hunters and food gatherers. By 5500 B.C., Neolithic farmers had learned to cultivate the Nile Valley and to domesticate animals. As farming spread across North Africa, Neolithic villages even appeared in the Sahara, which was then a well-watered area. Scientists have found ancient rock paintings that show a Sahara covered with rich grasslands and savanna.

About 2500 B.C., a climate change slowly dried the Sahara. As the land became parched, the desert spread. This process of **desertification** devoured thousands of acres of cropland and pastureland. The ever-expanding desert forced many people to move, or migrate, to seek new areas in order to maintain their ways of life.

The Bantu Migrations Over thousands of years, the migration of people throughout Africa contributed to the continent's rich diversity of cultures. Scholars have traced these migrations by studying language patterns. They have learned, for example, that West African farmers and herders migrated to the south and east between about 1000 B.C. and A.D. 1000. These West African peoples spoke a variety of languages deriving from a single common language. The root language is called **Bantu,** which gives this movement its name—the Bantu migrations.

As the Bantu-speakers migrated into southern Africa, they spread their skills in farming, ironworking, and domesticating animals. Some existing cultures merged with those of the Bantu-speakers wherever they settled. The influence of the

Bantu-speakers is still found in the languages of the region today.

☑ **ANALYZE INFORMATION** What was the effect of the Bantu migrations on African culture?

Egypt and Nubia Flourish

While Egyptian civilization was developing along the northern Nile River, another African civilization took shape on a ribbon of fertile land along the southern Nile. The ancient kingdom of **Nubia,** also called Kush, was located in present-day Sudan. Archaeologists and historians have just begun to document the shifting tides of Nubia's 4,000-year history.

Nubia and Egypt: Two Great Powers Nubia and Egypt were sometimes rivals and sometimes allies. From time to time, ambitious Egyptian pharaohs subdued Nubia, but the Nubians always regained their independence. As a result of conquest and trade, Nubian rulers adopted many Egyptian traditions. They built palaces and pyramids modeled on Egyptian style. They used Egyptian titles and worshiped Egyptian deities.

About 730 B.C., the Nubian king **Piankhi** (PYAHN kee) conquered Egypt. For a century, Nubian kings ruled Egypt. But Nubian armies could not match the iron weapons of the Assyrians who invaded from southwest Asia.

Nubian Trade and Iron By 500 B.C., Nubian rulers had moved their capital from Napata to **Meroë** (MEHR uh wee). Meroë eventually commanded both the Nile's north-south trade route and the east-west trade route from the Red Sea to Central Africa. Along this wide trade network, Nubia sent gold, ivory, animal skins, and perfumes to the Mediterranean world and Southwest Asia. Meroë's location helped make it a successful center of commerce.

Equally important, however, were the region's resources. Meroë was rich in iron ore. Fueled by the region's large quantities of timber, the smelting furnaces of Meroë produced the iron tools and weaponry needed to feed, control, and defend the kingdom. Today, giant heaps of iron waste remain as evidence of ancient Meroë's industry.

Splendor and Decline Although Nubia absorbed much from Egypt, Nubian culture later followed its own course. For example, after gaining independence from Egypt, Nubians worshiped their own gods, including Apedemak, a lion-headed

>> Nubians and Egyptians worshiped many of the same gods and goddesses, including Amon, the king of all the gods, who was often depicted as a ram.

🔵 BOUNCE to Activate Gallery

warrior god. At Meroë, artistic styles reflected a greater sense of freedom than Egyptian styles did. Nubians also created their own system of writing, using an alphabet instead of hieroglyphics. Unfortunately, the Nubian language is still not fully understood.

After the joint reign of King Natakamani and Queen Amanitere in the first century A.D., the splendor of Nubia's golden age dimmed. Finally, about A.D. 350, King Ezana's armies from the kingdom of Axum overwhelmed Nubia.

☑ **APPLY CONCEPTS** How did trade affect Nubia and North Africa?

North Africa in the Ancient World

Early African civilizations had strong ties to the Mediterranean world. Trade linked Egypt with Greece and Mesopotamia. Later, Egypt was ruled, in turn, by the Greeks and Romans. These powers also knew of the rich civilization that lay south of Egypt and valued Nubian exports. Over time, however, Nubia lost touch with the Mediterranean world.

Phoenicians and Carthage As Nubia thrived along the Nile, Carthage began to rise as a great North African power. Founded by Phoenician traders as a port on the Mediterranean coast, Carthage came to dominate trade in the western Mediterranean. From 800 B.C. to 146 B.C., Carthage forged an empire that stretched from present-day Tunisia, Algeria, and Morocco to southern Spain and beyond.

As Rome expanded, territorial and trade rivalries erupted between the two powers. After a series of fierce wars, Rome eventually defeated Carthage and totally destroyed the capital city.

Rome Controls North Africa Rome expanded its rule over much of North Africa from the coast to the Sahara and into Egypt. There, the Romans built roads, dams, aqueducts, and cities. They developed North African farmlands to harvest bumper crops of grain, fruit, and other foods. From North Africa, they imported lions and other fierce animals to Rome to do battle with gladiators. North Africa also provided soldiers for the Roman army, including **Septimius Severus,** who would later become a Roman emperor.

Under Roman rule, Christianity spread to the cities of North Africa. In fact, Augustine, the most influential Christian thinker of the late Roman empire, was born in present-day Algeria. From A.D. 395 to A.D. 430, Augustine was bishop of Hippo, a city located near the ruins of ancient Carthage.

Islam Spreads In the 690s, Muslim Arabs conquered and occupied the cities of North Africa. By the early 700s, they had successfully conquered the Berbers, a largely nomadic North African people. Islam also spread peacefully as, over time, Muslim traders from North Africa carried Islam into West Africa. Muslim civilization blossomed in cities such as Cairo, Fez, and Marrakesh, which became famous for their mosques and universities.

Muslim, Jewish, and Christian traders and merchants lived, bartered, and interacted with one another as commerce expanded throughout North and West Africa. Jewish communities formed near Muslim and Christian enclaves across North Africa. Some West African societies adopted Islam into their cultures, creating African varieties of Islam, while many Africans continued to practice traditional religions such as ancestor worship.

Islam eventually became the dominant religion in many regions of Africa, and Muslim rulers governed many African kingdoms. These rulers established centralized systems of government and a vast trade

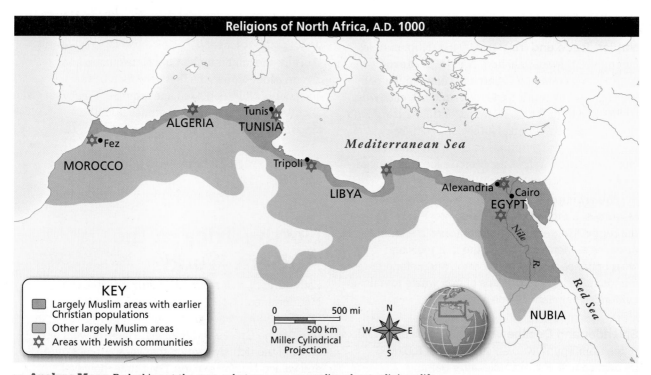

>> **Analyze Maps** By looking at the map, what can you generalize about religious life in North Africa?

network to India and China, which allowed the movement of goods into and out of Africa to flourish.

☑ **IDENTIFY CAUSE AND EFFECT** Describe the role trade played in the development of culture in Africa.

☑ **ASSESSMENT**

1. **Draw Conclusions** How did Africa's geographic features influence migration, cultural development, and trade?

2. **Identify** In what ways did outside influences affect Nubian development?

3. **Explain** What were some of the ways that Rome benefited from its control of North Africa?

4. **Identify Central Issues** What major changes occurred in North Africa from around 800 B.C. to A.D. 700?

5. **Determine Relevance** How did the Bantu migrations contribute to African cultural diversity?

6. **Connections to Today** How might the Arab conquest of North Africa—and the spread of the Arabic language there—have helped unify the region culturally?

8.6

Artists working in Benin sculpted many figures in bronze, including this warrior.

 BOUNCE to Activate Flipped Video

Objectives

Analyze how the gold and salt trade in Africa facilitated the spread of ideas and trade.

Describe how the rulers of Ghana, Mali, and Songhai built strong kingdoms.

Summarize how other West African societies developed.

Key Terms

surplus
commodity
Ghana
Sundiata
Mali
Mansa Musa
Songhai

Kingdoms of West Africa

As the Sahara dried out in Neolithic times, people were forced to migrate. Some moved into the savanna, the grasslands area that offered land for farming and pasturing herds. There, farmers grew beans, melons, and a variety of grains. Men cleared the land and prepared fields for planting. Women weeded, transplanted seeds, and threshed or ground grains.

Trade Grows Across the Sahara

By A.D. 100, settled farming villages were expanding, especially along the Senegal and Niger rivers and around Lake Chad. In time, these villages grew into towns with local rulers creating governments over growing populations.

Trading Patterns Emerge Farming villages began to produce a **surplus;** that is, more food than they needed. They began to trade their surplus food for products from other villages. Gradually, a trade network emerged across the savanna. It linked the savanna to the forest lands in the south and then funneled goods across the Sahara to the Mediterranean world and the Middle East. From West Africa, caravans crossed the Sahara carrying leather goods, kola nuts, cotton cloth, and enslaved people. From North Africa, Arab and Berber merchants brought silk, metal, beads, and horses to the peoples south of the Sahara. They also spread their beliefs and ideas.

Trading Gold for Salt Two products, gold and salt, dominated the Sahara trade. Gold was widely available in the area of present-day Ghana, Nigeria, and Senegal. The precious metal was found

in the soil along rivers in various forms, including nuggets and dust. The gold was carried to the markets of North Africa and eventually made its way into Europe.

In exchange, West Africans traded for an equally important **commodity,** or valuable product—salt. Salt was rare in some regions of Africa. However, people need salt in their diet to prevent dehydration, especially in tropical areas. Salt is also used to preserve food. The Sahara had an abundance of salt. In fact, at Taghaza, in the central Sahara, people built homes out of blocks of salt. But in the savanna, several hundred miles south, salt was scarce. It was easily worth its weight in gold, pound for pound.

As farming and trade prospered, cities developed on the northern edges of the savanna. Soon strong monarchs arose, gaining control of the most profitable trade routes, and building powerful kingdoms. As the gold and salt trade expanded, so did the spread of ideas and religion. Traders brought their customs and ideas with them as they traveled throughout Africa, helping to spread Islam and the Arabic language to many places. Neighboring kingdoms strengthened their trading partnerships, which helped the region maintain peaceful relationships.

☑ **EXPLAIN** In what ways did farming affect the growth of African villages and cities?

Ghana

Between about 800 and 1600, several powerful kingdoms won control of the prosperous Sahara trade. The first of these kingdoms was **Ghana,** located on the broad "V" made by the Niger and Senegal rivers.

Ghana means ruler and was the name used for this kingdom by Arab traders. The modern nation of Ghana is not located on the site of the ancient kingdom, but lies several hundred miles to the south. Ancient Ghana occupied lands in what are today western Mali and southern Mauritania.

Gold Wealth of Ghana By 800, the rulers of the Soninke people had united many farming villages to create the kingdom of Ghana. Given their favorable location, the rulers of Ghana controlled the gold-salt trade across West Africa. Two streams of trade came together in the marketplaces of Ghana, where the king collected tolls on all goods entering or leaving his land. So great was the flow of gold that Arab writers called Ghana "the land of gold."

The King and His Court Ghana may have had several large cities that served as capitals during its long history. The last great capital was called Kumbi Saleh, and according to the custom of the time, it included two separate walled towns. The first town

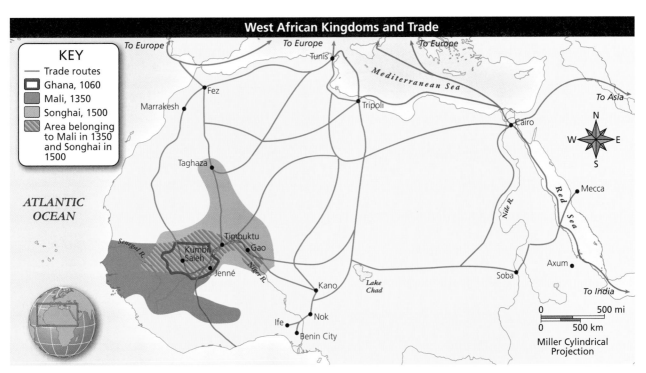

>> **Analyze Maps** What do the trade routes on this map suggest about the West African kingdoms?

🅑 **BOUNCE to Activate Map**

was the home of the king and included the royal palace. The second was home to Muslim merchants and traders.

The royal palace was surrounded by a complex of domed buildings. Here, in a court noted for its wealth and splendor, the king of Ghana presided over elaborate ceremonies. To his people, the king was a godlike figure who administered justice and kept order. In the second town of Kumbi Saleh, prosperous Muslim merchants from north of the Sahara lived in luxurious stone buildings. Lured by the gold wealth of Ghana, these merchants helped make Kumbi Saleh a bustling center of trade.

Islam's Influence Even before the rise of Ghana, Muslim traders had brought their faith to West Africa. As Ghana flourished, Muslim merchants and traders came to play an important role in the kingdom. The king employed Muslims as counselors and officials. Over time, Ghana's rulers adapted some military technology and ideas about government and law from the Muslim world.

The gold-salt trade and other trade with the Muslim world brought other ideas and customs to West Africa. Muslim merchants introduced their Arabic language and writing, coinage, and business methods. From the Islamic world came an emphasis on education and learning. Islamic clerics and scholars traveled with Muslim traders into West Africa and other parts of the continent. Muslim scholars built libraries and schools. Educated Muslims became advisors to West African rulers. Some rulers embraced Islam, which led their people to convert to the new religion. Many African converts to Islam combined aspects of their new faith with some of their traditional beliefs.

As Islam spread across Africa, its teachings and beliefs based on the Quran influenced how people lived. For example, some African Muslim rulers imposed the *zakat,* or a yearly tax on certain kinds of property that was used for charitable purposes. The zakat reflected the Islamic practice of alms giving, or charity.

Ghana Declines About 1050, the Almoravids (al muh RAH vuds), pious Muslims from North Africa, launched a campaign to spread their form of Islam and seize control of Ghana's trade routes. After conquering parts of North Africa and Spain, they pushed south across the Sahara. The Almoravids conquered Ghana, but were unable to maintain control over their extended empire for long. Ghana survived, but its empire declined in the late 1100s. In time, it was swallowed up by a rising new West African power, the kingdom of Mali.

☑ **DESCRIBE** What impact did trade have on the West African kingdom of Ghana?

Mali

Amid the turmoil of Ghana's collapse, the Mandinka people on the upper Niger suffered a bitter defeat by a rival leader. Their king and all but one of his sons were executed. According to tradition, the survivor was a sickly boy named **Sundiata,** regarded by his father's enemies as too weak to be a threat. By 1235, however, Sundiata had become a great king and crushed his enemies, seizing control of the lucrative gold trade routes, and founding the empire of **Mali.**

Mansa Musa: Mali's Greatest Ruler *Mali* is an Arab version of the Mandinka word that means "where the king dwells." The *mansas,* or kings of Mali, expanded their influence over the gold-mining regions to the south and the salt supplies of Taghaza. Where caravan routes crossed, towns such as Timbuktu mushroomed into great trading cities.

The greatest Mali ruler was **Mansa Musa** (MAHN sah MOO sah), who came to the throne around 1312. He expanded Mali's borders westward to the Atlantic Ocean and pushed northward to conquer many cities.

>> **Draw Conclusions** In this 1325 world map, Mali ruler Mansa Musa is offering gold to a trader. What does this image say about Mansa Musa and the Mali empire?

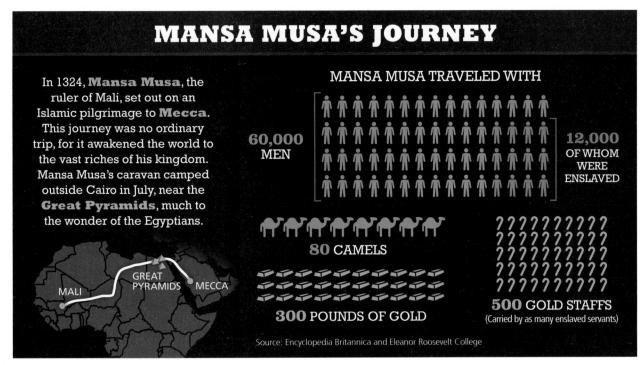

MANSA MUSA'S JOURNEY

In 1324, **Mansa Musa**, the ruler of Mali, set out on an Islamic pilgrimage to **Mecca**. This journey was no ordinary trip, for it awakened the world to the vast riches of his kingdom. Mansa Musa's caravan camped outside Cairo in July, near the **Great Pyramids**, much to the wonder of the Egyptians.

MALI — GREAT PYRAMIDS — MECCA

MANSA MUSA TRAVELED WITH

60,000 MEN

12,000 OF WHOM WERE ENSLAVED

80 CAMELS

300 POUNDS OF GOLD

500 GOLD STAFFS
(Carried by as many enslaved servants)

Source: Encyclopedia Britannica and Eleanor Roosevelt College

>> **Analyze Data** Mansa Musa's pilgrimage to Mecca in 1324 was a sight to behold as he traveled in grand style. Based on the numbers, what percentage of those who traveled with him were enslaved?

During his 25-year reign, Mansa Musa worked to ensure peace and order in his empire. A Muslim, he based his system of justice on the Quran. However, in order to ensure prosperity and peace in his kingdom, he did not impose Islam on the people, but promoted religious freedom and tolerance.

Mansa Musa's Pilgrimage In 1324, Mansa Musa fulfilled one of the Five Pillars of Islam by making the hajj, or pilgrimage, to Mecca. Through his pilgrimage, Mansa Musa showed his devotion to Islam, but the visit also allowed him to forge new diplomatic and economic ties with other Muslim states. Mansa Musa returned home with Muslim scholars, architects, and teachers. The newcomers introduced Arab styles in the palaces and mosques of Mali. They also helped promote Islamic education in Mali.

As a result of Mansa Musa's pilgrimage, word of Mali's great wealth spread across the Muslim world and filtered into Europe. The news sparked the interest of European rulers in African gold, especially since they had recently begun to use gold coins. Europeans began importing the gold, which primarily came to Mali from the south. The gold was then transported across the Sahara to North African cities along the Mediterranean. From there, the gold was shipped to Europe.

Growth of Timbuktu As he returned home from Mecca, Mansa Musa stopped in the busy city of Timbuktu, where he built a palace and mosque. Timbuktu had grown from a small settlement into a major center of trade and Islamic learning. Its diverse population included Muslim and non-Muslim merchants from West Africa and Arabs from North Africa and elsewhere.

For hundreds of years, the city drew some of the best scholars from the Muslim world, including doctors, religious scholars, and judges. Even before Mansa Musa, Timbuktu had won fame for its thriving university that reportedly had 25,000 students from Africa and the Muslim world. The university showed the Islamic emphasis on education and the peaceful spread of Islam through trade and learning.

☑ **DRAW CONCLUSIONS** What were some of Mansa Musa's accomplishments when he ruled Mali?

Songhai

In the 1400s, disputes over succession weakened Mali. Subject peoples broke away, and the empire shriveled. By the 1460s, the wealthy trading city of Gao (gow) had become the capital of the emerging West African kingdom of **Songhai** (SAWNG hy).

An Empire Expands Songhai developed on fertile ground at the bend of the Niger River in present-day Mali and Niger. Between 1464 and 1492, the soldier-king Sonni Ali built one of the largest states in West African history. Sonni Ali brought trade routes and wealthy cities like Timbuktu under his control. Unlike the rulers of Mali, he did not adopt Islam, but instead followed traditional religious beliefs.

Soon after Sonni Ali's death in 1492, however, the emperor Askia Muhammad set up a Muslim dynasty. He further expanded the territory of Songhai and improved its government.

To run the empire more efficiently, he set up a bureaucracy with separate departments for farming, the military, and the treasury. Officials appointed by the emperor supervised each department.

Like Mansa Musa, Askia Muhammad made a pilgrimage to Mecca that led to stronger ties with the wider Muslim world. Scholars from Muslim lands flocked to Askia Muhammad's court at Gao. In towns and cities across Songhai, he built mosques and opened schools for the study of the Quran.

Invaders from the North Songhai continued to prosper after Askia Muhammad died in 1528, but disputes over succession led to frequent changes in leadership. In 1586, a dispute erupted that led to civil war. Soon after, the ruler of Morocco sent his armies south to seize the West African gold mines. The invaders used gunpowder weapons to defeat the disunited forces of Songhai.

Like the Almoravids who conquered Ghana, the Moroccans were not able to rule an empire that reached so far south of the Sahara. With the downfall of Songhai, though, this part of West Africa splintered into many small kingdoms. Memories of the splendid gold-rich kingdoms of the region survived.

☑ **IDENTIFY** In which ways did Askia Muhammad shape the Songhai empire?

Small Societies and Kingdoms of West Africa

In the period from 500 to 1500, other kingdoms and societies flourished in various part of West Africa. The kingdom of Benin (beh NEEN) developed in

THE GREAT CITY OF TIMBUKTU	
Timbuktu was one of the grandest and greatest cities in West Africa. Founded around 1100, the city was a great cultural, religious, and economic center. The city reached the zenith of its power in the 1400s and 1500s.	
CENTER OF TRADE	Salt from Taghaza came into Timbuktu by camel in 200–pound (90.7 kg) blocks. Once it arrived, merchants in Timbuktu dispersed the salt throughout western Africa. Merchants from Ghudamis traveled to Timbuktu to buy gold with salt.
CENTER OF LEARNING	The University of Sankore encompassed 180 Quranic schools with 25,000 students. Sacred Muslim texts were carried into Timbuktu, so scholars from Cairo, Baghdad, and Persia could study them.
LOOKING TO THE STARS	Astronomers in Timbuktu charted the movement of the stars while physicians studied the healing properties of plants.
CITY OF READING	In the mid–1500s, an Islamic scholar named Mohammed abu Bakr al–Wangariai amassed thousands of manuscripts and books on subjects ranging from history to astronomy.
THE FALL	The city began its decline in the 1500s when Moroccan invaders arrested or exiled the Muslim scholars and trading patterns began to shift to the coasts.

>> Founded around 1100, Timbuktu was a great cultural, religious, and economic center. The city reached the height of its power in the 1400s and 1500s.

the rain forest, while the fertile northern lands of modern-day Nigeria were home to the Hausa (HOW suh) people. They were both successful farmers and traders.

Benin: A Forest Kingdom South of the savanna, Benin rose in the rain forests of the Guinea coast of what is now Nigeria. The forest peoples built farming villages and traded pepper and ivory—and later, enslaved people—to their neighbors in the savanna.

The rulers of Benin organized their kingdom in the 1300s, probably building on the achievements of earlier forest peoples. Their *oba*, or king, was a political, judicial, and religious leader. Still, much power was spread among other figures, including the queen mother and a council of hereditary chiefs.

A three-mile-long wall surrounded the capital, Benin City, where a great palace was decorated with elaborate brass plaques and sculptures. Artisans from Ife (EE fay), a neighboring forest state, taught the people of Benin how to cast bronze and brass. Benin sculptors developed their own unique style for representing the human face and form. Their works depicted warriors, queen mothers, and the oba himself. Later, the sculptures showed helmeted and bearded Portuguese merchants, who began to arrive in growing numbers in the 1500s.

Walled City-States of the Hausa By the 1300s, the Hausa had built a number of independent clay-walled cities. Walls were designed to protect the people from invasions.

While these cities remained independent of one another, in time, the walled cities expanded into thriving commercial centers. In the cities, cotton weavers and dyers, leatherworkers, and other artisans produced goods for sale. Merchants traded with Arab and Berber caravans from north of the Sahara. Hausa goods were sold as far away as North Africa and southern Europe.

Kano was the most prosperous Hausa city-state. Its walls, over 12 miles in circumference and up to 50 feet high, protected a population of more than 30,000. Kano's greatest king, Muhammad Rumfa, was a Muslim, as were many of the city's merchants and officials. During his reign, the Hausa developed a writing system influenced by Arabic script, and Islamic law influenced government.

Many Hausa rulers were women, including Amina of the city-state of Zazzau, located in present-day Nigeria. In the late 1500s, she conquered Kano and other regions, expanding the boundary of Zazzau

>> The mud and stone walls of Hausa cities have survived the centuries. The walls helped the cities expand into thriving centers of commerce.

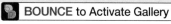
BOUNCE to Activate Gallery

as far as the Niger River. Under Amina, the Hausa came to dominate many Saharan trade routes.

☑ **SUMMARIZE** Describe how other cultures influenced Benin and the Hausa city-states.

☑ ASSESSMENT

1. **Identify Cause and Effect** Why did the gold-salt trade develop between West Africa and North Africa?

2. **Compare** How was the reign of Mansa Musa in Mali similar to that of Askia Muhammad in Songhai?

3. **Identify Central Ideas** What did Timbuktu contribute to Mali's importance as a kingdom?

4. **Check Understanding** How did the gold-salt trade affect the kingdom of Ghana?

5. **Connections to Today** How did the Arabic language contribute to the cultural development of West Africa?

Travels: Ibn Battuta

Moroccan *qadi*, or judge, Ibn Battuta (1304–c.1368) was born in Tangier to a Berber family of the Muslim faith. After he completed his education at the age of 21, Ibn Battuta decided to make the hajj, or Muslim pilgrimage to Mecca. He went on to spend nearly 30 years traveling, visiting much of Southwest Asia, West Africa, southern Russia, India, and China. Along the way he gained fame and wealth and met kings, sheiks, and holy men—including the Byzantine emperor and the sultan of Delhi—as well as ordinary people. In this excerpt from his book, the *Rihlah*, or *Travels*, Ibn Battuta describes the unique trading tradition of Mogadishu.

The second primary source is from the writings of Al-Bakri, a Muslim Spaniard who traveled through the kingdom of Ghana in the 11th century.

Travels of Ibn Battuta

>> Map showing the extent of Ibn Battuta's travels

Primary Source 1

On leaving Zayla we sailed for fifteen days and came to Maqdashaw [Mogadishu], which is an enormous town. Its inhabitants are merchants and have many camels, of which they slaughter hundreds every day [for food]. When a vessel [ship] reaches the port, it is met by sumbuqs, which are small boats, in each of which are a number of young men, each carrying a covered dish containing food. He presents this to one of the merchants on the ship saying "This is my guest," and all the others do the same.

☑ **SUMMARIZE** How are travelers greeted in Mogadishu?

Each merchant on disembarking [leaving] goes only to the house of the young man who is his host, except those who have made frequent journeys to the town and know its people well; these live where they please. The host then sells his goods for him and buys for him, and if anyone buys anything from him at too low a price, or sells to him in the absence of his host, the sale is regarded by them as invalid [not legally recognized]. This practice is of great advantage to them. . . . We stayed there three days, food being brought to us three times a day, and on the fourth, a Friday, the qadi [judge] and one of the wazirs [Arab official] brought me a set

of garments. We then went to the mosque and prayed...

—*Travels,* Ibn Battuta

☑ **COMPARE AND CONTRAST** How does trading in Mogadishu compare to trading elsewhere?

Primary Source 2

When he gives audience to his people, to listen to their complaints and set them to rights, he sits in a pavilion around which stand ten pages holding shields and gold-mounted swords: and on his right hand are the sons of the princes of his empire, splendidly clad and with gold plaited into their hair. The governor of the city is seated on the ground in front of the king, and all around him are his vizirs in the same position. The gate of the chamber is guarded by dogs of an excellent breed, who never leave the king's seat: they wear collars of gold and silver, ornamented with the same metals. The beginning of a royal audience is announced by the beating of a kind of drum which they call deba, made of a long piece of hollowed wood. The people gather when they hear this sound. . . .

The king [of Ghana] exacts the right of one dinar of gold on each donkey-load of salt that enters his country, and two dinars of gold on each load of salt that goes out.

—*The Book of Routes and Realms,* Al-Bakri

☑ **DESCRIBE** How would you describe the kingdom of Ghana at that time?

☑ ASSESSMENT

1. **Identify Supporting Details** What details in the text reveal to you that Ibn Battuta and other travelers were treated well by the people of Mogadishu?

2. **Determine Author's Purpose** Why do you think Ibn Battuta recorded this description of Mogadishu in his travels?

3. **Analyze Interactions** How did Ibn Battuta's faith affect his travels and his interactions with other Muslims?

4. **Identify** According to the primary source by Al-Bakri, what was one source of wealth for the Ghana empire?

8.7

A portrait of King Lalibela, ruler of Ethiopia in the early 1200s

 BOUNCE to Activate Flipped Video

Objectives

Explain how religion influenced the development of Axum and Ethiopia.

Understand how trade affected the city-states in East Africa.

Describe the economy of Great Zimbabwe.

Explain why Europeans began to explore Africa and interact with African societies.

Key Terms

Axum
Adulis
Ethiopia
Lalibela
Swahili
Great Zimbabwe
Prince Henry

Trading States of East Africa

After 100 B.C., the kingdom of **Axum** expanded across the northern Ethiopian highlands. By about A.D. 1, Axum had gained control of the Red Sea coast in present-day Eritrea. By controlling the Red Sea trade with Rome and Persia, Axum grew rich.

Axum

Located to the southeast of Nubia, Axum extended from the mountains of present-day Ethiopia to the sun-bleached shores of the Red Sea in present-day Eritrea. The peoples of Axum were descended from African farmers and people from the Middle East who brought Jewish traditions through Arabia. This merging of cultures gave rise to a unique written and spoken language, Geez (pronounced "gay EZ").

An Ideal Location for Trade The kingdom of Axum profited from the strategic location of its two main cities, the port of **Adulis** on the Red Sea, and the upland capital city of Axum. By A.D. 400, the kingdom commanded a triangular trade network that connected Africa, India, and the Mediterranean world.

A great variety of goods funneled in and out of the markets of these two cities. From the interior of Africa, traders brought ivory, animal hides, and gold to the markets of Axum. Goods from farther south and across the Indian Ocean came to the Red Sea harbor of Adulis. There, the traders and markets offered iron, spices, precious stones, and cotton cloth from India and other lands beyond the Indian Ocean. Ships carried these commodities up the Red Sea, where they collected goods from Europe and countries along the Mediterranean.

Christianity Takes Hold In these great centers of international trade, Greek, Egyptian, Arab, and Jewish merchants mingled with traders from Africa, India, and other regions. Ideas spread as these goods were traded. By the 300s, Christianity had reached the region. After converting to the new religion, Axum's King Ezana made Christianity the official religion of his kingdom. As Christianity took hold among Axum's people, they replaced older temples with Christian churches decorated with intricately designed religious images and murals painted on wood panels.

Islam Spreads At first, Christianity strengthened the ties between Axum, North Africa, and the Mediterranean world. In the 600s, however, Islam began to spread across North Africa and other regions surrounding Axum. Many African rulers embraced this new faith, creating strong cultural ties across much of the continent. Axum, which remained Christian, grew isolated from its own trade network—by distance from Europe and by religion from many former trading partners. As civil war and economic decline combined to weaken Axum, the kingdom slowly declined.

☑ **SYNTHESIZE** Describe how the spread of Christianity and Islam affected the kingdom of Axum.

Ethiopia

Though Axum's political and economic power faded, its cultural and religious influence did not disappear. This legacy survived among the peoples of the interior uplands, in what is today northern Ethiopia. Although Axum's empire was only a portion of the present-day nation, when referring to their kingdom as a whole, the Axumite kings frequently used **Ethiopia,** a term the Greeks used for the region.

A Distinctive Culture Medieval Ethiopia was protected by rugged mountains, and the descendants of the Axumites were able to maintain their independence for centuries. Their success was due in part to the unifying power of their Christian faith, which gave them a unique sense of identity and helped establish a culture distinct from that of neighboring peoples.

One example of Ethiopia's distinct culture is the unique churches of Lalibela. In the early 1200s, King **Lalibela** came to power in Ethiopia.

During his reign, he directed the building of eleven remarkable churches that workers carved from ground level downward into the solid rock of the mountains. These amazing structures still exist today and illustrate the architectural and artistic skill of the craftsmen who created them.

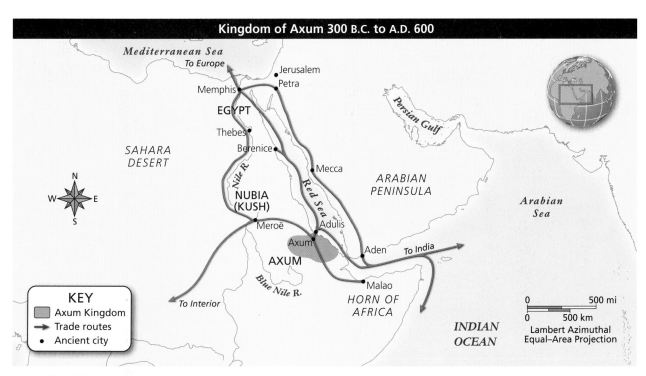

Kingdom of Axum 300 B.C. to A.D. 600

KEY
Axum Kingdom
Trade routes
Ancient city

>> **Analyze Maps** Axum's location allowed the kingdom to become a hub of trade in East Africa. Based on the map, why did the Axum kingdom become a favorite center for maritime traders?

Despite their isolation, Ethiopian Christians kept ties with the Holy Land. In fact, some made pilgrimages to Jerusalem. They also were in touch with Christian communities in Egypt. Over time, Ethiopian Christianity absorbed many local customs. Traditional East African music and dance were adapted, and their influence is still felt in Ethiopian church services today. In addition, the services are still conducted in the ancient language of Geez.

Judaism in Ethiopia The kings of Ethiopia claimed descent from the Israelite king Solomon and the queen of Sheba. This belief was recorded in an ancient Ethiopian book called *The Glory of Kings* and reinforced by the fact that Ethiopians observe some of the Jewish holidays and dietary laws.

Some Ethiopians practiced Judaism, not the predominant Christianity. These Ethiopian Jews lived in the mountains of Ethiopia until the late 1900s, when most evacuated to Israel due to famine and persecutions.

☑ **IDENTIFY** How did Ethiopia's geographic isolation shape its culture?

City-States of East Africa

While Axum declined, a string of commercial cities—including Kilwa, Mogadishu, Mombasa, and Sofala—gradually arose along the East African coast. Since ancient times, Phoenician, Greek, Roman, and Indian traders had visited this region. In the 700s, Arab traders began visiting this region more frequently, and Arab and Persian merchants set up Muslim trading centers beginning in the 900s. Port cities, as well as offshore islands such as Lamu and Zanzibar, were ideally located for trade with Asia. As a result, Asian traders and immigrants from as far away as Indonesia soon added to the rich cultural mix.

Trade in the Indian Ocean By the 600s, sailors had learned that the annual monsoon winds could carry sailing ships plying the waters of the Indian Ocean between India and Africa. On the East African coast, rulers took advantage of the opportunities for trade that these winds of the Indian Ocean provided.

They welcomed ships from Arabia, Persia, and China. Because of demand for these goods from customers, traders acquired ivory, leopard skins, iron, copper, and gold. From India, Southeast Asia, and China came cotton cloth, silk, spices, porcelain, glassware, and swords.

The traders from Arabia, Persia, and China also contributed to the development of the slave trade. Customers of these traders throughout Asia bought enslaved people to work as laborers or domestic servants. In every port, the traders purchased enslaved people who had been captured on raids into the interior of Africa, as well as from coastal regions.

>> Traders from Europe, Asia, and the interior of Africa met in East Africa to trade ivory, gold, and other goods. Some also bought and sold enslaved people.

Trade was beneficial to the merchants, and it also helped local rulers build strong, independent city-states. Although they competed for trade, relations between the city-states were generally peaceful. A Muslim visitor described Kilwa, the most successful city-state, as "one of the most beautiful and well-constructed towns in the world." Its royal palace still stands on cliffs that today overlook the ocean. The complex consists of courtyards, terraces, and nearly 100 rooms. Built of coral and cut stone, the structure is evidence of the old city's splendor.

Trade Influences Swahili The successful East African international trade system led to the emergence of a vibrant culture and language known as **Swahili.** By the 1000s, many East African coastal cities had not only grown in wealth but also in size. Traders from the Middle East and Asia began to settle permanently in flourishing trading cities such as Kilwa.

As more settlers arrived, the local East African culture absorbed cultural elements from these new residents. For example, the architecture of private houses and palaces displayed a blend of East African and Arabic designs that created unique and elegant Swahili buildings and furniture. Over time, many Arabic words were absorbed into the local Bantu-based language. In fact, the term *swahili* comes from an Arabic word meaning "of the coast." The language itself was eventually written in Arabic script.

The Travels of Ibn Battuta The journey of Ibn Battuta tells us much about travel and trade in East Africa, the Indian Ocean, and beyond. Ibn Battuta was born in Tangier to a Berber family of the Muslim faith. After completing his education at the age of 21, Ibn Battuta made the hajj, or the pilgrimage to Mecca that Muslims are expected to make if they are able. His trek became one of the greatest journeys of medieval times. The 30-year trip took Ibn Battuta to Southwest Asia, West Africa, Southern Russia, India, and China. Along the way, he gained fame and wealth and met kings, sheiks, and holy men. He wrote a book called the *Rihlah,* or *Travels,* in which the following passage describes the unique trading tradition of Mogadishu.

> . . . we sailed for fifteen days and came to Maqdashaw [Mogadishu], which is an enormous town. Its inhabitants are merchants . . . When

>> **Determine Point of View** Beta Ghiorgis, which means House of George, is one of King's Lalibela's solid rock churches. Why would King Lalibela build a church in the shape of a cross?

>> Trade brought great wealth and different cultural influences to the region. The Great Mosque in Kilwa reflects the prosperity and the spread of Islam that trade brought to the area.

 BOUNCE to Activate Gallery

a vessel reaches the port, it is met by *sumbuqs*, which are small boats, in each of which are a number of young men, carrying a covered dish containing food. He presents this to one of the merchants on the ship saying "This is my guest" . . . Each merchant on disembarking goes only to the house of the young man who is his host . . . the host then sells his goods for him and buys for him, and if anyone buys anything from him at too low a price, or sells to him in the absence of his host, the sale is regarded by them as invalid.

—Ibn Battuta, the *Travels*

☑ **IDENTIFY CENTRAL IDEAS** What was the impact of trade on the city-states of East Africa?

Great Zimbabwe

To the south and inland from the coastal city-states, massive stone ruins sprawl across rocky hilltops near the great bend in the Limpopo River. The looming walls, large palace, and cone-shaped towers were once part of the powerful and prosperous capital of a great inland empire. Today, these impressive ruins are known as **Great Zimbabwe.**

An Inland Trading Center The word *zimbabwe* comes from a Bantu-based word that means "stone houses." In fact, Great Zimbabwe was built by a succession of Bantu-speaking peoples who settled in the region between 900 and 1500. These newcomers brought iron, mining methods, and improved farming skills. Early settlers raised cattle and built stone enclosures to protect their livestock. In time, these settlers improved their building methods and erected large walls and palaces.

The capital probably reached its height about 1300. By then, it had tapped nearby gold resources and created profitable commercial links with coastal cities such as Sofala. Archaeologists have found beads from India and porcelain from China, showing that Great Zimbabwe was part of a trade network that reached across the Indian Ocean. In addition, they have found artifacts that indicate that Great

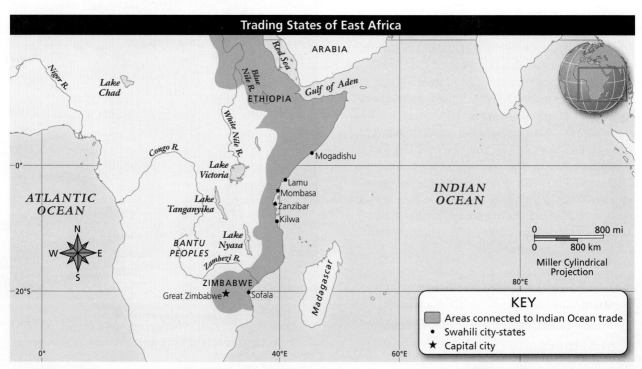

Trading States of East Africa

KEY
- ▨ Areas connected to Indian Ocean trade
- • Swahili city-states
- ★ Capital city

>> **Analyze Maps** What trade patterns does this map show?

🔲 **BOUNCE to Activate Map**

Zimbabwe had artisans skilled in making jewelry and weaving cotton cloth.

Very little is known about the government in Great Zimbabwe. However, after studying the architecture and artifacts of the ruins, some scholars have suggested that the ruler was a god-king who presided over a large court. Below the king, a central bureaucracy may have ruled an inner ring of provinces, while appointed governors had authority in more distant villages. Although there is much about Great Zimbabwe that remains unknown, as archaeologists continue their research, we are learning more about how the capital and empire developed.

Zimbabwe Declines By 1500, Zimbabwe was in decline. Some scholars suggest that the population had grown too great. Civil war and dwindling trade probably contributed as well.

By then, Portuguese traders were pushing inland to find the region's source of gold. They failed to discover the gold mines, but their attempts further weakened the small states that formed in the region as Zimbabwe declined. Some scholars believe that the environment also played a role in Great Zimbabwe's decline. Overgrazing and drought on the Zimbabwe Plateau, coupled with a decline in land productivity, may have eventually led to famine.

☑ **EXPLAIN** Explain how the ruins of Great Zimbabwe reflected the capital's wealth.

European Exploration of Africa

Portugal, a small nation on the western edge of Spain, led the way in European exploration. By the 1400s, Portugal was strong enough to expand into Muslim North Africa. In 1415, the Portuguese seized Ceuta (SAY oo tah) on the North African coast. The victory sparked the imagination of **Prince Henry,** known to history as Henry the Navigator.

The African Coast Mapped Prince Henry saw great promise in Africa. The Portuguese could convert Africans—most of whom practiced either Islam or native religions—to Christianity. He also believed that in Africa he would find the sources of the gold Muslim traders controlled.

Finally, Prince Henry hoped to find an easier way to reach Asia that bypassed the Mediterranean, which meant going around Africa. The Portuguese felt that with their expert knowledge

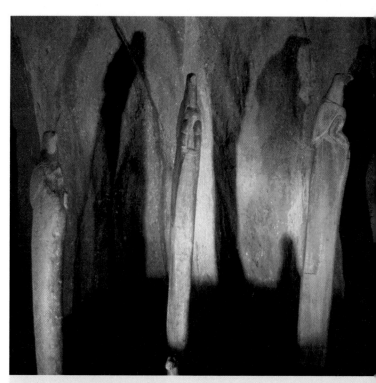

>> These figurines were crafted by artisans of Great Zimbabwe and show the wealth of detail in that advanced society.

and technology, they could accomplish this feat. At Sagres, in southern Portugal, Henry gathered scientists, cartographers, or mapmakers, and other experts. They redesigned ships, prepared maps, and trained captains and crews for long voyages.

Henry then sent ships that slowly worked their way south to explore the coast of West Africa. Henry died in 1460, but the Portuguese continued their quest.

Portuguese Footholds in Africa The Portuguese built small forts in West Africa to collect food and water and to repair their ships. They also established trading posts to trade muskets, tools, and cloth for gold, ivory, and hides. They also purchased enslaved Africans. These were not colonies peopled by settlers. Instead, the Portuguese left just enough men and firepower to defend their forts.

From West Africa, the Portuguese sailed around the continent. In 1488, Bartholomeu Dias rounded the southern tip of Africa. Despite the turbulent seas around it, the tip became known as the Cape of Good Hope because it opened the way for a trade route through the Indian Ocean to Asia.

The Portuguese continued to establish forts and trading posts, but they also attacked East African coastal cities such as Mombasa and Malindi, which were hubs of international trade. With cannons blazing, they expelled the Arabs who controlled the East African trade network and took over this thriving commerce for themselves. Each conquest added to their growing trade empire.

Over the next two centuries, some Portuguese explorers managed to reach parts of present-day Congo, Zambia, and Zimbabwe, establishing limited trade. In general, however, the Portuguese did not venture far from Africa's coasts. They knew little about the interior of Africa, and they lacked accurate maps or other resources to help them explore there. Furthermore, Africans in the interior, who wanted to control the gold trade, resisted such exploration.

Europeans Expansion into Africa Other European powers, such as Spain, France, England, and Holland also sought to expand their trade networks. These European countries used these footholds to protect and expand their trade routes in Africa, the Indian Ocean, and India.

Later, European countries would expand even further throughout Africa. The Dutch settled Cape Town at Africa's southern tip. Cape Town was the first permanent European settlement on the continent and supplied ships sailing to and from the East Indies. The French established a fort in the region of Senegal. These achievements would eventually allow European exploration of Africa to explode.

☑ **EXPLAIN** Why did Prince Henry encourage the Portuguese to explore Africa?

☑ ASSESSMENT

1. **Synthesize** How did geography and religion influence Ethiopia's development?

2. **Draw Conclusions** What was the main reason that European countries established outposts along Africa's coast?

3. **Test Conclusions** What does archeological evidence suggest about Great Zimbabwe's economy?

4. **Identify Central Ideas** How did religion and trade affect the development of East Africa?

5. **Identify Cause and Effect** What role did religion play in the rise and decline of Axum?

6. **Connections to Today** How did trade lead to the emergence of the Swahili language?

8.8

Griots, or traditional West African storytellers, memorize songs and stories that preserve the traditions of their people.

Diverse Peoples and Traditions in Africa

Across the immense African continent, a variety of cultures emerged, ranging from wealthy trading kingdoms to nomadic herding societies to small farming communities. As people adapted to different environments and landscapes, their ways of life differed. Across Africa, communities varied in size, economic activity, family patterns, and forms of government. Still, they all had these features as well as their own religious beliefs, art, and technology.

Many Cultures and Patterns of Life

Throughout Africa, communities varied in size, environment, and economics. However, each society developed around four common elements—family, government, religion, and art.

Early Communities As you have read, the worldwide Neolithic Revolution led to the beginning of settled farming communities located in areas with fertile soil and proximity to water. These farming settlements grew as surpluses increased, enabling artisans to develop specialized skills.

Advances in transportation, such as the use of the camel, increased a community's reach beyond its borders, and exchange allowed villages to grow into towns. Extended trade brought additional wealth, leading to the creation of states and kingdoms.

Family Patterns Across Africa, as elsewhere around the globe, the family was the basic unit of society. Patterns of family life varied greatly. In some small societies, the basic family unit was the **nuclear family,** or parents and children living and working

BOUNCE to Activate Flipped Video

Objectives

Identify the different ways that the family influenced medieval African cultures.

Describe the variety of forms of medieval African governments.

Understand the role of religion and art in medieval societies.

Key Terms

nuclear family
patrilineal
matrilineal
lineage
consensus
griot

>> This ornately crafted bronze wine bowl was made in eastern Nigeria around the 800s.

🅱 BOUNCE to Activate Gallery

>> In many African societies, older people were revered and looked upon as sources of wisdom. Today, family ties are often still an important part of modern African life.

🅱 BOUNCE to Activate Gallery

together as a unit. In other communities, family units included the extended family—parents, children, and several generations such as grandparents and uncles—who lived and worked together to ensure the success of the family group.

Women were valued as wives and mothers. Women contributed to the economy in settled farming societies, where they worked the fields.

Even in herding societies, women raised food in small gardens while men and boys tended the herds. Often, women were respected for their wisdom and skills in many areas. In a few societies, women served a soldiers, and, as you will read, served as rulers or in other government jobs.

Children were highly valued for the work they performed within the family and community and, most importantly, for the link they served between the past and future. Parents depended on children to care for them in old age and educated their children in the customs, skills, and ways of their society.

Kinship Ties Family organization varied in many ways across Africa. Some families were **patrilineal.** In these families, important kinship ties such as inheritance were passed through the father's side. Other families were **matrilineal,** with inheritance traced through the mother's side. In a patrilineal culture, a bride would move to her husband's village and become part of his family. In many matrilineal cultures, the husband joined his wife's family in her village.

Matrilineal cultures forged strong ties between brothers and sisters. Brothers were expected to protect their sisters, and sons were expected to help their mother's brothers whenever needed.

Wider Ties Each family belonged to a **lineage,** or group of households who claimed a common ancestor. Several lineages formed a clan that traced its descent to an even more remote and often legendary ancestor. Belonging to a particular family, lineage, or clan gave people a sense of community with shared responsibilities to that community.

An individual's place in some African societies was also determined by a system of age grades. An age grade included all girls or boys born in the same year. Each age grade had particular responsibilities and privileges. As they moved up from one age grade to another, children began to take part in village activities, which created social ties beyond the family.

☑ **IDENTIFY CENTRAL IDEAS** How did a person's kinship affect his or her place in society?

Government and Power

Farming peoples generally lived in tight-knit communities and helped one another in tasks such as clearing the land, planting, and harvesting. Both men and women planted, but usually were responsible for different crops. Political patterns varied, depending in part on the size of the community that the land could support.

Shared Power In farming societies, power was usually shared among a number of people rather than centralized in the hands of a single leader. In some villages, a chief had a good deal of authority, but in many others, elders made the major decisions. Sometimes, older men supervised religious ceremonies linked to the government, while younger men made decisions about war. In some places, especially in parts of West Africa, women took the dominant role in the marketplace or acted as official peacemakers in the village.

Villages often made decisions by a process known as **consensus,** or general agreement. In open discussions, people whose opinions were valued voiced their views before a final agreement was reached. Because of the experience and wisdom of older men and women, their opinions usually carried the greatest weight.

In villages that were part of a large kingdom such as Songhai, decisions made at a distant court had to be obeyed. These villagers, therefore, had to pay taxes and provide soldiers to the central, and frequently distant, government.

Kingdom of Kongo Many different forms of government developed in Africa. An example of one kind of government organization was the kingdom of Kongo. It flourished about A.D. 1500 in the forest zone of west-central Africa. The kingdom consisted of many villages grouped into districts and provinces and governed by officials appointed by the king. Each village had its own chief, a man chosen on the basis of the descent of his mother's family.

In theory, the king of Kongo had absolute power. In fact, that power was limited. The king was chosen by a board of electors and had to govern according to traditional laws. Unlike rulers of West Africa states, who maintained strong standing armies, kings of Kongo depended on a system of military service that called upon men to fight only in times of need. The king ruled through local governors who collected taxes either in goods or in cowrie shells, a common currency in Africa.

The organization of Kongo was just one type of African government. In many regions, people

>> King Alvaro II, ruler of Kongo, made alliances and trade agreements with Europeans, such as the Dutch depicted in this illustration.

belonged to small local societies without a centralized government.

☑ **EXPLAIN** How did power-sharing work in small African societies?

Religion

Across Africa, religious beliefs and practices were varied and complex. As elsewhere, religion helped to unite a society. Through religion, people learned about their origins. Oral traditions and myths taught important moral truths about right and wrong. Dancing, singing, and playing musical instruments were part of religious celebrations.

Africans of many ethnic backgrounds traditionally worshiped many gods and goddesses. Along with all ancient peoples, they identified the forces of nature with divine spirits and tried to influence those forces through rituals and ceremonies.

Traditional Beliefs Many African peoples believed that a single, unknowable supreme being stood above all the other gods and goddesses. This supreme being was the creator and ruler of the universe and was helped by the lesser gods and spirits, who were closer to the people.

Some African peoples believed, like the Chinese, that the spirits of their ancestors could help, warn, or punish their descendants on Earth. To honor and please their ancestors, they said prayers or performed rituals.

Like the followers of traditional religions in other parts of the world, many African peoples believed that every object on Earth is filled with a living spirit. They respected nature because they believed that the supreme being had created all things.

In some African societies, diviners and healers held places of honor. These men and women were well educated in the traditions of their societies. Diviners served as interpreters between people and the divine world. They might explain the cause of misfortune such as illness. The healer might then help a person find a solution to a problem. Diviners and healers also had knowledge of herbal medicines.

Christianity and Islam Spread By A.D. 1000, both Christianity and Islam had spread into Africa. African converts often associated the God of Christians and Muslims with their traditional supreme being. In this way, Christianity and Islam absorbed many local African practices and beliefs.

Over time, Islam played a dominant role in commerce, education, and government in large parts of Africa. Jewish communities had existed in North

>> Jews in many communities in Africa lived side by side with Muslims and Christians and worshiped in temples such as this one in Egypt.

Africa since ancient times. Later, many Jews moved to North Africa after they were expelled from Spain in 1492. As you have read, a community of Ethiopian Jews lasted for centuries, while Ethiopian Christian communities also survived for more than 1,500 years. In areas where Islam was dominant, Christians and Jews continued to practice their faiths as protected "people of the Book." Christians and Jews developed their own institutions within the context of the Islamic community, in some cases acting as advisors in the courts of the early caliphs.

☑ **DESCRIBE** Describe the various religious belief systems in medieval Africa.

Art and Literature

African artistic traditions extend far back in time to the ancient rock paintings of the Sahara, which were created by about 1000 B.C., and the over-4,000-year-old pyramids of Egypt and Nubia. More recently, but still about 1,000 years ago, the rock churches of Ethiopia and the palace of Great Zimbabwe were built. These accomplishments bear lasting witness to the creative power of these early and medieval civilizations.

Visual Arts African artists worked in many materials, including gold, ivory, wood, bronze, and cloth. They created many decorative items such as woven cloth, inscribed jugs and bowls, or jewelry simply for their beauty. Even so, art usually served social and religious purposes as well.

Art strengthened bonds within the community and linked the makers and the users of the work. Patterns used to decorate textiles, baskets, swords, and other objects had important meanings or special messages that the artisan or owner wanted to convey. Often, they identified an object as the work of a particular clan or the possession of royalty. One example is kente cloth, a traditional West African textile woven of silk and cotton. When it was made in bright gold and blue colors, the symbols of power, only the ruling elite and the wealthy were allowed to wear it.

In Africa, as elsewhere, much art was closely tied to religion. Statues and other objects were used in religious rites and ceremonies. In some rituals, for example, leaders wore elaborately carved masks decorated with cowrie shells or grass. Once the mask was in place, both the wearer and the viewers could feel the presence of the spiritual force it represented.

Literature Early African societies preserved their histories and values through both written and oral literature. Ancient Egypt, Nubia, and Axum left written records of their past. Later, Arabic provided a common written language in those parts of Africa influenced by Islam. African Muslim scholars gathered in cities such as Timbuktu and Kilwa. Documents in Arabic offer invaluable evidence about the law, religion, and history of the time.

Oral traditions date back many centuries. In West Africa, **griots** (GREE ohz), or professional storytellers, recited ancient stories. Griots preserved both histories and traditional folk tales in the same way that the epics of Homer or Vedic India were passed orally from generation to generation. The histories praised the heroic deeds of famous ancestors or rulers. Griots often used riddles to sharpen the wits of audiences.

Oral traditions also passed down folk tales, which blended fanciful stories with humor and sophisticated word play. Such stories often taught important moral lessons. Oral literature, like religion and art, thus encouraged a sense of community and common values in each of the diverse societies across the African continent.

☑ **IDENTIFY CENTRAL IDEAS** How did literature help to reinforce social ties?

☑ ASSESSMENT

1. **Identify Cause and Effect** How did an individual's family ties affect life in medieval African societies?

2. **Determine Relevance** What was the importance of art in medieval African cultures?

3. **Identify Central Ideas** How did religions develop and interact with one another in medieval African communities?

4. **Summarize** What were the forms of government in medieval Africa?

5. **Interpret** Why might it be beneficial for an African village to have more than one person sharing a leadership role?

6. **Connections to Today** How might Arabic and Swahili have helped to spread shared cultural features among Africa's diverse peoples?

Connections to Today

A market storefront in Sudan

Take Action to Learn About Languages in Africa

Centuries ago in Africa, Arabic and Swahili spread through conquest and trade to much of northern, central, and eastern Africa. Today, these languages continue to connect Africans across many national borders.

1. **Choose** Select one of these topics related to the cross-border roles of Arabic and Swahili today:

   - **Arabic:** How does Arabic promote trade, political cooperation, or cultural ties among African countries?

   - **Swahili:** How does Swahili link African countries economically, politically, or culturally?

2. **Ask Questions** What are some of the things you want to learn about Arabic or Swahili in Africa today? Write a list of questions.

3. **Learn** Research the topic you have chosen, collecting specific examples from reliable sources. Look for recent articles on the use of Arabic or Swahili in Africa.

4. **Raise Awareness** Create a written report or oral presentation on your findings about the ways Arabic or Swahili link Africans today. Be prepared to present your findings as directed by your teacher.

Use the texts, quizzes, interactivities, Quest Inquiries, Flipped Videos, and other resources from this Topic to prepare for the Topic Test.

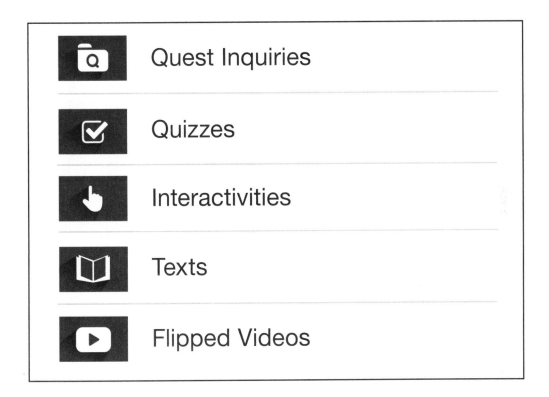

Quest Inquiries

Quizzes

Interactivities

Texts

Flipped Videos

While online you can also check the progress you've made learning the topic and course content by viewing your grades, test scores, and assignment status.

LESSON SUMMARIES
Use these Lesson Summaries, and the longer versions available online, to review the key ideas for each lesson in this Topic.

Lesson 1: The Origins of Islam
Muhammad, revered by Muslims as the messenger of God, introduced Islamic teachings to the peoples of Arabia. The Five Pillars of Islam, the Quran, and Sharia guide beliefs, daily conduct, and law in Islamic societies.

Lesson 2: A Muslim Empire
United by Islam, Arab Muslims conquered a large empire. Divisions over Muhammad's successor led to a split between Sunni and Shiite Muslims. The Umayyad and Abbasid caliphates built thriving capitals that became centers of trade and learning.

Lesson 3: Achievements of Muslim Civilization
Traders from the Muslim empire built a vast trade network stretching from China to Europe. Muslim scholars made important advances in science and mathematics.

Lesson 4: The Ottoman and Safavid Empires
After capturing Constantinople in 1453, the Ottoman Turks built a Muslim empire that ruled much of Eastern Europe and Southwest Asia. In the 1500s, the Safavid empire arose in Persia. Both the Ottoman and Safavid empires ruled diverse peoples.

Lesson 5: Early Civilizations of Africa
Geography and migrations contributed to cultural diversity in Africa. The earliest African civilizations arose in Egypt and Nubia. Later North African civilizations were influenced by Rome and by the spread of Islam.

Lesson 6: Kingdoms of West Africa

In West Africa, three strong kingdoms—Ghana, Mali, and Songhai—emerged. Their wealth came from the trans-Saharan gold-salt trade. This trade brought Islamic culture to many parts of West Africa.

Lesson 7: Trading States of East Africa
In East Africa, Ethiopia stood alone as a Christian kingdom. East African city-states such as Kilwa and Mogadishu became centers of a flourishing trade across the Indian Ocean.

Lesson 8: Diverse Peoples and Traditions in Africa
Family played a central role in African societies, which developed unique systems of government and rich artistic traditions. Christianity and Islam spread in Africa alongside traditional religions.

QUEST! FINDINGS

Hold Your Discussion on the Impact of the Battle of Tours Refer to your responses to the Quest Connections to help you prepare your discussion. Use the rubric and other Quest resources online to guide your work.

VISUAL REVIEW

Use these graphics to review some of the key terms, people, and ideas from this Topic.

Rise and Spread of Islam

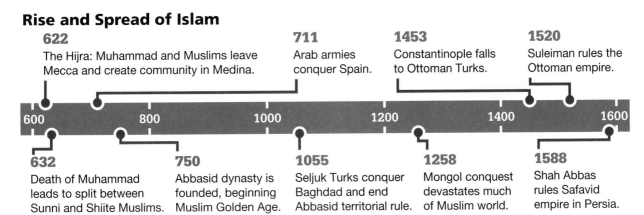

622
The Hijra: Muhammad and Muslims leave Mecca and create community in Medina.

711
Arab armies conquer Spain.

1453
Constantinople falls to Ottoman Turks.

1520
Suleiman rules the Ottoman empire.

632
Death of Muhammad leads to split between Sunni and Shiite Muslims.

750
Abbasid dynasty is founded, beginning Muslim Golden Age.

1055
Seljuk Turks conquer Baghdad and end Abbasid territorial rule.

1258
Mongol conquest devastates much of Muslim world.

1588
Shah Abbas rules Safavid empire in Persia.

The Five Pillars of Islam

First pillar	Declare faith that there is only one God and that Muhammad is God's messenger.
Second pillar	Pray five times a day while facing Mecca.
Third pillar	Give alms (charity) to the poor.
Fourth pillar	Fast from sunrise to sundown during holy month of Ramadan.
Fifth pillar	Make hajj, or pilgrimage, to Mecca (if physically able).

Empires and Trading States of Africa

EMPIRE OR STATE	DATES	ECONOMIC BASE
Northeastern Africa		
Egypt	2575 B.C.–1075 B.C.	Farming, trade
Nubia	1100 B.C.–A.D. 350	Trade, iron
West Africa		
Ghana	800–1050	Gold
Mali	1235–1400s	Gold-salt trade
Benin	1300s–1500s	Pepper, ivory, slave trade
Songhai	1460–1491	Trade
East Africa		
Axum	350–600s	Trade
Swahili city-states	600s–1000s	Trade
Great Zimbabwe	1300s–1500s	Trade

Topic 8 Assessment

KEY TERMS, PEOPLE, AND IDEAS

1. What role does the **mosque** play in Muslim worship?

2. What is the function of the **Sharia** in Islamic societies?

3. How did the selection of the **caliph** cause conflict between **Sunni** and **Shiite** Muslims?

4. What contributions did **Ibn Khaldun** and **Ibn Rushd** make to scholarship?

5. How did **janizaries** serve the Ottoman empire?

6. What are the geographic characteristics of African **savannas?**

7. According to tradition, what West African empire was founded by **Sundiata?**

8. How did **Swahili** originate?

9. What is the difference between a **matrilineal** family and a **patrilineal** family?

CRITICAL THINKING

10. **Draw Conclusions** What is the main significance of the hijra? Why do you think it became the starting point of the Muslim calendar?

11. **Summarize** Summarize three major factors that contributed to the growth of the Muslim empire.

12. **Draw Inferences** Muhammad taught that "the ink of the scholar is holier than the blood of the martyr." What do you think he meant? How might this attitude have contributed to the development of Muslim civilization?

13. **Compare** In what ways was the rule of Suleiman in the Ottoman empire similar to that of Shah Abbas in the Safavid empire?

14. **Identify Cause and Effect** What attracted invaders to the great kingdoms and cities of Africa?

15. **Cite Evidence** From your studies of both the Islamic world and Africa, cite at least two pieces of evidence that religious beliefs and practices often strongly influence artistic traditions.

16. **Use Visual Information** Look at the map. Based on the information on the map, what kind of relationship may have existed between cities such as Sofala and Great Zimbabwe? How were those two different?

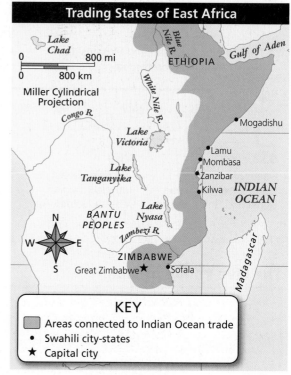

Trading States of East Africa

KEY
- Areas connected to Indian Ocean trade
- • Swahili city-states
- ★ Capital city

17. **Writing Activity: Write an Informative Essay** Write a two-paragraph essay based on the excerpt below. Explain (a) how the excerpt specifically relates to the Five Pillars of Islam, and (b) what other values are expressed or implied in the excerpt.

> O, believers! Fasting is prescribed [ordered] for you as it was prescribed for those before you so that you may learn self-restraint. Fast the prescribed number of days; except if any of you is ill or on a journey, then fast a similar number of days later. For those who can not endure it for *medical reasons,* there is a ransom [act of devotion]: the feeding of one poor person for each missed day. Whoever does more good *than this* voluntarily, it is better for him. However, if you truly understand *the rationale of fasting,* it is better for you to fast.
> —The Quran 2:183

18. **Connections to Today** Consider how Arabic and Swahili have linked Africans across history. What role might these languages play in building a more prosperous and peaceful future for northern, central, and eastern Africans?

DOCUMENT-BASED QUESTIONS

Muslim physicians of the Golden Age made many advances in diagnosis and treatment of disease. Read the documents below, then answer the questions that follow.

DOCUMENT A

"The knowledge of anything, since all things have causes, is not acquired or complete unless it is known by its causes. Therefore in medicine we ought to know the causes of sickness and health. And because health and sickness and their causes are sometimes manifest [obvious], and sometimes hidden and not to be comprehended except by the study of symptoms, we must also study the symptoms of health and disease."

    —From *On Medicine,* by Ibn Sina

DOCUMENT B

"The eruption of the smallpox is preceded by a continued fever, pain in the back, itching in the nose and terrors in the sleep. These are the more peculiar symptoms of its approach, especially a pain in the back with fever; . . . pain and heaviness of the head; inquietude, nausea and anxiety; (with this difference that the inquietude, nausea and anxiety are more frequent in the measles than in the smallpox; while on the other hand, the pain in the back is more peculiar to the smallpox than to the measles). . . . "

    —From *Treatise on Smallpox,* by Muhammad al-Razi

DOCUMENT C

This diagram of the human eye comes from an Arabic medical text written around 1200.

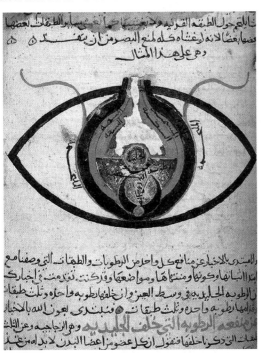

DOCUMENT D

"[Arab physician Ibn al-Nafis's] authoritative observations of anatomy and physiology are unlikely to have been founded on human dissections, as his grounding in Sharia law would have dictated otherwise. Other authors refute this conclusion, citing the prevalent practice of using the corpses of criminals to study disease as well as the strong belief among Muslims that anyone who undertook dissection was also increasing their faith in God....

"The enormous impact of [al-Razi, Ibn Sina, and al-Nafis] originated in their willingness to draw from the wisdom of others—Hellenic, Roman and Indian medical lore—and then to review and critique this wisdom, aided by their own experimentation and observations. In turn, their prodigious written records and later translations laid the foundations on which medicine was to thrive in the Renaissance period."

    —From "A Trio of Exemplars of Medieval Islamic Medicine: Al-Razi, Avicenna and Ibn Al-Nafis," Ritu Lakhtakia

19. Documents A and B both stress the need to
    A. understand the causes of diseases.
    B. understand the symptoms of diseases.
    C. find effective treatments for diseases.
    D. relieve the symptoms of diseases.

20. What Document C tells us about Muslim medical knowledge is that
    A. Muslim doctors had the ability to draw accurate diagrams.
    B. Muslim doctors drew diagrams that were not very accurate.
    C. Muslim doctors aimed for a detailed knowledge of the body's structure.
    D. Muslim doctors were better than modern doctors at treating the eye.

21. With which statement about Muslim medical knowledge would the author of Document D most agree?
    A. It was based on both prior learning and first-hand study.
    B. It was based on strict adherence to Sharia law.
    C. It had little influence outside the Muslim world.
    D. It was less advanced than that of India or Europe.

22. Writing Task Describe the way that Muslim physicians approached the study and treatment of disease. Use specific evidence from the documents above, along with information from this Topic, to support your answer.

GO ONLINE to access more practice

Civilizations of Asia (500–1650)

ESSENTIAL QUESTION What distinguishes one culture from another?

GO ONLINE for immersive experiences designed to bring China's Tang and Song dynasties to life through rich primary sources. Also access the eText, videos, Biographies, and other online resources.

Taj Mahal, India

Connections to Today

In our highly connected world, elements of culture—music, art, movies, food—can travel around the globe faster than ever before. In this topic, you'll learn about Asian civilizations between the years 500 and 1500. You'll also read about how their art, literature, science, technology, religious beliefs, and languages have spread. How do similar elements of culture spread from place to place today?

NBC LEARN

Learn about the life of Genghis Khan.

BOUNCE to Activate My Story Video

Topic 9 Overview

In this Topic, you will learn about the civilizations of Asia. Look at the lesson outline and explore the timeline. As you study this Topic, you will complete the Quest Inquiry.

LESSON OUTLINE

9.1 The Delhi Sultanate and Mughal India

9.2 Golden Ages in China: Tang and Song Dynasties

9.3 The Mongol Empire and Ming China

9.4 Korea and Its Traditions

9.5 The Island Kingdom of Japan

9.6 The Many Cultures of Southeast Asia

Key Events in Civilizations of Asia

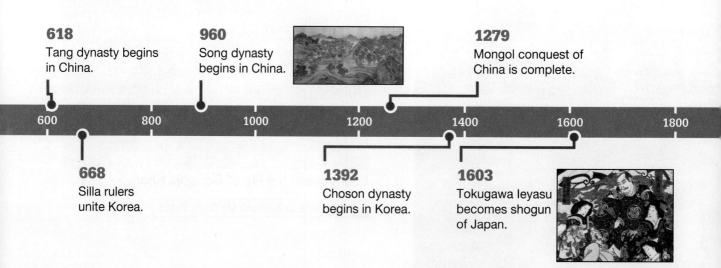

618
Tang dynasty begins in China.

960
Song dynasty begins in China.

1279
Mongol conquest of China is complete.

600   800   1000   1200   1400   1600   1800

668
Silla rulers unite Korea.

1392
Choson dynasty begins in Korea.

1603
Tokugawa Ieyasu becomes shogun of Japan.

QUEST! INQUIRY

The Historian's Round Table

Sometimes famous people are not remembered for their best accomplishments. In this Quest, you are part of a discussion group that is discussing the legacy of a famous conqueror: Genghis Khan. Consider the question: What can be learned about power and leadership from Genghis Khan?

STEP 1
Gather information about Genghis Khan. Ask questions. Make decisions based on your evidence. Choose the strongest supporting evidence.

STEP 2
Divide into two teams. One in support of Genghis Khan's legacy; the other against. Listen to the evidence for both sides. Discuss the conclusions.

STEP 3
Now switch sides. How successful is your team in supporting the opposing side? What conclusions have the teams reached? Discuss your findings.

STEP 4
Gathering evidence, evaluating it, and making decisions are important skills. People can lead in different ways. Consider some people today who lead differently.

 GO ONLINE to access complete Quest materials

9.1

Akbar's tolerance of different Indian cultures and his willingness to include them in government was one of his strengths as a ruler.

🅱 BOUNCE to Activate Flipped Video

Objectives

Describe the effects of the Delhi sultanate on India.

Explain how Muslim and Hindu civilizations interacted in India.

Describe the historical origins and central ideas of Sikhism.

Summarize the policies of Akbar that strengthened Mughal India.

Key Terms

sultan
Delhi
rajah
Sikhism
Babur
Mughal
Akbar
Nur Jahan
Shah Jahan
Taj Mahal

📶 **GO ONLINE** to access your digital course

The Delhi Sultanate and Mughal India

Invasions and migrations had long shaped the Indian subcontinent, contributing to its diverse cultures. Centuries after the rise of Islam in the Middle East, Muslim invaders conquered much of northern India. The arrival of Islam transformed the political and cultural landscape. As Muslim newcomers mingled with Indians, each civilization absorbed elements from the other.

The Delhi Sultanate

Struggles for Power After the Gupta empire fell in about 550, India again fragmented into many kingdoms of different sizes, which competed for power. Meanwhile, a rich Indian culture flourished. Hindu and Buddhist rulers spent huge sums to build and decorate magnificent temples, and to fund social services. Trade networks linked India to the Middle East, Southeast Asia, and China.

Although Muslims conquered the Indus Valley in 711, they advanced no farther into the subcontinent. After several failed attempts, around 1000, Muslim Turks and Afghans finally pushed further into other parts of India. They were fierce warriors with a tradition of conquest. Sultan Mahmud of Ghazni pillaged much of the north, but he did not settle there.

Muslim Invaders Triumph In the late 1100s, the **sultan,** or Muslim ruler, of Ghur defeated Hindu armies across the northern plain and made **Delhi** his capital. From there, his successors organized a sultanate, or land ruled by a sultan. The Delhi sultanate, which lasted from 1206 to 1526, marked the start of Muslim rule in northern India.

Why did the Muslim invaders triumph? They won on the battlefield in part because Muslim mounted archers had far greater mobility than Hindu forces, who rode slow-moving war elephants. Also, Hindu princes wasted resources battling one another instead of uniting against a common enemy. In some places, large numbers of Hindus, especially from low castes, converted to Islam.

By the time of the arrival of Islam, caste had become more rigid in parts of India than in previous eras, making social mobility more difficult for members of low castes. Some Hindus converted to Islam due to the simplicity of its message. Others did so because they sought political or economic advantage, because they were forcibly converted, or because they were fearful of the ways in which non-Muslims might be treated. Often, non-Muslims were treated as second-class citizens and forced to pay a special tax.

Changes Under the Delhi Sultanate Muslim rule brought significant changes to Indian government and society. Sultans introduced Muslim traditions of government. Many Turks, Afghans, Persians, and Arabs migrated to India to form a new Muslim ruling elite. Trade between India and Muslim lands increased. During the Mongol raids of the 1200s, many scholars and adventurers fled from Baghdad to India, bringing Persian and Greek learning. The

newcomers helped create a brilliant civilization at Delhi, where a new fusion of Indian and Persian art and architecture flourished.

Northern India Fragments The Delhi sultanate collapsed in 1398 when Mongol armies under the command of Tamerlane invaded India. He plundered the northern plain and smashed into Delhi. He targeted and killed over a hundred thousand Hindus. "Not a bird on the wing moved," reported stunned survivors.

Thousands of artisans were enslaved to build Tamerlane's capital at Samarkand. Delhi, an empty shell, slowly recovered. The sultans no longer controlled a large empire, however, and northern India again fragmented, this time into rival Hindu and Muslim states.

☑ **ANALYZE INFORMATION** How did the Delhi sultanate change Indian government and society?

The Meeting of Islam and Hinduism

At its worst, the Muslim conquest of northern India resulted in disaster for Hindus and Buddhists. The widespread destruction of Buddhist monasteries contributed to the drastic decline of Buddhism as

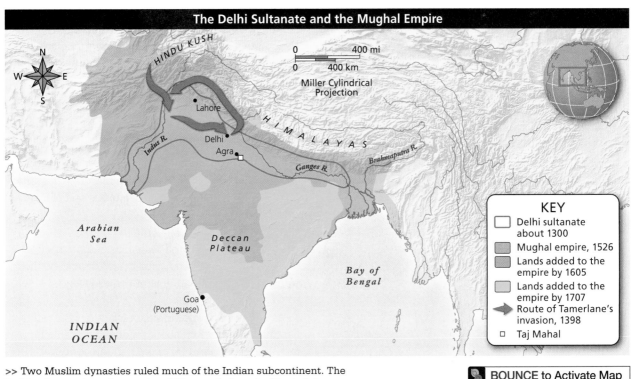

The Delhi Sultanate and the Mughal Empire

KEY
- Delhi sultanate about 1300
- Mughal empire, 1526
- Lands added to the empire by 1605
- Lands added to the empire by 1707
- Route of Tamerlane's invasion, 1398
- Taj Mahal

>> Two Muslim dynasties ruled much of the Indian subcontinent. The Delhi sultanate lasted more than 300 years before the Mughal dynasty replaced it. **Analyze Maps** Describe Tamerlane's route into India.

BOUNCE to Activate Map

>> Hindu worshipers leave offerings at a home altar for the elephant-headed God Ganesh, a form of Brahman symbolizing wisdom. Hindus revere Ganesh as the remover of obstacles. He is also known as "Lord of the People."

a major religion in India. During the most violent onslaughts, many Hindus were killed. Temples were destroyed and mosques built atop ruins. In time, though, relations became more peaceful.

Hindu-Muslim Differences The Muslim advance brought two utterly different religions and cultures face to face. Hinduism was an ancient religion that had evolved over thousands of years and offered many diverse paths to reach God. Hindus recognized many sacred texts and prayed or meditated before symbols and images representing many Gods and Goddesses. They believed these statues represented various forms of the Absolute, or God and helped them to focus prayer or meditation. Islam, by contrast, was a newer faith with a single sacred text. Muslims were devout monotheists who saw the statues and carvings in Hindu temples as an offense to their belief in one God and to the ban in Islam against worshiping images.

Hindus saw God in all humans and other beings but accepted differences in caste status and honored Brahmins as teachers and priests. Hindus celebrated religious occasions with music and dance, a practice condemned by many strict Muslims. Muslims taught the equality of all Muslims before God, but they also had a religious hierarchy. They recognized only one correct path to God.

Tolerance Grows Eventually, the Delhi sultans grew more tolerant of their Hindu subjects. Some Muslim scholars recognized that behind the many Hindu Gods and Goddesses was a single God. Hinduism was thus accepted as a monotheistic religion. This made them a protected subject group, and Hindus were allowed to practice their religion as long as they paid a special tax for non-Muslims. Some sultans even left **rajahs,** or local Hindu rulers, in place.

Cultural Sharing Indian converts to Islam kept many Hindu traditions, including marriage customs and caste. Living side by side, Hindus and Muslims developed a common life.

Hindus and Muslims came to honor each other's saints. Muslims adopted many Hindu practices, including clothing, food, music, and dance. At the same time, the Muslim custom of secluding women was adopted by Hindus.

In response to the spread of Islam, conservative Hindus strengthened some practices, especially rules around jati, or hereditary caste. In the centuries after the arrival of Islam, the Hindu caste system became more rigid. Muslims in India also became divided on the basis of caste.

>> Rajas in India often used specially trained elephants to hunt game. Muslim rulers adopted this form of hunting as well.

Finally, cultural blending led to a new language, Urdu, which added Persian and Arabic words to the Indian language spoken in Delhi. Artistic styles, too, changed as local Indian artisans applied Persian styles to Indian subjects.

☑ **EXPLAIN** How did Muslim and Hindu cultures interact?

Sikhism Emerges

In the late 1400s, a young man named Nanak founded the religion of **Sikhism** (SIK iz um) in the Punjab region of South Asia. According to Sikh beliefs, Nanak had entered a trance while swimming and was presumed drowned, but he emerged after three days and said that he had experienced a spiritual revelation. Based on his experience, Guru Nanak preached a faith recognizing one God for all humanity. He preached a powerful message proclaiming that men and women of all colors, races and religions should have equal rights and opportunities. He became known as Guru Nanak, after a word meaning spiritual guide.

Guru Nanak spent many years traveling throughout South Asia spreading the Sikh faith and way of life. During the 1500s and 1600s, his teachings and those of his successors shaped the core beliefs of Sikhism. Sikhism has grown into the world's fifth largest religion with 25 million followers.

A Message of Equality and Tolerance In the Punjabi language, the word *Sikh* (SIK) means "disciple." Sikhs consider themselves disciples of God who follow the teachings of the Ten Sikh Gurus and the guidance of the Sikh scripture, *Guru Granth Sahib*.

In addition to the belief in one God for all humanity, the basic Sikh beliefs include the equality of all people in the eyes of God, regardless of their race, gender, social class, or religion. This belief in equality and tolerance was also important in the Bhakti movement in Hinduism during the 1500s and 1600s, when Sikhism was developing and beginning to spread. At the time, strict division among social classes and inequality for women were common in India, as in other medieval societies. Guru Nanak's successors institutionalized his teachings by abolishing a discriminatory caste system among their followers, encouraging widow remarriage, and putting women in positions of authority.

Taking New Names During the early years of Sikhism in India, a person's last name often indicated

>> Portraits of Guru Nanak held places of honor in Sikh homes. This tradition continues today.

that person's social status, or caste. The tenth Sikh Guru, Gobind Singh, wanted to remove these barriers between people and promote tolerance of others. He sought to reinforce the idea of equality by giving all Sikh men the last name of Singh, which means *lion* in the Punjabi language. All women were given the last name Kaur, which means *princess*.

The "Five Ks" Some Sikhs aspire to take Amrit, which is a special initiation ceremony where individuals commit themselves to actively practicing the essential Sikh values of truthfulness, trust, loyalty, productive labor, sharing, integrity, and spirituality. Upon completing the Amrit, these Sikhs become part of the community of initiates called the Khalsa.

The Khalsa, as well as many Sikhs who have not been initiated, wear distinctive clothing that identifies them as Sikh. The clothing includes the five Sikh articles of faith, called the "Five Ks" among English-speaking Sikhs because they each begin with the English letter *k*.

The Five Ks are Kesh, which is uncut hair kept covered by a turban; the Kirpan (kir PAHN), a religious sword representing the responsibilities to fight oppression; the Kara (KUH rah), a metal bracelet; Kanga (KUN gah), a comb; and the Kachera (kuh CHEH rah), special underclothing.

As articles of faith, each object holds a deep personal and religious meaning for the Sikh wearing it. They are worn to honor the Sikh Gurus and to remind the wearer of the Sikh way of life. They also publicly proclaim the person to be a follower of Sikhism. This outward demonstration of faith has been a part of the spread of Sikhism through the centuries.

☑ **EXPLAIN** How did the Sikh beliefs challenge social norms and customs?

Mughal India

In 1526, Turkish and Mongol armies again poured through mountain passes into India. At their head rode **Babur** (BAH bur), who claimed descent from Genghis Khan and Tamerlane. Babur was a military genius, a poet, and the author of a detailed book of memoirs.

Babur Founds the Mughal Dynasty Just north of Delhi, Babur met a huge army led by the sultan Ibrahim. "I placed my foot in the stirrup of resolution and my hands on the reins of confidence in God," recalled Babur. His force was small but had cannons, which he put to good use.

>> An architectural masterpiece, the Taj Mahal is an enduring symbol of the glory of the Mughal empire and of India itself.

🔖 BOUNCE to Activate Gallery

In little time, Babur swept away the remnants of the Delhi sultanate and set up the **Mughal** dynasty, which ruled from 1526 to 1857. (*Mughal* is the Persian word for "Mongol.") Babur and his heirs conquered an empire that stretched from the Himalayas to the Deccan Plateau.

The chief builder of the Mughal empire was Babur's grandson **Akbar.** During his long reign, from 1556 to 1605, he created a strong central government and earned the title Akbar the Great.

Akbar the Great Akbar was a leader of unusual abilities. Although a Muslim, he won the support of Hindu subjects through his policy of tolerance, unlike earlier Muslim rulers. He opened government jobs to Hindus of all castes and recognized that he needed Hindu princes as his partners in order to rule the vast empire effectively. Akbar ended the special tax and other discriminatory practices toward non-Muslims, and he married a Hindu princess. As a result of these changes, Mughal art, music, food, literature, and religion incorporated Hindu features.

Akbar could not read or write, but he consulted leaders of many faiths, including Muslims, Hindus, Buddhists, and Christians. Like early Indian leaders such as Ashoka, he hoped to promote religious harmony through tolerance. By recognizing India's diversity, Akbar placed Mughal power on a firm footing.

Akbar strengthened his empire in other ways as well. To improve government, he used paid officials in place of hereditary officeholders. He modernized the army, encouraged international trade, standardized weights and measures, and introduced land reforms. While these policies increased the prosperity and harmony of his empire, Akbar also expanded his empire with sometimes brutal military force, waging wars that killed tens of thousands.

Akbar's Heirs Akbar's son Jahangir (juh HAHN geer) was a weaker ruler than his father. He left most details of government in the hands of his wife, **Nur Jahan.** Fortunately, she was an able leader whose shrewd political judgment was matched only by her love of poetry and royal sports. Nur Jahan was one of the most powerful women in Indian history until the 1900s.

The high point of Mughal literature, art, and architecture came with the reign of **Shah Jahan,** Akbar's grandson. When his wife, Mumtaz Mahal, died at age 39 after having borne 14 children, Shah Jahan was distraught. "Empire has no sweetness," he cried, "life itself has no relish left for me now."

Taj Mahal To honor his favorite wife, Shah Jahan ordered the building of a magnificent tomb, the **Taj Mahal** (TAHJ muh HAHL). Designed by a Persian architect and built mainly by Indian artisans, it has spectacular white domes and graceful minarets mirrored in clear blue reflecting pools. Verses from the Quran adorn its walls, and pleasant gardens surround the entire structure. The Taj Mahal stands as perhaps the greatest monument of the Mughal empire.

Shah Jahan planned to build a twin structure to the Taj Mahal as a tomb for himself. However, before he could do so, his son Aurangzeb usurped the throne in 1658. Shah Jahan was kept imprisoned until he died several years later.

Mughal Decline In the late 1600s, the emperor Aurangzeb rejected Akbar's tolerant policies and resumed persecution of Hindus. With this policy, the Mughals lost the support of India's majority Hindu population. Economic hardships grew worse under heavy taxes, and discontent sparked revolts.

Against this background, European traders began to gain small footholds in India. The Mughal empire survived into the 1800s, but was weakened by wars among rivals to the throne and local rulers who controlled their lands like independent kingdoms. In the end, the once-powerful empire dwindled to a small area around Delhi.

☑ **ANALYZE INFORMATION** How did the policies Akbar put in place help to strengthen his empire?

☑ ASSESSMENT

1. **Identify Cause and Effect** How did the Delhi Sultanate affect Indian government and society?

2. **Analyze Information** How did the relationship between Muslims and Hindus change over time?

3. **Analyze Information** Why might Sikhism appeal to many Indians during the 1600s?

4. **Determine Cause and Effect** How did Akbar win the support of his Hindu subjects, thus creating a more united society?

5. **Explain** What were some of Akbar's policies that resulted in a stronger government in Mughal India?

6. **Quest Connections** Compare and contrast the reigns of Akbar the Great and Aurangzeb.

9.2

⌨ **GO ONLINE to Project Imagine: Travel Through Time in Tang and Song China** for a firsthand view of key moments in the history of China's Golden Age.

▶ BOUNCE to Activate Flipped Video

Objectives

Summarize how the Tang dynasty reunified China.

Explain how the Song dynasty grew rich and powerful despite military setbacks.

Understand how China created an ordered society.

Describe the major cultural developments in the Tang and Song dynasties.

Key Terms

Tang dynasty
Tang Taizong
tributary state
land reform
Song dynasty
gentry
dowry
pagoda

Golden Ages in China: Tang and Song Dynasties

In the late 600s, Wu Zhao (woo jow) became the only woman to rule China in her own name. She proved herself to be a capable empress. Her strong rule helped guide China through one of its most brilliant periods. At a time when Europe was fragmented into many small feudal kingdoms, two powerful dynasties—the Tang and the Song—restored unity in China.

The Tang Dynasty Restores China to Glory

The Han Dynasty Collapses After the Han dynasty collapsed in 220, China broke apart and remained divided for nearly 400 years. Yet China escaped the decay that disrupted Western Europe after the fall of Rome. Farm production expanded and technology slowly improved. Buddhism spread, while learning and the arts continued to flourish. Even Chinese cities survived. Although invaders stormed into northern China, they often adopted Chinese civilization rather than demolishing it.

Meanwhile, various dynasties rose and fell in the south. During the brief Sui (sway) dynasty (589–618), the emperor Sui Wendi reunited the north and south. But China was not restored to its earlier glory until the emergence of the **Tang dynasty** in 618.

📶 **GO ONLINE to access** your digital course

Building an Empire The first Tang emperor, Li Yuan (lee yuahn), was a general under the Sui dynasty. When the Sui began to crumble, Li Yuan's ambitious 16-year-old son, Li Shimin, urged him to lead a revolt. Father and son crushed all rivals and established the Tang dynasty. Eight years later, Li Shimin compelled his aging father to step down and mounted the throne himself, taking the name **Tang Taizong** (ty dzung). A brilliant general, government reformer, historian, and master of the calligraphy brush, Tang Taizong would become China's most admired emperor.

Later Tang rulers carried empire-building to new heights, conquering territories deep into Central Asia. Chinese armies forced the neighboring lands of Vietnam, Tibet, and Korea to become **tributary states.** That is, while these states remained self-governing, their rulers had to acknowledge Chinese supremacy and send regular tribute to the Tang emperor. At the same time, students from Korea and Japan traveled to the Tang capital to learn about Chinese government, law, and arts.

Strengthening the Government and Economy
Tang rulers, such as Empress Wu Zhao, helped restore the Han system of uniform government throughout China. They rebuilt the bureaucracy and enlarged the civil service system to recruit talented officials trained in Confucian philosophy. They also set up schools to prepare male students for the exams and developed a flexible new law code.

Tang emperors instituted a system of **land reform** in which they broke up large agricultural holdings and redistributed the land to peasants. This policy strengthened the central government by weakening the power of large landowners. It also increased government revenues, since the peasants who farmed their own land would be able to pay taxes.

Decline of the Dynasty Like earlier dynasties, the Tang eventually weakened. Later Tang emperors lost territories in Central Asia to the Arabs. Corruption, high taxes, drought, famine, and rebellions all contributed to the downward swing of the dynastic cycle. In 907, a rebel general overthrew the last Tang emperor. This time, however, the chaos following the collapse of a dynasty did not last long.

☑ **ANALYZE INFORMATION** How did the Tang dynasty re-unify China?

>> Tang Taizong, the first Tang emperor, meets with his councilors at his court.

>> Bustling markets were important to the local economy. Food, tools, cloth, and other items were bought and sold at a market like this one.

![img_1]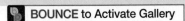

>> The invention of gunpowder made possible the cannon, such as this one with a dragon head at its mouth.

BOUNCE to Activate Gallery

>> The Song dynasty used a network of rivers and canals to improve local trade. Ships carried items from different parts of China to trading ports.

The Song Dynasty

In 960, a scholarly general named Zhao Kuangyin reunited much of China and founded the **Song** (sung) **dynasty.** The Song ruled for 319 years, slightly longer than the Tang, but they controlled less territory than the Tang. The Song also faced the constant threat of invaders in the north. In the early 1100s, the battered Song retreated south of the Huang River. There, the southern Song continued to rule for another 150 years. However, in the late 1200s Mongol invaders from the north attacked and overthrew the Song.

Song Achievements Despite military setbacks, the Song period was a time of great achievement. China's wealth and culture dominated East Asia even when its armies did not. Under the Song, the Chinese economy expanded because of improved farming methods and open border policy. The latter allowed a new type of faster-growing rice to be imported from Southeast Asia. Farmers were now able to produce two crops a year, one of rice and one of a cash crop to sell.

The rise in productivity created surpluses, allowing more people to pursue commerce, learning, or the arts. As people became more educated, they developed technology such as an improved compass, shipbuilding innovations, and gunpowder.

The Growth of Trade Under the Tang and Song, foreign trade flourished. Merchants arrived by land and seas from India, Persia, and the Middle East. The Chinese built better ships, and their merchants carried goods to Southeast Asia in exchange for spices and special woods. Tea was introduced to China from Southeast Asia, while Song porcelain has been found as far away as East Africa. To improve trade, the government issued paper money. China's cities, which had been mainly centers of government, now prospered as centers of trade. Several cities boasted populations over one million.

Trade spread ideas as well as goods. Merchants traveled in both directions along the 4,000-mile Silk Road, which linked China to India, Persia, and the Middle East. They helped spread technologies, advances in science and mathematics, religious beliefs, music, and artistic styles. Advances made in China were slowly carried westward to the Mediterranean world. At the same time, Chinese Buddhist monks headed west to India, the birthplace of Buddhism. There, they studied Indian culture.

Within China itself, the government promoted trade through a system of canals. From China's earliest history, rulers had supported the building of canals to improve transportation across large areas. The Grand Canal, completed under the Sui, linked areas in the south of China to the north. It allowed food, troops, and military supplies to reach the capital in the north. Under the Song, vast amounts of grain were shipped along the Grand Canal, spurring economic activity and the growth of cities along the route.

Advances in Science and Technology Under Tang and Song rulers, China enjoyed a golden age in science and technology. Using earlier advances, close observation, and analysis, the Chinese made breakthroughs in astronomy, agriculture, medicine, and military technology. Astronomers produced accurate star maps and calendars. Expert engineers developed irrigation and flood control projects. The human-operated water wheel was invented as well as new plows and rice-growing technologies.

By the mid-800s, the Chinese had discovered the chemistry of making explosives. At first, the new technology was used for fireworks. In time, gunpowder was put to military purposes for canons and other firearms. The Chinese pioneered the use of movable type to print books. The invention made printed books available more cheaply and spread learning, especially medical knowledge. During this time, the Chinese improved on their ancient practice of acupuncture to treat many ailments. The magnetic compass invented in China helped sailors at sea. The Chinese also developed mechanical clocks to tell exact time.

☑ **CHECK UNDERSTANDING** How was the Song dynasty able to continue its prosperity despite threats from the north?

An Ordered Society

Under the Tang and Song, China was a well-ordered society. At its head was the emperor, whose court was filled with aristocratic families. The court stood at the center of a huge bureaucracy from which officials fanned out to every province and county in China. The bureaucracy oversaw China's huge population, made up of the **gentry,** or wealthy landowners, and peasants.

The Bureaucracy Under the Tang and Song rulers, the Chinese bureaucracy, which had begun under the Han, continued to develop. Aristocratic families had less influence. Instead, officials came from the scholar-gentry, the educated landowning class.

>> Candidates take the rigorous civil service exam during the Song dynasty. Students studied for years in preparation for the exam, which usually led to an honored position as a civil servant in the bureaucracy.

The bureaucracy included a variety of government-funded departments. Some of these departments oversaw tax collecting and government revenue. Other departments were devoted to the study of disciplines such as medicine, astronomy, and mathematics.

Important mathematical texts were written during the Tang and Song dynasties that recorded existing arithmetic, algebra, and geometry knowledge and helped these ideas spread. Later mathematicians used these books as references for their own discoveries.

The Gentry China's gentry class stood at the top of Chinese society. They valued scholarship more than physical labor. Most scholar-officials at court came from this class because they alone could afford to spend years studying the Confucian ideas. Only a few lucky men passed the grueling civil service exam and won the most honored positions in government.

The Song scholar-gentry supported a revival of Confucian thought. Scholars searched out old Confucian texts and new schools of thinkers reinterpreted Confucian ideas that emphasized social order, duty, rank, and proper behavior. This Confucian revival stressed traditions of the past.

Although corruption and greed existed among the civil servants, the ideal Confucian official was a wise, kind, selfless, virtuous scholar who knew how to ensure harmony in society.

Peasants Most Chinese were peasants who worked the land, living on what they produced. Drought and famine were a constant threat, but new tools and crops did improve the lives of many peasants.

To add to their income, some families produced handicrafts such as baskets or embroidered items. They carried these products to nearby market towns to sell or trade for salt, tea, or iron tools.

Peasants lived in small, largely self-sufficient villages that managed their own affairs. "Heaven is high," noted one Chinese saying, "and the emperor far away." Peasants relied on one another rather than the government. When disputes arose, a village leader and council of elders put pressure on the parties to resolve the problem. Only if such efforts failed did villagers take their disputes to the emperor's county representative.

In China, even peasants could move up in society through education and government service. If a bright peasant boy received an education and passed the civil service examinations, both he and his family rose in status. Enslaved people in China at this time, however, did not have such opportunities. As in many other parts of the world, slavery played a role in early China, though a limited one.

Merchants: Prosperous but Lowly In market towns and cities, some merchants acquired wealth. Still, according to Confucian tradition, merchants had an even lower social status than peasants since their riches came from the labor of others. An ambitious merchant, therefore, might buy land and educate one son to enter the ranks of the scholar-gentry.

The Confucian attitude toward merchants affected economic policy. Some rulers favored commerce but sought to control it. They often restricted where foreign merchants could live and even limited the activities of private traders. Still, Chinese trade flourished during Song times.

Status of Women Women had higher status in Tang and early Song times than they did later. Within the home, women were called upon to run family affairs. A man's wife and his mother had great authority, managing servants and family finances. Still, families valued boys more than girls. When a young woman married, she became a part of her husband's family. She could not keep the **dowry,** or the payment a woman brings to a marriage. If widowed, she could never remarry.

Women's subordinate position was reinforced in late Song times when the custom of foot binding emerged. The custom probably began at the imperial court but later spread to the lower classes. The feet of young girls were bound with long strips of cloth, producing a lily-shaped foot about half the size of a foot that was allowed to grow normally. Tiny feet and a stilted walk became a symbol of nobility and beauty. Foot binding was extremely painful, yet the custom survived. Even peasant parents feared that they could not find a husband for a daughter with large feet.

Not all girls in China had their feet bound. Peasants who needed their daughters to work in the fields did not accept the practice. Yet most women did have to submit to foot binding. Women with bound feet often could not walk without help. Thus, foot binding reinforced the Confucian tradition that women should remain inside the home.

☑ **CHECK UNDERSTANDING** How did the Confucian attitude towards merchants affect some Chinese economic policies?

>> Despite the importance of trade, merchants had low social status in Chinese society. This was a result of the influence of Confucianism in Chinese life.

>> Homes of the nobility and wealthy were often designed along the lines of Buddhist temples. The homes included lovely courtyards and gardens, as well as guest rooms and banquet halls.

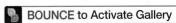
BOUNCE to Activate Gallery

The Rich Culture of Tang and Song China

A prosperous economy supported the rich culture of Tang and Song China. Writers produced brilliant works of poetry and prose, while the works of artists survived the centuries.

Seeking Balance and Harmony in Nature Along with poetry, painting and calligraphy were essential skills for the scholar-gentry. In both of these arts, they sought balance and harmony through the mastery of simple strokes and lines. The Song period saw the triumph of Chinese landscape painting. Steeped in the Daoist tradition, painters sought to capture the spiritual essence of the natural world. "When you are planning to paint," instructed a Song artist, "you must always create a harmonious relationship between heaven and earth."

Misty mountains and delicate bamboo forests dominated Chinese landscapes. Yet Chinese painters also produced realistic, vivid portraits of emperors or lively scenes of city life.

Sculpture and Architecture Buddhist themes dominated sculpture and influenced Chinese architecture. Chinese sculptors created striking statues of the Buddha. These statues created such a strong impression that many people today picture the Buddha as a Chinese god rather than an Indian holy man.

In China, the Indian stupa evolved into the graceful Chinese **pagoda,** a multistoried temple with eaves that curve up at the corners. Although the splendid royal palaces of Chinese emperors were long ago destroyed, statues and pagodas survived.

Porcelain The Chinese perfected techniques in making porcelain, a shiny, hard pottery that was prized as the finest in the world. They developed beautiful glazes to decorate vases, tea services, and other objects that Westerners would later call "chinaware."

Artists also produced porcelain figures of camels, elegant court ladies playing polo, and bearded foreigners newly arrived from their travels on the Silk Road.

Chinese Literature Prose and poetry flowed from the brushes of Tang and Song writers. Scholars produced works on philosophy, religion, and history. Short stories that often blended fantasy, romance, and adventure made their first appearance in Chinese literature. Among the gentry, poetry was the most respected form of Chinese literature. Confucian scholars were expected to master the skills of poetry. We know the names of some 200 major and 400 minor Tang and Song poets. Their works touched on Buddhist and Taoist themes as well as on social issues. Many poems reflected on the shortness of life and the immensity of the universe.

Probably the greatest Tang poet was Li Bo (lee boh). A zestful lover of life and freedom, he moved about from one place to another for most of his life.

He wrote some 2,000 poems celebrating harmony with nature or lamenting the passage of time. A popular legend says that Li Bo drowned when he tried to embrace the reflection of the moon in a lake.

> You ask me why I dwell in the green mountain; I smile and make no reply for my heart is free of care. As the peach-blossom flows down stream and is gone into the unknown, I have a world apart that is not among men.

—From "Green Mountain" by Li Bo

More realistic and less romantic were the poems of Li Bo's friend Du Fu. His verses described the horrors of war or condemned the lavishness of the court. A later poet, Li Qingzhao (lee ching jow), described the experience of women left behind when loved ones went off to war. Her poems reflect a time when invasion threatened to bring the brilliant Song dynasty to an end.

☑ **SUMMARIZE** What themes did Tang and Song arts address?

☑ ASSESSMENT

1. **Draw Conclusions** In what ways did the rise of the Tang dynasty unify and benefit China?

2. **Determine Relevance** What was the significance of the Grand Canal to the Song dynasty?

3. **Describe** Describe the social structure of China under the Tang and Song dynasties.

4. **Recognize Ideologies** How did the social structure of the Tang and Song dynasties reflect Confucian traditions?

5. **Analyze Information** What ideas and traditions were reflected in Chinese paintings?

6. **Connections to Today** During the Tang and Song dynasties, foreign trade led to the spread of ideas. How does economic activity today encourage the spread of culture?

Du Fu, "Song of Pengya," translated by Burton Watson

During the Tang Dynasty, which ruled China between 618 and 907, a series of wars affected the empire. The An Lushan Rebellion, which began in 755, was the greatest of these upheavals. Led by a Tang general, the revolt ended the reign of Emperor Xuanzong and weakened the dynasty itself.

The poem below describes the horrors experienced by those forced to flee the Tang capital city of Chang'an during the rebellion. It was written by Du Fu (712–770), a Tang poet often considered to be one of the greatest poets in China's history, who was influenced by his own experiences during the period. His works— over one thousand of which have survived— describe daily life, government actions, military tactics, the arts, and other aspects of Tang China.

>> This painting from the Tang Dynasty shows Emperor Xuanzong fleeing from Chang'an during the rebellion.

Primary Source

I remember when we first fled the rebels,
hurrying north over dangerous trails;
night deepened on Pengya Road,
the moon shone over White-water Hills.
A whole family endlessly trudging,
begging without shame from the people we met:
valley birds sang, a jangle of soft voices;
we didn't see a single traveler returning.
The baby girl in her hunger bit me;
fearful that tigers or wolves would hear her cries,
I hugged her to my chest, muffling her mouth,
but she squirmed and wailed louder than before
The little boy pretended he knew what
was happening;
importantly he searched for sour plums to eat.

☑ **DESCRIBE** What are the children doing? How are they reacting to the events the narrator describes?

Ten days, half in rain and thunder,
through mud and slime we pulled each other on.
There was no escaping from the rain,
trails slick, clothes wet and clammy;
getting past the hardest places,
a whole day advanced us no more than three or four li.

☑ **DRAW INFERENCES** A *li* is a Chinese measurement for 500 meters, or about 1,600 feet. How does this support the author's description of the challenges of the journey?

Mountain fruits served for rations,
low-hung branches were our rafter and roof.
Mornings we traveled by rock-bedded streams,
evenings camped in mists that closed in the sky.
We stopped a little while at the marsh of Tongjia,
thinking to go out by Luzi Pass;
an old friend there, Sun Zai,

ideals higher than the piled-up clouds;
he came out to meet us as dusk turned to darkness,
called for torches, opening gate after gate,
heated water to wash our feet,
cut strips of paper to call back our souls.

☑ **USE CONTEXT CLUES** "Cut strips of paper to call back our souls" refers to a ritual done to restore a person's soul, reflecting the belief that when a person is frightened their soul leaves their body. What does this phrase suggest about the travelers' experience?

Then his wife and children came;
seeing us, their tears fell in streams.
My little chicks had gone sound to sleep;
he called them to wake up and eat from his plate,
said he would make a vow with me,
the two of us to be brothers forever.
At last he cleared the room where we sat,
wished us goodnight, all he had at our command.
Who is willing, in the hard, bleak times,
to break open, lay bare his innermost heart?
Parting from you, a year of months has rounded,
Tartar tribes still plotting evil,
and I think how it would be to have strong wings
that would carry me away, set me down before you.

☑ **SUMMARIZE** How does the author describe the importance of friends and family in this poem?

☑ ASSESSMENT

1. **Analyze Style and Rhetoric** How does the author use metaphor and vivid description in the poem?

2. **Cite Evidence** What can you learn about the experiences of everyday people during Tang wars from this poem?

3. **Draw Conclusions** Why does the author dream of having "strong wings"?

4. **Determine Central Ideas** What would you identify as the main point of this poem?

9.3

Mongol archers on horseback, as shown in this Ming illustration, were tough warriors who could swiftly shoot arrows at enemies from all sides.

The Mongol Empire and Ming China

In the early 1200s, a new wave of invaders swept into China from the north and overran Song lands. The invaders were the Mongols, who had burst out of Central Asia to conquer a vast empire across Asia and Europe.

Mongols Build an Empire

The Mongols were a nomadic herding people who grazed their horses and sheep on the **steppes,** or vast, treeless plains, of Central Asia. Rival Mongol clans spent much of their time warring with one another. In the early 1200s, however, a brilliant Mongol chieftain united these warring tribes. This chieftain took the name **Genghis Khan,** meaning "Universal Ruler." Under his leadership, Mongol forces conquered a vast empire that stretched from the Pacific Ocean to Eastern Europe.

Mongols Conquer China Genghis Khan imposed strict military discipline and demanded absolute loyalty. His highly trained, mobile armies had some of the most skilled horsemen in the world. Genghis Khan had a reputation for fierceness. He could order the massacre of an entire city. Yet he also could be generous, rewarding the bravery of a single fighter.

Mongol armies conquered the Asian steppe lands with some ease, but as they turned on China, they encountered the problem of attacking walled cities. Chinese and Turkish military experts taught them to use cannons and other new weapons. The Mongols and Chinese launched missiles against each other from metal tubes filled with gunpowder. This use of cannons in warfare would soon spread westward to Europe.

BOUNCE to Activate Flipped Video

Objectives

Summarize how Mongol armies built an empire.

Describe China under Mongol rule.

Understand how the Ming restored Chinese rule.

Explain why the Ming explored the seas for only a brief period.

Key Terms

steppe
Genghis Khan
Kublai Khan
Yuan dynasty
Marco Polo
Ming dynasty
abacus
Zheng He

GO ONLINE to access your digital course

Genghis Khan did not live to complete the conquest of China. His heirs, however, continued to expand the Mongol empire. For the next 150 years, they dominated much of Asia. Their furious assaults toppled empires and spread destruction from southern Russia through Muslim lands in Southwest Asia to China. In China, the Mongols devastated the flourishing province of Sichuan (sih chwahn), and annihilated its great capital city of Chengdu.

Impact of Mongol Rule Once conquest was completed, the Mongols were not oppressive rulers. Often, they allowed conquered people to live much as they had before—as long as they regularly paid tribute to the Mongols.

Genghis Khan had set an example for his successors by ruling conquered lands with toleration and justice. Although the Mongol warrior had no use for city life, he respected scholars, artists, and artisans. He listened to the ideas of Confucians, Buddhists, Christians, Muslims, Jews, and Zoroastrians.

The Mongol Peace In the 1200s and 1300s, the sons and grandsons of Genghis Khan established peace and order within their domains. Today, many historians refer to this period of order as the *Pax Mongolica,* or Mongol Peace.

Political stability set the stage for economic growth. Under the protection of the Mongols, who now controlled the great Silk Road, trade flourished across Eurasia.

According to a contemporary, Mongol rule meant that people "enjoyed such a peace that a man might have journeyed from the land of sunrise to the land of sunset with a golden platter upon his head without suffering the least violence from anyone."

Cultural exchanges increased as foods, tools, inventions, and ideas spread along the protected trade routes. From China, the use of gunpowder moved westward into Europe. Techniques of papermaking also reached parts of Europe, and crops and trees from the Middle East were carried into East Asia.

☑ **DESCRIBE** How did the Mongol rulers change once their conquests were complete?

Mongols Rule China

Although Genghis Khan had subdued northern China, the Mongols needed nearly 70 more years to conquer the south. Genghis Khan's grandson, **Kublai Khan** (KOO bly KAHN), finally toppled the last Song emperor in 1279. From his capital at Khanbaliq, present-day Beijing, Kublai Khan ruled all of China as well as Korea, Tibet, and Vietnam.

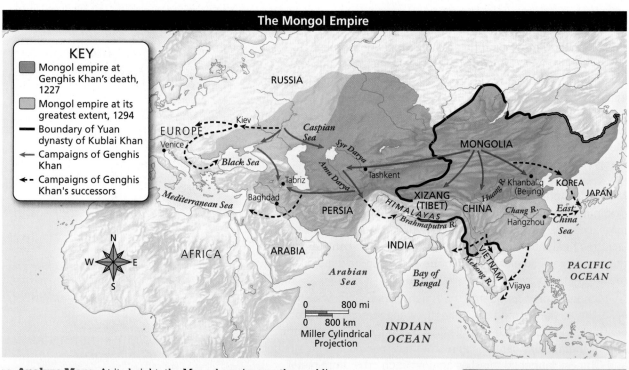

The Mongol Empire

KEY
- Mongol empire at Genghis Khan's death, 1227
- Mongol empire at its greatest extent, 1294
- Boundary of Yuan dynasty of Kublai Khan
- Campaigns of Genghis Khan
- Campaigns of Genghis Khan's successors

>> **Analyze Maps** At its height, the Mongol empire was the world's largest up to that time. Describe the growth of the empire between 1227 and 1294. Did Genghis Khan or his successors conquer the most land?

🔲 BOUNCE to Activate Map

Government Kublai Khan tried to prevent the Mongols from being absorbed into Chinese civilization as other conquerors of China had been. He decreed that only Mongols could serve in the military. He also reserved the highest government jobs for Mongols or for other non-Chinese officials whom he employed. Still, because there were too few Mongols to control so vast an empire, Kublai allowed Chinese officials to continue to rule in the provinces.

Under Mongol rule, an uneasy mix of Chinese and foreign customs developed. Kublai adopted a Chinese name for his dynasty, the **Yuan** (yuahn), and turned Khanbaliq into a Chinese walled city. At the same time, he had Arab architects design his palace, and many rooms reflected Mongol steppe dwellings. Kublai rebuilt and extended the Grand Canal to his new capital, which made the shipment of rice and other goods easier. He also welcomed many foreigners to his court.

As long as the Mongol empire prospered, contacts between Europe and Asia continued. The Mongols tolerated a variety of beliefs. The pope sent Christian priests to Beijing, while Muslims set up their own communities in China. Meanwhile, some Chinese products moved toward Europe. They included gunpowder, porcelain, and playing cards.

Marco Polo Describes China The Italian merchant **Marco Polo** was one of many visitors to China during the Yuan dynasty. Although there is some debate on whether Marco Polo reached China, most historians acknowledge that he did indeed reach Cathay (northern China). In 1271, Polo left Venice with his father and uncle. He crossed Persia and Central Asia to reach China. He then spent 17 years in Kublai's service. Finally, he returned to Venice by sea, visiting Southeast Asia and India along the way.

In his writings, Marco Polo left a vivid account of the wealth and splendor of China. He described the royal palace of Kublai Khan and also described China's efficient royal mail system, with couriers riding swift ponies along the empire's well-kept roads. Furthermore, he reported that the city of Hangzhou was 10 or 12 times the size of Venice, one of Italy's richest city-states. In the next centuries, Polo's reports sparked European interest in the riches of Asia.

☑ **DESCRIBE** How did Kublai Khan organize Mongol rule in China?

>> Marco Polo is welcomed at the court of Kublai Khan during the 1200s, as depicted in this hand-colored European illustration from the 1800s.

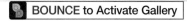 BOUNCE to Activate Gallery

>> Kublai Khan, the emperor of China, is portrayed as he was in the 1260s, an alert, vigorous, simply attired man. He wears the symbolic white robes of a Mongol shaman.

Chinese Rule Restored by the Ming

The Yuan dynasty declined after the death of Kublai Khan, which occurred in 1294. Most Chinese despised the foreign Mongol rulers. Confucian scholars retreated into their own world, seeing little to gain from the barbarians. Heavy taxes, corruption, and natural disasters led to frequent uprisings. Finally, Zhu Yuanzhang (dzoo yuahn jahng), a peasant leader, forged a rebel army that toppled the Mongols and pushed them back beyond the Great Wall. In 1368, he founded a new Chinese dynasty, which he called the **Ming,** meaning "brilliant."

Ming Policies Early Ming rulers sought to reassert Chinese greatness after years of foreign rule. They initially moved the capital to Nanjing, which they felt possessed more characteristics of the Chinese, but eventually moved it back to present-day Beijing. The Ming restored the civil service system, and Confucian learning again became the road to success. The civil service exams became more rigorous than ever. A board of censors watched over the bureaucracy, eliminating corruption and disloyalty.

Economic Revival Economically, Ming China was very productive. The fertile, well-irrigated plains of eastern China supported a population of more than 100 million. In the Chang River valley, peasants produced huge rice crops. Better methods of fertilizing helped to improve farming. Reshaping the landscape helped as well. Some farmers cut horizontal steps called terraces into steep hillsides to gain soil in which to grow crops. In the 1500s, new crops reached China from the Americas, especially corn and sweet potatoes.

Chinese cities, such as Nanjing, were home to many industries, including porcelain, paper, and tools. The Ming repaired the extensive canal system that linked various regions, made trade easier, and allowed cities to grow. New technologies increased output in manufacturing. Better methods of printing, for example, led to the production of a flood of books.

During this period, the Ming also carefully limited the extent and duration of trade with Europeans. Over time, one Chinese trade practice significantly impacted global trade. By accepting only silver or gold in exchange for goods in high demand in Europe, such as silk, tea, and porcelain, the Ming caused a massive flow of precious metals into China. First, China traded silk and tea for silver from Japan. Then, in the 1500s, vast quantities of silver from Spain's new territories in the Americas were shipped

>> Zhu Yuanzhang ousted the Mongols and led China as the Hongwu emperor, shown here, for 30 years. He founded the Ming dynasty, which ruled China for almost 300 years.

>> Asian and European markets greatly valued Ming porcelain, such as this dragon-figured vase. Such global trade helped fuel the flourishing Ming economy.

[ ] BOUNCE to Activate 3D Model

across the Pacific to the Philippines (claimed by Spain in 1565) to purchase Chinese goods.

Flourishing Culture Ming China also saw a revival of arts and literature. Ming artists developed their own styles of landscape painting and created brilliant blue and white porcelain. Ming vases were among the most valuable and popular Chinese products exported to the West.

Confucian scholars continued to produce classical poetry. At the same time, new forms of popular literature to be enjoyed by the common people began to emerge. Ming writers composed novels, including *The Water Margin* about an outlaw gang that tries to end injustice by corrupt officials. Ming writers also produced the world's first detective stories.

Ming Math, Science, and Technology In the late fifteenth century, China was the richest civilization in the world, possessing science and technology far beyond that of Europe. Gunpowder, papermaking, the magnetic compass, horse collars, cast iron, textile machinery, and many other technologies originated and were used in China long before spreading elsewhere.

In mathematics, after the brilliant Song and Yuan achievements in theory, research turned more to popular and practical application. Many earlier achievements were lost or forgotten. Taking the place of traditional Chinese counting rods for calculations, the **abacus,** invented much earlier, spread rapidly within and beyond China. The spread of the abacus is an example historians have identified of the diffusion of ideas about mathematics that occurred in China from the Tang to the Ming dynasties. To explain arithmetic on the abacus, Cheng Dawei wrote the *Suanfa tongzong* ("Systematic Treatise on Mathematics," 1592) and included his summary of contemporary mathematical knowledge.

Ming scholars at this time sought to integrate their own traditions with the Western mathematics and science they were learning from Jesuit missionaries. Knowing that the Chinese calendar had become increasingly inaccurate, the scholar Xu Guangqi thought of a way to repair it. In 1629, the emperor approved his plan to reform the Chinese calendar by employing Western astronomy and technology—including telescopes—to gather information about the heavenly bodies.

Xu Guangqi led the imperial research program. Telescopes and other instruments were constructed, allowing Chinese scholars, helped by Jesuit priests, to make observations, translate manuscripts, and

>> This illustration from an 1825 French book shows a Chinese merchant calculating with an abacus, or *suan pan* ("calculating plate").

>> Yang Lin, martial artist, one of 108 outlaw heroes of *The Water Margin,* strides through strong winds holding a barbed hooked pole in this Japanese print. His nickname: "Multicolored Leopard."

produce star atlases and a catalog. By using the new data and tools, movements of the sun, moon, and planets could be more accurately predicted and the calendar could be corrected.

☑ **IDENTIFY** How did Ming rulers restore an earlier style of Chinese government?

Chinese Fleets Explore the Seas

Early Ming rulers sent Chinese fleets into distant waters. The most extraordinary of these ventures were the voyages of the Chinese admiral and diplomat **Zheng He** (jung huh).

The Great Fleets of Zheng He Between 1405 and 1433, Zheng He made seven expeditions at the head of large fleets. His goal was to promote trade and collect tribute from lesser powers across the "western seas." He departed at the head of a fleet of 62 huge ships and over 200 smaller ones, carrying a crew of about 28,000 sailors. The largest ships measured 400 feet long.

Between 1405 and 1433, Zheng He explored the coasts of Southeast Asia and India and the entrances to the Red Sea and the Persian Gulf. He also visited many ports in East Africa.

In the wake of these expeditions, Chinese merchants settled in Southeast Asia and India and became a permanent presence in their trading centers. Exotic animals, such as giraffes, were imported from foreign lands as well. The voyages also showed local rulers the power and strength of the Chinese empire.

Zheng He set up an engraved stone tablet listing the dates, places, and achievements of his voyages. The tablet proudly proclaimed that the Ming had unified the "seas and continents" even more than the Han and Tang had done.

"The countries beyond the horizon and from the ends of the earth have all become subjects. . . . We have traversed immense waterspaces and have beheld in the ocean huge waves like mountains rising sky high, and we have set eyes on barbarian regions far away . . . while our sails loftily unfurled like clouds day and night continued their course, traversing those savage waves as if we were treading on a public throughfare."

—Zeng He, quoted in *The True Dates of the Chinese Maritime Expeditions in the Early Fifteenth Century* (Duyvendak)

The Ming Turn Inward In 1435, the Ming emperor suddenly banned the building of giant seagoing ships like the ones Zheng He had commanded.

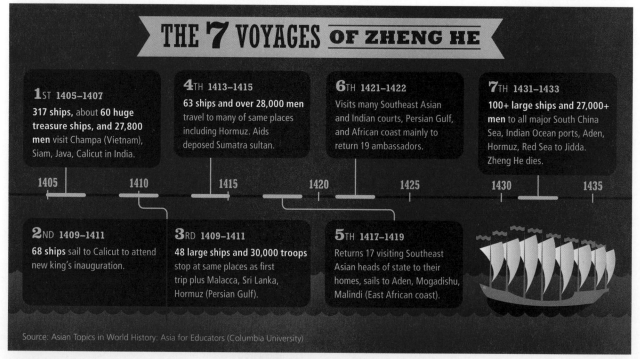

THE 7 VOYAGES OF ZHENG HE

1ST 1405–1407
317 ships, about 60 huge treasure ships, and 27,800 men visit Champa (Vietnam), Siam, Java, Calicut in India.

4TH 1413–1415
63 ships and over 28,000 men travel to many of same places including Hormuz. Aids deposed Sumatra sultan.

6TH 1421–1422
Visits many Southeast Asian and Indian courts, Persian Gulf, and African coast mainly to return 19 ambassadors.

7TH 1431–1433
100+ large ships and 27,000+ men to all major South China Sea, Indian Ocean ports, Aden, Hormuz, Red Sea to Jidda. Zheng He dies.

1405   1410   1415   1420   1425   1430   1435

2ND 1409–1411
68 ships sail to Calicut to attend new king's inauguration.

3RD 1409–1411
48 large ships and 30,000 troops stop at same places as first trip plus Malacca, Sri Lanka, Hormuz (Persian Gulf).

5TH 1417–1419
Returns 17 visiting Southeast Asian heads of state to their homes, sails to Aden, Mogadishu, Malindi (East African coast).

Source: Asian Topics in World History: Asia for Educators (Columbia University)

>> Zheng He's epic voyages were multipurpose expeditions of exploration, diplomacy, and trade to Southeast Asia, India, and Africa. **Analyze Data** Which voyage had the largest number of ships?

In time, ships with more than two masts were forbidden. In the 1500s, when Europeans first reached China by sea, the Ming carefully limited the extent and duration of trade. They did, however, demand silver or gold in exchange for Chinese products that Europeans wanted, such as silk, tea, and porcelain. This policy led to a flood of silver and gold into China.

Why did China, with its advanced naval technology, turn its back on overseas exploration? The fleets were costly and did not produce any profits. Also Confucian scholars at court had little interest in overseas ventures. To them, Chinese civilization was the most successful in the world. They wanted to preserve its ancient traditions, which they saw as the source of stability.

Eventually, this rigid loyalty to tradition would weaken China. Less than 60 years after China halted overseas expeditions, the explorer Christopher Columbus would sail west from Spain to find a sea route to Asia.

☑ **IDENTIFY** What occurred in 1435 that changed China's relationship with the rest of the world?

☑ ASSESSMENT

1. **Summarize** Summarize how Mongol armies built an empire.

2. **Describe** Describe China under Mongol rule.

3. **Draw Conclusions** How did the Ming restore Chinese rule?

4. **Identify Cause and Effect** How did Ming China impact global trade?

5. **Explain** Why did the Ming explore the seas for only a brief period?

6. **Connections to Today** Cultural exchanges led to the spread of inventions such as gunpowder and papermaking techniques. How do inventions and technological innovations spread today?

9.4

During the Silla dynasty, Buddhism expanded in Korea and stunning temples, such as the Pulguksa Temple shown here, were built. It is considered the most famous Buddhist temple in Korea.

 BOUNCE to Activate Flipped Video

Objectives

Describe how geography affected life on the Korean peninsula.

Understand the influence of China and Buddhism on Korea.

Explain the major achievements of the Choson dynasty.

Key Terms

Silla dynasty
Koryo dynasty
celadon
Choson dynasty
King Sejong
hangul
literacy rate

Korea and Its Traditions

As early as Han times, China expanded its influence to a ring of states and peoples on the border of the Middle Kingdom. To the northeast, Korea lay within the Chinese zone of influence. While Korea absorbed many Chinese traditions over the centuries, it also maintained its own identity.

The Geography of Korea

The Korean Peninsula Korea is located on a peninsula that juts south from the Asian mainland and points toward Japan. At the northern end of the peninsula, mountains and the Yalu River separate Korea from China.

An early visitor once compared Korea's landscape to "a sea in a heavy gale." Low but steep mountains cover nearly 70 percent of the Korean peninsula.

The most important range is the T'aebaek (ta bak). It runs from north to south along the eastern coast, with smaller chains branching off to form hilly areas. Because farming is difficult on the mountains, most people live along the western coastal plains, Korea's major farming region.

Korea has a 5,400-mile coastline with hundreds of good harbors. In addition, the offshore waters feature thousands of islands. Since early times, Koreans have depended upon seafood for most of the protein in their diet. Today, South Korea has one of the largest fishing industries in the world.

The Impact of Location Korea's location on China's eastern border has played a key role in its development. From its powerful

GO ONLINE to access your digital course

mainland neighbor, Korea received many cultural and technological influences. At various times in history, China extended political control over the Korean peninsula. Korea has also served as a cultural bridge linking China and Japan. Koreans have, from early times, adapted and transformed Chinese traditions before passing them on to the Japanese.

The earliest Koreans probably migrated southeastward from Siberia and northern Manchuria during the Stone Age. They spoke a language unrelated to Chinese and evolved their own ways of life long before any Chinese influences reached the peninsula.

About 108 B.C., the Han emperor, Wudi, conquered the northern part of the peninsula and set up a military colony there. For almost 400 years, the Han administered the area around what is today Pyongyang. From this outpost, Confucian traditions and Chinese ideas about government, as well as Chinese writing and farming methods, spread into Korea.

☑ **EXPLAIN** How did the relative location of the Korean peninsula influence the development of Korean civilization?

The Silla and Koryo Dynasties Develop

Between 100 B.C. and A.D. 676, powerful local rulers forged three separate kingdoms: Koguryo in the north, Paekche in the southwest, and Silla in the southeast. Although they were similar in language and cultural background, the three kingdoms often warred with one another or with China.

Chinese Influences Still, Chinese influences continued to arrive. Missionaries spread Mahayana Buddhism, which took root among the rulers and nobles. Korean monks then traveled to China and India to learn more about Buddhism. They brought home the arts and learning of China. A Korean writer of the time explained the benefits that he believed Buddhism could bring to his country:

"If you teach people to rely on this teaching [Buddhism] and practice it, then their minds can be corrected, and their bodies can be cultivated. You can regulate your family, you can

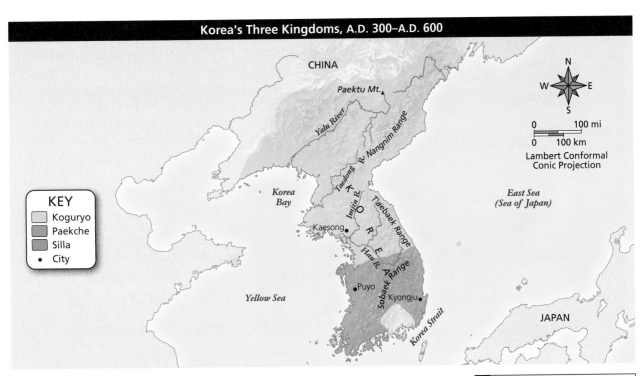

Korea's Three Kingdoms, A.D. 300–A.D. 600

KEY
- Koguryo
- Paekche
- Silla
- • City

>> The three early kingdoms of Korea shared an ethnic background and cultural similarities, although they were frequently at war with each other. **Analyze Maps** Which of these kingdoms was probably most influenced by Chinese civilization? Why?

BOUNCE to Activate Map

govern the state, and you can bring peace to the world."

—Gihwa, *The Exposition of the Correct*

The Silla Unite Korea By 688, backed by the Tang ruler Wu Zhao, the Silla kingdom had defeated Paekche and Koguryo and united Korea. From this time until 1910, Korea had only three dynasties. The **Silla dynasty** ruled a unified Korea from 668 to 935, the Koryo from 935 to 1392, and the Choson from 1392 to 1910. During much of its history, Korea was a tributary state, acknowledging Chinese power but preserving its independence.

Under Silla rule, Korea prospered and the arts flourished. Koreans made advances in medicine, astronomy, metal casting, and textile manufacturing.

Chinese influences remained strong, and Koreans adopted many features of Confucian China. Korean culture reflected the Confucian emphasis on the family as the foundation of the state. Women's public roles were restricted, and their position within the family became subordinate to the male head of the household.

The Silla built a capital city, Kyongju, modeled on the Tang capital. Buddhist influence grew and spread,

>> Celadon is created with a slip, or wash of liquid clay, that contains iron and is applied before glazing. When the pottery is fired at a high temperature, the iron colors the surface.

BOUNCE to Activate Chart

and the Silla supported the building of Buddhist temples. A brisk trade encouraged links between Korea and China. Koreans used Chinese written characters and studied Chinese ideas about government.

Koreans Adapt Chinese Influences At the same time, Koreans adapted and modified Chinese ideas. For example, the Silla set up a Confucian academy to train young men to become high officials. They even adapted the Chinese civil service examination, but the Korean civil service system reflected their own system of inherited ranks. In China, even a peasant could win political influence by passing the exam. In Korea, where rank was important, only aristocrats were permitted to take the test.

The Koryo Dynasty After a century of conflicts disrupted Silla rule, a rebel general finally seized power and set up the **Koryo dynasty** in 935. The English word "Korea" comes from the name of this dynasty.

During the Koryo age, Buddhism reached its greatest influence in Korea, while Korea developed more on its own than it had under the Silla. Confucian traditions remained strong, however. Koreans wrote histories and poems based on Chinese models, while artists created landscape paintings that reflected Chinese principles about harmony and balance.

Koreans used woodblock printing they had learned from China to produce a flood of Buddhist texts. In time, Korean investors took the Chinese invention one step further and created movable metal type, which allowed them to print large numbers of books.

Koreans also improved on other Chinese inventions. They learned to make porcelain from China, and then perfected the technique for making **celadon**, or porcelain with an unusual blue-green glaze. Korean celadon vases and jars were prized throughout Asia. In the 1200s, when the Mongols overran Korea and destroyed many industries, the secret of making celadon was lost forever.

☑ **SUMMARIZE** Summarize two technological achievements of the Koryo dynasty and explain how they showed Korea's cultural influences.

The Choson Dynasty

The Mongols invaded Korea between 1231 and the 1250s. In 1258, the Koryo made peace with the Mongols, but a lack of tax income weakened the kingdom. In 1392, the brilliant Korean general Yi Song-gye (yee sung gyeh) overthrew them and set

KOREAN AND CHINESE WRITING

KOREAN

HANGUL, THE KOREAN WRITING SYSTEM, HAS

24 LETTERS **14 CONSONANTS AND 10 VOWELS.**

THE LETTERS ARE COMBINED TO FORM SYLLABLES.

— ABOUT —
70% OF KOREAN VOCABULARY COMES FROM CHINESE.

KOREAN GRAMMAR IS SIMILAR TO JAPANESE.

CHINESE

CHINESE **HANJA**, HOWEVER, HAS MORE THAN

50,000 CHARACTERS.

A PERSON NEEDS TO KNOW ABOUT **3,000** — CHARACTERS —
TO READ A NEWSPAPER.

>> Korean hangul is used for nearly all written communication in both South and North Korea today. **Analyze Data** How might the introduction of hangul affect literacy rates?

up the **Choson dynasty.** This was the last and longest-lived of Korea's three dynasties. General Yi reduced Buddhist influence and set up a government based upon Confucian principles.

The Invention of Hangul Despite Chinese influence, Korea preserved its distinct identity. In 1443, **King Sejong** decided to replace the Chinese system of writing that had never worked well for the Korean language. "The language of this land," he noted, "is different from China's." Sejong had experts develop **hangul,** the Korean phonetic alphabet that uses symbols to represent the sounds of spoken Korean.

Although Confucian scholars and Koreans of the upper classes rejected hangul at the outset, its use quickly spread. Hangul was easier for Koreans to use than the thousands of characters of written Chinese. Its use led to an extremely high **literacy rate,** or percentage of people who can read and write.

Koreans Battle Japanese Invaders In the 1590s, an ambitious Japanese ruler decided to invade China by way of Korea. Japanese armies landed and for years looted and burned across the peninsula. To stop the invaders at sea, the Korean Admiral Yi Sun-shin used metal-plated "turtle ships" to beat back the invaders at sea. These turtle-shaped ships were the world's first ironclad warships. They had great mobility and firepower and helped Koreans win sea battles.

After six years of devastating war, the Japanese armies finally withdrew from Korea. As they left, however, they carried off many Korean artisans to introduce their skills to Japan.

☑ **EXPLAIN** Why did Korea want to develop its own system of writing?

☑ ASSESSMENT

1. **Make Generalizations** Why might Korea's location be of strategic importance to other countries?

2. **Identify Main Ideas** What are two examples of how Korea adapted or modified Chinese ideas?

3. **Evaluate Data** Today, Hangul Day is a holiday in South Korea. Why do you think Koreans celebrate this holiday?

4. **Identify Bias** Reread the quotation from the fourth-century writer Gihwa. What evidence can you find that he sympathized with the rulers and the upper class?

5. **Connections to Today** How are Korea's history and culture linked to those of China and Japan?

A New Alphabet for Korea

While Korea absorbed many traditions from China over the years, it also preserved its own distinct identity. But until the 1400s, there was no Korean alphabet—instead, Koreans had to use Chinese characters to capture their language, which did not work well. In 1443, a group of Korean scholars led by King Sejong introduced a 28-character Korean alphabet known as hangul. Although Confucian scholars and Koreans of the upper classes initially rejected hangul, it spread over time. Today the alphabet is still used, with some modifications.

The following sources provide two viewpoints on hangul. The first is from a Confucian scholar who wrote to the king arguing against the alphabet, while the second is from a scholar who worked on the alphabet project.

As you read, contrast their viewpoints on the need for a Korean alphabet. Then answer the questions to compare perspectives on the alphabet.

>> The base of this statue of King Sejong in Seoul, South Korea, displays the characters from hangul.

Primary Source 1

Ch'oe Malli, *Sejong Sillok*

We humbly believe that the invention of the Korean script is a work of divine creation unparalleled in history. There are, however, some questionable issues we wish to raise for Your Majesty's consideration.

1. Ever since the founding of the dynasty, our court has pursued the policy of respecting the senior state [China] with utmost sincerity and has consistently tried to follow the Chinese system of government. As we share with China at present the same writing and the same institutions, we are startled to learn of the invention of the Korean script. . . . If this becomes known to China and anyone argues against it, it would disgrace our policy of respecting China.

☑ **SUMMARIZE** Why does the author reject the new writing system?

2. Although winds and soils vary from region to region, there has been no separate writing system for local dialects. . . . It has been said that the barbarians are transformed only by means of adopting Chinese ways; we have never heard of Chinese ways being transformed by the barbarians. . . . Now, however, our country is devising a Korean script separately in order to discard the Chinese, and thus we are willingly being reduced to the status of barbarians. . . .

3. . . . If the Korean script is widely used, the cleric officials will study it exclusively and neglect scholarly literature. . . . Perhaps they could manage their clerical affairs using the Korean script, but if

they do not know the writings of the sages, they will become ignorant and unable to distinguish right from wrong. . . . This Korean script is nothing more than a novelty. It is harmful to learning and useless to the government. No matter how one looks at it, one cannot find any good in it.

☑ **ANALYZE WORD CHOICES** Why does the author use the word *barbarian*?

Primary Source 2

Chông Inji, *Hunim chôngûm*

[C]limates and soils in the four corners of the world are different, and enunciations and material force are likewise diverse. In general, the languages of different countries have their own enunciations but lack their own letters, so they borrowed the Chinese graphs to communicate their needs. This is, however, like trying to fit a square handle into a round hole. . . .

☑ **ANALYZE STYLE AND RHETORIC** What comparisons does the author make in this passage?

Although our country's rituals, music, and literature are comparable to those of China, our speech and language are not the same as China's. . . .
. . . His Majesty, the king, created twenty-eight letters of the Correct Sounds . . . These letters embrace the principles of heaven, earth, and men as well as the mysteries of yin and yang, and there is nothing they cannot express. With these twenty-eight letters, infinite turns and changes may be explained; they are simple and yet contain all the essence; they are refined and yet easily communicable. . . . They can be used whatever and wherever the occasion may be. Even the sounds of wind, the cries of cranes, the crowing of roosters, and the barking of dogs can all be transcribed in writing. . . .

☑ **SUMMARIZE** How does the author try to convince the reader of the usefulness of hangul?

As for the making of the Correct Sounds, it is not something that has been transmitted from our ancestors but has been achieved by nature. There is nothing in the Correct Sounds that is not based on the ultimate principle; there is no bias such as one finds in the things made by men.

☑ ASSESSMENT

Be sure to cite specific evidence from the sources as you answer the following questions.

1. **Determine Author's Purpose** Why do you think the author of the first source wrote it?

2. **Explain** Why does the author of the second source claim that hangul can be used to transcribe the sounds of wind, cranes, and other natural sounds?

3. **Compare and Contrast** How does the author of the second source disagree with the claims in the first source?

4. **Paraphrase** In one or two sentences, paraphrase both sources.

5. **Summarize** Both sources refer to climates and soils being different in different parts of the world, but they draw different conclusions from this. Explain their perspectives.

☐ **GO ONLINE** to access primary sources

9.5

Prince Shotoku was an advisor to Empress Suiko. He revolutionized Japan by creating a government based on Chinese practices and Buddhist teachings.

 BOUNCE to Activate Flipped Video

Objectives

Explain how geography set Japan apart.

Understand how China influenced Japan, and describe the Heian period.

Summarize the Japanese feudal system.

Explain how the Tokugawas united Japan.

Identify how Zen Buddhism shaped culture in Japan.

Key Terms

archipelago
tsunami
Shinto
selective borrowing
kana
Murasaki Shikibu
samurai
bushido
Zen

GO ONLINE to access your digital course

The Island Kingdom of Japan

Japan is an archipelago (ahr kuh **PEL** uh goh), or chain of islands, about 100 miles off the Asian mainland and east of the Korean peninsula. Its four main islands are Hokkaido, Honshu, Kyushu, and Shikoku.

Japan's Geography

Like Korea, Japan felt the powerful influence of Chinese civilization early in its history. At the same time, the Japanese continued to maintain their own distinct culture.

A Mountainous Land Japan is about the size of Montana, but most of its land is too mountainous to farm. As a result, most people settled in narrow river valleys and along the coastal plains. A mild climate and sufficient rainfall, however, helped Japanese farmers make the most of the limited arable land. As in ancient Greece, the mountainous terrain at first was an obstacle to unity.

The Sea Sets Japan Apart The surrounding seas have both protected and isolated Japan. The country was close enough to the mainland to learn from Korea and China, but too far away for the Chinese to conquer. Japan thus had greater freedom to accept or reject Chinese influences than did other East Asian lands. At times, the Japanese sealed themselves off from foreign influences, choosing to go their own way.

The seas that helped Japan preserve its identity also served as trade routes. The Inland Sea was an especially important link among various Japanese islands. The seas also offered plentiful food resources and the Japanese developed a thriving fishing industry.

The Pacific Ring of Fire Japan lies in a Pacific region known as the Ring of Fire, which also includes the Philippines, Indonesia, New Zealand, and western North and South America. The region is subject to frequent earthquakes and volcanoes.

Violent underwater earthquakes can launch killer tidal waves, called **tsunamis,** that sweep over the land without warning, wiping out everything in their path.

Throughout their long history, the Japanese came to fear and respect the dramatic forces of nature. Today, as in the past, soaring Mount Fuji, with its snow-capped volcanic crater, is a sacred symbol of the beauty and the majesty of nature.

☑ **INTEGRATE INFORMATION** How did Japan avoid being dominated by Chinese armies and influences?

Early Japan

The people we know today as the Japanese probably migrated from the Asian mainland more than 2,000 years ago. They slowly pushed the earlier inhabitants, the Ainu, onto the northernmost island of Hokkaido.

The Yamato Clan Early Japanese society was divided into *uji*, or clans. Each *uji* had its own chief and a special god or goddess who was seen as the clan's original ancestor. Some clan leaders were women, suggesting that women enjoyed a respected position in society.

By about A.D. 500, the Yamato clan came to dominate a corner of Honshu, the largest Japanese island. For the next 1,000 years, the Yamato Plain was the heartland of Japanese government. The Yamato set up Japan's first and only dynasty. They claimed direct descent from the sun goddess, Amaterasu, and chose the rising sun as their symbol. Later Japanese emperors were revered as living gods. While this is no longer the case, the current Japanese emperor still traces his roots to the Yamato clan.

Shinto: A Religion of Nature Early Japanese clans honored kami, or superior powers that were natural or divine beings. The worship of the forces of nature became known as **Shinto,** meaning "the way of kami." Although Shinto has not evolved into an international religion like Christianity, Buddhism, or Islam, its traditions survive to the present day in Japan. Hundreds of Shinto shrines dot the Japanese countryside. Though simple in design, they are

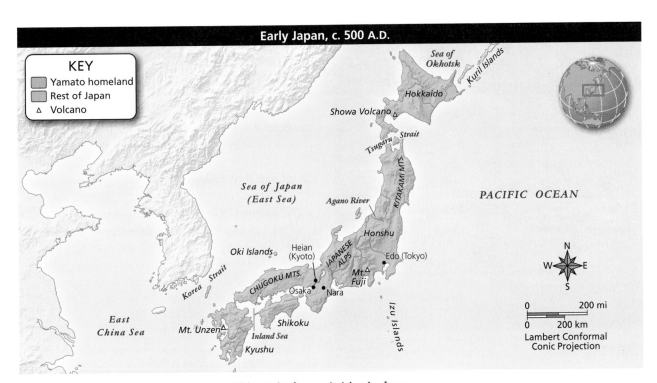

Early Japan, c. 500 A.D.

KEY
- Yamato homeland
- Rest of Japan
- △ Volcano

Sea of Okhotsk
Kuril Islands
Hokkaido
Showa Volcano △
Tsugaru Strait
KITAKAMI MTS.
Sea of Japan (East Sea)
Agano River
PACIFIC OCEAN
Honshu
Oki Islands
Heian (Kyoto)
JAPANESE ALPS
Edo (Tokyo)
CHUGOKU MTS.
Mt. Fuji △
Osaka
Nara
Korea Strait
Izu Islands
East China Sea
Mt. Unzen △
Shikoku
Inland Sea
Kyushu

N W E S

0   200 mi
0   200 km
Lambert Conformal Conic Projection

>> Japan is located on an archipelago. In addition to its four main islands, Japan includes over 3,000 smaller ones. **Analyze Maps** Explain how two geographic features might have influenced Japanese life.

generally located in beautiful, natural surroundings. Shinto shrines are dedicated to special sites or objects such as mountains or waterfalls, ancient gnarled trees, or even oddly shaped rocks.

Contact With Korea The Japanese language is distantly related to Korean but completely different from Chinese. From early on, Japan and Korea were in continuous contact with each other.

Korean artisans and metalworkers settled in Japan, bringing sophisticated skills and technology. Japanese and Korean warriors crossed the sea in both directions to attack each other's strongholds. Some of the leading families at the Yamato court claimed Korean ancestors.

By about A.D. 500, missionaries from Korea had introduced Buddhism to Japan. With it came knowledge of Chinese writing and culture that sparked a sustained period of Japanese interest in Chinese civilization.

☑ **CHECK UNDERSTANDING** What is Shinto, and how has it impacted Japan?

>> The Japanese government once cared for over 80,000 Shinto shrines. Today, however, private funds maintain these special places of worship of everyday things in nature.

Chinese Influence in Japan

In the early 600s, Prince Shotoku of the Yamato clan decided to learn about China directly instead of through Korean sources. He sent young nobles to study in China. Over the next 200 years, many Japanese students, monks, traders, and officials visited the Tang court.

Japan Imports Ideas from Tang China Each mission to China spent a year or more there—negotiating, trading, but above all studying. On their return to Japan, they were eager to spread Chinese thought, technology, and arts. They also imported Chinese ideas about government. Japanese rulers adopted the title "Heavenly Emperor" and claimed absolute power. They strengthened the central government, set up a bureaucracy, and adopted a law code similar to that of China. Still, the new bureaucracy had little real authority beyond the royal court. Out in the countryside, the old clans remained strong.

In 710, the Japanese emperor built a new capital at Nara, modeled on the Tang capital at Chang'an. There, Japanese nobles spoke Chinese and dressed in Chinese fashion. Their cooks prepared Chinese dishes and served food on Chinese-style pottery. Tea drinking, along with an elaborate tea ceremony, was imported from China. Japanese officials and scholars used Chinese characters to write official histories. Tang music and dances became very popular, as did gardens designed using Chinese influences.

As Buddhism spread, the Japanese adopted pagoda architecture. Buddhist monasteries grew rich and powerful. Confucian ideas and ethics also took root. They included an emphasis on filial piety, the careful management of relationships between superior and inferior, and respect for learning.

Selective Borrowing In time, the initial enthusiasm for everything Chinese died down. The Japanese kept some Chinese ways but discarded or modified others.

This process is known as **selective borrowing.** Japan, for example, never accepted the Chinese civil service examination to choose officials based on merit. Instead, they maintained their tradition of inherited status through family position. Officials were the educated sons of nobles.

By the 800s, as Tang China began to decline, the Japanese court turned away from its model. After absorbing all they could from China, the Japanese spent the next 400 years digesting and modifying these cultural borrowings to produce their own unique civilization. The Japanese asserted their identity by revising the Chinese system of writing and adding **kana,** or phonetic symbols representing syllables. Japanese artists developed their own styles.

☑ **GENERATE EXPLANATIONS** Why did Japanese nobles, students, monks, traders, and officials visit China?

Japanese Culture in the Heian Period

This blending of cultures of Chinese influences with Japanese culture occurred during the Heian (hay ahn) period in Japan, which lasted from 794 to 1185. During this time, the imperial capital was located in Heian, present-day Kyoto. There, emperors performed traditional religious ceremonies, while wealthy court families like the Fujiwara wielded real power. The Fujiwara married their daughters to the heirs of the throne, thus ensuring their authority.

An Elegant Court At the Heian court, an elegant and sophisticated culture blossomed. Noblewomen and noblemen lived in a fairy-tale atmosphere of beautiful pavilions, gardens, and lotus pools. Elaborate rules of etiquette governed court ceremony.

Courtiers dressed with extraordinary care in delicate, multicolored silk. Draping one's sleeve out a carriage window was a fine art.

Although men at court still studied Chinese, women were forbidden to learn the language. Despite these restrictions, it was Heian women who produced the most important works of Japanese literature of the period.

In the 900s, Sei Shonagon, a lady-in-waiting to the empress, wrote *The Pillow Book*. In a witty series of anecdotes and personal observations, she provides vivid details of court manners, amusements, decor, and dress.

Lady Murasaki Writes the World's First Novel
The best-known Heian writer was Shonagan's rival, **Murasaki Shikibu.** Her monumental work, *The Tale of Genji*, was the world's first full-length novel. Even though learning by girls was considered improper, she studied with her brother and learned how to read and write. She served as a lady-in-waiting at court, where she observed its customs.

Composed in 1010, *The Tale of Genji* recounts the adventures and loves of the fictional Prince Genji and his son. In one scene, Genji moves with ease through the festivities at an elaborate "Chinese banquet." After dinner, "under the great cherry tree of the Southern court," the entertainment begins. The main

>> During the Heian period, the wealthy aristocracy established a refined world that led to achievements in art and literature.

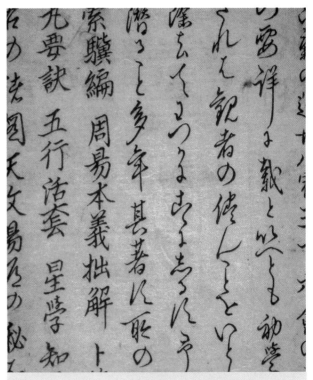

>> The adopted symbols of Chinese writing could not convey the various meanings of Japanese spoken language, so kana symbols were developed to add sounds.

event of the evening is a Chinese poetry contest. Genji and other guests are given a "rhyme word," which they must use to compose a poem in Chinese. Genji's poem is the hit of the banquet.

Heian Poetry The novel includes 800 poems about the Heian court, known as *waka*. They provide a detailed portrait of the life of the Japanese court at the time, including descriptions of members of the court creating poetry, music, and calligraphy. Lady Murasaki uses her complex tale to comment on life in the court.

The Heian romances like that of Murasaki are haunted by a sense of sadness. Writers of poems lament that love does not last, and beauty is soon gone. Perhaps this feeling of melancholy was prophetic. Outside the walls of the elegant Heian court, clouds of rebellion and civil war were gathering.

☑ **CHECK UNDERSTANDING** What was significant about the rise of Japanese literature during the Heian Period?

>> This illustration from *The Tale of Genji* shows the Heian court at leisure, a world Lady Murasaki depicted through her tale of human emotions and the beauty of nature.

Japan's Feudal Age

While the emperor presided over the splendid court at Heian, rival clans battled for control of the countryside. Local warlords and even some Buddhist temples formed armed bands loyal to them rather than to the central government. As these armies struggled for power, Japan evolved a feudal system. As in the feudal world of medieval Europe, a warrior aristocracy dominated Japanese society.

A Feudal Society Emerges In theory, the emperor stood at the head of Japanese feudal society. In fact, he was a powerless, though revered, figurehead. Real power lay in the hands of the shogun, or supreme military commander. Minamoto Yoritomo was appointed shogun in 1192. He set up the Kamakura shogunate, the first of three military dynasties that would rule Japan for almost 700 years.

Often the shogun controlled only a small part of Japan. He distributed lands to vassal lords who agreed to support him with their armies in time of need. These great warrior lords were later called daimyo (DY myoh). They, in turn, granted land to lesser warriors called **samurai,** meaning "those who serve." Samurai were the fighting aristocracy of a war-torn land.

Bushido: Way of the Warrior Like medieval Christian knights, samurai were heavily armed and trained in the skills of fighting. Over time, they developed their own code of values. Known as **bushido,** or the "way of the warrior," the code emphasized honor, bravery, and absolute loyalty to one's lord.

The true samurai had no fear of death. Samurai prepared for hardship by going hungry or walking barefoot in the snow. A samurai who betrayed the code of bushido was expected to commit seppuku (seh POO koo), or ritual suicide, rather than live without honor.

Bushido set values for the samurai and showed them how to live even when they were not fighting. It reflected ideas from Buddhism, Confucianism, and Shintoism. Bushido stressed Buddhist teachings about discipline and the importance of moderation along with Confucian emphasis on loyalty and duty.

Women in Feudal Society During the age of the samurai, the position of well-born women declined. At first, some women in feudal society trained in the military arts or supervised their family's estate. A few even became legendary warriors. As fighting increased, though, inheritance was limited to sons.

Unlike the European ideal of chivalry, the samurai code did not set women on a pedestal. The wife of a warrior had to accept the same hardships as her husband and owed the same loyalty to his overlord.

Other Classes Far below the samurai in the social hierarchy were the peasants, artisans, and merchants. Peasants, who made up 75 percent of the population, formed the backbone of feudal society in Japan. Peasant families cultivated rice and other crops on the estates of samurai. Some peasants also served as foot soldiers in feudal wars.

On rare occasions, an able peasant soldier might rise through the ranks to become a samurai himself.

Artisans, such as armorers and sword-makers, provided necessary goods for the samurai class. Merchants had the lowest rank in Japanese society, reflecting the Confucian view of them as people who were interested only in profits and who made these profits off the goods made by others. However, while peasants had a higher status, merchants often had much greater wealth.

Mongol Invaders Threaten Japan During the feudal age, most fighting took place between rival warlords, but the Mongol conquest of China and Korea also threatened Japan. When the Japanese refused to accept Mongol rule, Kublai Khan launched an invasion from Korea in 1274. A fleet carrying 30,000 troops arrived, but shortly afterwards a typhoon wrecked many Mongol ships and drove the invaders back to the mainland.

In 1281, the Mongols landed an even larger invasion force, but again a typhoon destroyed much of the Mongol fleet. The Japanese credited their miraculous delivery to the kamikaze (kah muh KAH zee), or divine winds. The Mongol failure reinforced the Japanese sense that they were a people set apart who enjoyed the special protection of the gods.

☑ **APPLY CONCEPTS** How did honor, bravery, and absolute loyalty to one's lord affect Japanese feudal society?

A United Japan

The Kamakura shogunate crumbled in the aftermath of the Mongol invasions. A new dynasty took power in 1338, but the level of warfare increased after 1450. To defend their castles, daimyo armed peasants as well as samurai, which led to even more ruthless fighting. A saying of the time declared, "The warrior does not care if he's called a dog or beast. The main thing is winning."

>> Over 13,000 invaders drowned in the first typhoon that saved Japan. Almost all of the 4,400 ships and 140,000 Chinese invaders were lost in the second typhoon.

>> After the Battle of Sekigahara in 1600, Tokugawa Ieyasau seized control of central Japan. He used strict administrative regulations to control anyone who challenged his power.

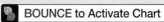
🔲 BOUNCE to Activate Chart

>> Edo, now called Tokyo, was once a small fishing village. This changed when Shogun Tokugawa made Edo his new capital, with his castle and palace at its center.

>> In addition to his Edo castle, Shogun Tokugawa built a castle in Kyoto to monitor the imperial court. Part of its fortification is shown here.

Warriors Gradually Unite Japan Gradually, several powerful warriors united large parts of Japan. By 1590, the ambitious and successful general Toyotomi Hideyoshi (hee day YOH shee), a commoner by birth, had brought most of Japan under his control. He then tried, but failed, to control Korea. After his death, another ambitious warrior, the daimyo Tokugawa Ieyasu (toh koo gah wah ee AY ah soo) defeated his rivals to become master of Japan.

Centralized Feudalism In 1603, Tokugawa was named shogun. The Tokugawa shogunate would last until 1868. The Tokugawa shoguns were determined to end feudal warfare. To do so, they kept the outward forms of feudal society, but imposed central government control on all of Japan. For this reason, their system of government is called centralized feudalism.

The Tokugawas created a unified, orderly society. To control the daimyo, they required these great lords to live in the shogun's capital at Edo (present-day Tokyo) every other year. A daimyo's wife and children had to remain in Edo full time, giving the shogun a powerful check on the entire family. The shogun also forbade daimyo to repair their castles or marry without permission.

New laws fixed the old social order rigidly in place and upheld a strict moral code. Only samurai were allowed to serve in the military or hold government jobs.

They were expected to follow the traditions of bushido. Peasants had to remain on the land. People in lower classes were forbidden to wear luxuries such as silk clothing.

A Booming Economy While the shoguns tried to hold back social change, the Japanese economy grew by leaps and bounds. With peace restored to the countryside, agriculture improved and expanded. New seeds, tools, and the use of fertilizer led to a greater output of crops.

Food surpluses supported rapid population growth. Towns sprang up on the lands around the castles of daimyo. Edo grew into a booming city, where artisans and merchants flocked to supply the needs of the daimyo and their families.

Trade flourished within Japan. New roads linked castle towns and Edo. Each year, daimyo and their servants traveled to and from the capital, creating a demand for food and services along the route. In the cities, a wealthy merchant class emerged. Despite their low social status under Confucian traditions, merchants gained influence by lending money to daimyo and samurai. Some merchants further improved their social position by marrying their daughters into the samurai class.

☑ **APPLY CONCEPTS** After the Tokugawas forced daimyo and their wives and children to live in certain places, what happened?

Japanese Feudal Culture Evolves

During Japan's feudal age, a Buddhist sect from China won widespread acceptance among samurai. Known in Japan as **Zen,** it emphasized self-reliance, meditation, and devotion to duty.

Zen Beliefs Zen had seemingly contradictory traditions. Zen monks were great scholars, yet they valued the uncluttered mind and stressed the importance of reaching a moment of "non-knowing." Zen stressed compassion for all, yet samurai fought to kill. In Zen monasteries, monks sought to experience absolute freedom, yet rigid rules gave the Zen master complete authority over his students.

Zen Buddhists believed that people could seek enlightenment through meditation and through the precise performance of everyday tasks. For example, the elaborate rituals of the tea ceremony reflected Zen values of peace, simplicity, and love of beauty. Zen reverence for nature also influenced the development of fine landscape paintings.

Artistic Traditions Change Under the Tokugawas, cities such as Edo and Osaka were home to an explosion in the arts and theater. At stylish entertainment quarters, sophisticated nobles mixed with the urban middle class. Urban culture emphasized luxuries and pleasures and differed greatly from the feudal culture that had dominated Japan for centuries.

New Drama Develops In the 1300s, feudal culture had produced Noh plays performed on a square, wooden stage without scenery. Men wore elegant carved masks while a chorus chanted important lines to musical accompaniment. The action was slow, and each movement had a special meaning. Many Noh plays presented Zen Buddhist themes, emphasizing the need to renounce selfish desires. Others recounted fairy tales or the struggles between powerful feudal lords.

In the 1600s, towns gave rise to a popular new form of drama called Kabuki. Kabuki was influenced by Noh plays, but it was less refined and included comedy or melodrama in portraying family or

>> This painting, *Flowers of the Four Seasons* (ink and watercolor on gold leafed paper), by Shiko Watanabe (1683–1755) demonstrates the taste for luxury that developed under the Tokugawa.

>> These modern performers of Noh theater are storytellers who do not act, but instead use visual appearance and movements to suggest symbols and refer to classic stories.

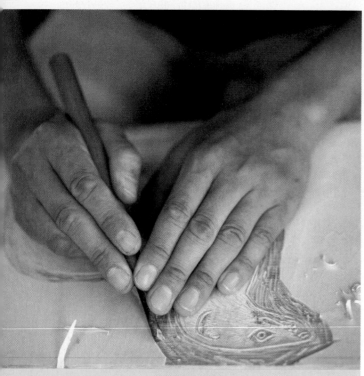

>> Japanese wildlife artist Ichiro Kikuta carves an image of a mongoose to make a woodblock print.

BOUNCE to Activate Gallery

historical events. Dressed in colorful costumes, actors used lively movements and exaggerated facial expressions. Kabuki originated with a temple dancer named Okuni, who became famous for her performances of warrior roles. However, the government soon banned women from performing on stage.

Puppet plays, known as bunraku, were also enormously popular in towns. A narrator told a story while handlers silently manipulated near-life-sized puppets. Bunraku plays catered to popular middle-class tastes.

Literature The feudal age produced stories like the *Tale of the Heike* about a violent conflict between two families. Other prose works dealt with Buddhist themes such as the fleeting nature of worldly things.

The Japanese also adapted Chinese poetry models, creating miniature poems, called haiku. In only three lines—totaling 17 syllables in the Japanese language—these tiny word pictures express a feeling, thought, or idea.

Painting and Printmaking Japanese paintings often reflected the influence of Chinese landscape paintings, yet Japanese artists developed their own styles. On magnificent scrolls, painters boldly recreated historical events, such as the Mongol invasions.

In the 1600s, the vigorous urban culture produced a flood of colorful woodblock prints to satisfy middle-class tastes. Some woodblock artists produced humorous prints. Their fresh colors and simple lines give us a strong sense of the pleasures of town life in Japan.

☑ **RECALL** Why did Kabuki and Noh theater as well as puppet plays and colorful woodblock prints gain popularity?

☑ ASSESSMENT

1. **Identify Cause and Effect** How did geography affect the development of Japan and set it apart from its neighbors?

2. **Check Understanding** Describe some of the ways China influenced Japan's political and cultural development.

3. **Analyze Information** Describe the structure of Japanese society under the feudal system.

4. **Check Understanding** How did the Tokugawas unite Japan, and what was the effect on the economy?

5. **Generate Explanations** How did Zen Buddhism help shape Japanese culture?

6. **Connections to Today** How does selective borrowing shape our world today? List examples from your own life.

GO ONLINE to access this biography: Prince Shotoku

Indian styles are evident in this Buddhist monument, the Borobudur temple in Central Java, which was long overgrown and covered in volcanic ash before its intricate carvings were rediscovered.

The Many Cultures of Southeast Asia

Located between China and India, the region known today as Southeast Asia was strongly influenced by both of these powerful neighbors. Even so, the distinct cultures of Southeast Asia retained their own unique identities.

The Geography of Southeast Asia

Two Major Regions Southeast Asia is made up of two major regions. The first, mainland Southeast Asia, includes several peninsulas that jut south between India and China. Today, this region is home to Myanmar, Thailand, Cambodia, Laos, Vietnam, and part of Malaysia. The second region, island Southeast Asia, consists of more than 20,000 islands scattered between the Indian Ocean and the South China Sea. It includes the present-day nations of Indonesia, Singapore, Brunei (broo NY), and the Philippines.

Separated by Mountains The mainland is separated from the rest of Asia by mountains and high plateaus. Still, traders and invaders did push overland into the region. Mountains also separate the four main river valleys of Southeast Asia—the Irrawaddy (ihr uh WAH dee), Chao Phraya (chow PRY uh), Mekong, and Red. These river valleys were home to early civilizations.

Trade in the Southern Seas Island Southeast Asia has long been of strategic importance. All seaborne trade between China

 BOUNCE to Activate Flipped Video

Objectives

Describe the geography of Southeast Asia.

Understand the impact of India on the history of Southeast Asia.

Summarize the characteristics of the new kingdoms and empires in Southeast Asia.

Explain the emergence of Vietnam.

Key Terms

stupa
King Suryavarman II
paddy

GO ONLINE to access your digital course

and India had to pass through either the Malacca or Sunda straits. Whoever commanded these straits controlled rich trade routes.

The monsoons, or seasonal winds, shaped trading patterns in the southern seas. Ships traveled northeast in summer and southwest in winter. Between seasons, while waiting for the winds to shift, merchants harbored their vessels in Southeast Asian ports, which became important centers of trade and culture. Soon, an international trade network linked India, Southeast Asia, and China to East Africa and the Middle East.

The key products of Southeast Asia were spices. In coastal towns from India to Southeast Asia, merchants bought and sold cloves, nutmeg, ginger, pepper, and other spices. Only a fraction of the spices traded in the region went to markets in Europe. Most cargoes were carried to East Asia, the Middle East, and East Africa.

Early Traditions The peoples of Southeast Asia developed their own cultures before Indian or Chinese influences shaped the region. At Bang Chiang in Thailand, archaeologists have found jars and bronze bracelets at least 5,000 years old. This evidence is challenging old theories about when civilization began in the region.

Over the centuries, diverse ethnic groups speaking many languages settled in Southeast Asia. Living in isolated villages, they followed their own religious and cultural patterns. Many societies were built around the nuclear family rather than the extended families of India and China.

Role of Women Women had greater equality in Southeast Asia than elsewhere in Asia. Female merchants took part in the spice trade, gaining fame for their skill in bargaining, finance, and languages. In some port cities, they gained enough wealth and influence to become rulers.

Matrilineal descent, or inheritance through the mother, was an accepted custom in Southeast Asia. Women also had some freedom in choosing or divorcing their marriage partners. Even after Indian and Chinese influences arrived, women retained their traditional rights.

☑ **IDENTIFY CAUSE AND EFFECT** How did Southeast Asia's location and climate affect the region's development and significance?

>> King Anawrahta built the Shwezigon Pagoda with an Indian bell-shaped stupa design above a terraced pyramid topped with a golden umbrella encrusted with jewels. The interior of the pagoda is also richly decorated.

Indian Culture Spreads

Indian merchants and Hindu priests filtered into Southeast Asia, slowly spreading their culture. Later, Buddhist monks and scholars introduced Theravada beliefs. Following the path of trade and religion came the influence of writing, law, government, art, architecture, and farming.

Indian Influence Increases In the early centuries A.D., Indian traders settled in Southeast Asian port cities in growing numbers. They gave presents to local rulers and married into influential families. Trade brought prosperity as merchants exchanged products such as cotton cloth, jewels, and perfume for raw materials such as timber, spices, and gold.

In time, local Indian families exercised considerable power. Also, people from Southeast Asia visited India as pilgrims or students. As these contacts increased, Indian beliefs and ideas won widespread acceptance. Indian influence reached its peak between 500 and 1000. Hinduism and Buddhism were often practiced together, with many families practicing both or intermarrying. Though Hindu influence would decline in later years, the impact of Hinduism can still be seen in Southeast Asia today.

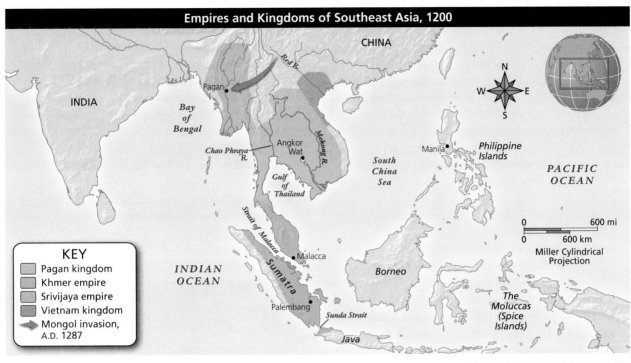

Empires and Kingdoms of Southeast Asia, 1200

KEY
- Pagan kingdom
- Khmer empire
- Srivijaya empire
- Vietnam kingdom
- Mongol invasion, A.D. 1287

>> **Analyze Maps** From which direction did the Mongol invasion take place?

BOUNCE to Activate Map

Arrival of Islam Long after Hinduism and Buddhism took root in Southeast Asia, Indians carried a third religion, Islam, into the region. By the 1200s, Muslims ruled northern India. From there, traders spread Islamic beliefs and Muslim culture throughout the islands of Indonesia and as far east as the Philippines. Today, Indonesia has the largest Muslim population of any nation in the world.

Arab merchants, too, spread the new faith. The prevalence of Islam in lands surrounding the Indian Ocean contributed to the growth of a stable, thriving trade network.

☑ **GENERATE EXPLANATIONS** How did Hinduism, Buddhism, and Islam become established in Southeast Asia?

Kingdoms and Empires

The blend of Indian influences with local cultures in time produced a series of kingdoms and empires in Southeast Asia. Some of these would rival those of India.

The Pagan Kingdom The kingdom of Pagan (puh GAHN) arose in the fertile rice-growing Irrawaddy Valley in present-day Myanmar. In 1044, King Anawrahta (an ow RAHT uh) united the region. He

is credited with bringing Buddhism to the Burman people. Buddhism had reached nearby cultures long before, but Anawrahta made Pagan a major Buddhist center.

Anawrahta filled his capital city with magnificent **stupas,** or dome-shaped shrines, at about the same time that people in medieval Europe were beginning to build Gothic cathedrals. Stupas originated in India, but in Pagan they took on a distinctly different form. These stupas were designed as sacred mountains of bricks and stone with stairways and terraces that turned them into large temples.

Painting, carvings, and sculpture told the life of the Buddha. The great Ananda temple at Pagan dates from A.D. 1090 and is still in use. Over time, many stupas have been built over smaller stupas.

Pagan flourished for some 200 years after Anawrahta's death, but fell in 1287 to conquering Mongols. When the Burmans finally threw off foreign rule, they looked back with pride to the great days of Pagan.

The Khmer Empire Indian influences also helped shape the Khmer (kuh MEHR) empire, which reached its peak between 800 and 1350. Its greatest rulers controlled much of present-day Cambodia, Thailand, and Vietnam. The Khmer people adapted Indian writing, mathematics, architecture, and art. Khmer rulers became pious Hindus. Like the princes and emperors of India, they saw themselves as god-kings. Most ordinary people, however, preferred Buddhism.

In the 1100s, **King Suryavarman II** (sur yuh VAHR mun) built the great temple complex at Angkor Wat. The ruins that survive today, though overgrown with jungle and pocked by the bullets of recent wars, are among the most impressive in the world. Hundreds of carved figures tell Hindu stories and glorify the king. Although the images of Vishnu, Shiva, and the Buddha reflect strong Indian influence, the style is uniquely Khmer.

The temples at Angkor Wat were intended to be Suryavarman's tomb. He and other royal family members wanted to be associated with the gods to ensure their immortality. Many of the carvings and sculptures there show the Hindu god Vishnu with Suryavarman's features.

Angkor Wat is part of a larger city, Angkor, which served as the center of the Khmer empire and was at one time one of the wealthiest and most sophisticated capitals in the world. Its artwork and design have been preserved despite being abandoned to the jungles in the 1300s.

The Srivijaya Empire In Indonesia, the trading empire of Srivijaya (sree wih JAW yuh) flourished

from the 600s to the 1200s. Srivijaya controlled the Strait of Malacca, which was vital to shipping. Both Hinduism and Buddhism reached this island empire. As elsewhere in Southeast Asia, however, the local people often blended Indian beliefs into their own forms of worship based on nature spirits.

Later, Islam spread to Sumatra, Java, and other islands. Local rulers adopted the new religion, which cemented commercial links with other Muslim trading centers around the Indian Ocean.

☑ CITE EVIDENCE How did India influence the Pagan kingdom and the Khmer and Srivijaya empires?

The Rise of Vietnam

In most of Southeast Asia, Indian influence was stronger than Chinese influence. Indian traditions spread mostly through trade rather than conquest. China, however, sent military forces to conquer the neighboring state of Annam (now the northern part of Vietnam).

The heart of northern Vietnam was the Red River delta, around present-day Hanoi. There, the river irrigated fertile rice **paddies,** or fields, which provided food for a growing population.

Chinese Domination In 111 B.C., Han armies conquered the region, and China remained in control for the next 1,000 years. During that time, the Vietnamese absorbed Confucian ideas. They adopted the Chinese civil service system and built a government bureaucracy similar to that found in China. Vietnamese nobles learned to speak and read Chinese.

Unlike the rest of Southeast Asia, where Theravada Buddhism had the strongest impact, Vietnam adopted Mahayana Buddhist beliefs from China. Taoism also helped shape Vietnamese society.

Resistance Despite these powerful Chinese influences, the Vietnamese preserved a strong sense of their separate identity. In A.D. 39, two noble sisters, Trung Trac and Trung Nhi, led an uprising that briefly drove the Chinese occupiers from the land. They tried to restore a simpler form of government based on ancient Vietnamese traditions. To this day, the Trung sisters are remembered as great martyrs and heroes.

Finally, in 939, as the Tang dynasty collapsed in China, Vietnam was able to break free from China. The Vietnamese turned back repeated Chinese

>> The magnificent temple complex at Angkor Wat in northern Cambodia is a striking blend of Indian and Khmer, as well as Hindu and Buddhist, artistic influences.

 BOUNCE to Activate Gallery

efforts to reconquer their land, but Vietnam still remained a tributary state of China. Ties between the two lands remained so strong that, while China was the "large dragon" of East Asia, Vietnam became known as the "smaller dragon."

☑ **IDENTIFY CAUSE AND EFFECT** How did the government and religion of Vietnam show outside influences?

>> The Trung sisters and other Vietnamese led revolts against China, but without peasant support, supplies, or trained troops, they only briefly freed Vietnam.

☑ ASSESSMENT

1. **Compare** What role did religion play in the Pagan kingdom and Khmer empire?

2. **Identify Cause and Effect** What key difference separated Vietnam's development from that of other parts of Southeast Asia?

3. **Generate Explanations** How did the geography of Srivijaya affect its cultural and religious development?

4. **Summarize** What are some ways India influenced the countries of Southeast Asia?

5. **Identify Central Ideas** Describe the geography of Southeast Asia and explain how geographic features affected the development of the region.

6. **Quest Connections** What do the actions of Anawrahta and Suryavarman II described in this lesson demonstrate about their priorities as leaders?

Connections to Today

This celebration of Chinese New Year in New York City is one example of the spread of elements of Asian cultures.

Take Action by Learning About Cultural Exchange

With modern technology, art, music, ideas, and other elements of culture can travel around the world almost instantaneously. How does Asian historical and contemporary culture influence other parts of the world today?

1. **Choose** one of the following elements of historical or contemporary culture from a region of Asia you studied in this topic:

   • Music; Art and architecture; Movies; Literature; Food

2. **Ask Questions** What are some of the things you want to know about how Asian cultures influence other parts of the world? Write a list of questions you want to answer or ideas you want to learn more about.

3. **Learn** Research the topic you have chosen. In addition to online sources, find at least one or two print sources.

4. **Design a Museum Exhibit** Plan a museum exhibit about the element of culture you have chosen. The exhibit should be fun and educational, and it should teach visitors of all ages about the cultural element you studied. Be sure to answer the questions museum visitors might have about the origins, spread, and influence of this cultural element. Share your exhibit with community members.

Use the texts, quizzes, interactivities, Quest Inquiries, Flipped Videos, and other resources from this Topic to prepare for the Topic Test.

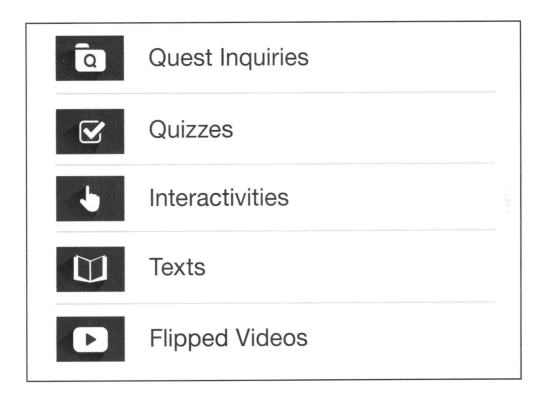

Quest Inquiries

Quizzes

Interactivities

Texts

Flipped Videos

While online you can also check the progress you've made learning the topic and course content by viewing your grades, test scores, and assignment status.

LESSON SUMMARIES
Use these Lesson Summaries, and the longer versions available online, to review the key ideas for each lesson in this Topic.

Lesson 1: The Delhi Sultanate and Mughal India
In 1206, Muslim armies captured the city of Delhi. Muslim generals established the Delhi sultanate. Eventually, religious tolerance grew and led to a blending of Hindu and Islamic religious practices and traditions.

Lesson 2: Golden Ages in China: Tang and Song Dynasties
After years of dynasties that rose and fell, two dynasties—the Tang and the Song—moved China into prolonged prosperity and technological innovation.

Lesson 3: The Mongol Empire and Ming China
The Mongols defeated the Song dynasty and established the Yuan dynasty in 1279. As Mongol rule declined, a new dynasty, the Ming, rose and conquered the Mongols. For nearly three hundred years, Ming China thrived.

Lesson 4: Korea and Its Traditions

Located near China and Japan, Korea absorbed many of their traditions. However, Koreans have also maintained their own separate and distinct culture.

Lesson 5: The Island Kingdom of Japan
Similar to Korea, Japan, because of its location, was influenced by China. Still, while borrowing some Chinese ways and modifying others, Japan established its own distinct culture. A blending of Chinese and Japanese culture during the Heian period ushered in significant cultural achievement and the establishment of a strong Japanese identity.

Lesson 6: The Many Cultures of Southeast Asia
Southeast Asia consists of both mainland areas and thousands of islands. A strong trading relationship between Southeast Asia and India resulted in Hindu, Buddhism, Islam, and other Indian influences filtering into the region. In fact, with the exception of Vietnam, Indian influences outweigh Chinese influence in Southeast Asia.

GO ONLINE to access lesson summaries

VISUAL REVIEW

Use these graphics to review some of the key terms, people, and ideas from this Topic.

Key Events of the Mughal Dynasty

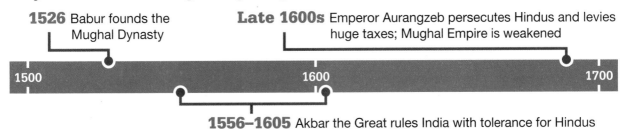

1526 Babur founds the Mughal Dynasty

Late 1600s Emperor Aurangzeb persecutes Hindus and levies huge taxes; Mughal Empire is weakened

1500   1600   1700

1556–1605 Akbar the Great rules India with tolerance for Hindus

Cultural Achievements of the Tang and Song Dynasties

- **Calligraphy** Artists sought balance and harmony through the mastery of simple brush strokes.
- **Chinese landscape painting** Painters sought to capture the spiritual essence of nature.
- **Porcelain** The Chinese perfected porcelain-making techniques that were prized around the world.
- **Architecture** Pagodas, influenced by Indian Buddhism, graced the landscape.
- **Literature** Writers created short stories and thousands of poems.

China's Influence on Its Neighbors

Language
- Writing (later replaced by hangul)
- Woodblock printing

Language
- Chinese spoken in the capital
- Official histories written in Chinese; kana later added

Government
- United with help of Tang China
- Chinese principles of government
- Restricted role of women
- Civil service examinations

Government
- Code of laws
- Absolute authority of emperor
- Strong central government

Korea ← **CHINESE INFLUENCE** → **Japan**

Belief systems
- Buddhism
- Confucianism
- Emphasis on family

Belief systems
- Buddhism
- Confucianism

Arts
- Landscape paintings
- Porcelain
- Histories and poems based on Chinese models

Arts
- Tang music, dance, and gardens
- Tea ceremony
- Architecture of the capital
- Pagoda architecture

Topic 9 Assessment

KEY TERMS, PEOPLE, AND IDEAS

1. How did the rise of the **Delhi** sultanate change life in India?

2. Why was there conflict between Hindus and Muslims in northern India?

3. What is the importance of the **pagoda** in Chinese culture?

4. What was the relationship between **tributary states** and rulers of the Tang dynasty?

5. How did **Marco Polo** impact relations between Europe and China?

6. How did rulers of the **Ming dynasty** try to restore Chinese culture?

7. What was Japan's cultural relationship to China and Korea?

8. What is Zen Buddhism, how and when did it come to Japan, and how did it influence Japanese culture?

9. What was the impact of Japan's geography on its economic and political development?

CRITICAL THINKING

10. **Predict Consequences** Rulers after Akbar rejected the policy of toleration of other religious beliefs. How do you think this rejection of toleration affected relations between Hindus and Muslims?

11. **Understand Geography** How might a map of China before the Tang dynasty differ from a map of China afterward? Give two examples.

12. **Recognize Cause and Effect** Describe one effect of each of the following on China: (a) the Mongol invasion (b) the expulsion of the Mongols (c) the rise of the Ming dynasty.

13. **Synthesize Information** How was the Mongol period both destructive and constructive?

14. **Analyze Information** How are Korea's history and culture linked to those of China and Japan?

15. **Make Comparisons** Discuss the differences between Japanese feudalism and Western European feudalism.

16. **Use Primary Sources** The selection below is from the essay collection of Kenko, a Zen Buddhist priest in feudal Japan. He wrote about the fleeting nature of worldly things. As you read, think about what you learned about Buddhist beliefs. (a) How does Kenko's essay reflect those beliefs?

> "If we were never to fade away . . . but linger on forever in the world, how things would lose their power to move us! The most precious thing in life is its uncertainty. The May fly waits not for the evening, the summer cicada knows neither spring nor autumn. What a wonderfully unhurried feeling it is to live even a single year in perfect serenity! If that is not enough for you, you might live a thousand years, and still feel it was but a single night's dream. We cannot live forever in this world.
> —*Kenko, Essays in Idleness*

Read the next selection, which is from a Confucian book of regulations for Chinese students.

> "Only after a book has been thoroughly learned should you go on to another. Do not read too many things on a superficial level. Do not attempt to memorize a piece without understanding it. Read only those books which expound virtues. Do not look into useless writings.
> —*Chieng Tuan-li, A Schedule for Learning*

(b) What does this suggest about the goal for a student's education? (c) Write a short paragraph comparing the goals of one who follows Zen Buddhism and one who follows Confucianism.

17. **Writing Activity: Write a Research Paper** Conduct research to learn more about the process for civil service examinations during China's Song Dynasty. What two accomplishments must a candidate for the exams possess? What aspect(s) of China's civil service system might inspire feelings of anxiety, nervousness, and awe in a candidate? Write a research paper about your findings, citing reliable sources.

18. **Connections to Today** During the period you read about in this topic, increasing trade between Asia and other parts of the world meant that ideas and culture began to travel more easily from one place to another. How much faster can culture spread today as compared to 1,000 years ago? What enables this spread of culture? What might limit or restrict it?

DOCUMENT-BASED QUESTIONS

Akbar the Great ruled India from 1556–1605. Read the documents below, then answer the questions that follow.

DOCUMENT A

In this letter, Akbar explains why he wishes to study many religions.

"As most men are fettered by the bonds of tradition . . . without investigating the arguments and reasons, to follow the religion in which he was born, thus excluding himself from the possibility of ascertaining the truth which is the noblest aim of the human intellect. Therefore we associate . . . with learned men of all religions, and thus derive profit from their exquisite discourses and exalted aspirations."

—Akbar the Great, Letter to King Philip II of Spain, 1582

DOCUMENT B

This 16th century miniature shows Emperor Akbar in conversation with Roman Catholic (Jesuit) missionaries.

DOCUMENT C

At Akbar's request, Portuguese missionaries traveled to his court in 1591 to teach him about Christianity. This letter explains why the mission ended.

"And the principal of all the reasons was that the haughtiness of [Akbar] had attained to such a degree that he considered himself as a prophet and a legislator saying that the period of the law of Muhammad had now come to an end and that . . . therefore another prophet has to come, who will establish it, and that he is the one man to do it. . . . [P]eople worship him in public as a prophet with such shameless praises that I heard him called God, many times and in public."

—Father Christoval de Vega of the Jesuits, Letter of December 2, 1593

DOCUMENT D

This is part of a law passed by Akbar. It revoked one that required Hindus to pay a tax because of their religion.

". . . certain community councils in India which during the reign of the Muslim sultans, before my reign, were charged certain taxes, are now being excused. . . . Both Hindus and Muslims are one in my eyes, so I give freedom [of action] to these councils. They are exempt from the payment of *jazia* [religious tax] and other taxes."

—Order issued by Emperor Akbar, 1580

19. Which document contradicts the information contained in Document D?
   A. Document A
   B. Document B
   C. Document C
   D. None of the above

20. Which of the following best summarizes Document A?
   A. India is home to the one true religion.
   B. People should explore all religions in order to arrive at the truth.
   C. It is best to follow the religion of one's ancestors in order to arrive at the truth.
   D. The noblest aim of humans is to follow tradition.

21. Examine Evidence Document A gives a certain impression of Emperor Akbar. What is this impression and which document(s) corroborate this impression? In what way?

22. Writing Task One of these documents expresses a different view of Emperor Akbar than the other three. Identify which document that is and what viewpoint it expresses. Then write a paragraph exploring possible reasons for the discrepancy. Consider such details as the date when each document was written, the author of each, and other facts, including information from this topic, to support your answer.

The Renaissance and Reformation (1300–1650)

ESSENTIAL QUESTION Why is Culture Important?

GO ONLINE for immersive experiences designed to help you feel the exciting spirit of the Renaissance through rich primary sources. Also access the eText, videos, Biographies, and other online resources.

The *Mona Lisa*, a painting by Leonardo da Vinci

Connections to Today

You have a world of information at your fingertips. With a computer or a phone, you can find almost anything. Now, imagine a world where there are few computers—and you don't know how to use one anyway. That was the world before the Information Revolution of the late 20th Century.

And that was the world before the rise of printing in the 1400s. There were relatively few books, and few people could read. In this topic, you will learn about the Printing Revolution. How can information technology change the world?

NBC LEARN

Learn more about Leonardo da Vinci, a true Renaissance man.

 BOUNCE to Activate My Story Video

415

In this Topic, you will learn about the events of the Renaissance and Reformation. Look at the lesson outline and explore the timeline. As you study this Topic, you will complete the Quest Inquiry.

LESSON OUTLINE

10.1 The Italian Renaissance

10.2 The Renaissance in Northern Europe

10.3 The Protestant Reformation

10.4 Reformation Ideas Spread

10.5 Scientific Revolution

Key Events of the Renaissance and Reformation

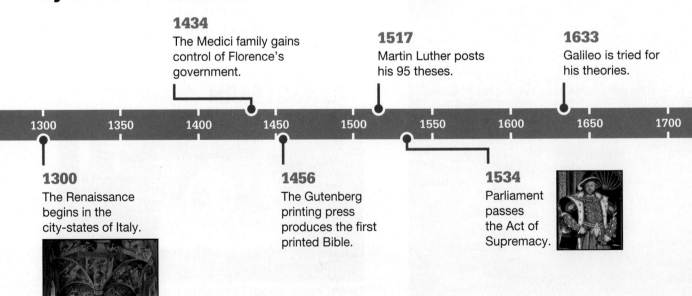

1434 The Medici family gains control of Florence's government.

1517 Martin Luther posts his 95 theses.

1633 Galileo is tried for his theories.

1300 The Renaissance begins in the city-states of Italy.

1456 The Gutenberg printing press produces the first printed Bible.

1534 Parliament passes the Act of Supremacy.

QUEST! INQUIRY

Building a "Hall of Fame" Website

Who were the influential figures in the Renaissance and the Scientific Revolution who helped shape a new worldview? In this Quest, you will create a Hall of Fame Website to honor those individuals.

STEP 1
With your team, identify, then create a list of possible nominees.

STEP 2
Consider the criteria you will use to select the final group of nominees. Then research the nominees. What were their accomplishments? What changes occurred because of these accomplishments?

STEP 3
Write and edit the Hall of Fame entries. Create elements for the website.

STEP 4
Build your website. Reflect on the chosen members. Think about individuals today who have made an impact on the world.

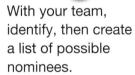 **GO ONLINE** to access complete Quest materials

10.1

 GO ONLINE to Project Imagine: Step into Life in Renaissance Florence for perspectives on the Italian Renaissance.

BOUNCE to Activate Flipped Video

Objectives

Describe the characteristics of the Renaissance and understand why it began in Italy.

Identify Renaissance artists and explain how new ideas affected the arts of the period.

Understand how writers of the time addressed Renaissance themes.

Explain the impact of the Renaissance.

Key Terms

humanism
humanities
Petrarch
vernacular
Florence
patron
perspective
Leonardo da Vinci
Michelangelo
Raphael
Baldassare
  Castiglione
Niccolò Machiavelli

The Italian Renaissance

From the 1300s to the 1500s, Western Europe enjoyed a golden age in the arts and literature, known as the Renaissance. The word literally means "rebirth." The Renaissance was a time of great creativity and change in many areas—economic, political, social, and above all, cultural.

The Italian Renaissance

The Renaissance marked the transition between medieval and early modern times. During the Renaissance, Western Europe witnessed the growth of cities and trade, which greatly extended people's horizons.

A New Worldview Most important, the Renaissance changed the way Europeans saw themselves and their world. Through contacts in Spain and Sicily, Christian European scholars began to study Muslim philosophy, art, and science. Muslim scholars also reintroduced knowledge of Greco-Roman civilization to later Europeans. Spurred by a reawakened interest in the learning of ancient Greece and Rome, creative Renaissance minds set out to transform their own age. Their era, they felt, was a time of rebirth after the disorder and disunity of the medieval world.

Renaissance Europe did not really break with its medieval past. Much of the classical heritage had survived, including the Latin language and knowledge of ancient thinkers such as Euclid and Aristotle. Yet the Renaissance did produce new attitudes toward culture and learning. Unlike medieval scholars, who debated the nature of life after death, Renaissance thinkers were eager to explore the richness and variety of human experience in the here and now.

During the Renaissance, there was a new emphasis on individual achievement. Indeed, the Renaissance ideal was a person with talents and skills in many fields.

A Spirit of Adventure and Curiosity The Renaissance supported a spirit of adventure and curiosity that led Europeans to explore unfamiliar worlds or to reexamine familiar ones. Navigators who sailed uncharted seas represented that spirit. So, too, did the scientists who looked at the universe in new ways.

An Italian thinker, Pico della Mirandola, captured this spirit of adventure and confidence in human abilities when he wrote: "To [man] it is granted to have whatever he chooses, to be whatever he wills."

Renaissance Humanism At the heart of the Italian Renaissance was an intellectual movement known as **humanism**. Humanist scholars studied classical Greek and Roman cultures, hoping to use the wisdom of the ancients to increase their understanding of their own times. Though most humanists were pious Christians, they focused on worldly, or secular, subjects rather than on the religious issues that had occupied medieval thinkers.

Humanists believed that education should stimulate the individual's creative powers. They emphasized the **humanities**—subjects such as grammar, rhetoric (the study of using language effectively), poetry, and history—that had been taught in ancient Greek and Roman schools.

Francesco **Petrarch** (PEE trahrk), who lived in Florence, a city in north Italy in the 1300s, was an early Renaissance humanist. From monasteries and churches, he hunted down and assembled a library of Greek and Roman manuscripts. Through his efforts, and those who followed his example, the speeches of Cicero, the poems of Homer and Virgil, and Livvy's *History of Rome* again became known to Western Europeans.

Petrarch also wrote poetry. His *Sonnets to Laura* are love poems, inspired by a woman he knew only at a distance, but their style greatly influenced writers of his time. Petrarch wrote in the **vernacular**, or everyday language of ordinary people, as well as in Latin.

☑ **DESCRIBE** What were some important characteristics of the Renaissance?

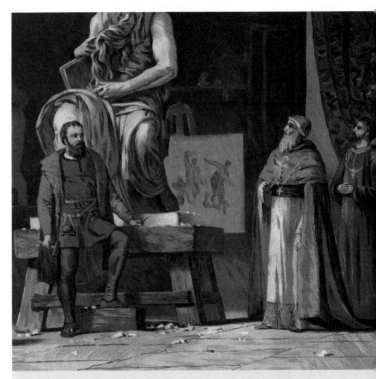

>> The Church was an important patron of Renaissance art, commissioning paintings and sculptures. Here, the pope meets with artist Michelangelo.

>> Francesco Petrarch, an Italian Renaissance scholar, poet, and humanist.

The Renaissance Begins in Italy

The Renaissance began in Italy in the mid-1300s and later spread north to the rest of Europe. It reached its height in the 1500s. The Renaissance emerged in Italy for several reasons.

Italy's History and Geography The Renaissance was marked by a reawakened interest in the culture of ancient Rome. Since Italy was the center of ancient Roman civilization, it was only natural for this reawakening to begin there. Architectural remains, antique statues, coins, and inscriptions were all daily reminders of the glory of ancient Rome.

Italy differed from the rest of Europe in another important way. Italy's cities had thrived during the Middle Ages. In the north, city-states like Florence, Milan, Venice, and Genoa grew into prosperous centers of trade and manufacturing. Rome and Naples also contributed to the Renaissance cultural revival.

At trading ports along Italy's coastlines, ships brought goods, people, and ideas from the Muslim world, which had preserved much learning from ancient Greece and Rome. Many texts—and much knowledge—that had been lost in Europe were recovered through these trading contacts.

A class of wealthy and powerful merchants emerged in Italy's city-states, and they promoted the cultural rebirth. These merchants exerted both political and economic leadership, and their attitudes and interests helped to shape Renaissance Italy. They stressed individual achievement and spent lavishly to support the arts.

Florence and the Medicis **Florence**, perhaps more than any other city, came to symbolize the Italian Renaissance. Like ancient Athens, it produced a dazzling number of gifted poets, artists, architects, scholars, and scientists in a short space of time.

In the 1400s, the Medici (MED dee chee) family of Florence organized a banking business. Their business prospered, and the family expanded into manufacturing, mining, and other ventures. Money translated into cultural and political power. Cosimo de' Medici gained control of the Florentine government in 1434, and the family continued as uncrowned rulers of the city for many years.

The best known Medici was Cosimo's grandson, Lorenzo, known as "the Magnificent." Lorenzo represented the Renaissance ideal. A clever politician, he held Florence together through difficult times. He was also a generous **patron**, or financial supporter, of the arts. At Lorenzo's invitation, poets

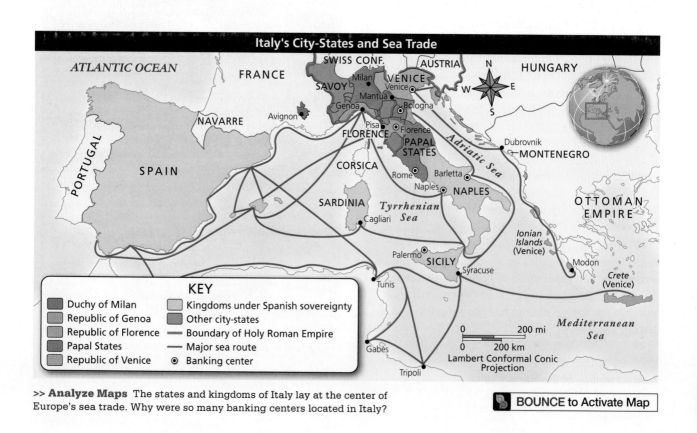

>> **Analyze Maps** The states and kingdoms of Italy lay at the center of Europe's sea trade. Why were so many banking centers located in Italy?

BOUNCE to Activate Map

and philosophers frequently visited the Medici palace. Artists learned their craft by sketching ancient Roman statues displayed in the Medici gardens.

☑ **IDENTIFY CAUSE AND EFFECT** Why did Italy's historic legacy make it an ideal place for the Renaissance to begin?

Art Flourishes in the Renaissance

The Renaissance attained its most glorious expression in its paintings, sculpture, and architecture. Wealthy patrons played a major role in this artistic flowering. Popes and princes, along with successful merchants, supported the work of hundreds of artists.

Art Reflects New Ideas and Attitudes

Renaissance art reflected humanist concerns. Like the artists of the Middle Ages, Renaissance artists portrayed religious figures, such as Mary and Jesus. However, they often set these figures against Greek or Roman backgrounds.

Painters also produced portraits of well-known figures of the day, reflecting the humanist interest in individual achievement. Renaissance artists also painted scenes from Greek and Roman mythology and depicted historical events.

Renaissance artists studied ancient Greek and Roman works and revived many classical forms. The sculptor Donatello, for example, created a life-size statue of a soldier on horseback. It was the first such figure done since ancient times.

New Techniques and Styles Ancient Roman art was realistic, a style that was abandoned in the Middle Ages. Renaissance painters developed new techniques for representing humans and landscapes in a realistic way. They discovered the rules of **perspective**, which allowed them to represent a three-dimensional world—what people see—onto a two-dimension surface, such as wood or canvas. By making distant objects smaller than those close to the viewer, artists gave the impression of space and depth on a flat surface.

Artists also used shadings of light and dark to make objects look round and real, making scenes more dramatic. Renaissance artists studied human anatomy and drew from live models. This made it possible to portray the human body more accurately than medieval artists had done.

>> In this painting by Italian Renaissance artist Tintoretto, Mary Magdalene anoints the feet of Jesus. Classical columns in the background reflect the Renaissance style.

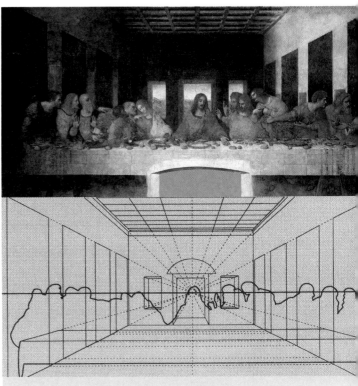

>> **Analyze Information** Leonardo da Vinci used perspective in his painting, *The Last Supper,* completed in 1498. What techniques bring the viewer's eye to the central figure of Jesus?

🅑 BOUNCE to Activate Illustration

>> The Duomo, a dome atop a cathedral in Florence, was designed by Renaissance architect Filippo Brunelleschi. Completed in 1496, it was modeled on the dome of the Pantheon, built in ancient Rome.

BOUNCE to Activate 3D Model

>> Michelangelo was the greatest Renaissance sculptor. The realistic depiction of human anatomy in his *Pieta* reflects classical influence.

Renaissance Architecture Renaissance architects rejected the Gothic style of the late Middle Ages. To them, it was disorderly. Instead, they adopted the columns, arches, and domes used by the ancient Greeks and Romans. To top the cathedral in Florence, Filippo Brunelleschi (broo nay LAYS kee) created a majestic dome, modeled on the dome of the ancient Pantheon in Rome.

Like so many other Renaissance artists, Brunelleschi had many talents. He had studied sculpture with Donatello and was an accomplished engineer, inventing many of the machines used to construct his dome.

Leonardo da Vinci Florence was home to many outstanding painters and sculptors. Among the most brilliant was **Leonardo da Vinci** (DAH VIHN chee), who was born in 1452. His endless curiosity fed a genius for invention. He sketched objects in nature and dissected corpses to learn how bones and muscles work. Today, people admire Leonardo's paintings for their freshness and realism. Most popular is the *Mona Lisa*, a portrait of a woman whose mysterious smile has baffled viewers for centuries.

Another masterpiece, *The Last Supper*, which shows Jesus and his disciples, is a deceptively simple painting and a brilliant example of the use of perspective. To create it, Leonardo used a new type of paint, which decayed over time. However, the painting has been restored.

Although Leonardo thought of himself as an artist, his interests extended to botany, anatomy, optics, music, architecture, and engineering. He sketched flying machines and undersea boats centuries before the first airplane or submarine was built. His many notebooks filled with sketches are a testament to his genius.

Michelangelo Like Leonardo, **Michelangelo** was a many-sided genius. He was a sculptor, engineer, painter, architect, and poet. Born in 1475, he came under the wing of the Medicis in Florence. As a young man, he shaped marble into masterpieces like the *Pieta,* which captures the sorrow of Mary as she cradles the dead Jesus on her knees. *David,* Michelangelo's statue of the biblical shepherd who killed the giant Goliath, recalls the harmony and grace of ancient Greek sculptures.

In 1508, Michelangelo started a new project, painting a series of murals on the vast curved ceiling of the Sistine Chapel in Rome. During the next four years, he worked to complete scenes from the biblical book of *Genesis* along with figures of prophets who had foretold the coming of Jesus.

Later, as an architect, Michelangelo drew a design for the enormous dome of St. Peter's Cathedral in Rome. Although he did not live to see it, the dome was completed based on his exact design. The dome served as a model for many later structures, including the Capitol in Washington, D.C.

Raphael A few years younger than Leonardo and Michelangelo, **Raphael** (rah fah EL) studied the works of those great masters. His paintings blend Christian and classical styles. Among his best-known works is *School of Athens*, which pictures an imaginary gathering of great thinkers and scientists, including Plato, Aristotle, Socrates, and the Arab philosopher Averroës. In typical Renaissance fashion, Raphael included Michelangelo, Leonardo, and himself.

☑ **IDENTIFY** Which artistic technique was developed during the Renaissance and used in *The Last Supper*?

New Books Reflect Renaissance Themes

Poets, artists, and scholars mingled with politicians at the courts of Renaissance rulers. A literature of "how to" books sprang up to help ambitious men and women who wanted to rise in the Renaissance world.

Castiglione's Ideal Courtier The most widely read of these handbooks was *The Book of the Courtier*, by **Baldassare Castiglione** (kahs teel YOH nay). In it, he describes the manners, skills, learning, and virtues that a member of the court should have.

The ideal differed for men and women. The ideal man, wrote Castiglione, is athletic but not overactive. He is good at games but not a gambler. He plays a musical instrument and knows literature and history but is not arrogant. The ideal woman offers a balance to men. She is graceful and kind, lively but reserved. She is beautiful, "for outer beauty," wrote Castiglione, "is the true sign of inner goodness."

Machiavelli's Advice to Princes **Niccolò Machiavelli** (mahk ee uh VEL ee) wrote a different kind of handbook. He had served Florence as a diplomat and had observed kings and princes in foreign courts. He had also studied ancient Roman history. In *The Prince*, published in 1513, Machiavelli offered a guide to rulers on how to gain and maintain

>> **Analyze Information** In *School of Athens,* Italian painter Raphael imagines a gathering of great thinkers and scientists. Why did he include Renaissance artists in the scene?

>> This 1474 painting by Italian Renaissance artist Andrea Mantegna is called *The Court of Mantua.* An Italian nobleman was Mantegna's patron and commissioned art works like this.

NICCOLO MACCHIAVELLI.

From a Print by Raphael Morghen, after a Picture by Bronzino

>> **Analyze Information** Niccolò Machiavelli, the Italian Renaissance political philosopher and writer. Would Machiavelli have considered *The Court of Mantua* painting as realistic or not? Why?

power. It combined his personal experience of politics with his knowledge of the past.

The Prince did not discuss leadership in terms of high ideals, as Plato had. Instead, it looked at real rulers in an age of ruthless power politics. Machiavelli stressed that the end justifies the means.

He urged rulers to use whatever methods were necessary to achieve their goals.

Machiavelli saw himself as an enemy of oppression and corruption, but critics attacked his cynical advice. (In fact, the term "Machiavellian" came to refer to the use of deceit in politics.) Later students of government, however, argued that Machiavelli provided a realistic look at politics. His work continues to spark debate because it raises important ethical questions about the nature of government and the use of power.

☑ **IDENTIFY** How did Renaissance writings express realism?

☑ ASSESSMENT

1. **Analyze Information** What were some of the characteristics of the Italian Renaissance?

2. **Identify Cause and Effect** How did Italy's trade with the Muslim world contribute to the Italian Renaissance?

3. **Analyze Information** What new ideas and techniques resulted in more realistic and accurate portrayals of people in Renaissance paintings?

4. **Draw Conclusions** What Renaissance theme appears in Machiavelli's book *The Prince*?

5. **Identify Central Ideas** What was the impact of the Italian Renaissance in the field of architecture?

6. **Quest Connections** How did the accomplishments of Leonardo da Vinci and Michelangelo reflect Renaissance ideals and values?

GO ONLINE to access these biographies: Michelangelo, Machiavelli

Oration on the Dignity of Man, Pico della Mirandola

At the heart of the Italian Renaissance was humanism, a classical philosophy that emphasized the potential of each individual. In 1486, at age 23, Italian philosopher Giovanni Pico della Mirandola wrote "Oration on the Dignity of Man," which is now considered the model of Renaissance humanist thought. (As was traditional at the time, Pico uses "man" to indicate humanity.)

Pico's ideas were based partly on classical thought, but also on the medieval Christian concept of the Chain of Being: a hierarchy with God at the top, continuing through angels down to animals and plants. For humanists like Pico, humans occupied a special and honored place in this chain.

>> Pico's ideas reflected the medieval ideal of the Chain of Being, which placed humans lower than angels and higher than animals.

Primary Source

I once read that Abdala the Muslim, when asked what was most worthy of awe and wonder in this theater of the world, answered, "There is nothing to see more wonderful than man"; Hermes Trismegistus concurs with this opinion: "A great miracle, Asclepius, is man!" ... After thinking a long time, I have figured out why man is the most fortunate of all creatures and as a result worthy of the highest admiration and earning his rank on the chain of being, a rank to be envied not merely by the beasts but by the stars themselves and by the spiritual natures [angels] beyond and above this world....

☑ **DRAW INFERENCES** Pico begins by quoting both Muslim and Greek sources. What does this tell you about his background?

[God] made man a creature of indeterminate [uncertain] and indifferent [able to develop in various ways] nature, and, placing him in the middle of the world, said to him, "Adam, we give you no fixed place to live, no form that is peculiar to you, nor any function that is yours alone. According to your desires and judgement, you will have and possess whatever place to live, whatever form, and whatever functions you yourself choose. All other things have a limited and fixed nature prescribed and bounded by Our laws. You, with no limit or no bound, may choose for yourself the limits and bounds of your nature. We have placed you at the world's center so that you may survey everything else in the world. We have made you neither of heavenly nor of earthly stuff, neither mortal nor immortal, so that with free choice and dignity, you may fashion yourself into whatever form you choose. To you is granted the power of degrading yourself into the lower forms of life, the beasts, and to you is granted the power, contained in your intellect and judgement, to be reborn into the higher forms, the divine."

☑ **UNDERSTAND THE MAIN IDEA** Pico here imagines what God might say to humans. In one sentence, summarize the main idea of this speech.

Imagine! The great generosity of God! The happiness of man! To man it is allowed to be whatever he chooses to be! As soon as an animal is born, it brings out of its mother's womb all that it will ever possess. Spiritual beings from the beginning become what they are to be for all eternity. Man, when he entered life, the Father gave the seeds of every kind and every way of life possible. Whatever seeds each man sows and cultivates will grow and bear him their proper fruit. If these seeds are vegetative, he will be like a plant. If these seeds are sensitive, he will be like an animal. If these seeds are intellectual, he will be an angel and the son of God. And if, satisfied with no created thing, he removes himself to the center of his own unity, his spiritual soul, united with God, alone in the darkness of God, who is above all things, he will surpass every created thing. Who could not help but admire this great shape-shifter? In fact, how could one admire anything else? . . .

☑ **ANALYZE STYLE AND RHETORIC** What effect does the use of exclamation points have on the tone of this passage?

Considering that we are born with this condition, that is, that we can become whatever we choose to become, we need to understand that we must take earnest care about this, so that it will never be said to our disadvantage that we were born to a privileged position but failed to realize it and became animals and senseless beasts. Instead, the saying of Asaph the prophet should be said of us, "You are all angels of the Most High"; Above all, we should not make that freedom of choice God gave us into something harmful, for it was intended to be to our advantage. Let a holy ambition enter into our souls; let us not be content with mediocrity, but rather strive after the highest and expend all our strength in achieving it.

☑ **IDENTIFY CENTRAL IDEAS** What kind of people does Pico admire? What kind does he condemn?

☑ ASSESSMENT

1. **Compare and Contrast** How does Pico think humans differ from both animals and "spiritual beings" such as angels?

2. **Analyze Arguments** According to Pico, what is the source of human potential? What are its limits? What responsibilities do humans have as a result?

3. **Determine Author's Purpose** What impact do you think Pico wanted his oration to have?

4. **Integrate Information from Diverse Sources** How do the ideas expressed here relate to what you have learned about the values and achievements of the Italian Renaissance?

GO ONLINE to access primary sources

10.2

☐ **GO ONLINE** to Project Imagine: See Life Through an Artist's Eyes to show how a Northern Renaissance artist depicted daily life.

The Renaissance in Northern Europe

In the mid-1300s, the Black Death had reduced the population of Europe by one-third and brought the economy to a standstill. Italy recovered fairly quickly and was soon the center of the Renaissance and its creative upsurge. Only after 1450 did northern Europe enjoy the economic growth that had earlier supported the Renaissance in Italy.

Artists of the Northern Renaissance

The northern Renaissance began in the prosperous cities of **Flanders**, a region that included parts of what is today northern France, Belgium, and the Netherlands. Flanders was a thriving center of trade for northern Europe. From Flanders, the Renaissance spread to Spain, France, Germany, and England, which enjoyed cultural rebirths during the 1500s.

Flemish Painters Among the many talented artists of Flanders in the 1400s, Jan van Eyck stands out. His portrayals of townspeople as well as religious scenes abound in rich details that add to the realism of his art. Van Eyck developed new techniques for using oil paint. He and other Flemish artists used these new methods to produce strong colors and a hard-surfaced paint that could survive for centuries.

A leading Flemish painter of the 1500s was Pieter Bruegel (BROY gul). He used vibrant colors to portray lively scenes of peasant life, earning him the nickname "Peasant Bruegel." Although Bruegel produced works on religious and classical

BOUNCE to Activate Flipped Video

Objectives

Describe the themes that northern European artists, humanists, and writers explored.

Explain how the printing revolution shaped European society.

Key Terms

Flanders
Albrecht Dürer
engraving
Erasmus
Sir Thomas More
utopian
William Shakespeare
Johannes Gutenberg

>> This 1511 woodcut print by Albrecht Dürer is called *St. Christopher.*

🅑 BOUNCE to Activate Gallery

>> Desiderius Erasmus was a Dutch priest and humanist scholar who was active during the Northern European Renaissance. He believed an individual's chief duties were to be open-minded and to show good will toward others.

themes, his secular art influenced later Flemish artists, who painted scenes of ordinary people in their daily lives.

Albrecht Dürer: A "German Leonardo" Among the most influential artists of the northern Renaissance was the German painter and printmaker **Albrecht Dürer** (DYOOR ur). In 1494, he made the first of several trips to Italy to study the works and techniques of Italian masters. At home, he employed the new methods in his own paintings, engravings, and prints. Through these works as well as his essays, Dürer helped spread Renaissance ideas to northern Europe.

Dürer had a keen, inquiring mind. Because of his wide-ranging interests, which extended far beyond art, he is sometimes called the "German Leonardo."

Dürer is well-known for applying the painting techniques he had learned in Italy to **engraving**, a method of making prints from metal plates. In an engraving, an artist etches a design on a metal plate with acid. The artist then uses the plate to make prints. Many of Dürer's engravings and paintings portray religious upheaval of the time.

☑ **IDENTIFY** What were some important artistic themes in the Northern European Renaissance?

Northern Renaissance Humanists and Writers

Like the Italian humanists, northern European humanist scholars stressed education and classical learning. At the same time, they emphasized religious themes. They believed that the revival of ancient learning should be used to bring about religious and moral reform.

Although most humanist scholars wrote mainly in Latin, other writers began to write in the vernacular, or everyday language of ordinary people. In this way, their works were accessible to the new middle class audience living in towns and cities.

Erasmus The great Dutch humanist Desiderius **Erasmus** (ih RAZ mus), became a priest in 1492. He used his knowledge of classical languages to produce a new Greek edition of the New Testament and a much-improved Latin translation of the Bible. At the same time, Erasmus called for a translation of the Bible into the vernacular.

"I disagree very much with those who are unwilling that Holy Scripture, translated into the vernacular, be read by the uneducated." For him, "the strength of the Christian religion" should not be based on people's ignorance of it, but on their ability to study it on their own.

Erasmus used his pen to call for reforms in the Church. He challenged the worldliness of the Church and urged a return to early Christian traditions. His best-known work, *In Praise of Folly*, uses humor to explore the ignorant, immoral behavior of people. Erasmus taught that an individual's chief duties were to be open-minded and show good will toward others.

Sir Thomas More Erasmus's friend, the English humanist **Sir Thomas More**, also pressed for social and economic reforms. In *Utopia*, More describes an ideal society in which men and women live in peace and harmony. Private property does not exist. No one is idle, all are educated, and justice is used to end crime rather than to eliminate criminals. Today, the word **utopian** has come to describe any ideal society, with the implication that such a society is impractical.

Rabelais's Comic Masterpiece The French humanist François Rabelais (rab uh LAY) had a varied career as a monk, a physician, a Greek scholar, and an author. Unlike Erasmus and More, Rabelais wrote in the French vernacular. In *Gargantua and Pantagruel*, he chronicles the adventures of two gentle giants. On the surface, the novel is a comic tale of travel and war. But Rabelais uses his characters to offer opinions on religion, education, and other serious subjects.

Shakespeare Explores Universal Themes The towering figure of Renaissance literature was the English poet and playwright **William Shakespeare**. Between 1590 and 1613, he wrote 37 plays that are still performed around the world. Shakespeare's genius was in expressing universal themes in everyday realistic settings. His work explores Renaissance ideals such as the complexity of the individual and the importance of the classics.

At the same time, his characters speak in language that common people can understand and appreciate. Shakespeare's comedies, such as *A Midsummer Night's Dream*, laugh at the follies and joys of young people in love. His history plays, such as *Richard III*, chronicle the power struggles of English kings. His tragedies show human beings crushed by powerful forces or their own weakness. In *Romeo and Juliet*, two teenagers fall victim to an old family feud, while *Macbeth* depicts an ambitious

>> Boats sit in front of the island Utopia, from More's 1516 book *Utopia*. On the island, "...men and women of all ranks, go to hear lectures of one sort or other." More advocated for an education system available to all.

>> William Shakespeare (1564–1616), English author, playwright, and poet

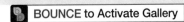 BOUNCE to Activate Gallery

couple whose desire for political power leads them to murder.

Shakespeare's love of words vastly enriched the English language. More than 1,700 words appeared for the first time in his works, including *bedroom*, *lonely*, *generous*, *gloomy*, *heartsick*, *hurry*, and *sneak*.

☑ **COMPARE** What Renaissance themes are explored in Shakespeare's works?

The Printing Revolution

The great works of Renaissance literature reached a large audience. The reason for this was a crucial breakthrough in technology—the development of printing in Europe.

The New Technology In 1456, **Johannes Gutenberg** (GOOT un burg) of Mainz, Germany, printed a complete edition of the Christian Bible. Gutenberg may have heard reports of the use of movable ceramic type in China. He developed his own, more durable metal type and combined it with a printing press, a machine that allowed fast production of printed pages. With the Gutenberg Bible, the European age of printing had begun. Within a few years, printing presses using Gutenberg's technology sprang up in Italy, Germany, the Netherlands, and England.

The development of printing set off revolutionary changes that would transform Europe. Before the printing press, there had been only a few thousand books in all of Europe. These books had been slowly copied out by hand. By 1500, according to some estimates, 15 to 20 million volumes had been produced on new printing presses. In the next century, between 150 and 200 million books went into circulation.

The Impact of the Printed Book The printing revolution ushered in a new era of mass production of books. It also affected the price of books. Books printed with movable type on rag paper were easier to produce and cheaper than hand-copied works. As books became readily available, more people learned to read and write. They thus gained access to a broad range of knowledge as presses churned out books on topics from medicine and law to astrology, mining, and geography.

Printing influenced both religious and secular, or nonreligious, thought. "The preaching of sermons is speaking to a few of mankind," noted an English author, "but printing books is talking to the whole world." With printed books, educated Europeans were exposed to new ideas that greatly expanded their horizons.

The new printing presses contributed to the religious turmoil that engulfed Europe in the 1500s. By then, many Christians could read the Bible

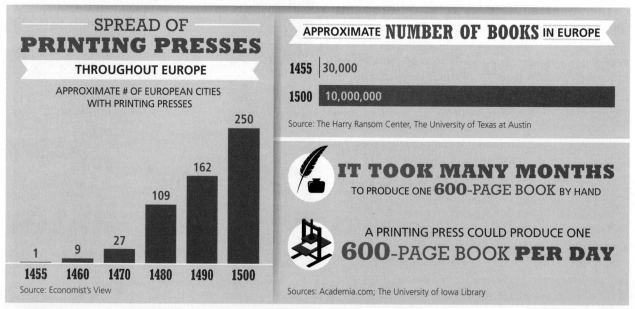

EFFECTS OF THE **PRINTING PRESS**

SPREAD OF **PRINTING PRESSES**
THROUGHOUT EUROPE

APPROXIMATE # OF EUROPEAN CITIES WITH PRINTING PRESSES

Year	Number
1455	1
1460	9
1470	27
1480	109
1490	162
1500	250

Source: Economist's View

APPROXIMATE **NUMBER OF BOOKS** IN EUROPE

Year	Number
1455	30,000
1500	10,000,000

Source: The Harry Ransom Center, The University of Texas at Austin

IT TOOK MANY MONTHS TO PRODUCE ONE **600**-PAGE BOOK BY HAND

A PRINTING PRESS COULD PRODUCE ONE **600**-PAGE BOOK **PER DAY**

Sources: Academia.com; The University of Iowa Library

>> **Analyze Charts** The chart shows the effects of the printing press in Europe. Is it likely or unlikely that in 1500, only the largest European capital cities had printing presses?

for themselves. As a result, the ideas of religious reformers spread faster and to a larger audience than ever before.

☑ **CHECK UNDERSTANDING** Why was it hard for the general population to access books before the printing press?

☑ ASSESSMENT

1. **Identify Cause and Effect** What effects did the invention of the printing press have on European society?

2. **Draw Conclusions** How did the Flemish painters Jan van Eyck and Pieter Bruegel's realistic portrayals of townspeople and peasants reflect common themes in Renaissance art?

3. **Compare** Why is the German artist Albrecht Dürer compared to the Italian Renaissance figure Leonardo da Vinci?

4. **Identify Central Ideas** What intellectual topics did the Renaissance humanist Sir Thomas More explore?

5. **Analyze Information** Shakespeare wrote plays about historical figures such as the Roman general Julius Caesar. How does this reflect an important aspect of the Renaissance?

6. **Connections to Today** Which do you think had a greater impact on its time, the printing revolution or today's information revolution?

>> Johannes Gutenberg with the first printing press in 1450s Mainz, Germany

🖥 **GO ONLINE** to access these biographies: Desiderius Erasmus, William Shakespeare

10.3

Although the clergy had been selling indulgences for years, this practice sparked the first serious steps toward reform.

 BOUNCE to Activate Flipped Video

Objectives

Summarize the factors that encouraged the Protestant Reformation.

Explain the impact of the printing press on the Reformation.

Analyze Martin Luther's role in shaping the Protestant Reformation.

Explain the teachings and impact of John Calvin.

Key Terms

indulgence
Martin Luther
Wittenberg
Charles V
diet
John Calvin
predestination
Geneva
theocracy

The Protestant Reformation

During the Renaissance, Christians from all levels of society grew impatient with the corruption of the clergy and the worldliness of the Roman Catholic Church. In the words of one unhappy peasant, "Instead of saving the souls of the dead and sending them to Heaven, [the clergy] gorge themselves at banquets after funerals . . . They are wicked wolves! They would like to devour us all, dead or alive."

Causes of the Reformation

From such bitterness sprang new calls for reform. During the Middle Ages, the Church had renewed itself from within. In the 1500s, however, the movement for reform unleashed forces that would shatter Christian unity in Europe. This reform movement is known as the Protestant Reformation.

Abuses Within the Church Beginning in the late Middle Ages, the Church had become increasingly caught up in worldly affairs. Popes competed with Italian princes for political power. They fought long wars to protect the Papal States against invasions by secular rulers. They plotted against powerful monarchs who tried to seize control of the Church within their lands.

Popes, like other Renaissance rulers, led lavish lives. When Leo X, a son of Lorenzo the Magnificent, was elected pope, he is said to have exclaimed, "God has given us the papacy—let us enjoy it." Like other Renaissance rulers, popes were patrons of the arts. They hired painters and sculptors to beautify churches and spent vast sums to rebuild the Cathedral of St. Peter in Rome.

To finance such projects, the Church increased fees for services such as marriages and baptisms. Some clergy also promoted the sale of indulgences. An **indulgence** was a type of pardon that the Church said lessened the time of punishment a soul faced for sins committed during a person's lifetime. In the Middle Ages, the Church had granted indulgences only for good deeds. By the late 1400s, however, indulgences could be bought with money or a gift to the Church.

Many Christians protested such practices. In Northern Europe, especially, religious piety deepened even as interest in secular things was growing. Christian humanists such as Erasmus urged a return to the simplicity of the early Christian church. They stressed Bible study and rejected Church pomp.

Early Reformers Even before the Protestant Reformation, a few religious thinkers had called for change. In England in the late 1300s, John Wycliffe attacked corruption in the Church. He also questioned some Church doctrines. He is probably best remembered for supporting the translation of the Bible into English. After his death, Wycliffe was condemned for heresy, but not before his ideas had spread to other lands.

A Czech priest and philosopher, John Hus, was a follower of Wycliffe. Like Wycliffe, Hus believed Christians should be allowed to read the Bible in their own language. He rejected some Church teachings, including indulgences. Put on trial for his activities, he was condemned and burned at the stake. His followers continued to operate in Eastern Europe, despite Church efforts to destroy the movement.

☑ **ANALYZE INFORMATION** What factors worked together to set the groundwork for the Protestant Reformation?

Martin Luther's Protests Bring Change

Protests against the Church continued to grow. In 1517, these protests erupted into a full scale revolt. The man who triggered the revolt was a German monk and professor of theology named **Martin Luther**.

Raised in a middle-class German family, Martin Luther had been slated by his father for a career as a lawyer. As a youth, however, he had a powerful religious experience that changed his life. One day, during a violent storm, a terrified Luther cried out to

St. Anne for help. He promised to become a monk if he were spared.

True to his word, Luther entered a monastery. There, he prayed, fasted, and tried to lead a holy life. Still, he suffered from doubts. He believed he was a sinner, doomed to eternal damnation.

He also grew increasingly disillusioned with what he saw as the corruption and worldliness of the Church. An incident in his native town of **Wittenberg,** Germany, prompted him to act.

95 Theses Challenge the Church In 1517, a German priest, Johann Tetzel, set up a pulpit on the outskirts of Wittenberg. With the approval of the pope, he sold indulgences to any Christian who contributed money for the rebuilding of the Cathedral of St. Peter in Rome. Tetzel claimed that purchase of these indulgences would assure entry into heaven not only for the buyers but for their dead relatives as well.

To a pious man like Luther, Tetzel's actions were an outrage. Luther was furious that people could pay for indulgences and think they were saved instead of seeking true repentance for their sins. Besides, only the rich could afford indulgences.

>> Martin Luther nails his 95 Theses to the church door in Wittenberg. The theses also contained an invitation to church leaders to debate Luther on the issues raised by his theses. The invitation was ignored.

 BOUNCE to Activate Illustration

In response, Luther drew up a list of 95 Theses, or arguments, against indulgences. Following the custom of the time, he posted the list on the door of Wittenberg's All Saints Church. In the 95 Theses, he argued that indulgences had no basis in the Bible, that the pope had no authority to release souls from purgatory (a place where, according to Church teachings, sinners atoned for their sins after death), and that Christians could be saved only through faith.

A Firestorm Begins Almost overnight, copies of Luther's 95 Theses were printed and distributed across Europe, where they stirred furious debate. The Church called on Luther to recant, or give up his views. Luther refused. Instead, he developed even more radical doctrines. Before long, he was urging Christians to reject the tyranny of Rome. He wrote that the Church could only be reformed by secular, or non-Church, authorities.

> I have cast the die. . . . I will not reconcile myself to them [the Roman Catholic Church] for all eternity. . . . Let them condemn and burn all that belongs to me; in return I will do as

>> Charles V summoned the excommunicated Luther to the Diet of Worms. When Luther refused to recant, Charles V declared him an outlaw. This made it a criminal offense for anyone to help Luther in any way.

much for them. . . . Now I no longer fear, and I am publishing a book in the German tongue about Christian reform, directed against the pope, in language as violent as if I were addressing the Antichrist.

—Martin Luther, 1520

In 1521, Pope Leo X excommunicated Luther. Later that year, the new Holy Roman emperor, **Charles V**, summoned Luther to the **diet**, or assembly, of German princes at the city of Worms (vohrms). Luther went, expecting to defend his writings. Instead, the emperor simply ordered him to give them up. Luther again refused.

Charles declared Luther an outlaw, making it a crime for anyone in the empire to give him food or shelter. Still, Luther had many powerful supporters. One of them let Luther hide in his castle. Throughout Germany, thousands hailed him as a hero. They accepted his teachings and, following his lead, renounced the authority of the pope.

Luther's Teachings At the heart of Luther's teachings were several beliefs. First, he argued that salvation could be achieved through faith alone. He thus rejected the Church doctrine that good deeds were necessary for salvation. Second, Luther declared that the Bible was the sole source of religious truth. He denied other traditional authorities, such as Church councils or the pope.

Third, Luther rejected the idea that priests and the Church hierarchy had special powers. He talked, instead, of the "priesthood of all believers." All Christians, he said, have equal access to God through faith and the Bible. Luther translated the Bible into the German vernacular so that ordinary people could study it. Every town, he said, should have a school where children could learn to read the Bible.

Luther wanted to change or modify other church practices. He rejected five of the seven sacraments because the Bible did not mention them. He banned indulgences, confession, pilgrimages, and prayers to saints. He simplified the elaborate ritual of the mass and instead emphasized the sermon. And Luther permitted the clergy to marry. These, and other changes, were adopted by the Lutheran churches set up by his followers.

Luther's Reforms Gain Support The new printing presses spread Luther's writings throughout Germany and Scandinavia, prompting him to declare that "printing was God's highest act of grace." Fiery preachers denounced Church abuses. By 1530, the Lutherans were using a new name, *Protestant*, for those who "protested" papal authority.

The "protests" were also expressed in some artists' work. Lucas Cranach was a court painter to Frederick the Wise, one of the electors of Saxony. Cranach befriended Luther and painted portraits of him and other Protestant notables. Cranach's work promoted the Protestant cause and its leaders.

Luther's ideas won widespread support for many reasons. Many clergy saw Luther's reforms as the answer to corruption in the Roman Catholic Church.

A number of German princes, however, embraced Lutheran beliefs for more selfish reasons. Some saw Lutheranism as a way to throw off the rule of both the Church and the Holy Roman emperor. Others welcomed a chance to seize valuable Church property in their territories. Still other Germans supported Luther because of feelings of national loyalty. They were tired of German money going to support churches and clergy in Italy.

The Peasants' Revolt Many peasants also took up Luther's call for reform. They hoped to gain his support for social and economic change as well. In 1524, a Peasants' Revolt erupted across Germany. The rebels demanded an end to serfdom and for other changes to ease their harsh lives. However, Luther strongly favored social order and respect for political authority. As the Peasants' Revolt grew more violent, Luther denounced it. With his support, nobles suppressed the rebellion with great brutality, killing as many as 100,000 people and leaving thousands more homeless.

The Peace of Augsburg During the 1530s and 1540s, Charles V tried to force Lutheran princes back into the Catholic Church, but with little success. Finally, after a number of brief wars, Charles and the princes reached a settlement. The Peace of Augsburg, signed in 1555, allowed each prince to decide which religion—Catholic or Lutheran—would be followed in his lands. Most northern German states chose Lutheranism. The southern German states remained largely Catholic.

☑ **DRAW CONCLUSIONS** What effects did Martin Luther's teachings have on Northern Europe?

>> This 1545 woodcut by Lucas Cranach the Elder is an example of how Reformation art expressed the differences between Protestantism and Catholicism. Cranach wrote that the work was meant to show the difference between the "true religion" and the "false idolatrous teaching."

 BOUNCE to Activate Gallery

>> The leaders of Germany's Peasants' Revolt of 1524 hoped for Luther's support. Instead, Luther sided with the authorities because of his belief in social order and the rule of law.

John Calvin Challenges the Church

In the wake of Luther's revolt against the Church, other reformers challenged Church authority. The most important was **John Calvin**, who lived in what is today Switzerland. Calvin had a razor-sharp mind, and his ideas had a profound effect on the direction of the Protestant Reformation.

Calvin's Teachings Calvin was born in France and trained as a priest and lawyer. In 1536, Calvin published the *Institutes of the Christian Religion*, which was widely read. In it, he set forth his religious beliefs. He also provided advice on how to organize and run a Protestant church.

Like Luther, Calvin believed that salvation was gained through faith alone. He, too, regarded the Bible as the only source of religious truth. But Calvin put forth a number of ideas of his own.

Calvin taught that God was all-powerful and that humans were by nature sinful. God alone, he said, decided whether an individual achieved eternal life. This idea that God had long ago determined who would gain salvation was known as **predestination**.

To Calvinists, the world was divided into two kinds of people—saints and sinners. Calvinists tried to live like saints, believing that only those who were saved could live truly Christian lives.

Calvin's Geneva In 1541, Protestants in the city-state of **Geneva** in Switzerland asked Calvin to lead their community. In keeping with his teachings, Calvin set up a **theocracy**, or government run by church leaders.

Calvin's followers in Geneva came to see themselves as a new "chosen people" entrusted by God to build a truly Christian society. Calvinists stressed hard work, discipline, thrift, honesty, and morality. Citizens faced fines or other harsher punishments for offenses such as fighting, swearing, laughing in church, or dancing. To many Protestants, Calvinist Geneva seemed like a model community.

Calvinist Ideas Spread Reformers from all over Europe visited Geneva and then returned home to spread Calvinist ideas. By the late 1500s, Calvinism had taken root in Germany, France, the Netherlands, England, and Scotland. This new challenge to the Roman Catholic Church set off bloody wars of religion across Europe.

In Germany, Catholics and Lutherans opposed Calvinists. In France, wars raged between French Calvinists and Catholics. Calvinists in the Netherlands organized the Dutch Reformed Church.

Beliefs and Practices of Catholicism, Lutheranism, and Calvinism

	CATHOLICISM	LUTHERANISM	CALVINISM
SALVATION	Salvation is achieved through faith and good works.	Salvation is achieved through faith alone.	God alone predetermines who will be saved.
SACRAMENTS	Priests perform seven sacraments, or rituals—baptism, confirmation, marriage, ordination, communion, anointing of the sick, and penance.	Accepts some of the sacraments, but rejects others because rituals cannot erase sin—only God can.	Accepts some of the sacraments, but rejects others because rituals cannot erase sin—only God can.
HEAD OF CHURCH	Pope	Elected councils	Council of elders
IMPORTANCE OF THE CHRISTIAN BIBLE	Bible is one source of truth; Church tradition is another.	Bible alone is source of truth.	Bible alone is source of truth.
HOW BELIEF IS REVEALED	Priests interpret the Bible and Church teachings for the people.	People read and interpret the Bible for themselves.	People read and interpret the Bible for themselves.

>> **Analyze Charts** Who served as head of the Lutheran Church? Why was this an important difference from the organization of the Catholic Church?

In Scotland, a Calvinist preacher named John Knox led a religious rebellion, overthrowing the Catholic queen and establishing the Scottish Presbyterian Church.

☑ **SUMMARIZE** How did Calvin and his supporters implement his ideas?

☑ ASSESSMENT

1. **Identify Central Ideas** How did rebellions against the Roman Catholic Church affect northern European society?

2. **Analyze Information** Why did the sale of indulgences become a critical point of focus during the Renaissance but not during the Middle Ages?

3. **Analyze Information** How did Luther's ideas provide the catalyst for the Protestant Reformation?

4. **Summarize** How did Calvin see predestination as a means to a Christian life?

5. **Connections to Today** (a) Why was the printing press essential to the success of the Protestant Reformation? (b) What role does the Internet play in political and social movements today?

The Peasants' Revolt

The Renaissance brought great changes to Europe. But for German peasants, little had changed since the medieval days of serfdom. Inspired by the Reformation, they demanded change. This led to the Peasants' Revolt of 1524–1525. Some Protestant reformers supported the revolt.

At first, Martin Luther was also sympathetic to many of the peasants' grievances. But he was appalled by the Peasants' Revolt and called on German princes to respond harshly and swiftly.

The first Primary Source below is from a list of demands drawn up by German peasants in 1525. The second is from Luther's response the same year. **As you read them, contrast their attitudes toward the peasants' right to revolt.**

>> The 1524 revolt was not the first in German history. In this image from an earlier Peasants Revolt, a knight is captured by peasants.

Primary Source 1

The Twelve Articles of the Swabian Peasants

First, it is our humble petition and desire, as also our will and desire, that in the future we should have power and authority so that each community should choose and appoint a pastor, and that we should have the right to depose him should he conduct himself improperly. The pastor thus chosen should teach us the gospel pure and simple, without any addition, doctrine, or ordinance of man....

☑ **DRAW INFERENCES** What relationship did peasants have to their pastors before the revolt?

It has been the custom hitherto for men to hold us as their own property, which is pitiable enough, considering that Christ has delivered and redeemed us all, without exception, by the shedding of his precious blood, the lowly as well as the great.

Accordingly it is consistent with Scripture that we should be free.

☑ **ANALYZE ARGUMENTS** How does the author attack the medieval institution of serfdom?

In the fourth place, it has been the custom heretofore that no poor man should be allowed to touch venison or wild fowl, or fish in flowing water, which seems to us quite unseemly and unbrotherly as well as selfish and not agreeable to the word of God. In some places the authorities preserve the game to our great annoyance and loss, recklessly permitting the unreasoning animals to destroy to no purpose our crops....

In the fifth place, we are aggrieved in the matter of woodcutting, for the noble folk have appropriated all the woods to themselves alone. If a poor man requires wood, he must pay double for it....

☑ **IDENTIFY THE MAIN IDEA** Write a single sentence that expresses the main concern of the Fourth and Fifth articles.

Seventh, we will not hereafter allow ourselves to be further oppressed by our lords, but will let them demand only what is just and proper according to the word of the agreement between the lord and the peasant. The lord should no longer try to force more services or other dues from the peasant without payment, but permit the peasant to enjoy his holding in peace and quiet. The peasant should, however, help the lord when it is necessary, and at proper times, when it will not be disadvantageous to the peasant, and for a suitable payment....

☑ **ANALYZE INTERACTIONS** What does the author consider the proper relationship between peasants and lords? How might a lord respond?

Primary Source 2

Against the Robbing and Murdering Hordes of Peasants, Martin Luther

In the former book I did not venture to judge the peasants, since they had offered to be set right and to be instructed, and Christ's command, in Matthew VII, says that we are not to judge. But before I look around they go on, and, forgetting their offer, they betake themselves to violence, and rob and rage and act like mad dogs. By this it is easy to see what they had in their false minds, and that the pretenses which they made in their twelve articles, under the name of the Gospel, were nothing but lies....

☑ **IDENTIFY CAUSE AND EFFECT** Why did Luther's attitude toward the peasants change?

The peasants have taken on themselves the burden of three terrible sins against God and man, by which they have abundantly merited death in body and soul. In the first place they have sworn to be true and faithful, submissive and obedient, to their rulers, as Christ commands. . . . Because they are breaking this obedience, and are setting themselves against the higher powers, willfully and with violence, they have forfeited body and soul, as faithless, perjured, lying, disobedient knaves and scoundrels are wont [inclined] to do.... In the second place, they are starting a rebellion, and violently robbing and plundering monasteries and castles which are not theirs, by which they have a second time deserved death in body and soul, if only as highwaymen and murderers....

I will not oppose a ruler who, even though he does not tolerate the Gospel, will smite and punish these peasants without offering to submit the case to judgement. For he is within his rights, since the peasants are not contending any longer for the Gospel, but have become faithless, perjured, disobedient, rebellious murderers, robbers and blasphemers [people who mock God]....

☑ **DETERMINE AUTHOR'S POINT OF VIEW** What is Luther's attitude toward the established social order?

☑ ASSESSMENT

1. **Make Connections** How do their demands of the peasants regarding their pastors reflect some of the ideas of the Protestant Reformation?

2. **Analyze Word Choices** What is the emotional impact of the words Luther uses to describe the peasants?

3. **Analyze Arguments** Why does Luther believe that the arguments put forth in the Twelve Articles were lies?

4. **Compare and Contrast** How do these two sources reflect different concepts of social order and duty?

10.4

This portrait of King Henry VIII of England was painted by the famous court artist, Hans Holbein. Henry broke with the Catholic Church over differences concerning his marriage to Catherine of Aragon.

 BOUNCE to Activate Flipped Video

Objectives

Describe the new ideas that Protestant sects embraced.

Understand why England formed a new church.

Analyze how the Catholic Church reformed itself.

Explain why many groups faced persecution during the Reformation.

Explain the impact of the Reformation.

Key Terms

sect
Henry VIII
Mary Tudor
Thomas Cranmer
Elizabeth
canonize
compromise
Council of Trent
Ignatius of Loyola
St. Teresa of Avila
ghetto

Reformation Ideas Spread

Henry III, the Catholic king of France, was deeply disturbed by the Calvinist reformers in Geneva. "It would have been a good thing," he wrote, "if the city of Geneva were long ago reduced to ashes, because of the evil doctrine which has been sown from that city throughout Christendom."

An Explosion of Protestant Sects

Henry was not alone in his anger. Across Europe, Catholic monarchs and the Catholic Church fought back against the Protestant challenge. They also took steps to reform the Church and to restore its spiritual leadership in the Christian world.

As the Reformation continued, hundreds of new Protestant **sects**, or religious groups, sprang up. Some sects developed their own versions of the teachings of Luther or Calvin, or followed the teachings of another Swiss reformer, Ulrich Zwingli. Others developed ideas that were increasingly radical.

Radical Reformers A number of groups, for example, rejected the practice of infant baptism. Infants, they argued, are too young to understand what it means to accept the Christian faith. Only adults, they felt, should receive the sacrament of baptism. Because of this belief, they became known as Anabaptists.

Most Anabaptists, however, were peaceful. In an age of religious intolerance, they called for religious toleration. They also put forward the idea of the separation of church and state. Despite harsh persecution for their threat to the traditional order, these groups influenced Protestant thinking in many countries. Today,

GO ONLINE to access your digital course

the Baptists, Mennonites, and Amish all trace their religious ancestry to the Anabaptists.

☑ **EXPLAIN** In what ways did Anabaptist sects differ from other Protestant sects?

The English Reformation

In England, religious leaders like John Wycliffe had called for Church reform as early as the 1300s. By the 1520s, some English clergy were exploring Protestant ideas. The break with the Catholic Church, however, was the work not of religious leaders but of King **Henry VIII**. For political reasons, Henry wanted to end papal control over the English Church.

Henry VIII Seeks an Annulment At first, Henry VIII stood firmly against the Protestant revolt. The pope even awarded him the title "Defender of the Faith" for a pamphlet that Henry wrote denouncing Luther.

In 1527, however, an issue arose that set Henry at odds with the Church. After 18 years of marriage, Henry and his Spanish wife, Catherine of Aragon, had only one surviving child, **Mary Tudor**. Henry felt that England's stability depended on his having a male heir. He wanted to divorce Catherine and marry a new wife, hoping she would bear him a son. Because Catholic law does not permit divorce, he asked the pope to annul, or cancel, his marriage.

Popes had annulled royal marriages before. But this pope refused. He did not want to offend the Holy Roman emperor Charles V, Catherine's nephew. He therefore refused Henry's request.

Henry VIII Breaks with the Church Henry was furious. Spurred on by his advisers, many of whom leaned toward Protestantism, he decided to take over the English Church. Henry had Parliament pass a series of laws that took the English Church from the pope's control and placed it under Henry's rule. The most notable of these laws was the Act of Supremacy, passed in 1534. It made Henry "the only supreme head on Earth of the Church of England."

By then, Henry had appointed **Thomas Cranmer** archbishop. Cranmer had annulled the king's marriage to Catherine. Henry married Anne Boleyn, a noble lady-in-waiting to Catherine. Soon, Anne gave birth to a daughter, **Elizabeth**. In the years that followed, Henry married four more times, but had only one son, Edward.

Many loyal Catholics refused to accept the Act of Supremacy and were executed for treason.

Among them was the well-known English humanist, Sir Thomas More. More was later **canonized**, or recognized as a saint, by the Catholic Church.

The Church of England Between 1536 and 1540, Henry ordered the closing of all convents and monasteries in England and seized their lands and wealth for the crown. This became know as the dissolution, the dissolving, or ending, of Catholic monasteries in England.

This move brought new wealth to the royal exchequer. Henry shrewdly granted some church lands to nobles and other high-ranking citizens, thereby securing their support for the Anglican Church, as the new Church of England was called. Henry used much of his newly acquired wealth to pursue wars in Europe.

Despite Henry's actions in rejecting the pope's authority, he was not a religious radical. He had no use for most Protestant doctrines. Aside from breaking away from Rome and allowing use of the English Bible, he kept most Catholic forms of worship.

Religious Turmoil When Henry died in 1547, his nine-year-old son, Edward VI, inherited the throne.

>> Monks were forced to leave monasteries as part of the dissolution ordered by King Henry VIII. Henry ordered that Catholic convents and monasteries be closed, claiming they were centers of immorality.

🅑 BOUNCE to Activate Timeline

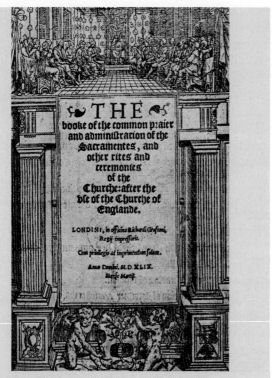

>> The *Book of Common Prayer* was written in English, rather than Latin. This is the title page from the 1549 first edition.

>> Although Protestant, Queen Elizabeth showed more tolerance for Catholics and other Protestant sects in an effort to end religious conflicts. The Elizabethan settlement went far in achieving that goal.

The young king's advisers were devout Protestants who pushed for Calvinist reforms. Thomas Cranmer drew up the *Book of Common Prayer* to be used in the Anglican Church. It imposed a moderate form of Protestant service but preserved many Catholic doctrines. Even so, it sparked uprisings that were harshly suppressed.

When Edward died in his teens, his half-sister Mary Tudor came to the throne. A pious Catholic, she was determined to make England Catholic once more. She failed, but not before hundreds of English Protestants, including Archbishop Cranmer, were burned at the stake for heresy.

The Elizabethan Settlement On Mary's death, the throne passed to her Protestant half-sister, Elizabeth. For years, Elizabeth had survived court intrigues, including the religious swings under Edward and Mary. As queen, Elizabeth adopted a policy of religious **compromise**, or acceptable middle ground. She moved cautiously at first but gradually enforced reforms that both moderate Catholics and Protestants could accept. This policy of compromise was later known as the Elizabethan settlement.

Under Elizabeth, English replaced Latin as the language of the Anglican service. The *Book of Common Prayer* was restored, although it was revised to make it more acceptable to Catholics. Much of the Catholic ritual was kept. The Church of England also kept the old hierarchy of bishops and archbishops, but Elizabeth quickly affirmed that the monarch, not the pope, was the head of the Anglican Church.

Even though Elizabeth preserved many traditional Catholic ideas, she firmly established England as a Protestant nation. During a long and skillful reign, she worked to restore unity, and England escaped the kinds of religious wars that tore apart other European countries in the 1500s.

☑ **ANALYZE INFORMATION** What factors led to the formation of the Church of England?

The Catholic Reformation

As the Protestant Reformation swept across northern Europe, a vigorous reform movement took hold within the Catholic Church. The leader of this movement, known as the Catholic Reformation, was Pope Paul III. (Protestants often called it the Counter-Reformation.)

During the 1530s and 1540s, the pope set out to revive the moral authority of the Church and roll back the Protestant tide. To end corruption within the papacy, he appointed reformers to top posts. They and their successors led the Catholic Reformation for the rest of the century.

The Council of Trent Passes Reforms To establish the direction that reform should take, the pope called the **Council of Trent** in 1545. It met off and on for almost 20 years. The council reaffirmed the traditional Catholic views that Protestants had challenged. The council believed that salvation comes through faith and good works. It declared that the Christian Bible, while a major source of religious truth, is not the only source.

The council also took steps to end abuses in the Church. It provided stiff penalties for worldliness and corruption among the clergy. It also established schools to create a better-educated clergy who could challenge Protestant teachings.

The Inquisition Is Strengthened To deal with the Protestant threat more directly, Pope Paul strengthened the Inquisition. The Inquisition was a Church court set up during the Middle Ages. To battle Protestant ideas, the Inquisition used secret testimony, torture, and execution to root out what the Church considered heresy. It also prepared the *Index of Forbidden Books*, a list of works considered too immoral for Catholics to read. The list included books by Luther and Calvin and even some books by Italian humanists.

The Jesuits In 1540, the pope recognized a new religious order, the Society of Jesus, or Jesuits. Founded by **Ignatius of Loyola**, the Jesuit order was dedicated to combating heresy and spreading the Catholic faith.

Ignatius was a Spanish knight whose military career ended abruptly when his leg was shattered in battle. During a long and painful recovery, he found comfort reading about Christian saints who had overcome mental and physical torture. He then vowed to become a "soldier of God."

Ignatius drew up a strict program for the Jesuits. It included spiritual and moral discipline, rigorous religious training, and absolute obedience to the Church. Led by Ignatius, the Jesuits embarked on a crusade to defend and spread the Catholic faith worldwide.

To further the Catholic cause, Jesuits became advisers to Catholic rulers, helping them combat heresy in their lands. They set up schools that taught humanist and Catholic beliefs and enforced discipline and obedience. Daring Jesuits slipped into Protestant lands in disguise to minister to Catholics.

>> Pope Paul III meets with Catholic religious leaders at the Council of Trent, where he called for a series of reforms to correct abuses within the Church.

>> Ignatius of Loyola founded the Jesuits and was one of the key individuals of the Catholic Reformation. He represented the Church's new commitment to religious education, moral reform, and strict obedience to Church teachings.

Jesuit missionaries spread their Catholic faith to Asia, Africa, and the Americas.

Teresa of Avila As the Catholic Reformation spread, many Catholics experienced renewed feelings of intense faith. Among those who experienced religious renewal was **Teresa of Avila**. Born into a wealthy Spanish family, Teresa entered a convent in her youth. The convent routine was not strict enough for her strong religious nature. So she set up her own order of nuns. They lived in isolation, eating and sleeping very little and dedicating themselves to prayer and meditation.

Impressed by her spiritual life, her superiors in the Church asked Teresa to reorganize and reform Spanish convents and monasteries. Teresa was widely honored for her work, and after her death the Church declared her a saint. Her spiritual writings rank among the most important Christian texts of her time and are still widely read today.

Results of the Catholic Reformation By 1600, the majority of Europeans remained Catholic. Tireless Catholic reformers, like Francis de Sales in France, had succeeded in bringing Protestants back into the Catholic Church. Across Catholic Europe, piety,

charity, and religious art flourished, and church abuses were reduced from within.

The reforms of the Catholic Reformation did stop the Protestant tide and even returned some areas to the Catholic Church. Still, Europe remained divided into a Catholic south and a Protestant north. This division would fuel conflicts that lasted for centuries, although later, the goals were more political than religious.

☑ **ANALYZE INFORMATION** What were some of the specific results of the Catholic Reformation?

Religious Persecution Continues

During this period of heightened religious passion, persecution was widespread. Both Catholics and Protestants fostered intolerance. The Inquisition executed many people accused of heresy. Catholic mobs attacked and killed Protestants. Protestants killed Catholic priests and destroyed Catholic churches. Both Catholics and Protestants persecuted radical sects like the Anabaptists.

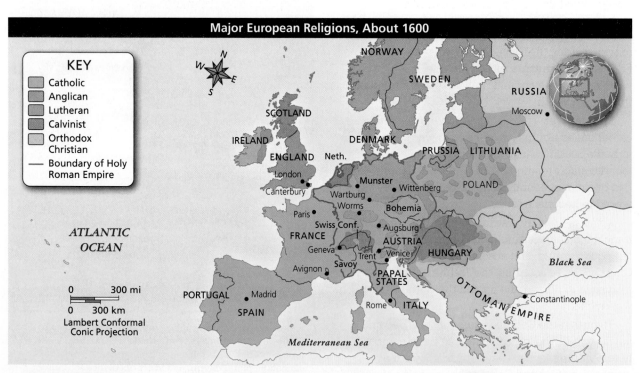

Major European Religions, About 1600

KEY
- Catholic
- Anglican
- Lutheran
- Calvinist
- Orthodox Christian
- Boundary of Holy Roman Empire

ATLANTIC OCEAN

0   300 mi
0   300 km
Lambert Conformal Conic Projection

NORWAY
SWEDEN
RUSSIA
Moscow
SCOTLAND
IRELAND
DENMARK
ENGLAND   Neth.
PRUSSIA   LITHUANIA
London
Canterbury   Munster   Wittenberg   POLAND
Wartburg
Worms   Bohemia
Paris
Swiss Conf.   Augsburg
FRANCE   AUSTRIA
Geneva   Trent   Venice   HUNGARY
Avignon   Savoy
PAPAL STATES   Black Sea
PORTUGAL   Madrid   OTTOMAN EMPIRE
SPAIN   Rome   ITALY   Constantinople
Mediterranean Sea

>> **Analyze Maps** By 1600, the spread of Protestantism had transformed Catholic Europe. What was the main religion in France? Why were most people in each region practicing that religion by 1600?

🔲 BOUNCE to Activate Map

Witch Hunts The religious fervor of the time contributed to a wave of witch hunting. Between 1450 and 1750, tens of thousands of women and men died as victims of witch hunts. Often, those accused of being witches, or agents of the devil, were women.

Scholars have offered various reasons for this savage persecution, but most agree that it had to do with people's beliefs in magic and spirits. At the time, people saw a close link between magic and heresy. Witches, they believed, were in league with the devil and were thus anti-Christian.

In troubled times, people looked for scapegoats. Typically, people accused of witchcraft were social outcasts—beggars, poor widows, midwives blamed for infant deaths, or herbalists whose potions and cures were seen as gifts of the devil.

In the charged religious atmosphere of the Reformation, many people were convinced that witchcraft and devil worship were on the rise. Most victims of witch hunts died in the German states, Switzerland, and France, all centers of religious conflict. When the wars of religion came to an end, the persecution of witches also declined.

Persecution of Jews The Reformation brought hard times to Europe's Jews. For many Jews in Italy, the early Renaissance had been a time of relative prosperity. Unlike Spain, which had expelled its Jews in 1492, Italy allowed them to remain. Some Jews followed the traditional trades they had been restricted to in medieval times. They were goldsmiths, artists, traders, and moneylenders. Others expanded into law, government, and business. A few well-educated Jews served as advisers to powerful rulers.

Yet the pressure remained strong on Jews to convert. By 1516, Jews in Venice had to live in a separate quarter of the city called the **ghetto**. Other Italian cities set up walled ghettos in which Jews were forced to live.

At first, Luther hoped that Jews would be converted to his teachings. When they did not convert, he called for them to be expelled from Christian lands and for their synagogues to be burned.

During the Reformation, restrictions on Jews increased. Some German princes expelled Jews from their lands. All German states confined Jews to ghettos or required them to wear a yellow badge if they traveled outside the ghetto.

In the 1550s, Pope Paul IV reversed the lenient policy of Renaissance popes and restricted Jewish activities. After 1550, many Jews migrated to Poland-

>> People gather on a street in a Jewish ghetto in Rome. The gate at the end of the street would likely be closed and locked at sundown. This was for the protection of the Jewish residents from mobs bent on violence.

Lithuania and to parts of the Ottoman Empire. Dutch Calvinists also tolerated Jews, taking in families who were driven out of Portugal and Spain.

☑ **SYNTHESIZE** How did increased religious fervor lead to persecutions?

☑ ASSESSMENT

1. **Explain** Why did some consider the Anabaptist sects radical?

2. **Identify Cause and Effect** What roles did Henry VIII and Elizabeth I play in bringing the Reformation to England?

3. **Analyze Information** What steps did the Catholic Church take to reform and to stop the growth of Protestantism?

4. **Distinguish** Why did the Reformation see an increase in persecution of people of different beliefs or religions?

5. **Connections to Today** What long-term effects of the Protestant Reformation can you see in the United States today?

GO ONLINE to access this biography: Ignatius of Loyola

10.5

The ancient Greek astronomer Ptolemy believed that the Earth was at the center of the universe and the sun and stars revolved around it. This is an image of Ptolemy's Geocentric Universe.

 BOUNCE to Activate Flipped Video

Objectives

Explain how new discoveries in astronomy changed the way people viewed the universe.

Understand the new scientific method and how it developed.

Identify the contributions that Galileo, Copernicus, Newton, and other scientists made to the Scientific Revolution.

Key Terms

Nicolaus Copernicus
heliocentric
Tycho Brahe
Johannes Kepler
Galileo
scientific method
Francis Bacon
René Descartes
hypothesis
Robert Boyle
Isaac Newton
calculus
gravity

The Scientific Revolution

Both the Renaissance and the Reformation looked to the past for models. Humanists turned to ancient classical learning. Religious reformers looked to the Bible and early Christian times for inspiration. The Renaissance spirit of inquiry led scientists to explore beyond the knowledge of the ancients.

Changing Views of the Universe

Beginning in the 1500s, profound changes took place in the sciences that pointed toward a future shaped by a new way of thinking about the physical universe. These new understandings about the physical world became part of what is now called the Scientific Revolution.

Old Views Until the mid-1500s, European scholars accepted the ideas set out by ancient Greek thinkers like Aristotle. The Greek astronomer Ptolemy had taught that Earth was the center of the universe.

European scholars long accepted this view because it seemed to agree with common sense. It also followed the teachings of the Church. In the 1500s and 1600s, startling discoveries radically changed the way Europeans viewed the physical world.

Copernicus Offers a New Theory In 1543, Polish scholar **Nicolaus Copernicus** (koh PUR nih kus) published *On the Revolutions of the Heavenly Spheres*. In it, he proposed a **heliocentric**, or sun-centered, model of the universe. The sun,

GO ONLINE to access your digital course

he said, stands at the center of the universe. Earth is just one of several planets that revolve around the sun.

Most experts rejected this revolutionary theory, which contradicted both Church teachings and the teachings of Ptolemy. In Europe, all scientific knowledge and many religious teachings were based on the arguments developed by classical thinkers. If Ptolemy's reasoning about the planets was wrong, then the whole system of human knowledge might be called into question.

In the late 1500s, the Danish astronomer **Tycho Brahe** (TEE koh BRAH uh) provided evidence to support Copernicus's theory. Brahe set up an astronomical observatory. Every night for years, he carefully observed the sky, accumulating data about the movement of the heavenly bodies.

After Brahe's death, his assistant, the brilliant German astronomer and mathematician **Johannes Kepler** used Brahe's data to calculate the orbits of the planets revolving around the sun. His calculations supported Copernicus's heliocentric view. At the same time, however, they showed that each planet does not move in a perfect circle, as both Ptolemy and Copernicus believed, but in an oval-shaped orbit called an ellipse.

The Church Rejects Galileo's Discoveries

Scientists from many different lands built on the work of Copernicus and Kepler. In Italy, **Galileo Galilei** used new technology to assemble an astronomical telescope. With this instrument he became the first person to see mountains on the moon. He observed that the four moons of Jupiter move slowly around that planet—exactly, he realized, the way Copernicus said that Earth moves around the sun.

Galileo's discoveries caused an uproar. Other scholars attacked him because his observations contradicted ancient views about the world. The Church condemned him because his ideas challenged the Christian teaching that the heavens were fixed, unmoving, and perfect.

In 1633, Galileo was tried before the Inquisition, and spent the rest of his life under house arrest. Threatened with death unless he withdrew his "heresies," Galileo agreed to state publicly in court that Earth stood motionless at the center of the universe. However, legend has it that as he left the court he muttered, "And yet it moves."

☑ **ANALYZE INFORMATION** Why were the discoveries of astronomers like Galileo seen as radical and a threat to Church authority?

A New Scientific Method

Despite the opposition of the Church, by the early 1600s a new approach to science had emerged. Unlike most earlier approaches, it started not with Aristotle or Ptolemy or even the Bible but with observation and experimentation. Most important, complex mathematical calculations were used to convert the observations and experiments into scientific laws. In time, this approach became known as the **scientific method.**

Revolutionary Scientific Thinkers The new scientific method was really a revolution in thought. Two giants of this revolution were the Englishman **Francis Bacon** and the Frenchman **René Descartes** (day KAHRT). Each devoted himself to understanding how truth is determined.

Both Bacon and Descartes, writing in the early 1600s, rejected Aristotle's scientific assumptions. They also challenged the medieval scholars who sought to make the physical world fit in with the teachings of the Church. Both argued that truth is not known at the beginning of inquiry but at the end, after a long process of investigation.

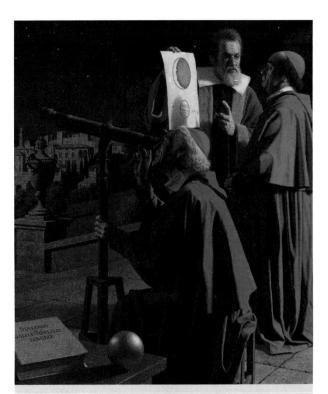

>> Galileo explains to skeptical church officials that the moon's phases reflect its relation to the earth and the sun. Galileo studied the moon through a special telescope he built for the purpose.

 BOUNCE to Activate Gallery

Bacon and Descartes differed in their methods, however. Bacon stressed experimentation and observation. He wanted science to make life better for people by leading to practical technologies. Descartes emphasized human reasoning as the best road to understanding. His *Discourse on Method* explains how he decided to discard all traditional authorities and search for provable knowledge. Left only with doubt, he concluded that doubt was the only thing he could not question, and that in order to doubt he had to exist as a rational, thinking being. At that point, he made his famous statement, "I think, therefore I am."

A Step-By-Step Process Over time, the scientific method evolved into a step-by-step process of discovery. Scientists collected and accurately measured data. To explain the data, scientists used reasoning to propose a logical **hypothesis,** or possible explanation. They then tested the hypothesis with further observation or experimentation.

For the first time, mathematical calculations were used to convert the observations and experiments into scientific laws. After reaching a conclusion, scientists repeated their work at least once—and usually many times—to confirm and refine their hypotheses or formulate better ones.

Thinkers like Bacon and Descartes helped bring the scientific method to the pursuit of all knowledge. Their pioneering approaches to thought opened the way to even more revolutionary ways of thinking in the 1700s.

☑ **EXPLAIN** How did the ideas of Francis Bacon and René Descartes lead to a new scientific method?

Breakthroughs in Medicine and Chemistry

The 1500s and 1600s saw dramatic changes in many of the sciences, especially medicine and chemistry. Like Copernicus, Bacon, and Descartes, scientists rejected long-held assumptions. They relied on new technology, such as the microscope, and benefited from better communication, especially the availability of printed books.

Exploring Human Anatomy Medieval physicians relied on the works of the ancient Greek physician Galen. Galen, however, had made many errors, in

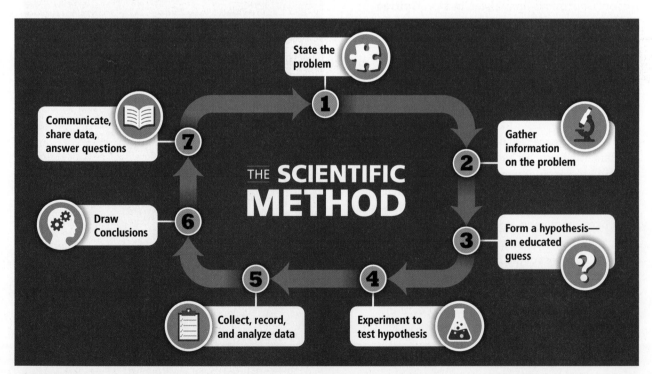

>> **Analyze Information** The scientific method, still used today, is based on careful observation and measurement of data. Why do you think it's critical to follow each step in sequence and to follow the same procedure for each step?

part because he had limited knowledge of human anatomy. During the Renaissance, physicians made new efforts to study the human body.

In 1543, Andreas Vesalius (vuh SAY lee us) published *On the Structure of the Human Body*, the first accurate and detailed study of human anatomy. Vesalius's careful and clear drawings corrected errors inherited from ancient classical authorities.

About the same time, French physician Ambroise Paré (pa RAY) made many practical advances. He developed a new, more effective ointment for preventing infection and better ways to seal wounds during surgery. He introduced the use of artificial limbs and invented several scientific instruments.

In the early 1600s, William Harvey, an English scholar, described the circulation of the blood for the first time. He showed how the heart serves as a pump to force blood through veins and arteries. Pioneering scientists like Harvey opened the way for further advances.

The Microscope Later in the 1600s, the Dutch inventor Anton van Leeuwenhoek (LAY wun hohk) perfected the single-lens microscope. Van Leeuwenhoek worked on grinding lenses as a hobby. He used them to examine tiny objects such as lice or the mouths of bees.

Peering through his microscope at drops of water, he was surprised to see tiny organisms, which he called "very little animalcules." Van Leeuwenhoek thus became the first human to see cells and microorganisms such as bacteria. For this work, he is often called the founder of microbiology. Over time, the microscope would lead to still more startling discoveries.

The New Science of Chemistry The branch of science today called chemistry was known as alchemy in medieval times. Alchemists believed that one substance could be transformed into another substance and tried to turn ordinary metals into gold. During the Scientific Revolution, chemistry slowly freed itself from the magical notions of alchemy. Still, scientists benefited from some of the alchemists' practical knowledge, such as the manipulation of metals and acids.

In the 1600s, English chemist **Robert Boyle** explained that all matter was composed of tiny particles that behave in knowable ways. Boyle distinguished between individual elements and chemical compounds and explained the effect of temperature and pressure on gases. Boyle's work opened the way to modern chemical analysis of the composition of matter.

>> English surgeon John Banister dissects a corpse to teach students about human anatomy. New approaches to scientific investigation helped to change how physicians learned about the human body.

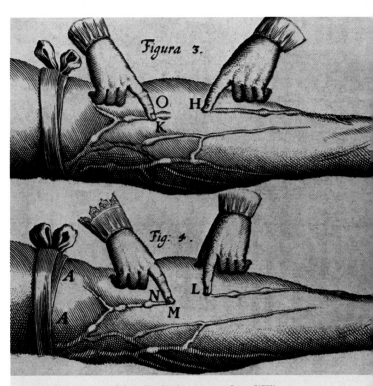

>> An illustration of the circulatory system from William Harvey's book, *On the Motions of the Heart and Blood*. Harvey revolutionized medicine by suggesting that blood circulates continuously throughout the body.

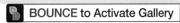

BOUNCE to Activate Gallery

>> Isaac Newton performs an experiment to analyze how light is made up of a spectrum of different colors.

Isaac Newton Links the Sciences As a student at Cambridge University in England, **Isaac Newton** devoured the works of the leading scientists of his day. By age 24, he had formed a brilliant theory to explain why the planets moved as they did. According to one story, Newton saw an apple fall from a tree. He wondered whether the force that pulled that apple to Earth also controlled the movements of the planets.

Over the next 20 years, Newton perfected his theory. To do so, he developed the basis for **calculus**, a branch of mathematics. Using mathematics, he showed that a single force keeps the planets in their orbits around the sun. He called this force **gravity**.

In 1687, Newton published *Mathematical Principles of Natural Philosophy*, explaining the law of gravity and other workings of the universe. Nature, argued Newton, follows uniform laws. All motion in the universe can be measured and described mathematically.

To many people, Newton's work seemed to link the sciences of physics and astronomy with mathematics, just as gravity bound the universe together.

For more than 200 years Newton's laws held fast, until the early 1900s, when a revolution in physics once more transformed the way people saw the universe. Still, Newton's work, ranging from the laws of motion and gravity to mathematics, makes him one of the most influential scientists of all time.

☑ **EXPLAIN** How did Boyle's research transform chemistry into a real science?

☑ ASSESSMENT

1. **Recognize Ideologies** How did the theories of Copernicus and Galileo change the way people understood the universe?

2. **Make Generalizations** In what ways did the scientific method differ from earlier approaches to learning?

3. **Identify Cause and Effect** What impact did Renaissance ideas have on medicine?

4. **Synthesize** How did Newton build on the ideas of earlier scientists?

5. **Infer** How did the Reformation help spur the Scientific Revolution?

6. **Quest Connections** Choose one of the following scientists and explain how you think their work helped shape modern medicine: Andreas Vesalius; Ambroise Paré; William Harvey; Anton van Leeuwenhoek.

GO ONLINE to access these biographies: Galileo, Isaac Newton

Connections to Today

An explosion of cell phones in Greece

Take Action About the Information Revolution

The printing press transformed life in Renaissance Europe as much as the computer and the Internet have transformed life today. But, like all revolutions, our Information Revolution has drawbacks as well as benefits.

1. **Choose** one of these issues related to today's online world.

   - **Misinformation:** Consider how the Internet and social media have made it easy to spread false information as well as true.

   - **Identity theft:** Research privacy and security issues, including the ways hackers can steal personal information.

   - **Cyberbullying:** Explore the use of social media to victimize people, especially young people.

2. **Ask Questions** What are some things you want to learn about the issue you have selected? Write a list of questions relating for further study.

3. **Learn** Do research on the topic you have chosen. Seek out at least one print source – such as a book, magazine, or newspaper–instead of depending solely on the Internet to research the Internet.

4. **Take Action** Create an informational poster about the topic you have chosen. (For example, if you chose the first topic, you might create a poster on Tips for Determining Reliable Internet Sources.) Include both text and appropriate images.

LESSON SUMMARIES

Use these Lesson Summaries, and the longer versions available online, to review the key ideas for each lesson in this Topic.

Lesson 1: The Italian Renaissance

The Renaissance that began in Italy in the 1300s was a time of creativity and interest in learning and the arts. The intellectual movement known as humanism stressed education, classical learning, and the development of the individual. Michelangelo, one of the celebrated painters of the Renaissance, represented artists of the time with his interest in classical and religious themes.

Lesson 2: The Renaissance in Northern Europe

By the 1400s, the Renaissance spread from Italy to cities in northern Europe. The English playwright William Shakespeare was the greatest writer of the Renaissance. The printing press, invented in Germany, quickened the spread of ideas and knowledge.

Lesson 3: The Protestant Reformation

The Renaissance in Northern Europe sparked ideas which led reformers like Martin Luther and John Calvin to challenge Church authority and corruption. Eventually, these reforms led to a breaking away from the Church.

Lesson 4: Reformation Ideas Spread

As ideas of the Reformation spread, religious conflict erupted in many nations. The Roman Catholic Church, in response, started its own reform movement.

Lesson 5: Scientific Revolution

During the Scientific Revolution, discoveries by Copernicus, Newton, and Galileo changed the way Europeans viewed the physical world. The scientific method used mathematics, experimentation, and observation to gain scientific knowledge.

QUEST! FINDINGS

Build Your "Hall of Fame" Website Refer to your responses to the Quest Connections to help you build your "Hall of Fame" website. Use the rubric and other Quest resources online to guide your work.

GO ONLINE to access lesson summaries

VISUAL REVIEW

Use these graphics to review some of the key terms, people, and ideas from this Topic.

Major Themes of the Renaissance

- Importance of classical learning
- Emphasis on the individual
- Adventurous spirit and willingness to experiment
- Focus on realism in art and literature
- Questioning of traditional religious ideas

Important Figures of the Scientific Revolution

PERSON	ACHIEVEMENT	DATE
Nicolaus Copernicus	Developed the sun-centered model of the universe	1543
Tycho Brahe and Johannes Kepler	Built astronomical observatory to calculate the planetal orbits; supported Copernicus's views	Late 1500s
Galileo Galilei	Developed telescope to view the planets and confirmed Copernicus's theory	1600
Francis Bacon	Called for new scientific method	Early 1600s
René Descartes	Developed new philosophy of human reasoning	Early 1600s
Isaac Newton	Developed laws of gravity and motion; invented calculus	Late 1600s
Robert Boyle	Identified basic building blocks of matter, opening the way for modern chemistry	Late 1600s

Causes and Effects of the Protestant Reformation

CAUSE AND EFFECT

LONG-TERM CAUSES	IMMEDIATE CAUSES
• Roman Catholic Church becomes more worldly. • Humanists urge a return to simple religion. • Shift to more uncertain, urban-based economies causes people to look for society that makes more sense to them. • Monarchs and other leaders question the pope's authority and wealth.	• Johann Tetzel sells indulgences in Wittenberg. • Martin Luther posts 95 Theses. • Luther translates the Bible into German. • The printing press spreads reform ideas. • Calvin and other reformers preach against Roman Catholic traditions.

PROTESTANT REFORMATION

IMMEDIATE EFFECTS	LONG-TERM EFFECTS
• Peasants' Revolt • Catholic Reformation • Strengthening of the inquisition • Luther's calls for Jewish expulsion result in Jewish migration to Eastern Europe	• Religious wars in Europe • Founding of Lutheran, Calvinist, Anglican, Presbyterian, and other Protestant churches • Weakening of Holy Roman Empire • Increased anti-Semitism

Topic 10 Assessment

KEY TERMS, PEOPLE, AND IDEAS

1. How did ideas from the Renaissance lead to the Scientific revolution?

2. How did **humanism** influence Renaissance painting and sculpture?

3. Why did the use of **vernacular** in literature spread during the Renaissance?

4. How did **Johann Gutenberg's** printing press impact Europe?

5. Why did **John Calvin** feel it necessary to establish a **theocracy**?

6. How did Queen **Elizabeth** try to achieve religious unity?

7. What spurred the rise of so many Protestant **sects** during the Reformation?

8. Why were the theories of **Galileo** and **Copernicus** considered dangerous by the Church?

CRITICAL THINKING

9. **Analyze Information** How did Italy's geography encourage the spread of Renaissance ideas?

10. **Analyze Visuals**

Look at Michelangelo's famous statue, the *Pietá,* commissioned by a cardinal and housed in the Vatican. (a) Why is the choice of this sculpture representative of the Renaissance? (b) How does the sculpture show Renaissance humanism?

11. **Making Comparisons** (a) Compare and contrast the Renaissance in Italy with the Renaissance in northern Europe (b) What differences existed between paintings done by Italian Renaissance painters and those done by painters from northern Europe?

12. **Identify Point of View** How did the philosophy of renaissance humanism differ from that of medieval scholasticism?

13. **Analyze Information** How did contributions from the Scientific Revolution change the people's world view?

14. **Draw Inference** (a) Why did peasants in Northern Europe draw inspiration from Martin Luther's ideas? (b) What was Luther's response to their revolt?

15. **Draw Conclusions** The Renaissance and Scientific Revolution are often described as eras of human progress. Evaluate whether or not this is an accurate description.

16. **Writing Activity: Write an Argument** The passage below is from the Council of Trent called by Pope Paul III in 1545 to establish the direction of Catholic reform.

> Therefore, following the example set by our fathers at the Council of Carthage, it is ordered that bishops shall content themselves not only with modest household furniture and simple food, but with regard to the rest of their manner of living. . .so that nothing appears that is alien to this holy institution of the Church and that does not show simplicity, zeal for God, and contempt for worldly things.
> —*Canons and Decrees of the Holy Council of Trent*

Use evidence from the passage to write a two-paragraph essay. In the first paragraph, describe what the audience was for this passage and what its purpose was. In the second, use evidence from the passage and your own knowledge to express your opinion of whether you think this was an effective response to the Reformation.

17. **Connections to Today** Some people think that the Internet has made printed books unnecessary. Do you agree? Why or why not?

DOCUMENT-BASED QUESTIONS

In a time when new ideas and discoveries were commonplace, the invention of the printing press was no less than astonishing in its impact. Read the documents below, then answer the questions that follow.

DOCUMENT A

"In 1455 all Europe's printed books could have been carried in a single wagon. Fifty years later, the titles ran to tens of thousands, the individual volumes to millions. Today, books pour off presses at the rate of 10,000 million *a year*. That's some 50 million tons of paper. Add in 8,000 to 9,000 daily newspapers, and the Sundays, and the magazines, and the figure rises to 130 million tons . . . It would make a pile 700 meters [2,297 feet] high—four times the height of the Great Pyramid."

—From *Gutenberg: How One Man Remade the World with Words* by John Man

DOCUMENT B

"Printing spread from Mainz to Strasbourg (1458), Cologne (1465), Augsburg (1468), Nuremberg (1470), Leipzig (1481), and Vienna (1482). German printers, or their pupils, introduced the 'divine' art to Italy in 1467, Switzerland and Bohemia in 1468, France and the Netherlands in 1470, Spain, England, Hungary, and Poland between 1474 and 1476, Denmark and Sweden in 1482–1483. By 1500 the presses had issued about six million books in approximately forty thousand editions, more books, probably, than had been produced in western Europe since the fall of Rome . . . Now individuals could afford to own books, where before they had normally been owned almost exclusively by institutions—monasteries, cathedral chapters, and colleges."

—From *The Foundation of Early Modern Europe, 1460–1559* by Eugene F. Rice, Jr.

DOCUMENT C

"As if to offer proof that God has chosen us to accomplish a special mission, there was invented in our land . . . the art of printing. This opened German eyes even as it is now bringing enlightenment to other countries. Each man became eager for knowledge, not without feeling a sense of amazement at his former blindness."

—From *Address to the Estates of the Empire* by Johann Sleidan

DOCUMENT D

The Spread of Printing in Renaissance Europe

KEY
- Printing presses before 1471
- Printing presses, 1471–1500

Azimuthal Equidistant Projection

18. According to Document B, the increased supply and lower cost of books had what effect?
   A. More people became teachers.
   B. More people became printers.
   C. More people bought books.
   D. More people bought printing presses.

19. What information about printing can be found only on Document D?
   A. dates printing presses were introduced
   B. areas where the concentration of printing presses was densest
   C. numbers of printing presses introduced into selected cities
   D. countries where printing presses were introduced

20. What does German historian Sleidan, in Document C, imply is the *most important* role of the printing press?
   A. spreading of the Protestant religion
   B. teaching German history to other countries
   C. making books cheaper
   D. giving Germans more knowledge

21. **Writing Tasks** How did the invention of the printing press affect the spread of the Reformation? Use specific evidence from the documents above, along with information from this Topic, to support your answer.

GO ONLINE to access more practice

New Global Connections
(1415–1796)

ESSENTIAL QUESTION Why do people move?

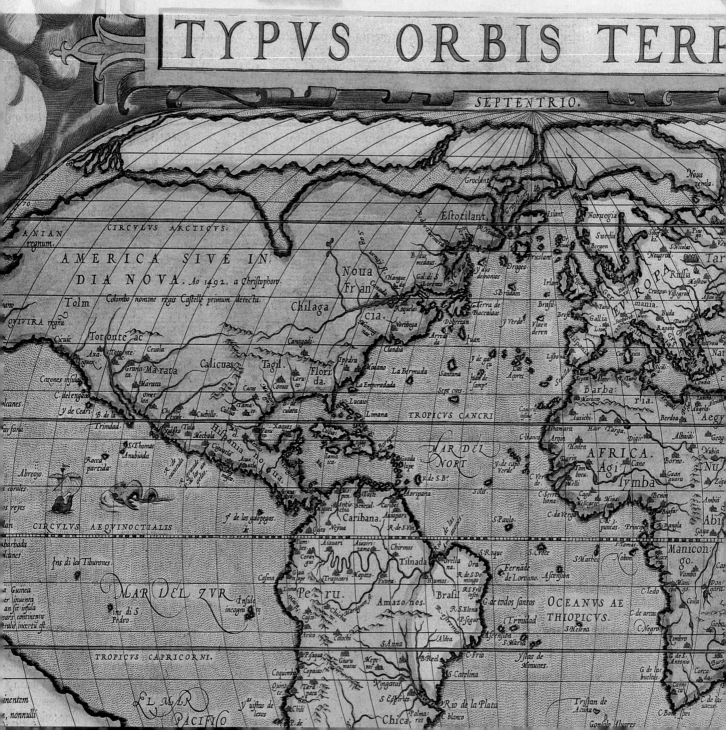

GO ONLINE to access the eText, videos, Interactive Primary Sources, Biographies, and other online resources.

Map of the world, late 1500s

Connections to Today

Slavery is a thing of the past. That's what many people think but, sadly, slavery still exists throughout the world. The United Nations reports that up to 40 million people are victims of human trafficking – the illegally finding, transportation and holding of forced laborers. Some work to pay off debts, some are tricked – others are simply kidnapped. And about 25% of the victims are children.

In this topic, you will learn about a global trade in enslaved people that arose in the 1500s. Why do you think trafficking in human beings has been so hard to end?

Learn about the Spanish conquest of Mexico.

BOUNCE to Activate My Story Video

Topic 11 Overview

In this Topic, you will learn about the events which took place during the era of new global connections. Look at the lesson outline and explore the timeline. As you study this Topic, you will complete the Quest Inquiry.

LESSON OUTLINE

11.1 Europeans Explore Overseas

11.2 Europeans Gain Footholds in Asia

11.3 European Conquests in the Americas

11.4 European Colonies in North America

11.5 The Slave Trade and Its Impact on Africa

11.6 Effects of Global Contact

Key Events of New Global Connections

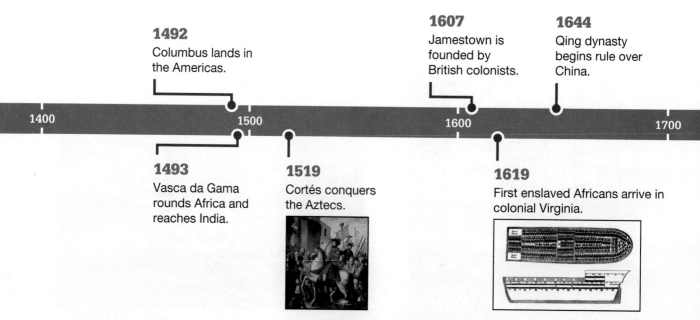

1492
Columbus lands in the Americas.

1493
Vasca da Gama rounds Africa and reaches India.

1519
Cortés conquers the Aztecs.

1607
Jamestown is founded by British colonists.

1619
First enslaved Africans arrive in colonial Virginia.

1644
Qing dynasty begins rule over China.

1400   1500   1600   1700

QUEST! INQUIRY

Exploring the Columbian Exchange

How did the Columbian Exchange affect both Europe and the Americas? In this Quest, you will explore documents related to the Columbian Exchange and its effects on Europe and the Americas.

STEP 1
Watch the flipped video on Cortés, Moctezuma, and the Columbian Exchange. Make a list of questions about how the Columbian Exchange affected Europe and the Americas.

STEP 2
Study the six documents you received. As you read, evaluate the information included and the viewpoints expressed in the written sources.

STEP 3
Write your essay. Identify documents from which you have used evidence. Respond to at least one argument that you do not agree with. Read, edit, and revise your article.

STEP 4
Share your completed essay with other class members. Reflect on the impact of the Columbian Exchange and human migration.

GO ONLINE to access complete Quest materials

11.1

On their way to the Indies, Vasco da Gama's ships rounded the southern tip of Africa, shown here in the distance.

 BOUNCE to Activate Flipped Video

Objectives

Understand the major causes of European exploration.

Analyze early Portuguese and Spanish explorations and expansion.

Describe how the Portuguese established footholds on Africa's coasts.

Describe European searches for a direct route to Asia.

Key Terms

Moluccas
Prince Henry
cartographer
Mombasa
Malindi
Vasco da Gama
Christopher
   Columbus
Line of Demarcation
Treaty of Tordesillas
Ferdinand Magellan
circumnavigate
Cape Town
Boers

Europeans Explore Overseas

Starting in the 1400s, Europeans undertook a flurry of exploration, mapping new sea routes around the world. This great age of exploration was fueled by many causes, but at first, the most important cause was the search for spices.

Causes of European Exploration

European Trade with Asia Europeans had traded with Asia long before the Renaissance. During the Middle Ages, the Crusades introduced Europeans to many luxury goods from Asia. When the Mongol empire united much of Asia in the 1200s and 1300s, Asian goods flowed to Europe along complex overland trade routes.

The Black Death and the breakup of the Mongol empire disrupted Asian trade routes, but by the 1400s, Europe's population was growing—as was the demand for goods from Asia. The most valued trade items were spices, such as cloves, cinnamon, and pepper. People used spices to preserve and add flavor to food, and to make medicines and perfumes.

The chief source of spices was the **Moluccas,** an island chain in present-day Indonesia. Europeans called the Moluccas the Spice Islands.

The Drive to Explore In the 1400s, Arab and Italian merchants controlled most trade between Asia and Europe. Muslim traders

GO ONLINE to access your digital course

brought spices and other goods to Mediterranean ports in Egypt, Syria, and Turkey. From there, Italian traders carried them to European markets. Each time goods passed from one trader to another, prices increased.

Western Europeans wanted to cut out the Muslim and Italian middlemen and gain direct access to the riches of Asia. To do so, the Atlantic powers sought a new route to Asia, one that bypassed the Mediterranean.

Many explorers hoped to get rich by entering the spice trade or conquering other lands. Yet the desire for wealth was not the only motive that lured them to sea. Some missionaries and soldiers ventured overseas to win new converts to Christianity. The Renaissance spirit of curiosity also fed a desire to learn more about lands beyond Europe.

Improved Technology Improvements in technology helped Europeans cross vast oceans. Cartographers, or mapmakers, created more accurate maps and sea charts. European sailors also learned how to use the astrolabe, an instrument used to determine latitude at sea. The astrolabe was first developed by the ancient Greeks and later perfected by the Arabs.

Along with more reliable navigational tools, Europeans designed larger and better ships. The Portuguese developed the caravel, which combined the square sails of European ships with Arab lateen, or triangular, sails. Caravels also adapted the sternpost rudder and numerous masts of Chinese ships. The new rigging made it easier to sail closer to upwind. Finally, European ships added more armaments, including sturdier cannons.

☑ **IDENTIFY** What were the major causes of European exploration?

Portugal Explores the Seas

Portugal, a small nation just west of Spain, led the way in exploration. As in Spain, Christian knights in Portugal had fought to end Muslim rule. By the 1400s, Portugal was strong enough to expand into Muslim North Africa. In 1415, the Portuguese seized Ceuta (SAY oo tah) on the North African coast. The victory sparked the imagination of **Prince Henry,** known to history as Henry the Navigator.

The African Coast Mapped Prince Henry saw great promise in Africa. The Portuguese could convert Africans—most of whom practiced either Islam or native religions—to Christianity. He also

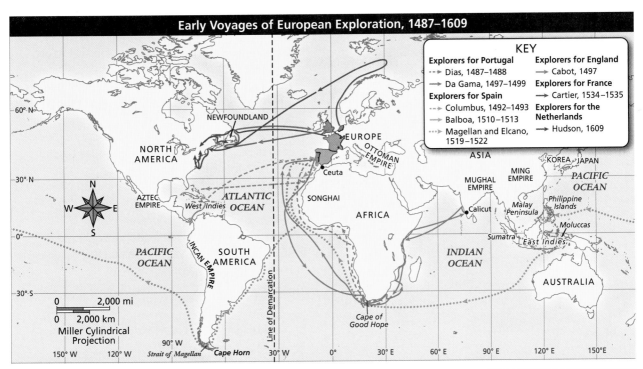

Early Voyages of European Exploration, 1487–1609

KEY

Explorers for Portugal
- ‑‑► Dias, 1487–1488
- ─► Da Gama, 1497–1499

Explorers for Spain
- ‑‑► Columbus, 1492–1493
- ─► Balboa, 1510–1513
- ····► Magellan and Elcano, 1519–1522

Explorers for England
- ─► Cabot, 1497

Explorers for France
- ─► Cartier, 1534–1535

Explorers for the Netherlands
- ─► Hudson, 1609

>> **Analyze Maps** Portugal led the way in exploring the world by ship. Spain and other countries soon followed. How did Magellan's route to Asia differ from the routes of other explorers?

🄱 BOUNCE to Activate Map

believed that in Africa he would find the sources of the gold Muslim traders controlled.

Finally, Prince Henry hoped to find an easier way to reach Asia that bypassed the Mediterranean, which meant going around Africa. The Portuguese felt that with their expert knowledge and technology, they could accomplish this feat. At Sagres, in southern Portugal, Henry gathered scientists, **cartographers,** or mapmakers, and other experts. They redesigned ships, prepared maps, and trained captains and crews for long voyages.

Henry then sent ships that slowly worked their way south to explore the coast of West Africa. Henry died in 1460, but the Portuguese continued their quest.

Portuguese Footholds in Africa The Portuguese built small forts in West Africa to collect food and water and to repair their ships. They also established trading posts to trade muskets, tools, and cloth for gold, ivory, hides, and slaves. These were not colonies peopled by settlers. Instead, the Portuguese left just enough men and firepower to defend their forts.

From West Africa, the Portuguese sailed around the continent. In 1488, Bartholomeu Dias rounded the southern tip of Africa.

Despite the turbulent seas around it, the tip became known as the Cape of Good Hope because it

>> **Identify** This colored woodcut, "World Map According to Ptolemy" (1541), shows premodern European geographic knowledge. Which regions are shown most inaccurately? Explain.

opened the way for a trade route through the Indian Ocean to Asia.

The Portuguese continued to establish forts and trading posts, but they also attacked East African coastal cities such as **Mombasa** and **Malindi,** which were hubs of international trade. With cannons blazing, they expelled the Arabs who controlled the East African trade network and took over this thriving commerce for themselves. Each conquest added to their growing trade empire.

Over the next two centuries, some Portuguese explorers managed to reach parts of present-day Congo, Zambia, and Zimbabwe, establishing limited trade. In general, however, the Portuguese did not venture far from Africa's coasts. They knew little about the interior of Africa, and they lacked accurate maps or other resources to help them explore there. Furthermore, Africans in the interior, who wanted to control the gold trade, resisted such exploration.

Beyond Africa: Reaching India In 1497, Portuguese navigator **Vasco da Gama** followed in Dias's footsteps, leading four ships around the Cape of Good Hope. Da Gama, however, had plans to go farther. After a ten-month voyage, da Gama reached the great spice port of Calicut on the west coast of India. On the long voyage home, the Portuguese lost half their ships, and many sailors died of hunger, thirst, and scurvy, a disease caused by a lack of vitamin C in the diet.

Despite the suffering, the venture proved highly profitable to survivors. In India, da Gama had acquired a cargo of spices that he sold at an enormous profit. He quickly outfitted a new fleet, seeking greater profits. In 1502, he forced a treaty on the ruler of Calicut. Da Gama then left Portuguese merchants there whose job was to buy spices when prices were low and store them until the next fleet could return. Before long, the Portuguese began seizing other outposts around the Indian Ocean, building a vast trading empire and making Portugal a world power.

☑ **EXPLAIN** How did the Portuguese create a trading empire stretching from Africa through the Indian Ocean to India?

Columbus Searches for a Route to Asia

The profitable Portuguese voyages spurred other European nations to seek a sea route to Asia. An Italian navigator from the port of Genoa,

The Treaty of Tordesillas, 1494

CAUSES	KEY PROVISIONS OF TREATY	EFFECTS
• Columbus explored Caribbean islands. • Spain, seeking wealth and power, claimed control of the islands. • Portugal, with its own ambitions, disputed Spain's claims. • Aided by Pope Alexander IV, Spain and Portugal negotiated a treaty.	• Lands west of a meridian 370 leagues west of the Cape Verde Islands would belong to Spain. • Lands east of a meridian 370 leagues west of the Cape Verde Islands would belong to Portugal.	• Treaty favored Spain: most of Americas were west of the line. • Spain claimed much of the Americas. • Spanish colonies yielded incredible wealth for Spain, especially silver and gold. • Spanish language and culture became key elements of Latin American culture. • Brazil became a Portuguese colony and retains much Portuguese culture today. • England, France, and other countries did not recognize the agreement and established their own colonies in the Americas.

>> **Analyze Charts** The Treaty of Tordesillas resolved a major territorial dispute between Spain and Portugal. Whose rights and claims were not addressed by this treaty?

Christopher Columbus, wanted to reach the East Indies—a group of islands in Southeast Asia, today mostly in Indonesia—by sailing west across the Atlantic. Like most educated Europeans, Columbus knew that Earth was a sphere. A few weeks sailing west, he reasoned, would bring a ship to eastern Asia. His plan made sense, but Columbus greatly underestimated Earth's size—and he had no idea that two continents, North and South America, lay in his path.

Reaching Faraway Lands Portugal refused to sponsor him, but Columbus persuaded Ferdinand and Isabella of Spain to finance his voyage. To increase their authority, the Spanish rulers had taken radical measures, including expelling Jews from Spain. They hoped their actions would strengthen Catholicism. However, the loss of some of Spain's most affluent and cultured people weakened the nation. The rulers hoped Columbus's voyage would bring wealth and prestige.

On August 3, 1492, Columbus sailed west with three small ships, the *Niña*, the *Pinta*, and the *Santa María*. Although the expedition encountered good weather and a favorable wind, no land came into sight for many weeks. Provisions ran low, and the crew became anxious. Finally, on October 12, land was spotted.

Columbus spent several months cruising the islands of the Caribbean. Because he thought he had reached the Indies, he called the people of the region "Indians." In 1493, he returned to Spain to a hero's welcome. In three later voyages, Columbus remained convinced that he had reached the coast of east Asia. Before long, though, other Europeans realized that Columbus had found a route to previously unknown continents.

Spain and Portugal Divide Up the World Spain and Portugal each pressed rival claims to the islands Columbus explored. With the support of the pope, the two countries agreed to settle their claims and signed the **Treaty of Tordesillas** in 1494. It set a **Line of Demarcation,** dividing the non-European world into two zones. Spain had trading and exploration rights in any lands west of the line, including most of the Americas. Portugal had the same rights east of the line. The actual Line of Demarcation was unclear because geography at the time was not precise. However, the treaty allowed Spain and Portugal to claim vast areas in their zones. It also spurred other European nations to challenge Spanish and Portuguese claims and build their own trade empires.

Naming the Western Hemisphere An Italian sea captain named Amerigo Vespucci wrote a journal describing his voyage to Brazil. In 1507, a German cartographer named Martin Waldseemüller used Vespucci's descriptions of his voyage to publish a map of the region, which he labeled "America." Over time, the term "Americas" came to be used for both continents of the Western Hemisphere. The islands Columbus had explored in the Caribbean became known as the West Indies.

☑ **INFER** Why were Spanish rulers pleased with the Treaty of Tordesillas and Line of Demarcation?

The Search for a Route to the Pacific

Once Europeans realized that the Americas blocked a sea passage to India, they hunted for a route around or through the Americas in order to reach Asia. The English, Dutch, and French explored the coast of North America unsuccessfully for a "northwest passage," or a route from the Atlantic Ocean to the Pacific through the Arctic islands. Meanwhile, in 1513, the Spanish adventurer Vasco Núñez de Balboa, helped by local Indians, hacked a passage westward through the tropical forests of Panama. From a ridge on the west coast, he gazed at a huge body of water. The body of water that he named the South Sea was in fact the Pacific Ocean.

Magellan Sets Sail On September 20, 1519, a minor Portuguese nobleman named **Ferdinand Magellan** set out from Spain with five ships to find a way to reach the Pacific. Magellan's ships sailed south and west, through storms and calms and tropical heat. At last, his fleet reached the coast of South America. Carefully, they explored each bay, hoping to find one that would lead to the Pacific. In November 1520, Magellan's ships entered a bay at the southern tip of South America. Amid brutal storms, rushing tides, and unpredictable winds, Magellan found a passage that later became known as the Strait of Magellan. The ships emerged into Balboa's South Sea. Magellan renamed the sea the Pacific, from the Latin word meaning *peaceful*.

The Long Way Home Their mission accomplished, most of the crew wanted to return to Spain the way they had come. Magellan, however, insisted that they push on across the Pacific to the East Indies. Magellan underestimated the size of the Pacific. Three more weeks, he thought, would bring them to the Spice Islands. Magellan was wrong.

For nearly four months, the ships plowed across the uncharted ocean. Finally, in March 1521, the fleet reached the Philippines, where Magellan was killed. On September 8, 1522, nearly three years after setting out, the survivors—one ship and 18 sailors—reached Spain. The survivors had been the first

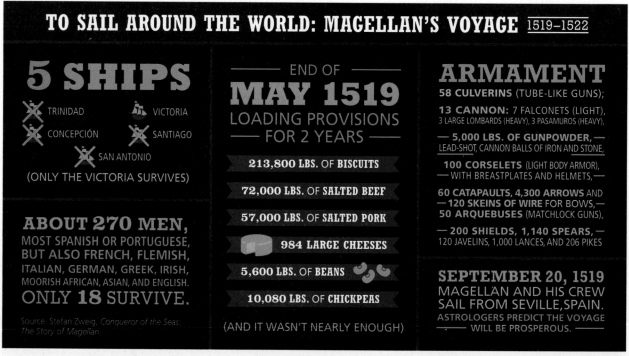

TO SAIL AROUND THE WORLD: MAGELLAN'S VOYAGE 1519–1522

5 SHIPS
✕ TRINIDAD   ⛵ VICTORIA
✕ CONCEPCIÓN   ✕ SANTIAGO
✕ SAN ANTONIO
(ONLY THE VICTORIA SURVIVES)

ABOUT 270 MEN,
MOST SPANISH OR PORTUGUESE, BUT ALSO FRENCH, FLEMISH, ITALIAN, GERMAN, GREEK, IRISH, MOORISH AFRICAN, ASIAN, AND ENGLISH.
ONLY **18** SURVIVE.

Source: Stefan Zweig, *Conqueror of the Seas: The Story of Magellan*.

— END OF —
MAY 1519
LOADING PROVISIONS
— FOR 2 YEARS —

213,800 LBS. OF BISCUITS
72,000 LBS. OF SALTED BEEF
57,000 LBS. OF SALTED PORK
984 LARGE CHEESES
5,600 LBS. OF BEANS
10,080 LBS. OF CHICKPEAS

(AND IT WASN'T NEARLY ENOUGH)

ARMAMENT
58 CULVERINS (TUBE-LIKE GUNS);
13 CANNON: 7 FALCONETS (LIGHT), 3 LARGE LOMBARDS (HEAVY), 3 PASAMUROS (HEAVY),
— **5,000 LBS. OF GUNPOWDER,** — LEAD-SHOT, CANNON BALLS OF IRON AND STONE,
100 CORSELETS (LIGHT BODY ARMOR), — WITH BREASTPLATES AND HELMETS, —
60 CATAPAULTS, 4,300 ARROWS AND — **120 SKEINS OF WIRE** FOR BOWS, — **50 ARQUEBUSES** (MATCHLOCK GUNS),
— **200 SHIELDS, 1,140 SPEARS,** — 120 JAVELINS, 1,000 LANCES, AND 206 PIKES

SEPTEMBER 20, 1519
MAGELLAN AND HIS CREW SAIL FROM SEVILLE, SPAIN.
ASTROLOGERS PREDICT THE VOYAGE — WILL BE PROSPEROUS. —

>> Months of careful planning, provisioning, and loading of supplies went into preparing for Magellan's voyage. Even so, during the long voyage, regular stops for fresh food and water were required.

🅑 BOUNCE to Activate 3D Model

people to **circumnavigate,** or sail around, the world. Antonio Pigafetta, one of the few survivors of the expedition, observed: "I believe of a certainty that no one will ever again make such a voyage."

☑ **INFER** What was the significance of Balboa's discovery?

European Expansion in Africa

Following the Portuguese and Spanish examples, several other European powers sought to expand their trade networks. By the 1600s, the French, English, and Dutch all had footholds along the coast of West Africa. These outposts often changed hands as European countries battled for control of the new trade routes. Like the Portuguese, they used these footholds to protect and expand their trade routes in Africa, the Indian Ocean, and India.

The Dutch Settle Cape Town In 1652, Dutch settlers began to arrive at the southern tip of the continent. They built **Cape Town,** the first permanent European settlement in Africa, to supply ships sailing to or from the East Indies.

Dutch farmers, called **Boers,** settled around Cape Town. Over time, they ousted, enslaved, or killed the people who lived there. The Boers held a Calvinist belief that they were the elect, or chosen, of God. They looked on Africans as inferiors. In the 1700s, Boer herders and ivory hunters began to push north from the Cape Colony. As they did so, they battled powerful African groups like the Zulus who had settled in southern Africa.

The British and French Explore By the mid-1600s, the British and French had both reached present-day Senegal. The French established a fort in the region around 1700. In the late 1700s, stories about British explorers' search for the source of the Nile River sparked an interest in Africa among Europeans, especially the French and British. In 1788, the British established the African Association, an organization that sponsored explorers to Africa. Over the next century, European exploration of Africa would explode.

☑ **IDENTIFY** Why did the European presence in Africa expand?

>> In the late 1600s, the Dutch colony at Cape Town was busy with arriving and departing ships.

☑ ASSESSMENT

1. **Identify Cause and Effect** Why did Europeans explore Africa, Asia, and the Americas beginning in the 1400s?

2. **Identify Steps in a Process** Describe how the Portuguese gained dominance of the spice trade.

3. **Draw Conclusions** How did competition between European countries such as Portugal and Spain affect overseas exploration and expansion?

4. **Summarize** Summarize European searches for a direct route across the Atlantic Ocean to Asia.

5. **Cite Evidence** How did religious beliefs encourage Dutch immigrants to aggressively expand their settlements in southern Africa?

6. **Quest Connections** How might the voyages of navigators like Columbus affect future trading patterns?

11.2

The experienced and ruthless admiral Afonso de Albuquerque spearheaded Portugal's efforts to build a trade empire around the Indian Ocean.

BOUNCE to Activate Flipped Video

Objectives

Summarize how Portugal built a trading empire in South and Southeast Asia.

Analyze the rise of Dutch and Spanish dominance in Asia and the Indian Ocean.

Understand how the decline of Mughal India affected European traders in the region.

Describe European contacts with Ming and Qing China.

Summarize Korea's and Japan's attitudes toward contact with the outside world.

Key Terms

Afonso de
  Albuquerque
Mughal empire
Goa
Malacca
outpost
Dutch East India
  Company
sovereign
Philippines
sepoy
Macao
Guangzhou

Matteo Ricci
Manchus
Qing
Qianlong
Lord Macartney
Tokugawa
Nagasaki

Europeans Gain Footholds in Asia

Portugal was the first European power to gain a foothold in Asia. The Portuguese ships were small in size and number, but the firepower of their shipboard cannons was unmatched. In time, this superior firepower helped them win control of the rich Indian Ocean spice trade and build a trading empire in Asia.

Portugal Builds an Empire in Asia

Albuquerque in India After Vasco da Gama's voyage, the Portuguese, under **Afonso de Albuquerque's** command, burst into the Indian Ocean. By that time, Muslim rulers, originally from central Asia, had established the **Mughal empire** throughout much of India.

The southern regions of India, however, were still controlled by a patchwork of local princes. The Portuguese won these princes to their side with promises of aid against other Europeans. With these southern footholds, Albuquerque and the Portuguese hoped to end Muslim power and turn the Indian Ocean into a "Portuguese lake."

Trading Outposts Around the Indian Ocean In 1510, the Portuguese seized the island of **Goa** off the coast of India, making it their major military and commercial base. Albuquerque burned coastal towns and crushed Arab fleets at sea. The Portuguese took

GO ONLINE to access your digital course

the East Indies port of **Malacca** in 1511, killing the city's Muslim inhabitants.

In less than 50 years, the Portuguese had built a trading empire with military and merchant **outposts,** or distant areas under their control, around the Indian Ocean. They used the cities they had seized on the east coast of Africa to resupply and repair their ships. For most of the 1500s, Portugal controlled the spice trade between Europe and Asia.

Limited Impact Despite their sea power, the Portuguese remained on the fringe of Asian trade. They had neither the strength nor the resources to conquer much territory on land. In India and China, where they faced far stronger empires, they merely sought permission to trade.

The intolerance of Portuguese missionaries caused resentment. In Goa, they attacked Muslims, destroyed Hindu temples, and introduced the Inquisition. Portuguese ships even sank Muslim pilgrim ships on their way to Mecca. While the Portuguese disrupted some older trade patterns, exchanges continued among the peoples of Asia. Some bypassed Portuguese-controlled towns. Others traded with the newcomers.

In the late 1500s, Portuguese power declined overseas. By the early 1600s, other Europeans were vying to replace the Portuguese in the rich spice trade.

☑ **INFER** How did the Portuguese use geographic factors to help them control the spice trade?

Rise of the Dutch and the Spanish

The Dutch were the first Europeans to challenge Portuguese domination of Asian trade. Their homeland (in the present-day Netherlands) was a group of provinces and prosperous trading cities which fell under Spanish rule in the early 1500s. Later, the Protestant northern provinces won independence and soon competed against Portugal to control the rich spice trade of the Indies.

Dutch Sea Power In 1599, a Dutch fleet returned to Amsterdam from Asia carrying a rich cargo of pepper, cloves, and other spices. This successful voyage led to a frenzy of overseas activity. Dutch warships and trading vessels soon made the Dutch leaders in European commerce. They used their sea power to set up colonies and trading posts

around the world, including a strategic settlement at Cape Town.

The Dutch Dominate Indian Ocean Trade In 1602, a group of wealthy Dutch merchants formed the **Dutch East India Company.** Unlike Portuguese and Spanish traders, whose expeditions were tightly controlled by government, the Dutch East India Company had full **sovereign** powers. With its power to build armies, wage war, negotiate peace treaties, and govern overseas territory, it came to dominate the region.

In 1641, the Dutch captured Malacca from the Portuguese, opened trade with China, and soon enforced a monopoly in the Spice Islands. They controlled shipments to Europe as well as much of the trade within Southeast Asia. Like the Portuguese, the Dutch used military force to further their trading goals. Yet they forged closer ties with local rulers than the Portuguese had. Many Dutch merchants married Asian women. In the 1700s, however, the growing power of England and France contributed to a decline in the Dutch overseas trading empire.

Spain Captures the Philippines While the Portuguese and Dutch set up bases on the fringes of

>> This hand-colored woodcut illustration shows Dutch merchant galleons at sea during the 1600s. Note these ships' great storage capacity for trade goods.

Asia, Spain took over the **Philippines.** Magellan had claimed the archipelago for Spain in 1521. Within about 50 years, Spain had conquered and colonized the islands, renaming them for the Spanish king Philip II. Unlike most other peoples of Southeast Asia, the Filipinos were not united. As a result, they could be conquered more easily.

In the spirit of the Catholic Reformation, Spanish priests set out to convert the Filipino people to Christianity. Later, missionaries from the Philippines tried to spread Catholic teachings in China and Japan.

The Spanish Trade Network The Philippines became a key link in Spain's overseas trading empire. The Spanish shipped silver mined in Mexico and Peru across the Pacific to the Philippines. From there, they used the silver to buy goods in China. In this way, large quantities of American silver flowed into the economies of East Asian nations.

☑ **COMPARE AND CONTRAST** How did Dutch expansion and trade in Asia differ from Portuguese and Spanish expansion and trade?

Europeans Trade in Mughal India

For two centuries, the Mughal empire had enjoyed a period of peace, strength, and prosperity. European merchants were dazzled by India's splendid Mughal court and its many luxury goods.

A Thriving Trade Center Mughal India was the center of the valuable spice trade. It was also the world leader in textile manufacturing, exporting large quantities of silk and cotton cloth. The Mughal empire was larger, richer, and more powerful than any kingdom in Europe. When Europeans sought trading rights, Mughal emperors saw no threat in granting them. The Portuguese—and later the Dutch, English, and French—thus were permitted to build forts and warehouses in Indian coastal towns.

Turmoil and Decline Over time, the Mughal empire weakened. Later rulers ended an earlier policy of religious toleration, rekindling conflicts between Hindu and Muslim princes. Civil war drained Mughal resources. Rulers then increased taxes, sparking peasant rebellions. Several weak rulers held the throne in the early 1700s. Corruption became widespread, and the central government slowly faded.

>> In this Mughal illustration painted on fine cotton, a servant is at work, standing on a richly decorated carpet. Indian carpets and other textiles were highly prized trade goods.

🔊 BOUNCE to Activate Chart

>> In 1712, the Mughal emperor Shah Jahan gave this reception for Jan Joshua Ketelaer, an envoy from the Dutch East India Company.

British-French Rivalry in India As Mughal power faltered, French and English traders fought for power. Like the Dutch, entrepreneurs in England and France had set up the English and French East India companies. These companies made alliances with local officials and independent rajahs, or princely rulers. Each company organized its own army of **sepoys,** or Indian troops.

By the mid-1700s, the British and the French had become locked in a bitter struggle for global power. The fighting involved both nations' lands in Asia and the Americas. In India, the British East India Company used an army of British troops and sepoys to drive out the French. The company then forced the Mughal emperor to recognize its right to collect taxes in the northeast. By the late 1700s, it had used its great wealth to dominate most of India.

☑ **EXPLAIN** How did the British gain power in India?

Ming China and Europe

Portuguese ships first reached China from their base in Malacca in 1514. The Chinese considered the Portuguese and all other foreigners barbarians, believing that they lacked the civilized ways of the Chinese. Europeans, by contrast, wrote enthusiastically about China. In 1590, a visitor described Chinese artisans "cleverly making devices out of gold, silver and other metals," and wrote with approval: "They daily publish huge multitudes of books."

Trade with Ming China European interest in China and other parts of East Asia continued to grow. The Ming, however, had no interest in Europe—since, as a Ming document proclaimed, "Our empire owns the world." The Portuguese wanted Chinese silks and porcelains, but had little to offer in exchange. European textiles and metalwork were inferior to Chinese products. The Chinese therefore demanded payment in gold or silver.

The Ming eventually allowed the Portuguese a trading post at **Macao** near Canton, present-day **Guangzhou** (GWAHNG joh). Later, they let the Dutch, English, and other Europeans trade with Chinese merchants. Foreigners could trade only at Canton under the supervision of imperial officials. When each year's trading season ended, they had to sail away.

Christian Missionaries Portuguese missionaries arrived in China along with the traders. In later years, the Jesuits—from Spain, Italy, and Portugal—arrived. Most Jesuits had a broad knowledge of many

>> Europeans desired fine Ming goods, such as porcelain vases with intricate designs.

🅑 **BOUNCE to Activate Map**

>> The Jesuit missionary priest Matteo Ricci impressed Chinese scholars with his knowledge and appreciation for Chinese culture.

subjects, and the Chinese welcomed the chance to learn about Renaissance Europe from these scholars. A few European scholars, like the brilliant Jesuit priest **Matteo Ricci** (mah TAY oh REE chee) did make an impression on Ming China. In the 1580s, Ricci learned to speak Chinese and adopted Chinese clothing. His goal was to convert upper-class Chinese to Christianity. He hoped that they, in turn, would spread Christian teachings to the rest of China.

Ricci won friends among the scholarly class in China by sharing his knowledge of the arts and sciences of Renaissance Europe. The Chinese were fascinated by new European technologies, including maps. They were also open to European discoveries in astronomy and mathematics. While Chinese rulers welcomed Ricci and other Jesuits from Europe for their learning, the priests had little success in spreading their religious beliefs.

☑ **IDENTIFY CAUSE AND EFFECT** How did Ming China's policies toward Europeans affect global trade?

The Manchus Conquer China

By the early 1600s, the aging Ming dynasty was decaying. Revolts erupted, and Manchu invaders from the north pushed through the Great Wall.

The **Manchus** ruled a region in the northeast, Manchuria, that had long been influenced by Chinese civilization. In 1644, the Manchus seized Beijing and made it their capital.

The Qing Dynasty Rises The Manchus set up a new dynasty called the **Qing** (ching), which means "pure." The Manchus won the support of Chinese scholar-officials because they adopted the Confucian system of government. For each top government position, the Qing chose two people, one Manchu and one Chinese. Local government remained in the hands of the Chinese, but Manchu troops stationed across the empire ensured loyalty.

Two rulers oversaw the most brilliant age of the Qing. Kangxi (kahng shee), who ruled from 1661 to 1722, was an able administrator and military leader. He extended Chinese power into central Asia and promoted Chinese culture. Kangxi's grandson **Qianlong** (chen lung) had an equally successful reign from 1736 to 1796. He expanded China's borders to rule the largest area in the nation's history. Qianlong retired after 60 years because he did not want to rule longer than his grandfather had.

Peace and Prosperity Spread The Chinese economy expanded under both emperors. New crops from the Americas, such as potatoes and corn, had been introduced into China. These crops boosted farm output, which in turn contributed to a

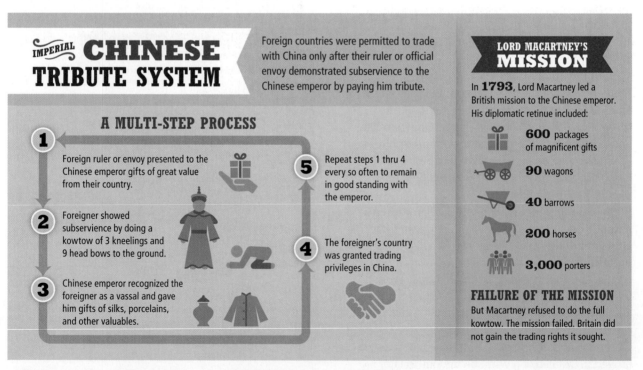

>> European trade activities in China were strictly limited. Only countries that observed the rules of the imperial tribute system could hope for permission to trade.

population boom. China's population rose from 140 million in 1740 to over 300 million by 1800. The silk, cotton, and porcelain industries expanded. Internal trade grew, as did the demand for Chinese goods from all over the world.

The Qing Limit Foreign Traders The Qing maintained the Ming policy of restricting foreign traders. Still, Europeans kept pressing to expand trade to cities other than Guangzhou. In 1793, **Lord Macartney** arrived in China at the head of a British diplomatic mission. He brought samples of British-made goods to show the Chinese the advantages of trade with Westerners. The Chinese, who looked on the goods as rather crude products, thought they were gifts offered as tribute to the emperor.

Further misunderstandings followed. Macartney insisted on an audience with the emperor. The Chinese told Macartney he would have to perform the traditional kowtow, touching his head to the ground to show respect to the emperor. Macartney refused. He also offended the Chinese by speaking of the natural superiority of the English. The negotiations faltered.

At the time, Qianlong's attitude seemed justified by China's successes. After all, he already ruled the world's greatest empire. Why should he negotiate with a nation as distant as Britain?

In the long run, however, his policy proved disastrous. Even in the late 1700s, there was much the Chinese could have learned from the West. In the 1800s, China would discover to its regret the cost of ignoring the West and rejecting its advances—especially in military technology.

☑ **SUMMARIZE** How did the Qing respond to Britain's diplomatic mission?

Korea and Japan Choose Isolation

Before the 1500s, Korean traders had far-reaching contacts across East Asia. A Korean map from the 1300s accurately outlines lands from Japan to the Mediterranean. Koreans probably acquired this knowledge from Arab traders who had visited Korea.

Invaders Attack Korea In 1592, and again in 1597, the Japanese invaded Korea. The Japanese were driven out in 1598, but the invasions proved disastrous for Korea. Villages were burned to the ground, famine and disease became widespread, and the population decreased. Then, in 1636, before

>> A brightly colored formal portrait of Kangxi, a Qing dynasty emperor. Kangxi ascended the throne as a boy and reigned from 1662 to 1722.

>> Outnumbered Korean ships destroy an invading Japanese fleet at the Battle of Myeongnyang in 1597, as depicted by an artist in the 1900s.

>> This painted Japanese screen shows Portuguese merchants visiting Japan in the 1500s.

the country was fully recovered, the Manchus invaded Korea. When the Manchus set up the Qing dynasty in China, Korea became a tributary state. It was run by its own government but forced to acknowledge China's supremacy.

Korea Limits Contact With the World Devastated by the two invasions, Korean rulers adopted a policy of isolation, excluding foreigners except the Chinese and a few Japanese. When European sailors were shipwrecked on Korean shores, they were imprisoned and held as spies. Although Korea had few contacts with much of the world for almost 250 years, Koreans on tribute missions brought back maps, as well as books on scientific discoveries. This was also a great age for Korean arts and literature.

Westerners Arrive in Japan Unlike the Chinese or Koreans, the Japanese at first welcomed Western traders. In 1543, the Portuguese reached Japan, followed by the Spanish, Dutch, and English. They arrived at a turbulent time, when Japanese daimyo were struggling for power. The daimyo, powerful warrior lords, quickly adopted Western firearms, which may have helped the **Tokugawa** shoguns centralize power and impose order.

Japan was much more open to Christian missionaries than China. Jesuits, such as the

Spanish priest Francis Xavier, found the Japanese curious and eager to learn about Christianity.

A growing number of Japanese adopted the new faith. The Japanese also welcomed the printing press the Jesuits brought.

The Tokugawa shoguns, however, grew increasingly hostile toward foreigners. After learning that Spain had seized the Philippines, they may have seen the newcomers as threats. They also worried that Japanese Christians—who may have numbered as many as 300,000—owed their allegiance to the pope, rather than to Japanese leaders. In response, the Tokugawas expelled foreign missionaries. They brutally persecuted Japanese Christians, killing many thousands of people.

Tokugawas Bar Foreigners By 1638, the Tokugawas had turned against European traders as well. Japan barred all European merchants and forbade Japanese citizens from traveling abroad. To further their isolation, the Japanese outlawed the building of large ships, thereby ending foreign trade. In order to keep informed about world events, they permitted just one or two Dutch ships each year to trade at a small island in **Nagasaki** harbor.

Japan remained isolated for more than 200 years. Art and literature flourished, and internal trade boomed. Cities grew in size and importance, and some merchant families gained wealth and status. By the early 1700s, Edo (present-day Tokyo) had a million inhabitants, more than either London or Paris.

☑ **IDENTIFY PATTERNS** Why did both Korea and Japan pursue a policy of isolationism?

☑ ASSESSMENT

1. **Identify Steps in a Process** Summarize the steps by which Portugal built a trading empire in Asia around the Indian Ocean.

2. **Identify Cause and Effect** How did dominating the Philippines benefit Spain?

3. **Draw Conclusions** How did the decline of Mughal India aid European traders in the region?

4. **Synthesize** How successful were European attempts to establish missions and trade in Ming and Qing China?

5. **Connections to Today** Why would it be difficult for a nation today to isolate itself the way Korea and Japan did in the 1600s?

Emperor Qianlong's Letter to King George III

Since early in its history, China's leaders had considered their land the center of the world, a "Middle Kingdom" that was the source of all civilization. This view persisted through many changes in dynasty. The Manchu emperor Qianlong, who ruled from 1736 to 1796, certainly shared this belief in Chinese superiority.

By the late 1700s, European powers had exerted their power over much of the globe, but they at first made little headway in China. When British diplomat Lord Macartney applied for the right to send a permanent British trade representative to China, Qianlong sent this reply to King George III of England.

>> Emperor Qianlong

Primary Source

You, O King, live beyond the confines of many seas, nevertheless, impelled by your humble desire to partake of the benefits of our civilisation, you have dispatched a mission respectfully bearing your memorial [letter]. Your Envoy has crossed the seas and paid his respects at my Court on the anniversary of my birthday. To show your devotion, you have also sent offerings of your country's produce.

I have perused [carefully read] your memorial: the earnest terms in which it is couched reveal a respectful humility on your part, which is highly praiseworthy. In consideration of the fact that your Ambassador and his deputy have come a long way with your memorial and tribute, I have shown them high favour and have allowed them to be introduced into my presence. To manifest [make clear] my indulgence, I have entertained them at a banquet and made them numerous gifts. I have also caused presents to be forwarded to the Naval Commander and six hundred of his officers and men, although they did not come to Peking [Beijing], so that they too may share in my all-embracing kindness.

☑ **DETERMINE AUTHOR'S POINT OF VIEW** What does Xianlong say is Britain's motive for seeking closer ties with China?

As to your entreaty to send one of your nationals to be accredited [authorized] to my Celestial Court and to be in control of your country's trade with China, this request is contrary to all usage of my dynasty and cannot possibly be entertained. It is true that Europeans, in the service of the dynasty, have been permitted to live at Peking, but they are compelled to adopt Chinese dress, they are strictly confined to their own precincts and are never permitted to return home. You are presumably familiar with our dynastic regulations. Your proposed Envoy to my Court could not be placed in a position similar to that of European officials in

Peking who are forbidden to leave China, nor could he, on the other hand, be allowed liberty of movement and the privilege of corresponding with his own country; so that you would gain nothing by his residence in our midst….

☑ **EXAMINE INFORMATION** What does Qianlong reveal about how foreigners in his capital city of Peking are treated and viewed?

Swaying [ruling] the wide world, I have but one aim in view, namely, to maintain a perfect governance and to fulfil the duties of the State: strange and costly objects do not interest me. If I have commanded that the tribute offerings sent by you, O King, are to be accepted, this was solely in consideration for the spirit which prompted you to dispatch them from afar. Our dynasty's majestic virtue has penetrated unto every country under Heaven, and Kings of all nations have offered their costly tribute by land and sea. As your Ambassador can see for himself, we possess all things. I set no value on objects strange or ingenious, and have no use for your country's manufactures.

☑ **ANALYZE WORD CHOICES** What attitude does Qianlong show by using the phrases "tribute offerings" and "strange or ingenious"?

This then is my answer to your request to appoint a representative at my Court, a request contrary to our dynastic usage, which would only result in inconvenience to yourself. I have expounded my wishes in detail and have commanded your tribute Envoys to leave in peace on their homeward journey. It behoves you, O King, to respect my sentiments and to display even greater devotion and loyalty in future, so that, by perpetual submission to our Throne, you may secure peace and prosperity for your country hereafter….

☑ **PARAPHRASE** Restate the last sentence of this excerpt in your own words.

☑ ASSESSMENT

1. **Analyze Style and Rhetoric** What is the overall tone of this letter? How does Qianlong's language reflect his attitude toward himself, China, and the outside world?

2. **Assess an Argument** What are the main reasons Qianlong gives for rejecting the British proposal? Do you think his reasons are valid?

3. **Determine Author's Purpose** What do you think was Qianlong's main goal in writing this letter the way he did?

4. **Analyze Interactions** How do you think King George would have reacted to this letter?

GO ONLINE to access primary sources

11.3

This 1892 Spanish painting presents a highly biased and romanticized view of the first meeting between Columbus and the Taínos.

European Conquests in the Americas

In 1492, Columbus landed in the islands that are now called the West Indies. In later voyages, he claimed all the lands he visited for Spain. Columbus's voyages set Spain on a course of exploration and colonization in the Americas. Before long, Spain conquered and ruled a vast empire that included the West Indies, much of South America, Central America, Mexico, and other parts of North America. The Spanish conquests transformed the Americas and would have a huge impact on Europe, and even on distant lands in Asia.

First Encounters

Columbus Conquers the Taínos When Columbus first arrived in the West Indies in 1492, he encountered the **Taíno** (TY noh) people. The Taínos lived in villages and grew corn, yams, and cotton, which they wove into cloth. They were friendly and open toward the Spanish. Columbus noted that they were "generous with what they have, to such a degree as no one would believe but he who had seen it."

Friendly relations soon evaporated. Columbus's men assaulted Taíno men and women, seized some to take back to the Spanish king, and claimed their land for Spain. The Spanish killed any Taínos who dared to resist. Columbus later required each Taíno to give him a set amount of gold. Any Taíno who failed to deliver was tortured or killed.

A wave of Spanish **conquistadors** (kahn KEES tuh dawrz), or conquerors, who soon arrived in the Americas continued Columbus's ruthless pattern. They first settled on the islands of

 BOUNCE to Activate Flipped Video

Objectives

Analyze the results of the first encounters between the Spanish and American Indians.

Explain how the Aztec and Inca empires were impacted by Spanish conquistadors and European colonization.

Describe how Portugal and other European nations challenged Spanish power.

Analyze the major features of Spanish colonial government, society and culture.

Describe the impact of Spanish colonization of the Americas.

Key Terms

Taíno	viceroy
conquistador	encomienda
immunity	Bartolomé de Las
Hernán Cortés	Casas
Tenochtitlán	peon
Malinche	peninsular
alliance	creole
Moctezuma	mestizo
Francisco Pizarro	
civil war	
privateer	

>> After fighting with Tlaxcalans, Cortés and his men were welcomed into Tlaxcala. The Tlaxcalans became allies of the Spanish in the conflict with the Aztecs.

>> A Spanish conquistador with his helmet, body armor, and sword rides on horseback in this hand-colored illustration from the 1800s.

Hispaniola (now the Dominican Republic and Haiti), Cuba, and Puerto Rico. Throughout the region, the conquistadors seized the American Indians' gold ornaments and then made them pan for more gold. At the same time, the Spanish forced the American Indians to convert to Christianity.

Guns, Horses, and Disease Although Spanish conquistadors only numbered in the hundreds as compared to millions of American Indians, they had many advantages. Their guns and cannons were superior to the American Indians' arrows and spears, and European metal armor provided them with better protection. They also had horses, which not only were useful in battle and in carrying supplies, but also frightened the American Indians, who had never seen a horse.

Most important, an invisible invader—disease— helped the conquistadors take control of the Taínos and other American Indians. Europeans unknowingly carried diseases, such as smallpox, measles, and influenza, to which American Indians had no **immunity,** or resistance. These diseases spread rapidly and wiped out village after village. As a result, the American Indian population of the Caribbean islands declined by as much as 90 percent in the 1500s. Millions of American Indians died from disease as Europeans made their way inland.

☑ **DESCRIBE** How did Spanish conquistadors treat the Taínos?

Cortés Conquers the Aztecs

From the Caribbean, Spanish explorers probed the coasts of the Americas. From local peoples, they heard stories of empires rich in gold, but the first explorers also told about fierce fighters they had encountered. Attracted by the promise of riches as well as by religious zeal, a flood of adventurers soon followed.

Cortés Arrives in Mexico Among the earliest conquistadors was **Hernán Cortés.** Cortés, a landowner in Cuba, heard of Spanish expeditions that had been repelled by Indians. He believed that he could succeed where none had before. In 1519, he landed on the coast of Mexico with about 600 men, 16 horses, and a few cannons. He began an inland trek toward **Tenochtitlán** (teh nawch tee TLAHN), the capital of the Aztec empire.

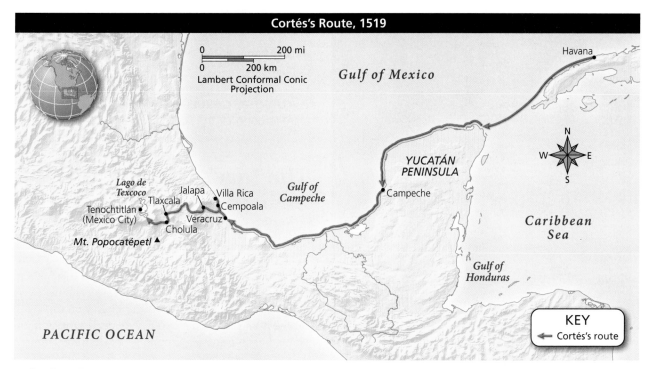

0   200 mi
0   200 km
Lambert Conformal Conic
Projection

Gulf of Mexico

Havana

YUCATÁN
PENINSULA

Gulf of
Campeche

Campeche

Caribbean
Sea

Lago de
Texcoco
Tenochtitlán
(Mexico City)
Tlaxcala
Jalapa
Villa Rica
Cempoala
Veracruz
Cholula
Mt. Popocatépetl ▲

Gulf of
Honduras

PACIFIC OCEAN

KEY
← Cortés's route

N
W   E
S

>> **Analyze Maps** Why do you think Cortés's ships sailed so close to the Mexican coast?

A young Indian woman named **Malinche** (mah LEEN chay), called Doña Marina by the Spanish, served as his translator and advisor. Malinche knew both the Maya and Aztec languages, and she learned Spanish quickly.

Malinche told Cortés that the Aztecs had gained power by conquering other groups of people. The Aztecs sacrificed thousands of their captives to the Aztec gods each year. Many conquered peoples hated their Aztec overlords, so Malinche helped Cortés arrange **alliances** with them. They agreed to help Cortés fight the Aztecs.

Moctezuma's Dilemma Meanwhile, messengers brought word about the Spanish to the Aztec emperor **Moctezuma** (mahk tih ZOO muh). The Aztec ruler hesitated. Was it possible, he wondered, that the leader of the pale-skinned, bearded strangers might be Quetzalcoatl (ket sahl koh AHT el), an Aztec god-king who had long ago vowed to return from the East? To be safe, Moctezuma sent gifts of turquoise, feathers, and other goods with religious importance, but urged the strangers not to continue to Tenochtitlán.

Cortés, however, had no intention of turning back. He was not interested in the Aztec religious objects, but was extremely interested in the gold and silver ornaments that Moctezuma began sending him.

Cortés became more determined than ever to reach Tenochtitlán. Fighting and negotiating by turns, Cortés led his forces inland toward the capital. At last, the Spanish arrived in Tenochtitlán, where they were dazzled by the grandeur of the city.

Cortés Takes Tenochtitlán Moctezuma welcomed Cortés to his capital. However, relations between the Aztecs and Spaniards soon grew strained. The Spanish scorned the Aztecs' religion and sought to convert them to Christianity. At the same time, as they remained in the city, they saw more of the Aztec treasure. They decided to imprison Moctezuma so they could gain control of the Aztecs and their riches.

Cortés compelled Moctezuma to sign over his land and treasure to the Spanish. In the meantime, a new force of Spanish conquistadors had arrived on the coast to challenge Cortés. In the confusion that followed—with various groups of Spanish, Aztecs, and American Indians all fighting for control—the Aztecs drove the Spanish from the city. More than half of the Spanish were killed in the fighting, as was Moctezuma.

Cortés retreated to plan an assault. In 1521, in a brutal struggle, Cortés and his American Indian allies captured and demolished Tenochtitlán. The Spanish later built Mexico City on the ruins of

>> Atahualpa, portrayed here by an unknown painter in the 1500s, was the thirteenth and last Incan ruler.

Tenochtitlán. As in the Caribbean, disease had aided their cause. Smallpox had spread among the Aztecs from the 1519 encounter, decimating the population.

☑ **IDENTIFY CAUSE AND EFFECT** Why did Cortés want to conquer the Aztecs?

The Incan Empire and Beyond

Cortés's success inspired other adventurers. Among them was Spaniard **Francisco Pizarro** (pee SAHR oh). Pizarro had heard rumors about a fabulously rich empire in Peru, with even more gold than the Aztecs. Pizarro arrived in Peru in 1532, just after the Incan ruler Atahualpa (ah tah WAHL puh) had won the throne from his brother in a bloody **civil war.** A civil war is fought between groups of people in the same nation. The war had weakened the Incas, and they had also begun to be affected by European diseases. In the end, however, it was trickery that helped Pizarro defeat the Incas.

Atahualpa Resists When Pizarro and his small force of about 200 men reached the Inca leader, they urged him to convert to Christianity and accept Charles V as sovereign. When Atahualpa refused, Pizarro tricked the Incan leader into meeting with him. Then with the help of Indian allies, he took the emperor prisoner and killed thousands of Incas.

For a time, the Spanish held Atahulpa captive. Pizarro's secretary described him as

> a man of thirty years, good-looking and poised, somewhat stout, with a wide, handsome, and ferocious face, and the eyes flaming with blood . . .
>
> —Francisco de Xerez

Pizarro Triumphs After several months, the Spanish executed Atahualpa. Despite continuing resistance, they then overran the Incan heartland. They had superior weapons, and the Incan people were weakened by European diseases. From Peru, Spanish forces surged across what are today Ecuador and Chile. Before long, Spain had added much of South America to its growing empire. Pizarro himself was killed by a rival Spanish faction a few years after he established the city of Lima.

>> The conquistador Francisco Pizarro appears in full armor in this hand-colored woodcut from the 1800s.

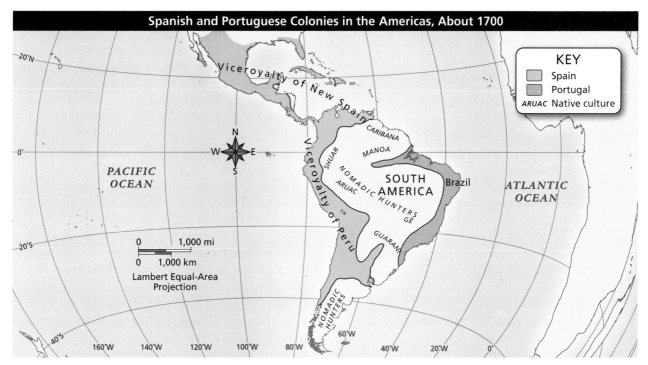

KEY
- Spain
- Portugal
- ARUAC Native culture

Viceroyalty of New Spain

Viceroyalty of Peru

PACIFIC OCEAN

ATLANTIC OCEAN

SOUTH AMERICA

Brazil

CARIBANA
MANOA
SHUAR
NOMADIC ARUAC
HUNTERS
GĚ
GUARANI
NOMADIC HUNTERS

0   1,000 mi
0   1,000 km
Lambert Equal-Area Projection

>> **Analyze Maps** What do all the European land claims in South America have in common? Which country settled the easternmost region?

BOUNCE to Activate Map

Beyond Spain's Empire As in the Spanish empire, the American Indians who lived in Brazil—the Tupian Indians—had been largely wiped out by disease. In the 1530s, Portugal began to issue grants of land to Portuguese nobles, who agreed to develop the land and share profits with the crown. Landowners sent settlers to build towns, plantations, and churches.

Unlike Spain's American colonies, Brazil offered no instant wealth from silver or gold. However, early settlers cut and exported brazilwood. The Portuguese named the colony after this wood, which was used to produce a valuable dye. Soon they turned to plantation agriculture and raising cattle.

Like the Spanish, the Portuguese forced Indians and Africans to clear land for plantations. As many as four million Africans were sent to Brazil. As in Spanish America, a new culture emerged in Brazil that blended European, American Indian, and African elements.

Challenges to Portugal and Spain In the 1500s, the wealth of the Americas helped make Spain the most powerful country in Europe, with Portugal not far behind. The jealous English and Dutch shared the resentment that French king Francis I felt when he declared, "I should like to see Adam's will, wherein he divided the Earth between Spain and Portugal."

To get around those countries' strict control over colonial trade, smugglers traded illegally with Portuguese and Spanish colonists. In the Caribbean and elsewhere, Dutch, English, and French pirates preyed on treasure ships from the Americas. Some pirates, called **privateers,** even operated with the approval of European governments. Other European explorers continued to sail the coasts of the Americas, hunting for gold and other treasure, as well as a northwest passage to Asia.

☑ **COMPARE AND CONTRAST** How was Pizarro's treatment of the Incas similar to Cortés's treatment of the Aztecs?

Governing the Spanish Empire

Spanish settlers and missionaries followed the conquistadors to the Americas. In time, the huge Spanish empire stretched from California in the north to Argentina in the south. Spain divided these lands into four provinces, including New Spain (Mexico) and Peru.

Spain imposed its culture, language, religion, and way of life on millions of new subjects in its empire. The Spanish built new Spanish-style cities on top of the ruins of American Indian cities. "Christianizing" American Indians, however, turned out to be more complex. In the end, though, Spain imposed its will by force.

Royal Officials Rule the Provinces Spain was determined to maintain strict control over its empire. To achieve this goal, the king set up the Council of the Indies to pass laws for the colonies. He also appointed **viceroys,** or representatives who ruled in his name, in each province. Lesser officials and audiencias (ow dee EN see ahs), or advisory councils of Spanish settlers, helped the viceroy rule. The Council of the Indies in Spain closely monitored these colonial officials to make sure they did not assume too much authority.

Missionaries Spread Christianity To Spain, winning souls for Christianity was as important as gaining land. The Catholic Church worked with the government to convert American Indians to Christianity. Church leaders often served as royal officials and helped to regulate the activities of Spanish settlers. As Spain's American empire expanded, Church authority expanded along with it.

Franciscans, Jesuits, and other missionaries baptized thousands of American Indians. They built mission churches and—backed by the power of the Spanish army—worked to turn new converts into loyal subjects of the Catholic king of Spain. They also introduced European clothing, the Spanish language, and crafts such as carpentry and locksmithing. Where they could, the Spanish missionaries forcibly imposed European culture over American Indian culture.

Regulation of Trade To make the empire profitable, Spain closely controlled its economic activities, especially trade. The most valuable resources shipped from Spanish America to Spain were silver and gold. Colonists could export raw materials only to Spain and could buy only Spanish manufactured goods. Laws forbade colonists from trading with other European nations or even with other Spanish colonies.

When sugar cane was introduced into the West Indies and elsewhere, it quickly became a profitable resource. The cane was refined into sugar, molasses, and rum. Sugar cane, however, had to be grown on plantations, large estates run by an owner or the owner's overseer. And plantations needed large numbers of workers to be profitable.

Forced Labor: The Encomienda System At first, Spanish monarchs granted the conquistadors

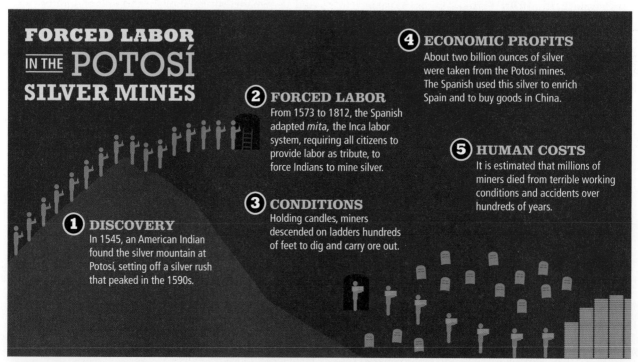

FORCED LABOR IN THE POTOSÍ SILVER MINES

① DISCOVERY
In 1545, an American Indian found the silver mountain at Potosí, setting off a silver rush that peaked in the 1590s.

② FORCED LABOR
From 1573 to 1812, the Spanish adapted *mita*, the Inca labor system, requiring all citizens to provide labor as tribute, to force Indians to mine silver.

③ CONDITIONS
Holding candles, miners descended on ladders hundreds of feet to dig and carry ore out.

④ ECONOMIC PROFITS
About two billion ounces of silver were taken from the Potosí mines. The Spanish used this silver to enrich Spain and to buy goods in China.

⑤ HUMAN COSTS
It is estimated that millions of miners died from terrible working conditions and accidents over hundreds of years.

>> While the process of extracting silver from the Potosí mines was terribly destructive for American Indian and other forced laborers, it proved immensely profitable for Spain.

encomiendas (en koh mee EN dahs), the right to demand labor or tribute from American Indians in a particular area. The conquistadors used this system to force American Indian to work under the most brutal conditions. Those who resisted were hunted down and killed. Disease, starvation, and cruel treatment caused drastic declines in the American Indian population.

The encomienda system was used in the mines as well as on plantations. By the 1540s, tons of silver from the Potosí region of Peru and Bolivia filled Spanish treasure ships. Year after year, thousands of American Indians were forced to extract the rich ore from dangerous shafts deep inside the Andes Mountains. As thousands of American Indians died from the terrible conditions, they were replaced by thousands more.

A Spanish Priest Condemns the Abuses A few bold priests, like **Bartolomé de Las Casas** (bahr toh loh MAY deh lahs KAHS ahs), condemned the evils of the encomienda system. In vivid reports to Spain, Las Casas detailed the horrors that Spanish rule had brought to American Indians and pleaded with the king to end the abuse.

Prodded by Las Casas, Spain passed the New Laws of the Indies in 1542. The laws forbade enslavement and abuse of American Indians, but Spain was too far away to enforce them. Many American Indians were forced to become **peons,** workers forced to labor for a landlord in order to pay off a debt. Landlords advanced them food, tools, or seeds, creating debts that workers could never pay off in their lifetime.

Enslaving People from Africa To fill the labor shortage, Las Casas urged colonists to import enslaved people from Africa to use as workers. He believed that Africans were immune to tropical diseases and had skills in farming, mining, and metalworking. Las Casas later regretted that advice because it furthered a brutal trade in enslaved Africans.

The Spanish began bringing African captives to the Americas by the 1530s. As demand for sugar products skyrocketed, the settlers imported millions of enslaved Africans. They were forced to work as field hands, miners, or servants in the houses of wealthy landowners. Others became skilled artists and artisans.

Within a few generations, Africans and their American-born descendants greatly outnumbered European settlers throughout the Americas. In the

>> This Mexican painting from the 1700s shows a Spanish man with his American Indian wife and their mestizo child, who is trying on a new pair of shoes.

cities, some enslaved Africans earned enough money to buy their freedom. Others resisted slavery by rebelling or running away. You will learn more about slavery in the Americas in a later lesson.

☑ **DEFINE** What was the encomienda system?

Society and Culture in Spanish America

In Spanish America, a diverse mix of peoples gave rise to a new society. The blending of American Indian, African, and European peoples and traditions resulted in a culture distinct to the Americas.

A Society of Unequal Classes Spanish colonial society was made of distinct social classes. At the top were **peninsulares** (peh neen soo LAY rayz), people born in Spain. (The term *peninsular* referred to the Iberian Peninsula, on which Spain is located.) Peninsulares filled the highest positions in both colonial governments and the Catholic Church. Next came **creoles,** American-born descendants of Spanish settlers. Creoles owned most of the plantations, ranches, and mines.

People of mixed backgrounds stood lower in the social order. People of American Indian and European ancestry were called **mestizos**. Those of African and European ancestry were called mulattoes, a term now considered offensive. American Indians and people of African descent formed the lowest social classes.

Thriving Towns and Cities Spanish settlers generally lived in towns and cities. The population of Mexico City grew so quickly that by 1550 it was the largest Spanish-speaking city in the world. Colonial cities were centers of government, commerce, and European culture. Around the central plaza, or square, stood government buildings and a Spanish-style church. Broad avenues and public monuments symbolized European power and wealth. Cities were also centers of intellectual and cultural life. Architecture and painting, as well as poetry and the exchange of ideas, flourished in Spanish cities in the Americas.

Educational Opportunities To meet the Church's need for educated priests, the colonies built universities. The University of Mexico was established as early as 1551. A dozen Spanish American universities were already educating young men long before Harvard was founded in 1636 as the first college in the 13 English colonies.

Women desiring an education might enter a convent. One such woman was Sor Juana Inés de la Cruz (sawr HWAN uh ee NES deh lah krooz). Refused admission to the University of Mexico because she was female, Juana entered a convent at around the age of 18. There, she devoted herself to study and the writing of poetry. She earned a reputation as one of the greatest poets ever to write in the Spanish language.

A Blending of Cultures Although Spanish culture was dominant in the cities, the blending of diverse traditions changed people's lives throughout the Americas. Settlers learned American Indian styles of building, ate foods native to the Americas, and traveled in Indian-style canoes. Indian artistic styles influenced the newcomers. At the same time, Europeans taught their religion to American Indians. They also introduced animals, especially the horse, thereby transforming the lives of many American Indians.

Africans contributed to this cultural mix with their farming methods, cooking styles, and crops. African drama, dance, and song heightened Christian services. In Cuba, Haiti, and elsewhere, Africans forged new religions that blended African and Christian beliefs.

☑ **DRAW CONCLUSIONS** In Spanish colonial society, what determined a person's social rank?

The Impact of Spanish Colonization

Spanish exploration, colonization, and expansion had a long-lasting impact on American Indians, Europeans, and others beyond these two groups. By establishing an empire in the Americas, Spain dramatically changed the pattern of global encounter first set in motion by European exploration of Africa's coasts. For the first time, much of the world was now connected by sea routes, on which traveled ships carrying goods, people, and ideas.

Spain Wins Wealth and Power In the 1500s, Spain acquired enormous wealth from its American colonies. Every year treasure fleets sailed to Europe loaded with gold and silver. These riches helped make Spain the most powerful country in Europe. At the same time, the French, English, and Dutch jealously eyed the Spanish treasure fleets and defied Spain's claims to the Americas.

>> Sor Juana Inés de la Cruz, a Catholic nun, appears at her desk in this painting from the 1700s by Miguel Cabrera. She defended women's right to learn and was recognized as an important writer.

American Indian Population of Central Mexico

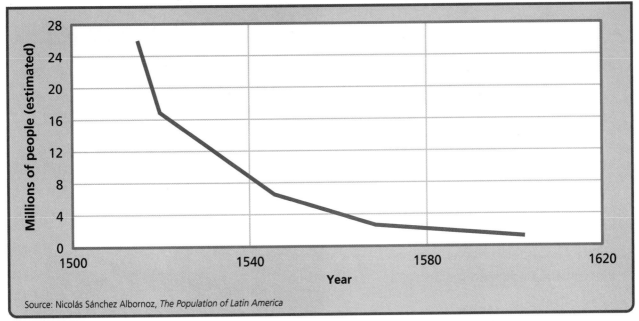

Source: Nicolás Sánchez Albornoz, *The Population of Latin America*

>> **Analyze Graphs** What is the estimated population decline between 1519 and 1540? How does it compare with the population change between 1540 and 1580? Why?

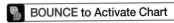

BOUNCE to Activate Chart

American Indian Suffering and Resistance The conquest of the Americas brought suffering and death to many American Indian peoples. Although many converted to Christianity and adopted some Spanish ways, others resisted Spanish rule for centuries. For centuries, the Maya fought Spanish rule in Mexico and Central America. Long after the death of Atahualpa, revolts erupted among the Incas.

Resistance did not always take the form of military action. Throughout the Americas, American Indians resisted Europeans by preserving their own cultures, languages, religious traditions, and skills, such as weaving and pottery. As you will read later, European exploration and colonization had tremendous global impact even beyond the Americas by connecting people, goods, and ideas around the world.

☑ **DESCRIBE** In what ways did American Indians resist European influence?

☑ **ASSESSMENT**

1. **Identify Patterns** Describe the common effects of the first encounters between the Spanish and American Indians in Mexico, Peru, and elsewhere.

2. **Draw Conclusions** Why were American Indians unable to defeat the Spanish conquistadors?

3. **Identify Main Ideas** Describe the main characteristics of government, religion, and economics in Spain's colonies in the Americas.

4. **Categorize** Explain how the people of Spanish colonial society were categorized into different social classes.

5. **Connections to Today** As in the encomienda system, debt slavery is a common form of forced labor today in nations such as India. Why is this form of slavery especially difficult to escape?

Spanish Rule in the Indies

On October 12, 1492, Christopher Columbus landed on an island in the Caribbean Sea. Soon after, he established a colony on an island he called Hispaniola. This marked the start of Spanish conquest of the Americas. Columbus was followed by soldiers, fortune hunters, and priests. One of these priests, Bartolomé de Las Casas, took part in the conquest of Cuba. But he later became horrified by the treatment of American Indians and dedicated the rest of his life to ending these abuses.

The first Primary Source below is from a letter Columbus wrote to the monarchs of Spain in 1494, listing his recommendations for how to rule the Indies. The second source was written by Las Casas in 1542. **As you read, compare their attitudes toward the relationship between the Spanish and the Indians.**

>> Caribbean workers are forced to wash gold under the eyes of Spanish conquerors.

Primary Source 1

Letter to the King and Queen of Spain, Christopher Columbus

1. That in the said island there shall be founded three or four towns, situated in the most convenient places, and that the settlers who are there be assigned to the aforesaid places and towns.
2. That for the better and more speedy colonization of the said island, no one shall have liberty to collect gold in it except those who have taken out colonists' papers, and have built houses for their abode, in the town in which they are, that they may live united and in greater safety.

☑ **CITE EVIDENCE** What evidence shows that Columbus did not think colonists should have much freedom?

3. That each town shall have its alcalde [Mayor] . . . and its notary public, as is the use and custom in Castile.
4. That there shall be a church, and parish priests or friars to administer the sacraments, to perform divine worship, and for the conversion of the Indians.
5. That one per centum of all the gold that may be found shall be set aside for building churches and adorning the same, and for the support of the priests or friars belonging to them; and, if it should be thought proper to pay any thing to the alcaldes or notaries for their services, or for ensuring the faithful perforce of their duties, that this amount shall be sent to the governor or treasurer who may be appointed there by your Highnesses.

☑ **DRAW INFERENCES** How did Columbus view the rights of the American Indians in the colonies?

Primary Source 2

The Destruction of the Indies, Bartolomé de las Casas

There are two main ways in which those who have traveled to this part of the world pretending to be Christians have uprooted these pitiful peoples and wiped them from the face of the earth. First, they have waged war on them: unjust, cruel, bloody and tyrannical [using power unjustly] war. Second, they have murdered anyone and everyone who has shown the slightest sign of resistance. . . . This latter policy has been instrumental [an important tool] in suppressing the native leaders, and, indeed, given that the Spaniards normally spare only women and children, it has led to the annihilation [complete destruction] of all adult males. . . .

☑ **CITE EVIDENCE** What evidence does Las Casas give to show the cruelty of the Spaniards?

The reason the [Spanish] have murdered on such a vast scale and killed anyone and everyone in their way is purely and simply greed. They have set out to line their pockets with gold. . . . The Spaniards have shown not the slightest consideration for these people, treating them (and I speak from first-hand experience, having been there from the outset) not as brute animals—indeed, I would to God they had done and had shown them the consideration they afford their animals—so much as piles of dung in the middle of the road. They have had as little concern for their souls as for their bodies, all the millions that have perished having gone to their deaths with no knowledge of God and without the benefit of the Sacraments [sacred right of the Christian church]. . . .

☑ **IDENTIFY CAUSE AND EFFECT** According to Las Casas, what caused the Spanish to treat American Indians unjustly?

The indigenous [native to a region or country] peoples never did the Europeans any harm whatever; on the contrary, they believed them to have descended from the heavens, at least until they or their fellow-citizens had tasted, at the hands of these oppressors, a diet of robbery, murder, violence, and all other manner of trials and tribulations [great sorrows].

☑ **IDENTIFY SUPPORTING DETAILS** Who did the American Indians first think the Europeans were, and why?

☑ ASSESSMENT

1. **Draw Inferences** What were Columbus's main concerns in suggesting this plan to the king and queen?

2. **Determine Author's Purpose** Why do you think Las Casas wrote this detailed account about the treatment of American Indians by the Spanish?

3. **Compare** Do you think Columbus and las Casas agreed or disagreed about Spain's right to claim and govern Hispaniola? Explain.

4. **Analyze Interactions** How do you think Columbus and other Spanish conquistadors might have responded to Las Casas's description of the conquistadors?

5. **Predict** Whose viewpoint do you think will have a greater influence on Spanish policy?

🔲 **GO ONLINE** to access primary sources

11.4

French explorer Jacques Cartier found that the St. Lawrence River was a gateway into a vast territory of rich forests, with an abundance of fish and animals that could provide wealth from trade.

 BOUNCE to Activate Flipped Video

Objectives

Explain why the colony of New France grew slowly.

Analyze the establishment and growth of the English colonies.

Understand why Europeans competed for power in North America and how their struggle affected American Indians.

Key Terms

New France
Jacques Cartier
revenue
Samuel de
   Champlain
John Cabot
Pilgrim
compact
French and Indian
   War
Treaty of Paris

European Colonies in North America

During the 1600s, France, the Netherlands, England, and Sweden joined Spain in settling North America. At first, Europeans were disappointed that North America did not yield gold treasure or offer a water passage to Asia, as they had hoped. Before long, though, the English and French were turning profits by growing tobacco in Virginia, fishing off the North Atlantic coast, and trading furs from New England and Canada with Europe.

New France

By 1700, France and England controlled large parts of North America. As their colonies grew, they developed their own governments that differed from each other and from that of Spanish America.

French Exploration Begins By the early 1500s, French fishing ships were crossing the Atlantic each year to harvest rich catches of cod off Newfoundland, Canada. Within 200 years, the French had occupied or claimed nearly half of North America.

French claims in Canada—which the French called **New France**—quietly grew while French rulers were distracted by wars at home in Europe. In 1534, **Jacques Cartier** (zhahk kahr tee AY) began exploring the coastline of eastern Canada, eventually becoming the first European to sail into the St. Lawrence River. Traveling inland on the river, he claimed much of present-day eastern Canada for France.

French explorers and fur traders gradually traveled inland with the help of American Indian allies, who sought support against rival American Indian groups. Jesuits and other missionaries soon followed the explorers. They advanced into the wilderness, trying with little success to convert the American Indians they met to Christianity.

New France Grows Slowly The population of New France grew slowly. The first permanent French settlement was not established until 1605. Then, in 1608, **Samuel de Champlain** established a colony in Quebec. Wealthy landlords bought huge tracts, or areas of land, along the St. Lawrence River. They sought settlers to farm the land, but the harsh Canadian climate, with its long winters, attracted few French peasants.

Many who went to New France soon abandoned farming in favor of the more profitable fur trapping and trading. They faced a hard life in the wilderness, but the soaring European demand for fur ensured good prices. Fishing was another industry that supported settlers, who exported cod and other fish to Europe.

Royal Power and Economic Growth In the late 1600s, the French king Louis XIV set out to strengthen royal power and boost **revenues,** or income, from taxes from his overseas empire. He appointed officials to oversee economic activities in New France.

He also sent soldiers and more settlers—including women—to North America. However, Louis, who was Catholic, prohibited Protestants from settling in New France.

By the early 1700s, French forts, missions, and trading posts stretched from Quebec to Louisiana, and the population was growing. Yet the population of New France remained small compared to that of the English colonies that were expanding along the Atlantic coast.

☑ **EXPRESS PROBLEMS CLEARLY** Why was the growth of New France slow?

The 13 English Colonies

At the time of Columbus and throughout the centuries ahead, the English sailed westward, hoping to find a sea passage to India. In 1497, **John Cabot,** an Italian explorer, commanded an English expedition that reached the rich fishing grounds off Newfoundland. He claimed the region for England. Dozens of other English explorers continued to search for a northwest passage to Asia, without success. In the 1600s, England turned its attention instead to building colonies along the Atlantic seaboard of North America.

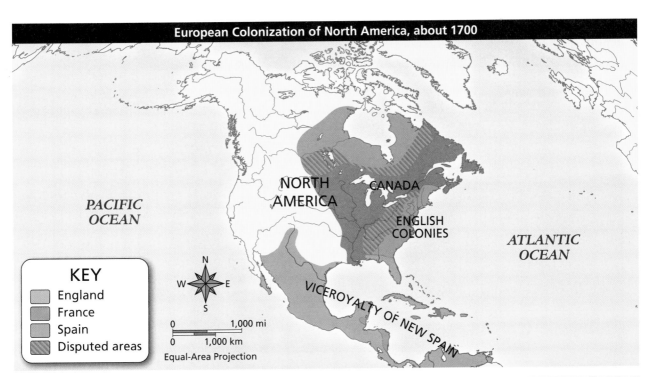

European Colonization of North America, about 1700

PACIFIC OCEAN

NORTH AMERICA

CANADA

ENGLISH COLONIES

ATLANTIC OCEAN

VICEROYALTY OF NEW SPAIN

KEY
England
France
Spain
Disputed areas

0   1,000 mi
0   1,000 km
Equal-Area Projection

>> England, France, and Spain controlled large parts of North America. Their colonies differed from each other in a number of ways.

BOUNCE to Activate Map

Jamestown The English built their first permanent colony at Jamestown, Virginia, in 1607. Its early years were filled with disaster. Many settlers died of starvation and disease. The rest survived with the help of friendly American Indians.

Plymouth In 1620, another group of English settlers landed at Plymouth, Massachusetts. They were **Pilgrims,** or English Protestants who rejected the Church of England. They sought religious freedom rather than commercial profit. Before coming ashore, the men signed the Mayflower Compact, in which they set out guidelines for governing their North American colony. A **compact** is an agreement among people. Today, we see this document as an important early step toward self-government.

Many Pilgrims died in the early years of the Plymouth colony. Local American Indians, however, taught them to grow corn and helped them survive in the new land. Soon, a new wave of English Protestant immigrants arrived to establish the Massachusetts Bay Colony.

Expansion and Prosperity In the 1600s and 1700s, other groups and individuals founded colonies for England. Some colonies, like Virginia and New York, were commercial ventures, organized for profit.

Others, like Massachusetts, Pennsylvania, and Maryland, were set up as havens for persecuted religious groups. Still others, like Georgia and South Carolina, were gifts from the king of England to loyal supporters.

Geographic conditions helped shape different ways of life in the New England, Middle, and Southern colonies. At first, settlers in each colony just struggled to survive. Early on, they abandoned dreams of finding riches like the Spanish had in Mexico and Peru. Instead, they learned to create wealth by using the resources native to their surroundings and, sometimes, by using the forced labor of others.

In New England, many settlers were farmers who recreated in North America their village life from England. They took advantage of fishing and timber resources, and some colonists set up shipbuilding industries. In the Middle Colonies, farmers grew large quantities of grain on the abundant land. In the Southern Colonies, a plantation economy emerged. Cash crops, such as rice and tobacco, grew well in the warm climate. They therefore developed a plantation economy to grow these crops.

As in New Spain, English colonists bought enslaved workers to clear land and raise crops. The English tried using American Indian labor, but the Indians fled or died of diseases. Before long, the colonists began to rely on the work of Africans who were brought to the colonies and sold as slaves. In several colonies in the South, enslaved Africans

THE MAYFLOWER COMPACT
NOVEMBER 21, 1620

- First written framework of government in English colonies

- Signed by all 41 adult males aboard the Mayflower

- Signers agreed to form a civil government and obey its laws

- Signers agreed to enact "just and equal laws" for the general good of the colony

- Based on English traditions of self-government

- Served as inspiration for later more complex frameworks of government

>> In the Mayflower Compact the Pilgrims agreed to form a government and obey its laws. The idea of self-government would later become a founding principle of the United States.

Roots of Democracy

TRADITIONS INFLUENCING ENGLISH COLONIAL SELF- GOVERNMENT

JUDEO-CHRISTIAN IDEALS

Jewish and Christian traditions emphasized the value of the individual, the importance of social responsibility, and the idea of free will, or the freedom of humans to make choices for themselves

GRECO-ROMAN MODELS

Ancient Greek democracy and Roman republicanism served as ancient models of limited self-government and influenced ideas about equality before the law and individual liberty

ENGLISH TRADITION OF GUARANTEED RIGHTS

The Magna Carta (1215) and the English Bill of Rights (1689) guaranteed certain rights to citizens, including the right to trial by jury and individual liberty

ENGLISH PARLIAMENTARY TRADITION

Beginning with the Magna Carta, the two houses of Parliament played an increasing role in representing the English people and making English laws

>> The ideas of democracy and representative government have a long history. They are based on traditions that are far older than the English colonies that gave birth to the United States.

 BOUNCE to Activate Chart

and their descendants would eventually outnumber people of European descent.

Limited Self-Government Like the rulers of Spain and France, English monarchs asserted control over their American colonies. They appointed royal governors to oversee colonial affairs and had Parliament pass laws to regulate colonial trade. Yet, compared with settlers in the Spanish and French colonies, male English colonists enjoyed a large degree of self-government. Each colony had its own representative assembly, elected by men who owned property, that advised the governor and made decisions on local issues.

The tradition of consulting representative assemblies grew out of the English experience. Beginning in the 1200s, Parliament had begun to play an important role in English affairs. Slowly, too, English citizens had gained certain legal and political rights. England's American colonists expected to enjoy the same rights. When colonists later protested British policies in North America, they viewed themselves as "freeborn Englishmen" who were defending their traditional rights.

☑ **IDENTIFY CENTRAL IDEAS** Why did the English colonies have a large degree of self-government?

A Power Struggle Begins

By the 1600s, Spain, France, England, and the Netherlands all had colonies in North America. They began to fight—both in the colonies and around the world—to protect and expand their interests.

A Race for Colonies By the late 1600s, French claims included present-day Canada as well as much of the present-day central United States. The Spanish claimed present-day Texas and Florida. Meanwhile, the English and Dutch maintained colonies along the East Coast. (In the 1670s, the British gained control of the Dutch colony of New Netherland, renaming it New York.) American Indians entered the conflict, hoping to play the Europeans against one another.

Competition was also fierce in the Caribbean, as European nations fought to acquire the profitable sugar-producing colonies. By the 1700s, the French and English Caribbean islands, worked by enslaved Africans, had surpassed the whole of North America in exports to Europe.

Britain and France in a Global Struggle By the 1700s, Britain and France emerged as bitter rivals for power around the globe. Their clashes in Europe ignited conflicts in the Americas, India, and Africa.

In 1754, fighting broke out between the French and British in North America. In the British colonies, it marked the beginning of the **French and Indian War.** By 1756, that regional conflict was linked to the Seven Years' War in Europe. The war soon spread to India and other parts of the globe.

Although France held more territory in North America, the British colonies had more people. Trappers, traders, and farmers from the British colonies were pushing west into the Ohio Valley, a region claimed by France. The French, who had forged alliances with American Indians, fought to oust the intruders.

During the war, British soldiers and colonial troops launched a series of campaigns against the French in Canada and on the Ohio frontier. In 1759, the British captured Quebec, capital of New France, and then Montreal. Although the war dragged on until 1763, the British had won control of Canada.

The 1763 **Treaty of Paris** officially ended the worldwide war and ensured British dominance in North America. France ceded all of Canada and its lands east of the Mississippi River to Britain. It handed the Louisiana Territory over to Spain. However, France did regain the rich sugar-producing islands in the Caribbean. They also regained outposts in Africa used for the trade in enslaved people, which the British had seized during the war.

☑ **SUMMARIZE** How did wars between European powers in the Americas affect American Indians?

☑ **ASSESSMENT**

1. **Generate Explanations** Why did European countries compete to expand their power in North America?

2. **Summarize** What obstacles did the Pilgrims face during their first years trying to establish Plymouth colony, and how did they overcome the obstacles?

3. **Compare and Contrast** How were conditions in New France and the English colonies different?

4. **Identify Patterns** How did the various regions of the British colonies become prosperous in different ways?

5. **Identify Central Issues** How was the French and Indian War caused by European expansion and competition on a global scale?

6. **Quest Connections** What products exported from North America were most valued in Europe by the 1700s?

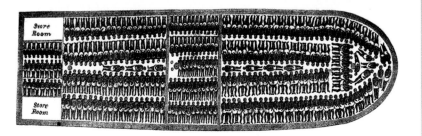

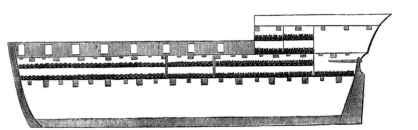

This 1800s diagram shows how enslaved Africans were so tightly crammed in small spaces that they had to lie side by side with little room to move for many hours at a time.

The Slave Trade and Its Impact on Africa

In the 1400s and 1500s, as you have read, Europeans set up small forts on the coast of West Africa in order to resupply their ships and profit from local trade, especially in gold. As Europeans built colonies in the Americas, they needed large numbers of laborers to make their colonies profitable. By the 1600s, they increasingly turned to Africa to provide that labor.

The Trade in Enslaved Africans Expands

Slavery Throughout History Slavery has existed all over the world since ancient times: ancient Egypt, Greece, and Rome, as well as China, Persia, the Aztecs, and other societies had enslaved people. The English word *slave* comes from *Slav*, the people of Eastern Europe who were often sold into slavery in the Middle Ages.

The institution of slavery occurred as a result of debt (a person's service was pledged until a debt was paid), a punishment for a crime, or enslavement as a prisoner of war. Most people enslaved in these ways were used for agricultural and industrial labor.

The Arabs also enslaved some of the people they conquered. In the Middle East, enslaved Africans worked on large farming estates or large-scale irrigation projects. Others became artisans, soldiers, or merchants.

By the 1400s, however, the Arabs gained a rival in the trade in enslaved people. The Portuguese began to explore the coast of Africa. They began to trade enslaved Africans in Portugal and Spain.

 BOUNCE to Activate Flipped Video

Objectives

Summarize the expansion of the African slave trade.

Explain how triangular trade worked.

Understand the nature of the Middle Passage and describe its effects.

Analyze the impact of the Atlantic slave trade on West Africa and the Americas.

Key Terms

plantation
Afonso I
missionary
Olaudah Equiano
triangular trade
Middle Passage
mutiny
Asante kingdom
Osei Tutu
monopoly
Oyo empire

GO ONLINE to access your digital course

>> The African slave trade expanded in response to Europeans' increasing use of enslaved workers on plantations in the Americas.

>> Portuguese soldiers and missionaries are received by the king of Kongo. Afonso I of Kongo welcomed Portuguese missionaries and scholars and sent his son to Portugal to learn about Christianity.

Europeans Enter the Slave Trade In the 1400s and early 1500s, the Portuguese and other Europeans brought enslaved Africans back to Europe. As European colonies in the Americas grew, Europeans and colonists also began to buy and sell enslaved Africans to clear **plantations,** or the large estates run by an owner or an owner's overseer.

Europeans lacked the resources to travel inland to enslave people. Instead, they relied on local African rulers and traders to bring captives—usually from other African nations—to coastal trading posts. There, the traders exchanged captured Africans for weapons, gunpowder, textiles, iron, and other goods.

In the 1500s, the trade in enslaved Africans was relatively small. Over the next 300 years, however, it grew into a huge, profitable business.

By the 1700s and 1800s, traders had shipped millions of enslaved Africans across the Atlantic to work on tobacco and sugar plantations in the Americas. These people were treated as property.

African Resistance As the trade in enslaved Africans grew, some African leaders tried to slow it down or even stop it altogether. They used different forms of resistance, but in the end, the system that supported the trade was too strong for them to resist.

An early critic of the trade was **Afonso I,** ruler of Kongo in west-central Africa. As a young man, Afonso had been tutored by Portuguese **missionaries,** who baptized him to Christianity.

Impressed by his early contacts with the Portuguese, Afonso hoped to build a Christian state in Kongo. After becoming king in 1505, he called on Portuguese missionaries, teachers, and technical experts to help him develop Kongo and increase his own power. He sent his sons to Portugal to be educated in Christian ways.

Afonso grew worried as more and more Portuguese came to Kongo to buy enslaved captives. Afonso wanted to maintain contact with Europe but end the slave trade. His appeal failed, and the trade continued.

In the late 1700s, another African ruler tried to halt the trade in human beings in his lands. He was the almany (religious leader) of Futa Toro, in present-day Senegal. Since the 1500s, French sea captains had bought captives from African traders in Futa Toro. To end this trade, the almany issued a law in 1788. It forbade anyone to transport enslaved people through his land to sell abroad. However, the inland traders simply worked out a new route to the coast. Sailing to this new market, the French captains easily purchased the captives that the almany had prevented them from buying in Futa Toro.

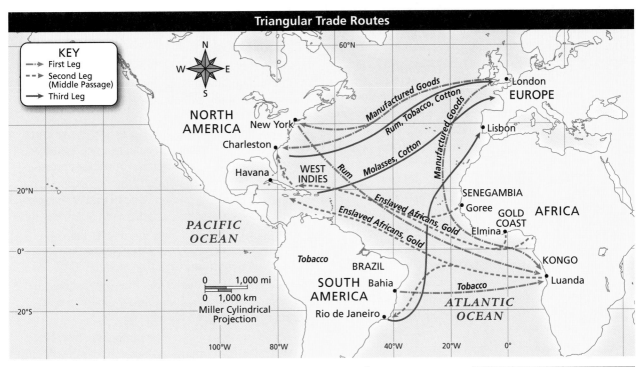

>> **Analyze Maps** This map shows triangular trade routes that started in the 1500s. What trade goods were enslaved Africans exchanged for in North America?

BOUNCE to Activate Map

☑ **IDENTIFY CAUSE AND EFFECT** Why did the African slave trade expand?

The Atlantic Slave Trade

In 1789, a formerly enslaved African American named **Olaudah Equiano** wrote an account of his life. In it, he described the experience of being captured as a child by slave traders and being transported as human cargo from West Africa to the Americas:

> The first object which saluted my eyes when I arrived on the coast was the sea, and a slave ship which was then riding at anchor and waiting for its cargo. These filled me with astonishment, which was soon converted into terror when I was carried on board.

> —Olaudah Equiano

Enslaved Africans like Olaudah Equiano formed part of an international trade network that arose during the 1500s. The Spanish were the first major European enslavers, buying enslaved Africans to labor in Spain's American colonies.

As other European powers established colonies in the Americas, the slave trade—and with it the entire international trade network—intensified.

Triangular Trade The Atlantic slave trade formed one part of a three-legged international trade network known as the **triangular trade.** This was a triangle-shaped series of Atlantic trade routes linking Europe, Africa, and the Americas.

The triangular trade worked in the following way. On the first leg, merchant ships brought European goods—including guns—to Africa. In Africa, the merchants traded these goods for enslaved people. On the second leg, known as the **Middle Passage,** the enslaved Africans were transported to the Americas. There, these people were exchanged for sugar, molasses, and other products manufactured at plantations owned by Europeans.

On the final leg, merchants carried sugar, molasses, cotton, and other American goods such as furs, salt fish, and rum made from molasses. These goods were shipped to Europe, where they were traded at a profit for the European commodities that merchants needed to return to Africa.

Merchants, Industries, and Cities Thrive

The triangular trade was immensely profitable for many people. Merchants grew wealthy. Even though there were risks such as losing ships at sea, the money to be made from valuable cargoes usually outweighed the risks. Certain industries that supported trade thrived. For example, a shipbuilding industry in New England grew to support the shipping industry. Other colonial industries, such as fishing, raising tobacco, and processing sugar, became hugely successful.

Thriving trade led to successful port cities. European cities such as Nantes, France, and Bristol, England, grew prosperous because of the triangular trade. In North America, even newly settled towns such as Salem, Massachusetts, and Newport, Rhode Island, quickly grew into thriving cities. Even though few enslaved people were imported directly to northern cities in North America, the success of the port cities there was made possible by the Atlantic slave trade.

☑ **IDENTIFY CAUSE AND EFFECT** How did the Atlantic slave trade affect colonial economies?

>> Europeans built fortresses in ports along the west coast of Africa, such as the town of Elmina in what is now Ghana, shown here. **Hypothesize** What was one probable use of the fortress?

Horrors of the Middle Passage

To merchants, the Middle Passage was just one leg of the triangular trade. For enslaved Africans, the Middle Passage was a horror.

Forced March to the Ships The terrible journey began before the slave ships set sail. Most Africans were taken from inland villages. After they were enslaved, they were forced to march to coastal ports. Men, women, and children were bound with ropes and chains, often to one another, and forced to walk distances as long as a thousand miles. They might be forced to carry heavy loads, and often the men's necks were encircled with thick iron bands.

Many captives died along the way. Others tried to escape, and were often quickly recaptured and brutally punished.

Those who survived the march were restrained in coastal holding pens and warehouses in shipping ports such as Elmina, in what is now Ghana, or Gorée, in what is now Senegal. They were held there until European traders arrived by ship.

Packed Aboard the "Floating Coffins" Once purchased, Africans were packed below the decks of slave ships, usually in chains. Hundreds of men, women, and children were crammed into a single vessel for voyages that lasted from three weeks to three months. The ships faced many perils, including storms at sea, raids by pirate ships, and **mutinies,** or revolts, by the captives.

Disease was the biggest threat to the lives of the captives and the profit of the merchants. Of the captives who died, most died of dysentery. Many died of smallpox. Many others died from apparently no disease at all. Whatever the cause, slave ships became "floating coffins" on which up to half the enslaved Africans on board died from disease or brutal mistreatment.

Some enslaved Africans resisted, and others tried to seize control of the ship and return to Africa. Suicide, however, was more common than mutiny. Many Africans believed that in death they would be returned to their home countries. So they hanged themselves, starved themselves, or leapt overboard.

☑ **SUMMARIZE** Why did so many enslaved Africans die during the Middle Passage?

THE ATLANTIC SLAVE TRADE 1514–1866

ANNUAL RATE OF FORCED MIGRATION
ENSLAVED AFRICANS SHIPPED TO AMERICAS EACH YEAR

1500s 2,000
1780s 80,000

THE TOTAL NUMBERS

MORE THAN 35,000 VOYAGES

11 MILLION
REACHED THE AMERICAS

2 MILLION
DIED DURING THE PASSAGE

Source: The Trans-Atlantic Slave Trade Database (Emory University, 2009)

FINAL DESTINATIONS

95% CARIBBEAN AND SOUTH AMERICA

4% NORTH AMERICA

1% EUROPE AND OTHER DESTINATIONS

1525 First transport of enslaved people direct from Africa to the Americas

1808 Abolition of British and U.S. slave trades takes effect

1867 Last trans-Atlantic shipment of enslaved Africans arrives in Americas

1780s Atlantic slave trade reaches its peak

1850 Brazil suppresses slave trade

1865 Slavery abolished in U.S. by 13th Amendment to the Constitution

>> **Analyze Charts** Based on this information, what percentage of enslaved Africans died during passage to the Americas? Where in the Americas did most enslaved Africans end up?

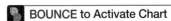
BOUNCE to Activate Chart

Impact of the Slave Trade

Historians continue to debate how many Africans were carried to the Americas during the Atlantic slave trade. Some historians estimate that about 2,000 Africans were sent to the Americas each year during the 1500s. In the 1780s, when the slave trade reached its peak, that number approached 80,000 a year. By the mid-1800s, when the overseas slave trade was finally ended, an estimated 11 million enslaved Africans had been forcibly carried to the Americas. Another 2 million probably died under the brutal conditions of the Middle Passage.

The slave trade brought great profits to many Europeans and Americans and provided the labor needed by colonial economies. Yet the slave trade had a devastating impact on African societies. Millions of people in Africa were brutalized by the slave trade and slavery itself. Many others died during the horrific Middle Passage.

The Asante Kingdom In some parts of Africa, the slave trade had little or no impact. In other areas, it disrupted whole societies. The slave trade triggered wars, increased tensions among neighboring peoples, and led to the rise of strong new states. The rulers of these states battled each other to control the capture and sale of Africans to European traders.

The **Asante kingdom** (uh SAHN teh) emerged in the area occupied by present-day Ghana. In the late 1600s, an able military leader, **Osei Tutu,** won control of the trading city of Kumasi. From there, he conquered neighboring peoples and unified the Asante kingdom. The Asante faced a great challenge in the Denkyera, a powerful neighboring enemy kingdom. Osei Tutu realized that in order to withstand the Denkyera, the people of his kingdom needed to be firmly united. To do this, he claimed that his right to rule came from heaven, and that people in the kingdom were linked by spiritual bonds. This strategy paid off when the Asante defeated the Denkyera in the late 1600s.

Under Osei Tutu, government officials, chosen by merit rather than by birth, supervised an efficient bureaucracy. They managed the royal monopolies on gold mining and the slave trade. A **monopoly** is the exclusive control of a business or industry. The Asante traded with Europeans on the coast, exchanging gold and enslaved people for firearms. They also played rival Europeans against one another to protect themselves. In this way, they built a wealthy, powerful state.

The Oyo Empire The **Oyo empire** arose from successive waves of settlement by the Yoruba people of present-day Nigeria. It began as a relatively small forest kingdom. Beginning in the late 1600s, however, its leaders used wealth from the slave trade to build up an impressive army. The Oyo empire used the army to conquer the neighboring kingdom of Dahomey. At the same time, it continued to gain wealth by trading with European merchants at the port city of Porto-Novo.

Slavery and the Americas The slave trade brought millions of Africans to the Americas. The descendants of the early captives knew life only under slavery. Many had limited or perhaps no specific information about their African ancestors. By the late 1700s and throughout the 1800s, reformers in Britain, the United States, and elsewhere called for abolition, or ending slavery and the slave trade.

In 1807, Britain abolished the slave trade throughout its empire and abolished slavery itself in 1833. In the United States, the issue of the spread of slavery into new territories helped fuel tensions that ultimately led to the Civil War. In 1865, when the Thirteenth Amendment was ratified, slavery was officially ended in all parts of the United States.

Slavery continued longer elsewhere in the Americas, notably in Brazil. Over the centuries, about 80 percent of all enslaved Africans were brought to Brazil or the Caribbean.

In Brazil, the profitable sugar industry along with other businesses relied on slave labor. Only in 1888 was slavery officially ended in Brazil.

The Atlantic slave trade brought people from different societies in Africa to the Americas.

Although most came from West Africa, that region was home to diverse communities from small chiefdoms to larger states and kingdoms. A rich variety of African traditions, languages, beliefs, stories, music, and other cultural elements were added to the emerging new cultures of the Americas.

☑ **CONTRAST** How did the slave trade damage some African states, but help others?

☑ ASSESSMENT

1. **Compare and Contrast** How was the trade in enslaved Africans before European involvement different from the trade after European involvement?

2. **Identify Cause and Effect** How did the Atlantic slave trade affect the Asante kingdom and the Oyo empire?

3. **Identify Steps in a Process** How did the three steps of the triangular trade network function?

4. **Infer** Why was disease the leading cause of death of enslaved Africans on the Middle Passage?

5. **Summarize** Write a short summary explaining how the Atlantic slave trade impacted West Africa and the Americas.

6. **Connections to Today** How do you think forms of enforced labor today differ from the Atlantic slave trade of the 1500s–1800s?

Two Slavery Narratives

In the first several chapters of his narrative, Olaudah Equiano describes how enslavers kidnapped him and his sister from their home in West Africa and transported them to the African coast. During this six- or seven-month journey, Equiano writes that he was separated from his sister and held at a series of way stations before being shipped with other captives to North America. The following account describes this horrifying journey.

The second primary source is from Mary Prince. Born into slavery in Brackish Pond, Bermuda, Prince's story is the first slave narrative from a Black British woman who would, as did Equiano, eventually escape slavery.

As you read, look for similarities in their descriptions of slavery.

>> Olaudah Equiano

Primary Source 1

The Interesting Narrative of the Life of Olaudah Equiano

At last when the ship we were in, had got in all her cargo, they made ready with many fearful noises, and we were all put under deck, so that we could not see how they managed the vessel. But this disappointment was the least of my sorrow. The stench of the hold [the cargo area of a ship, often below deck] while we were on the coast was so intolerably loathsome, that it was dangerous to remain there for any time, and some of us had been permitted to stay on the deck for the fresh air; but now that the whole ship's cargo were confined together, it became absolutely pestilential [deadly; disease-ridden]. The closeness of the place, and the heat of the climate, added to the number in the ship, which was so crowded that each

had scarcely room to turn himself, almost suffocated us.

☑ **ANALYZE WORD CHOICES** What specific words create the most vivid impression of conditions on the slave ship?

This produced copious [plentiful; abundant] perspirations, so that the air soon became unfit for respiration, from a variety of loathsome smells, and brought on a sickness among the slaves, of which many died—thus falling victims to the improvident [reckless, rash] avarice [greediness], as I may call it, of their purchasers. This wretched [deeply distressing; miserable] situation was again aggravated by the galling [chafing] of the chains, now become insupportable, and the filth of the necessary tubs, into which the children often fell, and were almost suffocated. The shrieks of the women, and the groans of the dying, rendered the whole a scene of horror almost inconceivable. Happily perhaps, for myself, I was soon reduced so low here that it was thought necessary to keep me almost always on deck; and from my extreme youth I was not put in fetters [chains]. In this situation I expected every hour to share the fate of my companions, some of whom were almost daily brought upon deck at the point of death, which I began to hope would soon put an end to my miseries. Often did I think many of the inhabitants of the deep much more happy than myself.

☑ **IDENTIFY SUPPORTING DETAILS** Why did Equiano find himself in a different position than other enslaved people?

Primary Source 2

The History of Mary Prince

Our mother, weeping as she went, called me away with the children Hannah and Dinah, and we took the road that led to Hamble Town, which we reached about four o'clock in the afternoon. We followed my mother to the market-place, where she placed us in a row against a large house, with our backs to the wall and our arms folded across our breasts. I, as the eldest, stood first, Hannah next to me, then Dinah; and our mother stood beside, crying over us. My heart throbbed with grief and terror so violently, that I pressed my hands quite tightly across my breast, but I could not keep it still, and it continued to leap as though it would burst out of my body.

☑ **DEVELOP EMPATHY** How does Prince try to stir her readers' feelings?

But who cared for that? Did one of the many by-standers, who were looking at us so carelessly, think of the pain that wrung the hearts of the negro woman and her young ones? No, no! They were not all bad, I dare say, but slavery hardens white people's hearts towards the blacks; and many of them were not slow to make their remarks upon us aloud, without regard to our grief—though their light words fell like cayenne on the fresh wounds of our hearts. Oh those white people have small hearts who can only feel for themselves.

☑ **UNDERSTANDING THE MAIN IDEA** What does this reveal about the lives of enslaved people and their enslavers?

☑ ASSESSMENT

1. **Analyze Style and Rhetoric** What sensory details does Olaudah Equiano use to tell his story? How effective are they in making the story come alive? Cite specific examples from the text in your answer.

2. **Analyze Style and Rhetoric** What is the effect of the two questions and the answer that Prince includes in the middle of this excerpt?

3. **Compare and Contrast** How do Equiano and Prince reach similar conclusions about those who participate in the slave trade? Cite specific examples.

4. **Determine Author's Purpose** Why do you think Equiano and Prince wrote these narratives? Explain your reasoning.

5. **Analyze Interactions** How might the narratives of Olaudah Equiano and Mary Prince have been used by opponents of slavery?

GO ONLINE to access primary sources

11.6

This 1592 engraving shows ships preparing to leave Lisbon, Portugal, bound for Asia and the Americas.

Effects of Global Contact

The European voyages of exploration in the 1500s and 1600s set off a chain of events that brought major changes to the world. Over the next centuries, European exploration and expansion overseas affected people from Asia, Africa, and the Americas to Europe itself.

The Columbian Exchange

A Global Exchange When Columbus returned to Spain in March 1493, he brought with him plants and animals that he had found in the Americas. Later that year, Columbus returned to the Americas with some 1,200 settlers and a collection of European animals and plants. In this way, Columbus began a vast global exchange that would profoundly affect the world. Because this exchange began with Columbus, we call it the **Columbian Exchange.**

Exchanging Foods and Animals In the Americas, Europeans found a variety of foods that were new to them, including tomatoes, pumpkins, and peppers. They eagerly transported these to Europe. Two of these new foods, corn and potatoes, became important foods in the Old World. Easy to grow and store, potatoes helped feed Europe's rapidly growing population. Corn spread all across Europe and to Africa and Asia, becoming one of the world's most important cereal crops.

Europeans also carried a wide variety of plants and animals to the Americas, including wheat and grapes from Europe and

BOUNCE to Activate Flipped Video

Objectives

Explain how European exploration led to the Columbian Exchange.

Explain new economic factors and principles that contributed to the success of the commercial revolution.

Understand the impact of mercantilism on European and colonial economies.

Key Terms

Columbian
  Exchange
Commercial
  Revolution
inflation
price revolution
capitalism
free enterprise
  system
entrepreneur
mercantilism
tariff

GO ONLINE to access your digital course

bananas and sugar cane from Africa and Asia. Cattle, pigs, goats, and chickens, unknown before the European encounter, joined the American Indian diet. Horses and donkeys transported people and goods quickly. Horses also provided the nomadic peoples of western North America with a new, more effective way to hunt buffalo.

Population Growth The transfer of food crops from continent to continent took time. By the 1700s, however, corn, potatoes, manioc, beans, and tomatoes were contributing to population growth around the world. While other factors help account for the population explosion that began at this time, the dispersal of new food crops from the Americas was certainly a key cause.

Movement of People and Ideas The Columbian Exchange resulted in the migration of millions of people. Shiploads of Europeans sailed to the Americas in search of new opportunities. Others settled on the fringes of Africa and Asia. As you have read, the Atlantic slave trade forcibly brought millions of Africans to the Americas. American Indian populations, however, declined drastically in the years after European arrival, largely as a result of diseases. Some American diseases traveled to Europe.

The vast movement of people led to the diffusion, or transfer, of ideas and technologies. Europeans

and Africans brought their beliefs and customs to the Americas. In Europe and elsewhere, people adapted ideas and inventions from distant lands. Language also traveled. Words such as *pajama* (from India) and *hammock* or *canoe* (from the Americas) entered European languages as evidence of the global exchange.

☑ **IDENTIFY CAUSE AND EFFECT** How did the Columbian Exchange affect global population?

A Commercial Revolution

The opening of direct links with Asia, Africa, and the Americas had far-reaching economic consequences for Europeans and their colonies. Europe underwent a period of economic growth and change known as the **Commercial Revolution,** which spurred the growth of modern capitalism, banking, and investing.

The Price Revolution By the 1500s, prices began to rise in many parts of Europe. At the same time, there was much more money in circulation. Earnings were often retained in banks or reinvested in the economy.

A rise in prices that is linked to a sharp increase in the amount of money available is called **inflation.** The period in European history when inflation rose

The Columbian Exchange

TRANSFERRED FROM THE WESTERN HEMISPHERE		TRANSFERRED FROM THE EASTERN HEMISPHERE	
Corn	Turkeys	Wheat	Coffee
Potatoes	Pineapples	Sugar	Horses
Sweet Potatoes	Tomatoes	Bananas	Pigs
Beans	Cocoa	Rice	Cows, oxen
Peanuts	Cassava/manioc	Oats	Goats
Squash	Silver	Barley	Chickens
Pumpkins	Quinine	Rye	Smallpox
Chili peppers	Sunflowers	Grapes	Typhus

>> **Analyze Charts** The Columbian Exchange affected people around the world. What livestock were introduced to the Americas by the Columbian Exchange?

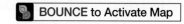 BOUNCE to Activate Map

TULIPMANIA PRICE BUBBLE 1636–1637

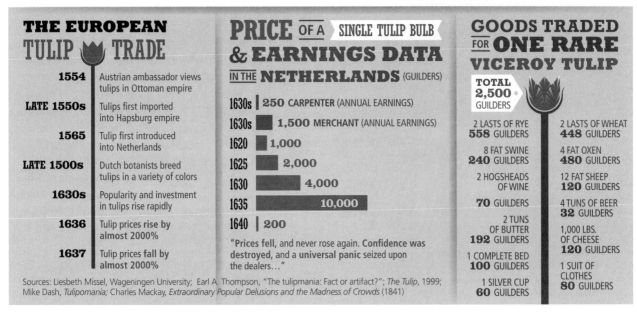

THE EUROPEAN TULIP TRADE

1554	Austrian ambassador views tulips in Ottoman empire
LATE 1550s	Tulips first imported into Hapsburg empire
1565	Tulip first introduced into Netherlands
LATE 1500s	Dutch botanists breed tulips in a variety of colors
1630s	Popularity and investment in tulips rise rapidly
1636	Tulip prices rise by almost 2000%
1637	Tulip prices fall by almost 2000%

Sources: Liesbeth Missel, Wageningen University; Earl A. Thompson, "The tulipmania: Fact or artifact?"; *The Tulip*, 1999; Mike Dash, *Tulipomania*; Charles Mackay, *Extraordinary Popular Delusions and the Madness of Crowds* (1841)

PRICE OF A SINGLE TULIP BULB & EARNINGS DATA IN THE NETHERLANDS (GUILDERS)

1630s	250 CARPENTER (ANNUAL EARNINGS)
1630s	1,500 MERCHANT (ANNUAL EARNINGS)
1620	1,000
1625	2,000
1630	4,000
1635	10,000
1640	200

"Prices fell, and never rose again. Confidence was destroyed, and a universal panic seized upon the dealers..."

GOODS TRADED FOR ONE RARE VICEROY TULIP

TOTAL 2,500 GUILDERS

2 LASTS OF RYE **558** GUILDERS	2 LASTS OF WHEAT **448** GUILDERS
8 FAT SWINE **240** GUILDERS	4 FAT OXEN **480** GUILDERS
2 HOGSHEADS OF WINE **70** GUILDERS	12 FAT SHEEP **120** GUILDERS
2 TUNS OF BUTTER **192** GUILDERS	4 TUNS OF BEER **32** GUILDERS
	1,000 LBS. OF CHEESE **120** GUILDERS
1 COMPLETE BED **100** GUILDERS	1 SUIT OF CLOTHES **80** GUILDERS
1 SILVER CUP **60** GUILDERS	

>> **Analyze Charts** Tulipmania is an example of an inflationary price bubble. From an investment standpoint, which year was the worst to buy a tulip? Explain. How many tuns of butter needed to be sold in order to purchase one tulip?

rapidly is known as the **price revolution.** Inflation was fueled by the enormous amount of silver and gold flowing into Europe from the Americas by the mid-1500s. When prices began to rise, output also increased.

Free Enterprise Expanded trade and the push for overseas empires spurred the growth of European **capitalism,** or the investment of money to make a profit. In a capitalist economy, also called a **free enterprise system,** most businesses are privately owned and economic decisions are made between buyers and sellers based on supply and demand. Other key elements of capitalism include the accumulation and investment of capital (money) and competition within a free market.

During the Commercial Revolution, **entrepreneurs,** or enterprising business people, organized, managed, and took on the risks of doing business. Entrepreneurs provided jobs for workers and paid for raw materials, transport, and other costs of production. They pushed for predictable laws and secure contracts to protect their property and investments from unfair seizure or taxes.

As trade increased, entrepreneurs sought to expand into overseas ventures. Distant markets could be risky since governments were often small or weak in those places, but capitalists, because of their resources, were more willing to take risks.

As a result, the price revolution of the early modern age gave a boost to capitalism. Supply and demand began to control markets and prices rather than the more traditional medieval concept of a just, or fair, price. Entrepreneurs and capitalists made up a new business class devoted to the goal of making profits. Together, they helped change local European economies into an international trading system.

New Business Methods Early European capitalists discovered new ways to create wealth. From the Arabs, they adapted methods of bookkeeping to show profits and losses from their ventures. During the late Middle Ages, as you have read, banks increased in importance, allowing wealthy merchants to lend money at interest. Businesses could more easily obtain short-term loans because of expanded credit.

The joint stock company, which had also emerged in the late Middle Ages, grew in importance. It allowed people to pool large amounts of capital needed for overseas trading voyages. Individuals who invested in a joint stock company shared in the profits a company made. If a venture failed, investors lost only the amount they had put into the voyage, not the entire cost of the voyage.

>> These Irish women are boiling flax and spinning yarn to make linen cloth. Enterprising capitalists employed peasant cottagers like these in the "putting-out" system.

BOUNCE to Activate Chart

>> As European rulers embraced mercantilism and expanded trade, their ports became thriving centers of commerce. This painting depicts the crowded port of Toulon, France, in the mid-1700s.

Entrepreneurs Bypass the Guilds The growing demand for goods led merchants to find ways to increase production. Traditionally, guilds controlled the manufacture of goods. But guild masters often ran small-scale businesses without the capital to produce for large markets. They also had strict rules regulating quality, prices, and working conditions.

Enterprising capitalists devised a way to bypass the guilds called the "putting-out" system. It was first used to produce textiles but later spread to other industries. Under this system, for example, a merchant capitalist distributed raw wool to peasant cottages. Cottagers spun the wool into thread and then wove it into cloth. Merchants bought the wool cloth from the peasants and sent it to the city for finishing and dyeing. Finally, the merchants sold the finished product for a profit.

The "putting-out" system, also known by the term "cottage industry," separated capital and labor for the first time. In the 1700s, this system would lead to the capitalist-owned factories of the Industrial Revolution.

☑ **COMPARE AND CONTRAST** How did capitalism, or free enterprise, differ from the medieval guild system?

Mercantilism

European monarchs enjoyed the benefits of the Commercial Revolution. In the fierce competition for trade and empire, they adopted a new economic policy, known as **mercantilism,** which was aimed at strengthening their national economies. Mercantilists believed that a nation's real wealth was measured in its gold and silver treasure. To build its supply of gold and silver, they said, a nation must export more goods than it imported.

The Value of Colonies To mercantilists, overseas colonies existed for the benefit of the parent country. They provided resources and raw materials not available in Europe. In turn, they enriched a parent country by serving as a market for its manufactured goods. To achieve these goals, European powers passed strict laws regulating trade with their colonies. Colonists could not set up their own industries to manufacture goods. They were also forbidden from buying goods from a foreign country. In addition, only ships from the parent country or the colonies themselves could be used to send goods into or out of the colonies.

Increasing National Wealth Mercantilists urged rulers to adopt policies that they believed would increase national wealth and government revenues. To boost production, governments exploited mineral and timber resources, built roads, and backed new industries. They imposed national currencies and established standard weights and measures.

Governments also sold monopolies to large producers in certain industries as well as to big overseas trading companies. Finally, they imposed **tariffs,** or taxes on imported goods. Tariffs were designed to protect local industries from foreign competition by increasing the price of imported goods. All of these measures led to the rise of national economies, in which national governments had a lot of control over their economies. However, modern economists debate whether mercantilist measures actually made nations wealthier.

Impact on European Society By the 1700s, European societies were still divided into distinct social classes. Merchants who invested in overseas ventures acquired wealth, while the price revolution hurt nobles, whose wealth was in land.

Economic changes took generations, even centuries, to be felt by the majority of Europeans, who were still peasants. The merchants and skilled workers of Europe's growing cities thrived. Middle-class families enjoyed a comfortable life. In contrast, hired laborers and those who served the middle and upper classes often lived in crowded quarters on the edge of poverty.

☑ **DESCRIBE** How did mercantilism and colonialism contribute to the success of Europe's Commercial Revolution?

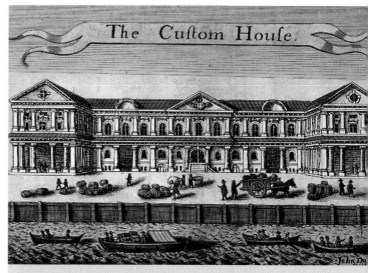

>> At the Customs House of London, government officials supervised regulations on overseas trade. Customs officers collected the tariffs that were due on imported goods.

☑ **ASSESSMENT**

1. **Identify Cause and Effect** What economic factors and principles contributed to the success of Europe's Commercial Revolution?

2. **Make Generalizations** What economic changes came during the Commercial Revolution?

3. **Identify Steps in a Process** How did the "putting out" system work?

4. **Compare Points of View** How did capitalists and mercantilists have different points of view on government regulation of the economy?

5. **Quest Connections** How was the impact of the Columbian Exchange positive in some ways, but negative in other ways?

Connections to Today

A 2017 protest in London against modern slavery.

Take Action About Forced Labor in Today's World

The Atlantic slave trade ended in the 1800s, but millions of people today continue to be victims of forced labor. Some are even smuggled into the United States.

1. **Choose** one of these topics related to human trafficking in today's world.

   - **Bonded labor:** Investigate how people are forced to work to pay off a debt.

   - **Domestic labor:** Examine how many domestic workers, such as nannies, are tricked into situations where they cannot leave.

   - **Child labor:** Research how children under the age of 18 are forced to work.

2. **Ask Questions** Write a list of questions relating to the topic you have chosen. What are some of the things you want to learn about that form of modern slavery and about efforts to end it?

3. **Learn** Do research on the topic you have chosen. A good source of information might be websites from the United Nations or other organizations that work to end human trafficking. You might also research recent articles on the subject. Make sure you collect specific statistics.

4. **Take Action** Create a website designed to raise awareness of slavery today. Write introductory text describing the problem. Include statistics and other information you learned through your research, as well as links to organizations involved in the fight against modern slavery.

Use the texts, quizzes, interactivities, Quest Inquiries, Flipped Videos, and other resources from this Topic to prepare for the Topic Test.

Quest Inquiries

Quizzes

Interactivities

Texts

Flipped Videos

While online you can also check the progress you've made learning the topic and course content by viewing your grades, test scores, and assignment status.

LESSON SUMMARIES

Use these Lesson Summaries, and the longer versions available online, to review the key ideas for each lesson in this Topic.

Lesson 1: Europeans Explore Overseas

Europeans traded with Asia before the Renaissance. But as Europeans were introduced to luxury goods from Asia, the desire for spices and goods increased. Portugal led the way in exploration.

Lesson 2: Europeans Gain Footholds in Asia

Portugal was the first European nation to establish a trade network in Asia. They soon faced challenges from the Dutch and Spanish traders. By the late 1500s, the Dutch replaced the Portuguese as the major European power in Asia. Spain developed a trade network in the Philippines.

Lesson 3: European Conquests in the Americas

In a search for a route to India, Columbus landed in the Americas in 1492. After this voyage, Spanish conquistadors defeated the Aztecs and the Incas. By the 1500s, Spain claimed a vast empire in the Americas.

Lesson 4: Europeans Colonize in North America

By the 1500s, the wealth of the Americas made Spain the most powerful country in Europe and spurred envy among other European nations. France, the Netherlands, England, and Sweden joined Spain in claiming part of North America. A bitter rivalry between France and Britain led to the French and Indian War. Britain emerged the victor and the dominant power in North America.

Lesson 5: The Slave Trade and Its Impact on Africa

In the 1500s, Europeans begin enslaving growing numbers of Africans. The Atlantic slave trade brought millions of enslaved Africans to the Americas to supply labor needs in the colonies. Those involved in the trade earned huge profits.

Lesson 6: Effects of Global Contact

European exploration and conquest between 1500 and 1700 changed the diets, plant and animal life, and economies of Asia, Africa, and the Americas. This global exchange of goods and ideas is known as the Columbian Exchange. Exploration also led the way to an expansion of trade that ushered in the growth of capitalism.

QUEST! FINDINGS

Write Your Essay Refer to your responses to the Quest Connections to help you write your essay to share with the class. Use the rubric and other Quest resources online to guide your work.

VISUAL REVIEW

Use these graphics to review some of the key terms, people, and ideas from this Topic.

Causes of European Exploration

- Desire for Asian luxury goods such as spices, gold, and silks
- Motivation to spread Christianity
- Strategic need to gain more direct access to trade
- Desire to gain glory for country
- Renaissance curiosity to explore new lands
- Competition with other European countries

Key Elements of Europe's Commercial Revolution

- **Columbian Exchange** Food, ideas, technologies, and diseases are exchanged between the hemispheres, resulting in population growth.
- **Inflation** Rising prices occur along with an increase in the money supply.
- **Price Revolution** Rising prices are coupled with inflation.
- **Capitalism** People invest money to make a profit.
- **Mercantilism** European countries adopt mercantilist policies—such as establishing colonies, increasing exports, and limiting imports—to compete for trade and empire.

Major European Settlements/Colonies in the Americas

DATE	REGION SETTLED	COUNTRY	PURPOSE
1520s	Mexico	Spain	Find gold
1530s	Peru	Spain	Find gold
1530s	Brazil	Portugal	Establish settlements and plantations
Early 1500s	New France (eastern Canada)	France	Take part in fur trade and fishing
Early 1600s	13 colonies (present-day eastern United States)	England	Various reasons including establishing settlements and escaping religious persecution

American Indian Population of Central Mexico Declines

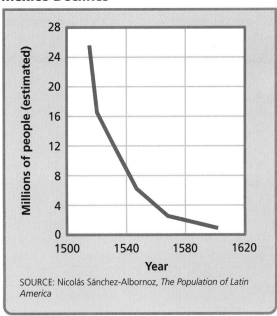

SOURCE: Nicolás Sánchez-Albornoz, *The Population of Latin America*

Topic 11 Assessment

KEY TERMS, PEOPLE, AND IDEAS

1. How did the **Treaty of Tordesillas** prevent war between Spain and Portugal?

2. What was the purpose of the **Dutch East India Company**?

3. What prompted European interest in trading with Asia?

4. What factors helped **Cortés** to defeat the Aztecs?

5. Compare the economic and political systems of **New France** and Spain in the Americas.

6. Why was the **Middle Passage** a critical part of the triangular trade?

7. What were the benefits of **mercantilism**?

8. What factors contributed to the growth of **capitalism**?

9. How did the **Treaty of Paris in 1763** change the map of North America?

CRITICAL THINKING

10. **Evaluate Information** How did Henry the Navigator spearhead the search for a route to Asia?

11. **Draw Conclusions** Initially, why were Mughal India and Ming China unconcerned about European contacts for trade? What later effect would this have on those empires?

12. **Summarize** Discuss the impact of the Atlantic slave trade between West Africa and the Americas.

13. **Identify Effects** What impact did American gold and silver have on European economies?

14. **Analyze Information** How did the Columbian Exchange shape global economies and societies?

15. **Predict Consequences** Describe the relationship between a parent country and its colonies in economic terms according to mercantilists. Why might this relationship be problematic for the people living in the colonies?

16. **Using Primary Sources** William Cowper, an English poet, wrote the following poem in the 1700s. How does he use irony to express his feelings about the slave trade?

> "I own I am shocked at the purchase of slaves,
>
> And fear those who buy them and sell them
>   are knaves.
>
> What I hear of their hardships, their tortures
>   and groans,
>
> Is almost enough to draw pity from stones.
>
> I pity them greatly but I must be mum,
>
> For how could we do without sugar and rum?"

(b) Cowper's poem refers to the triangular trade. What role did each of the following have in the trade—a factory owner in England, a New England merchant, an enslaved African, and a Southern plantation owner?

17. **Writing Activity: Write an Explanatory Essay** Columbus advised Isabella and Ferdinand how best to set up their first American colonies:

> "That for the better and more speedy colonization of the said island, no one shall have liberty to collect gold in it except those who have taken out colonists' papers."

Compare the establishment of the Spanish empire in the Americas with the establishment of the English empire in the Americas. Cite evidence from what you have read as you write your informative essay. Note differences and similarities in the following: political systems, economic systems, religion, and effects on the American Indian population.

18. **Connections to Today (a)** Identify three ways the world might have been different today if European powers had not sought out new trade routes to Asia in the 1400s and 1500s. Include examples that consider the long-term impact on the Americas, Europe, Africa, and Asia. **(b)** Overall, do you think the impact of the period has been mostly positive or mostly negative?

DOCUMENT-BASED QUESTIONS

Why did the age of exploration begin?

Read the documents below, then answer the questions that follow.

DOCUMENT A

"The discovery of the new Western World followed, as an incidental consequence, from the long struggle of the nations of Europe for commercial supremacy and control of the traffic with the East. In all these dreams of the politicians and merchants, sailors and geographers, who pushed back the limits of the unknown world, there is the same glitter of gold and precious stones, the same odour of far-fetched spices."

—*Sir Walter Raleigh, 1509*

DOCUMENT B

"The starting point for the European expansion out of the Mediterranean and the Atlantic continental shelf had nothing to do with, say, religion or the rise of capitalism—but it had a great deal to do with pepper. . . . . [Pepper] comprised more than half of all the spice imports into Italy over a period of more than a century. No other single spice came within one-tenth of the value of pepper. . . . However, since about 1470 the Turks had been impeding the overland trade routes east from the Mediterranean. As a result the great Portuguese, Italian, and Spanish explorers all sailed west or south in order to reach the Orient. The Americas were discovered as a by-product in the search for pepper."

—*From Seeds of Change by Henry Hobhouse*

DOCUMENT C

This 18th century Spanish painting depicts Francis Xavier performing a baptism in Japan.

DOCUMENT D

This page from a sixteenth-century book about navigation depicts England's Queen Elizabeth in the ship at the right.

19. Documents A and B both make the point that the discovery of new lands was motivated by
  A. religious fanaticism
  B. adventurous dreams
  C. wanting to make money
  D. Renaissance ideals

20. What motivation for exploration and expansion is implied in Document C?
  A. the search for spices
  B. the desire to please the king or country
  C. the desire to spread Christianity
  D. the desire to learn about other lands

21. What does Document D suggest about how European monarchs view exploration?
  A. as vitally important to their nations
  B. as interesting but unnecessary
  C. as important but not worth investing in
  D. without concern

22. **Writing Tasks** Review the motivations presented. Choose the motivation you think was the most compelling for Europeans. Use information from the topic and documents to support your argument.

Absolutism and Revolution (1550–1850)

ESSENTIAL QUESTION How much power should the government have?

GO ONLINE to access the eText, videos, Interactive Primary Sources, Biographies, and other online resources.

The execution of Queen Marie Antoinette during the French Revolution

Connections to Today

On May 19, 2018, Prince Harry, a member of the British royal family, and Meghan Markle married. The union was not a typical royal marriage. Meghan Markle was a former American actress, divorced, and biracial. While this was not the first marriage between a royal family member and a commoner, it does reflect the changing customs of royal marriage. In this topic, you will learn how kings emerged as absolute rulers with unlimited authority. How has the monarchy changed?

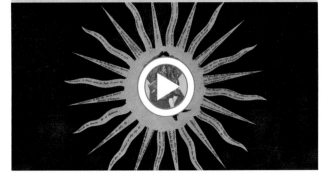

Learn about King Louis XIV of France, the greatest of the absolute monarchs.

 BOUNCE to Activate My Story Video

Topic 12 Overview

In this Topic, you will learn about the events of the age of Absolutism and Revolution. Look at the lesson outline and explore the timeline. As you study this Topic, you will complete the Quest inquiry.

LESSON OUTLINE

12.1 Absolute Monarchy in Spain and France

12.2 Rise of Austria, Prussia, and Russia

12.3 Triumph of Parliament in England

12.4 The Enlightenment

12.5 The American Revolution

12.6 The French Revolution Begins

12.7 A Radical Phase

12.8 The Age of Napoleon

Key Events of the Age of Absolutism and Revolution

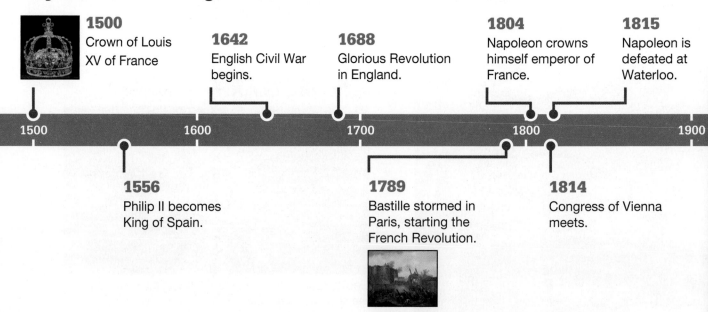

1500 Crown of Louis XV of France

1642 English Civil War begins.

1688 Glorious Revolution in England.

1804 Napoleon crowns himself emperor of France.

1815 Napoleon is defeated at Waterloo.

1500 — 1600 — 1700 — 1800 — 1900

1556 Philip II becomes King of Spain.

1789 Bastille stormed in Paris, starting the French Revolution.

1814 Congress of Vienna meets.

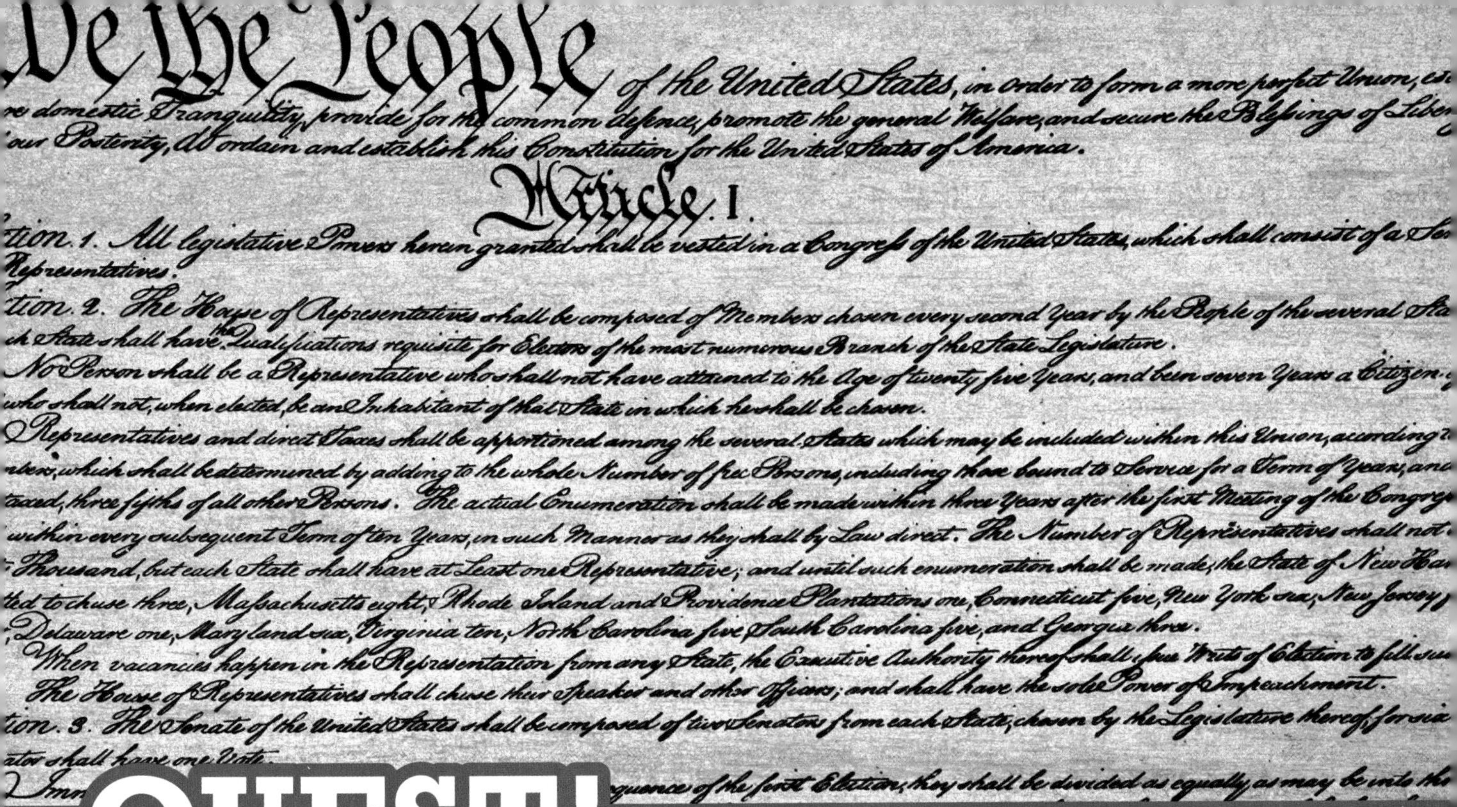

Background text (historical document, partially legible):

We the People *of the United States, in order to form a more perfect Union, establish... domestic Tranquility, provide for the common defence, promote the general Welfare, and secure the Blessings of Liberty... our Posterity, do ordain and establish this Constitution for the United States of America.*

Article. I.

Section. 1. All legislative Powers herein granted shall be vested in a Congress of the United States, which shall consist of a Senate and House of Representatives...

Becoming a Human Rights Advocate

What rights should everyone have? In this Quest, you will examine different ideas about what rights people are entitled to. Then your team will draft a human rights bill with the group's conclusion about the rights everyone should have.

STEP 1
Read the quotes from former President Barack Obama discussing human rights at a press conference with President Hu. What did you learn?

STEP 2
Examine the documents discussing human rights. What general conclusions can you make? What viewpoints are presented?

STEP 3
Draw up a list of human rights that you feel should be universal. Then write a letter to your senator stating why this human rights bill is needed.

STEP 4
Edit, then revise your bill and your letter. Reflect on how human rights have changed through the years.

This photo shows a jeweled crown worn by King Louis XV of France. Crowns were a symbol of the wealth, power, and prestige of the monarch.

BOUNCE to Activate Flipped Video

Objectives

Identify the characteristics of absolute monarchy, including the concept of divine right.

Explain how Spanish power grew under Charles V and Philip II.

Understand how France built a centralized monarchy after the wars of religion.

Evaluate Louis XIV as an absolute monarch.

Describe how the arts flourished in Spain and France.

Key Terms

absolute monarchy
divine right
Hapsburg empire
Charles V
Philip II
armada
El Greco
Miguel de Cervantes
Huguenots
Henry IV

Edict of Nantes
Cardinal Richelieu
Louis XIV
intendants
Jean-Baptiste Colbert
Versailles
levée
balance of power

Absolute Monarchy in Spain and France

During the Renaissance and Reformation, European rulers continued to centralize power at the expense of their nobles and the clergy. As wars of religion raged in many European lands, monarchs battled to impose royal law and restore order in their kingdoms.

Ruling with Absolute Power

Between about 1500 and 1800, the old feudal order gave way to individual nation-states with strong central governments. Monarchs presided over government bureaucracies that enforced the law and collected taxes. They used income not only to support lavish Renaissance courts but also to strengthen their military power.

Powerful States and Rulers The emergence of strong unified nation-states occurred at different times in different parts of Europe.

The rulers of some countries, such as Spain and France, set up **absolute monarchies.** The chief characteristic of this political system is that a ruler has complete authority over the government and the lives of the people.

During the Age of Absolutism, as this period is called, powerful new dynasties emerged. The Hapsburgs in Spain and the Bourbons in France passed power from generation to generation within the family while they added lands to their kingdoms through skillfully arranged marriages.

GO ONLINE to access your digital course

Absolute monarchs often had parliaments or other bodies, but these bodies had no real power. The ruler could dissolve them at will. In theory, absolute monarchs had total power, but in practice, to preserve power, they had to balance the interests of different groups from nobles and clergy to the middle class and peasants.

Divine Right to Rule During the Age of Absolutism, European monarchs embraced the idea of **divine right,** meaning that their authority to rule came directly from God. They used divine right theory to justify their power. As God's representative on Earth, monarchs could command absolute obedience from their subjects. This meant rulers could justify all of their actions with divine sanction or approval. In the 1600s, a French bishop and court preacher, Jacques Bossuet (bah soo WAY) defended the theory of divine right and royal absolutism, saying that absolute power was necessary to protect the people.

> "The royal power is absolute....Without this absolute authority the king could neither do good nor repress evil. It is necessary that his power be such that no one can escape him."
>
> —Jacques Bossuet, "Politics Drawn from the Very Words of Scripture," 1679

Still, absolute monarchs who claimed to rule by divine right were expected to act for the good of their people. Unlike divine right under Mandate of Heaven, the right to rule was not unconditional.

By 1700, absolute monarchs reigned over most of the great powers in Europe, except England. In time, however, thinkers and others challenged divine right theory along with the entire system of absolute monarchy. They called, instead, for limits on government power and for governments to be responsible to the people.

☑ **IDENTIFY** What are the characteristics of an absolute monarchy?

Spain and the Hapsburg Empire

By the 1500s, Spain had emerged as the first modern European power. Through their marriage, Queen Isabella and King Ferdinand had unified the country. They pursued a policy of imposing religious unity and financed Columbus's voyage, which would lead to the Spanish conquest of the Americas. Wealth from the Americas would help Spain to become the most powerful nation in Europe.

Charles V Wears Two Crowns In 1516, Ferdinand and Isabella's grandson, Charles I, became king of Spain, and thereby ruler of the Spanish colonies in the Americas as well. When his other grandfather died in 1519, Charles I also became heir to the sprawling **Hapsburg empire,** which included the German states of the Holy Roman Empire and the Dutch Netherlands. As ruler of the Hapsburg empire, Charles took the name **Charles V,** the title by which historians now usually refer to him.

Ruling two empires involved Charles in constant warfare. He continued a long Hapsburg struggle with France over rival claims in Italy.

As a devout Catholic, he fought to suppress Protestantism in the German states. After years of religious conflict, however, Charles was forced to allow the German princes to choose their own religion.

His greatest foe was the Ottoman empire, which at the time controlled the Balkans in southeastern Europe. Under Suleiman, Ottoman forces advanced across central Europe to the walls surrounding Vienna, Austria. Although Austria held firm during the siege, the Ottomans occupied much of Hungary following their crushing victory at the Battle of Mohács. Ottoman naval forces also continued to challenge Spanish power in the Mediterranean.

>> In the early 1500s, Charles V became ruler over both the Spanish and the Hapsburg empires. He faced constant warfare, particularly against the Ottomans.

>> This painting shows the abdication of Charles V in 1555. He divided the Hapsburg empire between his son, Philip II of Spain, and his brother, Holy Roman Emperor Ferdinand I. **Infer** What types of problems could have contributed to Charles V's decision to resign?

>> The Spanish fleet was victorious over the Ottomans at the Battle of Lepanto in 1571.

The Empire Is Divided The **Hapsburg empire** proved to be too scattered and cumbersome for any one person to rule. Exhausted, Charles gave up his titles in 1556 and entered a monastery. He divided his empire, leaving the Hapsburg lands in central Europe to his brother Ferdinand, who became Holy Roman emperor. He gave Spain, the Netherlands, some southern Italian states, and Spain's overseas empire to his son Philip, who became Philip II.

☑ **SUMMARIZE** Why did Charles V divide the Hapsburg Empire?

Philip II Becomes an Absolute Monarch

During his 42-year reign, **Philip II** expanded Spanish influence, strengthened the Catholic Church, and made his own power absolute. Thanks in part to silver from Spanish colonies in the Americas, he made Spain the foremost power in Europe.

A Dedicated Ruler Philip surpassed Ferdinand and Isabella in making every part of the government responsible to him. He reigned as an absolute monarch, claiming divine right. Like his father, he was hard working, devout, and ambitious. Unlike many other monarchs, Philip devoted most of his time to government work. He seldom hunted, never jousted, and lived as simply as a monk. The king's isolated, somber palace outside Madrid, known as the Escorial (es kohr YAHL), reflected his character. It served as a church, a residence, and a tomb for the royal family.

Philip saw himself as the guardian of the Roman Catholic Church. The great undertaking of his life was to defend the Catholic Reformation and turn back the rising Protestant tide in Europe. Within his empire, Philip enforced religious unity, turning the Inquisition against Protestants and other people thought to be heretics.

The Wars of Philip II Philip fought many wars to advance Spanish Catholic power. In the Mediterranean, Spain and its Italian allies soundly defeated an Ottoman fleet at the Battle of Lepanto in 1571. Although Christians hailed this as a great victory, the Ottoman empire would remain a major power in the Mediterranean region for three more centuries.

During the last half of his reign, Philip battled Protestants and other rebels in the Netherlands. At

The Wars of Philip II, 1571–1588

KEY
- Ottoman Empire
- Spanish Hapsburg possessions
- Boundary of Holy Roman Empire
- Battle site

>> **Integrate Information** Which country divided Philip's empire? Based on the map, why was England in a position to disrupt Spanish shipping?

the time, the region included 17 provinces that are today Belgium, the Netherlands, and Luxembourg. It was the richest part of Philip's empire.

Protestants in the region resisted Philip's efforts to crush their faith. Protestants and Catholics alike opposed high taxes and autocratic Spanish rule, which threatened local traditions of self-government.

In the 1560s, riots against the Inquisition sparked a general uprising in the Netherlands. Savage fighting raged for decades. In 1581, the northern, largely Protestant provinces declared their independence from Spain and became known as the Dutch Netherlands. They did not gain official recognition, however, until 1648. The southern, mostly Catholic provinces of the Netherlands remained part of the Spanish Empire.

The Spanish Armada By the 1580s, Philip saw England's Queen Elizabeth I as his chief Protestant enemy. First secretly, then openly, Elizabeth had supported the Dutch against Spain. She encouraged English captains, known as sea dogs, to plunder Spanish treasure ships and loot Spanish cities in the Americas. To Philip's dismay, Elizabeth made Francis Drake, the most daring sea dog, a knight instead of punishing him as a pirate.

To end English attacks and subdue the Dutch, Philip prepared a huge **armada,** or fleet, to carry a Spanish invasion force to England. In 1588, the

Spanish Armada sailed with more than 130 ships, 20,000 men, and 2,400 pieces of artillery. The Spanish were confident of victory. "When we meet the English," predicted one Spanish commander, "God will surely arrange matters so that we can grapple and board them, either by sending some strange freak of weather or, more likely, just by depriving the English of their wits."

This prediction did not come to pass. In the English Channel, lumbering Spanish ships were outmaneuvered by the lighter, faster English ships. Strong winds favored the English, scattering the Armada. After further disasters at sea, the tattered remnants limped home in defeat.

Decline of the Spanish Empire While the defeat of the Spanish Armada ended Philip's plan to invade England, it had little short-term effect on his power. In the long-term, however, Spanish power slowly faded. The decline was due in part to Philip's successors, who were less able rulers than he.

Economic problems were also to blame. Costly overseas wars drained wealth out of Spain almost as fast as it came in. Treasure from the Americas led Spain to neglect farming and commerce. The government heavily taxed the small middle class, weakening a group that in other European nations supported royal power. The expulsion of Muslims and Jews from Spain deprived the economy of many skilled artisans and merchants. Finally, the influx of American gold and silver led to soaring inflation. As Spain's power dwindled in the 1600s and 1700s, Dutch, English, and French fleets challenged—and eventually surpassed—Spanish power both in Europe and around the world.

☑ **SUMMARIZE** What were Philip II's motivations for waging war?

Arts and Literature of Spain's Golden Century

The century from 1550 to 1650 is often referred to as Spain's *siglo de oro* (SEEG loh day OHR oh), or "golden century," for the brilliance of its arts and literature. Philip II was an enthusiastic patron of the arts and also founded academies of science and mathematics.

Painting Among the famous painters of this period was a man known as **El Greco,** meaning "the Greek." Though not Spanish by birth, El Greco became a master of Spanish painting. Born on the Greek island of Crete, El Greco had studied in Italy before settling in Spain. He produced haunting

>> The Spanish painter El Greco was born Domenikos Theotokopoulos in Greece. The *View of Toledo,* shown here, was one of the very few landscapes done by El Greco. It shows his elongated, dramatic style.

BOUNCE to Activate Gallery

religious pictures and striking portraits of Spanish nobles, done in a dramatically elongated style.

El Greco's use of vibrant colors influenced the work of Diego Velázquez (vuh LAHS kes), court painter to King Philip IV. Velázquez is perhaps best known for his vivid portraits of Spanish royalty.

Literature Spain's golden century produced several outstanding writers. Lope de Vega (LOH pay duh VAY guh), a peasant by birth, wrote more than 1,500 plays, including witty comedies and action-packed romances.

During Spain's golden age, **Miguel de Cervantes** (sur VAN teez) wrote Europe's first modern novel. *Don Quixote* pokes fun at medieval tales of chivalry. The elderly Don Quixote has read too many tales of days when fictional knights were bold. Imagining himself a medieval knight, he sets out across the Spanish countryside dressed in rusty armor. By his side is his practical servant, Sancho Panza.

Don Quixote mocks the traditions of Spain's feudal past. At the same time, Cervantes depicts with affection both the earthy realism of Sancho and the foolish but heroic idealism of Don Quixote.

☑ **DESCRIBE** What was the *siglo de oro*?

Royal Power Expands in France

Like Philip II in Spain, French rulers were determined to expand royal power. France was torn apart by wars of religion in the late 1500s. Then a new dynasty, the Bourbons, rose to power and built the foundations for an absolute monarchy in France.

Wars of Religion After the Hundred Years' War, French kings slowly consolidated power over their lands. In the 1500s, rivalry with Spain and the Protestant Reformation posed new challenges for France. Religious wars between the Catholic majority and French Protestants, called **Huguenots** (HYOO guh nahts), tore France apart. Leaders on both sides used the strife to further their own ambitions.

Each side committed terrible acts of violence. The worst began on St. Bartholomew's Day (a Catholic holiday), August 24, 1572.

While Huguenot and Catholic nobles were gathered for a royal wedding, a Catholic plot led to the massacre of 3,000 Huguenots. In the next few days, thousands more were slaughtered. For many, the St. Bartholomew's Day Massacre symbolized the complete breakdown of order in France.

Henry IV Restores Order In 1589, a Huguenot prince inherited the French throne as **Henry IV.** Henry was the first ruler in the Bourbon dynasty. As a Huguenot, Henry had battled Catholic forces. Once on the throne, he realized he would face severe problems ruling a largely Catholic country, so he converted to Catholicism. "Paris is well worth a Mass," he is supposed to have said. To protect Protestants, however, he issued the **Edict of Nantes** in 1598. It granted the Huguenots religious toleration and other freedoms.

Henry IV then set out to restore royal power and rebuild a land shattered by war. His goal, he said, was not the victory of one sect over another, but "a chicken in every pot"—a good Sunday dinner for every peasant. Under Henry, the government reached into every area of French life.

Royal officials administered justice, improved roads, built bridges, and revived agriculture. By building the royal bureaucracy and reducing the influence of nobles, Henry IV laid the foundations for royal absolutism.

Richelieu Strengthens Royal Authority When Henry IV was killed by an assassin in 1610, his nine-year-old son, Louis XIII, inherited the throne. For a time, nobles reasserted their power. Then, in 1624, Louis appointed **Cardinal Richelieu** (ree shul YOO) as his chief minister. This cunning, capable leader devoted the next 18 years to strengthening the central government.

Richelieu was determined to destroy the power of two groups that defied royal authority—nobles and Huguenots. He defeated the private armies of the nobles and destroyed their fortified castles. While reducing their independence, Richelieu tied the nobles to the king by giving them high posts at court or in the royal army. At the same time, he smashed the walled cities of the Huguenots and outlawed their armies. Yet he allowed them to continue to practice their religion.

Richelieu handpicked his able successor, Cardinal Mazarin (ma za RAN). When five-year-old **Louis XIV** inherited the throne in 1643, the year after Richelieu's death, Mazarin was in place to serve as chief minister. Like Richelieu, Mazarin worked tirelessly to extend royal power.

☑ **IDENTIFY SUPPORTING DETAILS** How did the Edict of Nantes affect Huguenots?

>> The St. Bartholomew's Day Massacre began at a royal wedding in Paris in 1572. Thousands of French Huguenots were massacred.

>> Cardinal Richelieu, one of the architects of French absolutism, was principle advisor to Louis XIII. The Siege of La Rochelle, shown here, was a battle in Richelieu's campaign to bring the Huguenots under royal authority.

Louis XIV, an Absolute Monarch

Soon after Louis XIV became king, disorder again swept France. In an uprising called the *Fronde*, nobles, merchants, peasants, and the urban poor each rebelled in order to protest royal power or preserve their own. On one occasion, rioters drove the boy king from his palace. It was an experience Louis would never forget.

When Mazarin died in 1661, the 23-year-old Louis resolved to take complete control over the government himself. "I have been pleased to entrust the government of my affairs to the late Cardinal," he declared. "It is now time that I govern them myself."

"I Am the State" Like his great-grandfather Philip II of Spain, Louis XIV firmly believed in his divine right to rule. He took the sun as the symbol of his absolute power.

Just as the sun stands at the center of the solar system, he argued, so the Sun King stands at the center of the nation. Louis is often quoted as saying, "*L'état, c'est moi*" (lay TAH seh MWAH), which in English translates as "I am the state."

During his reign, Louis did not once call a meeting of the Estates General, the medieval assembly made up of representatives of all French social classes. In fact, the Estates General did not meet between 1614 and 1789. Thus, the Estates General played no role in checking royal power.

Louis Centralizes Power Louis spent many hours each day attending to government affairs. To strengthen the state, he followed the policies of Richelieu. He expanded the bureaucracy and appointed **intendants,** royal officials who collected taxes, recruited soldiers, and carried out his policies in the provinces.

The king often appointed wealthy middle-class men to government jobs. In this way, Louis cemented ties with the middle class and limited the influence of nobles.

Under Louis XIV, the French army became the strongest in Europe. The state paid, fed, trained, and supplied up to 300,000 soldiers. Louis used this highly disciplined army to enforce his policies at home and abroad.

Colbert Strengthens the Economy The French economy grew under the king's brilliant finance minister, **Jean-Baptiste Colbert** (kohl behr). Colbert had new lands cleared for farming, encouraged mining and other basic industries, and built up luxury trades such as lacemaking. To protect French manufacturers, Colbert put high tariffs on imported goods.

LOUIS XIV STRENGTHENS HIS ABSOLUTE MONARCHY

FOLLOWED THE PROVEN POLICIES OF CARDINAL RICHELIEU

SPENT **MANY HOURS** EACH DAY ATTENDING TO GOVERNMENT AFFAIRS

EXPANDED THE BUREAUCRACY

APPOINTED INTENDANTS WHO COLLECTED TAXES, RECRUITED SOLDIERS, AND CARRIED OUT POLICIES

GAVE MANY JOBS TO WEALTHY MIDDLE-CLASS MEN TO CEMENT HIS TIES WITH THE MIDDLE CLASS

BUILT THE FRENCH ARMY INTO THE STRONGEST IN EUROPE

>> **Make Generalizations** What do all Louis XIV's efforts to strengthen absolutism have in common?

Colbert also fostered overseas colonies, such as New France in North America and several colonies in India. Imposing mercantilist policies, he regulated trade with the colonies to enrich the royal treasury.

Colbert's policies helped make France the wealthiest state in Europe. Yet not even his financial genius could produce enough income to support the huge costs of Louis's court and his many foreign wars.

☑ **RECALL** Why did Louis XIV choose the sun as his symbol?

The Royal Palace at Versailles

In the countryside near Paris, Louis XIV turned a royal hunting lodge into the immense palace of **Versailles** (ver SY). There, he presided over both his court and the government. Versailles became the perfect symbol of the power of the Sun King.

Louis spared no expense in making Versailles the most magnificent building in Europe. Its halls and salons displayed the finest paintings and statues. Some depicted the king as Apollo, the ancient Greek god of the sun. Chandeliers and mirrors glittered with gold. In the royal gardens, millions of flowers, trees, and fountains were set out in precise geometric patterns, reflecting royal power over nature.

Elaborate Court Ceremonies Louis XIV perfected elaborate ceremonies that emphasized his own importance. Each day began in the king's bedroom with a ritual known as the **levée** (luh VAY), or rising. High-ranking nobles competed for the honor of holding the royal washbasin or handing the king his diamond-buckled shoes. At night, the ceremony was repeated in reverse. Wives of nobles vied to serve women of the royal family.

Rituals such as the levée served a serious purpose. French nobles were descendants of the feudal lords who had held power in medieval times. At liberty on their estates, these nobles were a threat to the power of the monarchy. By luring nobles to Versailles, Louis turned them into courtiers angling for privileges rather than rival warriors battling for power. His tactic worked because he carefully protected their prestige and continued their privilege of not paying taxes.

A Flowering of French Culture The king and his court supported a "splendid century" of the arts.

>> Louis XIV, who came to the throne at a young age, ruled France for more than 72 years. He believed in the divine right of kings and was a powerful absolute monarch.

>> The Hall of Mirrors is one of the most famous rooms at the Versailles Palace. This elaborate palace was the principal residence of Louis XIV and a monument to his power.

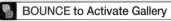 BOUNCE to Activate Gallery

>> English troops fight the French in this 1704 battle in the War of the Spanish Succession, one of the many foreign wars of Louis XIV.

The king sponsored musical entertainments and commissioned plays by the best writers. The age of Louis XIV came to be known as the classical age of French drama.

In painting, music, architecture, and decorative arts, French styles became the model for all Europe. A new form of dance drama, ballet, gained its first great popularity at the French court. As a leading patron of culture, Louis sponsored the French Academies, which set high standards for both the arts and the sciences.

☑ **SUMMARIZE** How did Louis XIV secure support from the nobility?

The Legacy of Louis XIV

Louis XIV ruled France for 72 years—far longer than any other monarch. During that time, French culture, manners, and customs set the standard for European tastes. The Sun King made France the strongest state in Europe. In both foreign and domestic affairs, however, many of Louis's policies were costly failures.

Costly Wars Louis XIV poured vast resources into wars meant to expand French borders. However, rival rulers joined forces to check these ambitions. Led by the Dutch or the English, these alliances fought to maintain the **balance of power.** The goal was to maintain a distribution of military and economic power to prevent any one country from dominating Europe.

In 1700, Louis's grandson Philip V inherited the throne of Spain. To maintain the balance of power, neighboring nations led by England fought to prevent the union of France and Spain.

The War of the Spanish Succession dragged on until 1713, when an exhausted France signed the Treaty of Utrecht (YOOtrekt). Philip remained on the Spanish throne, but France agreed never to unite the two crowns.

Huguenots Face Persecution Perhaps Louis's most costly mistake was his treatment of the Huguenots. Louis saw the Protestant minority as a threat to religious and political unity. In 1685, he revoked, or withdrew, the Edict of Nantes.

Facing renewed persecution, more than 100,000 Huguenots fled France. They settled mainly in England, the Netherlands, Germany, Poland, and the Americas. The Huguenots had been among the hardest working and most prosperous of Louis's subjects. Their loss was a serious blow to the French economy, just as the expulsion of Spanish Muslims and Jews had hurt Spain.

☑ **IDENTIFY CAUSE AND EFFECT** How did Louis's actions weaken the French economy?

☑ ASSESSMENT

1. **Identify** What factors led to the rise of absolute monarchies?

2. **Summarize** How did Spanish power grow under Charles V? under Philip II?

3. **Identify Supporting Details** How did France build a centralized monarchy after the wars of religion?

4. **Analyze** What impact did Spanish king Philip II and French king Louis XIV have on the arts?

5. **Connections to Today** Would you consider Louis XIV a successful absolute monarch? What qualities did Louis XIV possess as a monarch that many people would find unacceptable today?

12.2

At the Battle of White Mountain in 1620, forces led by the Holy Roman emperor destroyed the Bohemian army.

Rise of Austria, Prussia, and Russia

During the Reformation, the many German-speaking states within the Holy Roman Empire were plunged into religious wars. Some princes remained loyal to the Roman Catholic Church. Others accepted the teachings of Protestant reformers like Martin Luther or John Calvin. By the early 1600s, war raged across much of the Holy Roman Empire.

The Thirty Years' War

A Fragmented "Empire" By early modern times, as the French philosopher Voltaire later observed, the Holy Roman Empire was neither holy, nor Roman, nor an empire. Instead, by the seventeenth century it had become a patchwork of several hundred small, separate states.

In theory, these states were ruled by the Holy Roman emperor, who was chosen by seven leading German princes called **electors.** In practice, the emperor had little power over the many rival princes. This power vacuum contributed to the outbreak of the Thirty Years' War.

Religion further divided the German states. The north had become largely Protestant, while the south remained Catholic.

Conflict Erupts The Thirty Years' War was actually a series of wars. It began in Bohemia, the present-day Czech Republic. Ferdinand, the Catholic Hapsburg king of Bohemia, sought to suppress Protestants and to assert royal power over nobles.

 BOUNCE to Activate Flipped Video

Objectives

Outline the causes and results of the Thirty Years' War.

Understand how Austria and Prussia emerged as great powers.

Explain the steps Peter the Great took to modernize Russia.

Describe how Russia grew under Peter the Great and Catherine the Great.

Describe how European nations tried to maintain a balance of power.

Key Terms

elector	boyar
mercenary	autocratic
depopulation	warm-water port
Peace of Westphalia	St. Petersburg
Maria Theresa	Catherine the Great
War of the Austrian Succession	partition
Prussia	
Frederick William I	
Frederick II	
Peter the Great	
westernization	

 **GO ONLINE** to access your digital course

In May 1618, a few rebellious Protestant nobles tossed two royal officials out of a castle window in Prague. This act, known as the Defenestration of Prague, sparked a general revolt, which Ferdinand moved to suppress. As both sides sought allies, what began as a local conflict widened into a general European war.

The following year, Ferdinand was elected Holy Roman Emperor. With the support of Spain, Poland, and other Catholic states, he tried to roll back the Reformation by force. Early on, he defeated rebellious Bohemians and their Protestant allies. Alarmed, Protestant powers like the Netherlands and Sweden sent troops into Germany.

Political motives quickly outweighed religious issues. Catholic and Protestant rulers shifted alliances to suit their own interests. At one point, Catholic France joined Lutheran Sweden against the Catholic Hapsburgs.

A Time of Chaos The fighting took a terrible toll. Roving armies of **mercenaries,** or soldiers for hire, burned villages, destroyed crops, and killed without mercy. Murder and torture were followed by famine and disease. Wolves, not seen in settled areas since the Middle Ages, stalked the deserted streets of once-bustling villages.

The war led to a severe **depopulation,** or reduction in population. Exact statistics do not exist, but historians estimate that as many as one third of the people in the German states may have died as a result of the war.

Peace Is Restored Finally, in 1648, the exhausted combatants accepted a series of treaties, known as the **Peace of Westphalia.** Because so many powers had been involved in the conflict, the treaties ended with a general European peace and settled other international problems.

Among the combatants, France emerged a clear winner, gaining territory on both its Spanish and German frontiers. The Hapsburgs were not so fortunate. They had to accept the almost total independence of all the princes of the Holy Roman Empire. In addition, the Netherlands and the Swiss Federation (present-day Switzerland) won recognition as independent states.

The Thirty Years' War left German lands divided into more than 360 separate states—"one for every day of the year." These states still acknowledged the rule of the Holy Roman emperor. Yet each state had its own government, currency, church, armed forces, and foreign policy.

The German-speaking states, if united, had the potential to become the most powerful nation in

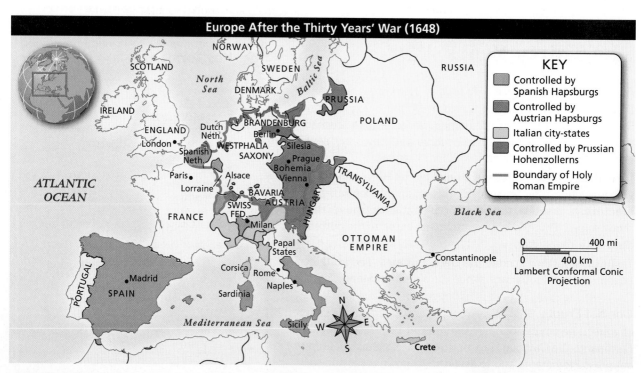

>> **Analyze Maps** After the Thirty Years' War, the Peace of Westphalia redrew the map of Europe. Who controlled Bohemia after 1648?

BOUNCE to Activate Map

Europe. They remained fragmented, however, and would not be joined into a single nation for another 223 years.

☑ **IDENTIFY CAUSE AND EFFECT** What were some effects of the Peace of Westphalia?

Hapsburg Austria Expands

The Thirty Years' War took a terrible toll on the people of the German states. Out of the ashes, however, rose two great German-speaking powers: Austria and Prussia. Like Louis XIV in France, their rulers tried to centralize power and rule as absolute monarchs.

A Diverse Empire Though weakened by war, the Hapsburgs still wanted to create a strong united state. They kept the title "Holy Roman emperor" but focused their attention on expanding their own lands. To Austria, their base of power, they added Bohemia, Hungary, and, later, parts of Poland and some Italian states.

Uniting these lands proved difficult. Not only were they divided by geography, they included a number of diverse peoples and cultures as well. By the 1700s, the Hapsburg Empire included Germans, Magyars, Slavs, and others. In many parts of the empire, people had their own languages, laws, political assemblies, and customs.

The Hapsburgs did exert some control over these diverse peoples. They sent German-speaking officials to Bohemia and Hungary and settled Austrians on lands they had seized in these provinces. They also put down revolts in Bohemia and Hungary. Still, the Hapsburgs never developed a fully centralized governmental system like that of France.

Empress Maria Theresa In the early 1700s, a new challenge threatened Hapsburg Austria. Emperor Charles VI had no male heir. His daughter, **Maria Theresa,** was intelligent and capable, but no woman had yet ruled Hapsburg lands in her own name. Charles persuaded other European rulers to recognize his daughter's right to succeed him. When he died, however, many ignored their pledge.

Shortly after Charles's death in 1740, Frederick II of Prussia seized the rich Hapsburg province of Silesia. This action sparked the eight-year **War of the Austrian Succession.**

>> The War of the Austrian Succession challenged Maria Theresa's right to rule the Holy Roman Empire. In 1745, French forces defeated British and Austrian troops at the Battle of Fontenoy, shown here.

Maria Theresa set off for Hungary to appeal for military help from her Hungarian subjects. The Hungarians were ordinarily unfriendly to the Hapsburgs. But she made a dramatic plea before an assembly of Hungarian nobles. According to one account, the nobles rose to their feet and shouted, "Our lives and blood for your Majesty!" She eventually got further help from Britain and Russia.

Reforms of an Absolute Monarch Maria Theresa never succeeded in forcing Frederick out of Silesia. Still, she did preserve her empire and win the support of most of her people. Equally important, she strengthened Hapsburg power by reorganizing the bureaucracy and improving tax collection. She forced nobles and clergy to pay taxes and tried to ease the burden of taxes and labor services on peasants.

Maria Theresa was an absolute monarch who believed that her decisions were for the good of her subjects. Like other rulers at the time, she strengthened royal authority by limiting the power of nobles and the Church.

☑ **IDENTIFY CAUSE AND EFFECT** What caused the War of the Austrian Succession?

Prussia Emerges

While Austria was molding a strong Catholic state, **Prussia** emerged as a new Protestant German-speaking power in the north. In the 1600s, the Hohenzollern (HOH un tsahl urn) family ruled scattered lands across north Germany. After the Peace of Westphalia, ambitious Hohenzollern rulers united their holdings by taking over states between them. Like absolute rulers elsewhere, they imposed royal power on all their subjects and reduced the independence of their nobles, called Junkers (YOON kerz).

Creating an Efficient Bureaucracy To achieve their goals, Hohenzollern rulers set up an efficient central bureaucracy and forged one of the best-trained armies in Europe. One Prussian military leader boasted, "Prussia is not a state which possesses an army, but an army which possesses a state."

Emperor **Frederick William I,** who came to power in 1713, gained the loyalty of the Junkers by giving them positions in the army and government. His tactic reduced the nobles' independence and increased his own control. By 1740, Prussia was strong enough to challenge its rival Austria.

>> Hohenzollern rulers united their lands to create a Prussian empire. This 18th-century print shows a Prussian army camp in Pomerania, territory that lay between East Prussia and West Prussia.

Frederick the Great That year, young **Frederick II** inherited the throne. From an early age, Frederick was trained in the art of war, as his father insisted.

> His tutor must take the greatest pains to imbue my son with a sincere love for the soldier's profession and to impress upon him that nothing else in the world can confer upon a prince such fame and honor as the sword.
> —Frederick William I

However, Frederick preferred playing the flute and writing poetry. His father despised these pursuits and treated the young prince so badly that he tried to flee the country. Discovering these plans, Frederick William put his son in solitary confinement. Then he forced the 18-year-old prince to watch as the friend who had helped him was beheaded.

Frederick's harsh military training had an effect. After becoming king in 1740, Frederick II lost no time in using his army. He boldly seized Silesia from Austria, sparking the War of the Austrian Succession.

In several later wars, Frederick continued to brilliantly use his disciplined army, forcing all to recognize Prussia as a great power. His exploits and his power as an absolute monarch earned him the name Frederick the Great.

☑ **SUMMARIZE** How did Frederick William increase his power?

Peter the Great Modernizes Russia

From 1604 to 1613, Russia was in a period of disorder, plagued by foreign invasions and internal rebellion. The rise of the first Romanov tsar restored a measure of order. Still, Russia remained a medieval state, untouched by the Renaissance or Reformation and largely isolated from Western Europe.

At the end of the century, a tsar emerged who was strong enough to regain the absolute power of earlier tsars. Just 10 years old when he took the throne in 1682, Peter I took control of the government seven years later. **Peter the Great,** as he came to be called, used his power to put Russia on the road to becoming a great modern power.

Peter Visits the West The young tsar was a striking figure, nearly seven feet tall, with a booming laugh and a furious temper. Although he was not well educated, he was immensely curious. He spent hours in the Moscow neighborhood where many Dutch,

Scottish, English, and other foreigners lived. There, he heard of the new technology that was helping Western European monarchs forge powerful empires.

In 1697, Peter set out to learn about Western technology and ways for himself. He spent hours walking the streets of European cities, noting the manners and homes of the people. He visited factories and art galleries, learned anatomy from a doctor, and even had a dentist teach him how to pull teeth.

In England, Peter was impressed by Parliament. "It is good," he said, "to hear subjects speaking truthfully and openly to their king."

The Westernization of Russia Returning to Russia, Peter brought a group of technical experts, teachers, and soldiers he had recruited in Europe. He then embarked on a policy of **westernization,** the adoption of Western ideas, technology, and culture.

Some changes had a symbolic meaning. He forced the **boyars,** or landowning nobles, to shave their traditional beards and wear Western-style clothes. To end the practice of secluding upper-class women in separate quarters, he held grand parties at which women and men were expected to dance together. Russian nobles opposed this radical mixing of the sexes in public, but they had to comply.

To impose his will, Peter became the most **autocratic** of Europe's absolute monarchs, meaning that he ruled with unlimited authority. Determined to centralize royal power, he brought the Russian Orthodox Church under his control. He forced the haughty boyars to serve the state in civilian or military jobs.

Extending Serfdom Peter knew that nobles would serve the state only if their own interests were protected. Therefore, he passed laws ensuring that nobles retained control over their lands. This included the serfs who were tied to those lands.

Under Peter's rule, serfdom spread in Russia at a time when it was dying out in Western Europe. Further, he forced some serfs to become soldiers or to work as laborers on roads, canals, and other government projects.

A Harsh, Effective Ruler Peter showed no mercy to any who resisted his new order. When elite palace guards revolted, he had more than 1,000 of the rebels tortured and executed. Then, as an example of his power, he left their rotting corpses outside the palace walls for months.

Peter was known not only for cruelty but also for remaking Russia. He imported Western technology,

>> In this image, Peter the Great is studying the building plans for St. Petersburg. The establishment of the city was one of his most important and long-lasting achievements.

BOUNCE to Activate Cartoon

>> While visiting the Netherlands, Peter the Great disguised himself as a ship carpenter's apprentice to study shipbuilding. **Draw Conclusions** Why might Peter disguise himself like this?

>> Peter wanted to gain access to a warm-water port and the open sea. His first step toward this goal was to capture Azov, a town in what is now southwestern Russia, from the Turks. This painting shows the successful capture of Azov in 1696.

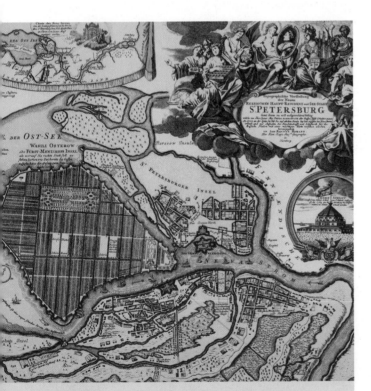

>> **Analyze Maps** This historical map shows the city of St. Petersburg, built by Peter the Great. What are the benefits of St. Petersburg's location? What are the challenges?

simplified the Russian alphabet, and set up academies for the study of mathematics, science, and engineering. To pay for his reforms, Peter adopted mercantilist policies, such as encouraging exports. He improved waterways and canals, developed mining and textile manufacturing, and backed new trading companies. Peter succeeded in refashioning Russia from a medieval backwater into a rising European—and Asian—power.

☑ **CATEGORIZE** What policies did Peter use to solidify his control over the nobles?

Expanding Russia's Borders

From his earliest days as tsar, Peter worked to build Russia's military power. He created the largest standing army in Europe, built a world-class navy from scratch, and set out to extend Russian borders to the west and south. To achieve these goals meant fighting Russia's neighbors.

Seeking a Warm-Water Seaport Peter's chief goal was to win a **warm-water port,** a port that was not frozen in winter. Russian seaports, located along the Arctic Ocean, were covered in ice most of the year. A warm-water port would increase Russia's ability to trade with the West.

The nearest warm-water coast was located along the Black Sea. To gain control of this territory, Peter had to push through the powerful Ottoman Empire. In the end, Peter was unable to defeat the Ottomans and gain his warm-water port. The drive to achieve this goal motivated future Russian tsars, and by the late 1700s, Catherine the Great would succeed.

The Great Northern War In 1700, Peter began a long war against the kingdom of Sweden, which at the time dominated the Baltic region. Early on, Russia suffered humiliating defeats. A Swedish force of only 8,000 men defeated a Russian army five times its size. Undaunted, Peter rebuilt his army, modeling it after European armies.

Finally, in 1709, he defeated the Swedes and won territory along the Baltic Sea. On this land, Peter would build a magnificent new capital city, **St. Petersburg.**

A "Window on the West" St. Petersburg became the great symbol of Peter's desire to forge a modern, Western-oriented Russia nation. Seeking to open a "window on the West," he located the city along the swampy shores of the Neva River, near the Baltic coast. He forced tens of thousands of serfs to drain the swamps. Many thousands died, but Peter's plan for the city succeeded.

On his journey to the West, Peter had visited Louis XIV's splendid new palace of Versailles. Like the Sun King, Peter invited the best European architects and artisans to design and build the palaces for his new city. Peter even planned the city's parks and boulevards himself, modeling them on those he had seen at Versailles.

Expanding to the East Peter also expanded the Russian empire eastward toward the Pacific. Russian traders and raiders also crossed the plains and rivers of Siberia. Under Peter, Russia signed a treaty with China that recognized Russia's claim to lands north of China and defined the common border of the two empires.

In the early 1700s, Peter hired the Danish navigator Vitus Bering to explore what became known as the Bering Strait between Siberia and Alaska. After Peter's death, Russian traders built outposts in Alaska and northern California. Few Russians moved east of the Ural Mountains at this time, but the expansion made Russia the largest country in the world. It still is today, nearly 300 years later.

A Mixed Legacy When Peter died in 1725, he left a mixed legacy. He had expanded Russian territory, gained ports on the Baltic Sea, and created a mighty army. He had also ended Russia's long period of isolation. From the 1700s on, Russia would be increasingly involved in the affairs of Western Europe. Yet many of Peter's ambitious reforms died with him. Nobles, for example, soon ignored his policy of service to the state.

Like earlier tsars, Peter the Great had used terror to enforce his absolute power. His policies contributed to the growth of serfdom, which served only to widen the gap between Russia and the West that Peter had sought to narrow.

☑ **IDENTIFY CAUSE AND EFFECT** What impact did Peter's defeat of Sweden have on Russia's expansion?

Catherine the Great

Peter's successors in the Romanov dynasty were ineffective rulers. Russian nobles quickly reasserted their independence. Then a new monarch took the

>> The Bering expedition brought the Russians to the west coast of North America.

>> Catherine the Great, shown here in a 1794 portrait, took over the rule of Russia after the assassination of her husband, Tsar Peter III.

reins of power firmly in hand. She became known to history as **Catherine the Great.**

A German Princess Becomes Tsar A German princess by birth, Catherine came to Russia at the age of 15 to wed the heir to the Russian throne. She learned Russian, embraced the Russian Orthodox faith, and won the loyalty of the people.

In 1762, a group of Russian army officers loyal to her deposed and murdered her mentally unstable husband, Tsar Peter III. Whether or not Catherine was involved in the assassination is uncertain. In any case, with the support of the military, she ascended the Russian throne.

Catherine Embraces Reform Catherine proved to be an efficient, energetic empress. She reorganized the provincial government, codified laws, and began state-sponsored education for both boys and girls.

Like Peter the Great, Catherine embraced Western ideas and worked to bring Russia fully into European cultural and political life. At court, she encouraged French language and customs, wrote histories and plays, and organized performances. She was also a serious student of the French thinkers who led the intellectual movement known as the Enlightenment.

An Absolute Monarch Like rulers in France and Spain, Catherine was an absolute monarch. Like them, she could be ruthless. She granted a charter to the boyars outlining important rights, such as exemption from taxes. She also allowed them to increase their stranglehold on the peasants. When peasants rebelled against the harsh burdens of serfdom, Catherine harshly suppressed the uprisings. Under Catherine, conditions grew even worse for Russian peasants and serfdom continued to spread.

Like Peter the Great, Catherine was determined to expand Russia's borders. After a war against the Ottoman Empire, she achieved the Russian dream of a warm-water port on the Black Sea. She also took steps to seize territory from neighboring Poland.

The Partitions of Poland Poland-Lithuania had once been a great European power. However, its rulers were unable to centralize their power or diminish the influence of the Polish nobility. In the 1770s, three powerful neighboring monarchs— Catherine of Russia, Frederick II of Prussia, and Joseph II of Austria—hungrily eyed Poland.

To avoid fighting one another, the three monarchs agreed in 1772 to **partition,** or divide up, Poland. Poland was partitioned three times between the 1770s and 1790s. Russia took the eastern part, where many Russians and Ukrainians lived. Austria and

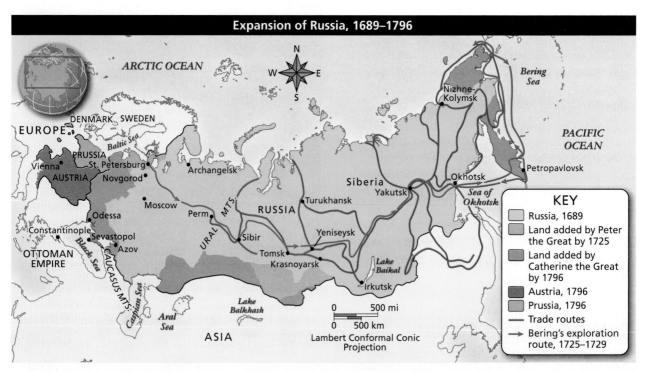

>> **Analyze Maps** Russia expanded its borders from 1689 to 1796. Which five cities could probably serve as warm-water ports?

Prussia divided up the rest. By 1795, the independent kingdom of Poland had vanished from the map. Not until 1919 would a free Polish state reappear.

☑ **COMPARE** How were Catherine's goals similar to those of Peter?

Five Great European Powers

By 1750, five European powers had come to dominate European affairs. They were Austria, Prussia, France, Britain, and Russia. All five had strong centralized governments. Although Spain and the Ottoman Empire ruled parts of Europe, these once powerful empires were in decline.

Struggles for Power As these five nation-states competed with one another, they formed various alliances to maintain the balance of power. Though nations sometimes switched partners, two basic rivalries persisted. Prussia battled Austria for control of the German-speaking states. At the same time, Britain and France competed for power and influence both in Europe and in their growing overseas empires.

On occasion, these rivalries resulted in worldwide conflict. The Seven Years' War, which lasted from 1756 until 1763, was fought on four continents.

In Europe, Prussia and Britain battled Austria, France, Russia, and Sweden. Britain and France also battled for power in India, Africa, and North America, where the conflict became known as the French and Indian War.

Absolutism at Its Peak Absolutism reached its peak in the mid-1700s. Four of the five great European powers were ruled by absolute monarchs. Britain, with its strong Parliament, was the only exception.

At the same time, new ideas were circulating about natural rights and the role of government. In time, demands for change and reform would topple French absolutism, revolutionize European societies, and transform the balance of power in Europe.

>> The Seven Years' War in Europe pitted Europe, Prussia, and Britain against Austria, France, Russia, and Sweden. This painting shows a December 1757 battle in which the Prussians defeated the Austrians.

☑ **DESCRIBE** How did European nations maintain a balance of power?

☑ ASSESSMENT

1. **Identify Cause and Effect** What were the causes and results of the Thirty Years' War?

2. **Identify** How were the goals of Austria and Prussia similar?

3. **Describe** How did European nations try to maintain a balance of power?

4. **List** What steps did Peter the Great take to modernize Russia?

5. **Describe** How did Russia grow under Peter the Great and Catherine the Great?

Henry VIII consulted with Parliament frequently. Here, he presides as chairmen over the House of Lords.

Objectives

Describe the relationship between Parliament and the monarchy under the Tudors and Stuarts.

Explain how English government developed after the English Civil War.

Identify the causes of the Glorious Revolution and the ideas contained in the English Bill of Rights.

Identify the characteristics of limited monarchy and constitutional government in England.

Key Terms

James I
dissenter
Puritan
Charles I
Oliver Cromwell
English Bill of Rights
limited monarchy
constitutional
  government
cabinet
prime minister
oligarchy

Triumph of Parliament in England

During the age of absolutism, English monarchs, like rulers on the continent, tried to increase royal power and claim the divine right to rule. Their efforts, however, ran into the obstacle of Parliament, which during the Middle Ages had acquired the power of the purse. Only Parliament could grant monarchs the funds they needed to pursue their ambitions. And Parliament at times stood firm against royal absolutism.

Tudor Monarchs Work with Parliament

Henry VIII From 1485 to 1603, England was ruled by Tudor monarchs. Although the Tudors believed in divine right, they shrewdly recognized the value of good relations with Parliament. When Henry VIII broke with the Roman Catholic Church, he turned to Parliament to legalize his actions. Parliament approved the Act of Supremacy, making the monarch head of the Church of England.

A constant need for money led Henry to consult Parliament frequently. Although he had inherited a bulging treasury, he quickly used up his funds fighting overseas wars. To levy new taxes, the king had to seek the approval of Parliament. Members of Parliament tended to vote as Henry's agents instructed. Still, they became accustomed to being consulted on important matters.

Elizabeth I When Henry's daughter Elizabeth I gained the throne, she too both consulted and controlled Parliament. In theory, the monarch called Parliament for advice. In practice, Elizabeth rarely asked for its view. During her 45-year reign, she summoned Parliament only 13 times. All but one time, she asked for money.

When Parliament met, the queen's advisers conveyed her wishes. Certain subjects, such as foreign policy or the queen's marriage, were forbidden. Her skill in handling Parliament helped make "Good Queen Bess" a popular and successful ruler.

✅ **CHECK UNDERSTANDING** Why did Henry VIII work with Parliament?

>> James I, the first Stuart king of England, ruled England from 1603 to 1625.

Stuart Monarchs Clash with Parliament

Elizabeth died childless in 1603. The throne passed to her relatives the Stuarts, the ruling family of Scotland. The Stuarts were neither as popular as the Tudors nor as skillful in dealing with Parliament. They also inherited problems that Henry and Elizabeth had long suppressed. The result was a "century of revolution" that pitted the Stuart monarchs against Parliament.

James I Asserts Divine Right When the first Stuart monarch, **James I,** took the throne, he agreed to rule according to English laws and customs. Soon, however, he was lecturing Parliament about divine right. In 1610, the king made a speech in Parliament.

> The state of Monarchy is the supremest thing upon earth; for kings are not only God's lieutenants upon earth and sit upon God's throne, but even by God himself they are called gods. . . . Kings are justly called gods for that they exercise a manner or resemblance of Divine power on earth . . . And to the King is due both the affection of the soul and the service of the body of his subjects....
>
> —King James I

Parliament was not impressed with the king's claim to rule by divine right. Instead, James faced

>> King James gave Greek and Hebrew scholars specific instructions for translating the Christian Bible into English. The King James Bible is considered a literary masterpiece.

repeated clashes with Parliament, mostly over money and foreign policy that involved the king's wars in Europe. James lived extravagantly and had to ask Parliament for funds to finance his lavish court.

More than once, when members wanted to discuss foreign policy before voting funds, James dissolved Parliament and raised money without their consent. These actions poisoned relations between the king and Parliament.

James also found himself embroiled in religious disputes. He clashed with **dissenters,** Protestants who differed with the Church of England. One group were called **Puritans** because they sought to "purify" the English church of Catholic practices. Puritans called for simpler services and a more democratic church without bishops. James rejected their demands, vowing to "harry them out of this land or else do worse."

Charles I Clashes with Parliament In 1625, **Charles I** inherited the throne. Like his father, Charles behaved like an absolute monarch. He imprisoned his foes without trial and squeezed the nation for money. By 1628, however, his need to raise taxes forced Charles to summon Parliament. Before voting any funds, Parliament insisted that Charles sign the Petition of Right.

This document prohibited the king from raising taxes without Parliament's consent or from jailing anyone without legal justification.

Charles did sign the Petition, but he then dissolved Parliament in 1629. For 11 years, he ignored the Petition and ruled without Parliament. During that time, he created bitter enemies, especially among Puritans. His Archbishop of Canterbury, William Laud, tried to force all clergy to follow strict Anglican rules, dismissing or imprisoning dissenters. Many people felt that the archbishop was trying to revive Catholic practices.

In 1637, Charles and Laud tried to impose the Anglican prayer book on Scotland. The Calvinist Scots revolted. To get funds to suppress the Scottish rebellion, Charles once again had to summon Parliament in 1640. When it met, however, Parliament launched its own revolt.

The Long Parliament Begins The 1640 Parliament became known as the Long Parliament because it lasted on and off until 1653.

Its actions triggered the greatest political revolution in English history. In a mounting struggle with Charles I, Parliament tried and executed his chief ministers, including Archbishop Laud. It called for the abolition of bishops and declared that the Parliament could not be dissolved without its own consent.

Charles lashed back. In 1642, he led troops into the House of Commons to arrest its most radical leaders. They escaped through a back door and soon raised their own army. The clash now moved to the battlefield.

☑ **DESCRIBE** What was the Petition of Right?

The English Civil War

The civil war that followed lasted from 1642 to 1651. Like the Fronde that occurred about the same time in France, the English Civil War posed a major challenge to absolutism. But while the forces of royal power won in France, in England the forces of revolution triumphed.

Cavaliers and Roundheads At first, the odds seemed to favor the supporters of Charles I, called Cavaliers. Many Cavaliers were wealthy nobles, proud of their plumed hats and fashionably long hair. Well trained in dueling and warfare, the Cavaliers expected a quick victory. But their foes proved to be tough fighters with the courage of their convictions.

>> Charles I and his troops stormed into the House of Commons to arrest radicals.

 BOUNCE to Activate Timeline

The forces of Parliament were composed of country gentry, town-dwelling manufacturers, and Puritan clergy. They were called Roundheads because their hair was cut close around their heads. The Roundheads found a leader of genius in **Oliver Cromwell.** A Puritan member of the lesser gentry, Cromwell proved himself to be a skilled general.

He organized the "New Model Army" for Parliament into a disciplined fighting force. Cromwell's army defeated the Cavaliers in a series of decisive battles. By 1647, the king was in the hands of parliamentary forces.

Execution of the King Eventually, Parliament set up a court to put the king on trial. It condemned him to death as "a tyrant, traitor, murderer, and public enemy." On a cold January day in 1649, Charles I stood on a scaffold surrounded by his foes. "I am a martyr of the people," he declared. Showing no fear, the king told the executioner that he himself would give the sign for him to strike. After a brief prayer, Charles knelt and placed his neck on the block. On the agreed signal, the executioner severed the king's neck with a single stroke.

The execution sent shock waves throughout Europe. In the past, a king had occasionally been assassinated or killed in battle. But for the first time, a ruling monarch had been tried and executed by his own people. The parliamentary forces had sent a clear message that, in England, no ruler could claim absolute power and ignore the rule of law.

☑ **IDENTIFY CAUSE AND EFFECT** What was the result of the English Civil War?

Cromwell and the Commonwealth

After the execution of Charles I, the House of Commons abolished the monarchy and the House of Lords, and established the Church of England. It declared England a republic, known as the Commonwealth, under the leadership of Oliver Cromwell.

Challenges to the Commonwealth The new government faced many threats. Supporters of Charles II, the uncrowned heir to the throne, attacked England by way of Ireland and Scotland. Cromwell led forces into Ireland and brutally crushed the uprising. He then took harsh measures against the Irish Catholic majority that are still vividly remembered in that nation today. In 1652, Parliament

>> Oliver Cromwell led parliamentary forces in the English Civil War.

>> Charles I was beheaded in January 1649. It was the first time a ruling monarch had been tried and executed by his own people.

passed a law exiling most Catholics to barren land in the west of Ireland. Any Catholic found disobeying this order could be killed on sight.

Squabbles also splintered forces within the Commonwealth. One group, called Levellers, thought that poor men should have as much say in government as the gentry, lawyers, and other leading citizens. "The poorest he that is in England hath a life to live as the greatest he," wrote one Leveller. In addition, woman Levellers asserted their right to petition Parliament. These ideas horrified the gentry, who dominated Parliament.

Cromwell suppressed the Levellers, as well as more radical groups who threatened ownership of private property. In 1653, as the challenges to order grew, Cromwell took the title Lord Protector. From then on, he ruled as a virtual dictator, using the army to back up his orders.

England Under the Puritans Under the Commonwealth, Puritan preachers tried to root out godlessness and impose a "rule of saints." The English Civil War thus ushered in a social revolution as well as a political one.

Parliament enacted a series of laws designed to make sure that Sunday was set aside for religious observance.

Anyone over the age of 14 who was caught "profaning the Lord's Day" could be fined. To the Puritans, theaters were frivolous. So, like John Calvin in Geneva, Cromwell closed all theaters. Puritans also frowned on taverns, gambling, and dancing.

Puritans felt that every Christian, rich and poor, must be able to read the Bible. To spread religious knowledge, they encouraged education for all people. By mid-century, families from all classes were sending their children to school, girls as well as boys.

Puritans pushed for changes in marriage to ensure fidelity. In addition to marriages based on business interests, they encouraged marriages based on love. Still, as in the past, women were seen mainly as subordinate to men.

Although Cromwell did not tolerate open worship by Roman Catholics, he believed in religious freedom for other Protestant groups. He even welcomed Jews back to England after more than 350 years of exile.

Puritan Rule Ends Oliver Cromwell died in 1658. Soon after, the Puritans lost their grip on England. Many people were tired of military rule and strict Puritan ways. In 1660, a newly elected Parliament invited Charles II to return to England from exile.

England's "kingless decade" ended with the Restoration, or return of the monarchy. Yet Puritan ideas about morality, equality, government, and

THE PURITAN INFLUENCE

After the execution of Charles I, Puritans and reformers controlled Parliament. They believed that it was time to encourage seriousness of purpose. Puritans did dance and sing, but they did so only in private gatherings. Their objection was not so much to the music and dancing as to the "public disorder" to which those frivolities contributed.

NO PUBLIC MUSIC

NO PUBLIC DANCING

PUBLIC THEATERS CLOSED

EDUCATION FOR ALL

MODEST CLOTHING

STRONG FAMILIES

>> **Analyze Information** The Puritans sought societal and moral reforms. How did Puritans feel about education?

education endured. These ideas were already shaping England's colonies in North America, where many Puritans had settled.

☑ **DESCRIBE** What was the Commonwealth?

From Restoration to Glorious Revolution

In late May 1660, cheering crowds welcomed Charles II back to London. An observer described the celebration as a triumph.

> This day came in his Majesties Charles the Second to London after a sad, and long Exile . . . with a Triumph of above 20,000 horse and [soldiers], brandishing their swords, and shouting with inexpressible joy; the [ways strewn] with flowers, the bells ringing, the streets hung with [tapestry].
>
> —John Evelyn, *Diary*

>> Crowds welcomed Charles II back after the monarchy was restored.

A Popular King With his charm and flashing wit, young Charles II was a popular ruler. He reopened theaters and taverns and presided over a lively court in the manner of Louis XIV.

Charles restored the official Church of England but encouraged toleration of other Protestants such as Presbyterians, Quakers, and Baptists. Although Charles accepted the Petition of Right, he shared his father's belief in absolute monarchy and secretly had Catholic sympathies. Still, he shrewdly avoided his father's mistakes in dealing with Parliament.

Charles was a strong supporter of science and the arts. He helped found the Royal Society, a group formed to advance scientific knowledge. Its early members, such as Isaac Newton, Robert Hooke, and Robert Boyle, advanced the study of mathematics, biology, physics, and chemistry. Charles was equally supportive of the arts, especially architecture. After the Great Fire of 1666 destroyed much of London, Charles appointed the great architect, Sir Christopher Wren, to rebuild the city.

The Glorious Revolution Charles's brother, James II, inherited the throne in 1685. Unlike Charles, James practiced his Catholic faith openly. He angered his subjects by suspending laws on a whim and appointing Catholics to high office. Many English Protestants feared that James would restore the Roman Catholic Church.

In 1688, alarmed parliamentary leaders invited James's Protestant daughter, Mary, and her Dutch Protestant husband, William III of Orange, to become rulers of England. When William and Mary landed with their army, James II fled to France. This bloodless overthrow of the king became known as the Glorious Revolution.

The English Bill of Rights Before they could be crowned, William and Mary had to accept several acts passed by Parliament in 1689 that became known as the **English Bill of Rights.** The Bill of Rights ensured the superiority of Parliament over the monarchy. It required the monarch to summon Parliament regularly and ensured that the House of Commons kept control over spending. A king or queen could no longer interfere in parliamentary debates or suspend laws. The Bill of Rights also barred any Roman Catholic from sitting on the throne.

The Bill of Rights also restated the traditional legal rights of English citizens, such as trial by jury. It abolished excessive fines and cruel or unjust punishment. It affirmed the principle of habeas corpus. That is, no person could be held in prison without first being charged with a specific crime. The legal ideas contained in the English Bill of Rights would later have a strong influence on the United States.

Soon after, the separate Toleration Act of 1689 granted limited religious freedom to Puritans, Quakers, and other Protestant dissenters. Still, only members of the Church of England could hold public office. And Catholics were allowed no religious freedom.

A Limited Monarchy The Glorious Revolution turned England into a **limited monarchy,** a type of government in which a constitution or legislative body limits the monarch's powers. English rulers still had much power, but they had to obey the law and govern in partnership with Parliament. In an age of absolute monarchy elsewhere in Europe, the limited monarchy in England was quite radical.

Among the people who lived at the time of the Glorious Revolution was the political thinker, John Locke. Events in England helped shape his philosophy. Much later, Locke's ideas about government and natural rights would influence the Americans who drew up the Declaration of Independence and the United States Constitution.

☑ **DEFINE** What was the Glorious Revolution?

England's Constitutional Government Evolves

In the century following the Glorious Revolution, three new political institutions arose in Britain: political parties, the cabinet, and the office of prime minister. The appearance of these institutions was part of the evolution of Britain's **constitutional government**—that is, a government whose power is defined and limited by law.

Political Parties In the late 1600s, political parties emerged in England as a powerful force in politics. At first, there were just two political parties—Tories and Whigs.

Tories were generally aristocrats who sought to preserve older traditions. They supported broad royal powers and a dominant Anglican Church.

Whigs backed the ideas embodied in the Glorious Revolution. They were more likely to reflect urban business interests, support religious toleration, and favor Parliament over the crown. For much of the 1700s Whigs dominated Parliament.

The Cabinet System The cabinet, another new feature of government, evolved in the 1700s after the British throne passed to a German prince. George I spoke no English and relied on the leaders

Influence of the Glorious Revolution

	English Bill of Rights	Writings of John Locke	Constitutional Government
OUTCOME IN ENGLAND	• People elect representatives to Parliament, which is supreme over the monarch. • All citizens have natural rights.	• People have natural rights such as life, liberty, and property. • There is a social contract between people and government.	• Government is limited and defined by law. • Political parties, the cabinet, and the office of prime minister arise.
	↓	↓	↓
IMPACT ON THE UNITED STATES	• Colonists believed that they too had rights, including the right to elect people to represent them.	• Locke's ideas shaped the American Revolution and the writing of the Declaration of Independence and the Constitution.	• Government is limited and defined by law. • The new nation formed a constitutional government with two parties and even stronger provisions for the separation of powers.

>> **Analyze Charts** A common protest during the American Revolution was "no taxation without representation." Which outcome in England influenced that idea?

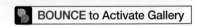 BOUNCE to Activate Gallery

in Parliament to help him rule. Under George I and his German-born son George II, a handful of parliamentary advisors set policy. They came to be referred to as the **cabinet** because of the small room, or "cabinet," where they met.

In time, the cabinet gained official status. It was made up of leaders of the majority party in the House of Commons. The cabinet remained in power so long as it enjoyed the support of the Commons.

If the Commons voted against a cabinet decision, the cabinet resigned. The cabinet system (also called a parliamentary system) was later adopted by other countries in Europe and elsewhere around the globe.

The Prime Minister Over time, the head of the cabinet came to be known as the **prime minister.** This person was always the leader of the majority party in the House of Commons.

Eventually, the prime minister became the chief official of the British government and the prime minister's power would exceed that of the monarch. From 1721 to 1742, the able Whig leader Robert Walpole molded the cabinet into a unified body by requiring all members to agree on major issues. Although the title was not yet in use, Walpole is often called Britain's first prime minister.

Rule by an Oligarchy Even as Parliament and the cabinet assumed new powers, British government was far from democratic. Rather, it was an **oligarchy**—a government in which the ruling power belongs to a few people.

Landowning aristocrats were believed to be the "natural" ruling class. The highest nobles held seats in the House of Lords. Other wealthy landowners and rich business leaders in the cities controlled elections to the House of Commons. The right to vote was limited to a relatively few male property owners, whose votes were often openly bought.

The lives of most people contrasted sharply with those of the ruling elite. The majority made a meager living from the land.

In the 1700s, even that poor existence was threatened. Wealthy landowners, attempting to increase agricultural production, bought up farms and took over common lands, evicting tenant farmers and small landowners. Because they controlled Parliament, they easily passed laws ensuring that their actions were legal. A small but growing middle class included successful merchants and manufacturers. These prosperous and often wealthy people controlled affairs in the towns and cities. Some improved their social standing by marrying

>> The marketplace brought different classes of people together, but the classes differed widely in terms of political power. **Interpret** In this painting, how can you tell the different classes apart?

into the landed gentry. The middle class also produced talented inventors and entrepreneurs who would soon help usher in the Industrial Revolution.

☑ **CHECK UNDERSTANDING** What were the new political institutions that developed as a result of Britain's constitutional government?

☑ **ASSESSMENT**

1. **Check Understanding** Why was James I resistant to working with Parliament?

2. **Define** What was the Long Parliament?

3. **Recall** Who was Oliver Cromwell?

4. **Identify Central Ideas** What is the main feature of a constitutional government?

5. **Quest Connections** How did the English Bill of Rights expand citizen rights? How did the English Bill of Rights influence the manner in which citizens are protected today?

The Monarchy and Parliament Fight for Power

When the Catholic king, James II, was forced from the English throne in 1688, Parliament offered the crown to his Protestant daughter Mary and her husband, William of Orange. Parliament, however, insisted that William and Mary submit to a bill of rights. The first primary source from The English Bill of Rights, written in 1689, sums up the powers that Parliament had been seeking since the Petition of Right in 1628. The second primary source is from The Petition of Right, in which Parliament protests the overreach of authority by KingCharles I.

>> William and Mary accept the crown.

As you read, compare their viewpoints on the rights of citizens.

Primary Source 1

The English Bill of Rights (1689)

Whereas, the late King James II . . .
did endeavor to subvert and extirpate
[eliminate] the Protestant religion and the
laws and liberties of this kingdom . . .
and whereas the said late king James II
having abdicated the government, and the
throne being vacant. . . . The said Lords
[Parliament] . . . being now assembled in a
full and free representative [body] of this
nation . . . do in the first place . . . declare.

- That the pretended [untruthfully claimed] power of suspending the laws or the execution of laws by regal authority without consent of Parliament is illegal;
- That the pretended power of dispensing with laws or the execution of laws by regal authority, as it hath been assumed and exercised of late, is illegal; . . .
- That levying [collecting] money for or to the use of the Crown by pretence of prerogative [a right exclusive to a king or queen], without grant of Parliament, for longer time, or in other manner than the same is or shall be granted, is illegal;
- That it is the right of the subjects to petition [make a request of] the king, and all commitments and prosecutions for such petitioning are illegal;

☑ **CITE EVIDENCE** On what grounds did Parliament draw up the English Bill of Rights?

- That the raising or keeping a standing army within the kingdom in time of peace, unless it be with consent of Parliament, is against law;
- That the subjects which are Protestants may have arms for their defence suitable to their conditions and as allowed by law;
- That election of members of Parliament ought to be free;
- That the freedom of speech and debates or proceedings in Parliament ought not to be impeached [discredited] or questioned in any court or place out of Parliament;

- That excessive bail ought not to be required, nor excessive fines imposed, nor cruel and unusual punishments inflicted;
- That jurors ought to be duly [done at a proper time] impaneled [registered on a panel of jurors] and returned [released from service], and jurors which pass upon men in trials for high treason ought to be freeholders [property owners with unconditional rights];
- That all grants and promises of fines and forfeitures of particular persons before conviction are illegal and void;
- And that for redress [correction] of all grievances, and for the amending, strengthening and preserving of the laws, Parliaments ought to be held frequently.

☑ **DRAW CONCLUSIONS** Why might Parliament have included the point that its members should be elected freely? What larger concept is supported by this point?

Primary Source 2

Petition of Right (1628)

III. And whereas also by the statute called 'The Great Charter of the Liberties of England,' it is declared and enacted, that no freeman may be taken or imprisoned or be disseized [deprived] of his freehold or liberties [or his free customs, or be outlawed or exiled, or in any manner destroyed] but by the lawful judgment of his peers, or by the law of the land.

VI. And whereas of late great companies of soldiers and mariners have been dispersed into divers counties of the realm, and the inhabitants against their wills have been compelled to receive them into their houses, and there to suffer them to sojourn against the laws and customs of this realm, and to the great grievance and vexation of the people.

X. They do therefore humbly pray your most excellent Majesty, that no man hereafter be compelled to make or yield any gift, loan, benevolence, tax, or such like charge, without common consent by act of parliament; and that none be called to make answer, or take such oath, or to give attendance, or be confined, or otherwise molested or disquieted concerning the same or for refusal thereof; and that no freeman, in any such manner as is before mentioned, be imprisoned or detained; and that your Majesty would be pleased to remove the said soldiers and mariners, and that your people may not be so burdened in time to come.

☑ **CITE EVIDENCE** How did the Petition of Right protect a person who is arrested?

☑ ASSESSMENT

1. **Analyze Interactions** Review the American Declaration of Independence. What similarities do you notice between the two documents?

2. **Determine Central Ideas** Which ideas in the English Bill of Rights and the Petition of Right influenced the formation of the United States government?

3. **Compare** How did the Magna Carta set the foundation for the English Bill of Rights?

4. **Determine Central Ideas** How did the English Bill of Rights make Parliament more powerful? Provide specific examples from the text in your response.

5. **Summarize** How does the Petition of Right recognize the rights of homeowners?

📶 **GO ONLINE** to access primary sources

Sir Isaac Newton was a key figure in the Scientific Revolution. Among his many discoveries were the laws of gravity.

Objectives

Describe how science led to the Enlightenment.

Explain the political philosophies of Hobbes, Locke, Voltaire, Montesquieu, and Rousseau.

Summarize the economic ideas of the physiocrats and Adam Smith.

Describe how Enlightenment ideas spread and influenced the arts.

Understand the role of enlightened despots.

Key Terms

natural law
Thomas Hobbes
John Locke
social contract
natural rights
philosophe
Montesquieu
Voltaire
Jean-Jacques
  Rousseau
laissez faire
Adam Smith

free market
free enterprise
  system
censorship
salon
baroque
rococo
enlightened despot
Joseph II

The Enlightenment

During the Scientific Revolution of the 1500s and 1600s, European scholars made advances in physics, chemistry, biology, and medicine. Like ancient scholars, the thinkers of the Scientific Revolution relied on reason, but they also developed a new "scientific method" to test their theories and observations. Using mathematics and the scientific method, they discovered a series of laws that governed the physical universe.

Scientific Revolution Leads to the Enlightenment

The Scientific Revolution, in turn, helped spark the Enlightenment in which thinkers emphasized the use of reason to uncover "natural" laws that governed human life. During the Enlightenment of the 1600s and 1700s, thinkers developed new ideas about government and basic human rights.

While scientists and mathematicians developed laws about natural phenomena like the law of gravity, European thinkers searched for similar laws that governed human life. Like scientists, they emphasized the power of reason, rather than religious beliefs. During the 1600s and 1700s, these thinkers developed new ideas about **natural laws**—unchanging principles, discovered through reason, that govern all human conduct.

Using the methods of the Scientific Revolution, European thinkers and reformers set out to study human behavior and solve the problems of society. The German philosopher Immanuel Kant used the word *enlightenment* to describe this new approach. During the Enlightenment, also called the Age of Reason, philosophers emphasized the power of human reason to uncover general laws of nature that shape all of human experience.

The Enlightenment continued a trend that began during the Renaissance. During the Middle Ages, Europe had been dominated by the Church. Feudal monarchs, like later absolute rulers, looked to the Church to justify their royal authority. The Renaissance placed a new emphasis on secularism and individual achievement.

The Scientific Revolution and Enlightenment also stressed science and natural law rather than religious authority. Enlightenment thinkers turned away from absolutism and divine right toward democracy and individual rights. Their ideas would encourage revolutionary leaders in Europe and the Americas. Though Christianity would remain a strong force in western culture, most governments became increasingly secular. The French Revolution in particular would see a radical decline in Church influence on government.

☑ **EXPLAIN** How was the Scientific Revolution directly related to the development of the concept of natural law?

Hobbes and Locke on the Role of Government

During the 1600s, two English thinkers, **Thomas Hobbes** and **John Locke,** set forth ideas that were to become key to the Enlightenment. Both men lived through the upheavals of the English Civil War. Yet they reached different conclusions about human nature and the purpose and proper role of government.

Hobbes Argues for Powerful Government In 1651, Thomas Hobbes outlined his ideas in a work titled *Leviathan.* In it, he argued that people were naturally cruel, greedy, and selfish. If not strictly controlled, they would fight, rob, and oppress one another. Life in the "state of nature"—without laws or other control—would be "solitary, poor, nasty, brutish, and short."

To escape that "brutish" life, said Hobbes, people entered into a **social contract,** an agreement by which they gave up their freedom for an organized society. Hobbes believed that only a powerful government could ensure an orderly society. For him, such a government was an absolute monarchy, which could impose order and compel obedience. Not surprisingly, Hobbes had supported the Stuart kings in their struggle against Parliament.

Locke Focuses on Natural Rights John Locke had a more optimistic view of human nature. He thought people were basically reasonable and moral.

Further, they had certain **natural rights,** or rights that belonged to all humans from birth. These included the right to life, liberty, and property.

In *Two Treatises of Government,* Locke argued that people formed governments to protect their natural rights. The best kind of government, he said, had limited power and was accepted by all citizens. Thus, unlike Hobbes, Locke rejected absolute monarchy.

Locke proposed a radical idea about this time. A government, he said, has an obligation to the people it governs. If a government fails its obligations or violates people's natural rights, the people have the right to overthrow that government. Given these ideas, Locke supported the overthrow of James II in the Glorious Revolution of 1688. In Locke's view, the king deserved to lose his throne because he had violated the rights of the English people.

Locke's idea would one day influence leaders of the American Revolution, such as Benjamin Franklin, Thomas Jefferson, and James Madison. Locke's idea of the right of revolution would also echo across Europe and Latin America in the centuries that followed.

>> This illustration from Thomas Hobbes's book *Leviathan* reflects his belief in a powerful ruler. The monarch rises above all society, just as the mythological Leviathan, or sea monster, rises above all the seas.

▶ BOUNCE to Activate Chart

☑ **CONTRAST** How did Hobbes and Locke differ in their views on the role of government?

The *Philosophes*

In the 1700s, France saw a flowering of Enlightenment thought. French **philosophes** (fee loh ZOHFS), or philosophers, felt that nothing was beyond the reach of human reason. As they examined ideas about government, law and society, they called for reforms to protect people's natural rights. Their ideas, like those of Locke, would shift political thought and strongly influence the development of democratic-republican government.

Montesquieu Calls for Separation of Powers An early and influential *philosophe* was Baron de **Montesquieu** (MAHN tus kyoo). Montesquieu studied the governments of Europe, from Italy to England. He read about ancient and medieval Europe, and learned about Chinese and Native American cultures. He sharply criticized absolute monarchy.

In 1748, Montesquieu published *The Spirit of the Laws,* in which he discussed governments throughout history. Montesquieu felt that the best way to protect liberty was to divide the various functions and powers of government among three branches: the legislative, executive, and judicial.

He also felt that each branch of government should be able to serve as a check on the other two, an idea that we call checks and balances. Montesquieu's beliefs would influence the Framers of the United States Constitution.

Voltaire Supports Freedom of Thought Probably the most famous of the *philosophes* was François-Marie Arouet, who took the name **Voltaire.** "My trade," said Voltaire, "is to say what I think." He used biting wit as a weapon to expose the abuses of his day. He targeted corrupt officials and idle aristocrats. With his pen, he battled inequality, injustice, and superstition. He detested the slave trade and deplored religious prejudice.

Voltaire's outspoken attacks offended both the French government and the Catholic Church. He was imprisoned and forced into exile. Even as he saw his books outlawed and sometimes even burned, he continued to defend the principle of freedom of speech.

Diderot Edits the *Encyclopedia* Denis Diderot (DEE duh roh) worked for years to produce a 28-volume set of books called the *Encyclopedia*. As the editor, Diderot did more than just compile articles. His purpose was "to change the general way

Montesquieu: Separation of Powers

	FUNCTION	EXAMPLES IN U.S. GOVERNMENT	EXAMPLES IN BRITISH GOVERNMENT
LEGISLATIVE	Creates law	Congress	Parliament
EXECUTIVE	Enforces law	President	Prime minister
JUDICIAL	Applies law	Supreme Court	U.K. Supreme Court

>> **Analyze Charts** Montesquieu believed in the separation of the powers of government into branches. Who currently heads the executive branch of government in the United States?

of thinking" by explaining ideas on topics such as government, philosophy, and religion.

Diderot's *Encyclopedia* included articles by leading thinkers of the day, including Montesquieu and Voltaire. In these articles, the *philosophes* denounced slavery, praised freedom of expression, and urged education for all. They attacked divine-right theory and traditional religions.

The French government viewed the *Encyclopedia* as an attack on public morals, and the pope threatened to excommunicate Roman Catholics who bought or read the volumes. Despite these and other efforts to ban the *Encyclopedia*, more than 4,000 copies were printed between 1751 and 1789.

Rousseau Promotes the Social Contract The most controversial *philosophe* was **Jean-Jacques Rousseau** (roo SOH). Rousseau believed that people in their natural state were basically good. This natural innocence, he felt, was corrupted by the evils of society, especially the unequal distribution of property.

In 1762, Rousseau set forth his ideas about government and society in *The Social Contract*. Rousseau felt that society placed too many limitations on people's behavior. He believed that some controls were necessary, but that they should be minimal. Additionally, only governments that had been freely elected should impose these controls. Rousseau put his faith in the "general will," or the best conscience of the people. The good of the community as a whole, he said, should be placed above individual interests. Woven through Rousseau's work is a hatred of all forms of political and economic oppression.

Women and the Enlightenment The Enlightenment slogan "free and equal" did not apply to women. Though the *philosophes* said women had natural rights, their rights were limited to the areas of home and family.

By the late 1700s, a small but growing number of women protested this view. Germaine de Staël in France and Mary Wollstonecraft in Britain argued that women were being excluded from the social contract itself. Their arguments, however, were ridiculed and often sharply condemned.

Wollstonecraft was a British writer and thinker. She accepted that a woman's first duty was to be a good mother but felt that a woman should be able to decide what was in her own interest without depending on her husband. In her book *A Vindication of the Rights of Woman*, Wollstonecraft

>> Writer Mary Wollstonecraft was a passionate advocate for social and educational equality for women.

called for equal education for girls and boys. Only education, she argued, could give women the tools they needed to participate equally with men in public life. Her ideas would influence the women's rights movement that emerged in the next century.

Enlightenment Thinkers and Slavery While Enlightenment philosophy declared that equality and the protection of natural rights belonged to all, this was not meant for everyone. These rights were often expressly applied to white males. Most Enlightenment thinkers saw no contradiction in this. Montesquieu, for example, did not support slavery, claiming it was "against nature's wishes." But he argued that enslavement of Africans was acceptable. In similar fashion, Immanuel Kant adhered to the same views. Diderot, however, felt slavery was morally wrong. "Slavery," he wrote, "violates religion, morality, natural laws, and all the rights of human nature."

☑ **IDENTIFY SUPPORTING DETAILS** What political philosophies did Jean-Jacques Rousseau set forth in *The Social Contract*?

New Economic Ideas

French thinkers known as physiocrats focused on economic reforms. Like the *philosophes*, physiocrats based their thinking on natural laws. The physiocrats claimed that their rational economic system was based on the natural laws of economics.

Laissez-Faire Economics Physiocrats rejected mercantilism, which required government regulation of the economy to achieve a favorable balance of trade. Instead, they urged a policy of **laissez faire** (les ay FEHR), allowing business to operate with little or no government interference. Physiocrats supported free trade and opposed tariffs.

Adam Smith and *The Wealth of Nations* Scottish economist **Adam Smith** greatly admired the physiocrats. In his influential work *The Wealth of Nations*, he argued that the **free market,** the natural forces of supply and demand, should be allowed to operate and regulate business. Smith favored a **free enterprise system** in which commerce and business compete for profit with little or no government interference.

Smith tried to show how manufacturing, trade, wages, profits, and economic growth were all linked to the market forces of supply and demand. Wherever there was a demand for goods or services, he said,

suppliers would seek to meet that demand in order to gain profits.

Smith was a strong supporter of laissez faire. However, he felt that government had a duty to protect society, administer justice, and provide public works. Adam Smith's ideas about free enterprise would help to shape productive economies in the 1800s and 1900s.

☑ **COMPARE AND CONTRAST** How is laissez-faire policy different from mercantilism?

Spread of Enlightenment Ideas

From France, Enlightenment ideas flowed across Europe and beyond. Everywhere, thinkers examined traditional beliefs and customs in the light of reason and found them flawed. Literate people eagerly read Diderot's *Encyclopedia* as well as small pamphlets turned out by printers that discussed a broad range of issues. More and more people came to believe that reform was necessary in order to achieve a just society.

During the Middle Ages, most Europeans had accepted without question a society based on divine-right rule, a strict class system, and a belief in heavenly reward for earthly suffering. In the Age of Reason, such ideas seemed unscientific and irrational. A just society, Enlightenment thinkers taught, should ensure social justice and happiness in this world. While many people embraced these new ideas, other groups rejected calls for change.

Writers Confront Censorship Most, but not all, government and church authorities felt they had a sacred duty to defend the old order. They believed that God had set up the old order.

To protect against the attacks of the Enlightenment, they waged a war of **censorship,** or restricting access to ideas and information. They banned and burned books and imprisoned writers.

To avoid censorship, writers like Montesquieu and Voltaire sometimes disguised their ideas in works of fiction. In the *Persian Letters*, Montesquieu used two fictional Persian travelers, named Usbek and Rica, to mock French society. The hero of Voltaire's satirical novel *Candide*, published in 1759, travels across Europe and even to the Americas and the Middle East in search of "the best of all possible worlds." Voltaire slyly uses the tale to expose the corruption and hypocrisy of European society.

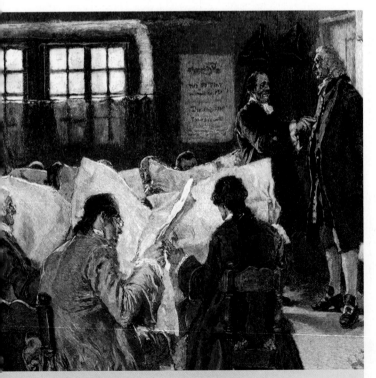

>> Enlightenment ideas spread through the printing of pamphlets and newspapers available to citizens.

In England, Jonathan Swift published *Gulliver's Travels* in 1726. The story uses fantasy to satirize, or make fun of, English political life.

In a famous scene, Gulliver is bound by the Lilliputians, tiny six-inch-tall characters, and is unable to move. The harder Gulliver tries to break free, the more the Lilliputians attack him. Swift uses the story to comment on the pettiness of nations and their rulers.

Salons Spread Ideas New literature, the arts, science, and philosophy were regular topics of discussion in **salons,** or informal social gatherings at which writers, artists, *philosophes*, and others exchanged ideas. The salon originated in the 1600s, when a group of noblewomen in Paris began inviting a few friends to their homes for poetry readings. By the 1700s, some middle-class women began holding salons. There, middle-class citizens met with nobles on an equal basis to discuss Enlightenment ideas.

Through the salons, Enlightenment ideas spread among the educated people of Europe. Madame Geoffrin (zhoh FRAN) ran one of the most respected salons. In her home on the Rue St. Honoré (roo sant ahn ur AY), she brought together the brightest and most talented people of her day.

The young musical genius Wolfgang Amadeus Mozart played for her guests, and Diderot was a regular at her weekly dinners for philosophers and poets.

Slow Change for the Majority At first, most Europeans were untouched by the spread of Enlightenment ideas. They remained what they had always been—peasants living in small rural villages. Echoes of serfdom still remained throughout Europe despite advances in Western Europe. Centuries-old traditions continued to shape European society, which only very slowly began to change.

By the late 1700s, ideas about equality and social justice had finally seeped into peasant villages across Europe. Some peasants welcomed ideas about equality and an end to the old order. Others did not. Upheavals in France and elsewhere quickened the pace of change. By the early 1800s, war and changing economic conditions began to transform life for people across Europe.

☑ **IDENTIFY CENTRAL IDEA** How did those opposed to Enlightenment ideas try to stop the spread of information?

>> During the Enlightenment, Madame Geoffrin's salons were popular gatherings for intellectual discussions.

Arts and Literature of the Enlightenment

In the 1600s and 1700s, the arts evolved to meet changing tastes. As in earlier periods, artists and composers had to please their patrons, the men and women who commissioned works from them or gave them jobs.

Changing Styles in Art and Architecture In the age of Louis XIV, courtly art and architecture were either in the Greek and Roman tradition or in a grand, ornate style known as **baroque.** Baroque paintings were huge, colorful, and full of excitement. They glorified historic battles or the lives of saints. Such works matched the grandeur of European courts at that time.

By the mid-1700s, architects and designers developed a new style that reflected changing tastes. Unlike the heavy splendor of the baroque, **rococo** art was lighter, more personal, elegant and charming. Rococo furniture and tapestries featured delicate shells and flowers, and more pastel colors were used. Portrait painters showed noble subjects in charming rural settings, surrounded by happy servants and pets. Although this style was criticized by the *philosophes* for its superficiality, it was popular with the upper and middle classes.

New Trends in Music During the Enlightenment, composers and musicians developed new forms of music. Their music followed ordered structured forms well suited to the Age of Reason. At the same time, their work transcended, or rose above, the culture of the Enlightenment and remains popular all over the world today.

Ballets and opera—plays set to music—were performed at royal courts, and opera houses sprang up from Italy to England. In the past, only the highest people in society could afford to commission new works of music. By the mid-1700s, wealthy middle class people commissioned works and hired musicians to perform them. Among the towering musical figures of the era was Johann Sebastian Bach.

A devout German Lutheran, Bach wrote beautiful religious works for organ and choirs. His skills playing the organ and harpsichord were recognized during his lifetime, but he is now generally regarded as one of the greatest composers in history. Bach was a master of counterpoint, a technique that weaves two or more independent melodies together to create a new harmony.

Another German-born composer, George Frideric Handel, spent much of his life in England, where his music was extremely popular with the general public. There, he wrote *Water Music* and other pieces for King George I, as well as more than 30 operas. His most celebrated choral work, the *Messiah*, is often performed at Christmas and Easter. The stirring "Hallelujah Chorus" from the *Messiah* conveys universal themes of joy and celebration.

In 1761, a six-year-old prodigy, Wolfgang Amadeus Mozart, burst onto the European scene. He gained instant celebrity as a composer and performer.

During his brief life, the young man from Salzburg in Austria composed an amazing variety of music with remarkable speed. His operas reflected Enlightenment criticism of a class-ridden world full of hypocrisy and lies. At age 35, Mozart died in poverty, leaving a musical legacy that thrives today.

The Novel Takes Shape By the 1700s, literature developed new forms and a wider audience. Middle-class readers, for example, liked stories about their own times told in straightforward prose. One result was an outpouring of novels, or long works of prose fiction.

English novelists wrote many popular stories. Daniel Defoe wrote *Robinson Crusoe*, an exciting tale about a sailor shipwrecked on a tropical island. In a novel called *Pamela*, Samuel Richardson used a series of letters to tell a story about a servant girl. This technique was adopted by other authors of the period.

☑ **DRAW CONCLUSIONS** How did literature change as Enlightenment ideas spread?

>> Johann Sebastian Bach plays the piano with his family in an 1870 painting. Many of Bach's children became important musicians.

🔲 BOUNCE to Activate Gallery

The Enlightened Despots

Discussions of Enlightenment theories enlivened the courts of Europe. *Philosophes* hoped to convince European rulers to adopt their ideas and introduce reforms. Some monarchs did accept Enlightenment ideas. They became **enlightened despots,** or absolute rulers who used their power to bring about political and social change.

Frederick the Great As king of Prussia from 1740 to 1786, Frederick II exerted extremely tight control over his subjects. Still, he saw himself as the "first servant of the state," with a duty to work for the common good.

Frederick openly praised Voltaire's work and invited him to Berlin. He asked French scientists to help him set up a Prussian academy of science. As king, he tried to reduce the use of torture and allowed a free press. He also tolerated religious differences, welcoming victims of religious persecution. "In my kingdom," he said, "everyone can go to heaven in his own fashion."

Most of Frederick's reforms were directed at making the Prussian government more efficient. To do this, he reorganized the government's civil service and simplified laws. Although Frederick did believe in enlightened reform, his efforts to improve government meant more power for himself.

Catherine the Great Catherine II, empress of Russia, read the works of the *philosophes* and exchanged letters with Voltaire and Diderot. She praised Voltaire as someone who had "fought the united enemies of humankind: superstition, fanaticism, ignorance, trickery." Catherine admired the Enlightenment ideas of equality and liberty.

Catherine experimented with implementing Enlightenment ideas. Early in her reign, she made some limited reforms in law and government. Catherine abolished torture and granted some religious tolerance for Christians and Muslims in her lands. However, she increased restrictions and taxes on Jews. She granted nobles a charter of rights and spoke out against serfdom. Still, like Frederick in Prussia, Catherine did not intend to give up power. Her main political contribution to Russia was an expanded empire.

Joseph II The most radical of the enlightened despots was **Joseph II** of Austria, the son and successor of Maria Theresa. Joseph was an eager student of the Enlightenment, and he traveled in disguise among his subjects to learn of their problems.

Like his mother, Joseph worked to modernize Austria's government. He chose talented middle-class officials rather than nobles to head departments and imposed a range of political and legal reforms. Despite opposition, Joseph granted more rights to and eased some restrictions on Protestants and Jews in his Catholic empire. He ended censorship by allowing a free press and attempted to bring the Catholic Church under royal control. He sold the property of many monasteries that were not involved in education or care of the sick and used the proceeds to build hospitals. Joseph even abolished serfdom. Like many of his other reforms, however, this measure was canceled after his death.

☑ **ANALYZE INFORMATION** What did Frederick the Great mean by, "In my kingdom, everyone can go to heaven in his own fashion"?

>> Catherine the Great expressed an interest in many Enlightenment ideas. She often met with scholars to learn more. **Interpret** What type of scholar do you think she is meeting in this painting? Explain.

☑ ASSESSMENT

1. **Explain** Explain the influence of scientific ideas on the progression of thought from the Scientific Revolution to the Enlightenment.

2. **Identify Central Ideas** What are some ways in which Enlightenment ideas spread?

3. **Identify Central Ideas** Explain the components of the free-enterprise system.

4. **Draw Conclusions** Why might some absolute monarchs have been willing to consider Enlightenment ideas, while others were not?

5. **Identify Central Ideas** In what way were the ideas of John Locke and Jean-Jacques Rousseau similar?

6. **Connections to Today** How did the Enlightenment change the way some monarchs ruled? How do you think most monarchs rule today?

📶 **GO ONLINE** to access this biography: John Locke

The Enlightenment and Slavery

Enlightenment philosophers supported the idea of individual freedoms and liberties. At the time, the existence of a flourishing slave trade contradicted those ideals. The views presented here represent the differing views on slavery and race held by Enlightenment thinkers.

The *Encyclopedia*, edited by French philosopher and writer Denis Diderot, was published between 1751 and 1772. This *Encyclopedia* article presents Louis de Jaucourt's viewpoint on the slave trade. The second excerpt, from *Observations on the Feeling of the Beautiful and the Sublime,* was written by Immanuel Kant, a German Enlightenment philosopher. It states his views about Africans.

Note: Both authors use the term *Negro* in these excerpts. The term *Negroes* is an outdated term describing Black people.

As you read, consider the arguments presented by both philosophers to support their different views. Then answer the questions to compare their perspectives.

>> Encyclopedia title page, first edition 1751

Primary Source 1

Article from the *Encyclopedia*, "Slave Trade" by Louis de Jaucourt

The Slave Trade (Commerce of Africa) is the buying of unfortunate Negroes by Europeans on the coast of Africa to use as slaves in their colonies.

Negroes, says a modern Englishman full of enlightenment and humanity, have not become slaves by the right of war; neither do they deliver themselves voluntarily into bondage.... Nobody is unaware that they are bought from their own princes..., and that traders have them transported in the same way as their other goods, either in their colonies or in America, where they are displayed for sale.

If commerce of this kind can be justified by a moral principle, there is no crime, however atrocious it may be, that cannot be made legitimate. Kings, princes, and magistrates are not the proprietors of their subjects: they do not, therefore, have the right to dispose of their liberty and to sell them as slaves.

☑ **DETERMINE AUTHOR'S POINT OF VIEW**
According to Jaucourt, is it acceptable for Europeans to buy Africans to use as slaves? Explain why or why not.

On the other hand, no man has the right to buy them or to make himself their master. Men and their liberty are not objects of commerce; they can be neither sold nor bought nor paid for at any price. We must conclude from this that a man whose slave has run away should only blame himself, since he had acquired for money illicit goods whose acquisition is prohibited by all the laws of humanity and equality.

There is not, therefore, a single one of these unfortunate people regarded only as slaves who does not have the right to be declared free, since he has never lost his freedom. Consequently the sale that has been completed is invalid in itself. This Negro does not divest himself and can never divest himself of his natural right; he carries it everywhere with him, and he can demand everywhere that he be allowed to enjoy it.

☑ **EXPLAIN AN ARGUMENT** What does Jaucourt say about the right of traders to buy and sell slaves? How does he argue that all slaves have the right to be declared free?

Primary Source 2

From *Observations on the Feeling of the Beautiful and the Sublime* by Immanuel Kant

The Negroes of Africa have by nature no feeling that rises above the trifling. Mr. Hume [a Scottish philosopher] challenges anyone to cite a single example in which a Negro has shown talents, and asserts that among the hundreds of thousands of blacks who are transported elsewhere from their countries, although many of them have even been set free, still not a single one was ever found who presented anything great in art or science or any other praiseworthy quality, even though among the whites some continually rise aloft from the lowest rabble, and through superior gifts earn respect in the world.

☑ **CITE EVIDENCE** What evidence does Kant provide to show the inferiority of "the Negroes of Africa"?

So fundamental is the difference between these two races of man, and it appears to be as great in regard to mental capacities as in color. The religion of fetishes so widespread among them is perhaps a sort of idolatry that sinks as deeply into the trifling as appears to be possible to human nature. A bird's feather, a cow's horn, a conch shell, or any other common object, as soon as it becomes consecrated by a few words, is an object of veneration and of invocation in swearing oaths. The blacks are very vain but in the Negro's way, and so talkative that they must be driven apart from each other with thrashings.

☑ **DRAW INFERENCES** How does Kant view the religion of African cultures?

☑ ASSESSMENT

1. **Identify** According to Jaucourt, do Europeans know how Africans become slaves? Identify the stages of the enslavement process.

2. **Summarize** How does Kant characterize the "Negroes of Africa"?

3. **Compare and Contrast** How does each author address the question of slavery? What arguments are used to justify the conclusions?

4. **Analyze** As a philosopher of the Enlightenment, could Kant's observations in his essay be justified as scientific? Explain.

5. **Draw Conclusions** Why do you think some enlightenment thinkers supported slavery?

12.5

England had a vast trading network that included its thirteen North American colonies. This image shows the busy port of Charleston, South Carolina.

 BOUNCE to Activate Flipped Video

Objectives

Describe how Britain became a global power.

Understand the events and ideas leading up to the American Revolution, including the impact of the Enlightenment.

Summarize key events of the American Revolution.

Identify the political and legal ideas in the Declaration of Independence and the United States Constitution.

Key Terms

George III
Stamp Act
George Washington
Benjamin Franklin
Thomas Jefferson
popular sovereignty
Yorktown, Virginia
Treaty of Paris
James Madison
federal republic
checks and balances

The American Revolution

By the 1770s, Britain was a major power in Europe with territories around the globe. Although upheavals in the 1600s had created a limited monarchy, a new king was eager to recover powers the crown had lost.

Britain Becomes a Global Power

Trade and Commerce Britain's rise to global prominence had multiple causes. England's location and long seagoing tradition placed it in a position to build a vast trading network. By the 1600s, England had trading outposts and colonies in the West Indies, North America, and India. A new merchant class expanded trade and competed vigorously with Spanish, Portuguese, and Dutch traders.

During the 1700s, thousands of settlers sailed to North America to build colonies. At the same time, British merchants expanded into the profitable slave trade, carrying enslaved people from West Africa to the Americas.

Britain's economic policies added to its prosperity. England offered a climate favorable to business and commerce. It put fewer restrictions on trade than some of its neighbors, such as France.

Territorial Expansion In the 1700s, Britain was generally on the winning side in European conflicts. In the Treaty of Utrecht, which ended the War of the Spanish Succession, France gave

Nova Scotia and Newfoundland to Britain. As a result of the French and Indian War, Britain gained all of French Canada, as well as rich islands in the Caribbean in 1763.

At home, England grew by merging with neighboring Scotland. In 1701, the Act of Union united the two countries in the United Kingdom of Great Britain. The union brought economic advantages.

Free trade between both lands created a larger market for farmers and manufacturers. The United Kingdom also included Wales, and in 1801 Ireland would be added to Great Britain.

George III Takes Power In 1760, **George III** began a 60-year reign. Unlike his German father and grandfather, the new king was born in England. He spoke English and loved Britain. But George was eager to recover the powers the crown had lost since the Glorious Revolution. Following his mother's advice, "George, be a king!" he set out to reassert royal power. He wanted to end Whig domination, choose his own ministers, dissolve the cabinet system, and make Parliament follow his will.

Gradually, George found seats in Parliament for "the king's friends." With their help, he began to assert his leadership. Many of his policies, however, would prove disastrous. He angered colonists in North America, leading 13 English colonies to declare independence.

Britain's loss of its American colonies discredited the king. Increasingly, too, he suffered from bouts of mental illness. By 1788, cabinet rule was restored in Britain.

☑ **ANALYZE INFORMATION** What were some of the elements that led to Britain's rise to global prominence in the 1700s?

The British Colonies in America

By 1750, a string of prosperous colonies stretched along the eastern coast of North America. They were part of Britain's growing empire. Colonial cities such as Boston, New York, and Philadelphia were busy commercial centers that linked North America to the West Indies, Africa, and Europe. Colonial shipyards produced many vessels for this trade.

Britain applied mercantilist policies to its colonies in an attempt to strengthen its own economy by exporting more than it imported. To this end, in the 1600s, Parliament had passed the Navigation Acts to regulate colonial trade and manufacturing. For the most part, however, these acts were not rigorously enforced. Therefore, activities like smuggling were common and not considered crimes by the colonists.

By the mid-1700s, the colonies were home to diverse religious and ethnic groups. Social

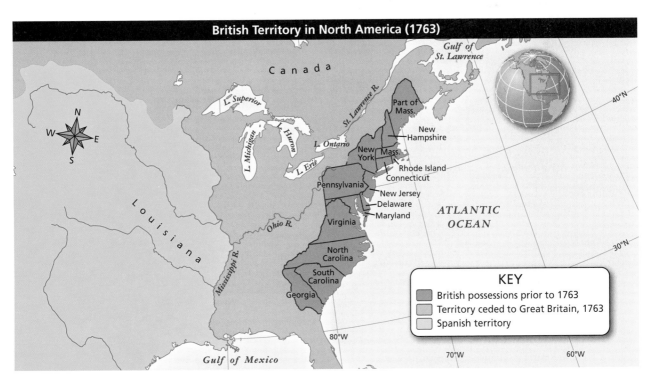

British Territory in North America (1763)

KEY
British possessions prior to 1763
Territory ceded to Great Britain, 1763
Spanish territory

>> **Analyze Maps** What do all of the colonies on this map have in common?

distinctions were more blurred than in Europe, although wealthy landowners and merchants dominated government and society. In politics, as in much else, there was a good deal of free discussion.

Colonists felt entitled to the rights of English citizens, and their colonial assemblies exercised much control over local affairs. Many also had an increasing sense of their own destiny separate from Britain.

☑ **DESCRIBE** Why did Americans believe they had the same rights as English citizens?

Discontent in the Colonies

The French and Indian War had drained the British treasury. George III and his advisors insisted that colonists pay the costs of their own defense, including troops still stationed in frontier posts.

Growing Tensions Parliament passed new taxes on the colonies. The Sugar Act of 1764 taxed imports, while the **Stamp Act** of 1765 taxed items such as newspapers and pamphlets. Although the new taxes were not burdensome, colonists bitterly resented them as an attack on their rights. "No taxation

>> Benjamin Franklin, Thomas Jefferson, John Adams, Robert R. Livingston, and Roger Sherman served as the committee to draft the Declaration of Independence.

 BOUNCE to Activate Illustration

without representation," they protested. Since they had no representatives in Parliament, they believed that Parliament had no right to tax them. Parliament repealed the Stamp Act, but asserted its right to tax the colonists.

A series of violent clashes intensified the colonists' anger. In March 1770, British soldiers in Boston opened fire on a crowd that was pelting them with stones and snowballs. Colonists called the death of five protesters the Boston Massacre.

Then, in December 1773, a handful of colonists hurled a cargo of recently arrived British tea into the harbor to protest a tax on tea. The incident became known as the Boston Tea Party. When Parliament passed harsh laws to punish Massachusetts, other colonies rallied to help Massachusetts.

As tensions rose, representatives from 12 colonies gathered in Philadelphia in 1774. At the First Continental Congress, representatives discussed how to respond to Britain's harsh moves against Massachusetts.

Among the participants were the radical but fair-minded John Adams, the Virginia planter and soldier **George Washington,** and **Benjamin Franklin,** a leading figure of the Enlightenment in America.

Declaring Independence In April 1775, the crisis between the colonists and the British exploded into war. At the battles of Lexington and Concord in Massachusetts, colonists clashed with British troops—the opening shots of the American Revolution. Soon after, the Second Continental Congress met and set up a Continental Army with George Washington in command.

In 1776, Congress took a momentous step, voting to declare independence from Britain. Young **Thomas Jefferson** of Virginia was the principal author of the Declaration of Independence. Jefferson's political philosophy was heavily influenced by Enlightenment thinkers, especially John Locke. The document clearly reflects Locke's political and legal ideas, including the idea of natural law. It announced that people have "certain inalienable rights, that among them are life, liberty, and the pursuit of happiness."

In the Declaration, Jefferson further stated that people had the right "to alter or to abolish" unjust governments, echoing Locke's ideas about the right to revolt. He then carefully detailed the colonists' grievances against Britain, such as imposing taxes without consent, dissolving colonial legislatures at will, and depriving many colonists of their legal right to trial by jury. Because Parliament had trampled colonists' natural rights, he argued, the colonists had the right to rebel and set up a new government to protect them.

The document spelled out the political principle of **popular sovereignty,** the idea that all government power comes from the people. Aware of the risks involved, on July 4, 1776, American leaders signed the Declaration, pledging "our lives, our fortunes, and our sacred honor" to the cause of the United States of America.

☑ **DRAW CONCLUSIONS** Why did the colonists object so strongly to the idea of taxation without representation?

The American Revolution

At first, the American cause looked bleak. The colonists themselves were divided. About one third of the American colonists were Loyalists, or those who supported Britain. Many others refused to fight for either side.

Military Strengths and Weaknesses The colonists faced severe military disadvantages as well. The British had a large number of trained soldiers, a huge fleet, and plentiful money. They occupied most major American cities. The Americans lacked military resources, had little money to pay soldiers, and did not have a strategic plan.

Still, the colonists had some advantages. They were battling for their own independence on their own familiar home ground. Although the British held New York and Philadelphia, colonists controlled the countryside. And they had a strong, inspiring military leader in George Washington.

As the war unfolded, the British relied on Loyalists as well as Native American groups, some of whom sided with them. The British also sought support among African Americans held in slavery. They offered freedom to any who would join their side.

Alliance with France The first turning point in the war came in 1777, when the Americans triumphed over the British at the Battle of Saratoga. This victory persuaded France to join the Americans against its old rival, Britain. The alliance brought the Americans desperately needed supplies, trained soldiers, and French warships. Spurred by the French example,

>> George Washington encouraged his men to fight on despite heavy odds.

the Netherlands and Spain added their support.

Hard times continued, however. In the brutal winter of 1777–1778, Continental troops at Valley Forge suffered from cold, hunger, and disease. Throughout this crisis and others, Washington was patient, courageous, and determined. He held the ragged army together.

Victory for the Americans Finally, in 1781, with the help of a French fleet, Washington forced the surrender of a British army at **Yorktown, Virginia.** With that defeat, the British war effort crumbled.

Two years later, American, British, and French diplomats signed the **Treaty of Paris,** ending the war. Britain formally recognized the independence of the United States of America. Britain also accepted the new nation's western frontier as the Mississippi River.

☑ **GENERATE EXPLANATIONS** Why was the selection of George Washington as head of the American army essential to the ultimate success of the American Revolution?

>> James Madison is known as the father of the U.S. Constitution because he was instrumental in drafting the document.

>> The U.S. Constitution, shown here, set up a series of checks and balances in which each branch of government can limit the powers of the other branches.

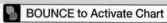

BOUNCE to Activate Chart

The United States Constitution

The Articles of Confederation was the new nation's first constitution. It proved to be too weak to rule effectively. To address this problem, the nation's leaders gathered once more. Among them were George Washington, **James Madison,** and Benjamin Franklin. During the hot summer of 1787, they hammered out the Constitution of the United States. This framework for a strong, flexible government has remained in place for more than 200 years.

The Impact of the Enlightenment The Framers of the Constitution had absorbed the ideas of Locke, Montesquieu, and Rousseau. Like Rousseau, the framers saw government in terms of a social contract among members of the community. A central feature of the new federal government—the separation of powers among the legislative, executive, and judicial branches—was borrowed directly from Montesquieu.

The Framers were also influenced by the ideas of an English legal scholar of the 1700s, William Blackstone, who shared many of Locke's ideas. Blackstone's writings greatly informed the legal ideas contained in the Constitution and a good portion of American law to the present day. For example, his famous statement that "the law holds it better that ten guilty persons escape, than that one innocent party suffer" is reflected in the Constitutional rights given to people accused of crimes.

A Framework of Government The Constitution created a **federal republic,** with power divided between the federal, or national, government and the states. It provided for both an elected legislature and an elected president.

To prevent any branch of government from becoming too powerful, the Constitution set up a series of **checks and balances.** Under this system, each branch of the government has the right to monitor and limit each of the other branches.

The Bill of Rights, or the first ten amendments to the Constitution, recognized the idea that citizens have basic rights that the government must protect. These included freedom of religion, speech, and the press.

It also affirmed legal ideas, such as the right to trial by jury and the principle that no one may be forced to testify against him- or herself. The Bill of Rights, like the Constitution, put Enlightenment ideas into practice.

Symbol of Freedom From the start, the new republic was a symbol of freedom for many. The Declaration of Independence, along with the Bill of Rights, put forth the idea that there are certain rights that belong to everyone. The American Revolution became the example to follow. Nationalists in other countries demanded freedom. Today, it is still a prototype for wars of independence.

In 1789, most countries in Europe were ruled by hereditary absolute monarchs. The United States stood out as a beacon to Europeans who took up the cry for liberty and freedom.

Demands for written constitutions and a limit to royal power would bring great changes to Europe in the decades ahead. Revolutionaries in Latin America were also inspired by the example of the United States.

Under the Constitution, citizens enjoy many rights, but they also have many responsibilities. They are expected to vote, sit on juries, and keep informed on topics of local and national interest. Noncitizens who reside in the United States also enjoy its constitutional rights and protections and have responsibilities such as paying taxes and abiding by local, state, and federal laws.

☑ **ANALYZE CONTEXT** How did the ideas of the Enlightenment influence the United States Constitution and the Bill of Rights?

☑ ASSESSMENT

1. **Identify Main Ideas** How did trade play a role in Britain's becoming a global power?

2. **Identify Cause and Effect** Why did North America's geography make it difficult for the British to win the war?

3. **Check Understanding** Why did colonists wait to declare independence from Britain?

4. **Hypothesize** Why do you think many countries over time have emulated the principles outlined in the Declaration of Independence and the U.S. Constitution?

5. **Describe** In what way does the Bill of Rights put the ideas of the Enlightenment into practice?

6. **Connections to Today** Why did the colonists look to the establishment of a republic as an alternative to the monarchy in Britain? What safeguards against an individual gaining too much power remain in place today?

Declaration of Independence

By signing the Declaration of Independence, members of the Continental Congress sent a clear message to Britain that the American colonies were free and independent states. Starting with its preamble, the document spells out all the reasons the people of the United States have the right to break away from Britain.

>> Presenting the Declaration of Independence

Primary Source

When in the Course of human events, it becomes necessary for one people to dissolve the political bands which have connected them with another, and to assume among the powers of the earth, the separate and equal station to which the Laws of Nature and of Nature's God entitle them, a decent respect to the opinions of mankind requires that they should declare the causes which impel [force] them to the separation.

We hold these truths to be self-evident, that all men are created equal, that they are endowed [gifted] by their Creator with certain unalienable [cannot be taken away] Rights, that among these are Life, Liberty and the pursuit of Happiness. That to secure these rights, Governments are instituted among Men, deriving their just powers from the consent of the governed. That whenever any Form of Government becomes destructive of these ends, it is the Right of the People to alter or to abolish it, and to institute new Government, laying its foundation on such principles and organizing its powers in such form, as to them shall seem most likely to effect their Safety and Happiness. Prudence [cautiousness],

indeed, will dictate that Governments long established should not be changed for light and transient causes; and accordingly all experience hath shown that mankind are more disposed to suffer, while evils are sufferable, than to right themselves by abolishing the forms to which they are accustomed. But when a long train of abuses and usurpations [unjust uses of power], pursuing invariably the same Object evinces a design to reduce them under absolute Despotism [rule of absolute power], it is their right, it is their duty, to throw off such Government, and to provide new Guards for their future security. Such has been the patient sufferance of these Colonies; and such is now the necessity which constrains them to alter their former Systems of Government. The history of the present King of Great Britain is a history of repeated injuries and usurpations, all having in direct object the establishment of an absolute Tyranny over these States. To prove this, let Facts be submitted to a candid world.

He has refused his Assent to Laws, the most wholesome and necessary for the public good. . . . He has refused to pass other Laws for the accommodation of large districts of people, unless those people would relinquish [give up] the right of Representation in the Legislature, a right inestimable [priceless] to them and formidable to tyrants only. . . . He has dissolved Representative Houses repeatedly, for opposing with manly firmness his invasions on the rights of the people. . . .

He has kept among us, in times of peace, Standing Armies without the Consent of our legislatures. . . . He has combined with others to subject us to a jurisdiction foreign to our constitution, and unacknowledged by our laws; giving his Assent to their Acts of pretended Legislation: For quartering [lodging] large bodies of armed troops among us: For protecting them, by a mock Trial, from punishment for any Murders which they should commit on the Inhabitants of these States: For cutting off our Trade with all parts of the world: For imposing Taxes on us without our Consent: For depriving us in many cases, of the benefits of Trial by Jury: For transporting us beyond Seas to be tried for pretended offences: For abolishing the free System of English Laws in a neighbouring Province, establishing therein an Arbitrary government, and enlarging its Boundaries so as to render it at once an example and fit instrument for introducing the same absolute rule into these Colonies:

. . . He has abdicated Government here, by declaring us out of his Protection and waging War against us . . .

In every stage of these Oppressions We have Petitioned for Redress [correction of wrongs] in the most humble terms: Our repeated Petitions have been answered only by repeated injury. A Prince, whose character is thus marked by every act which may define a Tyrant, is unfit to be the ruler of a free people.

Nor have We been wanting in attentions to our British brethren. We have warned them from time to time of attempts by their legislature to extend an unwarrantable jurisdiction over us. They too have been deaf to the voice of justice and of consanguinity [relation by blood].

We, therefore, the Representatives of the United States of America, in General Congress, Assembled, appealing to the Supreme Judge of the world for the rectitude [justness] of our intentions, do, in the Name, and by Authority of the good People of these Colonies, solemnly publish and declare, That these United Colonies are, and of Right ought to be Free and Independent States; that they are Absolved from all Allegiance to the British Crown, and that all political connection between them and the State of Great Britain, is and ought to be totally dissolved; and that as Free and Independent States, they have full Power to levy War, conclude Peace, contract Alliances, establish Commerce, and to do all other Acts and Things which Independent States may of right do.

☑ ASSESSMENT

1. **Identify Cause and Effect** How might the ideas about equality expressed in the Declaration of Independence have influenced later historical movements, such as the abolitionist movement and the women's suffrage movement?

2. **Identify Key Steps in a Process** Why was the Declaration of Independence a necessary document for the founding of the new nation?

3. **Draw Inferences** English philosopher John Locke wrote that government should protect "life, liberty, and estate." How do you think Locke's writing influenced ideas about government put forth in the Declaration of Independence?

4. **Analyze Structure** How does the declaration organize its key points from beginning to end?

12.6

Delegates of the Third Estate took the Tennis Court Oath in June 1789 and vowed to create a new constitution.

 BOUNCE to Activate Flipped Video

Objectives

Describe the social divisions of France's old order.

Trace the causes of the French Revolution.

Identify the reforms enacted by the National Assembly, including the Declaration of the Rights of Man and the Citizen.

Key Terms

ancien régime
estates
bourgeoisie
deficit spending
Louis XVI
Jacques Necker
Estates-General
cahiers
Tennis Court Oath
Bastille
faction
Marquis de Lafayette
Olympe de Gouges
Marie Antoinette

The French Revolution Begins

On April 28, 1789, unrest exploded at a Paris wallpaper factory. A rumor had spread that the factory owner was planning to cut wages even though bread prices were soaring. Enraged workers vandalized the owner's home and then rioted through the streets.

The Old Regime in France

The rioting reflected growing unrest in Paris and throughout France. In 1789, France faced not only an economic crisis but also widespread demands for far-reaching changes. By July, the hungry, unemployed, poorly paid people of Paris were taking up arms against the government, a move that would trigger the French Revolution.

In 1789, France, like the rest of Europe, still clung to an outdated social system that had emerged in the Middle Ages. Under this **ancien régime,** or old order, everyone in France belonged to one of three social classes, or **estates.** The First Estate was made up of the clergy; the Second Estate was made up of the nobility; and the Third Estate comprised the vast majority of the population.

First Estate: the Clergy During the Middle Ages, the Church had exerted great influence throughout Christian Europe. In 1789, the French clergy still enjoyed enormous wealth and privilege. The Church owned about 10 percent of the land, collected tithes, and paid no direct taxes to the state. High Church leaders such as

GO ONLINE to access your digital course

bishops and abbots were usually nobles who lived very well. Parish priests, however, often came from humble origins and might be as poor as their peasant congregations.

The First Estate did provide some social services. Nuns, monks, and priests ran schools, hospitals, and orphanages. But during the Enlightenment, *philosophes* targeted the Church for reform.

They criticized the idleness of some clergy, the Church's interference in politics, and its intolerance of dissent. In response, many clergy condemned the Enlightenment for undermining religion and moral order.

Second Estate: the Nobility The Second Estate was the titled nobility of French society. In the Middle Ages, noble knights had defended the land. In the 1600s, Richelieu and Louis XIV had crushed the nobles' military power but had given them other rights—under strict royal control. Those rights included top jobs in government, the army, the courts, and the Church.

At Versailles, ambitious nobles competed for royal appointments while idle courtiers enjoyed endless entertainments. Many nobles, however, lived far from the center of power. Though they owned land, they received little financial income. As a result, they felt the pinch of trying to maintain their status in a period of rising prices.

Many ambitious nobles came to hate absolutism and resented the royal bureaucracy that employed middle-class men in positions that once had been reserved for them. They feared losing their traditional privileges, especially their freedom from paying taxes.

Third Estate: From Middle Class to Peasantry The Third Estate was the most diverse social class. At the top sat the **bourgeoisie** (boor zhwah ZEE), or middle class. The bourgeoisie included prosperous bankers, merchants, and manufacturers, as well as lawyers, doctors, journalists, and professors.

The bulk of the Third Estate, however, consisted of rural peasants. Some were prosperous landowners who hired laborers to work for them. Others were tenant farmers or day laborers.

Among the poorest members of the Third Estate were urban workers. They included apprentices, journeymen, and others who worked in industries such as printing or cloth making.

Many women and men earned a meager living as servants, construction workers, or street sellers of everything from food to pots and pans. A large

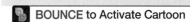

>> **Analyze Political Cartoons** What does this cartoon say about the relationship between the three social classes in France?

🅱 BOUNCE to Activate Cartoon

>> Merchants were among the bourgeoisie, France's middle class.

number of the urban poor were unemployed. To survive, some turned to begging or crime.

Widespread Discontent From rich to poor, members of the Third Estate resented the privileges enjoyed by their social "betters." Wealthy bourgeois families in the Third Estate could buy political office and even titles, but the best jobs were still reserved for nobles. Urban workers earned miserable wages. Even the smallest rise in the price of bread, their main food, brought the threat of greater hunger or even starvation. In 1775, before the French Revolution, peasants rioted over the high price of bread in an event called the "Flour War."

Because of traditional privileges, the First and Second Estates paid almost no taxes. Peasants were burdened by taxes on everything from land to soap to salt. Though they were technically free, many owed fees and services that dated back to medieval times, such as the corvée (kawr VAY), which was unpaid labor to repair roads and bridges.

Peasants were also incensed when nobles, hurt by rising prices, tried to reimpose old manor dues. In towns and cities, Enlightenment ideas about equality led people to question the inequalities of the old regime. Why, people demanded, should the first two estates have such great privileges at the expense of the majority? Throughout France, the Third Estate called for the privileged classes to pay their share.

☑ **CONTRAST** How did the lives of the Third Estate differ from the lives of clergy and nobles?

France's Economic Crisis

Along with social unrest, France faced economic woes, especially a mushrooming financial crisis. The crisis was caused in part by years of **deficit spending.** This occurs when a government spends more money than it takes in.

A Nation in Debt Louis XIV had left France deeply in debt. The Seven Years' War and the American Revolution strained the treasury even further. Costs generally had risen in the 1700s, and the lavish court soaked up millions. To bridge the gap between income and expenses, the government borrowed more and more money. By 1789, half of the government's income from taxes went to paying the interest on this enormous debt.

To solve the financial crisis, the government would have to increase taxes, reduce expenses, or both. However, the nobles and clergy fiercely resisted any attempt to end their exemption from taxes.

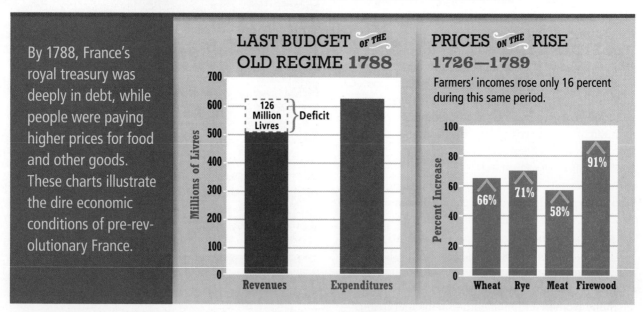

FRANCE IN ECONOMIC CRISIS

By 1788, France's royal treasury was deeply in debt, while people were paying higher prices for food and other goods. These charts illustrate the dire economic conditions of pre-revolutionary France.

LAST BUDGET OF THE OLD REGIME 1788

Millions of Livres

126 Million Livres } Deficit

Revenues   Expenditures

PRICES ON THE RISE 1726—1789

Farmers' incomes rose only 16 percent during this same period.

Percent Increase

Wheat 66%   Rye 71%   Meat 58%   Firewood 91%

>> **Analyze Charts** As France's deficit grew, so did the suffering of the poor. How much did the price of firewood rise between 1726 and 1789?

A Crumbling Economy Other economic woes added to the crisis. A general economic decline began in the 1770s. Then in the late 1780s, bad harvests set food prices soaring and brought hunger to poorer peasants and city dwellers.

Hard times and lack of food inflamed these people. In towns, people rioted, demanding bread. In the countryside, peasants began to attack the manor houses of nobles.

Failure of Reform The heirs of Louis XIV were not the right men to solve the economic crisis that afflicted France. Louis XV, who ruled from 1715 to 1774, pursued pleasure before serious business and ran up more debts.

The next king, **Louis XVI,** was well-meaning but weak and indecisive. He did wisely choose **Jacques Necker,** a financial expert, as an advisor. Necker urged the king to reduce extravagant court spending, reform government, and abolish burdensome tariffs on internal trade. When Necker proposed taxing the First and Second Estates, however, the nobles and high clergy forced the king to dismiss him.

As the crisis deepened, the pressure for reform mounted. The wealthy and powerful classes demanded, however, that the king summon the **Estates-General,** the legislative body consisting of representatives of the three estates, before making any changes. No French king had called the Estates-General for 175 years. They feared that nobles would try to recover the feudal powers they had lost under absolute rule.

To reform-minded nobles, the Estates-General seemed to offer a chance of carrying out changes like the ones the English had achieved through the Glorious Revolution. They hoped to bring the absolute monarch under the control of nobles and guarantee their own privileges.

☑ **DESCRIBE** What were some of the main reasons France was in serious economic trouble in the late 1700s?

Louis XVI Calls the Estates-General

As 1788 came to a close, France tottered on the verge of bankruptcy. Bread riots were spreading, and nobles, fearful of taxes, were denouncing royal tyranny. A baffled Louis XVI finally summoned the Estates-General to meet at Versailles the following year.

>> The poor made up the majority of the Third Estate. Here, they are shown rioting during the "Flour War," a brief 1775 uprising brought on by higher bread prices.

The Cahiers In preparation, Louis had all three estates prepare **cahiers** (kah YAYZ), or notebooks, listing their grievances. Many cahiers called for reforms such as fairer taxes, freedom of the press, or regular meetings of the Estates-General. In one town, shoemakers denounced regulations that made leather so expensive they could not afford to make shoes. Servant girls in the city of Toulouse demanded the right to leave service when they wanted and insisted that "after a girl has served her master for many years, she receive some reward for her service."

The cahiers testified to boiling class resentments. One called tax collectors "bloodsuckers of the nation who drink the tears of the unfortunate from goblets of gold." Another one of the cahiers condemned the courts of nobles as "vampires pumping the last drop of blood" from the people. Yet another complained that "20 million must live on half the wealth of France while the clergy . . . devour the other half."

The Tennis Court Oath Delegates to the Estates-General from the Third Estate were elected, though only propertied men could vote. Thus, the delegates were mostly lawyers, middle-class officials, and writers. They were familiar with the writings of

Voltaire, Rousseau, and other *philosophes*, as well as with the complaints in the cahiers. They went to Versailles not only to solve the financial crisis but also to insist on reform.

The Estates-General convened in May 1789. From the start, the delegates were deadlocked over the issue of voting. Traditionally, each estate had met and voted separately. Each group had one vote.

Under this system, the First and Second Estates always outvoted the Third Estate two to one. This time, the Third Estate wanted all three estates to meet in a single body, with votes counted "by head." After weeks of stalemate, delegates of the Third Estate took a daring step. In June 1789, claiming to represent the people of France, they declared themselves to be the National Assembly. A few days later, the National Assembly found its meeting hall locked and guarded. Fearing that the king planned to dismiss them, the delegates moved to a nearby indoor tennis court.

As curious spectators looked on, the delegates took their famous **Tennis Court Oath.** They swore "never to separate and to meet wherever the circumstances might require until we have established a sound and just constitution." When reform-minded clergy and nobles joined the Assembly, Louis XVI grudgingly accepted it.

At the same time, though, royal troops gathered around Paris. Rumors spread that the king planned to dissolve the Assembly.

☑ **DESCRIBE** Why did the Third Estate want the Estates-General to meet as a single body?

Storming the Bastille

On July 14, 1789, the city of Paris seized the spotlight from the National Assembly meeting in Versailles. The streets buzzed with rumors that royal troops were going to occupy the capital. More than 800 Parisians assembled outside the **Bastille,** a grim medieval fortress used as a prison for political and other prisoners. The crowd demanded weapons and gunpowder believed to be stored there.

The commander of the Bastille refused to open the gates and opened fire on the crowd. In the battle that followed, many people were killed. Finally, the enraged mob broke through the defenses. Thomas Jefferson was at the time American minister to France and described the scene as one of chaos and violence.

> The people rushed against the place, and almost in an instant were in possession of a fortification, defended by 100 men, of infinite strength, which in other times had stood several regular sieges and had never been taken. . . . They took all the arms, discharged the prisoners and such of the garrison as were not killed in the first moment of fury, carried the Governor and Lieutenant governor to the Greve (the place of public execution), cut off their heads, and set them through the city in triumph to the Palais royal.
>
> —Thomas Jefferson, letter to John Jay, July 14, 1789

The mob killed the commander and five guards and released the handful of prisoners who were being held there. However, they found no weapons.

For the French, the Bastille was a powerful symbol of the tyranny, inequalities, and injustices of the old order. The storming of the Bastille signaled the end of the absolute monarchy and a step toward freedom. It also marked the beginning of the French

>> The storming of the Bastille on July 14, 1789, was the opening event of the French Revolution.

Revolution. Today, July 14 is a national holiday when the French celebrate the birth of modern France.

☑ **IDENTIFY CENTRAL IDEAS** What was the main motivation behind the Parisians' attack on the Bastille?

Revolts in Paris and the Provinces

The political crisis of 1789 coincided with the worst famine in memory. Starving peasants roamed the countryside or flocked to towns, where they swelled the ranks of the unemployed. As grain prices soared, even people with jobs had to spend as much as 80 percent of their income on bread.

The "Great Fear" In such desperate times, rumors ran wild and set off what was later called the "Great Fear." Tales of attacks on villages and towns spread panic. Other rumors asserted that government troops were seizing peasant crops.

Inflamed by famine and fear, peasants unleashed their fury on nobles who were trying to reimpose medieval dues. Defiant peasants set fire to old manor records and stole grain from storehouses. The attacks eventually died down, but they clearly showed peasant anger with the injustice of the old order.

Paris in Arms Paris, too, was in turmoil. As the capital and chief city of France, it was the revolutionary center. A variety of factions competed to gain power. A **faction** is a group or clique within a larger group that has different ideas and opinions than the rest of the group.

Moderates looked to the **Marquis de Lafayette,** the aristocratic "hero of two worlds" who had fought alongside George Washington in the American Revolution. Lafayette headed the National Guard, a largely middle-class militia organized in response to the arrival of royal troops in Paris. The Guard was the first group to don the tricolor—a red, white, and blue badge that was eventually adopted as the national flag of France.

A more radical group, the Paris Commune, replaced the royalist government of the city. It could mobilize whole neighborhoods for protests or violent action to further the revolution. Newspapers and political clubs—many even more radical than the Commune—blossomed everywhere.

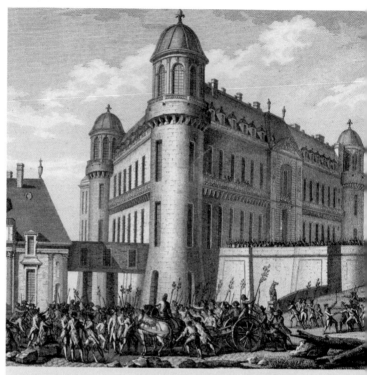

>> Peasant rebellions during the Great Fear began amid rumors that the king and other aristocrats wanted to overthrow the Third Estate.

Some demanded an end to the monarchy and spread scandalous stories about the royal family and members of the court.

☑ **IDENTIFY MAIN IDEAS** What stoked the "Great Fear"?

The National Assembly

Peasant uprisings and the storming of the Bastille stampeded the National Assembly into action. On August 4, in a combative all-night meeting, nobles in the National Assembly voted to end their own privileges. They agreed to give up their old manorial dues, exclusive hunting rights, special legal status, and exemption from taxes.

An End to Special Privilege "Feudalism is abolished," announced the proud and weary delegates at 2 A.M. As the president of the Assembly later observed, "We may view this moment as the dawn of a new revolution, when all the burdens weighing on the people were abolished, and France was truly reborn."

Were nobles sacrificing much with their votes on the night of August 4? Both contemporary observers

>> The ideals of the Enlightenment inspired the Declaration of the Rights of Man and the Citizen.

B BOUNCE to Activate Illustration

>> On October 5, 1789, thousands of women marched on the royal palace at Versailles hoping to draw attention to their poor living conditions.

and modern historians note that the nobles gave up nothing that they had not already lost. In the months ahead, the National Assembly turned the reforms of August 4 into law, meeting a key Enlightenment goal—the equality of all male citizens before the law.

Declaration of the Rights of Man In late August, as a first step toward writing a constitution, the Assembly issued the Declaration of the Rights of Man and the Citizen. The document was modeled in part on the American Declaration of Independence, written 13 years earlier. All men, the French declaration announced, were "born and remain free and equal in rights." They enjoyed natural rights to "liberty, property, security, and resistance to oppression." Like the writings of Locke and the *philosophes*, the declaration insisted that governments exist to protect the natural rights of citizens.

The declaration further proclaimed that all male citizens were equal before the law. Every French man had an equal right to hold public office "with no distinction other than that of their virtues and talents."

It affirmed the legal idea that no person could be arrested, tried or imprisoned except according to the law. In addition, the declaration asserted freedom of religion and called for taxes to be levied according to ability to pay. Its principles were captured in the enduring slogan of the French Revolution, "Liberty, Equality, Fraternity."

Some women were disappointed that the Declaration of the Rights of Man did not grant equal citizenship to them. In 1791, **Olympe de Gouges** (oh LAMP duh GOOZH) demanded equal rights in her Declaration of the Rights of Woman and the Female Citizen. "Woman is born free," she proclaimed, "and her rights are the same as those of man." She called for all citizens, men or women, to be equally eligible for all public offices. De Gouges and other women who pushed the cause of women's rights were often ridiculed or sometimes imprisoned and executed.

Women March on Versailles Louis XVI did not want to accept the reforms of the National Assembly. Nobles continued to enjoy gala banquets while people were starving.

By autumn, anger again turned to action. On October 5, about six thousand women marched 13 miles in the pouring rain from Paris to Versailles. "Bread!" they shouted. They demanded to see the king.

Much of the crowd's anger was directed at the queen, **Marie Antoinette.** She was the daughter

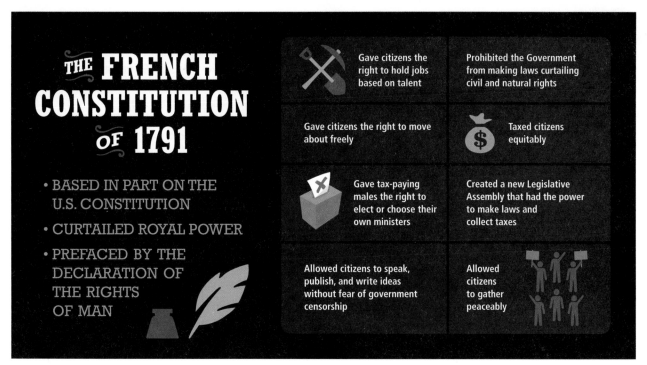

THE FRENCH CONSTITUTION OF 1791

- BASED IN PART ON THE U.S. CONSTITUTION
- CURTAILED ROYAL POWER
- PREFACED BY THE DECLARATION OF THE RIGHTS OF MAN

Gave citizens the right to hold jobs based on talent

Prohibited the Government from making laws curtailing civil and natural rights

Gave citizens the right to move about freely

Taxed citizens equitably

Gave tax-paying males the right to elect or choose their own ministers

Created a new Legislative Assembly that had the power to make laws and collect taxes

Allowed citizens to speak, publish, and write ideas without fear of government censorship

Allowed citizens to gather peaceably

>> **Analyze Charts** The Constitution of 1791 turned France upside down by destroying the old order. What powers did the Legislative Assembly now have?

of Maria Theresa of Austria. Ever since she had married Louis, she had come under attack for being frivolous and extravagant. She eventually grew more serious and even advised the king to compromise with moderate reformers. Still she remained a source of scandal. "Death to the Austrian!" the women who marched on Versailles shouted.

Lafayette and the National Guard eventually calmed the crowd. Still the women refused to leave Versailles until the king met their most important demand—to return to Paris. Not too happily, the king agreed. The next morning, the crowd, with the king and his family in tow, set out for the city. At the head of the procession rode women perched on the barrels of seized cannons. Crowds along the way cheered the king, who now wore the tricolor.

In Paris, the royal family moved into the Tuileries (TWEE luh reez) palace. For the next three years, Louis was a virtual prisoner.

☑ **DESCRIBE** Why did the women who marched on Versailles want King Louis XVI to return to Paris?

Reforms of the National Assembly

The National Assembly soon followed the king to Paris. Its largely bourgeois members worked to draft a constitution and to solve the continuing financial crisis.

Controlling the Church To pay off the huge government debt—much of it owed to the bourgeoisie—the Assembly voted to take over and sell Church lands. In an even more radical move, the National Assembly put the French Catholic Church under state control. Under the Civil Constitution of the Clergy, issued in 1790, bishops and priests became elected, salaried officials. The Civil Constitution ended papal authority over the French Church and dissolved convents and monasteries.

Reaction to the Civil Constitution was swift and angry. Many bishops and priests refused to accept the document while the pope condemned it.

Large numbers of French peasants, who were conservative concerning religion, also rejected the changes. When the government punished clergy who refused to support the Civil Constitution, a huge gulf opened between revolutionaries in Paris and the peasantry in the provinces.

>> Revolutionaries captured King Louis XVI as he tried to escape.

The Constitution of 1791 The National Assembly completed its main task by producing a constitution. The Constitution of 1791 set up a limited monarchy in place of the absolute monarchy that had ruled France for centuries. A new Legislative Assembly had the power to make laws, collect taxes, and decide on issues of war and peace. Lawmakers would be elected by tax-paying male citizens over age 25.

To make government more efficient, the constitution replaced the old provinces with 83 departments of roughly equal size. It abolished the old provincial courts, and it reformed laws.

To moderate reformers, the Constitution of 1791 seemed to complete the revolution. Reflecting Enlightenment goals, it ensured equality before the law for all male citizens and ended Church interference in government. At the same time, it put power in the hands of men with the means and leisure to serve in government.

The Royal Family Tries to Escape Meanwhile, Marie Antoinette and others had been urging the king to escape their humiliating situation. Louis finally gave in. One night in June 1791, a coach rolled north from Paris toward the border. Inside sat the king disguised as a servant, the queen dressed as a governess, and the royal children.

The attempted escape failed. In a town along the way, Louis's disguise was uncovered by someone who held up a piece of currency with the king's face on it. A company of soldiers escorted the royal family back to Paris, as onlooking crowds hurled insults at the king. In place of the old shouts of "Long Live the King!" people cried, "Long Live the Nation." To many, Louis's dash to the border showed that he was a traitor to the revolution. As new crises arose, the French Revolution entered a new, more radical phase.

☑ **DESCRIBE** How did the National Assembly try to reform the French Catholic Church?

☑ ASSESSMENT

1. **Apply Concepts** How did France's social divisions in the late 1700s contribute to the revolution?

2. **Draw Conclusions** Why was the conflict between the clergy and the Third Estate the most divisive in the course of the revolution?

3. **Compare** How might the complaints of a peasant and a merchant compare during the revolution?

4. **Identify Cause and Effect** What characteristics of the Third Estate helped fuel the Revolution?

5. **Describe** What did the Tennis Court Oath foretell about the coming events of the French Revolution?

Declaration of the Rights of Man and the Citizen

The National Assembly issued this document in 1789 after having overthrown the established government in the early stages of the French Revolution. The document was modeled in part on the English Bill of Rights and on the American Declaration of Independence. The basic principles of the French declaration were those that inspired the revolution, such as the freedom and equality of all male citizens before the law. The Articles below identify additional principles.

In 1791, Olymphe de Gouge presented the Declaration of the Rights of Woman and the Female Citizen to challenge the Declaration of the Rights of Man and the Citizen. The second primary source lists some of the ideas in the document.

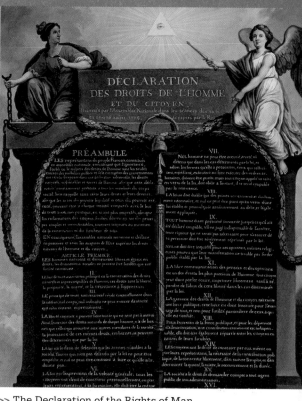

>> The Declaration of the Rights of Man

Primary Source 1

Therefore the National Assembly recognizes and proclaims, in the presence and under the auspices [approval and support] of the Supreme Being, the following rights of man and of the citizen:
1. Men are born and remain free and equal in rights. Social distinctions may be founded only upon the general good.
2. The aim of all political association is the preservation of the natural and imprescriptible [that which cannot be rightfully taken away] rights of man. These rights are liberty, property, security, and resistance to oppression. . . .
4. Liberty consists in the freedom to do everything which injures no one else. . . .
5. Law can only prohibit such actions as are hurtful to society. . . .
6. Law is the expression of the general will. Every citizen has a right to participate personally, or through his representative, in its formation. It must be the same for all, whether it protects or punishes. All citizens, being equal in the eyes of the law, are equally eligible to all dignities and to all public positions and occupations, according to their abilities, and without distinction except that of their virtues and talents.
7. No person shall be accused, arrested, or imprisoned except in the cases and according to the forms prescribed by law. . . .
11. The free communication of ideas and opinions is one of the most precious of the rights of man. Every citizen may, accordingly, speak, write, and print with freedom. . . .
13. A common contribution is essential for the maintenance of the public [military] forces and for the cost of administration. This should be equitably distributed among all the citizens in proportion to their means.

Primary Source 2

1. Woman is born free and remains equal to man in rights. Social distinctions may be based only on common utility.

2. The purpose of all political association is the preservation of the natural rights of woman and man. These rights are liberty, property, security, and especially resistance to oppression.

3. The principle of all sovereignty rests essentially in the nation, which is but the reuniting of woman and man. No body and no individual may exercise authority which does not emanate expressly from the nation.

6. The law should be the expression of the general will. All citizenesses and citizens should take part. . . .All citizenesses and citizens being equal in its eyes, should be equally admissible to all public dignities, offices and employments, according to their ability, and with no other distinction than that of their virtues and talents.

13. For maintenance of public authority and for expenses of administration, taxation of women and men is equal; she takes part in all forced labor service, in all painful tasks; she must therefore have the same proportion in the distribution of places, employments, offices, dignities and in industry.

17. Property belongs to both sexes whether united or separated; it is for each of them an inviolable and sacred right, and no one may be deprived of it . . .

☑ **ANALYZE ARGUMENTS** In what ways does de Gouge demand that women be regarded as equal citizens?

☑ ASSESSMENT

1. **Draw Conclusions** Many of the Declaration's principles are broad and idealistic. Choose one to analyze, addressing the potential problems that could arise when it becomes implemented as a law.

2. **Paraphrase** Tell in your own words what the Declaration says about law and fairness. Pay particular attention to Article 6 as you formulate your answer.

3. **Summarize** Explain how the Declaration protects individual liberties. Cite details in the text to support your response.

4. **Explain** According to de Gouges, what is a sovereign nation?

5. **Draw Conclusions** How did de Gouges hope to show the failings of the French Revolution in terms of rendering equality for men and women?

GO ONLINE to access primary sources

12.7

The September massacres lasted six days and resulted in more than 1,368 deaths.

A Radical Phase

The outbreak of the French Revolution stirred debate all over Europe and the United States. Supporters of the Enlightenment, such as Thomas Jefferson, saw the French experiment as the dawn of a new age for justice and equality. European rulers and nobles, however, denounced the French Revolution.

Radicals Gain Strength

Fear of the "French Plague" European rulers were horrified by the French Revolution, which threatened absolute monarchy. They increased border patrols to stop the spread of the "French plague." Fueling those fears were the horror stories that were told by **émigrés** (EM ih grayz)—nobles, clergy, and others who had fled France. Émigrés reported attacks on their privileges, their property, their religion, and even their lives. Even "enlightened" rulers turned against France. Catherine the Great of Russia burned Voltaire's letters and locked up critics.

Edmund Burke, a British statesman who earlier had defended the American Revolution, bitterly condemned revolutionaries in Paris. He predicted all too accurately that the revolution would become more violent. "When ancient opinions and rules of life are taken away," he warned, "we have no compass to govern us."

Threats from Abroad The failed escape of Louis XVI brought further hostile rumblings from abroad. In August 1791, the king of Prussia and the emperor of Austria—who was Marie Antoinette's brother—issued the Declaration of Pilnitz. In this document, the two monarchs threatened to protect the French monarchy.

BOUNCE to Activate Flipped Video

Objectives

Explain why the French Revolution entered a more radical phase.

Understand how radicals abolished the French monarchy.

Analyze the causes and course of the Reign of Terror.

Describe France under the Directory.

Identify how the French Revolution changed life in France.

Key Terms

émigré
sans-culottes
Jacobin
suffrage
Maximilien
  Robespierre
Reign of Terror
guillotine
Napoleon Bonaparte
Nationalism
Marseilles

The declaration may have been mostly a bluff, but revolutionaries in France took the threat seriously and prepared for war. The revolution was about to enter a new, more radical phase.

Radicals Seek Power In October 1791, the newly elected Legislative Assembly took office. Faced with crises at home and abroad, it survived for less than a year. Economic problems fed renewed turmoil.

Assignats (AS ig nats), the revolutionary currency, dropped in value, causing prices to rise rapidly. Uncertainty about prices led to hoarding and caused additional food shortages.

In Paris and other cities, working-class men and women, called **sans-culottes** (sanz koo LAHTS), pushed the revolution into more radical action. Sans-culottes means "without breeches." Men wore long trousers instead of the fancy knee breeches that men of the upper class wore. By 1791, many sans-culottes demanded an end to the monarchy and the creation of a republic. They also wanted the government to guarantee them a living wage.

Within the Legislative Assembly, several hostile factions competed for power. The sans-culottes found support among radicals, especially the Jacobins. A revolutionary political club, the **Jacobins** were mostly middle-class lawyers or intellectuals. They used pamphleteers and sympathetic newspaper editors to advance the republican cause.

Opposing the radicals were moderate reformers and officials who wanted no more reforms at all. The radicals soon held the upper hand in the Legislative Assembly.

War Breaks Out In April 1792, the war of words between French revolutionaries and European monarchs moved onto the battlefield. Eager to spread the revolution and destroy tyranny abroad, the Legislative Assembly declared war first on Austria and then on Prussia, Britain, and other states. The great powers expected to win an easy victory against France, a land divided by revolution. In fact, the fighting that began in 1792 lasted on and off until 1815.

The war abroad heightened tensions in Paris. Well-trained Prussian forces were cutting down raw French recruits. In addition, royalist officers were deserting the French army, joining émigrés and others hoping to restore the king's power.

☑ **CITE EVIDENCE** How did the monarchs of Europe react to the French Revolution?

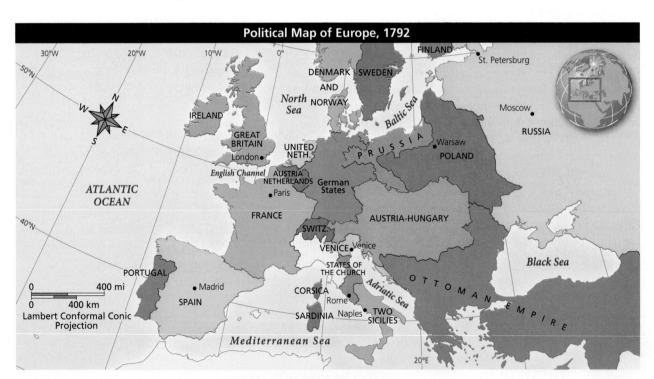

Political Map of Europe, 1792

>> Europe in the 1790s was dominated by monarchies. **Analyze Maps** Why do you suppose France's neighbors were afraid of the French Revolution?

The Monarchy Is Abolished

In 1793, the Revolution entered a radical phase. For a year, France experienced one of the bloodiest regimes in its long history as determined leaders sought to extend and preserve the Revolution.

New Outbreaks of Violence Battle disasters overseas quickly inflamed revolutionaries in Paris. They thought the king was in league with the enemies. On August 10, 1792, a crowd of Parisians stormed the royal palace of the Tuileries and slaughtered the king's guards. The royal family fled to the Legislative Assembly.

A month later, citizens attacked prisons that held nobles and priests accused of political offenses. More than 1,000 prisoners were killed, including many ordinary criminals.

Historians disagree about the people who carried out these "September massacres." Some call them bloodthirsty mobs. Others describe them as patriots defending France. In fact, most were ordinary citizens fired to fury by real and imagined grievances.

The National Convention Backed by Paris crowds, radicals then took control of the Assembly. Radicals called for the election of a new legislative body called the National Convention. **Suffrage,** the right to vote, was to be extended to all male citizens, not just to property owners.

The Convention that met in September 1792 was a more radical body than earlier Assemblies. It voted to abolish the monarchy and establish a republic. Deputies then drew up a new constitution. The Jacobins, who controlled the Convention, set out to erase all traces of the old order. They seized lands of nobles and abolished titles of nobility. All men and women were called "Citizen." Louis XVI became Citizen Capet, from the dynasty that ruled France during the Middle Ages.

Execution of a King and Queen During the early months of the Republic, the Convention also put Louis XVI on trial as a traitor to France. The king was convicted by a single vote and sentenced to death.

On a foggy morning in January 1793, Louis mounted a scaffold in a public square in Paris. He started to speak, "Frenchmen, I die innocent. I pardon the authors of my death. I pray God that the blood about to be spilt will never fall upon the head of France. . . ." Then a roll of drums drowned out his

>> Marie Antoinette's lavish lifestyle and disregard for the masses contributed to her unpopularity and later execution.

words. Moments later, the king was beheaded. The executioner lifted the king's head by its hair and held it before the crowd.

In October, Marie Antoinette was also executed. The popular press celebrated her death. The queen, however, showed great dignity as she went to her death. Her son, who might once have become Louis XVII, died of unknown causes in the dungeons of the Revolution.

☑ **CONTRAST** What was the main difference between earlier Assemblies and the National Convention, which met in September 1792?

The Reign of Terror

By early 1793, danger threatened France on all sides. The country was at war with much of Europe, including Britain, the Netherlands, Spain, and Prussia. In the Vendée (vahn DAY) region of France, royalists and priests led peasants in rebellion against the government.

In Paris, the sans-culottes demanded relief from food shortages and inflation. The Convention itself was bitterly divided between Jacobins and a rival group, the Girondins.

Committee of Public Safety To deal with the threats to France, the Convention created the Committee of Public Safety. The 12-member committee had almost absolute power. Preparing France for all-out war, it ordered all citizens to contribute to the war effort. They urged young men to go into battle, women to make tents or serve in hospitals, and children to turn old lint into linen.

Spurred by revolutionary fervor, recruits marched off to defend the republic. Young officers developed effective tactics to win battles with masses of ill-trained but patriotic forces. Soon, French armies overran the Netherlands. They later invaded Italy. At home, they crushed peasant revolts. European monarchs shuddered as the revolutionaries carried "freedom fever" into conquered lands.

Robespierre, the Incorruptible At home, the government battled counterrevolutionaries under the guiding hand of **Maximilien Robespierre** (ROHBZ pyehr). Robespierre, a shrewd lawyer and politician, quickly rose to the leadership of the Committee of Public Safety. Among Jacobins, his selfless dedication to the revolution earned him the nickname "the incorruptible." His enemies called him a tyrant.

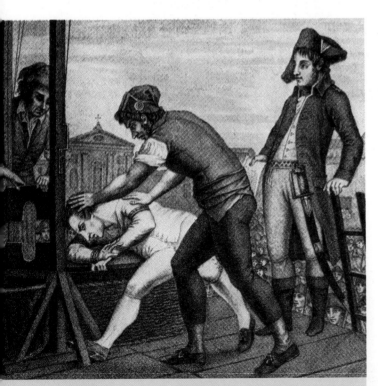

>> Robespierre was beheaded on July 28, 1794, a victim of the Terror he helped create.

B **BOUNCE to Activate Gallery**

"Death to the Traitors" Robespierre was one of the chief architects of the **Reign of Terror**, which lasted from September 1793 to July 1794. Revolutionary courts conducted hasty trials. Spectators greeted death sentences with cries of "Hail the Republic!" or "Death to the traitors!" In a speech given on February 5, 1794, Robespierre explained that the terror was necessary to protect the Revolution and achieve its goals.

During the Reign of Terror, about 300,000 citizens were arrested. About 17,000 were executed. They included nobles and clergy, peasants, and sans-culottes, along with middle-class citizens who had once supported the Revolution.

> It is necessary to stifle the domestic and foreign enemies of the Republic or perish with them. . . . The first maxim of our politics ought to be to lead the people by means of reason and the enemies of the people by terror.
>
> —Maximilien Robespierre

Many were victims of mistaken identity or were falsely accused by their neighbors. Many more were packed into hideous prisons, where deaths from disease were common.

The engine of the Terror was the **guillotine** (GIL uh teen). Its fast-falling blade extinguished life instantly. A member of the legislature, Dr. Joseph Guillotin (gee oh TAN), had introduced it as a more humane method of beheading than the uncertain ax. Still, the guillotine quickly became a symbol of horror.

Within a year, the Terror consumed those who initiated it. Weary of bloodshed and fearing for their own lives, members of the Convention turned on the Committee of Public Safety. On the night of July 27, 1794, Robespierre was arrested. The next day he was executed. After the heads of Robespierre and other radicals fell, executions slowed dramatically.

☑ **DRAW CONCLUSIONS** How did radicals such as Robespierre justify the use of terror?

Reaction and the Directory

In reaction to the Terror, the Revolution entered a third stage. Middle class and professional people dominated this stage of the Revolution.

A REVOLUTIONARY REVOLUTION

Born out of the ideas of the Enlightenment, the French Revolution changed the country's political and social landscape. It uprooted centuries-old institutions, created a new social order, and put into practice the idea that governments are formed by the will of the people.

- ABOLISHED THE MONARCHY
- CURTAILED THE POWER OF THE **FRENCH ROMAN CATHOLIC CHURCH**
- ABOLISHED THE FEUDAL SYSTEM
- CREATED EQUALITY BEFORE THE LAW
- GAVE TALENTED PEOPLE GREATER ACCESS TO JOBS
- CREATED A SENSE OF NATIONAL PRIDE
- CREATED POPULAR SOVEREIGNTY

>> **Analyze Charts** The French Revolution changed the country's political and social landscape. How did the Revolution change the social order?

BOUNCE to Activate Timeline

Moving away from the excesses of the Convention, moderates produced another constitution, the third since 1789. The Constitution of 1795 set up a five-man Directory and a two-house legislature elected by male citizens of property. The Directory held power from 1795 to 1799.

Weak, but willing to use force against its enemies, the Directory faced many challenges. Although France made peace with Prussia and Spain, the war continued with Austria and Great Britain. Corrupt leaders lined their own pockets but failed to solve pressing problems. When rising bread prices stirred hungry sans-culottes to riot, the Directory quickly suppressed them.

Another threat to the Directory was the revival of royalist feeling. Many émigrés were returning to France, and devout Catholics, who resented measures that had been taken against the Church, were welcoming them. In the election of 1797, supporters of a constitutional monarchy won the majority of seats in the legislature.

Despite its failings, the Directory consolidated many reforms of the National Convention. It set up a system of elite schools and helped the French economy to recover from the upheavals of the Terror. During the Directory, France had strengthened its armies and won several important battles.

As chaos threatened, politicians turned to **Napoleon Bonaparte,** a popular military hero who had won a series of brilliant victories against the Austrians in Italy. The politicians planned to use him to advance their own goals. To their dismay, however, before long Napoleon would outwit them all to become ruler of France.

☑ **IDENTIFY CAUSE AND EFFECT** Why did Catholics welcome the return of the émigrés?

The Revolution Transforms France

By 1799, the 10-year-old French Revolution had dramatically changed France. It had dislodged the old social order, overthrown the monarchy, and brought the Church under state control.

New symbols such as the red "liberty caps" and the tricolor confirmed the liberty and equality of all male citizens. The new title "citizen" applied to people of all social classes. Elaborate fashions and powdered wigs gave way to the practical clothes and simple haircuts of the sans-culottes.

Nationalism Spread Revolution and war gave the French people a strong sense of national identity. In earlier times, people had felt loyalty to local authorities. As monarchs centralized power, loyalty shifted to the king or queen. Instead, the government rallied sons and daughters of the Revolution to defend the nation itself.

Nationalism, a strong feeling of pride in and devotion to one's country, spread throughout France. The French people attended civic festivals that celebrated the nation and the Revolution. A variety of dances and songs on themes of the Revolution became immensely popular.

By 1793, France was a nation in arms. From the port city of **Marseilles** (mahr say), troops marched to a rousing new song. It urged the "children of the fatherland" to march against the "bloody banner of tyranny." This song, "La Marseillaise" (mahr say ez), would later become the French national anthem.

Social Reform Revolutionaries pushed for social reform and religious toleration. They set up state schools to replace religious ones and organized systems to help the poor, old soldiers, and war widows. With a major slave revolt raging in the

colony of St. Domingue (Haiti), the government also abolished slavery in France's Caribbean colonies.

Religion and the Revolution During the Revolution, different governments pursued different policies toward religion. The Civil Constitution of the Clergy put the Catholic Church under state control. Unlike the United States whose Constitution forbade the establishment of any official state church, France supported the French Catholic Church by paying the salaries of the clergy.

Many revolutionaries embraced the ideas of religious toleration. Yet this Enlightenment ideal often fell victim to politics. During the radical phase, leaders banned public religious worship and removed the names of saints from streets and buildings. Any who opposed these moves faced persecution or death. This effort to de-Christianize France had little popular support. In the end, the Catholic Church was restored with limited rights.

Comparison with the American Revolution The French Revolution came on the heels of the American Revolution. The two revolutions had both similarities and differences.

Both grew out of Enlightenment ideals such as liberty, freedom, and the rights of citizens. Both began with calls for reform, but ended up with a complete change of government. In the colonies and in France, people rose up against oppressive monarchies and high taxes. Each revolution broke out after years of increasing discontent with powerful rulers who imposed their will on the people.

Historians have compared the causes of the American and French Revolutions, and emphasized the role of the ideas behind the Glorious Revolution in helping to inspire both later events. Although the political traditions and social climate of France and the colonies differed, both the French and American colonists wanted a government that was responsible to its people. The colonists saw themselves as citizens of Britain, entitled to the same rights. The British people had won these rights by limiting the power of their monarch through the Magna Carta in 1215 and the Glorious Revolution of 1688. The violation of these rights by Parliament, over 70 years later, was one cause of the American Revolution.

France was an absolute monarchy, but here too the ideas behind the Glorious Revolution played a role. The Glorious Revolution had confirmed the supremacy of Parliament over the monarch in Britain. French revolutionary leaders were influenced by this political development, as well as by the ideals behind the American Revolution and the U.S. Constitution.

>> During the radical phase of the French Revolution, many Christian churches were renamed Temples of Reason. Religious symbols were covered. On some churches, the revolutionary motto "Liberté, egalité, fraternité" was inscribed on the stone facade.

In both countries, the people set up a republican form of government. In France, the first republic did not last, but in the United States, it has lasted until the present.

The short-lived republic of France had a government organized with separation of powers. The National Assembly became the legislative branch, and the king would represent the executive branch. Citizen rights were protected, but equal rights were not fully extended to women.

In both England and pre-revolutionary France, the state supported an official church. In America, although many of the leaders of the Revolution were deeply religious, the First Amendment to the Constitution forbade the establishment of any state-supported church. In France, a state-supported Catholic Church remained a powerful force for more than a century.

☑ **ANALYZE INFORMATION** Describe several ways the Revolution changed French society.

☑ **ASSESSMENT**

1. **Compare and Contrast** Compare and contrast the views of France's radical revolutionaries to the views of its moderates.

2. **Check Understanding** Why was the Committee of Public Safety allowed to terrorize France during the Reign of Terror?

3. **Describe** How did the Directory's actions ultimately lead to the rise of Napoleon?

4. **Describe** What actions did the French take after the Revolution to show their patriotism?

5. **Identify Cause and Effect** What was it about the nature of the French Revolution that led to political and social reform?

12.8

Napoleon was a military genius who dominated Europe for more than a decade.

 BOUNCE to Activate Flipped Video

Objectives

Describe how Napoleon Bonaparte rose to power.

Explain the impact of Napoleon and the Napoleonic Wars.

Identify the reasons for Napoleon's fall from power.

Understand how the Congress of Vienna tried to restore order to Europe.

Key Terms

plebiscite
Napoleonic Code
Napoleonic Wars
annex
Continental System
guerrilla warfare
abdicate
Congress of Vienna
legitimacy
Concert of Europe

The Age of Napoleon

From 1799 to 1815, Napoleon Bonaparte dominated France and Europe. A hero to some, an evil force to others, he gave his name to the final phase of the French Revolution—the Age of Napoleon.

Napoleon on the Rise

Early Years Napoleon was born in Corsica, a French-ruled island in the Mediterranean. At age nine, he was sent to France to be trained for a military career. When the revolution broke out, he was an ambitious 20-year-old lieutenant, eager to make a name for himself.

Napoleon favored the Jacobins and republican rule. However, he found the conflicting ideas and personalities of the French Revolution confusing. He wrote to his brother in 1793: "Since one must take sides, one might as well choose the side that is victorious, the side which devastates, loots, and burns. Considering the alternative, it is better to eat than be eaten."

Military Success During the turmoil of the Revolution, Napoleon rose quickly in the army. In December 1793, he drove British forces out of the French port of Toulon (too LOHN).

He then went on to win several dazzling victories against the Austrians, capturing most of northern Italy and forcing the Hapsburg emperor to make peace. Hoping to disrupt British trade with India, he led an expedition to Egypt in 1798. The Egyptian campaign proved to be a disaster, but Napoleon managed to hide stories of the worst losses from his admirers in France.

Success fueled Napoleon's ambition. By 1799, he moved from victorious general to political leader. That year, he helped overthrow the weak Directory and set up a three-man governing board known as the Consulate. Another constitution was drawn up, but Napoleon soon took the title First Consul. In 1800, he forced Spain to return Louisiana Territory to France. In 1802, Napoleon had himself named consul for life.

Napoleon Crowns Himself Emperor Two years later, Napoleon had acquired enough power to assume the title Emperor of the French. He invited the pope to preside over his coronation in Paris. During the ceremony, however, Napoleon took the crown from the pope's hands and placed it on his own head. By this action, Napoleon meant to show that he owed his throne to no one but himself.

At each step on his rise to power, Napoleon had held a **plebiscite** (PLEB uh syt), or popular vote by ballot. Each time, the French strongly supported him, even after he had assumed absolute power as emperor. To understand why, we must look at his policies.

✓ **CITE EVIDENCE** How did Napoleon rise to power so quickly in France?

Napoleon Reforms France

Napoleon consolidated his power by strengthening the central government. Order, security, and efficiency replaced liberty, equality, and fraternity as the slogans of the new regime.

Social and Economic Reforms To restore economic prosperity, Napoleon controlled prices, encouraged new industry, and built roads and canals. He set up a system of public schools under strict government control to ensure well-trained officials and military officers.

At the same time, Napoleon backed off from some of the Revolution's social reforms. He made peace with the Catholic Church in the Concordat of 1801. The Concordat kept the Church under state control but recognized religious freedom for Catholics. Revolutionaries who opposed the Church denounced the agreement, but Catholics welcomed it.

Napoleon won support across class lines. He encouraged émigrés to return, provided they take an oath of loyalty. Peasants were relieved when he recognized their right to lands they had bought from the Church and nobles during the Revolution.

The middle class, who had benefited most from the Revolution, approved of Napoleon's economic reforms and the restoration of order after years of chaos. Napoleon also opened jobs to all, based on talent, a popular policy among those who remembered the old aristocratic monopoly of power.

The Napoleonic Code Among Napoleon's most lasting reforms was a new code of laws, popularly called the **Napoleonic Code.** It embodied Enlightenment principles such as the equality of all citizens before the law, religious toleration, and the abolition of feudalism.

At the same time, the Napoleonic Code undid some reforms of the French Revolution. Women, for example, lost most of their newly gained rights and could not exercise the rights of citizenship. Male heads of households regained complete authority over their wives and children. Again, Napoleon valued order and authority over individual rights.

>> At Napoleon's coronation, he placed the crown on his own head to show that he was the source of his own power, not the pope.

The Napoleonic Wars

From 1804 to 1812, Napoleon furthered his reputation on the battlefield. In a series of conflicts known as the **Napoleonic Wars,** he battled the combined forces of the greatest European powers. He took great risks and even suffered huge losses. "I grew up on the field of battle," he once said, "and a man such as I am cares little for the life of a million men." By 1812, his Grand Empire reached its greatest extent.

As a military leader, Napoleon valued rapid movements and made effective use of his large armies. He developed a new plan for each battle so opposing generals could never anticipate what he would do next. His enemies paid tribute to his leadership. Napoleon's presence on the battlefield, said one, was "worth 40,000 troops."

Redrawing the Map of Europe As Napoleon created a vast French empire, he redrew the map of Europe. He **annexed,** or incorporated, into his empire the Netherlands, Belgium, and parts of Italy and Germany.

He also abolished the tottering Holy Roman Empire and created a 38 member Confederation of the Rhine under French protection. He cut Prussian territory in half, turning part of old Poland into the Grand Duchy of Warsaw.

Napoleon controlled much of Europe through forceful diplomacy. One tactic was placing friends and relatives on the thrones of Europe. For example, after unseating the king of Spain, he placed his own brother, Joseph Bonaparte, on the throne. He also forced alliances on European powers from Madrid to Moscow. At various times, the rulers of Austria, Prussia, and Russia reluctantly signed treaties with the "Corsican ogre," as defeated monarchs called him.

In France, Napoleon's successes boosted the spirit of nationalism. Great victory parades filled the streets of Paris with cheering crowds. The people celebrated the glory and grandeur that Napoleon had gained for France.

The Continental System Of all the major European powers, Britain alone remained outside Napoleon's European empire. With only a small army, Britain relied on its sea power to stop Napoleon's drive to rule the continent. In 1805, Napoleon prepared to invade England. But at the Battle of Trafalgar, fought

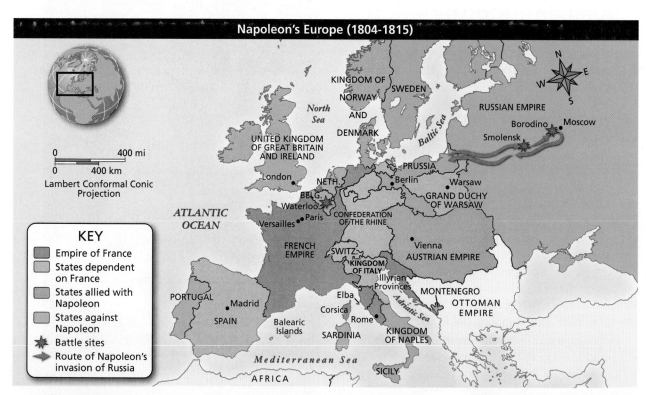

Napoleon's Europe (1804-1815)

KINGDOM OF NORWAY AND DENMARK · SWEDEN · North Sea · Baltic Sea · RUSSIAN EMPIRE · Borodino · Moscow · Smolensk · UNITED KINGDOM OF GREAT BRITAIN AND IRELAND · London · NETH. · PRUSSIA · Berlin · Warsaw · ATLANTIC OCEAN · BELG. · Waterloo · Paris · Versailles · CONFEDERATION OF THE RHINE · GRAND DUCHY OF WARSAW · FRENCH EMPIRE · SWITZ. · KINGDOM OF ITALY · Vienna · AUSTRIAN EMPIRE · Illyrian Provinces · PORTUGAL · Madrid · SPAIN · Balearic Islands · Corsica · Elba · Rome · SARDINIA · KINGDOM OF NAPLES · Adriatic Sea · MONTENEGRO · OTTOMAN EMPIRE · Mediterranean Sea · AFRICA · SICILY

0 400 mi
0 400 km
Lambert Conformal Conic Projection

KEY
- Empire of France
- States dependent on France
- States allied with Napoleon
- States against Napoleon
- ✦ Battle sites
- ➡ Route of Napoleon's invasion of Russia

>> **Analyze Maps** Napoleon reshaped the map of Europe with his military and political conquests. Who were Napoleon's allies?

🅑 **BOUNCE to Activate Map**

off the southwest coast of Spain, British Admiral Horatio Nelson smashed the French fleet.

With an invasion ruled out, Napoleon struck at Britain's lifeblood, its commerce. He waged economic warfare through the **Continental System**, which closed European ports to British goods. Britain responded with its own blockade of European ports. A blockade involves shutting off ports to keep people or supplies from moving in or out.

During their long struggle, both Britain and France seized neutral ships suspected of trading with the other side. British attacks on American ships sparked anger in the United States and eventually triggered the War of 1812.

In the end, Napoleon's Continental System failed to bring Britain to its knees. Although British exports declined, Britain's powerful navy kept vital trade routes open to the Americas and India. Meanwhile, trade restrictions created a scarcity of goods in Europe, sent prices soaring, and intensified resentment against French power.

Impact of Napoleon's Conquests French armies under Napoleon spread ideas of the revolution across Europe. They backed liberal reforms in the lands they conquered. In some places, they helped install revolutionary governments that abolished titles of nobility, ended Church privileges, opened careers to men of talent, and ended serfdom and manorial dues. The Napoleonic Code, too, influenced countries in continental Europe and Latin America.

☑ **IDENTIFY CAUSE AND EFFECT** How did Napoleon come to dominate most of Europe by 1812?

Challenges to the French Empire

In 1812, Napoleon continued his pursuit of European domination and invaded Russia. This campaign began a chain of events that eventually led to his downfall. Napoleon's final defeat brought an end to the era of the French Revolution.

Seeds of Defeat Napoleon's successes contained seeds of defeat. Although nationalism spurred French armies to success, it worked against them, too. Many Europeans who had welcomed the ideas of the French Revolution nevertheless saw Napoleon and his armies as foreign oppressors. They resented the Continental System and Napoleon's effort to impose French culture on them.

>> This painting depicts the Battle of Trafalgar, in which the British navy defeated the French on October 21, 1805.

>> Napoleon, shown here crossing the Alps on horseback, attempted to spread French culture across Europe.

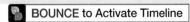
BOUNCE to Activate Timeline

>> Spanish patriots bravely resisted French invaders. In his famous painting *Third of May 1808*, Spanish artist Francisco Goya shows the execution of Spanish resistance leaders by French troops.

>> The French invasion of Russia became a disaster when the lack of food and supplies combined with a hard winter to nearly destroy Napoleon's army.

From Rome to Madrid to the Netherlands, nationalism unleashed revolts against France. In the German states, leaders encouraged national loyalty among German-speaking people to counter French influence.

Resistance in Spain Resistance to foreign rule bled French-occupying forces dry in Spain. Napoleon introduced reforms that sought to undermine the Spanish Catholic Church. But many Spaniards remained loyal to their former king and devoted to the Church. When the Spanish resisted the invaders, well-armed French forces responded with brutal repression. Far from crushing resistance, however, the French response further inflamed Spanish nationalism. Efforts to drive out the French intensified.

Spanish patriots conducted a campaign of **guerrilla warfare,** or hit-and-run raids, against the French. (In Spanish, guerrilla means "little war.") Small bands of guerrillas ambushed French supply trains or troops before retreating into the countryside. These attacks kept large numbers of French soldiers tied down in Spain when Napoleon needed them elsewhere.

Austria Seeks Revenge Spanish resistance encouraged Austria to resume hostilities against the French. In 1805, at the Battle of Austerlitz, Napoleon had won a crushing victory against an Austro-Russian army of superior numbers. Now, in 1809, the Austrians sought revenge. But once again, Napoleon triumphed—this time at the Battle of Wagram. By the peace agreement that followed, Austria surrendered lands populated by more than three million subjects.

Napoleon Invades Russia Tsar Alexander I of Russia was once an ally of Napoleon. The tsar and Napoleon planned to divide Europe if Alexander helped Napoleon in his Continental System. Many countries objected to this system, and Russia became unhappy with the economic effects of the system as well. Yet another cause for concern was that Napoleon had enlarged the Grand Duchy of Warsaw that bordered Russia on the west.

These and other issues led the tsar to withdraw his support from the Continental System. Napoleon responded to the tsar's action by assembling an army with soldiers from 20 nations, known as the Grand Army.

In 1812, with about 600,000 soldiers and 50,000 horses, Napoleon invaded Russia. To avoid battles with Napoleon, the Russians retreated eastward, burning crops and villages as they went. This scorched-earth policy left the French hungry and cold as winter came.

Napoleon entered Moscow in September. His triumph, however, was short-lived.

The Retreat from Moscow Even as French troops entered Moscow, Napoleon realized that he would not be able to feed and supply his army through the long Russian winter. In October, he turned homeward.

The 1,000-mile retreat from Moscow turned into a desperate battle for survival. Russian attacks and the brutal Russian winter took a terrible toll. Fewer than 20,000 soldiers of the once-proud Grand Army survived. Many died. Others deserted. French general Michel Ney sadly concluded, "General Famine and General Winter, rather than Russian bullets, have conquered the Grand Army."

Napoleon rushed to Paris to raise a new force to defend France. His reputation for success had been shattered.

☑ **ANALYZE INFORMATION** What led to Napoleon's disaster in Russia?

>> Once the scourge of Europe, Napoleon eventually fell from power. This painting shows Napoleon in exile.

Napoleon Falls from Power

The disaster in Russia changed the course of the Napoleonic Wars. Russia, Britain, Austria, and Prussia formed a new alliance against a weakened France. In 1813, they defeated Napoleon in the Battle of the Nations at Leipzig.

Napoleon Abdicates Briefly The next year, Napoleon **abdicated,** or stepped down from power. The victors exiled him to Elba, an island in the Mediterranean. They then recognized Louis XVIII, brother of Louis XVI, as king of France.

The restoration of Louis XVIII did not go smoothly. He agreed to accept the Napoleonic Code and honor the land settlements made during the Revolution. However, many émigrés rushed back to France bent on revenge. An economic depression and the fear of a return to the old regime helped rekindle loyalty to Napoleon.

As the victorious allies gathered in Vienna for a general peace conference, Napoleon escaped his island exile and returned to France. Soldiers flocked to his banner. As citizens cheered Napoleon's

advance, Louis XVIII fled. In March 1815, Napoleon entered Paris in triumph.

Napoleon Is Defeated at Waterloo Napoleon's triumph was short-lived. His star soared for only 100 days, while the allies reassembled their forces. On June 18, 1815, the opposing armies met near the town of Waterloo in Belgium. British forces under the Duke of Wellington and a Prussian army commanded by General Blücher crushed the French in an agonizing day-long battle. Once again, Napoleon was forced to abdicate and to go into exile on St. Helena, a lonely island in the South Atlantic. This time, he would not return.

Napoleon's Legacy Napoleon died in 1821, but his legend lived on in France and around the world. His contemporaries as well as historians today have long debated his legacy. Was he "the Revolution on horseback," as he claimed? Or was he a traitor to the Revolution?

No one, however, questions Napoleon's impact on France and on Europe. The Napoleonic Code consolidated many changes of the Revolution. The France of Napoleon was a centralized state with a constitution. Elections were held with expanded, though limited, suffrage. Many more citizens had rights to property and access to education than under the old regime. Still, French citizens lost many rights promised so fervently by republicans during the Convention.

On the world stage, the Napoleonic Wars spread the ideas of the French Revolution. He failed to make Europe into a French empire. Instead, he sparked nationalist feelings across Europe. The abolition of the Holy Roman Empire would eventually help in creating a new Germany.

Napoleon's impact also reached across the Atlantic. In 1803, his decision to sell France's vast Louisiana Territory to the American government doubled the size of the United States and ushered in an age of American expansion.

☑ **ANALYZE INFORMATION** Why were the French so eager for Napoleon to return to France after his escape from Elba?

The Congress of Vienna

After Waterloo, diplomats and heads of state again sat down at the **Congress of Vienna.** They faced the monumental task of restoring stability and order in Europe after years of war.

The Congress met for 10 months, from September 1814 to June 1815. It was a brilliant gathering of European leaders. Diplomats and royalty dined and danced, attended concerts and ballets, and enjoyed parties arranged by their host, Emperor Francis I of Austria. The work fell to Prince Clemens von Metternich of Austria, Tsar Alexander I of Russia, and Lord Robert Castlereagh of Britain. Defeated France was represented by Prince Charles Maurice de Talleyrand.

Goals of the Congress The chief goal of the Vienna decision makers was to create a lasting peace by establishing a balance of power and protecting the system of monarchy. Each of the leaders also pursued his own goals. Metternich, the dominant figure at the Congress, wanted to restore things to the way they were in 1792. Alexander I urged a "holy alliance" of Christian monarchs to suppress future revolutions.

Lord Castlereagh was determined to prevent a revival of French military power. The aged diplomat Talleyrand shrewdly played the other leaders against one another so France would be accepted as an equal partner.

Restoring Peace and Order The peacemakers redrew the map of Europe. To contain French

KEY
— Boundary of the German Confederation
Quadruple Alliance, 1815
- Great Britain
- Prussia
- Austrian Empire
- Russian Empire

Europe after the Congress of Vienna

>> **Analyze Maps** Why did the Congress of Vienna enlarge some of the countries around France?

ambitions, they ringed France with strong countries. In the north, they added Belgium and Luxembourg to Holland to create the kingdom of the Netherlands. To prevent French expansion eastward, they gave Prussia lands along the Rhine River. They also allowed Austria to reassert control over northern Italy.

To turn back the clock to 1792, the architects of the peace promoted the principle of **legitimacy,** restoring hereditary monarchies that the French Revolution or Napoleon had unseated. Even before the Congress began, they had put Louis XVIII on the French throne. Later, they restored "legitimate" monarchs in Portugal, Spain, and the Italian states.

Successes and Failures To protect the new order, Austria, Russia, Prussia, and Great Britain extended their wartime alliance. In the Quadruple Alliance, the four nations pledged to act together to balance power and suppress uprisings. They then set up the **Concert of Europe,** a loose organization whose goal was to preserve the agreements set up by the Congress of Vienna. The four great powers—and later France—worked to suppress any uprising inspired by the French Revolution. The Concert of Europe was the first modern international peace keeping organization.

The Vienna statesmen achieved their immediate goals in creating a lasting peace. Peace lasted in Europe for the next 100 years. Although smaller wars broke out, Europe would not see war on a Napoleonic scale until 1914. They failed, however, to foresee how powerful new forces such as nationalism would shake the foundations of Europe and Latin America in the future.

☑ **ANALYZE INFORMATION** What was the chief goal of the Congress of Vienna?

☑ **ASSESSMENT**

1. **Identify** What political views did Napoleon spread in Europe that angered monarchs?

2. **Describe** In what way was the Continental System an act of economic warfare? Why did it fail?

3. **Describe** In what way did Napoleon's actions doom his dream of creating a French empire in Europe?

4. **Compare and Contrast** Compare and contrast the goals of Prince Clemens von Metternich of Austria and Britain's Lord Castlereagh during the Congress of Vienna.

5. **Draw Conclusions** Why might some of the French have resisted a return to a monarchy?

🔊 **GO ONLINE** to access this biography: Napoleon Bonaparte

Connections to Today

On April 30, 2019, Emperor Akihito of Japan became the first Japanese monarch to abdicate, or give up the throne, in two hundred years.

Take Action About the Changes in the Monarchy

Monarchies have existed since 3000 B.C. Throughout history, the amount of power assumed by monarchies has varied. How has the monarchy changed in modern times?

1. **Choose** one of the following topics about the monarchy.
   - What is succession? How have the laws of succession changed in most European monarchies?

   - Compare the monarchies of the past with the monarchies of today. Consider divine right, marriages, royal rule, and the public life of members of the royal family.

2. **Ask Questions** What are some of the things you want to know about the monarchy today? Write a list of questions.

3. **Learn** Research the topic you have chosen. In addition to online sources, seek out at least one or two print sources.

4. **Raise Awareness** Create a chart which compares monarchies of the past with monarchies today. Share your chart with your class.

Use the texts, quizzes, interactivities, Quest Inquiries, Flipped Videos, and other resources from this Topic to prepare for the Topic Test.

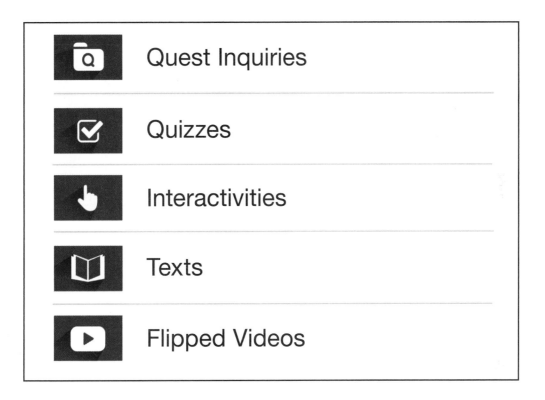

Q	Quest Inquiries
✓	Quizzes
👆	Interactivities
📖	Texts
▶	Flipped Videos

While online you can also check the progress you've made learning the topic and course content by viewing your grades, test scores, and assignment status.

LESSON SUMMARIES

Use these Lesson Summaries, and the longer versions available online, to review the key ideas for each lesson in this Topic.

Lesson 1: Absolute Monarchy in Spain and France

Both King Philip of Spain and Louis XIV ruled as absolute monarchs. Claiming rule by divine right, both rulers unified their nations and centralized power.

Lesson 2: Rise of Austria, Prussia, and Russia

After the brutal Thirty Years' War, Austria and Prussia emerged as great powers. In Russia, Peter the Great centralized royal power, sought to expand Russia, and started a program to modernize the nation.

Lesson 3: Triumph of Parliament in England

English monarchs attempted to expand royal power, but the British Parliament asserted its rights against royal claims to absolute power. The monarchy was abolished and then restored.

Lesson 4: The Enlightenment

The Scientific Revolution of the 1500s and 1600s changed the way people in Europe viewed the world. Enlightenment thinkers believed that social, political, and economic problems could be solved through the use of reason.

Lesson 5: The American Revolution

By 1750, thirteen prosperous colonies in North America were part of Britain's growing empire. As relations became strained with Britain, colonists bitterly resented what they saw as restrictions on their rights. The opposition would lead to revolution, independence, and the founding of the United States of America.

Lesson 6: The French Revolution Begins

Enlightenment ideas led people to question the social, economic, and political inequalities of the old regime. As social unrest increased, citizens stormed the Bastille, a prison for political prisoners. The revolution had begun.

Lesson 7: A Radical Phase

The moderate, first phase of the revolution which attempted to limit the power of the monarchy and guarantee basic rights gave way to the radical phase during which the monarchy was abolished, the king and queen were executed, and a Reign of Terror began.

Lesson 8: The Age of Napoleon

From 1799 to 1815, Napoleon Bonaparte gained power and built an empire that included much of Europe.

QUEST! FINDINGS

Create A Human Rights Bill
Refer to your responses to the Quest Connection to help you and your team create a Human Rights Bill. Present your finished work to the class. Use the rubric and other Quest resources online to guide your work.

GO ONLINE to access lesson summaries

VISUAL REVIEW

Use these graphics to review some of the key terms, people, and ideas from this Topic.

Key Rulers

- **Spain:** Charles V (Charles I of Spain); Philip II
- **France:** Henry IV; Louis XIV
- **Britain:** Henry VIII; Elizabeth I; James I; Charles I; Oliver Cromwell; Charles II; James II; William and Mary
- **Austria:** Ferdinand; Charles VI; Maria Theresa
- **Prussia:** Frederick William; Frederick the Great
- **Russia:** Peter the Great; Catherine the Great

American Declaration of Independence

Main Ideas
• All men are created equal and have natural rights to life, liberty, and the pursuit of happiness.
• It is the government's obligation to protect these rights.
• If a government fails to protect these rights, the people can revolt and set up a new government.

Enlightenment Ideas Influence Democracy

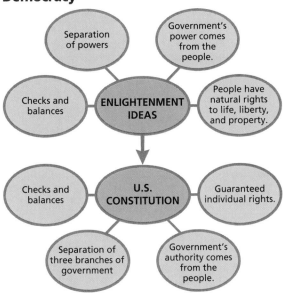

Causes and Effects of the French Revolution

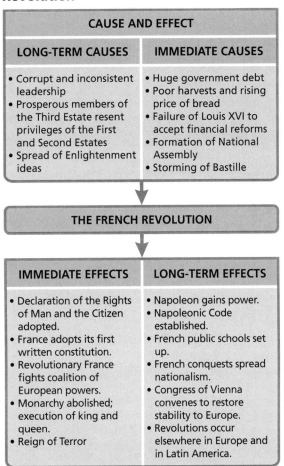

589

Topic 12 Assessment

KEY TERMS, PEOPLE, AND IDEAS

1. How did monarchs use the concept of **divine right** to support absolute rule?

2. How did **Peter the Great** envision Russia's future?

3. What is the connection between the policy of **laissez faire** and natural economic laws?

4. According to John Locke what is the purpose of government?

5. Compare the development of constitutional monarchy in England with that of France.

6. How did the Declaration of Independence influence the writing of the Declaration of the Rights of Man and the Citizen?

7. What role did **Robespierre** assume in the French Revolution?

8. After the fall of Napoleon, how did the Congress of Vienna affect nationalism in Europe?

9. How did the Glorious Revolution change English government?

CRITICAL THINKING

10. **Summarize** Why was the government of Britain an oligarchy rather than a democracy?

11. **Compare** How did Thomas Hobbes's view of government differ from John Locke's? Did the ideas of either influence the new government of the United States? Explain.

12. **Explain** Trace the shift in ideas that moved the French Revolution from constitutional monarchy to democratic despotism.

13. **Draw Conclusions** How did the ideas of a "just society" change during the Age of Reason?

14. **Synthesize Information** How did the Enlightenment impact both the American and French revolutions?

15. **Analyze Information** How did the American Revolution impact the way rebellions were fought? How did it affect expected outcomes?

16. **Analyze Cartoons** Look at the cartoon below. The figure on the left represents the British; the other figure represents Napoleon. What are both men carving? Explain.

17. **Writing Activity: Write an Informative Essay** The English Bill of Rights of 1688 granted basic rights to citizens, limited power of the monarch, and gave Parliament "power of the purse." These were critical steps in reducing the power of the monarchy and expanding the rights of the people. Using information from the topic, write a short essay that summarizes how these developments led to increased democracy in England.

18. **Connections to Today** Consider the role of the monarchy today. Are monarchies still relevant? Will monarchies survive as an institution? Take a stand.

DOCUMENT-BASED QUESTIONS

The struggle between English monarchs and Parliament raged through the seventeenth century, and was fought on battlefields and legal fronts. Read the documents below, then answer the questions that follow.

DOCUMENT A

"THE KINGS THEREAFTER in Scotland were before any estates or ranks of men within the same, before any Parliaments were holden or laws made; and by them was the land distributed (which at first was wholly theirs), states erected and decerned, and forms of government devised and established. And it follows of necessity that the Kings were the authors and makers of the laws and not the laws of the Kings."
—*True Law of Free Monarchies, 1598*

DOCUMENT B

"The Petition exhibited to his Majesty by the lords Spiritual and Temporal, and Commons, in this present Parliament assembled, concerning divers Rights and Liberties of the Subjects, with the King's Majesty's royal answer thereunto in full Parliament. . . . Your subjects have inherited this freedom, that they should not be compelled to contribute to any tax, tallage, aid, or other like charge not set by common consent, in parliament. . . . No man, of what estate or condition that he be, should be put out of his land or tenements, nor taken, nor imprisoned, nor disinherited nor put to death without being brought to answer by due process of law."
—*The Petition of Right, 1628*

DOCUMENT C

"Men, being, as has been said, by nature all free, equal, and independent, no one can be . . . subjected to the political power of another without his own consent. The only way whereby anyone divests himself of his natural liberty, and puts on the bonds of civil society is by agreeing with other men to join and unite into a community. . . .

It is evident, that *absolute monarchy*, which by some men is counted the only government in the world, is indeed *inconsistent with civil society.*"
—*Two Treatises on Government* by John Locke, 1690

DOCUMENT D

A mid-1600s engraving depicts Charles I as a political and religious martyr.

19. What is the main point of Document A?
    A. Kings are subject only to laws of parliament.
    B. Kings make laws but are not subject to them.
    C. Kings no longer have the power of life and death over subjects.
    D. Parliament now has the power of life and death over subjects.

20. Document B is a declaration of whose rights?
    A. the kings rights
    B. Parliament's rights
    C. subjects' rights
    D. the landed aristocracy's rights

21. Document C
    A. supports Document A.
    B. supports Document B.
    C. supports both Document A and Document B.
    D. supports Documents A and D.

22. **Writing Tasks** Would you describe the rise of Parliament in England as an evolution or a revolution? Use the documents along with information from this topic in your response.

The Industrial Revolution (1750–1914)

ESSENTIAL QUESTION How do science and technology affect society?

GO ONLINE for immersive experiences designed to help you explore perspectives on the early Industrial Revolution through rich primary sources. Also access the eText, videos, Biographies, and other online resources.

A furnace for manufacturing iron in England

Connections to Today

Coal powered the Industrial Revolution. It played a pivotal role in the successful growth of the economy during the later 18th and early 19th centuries. Today, coal, along with oil and natural gas, is one of the fossil fuels that provide the energy for everything from our transportation to the lights in our homes. In this Topic, you will learn how energy changes during the Industrial Revolution impacted the world. Today, what are the advantages and disadvantages of using fossil fuels? Are there other forms of energy that can be used?

Share the experiences of a worker in an early 19th century textile mill.

 BOUNCE to Activate My Story Video

In this Topic, you will learn about the events of The Industrial Revolution. Look at the lesson outline and explore the timeline. As you study this Topic, you will complete the Quest inquiry project.

LESSON OUTLINE

13.1 The Industrial Revolution Begins

13.2 Social Impact of Industrialism

13.3 The Second Industrial Revolution

13.4 Changing Ways of Life and Thought

Key Events of the Industrial Revolution

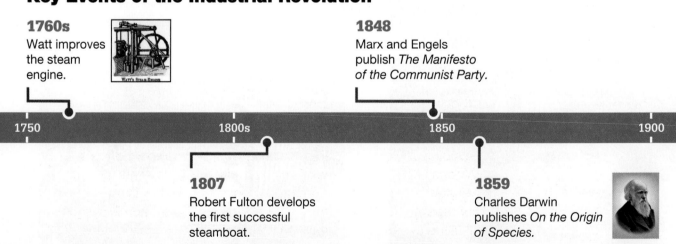

1760s
Watt improves the steam engine.

1848
Marx and Engels publish *The Manifesto of the Communist Party.*

1750   1800s   1850   1900

1807
Robert Fulton develops the first successful steamboat.

1859
Charles Darwin publishes *On the Origin of Species.*

QUEST! INQUIRY

Making Policy Decisions

Your team is part of a government think tank on economics. You will do important research that will be used to make important decisions. Your current study is about economic policies that will help improve the nation's living standards. There are many questions. In this Quest you will explore one: Who Should Control Economic Decisions?

STEP
Gather the documents. Analyze the content of each. List the conclusions. Then have a discussion about the different systems.

STEP
Choose the documents with a viewpoint the team will consider and evaluate. Outline your report. Then, still using evidence, consider arguments that could be used to oppose the team's decision.

STEP 3
Review, edit, and revise the report. Remember to support your decision with evidence. Then consider why the team's choice might be opposed.

STEP
Present your final report to the class. Reflect on what you have researched. How is the current economic system affecting the nation's families? Should changes be made?

 GO ONLINE to access complete Quest materials

13.1

🖵 **GO ONLINE to Project Imagine: Trace the Growth of Early Industry** to learn about the steam engine and other innovations that kicked off the Industrial Revolution.

 BOUNCE to Activate Flipped Video

Objectives

Describe how changes in agriculture helped spark the Industrial Revolution.

Analyze why the Industrial Revolution began in Britain.

Explain the role of steam technology and textile manufacturing in the Industrial Revolution.

Describe how the factory system and transportation revolution advanced industry.

Trace how the Industrial Revolution spread.

Key Terms

Industrial Revolution
anesthetic
enclosure
James Watt
smelt
capital
enterprise
entrepreneur
putting-out system
Eli Whitney
turnpike
Liverpool
Manchester

The Industrial Revolution Begins

For thousands of years following the rise of civilization, most people lived and worked in small farming villages. Then a chain of events set in motion in the mid-1700s changed that way of life. Today, we call this period of economic change the Industrial Revolution. Production shifted from simple hand tools to complex machines, and sources of energy shifted from human and animal power to steam and, later, electricity.

New Ways of Working Change Life

Like the Enlightenment, which occurred around the same time, the Industrial Revolution was partly an outgrowth of the Scientific Revolution of the 1600s and 1700s. The Scientific Revolution focused attention on the physical world, and thinkers used the scientific method to conduct controlled experiments. This scientific approach helped inventors to devise new technologies to improve life. These technologies would change the way work was done.

In contrast with most political revolutions, the Industrial Revolution was neither sudden nor swift. It was a long, slow, uneven process. Yet it affected people's lives as much as previous political changes and revolutions had. From its beginnings in Britain, it spread to the rest of Europe, to North America, and around the globe.

A Rural Way of Life In 1750, most people worked the land, using handmade tools. They lived in simple cottages lit by firelight and candles. They made their own clothing and grew their own food.

In nearby towns, they might exchange goods at a weekly outdoor market.

Like their ancestors, these people knew little of the world that existed beyond their village. The few who left home traveled only as far as their feet or a horse-drawn cart could take them. Those bold adventurers who dared to cross the seas were at the mercy of the winds and tides.

Growing Cities With the onset of the Industrial Revolution, the rural way of life began to disappear. By the 1850s, many country villages had grown into industrial towns and cities. Those who lived there were able to buy clothing and food that someone else produced.

Industrialization Brings Great Change Unlike earlier times, industrial-age travelers were able to move rapidly between countries and continents by train or steamship. Urgent messages flew along telegraph wires. New inventions and scientific "firsts" poured forth each year.

Between 1830 and 1855, for example, an American dentist first used an **anesthetic,** or drug that prevents pain during surgery; an American inventor patented the first sewing machine; a French physicist measured the speed of light; and a Hungarian doctor introduced antiseptic methods to reduce the risk of women dying in childbirth. By the early 1900s, our familiar world of skyscraper cities and carefully planned suburbs had begun to emerge.

How and why did these great changes occur? Historians point to a series of interrelated causes that helped trigger the industrialization of the West. The "West" referred originally to the industrialized countries of western Europe and North America, but today includes many more.

☑ **IDENTIFY MAIN IDEAS** How did the Industrial Revolution lead to social and economic changes in Europe?

A New Agricultural Revolution

Oddly enough, the Industrial Revolution was made possible in part by a change in the farming fields of western Europe. The first agricultural revolution took place some 11,000 years ago, when people learned to farm and domesticate animals. Then, about 300 years ago, a second agricultural revolution took place that greatly improved the quality and quantity of farm products.

Farmers Reclaim Land and Renew Soil The Dutch led the way in this new agricultural revolution. They built earthen walls known as dikes to reclaim land from the sea. They also combined smaller fields into larger ones to make better use of the land, and they used fertilizer from livestock to renew the soil.

In the 1700s, British farmers expanded on Dutch agricultural experiments. Educated farmers exchanged news of experiments through farm journals. Some farmers mixed different kinds of soils to get higher crop yields. Others tried out new methods of crop rotation.

Lord Charles Townshend urged farmers to grow turnips, which restored exhausted soil. Jethro Tull invented a new mechanical device, the seed drill, to aid farmers. It deposited seeds in rows to maximize land use rather than scattering them over land, a practice that wasted seeds by spacing plants irregularly.

Wealthy Landowners Enclose Lands Meanwhile, wealthy landowners pushed ahead with a practice called **enclosure.** Enclosure is the process of taking over and consolidating, or combining, lands formerly shared by peasant farmers. In the 1500s, landowners had enclosed land to gain more pastures for sheep in order to increase wool output. By the 1700s,

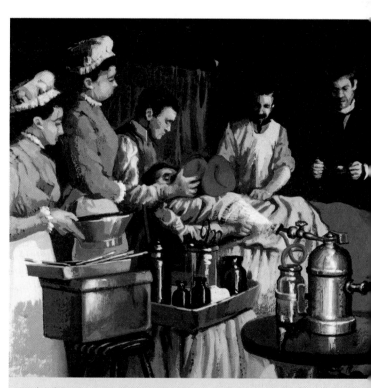

>> An American dentist demonstrates the use of ether as a surgical anesthetic in 1846.

they wanted to create larger fields that could be cultivated more efficiently. The British Parliament passed laws that made it easier for landowners to enclose lands.

As millions of acres were enclosed, farm output rose. Profits also rose because consolidated fields needed fewer workers. However, such progress had a human cost. Many farm laborers were thrown out of work, and small farmers were forced off their land because they could not compete with large landholders. Villages shrank when people left in search of work.

This shift in the labor force became a key factor in industrialization. Jobless farm workers migrated to towns and cities. Many found work in the new factories, tending to the machines of the Industrial Revolution.

Population Grows Because of Better Farming Not only did people move to towns and cities, but an overall boom in population also occurred. The improved farming practices of the agricultural revolution contributed to this rapid population growth. Precise population statistics for the 1700s are rare, but those that do exist are striking. Britain's population, for example,

soared from about 5 million in 1700 to almost 9 million in 1800.

The population of Europe as a whole shot up from roughly 120 million to about 180 million during the same period. Such growth had never before been seen.

Why did this population increase occur? The population boom was due more to declining death rates than to rising birth rates. The agricultural revolution reduced the risk of famine. Since people ate better, they were healthier. Also, by the late 1800s, better hygiene and sanitation, along with improved medical care, further slowed deaths from disease. During the Industrial Revolution, this growing population tended the machines and bought the goods produced by factories.

☑ **CHECK UNDERSTANDING** How did an agricultural revolution contribute to population growth?

Coal, Steam, and the Energy Revolution

Another major factor that contributed to the Industrial Revolution was an "energy revolution." In the past, the energy for work came mostly from the muscles of humans and animals. In the 1700s, inventive minds found ways to use water power more efficiently and harnessed new sources of energy. Among the most important energy sources was coal, which was used to develop the steam engine.

James Watt and the Steam Engine In 1712, inventor Thomas Newcomen developed a steam engine powered by coal to pump water out of mines. Later, in 1764, Scottish engineer **James Watt** looked at Newcomen's invention and set out to make improvements on the engine in order to make it more efficient. Watt's engine would become a vital power source of the Industrial Revolution.

The steam engine was first used to power machines, but later was adapted to power locomotives and steamships.

Producing Better Iron Coal was also a vital source of fuel in the production of iron, a material needed for the construction of machines and steam engines. The Darby family of Coalbrookdale, England, pioneered new methods of producing iron. In 1709, Abraham Darby used coal instead of charcoal to **smelt** iron, or separate iron from its ore.

WATT'S STEAM-ENGINE

>> Watt's engine used steam and atmospheric pressure to power pistons and rods that moved machinery. It had a separate condenser to keep the water hot, conserving energy.

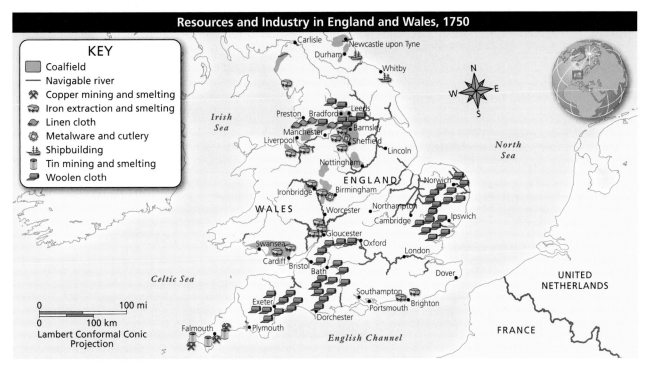

Resources and Industry in England and Wales, 1750

KEY
- ▢ Coalfield
- — Navigable river
- ✳ Copper mining and smelting
- 🛢 Iron extraction and smelting
- ◿ Linen cloth
- ◎ Metalware and cutlery
- ⚓ Shipbuilding
- 🛢 Tin mining and smelting
- ◿ Woolen cloth

>> **Analyze Maps** Notice where various resources and industries were located in 1750. Why is the location of navigable rivers important to resources and industry?

Darby's experiments led him to produce less expensive and better-quality iron, which was used to produce parts for the steam engines. Both his son and grandson continued to improve on his methods. In fact, Abraham Darby III built the world's first iron bridge. In the decades that followed, high-quality iron was used more and more widely, especially after the world turned to building railroads.

☑ **IDENTIFY SUPPORTING DETAILS** What did the Darby family contribute to the Industrial Revolution?

Why Did the Industrial Revolution Start in Britain?

Historians have fiercely debated why the Industrial Revolution began in Britain in the 1700s. They have identified a number of advantages Britain had. No single one was unique to Britain, but taken together they helped Britain take an early lead. This complex combination included natural resources, labor, capital, and entrepreneurship. Economists call these the four factors of production; that is, the elements necessary to produce goods. In addition to these factors, growing demand for goods and new technology provided the essential building blocks for Britain's leap forward.

Natural Resources and Geography During the 1700s, Britain began to take greater advantage of its abundant natural resources. Although Britain was a relatively small nation, it had large supplies of coal to power steam engines. Britain also had plentiful iron, which was used to build machines.

Britain's geography also provided an advantage. As an island nation with many ports, Britain had long benefited from trade. Its ships brought raw materials from its overseas empire and exported finished goods. Britain also had streams and rivers that could be harnessed to provide water power. Many rivers were later connected with canals and then used to transport goods to internal markets.

Labor and Capital A large number of workers were needed to mine the coal and iron, build the factories, and run the machines. The agricultural revolution of the 1600s and 1700s freed many men and women from farm labor. The population boom that resulted from changes in agriculture further swelled the available work force. The growing population also increased the demand for goods, which industry supplied.

To develop mining and other industries, capital was needed. **Capital** is money used to invest in enterprises. An **enterprise** is a business organization in an area such as shipping, mining, railroads, or factories. Many businesspeople were ready to risk their profits in new ventures. The capital that helped Britain industrialize came from landowners, banks, and merchants who profited from overseas trade, including the slave trade.

Entrepreneurs and Inventors Britain also had plenty of skilled mechanics. They developed practical new inventions and partnered with entrepreneurs to profit from them. An **entrepreneur** is someone who manages and assumes the financial risks of starting new businesses.

Technology was important to the Industrial Revolution, but did not cause it. Only when other necessary conditions existed, including demand and capital, did technology pave the way for industrialization.

A Favorable Climate for Business In addition to the advantages already cited, Britain had a stable government that supported economic growth. Other countries in Europe imposed heavy river tolls and other barriers to growth. Britain had far fewer blocks to the movement of goods. The government built a strong navy that protected its empire, including shipping and overseas trade.

Social attitudes adjusted to changing economic conditions. Although members of the upper class looked down on business and business people, they did not reject the great wealth produced by the new entrepreneurs. Religious groups encouraged thrift and hard work. These goals led inventors, bankers, and other risk-takers to devote their energies to new enterprises.

☑ **CHECK UNDERSTANDING** What conditions in Britain paved the way for the Industrial Revolution?

Textile Industry Initiates Industrialization

The Industrial Revolution first took hold in Britain's largest industry—textiles. In the 1600s, cotton cloth imported from India had become popular. British merchants tried to organize a cotton cloth industry at home. They developed the **putting-out system,** also known as the cottage industry, in which raw cotton was distributed to peasant families who spun it into thread and then wove the thread into cloth in their own homes. Skilled artisans in the towns then finished and dyed the cloth.

Technology Speeds Production Under the putting-out system, production was slow. The process of using manually operated machines for spinning and weaving took time. As the demand for cloth grew, inventors came up with a series of remarkable devices that revolutionized the British textile industry. For example, John Kay's flying shuttle enabled weavers to work so fast that they soon outpaced spinners. James Hargreaves solved that problem by producing the spinning jenny in 1764, which spun many threads at the same time. Five years later, Richard Arkwright patented the water frame, a spinning machine that could be powered by water.

Meanwhile, in America, these faster spinning and weaving machines presented a challenge—how to produce enough cotton to keep up with England. Raw cotton grown in the South had to be cleaned of dirt and seeds by hand, which is a time-consuming task. To solve this, **Eli Whitney** invented a machine called the cotton gin that separated the seeds from the raw cotton at a fast rate. He finished the cotton gin in 1793, and cotton production increased at a rapid rate.

The First Factories The new machines doomed the putting-out system. They were too large

Raw Cotton, Great Britain 1710–1849 in millions of pounds

ANNUAL AVERAGE CONSUMPTION		ANNUAL AVERAGE CONSUMPTION	
1710–19	1.3	1780–89	15.5
1720–29	1.5	1790–99	28.6
1730–39	1.7	1800–09	59.6
1740–49	2.1	1810–19	93.4
1750–59	2.8	1820–29	166.5
1760–69	3.5	1830–39	320.7
1770–79	4.8	1840–49	526.3

SOURCE: 1697–1780: Wadsworth and Mann [1931], 1780–1810: Baines [1835] 1810–1849: Ellison [1886]

>> **Analyze Charts** This chart shows the gradual increase in cotton use in Britain during the Industrial Revolution. What factors changed the British cotton industry and helped to make it the "workshop of the world"?

and expensive to be operated at home. Instead, manufacturers built long sheds to house the machines. At first, they located the sheds near rapidly moving streams, harnessing the water power to run the machines. Later, machines were powered by steam engines.

Spinners and weavers now came each day to work in these first factories, which brought together workers and machines to produce large quantities of goods. Early observers were awed at the size and output of these establishments. One onlooker noted: "The same [amount] of labor is now performed in one of these structures which formerly occupied the industry of an entire district."

☑ **IDENTIFY CAUSE AND EFFECT** What technology brought about advances in the British textile industry?

A Revolution in Transportation

As production increased, entrepreneurs needed faster and cheaper methods of moving goods from place to place. Some capitalists invested in **turnpikes,** private roads built by entrepreneurs who charged travelers a toll, or fee, to use them. Goods traveled faster as a result, and turnpikes soon linked every part of Britain. Other entrepreneurs had canals dug to connect rivers together or to connect inland towns with coastal ports. Engineers also built stronger bridges and upgraded harbors to help the expanding overseas trade.

Canals Improve Transportation During the late 1700s and early 1800s, British factories needed an efficient, inexpensive way to receive coal and raw materials and then to ship finished goods to market. In 1763, when the Bridgewater Canal opened, it not only made a profit from tolls, but it shortened the trip enough to cut in half the price of coal in Manchester.

The success of this canal set off a canal-building frenzy. Entrepreneurs formed companies to construct canals for profit. Not all the canals that were built had enough traffic to support them, however, and bankruptcy often resulted. Then, beginning in the 1830s, canals lost their importance as steam locomotives made railroads the new preferred form of transportation.

The Steam Locomotive Drives Railroads It was the invention of the steam locomotive that made the growth of railroads possible. In the early 1800s,

>> Workers and machines filled the early factories of the Industrial Revolution. Machines dramatically increased the quantity of goods that could be produced.

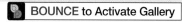
🅑 BOUNCE to Activate Gallery

>> Steam locomotives made travel faster than ever before. The locomotives burned coal to produce steam and traveled overland routes on iron rails.

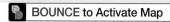
🅑 BOUNCE to Activate Map

pioneers like George Stephenson developed steam-powered locomotives to pull carriages along iron rails. The railroad did not have to follow the course of a river. This meant that tracks could go places where rivers did not, allowing factory owners and merchants to ship goods swiftly and cheaply over land. The world's first major rail line, from **Liverpool** to **Manchester,** opened in England in 1830.

In the following decades, railroad travel became faster and railroad building boomed. By 1870, rail lines crisscrossed Britain, Europe, and North America.

Cheaper Goods Lead to More Demand As the Industrial Revolution got under way, it triggered a chain reaction. Once inventors developed machines that could produce large quantities of goods more efficiently, prices fell. Lower prices made goods more affordable and thus attracted more consumers. Additional consumers then further fed the demand for goods. This new cycle caused a wave of economic and social changes that dramatically affected the way people lived.

☑ **DRAW CONCLUSIONS** How did the development of railroads advance the Industrial Revolution?

Industrialization Spreads

The start of industrialization had largely been forged from iron, powered by steam engines, and driven by the British textile industry. By the mid-1800s, the Industrial Revolution entered a second phase. By then, it had spread outside Britain. New industrial powers emerged. Factories powered by electricity used innovative processes to turn out new products. Changes in business organization contributed to the rise of giant companies. As the twentieth century dawned, this second Industrial Revolution transformed the economies of the Western world.

Other Nations Industrialize During the early Industrial Revolution, Britain stood alone as the world's industrial giant. To protect its head start, Britain tried to enforce strict rules against exporting inventions.

For a while, the rules worked. Then, in 1807, British mechanic William Cockerill opened factories in Belgium to manufacture spinning and weaving machines. Belgium became the first European nation after Britain to industrialize. By the mid-1800s, other nations had joined the race, and several newcomers were challenging Britain's industrial supremacy.

How were other nations able to catch up with Britain so quickly? First, nations such as Germany,

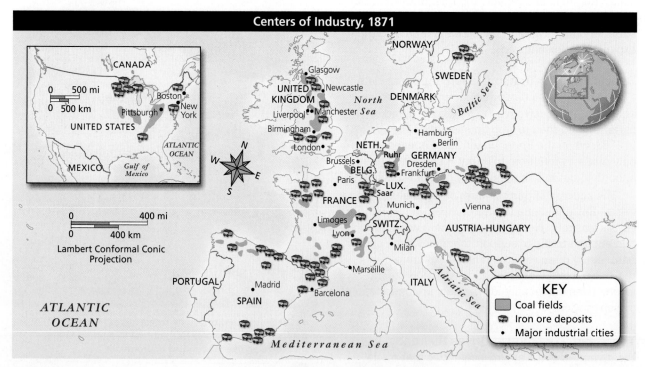

Centers of Industry, 1871

>> **Analyze Maps** By 1871, industrialization had spread through Europe and across the Atlantic to America. Which major industrial cities were probably shipping centers as well? Identify two nations that were at a disadvantage for industrialization.

France, and the United States had more abundant supplies of coal, iron, and other resources than Britain did. Also, they had the advantage of being able to follow Britain's lead. Like Belgium, latecomers often borrowed British experts or technology. The first American textile factory was built in Pawtucket, Rhode Island, with plans smuggled out of Britain. American inventor Robert Fulton powered his steamboat with one of James Watt's steam engines.

Two countries in particular—Germany and the United States—thrust their way to industrial leadership. Germany united into a powerful nation in 1871. Within a few decades, it became Europe's leading industrial power. Across the Atlantic, the United States advanced even more rapidly, especially after the Civil War.

With a large labor force, plenty of resources, and entrepreneurs who had capital, by 1900 the United States was manufacturing about 30 percent of the world's industrial goods. It had surpassed Britain as the leading industrial nation.

Industry Spreads Unevenly Other nations industrialized more slowly, particularly those in eastern and southern Europe. These nations often lacked natural resources or the capital to invest in industry. Although Russia did have resources, social and political conditions slowed its economic development. Only in the late 1800s, more than 100 years after Britain, did Russia move toward industrialization.

In East Asia, however, Japan offered a remarkable success story. Although Japan lacked many basic resources, it industrialized rapidly after 1868 because of a political revolution that made modernization a priority. Canada, Australia, and New Zealand also built thriving industries during this time.

Social, Economic, and Political Changes Like Britain, the new industrial nations underwent social changes, such as rapid urbanization. Early in the history of industrialization, men, women, and children worked long hours in difficult and dangerous conditions. By 1900, however, these conditions had begun to improve in many industrialized nations.

The factory system produced huge quantities of new goods at lower prices than ever before. In time, ordinary workers were buying goods that in earlier days only the wealthy could afford. The demand for goods created jobs, as did the building of cities, railroads, and factories. Politics changed, too, as leaders had to meet the demands of an industrial society.

Globally, industrial nations competed fiercely, altering patterns of world trade. Because of their

>> A street scene in Chicago, Illinois, from the early 1900s shows how the urban landscape was altered by industrialization. **Compare and Contrast** How is the scene similar to and different from a typical city street today?

technological and economic advantage, the Western powers came to dominate the world more than ever before.

☑ **ANALYZE INFORMATION** What factors allowed other nations to industrialize after Britain?

☑ ASSESSMENT

1. **Identify Cause and Effect** How did technological advances in agriculture affect the Industrial Revolution?

2. **Generate Explanations** Why was a supply of coal crucial to the Industrial Revolution?

3. **Synthesize** How did the four factors of production determine which nations were able to industrialize after Britain? Cite specific examples from the text.

4. **Cite Evidence** How did industrialization enable Western powers to dominate world affairs?

5. **Connections to Today** The Industrial Revolution resulted in important changes in human life. How has technology changed the lives of people today?

📡 **GO ONLINE to Project Imagine: Make Your Fortune in Industry** to see the choices facing entrepreneurs, including those affecting their workers.

 BOUNCE to Activate Flipped Video

Objectives

Outline the growth of industrial cities and the emergence of new social classes.

Describe the working conditions in factories and mines.

Analyze the benefits and challenges of industrialism.

Describe the ideas of Adam Smith and other thinkers regarding free enterprise.

Identify the origins and characteristics of socialism and communism

Key Terms

urbanization
tenement
labor union
standard of living
social mobility
free market
Thomas Malthus
Jeremy Bentham
utilitarianism
socialism
means of production
Robert Owen
Karl Marx
communism
proletariat
social democracy

Social Impact of Industrialism

The Industrial Revolution brought great riches to most of the entrepreneurs who helped set it in motion. It also provided employment for farmers and farmhands displaced by the changes in agriculture. But these jobs came with a heavy price. Millions of workers who crowded into the new factory towns endured dangerous working conditions, unsanitary and overcrowded housing, and unrelenting poverty.

Industry Causes Urban Growth

In time, reforms would curb many of the worst abuses of the early Industrial Age in Europe and the Americas. As standards of living increased, people at all levels of society would benefit from industrialization.

The Industrial Revolution brought rapid **urbanization,** or the movement of people to cities. Changes in farming, soaring population growth, and an ever-increasing demand for workers led masses of people to migrate from farms to cities. Almost overnight, small towns around coal or iron mines mushroomed into cities. Other cities grew up around the factories that entrepreneurs built in once-quiet market towns.

The British market town of Manchester numbered 17,000 people in the 1750s. Within a few years, it exploded into a center of the textile industry. Its population soared to 40,000 by 1780 and 70,000 by 1801. Visitors described the "cloud of coal vapor" that polluted the air, the pounding noise of steam engines, and the filthy stench of its river. This growth of industry and rapid population growth dramatically changed the location and distribution of two resources—labor and people.

📡 **GO ONLINE to access** your digital course

☑ **IDENTIFY SUPPORTING DETAILS** What led to the massive migration of people from farms to cities?

The Rise of New Social Classes

The Industrial Revolution helped create both a new middle class and a new urban working class. The middle class included entrepreneurs and others who profited from the growth of industry and the rise of cities. The middle class enjoyed a comfortable lifestyle.

When farm laborers and others moved to the new industrial cities, they took jobs in factories or mines. In rural villages, they had strong ties to a community, where their families had lived for generations. In the cities, they felt lost and bewildered. In time, though, factory and mine workers developed their own sense of community.

The Lives of the New Middle Class Those who benefited most from the Industrial Revolution were the entrepreneurs who set it in motion. The Industrial Revolution created this new middle class, or bourgeoisie (boor zhwah ZEE), whose

members came from a variety of backgrounds. Some were merchants who invested their profits in factories. Others were inventors or skilled artisans who developed new technologies. Some rose from "rags to riches," a pattern that the age greatly admired. Middle-class families lived in well-built, well-furnished homes. In time, middle-class neighborhoods had paved streets and a steady water supply. These families dressed and ate well. The new middle class took pride in their hard work and their determination to "get ahead." Only a few had sympathy for the poor.

As a sign of their new and improved status, middle-class women sought to imitate the wealthy women of the upper classes. They did not do physical labor or work outside the home. They hired maidservants to care for their homes and look after their children.

The Lives of the Working Class While the wealthy and the middle class lived in pleasant neighborhoods, vast numbers of poor struggled to survive in foul-smelling slums. They packed into tiny rooms in **tenements,** or multistory buildings divided into apartments. These tenements had no running water, only community pumps. Early

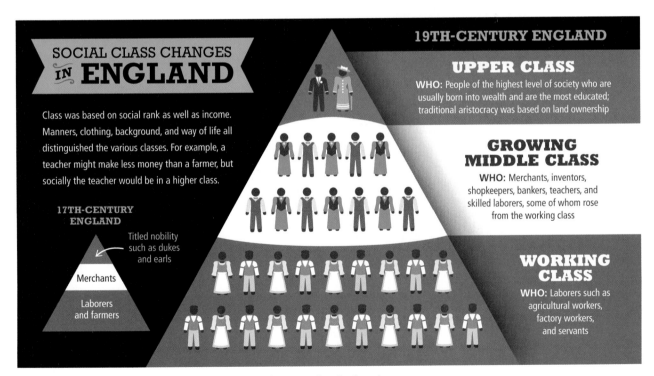

>> The expanding middle class included working-class people who found new opportunities because of industrialization. **Analyze Charts** Which class changed the least due to industrialization?

industrial cities had no sewage or sanitation systems, so waste and garbage rotted in the streets.

Sewage was also dumped into rivers, which created an overwhelming stench and contaminated drinking water. This led to the spread of diseases such as cholera.

Workers' Protests During the early Industrial Revolution, there were no **labor unions,** organizations of workers who bargained for better pay and working conditions. As the Industrial Revolution began, weavers and other skilled artisans resisted the new "labor-saving" machines that were replacing their jobs.

From 1811 to 1813, protesting workers, called Luddites (LUD yts), smashed machines and burned factories. The Luddites were harshly crushed. Although frustrated workers continued to protest, they were forbidden to form worker associations and strikes were outlawed.

Methodists Help the Poor Many working-class people found comfort in a religious movement called Methodism. John Wesley had founded the Methodist movement in the mid-1700s. Wesley stressed the need for a personal sense of faith. He encouraged his

followers to improve themselves by adopting sober, moral ways.

Methodist meetings featured hymns and sermons promising forgiveness of sin and a better life to come. Methodist preachers took this message of salvation into the slums. There, they tried to rekindle hope among the working poor. They set up Sunday schools where followers not only studied the Bible but also learned to read and write. Methodists helped channel workers' anger away from revolution and toward reform.

☑ **MAKE GENERALIZATIONS** How did members of the working class react to their new experiences in industrial cities?

Harsh Conditions in Factories and Mines

The heart of the new industrial city was the factory. There, the technology of the machine age imposed a harsh and dangerous way of life on workers. The miners who supplied the coal and iron for the Industrial Age faced equally unsafe working conditions.

Hazards of the Factory System Working in a factory system differed greatly from working on a farm. In rural villages, people worked long hours for low wages, but their work varied according to the season. Life was also hard for poor rural workers who were part of the putting-out system. If they worked too slowly, they did not earn enough, but at least they worked at their own pace. In the factories of industrial towns, workers faced a rigid schedule set by the factory whistle.

Working hours in early factories were long, with shifts lasting from 12 to 16 hours, six or seven days a week. A factory whistle announced time to eat a hasty meal, then quickly sent them back to the machines. Exhausted workers suffered accidents from machines that had no safety devices. They might lose a finger, a limb, or even their lives.

In textile mills, workers constantly breathed air filled with lint, which damaged their lungs. Those workers who became sick or injured lost their jobs.

At first, women made up much of the new industrial work force. Employers often preferred to hire women workers. They thought women could adapt more easily to machines and were easier to manage than men. More important, they were able to pay women less than men, even for the same work.

>> John Wesley, founder of Methodism, is shown preaching at his father's grave in a churchyard in Epworth, Lincolnshire, where he was born and raised.

Factory work created a double burden for women. Their new jobs took them out of their homes for 12 hours or more a day. They then returned to their tenements, which might consist of one damp room with a single bed. They had to feed and clothe their families, clean, and cope with such problems as sickness and injury.

Dangers in the Mines As the demand for coal and iron grew, more mines were opened. Although miners were paid more than factory workers, conditions in the mines were even harsher than in the factories. Miners worked in darkness, and the coal dust destroyed their lungs. There were always the dangers of explosions, flooding, and collapsing tunnels.

Women and children worked in mines, carting heavy loads of coal. Children were frequently hired to work in mines because they could climb through narrow shafts. Many spent their days on all fours or carried heavy baskets of coal up flimsy ladders.

Children Perform Risky Work Children had always worked on rural farms or as servants and apprentices. However, child labor took on new dimensions during the Industrial Revolution. Since children had helped with farm work, parents accepted the idea of child labor. The wages children earned were needed to keep their families from starving.

Factories and mines hired many boys and girls. These children often started working at age seven or eight, a few as young as five. Nimble-fingered and quick-moving, they changed spools in the hot and humid textile mills where sometimes they could not see because of all the dust. They also crawled under machinery to repair broken threads in the mills.

Conditions were even worse for children who worked in the mines. Some sat all day in the dark, opening and closing air vents. Others hauled coal carts in the extreme heat.

In the early 1800s, Parliament passed a series of laws, called "factory acts," to reform child labor practices. These early efforts were largely ignored. Then, in 1833, Michael Sadler headed up a committee to look into the conditions of child workers in the textile industry. The Sadler Report contained firsthand accounts of child labor practices and helped bring the harsh labor conditions to light. As a result, Parliament passed new regulations to ease working conditions for children.

An 1833 law forbade the hiring of children under the age of nine and limited the working hours of older children in the textile industry. Over time, Parliament passed other laws to improve working

>> Before child labor laws, working-class children like these boys in Pennsylvania worked long hours on hazardous jobs. Many of these mineworkers were aged 10 or even younger. **Hypothesize** Why did mine owners hire children for certain jobs?

BOUNCE to Activate Gallery

conditions in both factories and mines and to limit the work day of both adults and children to 10 hours. It also enacted laws to require the education of children and to stop the hiring of children and women in mines.

☑ **DRAW CONCLUSIONS** How did the Industrial Revolution change the lives of men, women, and children?

Benefits of the Industrial Revolution

Since the 1800s, people have debated whether the Industrial Revolution was a blessing or a curse. The early Industrial Age brought great hardships and much misery. Although the first factories did provide jobs and wages to displaced farm workers, the conditions under which they labored were generally terrible. In time, however, reformers, along with labor unions, pushed for laws to improve working conditions in factories, mines, and other industries. Despite the negative aspects of industrialization, the new industrial world eventually brought many advantages.

Better Standards of Living The factory system produced huge quantities of new goods at lower prices than ever before. In time, as wages and working conditions improved, ordinary workers were able to buy goods that in earlier days only the wealthy had been able to afford. Slowly, too, the **standard of living** rose for workers. The standard of living refers to the level of material goods and services available to people in a society. Families ate more varied diets, lived in better homes, and dressed in inexpensive, mass-produced clothing. Advances in medicine ensured healthier lives.

New job opportunities opened up for skilled and unskilled workers. The building of cities, railroads, and factories provided jobs. The demand for goods and the growth of new industries, such as railroads and eventually automobiles, created more job opportunities.

New Worlds for Entrepreneurs The new industrial world was more open to change and innovation than the old rural world. Enterprising people opened new businesses and invented new products. The British potter Josiah Wedgwood, for example, was an entrepreneur who combined science and new industrial methods of production. Wedgwood experimented with new materials to improve the quality of his pottery. He set up a factory that gave each different job to a specially skilled worker. Wedgwood also used his pottery to spread ideas about social justice, especially the abolition of the slave trade. His factory cast antislavery medallions, worn by many, that carried the image of a slave in chains with the words "Am I not a man and a brother?"

Social and Political Impact The Industrial Revolution opened new opportunities for success and increased **social mobility,** or the ability of individuals or groups to move up the social scale. In the past, birth determined a person's rank in society. Although birth still gave nobles their status, some families were able to move up the social ladder through successful enterprise. By the late 1800s, many people embraced the "rags to riches" idea, whereby a person could achieve great wealth and status through hard work and thrift.

With social mobility came greater political rights. As the middle class expanded, its members pushed for political influence. Gradually throughout the 1800s, working-class men gained the right to vote. From 1831 to 1885, the number of voters in England and Wales increased from 366,000 to almost 8 million. The growing number of voters gave the working class more power as politicians began to have to appeal to their concerns. Later, women also earned the right to vote. Labor unions won the right to bargain with employers for better wages, hours, and working conditions.

☑ **CHECK UNDERSTANDING** Why was the Industrial Revolution seen as both a blessing and a curse?

Laissez-Faire Economics

Many thinkers and economists tried to understand the staggering changes taking place in the early Industrial Age. As heirs to the Enlightenment, these thinkers looked for natural laws to explain the world of business and economics. Their ideas would influence governments down to the present. Among the most influential schools of thought were laissez-faire economics, utilitarianism, and socialism.

Adam Smith and Laissez-Faire Economics During the Enlightenment, thinkers looked for natural laws that governed the world of business

>> In *The Wealth of Nations,* Adam Smith proposed ideas about free market competition that are still applied today.

and economics. Physiocrats argued that natural laws should be allowed to operate without interference. As part of this philosophy, they believed that government should not interfere in the free operation of the economy. In the early 1800s, middle-class business leaders embraced this laissez-faire, or "hands-off," approach.

The main proponent of laissez-faire economics was Adam Smith, author of the bestseller *The Wealth of Nations*. Smith asserted that a **free market,** or unregulated exchange of goods and services, would come to help everyone, not just the rich. The free market, Smith said, would produce more goods at lower prices, making them affordable to everyone. A growing economy would also encourage capitalists to reinvest profits in new ventures.

As the Industrial Revolution spread, later supporters of this free-enterprise capitalism pointed to the successes of the early Industrial Revolution, in which government had played a limited role. Governments had taken steps to create a favorable atmosphere for business, such as Britain's laws to outlaw the export of inventions or the tariffs passed by the United States in 1789 to protect American industry, but played little role in the day-to-day operation of industry.

Malthus on Population Growth Like Smith, **Thomas Malthus** was a laissez-faire thinker whose writings influenced economic ideas for generations. In his 1798 book *An Essay on the Principle of Population*, he grimly predicted that poverty was unavoidable because the population was increasing faster than the food supply.

Malthus wrote: "The power of population is [far] greater than the power of the Earth to produce subsistence for man." He thought that the only checks on population growth were nature's "natural" methods of war, disease, and famine. As long as population kept increasing, he went on, the poor would suffer. He thus urged families to have fewer children and discouraged charitable handouts and vaccinations.

During the early 1800s, with industrial workers living and working in harsh conditions, many people accepted Malthus's bleak view. His view was proved wrong, however. Although the population boom did continue, the food supply grew even faster.

As the century progressed, living conditions in the Western world slowly improved, and people eventually did begin to have fewer children. By the 1900s, population growth was no longer a problem in the West, but it did continue to afflict many nations elsewhere.

>> Laissez-faire thinker Thomas Malthus believed that the increasing population put too great a strain on the food supply. He suggested smaller family sizes as a solution to ending poverty.

Ricardo and the "Iron Law of Wages" Another influential British laissez-faire economist, David Ricardo, dedicated himself to economic studies after reading Smith's *The Wealth of Nations*. Like Malthus, Ricardo claimed that the poor had too many children and had little chance to escape poverty. In his "Iron Law of Wages," Ricardo noted that when wages were high, families had more children. But more children increased the supply of labor, which led to lower wages and higher unemployment. Because of such gloomy predictions, economics became known as the "dismal science."

Neither Malthus nor Ricardo was a cruel man. Still, both opposed any government help for the poor. In their view, the best cure for poverty was not government relief but the unrestricted "laws of the free market." They felt that individuals should be left to improve their lot through thrift, hard work, and limiting the size of their families.

☑ **IDENTIFY CAUSE AND EFFECT** How did the ideas that Adam Smith discussed in *The Wealth of Nations* support the free enterprise system?

>> Philosopher and economist John Stuart Mill supported extending suffrage. Mill believed that political power through voting could lead to necessary reforms.

>> Widespread poverty, as shown here, motivated socialists to seek a more equitable economic system.

Utilitarians Support Limited Government

Other thinkers sought to modify laissez-faire doctrines to justify some government intervention. By 1800, British philosopher and economist **Jeremy Bentham** was advocating **utilitarianism,** or the idea that the goal of society should be "the greatest happiness for the greatest number" of its citizens. To Bentham, all laws or actions should be judged by their "utility." In other words, did they provide more pleasure or happiness than pain? Bentham strongly supported individual freedom, which he believed guaranteed happiness. Still, he saw the need for government to become involved under certain circumstances.

Bentham's ideas influenced the British philosopher and economist John Stuart Mill. Although he believed strongly in individual freedom, Mill wanted the government to step in to improve the hard lives of the working class.

"The only purpose for which power can be rightfully exercised over any member of a civilized community, against his will," Mill wrote, "is to prevent harm to others." Therefore, while middle-class business and factory owners were entitled to increase their own happiness, the government should prevent them from doing so in a manner that would harm workers.

Mill further called for giving the vote to workers and women. These groups could then use their political power to win reforms. Most middle-class people rejected Mill's ideas. Only in the later 1800s were his views slowly accepted. Today's democratic governments, however, have absorbed many ideas from Mill and the other utilitarians.

☑ **CHECK UNDERSTANDING** What did John Stuart Mill see as the proper role of government?

Socialist Thought Emerges

While the champions of laissez-faire economics favored the free market and individual rights, other thinkers focused on social inequality and what they claimed were the evils of industrial capitalism. They argued that industrialization had created an unjust gulf between rich and poor.

The Socialist Point of View To end poverty and injustice, some thinkers offered a radical solution—socialism. Under **socialism,** the people as a whole rather than private individuals would own and operate the **means of production**—the farms, factories, railways, and other large businesses that produced and distributed goods. In practice, when socialist governments gained power in the 1900s, they tended to regulate the production and distribution of goods, which often proved inefficient.

Socialism grew out of the Enlightenment faith in progress and human nature and its concern for social justice. Socialist thinkers developed a number of different ideas about how to achieve their goals. The early experiments in socialism differed greatly from what later socialist governments would do.

Owen and Utopian Socialism A number of early socialists established communities in which all work was shared and all property was owned in common. When there was no difference between rich and poor, they said, fighting between people would disappear. These early socialists were called Utopians. To critics, the name implied that they were impractical dreamers.

One of these social reformers was **Robert Owen.** Owen himself was an industrial success story. He started life as a poor Welsh boy and became a successful mill owner. Unlike most industrialists at the time, Owen refused to use child labor. He campaigned vigorously for laws that limited child labor and encouraged the organization of labor unions.

Like other Utopians, Owen believed there was a way he could change society for the better. To prove his point, he set up a model community around a mill in New Lanark, Scotland, to put his own ideas into practice. At his factory in New Lanark, he built homes for workers, opened a school for children, and generally treated employees well. He wanted to show that an employer could offer decent living and working conditions and still run a profitable business.

☑ **IDENTIFY** What were the characteristic beliefs of early socialists?

Marx and the Origins of Communism

In the 1840s, **Karl Marx,** a German philosopher, condemned the ideas of the Utopians as unrealistic idealism. He formulated a new theory, "scientific socialism," which he claimed was based on a scientific study of history. He teamed up with another German socialist, Friedrich Engels, whose father owned a textile factory in England.

Marxist Theory Marx and Engels wrote a pamphlet, *The Communist Manifesto*, which they published in 1848. "A spectre [ghost] is haunting Europe," it

>> This well-known Marxist poster proclaims in German, "Workers of all countries, unite!" **Determine Point of View** Why should workers unite, according to Marx?

▶ BOUNCE to Activate Chart

began, "the spectre of communism." According to Marx, **communism** would bring a classless society in which the means of production would be owned in common for the good of all.

In fact, wherever communism came to be practiced in the 1900s, it brought a system of government in which the state led by a small elite controlled all economic and political life and exercised authoritarian control over the people.

In *The Communist Manifesto*, Marx theorized that economics was the driving force in history. He argued that there was "the history of class struggles" between the "haves" and the "have-nots." The "haves" had always owned the means of production and thus controlled society and all its wealth. In industrialized Europe, Marx said, the "haves" were the bourgeoisie. The "have-nots" were the **proletariat,** or working class.

According to Marx, the modern class struggle pitted the bourgeoisie against the proletariat. In the end, he predicted, the proletariat would be triumphant. Workers would then take control of the means of production and set up a classless, communist society. In such a society, the struggles of the past would end because wealth and power would be shared equally.

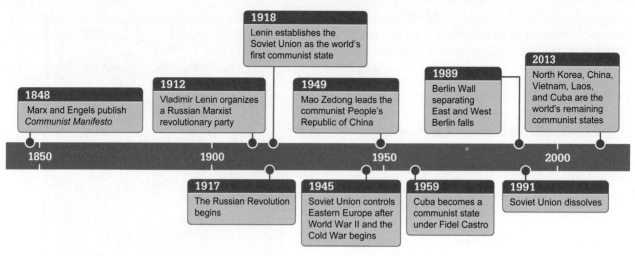

1848
Marx and Engels publish *Communist Manifesto*

1912
Vladimir Lenin organizes a Russian Marxist revolutionary party

1949
Mao Zedong leads the communist People's Republic of China

1989
Berlin Wall separating East and West Berlin falls

2013
North Korea, China, Vietnam, Laos, and Cuba are the world's remaining communist states

1850 · 1900 · 1950 · 2000

1917
The Russian Revolution begins

1945
Soviet Union controls Eastern Europe after World War II and the Cold War begins

1959
Cuba becomes a communist state under Fidel Castro

1991
Soviet Union dissolves

>> Since Marx's lifetime, communism has spread globally and then declined. **Analyze Charts** How much time elapsed between the Soviet Union's gaining control of Eastern Europe and the end of the Soviet Union?

Marx despised capitalism. He believed it created prosperity for only a few and poverty for many. He called for an international struggle to bring about its downfall. "Workers of all countries," he urged, "unite!"

Marxism Finds Support At first, Marxist ideas had little impact. In time, however, they would gain supporters around the world. In western Europe, communist political parties emerged and promoted the goals of violent revolution to achieve a classless society. Marx's ideas would never be practiced exactly as he imagined. Even so, Karl Marx remains a key historic figure, not only in his lifetime but in the century to come.

In the 1860s, German socialists adapted Marx's beliefs to form **social democracy,** a political ideology in which there is a gradual transition from capitalism to socialism instead of a sudden violent overthrow of the system. By the late 1800s, a rift formed between strict Marxists, who believed in revolution to end capitalism, and social democrats, who believed in the possibility of peaceful reform.

In the late 1800s, Russian socialists embraced Marxism and formed a communist party to bring about revolution. In 1917, the Russian Revolution set up a communist government there that lasted until 1991. During the 1900s, revolutionaries in countries from China to Cuba adapted Marxist ideas to their own situations and needs. Independence leaders in Asia, Latin America, and Africa often experimented with Marxist ideas.

Marxism Loses Its Appeal Marx claimed that his ideas were based on scientific laws. However, many of his ideas turned out to be wrong. He predicted that the misery of the proletariat would touch off a world revolution. Instead, by 1900, the standard of living of the working class improved in industrially developed countries. He also predicted that workers would unite across national borders to wage class warfare.

Instead, people continued to feel stronger ties to their own countries than to any international workers' movement. Finally, by the late 1900s, the few nations that had experimented with communism were moving away from government control of the economy and were adding elements of free-market capitalism.

☑ **CHECK UNDERSTANDING** What did Marx predict was the future of the proletariat?

☑ ASSESSMENT

1. **Summarize** How did the middle class live during the Industrial Revolution?

2. **Cite Evidence** What key social and economic changes did industrialization bring about, both for the better and for the worse? Explain your answer with evidence from the text.

3. **Identify Main Ideas** What were the historical origins and characteristics of the free enterprise system?

4. **Identify Patterns** How did the Industrial Revolution impact the development of modern economic systems? In your answer, identify the economic systems that arose during that period.

5. **Connections to Today** What was life like for working-class women during the Industrial Revolution? Discuss the role of women in today's workplace.

Child Labor Laws

Throughout history, child labor was acceptable to most people. Children were not required by law to go to school. Often, young boys became apprentices between the ages of ten and fourteen to gain skill in a specific trade. Young girls left home to become domestic servants. But, during the Industrial Revolution conditions for child workers in factories became increasingly dangerous. Child labor became a matter of intense debate in Britain during the Industrial Revolution. Two arguments regarding child labor are presented here. The first is a *Report From the Committee on Employment of Boys Sweeping Chimneys,* in 1817. The second is a report from *The Philosophy of Manufacturers,* by Andrew Ure, in 1835. Ure had observed the conditions of child workers in factories.

As you read, look for contrasts in their viewpoints. Then answer the questions that follow.

>> Child workers in the mines

Primary Source 1

Report From the Committee on Employment of Boys Sweeping Chimneys (1817)

Your Committee have also heard, from one of the Master Chimney Sweepers, that it is the custom of the trade to take the parent's word for the age of the apprentice—that no other evidence is asked for—that he never heard of it being the practice of the Masters to get a certificate of the age, and he was ignorant that the Act of Parliament required it. Your Committee refer generally to the evidence for proofs of the cruelties that are practiced, and of the ill-usage, and the particular hardships that are the lot of the wretched children who are employed in this trade. It is in evidence that they are stolen from their parents, and inveigled [tricked] out of workhouses; that in order to conquer the natural repugnance of the infants to ascend the narrow and dangerous chimneys, to clean which their labour is required, blows are used; that pins are forced into their feet by the boy that follows them up the chimney, in order to compel them to ascend it; and that lighted straw has been applied for that purpose; that the children are subject to sores and bruises, and wounds and burns on their thighs, knees, and elbows. . . .

☑ **DRAW CONCLUSIONS** Why do you think parents were reluctant to reveal the age of the boys?

Do you find that many boys show great repugnance to go up at first?—Yes, most of them. And if they resist and reject, in what way do you force them up?—By telling them we must take them again to their father and mother, and give them up again; and the parents are generally people who cannot maintain them.

So that they are afraid of going back to their parents for fear of being starved?—Yes, they go through a deal of hardship before they come to our trade.

☑ **DRAW CONCLUSIONS** Why might some boys choose to remain chimney sweepers?

Primary Source 2

The Philosophy of Manufacturers, Andrew Ure, (1835)

No master would wish to have any wayward children to work within the walls of his factory, who do not mind their business without beating, and he therefore usually fines or turns away any spinners who are known to maltreat their assistants. Hence, ill usage of any kind is a very rare occurrence. I have visited many factories, both in Manchester and in the surrounding districts, during a period of several months, entering the spinning rooms, unexpectedly, and often alone, at different times of the day, and I never saw a single instance of corporal chastisement [severe physical punishment] inflicted on a child, nor indeed did I ever see children in ill-humor.

☑ **CITE EVIDENCE** How does Ure suggest that his report is a fair assessment of child labor practices in British factories?

The scene of industry, so far from exciting sad emotions in my mind, was always exhilarating. It was delightful to observe the nimbleness with which they pieced the broken ends, as the mule carriage began to recede from the fixed roller-beam, [a part of the textile machine] and to see them at leisure, after a few seconds' exercise of their tiny fingers, to amuse themselves in any attitude they chose, till the stretch and winding-on were once more completed.

As to exhaustion by the day's work, they evinced [showed] no trace of it on emerging from the mill in the evening; for they immediately began to skip about any neighboring play-ground, and to commence their amusements with the same alacrity [joy] as boys issuing from a school. It is moreover my firm conviction, that if children are not ill-used by bad parents or guardians, but receive in food and raiment [clothing] the full benefit of what they earn, they would thrive better when employed in our modern factories, than if left at home in apartments too often ill-aired, damp, and cold.

☑ **EXPLAIN** Why does Ure feel the factory is a safe place for children?

☑ ASSESSMENT

Be sure to cite specific evidence from the sources as you answer the following questions.

1. **Analyze Arguments** How would the committee report on chimney sweeps support the reform bill?

2. **Draw Conclusions** Based on Ure's report, why is a child factory worker happier than a child chimney sweep?

3. **Identify Author's Point of View** Discuss the views on child labor as presented in both primary sources.

4. **Analyze Information** How does Ure support the factory owner's view of the Industrial Revolution?

GO ONLINE to access primary sources

GO ONLINE to Project Imagine: Visit the Crystal Palace to explore the innovations of the early Industrial Revolution, just as a second phase was about to begin.

The Second Industrial Revolution

The first phase of industrialization was forged from iron, powered by steam engines, and driven by the British textile industry. By the mid-1800s, the Industrial Revolution was entering a new phase in which new factories powered by new sources of energy used new processes to turn out new products. At the same time, new forms of business organization led to the rise of giant new companies.

Science and Technology Change Industry

During the early Industrial Revolution, inventions such as the steam engine were generally the work of gifted tinkerers. They experimented with simple machines to make them better.

During the second Industrial Revolution, the pace of change quickened as companies hired professional chemists and engineers to create new products and machinery. The union of science, technology, and industry spurred economic growth.

The Bessemer Process Transforms Steel British engineer **Henry Bessemer** and American inventor William Kelly independently developed a new process for making steel from iron. In 1856, Bessemer patented this process. Steel was lighter, harder, and more durable than iron, so it could be produced very cheaply. Steel quickly became the major material used in tools, bridges, and railroads. As steel production soared, industrialized countries measured their success in steel output. In 1880, for example,

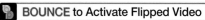

BOUNCE to Activate Flipped Video

Objectives

Describe the impact of new technology on industry, transportation, and communication.

Understand how big business emerged.

Summarize the impact of medical advances in the later 1800s.

Describe how cities changed and grew.

Explain how conditions for workers gradually improved.

Key Terms

Henry Bessemer	germ theory
Alfred Nobel	Louis Pasteur
Michael Faraday	Robert Koch
dynamo	Florence Nightingale
Thomas Edison	Joseph Lister
interchangeable parts	urban renewal
assembly line	mutual-aid society
Orville and Wilbur Wright	
Guglielmo Marconi	
stock	
corporation	
cartel	

the average German steel mill produced fewer than 5 million metric tons of steel a year. By 1910, that figure had reached nearly 15 million metric tons.

Innovations in Chemistry During the same period, chemists created hundreds of new products, from medicines such as aspirin to perfumes and soaps. Newly developed chemical fertilizers played a key role in increasing food production.

In 1866, the Swedish chemist **Alfred Nobel** invented dynamite, an explosive much safer than others used at the time. It was widely used in construction and, to Nobel's dismay, in warfare. Dynamite earned Nobel a huge fortune, which he willed to fund the famous Nobel prizes that are still awarded today.

Electricity Replaces Steam Power In the late 1800s, a new power source—electricity—replaced steam as the dominant source of industrial power. Scientists like Benjamin Franklin had tinkered with electricity a century earlier. The Italian scientist Alessandro Volta developed the first battery around 1800. Later, the English chemist **Michael Faraday** created the first simple electric motor and the first **dynamo,** a machine that generates electricity. Today, all electrical generators and transformers work on the principle of Faraday's dynamo.

>> After inventing the light bulb, Thomas Edison supervised the building of the first electric power system in New York City.

In the 1870s, the American inventor **Thomas Edison** made the first electric light bulb. Soon, Edison's "incandescent lamps" illuminated whole cities. The pace of city life quickened, and factories could continue to operate after dark. By the 1890s, cables carried electrical power from dynamos to factories.

Improved Methods of Production The basic features of the factory system remained the same during the 1800s. Factories still used large numbers of workers and power-driven machines to mass-produce goods. To improve efficiency, however, manufacturers designed products with **interchangeable parts,** identical components that could be used in place of one another. Interchangeable parts simplified both the assembly and repair of products. By the early 1900s, manufacturers had introduced another new method of production, the **assembly line.**

Workers on an assembly line add parts to a product that moves along a belt from one work station to the next. A different person performs each task along the assembly line. While not all factories used assembly lines, the factory system always relied on the division of labor. Each worker was assigned one task, such as putting the sole on a shoe or sewing a collar on a shirt. Once that task was done, the worker handed the product to the next person, who then performed his or her task. Interchangeable parts, the division of labor, and the assembly line all made production more efficient. They also lowered the price of factory goods, making them affordable to more people.

☑ **IDENTIFY CAUSE AND EFFECT** How did the assembly line and division of labor affect manufacturing?

Advances in Transportation and Communication

During the second Industrial Revolution, transportation and communications were transformed by technology. Steamships replaced sailing ships, and railroad building took off. In Europe and North America, rail lines connected inland cities and seaports, mining regions, and industrial centers. In the United States, a transcontinental railroad provided rail service from the Atlantic to the Pacific. In the same way, Russians built the Trans-Siberian Railroad, linking Moscow in European Russia to Vladivostok on the Pacific. Railroad tunnels and bridges crossed the Alps in Europe and the Andes in South America.

Passengers and goods rode on rails in India, China, Egypt, and South Africa.

The Age of the Automobile The transportation revolution took a new turn when a German engineer, Nikolaus Otto, invented a gasoline-powered internal combustion engine. In 1886, Karl Benz received a patent for the first automobile, which had three wheels. A year later, Gottlieb Daimler (DYM lur) introduced the first four-wheeled automobile. People laughed at the "horseless carriages," but they quickly changed the way people traveled.

The French nosed out the Germans as early automakers. Then the American Henry Ford started making models that reached the breathtaking speed of 25 miles per hour. In the early 1900s, Ford began using the assembly line to mass-produce cars, making the United States a leader in the automobile industry.

The First Airplane The invention of the internal combustion engine changed life and industry in other ways. Motorized threshers and reapers boosted farm production. Even more dramatically, the internal combustion engine made possible sustained, pilot-controlled flight. In 1903, American bicycle makers **Orville and Wilbur Wright** designed and flew a flimsy airplane at Kitty Hawk, North Carolina. Although their flying machine stayed aloft for only a few seconds, it ushered in the air age.

Soon, daredevil pilots were flying airplanes across the English Channel and over the Alps. Commercial passenger travel, however, would not begin until the 1920s.

A Communications Revolution A revolution in communications also made the world smaller. An American inventor, Samuel F. B. Morse, developed the telegraph, which could send coded messages over wires by means of electricity. His first telegraph line went into service between Washington, D.C., and Baltimore in 1844. By the 1860s, an undersea cable was relaying messages between Europe and North America. This trans-Atlantic cable was an amazing engineering accomplishment for its day.

Communication soon became even faster. In 1876, the Scottish-born American inventor Alexander Graham Bell patented the telephone. By the 1890s, the Italian pioneer **Guglielmo Marconi** had invented the radio, which allowed wireless communication over long distances. In 1901, Marconi received a radio message, using Morse code, sent from Britain to Canada. As Marconi had predicted, radio soon became a key part of a global communications network that linked every corner of the world.

>> In 1903, Orville and Wilbur Wright tested their flying machine at Kitty Hawk, North Carolina. By 1905, they had built an airplane that could stay in the air for 39 minutes.

BOUNCE to Activate Timeline

☑ **IDENTIFY CAUSE AND EFFECT** How did Nikolaus Otto's invention of the internal combustion engine affect the Industrial Revolution? What can you infer about its impact on Western nations?

The Rise of Big Business

By the late 1800s, what we call "big business" came to dominate industry. Big business refers to an establishment that is run by entrepreneurs who finance, manufacture, and distribute goods or services on a large scale. As time passed, some big businesses came to control entire industries.

Investors Form Corporations The latest technologies required the investment of large amounts of money, or capital. To get the needed capital, owners sold **stock,** or shares in their companies, to investors. Each stockholder became owner of a tiny part of a company. Large-scale companies, such as steel foundries, needed so much capital that they sold hundreds of thousands of shares. These businesses formed giant **corporations,** businesses that are owned by many investors who buy shares of stock. With large amounts of capital, corporations could expand into many areas.

Monopolies Dominate Industry Some powerful business leaders created monopolies and trusts, huge corporate structures that controlled entire industries or areas of the economy. In Germany, Alfred Krupp inherited a steelmaking business from his father. He bought up coal and iron mines along with the supply lines that carried raw materials to feed the steel business. Later, he and his son acquired plants that made tools, railroad cars, and weapons.

In the United States, John D. Rockefeller dominated the petroleum industry by gaining control of oil wells, oil refineries, and oil pipelines. Andrew Carnegie, who started out as a poor immigrant from Scotland, worked his way up to build an American steel empire. He later used his wealth to fund libraries, universities, and other charities.

Sometimes, a group of corporations would join forces and form a **cartel**, an association to fix prices, set production quotas, or control markets. In Germany, a single cartel fixed prices for 170 coal mines.

Opposing Views of Big Business The rise of big business sparked a stormy debate. Admirers saw the Krupps, Rockefellers, and Carnegies as "captains of industry" and praised their vision and skills. They pointed out that capitalists invested their wealth

in worldwide ventures, such as railroad building, that employed thousands of workers and added to the general prosperity. They also claimed that monopolies increased efficiency by driving out less efficient corporations.

To critics, the aggressive magnates were "robber barons" who ruthlessly destroyed competing companies in pursuit of profit. With the competition gone, they were free to raise prices. Destroying competition, critics argued, damaged the free-enterprise system. Reformers called for laws to prevent monopolies and regulate large corporations. By the early 1900s, some governments did move against monopolies. However, the political and economic power of business leaders often hindered efforts at regulation.

☑ **DRAW CONCLUSIONS** Why was there a move toward developing monopolies?

Better Medicine, Nutrition, and Health

The population explosion that had begun during the 1700s continued through the 1800s. Between 1800 and 1900, the population of Europe more than doubled. This rapid growth was not due to larger families. In fact, families in most industrializing countries had fewer children. Instead, populations soared because the death rate fell. Nutrition improved, thanks in part to improved methods of farming, food storage, and distribution. Medical advances and improvements in public sanitation also slowed death rates.

Combating Disease Since the 1600s, scientists had known of microscopic organisms, or microbes. Some scientists speculated that certain microbes might cause specific infectious diseases. Yet most doctors scoffed at this **germ theory.** Not until 1870 did French chemist **Louis Pasteur** (pas TUR) clearly show the link between microbes and disease. Pasteur went on to make other major contributions to medicine, including the development of vaccines against rabies and anthrax. He also discovered a process called pasteurization that killed disease-carrying microbes in milk.

In the 1880s, the German doctor **Robert Koch** identified the bacterium that caused tuberculosis, a respiratory disease that claimed about 30 million human lives in the 1800s. The search for a tuberculosis cure, however, took half a century. By 1914, yellow fever and malaria had been traced to microbes carried by mosquitoes.

>> This 1899 American political cartoon shows a monopoly as an octopus-like monster covering a city. **Analyze Political Cartoons** Which side of the debate about the effects of monopolies does this cartoon support? Explain.

Population Growth of Major Cities During the Industrial Revolution

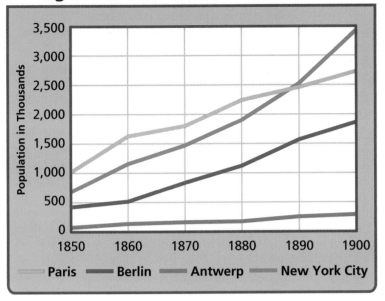

Life Expectancy During the Industrial Revolution

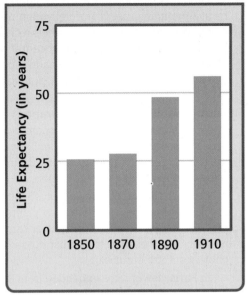

BOUNCE to Activate Gallery

>> Longer life expectancies contributed to population booms in major cities. **Analyze Graphs** Which city's population grew the most? How did life expectancy change between 1850 and 1910?

As people understood how germs caused disease, they bathed and changed their clothes more often. In European cities, better hygiene helped decrease the rate of disease.

Improving Hospital Care By the 1840s, anesthesia was being widely used to relieve pain during surgery. The use of anesthetic gas allowed doctors to experiment with operations that had never before been possible.

Yet, throughout the century, hospitals could be dangerous places. Surgery was performed with dirty instruments in dank rooms. Often, a patient would survive an operation, only to die days later of infection. For the poor, being admitted to a hospital was often a death sentence. Wealthy or middle-class patients insisted on treatment in their own homes.

"The very first requirement in a hospital," said British nurse **Florence Nightingale,** "is that it should do the sick no harm." As an army nurse during the Crimean War, Nightingale insisted on better hygiene in field hospitals. After the war, she worked to introduce sanitary measures in British hospitals. She also founded the world's first school of nursing.

The English surgeon **Joseph Lister** discovered how antiseptics prevented infection. He insisted that surgeons sterilize their instruments and wash their hands before operating. Eventually, the use of antiseptics drastically reduced deaths from infection.

☑ **DRAW CONCLUSIONS** Why was the improvement in hospital care especially important to the poor?

City Life Changes

As industrialization progressed, cities came to dominate the West. Cities grew as rural people streamed into urban areas for work. By the end of the 1800s, European and American cities had begun to take on many of the features of cities today.

New Cityscapes Growing wealth and industrialization altered the basic layout of European cities. City planners created spacious new squares and boulevards. They lined these avenues with government buildings, offices, department stores, and theaters.

The most extensive **urban renewal,** or rebuilding of the poor areas of a city, took place in Paris in the 1850s. Georges Haussmann, chief planner for Napoleon III, destroyed many tangled medieval streets full of tenement housing. In their place, he built wide boulevards and splendid public buildings.

The project was designed after Paris had experienced frequent uprisings, where poor city dwellers and their leaders set up barricades across narrow streets to battle the authorities. Haussmann's plan provided jobs, and the wide new boulevards made it harder for rebels to block streets and easier for troops to move around the city.

Gradually, settlement patterns shifted. In most American cities, the rich lived in pleasant neighborhoods on the outskirts of the city. The poor crowded into slums near the city center, within reach of factories. Trolley lines made it possible to live in one part of the city and work in another.

Safety, Sanitation, and Skyscrapers
Paved streets made urban areas much more livable. First gas lamps, and then electric street lights, illuminated the night, increasing safety. Cities organized police forces and expanded fire protection.

Beneath the streets, sewage systems made cities much healthier places to live. City planners knew that clean water supplies and better sanitation methods were needed to combat epidemics of cholera and tuberculosis.

In Paris, sewer lines expanded from 87 miles (139 kilometers) in 1852 to more than 750 miles (1200 kilometers) by 1911. The massive new sewer systems of London and Paris were costly, but they cut death rates dramatically.

By 1900, architects were using steel to construct soaring buildings. The Eiffel Tower became the symbol of Paris and the heights to which modern structures could reach. American architects like Louis Sullivan pioneered a new structure, the skyscraper. In large cities, single-family middle-class homes gave way to multistory apartment buildings.

Life in the Slums
Despite efforts to improve cities, urban life remained harsh for the poor. Some working-class families could afford better clothing, newspapers, or tickets to a music hall. But they went home to small, cramped row houses or tenements in overcrowded neighborhoods.

In the worst tenements in cities such as London and New York, whole families were often crammed into a single room that had little light and almost no ventilation. Less than one foot of space separated the buildings, and most tenements did not have running water. Bathrooms outside in the back might be shared by as many as twenty people.

Unsanitary conditions and overcrowding meant diseases spread quickly. Unemployment or illness meant lost wages that could ruin a family, leaving it homeless. High rates of crime and alcoholism were a constant curse. Conditions had improved somewhat from the early Industrial Revolution, but slums remained a fact of city life.

The Lure of City Life
Despite their drawbacks, cities attracted millions. New residents were drawn as much by the excitement as by the promise of work. For tourists, too, cities were centers of action.

Music halls, opera houses, and theaters provided entertainment for every taste. Museums and libraries offered educational opportunities. Sports, from tennis to bare-knuckle boxing, drew citizens of all classes. Tree-lined parks offered a chance for fresh air, walks, and picnics, while reminding people of life in the country.

☑ **DRAW CONCLUSIONS** How did industrialization change the face of cities?

The Working Class Wins New Rights

Workers tried to improve the harsh conditions of industrial life. They protested low wages, long hours, unsafe conditions, and the constant threat of unemployment. At first, business owners and governments tried to silence protesters. By mid-century, however, workers began to make progress.

The Growth of Labor Unions
Workers formed **mutual-aid societies,** self-help groups to aid sick or injured workers. Men and women joined socialist

>> It was not uncommon for more than one family to share a tiny apartment in tenement buildings. **Analyze Images** What evidence does this photograph provide about the lives of the urban poor?

parties or organized unions. In 1830 and 1848, revolutions had broken out across Europe, sparked by political and social unrest. The revolts left vivid images of widespread worker discontent that governments could no longer ignore.

By the late 1800s, most Western countries had granted all men the vote. Workers also won the right to organize unions to bargain on their behalf. Germany legalized labor unions in 1869. Britain, Austria, and France followed. By 1900, Britain had about three million union members, and Germany had about two million.

The main tactic of unions was the strike, or work stoppage. Workers used strikes to demand better working conditions, wage increases, or other benefits from their employers. Violence was often a result of strikes, particularly if employers called in the police or hired nonunion workers to keep their operations going.

Pressured by unions, reformers, and working-class voters, governments passed laws to regulate working conditions. Early laws forbade employers to hire very young children. Later laws outlawed child labor entirely and banned the employment of women in mines. Other laws limited work hours and improved safety. By 1909, British coal miners had won an eight-hour day, setting a standard for workers in other countries.

In Germany, and then elsewhere, Western governments established old-age pensions, as well as disability insurance for workers who were hurt or became ill. These programs protected workers from dying in poverty once they were no longer able to work.

An Improved Standard of Living Wages varied throughout the industrialized world, with unskilled laborers earning less than skilled workers. Women received less than half the pay of men doing the same work. Farm laborers barely scraped by during the economic slump of the late 1800s. Periods of unemployment brought desperate hardships to industrial workers and helped boost union membership.

Overall, though, standards of living for workers did rise. Working-class people began to benefit from higher wages and better working conditions. They, too, were able to afford a larger variety of goods and services. Many benefited from the growing movement to provide public education. Some were able to get access to health care. Efforts to curb diseases led to vaccination programs that reached into poor communities. Some workers were able to move out of overcrowded slums into the outer ring of cities and travel to work on subways and trolleys. Despite improvements in the standard of

>> Miners and steelworkers go on strike in Belgium. **Draw Conclusions** Who do you think the men on horseback are? Why are they there? Explain.

living, however, a large gap divided workers from the middle class.

☑ **DRAW CONCLUSIONS** What were some ways that life improved for workers?

☑ ASSESSMENT

1. **Identify Main Ideas** Identify the major effects of new technology and transportation on industry during the Industrial Revolution.

2. **Draw Conclusions** Why did big business emerge during the Industrial Revolution, and how did it affect free enterprise?

3. **Identify Central Issues** How did the Industrial Revolution bring about important changes to human life in cities? Identify changes for the better and for the worse.

4. **Apply Concepts** How did the working class begin to improve its conditions during the late 1800s?

5. **Quest Connections** How has technology changed the way we buy and sell goods?

GO ONLINE to access this biography: John D. Rockefeller

How the Other Half Lives:
Jacob Riis

Jacob Riis immigrated to the United States from Denmark in 1870. After living for several years in extreme poverty, he found a job as a police reporter for the *New York Tribune.* He became a leading muckraker, or journalist who worked to expose social problems. Riis's writing and photographs helped expose the harsh living conditions in the crowded tenements of New York City. This excerpt is from Riis's 1890 book, *How the Other Half Lives.*

Annie Daniel, a physician and public health reformer in New York, worked to both educate the public about and improve living conditions in tenements. The second primary source is from her speech "The Wreck of the Home: How Wearing Apparel is Fashioned in the Tenements".

>> A city tenement

Primary Source 1

The problem of the children becomes, in these swarms, to the last degree perplexing. Their very number make one stand aghast [horrified]. I have already given instances of the packing of the child population in East Side tenements. They might be continued indefinitely until the array [orderly arrangement] would be enough to startle any community. For, be it remembered, these children with the training they receive—or do not receive—with the instincts they inherit and absorb in their growing up, are to be our future rulers, if our theory of government is worth anything. More than a working majority of our voters now register from the tenements.

☑ **DETERMINE CENTRAL IDEAS** According to Riis, why should all Americans be concerned about tenement children?

I counted the other day the little ones, up to ten years or so, in a Bayard Street tenement that for a yard has a triangular space in the center with sides fourteen or fifteen feet long, just room enough for a row of ill-smelling closets [toilets] at the base of the triangle and a hydrant at the apex [highest point]. There was about as much light in this "yard" as in the average cellar. I gave up my self-imposed task in despair when I had counted one hundred and twenty-eight in forty families. . . .

☑ **SUMMARIZE** What is the tenement like on Bayard Street that Riis describes?

Bodies of drowned children turn up in the rivers right along since summer whom no one seems to know anything about. When last spring some workmen, while moving a pile of lumber on a North River pier, found under the last plank the body of a little lad crushed to death, no one had missed a boy, though his parents afterward turned up. The truant [a pupil who misses school without permission] officer assuredly does not know, though he spends his life trying to find out, somewhat illogically, perhaps, since the department that employs him admits that thousands of poor children are crowded out of the schools year by year for want of room.

SUMMARIZE What is Riis's complaint about the education received by tenement children?

Primary Source 2

". . . The new law relating to manufacturing in tenement-houses, provides that thirty- three distinct industries may be carried on in the living rooms of the workers–manufacturing all of which requires hand work or simple machinery. Every garment worn by a woman is found being manufactured in tenement rooms. The coarsest home-wrappers to the daintiest lace gown for a fine evening function are manufactured in these rooms. Corsets and shoes are the most uncommon. The adornments of woman's dress, the flowers and feathers for her hats, the hats themselves–these I have seen being made in the presence of small-pox, on the lounge with the patient. In this case the hats belonged to a Broadway firm. All clothing worn by infants and young children–dainty little dresses–I have seen on the same bed with children sick of contagious diseases and into these little garments is sewed some of the contagion. . . ."

DRAW CONCLUSIONS What conditions detailed in this excerpt might have resulted in laws to protect the consumer and the worker?

A child from 3 to 10 or 12 years adds by its labor from 50 cents to $1.50 per week to the family income. The hours of the child are as long as its strength endures or the work remains. A child 3 years old can work continuously from 1½ to 2 hours at a time; a child 10 years old can work 12 hours. Obviously under such conditions the child is deprived of the two greatest

rights which the parents and the state are bound to give each child; health and an education.

☑ ASSESSMENT

1. **Identify Supporting Details** What details in either one of these excerpts may have shocked readers of the time period? Why do you think muckrakers sought to shock their audience?

2. **Determine Meaning** To whom does the "Other Half" in the title refer? Why do you think Riis uses this phrase?

3. **Identify Cause and Effect** How do you think Riis's account might have contributed to social reforms for tenement housing?

4. **Explain** What advantage might the "putting out system" described by Daniel provide the manufacturer? Why does Daniel see the worker as abused?

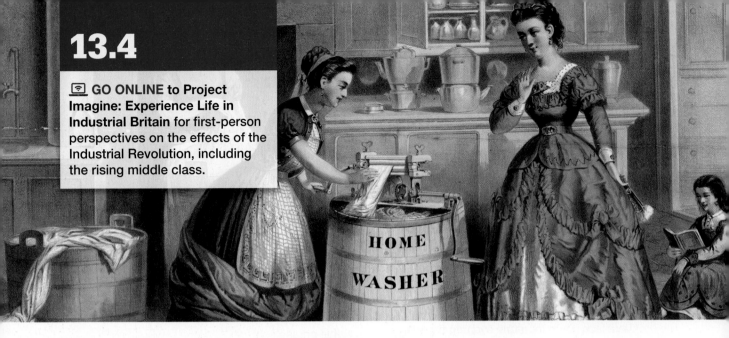

13.4

💻 **GO ONLINE to Project Imagine: Experience Life in Industrial Britain** for first-person perspectives on the effects of the Industrial Revolution, including the rising middle class.

 BOUNCE to Activate Flipped Video

Objectives

Identify what values shaped the new social order.

Describe how the role of women changed in the Industrial Revolution.

Explain the impact of education, new scientific ideas, and religion.

Analyze how romanticism, realism, and impressionism reflected the culture of the Industrial Age.

Key Terms

cult of domesticity
temperance
   movement
Elizabeth Cady
   Stanton
women's suffrage
Sojourner Truth
John Dalton
Charles Darwin
racism
social gospel
William Wordsworth
romanticism
Lord Byron

Victor Hugo
Ludwig van
   Beethoven
realism
Charles Dickens
Gustave Courbet
Louis Daguerre
impressionism
Claude Monet
Vincent van Gogh

Changing Ways of Life and Thought

The Industrial Revolution slowly changed the old social order in the Western world. For centuries, the two main classes were nobles and peasants. While middle-class merchants, artisans, and lawyers played important roles, they still had a secondary position in society. With the spread of industry, a more complex social structure emerged.

The New Social Order

The New Class Structure By the late 1800s, a new upper class emerged in western Europe. It came to include not only the old nobility but also wealthy families who had acquired their riches from business and industry. Rich entrepreneurs married into aristocratic families, gaining the status of noble titles. Nobles needed the money brought by the industrial rich to support their lands and lifestyle. By tradition, the upper class held the top jobs in government and the military.

Below this tiny elite, a growing middle class was pushing its way up the social ladder. At its highest rungs were the upper middle class, made up of mid-level business people and professionals such as doctors and scientists. With comfortable incomes, they enjoyed a wide range of material goods. Next came the lower middle class, which included teachers, office workers, shop owners, and clerks. On much smaller incomes, they struggled to keep up with their "betters."

Industrial workers and rural peasants were at the base of the social ladder. The size of this working class varied across Europe. In highly industrialized Britain, workers made up more than

30 percent of the population in 1900. In western Europe and the United States, the number of farmworkers dropped, but many families still worked the land. The rural population was higher in eastern and southern Europe, where industrialization was more limited.

Middle Class Values By midcentury, the growing middle class had developed its own way of life. A strict code of etiquette governed social behavior.

Rules dictated how to dress for every occasion, how to give a dinner party, how to pay a social call, when to write letters, and how long to mourn for relatives who had died.

Parents strictly supervised their children, who were expected to be "seen but not heard." A child who misbehaved was considered to reflect badly on the entire family. Servants, too, were seen as a reflection of their employers. Even a small middle-class household was expected to have at least a cook and a housemaid.

The Ideal Home and Family Middle-class families tended to include just the nuclear family, made up of parents and their children, rather than the larger extended families of the past. They lived in a large house, or perhaps one of the new apartment houses. Rooms were crammed with large, overstuffed furniture. Clothing reflected middle-class tastes for luxury and respectability.

Within the family, the division of labor between wife and husband changed. Earlier, middle-class women had helped run family businesses out of the home.

By the later 1800s, most middle-class husbands went to work in an office or shop. A successful husband was one who earned enough to keep his wife at home. Women spent their time raising children, directing servants, and doing religious or charitable service.

Books, magazines, and popular songs supported a **cult of domesticity** that idealized women and the home. Women and girls stitched sayings like "home, sweet home" into needlework that was hung on parlor walls. The ideal woman was seen as a tender, self-sacrificing caregiver who provided a nest for her children and a peaceful refuge for her husband to escape from the hardships of the working world.

This ideal rarely applied to the bottom rungs of the social ladder. Lower-middle-class women might work alongside their husbands in stores. Working-class women labored for low pay in garment factories or worked as domestic servants. Young women might leave domestic service after they married, but often had to seek other employment. Despite long days

working for wages, they were still expected to take full responsibility for child care and homemaking.

☑ **IDENTIFY MAIN IDEA** How did the roles of men and women in middle-class households change as a result of the Industrial Revolution?

The Struggle for Women's Rights

Some individual women and women's groups protested restrictions on women's lives. They sought a broad range of rights. Across Europe and the United States, politically active women campaigned for fairness in marriage, divorce, and property laws. Women's groups also supported the **temperance movement,** a campaign to limit or ban the use of alcoholic beverages. Temperance leaders pointed out that drinking threatened family life. They also argued that banning alcohol would create a more productive and efficient workforce.

These reformers faced many obstacles. In Europe and the United States, women could not vote. They were barred from most schools and had little, if any, protection under the law. A woman's husband or father controlled all of her property.

>> In industrialized cities, many members of the working class lived in tenement buildings like this. **Infer** What can you infer about working-class life from the way these people are dressed indoors?

The Campaign Begins In the late 1700s, women such as Olympe de Gouges in France and Mary Wollstonecraft in England had begun to call for women's rights. Later, their successors—mostly from the middle class—took up the struggle. In the United States, Lucretia Mott, **Elizabeth Cady Stanton,** and Susan B. Anthony campaigned for the abolition of slavery. In the process, they realized the severe restrictions on their own lives. They became the founders of the American women's rights movement.

Over time, women began to break the barriers that kept them out of universities and professions. By the late 1800s, a few women trained as doctors or lawyers. Others became explorers, researchers, or inventors, often without recognition. For example, Julia Brainerd Hall worked with her brother to develop an aluminum-producing process. Their company became hugely successful, but Charles Hall received almost all of the credit.

The Suffrage Movement By the late 1800s, married women in some countries had won the right to control their own property. The struggle for political rights proved far more difficult. In the United States, the Seneca Falls Convention of 1848 demanded that women be granted the right to vote. In Europe, groups dedicated to **women's suffrage,** or women's right to vote, emerged in the later 1800s.

Among men, some liberals and socialists supported women's suffrage. In general, though, suffragists faced intense opposition. Some critics claimed that women were too emotional to be allowed to vote. Others argued that women needed to be "protected" from grubby politics or that a woman's place was in the home, not in government.

To such claims, **Sojourner Truth,** an African American suffragist, is credited with replying, "Nobody ever helps me into carriages, or over mud puddles, or gives me any best place! And ain't I a woman?"

On the edges of the Western world, women made faster strides. In New Zealand, Australia, and some western territories of the United States, women won the vote by the early 1900s. There, women who had "tamed the frontier" alongside men were not dismissed as weak and helpless. In the United States, Wyoming became the first state to grant women the right to vote. In much of the Western world, however, the women's suffrage struggle took much longer. By 1920, women in Britain and the United States had finally won the vote.

☑ **IDENTIFY MAIN IDEAS** What were the arguments against women's suffrage?

The Rise of Public Education

By the late 1800s, reformers persuaded many governments to set up public schools and require basic education for all children. Teaching "the three Rs"—reading, writing, and 'rithmetic—was thought to produce better citizens. In addition, industrialized societies recognized the need for a literate workforce. Schools taught punctuality, obedience to authority, disciplined work habits, and patriotism. In European schools, children also received basic religious education.

Improving Public Schools At first, elementary schools were primitive. Many teachers had little schooling themselves. In rural areas, students attended class only during the times when they were not needed on the farm or in their parents' shops.

By the late 1800s, a growing number of children were in school, and the quality of elementary education improved. Teachers received training

>> In Britain, the first petition for women's suffrage was presented to Parliament in 1867. The suffragist movement continued until Parliament finally granted women over 30 the right to vote in 1918. Women gained the same voting rights as men in 1928.

🅑 BOUNCE to Activate Gallery

at normal schools, where the latest "norms and standards" of educational practices were taught. By the late 1800s, more schools were being set up in western Europe and elsewhere to train teachers.

In England, schooling girls and boys between the ages of five and ten became compulsory after 1881. At the same time, governments began to expand secondary schools, known as high schools in the United States. In secondary schools, students learned the "classical languages," Latin and Greek, along with history and mathematics.

In general, only middle-class families could afford to have their sons attend these schools, which trained students for more serious study or for government jobs. Middle-class girls were sent to school primarily in the hope that they might marry well and become better wives and mothers. Generally, girls' schools did not teach much science or mathematics, which were considered unnecessary and inappropriate for young women.

Higher Education Grows Colleges and universities expanded in this period, too. Most university students were the sons of middle or upper-class families. The university curriculum emphasized ancient history and languages, philosophy, religion, and law. By the late 1800s, universities added courses in the sciences, especially in chemistry and physics. At the same time, engineering schools trained students who would have the knowledge and skills to build the new industrial society.

Some women sought greater educational opportunities. By the 1840s, a few small colleges for women opened, including Bedford College in England and Mount Holyoke in the United States. In 1863, the British reformer Emily Davies campaigned for female students to be allowed to take the entrance examinations for Cambridge University. She succeeded, but as late as 1897, male Cambridge students rioted against granting degrees to women.

☑ **DRAW CONCLUSIONS** Why did more children attend school in the late 1800s than before?

New Directions in Science

Science in the service of industry brought great changes in the later 1800s. At the same time, researchers advanced new theories about the natural world. These ideas challenged long-held beliefs.

Modern Atomic Theory A crucial breakthrough in chemistry came in the early 1800s when the English Quaker schoolteacher **John Dalton** developed modern atomic theory. The ancient Greeks had

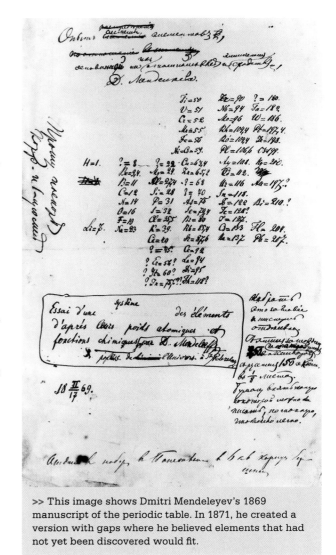

>> This image shows Dmitri Mendeleyev's 1869 manuscript of the periodic table. In 1871, he created a version with gaps where he believed elements that had not yet been discovered would fit.

speculated that all matter was made of tiny particles called atoms. Dalton showed that each element has its own kind of atoms. Earlier theories put forth the idea that all atoms were basically alike. Dalton also showed how different kinds of atoms combine to make all chemical substances. In 1869, the Russian chemist Dmitri Mendeleyev (men duh LAY ef) drew up a table that grouped elements according to their atomic weights. His table became the basis for the periodic table of elements used today.

The Question of Earth's Age The new science of geology opened avenues of debate. In *Principles of Geology*, Charles Lyell offered evidence to show that Earth had formed over millions of years. His successors concluded that Earth was at least two billion years old and that life had not appeared until long after Earth was formed. These ideas did not seem to agree with biblical accounts of creation.

Archaeology added other pieces to an emerging debate about the origins of life on Earth. In 1856, workers in Germany accidentally uncovered fossilized Neanderthal bones. Later scholars found fossils of other early modern humans. These archaeologists had limited evidence and often drew mistaken conclusions. But as more discoveries were made, scholars developed new ideas about early humans.

Darwin's Theory of Natural Selection Some of the most controversial new ideas came from the British naturalist **Charles Darwin.** In 1859, after years of research, he published *On the Origin of Species.* Darwin argued that all forms of life, including human beings, had evolved into their present state over millions of years. To explain the extremely long, slow process of evolution, he put forward a startling new theory.

Darwin adopted Thomas Malthus's idea that all plants and animals produced more offspring than the food supply could support. As a result, he said, members of each species constantly competed to survive. Natural forces "selected" those with physical traits best adapted to their environment to survive and to pass the trait on to their offspring. Darwin

>> Darwin's theories about evolution sparked much debate. **Analyze Political Cartoons** How does the portrayal of Darwin as a monkey relate to his theories? Do you think the cartoonist accepts the theories?

called this process natural selection. Later, some people called it "survival of the fittest."

The Uproar Over Darwin Like the ideas of Nicolaus Copernicus and Isaac Newton in earlier times, Darwin's theory ignited a furious debate between scientists and theologians. To many Christians, the Bible contained the only true account of creation. It told that God created the world and all forms of life within seven days. Darwin's theory, they argued, reduced people to the level of animals and undermined belief in God and the soul. While some Christians eventually came to accept the idea of evolution, others did not. Controversy over Darwin's theories has continued to the present day.

Social Darwinism Although Darwin himself never promoted any social ideas, some thinkers used his theories to support their own beliefs about society. The idea that natural selection applied to human society, especially to warfare and economic competition, became known as Social Darwinism. It was British philosopher Herbert Spencer who coined the phrase "survival of the fittest."

Social Darwinists argued that industrial tycoons earned their success because they were more "fit" than those they put out of business. War brought progress by weeding out weak nations. Victory was seen as proof of superiority.

Social Darwinism encouraged **racism,** the unscientific belief that one racial group is superior to another, and had horrific consequences for people throughout the world. For example, Social Darwinism was used to justify harsh treatment of the mentally ill and countless acts of violence toward people of "different" religions, races, and ethnicities. By the late 1800s, many Europeans and Americans claimed that the success of Western civilization was due to the supremacy of the white race. Such powerful ideas would have a long-lasting impact on world history.

☑ **IDENTIFY CENTRAL IDEAS** How did science begin to challenge existing beliefs in the late 1800s?

The Role of Religion

Despite the challenge of new scientific ideas, religion continued to be a major force in Western society. Christian churches and Jewish synagogues remained at the center of communities. Religious leaders influenced political, social, and educational developments.

The grim realities of industrial life stimulated feelings of compassion and charity. Christian and Jewish labor unions and political parties pushed for reforms. Individuals, church groups, and Jewish organizations all tried to help the working poor. Catholic priests and nuns set up schools and hospitals in urban slums. Many Protestant churches backed the **social gospel,** a movement that urged Christians to social service. They campaigned for reforms in housing, healthcare, and education.

Motivated by their religious values, Christians and Jews founded many organizations to help those in need. In Paris, Frédéric Ozanum established the St. Vincent de Paul Society in 1833. By 1878, William and Catherine Booth had set up the Salvation Army in London.

It both spread Christian teachings and provided social services. Their daughter, Evangeline Booth, later helped bring the Salvation Army to North America. In 1881, the Jewish community in New York founded the Hebrew Immigrant Aid Society, which provided shelter, food, employment, and education to many new immigrants.

☑ **IDENTIFY SUPPORTING DETAILS** What social services did religious organizations provide?

>> The hardships of industrial life led to the creation of numerous charitable organizations, including the Salvation Army, which provided many services to the needy.

The Romantics Turn from Reason

The Industrial Age shaped the arts as well as society and science. Many writers turned away from the harsh realities of industrial life to celebrate the peace and beauty of nature. These writers were part of a cultural movement called romanticism. **Romanticism** emphasized imagination, freedom, and emotion. (Romance, in the sense of romantic love, was not the focus of the movement.) From the late 1700s to 1850, romanticism shaped much of Western literature and arts.

Romantic Poetry Romantic writers, artists, and composers rebelled against the Enlightenment emphasis on reason, order, and emotional restraint. Instead, romantic writers focused on simple, direct language that conveyed intense feelings and glorified nature.

English poet **William Wordsworth** helped launch this cultural movement with the publication of *Lyrical Ballads* in 1789. Wordsworth rejected formal styles and conventions, and instead experimented with poetic forms and focused on

>> Romantic paintings often focused on nature and emotion. Note the romantic features of this portrait of William Wordsworth. His arms are crossed, and his head is down as though he is brooding about something. A dramatic landscape looms behind him.

common people and subjects, like the peace and beauty of the sunset.

> It is a beauteous evening, calm and free,
>
> The holy time is quiet as a Nun
>
> Breathless with adoration; the broad sun
>
> Is sinking down in its tranquility
>
> —William Wordsworth, *Complete Poetical Works*

Poets such as William Blake, Samuel Taylor Coleridge, John Keats, and Percy Bysshe Shelley were also leading lights of the romantic movement.

Mysterious Heroes Romantic writers created a new kind of hero—a mysterious, melancholy figure who felt out of step with society. "My joys, my grief, my passions, and my powers, / Made me a stranger," wrote Britain's George Gordon, **Lord Byron.** He himself was a larger-than-life figure equal to those he created.

>> In many of his paintings, romantic artist J.M.W. Turner focused on the effects of light and color. **Analyze Images** How does *A View on the Rhine* exemplify the characteristics of romantic art?

After a rebellious, wandering life, he joined Greek forces battling for independence from Turkish rule. When he died of a fever there, his legend bloomed. Moody, isolated romantic heroes came to be described as "Byronic."

The romantic hero often hid a guilty secret and faced a grim destiny. German writer Johann Wolfgang von Goethe (GUR tuh) wrote the dramatic poem *Faust*. The aging scholar Faust makes a pact with the devil, exchanging his soul for youth. After much agony, Faust wins salvation by accepting his duty to help others. In *Jane Eyre*, British novelist Charlotte Brontë weaves a tale about a quiet governess and her brooding, Byronic employer, whose large mansion conceals a terrifying secret.

Glorifying the Past Romantic writers combined history, legend, and folklore. Sir Walter Scott's novels and ballads evoked the turbulent history of Scottish clans or medieval knights. Novels such as *The Three Musketeers* by Alexandre Dumas (doo MAH) and *The Hunchback of Notre Dame* by **Victor Hugo** re-created France's past.

Architects, too, were inspired by old styles. Churches and other buildings, including the British Parliament, were modeled on medieval Gothic styles. To people living in the 1800s, medieval towers and lacy stonework conjured up images of a glorious past.

Romanticism in Music The orchestra, as we know it today, took shape in the early 1800s. The first composer to take full advantage of the broad range of instruments was the German composer **Ludwig van Beethoven.** Beethoven's stirring music transcended his own time and culture by conveying universal emotions such as love, loss, death, joy, and fear. For example, the famous opening of his Fifth Symphony conveys the sense of fate knocking on one's door.

His Sixth Symphony captures a joyful day in the countryside, interrupted by a violent thunderstorm. In all, Beethoven produced nine symphonies, five piano concertos, a violin concerto, an opera, two masses, and dozens of shorter pieces that are still popular today.

Romantic composers also tried to stir deep emotions. The piano music and passionate playing of the Hungarian composer Franz Liszt moved audiences to laugh or weep. Other composers wove traditional folk music into their works to glorify their nations' past. In his piano works, Frederic Chopin (shoh PAN) used Polish peasant dances to convey the sorrows and joys of people living under foreign occupation.

Romanticism in Art Painters, too, broke free from the discipline and strict rules of the Enlightenment. Landscape painters like J.M.W. Turner sought to capture the beauty and power of nature. Using bold brush strokes and colors, Turner often showed tiny human figures struggling against sea and storm.

Romantics painted many subjects, from simple peasant life to medieval knights to current events. Bright colors conveyed violent energy and emotion. The French painter Eugène Delacroix (deh luh KRWAH) filled his canvases with dramatic action. In *Liberty Leading the People,* the Goddess of Liberty carries the revolutionary tricolor as French citizens rally to the cause.

☑ **IDENTIFY CAUSE AND EFFECT** How was romanticism a reaction to the Enlightenment and the Industrial Revolution?

Artists Represent Real Life

By the mid-1800s, a new artistic movement, **realism,** took hold in the West. Realism was an attempt to represent the world as it was, without the heightened sentiment and idealized emotions of the romantics. Realists often stressed the harsh side of life in urban slums or peasant villages. Many writers and artists were committed to improving the lot of the unfortunates whose lives they depicted.

Novelists Expose Social Wrongs The English novelist **Charles Dickens** vividly portrayed the lives of slum dwellers and factory workers, including children. In *Oliver Twist,* Dickens tells the story of a nine-year-old orphan raised in a grim poorhouse. When a desperately hungry Oliver asks for more food, he is smacked in the head by his well-fed master and sent off to work. Later, he runs away to London. There he is taken in by Fagin, a villain who trains homeless children to become pickpockets.

The book shocked many middle-class readers with its picture of poverty, mistreatment of children, and urban crime. Yet Dickens's humor and colorful characters made him one of the most popular novelists in the world.

French novelists also portrayed the ills of their time. With *Les Misérables* (lay miz ehr AHB), Victor Hugo moved from romanticism to realism. The novel showed how hunger drove a good man to crime and

>> Romantic painter Eugene Delacroix turned to foreign lands and ancient times to portray the exotic or simpler ways of life. Although the painting focuses on peasant musicians rather than nature, it still seems idealized rather than harshly realistic.

>> This poster shows characters from a play based on Victor Hugo's novel *Les Misérables.* In the center is Jean Valjean, who was arrested for stealing a loaf of bread to keep his sister's child from starving.

>> In 1839, Louis Daguerre perfected an effective method of photography. His camera changed both art and society.

>> Realist painters focused on everyday subjects. *The Gross Clinic,* shown here, shows medical students dissecting a body. It is considered Eakins's masterpiece. **Analyze Images** Why were viewers so shocked by this painting? Why might Eakins have chosen this subject?

how the law hounded him ever after. The novels of Émile Zola painted an even grimmer picture. In *Germinal,* Zola exposed class warfare in the French mining industry. To Zola's characters, neither the Enlightenment faith in reason nor the romantic emphasis on feelings mattered at all.

Realism on Stage Norwegian dramatist Henrik Ibsen brought realism to the stage. His plays attacked the hypocrisy he observed around him. *A Doll's House* shows a woman caught in a straitjacket of social rules. In *An Enemy of the People,* a doctor discovers that the water in a local spa is polluted. Because the town's economy depends on its spa, the citizens denounce the doctor and suppress the truth. Ibsen's realistic dramas had a wide influence in Europe and the United States.

Realism in Art Realist painters also rejected the romantic emphasis on imagination. Instead, they focused on ordinary subjects, especially working-class men and women. "I cannot paint an angel," said the French realist **Gustave Courbet** (koor BAY), "because I have never seen one." Instead, he painted works such as *The Stone Breakers,* which shows two rough laborers on a country road. Later in the century, *The Gross Clinic,* by American painter Thomas Eakins, shocked viewers with its realistic depiction of an autopsy conducted in a medical classroom.

☑ **CONTRAST** How did realism differ from romanticism?

New Directions in the Visual Arts

By the 1840s, a new art form, photography, was emerging. **Louis Daguerre** (dah GEHR) in France and William Fox Talbot in England had improved on earlier technologies to produce successful photographs. At first, many photos were stiff, posed portraits of middle-class families or prominent people. Other photographs reflected the romantics' fascination with faraway places.

In time, photographers used the camera to present the grim realities of life. During the American Civil War, Mathew B. Brady preserved a vivid, realistic record of the corpse-strewn battlefields. Other photographers showed the harsh conditions in industrial factories or slums.

The Impressionists Photography posed a challenge to painters. Why try for realism, some artists asked, when a camera could do the same thing better?

By the 1870s, a group of painters took art in a new direction, seeking to capture the first fleeting impression made by a scene or object on the viewer's eye. The new movement, known as **impressionism**, took root in Paris, capital of the Western art world.

Since the Renaissance, painters had carefully finished their paintings so that no brush strokes showed. But impressionists like **Claude Monet** (moh NAY) and Edgar Degas (day GAH) brushed strokes of color side by side without any blending. According to new scientific studies of optics, the human eye would mix these patches of color.

By concentrating on visual impressions rather than realism, artists achieved a fresh view of familiar subjects. Monet, for example, painted the cathedral of Rouen (roo AHN), France, dozens of times from the same angle, capturing how it looked in different lights at different times of day.

The Postimpressionists Later painters, called postimpressionists, developed a variety of styles. Georges Seurat (suh RAH) arranged small dots of color to define the shapes of objects.

Vincent van Gogh experimented with sharp brush lines and bright colors. His unique brushwork lent a dreamlike quality to everyday subjects. Desperately poor, he sold few paintings in his short, unhappy life. Today, Van Gogh's masterpieces sell for millions of dollars each.

Paul Gauguin (goh GAN) also developed a bold, personal style. He rejected the materialism of Western life and went to live on the island of Tahiti in the South Pacific. His most famous works depict the people of Tahiti. In his paintings, people look flat, as in "primitive" folk art. But his brooding colors and black outlining of shapes convey intense feelings and images.

☑ **CONNECT** How did photography influence the development of painting?

>> After being rejected by France's most prestigious art exhibition, a group of painters held their own exhibition in 1874. One of the paintings, Claude Monet's *Impression: Sunrise,* gave the impressionist movement its name.

 BOUNCE to Activate Gallery

☑ ASSESSMENT

1. **Identify Cause and Effect** In what ways were the new artistic styles of the 1800s a reaction to changes in society?

2. **Draw Conclusions** Why did the movement to change women's roles in society face strong opposition?

3. **Infer** Why did reformers think free public education would lead to social change?

4. **Identify Supporting Details** How did the Industrial Revolution change the old social order and long-held traditions in the Western world?

5. **Infer** Referring to *Oliver Twist*, Charles Dickens wrote that "to show [criminals] as they really are, for ever skulking uneasily through the dirtiest paths of life . . . would be a service to society." How does his claim reflect the goals of realism?

GO ONLINE to access this biography: Sojourner Truth

Lord Byron's speech on the "Framework Bill", February 1812

From 1811 to 1812, a group of British weavers and textile workers began months of "machine breaking". They broke into factories and destroyed the new machines. It was a final effort to protest the arrival of machines which workers felt threatened their livelihoods. In addition, it showed their frustration with failed negotiations between workers and factory owners. They also attacked employers, magistrates [city officials], and food merchants. The riots spread to such an extent that 12,000 troops were called in to end the riots. In response, the British Parliament declared "machine breaking" a capital offense that was punishable by death.

>> Angry workers destroying machines

The Luddites had supporters. In 1812, one of the more prominent supporters, a well-known poet and a member of the House of Lords, Lord George Gordon Byron (known as Lord Byron) spoke before the House of Lords during a debate on the Frame Work Bill. This bill would make the destruction of mechanical knitting machines or stocking frames a major crime. Below is an excerpt from Byron's speech.

Primary Source

To enter into any detail of these riots would be superfluous; the House is already aware that every outrage short of actual bloodshed has been perpetrated, and that the proprietors of the frames obnoxious to the rioters, and all persons supposed to be connected with them, have been liable to insult and violence. During the short time I recently passed in Notts, not twelve hours elapsed without some fresh act of violence and, on the day I left the county, I was informed that forty frames had been broken the preceding evening as usual, without resistance and without detection.

☑ **EXPLAIN** How was Byron aware of the riots?

Such was then the state of that county, and such I have reason to believe it to be at this moment. But whilst these outrages must be admitted to exist to an alarming extent, it cannot be denied that they have arisen from circumstances of the most unparalleled distress. The perseverance of these miserable men in their proceedings, tends to prove that nothing but absolute want could have driven a large and once honest and industrious body of the people into the commission of excesses so hazardous to themselves, their families, and the community.

☑ **DESCRIBE** What, according to Byron, motivated the men to act as they did?

At the time to which I allude, the town and county were burdened with large detachments of the military; the police was in motion, the magistrates assembled, yet all these movements, civil and military had led to—nothing. Not a single instance had occurred of the apprehension of any real delinquent actually taken in the fact, against whom there existed legal evidence sufficient for conviction. But the police, however useless, were by no means idle: several notorious delinquents had been detected; men liable to conviction, on the clearest evidence, of the capital crime of poverty; men, who had been nefariously guilty of lawfully begetting several children, whom, thanks to the times! they were unable to maintain.

☑ **DETERMINE AUTHOR'S POINT OF VIEW** Discuss the role of the police in stopping the riots. What does Byron think of their presence?

Considerable injury has been done to the proprietors of the improved frames. These machines were to them an advantage, inasmuch as they superseded the necessity of employing a number of workmen, who were left in consequence to starve. By the adoption of one species of frame in particular, one man performed the work of many, and the superfluous labourers were thrown out of employment. Yet it is to be observed, that the work thus executed was inferior in quality, not marketable at home, and merely hurried over with a view to exportation. It was called, in the cant of the trade, by the name of Spider-work.

☑ **DETERMINE MEANING** What is Spider-work? Why might this term have been used?

The rejected workmen, in the blindness of their ignorance, instead of rejoicing at these improvements in arts so beneficial to mankind, conceived themselves to be sacrificed to improvements in mechanism. In the foolishness of their hearts, they imagined that the maintenance and well doing of the industrious poor, were objects of greater consequence than the enrichment of a few individuals by any improvement in the implements of trade which threw the workmen out of employment, and rendered the labourer unworthy of his hire.

And, it must be confessed that although the adoption of the enlarged machinery, in that state of our commerce which the country once boasted, might have been beneficial to the master without being detrimental to the servant, yet, in the present situation of our manufactures, rotting in warehouses without a prospect of exportation, with the demand for work and workmen equally diminished, frames of this construction tend materially to aggravate the distresses and discontents of the disappointed sufferers. But the real cause of these distresses, and consequent disturbances, lies deeper.

☑ **DESCRIBE** At the time of Byron's speech, what was the situation with the new machinery in factories?

☑ **ASSESSMENT**

1. **Analyze Style and Rhetoric** How does Byron use irony (a different outcome from what is expected) to describe the reaction of the workers to the new machines?

2. **Determine Central Ideas** Reread the paragraph beginning "The rejected workmen…". What other factor, aside from the machines, disturbed the textile workers?

3. **Explain** In his speech, Byron describes one of the ill effects of the Industrial Revolution. Were there benefits to having the new technology?

4. **Predict** The Framework Bill was passed. What effect do you think this had on workers?

Connections to Today

Wind turbines and solar panels, as shown here, are renewable sources of energy.

Take Action by Learning About Energy Sources

As the Industrial Revolution showed, inexpensive energy sources are vital to economic growth. What new forms of energy might drive the economy of the future?

1. **Choose** one of the following topics:

   - Solar Power

   - Wind Power

   - Electric Power

2. **Ask Questions** Generate a list of questions you have about the topic.

3. **Learn** about the topic and the major issues related to the topic. What major advances have been made with this source of energy? What are the major drawbacks? What are the primary uses for this form of energy at present? Take notes as you conduct your research and continue to generate questions as you learn more.

4. **Raise Awareness** Create a digital or print poster educating people about the form of energy you studied. What is its potential? What are its drawbacks? Share your poster with classmates and with the wider community.

Use the texts, quizzes, interactivities, Quest Inquiries, Flipped Videos, and other resources from this Topic to prepare for the Topic Test.

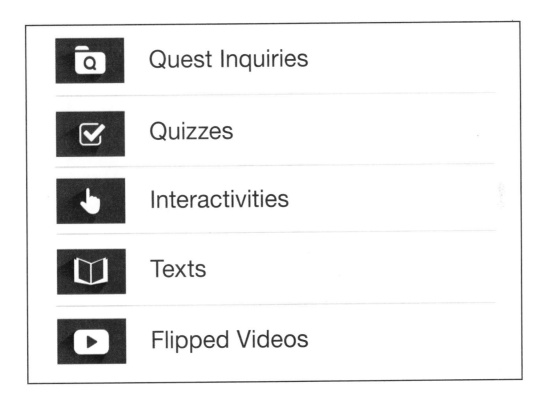

Quest Inquiries

Quizzes

Interactivities

Texts

Flipped Videos

While online you can also check the progress you've made learning the topic and course content by viewing your grades, test scores, and assignment status.

LESSON SUMMARIES
Use these Lesson Summaries, and the longer versions available online, to review the key ideas for each lesson in this Topic.

Lesson 1: The Industrial Revolution Begins
Life in farming villages that sustained most people for centuries underwent changes in the mid-1700s. This time of change is called the Industrial Revolution. It would have an impact on every aspect of life in Western Europe and the United States.

Lesson 2: Social Impact of Industrialism
With changes in farming, many people moved to the city. This movement or urbanization had benefits and problems. In addition, workers had to adjust to the difficulties of a factory system.

Lesson 3: The Second Industrial Revolution
Advances in science—the Bessemer Process, the use of electricity, along with numerous inventions to improve factory production—advances in transportation and communication, changed the way people worked and lived.

Lesson 4: Changing Ways of Life and Thought

The Industrial Revolution challenged long-held values and traditions. The rise of the middle class brought new social values and a strict etiquette code. Women campaigned for voting rights and reformers worked to make education accessible to all children. New cultural ideas embraced romanticism, then realism, in the arts.

QUEST! FINDINGS

Making Policy Decisions Refer to your Quest Connections to help you write a report about making economic decisions to present to the class. Use the rubric and other Quest resources online to guide your work.

VISUAL REVIEW

Use these graphics to review some of the key terms, people, and ideas from this Topic.

Key People

INVENTORS/DEVELOPERS

Henry Bessemer—steel processing
Michael Faraday—dynamo
Thomas Edison—electric light bulb
Gottlieb Daimler—automobile
Samuel F.B. Morse—telegraph
Alexander Graham Bell—telephone
Guglielmo Marconi—radio

SCIENTISTS

Louis Pasteur—vaccinations, pasteurization
Joseph Lister—antiseptics
John Dalton—modern atomic theory
Charles Darwin—theory of natural selection

REFORMERS

Florence Nightingale—sanitary measures in hospitals
Elizabeth Cady Stanton—women's rights
Susan B. Anthony—women's rights
William and Catherine Booth—Salvation Army

ARTISTS, WRITERS, AND COMPOSERS

William Wordsworth—romantic writer
Lord Byron—romantic writer
Ludwig van Beethoven—romantic composer
Charles Dickens—realist writer
Émile Zola—realist writer
Gustave Courbet—realist painter
Claude Monet—impressionist painter
Edgar Degas—impressionist painter
Vincent van Gogh—postimpressionist painter

Impact of the Industrial Revolution

KEY EFFECTS OF THE INDUSTRIAL REVOLUTION

INDUSTRIALIZATION

- Germany, France, and the U.S. join Great Britain as Industrial powers.
- Rise of factories; new production methods
- Advances in transportation and communication
- Rise of big business
- Growth of labor unions

URBANIZATION

- Advances in medicine and science
- Population growth due to falling death rates
- Higher standard of living

SOCIAL STRUCTURE

- Three social classes emerge
- Middle class expands
- Rise of urban working class
- Reform movements grow
- Public education expands

Topic 13 Assessment

KEY TERMS, PEOPLE, AND IDEAS

1. What is the practice of **enclosure**? How were small farmers affected?

2. How did **James Watt's** invention contribute to the technology of the Industrial Revolution?

3. How did the division of labor affect manufacturing?

4. How did natural resources in Britain contribute to the rise of the Industrial Revolution?

5. How did the Industrial Revolution affect the **standard of living**?

6. What policy did **Thomas Malthus** advocate for ending poverty?

7. According to Adam Smith, what were the benefits of a **free market**?

8. How did **Romanticism** reflect a new way of thinking?

9. What were the goals of social reformers in the United States?

CRITICAL THINKING

10. **Describe** How did industrialization gradually spread to other nations? What were the effects?

11. **Summarize** How did Robert Owen seek to improve social conditions?

12. **Synthesize Information** How did the rise of cities challenge the economic and social order of the time?

13. **Summarize Information** What laws helped workers in the late 1800s?

14. **Draw Conclusions** During the early years of the Industrial Revolution, the government exercised a policy of laissez faire economics. What were the effects on business? Were there benefits to this policy? Explain.

15. **Recognize Cause and Effect** Why did life expectancy rise steadily between 1850 and 1900?

16. **Use Primary Sources** Read the excerpt below from Karl Marx and Friedrich Engels. It gives their view on workers in the Industrial Revolution. Discuss how Marx feels a worker might regard his or her job. How does it support Marx's view of the worker as alienated or lost?

> "Owing to the extensive use of machinery and to division of labor, the work of the proletarians has lost all individual character, and consequently, all charm for the workman. He becomes [a limb] of the machine, and it is only the most simple, most monotonous, and most easily acquired knack that is required of him. Hence, the cost of production of a workman is restricted entirely to the means of [survival] that he requires for his maintenance. . . . . ."
> —*Karl Marx and Friedrich Engels, The Communist Manifesto*

17. **Writing Activity: Write an Informative Essay**
After James Watt decided to produce and market an improved steam engine, he needed money to carry out his dream. He found a partner—Matthew Boulton. Extremely pleased Boulton declared:

> "I have at my disposal what the whole world demands, something which will uplift civilization more than ever by relieving man of all undignified drudgery. I have *steam power*."

Discuss the significance of this technology in starting the Industrial Revolution. How did it impact the spread of the Industrial Revolution? Use your knowledge of the topic to explain the significance of steam power.

18. **Connections to Today** The invention of the steam engine marked the beginning of the Industrial Revolution and led to the use of coal as a major energy source. Today, energy needs have changed and greatly increased. What should be the main features of any energy source used today? Describe the features you think are needed. Do you think the fossil fuels currently used will support future needs? Explain.

DOCUMENT-BASED QUESTIONS

The birth of the modern city helped to define the Industrial Age. Read the documents below, then answer the questions that follow.

DOCUMENT A

"The first shock of a great earthquake had, just at that period, rent the whole neighborhood to its center. Traces of its course were visible on every side. Houses were knocked down; streets broken through and stopped; deep pits and trenches dug in the ground; enormous heaps of earth and clay thrown up; buildings that were undermined and shaking, propped by great beams of wood. . . . In short, the yet unfinished and unopened Railroad was in progress; and, from the very core of all this dire disorder, trailed smoothly away, upon its mighty course of civilization and improvement."

—*from Dombey and Son by Charles Dickens*

DOCUMENT B

SELECTED INVENTIONS, 1824–1911	
Cement	1824
Locomotive	1830
Dynamite	1866
Telephone	1876
Cash register	1879
Electric trolley car	1884–1887
Steel alloy	1891
Self-starting auto	1911

SOURCE: *The World Almanac*, 2004

DOCUMENT C

POPULATION OF MAJOR CITIES		
CITY	1850	1900
Berlin, Germany	419,000	1,889,000
London, England	2,685,000	6,586,000
Moscow, Russia	365,000	989,000
New York, United States	696,000	3,437,000
Paris, France	1,053,000	2,714,000

SOURCE: *International Historical Statistics*

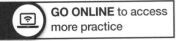 **GO ONLINE** to access more practice

DOCUMENT D
Brooklyn Bridge, 1883

19. The cause of the earthquake described in Document A was
   A. an underground fault in London.
   B. poorly constructed tall buildings.
   C. construction of a railroad.
   D. deep pits and trenches in the ground.

20. Which inventions from Document B had the most impact on New York City at the time Document D was created?
   A. trolley cars, steel alloy, cash registers
   B. dynamite, telephones, cash registers
   C. cement, locomotives, telephones
   D. cement, locomotives, dynamite

21. Which trend does Document C illustrate?
   A. the shift in population from Europe to the United States
   B. the shift in population from East Coast to West Coast
   C. the increase in population of cities
   D. the decease in rural population

22. **Writing Tasks** What were the most significant features of the modern city? Why? Use the information from Documents A through D as well as what you have learned in this Topic to support your opinion.

Nationalism and the Spread of Democracy (1790–1914)

ESSENTIAL QUESTION What are the challenges of diversity?

A statue of Simón Bolívar

Connections to Today

In many countries today, there is a conflict between nationalism and democracy. Countries that define their nationality in terms of ethnicity and culture sometimes deny democratic rights to ethnic minorities. The country's majority may discriminate against members of these minorities.

In this Topic you'll read how the ideals of democracy and nationalism first spread around the world. How do those ideals still sometimes contradict each other today?

Learn more about The Liberator, Simón Bolívar.

BOUNCE to Activate My Story Video

In this Topic, you will learn more about the events that occurred during the era of nationalism and the spread of democracy. As you study this Topic, you will complete the Quest team project.

LESSON OUTLINE

14.1 Revolutions Sweep Europe

14.2 Latin American Nations Win Independence

14.3 The Unification of Germany

14.4 The Unification of Italy

14.5 Democratic Reforms in Britain

14.6 Divisions and Democracy in France

14.7 Growth of the United States

14.8 Nationalism in Eastern Europe and Russia

Key Events of Nationalism and the Spread of Democracy

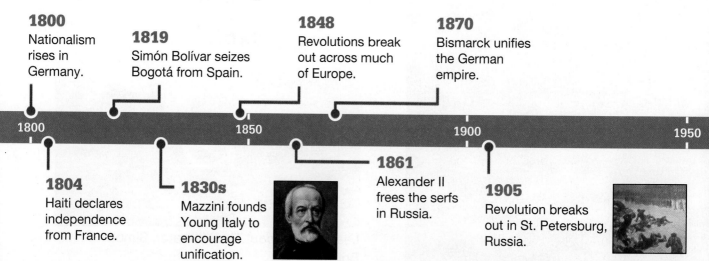

1800 Nationalism rises in Germany.

1819 Simón Bolívar seizes Bogotá from Spain.

1848 Revolutions break out across much of Europe.

1870 Bismarck unifies the German empire.

1800

1850

1900

1950

1804 Haiti declares independence from France.

1830s Mazzini founds Young Italy to encourage unification.

1861 Alexander II frees the serfs in Russia.

1905 Revolution breaks out in St. Petersburg, Russia.

QUEST! INQUIRY

Prepare for a Debate

What caused the Irish potato famine is a question that has sparked and still sparks controversy. Was British policy to blame for the famine that took the lives of over one million people? In this Quest, you will read different viewpoints. Then you will take a stand and defend your position.

 STEP 1
Review what you know about the political and economic situation in Britain and Ireland during the nineteenth century.

 STEP 2
Turn to the different sources and consider the varying viewpoints and the supporting evidence. Evaluate the sources.

 STEP 3
Team members will choose YES or NO positions. Write your position outlines. Use strong supporting evidence. Review, edit, and revise your position paper.

 STEP 4
In 1997, British prime minister Tony Blair apologized for Britain's role in the famine. Was the apology needed? Reflect on what you have learned as the discussion begins.

GO ONLINE to access complete Quest materials

Prince Metternich served as the foreign minister of Austria from 1809 to 1848. To suppress revolutionary ideas, he urged conservatives to censor the press and crush protests in their countries.

BOUNCE to Activate Flipped Video

Objectives

Compare the goals of conservatives and liberals in 19th-century Europe.

Identify the influence of liberty, equality, and nationalism on political revolutions.

Describe the causes and results of the revolutions of 1830 and 1848.

Key Terms

ideology
universal manhood
  suffrage
autonomy
radical
Louis Philippe
recession
Napoleon III
Louis Kossuth
absolutism

GO ONLINE to access your digital course

Revolutions Sweep Europe

At the Congress of Vienna in 1815, the powerful rulers of Europe sought to suppress revolutionary ideas, preserve their own power, and set up a lasting peace. Prince Klemens von Metternich, a commanding force at the congress, warned of the dangers of the "revolutionary seed" spread by the French Revolution and Napoleon. Revolutionary ideas, he warned, not only threatened Europe's monarchs, but also undermined the values of the old social order.

A Clash of Ideologies

> Passions are let loose . . . to overthrow everything that society respects as the basis of its existence: religion, public morality, laws, customs, rights, and duties, all are attacked, confounded [defeated], overthrown, or called in question.
>
> —Prince Klemens von Metternich

Unlike the monarchs attending the Congress of Vienna, other voices loudly opposed Metternich's views. In the decades after 1815, people with opposing **ideologies,** or systems of thought and belief, plunged Europe into turmoil.

Conservatives Favor Old Order The Congress of Vienna was a victory for the conservative forces, which included monarchs and their officials, noble landowners, and church leaders. To preserve the old political and social order, European monarchs worked together to ensure stability and prevent revolution. This arrangement is sometimes called the Concert of Europe. In addition to the conservative ruling class of Europe, conservative ideas appealed to peasants, who wanted to preserve traditional ways.

Conservatives of the early 1800s wanted to return to the way things had been before 1789. They had benefited under the old order. They wanted to restore royal families to the thrones they had lost when Napoleon swept across Europe. They supported a social hierarchy in which lower classes respected and obeyed their social superiors.

Conservatives also backed an established church—Catholic in Austria and southern Europe, Protestant in northern Europe, and Eastern Orthodox in eastern Europe.

Conservatives believed that talk about natural rights and constitutional government could lead only to chaos, as in France in 1789. If change had to come, they argued, it must come slowly. Conservatives felt that their own interest in peace and stability benefited everyone. Conservative leaders like Metternich opposed freedom of the press, which could spread revolutionary ideas. Metternich urged monarchs to crush protests in their own lands and help others to douse the flames of rebellion wherever they erupted.

☑ **IDENTIFY MAIN IDEAS** What was the primary goal of conservatives in the Concert of Europe?

Liberalism and Nationalism Spur Revolts

Challenging the conservatives at every turn were the liberals. Liberals embraced the ideas of the Enlightenment and the French Revolution. Their goals, and the rising tide of nationalism, ignited revolts across Europe.

Liberals Defend Natural Rights Because liberals spoke mostly for the bourgeoisie, or middle class, their ideas are sometimes called "bourgeois liberalism." Liberals included business owners, bankers, and lawyers, as well as politicians, newspaper editors, writers, and others who helped to shape public opinion.

Liberals wanted governments to be based on written constitutions and separation of powers. They opposed the old notion of the divine right of monarchs and the tradition of a ruling aristocracy. Liberals called for rulers elected by the people and responsible to them. Thus, most liberals favored a

>> **Analyze Political Cartoons** A determined Prince Metternich stands firm, with an angry crowd behind him. Whom does the crowd represent, and what do they want?

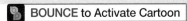
🅱 BOUNCE to Activate Cartoon

>> **Compare** After the Congress of Vienna, liberals repeatedly challenged the conservative order. How do the liberal protesters in this image differ in appearance from the image of the conservative leader Metternich in the previous text?

republican form of government over a monarchy, or at least wanted the monarch to be limited by a constitution.

Liberals defended natural rights such as liberty and equality. They stood for property rights and freedom of religion. Liberals of the early 1800s saw the role of government as limited to protecting these basic rights. In their view, only male property owners or others with a financial stake in society should have the right to vote. Not until later in the 1800s did liberals support the principle of **universal manhood suffrage,** giving all adult men the right to vote.

Liberals also strongly supported the laissez-faire economics of Adam Smith and David Ricardo. They saw the free market as an opportunity for capitalist entrepreneurs to succeed. As capitalists, and often employers, liberals had different goals from those of workers laboring in factories, mines, and other enterprises of the early Industrial Revolution.

Nationalism Grows Another challenge to Metternich's conservative order came from the rise of nationalist feelings. Like liberalism, nationalism was an outgrowth of the Enlightenment and the French Revolution. Nationalism, like liberalism, would feed the flames of revolt against the established order.

For centuries, European rulers had gained or lost lands through wars, marriages, and treaties. They exchanged territories and the people in them like pieces in a game. As a result, by 1815 Europe had several empires that included many nationalities. The Austrian, Russian, and Ottoman empires, for example, each included diverse peoples.

During the 1800s, national groups who shared a common heritage demanded their own states. Each group had its own leaders who inspired and organized the struggle. Although nationalism gave people a sense of identity and the goal of achieving an independent homeland, it also had negative effects. It often bred intolerance and led to persecution of other ethnic or national groups.

☑ **HYPOTHESIZE** Why would nationalism lead to intolerance and persecution of other ethnic or national groups?

Rebellions Erupt in Eastern Europe

Spurred by the ideas of liberalism and nationalism, revolutionaries fought against the old order. Although these ideas stirred unrest in Western Europe, the first successful nationalist revolts occurred in Eastern Europe. Eastern Europe was home to a mix of peoples and religions. In the early 1800s, several Balkan peoples in southeastern Europe rebelled against the Ottomans, who had ruled them for more than 300 years.

Goals of Liberals and Conservatives

LIBERALS	CONSERVATIVES
Ideas appealed to middle class of educated business people and professionals.	Ideas appealed to royalty, nobility, church leaders, and uneducated peasants.
GOALS:	**GOALS:**
Governments based on written constitutions	Royal families on their thrones
Separation of powers	Traditional social hierarchy
Natural rights of individuals (liberty, equality, and property)	Authority of established churches
Republican form of government	Respect and obedience to authority
Laissez-faire economics	Stability and order
Revolution, if necessary, to achieve goals	Suppression of revolutions

>> **Analyze Charts** Conservatives and liberals had very different ideas about the role of government. How did their different ideologies affect European politics in the early to mid-1800s?

Serbia Gains Independence The first Balkan people to revolt were the Serbs. From 1804 to 1817, the Serbian independence leaders Karageorge (ka rah JAWR juh) and Milos Obrenovic (oh BRAY noh vich) battled Ottoman forces in two major uprisings.

Although Serbs had support from Russia, which shared its Slavic heritage and Eastern Orthodox Christianity, the Serbs faced a terrible struggle. The fighting took a huge toll. During this period, Serbian literature and culture flourished, further strengthening Serbian nationalism.

Gradually, Serbia gained a degree of **autonomy,** or self-rule, within the Ottoman empire. An 1830 agreement gave Serbs complete control over their own internal affairs, although European countries did not recognize Serbia's independence until 1878. Serbia continued its close ties with Russia, which it saw as a protector of its hard-won freedom.

Greeks Revolt Against Ottoman Rule In 1821, the Greeks revolted, seeking to end centuries of Ottoman rule. At first, the Greeks were badly divided. But years of suffering in long, bloody wars of independence helped shape a national identity. Leaders of the rebellion justified their struggle as "a national war, a holy war, a war the object of which is to reconquer the rights of individual liberty." The Greeks had the support of romantic writers such as English poet Lord Byron, who went to Greece to aid the fight for independence.

The Greek rebels won the sympathy of even the conservative powers of Europe. In the late 1820s, Britain, France, and Russia forced the Ottomans to grant independence to some Greek provinces. By 1830, Greece was independent. The European powers, however, pressured the Greeks to accept Otto von Wittelsbach, a German prince, as their king. This move was meant to show that the European powers did not support nationalist revolutions.

Other Challenges to the Old Order During the 1820s, other revolts erupted along the fringe of Europe. In Spain, Portugal, and several Italian states, rebels demanded constitutional governments. The unrest posed a challenge to the conservative rulers of Europe. Spurred on by Metternich, a French army marched over the Pyrenees to suppress a revolt in Spain. Austrian forces crossed the Alps to smash Italian rebels.

Troops dampened the fires of liberalism and nationalism, but could not smother them. In the next decades, sparks would flare anew. Added to liberal and nationalist demands were the goals of

>> Uprisings flared up repeatedly across Europe, especially in Paris.

the new industrial working class. By the mid-1800s, social reformers and agitators were urging workers to support socialism or other ways of reorganizing property ownership, further contributing to the unrest of this period.

☑ **HYPOTHESIZE** Why would a monarch order his army to suppress an uprising in another country?

Revolutions of 1830 and 1848

In the 1820s, conservative forces quickly suppressed the liberal uprisings in Spain, Portugal, and the Italian states. They could not, however, end Europe's age of revolutions. Liberal French leader Alexis de Tocqueville warned that the revolutions of the 1820s were not over.

We are sleeping on a volcano . . . Do you not see that the Earth trembles anew? A wind of revolution blows, the storm is on the horizon.

—Alexis de Tocqueville

Conservatives and Liberals in France The Congress of Vienna had restored Louis XVIII to the French throne. The new ruler wisely issued a constitution, the Charter of French Liberties. It created a two-house legislature and allowed limited freedom of the press. Still, the king retained much power.

Louis's efforts at compromise satisfied few people. Ultra royalists despised constitutional government and wanted to restore the old regime. These "ultras" included many high clergy and émigré nobles who had returned to France after the revolution.

Opposing the ultras were the liberals. They wanted to extend suffrage and win a share of power for middle-class citizens like themselves. Another group, the **radicals,** or people who favor extreme change, called for a republic like France had in the 1790s. The working class still wanted what it had hoped to win in 1789: decent pay and bread the people could afford.

Citizens Lead the July Revolution When Louis XVIII died in 1824, his younger brother, Charles X, inherited the throne. Charles, a strong believer in **absolutism,** rejected the very idea of the charter. In July 1830, he suspended the legislature, limited the right to vote, and restricted the press.

In Paris, angry citizens threw up barricades across the narrow streets. From behind the barricades, people fired on the soldiers and pelted them with stones and roof tiles. Within days, rebels controlled Paris. The revolutionary tricolor flew from the towers of Notre Dame cathedral. A frightened Charles X abdicated and fled to England.

Louis Philippe, the "Citizen King" Radicals and liberals who had united against Charles X disagreed over a new government. Radicals wanted to set up a republic. Liberals, however, insisted on a constitutional monarchy and chose **Louis Philippe** as king. Louis Philippe was a cousin of Charles X and in his youth had supported the revolution of 1789.

The French called Louis Philippe the "citizen king" because he owed his throne to the people. Louis got along well with the liberal bourgeoisie. He dressed like them in a frock coat and top hat. Sometimes he strolled the streets, shaking hands with well-wishers. Liberal politicians filled his government.

Under Louis Philippe, the upper bourgeoisie prospered. Louis extended suffrage, but only to France's wealthier citizens. The vast majority of the people still could not vote. The king's other policies also favored the middle class at the expense of the workers.

☑ **RECALL** What actions did Charles X take in 1830, and how did French rebels respond?

Demands for Reform Spread

The July Revolution in Paris inspired uprisings elsewhere in Europe. Metternich later said, "When France sneezes, Europe catches cold." Most of the uprisings were suppressed. But here and there, rebels did force changes on conservative governments. Even when they failed, revolutions frightened rulers badly enough to encourage reforms later in the century.

Belgium Wins Independence The one notable success in 1830 took place in Belgium. In 1815, the Congress of Vienna had united the Austrian Netherlands (present-day Belgium) and the Kingdom of Holland under the Dutch king. The Congress had

>> French rebels erected barricades in the streets using household items and whatever else they could find that might offer protection during battles with government soldiers.

KEY

■ Gained independence, 1830–1831

✷ Revolutions of 1830

☇ Revolution suppressed

♛ New government established (constitutional monarchy)

North Sea

Baltic Sea

BELGIUM

PRUSSIA

Warsaw

RUSSIA

Paris

FRANCE

AUSTRIA

Black Sea

ATLANTIC OCEAN

ITALY

OTTOMAN EMPIRE

Mediterranean Sea

GREECE

0   400 mi
0   400 km
Albers Conic Equal-Area Projection

>> **Analyze Maps** What were the results of the revolutions of 1830?

wanted to create a strong barrier to help prevent French expansion in the future.

The Belgians resented the new arrangement. The Belgians and Dutch had different languages, religions, and economic interests. The Belgians were Catholic, while the Dutch were largely Protestant. The Belgian economy was based on manufacturing, while the Dutch relied on trade.

News of the 1830 Paris uprising ignited a revolutionary spark in Belgium. Students and workers, along with other citizens, threw up barricades in Brussels, the capital. The Dutch king hoped for help from Britain and France. These two countries backed Belgian demands for independence, expecting to benefit from the separation of Belgium and Holland. As a result, in 1831, Belgium became an independent state with a liberal constitution. Soon after, the major European powers signed a treaty recognizing Belgium as a "perpetually neutral state."

Polish Nationalists Defeated Nationalists in Poland also staged an uprising in 1830. But, unlike the Belgians, the Poles failed to win independence for their country.

In the late 1700s, Russia, Austria, and Prussia had divided up Poland. Poles had hoped that the Congress of Vienna would restore their homeland

in 1815. Instead, the great powers confirmed the division of Poland among those three powers.

In 1830, Polish students, army officers, and landowners rose in revolt. The rebels failed to gain widespread support, however, and were brutally crushed by Russian forces. Some survivors fled to Western Europe and the United States, where they kept alive the dream of freedom.

☑ **COMPARE AND CONTRAST** How were the Belgian and Polish revolutions of 1830 different?

The Revolution of 1848 in France

By the 1840s, discontent in France was again reaching a boiling point. The Industrial Revolution was changing life in France, especially in the cities. Politically, France remained divided. Radicals still wanted a republic. Utopian socialists called for an end to private ownership of property. Even liberals denounced Louis Philippe's government for corruption.

Discontent grew when a **recession,** or period of reduced economic activity, hit France. Factories closed and workers lost their jobs. Poor harvests led to rising food prices. In Paris, conditions were ripe for revolution.

Violence Erupts During "February Days" In February 1848, the government took steps to silence critics and prevent public meetings. This action sent angry crowds into the streets of Paris. During the "February Days," overturned carts, paving stones, and toppled trees again blocked the streets. Church bells rang alarms, while women and men on the barricades sang the revolutionary anthem "La Marseillaise." A number of demonstrators clashed with royal troops and were killed.

As the turmoil spread, Louis Philippe abdicated. A group of liberal, radical, and socialist leaders proclaimed the Second Republic. The First Republic had lasted from 1792 until 1804, when Napoleon became emperor.

From the start, deep differences divided the new government. Middle-class liberals wanted moderate political reforms. Socialists wanted far-reaching social and economic change and forced the government to set up national workshops to provide jobs for the unemployed.

Workers Lose Out During "June Days" By June, however, upper- and middle-class interests had won control of the government. They saw the national workshops as a waste of money and shut them down. Furious, workers again took to the streets of

Paris. This time, however, bourgeois liberals turned violently against the protesters. Peasants, who feared that socialists might take their land, also attacked the rioting workers. At least 1,500 people were killed before the government crushed the rebellion.

The fighting of the "June Days" left a bitter legacy. The middle class both feared and distrusted the socialists, while the working class harbored a deep hatred for the bourgeoisie.

Louis Napoleon Is Elected President By the end of 1848, the National Assembly was dominated by members who wanted to restore order. They issued a constitution for the Second Republic. It created a strong president and a one-house legislature. But it also gave the vote to all adult men, the widest suffrage in the world at the time. Nine million Frenchmen could now vote, compared with only 200,000 who had that right before.

When elections for president were held, the overwhelming winner was Louis Napoleon, nephew of Napoleon Bonaparte. The "new" Napoleon attracted the working classes by presenting himself as a man who cared about social issues such as poverty. At the same time, his famous name, linked with order and past French glory, helped him with conservatives.

Napoleon III Establishes the Second Empire Once in office, Louis Napoleon used his position as a stepping-stone to greater power. By 1852, he had proclaimed himself emperor, taking the title **Napoleon III.** Thus ended the short-lived Second Republic.

Like his celebrated uncle, Napoleon III used a plebiscite, or ballot in which voters have a direct say on an issue, to win public approval for his seizure of power. A stunning 90 percent of voters supported his move to set up the Second Empire. Many thought that a monarchy was more stable than a republic or hoped that Napoleon III would restore the glory days of Napoleon Bonaparte.

Napoleon III, like Louis Philippe, ruled at a time of rapid economic growth. For the bourgeoisie, the early days of the Second Empire brought prosperity and contentment. In time, however, Napoleon III would embark on foreign adventures that would bring down his empire and end French leadership in Europe.

☑ **CONTRAST** How did the French governments created after the Revolutions of 1830 and 1848 differ?

>> During the 1848 revolution, people in Paris blocked the streets with massive barricades to keep government troops from controlling the city.

Revolutionary Uprisings of 1848

KEY
→ Repression of revolutions in 1848
✳ Revolutions of 1848

>> **Analyze Maps** France's successful 1848 uprising sparked revolutions throughout Europe. How does the map show the difficulties conservatives had in stopping the spread of revolutionary ideas?

BOUNCE to Activate Map

Revolution Spreads Across Europe

The Revolution of 1848 in France triggered a wave of revolutions across Europe, just as it had in 1830. For opponents of the old order, it was a time of such hope that they called it the "springtime of the peoples." Although events in France touched off the revolts, grievances had been piling up for years.

European middle-class liberals wanted a greater share of political power, as well as protections for the basic rights of all male citizens. Workers demanded relief from the miseries of the Industrial Revolution. And nationalists of all classes ached to throw off foreign rule.

Revolts Shake the Austrian Empire In the Austrian empire, revolts broke out in the major cities, starting in Vienna. Metternich, who had long dominated Austrian politics, tried to suppress the revolts. Even though he censored the press, books were smuggled to universities throughout the empire. Students demanded change. When workers joined the students on the streets of Vienna, Metternich resigned and fled in disguise.

Revolution quickly spread to other parts of the Austrian empire. In Budapest, Hungarian nationalists

led by journalist **Louis Kossuth** demanded an independent government, an end to serfdom, and a written constitution. In Prague, the Czechs made similar demands. Overwhelmed by events, the Austrian government agreed to the reforms. The gains were temporary, however. Austrian troops soon regained control of Vienna and Prague and smashed the rebels in Budapest.

Revolts in Italy Uprisings also erupted in the Italian states. Nationalists wanted to end Austrian domination. As elsewhere, nationalist goals were linked to demands for liberal reforms such as constitutional government. Workers suffering economic hardships demanded even more radical changes.

From Venice in the north to Naples in the south, Italians set up independent republics. Revolutionaries expelled the pope from Rome. Before long, the forces of reaction returned, backed by military force. Austrian troops ousted the new governments in northern Italy. A French army restored the pope to power. Elsewhere, liberal reforms were canceled.

Rebellion in the German States In the German states, university students demanded national unity and liberal reforms. Economic hard times and a potato famine brought peasants and workers into the struggle. In Prussia, liberals forced King Frederick William IV to accept a constitution written by an elected assembly. Within a year, though, he dissolved the assembly.

Throughout 1848, delegates from German states met in the Frankfurt Assembly. Divisions soon emerged over whether Germany should be a republic or a monarchy and whether to include Austria in a united German state.

Finally, the assembly offered Prussia's Frederick William IV the crown of a united Germany. To their dismay, the conservative king rejected the offer because it came not from the German princes but from the people—"from the gutter," as he described it.

Failed Revolutions By 1850, rebellions faded, ending the age of liberal revolution that began in 1789. Why did the uprisings fail? In general, revolutionaries did not have mass support. Also, opposing goals divided liberals, who wanted moderate political reforms, and workers, who sought radical economic changes. And rulers did not hesitate to use force to crush the uprisings.

At mid-century, although Metternich was gone, his conservative system remained largely in force. In the decades ahead, liberalism, nationalism, and socialism would win successes not through revolution, but through political activity.

☑ **INTEGRATE INFORMATION** Describe the role nationalism played in European revolutions in 1848.

☑ ASSESSMENT

1. **Explain** Explain why peasants might support conservative control of government.

2. **Draw Conclusions** What conditions led the French people to revolt?

3. **Cite Evidence** Why did most of the revolutions of 1848 fail to achieve their goals?

4. **Identify Main Ideas** Explain the main ideologies that led to the uprisings throughout Europe.

5. **Connections to Today** Many parts of the Austrian empire were ethnically mixed. How might ethnic minorities in each region have felt about nationalist movements led by the region's majority?

GO ONLINE to access this biography: Alexis de Tocqueville

14.2

Simón Bolívar was a Venezuelan-born military and political leader. Inspired by Enlightenment ideals, he led revolutions to end Spanish rule in Latin America.

Latin American Nations Win Independence

In the late 1700s, the revolutionary fever that gripped Western Europe spread to Latin America. There, discontent was rooted in the social, racial, and political system that had emerged during 300 years of European rule. By 1825, most of Latin America was freed from colonial rule.

Spanish America Rises Up

Discrimination and social inequality bred resentment of Spain's rule in its American colonies. Opposition to Spanish rule grew.

A Complex Social Structure Spanish-born **peninsulares** dominated Spanish America. Only they could hold top jobs in government and the Church. Many **creoles**—the European-descended Latin Americans who owned the haciendas, ranches, and mines—bitterly resented their second-class status. Merchants fretted under mercantilist policies that tied the colonies to Spain.

Meanwhile, a growing population of **mestizos,** people of American Indian and European descent, as well as people of African and European descent, were angry at being denied the status, wealth, and power that were available to whites. American Indians suffered economic misery under the Spanish, who had conquered the lands of their ancestors. In the Caribbean region and parts of South America, masses of enslaved Africans who worked on plantations longed for freedom.

BOUNCE to Activate Flipped Video

Objectives

List the causes of growing discontent in Latin America, including the influence of the Enlightenment.

Trace the influence of the American and French Revolutions on Latin America.

Describe the revolutions in Haiti, Mexico, and Central America.

Explain how South American nations won independence, including the role of Simón Bolívar.

Key Terms

peninsular
creole
mestizo
Simón Bolívar
Toussaint
   L'Ouverture
Father Miguel
   Hidalgo
Father José Morelos
José de San Martín
Dom Pedro

GO ONLINE to access your digital course

Enlightenment Ideas Reach Spanish America In the 1700s, educated creoles read the works of Enlightenment thinkers. They watched colonists in North America throw off British rule and were inspired by their success. Translations of the Declaration of Independence and the Constitution of the United States circulated among the creole elite.

During the French Revolution, young creoles like **Simón Bolívar** (boh LEE vahr) traveled in Europe and were inspired by the ideals of "liberty, equality, and fraternity." Yet, despite their admiration for Enlightenment ideas and revolutions in other lands, most creoles were reluctant to act.

The Uprisings Begin The spark that finally ignited widespread rebellion in Spanish America was Napoleon's invasion of Spain in 1808. Napoleon ousted the Spanish king and placed his brother Joseph on the Spanish throne. In Spain's colonies, leaders saw Spain's weakness as an opportunity to reject foreign domination and demand independence from colonial rule.

☑ **CHECK UNDERSTANDING** In what ways did the American and French Revolutions influence Spanish Americans?

Haiti Fights for Freedom

Even before Spanish colonists hoisted the flag of freedom, revolution had erupted in a French-ruled colony on the island of Hispaniola. In Haiti, as the western part of the island is now called, French planters owned very profitable sugar plantations worked by nearly a half million enslaved people of African descent. These enslaved people were overworked and underfed.

Haitians Revolt Against Slavery Embittered by suffering and inspired by the talk of liberty and equality, enslaved islanders rebelled in 1791. The rebels were fortunate to find an intelligent and skillful leader in **Toussaint L'Ouverture** (too SAN loo vehr TOOR), who had gained an education and freedom from slavery. Although untrained, L'Ouverture was a brilliant and inspiring general.

The rebels faced a complicated struggle. Some free people of African descent, angry at discrimination, fought for the rebels. Others, often enslavers themselves, sided with the plantation owners. France and Britain sent armies against the rebels.

The fighting took more lives than any other revolution in the Americas. But by 1798, the rebels had achieved their goal: Slavery was abolished, and L'Ouverture's forces controlled most of the island.

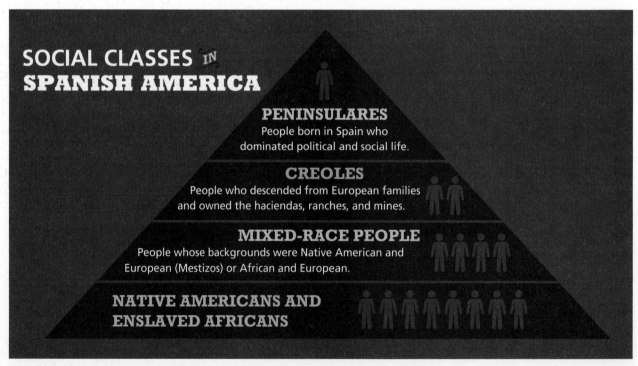

SOCIAL CLASSES IN SPANISH AMERICA

PENINSULARES
People born in Spain who dominated political and social life.

CREOLES
People who descended from European families and owned the haciendas, ranches, and mines.

MIXED-RACE PEOPLE
People whose backgrounds were Native American and European (Mestizos) or African and European.

NATIVE AMERICANS AND ENSLAVED AFRICANS

>> **Analyze Charts** In Spain's Latin American colonies, the social structure reflected inequality among the classes. Why would creoles be likely to support and lead revolutions in Spanish America?

Haitian Independence In 1802, Napoleon Bonaparte sent a large army to reconquer the former colony. L'Ouverture urged his countrymen to take up arms once again to resist the invaders. In April 1802 the French agreed to a truce, but then they captured L'Ouverture and carried him in chains to France. He died there in a cold mountain prison a year later.

The struggle for freedom continued, however, and late in 1803, with yellow fever destroying their army, the French surrendered. In January 1804, the island declared itself an independent country under the name of Haiti. In the following years, rival Haitian leaders fought for power. Finally, in 1820, Haiti became a republic.

☑ **CHECK UNDERSTANDING** What conditions led to the Haitian fight for independence?

Revolts in Mexico and Central America

The revolt by enslaved Haitians frightened creoles in Spanish America. Although they wanted power themselves, few wanted economic or social changes that might threaten their way of life. In 1810, however, a creole priest in Mexico, **Father Miguel Hidalgo** (hee DAHL goh), raised his voice for freedom.

Mexico's Battle for Independence Begins Father Hidalgo presided over the poor rural parish of Dolores. On September 15, 1810, he rang the church bells summoning the people to prayer. When they gathered, he startled them with an urgent appeal, "My children, will you be free?" Father Hidalgo's speech became known as "el Grito de Dolores"—the cry of Dolores. It called Mexicans to fight for independence.

A ragged army of poor mestizos and American Indians rallied to Father Hidalgo and marched to the outskirts of Mexico City. At first, some creoles supported the revolt. However, they soon rejected Hidalgo's call for an end to slavery and his plea for reforms to improve conditions for Native Americans. They felt that these policies would cost them power.

After some early successes, the rebels faced growing opposition. Less than a year after he issued the "Grito," Hidalgo was captured and executed, and his followers scattered.

José Morelos Continues the Fight Another priest picked up the banner of revolution. **Father José Morelos** was a mestizo who called for wide-ranging social and political reform. He wanted to improve conditions for the majority of Mexicans, abolish slavery, and give the vote to all men. For four years,

>> **Draw Conclusions** L'Ouverture's army defeated British, Spanish, and French armies to end slavery in Haiti and win independence from France. Why would the British and Spanish join the fight against the rebels?

>> Father Hidalgo led the Mexican independence movement, battling Spanish forces for almost a year before his capture and execution.

Morelos led rebel forces before he, too, was captured and shot in 1815.

Spanish forces, backed by conservative creoles, hunted down the surviving guerrillas. They had almost succeeded in ending the rebel movement when events in Spain had unexpected effects.

Mexico Wins Independence In Spain in 1820, liberals forced the king to issue a constitution. This move alarmed Agustín de Iturbide (ee toor BEE day), a conservative creole in Mexico. He feared that the new Spanish government might impose liberal reforms on the colonies as well.

Iturbide had spent years fighting Mexican revolutionaries. Suddenly, in 1821, he reached out to them. Backed by creoles, mestizos, and American Indians, he overthrew the Spanish viceroy. Mexico was independent at last. Iturbide took the title Emperor Agustín I. Soon, however, liberal Mexicans toppled the would-be monarch and set up the Republic of Mexico.

New Republics in Central America Spanish-ruled lands in Central America declared independence in the early 1820s. Iturbide tried to add these areas to his Mexican empire. After his overthrow, local leaders set up a republic called the United Provinces of Central America. The union soon fragmented into the separate republics of Guatemala, Nicaragua, Honduras, El Salvador, and Costa Rica.

☑ **HYPOTHESIZE** Why do you think Mexico's first two independence leaders were priests?

Discontent Sparks Revolts in South America

In South America, Native Americans had rebelled against Spanish rule as early as the 1700s, though with limited results. It was not until the 1800s that discontent among the creoles sparked a widespread drive for independence.

Bolívar Fights for Independence In the early 1800s, discontent spread across South America. As you read earlier, educated creoles like Simón Bolívar admired the French and American revolutions. They dreamed of winning their own independence from Spain.

In 1808, when Napoleon Bonaparte occupied Spain, Bolívar and his friends saw the occupation as a signal to act. In 1810, Bolívar led an uprising that established a republic in his native Venezuela. Bolívar's new republic was quickly toppled by conservative forces, however. For years, civil war raged in Venezuela. The revolutionaries suffered many setbacks. Twice Bolívar was forced into exile on the island of Haiti.

Then, Bolívar conceived a daring plan. He would march his army across the Andes and attack the Spanish at Bogotá, the capital of the viceroyalty of New Granada (present-day Colombia). First, he cemented an alliance with the hard-riding llaneros, or Venezuelan cowboys. Then, in a grueling campaign, he led an army through swampy lowlands and over the snowcapped Andes. Finally, in August 1819, he swooped down to take Bogotá from the surprised Spanish.

Other victories followed. By 1821, Bolívar had succeeded in freeing Caracas, Venezuela. "The Liberator," as he was now called, then moved south into Ecuador, Peru, and Bolivia. There, he joined forces with another great leader, **José de San Martín.**

San Martín Joins the Fight Like Bolívar, San Martín was a creole. He was born in Argentina but went to Europe for military training. In 1816, this gifted general helped Argentina win freedom from Spain. He then joined the independence struggle in other areas.

>> Bolívar leads his army against Spanish troops in the struggle to free South America from Spanish control.

 BOUNCE to Activate Gallery

Latin American Independence

KEY
Dates of independence appear next to country names.
- European colonies after 1830
- Countries within Gran Colombia, 1819–1830
- Countries within the United Provinces of Central America, 1823–1838
- Other newly independent countries

>> **Analyze Maps** What was Gran Colombia? Why is it not on maps of present-day South America?

BOUNCE to Activate Map

He, too, led an army across the Andes, from Argentina into Chile. He defeated the Spanish in Chile before moving into Peru to strike further blows against colonial rule. San Martín turned his command over to Bolívar in 1822, allowing Bolívar's forces to win the final victories against Spain.

Civil Wars Break Out The wars of independence ended by 1824. Bolívar then worked tirelessly to unite the lands he had liberated into a single nation, called Gran Colombia. Bitter rivalries, however, made that dream impossible. Before long, Gran Colombia split into three independent countries: Colombia, Venezuela, and Ecuador.

Bolívar faced another disappointment as power struggles among rival leaders triggered destructive civil wars. Before his death in 1830, a discouraged Bolívar wrote, "We have achieved our independence at the expense of everything else." Contrary to his dreams, South America's common people had simply exchanged one set of masters for another.

Brazil Gains Independence When Napoleon's armies conquered Portugal, the Portuguese royal family fled to Brazil. When the king returned to Portugal, he left his son **Dom Pedro** to rule Brazil. "If Brazil demands independence," the king advised Pedro, "proclaim it yourself and put the crown on your own head."

In 1822, Pedro followed his father's advice. A revolution had brought new leaders to Portugal who planned to abolish reforms and demanded that Dom Pedro return. Dom Pedro refused to leave Brazil. Instead, he became emperor of an independent Brazil. He accepted a constitution that provided for freedom of the press, freedom of religion, and an elected legislature. Brazil remained a monarchy until 1889, when it became a republic.

☑ **COMPARE AND CONTRAST** How did the goals of the Latin American revolutions differ from their results?

☑ ASSESSMENT

1. **Draw Conclusions** How did the social structure contribute to discontent in Latin America?

2. **Identify Central Issues** Explain why creoles did not support Hidalgo or Morelos and how this affected the fight for independence.

3. **Draw Conclusions** What advantages did the enslaved Haitians have over French soldiers?

4. **Identify Main Ideas** Describe the challenges Simón Bolívar faced while liberating South America.

5. **Connections to Today** How might Latin Americans of African and Indian descent have felt about creole dominance of the region's independence movements?

GO ONLINE to access this biography: Simón Bolívar

"Letter From Jamaica," Simón Bolívar, 1815

Simón Bolívar led the struggle for independence in Spanish-speaking South America. After winning some military victories against the Spanish, Bolívar faced temporary defeat in 1814. He fled to the British-ruled island of Jamaica, where he tried to win British support for the independence struggle. This excerpt comes from a letter that he wrote in 1815 to Henry Cullen, a British merchant living in Jamaica. He meant for the letter to be read by a wide audience. In it, he makes his case for independence and outlines the kind of government he hopes the Latin American countries will achieve. Bolívar later defeated Spanish forces and won independence for several South American countries.

>> Simón Bolívar

Primary Source

. . . Success will crown our efforts, because the destiny of America [that is, Spanish America] has been irrevocably decided; the tie that bound her to Spain has been severed. Only a concept maintained that tie and kept the parts of that immense monarchy together. That which formerly bound them now divides them. The hatred that the Peninsula [that is, Spain] has inspired in us is greater than the ocean between us. It would be easier to have the two continents meet than to reconcile the spirits of the two countries. The habit of obedience; a community of interest, of understanding, of religion; mutual goodwill; a tender regard for the birthplace and good name of our forefathers; in short, all that gave rise to our hopes, came to us from Spain. As a result there was born principle of affinity [relatedness] that seemed eternal, notwithstanding the misbehavior of our rulers, which weakened that sympathy, or, rather, that bond enforced by the domination of their rule.

☑ **ANALYZE WORD CHOICES** How does Bolívar use his wording to contrast the current attitude of people in the Spanish colonies with their earlier attitude?

At present the contrary attitude persists: we are threatened with the fear of death, dishonor, and every harm; there is nothing we have not suffered at the hands of that unnatural stepmother—Spain. The veil has been torn asunder. We have already seen the light, and it is not our desire to be thrust back into darkness. The chains have been broken; we have been freed, and now our enemies seek to enslave us anew. For this reason America fights desperately, and seldom has desperation failed to achieve victory.
. . .

☑ **USE CONTEXT CLUES** In the preceding sentence, is Bolívar predicting victory or failure to achieve victory for those seeking Latin American independence? How does the context make this clear?

More than anyone, I desire to see America fashioned into the greatest nation in the world, greatest not so much by virtue of her area and wealth as by her freedom and glory. Although I seek perfection for the government of my country, I cannot persuade myself that the New World can, at the moment, be organized as a great republic. Since it is impossible, I dare not desire it; yet much less do I desire to have all America a monarchy because this plan is not only impracticable but also impossible. Wrongs now existing could not be righted, and our emancipation would be fruitless. . . .

The party spirit [divisiveness] that today keeps our states in constant agitation would assume still greater proportions were a central power established, for that power—the only force capable of checking this agitation—would be elsewhere. Furthermore, the chief figures of [each country] would not tolerate the preponderance of leaders [in the central capital], for they would regard these leaders as so many tyrants. Their resentments would attain such heights that they would compare the latter to the hated Spaniards. Any such monarchy would be a misshapen colossus that would collapse of its own weight at the slightest disturbance.

☑ **ANALYZE ARGUMENTS** What arguments lead Bolívar to conclude that Latin America could not succeed as a unified republic or monarchy?

Mr. de Pradt [a French writer] has wisely divided America into fifteen or seventeen mutually independent states, governed by as many monarchs. I am in agreement on the first suggestion, as America can well tolerate seventeen nations; as to the second, though it could easily be achieved, it would serve no purpose. Consequently, I do not favor American monarchies. My reasons are these: The well-understood interest of a republic is limited to the matter of its preservation, prosperity, and glory.

Republicans, because they do not desire powers, which represent a directly contrary viewpoint, have no reason for expanding the boundaries of their nation to the detriment of their own resources, solely for the purpose of having their neighbors share a liberal constitution. . . .

For these reasons I think that the Americans . . . would prefer republics to kingdoms.

☑ **IDENTIFY SUPPORTING DETAILS** What observations support Bolívar's argument against monarchies?

☑ **ASSESSMENT**

1. **Determine Author's Point of View** What is Bolívar's view of Spanish colonial rule? Cite specific passages from the source.

2. **Integrate Information From Diverse Sources** How much does Bolívar's thinking reflect that of Enlightenment thinkers and European liberals, which you have read about in previous topics and lessons?

3. **Determine Author's Purpose** Considering that Bolívar wrote this letter after the independence struggle had faced setbacks, what do you think he hoped to accomplish with this letter?

4. **Explain an Argument** What is the main reason that Bolívar opposes monarchies?

5. **Identify Cause and Effect** Based on your text, how did independence unfold in Latin America? How might the views Bolívar expressed in this letter have helped shape that outcome?

14.3

Napoleon rides triumphantly into Berlin. French rule inspired German nationalism and demands for a unified German state.

 BOUNCE to Activate Flipped Video

Objectives

Identify the factors that promoted German nationalism.

Analyze how Bismarck achieved German unification.

Describe the German empire under Bismarck.

Explain the policies of Kaiser William II.

Key Terms

Otto von Bismarck
chancellor
Realpolitik
annex
kaiser
Reich
Kulturkampf
William II
social welfare

The Unification of Germany

In the early 1800s, German-speaking people lived in a number of small and medium-sized states, as well as in Prussia and the Austrian Hapsburg empire. Napoleon's invasions unleashed new forces in these lands, especially a sense of German nationalism. Early efforts to unify Germany failed, but by 1862 a strong-willed Prussian official, Otto von Bismarck, set out to build a strong, unified German state.

Moving Toward a Unified Germany

During much of history, Germans identified with their regional states and felt no need for political union. Napoleon helped change that.

Impact of Napoleonic Invasions Between 1806 and 1812, Napoleon annexed lands along the Rhine River for France. He dissolved the Holy Roman Empire. He also forced a number of German states into a Rhine Confederation allied with France.

At first, some Germans welcomed the French emperor as a hero with enlightened, modern policies. He encouraged freeing the serfs, made trade easier, and abolished laws against Jews. However, many Germans fought to free their lands from French rule, and a sense of German nationalism emerged. They began to demand a unified German state.

Napoleon's defeat did not resolve the issue. At the Congress of Vienna, Metternich opposed nationalist demands. A united Germany, he argued, would require dismantling the governments of the many German states. Instead, conservative peacemakers

GO ONLINE to access your digital course

created the German Confederation, a weak alliance headed by Austria.

New Efforts to Bring Unity In the 1830s, Prussia created an economic union called the Zollverein (TSAWL fur yn). It dismantled tariff barriers among many German states. Still, Germany remained politically fragmented.

In 1848, liberals meeting in the Frankfurt Assembly again demanded German political unity. They offered the throne of a united German state to Frederick William IV of Prussia. As you have learned, the Prussian ruler rejected the notion of a throne offered by "the people."

☑ **DESCRIBE** What impact did the Napoleonic Wars have on Germany?

Bismarck Becomes the Architect of German Unity

Where others had failed in uniting Germany, **Otto von Bismarck** succeeded. Bismarck came from Prussia's Junker (YOONG kur) class, made up of conservative landowning nobles. Bismarck first

served Prussia as a diplomat in Russia and France, and then as prime minister to King William I. In 1871, he became **chancellor,** or the highest official, of a united Germany.

Blood and Iron In his "blood and iron" speech delivered in 1862, Otto von Bismarck set the tone for his future policies. He wanted Prussian legislators to vote for more money to build up the army. Liberal members opposed the move. Bismarck rose and dismissed their concerns with a speech that has become known as the "blood and iron" speech.

> Germany does not look to Prussia's liberalism, but to her power . . . . The great questions of the day are not to be decided by speeches and majority resolutions—that was the mistake of 1848 and 1849—but by blood and iron!
>
> —Otto von Bismarck, 1862

Master of Realpolitik Bismarck's success was due in part to his strong will. He was a master of **Realpolitik** (ray AHL poh lee teek), or realistic politics based on the needs of the state. In the case

Bismarck Unites Germany, 1865–1871

KEY
- Kingdom of Prussia, 1865
- States added to Prussia, 1866
- States added to form North German Confederation, 1867
- States added to form German Empire, 1871
- Boundary of German Empire, 1871

>> **Analyze Maps** By 1871, Germany had been unified. In what year was the North German Confederation formed?

🅑 BOUNCE to Activate Timeline

of Realpolitik, power was more important than principles.

Although Bismarck was the architect of German unity, he was not really a German nationalist. His main goal was to increase Prussia's power, not to fulfill German nationalist aims. Bismarck's primary loyalty was to the Hohenzollerns (hoh un TSAWL urnz), the ruling dynasty of Prussia. Through unification, he hoped to bring more power to the Hohenzollerns.

A Powerful Military As Prussia's prime minister, Bismarck first moved to build up the Prussian army. Despite Bismarck's "blood and iron" speech, the liberal legislature refused to vote for funds for the military. In response, Bismarck strengthened the army with money that had been collected for other purposes. With a powerful, well-equipped military, he was then ready to pursue an aggressive foreign policy. Over the next decade, Bismarck led Prussia into three wars. Each war increased Prussian prestige and power and paved the way for German unity.

War with Denmark and Austria Bismarck's first maneuver was to form an alliance in 1864 with Austria. Prussia and Austria then seized the

>> Bismarck used war with France as a way to unite the German states. Here, a triumphant Prussian army enters Paris.

provinces of Schleswig and Holstein from Denmark. After a brief war, Prussia and Austria "liberated" the two provinces and divided up the spoils. Austria was to administer Holstein and Prussia was to administer Schleswig.

In 1866, Bismarck invented an excuse to attack Austria. The Austro-Prussian War lasted just seven weeks and ended in a decisive Prussian victory. Prussia then **annexed,** or took control of, several other north German states.

Bismarck dissolved the Austrian-led German Confederation and created a new confederation dominated by Prussia. Austria and four other southern German states remained independent. Bismarck's motives, as always, were strictly practical. Attempting to conquer Austria might have meant a long and risky war for Prussia.

The Franco-Prussian War In France, the Prussian victory over Austria angered Napoleon III. A growing rivalry between the two nations led to the Franco-Prussian War of 1870.

Germans recalled only too well the invasions of Napoleon I some 60 years earlier. Bismarck played up the image of the French menace to spur German nationalism. For his part, Napoleon III did little to avoid war, hoping to mask problems at home with military glory.

Bismarck furthered the crisis by rewriting and then releasing to the press a telegram that reported on a meeting between King William I and the French ambassador. Bismarck's editing of the "Ems dispatch" made it seem that William I had insulted the Frenchman. Furious, Napoleon III declared war on Prussia, as Bismarck had hoped.

A superior Prussian force, supported by troops from other German states, smashed the badly organized and poorly supplied French soldiers. Napoleon III, old and ill, surrendered within a few weeks. France had to accept a humiliating peace. The Franco-Prussian War left a bitter legacy for the French and a strong desire for revenge against Germany.

The German Empire Is Created Delighted by the victory over France, princes from the southern German states and the North German Confederation persuaded William I of Prussia to take the title **kaiser** (KY zur), or emperor. In January 1871, German nationalists celebrated the birth of the Second **Reich,** or empire. They called it that because they considered it heir to the Holy Roman Empire, set up in the 900s and abolished by Napoleon I in 1806.

A constitution drafted by Bismarck set up a two-house legislature. The Bundesrat (BOON dus raht), or upper house, was appointed by the rulers of the German states. The Reichstag (RYKS tahg), or lower house, was elected by universal male suffrage. Men's votes, though, were weighted by their income and property, giving control to the wealthy. Because the Bundesrat could veto any decisions of the Reichstag, real power remained in the hands of the emperor and his chancellor.

☑ **EXPLAIN** How did Bismarck unify Germany?

Germany Becomes an Industrial Giant

In January 1871, German princes gathered in the glittering Hall of Mirrors at the French palace of Versailles. They had just defeated Napoleon III in the Franco-Prussian War. Once home to French kings, the palace seemed the perfect place to proclaim the new German empire. To the winners as well as to the losers, the symbolism was clear: French domination of Europe had ended. Germany was now the dominant power in Europe.

In the aftermath of unification, the German empire emerged as the industrial giant of the European continent. By the late 1800s, German chemical and electrical industries were setting the standard worldwide. Among the European powers, German shipping was second only to Britain's.

Economic Progress Germany, like Great Britain, had several factors that helped it industrialize. Germany's spectacular growth was due in part to ample iron and coal resources, the basic ingredients for industrial development. A disciplined and educated workforce also helped the economy. The German middle class and educated professionals helped to create a productive and efficient society that prided itself on its sense of responsibility and deference to authority. Germany's rapidly growing population—from 41 million in 1871 to 67 million by 1914—also provided a huge home market along with a larger supply of industrial workers.

The new nation also benefited from earlier progress. During the 1850s and 1860s, German entrepreneurs had founded large companies and built many railroads. The house of Krupp (kroop) boomed after 1871, becoming an enormous industrial complex that produced steel and weapons for a world market.

>> Germany became a leader in various industries, including the production of chemicals, electronics, steel, weapons, and optical equipment.

Between 1871 and 1914, the business tycoon August Thyssen (TEES un) built a small steel factory of 70 workers into a giant empire with 50,000 employees. Optics was another important industry. German industrialist and inventor Carl Zeiss built a company that became known for its telescopes, microscopes, and other optical equipment.

Promoting Economic Growth German industrialists were the first to see the value of applied science in developing new products such as synthetic chemicals and dyes. Industrialists, as well as the government, supported research and development in the universities and hired trained scientists to solve technological problems in their factories.

The German government promoted economic development. After 1871, it issued a single currency for Germany, reorganized the banking system, and coordinated railroads built by the various German states. When a worldwide depression hit in the late 1800s, Germany raised tariffs to protect home industries from foreign competition. The leaders of the new German empire were determined to

>> Bismarck was a leader in international affairs, using a mix of force and diplomacy to further German interests. Bismarck (center) at the 1878 Congress of Berlin.

>> **Analyze Political Cartoons** In this political game of chess, Bismarck and Pope Pius IX try to checkmate each other. How does this image reflect the relationship between Bismarck and the Pope? How would each player define victory?

 BOUNCE to Activate Cartoon

maintain economic strength as well as military power.

☑ **DESCRIBE** What factors did Germany possess that made industrialization possible?

The Iron Chancellor

As chancellor of the new German empire, Bismarck pursued several foreign-policy goals. He wanted to keep France weak and isolated while building strong links with Austria and Russia. He respected British naval power but did not seek to compete in that arena. "Water rats," he said, "do not fight with land rats." Later, however, he would take a more aggressive stand against Britain as the two nations competed for overseas colonies.

On the domestic front, Bismarck applied the same ruthless methods he had used to achieve unification. The Iron Chancellor, as he was called, sought to erase local loyalties and crush all opposition to the imperial state. He targeted two groups—the Catholic Church and the Socialists. In his view, both posed a threat to the new German state.

Bismarck Challenges the Catholic Church After unification, Catholics made up about a third of the German population. Bismarck, who was Lutheran, distrusted Catholics—especially the clergy— whose first loyalty, he believed, was to the pope instead of to Germany.

In response to what he saw as the Catholic threat, Bismarck launched the **Kulturkampf** (kool TOOR kahmpf), or "battle for civilization," which lasted from 1871 to 1878. His goal was to make Catholics put loyalty to the state above allegiance to the Church. The chancellor had laws passed that gave the state the right to supervise Catholic education and approve the appointment of priests. Other laws closed some religious orders, expelled the Jesuits from Prussia, and made it compulsory for couples to be married by civil authority.

Bismarck's moves against the Catholic Church backfired. The faithful rallied behind the Church, and the Catholic Center party gained strength in the Reichstag. A realist, Bismarck saw his mistake and worked to make peace with the Church.

Bismarck Attacks the Socialists Bismarck also saw a threat to the new German empire in the growing power of socialism. Under socialism, the people are supposed to own and operate the means of production. Socialism had support among some Germans. By the late 1870s, German

Marxists had organized the Social Democratic party, which called for parliamentary democracy and laws to improve conditions for the working class. Bismarck feared that socialists would undermine the loyalty of German workers and turn them toward revolution. Bismarck had laws passed that dissolved socialist groups, shut down their newspapers, and banned their meetings. Once again, repression backfired. It served to unite workers to support the socialist cause.

Bismarck Changes Course Bismarck then changed course. He set out to woo workers away from socialism by sponsoring laws to protect them. By the 1890s, Germans had health and accident insurance as well as old-age insurance to provide retirement benefits. Thus, under Bismarck, Germany was a pioneer in social reform. Its system of economic safeguards became the model for other European nations.

Although workers benefited from Bismarck's plan, they did not abandon socialism. In fact, the Social Democratic party continued to grow. By 1912, it held more seats in the Reichstag than any other party. Yet Bismarck's program showed that conditions for workers could be improved without a revolution. Later, Germany and other European nations would build on Bismarck's social policies, greatly increasing government's role in providing for the needs of its citizens.

☑ **CHECK UNDERSTANDING** Why did Bismarck try to dissolve socialist groups?

Kaiser William II

In 1888, **William II** succeeded his grandfather as kaiser. The new emperor, supremely confident, wished to put his own stamp on Germany. In 1890, he shocked Europe by asking the dominating Bismarck to resign. "There is only one master in the Reich," he said, "and that is I." William II seriously believed that his right to rule came from God.

> My grandfather considered that the office of king was a task that God had assigned to him. . . . That which he thought I also think. . . . Those who wish to aid me in that task . . . I welcome with all my heart; those who oppose me in this work I shall crush.
>
> —William II

>> **Analyze Political Cartoons** Bismarck tries to push the scary looking "Socialist Jack" back into the box. What did Bismarck do after his anti-socialist laws strengthened the socialist cause?

>> Otto von Bismarck leaves his Berlin office in 1890 after Kaiser William II forced him to resign as chancellor.

>> Kaiser William II wanted a German navy strong enough to build an overseas empire. His decision to expand German military and naval power contributed to international tensions.

His government also provided services such as cheap transportation and electricity. An excellent system of public schools, which had flourished under Bismarck, taught students obedience to the emperor along with reading, writing, and mathematics.

Strengthening the Military Like his grandfather, William II lavished funds on the German army, already the most powerful in Europe. He also launched an ambitious campaign to expand the German navy and win an overseas empire to rival those of Britain and France. William's nationalism and aggressive military stance helped increase tensions on the eve of World War I.

☑ **RECALL** Why did William II ask Bismarck to resign?

☑ ASSESSMENT

1. **Recall** Describe Germany's economic changes after unifying in 1871.

2. **Describe** Why did Germany pioneer social reform under Bismarck?

3. **Compare** How did Kaiser William II continue Bismarck's policies?

4. **Identify Main Ideas** Why do you think the German empire was committed to maintaining its economic strength?

5. **Connections to Today** A large Polish ethnic minority lived within the German kingdom of Prussia. How might Prussian Poles have viewed German nationalism?

Social Welfare Not surprisingly, William resisted efforts to introduce democratic political reforms. At the same time, however, his government continued the idea of **social welfare,** or programs provided by the state for the benefit of its citizens. These programs, designed to combat support for socialists, helped improve conditions not only for workers and the elderly, but also German society in general.

The Unification of Italy

Although the peoples of the Italian peninsula shared a language, they had not been politically united since Roman times. Over the centuries, ambitious foreign conquerors had turned Italy into a battleground, occupying parts of the peninsula. By the early 1800s, nationalism inspired Italian patriots to dream of ousting foreign rulers and reuniting Italy.

First Steps to Italian Unity

The spread of nationalist ideas also found fertile ground in Italy. The path to Italian unification would not be easy, though.

Obstacles to Unity Political division had led people to identify with local regions. The people of Florence considered themselves Tuscans, those of Venice Venetians, those of Naples Neapolitans, and so on. Napoleon's occupation of Italy, however, provoked opposition to foreign rule.

The Congress of Vienna restored the division of Italy among small states and foreign territories. To Prince Metternich of Austria, Italy was merely a "geographical expression," not a nation. Moreover, a divided Italy suited Austrian interests. At Vienna, Austria took control of much of northern Italy, while Hapsburg rulers kept other Italian states under Austrian influence. In the south, a French Bourbon took the throne of Naples and Sicily.

Resentment of foreign rule promoted the spread of Italian nationalism. Between 1820 and 1848, nationalist revolts exploded across the region. Each time, Austria sent in troops to crush the rebels.

BOUNCE to Activate Flipped Video

Objectives

List the key obstacles to Italian unity.

Evaluate the roles played by Cavour and Garibaldi in Italian unification.

Describe the challenges that faced the new nation of Italy.

Key Terms

Camillo Cavour
Giuseppe Garibaldi
anarchist
emigration

GO ONLINE to access your digital course

>> Giuseppe Mazzini, the founder of Young Italy, dreamed of a unified Italian republic. Due to his failed attempts at revolution, he spent many years in exile but continued to inspire Italian nationalism.

🅑 BOUNCE to Activate Map

>> Prime Minister Cavour (middle) served Sardinia's King Victor Emmanuel II (right) with great success. Cavour improved the economy and brought other Italian states under Sardinian rule.

🅑 BOUNCE to Activate Gallery

Mazzini's Young Italy In the 1830s, the nationalist leader Giuseppe Mazzini founded Young Italy. The goal of this secret society was "to constitute Italy, one, free, independent, republican nation." In 1849, Mazzini helped set up a revolutionary republic in Rome, but French forces soon toppled it. Like many other nationalists, Mazzini spent much of his life in exile, plotting and dreaming of a united Italy.

Nationalism Spreads "Ideas grow quickly," Mazzini once said, "when watered by the blood of martyrs." Although revolution had failed, nationalist agitation had planted seeds for future harvests.

To nationalists like Mazzini, a united Italy made sense not only because of geography, but also because of a common language and shared traditions. Nationalists reminded Italians of the glories of ancient Rome and the medieval papacy. To others, unity made practical economic sense. It would end trade barriers among the Italian states and stimulate industry.

☑ **CHECK UNDERSTANDING** What forces hindered Italian unity?

The Struggle for Italy

After 1848, leadership of the Risorgimento (ree sawr jee MEN toh), or Italian nationalist movement, passed to the kingdom of Sardinia, which included Piedmont, Nice, and Savoy as well as the island of Sardinia. Its constitutional monarch, Victor Emmanuel II, hoped to join other states to his own, thereby increasing his power.

Cavour, a Crafty Politician In 1852, Victor Emmanuel made Count **Camillo Cavour** (kah VOOR) his prime minister. Cavour came from a noble family but favored liberal goals. He was a flexible, practical, crafty politician, willing to use almost any means to achieve his goals. Like Bismarck in Prussia, Cavour was a monarchist who believed in Realpolitik.

Once in office, Cavour moved first to reform Sardinia's economy. He improved agriculture, had railroads built, and encouraged commerce by supporting free trade. Cavour's long-term goal, however, was to end Austrian power in Italy and annex the provinces of Lombardy and Venetia.

Cavour Plots with France In 1855, Sardinia, led by Cavour, joined Britain and France against Russia in the Crimean War. Sardinia did not win territory, but it did have a voice at the peace conference. Sardinia also gained the attention of Napoleon III.

In 1858, Cavour negotiated a secret deal with Napoleon, who promised to aid Sardinia in case it faced a war with Austria. A year later, the shrewd Cavour provoked that war. With help from France, Sardinia defeated Austria and annexed Lombardy. Meanwhile, nationalist groups overthrew Austrian-backed rulers in several other northern Italian states. These states then joined with Sardinia.

Garibaldi's "Red Shirts" Next, attention shifted to the Kingdom of the Two Sicilies in southern Italy. There, **Giuseppe Garibaldi** (gah ree BAHL dee), a longtime nationalist and an ally of Mazzini, was ready for action.

Like Mazzini, Garibaldi wanted to create an Italian republic. He did not hesitate, however, to accept aid from the monarchist Cavour. By 1860, Garibaldi had recruited a force of 1,000 red-shirted volunteers. Cavour provided weapons and allowed two ships to take Garibaldi and his "Red Shirts" south to Sicily. With surprising speed, Garibaldi's forces won control of Sicily, crossed to the mainland, and marched triumphantly north to Naples.

Unity Achieved Garibaldi's success alarmed Cavour, who feared that the nationalist hero would set up his own republic in the south. To prevent this, Cavour urged Victor Emmanuel to send Sardinian troops to deal with Garibaldi. Instead, the Sardinians overran the Papal States and linked up with Garibaldi and his forces in Naples.

In a patriotic move, Garibaldi turned over Naples and Sicily to Victor Emmanuel. Shortly afterward, southern Italy voted to approve the move, and in 1861, Victor Emmanuel II was crowned king of Italy.

Two areas remained outside the new Italian nation: Rome and Venetia. Cavour died in 1861, but his successors completed his dream. Italy formed an alliance with Prussia in the Austro-Prussian War and won the province of Venetia. Then, during the Franco-Prussian War in 1870, France was forced to withdraw its troops from Rome. For the first time since the fall of the Roman empire, Italy was a united land.

☑ **DESCRIBE** What steps did Cavour take to promote Italian unity?

Italy Faces New Challenges

The new Italian nation faced a host of problems. Like the German empire that Bismarck cemented together out of many states, Italy had no tradition

>> **Analyze Political Cartoons** Garibaldi suggests that Pope Pius IX trade his papal cap for the cap of "liberty" that he offers. What does Garibaldi want? How do you think the Pope feels about the offer?

of political unity. Few Italians felt ties to the new nation. Strong regional rivalries left Italy unable to solve critical national issues.

Regional Differences The greatest regional differences were between the north and the south. The north was richer and had more cities than the south. For centuries, northern Italian cities had flourished as centers of business and culture. The south, on the other hand, was rural and poor. Its population was booming, but illiterate peasants could extract only a meager existence from the exhausted farmland.

Conflict with the Papal States Hostility between Italy and the Roman Catholic Church further divided the nation. Popes bitterly resented the seizure of the Papal States and of Rome. The government granted the papacy limited rights and control over church properties. Popes, however, saw themselves as "prisoners" and urged Italian Catholics—almost all Italians—not to cooperate with their new government.

Political and Social Turmoil Under Victor Emmanuel, Italy was a constitutional monarchy

>> Italian emigrant families with their baggage and belongings wait to board a ship at this crowded port. **Draw Conclusions** Why did many Italians emigrate to other countries in the early 1900s?

with a two-house legislature. The king appointed members to the upper house, which could veto bills passed by the lower house. Although the lower house consisted of elected representatives, only a small number of men had the right to vote.

In the late 1800s, unrest increased as radicals on the left struggled against a conservative government. Socialists organized strikes while **anarchists,** people who want to abolish all government, turned to sabotage and violence.

Slowly, the government extended suffrage to more men and passed laws to improve social conditions. Still, the turmoil continued. To distract attention from

troubles at home, the government set out to win an overseas empire in Ethiopia.

Economic Progress Despite its problems, Italy did develop economically, especially after 1900. Although the nation lacked important natural resources such as coal, industries did sprout up in northern regions. Industrialization, of course, brought urbanization as peasants flocked to the cities to find jobs in factories. As in other countries, reformers campaigned to improve education and working conditions.

The population explosion of this period created tensions, but an important safety valve was **emigration,** or movement away from their homeland. Many Italians left for the United States, Canada, and Latin American nations.

By 1914, the country was significantly better off than it had been in 1861. But it was hardly prepared for the great war that broke out in that year.

☑ **DESCRIBE** What problems did Italians face after unification?

☑ ASSESSMENT

1. **Analyze Context** Why would Prince Metternich of Austria oppose the idea of Italian unification?

2. **Describe** How did Cavour's appointment as prime minister of the kingdom of Sardinia help the cause of Italian unification?

3. **Analyze Information** Garibaldi could easily have kept the Kingdom of the Two Sicilies with himself as king. Why do you think he turned over control to Victor Emmanuel II instead?

4. **Cite Evidence** Why did conflict in Italy continue even after unification?

5. **Connections to Today** How might regional differences within Italy have posed challenges for Italian nationalists?

14.5

Reflecting Britain's gap between rich and poor in the 1800s, a wealthy man reads to people living in a London homeless shelter.

Democratic Reforms in Britain

In the early 1800s, only the wealthiest Britons could vote, while millions lived in severe poverty. By the end of that century, Britain had become more democratic.

Two Nations

In a scene from Benjamin Disraeli's 1845 novel, *Sybil*, or *The Two Nations*, a man boasts to a stranger that Queen Victoria

> ". . . reigns over the greatest nation that ever existed."
>
> "Which nation?" asked the . . . stranger, "for she reigns over two . . . Two nations; between whom there is no [communication] and no sympathy; who are as ignorant of each other's habits, thoughts, and feelings, as if they were . . . inhabitants of different planets."
>
> "You speak of—" said Egremont, hesitatingly, "The Rich and the Poor."
>
> —Benjamin Disraeli, *Sybil*

Benjamin Disraeli and other British leaders worked to bridge the gap between the "two nations" by expanding democratic

 BOUNCE to Activate Flipped Video

Objectives

Understand how political reforms in Britain affected suffrage and the nature of Parliament.

Identify the influence of Queen Victoria and the values she represented.

Describe social and economic reforms enacted by Parliament in the 1800s.

Describe the efforts by British women to win the vote.

Explain the struggle for Irish home rule and the impact of famine on Ireland.

Key Terms

Benjamin Disraeli
rotten borough
electorate
secret ballot
Queen Victoria
William Gladstone
parliamentary
  democracy
free trade
repeal
abolition
capital offense
penal colony
absentee landlord
home rule

rights and introducing social reforms to end deeply rooted inequalities. Unlike some of its neighbors in Europe, Britain generally achieved change through reform rather than revolution.

Parliament In Need of Reform In 1815, Britain was a constitutional monarchy with a parliament and two political parties. Still, it was far from democratic. Parliament was made up of the House of Lords and the House of Commons. The House of Lords were hereditary nobles and high-ranking clergy in the Church of England. They had the right to veto any bill passed by the House of Commons.

Members of the Commons were elected, but less than five percent of the people could vote. Wealthy country squires, or landowners, along with nobles, dominated politics and heavily influenced voters. In addition, old laws banned Catholics and non-Anglican Protestants from voting or serving in Parliament. In the 1820s, after fierce debates, Parliament finally ended these religious restrictions.

Pressure for Reform Builds An even greater battle soon erupted over making Parliament more representative. During the Industrial Revolution, centers of population shifted. Some rural towns lost so many people that they had few or no voters. Yet local landowners in these **rotten boroughs** still sent members to Parliament.

At the same time, populous new industrial cities like Manchester and Birmingham had no seats in Parliament because they had not existed as population centers in earlier times.

Reform Act of 1832 In the 1830s, as revolts flared in France and elsewhere, Whigs and Tories were battling over a bill to reform Parliament.

The Whig Party largely represented middle-class and business interests. The Tory Party spoke for nobles, landowners, and others whose interests and income were rooted in agriculture. In the streets, supporters of reform chanted, "The Bill, the whole Bill, and nothing but the Bill!" Their shouts seemed to echo the cries of revolutionaries on the continent.

Parliament finally passed the Great Reform Act in 1832. It redistributed seats in the House of Commons, giving representation to large towns and cities and eliminating rotten boroughs. It also enlarged the **electorate,** the body of people allowed to vote, by granting suffrage to more men. The act did, however, keep a property requirement for voting.

The Reform Act of 1832 did not bring full democracy, but it did give a greater political voice to middle-class men. Land-owning nobles, however, remained a powerful force in the government and in the economy.

The Chartist Movement The reform bill did not satisfy the demands of more radical reformers like the Chartists, who stood for working class interests. In the 1830s, they drew up the People's Charter, a petition setting out their goals. They demanded universal male suffrage, annual parliamentary elections, and salaries for members of Parliament. Another key demand was for a **secret ballot,** which would allow people to cast their votes without announcing them publicly.

Twice the Chartists presented petitions with over a million signatures to Parliament. Both petitions were ignored. In 1848, as revolutions swept Europe, the Chartists prepared a third petition and organized a march on Parliament. Fearing violence, the government banned the march.

Soon after, the unsuccessful Chartist movement declined. In time, however, Parliament would pass most of the major reforms proposed by the Chartists.

>> During the early 1800s, the British Parliament was not very democratic. The unelected House of Lords, shown here around 1830, could veto any bill passed by the elected House of Commons.

☑ **ANALYZE INFORMATION** How did reformers' efforts make the British parliament more democratic?

The Victorian Age

From 1837 to 1901, the great symbol in British life was **Queen Victoria.** Her reign was the longest in British history at that time. Although she exercised little real political power, she set the tone for what is now called the Victorian age.

Victorian Ideals As queen, Victoria came to embody the values of her age. These Victorian ideals included duty, thrift, honesty, hard work, and above all respectability. Victoria herself embraced a strict code of morals and manners. As a young woman, she married a German prince, Albert, and they raised a large family.

Although she outranked Albert, she treated him with the devotion a dutiful wife was expected to have for her husband. When he died in 1861, Victoria went into deep mourning and dressed in black for the rest of her long reign. She was fond of her 36 grandchildren, some of whom later became ruling monarchs.

Growing British Confidence Under Victoria, the British middle class—and growing numbers of the working class—felt great confidence in the future. That confidence grew as Britain expanded its already huge empire. Victoria, the empress of India and ruler of some 300 million subjects around the world, became a revered symbol of British might.

During her reign, Victoria witnessed growing agitation for social reform. The queen herself commented that the lower classes "earn their bread and riches so deservedly that they cannot and ought not to be kept back." As the Victorian era went on, reformers continued the push toward greater social and economic justice.

☑ **DRAW CONCLUSIONS** When Queen Victoria stated that the lower classes "earn their bread and riches so deservedly that they cannot and ought not to be kept back," what did she mean?

Reforms Increase Parliamentary Democracy

In the 1860s, a new era dawned in British politics. The old political parties regrouped under new leadership. Benjamin Disraeli forged the Tories into the modern Conservative Party. The Whigs, led by **William Gladstone,** evolved into the Liberal Party. Between 1868 and 1880, as the majority in Parliament swung between the two parties,

>> Queen Victoria in 1887. Her reign began in 1837 and lasted till her death at age 81 in 1901.

>> **Hypothesize** In the 1800s and early 1900s, Parliament passed laws to extend and protect suffrage for men. Why were private booths and a police officer needed in this English polling station?

 BOUNCE to Activate Timeline

Gladstone and Disraeli alternated as prime minister. Both fought for important reforms.

Expanding Male Suffrage Disraeli and the Conservative Party pushed through the Reform Bill of 1867. By giving the vote to many working-class men, the new law almost doubled the size of the electorate.

In the 1880s, it was the turn of Gladstone and the Liberal Party to extend suffrage. Their reforms gave the vote to farmworkers and most other men.

By century's end, almost-universal male suffrage, the secret ballot, and other Chartist ambitions had been achieved. Britain had truly transformed itself from a constitutional monarchy to a **parliamentary democracy,** a form of government in which the executive leaders (usually a prime minister and cabinet) are chosen by and responsible to the legislature (parliament), and are also members of it.

Victory for Democracy In the early 1900s, many bills passed by the House of Commons met defeat in the House of Lords. In 1911, a Liberal government passed measures to restrict the power of the Lords, including their power to veto tax bills. The Lords resisted. Finally, the government threatened to create enough new lords to approve the law, and the Lords backed down.

People hailed the change as a victory for democracy. In time, the House of Lords would become a largely ceremonial body with little power. The elected House of Commons would reign supreme.

☑ **COMPARE AND CONTRAST** What were the origins of the Liberal and Conservative parties? Which groups did they represent?

Economic and Social Reforms

During the early and mid-1800s, Parliament passed a series of social and economic reforms. Many laws were designed to help working class families whose labor supported the new industrial society. Among the most controversial reforms was the issue of **free trade,** or trade between countries without quotas, tariffs, or other restrictions. It pitted landowners and farmers against the middle and working classes.

Abolishing the Corn Laws Britain, like other European nations, taxed foreign imports in order to protect local economies. By the early 1800s however, supporters of free trade, usually middle-class business leaders, wanted to end these protective tariffs. Like Adam Smith, they argued that a laissez-faire policy would increase prosperity for all. Without tariffs they said, merchants would have larger markets in which to sell their goods, and consumers would benefit from open competition.

Some British tariffs were repealed in the 1820s. However, fierce debate erupted over the Corn Laws, which imposed high tariffs on imported grain. (In Britain, "corn" refers to all cereal grains, such as wheat, barley, and oats.) Farmers and wealthy landowners supported the Corn Laws because they kept the price of British grain high. Free traders, however, wanted Parliament to **repeal,** or cancel, the Corn Laws. They argued that repeal of these laws would lower the price of grain, make bread cheaper for workers, and open up trade in general.

Parliament finally repealed the Corn Laws in 1846, after widespread crop failures swept many parts of Europe. Liberals hailed the repeal as a victory for free trade and laissez-faire capitalism. However, in the late 1800s, economic hard times led Britain and other European countries to impose protective tariffs on many goods again.

>> London dock workers unload tea from cargo ships. British customs officials monitored such activities and collected tariffs on foreign imports. **Summarize** Who opposed tariffs, and why?

Abolition of Slavery During the 1700s, Enlightenment thinkers had turned the spotlight on the evils of the trade in enslaved Africans. At the time, British ships were carrying more Africans to the Americas than any other European country. Middle-class reformers in Britain increased pressure for **abolition,** calling for an end to slavery and the slave trade.

In Parliament, William Wilberforce led the movement to end the slave trade. A dedicated social reformer, Wilberforce also held strong religious convictions. Wilberforce helped shift political thought by persistently introducing anti-slavery motions for decades in Parliament. Finally, in 1807, Britain became the first European power to abolish the slave trade.

Banning the slave trade did not end slavery. Although the Congress of Vienna condemned slavery, it had taken no action. In Britain, liberals preached the immorality of slavery. Finally, in 1833, Parliament passed a law banning slavery in all British colonies.

Crime and Punishment Other reforms were aimed at the criminal justice system. In the early 1800s, more than 200 crimes were punishable by death. Such **capital offenses** included not only murder but also shoplifting, sheep stealing, and impersonating an army veteran.

In practice, some juries refused to convict people charged with crimes, because the punishments were so harsh. Executions were public occasions, and the hanging of a well-known murderer might attract thousands of curious spectators. By 1868 however, Parliament banned public hangings, and executions then took place behind prison walls. Afterward, instead of receiving a proper burial, the criminal's body might be given to a medical college for dissection.

Reformers began to reduce the number of capital offenses. By 1850, the death penalty was reserved for murder, piracy, treason, and arson. Many petty criminals were instead transported to **penal colonies,** or settlements for convicts, in the new British territory of Australia. Additional reforms improved prison conditions and outlawed imprisonment due to debt.

☑ **DRAW CONCLUSIONS** How did the Corn Laws affect the lower classes?

>> **Analyze Political Cartoons** In this cartoon, the British prime minister opens a particular gate. What change in policy does the cartoon depict? Explain.

>> Harsh working conditions and deadly accidents were common in British coal mines. With the Mines Act of 1842, Parliament prohibited all females and boys under age 10 from working in underground mines.

Victories for the Working Class

"Four [ghosts] haunt the Poor: Old Age, Accident, Sickness and Unemployment," declared Liberal politician David Lloyd George in 1905. "We are going to [expel] them."

As early as the 1840s, Parliament passed some laws aimed at improving conditions for workers. Later in the 1800s and early 1900s, Parliament passed additional reforms, designed to help the working class whose labor supported the new industrial society.

Working Conditions Improve As you have read, working conditions in the early industrial age were grim and often dangerous. Gradually, Parliament passed laws to regulate conditions in factories and mines. In 1842, for example, mine owners were forbidden to employ women or children under age 10. An 1847 law limited women and children to a 10-hour day. Later in the 1800s, the government regulated many safety conditions in factories and mines—and sent inspectors to see that the laws were enforced. Other laws set minimum wages and maximum hours of work.

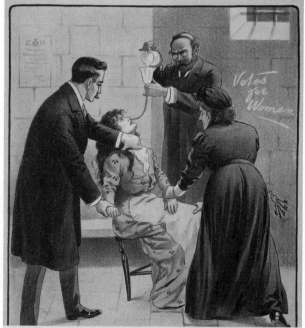

>> When some jailed English suffragists went on hunger strikes, prison officials force-fed them to keep them alive. The suffragists used posters like this to gain popular support for their cause.

Labor Unions Expand Early in the Industrial Revolution, labor unions were outlawed. Under pressure, government and business leaders slowly accepted worker organizations. Trade unions were made legal in 1825 but it remained illegal to go on strike until later in the century.

Despite restrictions, unions spread, and gradually they won additional rights. Between 1890 and 1914, union membership soared. Besides winning higher wages and shorter hours for workers, unions pressed for other laws to improve the lives of the working class.

Other Social Reforms During the late 1800s and early 1900s, both political parties enacted social reforms to benefit Britain's citizens. Disraeli sponsored laws to improve public health and housing for workers in cities. Under Gladstone, an education act called for free elementary education for all children. Gladstone also pushed to open up government jobs based on merit rather than on birth or wealth.

Another force for reform was the Fabian Society, a socialist organization founded in 1883. The Fabians promoted gradual change through legal means rather than by violence. Though small in number, the Fabians had a strong influence on British politics.

The Labour Party Emerges In 1900, socialists and union members backed the formation of a new political party, which became the Labour Party. (*Labour* is the British spelling of *labor*.) The Labour Party would quickly grow in power and membership until, by the 1920s, it surpassed the Liberal Party and became one of Britain's two major parties.

In the early 1900s, Britain began to pass social welfare laws modeled on those Bismarck had introduced in Germany. They protected workers with accident, health, and unemployment insurance as well as old-age pensions. One result of such reforms was that the Marxist idea of a communist revolution gained only limited support among the British working class. The middle class hailed reforms as proof that democracy was working.

☑ **IDENTIFY CENTRAL IDEAS** What reforms improved the lives of children in Britain?

Women Struggle for the Vote

In Britain, as elsewhere, women struggled against strong opposition for the right to vote. Women themselves were divided on the issue. Some women opposed suffrage altogether. Queen Victoria, for example, called the women's suffrage struggle "mad, wicked folly." Even women in favor of suffrage disagreed about how best to achieve it.

Radicals Take Action By the early 1900s, Emmeline Pankhurst, a leading suffragist, had become convinced that even more aggressive tactics were necessary to bring victory. Pankhurst and other radical suffragists interrupted speakers in Parliament, shouting, "Votes for women!" until they were carried away. They collected petitions and organized huge public demonstrations.

When mass meetings and other peaceful efforts brought no results, some women turned to more drastic, violent protests. They smashed windows or even burned buildings. Pankhurst justified such tactics as necessary to achieve victory. "There is something that governments care for far more than human life," she declared, "and that is the security of property, so it is through property that we shall strike the enemy." Many suffragists went on hunger strikes, risking their lives to achieve their goals.

Some titled women, like Lady Constance Lytton, joined the protests. Imprisoned after a demonstration, Lytton gave a false name and vowed to stay on a hunger strike until women won the vote. A doctor, unaware of her identity, force-fed Lytton through a tube. The painful ordeal failed to weaken Lytton's resolve. "No surrender," she whispered. "No surrender."

The Tide Turns Even middle-class women who disapproved of such radical and violent actions increasingly demanded votes for women. Still, Parliament refused to grant women's suffrage. Not until 1918 did Parliament finally grant suffrage to women over age 30. Younger women did not win the right to vote for another decade.

☑ **DRAW CONCLUSIONS** Why might some women have disagreed with the idea of giving women the vote?

The Irish Question

Throughout the 1800s, Britain faced the ever-present "Irish question." The English had begun conquering Ireland in the 1100s. In the 1600s, English and

>> The Irish potato blight caused great hardship, famine, and death. Without potatoes to sell, thousands of tenants could not pay rent and were evicted.

▶ BOUNCE to Activate Gallery

Scottish settlers colonized Ireland, taking possession of much of the best farmland.

The Irish never accepted English rule. They bitterly resented settlers and **absentee landlords** who owned large estates but did not live on them. Many Irish peasants had to pay these landlords high rents and live off of the potatoes they could grow for themselves. In addition, the Irish, most of whom were Catholic, had to pay tithes to support the Church of England. Under these conditions, resistance and rebellion were common.

Irish Nationalism Grows Like the national minorities in the Austrian empire, Irish nationalists campaigned vigorously for freedom and justice in the 1800s. Nationalist leader Daniel O'Connell, nicknamed "the Liberator," organized an Irish Catholic League and held mass meetings to demand repeal of unfair laws. "My first object," declared O'Connell, "is to get Ireland for the Irish."

Under pressure from O'Connell and other Irish nationalists, Britain slowly moved to improve conditions in Ireland. In 1829, Parliament passed the Catholic Emancipation Act, which allowed Irish Catholics to vote and hold political office. Yet many injustices remained. Absentee landlords could evict tenants almost at will. Other British laws forbade the teaching and speaking of the Irish language. Finally, when a potato famine caused starvation across Ireland in the 1840s, the British government offered little help.

Irish Home Rule The famine in Ireland caused by the potato blight left the Irish with a legacy of bitterness and distrust toward Britain. The Great Hunger fueled movements in Ireland that pitted radicals, such as the Fenians, who wanted an independent Ireland, against moderates who called for **home rule,** or local self-government.

In the 1870s, moderates found a rousing leader in the Irish nationalist, Charles Stewart Parnell. He rallied Irish members of Parliament to work for home rule. The "Irish question" disrupted British politics for decades. At times, political parties were so deeply split over the Irish question that they could not take care of other business.

As prime minister, Gladstone pushed for reforms in Ireland. He ended the use of Irish tithe money to support the Anglican church and tried to ease the hardships of Irish tenant farmers. New laws prevented landlords from charging unfair rents and protected the rights of tenants to the land they worked.

Finally, in 1914, Parliament passed a home rule bill that would give an Irish parliament the power to control Ireland's internal affairs. But Britain's parliament delayed putting the new law into effect when World War I broke out that year. As you will read, the dream of the Fenians was partly achieved in 1921, when the southern counties of Ireland finally became an independent nation.

☑ **MAKE GENERALIZATIONS** How did absentee landlords promote Irish nationalism?

☑ ASSESSMENT

1. **Identify Central Issues** Which groups would benefit from repealing the high tariffs known as the Corn Laws? Why?

2. **Draw Conclusions** How did the political, social, and economic reforms of the early 1800s in Britain reflect the growing power of the middle class?

3. **Support Ideas with Examples** Why did many people view the criminal justice system in Britain during the 1800s as unjust? Provide specific examples.

4. **Draw Conclusions** How did the Fabian Society reflect Victorian ideals?

5. **Identify Central Issues** What were two of the reforms that improved conditions in Ireland?

6. **Quest Connections** In what ways was the British government responsible for the Irish potato famine?

GO ONLINE to access this biography: William Gladstone

Napoleon III hoped to restore glory to France. Here he commands victorious French troops at the Battle of Solferino during the second Italian War of Independence in 1859.

Divisions and Democracy in France

During the late 19th century, France faced several challenges. At the same time, the French struggled to achieve a just democracy.

Napoleon III and the Second Empire

After the revolution of 1848, **Napoleon III,** nephew of Napoleon Bonaparte, rose to power and set up the Second Empire. He had wide appeal. The bourgeoisie trusted him to restore order. His promise to end poverty gave hope to the lower classes. People of all classes were attracted by his name, a reminder of French greatness. Unlike his famous uncle, however, Napoleon III would bring France neither glory nor an empire.

Limited Democracy On the surface, the Second Empire looked like a constitutional monarchy. In fact, Napoleon III ruled almost as a dictator, with the power to appoint the upper house of the legislature and many officials. Although the assembly was elected by universal male suffrage, officials "managed" elections so that supporters of the emperor would win. Debate was limited, and newspapers faced strict censorship.

In the 1860s, Napoleon III began to ease controls. He lifted some censorship and gave the legislature more power. He even issued a new constitution that extended democratic rights.

Economic Growth Like much of Europe, France prospered at mid-century. Napoleon III promoted investment in industry and

 BOUNCE to Activate Flipped Video

Objectives

List the domestic and foreign policies of Napoleon III.

Describe the challenges and political reforms of the Third Republic.

Explain how the Dreyfus Affair divided France and contributed to the growth of the Zionist movement.

Key Terms

Napoleon III
Suez Canal
premier
coalition
Dreyfus Affair
libel
Zionism

GO ONLINE to access your digital course

large-scale ventures such as railroad building and the urban renewal of Paris. During this period, a French entrepreneur, Ferdinand de Lesseps (luh SEPS), organized the building of the **Suez Canal** in Egypt to link the Mediterranean with the Red Sea and the Indian Ocean.

Workers enjoyed some benefits of economic growth. Napoleon legalized labor unions, extended public education to girls, and created a small public health program. Still, in France, as in other industrial nations, many people lived in great poverty.

Foreign Affairs Napoleon's worst failures were in warfare and foreign affairs. In the 1860s, he tried to place Maximilian, an Austrian Hapsburg prince, on the throne of Mexico. Through Maximilian, Napoleon hoped to turn Mexico into a French satellite. But after a large commitment of troops and money, the venture failed. Mexican patriots resisted fiercely, and the United States protested. After four years, France withdrew its troops. Maximilian was overthrown and shot by Mexican patriots.

Napoleon's successes were almost as costly as his failures. He helped Italian nationalists defeat Austria, and in return, the regions of Nice (nees) and Savoy were ceded to France. But this victory soon backfired when a united Italy emerged as a rival on France's border. And, though France and Britain won the Crimean War, France had little to show for its terrible losses except a return to the status of a great power.

Defeat in the Franco-Prussian War At this same time, France was growing increasingly concerned about the rise of a great European rival, Prussia. The Prussian leader Otto von Bismarck shrewdly manipulated the French and lured Napoleon into war in July 1870.

The Franco-Prussian War was a disaster for France. Napoleon III was forced to surrender to the Germans, ending the Second Empire. A brutal four-month siege of Paris by Prussian forces reduced residents to near starvation. People ate rats and killed circus animals for food. During the siege, Parisians used carrier pigeons and balloons to communicate with the outside world.

In 1871, a newly elected French Assembly accepted a harsh peace with Germany. France had to surrender the provinces of Alsace and Lorraine and pay a huge sum to Germany. The sting of defeat left the French burning to avenge their loss.

The Franco-Prussian War ended a long period of French domination of Europe that had begun under Louis XIV. Yet a Third Republic rose from the ashes of the Second Empire of Napoleon III. Economic growth, democratic reforms, and fierce nationalism all played a part in shaping modern France.

☑ **DESCRIBE** the government of France during the Second Empire.

The Third Republic Faces New Struggles

At the end of the Franco-Prussian War, a new government, known as the Third Republic, was set up in France. Even as a new National Assembly took power and made peace with Germany, France was plunged into a new crisis. Once again, the crisis was centered in Paris.

The Paris Commune In early 1871, an uprising broke out in Paris. Rebels set up the Paris Commune. Like the radical government during the French Revolution, its goal was to save the Republic from royalists. Communards, as the rebels were called, included workers and socialists as well as bourgeois republicans. As patriots, they rejected the harsh

>> Prussian troops stand in front of a ruined fort outside of Paris after defeating France in the Franco-Prussian War.

🅑 BOUNCE to Activate Gallery

peace that the National Assembly had signed with Germany. Radicals dreamed of creating a new socialist order.

The National Assembly ordered the Paris Commune to disband. When the Communards refused, the government sent troops to retake Paris. For weeks, civil war raged. As government troops advanced, the rebels set fire to several government buildings, toppled Paris monuments, and slaughtered a number of hostages. Finally, government forces butchered some 30,000 Communards. The suppression of the Paris Commune left bitter memories that deepened social divisions within France.

Coalition Governments Despite its shaky beginnings, the Third Republic remained in place for 70 years. The new republic had a two-house legislature. The powerful lower house, or Chamber of Deputies, was elected by universal male suffrage. Together with the Senate, it elected the president of the republic. However, the president had little power and served mostly as a figurehead. Real power was in the hands of the **premier** (prih MIR), or prime minister.

Unlike Britain, with its two-party system, France had many parties, reflecting the wide splits within the country. Among them were royalists, constitutional monarchists, moderate republicans, and radicals. With so many parties, no single party could win a majority in the legislature. In order to govern, politicians had to form **coalitions,** or alliances of various parties. Once a coalition controlled enough votes, it could then name a premier and form a cabinet.

Multiparty systems and coalition governments are common in Europe. Such alliances allow citizens to vote for a party that most nearly matches their own beliefs. Coalition governments, however, are often unstable. If one party deserts a coalition, the government might lose its majority in the legislature. The government then falls, and new elections must be held. In the first 10 years of the Third Republic, 50 different coalition governments were formed and fell.

Scandals Rock the Third Republic Despite frequent changes of governments, France made economic progress. It paid Germany the huge sum required by the peace treaty and expanded its overseas empire. By 1900, France was the largest democratic country in continental Europe, with a constitution that protected basic rights. Its overseas empire was second only to that of Britain. But in the 1880s and 1890s, a series of political scandals shook public trust in the government.

>> The Paris Commune, determined to save the Republic from royalists, rebelled against the new National Assembly. The Communards erected barricades throughout Paris.

>> **Analyze Political Cartoons** The Boulanger scandal rocked France. Boulanger leads as his supporters follow. What does the image of the man with the large banner suggest about Boulanger's goals?

BOUNCE to Activate Cartoon

One crisis involved the minister of war, General Georges Boulanger (boo lahn zhay), who rallied royalists, workers, the military, and ultranationalists eager for revenge on Germany. Accused of plotting to overthrow the republic, Boulanger fled to Belgium. In another scandal, a nephew of the president was caught selling nominations for the Legion of Honor, France's highest award. The president was forced to resign.

Even more disturbing was a crisis that began in 1894. Known as the Dreyfus Affair, it scarred French politics and society for decades.

☑ **DESCRIBE** a coalition government.

The Dreyfus Affair

The most serious and divisive scandal began in 1894. The scandal involved a French army officer, Captain Alfred Dreyfus, who was charged with treason. His trial and conviction ignited a decades-long controversy known as the **Dreyfus Affair.**

Dreyfus on Trial Alfred Dreyfus was accused of spying for Germany. After a military trial, Dreyfus

>> **Analyze Political Cartoons** This 1899 caricature, *The Traitor,* shows Dreyfus as a lindworm, a mythical dragon or serpent with a poisonous bite. Why was this figure used to represent Dreyfus?

was convicted of treason. The military claimed to have plenty of written evidence against Dreyfus. Yet neither Dreyfus nor his lawyer was allowed to see it. The army claimed secrecy was needed to protect France.

The injustice was rooted in anti-Semitism. The military elite detested Dreyfus, the first Jewish person to reach such a high position in the army. Although Dreyfus proclaimed his innocence, he was convicted and condemned to life imprisonment on Devil's Island, a desolate penal colony off the coast of South America.

A Long Struggle for Justice The Dreyfus Affair scarred French politics and society for decades. Royalists, ultranationalists, and Church officials charged Dreyfus supporters, or "Dreyfusards," with undermining France. Paris echoed with cries of "Long live the army!" and "Death to traitors!" Dreyfusards, mostly liberals and republicans, upheld ideals of justice and equality in the face of massive public anger.

By 1896, new evidence pointed to another officer, Ferdinand Esterhazy, as the spy. Still, the army refused to grant Dreyfus a new trial.

In 1898, French novelist Émile Zola joined the battle. In an article headlined *J'Accuse!* (I Accuse!), he charged the army and government with suppressing the truth. As a result, Zola was convicted of **libel,** or the knowing publication of false and damaging statements. He fled into exile.

Eventually, the Dreyfusards made progress, and the army had to release its evidence against Dreyfus. Much of it turned out to be forged. In 1906, a French court cleared Dreyfus of all charges and reinstated him in the army. Even though justice had triumphed, the Dreyfus Affair left lasting scars.

Growing Anti-Semitism The Dreyfus case reflected the rise of anti-Semitism in Europe. The Enlightenment and the French Revolution had spread ideas about religious toleration. In Western Europe, some Jews had gained jobs in government, universities, and other areas of life. Others had achieved success in banking and business, but most struggled to survive in the ghettos of Eastern Europe or the slums of Western Europe.

By the late 1800s, however, anti-Semitism was again on the rise. Anti-Semites were often members of the lower middle class who felt insecure in their social and economic position. Steeped in the new nationalist fervor, they adopted an aggressive intolerance for outsiders and a violent hatred of Jews.

The Rise of Zionism The Dreyfus case and growing anti-Semitic violence in Russia stirred Theodor Herzl (HAIRT sul), a Hungarian Jewish journalist living in France. Herzl called for Jews to set up their own nation state. He helped spur the growth of **Zionism**, a nationalist movement devoted to rebuilding a Jewish state in the Jews' ancient homeland. Many Jews had kept this dream alive since the destruction of the temple in Jerusalem by the Romans. In 1897, Herzl organized the First Zionist Congress in Basel, Switzerland.

☑ **DRAW CONCLUSIONS** What solution did Zionists propose to address widespread anti-Semitism?

Reforms in France

Although shaken by the Dreyfus affair, France achieved serious reforms in the early 1900s. Like Britain, France passed laws regulating wages, hours, and safety conditions for workers. It set up a system of free public elementary schools. Creating public schools was also part of a campaign to reduce the control of the Roman Catholic Church over education in France.

Separation of Church and State Like Bismarck in Germany, French reformers tried to limit or even end Church involvement in government. Republicans viewed the Church as a conservative force that opposed progressive policies. In the Dreyfus Affair, it had backed the army and ultranationalists.

From 1899 to 1905, the government enacted a series of reforms. It closed Church schools, along with many convents and monasteries. In 1905, it passed a law to separate church and state and stopped paying the salaries of the clergy. Catholics, Protestants, and Jews all enjoyed freedom of worship, but the new laws ensured that none had any special treatment from the government.

Rights for Women Under the Napoleonic Code, French women had few rights. By the 1890s, a growing women's rights movement in France sought legal reforms. It made some gains, such as an 1896 law giving married women the right to their own earnings.

In 1909, Jeanne-Elizabeth Schmahl founded the French Union for Women's Suffrage. Schmahl and other women sought to win the vote through legal means. Yet even liberal men were reluctant to grant

>> One of the many reforms in early 1900s France was the establishment of free public elementary schools.

women suffrage. They feared that women would vote for Church and conservative causes. In the end, French women did not win the vote until 1946.

☑ **DESCRIBE** How did French women try to change their role in French society in the late 1800s?

☑ ASSESSMENT

1. **Identify Main Ideas** What political changes did the end of the Franco-Prussian War bring to France?

2. **Draw Conclusions** Explain the effect of Napoleon III's foreign policy failures.

3. **Explain** How did coalition governments affect France?

4. **Draw Conclusions** Why was the Dreyfus Affair an important event in French history?

5. **Connections to Today** How does the Dreyfus affair show the contradictions between democratic rights and nationalism based on ethnicity or religion?

14.7

Many of the earliest settlers migrating west traveled in wagons, like the settlers moving through this mountain pass.

 BOUNCE to Activate Flipped Video

Objectives

Describe the territorial expansion of the United States.

Summarize the causes and effects of the Civil War.

Explain how American democracy grew in the 1800s.

Analyze the impact of economic growth and social reform on the United States.

Key Terms

expansionism
Louisiana Purchase
Manifest Destiny
secede
segregation

Growth of the United States

In the 1800s, the United States was a beacon of hope for many people. The American economy was growing rapidly, offering jobs to newcomers. The Constitution and the Bill of Rights held out the hope of political and religious freedom. Not everyone shared in the prosperity or the freedom to vote promised by the Constitution. Still, by the early 1900s, the United States had undertaken reforms to promise equality for all its citizens.

The United States Expands

From the earliest years of its history, the United States had followed a policy of **expansionism,** or extending the country's boundaries. At first, the United States stretched only from the Atlantic coast to the Mississippi River. In 1803, President Thomas Jefferson bought the Louisiana territory from France. In one stroke, the **Louisiana Purchase** virtually doubled the size of the country.

By 1846, the United States had expanded to include Florida, Oregon, and the Republic of Texas. The Mexican War (1846–1848) added California and the Southwest.

With growing pride and confidence, Americans claimed that their nation was destined to spread across the entire continent, from sea to sea. This idea became known as **Manifest Destiny.** Some expansionists even hoped to absorb Canada and Mexico. In fact, the United States did go far afield. In 1867, it bought Alaska from Russia and in 1898, annexed the Hawaiian Islands.

☑ **DESCRIBE** Describe the territorial gains of the United States during the 1800s.

🛜 **GO ONLINE** to access your digital course

Expanding Democracy

In 1800, the United States had the most liberal suffrage in the world, but still only white men who owned property could vote. States slowly chipped away at requirements. By the 1830s, most white men had the right to vote. Democracy was still far from complete, however.

By mid-century, reformers were campaigning for many changes. Some demanded a ban on the sale of alcoholic beverages. Others pushed for free elementary schools. But two campaigns stood out because they highlighted the limits of American democracy—the abolition movement and the women's rights movement.

The Abolition Movement In the early 1800s, a few Americans began to call for a complete end to slavery. One of these abolitionists was William Lloyd Garrison, who pressed the antislavery cause through his newspaper, the *Liberator*. Another was Frederick Douglass. He had been born into slavery and escaped, and he spoke eloquently in the North about the evils of the system.

By the 1850s, the battle over slavery had intensified. As territories moved toward statehood, proslavery and antislavery forces met in sometimes violent confrontations. Harriet Beecher Stowe's novel *Uncle Tom's Cabin* helped convince many northerners that slavery was evil.

Women Seek Equality Women worked hard in the antislavery movement. Lucretia Mott and Elizabeth Cady Stanton traveled to London for the World Antislavery Convention—only to find they were forbidden to speak because they were women. Gradually, American women began to protest the laws and customs that limited their lives. In 1848, Mott and Stanton organized the Seneca Falls Convention, the first women's rights convention, to address the problems faced by women.

The convention passed a resolution, based on the Declaration of Independence. It began, "We hold these truths to be self evident: that all men and women are created equal."

The women's rights movement sought equality before the law, in the workplace, and in education. Some women also demanded the right to vote. Many Americans, both women and men, ridiculed the idea of women voting. Support for this idea, however, slowly grew.

☑ **DRAW CONCLUSIONS** How did the abolitionist and women's rights movements highlight the limits of American democracy?

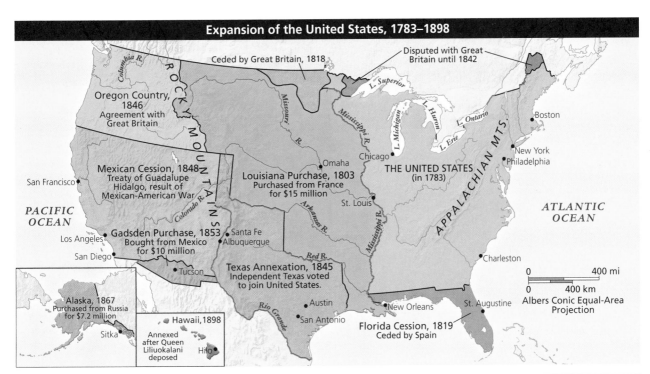

Expansion of the United States, 1783–1898

>> **Analyze Maps** Over the course of two centuries, the United States expanded its territory from east of the Mississippi River to the Pacific Ocean and beyond. How did the United States acquire territory on the Pacific coast?

🔲 BOUNCE to Activate Map

>> Lucretia Mott organized the Seneca Falls Convention with Elizabeth Cady Stanton in 1848.

BOUNCE to Activate Timeline

>> In the Union army, African Americans served in units commanded by white officers. Here, the famous Black 54th Massachusetts Regiment attacks Fort Wagner in South Carolina.

The Civil War

By the mid-1800s, the South and the North were developing along different paths. While the South remained largely rural and agricultural, the North was industrializing and had rapidly growing cities. Along with economic differences, the issue of slavery was increasingly driving a wedge between North and South.

The division reached a crisis in 1860 when Abraham Lincoln was elected president. Lincoln opposed extending slavery into new territories. Southerners feared that he would eventually abolish slavery altogether.

A Costly Civil War Soon after Lincoln's election, most southern states **seceded,** or withdrew, from the Union and formed the Confederate States of America. This action sparked the Civil War, which lasted from 1861 to 1865, and was an agonizing ordeal, dividing families as well as the nation.

The South had fewer resources, fewer people, and less industry than the North. Still, Southerners fought on. At first, the South won victories. At one point, Confederate armies under General Robert E. Lee drove northward as far as Gettysburg, Pennsylvania, before being driven back. In the last years of the war, Lincoln's most successful general, Ulysses S. Grant, used the massive resources of the North in a full-scale offensive against the South.

After devastating losses, the Confederacy finally surrendered in 1865. The struggle cost more than 600,000 lives—the largest casualty figures of any American war. Although the war left a bitter legacy, it did guarantee that the nation would remain undivided.

African Americans After the Civil War During the war, Lincoln issued the Emancipation Proclamation, a declaration freeing enslaved African Americans in the Confederate states. After the war, three amendments to the Constitution banned slavery throughout the country and granted political rights to African Americans. Under the Fifteenth Amendment, African American men won the right to vote.

Despite these amendments, African Americans faced many restrictions. In the South, state laws imposed **segregation,** or legal separation of the races, in hospitals, schools, and other public places. These laws were often called "Jim Crow laws." Other state laws imposed conditions for voter eligibility

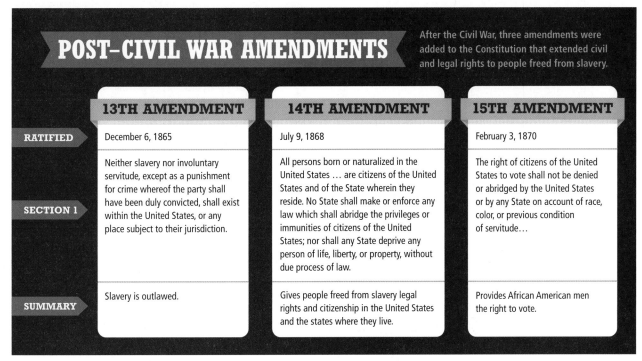

POST-CIVIL WAR AMENDMENTS

After the Civil War, three amendments were added to the Constitution that extended civil and legal rights to people freed from slavery.

	13TH AMENDMENT	14TH AMENDMENT	15TH AMENDMENT
RATIFIED	December 6, 1865	July 9, 1868	February 3, 1870
SECTION 1	Neither slavery nor involuntary servitude, except as a punishment for crime whereof the party shall have been duly convicted, shall exist within the United States, or any place subject to their jurisdiction.	All persons born or naturalized in the United States … are citizens of the United States and of the State wherein they reside. No State shall make or enforce any law which shall abridge the privileges or immunities of citizens of the United States; nor shall any State deprive any person of life, liberty, or property, without due process of law.	The right of citizens of the United States to vote shall not be denied or abridged by the United States or by any State on account of race, color, or previous condition of servitude…
SUMMARY	Slavery is outlawed.	Gives people freed from slavery legal rights and citizenship in the United States and the states where they live.	Provides African American men the right to vote.

>> After the Civil War, three amendments to the Constitution changed America.
Analyze Charts What was the purpose of these amendments, and why were they necessary?

that, despite the Fifteenth Amendment, prevented African Americans from voting.

African Americans also faced economic hardships. Newly freed African Americans had no land, and many ended up working as tenant farmers. Some headed west to work as cowhands or buy farmland. Others migrated to northern cities to find jobs in factories.

☑ **SYNTHESIZE** How did the 15th Amendment aim to expand democracy in the United States?

Economic Growth and Reform

As in Western Europe, the Industrial Revolution was transforming the United States at mid-century. By 1900, it led the world in industrial and agricultural output, thanks to many factors. It had vast natural resources, a stable government, and a growing population—including many immigrants.

The free enterprise system and the protection of property rights allowed entrepreneurs to invest in expanding businesses. The building of railroads and new technologies that improved communication further helped farming and industry.

Business and Labor By 1900, giant monopolies controlled whole industries. Scottish-born Andrew Carnegie built the nation's largest steel company, while John D. Rockefeller's Standard Oil Company dominated the world's petroleum industry. Big business enjoyed tremendous profits. The growing prosperity was not shared by all. In factories, wages were low and conditions were often brutal. To defend their interests, American workers organized labor unions such as the American Federation of Labor. Unions sought better wages, hours, and working conditions. Struggles with management sometimes erupted into violent confrontations. Slowly, however, workers made gains.

The Push for Reform When economic hard times hit in the late 1800s, the farmers also organized to defend their interests. In the 1890s, they joined city workers to support the new Populist party. The Populists never became a major party, but their platform of reforms, such as an eight-hour workday, eventually became law.

By 1900, reformers known as Progressives pressed for change. They sought laws to ban child labor, limit working hours, regulate monopolies, and give voters more power. In addition Progressives backed women's suffrage. After a long struggle, American suffragists finally won the vote in 1920, when the Nineteenth Amendment went into effect.

☑ **DRAW CONCLUSIONS** How did immigration help economic growth after the Civil War?

☑ ASSESSMENT

1. **Describe** What was Manifest Destiny and how did it affect the United States?

2. **Connect** How did the expansion of the United States set the stage for the Civil War?

3. **Analyze Information** What was the impact of economic growth on the United States?

4. **Synthesize** What problems did workers face during the late 1800s and early 1900s and how did they try to enact change?

5. **Connections to Today** How did ethnic and racial injustice conflict with democratic ideals in the history of the United States?

14.8

During the Revolution of 1848, nationalists challenged the multinational Austrian empire. Hungarian nationalists briefly had their own parliament, shown here.

Nationalism in Eastern Europe and Russia

In Eastern and Central Europe, the Austrian Hapsburgs and the Ottoman Turks ruled diverse ethnic groups. During the 1800s, the spread of nationalism among these groups contributed to tensions in Europe.

Nationalism Endangers Old Empires

Nationalism, which had brought unity to countries like Germany and Italy, would undermine multi-ethnic empires like those of the Austrian Hapsburgs and the Ottoman Turks. Why did nationalism bring new strength to some countries and weaken others?

The Lands of the Hapsburg Empire The Hapsburgs were the oldest ruling house in Europe. In addition to their base in Austria, over the centuries they had acquired the territories of Bohemia and Hungary, as well as parts of Romania, Poland, Ukraine, and northern Italy. By the 1800s, ruling such a vast empire made up of many nationalities posed a challenge for the Hapsburg monarchs, especially as the tide of nationalism rose.

Austrian Hapsburgs Face Challenges Since the Congress of Vienna, the Austrian emperor Francis I and his foreign minister Metternich had upheld conservative goals against liberal forces. "Rule and change nothing," the emperor told his son. Under Francis and Metternich, newspapers could not even use the word

 BOUNCE to Activate Flipped Video

Objectives

Explain how nationalism challenged the Austrian and Ottoman empires.

Summarize major obstacles to progress in Russia.

Describe the cycle of absolutism, reform, and reaction followed by the tsars.

Explain how industrialization contributed to the outbreak of revolution in 1905.

Key Terms

Francis Joseph
Ferenc Deák
Dual Monarchy
colossus
Alexander II
Crimean War
emancipation
zemstvo
pogrom
refugee
Duma
Peter Stolypin

constitution, much less discuss this key demand of liberals. The government also tried to limit industrial development, which would threaten traditional ways of life.

The Hapsburgs, however, could not hold back the changes that were engulfing Europe. By the 1840s, factories were springing up. Soon, the Hapsburgs found themselves facing the problems of industrial life that had long been familiar in Britain—the growth of cities, worker discontent, and the stirrings of socialism.

Nationalist Demands Equally disturbing to the old order were the urgent demands of nationalists. The Hapsburgs presided over a multinational empire. Of its 50 million people at mid-century, fewer than a quarter were German-speaking Austrians. Almost half belonged to different Slavic groups, including Czechs, Slovaks, Poles, Ukrainians, Serbs, Croats, and Slovenes. Often, rival groups shared the same region. The empire also included large numbers of Hungarians and Italians. The Hapsburgs ignored nationalist demands as long as they could. When nationalist revolts broke out in 1848, the government crushed them.

>> Francis Joseph inherited the Hapsburg throne while still a teenager. He made some reforms, but not enough to save his empire.

Reforms of Francis Joseph Amid the turmoil, 18-year-old **Francis Joseph** inherited the Hapsburg throne. He would rule until 1916, presiding over the empire during its fading days.

An early challenge came when Austria suffered its humiliating defeat at the hands of France and Sardinia in 1859. Francis Joseph realized he needed to strengthen the empire at home. Accordingly, he made some limited reforms. He granted a new constitution that set up a legislature. This body, however, was dominated by German-speaking Austrians.

The reforms thus satisfied none of the other national groups that populated the empire. The Hungarians, especially, were determined to settle for nothing less than self-government.

☑ **HYPOTHESIZE** What alternatives might Francis Joseph have had in responding to nationalist demands?

The Dual Monarchy

Austria's disastrous defeat in the 1866 war with Prussia brought renewed pressure for change from Hungarians within the empire. One year later, **Ferenc Deák** ((FAIR ents DEH ahk), a moderate Hungarian leader, helped work out a compromise that created a new political power known as the **Dual Monarchy** of Austria-Hungary.

The Creation of Austria-Hungary Under the agreement, Austria and Hungary were separate states. Each had its own constitution and parliament. Francis Joseph ruled both, as emperor of Austria and king of Hungary. The two states also shared ministries of finance, defense, and foreign affairs, but were independent of each other in all other areas.

Nationalist Unrest Increases Although Hungarians welcomed the compromise, other subject peoples resented it. Restlessness increased among various Slavic groups, especially the Czechs in Bohemia.

Some nationalist leaders called on Slavs to unite, insisting that "only through liberty, equality, and fraternal solidarity" could Slavic peoples fulfill their "great mission in the history of mankind." By the early 1900s, nationalist unrest often left the

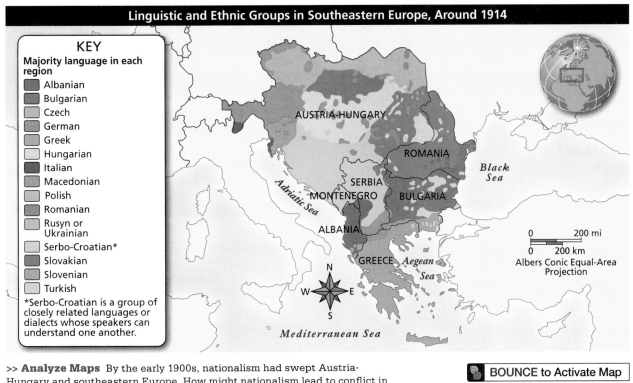

KEY

Majority language in each region

- Albanian
- Bulgarian
- Czech
- German
- Greek
- Hungarian
- Italian
- Macedonian
- Polish
- Romanian
- Rusyn or Ukrainian
- Serbo-Croatian*
- Slovakian
- Slovenian
- Turkish

*Serbo-Croatian is a group of closely related languages or dialects whose speakers can understand one another.

>> **Analyze Maps** By the early 1900s, nationalism had swept Austria-Hungary and southeastern Europe. How might nationalism lead to conflict in this region?

BOUNCE to Activate Map

government paralyzed in the face of pressing political and social problems.

☑ **DRAW CONCLUSIONS** Why did the Dual Monarchy fail to end nationalist demands?

The Ottoman Empire Declines

Like the Hapsburgs, the Ottomans ruled a multinational empire. It stretched from Eastern Europe to North Africa and the Middle East. There, as in Austria, nationalist demands tore at the fabric of the empire.

Nationalism in the Balkans In the Balkans, or the lands of southeastern Europe, Serbia won autonomy in 1830, and southern Greece won independence during the 1830s. But many Serbs and Greeks still lived in the Balkans under Ottoman rule. The Ottoman empire was also home to other national groups, such as Bulgarians and Romanians. During the 1800s, various subject peoples staged revolts against the Ottomans, hoping to set up their own independent states.

Dividing Ottoman Lands Such nationalist stirrings became mixed up with the ambitions of the great European powers. In the mid-1800s, Europeans came to see the Ottoman empire as "the sick man of Europe." Eagerly, they scrambled to divide up Ottoman lands. Russia pushed south toward the Black Sea and Istanbul, which Russians still called Constantinople.

Austria-Hungary took Bosnia and Herzegovina, angering Serbs. They had ambitions to expand their influence in the area. Meanwhile, Britain and France set their sights on other Ottoman lands in the Middle East and North Africa.

Balkan Wars In the end, a complex web of competing interests contributed to a series of crises and wars in the Balkans. Russia fought several wars against the Ottomans. France and Britain sometimes joined the Russians and sometimes the Ottomans.

Germany supported Austrian authority over the discontented national groups. But Germany also encouraged the Ottomans because of their strategic location in the eastern Mediterranean. In between, the subject peoples revolted and then fought among themselves. By the early 1900s, observers were referring to the region as the "Balkan powder keg."

The explosion that came in 1914 helped set off World War I.

☑ **DRAW CONCLUSIONS** How did Balkan nationalism contribute to the decline of the Ottoman Empire?

Russia Tries Reform

During the 1800s, Russia expanded its empire eastward into Asia but faced rising demands for reform at home. Reformers hoped to bring Enlightenment ideals such as constitutional government and social justice. They called for an end to autocratic rule and urged the tsar to modernize Russia. Under pressure, tsars introduced some reforms, but soon reverted to repression when ongoing unrest threatened their throne.

Russia Expands By 1815, Russia was not only the largest, most populous nation in Europe but also a great world power. Since the 1600s, explorers, soldiers, and traders seeking furs had expanded Russia's empire eastward across Siberia to the Pacific.

>> Russian nobles celebrate the coronation of Tsar Nicholas II in 1896. Russian royalty and nobility lived lives of wealth and luxury.

In their efforts to gain warm water ports, Peter the Great and Catherine II added lands on the Baltic and Black seas. During the 1800s, as tsars sought to contain the Ottoman and British empires, they expanded into the Caucasus region and Central Asia. In the process, Russia acquired a vast multi-national empire over parts of Europe and Asia.

Other European powers, including Britain and France, watched the Russian **colossus,** or giant, anxiously. Russia had immense natural resources. Its vast size gave it global influence. But Western Europeans disliked its autocratic government and feared its expansionist aims. At the same time, Russia remained economically undeveloped.

Obstacles to Progress By the 1800s, tsars saw the need to modernize but resisted reforms that would undermine their absolute rule. While they wavered, Russia fell further behind the West in economic and social developments.

A great obstacle to progress was the rigid social structure. Landowning nobles dominated society and rejected any change that would threaten their privileges. The middle class was small and weak.

Most Russians were serfs, or laborers bound to the land and to the landowners who controlled them. While serfdom had almost disappeared in Western Europe by the 1700s, it had survived and even spread in Russia.

Russian Serfdom Most serfs were peasants. Others were servants, artisans, or soldiers forced into the tsar's army. As industry expanded, some masters sent serfs to work in factories but took much of their pay.

Enlightened Russians knew that serfdom was inefficient. As long as most people had to serve the whim of their masters, Russia's economy would remain backward. Landowning nobles had no reason to improve agriculture and took little interest in industry.

The Tsars Have Absolute Power For centuries, tsars had ruled with absolute power, imposing their will on their subjects. On occasion, the tsars made limited attempts at liberal reform, such as easing censorship or making legal and economic reforms to improve the lives of serfs. However, in each instance the tsars drew back from their reforms when they began to fear losing the support of nobles.

In short, the liberal and nationalist changes brought about by the Enlightenment and the French Revolution had almost no effect on Russian autocracy.

The tsarist motto was the "three pillars of absolutism." They were: orthodoxy, or strong ties between the Russian Orthodox Church and the government; autocracy, or absolute government; and nationality, or Russian nationalism, which called for respect for Russian traditions and suppression of non-Russian groups within the empire.

☑ **IDENTIFY CENTRAL ISSUES** Why did industrialization and reform come more slowly to Russia than to Western Europe?

Emancipation and Stirrings of Revolution

During much of the 1800s, tsars moved back and forth between reform and repression. In mid-century, the tsar **Alexander II** moved toward reform, but his death at the hands of an assassin led to a return to repression.

The Crimean War Alexander II came to the throne during the **Crimean War.** The war had broken out after Russia tried to seize Ottoman lands along the Danube River. Britain, France, and Sardinia stepped in to help the Ottomans by sending armies into the Russian Crimea, a peninsula that juts into the Black Sea.

The war, which ended in a Russian defeat, revealed the country's backwardness. Russia had only a few miles of railroads, and the military bureaucracy was hopelessly inefficient.

Emancipation of the Serfs Russia's defeat in the Crimean War triggered widespread calls for change. Russian liberals demanded changes, and students demonstrated, seeking reform. Pressed from all sides, Alexander II finally agreed to reforms. In 1861, he issued a royal decree that required **emancipation,** or freeing, of the serfs.

Freedom brought problems. Former serfs had to buy the land they had worked, but many were too poor to do so. Also, the lands allotted to peasants were often too small to farm efficiently or to support a family. Peasants remained poor, and discontent festered.

Still, emancipation was a turning point. Many peasants moved to the cities, taking jobs in factories and building Russian industries. Equally important, freeing the serfs boosted the drive for further reform.

Limited Reforms Along with emancipation, Alexander II set up a system of local government.

>> The 1881 assassination of Alexander II prompted further repression by his son and successor, Alexander III.

🅑 BOUNCE to Activate Gallery

Elected assemblies, called **zemstvos,** were made responsible for matters such as road repair, schools, and agriculture. Through this system, Russians gained some experience of self-government at the local level.

The tsar also introduced legal reforms such as trial by jury. He eased censorship and tried to reform the military. A soldier's term of service was reduced from 25 years to 15, and brutal discipline was limited. Alexander also encouraged the growth of industry in Russia.

Dissent Continues Alexander's reforms failed to satisfy many Russians. Peasants had freedom but not land. Liberals wanted a constitution and an elected legislature. Radicals, who had adopted socialist ideas from the West, demanded even more revolutionary changes. The tsar, meanwhile, moved away from reform and toward repression.

In the 1870s, some socialists went to live and work among peasants, preaching reform and revolution. They had little success. The peasants scarcely understood them and sometimes turned them over to the police.

The failure of this movement, combined with renewed government repression, sparked anger

>> Jewish men view the damage done to their sacred Torah scrolls during an 1881 pogrom. Pogroms targeted Jewish communities in Russia.

>> An iron foundry in Lysva, Russia, in 1900. **Draw Conclusions** How did industrialization affect demands for reform in Russia?

among radicals, leading some to embrace violence. On March 13, 1881, terrorists assassinated Alexander II.

Return to Repression Alexander III responded to his father's assassination by returning to repression. To wipe out liberals and revolutionaries, he increased the power of the secret police, restored strict censorship, and exiled critics to Siberia.

The tsar also launched a program of Russification aimed at suppressing the cultures of non-Russian peoples within the empire. Alexander insisted on one language, Russian, and one church, the Russian Orthodox Church. Poles, Ukrainians, Finns, Armenians, Muslims, Jews, and many others suffered persecution.

Persecution and Pogroms Russia had acquired a large Jewish population when it carved up Poland and expanded into Ukraine. Under Alexander III, the persecution of Russia's Jewish population increased.

The tsar limited the number of Jews allowed to study in universities or practice certain professions. He revived old laws that forced Jews to live in restricted areas.

Official persecution encouraged **pogroms,** or violent mob attacks on Jewish people. Gangs beat and killed Jewish people and looted and burned their homes and stores. Faced with savage persecution, many left Russia. They became **refugees,** or people who flee their homeland to seek safety elsewhere. Large numbers of Russian Jews went to the United States.

☑ **IDENTIFY CAUSE AND EFFECT** Why did emancipation fail to meet the needs of the serfs and lead to continued discontent?

The Beginnings of Industrialization

By the late 1800s, Russia had finally entered the industrial age under Alexander III and his son Nicholas II. Russia had several factors of production needed to industrialize. It had vast natural resources, including land and minerals. Its large population included peasants and the beginnings of an urban working class. Over time, a new industrial class emerged with the capital and drive to invest in economic development.

In the 1890s, the government focused on economic development. It encouraged the building of railroads to connect iron and coal mines with factories and to transport goods across Russia.

It secured foreign capital to invest in transportation and industry. Loans from France helped Russia build the Trans-Siberian Railway, which stretched 5,000 miles from European Russia to the Pacific Ocean.

Political Turmoil Grows Industrialization increased social and political problems. Government officials and business leaders applauded economic growth. Nobles opposed it, fearing the changes it brought.

Industrialization also created new social ills as peasants flocked to cities to work in factories. Instead of a better life, they found long hours and low pay in dangerous conditions. In the slums around the factories, poverty, disease, and discontent multiplied. These conditions provided fertile ground for radicals, who sought supporters among the new industrial workers. At factory gates, Socialists often handed out pamphlets that preached the revolutionary ideas of Karl Marx, who won support among the new industrial workers.

☑ **HYPOTHESIZE** Why did industrialization increase radicalism among Russian peasants?

The Road to Revolution

When war broke out between Russia and Japan in 1904, Nicholas II called on his people to fight for "the Faith, the Tsar, and the Fatherland." Despite patriotic slogans and great sacrifices, the Russians suffered one humiliating defeat after another.

Bloody Sunday News of the military disasters unleashed pent-up discontent created by years of oppression. Protesters poured into the streets. Workers went on strike, demanding shorter hours and better wages. Liberals called for a constitution and reforms to overhaul the government.

As the crisis deepened, a young Orthodox priest, Father George Gapon, organized a peaceful march for Sunday, January 22, 1905. He felt certain that the tsar would help his people if only he understood their sufferings. Marchers flowed through the streets of St. Petersburg toward the tsar's Winter Palace. Chanting prayers and singing hymns, workers carried holy icons and pictures of the tsar. They also brought a petition for justice and freedom.

Fearing the marchers, the tsar had fled the palace and called in soldiers. As the people approached, they saw troops lined up across the square. Suddenly, gunfire rang out. Hundreds of men and women fell dead or wounded in the snow. One

>> Russian soldiers fire on peaceful protesters in front of the Winter Palace in St. Petersburg in January 1905. This event came to be known as Bloody Sunday.

>> Protesters march in St. Petersburg in 1905. Bloody Sunday led to uprisings against the tsar throughout Russia.

>> In this demonstration during the Russian Revolution of 1905, Russians demand a constitutional monarchy and democratic rule.

woman stumbling away from the scene moaned: "The tsar has deserted us! They shot away the orthodox faith." Indeed, the slaughter marked a turning point for Russians. "Bloody Sunday" killed the people's faith and trust in the tsar.

Unrest Explodes into Revolution In the months that followed Bloody Sunday, discontent exploded across Russia. Strikes multiplied. In some cities, workers took over local government. In the countryside, peasants revolted and demanded land. Minority nationalities called for autonomy. Terrorists targeted officials, and some assassins were cheered as heroes by discontented Russians.

At last, the clamor grew so great that Nicholas was forced to announce sweeping reforms. In the October Manifesto, he promised "freedom of person, conscience, speech, assembly, and union." He agreed to summon a **Duma,** or elected national legislature. No law, he declared, would go into effect without approval by the Duma.

Post-Revolution Reforms The manifesto won over moderates, leaving Socialists isolated. These divisions helped the tsar, who had no intention of letting strikers, revolutionaries, and rebellious peasants challenge him.

In 1906, the first Duma met, but the tsar quickly dissolved it when leaders criticized the government. Nicholas then appointed **Peter Stolypin** (stuh LIP yin) a conservative, as his prime minister. Arrests, pogroms, and executions followed as the conservative Stolypin sought to restore order.

Stolypin realized that Russia needed reform, not just repression. To regain peasant support, he introduced moderate land reforms. He strengthened the zemstvos and improved education before he was assassinated in 1911.

Several more Dumas met during this period, but new voting laws made sure they were conservative. By 1914, Russia was still an autocracy, but one simmering with unrest.

☑ **DRAW CONCLUSIONS** What does Bloody Sunday suggest about the relationship between the tsar and the Russian people?

☑ ASSESSMENT

1. **Identify Cause and Effect** What effect did nationalism have on the Hapsburg and Ottoman empires?

2. **Synthesize** How did the concept of liberty influence nationalism and revolution in Eastern Europe?

3. **Analyze Information** Tsar Alexander II declared that it is "better to abolish serfdom from above than to wait until it will be abolished by a movement from below." Explain his statement.

4. **Hypothesize** Why would a policy such as "Russification" lead to increased nationalism?

5. **Connections to Today** What was the impact of the Russian ethnic nationalism of Tsar Alexander III on other ethnic groups in Russia?

Connections to Today

Deadly attacks by the military of Myanmar forced hundreds of thousands of ethnic minority Rohingya to flee across the border. This refugee camp in Bangladesh provides emergency housing for the Rohingya.

Take Action to Explore Nationalism and Ethnic Discrimination

During the 19th century, nationalism spread around the world, often combined with a push for greater democracy. Today, we see that these two ideals can conflict when nations are defined in ethnic terms and ethnic minorities face discrimination.

1. **Choose** Select one of these topics related to nationalism and ethnic discrimination:

   - **Myanmar:** How did Burmese nationalism lead to ethnic discrimination in Myanmar despite moves toward democracy in that country?

   - **Europe:** How has ethnic nationalism in some democratic European countries fueled discrimination toward minorities in those countries in recent years?

   - **Elsewhere:** How has nationalism hurt the democratic rights of minorities in a country of your choice?

2. **Ask Questions** What are some of the things you want to learn about conflicts between nationalism and democratic rights today? Write a list of questions.

3. **Learn** Research the topic you have chosen, collecting specific examples from reliable sources. Look for recent news articles.

4. **Raise Awareness** Create a presentation of your findings. Be prepared to present your findings to your class or another audience in your school or community.

LESSON SUMMARIES

Use these Lesson Summaries, and the longer versions available online, to review the key ideas for each lesson in this Topic.

Lesson 1: Revolutions Sweep Europe

After 1815, opposing ideologies between conservatives, liberals and nationalists thrust Europe into turmoil for more than thirty years. Conservatives strongly denounced the ideals of natural rights and constitutional government. Liberals favored constitution-based governments, and nationalists hoped to regain lost territories and establish new homelands.

Lesson 2: Latin American Nations Win Independence

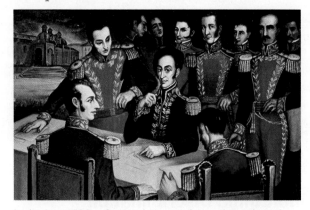

In the late 1700s, the revolutionary fervor that gripped Western Europe spread to Latin America. There, colonies that had endured years of social, racial, and political injustice revolted.

Lesson 3: The Unification of Germany

Otto von Bismarck, the chancellor of Prussia, was determined to build a strong, unified German state. In 1871, he became chancellor of a unified German Empire.

Lesson 4: The Unification of Italy

Nationalism spread to Italy as well during the early 1800s. By 1871, Italy was a united nation with its capital in Rome. Long-time nationalist Giuseppe Garibaldi and his Red Shirts played an important role in achieving this goal.

Lesson 5: Democratic Reforms in Britain

In 1815, Britain was a constitutional monarchy with a parliament and two political parties. With the support of Queen Victoria, Parliament passed a wide variety of reform measures that included the abolition of the slave trade, laws to benefit the working class, and the expansion of suffrage to most men. However, women contined to fight for suffrage.

Lesson 6: Divisions and Democracy in France

The Franco-Prussian War ended a long period of French leadership in Europe. Under Napoleon III, democratic reform, economic growth, and nationalism shaped modern France.

Lesson 7: Growth of the United States

In the 1800s, the United States represented hope for many people. During this time, the nation was expanding, developing industry, and moving to promise democratic rights to more of its citizens.

Lesson 8: Nationalism in Eastern Europe and Russia

In Eastern Europe, the Austrian Hapsburgs and the Ottoman Turks ruled lands that included diverse ethnic groups. Strong nationalist feelings among these subject people contributed to tensions building across the region. In Russia, reformers hoped to free Russia from autocratic rule and social injustice.

GO ONLINE to access lesson summaries

VISUAL REVIEW

Use these graphics to review some of the key terms, people, and ideas from this Topic.

Effects of Nationalism

NATIONALISM BY REGION				
GERMANY	**ITALY**	**AUSTRIA**	**BALKANS**	**RUSSIA**
• German states unite under William I in 1871. • Empire takes leading role in continental Europe. • Bismarck becomes known as the Iron Chancellor.	• Mazzini founds Young Italy. • Garibaldi leads Red Shirts. • Victor Emmanuel II makes Cavour prime minister of Sardinia. • Italian states become unified by 1871.	• Francis I and Metternich uphold conservative goals. • Dual Monarchy with Hungary is set up. • Nationalist groups grow restless. • Empire becomes weakened.	• Serbians achieve autonomy in 1830. • Greeks achieve independence in 1830. • New nations form in Ottoman lands. • "Balkan powder keg" helps set off World War I.	• Serfs are freed in 1861. • Alexander III encourages persecution and pogroms. • Russia enters the industrial age late. • Bloody Sunday leads to revolution in 1905. • Duma has limited power.

Independence Movements in Latin America

CAUSE AND EFFECT	
LONG-TERM CAUSES	**IMMEDIATE CAUSES**
• European domination • Spread of Enlightenment ideas • American and French Revolutions • Growth of nationalism	• Social injustices • Revolutionary leaders emerge • Napoleon invades Spain.

INDEPENDENCE MOVEMENTS

IMMEDIATE EFFECTS	LONG-TERM EFFECTS
• Haitians revolt against slavery. • Bolívar, San Martín, and others lead successful revolts. • Colonial rule ends in much of Latin America.	• Numerous independent nations in Latin America • Continuing efforts to achieve stable democratic governments and to gain economic independence

Key Events in the United States 1800s–Early 1900s

1803	Louisiana Purchase
1846–1848	Mexican War
1849	California Gold Rush
1861–1865	Civil War
1865	Slavery ended by 13th Amendment
1867	Purchase of Alaska
1869	Completion of Transcontinental Railroad
1882	Formation of Standard Oil Trust
1898	Spanish-American War; Hawaiian islands annexed
1908	Development of Henry Ford's Model T

Topic 14 Assessment

KEY TERMS, PEOPLE, AND IDEAS

1. How did reforms affect the social and political life of Britain?

2. What was the first step on Haiti's road to independence?

3. Is the term Iron Chancellor an appropriate title for **Otto von Bismarck**? Explain.

4. How did regional differences in Italy initially prevent the country's unification?

5. How did the British Great Reform Act of 1832 affect the **electorate**?

6. What effect did the **Dreyfus Affair** have on France?

7. Was **Manifest Destiny** in the United States accepted by everyone? Explain.

8. What was the **Dual Monarchy**?

9. Discuss the causes of the Latin American independence movement.

CRITICAL THINKING

10. **Synthesize Information** How did ideas from the Enlightenment and the Napoleonic Code influence nationalist movements in Europe during the 1840s?

11. **Summarize** How did Britain and France slowly extend democratic rights during the 1800s and early 1900s?

12. **Comparing** (a) How did the French system of political parties differ from the American system? (b) How did these differences affect the stability of governments under each system?

13. **Summarize** What sparked the Irish nationalist movement?

14. **Draw Conclusions** What social changes in the United States after the Civil War prompted political reform?

15. **Find the Main Idea** What economic changes promoted German unity?

16. **Analyze Cartoons** Look at the cartoon below. (a) What event is represented? (b) What does the cartoon suggest about the goals of nationalists?

17. **Writing Activity: Write a Research Paper** How were the outcomes of Latin American revolutions similar to, and different from, the American Revolution? Do research on the Latin American revolutions using reliable sources. Then write an essay in which you consider social classes, constitutions, and cooperation between colonies. Cite evidence from your research.

18. **Connections to Today** Consider how democratic ideals and nationalism, defined in ethnic terms, have sometimes come into conflict, resulting in discrimination against ethnic minorities. How might people in democracies today work to prevent such discrimination?

DOCUMENT-BASED QUESTIONS

The Dreyfus Affair divided and scarred French society and politics. Read the documents below, then answer the questions that follow.

DOCUMENT A

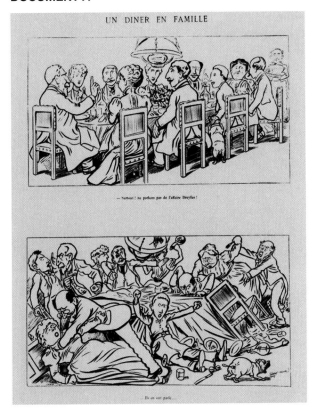

"Un Diner En Famille" [A Family Dinner]

Translation: "It is agreed that there should be no talk of the affair! But they did talk about it . . ."

—*From* Le Figaro *by Caran d'Ache, February, 1898*

DOCUMENT B

". . . if my voice ceased to be heard, it would mean that it had been extinguished forever, for if I have survived, it has been in order to insist on my honor—my property and the patrimony of our children—and in order to do my duty, as I have done it everywhere and always, and as it must always be done, when right and justice are on one's side, without ever fearing anything or anyone."

—*From a letter to his wife Lucie, by Alfred Dreyfus, September 1898, published in* Cinq Années

DOCUMENT C

"I accuse the offices of War of having conducted in the press, particularly in *L'Eclair* and in *L'Echo de Paris,* an abominable campaign designed to mislead public opinion and to conceal their wrongdoing."

"Finally, I accuse the first Court Martial of having violated the law in convicting a defendant on the basis of a document kept secret, and I accuse the second Court Martial of having covered up . . . [and] knowingly acquitting a guilty man."

—*From "J'Accuse," a letter to the President of the Republic by Émile Zola*

19. Document A illustrates
    A. why many French families believed Dreyfus was guilty.
    B. why Dreyfus was unfairly convicted of treason.
    C. how the Dreyfus case divided France.
    D. how anti-Semitism was a factor in the Dreyfus case.

20. In Document B, Dreyfus suggests that his wish to prove his innocence helped to
    A. keep him close to his family.
    B. keep him alive.
    C. make the Army take illegal actions.
    D. make anti-Semitic groups angry.

21. Which statement best summarizes Zola's letter in Document C?
    A. Although the French military convicted the wrong man, they attempted to carry out a fair trial.
    B. The French military was fooled by handwriting experts, who tried to convict the wrong man.
    C. The French military knowingly and illegally convicted an innocent man.
    D. The French military showed that the army was anti-Semitic at the highest levels.

22. **Writing Tasks** On July 21, 1906, a French general knighted Alfred Dreyfus a member of the Legion of Honor. Well-wishers attended the ceremony in the courtyard of the national military academy. Suppose you are reporting on the event for an American newspaper. Write a news story about the event, using the documents on this page along with information from the Topic.

The Age of Imperialism (1800–1914)

ESSENTIAL QUESTION Why Do People Move?

GO ONLINE to access the eText, videos, Interactive Primary Sources, Biographies, and other online resources.

Hafiz Abdul Karim attends to Queen Victoria, 1893

Connections to Today

Look at what you're wearing. Look at your phone or your computer. The odds are that something—or part of it—was manufactured, mined, or grown outside the United States. The shirt you're wearing may have been made by workers in Bangladesh or Cambodia. The cobalt that powers your phone probably came from a mine in Africa.

Today's global economy has roots in the Age of Imperialism, when western powers sought to control raw materials from Africa, Asia, and Latin America. What are the benefits and drawbacks of a global economy?

NBC LEARN

Learn how Menelik II helped Ethiopia resist colonization during the Age of Imperialism.

 BOUNCE to Activate My Story Video

Topic 15 Overview

In this Topic, you will learn about the events of the Age of Imperialism. Look at the lesson outline and explore the timeline. As you study this Topic, you will complete the Quest Inquiry.

Key Events of the Age of Imperialism

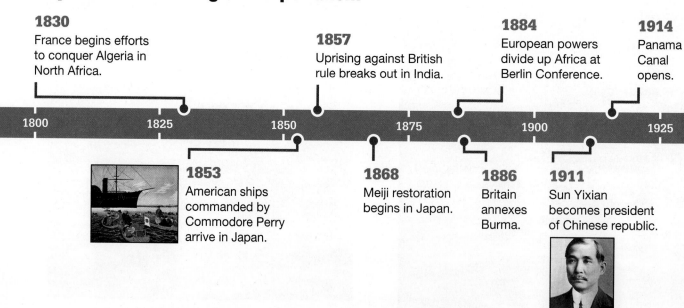

1830 France begins efforts to conquer Algeria in North Africa.

1857 Uprising against British rule breaks out in India.

1884 European powers divide up Africa at Berlin Conference.

1914 Panama Canal opens.

1800 1825 1850 1875 1900 1925

1853 American ships commanded by Commodore Perry arrive in Japan.

1868 Meiji restoration begins in Japan.

1886 Britain annexes Burma.

1911 Sun Yixian becomes president of Chinese republic.

QUEST!

Explore the Impact of Imperialism

How did imperialism affect India? In this Quest, you will write an essay that addresses the effects.

STEP 1

Examine the photo of the polo team in India in 1880. What does it tell you about British rule in India? What does it tell you about Indian traditions?

STEP 2

Study the documents on imperialism. Prepare a chart listing what you have learned. Ask questions, evaluate the sources. Draft an outline for your essay.

STEP 3

Write your essay. Begin by writing one or two sentences that give a basic answer to the question. Then create an outline that expands on that answer and incorporates details from the documents.

STEP 4

Share your essay with your classmates. Reflect on the impact of British imperialism in India. Are there still effects of imperialism on India and other countries today?

GO ONLINE to access complete Quest materials

The Netherlands played a leading role in the first phase of imperialism, from 1500 to 1800. The Dutch East India Company protected Dutch trade in the Indian Ocean and even had the right to make treaties and maintain its own armed forces.

 BOUNCE to Activate Flipped Video

Objectives

Explain the political, economic, and social causes of European imperialism.

Understand how technology and other factors contributed to the spread of imperialism.

Describe the characteristics of imperial rule.

Summarize the cultural, political, and social effects of imperialism.

Key Terms

imperialism
protectorate
sphere of influence

The New Imperialism

During the Industrial Revolution, the Western world was transformed. Advances in science and technology, industry, transportation, and communication strengthened the West, making it one of the most powerful societies in history.

Motivations for the New Imperialism

Armed with new economic and political power, Western nations set out to expand their overseas empires. Between 1870 and 1914, European nations brought much of the world and its people under their control.

European Expansion During the Age of Discovery European imperialism did not begin in the 1800s. **Imperialism** is the policy of one country's political, economic, or cultural domination over other lands and territories. During the Age of Discovery from the 1400s to the 1600s, Spain, Portugal, Britain, and France set up colonies in the Americas. Spain also seized control of the Philippine Islands.

Elsewhere, European nations gained only small outposts overseas. Portugal, Spain, and the Netherlands won footholds in Southeast Asia. The British and French were fierce rivals for trading rights in India. Europeans built trading forts on the coasts of Africa and negotiated limited trade with China and Japan.

GO ONLINE to access your digital course

Between 1500 and 1800, Europe had relatively little influence on the lives of the peoples in China, India, or Africa. Europeans traded with merchants in these lands but did not control any large territory, except in the Americas.

Expansion Turns into Empire Building By the 1800s, European nations with strong central governments had become more powerful. As the Industrial Revolution took off, some European nations grew rich. Spurred on by their new economic and military strength, these nations embarked on a path of aggressive expansion that modern historians call the "new imperialism." The new imperialism was a period in which industrial nations scrambled for territories that would provide them with raw materials and serve as markets for their manufactured goods.

In just a few decades, beginning in the 1870s, Europeans brought much of the world under their control. The new imperialism exploded out of a combination of causes. The main causes can be categorized as: economic, political, military, humanitarian, and religious.

Need for Resources Drives Further Expansion The Industrial Revolution created needs and desires that spurred overseas expansion. Manufacturers wanted access to natural resources such as rubber, petroleum, manganese for steel, and palm oil for machinery. They also wanted to expand their global markets by increasing the number of consumers to whom they could sell their manufactured goods.

Bankers, too, backed overseas expansion, which would provide new opportunities for investments. For some countries, colonies offered a valuable outlet for rapidly growing populations.

Political and Military Motives Political and military issues were closely linked to economic motives. Steam-powered merchant ships and naval vessels needed bases around the world to take on coal and supplies. Industrial powers seized islands or harbors to satisfy these needs.

Nationalism, a driving force in Europe throughout the 1800s, played a major role too. As Europeans started seizing territories overseas, it set off a race among rival nations. When France moved into West Africa, rival nations like Britain and Germany seized nearby African lands to halt further French expansion.

Western leaders claimed that colonies were needed to protect their national security interests. Sometimes, Western nations acquired colonies for the prestige of ruling a global empire.

Humanitarian and Religious Goals Many Westerners sincerely felt that people in other parts of the world needed their help and guidance. Missionaries, doctors, and colonial officials believed they had a duty to spread what they saw as the blessings of Western civilization, including its medicine, law, and the Christian religion.

Influence of Social Darwinism Behind the idea that the West had a civilizing mission was a growing sense of racial superiority in the West. Many Westerners had embraced the ideas of Social Darwinism. They applied Darwin's ideas about natural selection and survival of the fittest to human societies. European races, they argued, were superior to all others, and imperial conquest of weaker races was simply nature's way of improving the human species.

Although this reasoning was never part of Darwin's ideas, it became popular among many people in the West. As a result, the cultural heritage of millions of non-Westerners was destroyed because their societies were deemed inferior.

☑ **SUMMARIZE** What main factors contributed to European imperialism in the 1800s?

>> The growth of European industrial economies required raw materials to fuel its factories. New colonies provided both natural resources and new markets for European manufactured goods.

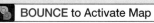
BOUNCE to Activate Map

Western Imperialism Spreads Rapidly

Starting in the late 1800s, the great powers of Europe divided up almost all of Africa along with large chunks of Asia. The European powers included Britain, France, Germany, Austria-Hungary, Russia, and Italy. The United States acquired the Philippines and gained influence in parts of Latin America.

Western nations claimed land in every corner of the globe. Leading the way were explorers, missionaries, merchants, soldiers, and settlers. The reasons for the success of Western imperialism in the late 1800s and early 1900s varied and so did the kinds of governments imposed by Western powers on their newly acquired territories.

Vulnerable Non-Western States As European nations grew stronger in the 1800s, several older civilizations were in decline. In the Middle East, the once powerful Ottomans faced many challenges within their diverse empire. In Mughal (MOO gul) India, weak rulers enforced less tolerant policies toward Hindus that triggered internal unrest. In China, Qing (ching) rulers resisted calls for modernization with disastrous consequences.

>> American author Mark Twain was an outspoken critic of both imperialism and the brutal Belgian rule in the Congo. In 1905, he published *King Leopold's Soliloquy,* which brought international attention to the situation.

🅑 BOUNCE to Activate Gallery

In West Africa, wars among African peoples and the damaging effects of the trade in enslaved Africans had undermined long-established kingdoms and city-states. Newer African states were not strong enough to resist the Western onslaught. Many Africans lived in small communities with no strong, centralized kingdom to protect them.

Western Advantages European powers had the advantages of strong economies, well-organized governments, and powerful armies and navies. Superior technology, including riverboats and the telegraph, as well as improved medical knowledge also played a role. The discovery of quinine in 1817 and other new medicines helped Europeans survive deadly tropical diseases such as malaria that had prevented them from exploring tropical regions in the interior of Africa.

Equally important, new weaponry gave Westerners a huge advantage. Advances such as Maxim guns—the earliest machine guns—along with repeating rifles and steam-driven warships were very strong arguments in persuading Africans and Asians to accept Western control.

Finally, Europeans often played rival groups within a region against one another. In India, the British successfully used rivalries between Hindu and Muslim princes to their advantage. In Africa, Europeans encouraged divisions among local rulers to keep them from joining forces against the newcomers.

Some Resist Imperialism People in Africa and Asia strongly resisted Western expansion. Many people fought the invaders, even though they had no weapons to equal the Maxim gun. Rulers in some areas tried to strengthen their societies against outsiders by reforming their own Muslim, Hindu, or Confucian traditions.

Although European powers defeated almost all the armed resistance, the struggle against imperialism continued. European rule turned many native peoples into forced laborers with no freedom of movement. By the early 1900s, nationalist movements were emerging. Western-educated Africans and Asians used Enlightenment ideas about freedom and liberty to call for an end to colonial rule. Tens of thousands in colonies around the world joined national liberation movements.

Critics at Home In the West, a small group of anti-imperialists emerged. Some argued that colonialism was a tool of the rich. Others opposed imperialist expansion because they wanted to focus on improving conditions for people in the West rather than imposing change on other cultures. Still others called imperialism immoral. Westerners, they pointed out, were moving toward greater democracy at home but were imposing undemocratic rule on other peoples.

☑ **EXPLAIN** How did Western imperialism spread through Africa and Asia so quickly?

Types of Imperial Rule

The new imperialism took several forms. In many areas, imperial powers established colonies. They sent governors, officials, and soldiers to control the people and set up a colonial bureaucracy. France and Britain, the leading imperial powers, developed different kinds of colonial rule.

Direct and Indirect Rule The French practiced direct rule, sending officials and soldiers from France to administer their colonies. Their goal was to impose French culture on their colonies and turn them into French provinces. Direct rule reflected the European belief that colonial people were incapable of ruling themselves.

The British, by contrast, used indirect rule. Under the system of indirect rule, a British governor and council of advisers made laws for each colony. Local rulers loyal to the governor retained some authority and served as agents for the British. The British encouraged the children of the local ruling class to get an education in Britain. In that way, a new generation was groomed to become agents of indirect rule—and of Western civilization.

Indirect rule differed from direct rule because it did not replace traditional rulers with European officials. Yet local rulers had only limited power and did not influence government decisions. Under both direct and indirect rule, the result was the same. Traditional rulers no longer had power or influence.

Other Types of Imperial Rule In some places, Western powers established a protectorate. In a **protectorate,** local rulers were left in place but were expected to follow the advice of European advisers on issues such as trade or missionary activity. For the Western powers, a protectorate had certain advantages over a colony. It cost less to run than a colony and usually did not require a large commitment of military forces unless a crisis occurred.

A third form of Western control was the **sphere of influence,** an area in which an outside power claimed exclusive investment or trading privileges.

>> The French practiced direct rule in their colonies. Here, French soldiers speak with an Algerian man. **Infer** What were the costs and benefits of direct rule?

Europeans carved out spheres of influence in China and elsewhere to prevent conflicts among themselves. The United States claimed parts of Latin America as its sphere of influence, holding off European powers that might compete with its interest.

☑ **COMPARE AND CONTRAST** Compare and contrast how Britain and France ruled their colonies.

The Effects of Imperialism

The new imperialism profoundly affected the political, economic, and social life of societies around the world. Colonial rule disrupted old civilizations and ways of life. European powers imposed Western culture on people who had different values and religious beliefs.

Another effect of imperialism was the continuous spread of early globalization. The term "globalization" may be recent but the changes represented by the term are historical and occurred long before the twenty-first century. The Industrial Revolution and imperialism were developments that had worldwide consequences. New inventions replaced the old models of transportation and communication which not only changed life during the Industrial Revolution but affected colonization and imperialism. With powerful weapons and sea vessels, Western countries were able to conquer areas in other parts of the world. These events changed trade, political systems, cultures, economies, and populations. A new age of global migration and economic exchange had begun.

Political Changes In conquered territories, European nations set up governments that reflected their own traditions. They introduced European legal systems that relied on abstract principles of right and wrong. By contrast, traditional African forms of justice had emphasized consensus, or general agreement. Many African societies saw these foreign principles as unjust, especially when Europeans used these laws to take land from local people.

As Europeans carved up the world, they drew borders around the territories they claimed. Often, these artificially-drawn borders split ethnic or cultural groups. Or they lumped people who shared no common heritage together into one colony.

>> Missionaries brought not only religion, but cultural change. Girls at this French missionary school in China learn Christmas carols. **Analyze Context** What evidence can you find in the photo that this is a missionary school?

Economic Changes European powers expected their colonies to be profitable. Colonial rulers therefore tapped local mineral and agricultural resources. Where mineral resources were lacking, colonial powers developed cash crops, such as rubber, cotton, palm oil, and peanuts. A cash crop is raised to be sold for money on the world market. The rise or fall of prices for cash crops affected standards of living in the colonies.

During the Age of Imperialism, a new global economic pattern emerged. Colonies provided raw materials for the factories of the industrial powers. European colonial powers then sold their manufactured goods to their colonies. The export of cash crops and natural resources in exchange for manufactured goods left colonies dependent on markets in the industrial world. Imports of machine-made goods destroyed indigenous cottage industries, or products made in people's homes.

Growth of a Money Economy The costs of governing colonies were huge, from salaries for officials and the military, to the costs of building roads, railroads, and schools. To pay for these costs, colonial governments required local people to pay taxes in cash.

The only way people could earn cash was to sell their labor, working on large plantations or in factories and mines owned by Europeans. Some became indentured servants or forced laborers who were shipped to other parts of the world to work on plantations or building projects.

Social and Cultural Changes The rise of the money economy contributed to the breakdown of traditional cultures. Until Europeans arrived, most people lived in close-knit villages that had subsistence economies. People produced the goods they needed or traded for goods they could not produce. As the money economy grew, people needed to have cash.

To earn money, men often took jobs in distant mines or plantations. Their long absences undermined family life. Some families moved to colonial cities, hoping to improve their positions. As a result, the close-knit village life declined.

Christian missionaries worked hard to win converts, urging newcomers to the faith to reject traditional beliefs and customs. Missionaries set up schools that emphasized the superiority of Western civilization. Impressed by European wealth, power, and teachings, many colonial people embraced Christianity, rejected their traditional cultures, and accepted the idea of European superiority.

Change Brings Benefits and Disadvantages

Although the new imperialism broke down traditional patterns of life, some people argue that colonial rule brought important benefits. Europeans developed their colonies economically, building roads and railroads and setting up telegraph systems.

Improvements in transportation and communication had advantages and disadvantages. They made travel easier and faster. Economic development created jobs that enabled colonial people to acquire new skills, although most were forced to work for very low wages.

Roads and railroads were built to benefit colonial rulers, not the people they controlled. Railroads linked plantations and mines to ports, where cash crops and raw materials were shipped overseas. New transportation systems allowed colonial governments to extend their control and encouraged the migration of workers.

Colonial governments and missionaries introduced improved medical care and better methods of sanitation. Missionaries set up hospitals and clinics and dedicated their lives to improving healthcare. New crops, tools, and farming methods increased food production. In many places, colonial rule secured peace by ending local warfare.

☑ **CATEGORIZE** How is migrating to find work a cultural as well as an economic effect of imperialism?

>> Coffee and tea were grown on plantations for the export market. Land used for these and other cash crops was not used to grow food. **Summarize** How did growing cash crops like coffee change colonized people's lives?

☑ ASSESSMENT

1. **Identify Cause and Effect** How did the Industrial Revolution lead to the new imperialism?

2. **Cite Evidence** How did Western nations come to dominate much of the world in the late 1800s?

3. **Distinguish** Why was Social Darwinism important to the new imperialism?

4. **Predict Consequences** How might grouping several rival ethnic groups into one political unit cause friction once that region gains independence?

5. **Quest Connections** What were the long-term effects of imperialism on the colonized peoples?

15.2

Europeans began trading along the African coast in the 1500s. Centuries later, they began moving into the continent's interior.

 BOUNCE to Activate Flipped Video

Objectives

Describe the forces that shaped Africa in the early 1800s.

Explain why European contact with Africa increased.

Analyze how European nations carved up Africa.

Describe African resistance to imperialism.

Key Terms

Usman dan Fodio
Shaka
paternalistic
David Livingstone
Henry Stanley
Leopold II
Boer War
Samori Touré
Yaa Asantewaa
Nehanda
Menelik II
elite

European Colonies in Africa

Between 1870 and 1914, Britain, France, Germany, and other European powers scrambled to carve up the African continent. They set up dozens of colonies and ruled over the lives of millions of people. Although people in Africa resisted, they could not hold back the tide of European conquest.

Africa Before Imperialism

Africa is a huge continent, nearly three times the size of Europe, with diverse regions and cultures. Before the scramble for Africa, people living on the continent spoke hundreds of languages and had developed varied governments. Some people lived in large centralized states, while others lived in village communities. Many still lived in nomadic societies.

North Africa North Africa includes the fertile land along the Mediterranean and the enormous Sahara. For centuries before 1800, the region had been part of the Muslim world. In the early 1800s, much of North Africa, including Egypt, was still ruled by the weakening Ottoman empire.

Islamic Revival in West Africa In the great savanna region of West Africa, an Islamic reform movement brought change. It began among the Fulani people in what is today northern Nigeria. There, the scholar and preacher **Usman dan Fodio** (oos MAHN dahn FOH dee oh) denounced the corruption of the local Hausa rulers. He called for social and religious reforms to purify and

GO ONLINE to access your digital course

revive Islam. Under Usman and other leaders, several new Muslim states arose, built on trade, farming, and herding.

Usman dan Fodio ruled the Sokoto Caliphate, the largest empire in Africa since the fall of Songhai in the 1500s. At its height in the mid-1800s, it stretched for 1,500 miles and included 30 emirates, or smaller states. During this time, literacy increased, local wars were quieted, and trade improved. Their success inspired other Muslim reform movements in West Africa. Between about 1780 and 1880, other Islamic leaders replaced old rulers or set up new states in West Africa.

In the forest regions, strong states like the Asante (uh SAHN teh) kingdom had emerged. The Asante traded with both Europeans and Muslims. Asante power was limited, however. They controlled several smaller states that felt no loyalty to the central government. These tributary states were ready to turn to other protectors who might help them defeat their Asante rulers. European powers would exploit this lack of unity.

East Africa The coastal regions of East Africa had long been a center of major trade routes, from the Red Sea to port cities like Mombasa (mahm BAH suh) and Kilwa (KEEL wah). These cities had suffered setbacks when the Portuguese arrived in the early 1500s.

Yet East African cities remained centers of trade. Merchants sent trading ships to the Red Sea or Persian Gulf. They exchanged ivory and copper from Central Africa for goods such as cloth and firearms. Other ships carried human captives, who had been seized in the interior and marched to the coast. From there, they were shipped as enslaved people to the Middle East.

Southern Africa In the early 1800s, southern Africa was in turmoil as a result of the Zulu wars. The Zulu people had migrated into southern Africa in the 1500s. By the 1800s, they had emerged as a major force in southern Africa under a ruthless and brilliant leader, **Shaka.**

Shaka's war disrupted life across southern Africa. Groups driven from their homelands by the Zulus then adopted Shaka's tactics.

They migrated north, conquering still other peoples and creating their own powerful states. By the 1830s, the Zulus faced a new threat, the arrival of well-armed, mounted Boers, descendants of Dutch farmers who were migrating north from the Cape Colony.

>> When Europeans arrived in Tanzania, they encountered small village communities like this Utiri village.

BOUNCE to Activate Map

>> East African port cities often served as centers for the trade in enslaved Africans. This market was on the island of Zanzibar.

In 1806, the Cape Colony had passed from the Dutch to the British. Many Boers resented British laws that abolished slavery and otherwise interfered with their way of life. To escape British rule, they loaded their goods into covered wagons and started north. Several thousand Boer families joined this "Great Trek."

As the migrating Boers came into contact with Zulus, fighting quickly broke out. At first, Zulu regiments held their own. But in the end, Zulu spears could not defeat Boer guns. The struggle for control of the land would rage until the end of the century.

Impact of the Slave Trade For centuries, Europeans had enslaved Africans, transporting them in horrible conditions on ships across the Atlantic to work plantations and mines in the Americas. Arabs and Africans had also traded in enslaved people. In the early 1800s, European nations slowly began to outlaw the slave trade, though it took years to end.

Some British and American abolitionists promoted the idea of resettling people freed from slavery in Africa. In 1787, the British organized Sierra Leone in West Africa as a colony for formerly enslaved people. Later, some free Black people from the United States founded a settlement in nearby Liberia. By 1847, Liberia had become an independent state.

Slavery still existed, however. Arab and African slave traders continued to seize captives from East and Central Africa to work as enslaved people in the Middle East and Asia well into the 1800s. The demand for enslaved people remained and the slave trade continued in Africa. As reports of this slave trade spread, abolitionists and European explorers demanded action to end it.

☑ **SUMMARIZE** What factors shaped each of the main regions of Africa during the early 1800s?

European Contact Increases

From the 1400s through the 1700s, Europeans traded along the African coast, but knew very little about the continent. They relied on Africans to bring enslaved people and trade goods, such as ivory and gold, from the interior to coastal trading posts.

European interest in Africa increased during the Age of Imperialism. Spurred on by trading companies and a desire for adventure, Europeans explored the rivers of Africa. In the past, difficult geography, resistance by Africans, and diseases had all kept Europeans from moving into the interior of Africa. In the 1880s, medical advances and river steamships helped Europeans move inland.

Explorers Push into Africa's Interior In the early 1800s, European explorers began pushing into the interior of Africa. Daring adventurers like Mungo Park and Richard Burton set out to map the course and sources of the great African rivers such as the Niger, the Nile, and the Congo.

Some explorers were self-promoters who wrote glowing accounts of their bold deeds. While they were fascinated by African geography, they had little understanding of the peoples they met. All, however, endured great hardships while exploring Africa.

Missionaries Follow Explorers Catholic and Protestant missionaries followed the explorers. All across Africa, they sought to win people to Christianity. The missionaries were sincere in their desire to help Africans. They built schools and medical clinics alongside churches. They also focused attention on the evils of the trade in enslaved Africans.

Still, missionaries, like most Westerners, took a **paternalistic** view of Africans, meaning they saw them as children in need of guidance. To them, African cultures and religions were "degraded." They urged Africans to reject their own traditions in favor of Western civilization.

>> Freetown, Sierra Leone, was settled by freed slaves from all over the world. Many had their origins in regions of Africa. Sierra Leone became a center of education for Africans.

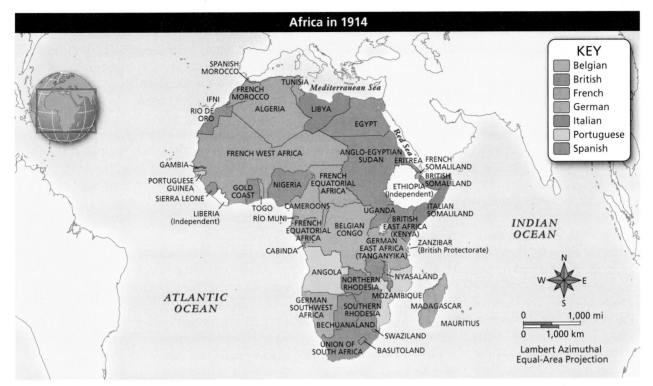

Africa in 1914

KEY
- Belgian
- British
- French
- German
- Italian
- Portuguese
- Spanish

>> **Analyze Maps** One goal of British imperialists in Africa was to gain control "from Cairo to the Cape" (South Africa). Which colony stood in the way of that plan? Which European country controlled that colony?

 BOUNCE to Activate Map

Livingstone's Explorations More than anyone else, **David Livingstone,** a British doctor and missionary, captured the imaginations of Westerners. For 30 years, he crisscrossed Africa. He wrote about the many peoples he met with more sympathy and less bias than did most Europeans. He relentlessly opposed the trade in enslaved Africans, which remained a profitable business for some. The only way to end this cruel traffic, he believed, was to open up the interior of Africa to Christianity and trade.

Europeans credited Livingstone with "discovering" the huge waterfalls on the Zambezi River. He named them Victoria Falls, after Britain's Queen Victoria. The Africans who lived nearby, however, had long known the falls as Mosi oa Tunya, "the smoke that thunders."

Livingstone blazed a trail that others soon followed. In 1869, the journalist **Henry Stanley** trekked into Central Africa to find Livingstone, who had not been heard from for years. He finally tracked him down in 1871 in what is today Tanzania, greeting him with the now-legendary question "Dr. Livingstone, I presume?"

☑ **RECALL** Why did European contact with Africa increase in the late 1800s?

European Nations Scramble for Colonies

Shortly after Stanley met up with Livingstone, King **Leopold II** of Belgium hired Stanley to explore the Congo River basin and arrange trade treaties with African leaders. Publicly, Leopold spoke of a civilizing mission to carry the light "that for millions of men still plunged in barbarism will be the dawn of a better era." Privately, he dreamed of conquest and profit.

Leopold's activities in the Congo set off a scramble by other nations. Before long, Britain, France, and Germany were pressing rival claims to the region. The scramble for Africa had begun. It would end with the partition of virtually the entire continent among the great powers of Europe.

The Berlin Conference To avoid bloodshed, European powers met at an international conference in 1884. It took place not in Africa but in Berlin, Germany. No Africans were invited to the conference.

At the Berlin Conference, European powers recognized Leopold's private claims to the Congo Free State but called for free trade on the Congo and Niger rivers.

They further agreed that a European power could not claim any part of Africa unless it had set up a government office there. Europeans quickly sent officials who would exert their power over local African rulers and peoples.

The rush to colonize Africa was on. In the 20 years after the Berlin Conference, the European powers partitioned almost the entire continent. As Europeans carved out their claims, they established new borders and frontiers. They redrew the map of Africa with little regard for traditional patterns of settlement or ethnic boundaries.

Leopold's Horror in the Congo Leopold and other wealthy Belgians exploited the riches of the Congo, including its copper, rubber, and ivory. Soon, horrifying reports filtered out of the region. They told of Belgian overseers torturing and brutalizing villagers. Forced to work for almost nothing, unwilling laborers were savagely beaten or mutilated. The population in some areas declined drastically.

Eventually, international outrage forced Leopold to turn over his personal colony to the Belgian government. It became the Belgian Congo in 1908. Under Belgian rule, the worst abuses were ended.

>> A major resource that the Belgians wanted from the Congo was rubber. **Cite Evidence** What evidence in the photo indicates that these rubber workers were enslaved?

Still, the Belgians regarded the Congo as a possession to be exploited for their own enrichment. African inhabitants of the Congo were given little or no role in the government, or the economy of the country. The rich resources of their mines went to Western investors in the mines.

France Expands Its Territory France took a giant share of Africa. In the 1830s, it had invaded and conquered Algeria in North Africa. The victory cost tens of thousands of French lives and killed many times more Algerians. In the late 1800s, France extended its influence along the Mediterranean into Tunisia.

France also gained colonies in West and Central Africa. At its height, the French empire in Africa was as large as the continental United States.

Britain's Share Britain's share of Africa was smaller and more scattered than that of France. However, it included more heavily populated regions with many rich resources. Britain took chunks of West and East Africa. It gained control of Egypt, pushed south into the Sudan, and ruled much of southern Africa.

The British industrialist Cecil Rhodes was a passionate imperialist who had made a fortune in mining in southern Africa. Rhodes dreamed of building a "Cape to Cairo" railway to link British possessions from Cape Town, South Africa, to Cairo, Egypt.

"I care nothing about money for its own sake," he once wrote, "but it is a power—and I do like power." Rhodes helped Britain extend its African empire by one million square miles. The British colony of Rhodesia (now Zimbabwe), was named after him.

The Boer War In southern Africa, Britain clashed with the Boers, who were descendants of Dutch settlers. Britain had acquired the Cape Colony from the Dutch in 1806. The Boers—Dutch farmers—resented British rule and many had migrated north to set up their own republics.

In the late 1800s, however, the discovery of gold and diamonds in the Boer republics led to conflict with Britain. The **Boer War,** which lasted from 1899 to 1902, involved bitter guerrilla fighting. The British won, but at great cost.

In 1910, the British united the Cape Colony and the former Boer republics into the Union of South Africa. The new constitution set up a government run by whites and laid the foundation for a system of complete racial segregation that would remain in force until 1993.

Others Nations Join the Scramble Other European powers joined the scramble for African colonies. They wanted to bolster their national image and further their economic growth and influence. The Portuguese carved out colonies in Angola and Mozambique. Italy reached across the Mediterranean to occupy Libya and then pushed into the "horn" of Africa, at the southern end of the Red Sea.

Germany was newly united in 1871 under the expert leadership of Bismarck. At first, Bismarck had little interest in overseas expansion, but eventually realized the importance of colonies. In the 1880s, Germany took lands in Southwest Africa (now Namibia) and East Africa (now part of Tanzania) as well as what are today Cameroon and Togo. A German politician, trying to ease the worries of European rivals, explained, "We do not want to put anyone in the shade, but we also demand our place in the sun."

☑ **IDENTIFY CAUSE AND EFFECT** How did King Leopold II set off a scramble for colonies in Africa?

African Resistance

Europeans met armed resistance across the continent. In North Africa, the Algerians fought French expansion for years. In West Africa, **Samori Touré** (sah MAWR ee too RAY) fought French forces. Elsewhere in West Africa, the Ibo and Fulani struggled for years against the British advance. In southern Africa, the Zulus resisted British domination, handing them several grave defeats before the British finally succeeded.

Women Leaders of the Resistance In West Africa, the British faced the powerful Asante kingdom in a series of wars. When their king was exiled, the Asante people put themselves under the command of their queen, **Yaa Asantewaa (**YA uh ah sahn TAY wuh). She led the fight against the British in the last Asante war.

Another woman, **Nehanda** (neh HAHN duh), was a spiritual leader of the Shona people in what is today Zimbabwe. Nehanda inspired the Shona to resist British rule. In the 1890s, she and her husband were captured and executed by the British. Her courage, however, inspired later generations to fight for freedom.

Ethiopia Remains Independent In East Africa, the ancient Christian kingdom of Ethiopia successfully resisted European colonization and remained

>> French troops capture the city of Mascara in December 1835, during the French–Algerian War. **Infer** What advantages do the Algerian troops have? What advantages do the French troops have?

independent. Like feudal Europe, Ethiopia had been divided up among a number of rival princes who ruled their own domains.

In the late 1800s, however, a reforming ruler, **Menelik II,** began to modernize his country. He hired European experts to plan modern roads and bridges and set up a Western school system. He imported the latest weapons and European officers to help train his army. Thus, when Italy invaded Ethiopia in 1896, Menelik was prepared. At the battle of Adowa (AH duh wuh), the Ethiopians smashed the Italian invaders. Ethiopia, along with Liberia, were the only African nations to preserve independence.

Resistance Against Germany In East Africa, the Germans fought wide-ranging wars against groups resisting foreign rule. During the 1890s, the Uhehe harried German forces. The Germans gained control by using terror. Any groups linked to the resistance were killed or driven off the land. Some were turned into forced laborers for settlers. In 1905, another rebellion, the Maji Maji War, erupted. In that conflict too, the Germans triumphed only after burning acres and acres of farmland, leaving thousands of local people to die of starvation.

>> During the Age of Imperialism, some Africans adopted Western dress. The man wearing a Western jacket behind the Asante king was an Asante official.

Two factors limited African resistance in East Africa. First, the slave trading states in East Africa had disrupted many small societies and made some Africans more sympathetic to European expansion. Second, the outbreak of rinderpest, a cattle disease, caused a disastrous famine. The epidemic, which killed 95 percent of all cattle in some areas, led to malnutrition and other diseases that affected people's ability to fight the invaders.

A New African Elite During the Age of Imperialism, a Western-educated African **elite,** or upper class, emerged in both Africa and other parts of the world. Some middle-class people in Africa admired Western ways and rejected their own culture. Others valued their ancient traditions and condemned Western societies that upheld liberty and equality for white Western people only. By the early 1900s, African leaders were forging nationalist movements to pursue self-determination and independence.

☑ **DESCRIBE** How did Ethiopians resist imperialism?

☑ ASSESSMENT

1. **Describe** Name one development in each region of Africa in the early 1800s.

2. **Identify Cause and Effect** How did imperialist European powers claim control over most of Africa by the end of the 1800s?

3. **Analyze Information** What impact did explorers and missionaries have on Africa?

4. **Infer** Why do you think the Europeans did not invite Africans to the Berlin Conference?

5. **Summarize** How did Africans resist European imperialism?

6. **Connections to Today** Do you think an event like the Berlin Conference could take place today? Why or why not?

Letter to King Leopold of Belgium, George Washington Williams

As a colony, the Congo Free State was under the personal control of King Leopold of Belgium. In 1889, Leopold was interviewed by George Washington Williams—a journalist, minister, and one of the first African American historians. Williams was favorably impressed by Leopold, who painted the Congo as a benevolent state where Africans were well cared for. But when Williams visited the Congo, he soon found out that the reality was far different. Outraged, he wrote an open, or public, letter to Leopold. It brought attention to the brutal conditions in the Congo and eventually led to the removal of the Congo from Leopold's control.

>> This 1905 cartoon shows King Leopold hoarding his wealth from the Congo.

Primary Source

Good and Great Friend,

I have the honor to submit for your Majesty's consideration some reflections respecting the Independent State of Congo, based upon a careful study and inspection of the country and character of the personal Government you have established upon the African Continent.

It afforded me great pleasure to avail myself of the opportunity afforded me last year, of visiting your State in Africa; and how thoroughly I have been disenchanted, disappointed and disheartened, it is now my painful duty to make known to your Majesty in plain but respectful language. Every charge which I am about to bring against your Majesty's personal Government in the Congo has been carefully investigated; a list of competent and

veracious witnesses, documents, letters, official records and data has been faithfully prepared, which will be deposited with Her Britannic Majesty's Secretary of State for Foreign Affairs, until such time as an International Commission can be created with power to send for persons and papers, to administer oaths, and attest the truth or falsity of these charges.
. . .

☑ **DRAW INFERENCES** At the start of the letter, what seems to be Williams's attitude toward Leopold?

I was anxious to see to what extent the natives had "adopted the fostering care" of your Majesty's "benevolent enterprise," and I was doomed to bitter disappointment. Instead of the natives of the Congo "adopting the fostering care" of your Majesty's Government, they everywhere complain that their land has been taken from them by force; that the Government is cruel and arbitrary, and declare that they neither love nor respect the Government and its flag. Your Majesty's Government has sequestered their land, burned their towns, stolen their property, enslaved their women and children, and committed other crimes too numerous to mention in detail. It is natural that they everywhere shrink from "the fostering care" your Majesty's Government so eagerly proffers them. . . .

USE CONTEXT CLUES Why does Williams place the phrase "fostering care" in quotation marks?

The Courts of your Majesty's Government are . . . unjust, partial and delinquent. I have personally witnessed and examined their clumsy operations. The laws printed and circulated in Europe "for the Protection of the blacks" in the Congo, are a dead letter and a fraud. I have heard an officer of the Belgian Army pleading the cause of a white man of low degree who had been guilty of beating and stabbing a black man, and urging race distinctions and prejudices as good and sufficient reasons why his client should be adjudged innocent. I know of prisoners remaining in custody for six and ten months because they were not judged. . . .

CITE EVIDENCE How does Williams support his generalizations about the laws in the Congo?

Your Majesty's Government is excessively cruel to its prisoners, condemning them, for the slightest offences, to the chain gang, the like of which cannot be seen in any other Government in the civilized or uncivilized world. Often these ox-chains eat into the necks of the prisoners and produce sores about which the flies circle, aggravating the running wound; so the prisoner is constantly worried. These poor creatures are frequently beaten with a dried piece of hippopotamus skin, called a "chicote", and usually the blood flows at every stroke when well laid on. . . .

Your Majesty's Government has violated the General Act of the Conference of Berlin by firing upon native canoes; by confiscating the property

of natives; by intimidating native traders, and preventing them from trading with white trading companies; by quartering troops in native villages when there is no war. . . .

UNDERSTAND MEANING What does Williams mean by "the General Act of the Conference of Berlin?"

Your Majesty's Government is engaged in the slave-trade, wholesale and retail. It buys and sells and steals slaves. . . .

All the crimes perpetrated in the Congo have been done in your name, and you must answer at the bar of Public Sentiment for the misgovernment of a people, whose lives and fortunes were entrusted to you by the august Conference of Berlin, 1884—1885. I now appeal to the Powers which committed this infant State to your Majesty's charge, and to the great States which gave it international being; and whose majestic law you have scorned and trampled upon, to call and create an International Commission to investigate the charges herein preferred in the name of Humanity, Commerce, Constitutional Government and Christian Civilization.

DETERMINE AUTHOR'S PURPOSE What was Williams's main goal in writing this letter?

✅ ASSESSMENT

1. **Compare and Contrast** Compare the attitude Williams expresses toward Leopold in the opening and closing paragraphs.

2. **Draw Conclusions** What specific details in this excerpt do you think would have outraged world opinion the most? Why?

3. **Draw Inferences** Based on this letter, do you think Williams opposed European colonization in Africa in general? Give reasons for your answer.

4. **Analyze interactions** How does the cartoon on the previous page reflect Williams's viewpoint?

15.3

During the Battle of the Pyramids in 1798, Napoleon and his army captured the Egyptian city of Cairo.

Europe and the Muslim World

In 1800, the Muslim world extended from North Africa to Southeast Asia. Much of this world was ruled by three giant Muslim empires—the Ottomans in the Middle East, the Mughals in India, and the Safavids (sah FAH vidz) in Persia. By this time, however, all three empires were in decline.

Unrest in Muslim Regions

Napoleon Bonaparte's 1798 invasion of Egypt opened a new era in European contact with the Muslim world. It focused attention on the fading power of the Ottoman empire. By the early 1800s, European countries were nibbling at the fringes of the Muslim world. Before long, they would strike at its heartland.

Declining Empires The decay of these once-mighty empires had many causes. Central governments had lost control over powerful groups such as landowning nobles, military elites, and urban craft guilds. Corruption was widespread. In some places, Muslim scholars and religious leaders were allied with the state. In other areas, they helped to stir discontent against governments.

Muslim Reform Efforts In the 1700s and 1800s, reform movements sprang up across the Muslim world. Reformers in parts of Africa and Asia generally stressed religious piety and strict rules of behavior. Efforts to reform the practice of Islam touched off revolts and demands for political change.

 BOUNCE to Activate Flipped Video

Objectives

Explain how internal and external pressures shaped the Muslim world.

Identify the challenges facing the Ottoman empire and Persia.

Describe the ways Egypt tried to modernize, including the opening of the Suez Canal.

Key Terms

Muhammad Ahmad
Mahdi
pasha
sultan
genocide
Muhammad Ali
concession

Islamic revivals arose in Africa. Usman dan Fodio struggled to reform Muslim practices in northern Nigeria. In the Sudan, south of Egypt, **Muhammad Ahmad** (AHK mud) announced that he was the **Mahdi** (mahk DEE), the long-awaited savior of the faith according to some Muslim traditions. In the 1880s, the Mahdi and his followers fiercely resisted British expansion into the region. In modern Sudan, followers of the Mahdi still have much influence.

Another Islamic reform movement, the Wahhabi (wah HAHB ee) movement in Arabia, rejected the schools of theology and law that had emerged in the Ottoman empire. In their place, they wanted to recapture the purity and simplicity of Muhammad's original teachings.

In a true Islamic society, they declared, the government furthered the goals of Islam. An Arab prince led a Wahhabi revolt against Ottoman rule. Although the revolt was put down, the Wahhabi movement survived. Its teachings remain influential in the kingdom of Saudi Arabia today.

European Imperialism In addition to internal decay and stresses, the old Muslim empires faced the threat of Western imperialism. Through a mix of diplomacy and military threats, European powers won treaties giving them favorable trading terms. They then demanded special rights for Europeans residing in Muslim lands. They used the need to protect their citizens' rights as an excuse to intervene in local affairs. At times, they took over an entire region.

☑ **EXPLAIN** How did Western powers gain the upper hand in Muslim regions of the world?

The Ottoman Empire Declines

At its height, the Ottoman empire extended across the Middle East, North Africa, and parts of Eastern Europe. By 1800, however, it faced serious challenges. Ambitious **pashas,** or provincial rulers, had increased their power. Economic problems and corruption added to Ottoman decay.

Nationalist Revolts As ideas of nationalism spread from Western Europe, internal revolts weakened the multi-ethnic Ottoman empire. Subject peoples in Eastern Europe, North Africa, and the Middle East threatened to break away.

In the Balkans, Greeks, Serbs, Bulgarians, and Romanians gained independence. Revolts against Ottoman rule also erupted in Arabia, Lebanon, and Armenia. The Ottomans suppressed these uprisings, but another valuable territory, Egypt, slipped out of their control.

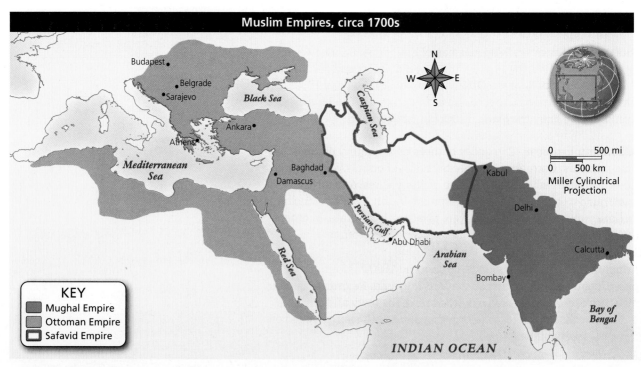

Muslim Empires, circa 1700s

KEY
- Mughal Empire
- Ottoman Empire
- Safavid Empire

>> **Analyze Maps** Western imperialism gained steam at a time when the three major Muslim empires were in decline. In which empire might ethnic diversity have created internal challenges? Why?

Increasing European Pressure Britain, France, and Russia each sought to benefit from the slow crumbling of the Ottoman empire. After seizing Algeria in the 1830s, France cast its attention on other Ottoman-ruled lands. Russia schemed to gain control of the Turkish straits—the Bosporus (BAHS puh rus) and the Dardanelles. Control of these straits would give the Russians access to the Mediterranean Sea.

Britain tried to thwart Russia's ambitions, which it saw as a threat to its own power in the Mediterranean and beyond to India. During the Crimean War in the 1850s, Britain and France joined forces to help the Ottoman empire resist Russian expansion. By the late 1880s, however, France and Britain had extended their own influence over Ottoman lands. Finally, in 1898, the newly united German empire hoped to increase its influence in the region by building a Berlin-to-Baghdad railway.

Efforts to Westernize Since the late 1700s, several Ottoman rulers had seen the need for reform and looked to the West for ideas. They reorganized the bureaucracy and system of tax collection. They built railroads, improved education, and hired Europeans to train a modern military. Young men were sent to the West to study science and technology. Many returned with Western political ideas about democracy and equality.

The reforms also brought improved medical care and revitalized farming. These improvements, however, were a mixed blessing. Better health care resulted in a population explosion. The growing population increased competition for the best land, which led to unrest.

The adoption of Western ideas about government increased tension. Many officials objected to changes that were inspired by a foreign culture. For their part, repressive **sultans,** rulers of the Ottoman Turkish empire, rejected reform and tried to rebuild the autocratic power enjoyed by earlier rulers.

The Young Turks In the 1890s, a group of liberals formed a movement called the Young Turks. They insisted that reform was the only way to save the Ottoman empire. In 1908, the Young Turks overthrew the sultan. Before they could achieve their planned reforms, however, the Ottoman empire was plunged into the world war that erupted in 1914.

Armenian Genocide By the late 1800s, Turkish nationalism had grown stronger. In the 1890s, it took an ugly, intolerant course.

Thanksgiving on the other side—No. 1   Thanksgiving on the other side—No. 2
THE POWERS WAITING TO DIVIDE THE TURKEY WHICH RUSSIA IS STILL PURSUING

>> **Analyze Political Cartoons** The European powers hoped to carve up the crumbling Ottoman empire for themselves. How do you know which figure in the cartoon represents the Ottoman empire?

🔊 BOUNCE to Activate Cartoon

Traditionally, the Ottomans allowed its diverse religious and ethnic groups to live in their own communities and practice their own religions. By the 1890s, however, nationalism was igniting new tensions between Ottoman rulers and minority peoples. Spurred by Turkish nationalism, Ottoman rulers feared a further breakup of the empire. These tensions led to increasing persecution and eventually a brutal genocide of the Armenians, a Christian people concentrated in the eastern mountains of the empire. **Genocide** is a deliberate and systematic killing of people who belong to a particular racial, ethnic, or cultural group.

The Muslim Turks accused Christian Armenians of supporting Russian plans against the Ottoman empire. Using this as a pretext, they installed repressive policies against the Armenians in the 1890s. When Armenians protested, the sultan had tens of thousands of them slaughtered. Survivors fled, many of them to the United States. Still, over the next 25 years, another million or more Armenians were killed by the Turks or died from disease and starvation. The Armenian genocide would reach new heights during World War I.

✓ **DESCRIBE** How were efforts to Westernize problematic for the Ottoman empire?

Modernization in Egypt

Egypt in 1800 was a semi-independent province of the Ottoman empire. In the early 1800s, it made great strides toward reform. Its success was due to **Muhammad Ali,** an Albanian Muslim soldier who was appointed governor of Egypt in 1805.

Ali had helped to oust the French from Egypt. They were remnants of Napoleon's forces that had occupied the land for several years. The French occupation had disrupted Egypt's traditional government, which gave Muhammad Ali an opportunity to remake Egypt.

Reform Efforts Muhammad Ali is sometimes called the "founder of modern Egypt." He introduced a number of political and economic reforms. First, he ended the power of the old ruling oligarchy and seized huge farms from the old landowning class. He reduced the power of religious leaders and crushed any protest against his rule. He then set out to rebuild Egypt along modern lines. He improved tax collection and backed large irrigation projects to increase farm output.

Muhammad Ali ordered Egyptian farmers to plant a new kind of cotton, to be sold as a cash crop. By expanding cotton production and encouraging the development of many local industries, Ali brought Egypt into the growing network of world trade.

Muhammad Ali also brought Western military experts to Egypt to help him build a well-trained, modernized army. He promoted education and the study of medicine. Before he died in 1849, he had set Egypt on the road to becoming a major Middle Eastern power.

The Suez Canal Muhammad Ali's successors lacked his skills, and Egypt came increasingly under foreign control. In 1858, a French entrepreneur, Ferdinand de Lesseps (LAY seps), organized a company to build the Suez Canal, a waterway connecting the Mediterranean and Red seas. Europe hailed its opening in 1869 because it greatly reduced the travel time between Europe and Asia. To Britain, especially, the canal was a "lifeline" to India, where its influence was increasing.

In 1875, the ruler of Egypt was unable to repay loans he had contracted for the canal and other modernization projects. To pay his debts, he sold his shares in the canal. The British prime minister Disraeli quickly bought them, giving Britain a controlling interest in the canal.

Becoming a British Protectorate Britain soon expanded its influence in Egypt. When a nationalist revolt erupted in 1882, Britain made Egypt a protectorate. In theory, the governor of Egypt was still an official of the Ottoman government. In fact, he followed policies dictated by Britain.

Under British influence, Egypt continued to modernize. At the same time, nationalist discontent simmered and flared into protests and riots well into the next century.

☑ **GENERATE EXPLANATIONS** How did Egypt fall under British control?

European Imperialism in Persia

Like the Ottoman empire, Persia faced major challenges in the 1800s. At first, the Qajar (kah JAHR) shahs, who ruled Persia from 1794 to 1925, exercised absolute power like the Safavids before them. Still, they did take steps to introduce reforms. The government improved finances and sponsored the building of railroads and telegraph lines. By the early 1900s, it was even experimenting with liberal reforms.

>> The British used their military strength to protect their interest in the Suez Canal. These troops were sent to Egypt during the 1882 Anglo-Egyptian War. **Identify Cause and Effect** Why would the British want to protect their control of the Suez Canal?

🔲 BOUNCE to Activate Gallery

The Great Game Reform, however, did not save Persia from Western imperialism. Both Russia and Britain battled for influence in the area. Russia wanted to protect its southern frontier and expand into Central Asia. Britain wanted to protect its interests in India.

Throughout the 1800s, Britain was determined to stop Russia's southward expansion, fearing that Russia might win control of northern India. Cartoons of the time showed the British lion pitted against the Russian bear. The competition between Russia and Britain in the region became known as the "Great Game." During this time, the two European powers sought to increase their influence in the Ottoman empire, Persia, Afghanistan, and Tibet. Persia was a particular focus of their rivalry.

For a time, each nation set up its own sphere of influence in Persia. Russia operated in the north and Britain in the south. The discovery of oil in the early 1900s upset the balance and generally heightened foreign interest in the region. Both Russia and Britain plotted to win control of the Persian oil fields and gain other rights.

Tensions Within Persia During the Age of Imperialism, Persia experienced changes similar to those of other regions subject to European expansion. It became a supplier of raw materials for industrial Europe and a market for its manufactured goods. Local Persian industries declined, unable to compete with factory-made goods. Much land was converted into producing cash crops, reducing local food production.

To raise money, the Persian government granted **concessions,** or special rights given to foreign companies or individuals. The money was supposed to be used to modernize the country but was often wasted on the extravagant Persian court. Persian nationalists and reformers protested the concessions, even more so after Russia sent troops to protect its concessions.

Persian nationalists included two very different groups. Some Persians, especially from the growing urban middle classes, wanted to move swiftly to adopt Western ways. Others, led by Muslim religious leaders, condemned the Persian government and Western influences. The religious leaders often spoke for the masses of the people who lived in rural poverty and resented government interference in their traditional way of life.

>> The discovery of oil in Persia led to a greater British and Russian presence in the country, which sparked a nationalist backlash.

☑ **ANALYZE INFORMATION** For what reason did Persia attract foreign interest in the early 1900s?

☑ ASSESSMENT

1. **Make Generalizations** What was the goal of the Wahhabi reform movement?

2. **Identify Cause and Effect** What effect did nationalism have on the Ottoman empire during the 1800s?

3. **Express Ideas Clearly** Who was Muhammad Ali, and why was he a significant figure?

4. **Summarize** How did Britain gain control of the Suez Canal?

5. **Connections to Today** (a) What resource sparked increased foreign interest in Persia in the early 1900s? (b) What role does this resource play in international relations today?

Draw Conclusions An official of the British East India Company rides in an Indian procession in the early 1800s. How does the painting convey the power of the British?

🔲 **BOUNCE to Activate Flipped Video**

Objectives

Understand the causes and effects of the Uprising of 1857.

Explain the impact of British rule on India.

Describe how the British and Indians viewed one another.

Trace the origins of Indian nationalism.

Key Terms

sati
sepoy
viceroy
deforestation
Ram Mohun Roy
purdah

India Becomes a British Colony

During the 1500s and 1600s, the Mughals presided over a powerful empire in India. By the mid-1700s, however, the Mughal empire was in decline. When Mughal rulers were strong, the British East India Company gained only limited trading rights on the fringe of the empire.

The British East India Company

As Mughal power declined, the British East India company's influence grew and it drove its rival France out of India. By the mid-1800s, the company controlled three fifths of India. In the 1800s, Britain turned its commercial interests in India into political ones.

Exploitation of Indian Diversity Even when Mughal power was at its height, India was home to many peoples and cultures. As Mughal power crumbled, India became fragmented. Indians speaking dozens of different languages and with different traditions were not able to unite against the newcomers.

The British took advantage of Indian divisions by playing rival princes against each other. When local disputes led to conflict, the British stepped in. Where diplomacy or intrigue did not work, the British used their superior weapons to overpower local rulers.

Implementation of British Policies The East India Company's main goal in India was to make money, and leading officials often grew rich. In pursuit of this goal, the company also worked to improve roads, preserve peace, and reduce banditry.

📶 **GO ONLINE** to access your digital course

By the early 1800s, British officials introduced Western education and legal procedures, in part to create a loyal and subservient local population. Missionaries felt Christianity was superior to Indian religions. The British also pressed for social change. They worked to improve the position of women within the family. One law banned **sati** (SUH tee), a custom practiced mainly by the upper classes. It called for a widow to join her husband in death by throwing herself on his funeral pyre.

However, the British used caste differences to their advantage. Caste was used to determine how the native population could best serve British rule. The census the British implemented made caste distinctions more rigid and permanent.

Increasing Discontent In the 1850s, the British East India Company took several unpopular steps that deepened anger with the British. The company had relied on Indian soldiers, called **sepoys,** (SEE poyz), that it had recruited for service. Sepoys had helped the company expand its control of India. As its empire grew, the British required sepoys to serve anywhere, either in India or overseas. The East India Company, prompted by Indian reformers, also passed a law that allowed widows to remarry.

The final insult came in 1857 when the British issued new rifles to the sepoys. Troops had to bite off the tips of cartridges before loading them into the rifles. The cartridges, however, were greased with animal fat—either from cows, which Hindus considered sacred, or from pigs, which were forbidden to Muslims. When troops refused the order to "load rifles," they were dismissed without pay or imprisoned.

The Uprising of 1857 Angry sepoys rose up against their British officers. The Uprising of 1857 (which the British called the Sepoy Rebellion) swept across northern and central India. Several sepoy regiments, joined by other Indian leaders, marched off to Delhi, the old Mughal capital. There, they hailed the last Mughal ruler as their leader. Leaders called on both Hindus and Muslims to support the uprising.

In some places, the sepoys brutally massacred British men, women, and children. The British soon rallied and crushed the revolt. They then took terrible revenge for their earlier losses, torching villages and slaughtering thousands of unarmed Indians.

Impact of the Uprising The Uprising left a bitter legacy of fear, hatred, and mistrust on both sides. It also brought major changes in British policy.

>> **Infer** Indian sepoys were soldiers employed by the British East India Company in the mid-1800s. What item or items in the image reflect India's culture, and which show a British influence?

BOUNCE to Activate Gallery

>> During the Uprising of 1857, the British battled Indian forces around Delhi, a city that was alternately controlled by both the British and the sepoys.

In 1858, Parliament ended the rule of the East India Company and put India directly under the British crown. It sent more troops to India, taxing Indians to pay the cost of these occupying forces.

The rebellion slowed the "reforms" that had angered Hindus and Muslims. In India, discontent continued to feed a growing nationalist movement. Indian nationalists later called the 1857 uprising India's First War of Independence.

☑ **IDENTIFY CAUSE AND EFFECT** What was the primary cause of the Sepoy Rebellion?

India Under British Rule

After 1858, Parliament set up a system of colonial rule in India which became known as the British Raj. A British **viceroy** in India governed in the name of the queen, and British officials held the top positions in the civil service and army. Indians filled most other jobs. With their cooperation, the British made India the "brightest jewel" in the crown of their empire.

British policies were designed to fit India into the overall British economy. At the same time, British officials felt they were helping India to modernize. In their terms, modernizing meant adopting not only Western technology but also Western culture.

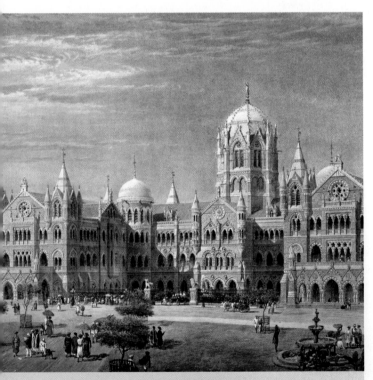

>> This railway station was built in India in 1878 during the British Raj. British architects incorporated traditional Indian architectural features into the design.

🎬 BOUNCE to Activate Illustration

An Unequal Partnership Britain saw India both as a market and as a source of raw materials. To this end, the British built roads and an impressive railroad network. Improved transportation let the British sell their factory-made goods across the subcontinent and carry Indian cotton, jute, and coal to coastal ports for transport to factories in England.

New methods of communication, such as the telegraph, also gave Britain better control of India. After the Suez Canal opened in 1869, British trade with India soared. But it remained an unequal partnership, favoring the British. The British flooded India with inexpensive, machine-made textiles, ruining India's once-prosperous hand-weaving industry.

Britain also transformed Indian agriculture. It encouraged nomadic herders to settle into farming and pushed farmers to grow cash crops, such as cotton, that could be sold on the world market. However, British land policies resulted in peasants losing property, leading to a steady decline in the standard of living for most Indians. Clearing new farmlands led to massive **deforestation,** or cutting of trees, and other environmental destruction.

The Strain of Population Growth The British introduced medical improvements as new farming methods increased food production. The result was rapid population growth.

The rising numbers put a strain on the food supply, especially as farmland was turned over to growing cash crops instead of food. In the late 1800s, terrible famines swept India.

Some Benefit from Colonial Rule On the positive side, British rule brought some degree of peace and order to the countryside. Railroads helped Indians move around the country, while the telegraph and postal system improved communication. Greater contact helped Indians bridge regional differences and develop a sense of national unity.

The upper classes, especially, benefited from some British policies. They sent their sons to British schools, where they were trained for posts in the civil service and military. Indian landowners and princes, who still ruled their own territories, grew rich from exporting cash crops.

☑ **IDENTIFY CAUSE AND EFFECT** What were some impacts of British colonial rule on agriculture in India?

SOME EFFECTS OF THE BRITISH RAJ

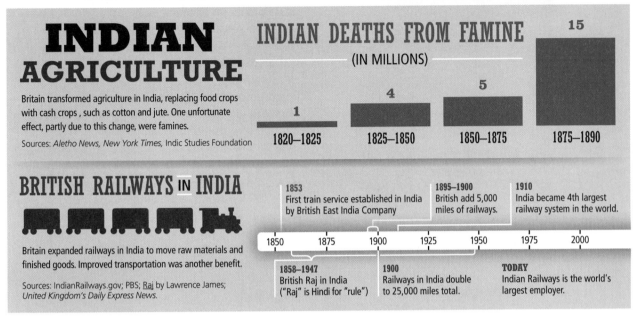

INDIAN AGRICULTURE

Britain transformed agriculture in India, replacing food crops with cash crops , such as cotton and jute. One unfortunate effect, partly due to this change, were famines.

Sources: *Aletho News, New York Times,* Indic Studies Foundation

INDIAN DEATHS FROM FAMINE
(IN MILLIONS)

1820–1825	1825–1850	1850–1875	1875–1890
1	4	5	15

BRITISH RAILWAYS IN INDIA

Britain expanded railways in India to move raw materials and finished goods. Improved transportation was another benefit.

Sources: IndianRailways.gov; PBS; <u>Raj</u> by Lawrence James; *United Kingdom's Daily Express News.*

1853 First train service established in India by British East India Company

1895–1900 British add 5,000 miles of railways.

1910 India became 4th largest railway system in the world.

1850   1875   1900   1925   1950   1975   2000

1858–1947 British Raj in India ("Raj" is Hindi for "rule")

1900 Railways in India double to 25,000 miles total.

TODAY Indian Railways is the world's largest employer.

>> **Support a Point of View with Evidence** The graph and timeline show some effects of the British Raj. How did British economic policies contribute to famine?

Diverse Views on Culture

Some educated Indians, impressed by British power and technology, urged India to follow a Western model of progress. These mostly upper-class Indians had learned English and adopted many Western ways. Other Indians felt that the path to freedom lay within their own Hindu or Muslim cultures.

Indian Attitudes In the early 1800s, **Ram Mohun Roy** combined both views. A great scholar, he knew Sanskrit, Persian, and Arabic classics, as well as English, Greek, and Latin works. Roy felt that India could learn from the West. At the same time, he wanted to revitalize and reform traditional Indian culture.

Roy condemned some traditions, such as rigid caste distinctions, child marriage, sati, and **purdah** (PUR duh), the isolation of women in separate quarters. But he also set up educational societies that helped revive pride in Indian culture. Because of his influence on later leaders, he is often hailed today as the founder of Indian nationalism.

Westerner Attitudes The British disagreed among themselves about India. A few admired Indian theology and philosophy. As Western scholars translated Indian classics, they acquired respect for India's ancient heritage. Western writers and philosophers borrowed ideas from Hinduism and Buddhism.

On the other hand, few British people knew about Indian achievements and dismissed Indian culture with contempt. In an essay on whether Indians should be taught in English or their own languages, British historian Thomas Macaulay arrogantly wrote that "a single shelf of a good European library is worth the whole native literature of India and Arabia." This view of Indian civilization was commonly accepted in Britain and elsewhere in Europe.

☑ **COMPARE AND CONTRAST** What were some differing views among British people about the culture of India?

The Growth of Indian Nationalism

Under British rule, a class of Western-educated Indians emerged. The British expected this elite class to support British rule. As it turned out, exposure to European ideas had another effect. By the late 1800s, Western-educated Indians were

>> AC Mazumdar served as president of the Indian National Congress, which pushed for self-rule for India.

Some members of the party began to call on Indians to boycott British goods in favor of Indian-made products. They reached out to India's diverse social classes. Overall, though, members of the Indian National Congress believed in peaceful protest to gain their objectives.

Formation of the Muslim League At first, Muslims and Hindus worked together for self-rule. In time, however, Muslim elites grew anxious that their interests were not being represented by the Congress party and worried that a government run by a Hindu majority would oppress Muslims.

In 1906, a group of Muslim leaders formed the Muslim League to protect the rights and interests of Muslims in India. The Muslim League initially favored British rule, but before long, it called for self-rule, as well as for Muslim-Hindu unity to achieve this goal. Eventually, by 1930, members of the league began talking of a separate Muslim country.

☑ **IDENTIFY CAUSE AND EFFECT** What was one cause of the Indian nationalist movement?

spearheading a nationalist movement. Seeing the contradiction between Western ideals of democracy and equality and the reality of domination and inequality under colonial rule, they were determined to seek independence.

Indian National Congress By the late 1800s, Indians, especially from the educated class, were discussing how to change British rule. In 1885, nationalist leaders organized the Indian National Congress, which became known as the Congress party.

At first, members of the Indian National Congress called for reforms in British rule. Over time, they called for greater democracy, which they felt should allow Indians to help rule the country. The Indian National Congress looked forward to eventual self-rule but supported Western-style modernization.

☑ ASSESSMENT

1. **Analyze Information** Why did the Uprising of 1857 leave "a bitter legacy of fear, hatred, and mistrust on both sides"?

2. **Analyze Information** What was one specific rule put in place by the East India Company that angered and offended sepoys?

3. **Analyze Information** Who benefited from British rule over India?

4. **Infer** How did Ram Mohun Roy view the British?

5. **Analyze Information** How did British rule contribute to the development of Indian nationalism?

6. **Quest Connections** What aspect of the British raj do you think had the greatest long-term impact on India?

15.5

The antiquated Chinese fleet was outmatched by larger, more technologically advanced British warships during the Opium War.

China and the West

For centuries, Chinese regulations had strictly controlled foreign trade, ensuring that China had a favorable balance of trade with other nations. **Balance of trade** refers to the difference in value between how much a country imports and how much it exports. By the 1800s, however, Western nations were using their growing power to weave a web of influence over East Asia, which tilted the balance of trade in their favor.

Economic Interest in China

Chinese rulers had limited the activities of foreign traders. European merchants were restricted to a small area in southern China. China sold them silk, porcelain, and tea in exchange for gold and silver. Under this arrangement, China enjoyed a **trade surplus,** exporting more than it imported. Westerners, on the other hand, had a **trade deficit** with China, buying more from the Chinese than they sold to them. In 1796, the British requested more trading rights. The emperor Qianlong refused, saying that there was nothing in the West that China needed.

By the late 1700s, two developments were underway that transformed China's relations with the Western world. First, China entered a period of decline.

Second, the Industrial Revolution created a need for expanded markets for European goods. At the same time, it gave the West superior military power.

The Opium War During the late 1700s, British merchants discovered they could make huge profits by trading opium grown in India for Chinese tea. Soon, many Chinese had become addicted to the drug. Silver flowed out of China in payment for the drug, disrupting the economy.

 BOUNCE to Activate Flipped Video

Objectives

Describe how Westerners tried to gain trade rights in China.

Explain how reformers tried to strengthen China.

Understand why the Qing dynasty fell.

Key Terms

balance of trade
trade surplus
trade deficit
Opium War
indemnity
extraterritoriality
Taiping Rebellion
Sino-Japanese War
Open Door Policy
Guang Xu
Boxer Uprising
Sun Yixian

GO ONLINE to access your digital course

The Chinese government outlawed opium and executed Chinese drug dealers. They called on Britain to stop the trade. The British refused, insisting on the right of free trade. In 1839, Chinese warships clashed with British merchants, triggering the **Opium War.** British gunboats, equipped with the latest in firepower, bombarded Chinese coastal and river ports. With outdated weapons and fighting methods, the Chinese were easily defeated.

Unequal Treaties In 1842, Britain made China accept the Treaty of Nanjing (nahn jing). It was the first of a series of "unequal treaties" that forced China to give up rights to Western powers. Under the Treaty of Nanjing, Britain received a huge **indemnity,** or payment for losses in the war. The British also gained the island of Hong Kong. China had to open five ports to foreign trade and grant British citizens in China **extraterritoriality,** the right to live under their own laws and be tried in their own courts.

Finally, the treaty included a "most favored nation" clause. It said that if the Chinese granted rights to another nation, Britain would automatically receive the same rights.

The Opium War was the first of a series of trading wars that set a pattern for later encounters between China and the West. France and the United States soon forced China to sign treaties, giving them rights similar to those the British had won. Western powers then continued to squeeze China to win additional rights, such as opening more ports to trade and letting Christian missionaries preach in China.

☑ **DESCRIBE** Describe how British trade with China triggered the Opium War.

The Taiping Rebellion and a Weakened China

By the 1800s, the Qing dynasty was in decline. Irrigation systems and canals were poorly maintained, leading to massive flooding of the Yellow River valley. The population explosion that had begun a century earlier created great hardships for China's peasants as they tried to feed more and more people.

An extravagant imperial court, tax evasion by the rich, and widespread official corruption added to the peasants' burden. Even the honored civil service was rocked by bribery and cheating scandals. As poverty and misery increased, peasants rebelled.

The Taiping Rebellion Throughout its long history, China was plagued by peasant uprisings, but the frequency and extent of revolts grew in the 1800s. The most shattering was the **Taiping Rebellion** (ty ping), which lasted from 1850 to 1864.

Its leader, Hong Xiuquan (shoh chwahn), was a village teacher who had failed the civil service exams several times. Inspired by religious visions, he set himself up as a revolutionary prophet.

He wanted to topple the hated Qing dynasty and set up a "Heavenly Kingdom of Great Peace"— the Taiping. Hong, influenced by both Confucian and Christian teachings, called for radical change. He wanted land reform, community ownership of property, equality of women and men, and strict morality.

Hong won followers among the poor and outcast. At first, some Westerners sympathized with the rebels but then realized that if the Qing dynasty fell, their trading rights could be lost. As the powerful Taiping movement spread, rebels won control of large parts of China. It took the government 15 years and vast sums of money to defeat the rebellion.

The Taiping Rebellion almost toppled the Qing dynasty. It is estimated that more than 20 million Chinese died in the fighting. The Qing government survived, but it had to share power with regional commanders who had helped crush the rebellion.

>> Troops from the Qing dynasty scale the walls to recapture the rebel capital during the Taiping Rebellion.

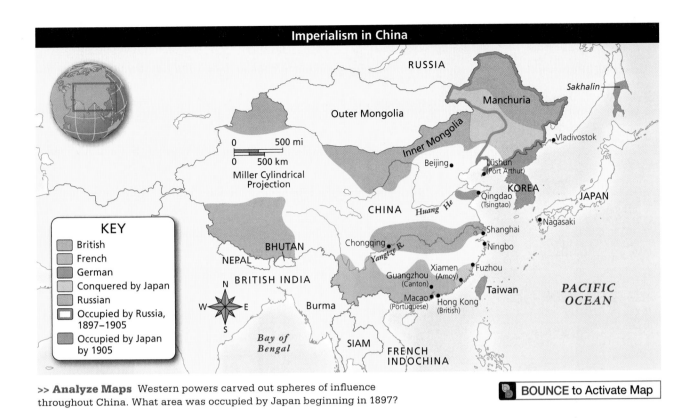

>> **Analyze Maps** Western powers carved out spheres of influence throughout China. What area was occupied by Japan beginning in 1897?

BOUNCE to Activate Map

During the rebellion, European powers kept up pressure on China. Russia seized lands in northern China. It then built the port of Vladivostok on the Pacific coast.

☑ **EXPLAIN** How did the Taiping Rebellion and other internal problems weaken the Qing dynasty?

Reform Efforts in China

By the mid-1800s, educated Chinese were divided over the need to reform China by adopting Western ways. Most saw no reason to build new industries because China's wealth came from land. Although Chinese merchants were allowed to do business, they were not seen as a source of economic prosperity for the country.

Scholar-officials also disapproved of the ideas of Western missionaries, whose emphasis on individual choice challenged the Confucian order. They saw Western technology as dangerous, too, because it threatened Confucian ways that had served China successfully for so long.

The imperial court was a center of conservative opposition. By the late 1800s, the empress Ci Xi (tsih shee) had gained power. A strong-willed ruler, she surrounded herself with advisers who were deeply committed to Confucian traditions.

Self-Strengthening Movement Some Chinese, however, wanted to adapt Western ideas. In the 1860s, reformers launched the "self-strengthening movement." They imported Western technology, setting up factories to make modern weapons.

They developed shipyards, railroads, mining, and light industry. The Chinese translated Western works on science, government, and the economy.

The movement made limited progress though, because the government did not rally behind it. Also, while China was undertaking a few selected reforms, the Western powers—and Japan—were moving ahead rapidly.

The Sino-Japanese War The island nation of Japan modernized rapidly after 1868. It then joined the Western imperialists in the competition for a global empire.

In 1894, Japanese pressure on China led to the **Sino-Japanese War.** It ended in disaster for China, with Japan gaining Korea and the island of Taiwan. When the two powers met at the peace table, there was a telling difference in outlook. Japanese officials dressed in Western-style clothing while the Chinese wore traditional robes.

Spheres of Influence The crushing defeat revealed China's weakness. Western powers moved swiftly

>> **Analyze Political Cartoons** The dogs represent the United States, Japan, and Britain. They guard an open door that says "China Trade." Which country opened the door?

>> Chinese rebels nicknamed Boxers wanted to drive out foreigners from their country. **Identify Cause and Effect** Why were the Boxers angry about the foreign presence in China?

BOUNCE to Activate Gallery

to carve out spheres of influence along the Chinese coast. The British took the Chang River valley.

The French acquired the territory near their colony of Indochina. Germany and Russia gained territory in northern China.

The United States, a longtime trader with the Chinese, did not take part in the carving up of China. It feared that European powers might shut out American merchants. In 1899, it called for a policy to keep Chinese trade open to everyone on an equal basis. The imperial powers more or less accepted the idea of an **Open Door Policy,** as it came to be called. No one, however, consulted the Chinese about the policy.

Hundred Days of Reform Defeated by Japan and humiliated by Westerners, Chinese reformers looked for a scapegoat. Reformers blamed conservative officials for not modernizing China. They argued that Confucius himself had been a reformer and that China could not look to a golden age in the past but must modernize as Japan had.

In 1898, a young emperor, **Guang Xu** (gwahng shoo), launched the Hundred Days of Reform. New laws set out to modernize the civil service exams, streamline government, and encourage new industries. Reforms affected schools, the military, and the bureaucracy.

Conservatives soon rallied against the reform effort. The emperor was imprisoned, and the aging empress Ci Xi reasserted control. Reformers fled for their lives.

☑ **IDENTIFY** Identify reformers' solutions for China's problems.

The Fall of the Qing Dynasty

By 1900, China was in turmoil. Anger against foreigners was growing. While the Chinese welcomed some Western ideas, they resented Christian missionaries who showed little respect for Chinese traditions and Confucian ideas. The presence of foreign troops was another source of discontent.

Protected by extraterritoriality, foreigners ignored Chinese laws and lived in their own communities. Chinese people were discriminated against in Western neighborhoods.

The Boxer Uprising Anti-foreign feeling finally exploded in the **Boxer Uprising.** In 1899, groups of

Chinese peasants had formed a secret society, the Righteous Harmonious Fists. Westerners watching them train in the martial arts dubbed them Boxers. Their goal was to drive out the "foreign devils" who were polluting the land with their non-Chinese ways, strange buildings, machines, and telegraph lines.

In late 1899 and throughout 1900, the Boxers attacked and killed foreigners across China. In response, the Western powers and Japan organized a multinational force.

After taking some losses, this force crushed the Boxers and rescued foreigners besieged in Beijing. The empress Ci Xi had at first supported the Boxers but reversed her policy as they retreated.

Consequences of the Uprising In the aftermath of the Boxer Uprising, foreign powers forced China to make still more concessions. The defeat, however, forced even Chinese conservatives to support Westernization. In a rush of reforms, China admitted women to schools and stressed science and mathematics in place of Confucian thought. More students were sent abroad to study.

During the early 1900s, China expanded economically. Mining, shipping, railroads, banking, and exports of cash crops grew. Small-scale Chinese industry developed with the help of foreign capital. A Chinese business class emerged, and a new urban working class began to press for rights in the same way Western workers had done.

Growth of Chinese Nationalism Although the Boxer Uprising failed, the flames of Chinese nationalism spread. Reformers who wanted to strengthen China's government introduced a constitutional monarchy. Some reformers called for a republic.

A passionate spokesman for a Chinese republic was **Sun Yixian** (soon yee shen), also known as Sun Yat-sen. In the early 1900s, he organized the Revolutionary Alliance to rebuild China on "Three Principles of the People." The first principle was nationalism, or freeing China from foreign domination. The second was democracy, or representative government. The third was livelihood, or economic security for all Chinese.

A Republic Is Born When Ci Xi died in 1908, a two-year-old boy inherited the throne. China slipped into chaos. In 1911, uprisings swiftly spread. Peasants, students, warlords, and even court politicians helped topple the Qing dynasty, ending China's 2000-year old monarchy.

>> Known as the Father of Modern China, Sun Yixian founded the Chinese Nationalist Party and became the first president of China after the fall of the Qing dynasty.

Sun Yixian hurried home from a trip to the United States. In early 1912, he was sworn in as president of the new Chinese republic. The republic faced overwhelming problems and was almost constantly at war with itself or foreign invaders.

☑ **IDENTIFY CAUSE AND EFFECT** What caused the Qing dynasty to fall?

☑ ASSESSMENT

1. **Generate Explanations** How did Western powers gain greater trading rights in China?

2. **Summarize** What internal problems threatened the Qing dynasty?

3. **Summarize** What were the goals of Chinese reformers?

4. **Synthesize** Describe how a republic replaced the Qing dynasty.

5. **Connections to Today** Why do you think U.S. balance of trade with large nations like China remains an important concern?

Generate Explanations Emperor Mutsuhito took the name "Meiji," or "enlightened rule," when he came to power. What made his rule "enlightened"?

 BOUNCE to Activate Flipped Video

Objectives

Identify the problems faced by Tokugawa Japan.

Explain how the United States opened Japan to the outside world.

Analyze the causes and effects of the Meiji Restoration.

Describe how Japan began to build an empire.

Key Terms

Matthew Perry
Mutsuhito
Tokyo
Meiji Restoration
Diet
zaibatsu
homogeneous
  society
First Sino-Japanese
  War
Russo-Japanese
  War

The Modernization of Japan

In 1853, United States warships arrived off the coast of Japan demanding Japan open its ports to trade. Japanese leaders debated how to respond. Some resisted giving up their longstanding policy of seclusion. Others felt that the wiser course was to learn from the foreigners.

Unrest in Tokugawa Japan

In the end, Japan abandoned its isolation. As a defense against Western imperialism, Japan decided to learn from the West. It swiftly transformed itself into a modern industrial power and then set out on its own imperialist path.

The Tokugawa Shoguns By 1603, Tokugawa Ieyasu had gained the office of shogun, the top military commander in Japan. This ended a long period of lawlessness and chaos in Japan. Although the emperor still lived in his capital of Kyoto, the shogun held the real power in Edo. The Tokugawa shoguns reimposed centralized feudalism on Japan, bringing the daimyo under their control and presiding over a long period of peace.

In 1637, the Tokugawas closed Japan to foreigners, and barred Japanese from traveling overseas. Their only window on the world was through Nagasaki, where the Dutch were allowed very limited trade.

For almost 250 years, Japan developed in isolation. During that time, the economy expanded, especially internal commerce. Farm output grew, and bustling cities sprang up.

Hardships Grow Economic growth, however, brought changes that put strains on the country. Daimyo suffered financial hardship because their wealth was in land. In a commercial economy, money was needed. Daimyo had the heavy expense of maintaining households in both Edo and their own domains.

Lesser samurai were unhappy, too, because they were no longer fighters. Many were government bureaucrats. Even though they were noble, they lacked the money to live as well as urban merchants. Merchants in turn resented their place at the bottom of the social ladder. No matter how rich they were, they had no political power. Peasants, meanwhile, suffered under heavy taxes.

The government responded by trying to revive old ways, emphasizing farming over commerce and praising traditional values. Efforts at reform failed. By the 1800s, many groups were discontent and had little loyalty to the old system.

☑ **IDENTIFY CAUSE AND EFFECT** By the mid-1800s, why did so many groups of people in Japan feel discontented?

The Opening of Japan

While the shogun faced troubles at home, disturbing news reached him from abroad. With alarm, he heard of how the British had defeated China in the Opium War and how imperialists had forced China to sign unequal treaties. Japanese officials realized it would not be long before Western powers sought trading rights in Japan.

External Pressure Leads to Internal Revolt In July 1853, a fleet of well-armed American ships commanded by Commodore **Matthew Perry** sailed into Tokyo Bay. Perry carried a letter from the president of the United States. It demanded that Japan open its ports to trade.

The shogun's advisers debated what to do. Japan did not have the ability to defend itself against the powerful United States Navy. In the Treaty of Kanagawa in 1854, the shogun Iesada agreed to open three Japanese ports to American ships, where they could take on supplies.

The United States soon won trading and other rights, including extraterritoriality. Britain, France, and Russia demanded and won similar rights. Like the Chinese, the Japanese deeply resented the humiliating terms of these unequal treaties. Some

bitterly criticized the shogun for not taking a strong stand against the foreigners.

Foreign pressure deepened the social and economic unrest. As the crisis worsened, many young, reform-minded samurai rallied around the emperor, long regarded as a figurehead.

In 1867, discontented daimyo and samurai led a revolt that unseated the shogun and "restored" the emperor, **Mutsuhito** to power. He moved from Kyoto, the old imperial capital, to the shogun's palace in Edo, which was renamed **Tokyo,** or "eastern capital." The emperor took the name Meiji (MAY jee), which means "enlightened rule."

The Meiji Restoration The young emperor, just 15 years old, began a long reign known as the **Meiji Restoration.** This period, which lasted from 1868 to 1912, was a major turning point in Japanese history.

The Meiji reformers, who ruled in the emperor's name, were determined to strengthen Japan against the West. Their goal was summarized in their motto, "A rich country, a strong military."

The new leaders set out to study Western ways, adapt them to Japanese needs, and eventually protect Japan from having to give in to Western demands. In 1871, members of the government

>> In this Japanese woodblock print, Japanese boats go out to meet one of Commodore Matthew Perry's ships in Tokyo Bay.

 BOUNCE to Activate Illustration

traveled abroad to learn about Western governments, economies, technology, and customs. The government brought experts from Western countries to Japan and sent young samurai to study in Europe and the United States.

☑ **SUMMARIZE** How did Japan react when it was forced to accept unequal treaties?

Transformation during the Meiji Period

The Meiji reformers faced an enormous task. They were committed to replacing the rigid feudal order with a completely new political and social system and to building a modern industrial economy. Change did not come easily. However, Japan adapted foreign ideas with great speed and success.

Reforming Government The reformers wanted to create a strong central government, equal to those of Western powers. After studying the governments of various European countries, they adapted the German model. In 1889, the emperor issued the Meiji constitution. It set forth the principle that all citizens were equal before the law. Like the German system, however, it gave the emperor autocratic, or unlimited, power. A legislature, called the **Diet,** was formed, made up of one elected house and one house appointed by the emperor. Suffrage, or the right to vote, was also limited.

Japan then set up a Western-style bureaucracy with separate departments to supervise finance, the army, the navy, and education. To strengthen the military, it turned to Western technology and ended the special privileges of samurai. In the past, samurai alone were warriors. In modern Japan, as in the modern West, all men were subject to military service.

Rapid Industrialization Meiji leaders made the economy a major priority. They encouraged Japan's business class to adopt Western methods. The government set up a modern banking system, built railroads, improved ports, and organized a telegraph and postal system.

To get industries started, the government typically built factories and then sold them to wealthy business families who developed them further. With such support, business dynasties like the Mitsubishi and Kawasaki families soon ruled over industrial empires that rivaled the Rockefellers in the United States or the Krupps in Germany. These powerful banking and industrial families were known as **zaibatsu** (zy baht soo).

By the 1890s, industry was booming. With modern machines, silk manufacturing soared. Shipyards, copper and coal mining, and steel making also helped make Japan an industrial powerhouse. As in other industrial countries, the population grew rapidly, and many peasants flocked to the growing cities for work.

Social Changes The constitution ended legal distinctions between classes, thus freeing more people to build the nation. The government set up schools and a university. It hired Westerners to teach modern technology to the new generation.

Despite the reforms, class distinctions survived in Japan as they did in the West. Also, although literacy increased and some women gained an education, women in general were still assigned a secondary role in society.

The reform of the Japanese family system, and women's position in it, became the topic of major debates in the 1870s. Reformers wanted women to become full partners in the process of nation building and to learn skills that would allow them to live on their own.

>> This woodblock print shows the announcement of the new Meiji constitution in 1889, which created a European-style government in Japan. **Analyze Images** What other European influences do you see in the print?

 BOUNCE to Activate Gallery

Investment in Meiji Japan

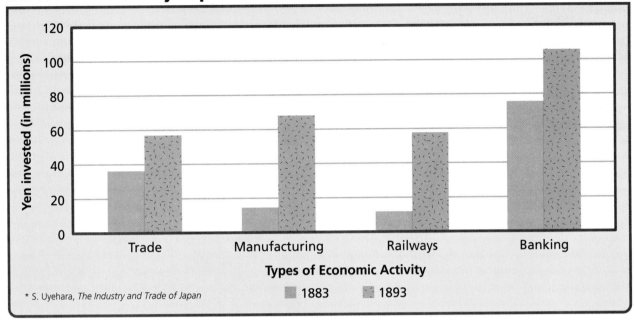

* S. Uyehara, *The Industry and Trade of Japan*

■ 1883 ■ 1893

>> **Analyze Charts** Meiji reformers worked to industrialize Japan. How does the chart reflect this goal?

While the government agreed to some increases in education for women, it dealt harshly with other attempts at change. It took away earlier political and legal rights that women had won. After 1898, Japanese women were forbidden any political participation and legally were placed in the same class as minors.

An Amazing Success Japan modernized with amazing speed during the Meiji period. Its success was due to a number of causes. It was a **homogeneous society**—that is, its people shared a common culture and language. Economic growth during Tokugawa times had set Japan on the road to development. Japan also had experience in learning and adapting ideas from foreign nations, such as China.

Like other people faced with Western imperialism, the Japanese were determined to resist foreign rule. By the 1890s, Japan was strong enough to force Western powers to revise the unequal treaties. By then, it was already competing with the West and acquiring its own overseas empire.

☑ **SUMMARIZE** What changes did the reforms of the Meiji Restoration bring about in Japan?

Japan Builds an Empire

As in Western industrial nations, Japan's economic needs fed its imperialist desires. As a small island nation, Japan lacked many basic resources, including coal, that were essential for industrial growth. Spurred by nationalism and a strong ambition to equal the West, Japan sought to build an empire. With its modern army and navy, it maneuvered for power in East Asia.

Japan Expands In 1894, competition between Japan and China for power in Korea led to the **First Sino-Japanese War.** ("Sino" means "Chinese.") Although China had far greater resources, Japan had benefited from modernization. To the surprise of China and the West, Japan won easily. It used its victory to gain treaty ports in China and control over the island of Taiwan. The war showed that Japan had joined the Western powers in the race for empire.

Ten years later, Japan successfully challenged Russia, its other rival for power in Korea and Manchuria. During the **Russo-Japanese War,** Japan's armies defeated Russian troops in Manchuria, and its navy destroyed almost an entire Russian fleet. For the first time in modern history, an Asian power humbled a European nation.

In the 1905 Treaty of Portsmouth, Japan gained control of Korea as well as rights in parts of Manchuria. This foothold on the mainland would fuel its ambitions in East Asia.

Korea Imperialist rivalries put the spotlight on Korea. Located at a crossroads of East Asia, the

>> **Analyze Political Cartoons** Japan began its imperialist agenda in Korea. Based on the cartoon, who else had imperialist ambitions in Korea?

>> Japan's victory in the Russo-Japanese War forced Russia to abandon its imperialist policies in East Asia.

Korean peninsula was a focus of competition among Russia, China, and Japan.

Korea had been a tributary state to China for many years. A tributary state is independent but acknowledges the supremacy of a stronger state. Although influenced by China, Korea had its own traditions and government. Like China and Japan, Korea had shut its doors to foreigners in the 1600s. It did, however, maintain relations with China and sometimes with Japan.

By the 1800s, Korea faced growing pressure from outsiders. As Chinese power declined, Russia expanded into East Asia. Then, as Japan industrialized, it too eyed Korea. Once again, Korea saw itself as "a shrimp among whales."

In 1876, Japan used its superior power to force Korea to open its ports to Japanese trade. Faced with similar demands from Western powers, Korea had to accept unequal treaties. After defeating China and then Russia, Japan made Korea a protectorate. In 1910, it annexed Korea outright, absorbing the kingdom into the Japanese empire.

Japanese Rule in Korea Japan ruled Korea for 35 years. Like Western imperialists, the Japanese set out to modernize their newly acquired territory. They built factories, railroads, and communications systems. Development, however, generally benefited the colonial power. Under Japanese rule, Koreans produced more rice than ever before, but most of it went to feed the Japanese.

The Japanese were as unpopular in Korea as Western imperialists were elsewhere. They imposed harsh rule on their colony and deliberately set out to erase the Korean language and identity. Repression bred resentment. And resentment, in turn, nourished a Korean nationalist movement.

Nine years after annexation, a nonviolent protest against the Japanese began on March 1, 1919, and soon spread throughout Korea. The Japanese crushed the uprising and massacred many Koreans. The violence did not discourage people who worked to end Japanese rule. Instead, the March First Movement became a rallying symbol for Korean nationalists.

The Koreans would have to wait many years to regain their freedom. By the early 1900s, Japan was the strongest power in Asia. In competition with Western nations, Japan continued to expand in East Asia. In time, Japanese ambitions to control a sphere of influence in the Pacific would put it on a collision course with several Western powers, especially Britain and the United States.

GENERATE EXPLANATIONS How did industrialization help start Japan on an imperialist course?

☑ ASSESSMENT

1. **Cite Evidence** What was one cause of discontent in Tokugawa Japan?

2. **Identify Main Ideas** What demand did the United States make on Japan in 1853?

3. **Make Generalizations** What was the goal of the Meiji reformers?

4. **Identify Cause and Effect** What was the main reason Japan become an imperialist power?

5. **Summarize** Why was the Russo-Japanese War significant?

6. **Connections to Today** Even though the March First Movement failed, March 1 is today celebrated as a national holiday in South Korea. Why do you think that is?

>> This sculpture in Tapgol Park in Seoul, South Korea, honors the struggle for Korean independence from Japanese rule.

15.7

The headquarters of the Dutch East India Company was called Batavia Castle. It was located in present-day Jakarta. The East India Company built trading and military bases throughout the Spice Islands.

🅑 BOUNCE to Activate Flipped Video

Objectives

Describe how Europe and the United States built colonies in Southeast Asia.

Explain how imperialism spread to the islands of the Pacific.

Analyze how Australia and New Zealand achieved self-rule.

Key Terms

French Indochina
Mongkut
Spanish-American
 War
Liliuokalani
indigenous
penal colony
Maori

Southeast Asia and the Pacific

By the mid-1800s, leaders throughout Southeast Asia faced the growing threat of Western imperialism. Before long, Western industrial powers divided up the region in their race for raw materials, new markets, and Christian converts.

European Imperialism in Southeast Asia

Southeast Asia commands the sea lanes between India and China. The region had long been influenced by both civilizations. In the 1500s and 1600s, European merchants gained footholds in Southeast Asia, but most of the peoples of the region remained independent.

When the Industrial Revolution set off the Age of Imperialism, the situation changed. Western powers, especially the Dutch, British, and French, used modern armies and technology to colonize much of Southeast Asia.

The Dutch East Indies In the 1600s, the Dutch East India Company gained control of the fabled riches of the Moluccas, or Spice Islands. The Dutch then reached out to dominate the rest of the East Indies—what is now Indonesia. The region included larger islands, such as Java, Sumatra, and Borneo, as well as many smaller islands.

By 1800, the Dutch government had taken over these areas from the Dutch East India Company. During the next century, the

📶 **GO ONLINE** to access your digital course

Dutch faced uprisings, but they gradually extended their control. Like other imperialist powers, the Dutch expected their Southeast Asia colonies to produce profitable crops of coffee, indigo, and spices. Under colonial rule, local people were enslaved and forced to work on plantations, raising anger and criticism.

The British in Burma and Malaya In the early 1800s, the rulers of Burma (present-day Myanmar) clashed with the British, who were expanding eastward from India. The Burmese misjudged British strength and suffered disastrous defeats in several wars. By 1886, Britain had annexed Burma. The Burmese, however, constantly resisted British rule.

At the same time, the British pushed south through the Malay Peninsula. The bustling port of Singapore grew up at the southern tip of the peninsula. Singapore stood on the sea route between the Indian Ocean and the China Sea. Soon, rubber and tin from Malaya, along with profits from Asian trade were flowing through Singapore to enrich Britain.

The French in Indochina The French, meanwhile, were building an empire on the Southeast Asian mainland. Like other imperialist powers, they wanted political influence, raw materials, and markets in the region.

In the early 1800s, French missionaries began winning converts in what is today Vietnam. In response to growing Western influence, Vietnamese officials tried to suppress Christianity by killing converts and priests. The French used the murders as a reason to invade.

Like the Burmese, the Vietnamese misjudged European power. Starting in 1858, the French attacked and took over parts of Vietnam. The Vietnamese fought fiercely but could not withstand superior European firepower. The French eventually seized all of Vietnam, Laos, and Cambodia. The West referred to these holdings as **French Indochina.**

Siam Stays Independent The kingdom of Siam (present-day Thailand) lay between British-ruled Burma and French Indochina. Siam escaped becoming a European colony partly because its rulers did not underestimate Western power and avoided incidents that might provoke invasion.

Although the king of Siam, **Mongkut** (mahng KOOT), had to accept some unequal treaties, he set Siam on the road to modernization. He and his son, Chulalongkorn, who ruled from 1868 to 1910, reformed the government, modernized the army, and hired Western experts to train Thais in the new technology. They abolished slavery and gave women some choice in marriage. Thai students

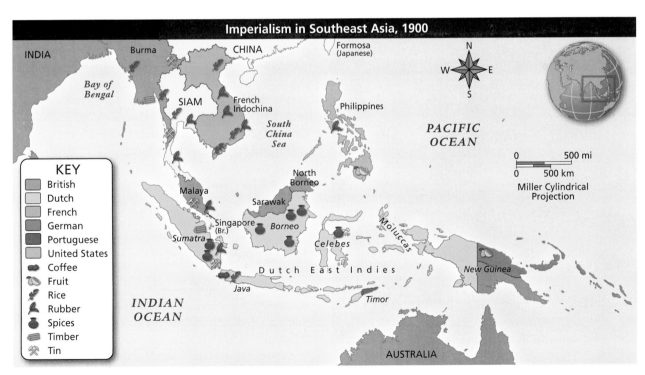

>> **Analyze Maps** Europeans sought to exploit the vast natural resources of Southeast Asia. According to the map, to which resources did the Dutch have exclusive access?

traveled abroad and spread Western ways when they returned home. As Siam modernized, Chulalongkorn bargained to remove the unequal treaties.

In the end, both Britain and France saw the advantage of making Siam a buffer, or neutral zone, between their colonies. In the early 1900s, they guaranteed its independence. But to prevent other imperialist powers from pushing into Siam, each set up its own sphere of influence there.

Characteristics of Colonial Southeast Asia By the 1890s, Europeans controlled most of Southeast Asia. They introduced modern technology and expanded commerce and industry. Europeans directed the mining of tin, the harvesting of rubber, and the building of harbors and railroads. But these changes benefited the European colonizers far more than they did the Southeast Asians.

☑ **DESCRIBE** How did the Burmese and the Vietnamese respond to colonization attempts?

>> During the Spanish-American War, the U.S. Navy destroyed Spanish ships in the Battle of Manila Bay in the Philippines.

▶ BOUNCE to Activate Map

Military Might and the Philippines

In the 1500s, Spain had seized the Philippines and extended its rule over the islands. Catholic missionaries spread Christianity among the Filipinos and the Catholic Church gained enormous power and wealth. Many Filipinos accused the Church of abusing its position. By the late 1800s, their anger fueled strong resistance to Spanish rule.

Leaders like José Rizal, a doctor who had studied abroad, called on Filipinos to use nonviolent means to win reforms. Although captured and executed by the Spanish, Rizal continued to inspire Filipinos eager to free their country from foreign rule.

Battles in the Philippines The United States became involved in the Philippines almost by accident. In 1898, war broke out between Spain and the United States over Cuba's effort to win independence from Spain. During the **Spanish-American War,** American battleships destroyed the Spanish fleet, which was stationed in the Philippines.

Seizing the moment, Filipino leaders declared independence from Spain. Rebel soldiers threw their support into the fight against Spanish troops. In return for their help, the Filipino rebels expected the United States to recognize their independence. Instead, the peace settlement with Spain placed the Philippines under American control.

Bitterly disappointed, Filipino nationalists renewed their struggle. From 1899 to 1901, Filipinos led by Emilio Aguinaldo (ah gee NAHL doh) battled American forces. Thousands of Americans and hundreds of thousands of Filipinos died. In the end, the Americans crushed the rebellion. The United States set out to modernize the Philippines, promising Filipinos self-rule some time in the future.

☑ **IDENTIFY MAIN IDEAS** How did the United States gain control of the Philippines?

Strategic Holdings in the Pacific Islands

In the 1800s, the industrialized powers began to take an interest in the islands of the Pacific. The thousands of islands splashed across the Pacific include the three regions of Melanesia, Micronesia, and Polynesia.

At first, American, French, and British whaling and sealing ships looked for bases to take on supplies while they were operating in the Pacific. Missionaries, too, moved into the region and opened the way for political involvement. For much of the 1800s, whalers, merchants, and missionaries were the only visitors to the Pacific Islands.

From Ports of Call to Colonies By the late 1800s, nationalist rivalries led European powers to claim Pacific islands as colonies. France set up a protectorate over Tahiti, but soon made it a colony. The race was on for control of the Pacific Islands.

In 1878, the United States secured an unequal treaty from Samoa, a group of islands in the South Pacific. The United States gained rights such as extraterritoriality and a naval station.

Other nations gained similar agreements. As their rivalry increased, the United States, Germany, and Britain agreed to a triple protectorate over Samoa.

Beginning in the mid-1800s, American sugar growers pressed for power in the Hawaiian Islands. When the Hawaiian queen **Liliuokalani** (lih lee uh oh kuh LAH nee) tried to reduce foreign influence, American planters overthrew her in 1893. They then asked the United States to annex Hawaii, which it did in 1898. Supporters of annexation argued that if the United States did not take Hawaii, Britain or Japan might do so.

>> Queen Liliuokalani reduced benefits to American businesses operating in Hawaii, generating opposition from businessmen like Sanford Dole of the pineapple industry.

Imperialist Rivalry By 1900, the United States, Britain, France, and Germany had claimed nearly every island in the Pacific. Japan, too, wanted a share of the region. Eventually, it would gain German possessions in the Pacific, setting the stage for a growing rivalry with the United States.

Although small in size, the Pacific Islands offered economic benefits to colonial powers. In Hawaii, sugarcane plantations were profitable. Elsewhere, imperial powers tapped into local resources such as nickel, or even guano, bird droppings used to make fertilizer. For imperialist powers locked in a global race for colonies, the Pacific Islands provided useful ports for their merchant ships and warships.

☑ **RECALL** Why did some Americans think the United States should control Hawaii?

Europeans in Australia

The Dutch in the 1600s were the first Europeans to reach Australia—the world's largest island and smallest continent. In 1770, Captain James Cook claimed Australia for Britain. For a time, however, Australia remained too distant to attract European settlers.

Australia's Indigenous People Like most regions claimed by imperialist powers, Australia had long been inhabited by other people. The first settlers had reached Australia about 40,000 years ago, probably from Southeast Asia. These **indigenous,** or original, inhabitants were called Aborigines, a European word for earliest people to live in a place. Today, many Australian Aborigines call themselves Kooris.

Isolated from the larger world, the Aborigines lived in small hunting and food-gathering bands, much as their Stone Age ancestors had. Aboriginal groups spoke as many as 250 distinct languages. The arrival of white settlers was a catastrophe for indigenous Australians, as it had been for the indigenous people of the Americas.

A Penal Colony Events in North America and Britain ended Australia's isolation. During the 1700s, Britain had sent convicts to its North American colonies, especially to Georgia. The American Revolution closed that outlet just as the Industrial Revolution was disrupting British society. British prisons were filled with poor people arrested for minor crimes such as stealing food, or serious crimes, such as murder.

To fill the need for prisons, Britain made Australia into a **penal colony,** a place to send people convicted of crimes. The first British ships, carrying about 700 convicts, arrived in Botany Bay, Australia, in 1788. The men, women, and children who survived the grueling eight-month voyage faced more hardships on shore. Many were city dwellers with no farming skills. Under the brutal discipline of soldiers, work gangs cleared land for settlement.

Emigration to Australia In the early 1800s, Britain encouraged free citizens to emigrate to Australia by offering them land and tools. As the newcomers occupied coastal lands, they thrust aside or killed the Aborigines.

In time, a prosperous wool industry grew up as settlers found that the land and climate suited sheepherding. In 1851, a gold rush in eastern Australia set off a population boom as gold hunters from around the world headed to the island continent. Many gold hunters stayed on to become ranchers and farmers.

They pushed into the rugged interior known as the Outback and displaced the Aborigines as they carved out huge sheep ranches and wheat farms.

>> Fireworks blaze over Perth, Australia, on Australia Day, which commemorates Australia's first European settlers. **Infer** How might Australia's aboriginal population feel about the celebration of Australia Day?

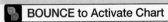
BOUNCE to Activate Chart

By the late 1800s, Australia had won a place in the growing world economy.

Self-Rule in Australia Australia was made up of separate colonies scattered around the continent. Britain worried about interference from other imperialist European powers. To counter this threat and to boost development, it responded to Australian demands for self-rule. In 1901, Britain helped the colonies unite into the independent Commonwealth of Australia. The new country kept its ties to Britain by recognizing the British monarch as its head of state.

The Australian constitution set up a federal system that limited the power of the central government. Its Parliament has a Senate and House of Representative, but its executive is a prime minister chosen by the majority party in Parliament.

Unlike Britain and the United States, Australia quickly granted women the right to vote. In 1856, some Australian states introduced the secret ballot, which became known as the Australian ballot. Later, other countries adopted this practice.

☑ **IDENTIFY CAUSE AND EFFECT** What effects did colonization have on Australia's indigenous population?

New Zealand's Story

About 1,000 miles southeast of Australia lies New Zealand. It consists of several islands. New Zealand was the last landmass in the world to be settled. Like Australia, New Zealand had its own indigenous people, the **Maori** (MAH oh ree).

Arrival of the Maori The ancestors of the Maori had reached New Zealand from Polynesia in the 1200s. These seafaring people were skilled navigators who relied on the winds, stars, and ocean currents to reach land.

In New Zealand, the Maori lived in small hunting bands and raised sweet potatoes and yams brought with them on their voyages. They had an extensive oral history, in which they recorded long genealogies, or family trees. They engaged in warfare but also traded with one another.

Arrival of Europeans In 1642, a Dutch explorer was the first European to reach New Zealand. Captain James Cook claimed the islands for Britain in 1769. The first Europeans arrived in New Zealand in the late 1700s.

Early settlements were outposts for whalers, seal hunters, and lumbering operations. In 1814, missionaries arrived to convert the Maori to Christianity.

White settlers were attracted to New Zealand by its mild climate and good soil. They introduced sheep and cattle and were soon exporting wool, mutton, and beef. Maori and Europeans traded in basic goods, exchanging potatoes and pork for European firearms.

Maori Struggles In 1840, Britain annexed New Zealand in part to keep the French from claiming any of it. Unlike Australia, where the Aborigines were spread thinly across a large continent, the Maori were concentrated in a smaller area. About 100,000 Maoris lived in New Zealand before the arrival of Europeans.

As colonists poured in, they took over more land. Disputes over land led to a series of fierce wars with the Maori. Even though Europeans offered to buy land, the Maori were unwilling to give up land they had farmed collectively for generations.

Many Maori died in clashes with settlers. Still more perished from disease brought by Europeans. By 1872, the Maori resistance had crumbled. The Maori population had fallen drastically, to less than 45,000. Only recently has the Maori population started to grow again.

The Nation of New Zealand Like settlers in Australia, white New Zealanders achieved self-rule. In 1893, New Zealand became the first modern country to give women the right to vote. In 1907, New Zealand became a dominion within the British empire with its own parliament, prime minister, and elected legislature.

Like Australia, New Zealand won independence faster than other territories claimed by the British. One reason was that both had large populations of white settlers. Imperialist nations like Britain felt that whites could govern themselves. Nonwhites in places like India were thought to be incapable of shouldering such responsibility.

☑ **COMPARE AND CONTRAST** Compare and contrast the European settlement of Australia and New Zealand.

>> Traditional Maori tattooing, which often covers the face, reveals important information about the wearer's family and identity, such as tribal affiliations and social status.

☑ **ASSESSMENT**

1. **Identify Supporting Details** How did industrialized powers divide up the various lands of Southeast Asia and the Pacific?

2. **Contrast** How was Siam different from the other nations of Southeast Asia?

3. **Draw Conclusions** Why were Filipino rebels disappointed when the United States took control of the Philippines?

4. **Synthesize** Describe how Hawaii became part of the United States.

5. **Identify Cause and Effect** Why did Britain grant self-rule to Australia and New Zealand?

6. **Connections to Today** Describe the relations of modern Hawaii and modern Australia to the nations that gained control of them in the 1800s.

Objectives

Identify the political problems faced by new Latin American nations.

Describe Mexico's struggle to achieve stability.

Explain why Latin America entered a cycle of economic dependence.

Analyze the influence of the United States on Latin America, including the opening of the Panama Canal.

Analyze how Canada achieved self-rule.

Key Terms

regionalism
caudillo
Benito Juárez
La Reforma
peonage
Monroe Doctrine
Panama Canal
confederation
dominion
métis

The Americas in the Age of Imperialism

After the wars of independence in the early 1800s, Latin American nations hoped to build democratic governments. That dream soon faded as power struggles erupted across the region. During the Age of Imperialism, Latin American economies became increasingly dependent upon those of more developed countries. Britain, and later the United States, invested heavily in Latin America.

Political Problems Linger

Simón Bolívar had hoped to create a single Latin American nation. After all, the people shared a common language, religion, and cultural heritage. But feuds among leaders, geographic barriers, and local nationalism shattered that dream of unity. In the end, 20 separate nations emerged.

These new nations wrote constitutions modeled on that of the United States. They set up republics with elected legislatures. During the 1800s, however, most Latin American nations were plagued by revolts, civil war, and dictatorships.

The Legacy of Colonialism Many problems facing the new nations had their origins in colonial rule. Spain and Portugal had kept tight control on their colonies, giving them little experience with self-government. The wars of independence barely changed the colonial social and political hierarchy. Creoles simply replaced *peninsulares* as the ruling class. The Roman Catholic Church kept its privileged position and still controlled huge amounts of land.

For most people—mestizos, other mixed-race people, Black people, and Indians—life did not improve after independence. The new constitutions guaranteed equality before the law, but deep-rooted inequalities remained. Voting rights were limited. Racial prejudice was widespread, and land remained in the hands of a few. Owners of haciendas ruled their estates, and the peasants who worked them, like medieval European lords.

The Rise of Dictators With few roads and no tradition of unity, the new nations were weakened by **regionalism,** or loyalty to a local area. Local strongmen, called *caudillos* (kow THEE yohs), assembled private armies to resist the central government.

At times, popular caudillos, sometimes former military leaders, gained national power. They looted treasuries and ignored constitutions. Supported by the military, they ruled as dictators.

Power struggles among competing strongmen led to frequent revolts that changed little except the name of the leader. In the long run, power remained in the hands of a privileged few who had no desire to share it.

Conservatives and Liberals As in Europe, the ruling elite in Latin America were divided between conservatives and liberals. Conservatives defended the traditional social order, favored press censorship, and strongly supported the Catholic Church. They wanted to maintain the rigid social distinctions between landowners and peasants, fearing that change would bring chaos and disorder.

Liberals backed Enlightenment ideas of liberty, equality, and popular sovereignty. They supported laissez-faire economics, opposing government interference in free enterprise. They also favored religious toleration and freedom of the press. They wanted to weaken the power of the Catholic Church by breaking up its vast landholdings and ending its monopoly on education. Liberals saw themselves as enlightened supporters of progress but often showed little concern for the needs of the majority of the people.

☑ **IDENTIFY CAUSE AND EFFECT** What political obstacles to democracy were caused by lingering effects of colonial rule in Latin America?

Mexico's Search for Stability

During the 1800s, each Latin American nation followed its own course. Mexico provides an example of the challenges facing many Latin American nations.

In the years after independence, large landowners, army leaders, and the Catholic Church dominated Mexican politics. Deep social divisions separated wealthy creoles from mestizos and Indians who lived in desperate poverty. Bitter battles between conservatives and liberals led to revolts and the rise of dictators.

Santa Anna and War With the United States Between 1833 and 1855, an ambitious and cunning *caudillo*, Antonio López de Santa Anna, gained and lost power many times. Allied with Spain during Mexico's war of independence, Santa Anna switched sides when he saw that Spain was losing.

Santa Anna followed a similar pattern as president of Mexico. At first, he portrayed himself as a liberal reformer. Then, after conservative critics opposed his reforms, he reversed his stand. When in power, Santa Anna ruled as a dictator.

Settlers in Mexico's northern territory of Texas took advantage of the chaos in Mexico to seek independence in 1835. Many settlers had moved to Texas from the United States and wanted to ensure a stable government. They also opposed Mexico's attempts to end slavery.

Santa Anna marched north to crush the rebels. Although he overwhelmed Texas forces at the Alamo, he was soon defeated and captured. In 1836, he was forced to recognize the independent Republic of Texas.

>> Life did not improve for many lower class Latin Americans after their countries gained independence. Here, peasant women process crops grown on a hacienda in Mexico in the 1800s.

Santa Anna returned to Mexico in disgrace, but reemerged as a hero in a brief conflict with France. In 1846, after the United States annexed Texas, war broke out between Mexico and the United States. Santa Anna took command of Mexican forces, but was again defeated.

In the Treaty of Guadalupe-Hidalgo, which ended the war in 1848, Mexico lost almost half its territory to the United States. The humiliating defeat forced Santa Anna into exile and triggered new violence between conservatives and liberals in Mexico.

La Reforma Brings Changes to Mexico In 1855, **Benito Juárez** (WAHR ez) and other liberals gained power and opened an era of reform known as **La Reforma.**

Juárez, of Zapotec Indian heritage, offered hope to the oppressed people of Mexico. He and his fellow reformers revised the Mexican constitution to strip the military of power and end the special privileges of the Church. They ordered the Church to sell unused lands to peasants.

Conservatives resisted La Reforma, unleashing a disastrous civil war. Juárez was elected president in 1861 and expanded his reforms. Conservative opponents turned to Europe for help. Mexico owed large debts to several European countries, including France. In 1863, Napoleon III sent troops to Mexico and set up Austrian archduke Maximilian as emperor.

For four years, Juárez's forces battled against Mexican conservatives and French forces. When France withdrew its troops, Maximilian was captured and shot. In 1867, Juárez returned to power and tried to renew reform, but opponents resisted. Juárez died in office in 1872 never achieving all the reforms he envisioned. He did, however, bring mestizos into politics, separate church and state, and help to unite Mexico.

A Dictator's Order, Progress, and Oppression
After Juárez died, General Porfirio Díaz, a hero of the war against the French, used the military to seize power. From 1876 to 1880 and 1884 to 1911, he ruled as a dictator. In the name of "Order and Progress," he strengthened the army, local police, and central government. Any opposition was brutally crushed.

Under his harsh rule, Mexico made impressive economic advances. It build railroads, increased foreign trade, developed some industry, and expanded mining. Growth, however, had a high cost. Capital for development came from foreign investors, to whom Díaz granted special rights. He also let wealthy landowners buy up Indian lands.

The rich prospered, but most Mexicans remained poor. Many Indians and mestizos fell into **peonage** to their employers. In the peonage system, hacienda owners would give workers advances on their wages and require them to stay on the hacienda until they had paid back what they owed. Wages remained low, and workers were rarely able to repay the hacienda owner.

Most Mexicans lived in desperate poverty even as they worked on haciendas or in the new factories. Many children died in infancy. Other children worked 12-hour days and never learned to read or write.

☑ **SUMMARIZE** What reforms did Juárez achieve to help Mexico attempt a more stable government and society?

The Economics of Latin America's Dependence

Under colonial rule, mercantilist policies made Latin America economically dependent on Spain and Portugal. Colonies sent raw materials such as cash

>> Benito Juárez, a Mexican lawyer and politician, brought reforms to Mexico and served several terms as president. His reforms helped unite Mexico and bring mestizos into politics.

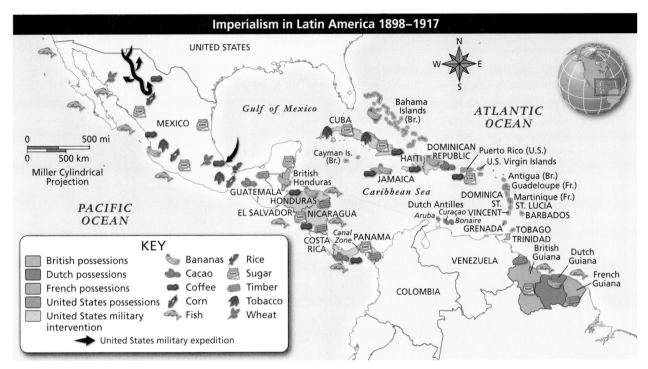

Imperialism in Latin America 1898–1917

KEY

- British possessions
- Dutch possessions
- French possessions
- United States possessions
- United States military intervention
- ➤ United States military expedition

- Bananas
- Cacao
- Coffee
- Corn
- Fish
- Rice
- Sugar
- Timber
- Tobacco
- Wheat

>> **Analyze Maps** The map shows European and U.S. possessions in Latin America in the early 1900s. Imperialists often acted to protect business interests. What explains the strong U.S. interest in Latin America?

crops or precious metals to the parent country and had to buy manufactured goods from them.

Strict laws kept colonists from trading with other countries. Other laws prohibited the building of local industries that would have competed with the parent country. Overall, these policies kept the colonies from developing their own economies.

The Cycle of Economic Dependence After independence, this pattern changed very little. The new Latin American republics did adopt free trade, welcoming all comers. Britain and the United States rushed into the new markets, replacing Spain as Latin America's chief trading partners. But the region remained as economically dependent as before.

Economic dependence occurs when less developed nations export raw materials and commodities to industrial nations and import manufactured goods, capital, and technological know-how. The relationship is unequal because the more developed nations control the prices and terms of trade.

Foreign Investment and Influence In the 1800s, foreign goods flooded Latin America, creating large profits for foreigners and for a handful of local

business people. Foreign investment, which could yield enormous profits, was often accompanied by local interference. Investors from Britain, the United States, and other nations pressured their governments to take action if political events or reform movements in a Latin American country seemed to threaten their interests.

Limited Economic Growth After 1850, some Latin American economies did grow. Industrial countries needed increasing quantities of raw materials and other products from Latin America. With foreign capital, Latin American countries were able to develop mining and agriculture. Chile exported copper and nitrates. Argentina expanded its livestock and wheat production. Brazil added coffee and rubber to its traditional cash crop of sugar. By the early 1900s, both Venezuela and Mexico were developing profitable oil industries.

Throughout the region, foreigners invested in modern ports and railroads to carry goods from the interior to coastal cities. As in the United States at the time, European immigrants poured into Latin America. The newcomers helped to promote economic activity, and a small middle class emerged.

Thanks to trade, investment, technology, and migration, Latin American nations moved into the world economy. Yet internal development was limited. Local industries grew slowly, in part because of the social structure.

The tiny elite at the top benefited from the economic upturn. Their wealth grew, but very little trickled down to the masses of people at the bottom. The poor earned too little to buy consumer goods. Without a strong consumer demand, many industries failed to develop.

☑ **IDENTIFY CAUSE AND EFFECT** What were some negative effects of foreign investment in Latin America?

The United States Wields Power and Influence

As Latin American nations tried to build stable governments and develop their economies, the United States expanded across North America. At first, the young republics in the Western Hemisphere looked favorably on each other. Simón Bolívar praised the United States as a "model of political virtues and moral enlightenment." In time however, Latin

COASTING.
The old horse was too slow for Uncle Sam.

>> **Analyze Political Cartoons** This cartoon portrays the early 1900s entry of the United States into competition with European powers for territory in the Eastern Hemisphere. Why are the Europeans shouting at Uncle Sam?

🔊 BOUNCE to Activate Cartoon

American nations began to feel threatened by the "Colossus of the North," the giant power that cast its shadow over the entire hemisphere.

The Monroe Doctrine of 1823 In the 1820s, Spain plotted to recover its American colonies. Britain opposed any move that might close the door to trade with Latin America. Britain asked the United States to join it in a statement opposing any new colonization of the Americas.

American President James Monroe, however, wanted to avoid any "entangling alliance" with Britain. Acting alone, he issued the **Monroe Doctrine** in 1823. "The American continents," it declared, "are henceforth not to be considered as subjects for future colonization by any European powers."

The United States lacked the military power to enforce the Monroe Doctrine. But with the support of Britain's strong navy, the doctrine discouraged European interference. For more than a century, the Monroe Doctrine would be the key to United States policy in the Americas.

The United States Expands As a result of the Mexican American War, the United States acquired the thinly populated regions of northern Mexico, gaining all or part of the present-day states of California, Arizona, New Mexico, Nevada, Utah, and Colorado. The victory fed dreams of future expansion. Before the century had ended, the United States controlled much of North America and was becoming involved in overseas conflicts.

Cuba and the Spanish American War For decades, Cuban patriots had battled to free their island from Spanish rule. As they began to make headway, the United States joined their cause, declaring war on Spain in 1898. The brief Spanish-American War ended in a crushing defeat for Spain.

In the peace treaty ending the war, the United States acquired Puerto Rico in the Caribbean and the Philippines and Guam in the Pacific. Cuba was granted independence, but in 1901, the United States forced Cubans to add the Platt Amendment to their constitution. The amendment gave the United States naval bases in Cuba and the right to intervene in Cuban affairs.

U.S. Intervention in Latin America American investments in Latin America soared in the early 1900s. Citing the need to protect those investments, in 1904 the United States issued the Roosevelt Corollary to the Monroe Doctrine. Under this policy, the United States claimed "international police power" in the Western Hemisphere. For example, when the Dominican Republic failed to pay its foreign debts, the United States sent in troops. Americans collected customs duties, paid off the debts, and remained for years.

In the next decades, the United States sent troops to Cuba, Haiti, Mexico, Honduras, Nicaragua, and other countries in Central America and the Caribbean. Like European powers in Africa and Asia, the United States intervened in Latin America to protect American lives and investments. Still, its actions triggered outrage and resentment across Latin America.

The Panama Canal From the late 1800s, the United States had wanted to build a canal across the isthmus of Panama in Central America. A canal would let American warships move between the Atlantic and Pacific coasts and protect its coastlines on either side of the continent. Shorter shipping times would also greatly reduce the cost of trade.

The isthmus of Panama, however, belonged to Colombia, which refused to sell the United States land for the canal. In 1903, the United States backed a revolt by Panamanians against Colombia. The Panamanians quickly won independence and gave the United States control of the land to build the canal.

Construction began in 1904. Engineers solved many difficult problems in the course of building the canal, including cutting through mountains and excavating about 232 million cubic yards of dirt, rocks, and debris.

The **Panama Canal** opened in 1914. It was an engineering marvel that boosted American trade and shipping worldwide. The canal cut the distance of a sea journey between cities such as New York and San Francisco by thousands of miles.

To people in Latin America, however, the canal was another example of "Yankee imperialism." During the 1900s, nationalist feeling in the hemisphere was often expressed as anti-Americanism. On December 31, 1999, Panama finally gained complete control over the canal, which now forms a vital part of the Panamanian economy.

☑️ **IDENTIFY CAUSE AND EFFECT** How did the United States influence the direction of Cuban history?

>> **Analyze Information** Two men stand inside one of the Panama Canal lock's enormous gates. The gates allow water to flow in and out, raising or lowering ships to different levels. What does the perspective of the photo indicate about the scale of the project?

 BOUNCE to Activate Gallery

>> By the late 1700s, there were still parts of Canada that had not yet been reached by European settlers. By the mid-1800s, the country had begun to grow, and settlements spread to new areas.

Canada Achieves Self-Rule

In North America, Canada developed slowly in the shadow of its powerful neighbor to the south. Canada's first European rulers were the French. When France lost Canada to Britain in 1763, thousands of French-speaking Catholic settlers remained there.

After the American Revolution, about 30,000 British loyalists fled from the United States to Canada. Unlike the earlier French settlers, they were English-speaking and Protestant. Rivalries between these two groups have been an ongoing issue in Canada ever since.

Native Americans formed another strand of the Canadian heritage. In the 1790s, various groups of Native American people lived in eastern Canada. Others, in the west and the north, remained largely undisturbed by white settlers. Canadians today refer to all these Native American groups as First Nations.

Unrest in the Two Canadas To ease ethnic tensions between European settlers, Britain passed the Constitutional Act of 1791. The act created two provinces: English-speaking Upper Canada (now Ontario) and French-speaking Lower Canada (now Quebec). Each had its own laws, legislature, and royal governor. French traditions and the Catholic Church were protected in Lower Canada while English traditions and laws guided Upper Canada.

During the early 1800s, unrest grew in both colonies. The people of Upper Canada resented the power held by a small British elite who controlled the government. In Lower Canada, people felt that British officials ignored their needs.

In 1837, discontent flared into rebellion in both Upper and Lower Canada. William Lyon Mackenzie led the revolt in Upper Canada, crying, "Put down the villains who oppress and enslave our country!" Louis Joseph Papineau, the head of the French Canadian Reform party, led the rebellion in Lower Canada.

Britain's Response The British had learned a lesson from the American Revolution. While they hurried to put down the disorder, they sent an able politician, Lord Durham, to compile a report on the causes of the unrest. In 1839, the Durham Report called for the two Canadas to be united and given control over their own affairs.

In 1840, Parliament passed the Act of Union, a major step toward self-government. It joined the two Canadas and gave Canada an elected legislature to determine domestic policies. Britain kept control of foreign policy and trade.

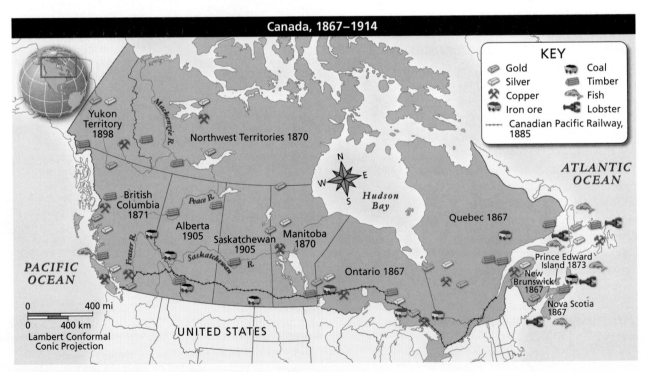

Canada, 1867–1914

KEY
Gold
Silver
Copper
Iron ore
Coal
Timber
Fish
Lobster
Canadian Pacific Railway, 1885

Yukon Territory 1898
Northwest Territories 1870
British Columbia 1871
Alberta 1905
Saskatchewan 1905
Manitoba 1870
Quebec 1867
Ontario 1867
New Brunswick 1867
Prince Edward Island 1873
Nova Scotia 1867

PACIFIC OCEAN
ATLANTIC OCEAN
Hudson Bay
UNITED STATES

Mackenzie R.
Peace R.
Fraser R.
Saskatchewan R.

0   400 mi
0   400 km
Lambert Conformal Conic Projection

>> **Analyze Maps** Canada grew throughout the late 1800s. This map shows Canadian provinces from 1867 to 1914 and their natural resources. List the natural resources of Manitoba and Nova Scotia.

The Dominion of Canada Like the United States, Canada expanded westward in the 1800s and new settlements were built. As the country grew, two Canadians, John Macdonald and George-Etienne Cartier, urged **confederation,** or unification, of British settlements in North America. They included Nova Scotia, New Brunswick, Prince Edward Island, and British Columbia, as well as the united Upper and Lower Canadas.

Like many Canadians at the time, the two leaders feared that the United States might try to dominate Canada. Confederation, they thought, would strengthen the new nation against American ambitions and help it develop economically.

Britain finally agreed to the plan. In 1867, it passed the British North America Act, which created the Dominion of Canada. A **dominion** is a self-governing nation. As a dominion, Canada had its own parliament, modeled on that of Britain. By 1900, Canada also controlled its own foreign policy. Still, Canada maintained close ties with Britain.

Like Australia and New Zealand, Canada won independence and self-rule faster and easier than British colonies in Africa or Asia. Many Canadians shared the same language and cultural heritage as Britain. Racial attitudes also played a part, as Britain considered white Canadians better able to govern themselves than the non-white populations elsewhere in their empire.

Canada Expands John MacDonald, Canada's first prime minister, encouraged expansion. To unite the far-flung regions of Canada, he called for a transcontinental railroad. In 1885, the Canadian Pacific Railway opened, linking eastern and western Canada. Wherever the railroad went, settlers followed. It moved people and products, such as timber, grain, minerals, and manufactured goods across the country.

As in the United States, westward expansion destroyed the way of life of American Indian people. Most were forced to sign treaties giving up their lands. Some resisted. Louis Riel led a revolt of the **métis,** people of mixed American Indian and French Canadian descent.

These French-speaking Catholics accused the government of stealing their land and trying to destroy their language and religion. Government troops put down the uprising and executed Riel.

In the late 1800s and early 1900s, more immigrants flooded into Canada from Germany, Italy, Poland, Russia, Ukraine, China, and Japan. They joined the English, Scottish, and Irish settlers who had arrived earlier. These groups enriched Canada economically and culturally.

By 1914, Canada was a flourishing independent nation. Still, two issues plagued Canada. First, French-speaking Canadians were determined to preserve their separate heritage, making it hard for Canadians to create a single national identity. Second, the United States exerted a powerful economic and cultural influence that threatened to dominate Canada. Both issues have continued to affect Canada to the present day.

☑ **ANALYZE INFORMATION** What were some reasons that Canada achieved self-rule faster and easier than other British colonies?

☑ ASSESSMENT

1. **Connect** How was Latin America's ruling elite similar to Europe's ruling class, and why was that a political problem?

2. **Identify Cause and Effect** How did dictator General Porfirio Díaz contribute to economic and political instability in Mexico?

3. **Identify Cause and Effect** How did colonial rule contribute to Latin America's continuing economic dependence after colonialism?

4. **Identify Cause and Effect** What effects did the Monroe Doctrine and Roosevelt Corollary have on Latin America?

5. **Summarize** How did the British respond to the Canadians' desire for self-rule?

6. **Connections to Today** Are the United States and Latin America still economically linked today? Explain.

Garment workers in Bangladesh

Take Action About the Global Economy

In the Age of Imperialism, colonizing nations controlled the emerging global economy. Today, large multinational corporations often play a similar role. And today, as in the past, raw materials and finished products are traded on a vast global scale.

1. **Choose** one of these categories of products that are produced and marketed on a global scale in our interdependent world economy.

   - Clothing

   - Food

   - Technology

2. **Ask Questions** Ask questions about the clothes you wear, the food you eat, or the technology you use. What do you want to know about the raw materials that went into these products or how they were manufactured?

3. **Learn** Do research on the products you have chosen. Trace the sources of the raw materials as well as the manufacture and identify anything that came from a country other than the United States.

4. **Take Action** Create an illustrated poster that shows the international nature of the product you have chosen. Make sure the poster includes a world map as well as informational text. Share the poster within your school or within a community setting to raise awareness about the global economy.

Use the texts, quizzes, interactivities, Quest Inquiries, Flipped Videos, and other resources from this Topic to prepare for the Topic Test.

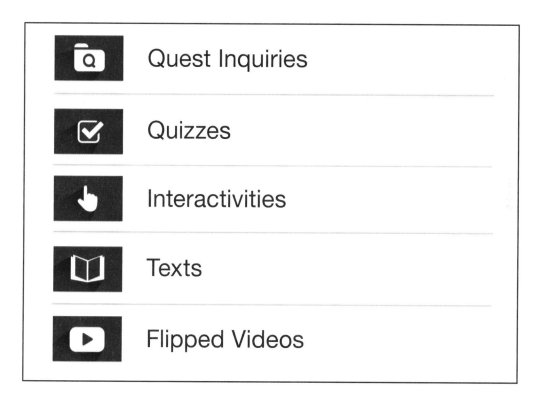

Quest Inquiries

Quizzes

Interactivities

Texts

Flipped Videos

While online you can also check the progress you've made learning the topic and course content by viewing your grades, test scores, and assignment status.

LESSON SUMMARIES

Use these Lesson Summaries, and the longer versions available online, to review the key ideas for each lesson in this Topic.

Lesson 1: The New Imperialism

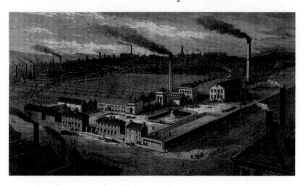

During the 1800s, some European nations set up colonies in Africa and Asia to acquire the natural resources needed to meet manufacturing demands. Claiming cultural superiority, Europeans felt Western culture should be spread, but colonial resistance to Western domination rose.

Lesson 2: European Colonies in Africa

In the late 1800s, Britain, France, and other European nations began a scramble for African territories. Within twenty years, Europeans had carved up the continent and dominated millions of Africans.

Lesson 3: Europe and the Muslim World

Napoleon's Egyptian campaign highlighted the decline of the Ottoman empire and opened a new era of European contact with the Muslim regions. European nations soon moved in to benefit from crumbling empires.

Lesson 4: India Becomes a British Colony

In the early 1600s, the British East India Company won trading rights on the fringe of the Mughal empire. As Mughal power declined, the company's influence grew. After the Uprising of 1857, Parliament ended the rule of the British East India Company and after 1858, set up colonial rule in India.

Lesson 5: China and the West

After defeat in the Opium Wars with Britain, China was forced to accept terms of an unequal treaty which resulted in concessions to Western powers. Qing China declined as Western powers used diplomacy and war to gain power in East Asia.

Lesson 6: The Modernization of Japan

Under military pressure from the United States, Japan ended its centuries of isolation and opened its markets to the West. During the Meiji Restoration, Japan rapidly modernized. By the early 1900s, Japan was the strongest empire in Asia.

Lesson 7: Southeast Asia and the Pacific

As they had in Africa, Western industrial powers pushed into Southeast Asia in their need to acquire raw materials, new markets, and to spread Christianity. They also took over nearly every island in the Pacific, as well as Australia.

Lesson 8: The Americas in the Age of Imperialism

The economies of Latin America became dependent on industrialized nations for investment, technology, and manufactured goods.

QUEST! FINDINGS

Write Your Essay Refer to your responses to the Quest Connections to help you write your essay. Use the rubric and other Quest resources online to guide your work.

GO ONLINE to access lesson summaries

VISUAL REVIEW

Use these graphics to review some of the key terms, people, and ideas from this Topic.

Western Imperialism

AFRICA

- Berlin Conference
- Raw materials exploited
- Boer War
- Racial segregation in South Africa
- Western-educated African elite
- Nationalism grows

MUSLIM REGIONS

- Islamic reform movements
- Internal revolts
- Armenian genocide
- Egypt modernizes

INDIA

- British East India Company
- Changes to legal and caste systems
- Uprising of 1857
- Indians forced to raise cash crops
- Population growth and famine
- Indian National Congress
- Muslim League

CHINA

- Opium War
- Unequal trade treaties
- Self-strengthening movement
- Sino-Japanese War
- Boxer Uprising

New Imperialism

CAUSES

- Industrial Revolution strengthens the West
- Newly industrialized nations seek new markets
- European nations compete for power

EFFECTS

- Europeans claim and conquer large empires in Africa and Asia
- Western powers spread their ideas and adopt elements of nonwestern cultures
- Local people resist European domination
- Some nonwestern leaders attempt reforms in an effort to modernize

KEY TERMS, PEOPLE, AND IDEAS

1. Why did Europeans seek to expand their overseas empires in the 1800s? What two European nations would colonize most of Africa?

2. What role did the **Boer War** play in Britain's bid for colonial power in Africa?

3. How did Social Darwinism become a factor in the New Imperialism?

4. What events sparked the **Boxer uprising** in China?

5. Why do people in India refer to the Uprising of 1857 as the First War of Independence?

6. What problems faced new nations in Latin America as a result of colonial rule?

7. What role did **Commodore Matthew Perry** assume in establishing relations with Japan?

8. How did the **Monroe Doctrine** affect Latin America?

9. Why did the United States want to build the **Panama Canal**?

CRITICAL THINKING

10. **Synthesize Information** How did the Industrial Revolution contribute to the new imperialism?

11. **Analyze Visuals** This 1892 cartoon from a British newspaper shows British colonialist Cecil Rhodes.

(a) How does this cartoon reflect what you have learned about the goals and activities of Rhodes? (b) Do you think the cartoonist was a supporter or critic of imperialism? Explain.

12. **Analyze Information** Describe the ideology of Sun Yixian in his quest for a new China.

13. **Draw Conclusions** How did European imperialism cause political conflict among peoples in different colonies?

14. **Analyze Information** How did the Monroe Doctrine establish new goals for U.S. foreign policy?

15. **Evaluate Information** How did British rule lead to growing Indian nationalism?

16. **Analyze Information** Both foreign and Chinese belief systems influenced China during the 1800s. Some Chinese wanted to adopt Western ways, while others wanted to maintain Confucian ways. How did the choices China made influence its future relationship with Western nations? Do you think China's history would have been different if if had made the same choices as Japan? Take a stand as to why or why not.

17. **Writing Activity: Write an Explanatory Essay** Read the following passage in which a Brazilian writer describes how the richer class dresses.

> "At that time . . . Brazil did not manufacture a yard of silk, a shoe, a spool of thread; everything was imported. . . . Men's clothing for a tropical climate was made of English wool suitable for life in the unheated homes of an English winter. I asked myself: how did they stand the heat? The ladies when they took off their shoes at home used slippers of heavy wool, as if they were in Siberia. . . . Except for the poor, I never saw in the Pernambuco [the writer's hometown] of my time anyone dressed in light clothing.
> —Gilbert Amado, Historia da Minha Infancia

Use the passage and what you have learned about imperialism to write a two-paragraph essay. In the first paragraph, explain how the elite in Pernambuco dressed so impractically. In the second paragraphy, use this evidence to explain what this suggests about the values of the colonial elite.

18. **Connections to Today** Compare the economic relationship between developed and developing countries today to the relationship between industrial powers and the lands they colonized durign the Age of Imperialism. How are they they similar? How are they different?

DOCUMENT-BASED QUESTIONS

The Armenian genocide has been called the "forgotten genocide." This genocide of the Christian Armenians of Turkey took place between 1895 and 1923, and was implemented by the Muslim Ottoman government. Read the documents below, then answer the questions that follow.

DOCUMENT A

"As it got worse, all of us, and all the people, began gathering in our school. The word came around that the Turks were going on the streets and killing all the Armenians and leaving them on the streets. I, myself, was in school already, so I simply stayed there. Then orders came from the school that we, too, should run away. But where? All the buildings were on fire! The Turks were burning everything. There was a whole group of us running away from the school."

— *Annalin, a survivor from Smyrna on events of 1922*

DOCUMENT B

"The massacre of Armenian subjects in the Ottoman Empire in 1896 . . . was amateur and ineffective compared with the largely successful attempt to exterminate [them] during the First World War in 1915. . . . [This] genocide was carried out under the cloak of legality by cold-blooded governmental action. These were not mass-murders committed spontaneously by mobs of private people. . . ."

— *Arnold Toynbee, British historian, cited in Experiences*

DOCUMENT C

"The 1,000 Armenian houses are being emptied of furniture by the police one after the other. The furniture, bedding and everything of value is being stored in large buildings about the city. . . . The goods are piled in without any attempt at labeling or systematic storage. A crowd of Turkish women and children follow the police about like a lot of vultures and seize anything they can lay their hands on and when the more valuable things are carried out of the house by the police they rush in and take the balance. . . . I suppose it will take several weeks to empty all the houses and then the Armenian shops and stores will be cleared out."

— *From a report to the American embassy by Oscar S. Heizer, American consul in Tebizond, July 1915*

DOCUMENT D

"The proportion of Armenians killed by the Turks in World War I out of the general number of Armenians in the Ottoman Empire was no less than that of the Jewish victims [during the Holocaust] out of the total Jewish population in Europe. Nor are the methods of killing unique. . . . The type of murder committed by the Germans in the USSR—mass machine-gunning—was the traditional method of mass murder in our century, and the death marches of Jews in the closing stages of the war had their precedent in the Armenian case as well. Nor is the fact that in the case of the Holocaust it was a state machine and a bureaucracy that was responsible for the murder unique, because there, too, the Young Turks had preceded the German Nazis in planning the execution of a population with such means as were modern at the time."

— *From Remembrance and Denial by Richard G. Hovannisian*

19. According to Document B, the 1915 genocide of Armenians

A. went unpunished.

B. was ineffective and unsuccessful.

C. was not as well documented as the 1896 massacre.

D. was committed with the knowledge of the Turkish government.

20. How Document C shows that the Turkish police

A. tried to protect the property of Armenian citizens despite their government's orders.

B. tried to help Armenian citizens as best they could.

C. took part in stealing the property of Armenian citizens.

D. protested to the American embassy to try to help their friends.

21. According to Document D, the Armenian Genocide and the Holocaust

A. were committed by the same people.

B. were carried out in a similar way.

C. had very few similarities, except for the large number of murders.

D. both took place in Germany.

22. Writing Tasks Ismayale Kemal Pasha, a governor in Marash, tried to save Armenian citizens, despite orders from his superiors to carry out the genocide without remorse. Suppose Ismayale Kemal Pasha explained his decision to help in a memoir. Write a brief explanation from his point of view. Use these documents along with information from the Topic in your writing.

GO ONLINE to access more practice

World War I and the Russian Revolution (1914–1924)

ESSENTIAL QUESTION When is war justified?

Barbed

creep

with Ha

project **Imagine**

GO ONLINE for immersive experiences designed to help you feel the drama of World War I through rich primary sources. Also access the eText, videos, Biographies, and other online resources.

American soldiers in World War I

Connections to Today

When you hear the word *drone,* do you think of choreographed light shows at the Super Bowl, tiny drones dropping an online shopping item at your doorstep, or military drones searching for terrorists?

Did you know that early predecessors of today's drones were created during World War I by Nicola Tesla and others? In this topic you'll read about many new deadly technologies that were developed and used during the war. How have these World War I technologies continued to impact our lives today?

NBC LEARN

See World War I through the eyes of an English soldier and poet.

 BOUNCE to Activate My Story Video

In this Topic, you will learn about the events of World War I. Look at the lesson outline and explore the timeline. As you study this Topic, you will complete the Quest Inquiry.

LESSON OUTLINE

16.1 World War I Begins

16.2 Fighting the Great War

16.3 World War I Ends

16.4 Revolution in Russia

Key Events of World War I

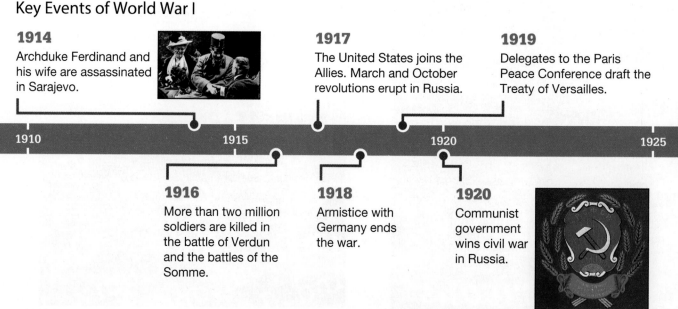

1914
Archduke Ferdinand and his wife are assassinated in Sarajevo.

1917
The United States joins the Allies. March and October revolutions erupt in Russia.

1919
Delegates to the Paris Peace Conference draft the Treaty of Versailles.

1910

1915

1920

1925

1916
More than two million soldiers are killed in the battle of Verdun and the battles of the Somme.

1918
Armistice with Germany ends the war.

1920
Communist government wins civil war in Russia.

QUEST!

INQUIRY

Create a Video Docudrama about World War I

How did the war change the lives of civilians, soldiers, and leaders? In this Quest, you will read about the changes, then create a docudrama of people's experiences during that time.

STEP 1

As you begin the project, review what you know about World War I. Assign topics to be researched. List questions. Prepare story outlines.

STEP 2

Become familiar with the requirements of making a docudrama. There are websites you can use.

STEP 3

After information is gathered and evaluated, start writing the first narrative draft. Review, edit, and revise your presentation.

STEP 4

Present your completed video to your classmates, and your family and friends. Use this opportunity to reflect on the impact of war as it affected people then and now.

GO ONLINE to access complete Quest materials

16.1

🖥 **GO ONLINE to Project Imagine: Follow the Paths to War** for first-person perspectives on the causes of war.

📼 **BOUNCE to Activate Flipped Video**

Objectives

Describe how imperialism, nationalism, and militarism pushed Europe closer to war.

Identify the key event that sparked World War I.

Trace how the alliance system drew nations into the war.

Key Terms

entente
militarism
Alsace and Lorraine
ultimatum
mobilize
neutrality

World War I Begins

By 1914, Europe had enjoyed a century of relative peace. Idealists hoped for a permanent end to the scourge of war. International events, such as the first modern Olympic games in 1896 and the First Universal Peace Conference in 1899, were steps toward keeping the peace. "The future belongs to peace," said French economist Frédéric Passy (pa SEE).

European Powers Form Alliances

Not everyone was so hopeful. "I shall not live to see the Great War," warned German Chancellor Otto von Bismarck, "but you will see it, and it will start in the east." It was Bismarck's prediction, rather than Passy's, that came true.

Nations Form Alliances Despite efforts to ensure peace, the late 1800s saw growing rivalries among the powers of Europe—Britain, France, Germany, Austria-Hungary, Italy, and Russia—as well as the Ottoman Empire and Japan. In an atmosphere of fear and distrust, the great powers set out to protect themselves by forming alliances. Nations signed treaties pledging to defend each other. These alliances were intended to create powerful combinations that no one would dare attack. Gradually, two rival alliances evolved.

The Triple Alliance The first major alliance had its origins in Bismarck's day. He knew that France longed to avenge its defeat in the Franco-Prussian War. Sure that France would not attack Germany without help, Bismarck signed treaties with other powers. By 1882, Germany had formed the Triple Alliance with Italy and Austria-Hungary. Although Bismarck had previously signed an alliance with Russia, Kaiser William II did not preserve that alliance, leaving Russia free to seek other allies.

In 1914, when war did erupt, Germany and Austria-Hungary fought on the same side. They became known as the Central Powers.

The Triple Entente A rival bloc took shape in 1893, when France and Russia signed a secret treaty. France was eager to end its isolation and balance the growing power of Germany. In 1904, France and Britain signed an **entente** (ahn TAHNT), a nonbinding agreement to follow common policies. Though not as formal as a treaty, the entente led to close military and diplomatic ties. Britain later signed a similar agreement with Russia, creating the Triple Entente. When war began, these powers became known as the Allies.

Britain and France had been rivals for hundreds of years, and France had invaded Russia during the Napoleonic Wars. Still, these three powers joined together in the Triple Entente because they feared Germany wanted to dominate Europe.

Other Alliances Other states were drawn into alliances. Germany signed a treaty with the Ottoman empire. As early as 1867, Britain had signed a treaty to protect Belgium's right to remain neutral in any European conflict. Italy had a secret treaty with France not to attack it. And Russia had agreed to protect Serbia. Britain forged ties with Japan.

Rather than easing tensions, the growth of rival alliance systems made governments increasingly nervous. A local conflict could mushroom into a general war. In 1914, that threat became a reality.

☑ **ANALYZE INFORMATION** Why did the European nations form opposing alliances?

Major Causes of World War I

During the late 1800s and early 1900s, tensions were increasing among the great powers of Europe. Aggressive nationalism, economic competition, imperialism, militarism, and an arms race all helped fuel an atmosphere of suspicion and distrust.

Economic and Imperial Rivalry Economic rivalries helped sour the international atmosphere. Germany, the newest of the great powers, was growing into an economic and military powerhouse. Britain felt threatened by Germany's rapid growth. Germany, in turn, thought the other great powers

>> Germany, led by Kaiser William II (left), and Austria-Hungary, led by Emperor Francis Joseph (right), became close allies in the years before World War I.

LA FRANCE VA POUVOIR PORTER LIBREMENT AU MAROC LA CIVILISATION LA RICHESSE ET LA PAIX

>> A Parisian newspaper presented this view of imperialism. The caption says "France freely gives Morocco civilization, peace, and wealth." **Hypothesize** Who might have opposed this viewpoint? Why?

did not give it enough respect. It also worried about future economic competition from Russia, which had a huge population and vast natural resources.

Imperialism also divided European nations. In 1905 and again in 1911, competition for colonies brought France and Germany to the brink of war in Morocco, then under France's influence. Although diplomats kept the peace, Germany did gain some territory in central Africa. As a result of the two Moroccan crises, Britain and France strengthened their ties against Germany.

Militarism and the Arms Race The late 1800s saw a rise in **militarism,** or the glorification of the military. Under militarism, the armed forces and readiness for war came to dominate national policy. Militarists painted war in romantic colors. Young men dreamed of blaring trumpets and dashing cavalry charges—not at all the sort of conflict they would soon face.

With international tensions on the rise, the great powers began to build up their armies and navies. The fiercest competition was the naval rivalry between Britain and Germany. To protect its vast overseas empire, Britain had built the world's most respected navy. As Germany began acquiring overseas colonies, it began to build up its own navy. Suspicious of Germany's motives, Britain in turn increased naval spending. Newspapers dramatized

the arms race and stirred national public opinion against rival countries.

The arms race helped military leaders gain influence. On matters of peace and war, civilian governments turned to military leaders for advice. Germany generals and British admirals enjoyed great respect and got more funds to build up their forces. As militarism and the arms race fed each other, tensions grew.

Nationalism Aggressive nationalism also caused tension. Nationalism was strong in both Germany and France. Germans were proud of their new empire's military power and industrial leadership. The French were bitter about their 1871 defeat in the Franco-Prussian War and yearned to recover the parts of the border provinces of **Alsace and Lorraine** that had been taken in the war.

In Eastern Europe, Russia sponsored a powerful form of nationalism called Pan-Slavism. It held that all Slavic peoples shared a common nationality. As the largest Slavic country, Russia felt that it had a duty to lead and defend all Slavs. By 1914, it stood ready to support Serbia, a proud young Slavic nation, against any threat.

Two old multinational empires particularly feared rising nationalism. Austria-Hungary worried that nationalism might foster rebellion among the many minority populations within its empire. Ottoman

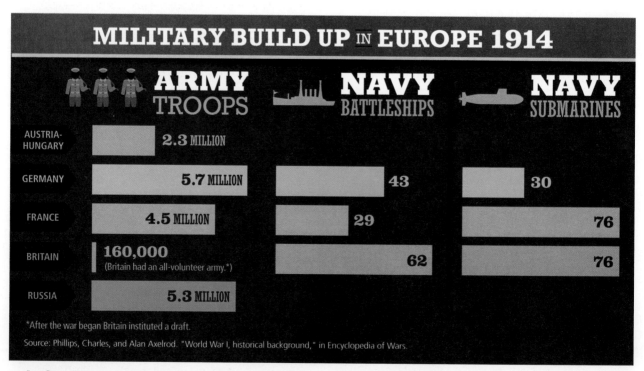

MILITARY BUILD UP IN EUROPE 1914

	ARMY TROOPS	NAVY BATTLESHIPS	NAVY SUBMARINES
AUSTRIA-HUNGARY	2.3 MILLION		
GERMANY	5.7 MILLION	43	30
FRANCE	4.5 MILLION	29	76
BRITAIN	160,000 (Britain had an all-volunteer army.*)	62	76
RUSSIA	5.3 MILLION		

*After the war began Britain instituted a draft.

Source: Phillips, Charles, and Alan Axelrod. "World War I, historical background," in Encyclopedia of Wars.

>> **Analyze Data** According to this infographic, which country had the most soldiers? Which country had the largest navy?

Turkey felt threatened by nearby new nations, such as Serbia. If realized, Serbia's dream of a South Slav state could take territory away from both Austria-Hungary and Turkey.

In 1912, several Balkan states—Serbia, Greece, Bulgaria and Montenegro—attacked Turkey and succeeded in taking a large area of land away from Turkish control. The next year, they fought among themselves over the spoils of war. These brief but bloody Balkan wars raised tensions to a fever pitch. By 1914, the Balkans were called the "powder keg of Europe"—a barrel of gunpowder that a tiny spark might cause to explode.

☑ **IDENTIFY CAUSE AND EFFECT** How did imperialism heighten tensions in Europe?

The Balkan Powder Keg Explodes

As Bismarck had predicted, the Great War began in Eastern Europe. A regional conflict between tiny Serbia and the huge empire of Austria-Hungary grew rapidly into a general war that would mark one of history's significant turning points.

Archduke Francis Ferdinand Is Assassinated

The crisis began when Archduke Francis Ferdinand of Austria-Hungary announced that he would visit Sarajevo (sa ruh YAY voh), the capital of Bosnia. Francis Ferdinand was the nephew and heir of the aging Austrian emperor, Francis Joseph. At the time of his visit, Bosnia was under the rule of Austria-Hungary. But it was also the home of many Serbs and other Slavs.

News of the royal visit angered many Serbian nationalists. They viewed the Austrians as foreign oppressors. Some members of Unity or Death, a Serbian terrorist group commonly known as the Black Hand, vowed to take action.

The archduke ignored warnings of anti-Austrian unrest in Sarajevo. On June 28, 1914, he and his wife, Sophie, rode through Sarajevo in an open car. As the car passed by, a conspirator named Gavrilo Princip (GAV ree loh PREEN tseep) seized his chance and fired twice into the car. Moments later, the archduke and his wife were dead.

Austria Declares War on Serbia

When news of the assassination of Francis Ferdinand reached Vienna, the government of Emperor Francis Joseph blamed Serbia. Austria-Hungary believed that Serbia

>> This political cartoon was published in 1912 in the British magazine *Punch*. **Analyze Political Cartoons** What view of the Balkans does this cartoon present?

🅱 BOUNCE to Activate Cartoon

would stop at nothing to achieve its goal of a South Slav empire. Austria decided its only course was to punish Serbia.

In Berlin, Kaiser William II was horrified at the assassination. He wrote to Francis Joseph, advising him to take a firm stand toward Serbia. Instead of urging restraint, Germany gave Austria a "blank check," or permission to undertake whatever action it chose.

For weeks, diplomats shuttled notes among the great powers, trying to head off a conflict. Backed by Germany, however, Austria-Hungary sent Serbia a harsh **ultimatum,** or final set of demands. To avoid war, said the ultimatum, Serbia must end all anti-Austrian agitation and punish any Serbian official involved in the murder plot. It must even let Austria join in the investigation. Austria-Hungary gave Serbia 48 hours to reply.

Serbia agreed to most, but not all, of the terms of Austria's ultimatum. This partial refusal gave Austria the opportunity it was seeking. On July 28, 1914, Austria declared war on Serbia.

☑ **INTEGRATE INFORMATION** How did Austria's alliance system influence Austria's decision to send Serbia an ultimatum?

>> To aid its ally Serbia, Russia mobilized its army, including these Cossacks. As World War I began, European armies still sent cavalry units into battle.

>> In August 1914, Germany invaded neutral Belgium to reach France. Here, the German infantry advances across a Belgian field filled with flowers.

The Alliance System Leads to War

The war between Austria and Serbia might have been another "summer war," like most European wars of the previous century. However, the carefully planned alliances soon drew the great powers into the conflict.

Russia and France Support Serbia After receiving Austria's ultimatum, Serbia turned to its ally, Russia. From St. Petersburg, Nicholas II telegraphed William II. The tsar asked the kaiser to urge Austria to soften its demands. When this plea failed, Russia began to **mobilize,** or prepare its military forces for war. On August 1, Germany responded by declaring war on Russia.

Russia, in turn, appealed to its ally France. In Paris, nationalists saw a chance to avenge France's defeat in the Franco-Prussian War. Though French leaders had some doubts, they gave Russia the same kind of backing Germany offered to Austria. When Germany demanded that France keep out of the conflict, France refused. Germany then declared war on France.

Germany Marches Through Belgium By early August, the battle lines were hardening. Italy and Britain still remained uncommitted. Italy chose to stay neutral for the time being. **Neutrality** is a policy of supporting neither side in a war. Britain had to decide quickly whether or not to support its ally France. Then, Germany's war plans suddenly made the decision for Britain.

Germany's worst fear was a war on two fronts, with France attacking from the west and Russia from the east. Years earlier, General Alfred Schlieffen (SHLEE fun) had developed a strategy to avoid a two-front war. Schlieffen reasoned that Russia's lumbering military would be slow to mobilize. Under the Schlieffen Plan, Germany first had to defeat France quickly. Then it would concentrate its forces against Russia.

To ensure a swift victory in the west, the Schlieffen Plan required German armies to march through neutral Belgium and then swing south behind French lines. The goal was to encircle and crush France's army. The Germans embarked on the plan by invading Belgium on August 3.

However, Germany had signed a treaty with Britain and France guaranteeing Belgian neutrality. Outraged by the invasion of Belgium, Britain declared war on Germany on August 4.

Once the machinery of war was set in motion, it seemed impossible to stop. Military leaders insisted that they must mobilize their forces immediately to accomplish their military goals. These military

KEY
- Central Powers
- Allies
- Neutral nations
- Neutral nations that later joined the Allies
- Neutral nations that later joined the Central Powers
- The Balkans

ATLANTIC OCEAN

0 400 mi
0 400 km
Lambert Conformal Conic Projection

>> **Analyze Maps** How does this map help explain the expansion of World War I from a localized to a global war?

BOUNCE to Activate Map

timetables made it impossible for political leaders to negotiate instead of fight.

Whose Fault? How did an assassination lead to all-out war in just a few weeks? During the war, each side blamed the other. Afterward, the victorious Allies blamed Germany. Today, most historians agree that all parties must share blame for a catastrophe nobody wanted.

Each great power believed its cause was just. Austria wanted to punish Serbia for encouraging terrorism. Germany felt that it must stand by its one dependable ally, Austria. Russia saw the Austrian ultimatum to Serbia as an effort to oppress Slavic peoples.

France feared that if it did not support Russia, it would have to face Germany alone later. Britain felt committed to protect Belgium, but also feared the growing power of Germany.

Once the machinery of war was set in motion with the Austrian ultimatum and mobilization of troops, political leaders could no longer save the peace. Although government leaders made the decisions, most people on both sides were committed to military action. Young men rushed to enlist, cheered on by women and their elders. Now that war had come at last, it seemed an exciting adventure.

British diplomat Edward Grey was less optimistic. As armies began to move, he predicted, "The lamps are going out all over Europe. We shall not see them lit again in our lifetime."

☑ **IDENTIFY CENTRAL ISSUES** How did Germany's invasion of Belgium bring Britain into the war?

☑ ASSESSMENT

1. **Generate Explanations** How were economic competition and imperialism causes of World War I?

2. **Identify Cause and Effect** Was nationalism a cause of World War I? Why or why not? Give examples.

3. **Identify Central Issues** What is militarism, and how did it influence the nations of Europe prior to World War I?

4. **Draw Conclusions** How did the alliance system spread the original conflict between Austria-Hungary and Serbia into a general war involving many countries?

5. **Connections to Today** Europeans romanticized war at the outbreak of World War I. Do you think Americans romanticize war today? Explain your reasoning and cite examples to support your answer.

16.2

🖥 GO ONLINE to Project
Imagine: Survive on the Front
Lines to glimpse daily life for
soldiers on the Western Front.

BOUNCE to Activate Flipped Video

Objectives

Understand how trench warfare led to a
stalemate on the Western Front.

Identify and describe the impact of modern
military technology on the fighting.

Outline the course of the war on multiple
European fronts.

Explain how World War I was a global
conflict.

Key Terms

stalemate
zeppelin
U-boat
convoy
Dardanelles
T. E. Lawrence

Fighting the Great War

World War I—known at the time as the "Great War"—was the
largest conflict in history up to that time. The French mobilized
almost 8.5 million men, the British nearly 9 million, the Russians
12 million, and the Germans 11 million. For those who fought, the
statistics were more personal. "One out of every four men who
went out to the World War did not come back again," recalled a
survivor, "and of those who came back, many are maimed and
blind and some are mad."

A New Kind of War

The early enthusiasm for the war soon faded. There were no
stirring cavalry charges, no quick and glorious victories. This was
a new kind of war, far deadlier than any before.

Stalemate on the Western Front As the war began, German
forces fought their way through Belgium toward Paris, following
the Schlieffen Plan. The Belgians resisted more than German
generals had expected, but the German forces prevailed. However,
Germany's plans for a quick defeat of France soon faltered.

The Schlieffen Plan failed for several reasons. First, Russia
mobilized more quickly than expected. After Russian forces won
a few small victories in eastern Prussia, German generals hastily
shifted some troops to the east. This move weakened their forces
in the west. Then, in September 1914, British and French troops
pushed back the German drive along the Marne River. The first
battle of the Marne ended Germany's hopes for a quick victory on
the Western Front.

Both sides then began to dig deep trenches to protect their armies from fierce enemy fire. They did not know that the conflict would turn into a long, deadly **stalemate,** a deadlock in which neither side is able to defeat the other. Battle lines in France would remain almost unchanged for four years.

Trench Warfare On the Western Front, the warring armies burrowed into a vast system of trenches, stretching from the Swiss frontier to the English Channel. An underground network linked bunkers, communications trenches, and gun emplacements.

There, millions of soldiers roasted under the broiling summer sun or froze through long bitter winters. They shared their food with rats and their beds with lice.

Between the opposing trench lines lay "no man's land," an empty tract, pocketed with shell holes. Through coils of barbed wire, soldiers peered over the edge of their trenches, watching for the next enemy attack. They themselves would have to charge into this man-made desert when officers gave the order.

Sooner or later, soldiers obeyed the order to go "over the top." With no protection but their rifles and helmets, they charged across no man's land toward the enemy lines. With luck, they might overrun a few trenches. In time, the enemy would launch a counterattack, with similar results. Each side then rushed in reinforcements to replace the dead and wounded. The struggle continued, back and forth, over a few hundred yards of territory.

High Casualty Rates To break the stalemate on the Western Front, both the Allies and the Central Powers launched massive offensives in 1916. German forces tried to overwhelm the French at Verdun (vur DUN). The French defenders held firm, sending up the battle cry "They shall not pass." The 11-month struggle cost more than a half a million casualties, or soldiers killed, wounded, or missing, on both sides.

An Allied offensive at the Somme River (sum) was even more costly. In a single grisly day, nearly 60,000 British soldiers were killed or wounded. In the five-month battle, more than one million soldiers were killed, without either side winning an advantage.

Some soldiers wrote about their experiences on the front lines:

> The blue French cloth mingled with the German grey upon the ground, and in some places the bodies were piled so high that one could take cover from shell-fire behind them. The noise was so terrific that orders had to be shouted by each man into the ear of the next. And whenever there

Europe in World War I, 1914

KEY
Allies
Central Powers
Neutral nations
Front line, 1914
Battle site

>> **Analyze Maps** Who do you think was in a better strategic position at the start of the war, the Allies or the Central Powers? Why?

BOUNCE to Activate Map

>> This German soldier was one of the many casualties of the fighting during World War I. Massive offenses and new military technology combined to produce extremely high casualty rates.

🅑 BOUNCE to Activate 3D Model

>> Poison gas and machine guns are two examples of the military technology that killed and wounded so many. These British machine gunners wear gas masks during the Battle of the Somme, in July 1916.

🅑 BOUNCE to Activate Gallery

was a momentary lull in the tumult of battle and the groans of the wounded, one heard, high up in the blue sky, the joyful song of birds! Birds singing just as they do at home in spring-time! It was enough to tear the heart out of one's body!

—German soldier Richard Schmieder, writing from the trenches in France

☑ **IDENTIFY CAUSE AND EFFECT** How did the failure of Germany's Schlieffen Plan to quickly defeat France affect the future course of the war?

Modern Military Technology

The enormous casualties suffered on the Western Front were due in part to the destructive power of modern weapons. Two significant weapons were the rapid-fire machine gun and the long-range artillery gun. Machine guns mowed down waves of soldiers. Artillery allowed troops to shell the enemy from more than 10 miles away. The shrapnel, or flying debris from artillery shells, killed or wounded even more soldiers than the guns.

Poison Gas Efforts to overcome the stalemate of trench warfare led to the use of poison gas. Early on, the French used tear gas grenades, but by 1915, the Germans began employing poison gas on a large scale. Even though the Allies condemned the use of poison gas, both sides developed and used different kinds of poison gases. Poison gas blinded or choked its victims or caused agonizing burns and blisters. It could be fatal. Though soldiers were eventually given gas masks, poison gas remained one of the most dreaded hazards of the war.

One British soldier recalled the effects of being gassed:

I suppose I resembled a kind of fish with my mouth open gasping for air. It seemed as if my lungs were gradually shutting down and my heart pounded away in my ears like the beat of a drum. . . . To get air into my lungs was real agony.

—William Pressey, quoted in *People at War 1914–1918*

Poison gas was an uncertain weapon. Shifting winds could blow the gas back on the soldiers who launched it. As both sides invented masks to protect against gas attacks, it became less useful. After the war, disgust and horror with the use of poison gas led to its ban in 1925, which is still in effect today.

Tanks, Airplanes, and Submarines During World War I, advances in technology, such as the gasoline-powered engine, led the opposing forces to use tanks, airplanes, and submarines against each other. In 1916, Britain introduced the first armored tank. Mounted with machine guns, the tanks were designed to move across no man's land. Still, the first tanks broke down often. They failed to break the stalemate.

Both sides also used aircraft. At first, planes were utilized simply to observe enemy troop movements. In 1915, Germany used **zeppelins** (ZEP uh linz), large gas-filled balloons, to bomb the English coast. Later, both sides equipped airplanes with machine guns. Pilots known as "flying aces" confronted each other in the skies. These "dogfights" were spectacular, but had little effect on the course of the war on the ground.

Submarines proved much more important. German **U-boats,** nicknamed from the German word for submarine, *Unterseeboot,* did tremendous damage to the Allied side, sinking merchant ships carrying vital supplies to Britain. To defend against the submarines, the Allies organized **convoys,** or groups of merchant ships protected by warships.

☑ **INFER** How did U-boat attacks affect the fighting on land?

Other European Fronts

From the outset of World War I, Germany and Austria-Hungary battled Russia on the Eastern Front. There, battle lines shifted back and forth, sometimes over large areas. Even though the armies were not mired in trench warfare, casualties rose even higher than on the Western Front. The results were just as indecisive.

Mounting Russian Losses in the East In August 1914, Russian armies pushed into eastern Germany. Then, the Russians suffered a disastrous defeat at Tannenberg. Reeling from the disaster, the Russians retreated. After Tannenberg, the warring armies in the east fought on Russian soil.

>> On the Italian front, soldiers trekked through the Alps using snowshoes and skis. At times, they even engaged in battle while wearing their skis. **Analyze Visuals** Based on this image, what else besides deadly weapons caused high casualty rates?

As the least industrialized of the great powers, Russia was poorly equipped to fight a modern war. Although Russian factories geared up to produce rifles and other machinery for war, Russia lacked the roads and railroads to carry goods to the front. As the war raged on, some troops even lacked rifles. Still, Russian commanders continued to send masses of peasant soldiers into combat.

War in Southern Europe Southeastern Europe was another battleground. In 1915, Bulgaria joined the Central Powers and helped defeat its old rival Serbia. Romania, hoping to gain some land in Hungary, joined the Allies in 1916, only to be crushed by the Central Powers.

Also in 1915, Italy declared war on Austria-Hungary and later on Germany. The Allies had agreed in a secret treaty to give Italy some Austrian-ruled lands on its northern border. Over the next two years, the Italians and Austrians fought numerous battles, with few major breakthroughs. In October 1917, Italy suffered a major setback during the battle of Caporetto, but French and British forces stepped in to stop the Central Powers from advancing into Italy. Still, Caporetto proved as disastrous for Italy as Tannenberg had been for Russia.

CONTRAST How was the Eastern Front different from the Western Front?

A Global Conflict

Though most of the fighting took place in Europe, World War I was a global conflict. In 1914, Japan joined the Allies by declaring war on Germany. Japan used the war as an excuse to seize German outposts in China and islands in the Pacific. Japan's advances in East Asia and the Pacific would have far-reaching consequences in the years ahead as ambitious Japanese leaders set out to expand their footholds in China.

The Ottoman Empire Joins the War Because of its strategic location, the Ottoman empire was a desirable ally. If the Ottoman Turks had joined the Allies, the Central Powers would have been almost completely encircled. However, the Turks joined the Central Powers in late October 1914. The Turks then cut off crucial Allied supply lines to Russia through the **Dardanelles,** a vital strait connecting the Black Sea and the Mediterranean.

In 1915, the Allies sent a massive force of British, Indian, Australian, and New Zealander troops to attempt to open up the strait. At the battle of Gallipoli (guh LIP uh lee), Ottoman troops trapped the Allies on the beaches of the Gallipoli peninsula. In January 1916, after 10 months and more than 200,000 casualties, the Allies finally withdrew from the Dardanelles.

Despite their victory at Gallipoli, the war did not go well for the Ottomans on a second front, the Middle East. The Ottoman empire included vast areas of Arab land. In 1916, Arab nationalists led by Husayn ibn Ali declared a revolt against Ottoman rule. The British government sent Colonel **T. E. Lawrence**—later known as Lawrence of Arabia—to support the Arab revolt. Lawrence led guerrilla raids against the Ottomans, dynamiting bridges and supply trains. Eventually, the Ottoman empire lost a great deal of territory to the Arabs, including the key city of Baghdad.

Deportation and Genocide Against Armenians Meanwhile, the Ottoman empire was fighting Russia on a third front in the Caucasus Mountains. This region was home to ethnic Armenians, some of whom lived under Ottoman rule and some of whom lived under Russian rule. As Christians, the Armenians were a minority in the Ottoman empire and did not have the same rights as Muslims. Still, they prospered—much to the resentment of their neighbors.

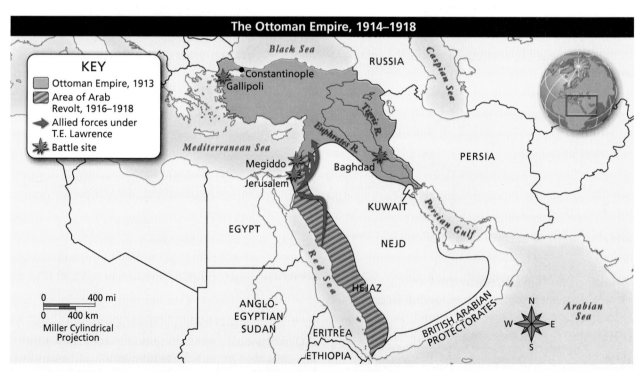

>> **Analyze Maps** How did the Arab revolt against the Ottoman empire affect the Allied cause?

Starting in 1915, the Ottoman government embarked on a brutal campaign against the Armenians, some of whom had joined the Russian forces. Claiming Armenians were traitors, the government ordered the deportation of the entire Armenian population from the war zone. But Henry Morgenthau, the U.S. ambassador to the Ottoman Empire, disputed Ottoman claims that the deportations were a wartime necessity:

". . . When the Turkish authorities gave the orders for these deportations, they were merely giving the death warrant to a whole race . . . in their conversations with me, they made no particular attempt to conceal the fact."

—Henry Morgenthau, *Ambassador Morgenthau's Story*

During barbarous forced marches, between 600,000 and 1.5 million Armenians were killed or died from hunger or thirst. A later wave of atrocities forced most of the remaining Armenians from Turkey. Many Armenians fled to other countries, including the United States.

Survivors of the genocide were not able to return to their homeland. Their property was seized by the new Turkish government. Today nearly ten million Armenians are part of the Armenian diaspora. At Morgenthau's urging, the United States government organized the Near East Relief Agency to aid genocide victims.

European Colonies and the War European colonies were also drawn into the struggle. The Allies overran scattered German colonies in Africa and Asia. They also turned to their own colonies and dominions for troops, laborers, and supplies. Colonial recruits from British India and French West Africa fought on European battlefields. Canada, Australia, and New Zealand sent troops to Britain's aid.

People in the colonies had mixed feelings about serving. Some were reluctant to serve rulers who did not treat them fairly. Other colonial troops volunteered eagerly. They expected that their service would be a step toward citizenship or independence. Such hopes would be dashed after the war.

☑ **SUMMARIZE** What were the major features and immediate effects of the war in the Middle East?

>> Troops from Europe's colonies fought in World War I. These soldiers in a dugout near Verdun in 1915 are from French Africa.

☑ **ASSESSMENT**

1. **Identify Central Issues** What is a stalemate, and why did one develop on the Western Front?

2. **Identify Cause and Effect** What were the effects of major new military technologies on World War I?

3. **Draw Conclusions** How did the Ottoman empire's entry into the war on the side of the Central Powers have a negative impact on Russia?

4. **Support Ideas with Evidence** How did the war contribute to the genocide against the Armenian people? Include details from the text.

5. **Synthesize** How did imperialism influence the war?

6. **Connections to Today** Why do you think the use of poison gas as a weapon was banned in 1925? Do you think the ban is enforceable today? Explain your answer.

The Costs of Total War

Soldiers of World War I suffered from the horrors of war on an unprecedented level due to widespread fighting and devastating new technology. But the impact on civilians was also significant, and sometimes even deadly. Total war is the channeling of a nation's entire resources into a war effort. Military attacks on ports and factories is one way in which total war affected civilians.

The following sources provide two viewpoints on total war during World War I. The first is a military perspective from German pilot Captain Peter Strasser. The second provides a civilian perspective from a young English boy, Jack Littenstein, who witnessed a German zeppelin (floating airship) attack on London. Littenstein wrote the account for a school assignment.

As you read, think about how you may have felt about these events if you had been living during this time. Then answer the questions to compare perspectives on total war.

>> A German zeppelin bombs Britain during World War I.

Primary Source 1

Letter From German Captain Peter Strasser To his Mother, March 1916

We who strike the enemy where his heart beats have been slandered as "baby-killers"and "murderers of women." . . . What we do is repugnant to us too, but necessary. Very necessary. Nowadays there is no such animal as a non-combatant; modern warfare is total warfare.

☑ **ANALYZE WORD CHOICES** What does the word *slandered* mean? Why does Captain Strasser use that word?

A soldier cannot function at the front without the factory worker, the farmer and all the other providers behind him. You and I, Mother, have discussed this subject, and I know you understand what I say. My men are brave and honourable. Their cause is holy, so how can they sin while doing their duty? If what we do is frightful, then may frightfulness be Germany's salvation.

☑ **DETERMINE AUTHOR'S POINT OF VIEW** How does Strasser feel about the work that he and his men are doing?

Primary Source 2

Account of a London Air Raid, J. Littenstein, September 1915

It was our Jewish New Year and I was sitting in my aunt's house reading the "Boy's Friends." My sister and my cousin were talking politics. One said the German Navy was afraid to come out, and the other said that Our fleet ought to go and fetch them. This she said with some emphasis on the "our."

☑ **CITE EVIDENCE** What evidence is there in this account that the war was having an effect on civilians?

Suddenly Bang! Crash! Tinkle! Tinkle! There was a splintering of wood and a crash of falling glass. We all sprang to our feet with surprising alacrity. At other times wild horses could not drag me from the paper I was reading. As it was I was dragged away from it this time. Baa-ang! There was another crash.

"Bombs and Zeppelins" said my aunt. She was cool but the other women were panic-stricken. They gave vent to shrieks and screams that would have done credit to a hyena. I was shivering like a jelly but I soon got over it. There was a pattering of feet and a knock and the boy from upstairs came down. He was a boy scout Edgar Brown by name. My aunt had snatched the baby from the bed in a blanket and had put [out] all the lights but one. "The basement" she said putting out the last light, and we all ran downstairs.

☑ **INTEGRATE INFORMATION FROM DIVERSE SOURCES** Why is it significant that this account came from a young civilian?

Boom! Boom! Boom! The short sharp bark of anti-aircraft guns smote upon our ears. "Those are our guns" said Edgar. "Coming up to have a look" said I. "Righto" said Edgar. We went up to the door and a sight that I shall never forget met my eyes. The "National Penny Bank" was blazing like a bonfire. . . .

Next morning I learnt that the casualties were 106.

☑ **SUMMARIZE** Based on Littenstein's descriptions, how did total war impact civilians?

☑ ASSESSMENT

Be sure to cite specific evidence from the sources as you answer the following questions.

1. **Determine Author's Purpose** What is Strasser's main argument? Do you agree with it?

2. **Determine Meaning** What is Littenstein trying to convey about the zeppelin attack?

3. **Compare and Contrast** How are the perspectives on total war similar and different in the selections?

4. **Draw Conclusions** Do you think Strasser may have had a different opinion about total war if he would have read Littenstein's account, or if he would have witnessed an attack on civilians up close? Explain your answer.

5. **Develop Empathy** How do these excerpts help you understand the perspectives of some soldiers and civilians during times of war? How do you think you would feel in these situations?

16.3

🖥 **GO ONLINE to Project Imagine: Do Your Bit for Britain** to explore women's contributions to the war effort.

🅱 BOUNCE to Activate Flipped Video

Objectives

Describe how World War I became a total war.

Explain how U.S. entry into the war led to an Allied victory.

List the effects of World War I in terms of financial costs, high casualty rates, and political impact.

Describe the issues at the Paris Peace Conference and the impact of Woodrow Wilson's Fourteen Points.

Summarize the terms and impact of the Treaty of Versailles.

Key Terms

total war
conscription
contraband
Lusitania
propaganda
atrocity
Fourteen Points
self-determination
armistice
pandemic
reparation
radical
collective security
mandate

World War I Ends

By 1917, European societies were cracking under the strain of war. Casualties on the fronts and shortages at home sapped morale. The stalemate dragged on, seemingly without end. Soon, however, the departure of one country from the war and the entry of another would tip the balance and end the stalemate.

Governments Direct Total War

As the struggle wore on, nations realized that a modern, mechanized war required the channeling of a nation's entire resources into the war effort, or **total war.** To achieve total war, governments began to take a stronger role in directing the economic and cultural lives of their people.

Recruiting and Supplying Huge Armies Early on, both sides set up systems to recruit, arm, transport, and supply armies that numbered in the millions. All of the warring nations except Britain immediately imposed universal military **conscription,** or "the draft," which required all young men to be ready for military or other service. Britain, too, instituted conscription in 1916. Germany set up a system of forced civilian labor as well.

Governments raised taxes and borrowed huge amounts of money to pay the costs of war. They rationed food and other products, from boots to gasoline. In addition, they introduced other economic controls, such as setting prices and forbidding strikes.

Blockades and Submarines Impact Economies At the start of the war, Britain's navy formed a blockade in the North Sea to keep ships from carrying supplies into and out of Germany. International law allowed wartime blockades to confiscate **contraband,** or military supplies and raw materials needed to

 GO ONLINE to access your digital course

make military supplies. Items such as food and clothing were exempt. Still, the British blockade stopped both types of goods from reaching Germany. As the war progressed, it became harder and harder to feed the German and Austrian people. In Germany, the winter of 1916 and 1917 was remembered as "the turnip winter," because the potato crop failed and people ate turnips instead.

To retaliate, Germany used U-boats to create its own blockade. In 1915, Germany declared that it would sink all ships carrying goods to Britain. In May 1915, a German submarine torpedoed the British liner **Lusitania** off the coast of Ireland. Almost 1,200 passengers were killed, including 128 Americans. Germany justified the attack, arguing that the *Lusitania* was carrying weapons.

When American President Woodrow Wilson threatened to cut off diplomatic relations with Germany, Germany agreed to restrict its submarine campaign. Before attacking any ship, U-boats would surface and give warning, allowing neutral passengers to escape to lifeboats. Unrestricted submarine warfare stopped—for the moment.

The Propaganda War Total war also meant controlling public opinion. Even in democratic countries, special boards censored the press. Their aim was to keep complete casualty figures and other discouraging news from reaching the public. Government censors also restricted popular literature, historical writings, motion pictures, and the arts.

Both sides waged a propaganda war. **Propaganda** is the spreading of ideas to promote a cause or to damage an opposing cause. Allied propaganda played up the brutality of Germany's invasion of Belgium.

The British and French press circulated tales of **atrocities,** horrible acts committed against innocent people. Although some atrocities did occur, often the stories were distorted by exaggerations or completely made up.

Governments also used propaganda to motivate military mobilization, especially in Britain before conscription started in 1916. In France and Germany, propaganda urged civilians to loan money to the government.

Women Contribute to the War Effort Women played a critical role in total war. As millions of men left to fight, women took over their jobs and kept national economies going. Many women worked in war industries, manufacturing weapons and supplies. Others joined women's branches of the

>> This painting portrays the sinking of the *Lusitania* by a German submarine. Unrestricted submarine warfare worsened American public opinion of Germany.

Daddy, what did YOU do in the Great War?

>> Posters such as this British one helped to stoke patriotic emotions. **Determine Author's Purpose** What did the creators of this poster hope that men would do after viewing this image?

 BOUNCE to Activate Gallery

armed forces. When food shortages threatened Britain, volunteers in the Women's Land Army went to the fields to grow their nation's food.

Nurses shared the dangers of the men whose wounds they tended. At aid stations close to the front lines, nurses often worked around the clock, especially after a big "push" brought a flood of casualties. In her diary, English nurse Vera Brittain describes sweating through 90-degree days in France, "stopping hemorrhages, replacing intestines, and draining and reinserting innumerable rubber tubes" with "gruesome human remnants heaped on the floor."

War work gave women a new sense of pride and confidence. After the war, most women had to give up their jobs to men returning home. Still, they had challenged the idea that women could not handle demanding and dangerous jobs. In many countries, including Britain, Germany, and the United States, women's support for the war effort helped them finally win the right to vote, after decades of struggle.

☑ **DRAW CONCLUSIONS** How can total war increase the power of government and have a lasting political impact?

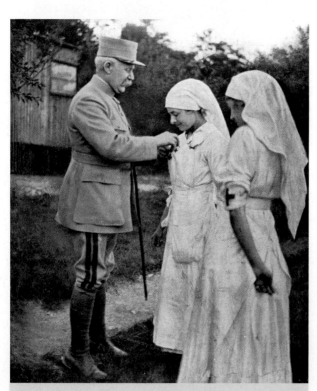

>> Women worked as nurses at the front in difficult and dangerous conditions. Here, a French general honors a nurse who took part in the battle of Verdun in 1916.

Morale Breaks Down

Despite inspiring propaganda, by 1917 the morale of troops and civilians had plunged. Germany was sending 15-year-old recruits to the front, and Britain was on the brink of bankruptcy.

War-Weary Civilians and Soldiers Long casualty lists, food shortages, and the failure of generals to win promised victories led to calls for peace. Instead of praising the glorious deeds of heroes, war poets like British soldier Siegfried Sassoon began denouncing the leaders whose errors wasted so many lives.

> You smug-faced crowds with kindling eye
>
> Who cheer when soldier lads march by,
>
> Sneak home and pray you'll never know
>
> The hell where youth and laughter go.
>
> —Siegfried Sassoon, "Suicide in the Trenches"

As morale collapsed, troops in some French units mutinied. In Italy, many soldiers deserted during the retreat at Caporetto. In Russia, soldiers left the front to join in a full-scale revolution back home.

Revolution in Russia Three years of war had hit Russia especially hard. Stories of incompetent generals and corruption eroded public confidence. In March 1917, bread riots in St. Petersburg erupted into a revolution that brought down the Russian monarchy. (You'll learn more about the causes and effects of the Russian Revolution in another lesson.) The new Russian government continued the war effort.

At first, the Allies welcomed the overthrow of the tsar. They hoped Russia would institute a democratic government and become a stronger ally. But in October of that year, a second revolution brought V. I. Lenin to power. Lenin had promised to pull Russian troops out of the war. Early in 1918, Lenin signed the Treaty of Brest-Litovsk (brest lih TAWFSK) with Germany. The treaty ended Russian participation in World War I.

Russia's withdrawal had an immediate impact on the war. With Russia out of the struggle, Germany could concentrate its forces on the Western Front. In the spring of 1918, the Central Powers stood ready to achieve the great breakthrough they had sought for so long. But by then, Germany faced a new opponent. The United States had entered the war.

☑ **CITE EVIDENCE** What evidence shows that soldiers' morale declined and negatively affected the war effort?

The United States Enters the War

Soon after the Russian Revolution began, another event altered the balance of forces. The United States declared war on Germany. Many factors contributed to the decision of the United States to exchange neutrality for war in 1917.

Unrestricted Submarine Warfare A major reason for the U.S. entry into the war was German submarine attacks. After the sinking of the Lusitania and under pressure from President Wilson, Germany had agreed to restrict its submarine campaign. By early 1917, however, Germany was desperate to break the stalemate in the war. On February 1, the German government announced that it would resume unrestricted submarine warfare. Wilson angrily denounced Germany.

Anti-German Sentiment Grows Many Americans supported the Allies because of cultural ties. The United States shared a cultural history and language with Britain and sympathized with France as another democracy. On the other hand, some German Americans favored the Central Powers. So did many Irish Americans, who resented British rule of Ireland, and Russian Jewish immigrants, who did not want to be allied with the tsar. The resumption of unrestricted submarine warfare, however, increased anger toward Germany and spurred support for the Allies.

Another German move also angered Americans. In early 1917, the British intercepted a message from the German foreign minister, Arthur Zimmermann, to his ambassador in Mexico. In the note, Zimmerman wrote that if Mexico joined Germany in the event of war with the United States, Germany would help Mexico "to reconquer the lost territory in New Mexico, Texas, and Arizona." Britain revealed the Zimmermann note to the American government. When the note became public, anti-German feeling intensified in the United States.

>> Soldiers ate, slept, fought and died in the trenches. As the war dragged on and casualties mounted, morale was severely tested.

>> Germany resumed unrestricted submarine warfare in 1917. Here, President Wilson reads a German message and ponders what to do. **Analyze Political Cartoons** What does the overflowing waste basket suggest?

Wilson Asks for a "War to End War" In April 1917, Wilson asked Congress to declare war on Germany. "We have no selfish ends to serve," he stated. Instead, he painted the conflict idealistically as a war "to make the world safe for democracy" and later as a "war to end war."

The United States needed months to recruit, train, supply, and transport a modern army across the Atlantic. But by 1918, about two million American soldiers had joined the war-weary Allied troops fighting on the Western Front. Although relatively few American troops engaged in combat, their arrival gave Allied troops a much-needed morale boost. Just as important to the debt-ridden Allies was American financial aid.

Wilson's Fourteen Points Though he had failed to maintain American neutrality, Wilson still hoped to be a peacemaker. In January 1918, he issued the **Fourteen Points,** a list of his terms for resolving both this war and future wars. He called for freedom of the seas, free trade, large-scale reductions of arms, and an end to secret treaties. For Eastern Europe, Wilson favored **self-determination,** the right of people to choose their own form of government. Finally, Wilson urged the creation of a "general association of nations" to keep the peace in the future.

☑ **INFER** Why did President Woodrow Wilson think that World War I was "the war to end wars"?

The Great War Ends

A final showdown on the Western Front began in early 1918. The Germans badly wanted to achieve a major victory before eager American troops arrived in Europe.

Final Offensives In March 1918, the Germans launched a huge offensive on the Western Front with troops newly freed from fighting in Russia. By July, the spring offensive had driven the Allies back 40 miles, the biggest German breakthrough in three years. The rapid push exhausted the German forces and cost heavy casualties.

By then, fresh American troops were pouring into the Western Front. The Allies launched a counter-offensive, slowly driving German forces back through France and Belgium. In September, German generals told the Kaiser that the war could not be won.

Germany Asks for Peace Uprisings exploded among hungry city dwellers across Germany. German commanders advised the kaiser to step down. William II did so in early November, fleeing into exile in the Netherlands.

WOODROW WILSON'S FOURTEEN POINTS	
1. No secret treaties	10. Peoples of Austria-Hungary should have freest opportunity for autonomous development.
2. Freedom of the seas	
3. Free trade	11. Occupation forces to be evacuated from Romania, Serbia and Montenegro; Serbia should have free and secure access to the sea
4. Large–scale reduction of arms	
5. Impartial adjustment of colonial claims based on interests of governments and native populations.	
6. Evacuation of all Russian territory; providing Russia the best opportunity for self–determination	12. Autonomous development for the non–Turkish peoples of the Ottoman Empire; free passage for all ships through the Dardanelles
7. Evacuation and restoration of Belgium as a sovereign nation	13. Independence for Poland, with free and secure access to the sea
8. Liberation of France; return of the region of Alsace–Lorraine to France	14. Formation of a general association of nations to guarantee to its members political independence and territorial integrity (the League of Nations)
9. Readjustment of Italy's frontiers based on recognizable lines of nationality	

>> **Analyze Information** Which of Wilson's Fourteen Points deal with countries having free access to international commerce? Why did Wilson consider this so important?

The Costs of World War I

COUNTRY	ALLIES				CENTRAL POWERS	
	RUSSIA	BRITISH EMPIRE	FRANCE	UNITED STATES	GERMANY	AUSTRIA-HUNGARY
MOBILIZED FORCES	12,000,000	8,904,467	8,410,000	4,355,000	11,000,000	7,800,000
KILLED	1,700,000	908,371	1,357,800	116,516	1,773,700	1,200,000
WOUNDED	4,950,000	2,090,212	4,266,000	204,002	4,216,058	3,620,000
PRISONERS AND MISSING	2,500,000	191,652	537,000	4,500	1,152,800	2,200,000
TOTAL CASUALTIES	9,150,000	3,190,235	6,160,800	323,018	7,142,558	7,020,000
CASUALTY RATE	76%	36%	73%	7%	65%	90%
FINANCIAL COSTS	$25 billion	$55 billion	$48 billion	$32 billion	$60 billion	$22 billion

SOURCE: *The Harper Encyclopedia of Military*, History, R. Ernest Dupuy and Trevor N. Dupuy; *The Great War*, www.pbs.org.

>> World War I ended in 1918, but its human and economic costs would be felt for decades. Many nations had thrown all their resources into the fight, and their losses were staggering.

By autumn, Austria-Hungary was also reeling toward collapse. As the government in Vienna tottered, the subject nationalities revolted, splintering the empire of the Hapsburgs. Bulgaria and the Ottoman empire also asked for peace.

The new German government sought an **armistice,** or agreement to end fighting, with the Allies. At 11 A.M. on November 11, 1918, the Great War at last came to an end.

The Human Toll The human and material costs of the war were staggering. More than 8.5 million men had died in battle. More than twice that number had been wounded, many of them disabled for life. Historians estimate that at least 6 million civilians also lost their lives as a result of the war.

The devastation was made even worse in 1918 by a deadly **pandemic** of influenza. A pandemic is the spread of a disease across a large area—in this case, the whole world. In just a few months, the flu killed more than 20 million people worldwide.

The Economic Toll In battle zones from France to Russia, homes, farms, factories, roads, and churches had been shelled into rubble. People had fled these areas as refugees. Now they had to return and start to rebuild. The costs of reconstruction and paying off huge war debts would burden an already battered Europe.

Shaken and disillusioned, people everywhere felt bitter about the war. The Allies blamed the conflict on their defeated foes and insisted that the losers make **reparations,** or payments for war damage. The stunned Central Powers, who had viewed the armistice as a cease-fire rather than a surrender, looked for scapegoats on whom they could blame their defeat.

The Political Toll Under the stress of war, governments had collapsed in Russia, Germany, Austria-Hungary, and the Ottoman empire. Political **radicals,** or people who wanted to make extreme changes, dreamed of building a new social order from the chaos. Conservatives warned against the spread of Bolshevism, or communism, as it was soon called.

Unrest also swept through Europe's colonial empires. African and Asian soldiers had discovered that the imperial powers were not as invincible as they seemed. Colonial troops returned home with a more cynical view of Europeans and renewed hopes for independence.

☑ **GENERATE EXPLANATIONS** Why might the war cause an economic recession or depression in Europe?

Making the Peace

Just weeks after the war ended, President Wilson boarded a steamship bound for France. He had decided to go in person to Paris, where Allied leaders would make the peace. Wilson was certain that he could bring a "just peace" to the world. "Tell me what is right," Wilson urged his advisors, "and I'll fight for it."

To a weary, angry world, Wilson seemed a symbol of hope. His talk of democracy and self-determination raised expectations for a just and lasting peace—even in defeated Germany. Sadly, it would not be that easy. Europe was a shattered continent. Its problems, and those of the world, would not be solved for many years afterward.

Allies Have Conflicting Goals The victorious Allies met at the Paris Peace Conference to discuss the fate of Europe, the former Ottoman empire, and various colonies around the world. The Central Powers and Russia, under its new communist government, were not allowed to take part in the negotiations.

Wilson was one of three strong leaders who dominated the Paris Peace Conference. He was a dedicated reformer and at times was so stubbornly convinced that he was right that he could be hard to work with. Wilson urged for "peace without victory" based on the Fourteen Points.

Two other Allied leaders at the peace conference had different aims. British Prime Minister David Lloyd George had promised to build a postwar Britain "fit for heroes"—a goal that would cost money. The chief goal of the French leader, Georges Clemenceau (KLEM un soh), was to weaken Germany so that it could never again threaten France. "Mr. Wilson bores me with his Fourteen Points," complained Clemenceau. "Why, God Almighty has only ten!"

Obstacles to Settlement Crowds of other representatives circled around the "Big Three" with their own demands. Among the most difficult issues were the secret agreements made by the Allies during the war. Italy had signed one such treaty. The Italian prime minister, Vittorio Orlando (awr LAN doh), insisted that the Allies honor their secret treaty to give former Austro-Hungarian lands to Italy. Such agreements often violated the idea of self-determination.

Self-determination posed other problems. Many people who had been ruled by Russia, Austria-Hungary, or the Ottoman empire now demanded national states of their own. The territories claimed by these peoples often overlapped, so it was impossible to satisfy them all. Some ethnic groups became unwanted minorities in newly created states.

Wilson had to compromise on his Fourteen Points. However, he stood firm on his goal of creating an international League of Nations. The League would be based on the idea of **collective security,** a system in which a group of nations acts as one to preserve the peace of all. Wilson felt sure that the League could correct any mistakes made in Paris.

The Treaty of Versailles In June 1919, the Allies ordered representatives of the new German Republic to sign the treaty they had drawn up at the palace of Versailles (vur SY) outside Paris. The German delegates were horrified. The Treaty of Versailles forced Germany to assume full blame for causing the war.

It also imposed huge reparations that would burden an already damaged German economy. The reparations covered not only the destruction caused by the war, but also pensions for millions of Allied soldiers or their widows and families. The total cost of German reparations would come to over $400 billion in today's money.

OVERWEIGHTED.

PRESIDENT WILSON. "HERE'S YOUR OLIVE BRANCH. NOW GET BUSY."
DOVE OF PEACE. "OF COURSE I WANT TO PLEASE EVERYBODY; BUT ISN'T THIS A BIT THICK?"

>> In this cartoon, President Wilson says to the dove, "Here's your olive branch. Now get busy." **Analyze Political Cartoons** Does the cartoonist think Wilson's solution will work?

Europe, 1920

>> **Analyze Maps** Based on this map and the text, why were many Germans unhappy with the territorial changes that occurred after World War I?

BOUNCE to Activate Map

Other parts of the treaty were aimed at weakening Germany. The treaty severely limited the size of the once-feared German military. It returned Alsace and Lorraine to France, removed hundreds of square miles of territory from western and eastern Germany, and stripped Germany of its overseas colonies. The treaty compelled many Germans to leave the homes they had made in Russia, Poland, Alsace-Lorraine, and the German colonies to return to Germany or Austria.

But, the Treaty of Versailles would ultimately fail. The Germans signed because they had no choice. However, German resentment of the Treaty of Versailles would poison the international climate for 20 years. That resentment helped to fuel support for the Nazis in the 1930s. It would help spark an even deadlier world war in the years to come.

☑ **COMPARE POINTS OF VIEW** How did the goals of the Big Three Leaders—Wilson, Lloyd George, and Clemenceau—conflict?

Effects of the Peace Settlements

The Allies drew up separate treaties with the other Central Powers. These treaties redrew the map of Eastern Europe and affected colonial peoples around the globe. Like the Treaty of Versailles, these treaties left widespread dissatisfaction.

New Nations in Europe A key principle of Wilson's Fourteen Points was self-determination. This goal helped a band of new nations emerge in Eastern Europe where the German, Austrian, Ottoman, and Russian empires had once ruled.

Poland became an independent nation after more than 100 years of foreign rule. The Baltic states of Latvia, Lithuania, and Estonia fought for and achieved independence. Three new republics— Czechoslovakia, Austria, and Hungary—rose in the old Hapsburg heartland. In the Balkans, the peacemakers created a new South Slav state, Yugoslavia, dominated by Serbia.

Despite the settlement, Eastern Europe remained a center of political conflict and unrest. The new nations were also relatively poor, with agricultural economies and little capital for industry.

The Mandate System European colonies in Africa, Asia, and the Pacific had looked to the Paris Peace Conference with high hopes. Nationalist leaders in these regions expected that the peace would bring new respect and an end to imperial rule. They took up Wilson's call for self-determination.

However, the leaders at Paris applied self-determination only to parts of Europe. Outside Europe, the victorious Allies added to their overseas empires.

>> Delegates attend the first meeting of the League of Nations on December 4, 1920, in the Hall of Reformation in Geneva, Switzerland.

The treaties created a system of **mandates,** territories administered by Western powers. Britain and France gained mandates over German colonies in Africa. Japan and Australia were given mandates over some Pacific islands. The treaties handled lands that used to be part of the Ottoman empire as if they were colonies, too.

In theory, mandates were to be held until they were able to stand alone. In practice, they became colonies, remaining under the political and economic control of the Allied powers. From Africa to the Middle East and across Asia, people living in the mandates felt betrayed by the peacemakers.

Widespread Discontent Germans and colonial peoples were not the only groups dissatisfied by the peace. Italy was angry because it did not get all the lands promised in its secret treaty with the Allies. Japan protested the refusal of the Western powers to recognize its claims in China. At the same time, China was forced to accept Japanese control over some former German holdings. Russia, excluded from the peace talks, resented the reestablishment of a Polish nation and three independent Baltic states on lands that had been part of the Russian empire.

All of these discontented nations bided their time. They waited for a chance to revise the peace settlements in their favor.

The League of Nations The Paris Peace Conference did offer one beacon of hope with the establishment of the League of Nations. More than 40 nations joined the League. They agreed to negotiate disputes rather than resort to war and to take common action against any aggressor state.

Wilson's dream had become a reality, or so he thought. On his return from Paris, Wilson faced resistance from his own Senate.

Some Republican senators, led by Henry Cabot Lodge, wanted to restrict the treaty so that the United States would not be obligated to fight in future wars. Wilson would not accept Lodge's compromises. In the end, the Senate refused to ratify the treaty, and the United States never joined the League. Congress's rejection robbed the treaty of its political authority leading other countries to lessen their commitment to it.

The loss of the United States weakened the League's power. In addition, the League had no power outside of its member states. As time soon revealed, the League could not prevent war. Still, it was a first step toward something genuinely new—an international organization dedicated to maintaining peace and advancing the interests of all peoples.

☑ **DRAW CONCLUSIONS** How did the refusal of the United States to join the League of Nations weaken the League's power?

☑ ASSESSMENT

1. **Identify Cause and Effect** How did World War I affect the role of women in society?

2. **Analyze Context** Why did it take so long for the United States to enter World War I?

3. **Compare and Contrast** After World War I, why were conditions ripe for social and political change in Russia, but not in the United States?

4. **Predict Consequences** How might the harsh provisions of the Treaty of Versailles affect conditions in Germany?

5. **Quest Connections** How can a long war with high casualties change the lives of civilians, soldiers, and leaders?

GO ONLINE to access this biography: Woodrow Wilson

Conflicting Goals for Peace

In a speech to Congress on January 8, 1918, President Wilson laid out America's war aims and his vision for peace after the war. His speech included fourteen key points upon which he believed the peace following the war must be based. However, not all of Wilson's ideas were adopted at the Paris Peace Conference.

The Fourteen Points speech is excerpted below. Following it is an excerpt from the opening speech of Premier Georges Clemenceau of France at the Versailles conference in 1919. It is his response to the Fourteen Points.

As you read, compare their viewpoints on postwar peace.

>> Woodrow Wilson

Primary Source 1

The Fourteen Points, Woodrow Wilson

. . . What we demand in this war, therefore, is nothing peculiar [unique] to ourselves. It is that the world be made fit and safe to live in; and particularly that it be made safe for every peace-loving nation which, like our own, wishes to live its own life, [and] determine its own institutions [choose its own government]. . . . The program of the world's peace, therefore, is our only program; and that program, the only possible program as we see it, is this:

☑ **DISTINGUISH AMONG FACT, OPINION, AND REASONED JUDGMENT** When Wilson says, "The program of the world's peace, therefore, is our only program, the only possible program as we see it, is this," is this a fact, an opinion, or a reasoned judgment? Explain your answer.

1. Open covenants [formal agreements] of peace, openly arrived at, after which there shall be no private international understandings of any kind but [instead] diplomacy shall proceed always frankly [openly and honestly] and in the public view.

☑ **EXPLAIN AN ARGUMENT** Why might Wilson think that prohibiting secret agreements between nations is necessary in order to avoid war?

2. Absolute freedom of navigation upon the seas, outside territorial waters, alike in peace and in war, except as the seas may be closed in whole or in part by international action for the enforcement of international covenants.

☑ **PARAPHRASE** Restate Point 2 in your own words.

3. The removal, so far as possible, of all economic barriers and the establishment of an equality of trade conditions among all the nations consenting to the peace and associating themselves for its maintenance.
4. Adequate guarantees given and taken that national armaments will be reduced to the lowest point consistent with domestic safety.

☑ **ANALYZE WORD CHOICES** What two things does Wilson leave unspecified in Point 4?

5. A free, open-minded, and absolutely impartial adjustment of all colonial claims, based upon a strict observance of the principle that in determining all such questions of sovereignty the interests of the populations concerned must have equal weight with the equitable claims of the government whose title is to be determined....

14. A general association [organization] of nations must be formed under specific covenants for the purpose of affording mutual guarantees of political independence and territorial integrity to great and small states alike.

☑ **INTEGRATE INFORMATION FROM DIVERSE SOURCES** Does such an association of nations exist today? If so, what is it?

Primary Source 2

Speech at Versailles, Georges Clemenceau

I come now to the order of the day. The first question is as follows: "The responsibility of the authors of the war." The second is thus expressed: "Penalties for crimes committed during the war." ... [The task at hand] is a very vast field. But we beg of you to begin by examining the question as to the responsibility of the authors of the war. I do not need to set forth our reasons for this. If we wish to establish justice in the world we can do so now, for we have won victory and can impose the penalties demanded by justice.

We shall insist on the imposition of penalties on the authors of the abominable crimes committed during the war. Has anyone any question to ask in regard to this? If not, I would again remind you that every delegation should devote itself to the study of this first question, which has been made the subject of reports by eminent jurists, and of a report which will be sent to you entitled, "An Inquiry into the Criminal Responsibility of the Emperor William II."

☑ ASSESSMENT

1. **Compare and Contrast** Points 6–13 deal with specific territorial issues, such as breaking up the Ottoman and Austro-Hungarian Empires and restoring sovereignty to Belgium and Poland. To an American in 1918, how would those points be different from the ones excerpted here?

2. **Explain** What demands, if met, would have convinced France to embrace the Fourteen Points?

3. **Integrate Information From Diverse Sources** Why might isolationists oppose some or all of Wilson's Fourteen Points?

4. **Draw Inferences** What political impact do you think Wilson's Fourteen Points had?

5. **Develop Empathy** Preventing war seems like an admirable goal. Why might people reject some or all of Wilson's points?

GO ONLINE to access primary sources

16.4

Vladimir Ilyich Lenin took his revolutionary ideas directly to the people, addressing crowds in the streets.

Revolution in Russia

The year 1913 marked the 300th anniversary of the Romanov dynasty. Everywhere, Russians honored the tsar and his family. Tsarina Alexandra felt confident that the people loved Nicholas too much to ever threaten him. "They are constantly frightening the emperor with threats of revolution," she told a friend, "and here,— you see it yourself—we need merely to show ourselves and at once their hearts are ours."

Causes of the February Revolution

Appearances were deceiving. In March 1917, the first of two revolutions would topple the Romanov dynasty and pave the way for even more radical changes. These revolutions are known to Russians as the February and October Revolutions, and to many westerners as the March and November Revolutions.

In 1917, Russia still used an old calendar, which was 13 days behind the one used in Western Europe. Russia did not adopt the Western calendar until 1918.

Roots of Discontent In 1914, the huge Russian empire stretched from Eastern Europe east to the Pacific Ocean. Unlike Western Europe, Russia was slow to industrialize despite its huge potential. Landowning nobles, priests, and an autocratic tsar controlled the government and economy. Much of the majority peasant population endured stark poverty. As Russia began to industrialize, a small middle class and an urban working class emerged.

 BOUNCE to Activate Flipped Video

Objectives

Explain the causes of the February (March) Revolution.

Describe the goals of Lenin and the Bolsheviks in the October Revolution.

Summarize the outcome of the civil war in Russia.

Analyze how Lenin built a Communist state in the Soviet Union.

Key Terms

proletariat
soviet
V. I. Lenin
Cheka
commissar

After the Revolution of 1905, Nicholas had failed to solve Russia's basic political, economic, and social problems. The elected Duma set up after the revolution had no real power. Moderates pressed for a constitution and social change. But Nicholas II, a weak and ineffective leader, blocked attempts to limit his authority. Like past tsars, he relied on his secret police and other enforcers to impose his will. A corrupt bureaucracy and an overburdened court system added to the government's problems.

Revolutionaries hatched radical plots. Some hoped to lead discontented peasants to overthrow the tsarist regime. Marxists tried to ignite revolution among the **proletariat**—the growing class of factory and railroad workers, miners, and urban wage earners. A revolution, they believed, would occur when the time was ripe.

World War I Intensifies Discontent The outbreak of war in 1914 fueled national pride and united Russians. Armies dashed to battle with enthusiasm. But like the Crimean and Russo-Japanese wars, World War I quickly strained Russian resources. Factories could not turn out enough supplies. The transportation system broke down, delivering only a trickle of crucial materials to the front. By 1915, many soldiers had no rifles and no ammunition. Badly

equipped and poorly led, they died in staggering numbers. In 1915 alone, Russian casualties reached two million.

In a patriotic gesture, Nicholas II went to the front to take personal charge. The decision proved a disastrous blunder. The tsar was no more competent than many of his generals. Worse, he left domestic affairs to the tsarina, Alexandra.

In Nicholas's absence, Alexandra relied on the advice of Gregory Rasputin, an illiterate peasant and self-proclaimed "holy man." The tsarina came to believe that Rasputin had miraculous powers after he helped her son, who suffered from hemophilia, a disorder in which any injury can result in uncontrollable bleeding.

By 1916, Rasputin's influence over Alexandra had reached new heights and weakened confidence in the government. Fearing for the monarchy, a group of Russian nobles killed Rasputin on December 29, 1916.

Tsar Nicholas II Steps Down By March 1917, disasters on the battlefield, combined with food and fuel shortages on the home front, brought the monarchy to collapse. In St. Petersburg (renamed Petrograd during the war), workers were going on strike. Marchers, mostly women, surged through the streets, shouting, "Bread! Bread!" Troops refused to fire on the demonstrators, leaving the government helpless. Finally, on the advice of military and political leaders, the tsar abdicated.

Duma politicians then set up a provisional, or temporary, government. Middle-class liberals in the government began preparing a constitution for a new Russian republic. At the same time, they continued the war against Germany.

☑ **IDENTIFY CAUSE AND EFFECT** What were the causes of the Russian Revolution of March 1917?

Lenin Leads the Bolsheviks

Outside the provisional government, revolutionary socialists plotted their own course. In Petrograd and other cities, they set up **soviets,** or councils of workers and soldiers. At first, the soviets worked democratically within the government. Before long, though, the Bolsheviks, a radical socialist group, took charge. The leader of the Bolsheviks was a determined revolutionary, V. I. Lenin.

>> Gregory Rasputin's followers, including the tsarina Alexandra, considered him a mystic and a faith healer. His opponents called him the "mad monk."

The Making of a Revolutionary **V. I. Lenin** was born Vladimir Ilyich Ulyanov (ool YAHN uf) in 1870 to a middle-class family. He adopted the name Lenin when he became a revolutionary.

When he was 17, his older brother was arrested and hanged for plotting to kill the tsar. The execution branded his family as a threat to the state and made the young Vladimir hate the tsarist government. As a young man, Lenin read the works of Karl Marx and participated in student demonstrations. He spread Marxist ideas among factory workers along with other socialists, including Nadezhda Krupskaya (nah DYEZ duh kroop SKY uh), the daughter of a poor noble family.

In 1895, Lenin and Krupskaya were arrested and sent to Siberia. During their imprisonment, they were married. After their release, they went into exile in Switzerland. There, they worked tirelessly to spread revolutionary ideas that would eventually succeed in shifting political thought in Russia and other nations.

Lenin Adapts Marxism Lenin adapted Marxist ideas to fit Russian conditions. Marx had predicted that the industrial working class would rise spontaneously to overthrow capitalism. But Russia did not have a large urban proletariat. Instead, Lenin called for an elite group to lead the revolution and set up a "dictatorship of the proletariat." Though this elite revolutionary party represented a small percentage of socialists, Lenin gave them the name Bolsheviks, meaning "majority."

In Western Europe, many leading socialists had come to think that socialism could be achieved through gradual and moderate reforms such as higher wages, increased suffrage, and social welfare programs.

A group of socialists in Russia, the Mensheviks, favored this approach. The Bolsheviks rejected it. To Lenin, reforms of this nature were merely capitalist tricks to repress the masses. Only revolution, he said, could bring about needed changes.

In March 1917, Lenin was still in exile. As Russia stumbled into revolution, Germany saw a chance to weaken its enemy by helping Lenin return home. Lenin rushed across Germany to the Russian frontier in a special train. He greeted a crowd of fellow exiles and activists with this cry: "Long live the worldwide Socialist revolution!"

☑ **EXPLAIN** Explain how Lenin adapted Marxist ideas to Russian society and government.

>> In this 1920 painting, "Bolshevik," by Boris Kustodiev, a giant carries a red banner through a Russian city. **Analyze Art** Who or what does the giant symbolize?

🅑 BOUNCE to Activate Chart

The October Revolution Brings the Bolsheviks to Power

Lenin threw himself into the work of furthering the revolution. Another dynamic Marxist revolutionary, Leon Trotsky, helped lead the fight. To the hungry, war-weary Russian people, Lenin and the Bolsheviks promised "Peace, Land, and Bread."

Causes of the October Revolution Meanwhile, the provisional government, led by Alexander Kerensky, continued the war effort and failed to deal with land reform. Those decisions proved fatal. Most Russians were tired of war. Troops at the front were deserting in droves. Peasants wanted land, while city workers demanded an end to the desperate shortages.

In July 1917, the government launched the disastrous Kerensky Offensive against Germany. By November, according to one official report, the army was "a huge crowd of tired, poorly clad, poorly fed, embittered men." Growing numbers of troops mutinied. Peasants seized land and drove off fearful landlords.

The Bolsheviks Seize Power Conditions were ripe for the Bolsheviks to make their move. In November 1917, squads of Red Guards—armed factory workers—joined mutinous sailors from the Russian fleet in attacking the provisional government. In just a matter of days, Lenin's forces overthrew the provisional government.

The Bolsheviks quickly seized power in other cities. In Moscow, it took a week of fighting to blast the local government out of the walled Kremlin, the former tsarist center of government. Moscow became the Bolsheviks' capital, and the Kremlin their headquarters.

"We shall now occupy ourselves in Russia in building up a proletarian socialist state," declared Lenin.

The Bolsheviks ended private ownership of land and distributed land to peasants. Workers were given control of the factories and mines. A new red flag with an entwined hammer and sickle symbolized union between workers and peasants. Throughout the land, millions thought they had at last gained control over their own lives. In fact, the Bolsheviks—renamed Communists—would soon become their new masters.

>> A crusading white knight slays the red dragon in this Russian civil war propaganda poster. Its title is "For a United Russia." **Draw Conclusions** Which side in the Russian civil war made this poster? Why?

☑ **DESCRIBE** Describe the reasons for the fall of Kerensky's government.

Civil War Erupts in Russia

After the Bolshevik Revolution, Lenin quickly sought peace with Germany. Russia signed the Treaty of Brest-Litovsk in March 1918, giving up a huge chunk of its territory and its population. The cost of peace was extremely high, but the Communist leaders knew that they needed all their energy to defeat a collection of enemies at home. Russia's withdrawal affected the hopes of both the Allies and the Central Powers.

The Opposing Forces For three years, civil war raged between the "Reds," as the Communists were known, and the counterrevolutionary "Whites." The "White" armies were made up of tsarist imperial officers, Mensheviks, democrats, and others, all of whom were united only by their desire to defeat the Bolsheviks. Nationalist groups from many of the former empire's non-Russian regions joined them in their fight. Poland, Estonia, Latvia, and Lithuania broke free, but nationalists in Ukraine, the Caucasus, and central Asia were eventually subdued.

The Allies intervened in the civil war. They hoped that the Whites might overthrow the Communists and support the fight against Germany. Britain, France, and the United States sent forces to help the Whites. Japan seized land in East Asia that tsarist Russia had once claimed. The Allied presence, however, did little to help the Whites. The Reds appealed to nationalism and urged Russians to drive out the foreigners. In the long run, the Allied invasion fed Communist distrust of the West.

Brutality was common in the civil war. Counterrevolutionary forces slaughtered Communist prisoners and tried to assassinate Lenin. The Communists shot the former tsar and tsarina and their five children in July 1918 to keep them from becoming a rallying symbol for counterrevolutionary forces.

Terror and War Communism The Communists used terror not only against the Whites, but also to control their own people. They organized the **Cheka,** a secret police force much like the tsar's. The Cheka executed ordinary citizens, even if they were only suspected of taking action against the revolution. The Communists also set up a network of forced labor camps in 1919—which grew under Stalin into the dreaded Gulag.

The Union of Soviet Socialist Republics, 1923

KEY
- Union of Soviet Socialist Republics, 1923
- - - - S.S.R. boundaries

>> **Analyze Maps** Russia was by far the largest of the various republics that made up the Soviet Union. How do you think nationalism affected the Soviet Union?

BOUNCE to Activate Map

The Communists adopted a policy known as "war communism." They took over banks, mines, factories, and railroads. Peasants in the countryside were forced to deliver almost all of their crops to feed the army and hungry people in the cities. Peasant laborers were drafted into the military or forced to work in factories.

Meanwhile, Trotsky turned the Red Army into an effective fighting force. He used former tsarist officers under the close watch of **commissars,** Communist party officials assigned to the army to teach party principles and ensure party loyalty. Trotsky's passionate speeches roused soldiers to fight. So did the order to shoot every tenth man if a unit performed poorly.

The Reds' position in the center of Russia gave them a strategic advantage. The White armies were forced to attack separately from all sides. They were never able to cooperate effectively with one another. By 1921, the Communists had managed to defeat their scattered foes.

☑ **INTEGRATE INFORMATION** How did Lenin and Trotsky use brutality and terror to win the Russian Civil War?

The Communist Soviet Union Emerges

Russia was in chaos. Millions of people had died since the beginning of World War I. Millions more perished from famine and disease. Lenin faced the enormous problem of rebuilding a shattered state and economy.

New Government, Old Problems In 1922, Lenin's Communist government united much of the old Russian empire into the Union of Soviet Socialist Republics (USSR), or Soviet Union. The Communists produced a constitution that seemed both democratic and socialist. It set up an elected legislature, later called the Supreme Soviet, and gave all citizens over 18 the right to vote. All political power, resources, and means of production would belong to workers and peasants. The Soviet Union was a multinational state made up of European and Asian peoples. In theory, all the member republics shared certain equal rights.

Reality, however, differed greatly from theory. The Communist party, not the people, reigned supreme. Just as the Russian tsars had, the party used the army and secret police to enforce its will. Russia, which was the largest republic, dominated the other republics.

>> Lenin (left) and Stalin (right) appear together here. But British art historian David King claims that Stalin's image was airbrushed into the photo. **Hypothesize** Why would Stalin want photos of him appearing with Lenin?

Stalin Comes to Power Lenin died in 1924 at the age of 54. His death set off a power struggle among Communist leaders. The chief contenders were Trotsky and Joseph Stalin. Trotsky was a brilliant Marxist thinker, a skillful speaker, and an architect of the Bolshevik Revolution. Stalin, by contrast, was neither a scholar nor an orator. He was, however, a shrewd political operator and behind-the-scenes organizer. Trotsky and Stalin differed on the future of communism. Trotsky urged support for a worldwide revolution against capitalism. Stalin, who was more cautious, wanted to concentrate on building socialism at home first.

Eventually, Stalin isolated Trotsky within the party and stripped him of party membership. Trotsky fled the country in 1929, but continued to criticize Stalin. In 1940, a Stalinist agent murdered Trotsky in Mexico.

In 1922, Lenin had expressed grave doubts about Stalin's ambitious nature: "Comrade Stalin . . . has concentrated an enormous power in his hands; and I am not sure that he always knows how to use that power with sufficient caution." Just as Lenin had warned, in the years that followed, Stalin used ruthless measures to win dictatorial power.

☑ **DESCRIBE** What capitalist measures did Lenin incorporate into his New Economic Policy?

Lenin Abandons War Communism On the economic front, Lenin retreated from his policy of "war communism," which had brought the economy to near collapse. Under party control, factory and mine output had fallen. Peasants stopped producing grain, knowing the government would only seize it.

In 1921, Lenin adopted the New Economic Policy, or NEP. It allowed some capitalist ventures. Although the state kept control of banks, foreign trade, and large industries, small businesses were allowed to reopen for private profit. The government also stopped squeezing peasants for grain. Under the NEP, peasants held on to small plots of land and freely sold their surplus crops.

Lenin's compromise with capitalism helped the Soviet economy recover and ended armed resistance to the new government. By 1928, food and industrial production climbed back to prewar levels. The standard of living improved, too. But Lenin always saw the NEP as just a temporary retreat from communism. His successor would soon return the Soviet Union to "pure" communism.

☑ ASSESSMENT

1. **Identify Cause and Effect** How did the actions of Tsar Nicholas II and his wife lead to revolution in Russia?

2. **Compare and Contrast** Compare and contrast Lenin's idealistic vision of a socialist state with the reality of communism in the new Soviet Union.

3. **Distinguish** Differentiate between the February Revolution and the October Revolution. What were the outcomes of each?

4. **Hypothesize** If World War I had not taken place, do you think the Russian Revolution would have happened? Support your argument with facts.

5. **Quest Connections** How did World War I help to pave the way for the Russian Revolution?

Connections to Today

Drones and other forms of technology have roots in past wars.

Take Action About the Impact of Technology

Technologies developed for war, like those used during World War I, often transfer into use in civilian life. Today's technologies are no different.

1. **Choose** one of the following technology-related topics:

   - **Regulating drones:** Research government regulations and the controversies surrounding civilian drone use.

   - **Artificial intelligence (AI):** Investigate the use of AI (computers designed to mimic human intelligence), and how such systems are regulated.

   - **Technology addition:** Explore the obsessive use of technology and its causes, effects, and treatment.

2. **Ask Questions** Generate a list of questions you have about the topic.

3. **Learn** about the topic and the major issues related to the topic. Are there any major debates related to the topic or issues? What are the strongest arguments on each side of the debate? Take notes as you conduct your research and continue to generate questions as you learn more.

4. **Take Action** Write a short summary of the topic or issue and create a poster advocating your position on the issue. Use the poster to educate your classmates and community about the topic.

Topic 16 Quick Study Guide

LESSON SUMMARIES
Use these Lesson Summaries, and the longer versions available online, to review the key ideas for each lesson in this Topic.

Lesson 1: World War I Begins
By the early 1900s, many efforts had been made to promote peace, but more powerful forces were pushing Europe to the brink of war. Aggressive nationalism, economic competition, militarism, and alliances were among the factors that could increase tension and start a war.

Lesson 2: Fighting the Great War
The "Great War" was the largest conflict in history up to that time. The early enthusiasm for the war soon disappeared. Modern weapons resulted in huge numbers of casualties and prevented either side from gaining an advantage.

Lesson 3: World War I Ends

The stalemate dragged on—until Russia left the war and the United States joined on the side of the Allied Powers. The Allies won the war in 1918, but the human and economic costs were staggering. The postwar treaties forced Germany to pay reparations to the Allies, redrew the map of Eastern Europe, and affected colonial peoples around the globe.

Lesson 4: Revolution in Russia
After the Revolution of 1905, Czar Nicholas II failed to solve Russia's basic political, economic, and social problems. Discontent sparked new eruptions. In March 1917, the first of two revolutions would destroy the Romanov dynasty and pave the way for even more radical changes.

QUEST! FINDINGS

Create Your Docudrama Refer to your responses to the Quest Connections to help you create your video docudrama to present to the class. Use the rubric and other Quest resources online to guide your work.

GO ONLINE to access lesson summaries

VISUAL REVIEW

Use these graphics to review some of the key terms, people, and ideas from this Topic.

Causes and Effects of World War I

CAUSE AND EFFECT	
LONG-TERM CAUSES	**IMMEDIATE CAUSES**
• Rivalries among European powers • European alliance system • Militarism and arms race • Nationalist tensions in the Balkans	• Austria-Hungary's annexation of Bosnia and Herzegovina • Fighting in the Balkans • Assassination of Archduke Francis Ferdinand • Russian mobilization • German invasion of Belgium

↓

WORLD WAR I

↓

IMMEDIATE EFFECTS	LONG-TERM EFFECTS
• Enormous cost in lives and property • Revolution in Russia • Creation of new nations in Eastern Europe • German reparations • German loss of overseas colonies • Balfour Declaration • League of Nations	• Economic impact of war debts on Europe • Stronger central governments • Emergence of United States and Japan as important powers • Growth of nationalism in colonies • Rise of fascism • Increased anti-Semitism in Germany • World War II

Key Events in the Russian Revolution

- **1914–1917** World War I pressures Russia.
- **March 1917** March Revolution causes tsar to abdicate; the provisional government takes power.
- **November 1917** Bolsheviks under Lenin topple provisional government (November Revolution).

Financial Costs of World War I

British empire	$ $ $ $ $ $
France	$ $ $ $ $
Russia	$ $ $
United States	$ $ $ ⊄
Germany	$ $ $ $ $ $
Austria-Hungary	$ $ ⊄
$ represents $10 billion	

SOURCE: *The Harper Encyclopedia of Military History*, R.Ernest Dupuy and Trevor N. Dupuy

Topic 16 Assessment

KEY TERMS, PEOPLE, AND IDEAS

1. Why did the United States enter WWI? How did this affect the outcome of the war?

2. How did the **Lusitania** incident affect relations between the United States and Germany?

3. What factors contributed to the **stalemate** on the Western Front?

4. Why do some historians label the strategy used in WWI as a **"total war"** effort?

5. How did imperialism affect WWI?

6. Why might some colonial troops have been willing to fight in the war?

7. How did Woodrow Wilson's goals at the Paris Peace Conference differ from those of the other Allied leaders?

8. What were the **Fourteen Points**?

9. How did the rise of nationalism in Turkey during WWI affect the Armenian population?

CRITICAL THINKING

10. **Analyzing Information** (a) What do you think Woodrow Wilson meant by "peace without victory"? (b) Why do you think European Allies were unwilling to accept this idea?

11. **Summarize** What measures did wartime governments take to control national economies and public opinion?

12. **Summarize** How did the peace treaties shift geographic borders in Europe and the Middle East after WWI?

13. **Recognize Causes and Effects** What were the causes and effects of the civil war in Russia?

14. **Predict Consequences** One member of the Paris Peace Conference said of the negotiations "This is not a peace; it is an armistice for twenty years." Do you agree or disagree? Explain

15. **Analyze Information** How did the loss of the United States as a member nation affect the League of Nations?

16. **Analyze Images** Look at the image below of a trench used during WW I. (a) How do you think soldiers were affected by this kind of warfare? (b) Why might some historians feel this was the best way to fight the war?

17. **Writing Activity: Write an Argument** Aggressive nationalism was among the causes of World War I. Helmuth von Moltke, a German military leader, described the strategy Germany should use at the beginning of World War I.

> "The German people must be made to see that we have to attack because of our enemy's provocation. Things must be so built up that war will seem as a deliverance from the great armaments, the financial burdens, the political tensions. . . Germany must regain what she formerly lost."

Some historians are of the opinion that the major cause of World War I was Germany's desire to be a world power. Is there evidence to support this view? Choose a side and then use your knowledge of this Topic and the quote to write a short argument essay. Be sure to support your claim with evidence.

18. **Connections to Today** Many new deadly weapons were used during World War I. What has been the legacy of the weapons developed during World War I? Have they been used for destructive purposes? Constructive purposes? Do governments control their use today? Cite one or two examples. Then think about military technology in use today. How might that technology affect the world in the future?

DOCUMENT-BASED QUESTIONS

The entry of the United States into the war in April 1917 was a turning point in World War I. Read the documents below, then answer the questions that follow.

DOCUMENT A

American Soldiers Arrive in Europe, 1918

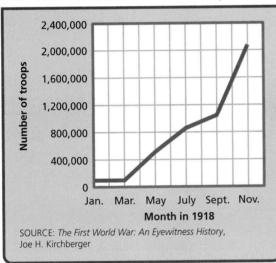

SOURCE: *The First World War: An Eyewitness History,* Joe H. Kirchberger

DOCUMENT B

"British shipping losses, especially since the declaration of unrestricted submarine warfare, had risen dangerously. . . . But the entry of the United States into the war made the German submarine warfare an evident failure, because thereafter the number of ships convoyed and the number of ships protecting the convoys was increased steadily. Convoys of ships transporting food, war materials, and troops arrived safely in Britain, and the rate of shipping construction soon exceeded the rate of loss."

— *The End of the European Era. 1890 to the Present. by Felix Gilbert and David Clay Large*

DOCUMENT C

Winston Churchill, who served in Britain's navy and army during World War I, wrote about the effect American troops had on their tired Allies.

"The impression made upon the hard-pressed French by this seemingly inexhaustible flood of gleaming youth in its first maturity of health and vigour was prodigious [amazing]. None were under twenty, and few were over thirty . . . the French Headquarters were thrilled with the impulse of new life. . . . Half trained, half organized, with only their courage, their numbers and their magnificent youth behind their weapons, they were to buy their experience at a bitter price. But this they were quite ready to do."

DOCUMENT D

Loans from the United States to Allies

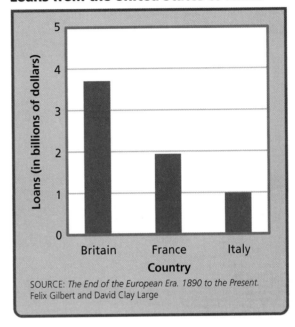

SOURCE: *The End of the European Era. 1890 to the Present.* Felix Gilbert and David Clay Large

19. How would you describe the arrival of American troops in Europe in 1918?
- **A.** slow at first, but rapid after March
- **B.** steady throughout the year
- **C.** rapid at first, but slow after March
- **D.** No American troops arrived in Europe in 1918.

20. How did the United States navy help break Germany's submarine blockade of Britain?
- **A.** by completely destroying the German submarine fleet
- **B.** by finding new routes around the German submarine fleet
- **C.** by strengthening the convoys
- **D.** by sending supplies to France rather than Britain

21. Based on Document C, how did Churchill feel about American soldiers?
- **A.** They were experienced but had a poor attitude toward the war.
- **B.** They were energetic and willing to fight, although not experienced.
- **C.** They were well-trained and energetic.
- **D.** They were neither energetic nor experienced.

22. **Writing Tasks** How did the United States help bring about the Allied victory in 1918? Use your knowledge of World War I and specific evidence from the documents to support your points.

The World Between the Wars (1910–1939)

ESSENTIAL QUESTION What should governments do?

Wealthy women attend the opera in Paris in the 1920s

Connections to Today

In 2016, Robert Duterte won the presidential election in the Philippines. His reputation as a crime-buster did raise human rights concerns. Still, he won the confidence of the citizens.

By 2018 and 2019, political shifts in the Philippines, Turkey, China, and Guatemala led to fear, repression, and increased violations of human rights. A strong anti-democratic trend took hold. In this topic, you will learn about the rise of authoritarian states after World War I. What led to the rise of authoritarian states today?

Explore the efforts of Mohandas Gandhi to win independence for India.

BOUNCE to Activate My Story Video

Topic 17 Overview

In this Topic, you will learn about the events that largely occurred between the world wars. Look at the lesson outline and explore the timeline. As you study this Topic, you will complete the Quest inquiry.

LESSON OUTLINE

17.1 Revolution and Nationalism in Latin America

17.2 Nationalist Movements in Africa and the Middle East

17.3 India Seeks Self Rule

17.4 New Forces in China and Japan

17.5 The West After World War I

17.6 Fascism Emerges in Italy

17.7 The Soviet Union Under Stalin

17.8 The Rise of Nazi Germany

Key Events of the World Between WWI and WWII

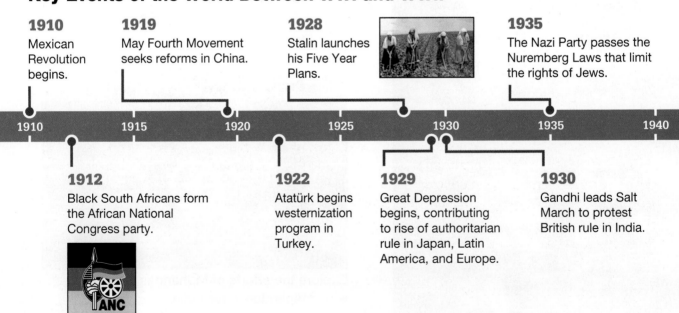

1910
Mexican Revolution begins.

1919
May Fourth Movement seeks reforms in China.

1928
Stalin launches his Five Year Plans.

1935
The Nazi Party passes the Nuremberg Laws that limit the rights of Jews.

1910 1915 1920 1925 1930 1935 1940

1912
Black South Africans form the African National Congress party.

1922
Atatürk begins westernization program in Turkey.

1929
Great Depression begins, contributing to rise of authoritarian rule in Japan, Latin America, and Europe.

1930
Gandhi leads Salt March to protest British rule in India.

QUEST! INQUIRY

Civic Discussion: Lenin and Stalin

After the death of Bolshevik leader Lenin, Stalin gained control of the Communist party. In this Quest, you will prepare a discussion to address whether Lenin sowed the seeds for Stalin's brutal dictatorship.

STEP 1
Begin the discussion about the question. Review what you know about the topic. List major points that can be used in answering the question.

STEP 2
Review the documents. Evaluate the evidence. Discuss the conclusions. Then have team members take sides. Outline discussion points.

STEP 3
Work with your group to determine the strongest arguments. Prepare your discussion. Review, edit, and revise.

STEP 4
Present your discussion. Reflect on the importance of understanding issues from multiple perspectives.

GO ONLINE to access complete Quest materials

17.1

Peasants joined the Mexican revolution in the hopes of improving their lives. Most were untrained and had few supplies, but they continued to fight for social, political, and economic change.

 BOUNCE to Activate Flipped Video

Objectives

Identify causes and effects of the Mexican Revolution.

Analyze the effects of economic and political nationalism on Latin America.

Trace the changing relationship between Latin America and the United States.

Key Terms

Porfirio Díaz
hacienda
Emiliano Zapata
Venustiano Carranza
nationalization
Lázaro Cárdenas
economic
   nationalism
cultural nationalism
Good Neighbor
   Policy

Revolution and Nationalism in Latin America

By 1910, the dictator **Porfirio Díaz** had ruled Mexico for almost 35 years, winning re-election as president again and again. On the surface, Mexico enjoyed peace and economic growth. Díaz welcomed foreign investors who developed mines, built railroads, and drilled for oil.

The Mexican Revolution

Seeds of Discontent However, underneath the surface, discontent rippled through Mexico. The country's prosperity benefited only a small group. The majority of Mexicans were mestizos or Indian peasants who lived in desperate poverty. Most of these peasants worked on **haciendas,** or large plantations, controlled by the landowning elite.

Some peasants moved to cities, where they found jobs in factories, or worked in mines. Everywhere, they earned meager wages. In Mexican cities, middle-class liberals, who embraced the ideals of democracy, opposed the Díaz dictatorship.

The unrest boiled over in 1910 when Francisco Madero, a liberal reformer from an elite family, demanded free elections. After being imprisoned by Diaz, he hoisted the flag of revolution. Soon, revolutionaries all across Mexico joined Madero's cause. Faced with rebellion in several parts of the country, Díaz resigned in 1911.

GO ONLINE to access your digital course

A Complex Struggle Madero became president of Mexico, but he turned out to be too liberal for conservatives and not radical enough for the revolutionaries. In 1913, he was murdered by one of his generals, Victoriano Huerta. Huerta ruled as a military dictator, but was quickly faced with rebellion.

During a long, complex power struggle, several radical leaders emerged. They sometimes joined forces but then fought each other. In southern Mexico, **Emiliano Zapata** led a peasant revolt. Zapata, an Indian peasant farmer, understood the misery of peasant villagers. The battle cry of the Zapatistas, as these rebels were called, was "Tierra y libertad!" which means "land and freedom."

Francisco "Pancho" Villa, a hard-riding rebel from the north, fought mostly for personal power but won the intense loyalty of his peasant followers. Villa and Zapata formed an uneasy coalition with **Venustiano Carranza,** a rich landowner who wanted political reform but opposed social change.

Fighting flared across Mexico for a decade, killing as many as a million Mexicans. Peasants, small farmers, ranchers, and urban workers were drawn into the violent struggle. Female soldiers known as soldaderas cooked, tended the wounded, and fought alongside men.

During the revolution, President Woodrow Wilson of the United States twice sent troops to Mexico. In 1914, U.S. forces helped depose, or remove, Huerta. In 1916, they tried to hunt down Pancho Villa, whose raid into New Mexico had killed 16 Americans. After the overthrow of Huerta, Carranza turned on Villa and Zapata and defeated them. In 1917, Carranza was elected president of Mexico. That year, he reluctantly signed a new constitution.

☑ **SEQUENCE EVENTS** Explain the events of the Mexican Revolution in order.

Economic and Social Reforms

Venustiano Carranza had called for a new constitution during the Mexican Revolution. But he did not like the one he had reluctantly signed in 1917 and did not institute its reforms. In 1920, rival revolutionaries arranged for his assassination. The constitution, however, survived. With some revisions, it is still in effect today.

The Constitution of 1917 The Constitution of 1917 addressed three major issues: land, religion, and

>> Francisco Madero served as president for less than two years before he was overthrown. Though he accomplished little, he remained an inspiration to revolutionaries.

🅱 BOUNCE to Activate Gallery

>> During the Constitutional Convention in Querétaro, Venustiano Carranza chaired the committee that drafted the Constitution of 1917. The Congress approved it on February 5, 1917.

labor. The constitution strengthened government control over the economy. It permitted the breakup of large estates, placed restrictions on foreigners owning land, and allowed **nationalization,** or government takeover, of natural resources. Church land was made "the property of the nation." The constitution set a minimum wage and protected the workers' right to strike.

Although the constitution gave suffrage only to men, it did give women some rights. Women doing the same jobs as men were entitled to the same pay. In response to women activists' efforts to change the Mexican government, Carranza also passed laws allowing married women to draw up contracts, take part in legal suits, and have equal authority with men in spending family funds.

The PRI Takes Control In 1929, the government organized what later became the Institutional Revolutionary Party (PRI). The PRI made political choices to accommodate many groups in Mexican society, including business and military leaders, peasants, and workers. Its leaders backed social reform, even while it kept power in its own hands and suppressed political opposition. It also boosted Mexican industry. Over time, the PRI brought stability to Mexico and carried out many desired reforms. The PRI dominated Mexican politics until 2000.

Social and Economic Reforms At first, the Constitution of 1917 was just a set of goals to be achieved in the future. But in the 1920s and 1930s, as the government finally restored order, it began to carry out reforms.

In the 1920s, the government helped some Indian communities regain lands that had been taken from them. In the 1930s, President **Lázaro Cárdenas** made the decision to redistribute millions of acres of land to peasants under a communal land program. The government supported labor unions and launched a massive effort to combat illiteracy. Schools and libraries were set up. For the first time, Mexicans in rural areas who grew up speaking various Indian languages learned Spanish.

Dedicated teachers, often young women, worked for low pay. While they taught basic skills, they also spread ideas of nationalism that began to bridge the gulf between the regions and the central government. As the revolutionary era ended, Mexico became the first Latin American nation to pursue real social and economic reforms for the majority of its people.

Under the PRI, the government also took a strong role in directing the economy. In 1938, labor disputes broke out between Mexican workers and the management of some foreign-owned petroleum companies. In response, President Cárdenas nationalized Mexico's oil resources. American and

Land Distributed in Mexico by President, 1915–1940

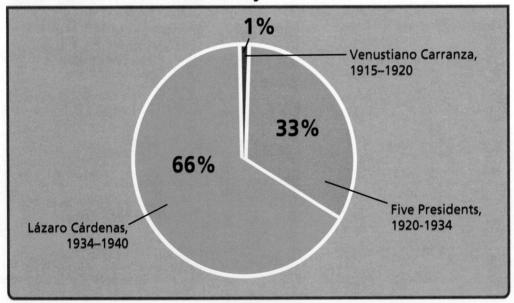

1%
Venustiano Carranza, 1915–1920

33%

66%

Five Presidents, 1920-1934

Lázaro Cárdenas, 1934–1940

>> **Analyze Graphs** Between 1915 and 1940, nearly 75 million acres of land were distributed to Mexico's people, fulfilling one goal of the constitution. Which president redistributed the most land?

British oil companies resisted Cárdenas's decision, but eventually accepted compensation for their losses. Mexicans felt that they were at last gaining economic independence from foreign influence.

☑ **IDENTIFY CENTRAL IDEAS** How did the PRI accommodate many groups in Mexican society while keeping power for itself?

Nationalism Spreads in Latin America

The issues facing Mexico were echoed in other Latin American nations. In the early 1900s, Latin America's economy was booming because of exports. Latin Americans sold their plentiful natural resources and cash crops to industrialized countries. In return, they bought products made in those countries.

Stable governments helped to keep the region's economy on good footing. Some Latin American nations, such as Argentina and Uruguay, had democratic constitutions. However, military dictators or small groups of wealthy landowners held the real power. The tiny ruling class kept the economic benefits of the booming economy for themselves. The growing middle class and the lower classes— workers and peasants—had no say in their own governments.

Economic Nationalism During the 1920s and 1930s, world events affected Latin American economies. After World War I, trade with Europe fell off. The Great Depression that struck the United States in 1929 spread around the world in the 1930s. Prices for Latin American exports plunged as demand dried up. At the same time, the cost of imported consumer goods rose. Latin American economies, dependent on export trade, declined rapidly.

A tide of **economic nationalism,** or emphasis on home control of the economy, swept Latin American countries. It was directed largely at ending economic dependence on the industrial powers, especially the United States and Britain. Since consumers could no longer afford costly imports, local entrepreneurs set up factories to produce goods at home. They urged their governments to raise tariffs, or taxes on imports, to protect these new industries. Following Mexico's lead, some nations nationalized resources or took over foreign-owned industries.

The drive to create domestic industries had limited success. In Mexico, Argentina, Brazil, and

>> The Institutional Revolutionary Party (PRI) created a more stable government in Mexico and increased the representation of peasants and urban laborers.

>> Students rally to support President Lázaro Cárdenas's nationalization of the foreign-owned oil industry. One of the signs reads: "We will collaborate enthusiastically in the betterment of Mexico."

a few other countries, some areas of manufacturing grew. Mexico and Venezuela also benefited from a growing demand for their oil. But most Latin American nations lacked the resources to build large industries. As in the past, the unequal distribution of wealth hurt efforts at economic development. Only a few in the wealthy ruling class benefited from economic growth.

Political Nationalism The Great Depression also triggered political changes in Latin America. The economic crisis caused people to lose faith in the ruling oligarchies and the ideas of liberal government. Liberalism, a belief in the individual and in limited government, was a European theory. People began to feel that it did not work in Latin America.

In the midst of economic crisis, authoritarian governments with strong nationalist goals gained power in many countries. Authoritarian rulers imposed stability and supported economic nationalism, but suppressed opposition political parties and silenced critics.

Cultural Nationalism By the 1920s, an upsurge of national feeling led Latin American writers, artists, and thinkers to reject European influences. Instead, they took pride in their own culture, with its blend of Western and Native American traditions.

In Mexico, **cultural nationalism,** or pride in one's own national culture, was reflected in the revival of mural painting, a major art form of the Aztecs and Maya. Diego Rivera, José Clemente Orozco (oh ROHS koh), and other muralists created magnificent works that reflected Mexican culture and history. On the walls of public buildings, they portrayed the struggles of the Mexican people for liberty. The murals have been a great source of national pride ever since.

Relations with the United States Nationalism affected how Latin American nations saw the United States. During and after World War I, investments by the United States in Latin America soared, while British influence declined. The United States continued to play the role of international policeman, intervening to restore order when it felt its interests were threatened.

During the Mexican Revolution, the United States stepped in with military force to support the leaders who favored American interests. This interference stirred up anti-American feelings, which increased throughout Latin America during the 1920s. For example, in Nicaragua, Augusto César Sandino led a guerrilla movement against United States forces occupying his country.

U.S. Intervention in Latin America, 1912–1934

COUNTRY	YEAR(S)	TYPE/REASON
Nicaragua	1912–1934	20-year occupation to fight guerrillas; from 1926–1933, sought to capture nationalistic forces led by Augusto César Sandino
Haiti	1914–1934	19–year occupation after revolutions
Dominican Republic	1916–1924	8-year Marine occupation
Cuba	1917–1933	Military occupation and establishment of economic protectorate under Platt Amendment
Panama	1918–1920	Police duty after elections; protection of United Fruit plantations
Guatemala	1920–1921	Two-week intervention against unionists; support of a coup
Costa Rica / Panama	1921	Troop intervention in border dispute
Mexico	1923	Air Force defense of Calles from rebellion
Honduras	1924–1925	Two landings during election unrest
Panama	1925	Marine suppression of general strike
El Salvador	1932	Warship support of ruling general during revolt

>> **Analyze Charts** During the early 1900s, the United States regularly intervened in Latin American conflicts. What was the most common form of intervention?

The Good Neighbor Policy In the 1930s, President Franklin Roosevelt took a new approach to Latin America. He pledged to follow "the policy of the good neighbor."

Under the **Good Neighbor Policy,** the United States agreed to stop interfering in the affairs of Latin American nations. The United States withdrew troops stationed in Haiti and Nicaragua and lifted the Platt Amendment, which had limited Cuban independence.

When Mexico nationalized its oil industry in 1938, Roosevelt resisted demands by some Americans to intervene. The Good Neighbor policy survived until 1945 when global tensions led the United States to intervene once again in the region.

☑ **SYNTHESIZE** How did political and cultural nationalism grow in Latin America?

☑ ASSESSMENT

1. **Identify Central Ideas** How did Mexican artists express cultural nationalism?

2. **Identify Central Issues** How did nationalism affect Latin America?

3. **Assess Credibility** How did the PRI fulfill some goals of the Mexican Revolution but not others?

4. **Cite Evidence** What role did the United States play after World War I and during the Mexican Revolution? Cite evidence to support your response.

5. **Connections to Today** Did the Constitution of 1917 protect the rights of Mexican citizens? Are the rights of U.S. citizens protected today? Explain.

>> Artist Diego Rivera portrayed the history of Mexico in this mural. The bottom represents Aztec civilization. The top half focuses on the Mexican Revolution and the future of Mexico.

BOUNCE to Activate Gallery

Throughout Africa, Europeans operated mines and paid Africans low wages to work in them. Here, South Africans are working in a diamond mine owned by a Dutch company.

BOUNCE to Activate Flipped Video

Objectives

Explain how Africans resisted colonial rule.

Describe the rise of nationalism in Africa.

Describe how Turkey and Persia modernized.

Understand how the mandate system contributed to Arab nationalism and to conflict between Jews and Arabs.

Key Terms

apartheid
Pan-Africanism
Marcus Garvey
négritude movement
Asia Minor
Atatürk
Reza Khan
Pan-Arabism
Balfour Declaration

Nationalist Movements in Africa and the Middle East

During the early 1900s, more and more Africans felt the impact of colonial rule. European nations exploited, or took advantage, of their colonies to produce profits for the parent country. Although the peoples of Africa had long tried to resist foreign imperialism, calls for change spread, fueling new nationalist movements.

Africans Protest Colonial Rule

Exploitation of African Colonies European governments expected their colonies to be profitable. To do so, they exploited the mineral resources of Africa, sending raw materials to feed European factories. In Kenya and Rhodesia, white settlers forced Africans off the best land. Also in Kenya, the British made all Africans carry identification cards, pay a tax, and live or travel only in certain areas.

Everywhere, farmers were forced to work on European-run plantations or in mines to earn money to pay taxes. Those farmers who kept their own land had to grow cash crops, like cotton, for the benefit of the colonizers instead of food. This led to famines in some regions. Increasingly, African people lost their self-sufficiency and became dependent on European goods.

GO ONLINE to access your digital course

Protesting Imperialism During World War I, more than one million Africans had fought on behalf of their colonial rulers. Many had hoped that their service would lead to more rights and opportunities. Instead, the situation after World War I remained mostly the same or even worsened.

Many Western-educated Africans criticized the injustice of imperial rule. Although they had trained for professional careers, the best jobs went to Europeans.

Inspired by President Woodrow Wilson's call for self-determination, Africans condemned the colonial system that excluded them from controlling their own lands. During the 1920s and 1930s, a new generation of leaders proud of their unique heritage struggled to restore Africa for Africans. Protests and opposition to imperialism multiplied. Some of this new generation turned to socialism or the writings of Marx and Lenin.

While large-scale revolts were rare, protests were common. In Kenya, the Kikuyu people protested the loss of their land to white settlers and denounced forced labor and heavy taxes. In the 1920s, Ibo women in Nigeria revolted against British policies that threatened their rights. The British eventually ended the "Women's War" with gunfire.

A Policy of Segregation in South Africa Between 1910 and 1940, whites strengthened their grip on South Africa. They imposed a system of racial segregation to ensure white economic, political, and social supremacy. New laws, for example, restricted better-paying jobs in mines to whites only.

Black South Africans were pushed into low-paid, less-skilled work. Black South Africans had to carry passes at all times. They were evicted from the best land and forced to live on crowded "reserves," which were located in dry, infertile areas.

Other laws chipped away at the rights of Black South Africans. In one South African province, educated Black South Africans who owned property had been allowed to vote in local elections. In 1936, the government abolished that right. The system of segregation would become even stricter after 1948, when **apartheid** (uh PAHR tayt), a policy of rigid racial segregation, became law.

Yet South Africa was also home to a vital nationalist movement. African Christian churches and African-run newspapers demanded rights for Black South Africans. In 1912, they formed a political party, later called the African National Congress (ANC), to protest unfair laws and demand a change to South Africa's white government. Their efforts had no immediate effect, but the ANC did build a framework for political action in later years.

☑ **IDENTIFY CAUSE AND EFFECT** How did Africans think that fighting on behalf of their colonial rulers during World War I would impact their lives?

A Rising Tide of African Nationalism

In the 1920s, a movement known as Pan-Africanism began to nourish the nationalist spirit and strengthen resistance. **Pan-Africanism** emphasized the unity of Africans and the people of African descent worldwide. Among its most inspiring leaders was Jamaica-born **Marcus Garvey.** He preached a forceful, appealing message of "Africa for Africans" and demanded an end to colonial rule. Garvey's ideas influenced a new generation of African and African American leaders.

The Pan-African Congress African American scholar and activist W.E.B. DuBois (doo BOYS) organized the first Pan-African Congress in 1919. It met in Paris, where the Allies were holding their peace conference.

>> Opposition to imperialism grew among Africans in the 1920s and 1930s. In 1929, Ibo market women in Nigeria demanded a voice in decisions that affected their markets. The "Women's War" soon became a full-fledged revolt.

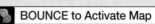

🔊 BOUNCE to Activate Map

>> Léopold Senghor inspired many writers of the négritude movement, including Birago Diop and Mongo Beti. He was admired throughout the world as a writer and statesman.

🔊 **BOUNCE to Activate Gallery**

>> In 1922, Faud I changed his title from Sultan to King of Egypt. He tried to increase his power with a new Constitution. Widespread protest led him to restore the earlier Constitution.

Delegates from African colonies, the West Indies, and the United States called on the Paris peacemakers to approve a charter of rights for Africans and an end to colonialism. Although the Western powers ignored their demands, the Pan-African Congress established cooperation among African and African American leaders.

Writers Celebrate African Culture A literary movement further awakened nationalism and self-confidence among Africans. French-speaking writers from West Africa and the Caribbean who were living in Paris founded the **négritude movement.** Writers of the négritude movement expressed pride in their African roots and culture and protested colonial rule. Their work often transcended their time and place to convey universal themes, such as the human desire for freedom and dignity.

The best known writer of the négritude movement was the Senegalese poet Léopold Senghor. Senghor celebrated Africa's rich cultural heritage. He fostered African pride by rejecting the negative views of Africa spread by colonial rulers. Later, Senghor would take an active role in Senegal's drive to independence, and he would serve as its first president in 1960.

Independence for Egypt African nationalism brought little political change, except to Egypt. During World War I, Egyptians had been forced to provided food and workers to help Britain. Simmering resistance to British rule flared as the war ended. Western-educated officials, peasants, landowners, Christians, and Muslims united behind the Wafd (WAHFT) party, which launched strikes and protests.

In 1922 Britain finally agreed to Egyptian independence. In fact, British troops stayed in Egypt to guard the Suez Canal and to back up the Egyptian monarch, King Faud. Displeased with this state of affairs, during the 1930s many young Egyptians joined an organization called the Muslim Brotherhood. This group fostered a broad Islamic nationalism that rejected Western culture and denounced corruption in the Egyptian government.

☑ **SYNTHESIZE** How did the négritude movement reflect the history of African culture, and how did this affect Africans?

Modernization of Turkey and Persia

Nationalist movements greatly affected the Middle East in the aftermath of World War I. The defeated Ottoman empire was near collapse in 1918. Its Arab lands were divided between Britain and France. However, in **Asia Minor,** a peninsula in western Asia between the Black Sea and the Mediterranean Sea, ethnic Turks resisted Western control and fought to build a modern nation.

Atatürk Takes Power In 1920, the Ottoman sultan reluctantly signed the Treaty of Sèvres, in which the empire lost its Arab and North African lands. The sultan also had to give up some land in Asia Minor to a number of Allied countries, including Greece. A Greek force landed in the city of Smyrna (now Izmir) to assert Greece's claims.

Turkish nationalists, led by the determined and energetic Mustafa Kemal, overthrew the sultan, defeated the Greeks, and declared Turkey a republic. Kemal later took the name **Atatürk** (ah tah TURK), meaning "father of the Turks." He negotiated a new treaty. Among other provisions, the treaty called for about 1.3 million Greeks to leave Turkey, while some 400,000 Turks left Greece.

Westernization of Turkey Between 1923 and his death in 1938, Atatürk forced through an ambitious program of radical reforms. His goals were to modernize Turkey along Western lines and to separate religion from government.

To achieve these goals, Atatürk mandated that Islamic traditions in several fields be replaced with Western alternatives. For example, he replaced Islamic law with laws based on a European model, replaced the Arabic alphabet with the Latin alphabet, and forced people to wear Western-style clothing. Under Atatürk, state schools replaced religious schools.

Atatürk's government encouraged industrial expansion. The government built railroads, set up factories, and hired westerners to advise on how to make Turkey economically independent.

To achieve his reforms, Atatürk ruled with an iron hand. To many Turks, he was a hero who was transforming Turkey into a strong, modern power. Some Turkish Muslims, however, rejected Atatürk's dictatorial powers and his formation of a secular government. To them, the Quran and Islamic customs provided all the guidance needed.

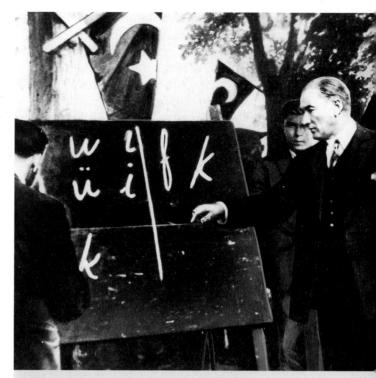

>> Atatürk stands before a crowd, pointing to letters of the Roman alphabet. He introduced the western alphabet to Turkey as one of his many modernizing reforms.

>> Reza Khan, seated here on the throne of the shahs, overthrew the reigning shah in 1925. On December 16, 1926, the Grand Council of Persia appointed Reza Khan king.

Persian Nationalism and Reform The success of Atatürk's reforms inspired nationalists in neighboring Persia (present-day Iran). Persian nationalists greatly resented the British and Russians, who had won spheres of influence over Persia in 1907. In 1925, an ambitious army officer, **Reza Khan,** overthrew the shah. He set up his own dynasty, with himself as shah.

Like Atatürk, Reza Khan rushed to modernize Persia and make it fully independent. He built factories, roads, and railroads and strengthened the army. He forced Persians to wear Western clothing and set up modern, secular schools. In addition, he moved to replace Islamic law with secular law and encouraged women to take part in public life. The shah had the support of wealthy urban Persians. However, Muslim religious leaders fiercely condemned his efforts to introduce Western ways.

Reza Khan also persuaded the British company that controlled Persia's oil industry to give Persia a larger share of the profits and insisted that Persian workers be hired at all levels of the company. In the decades ahead, oil would become a major factor in Persia's economy and foreign policy.

☑ **INFER** Why did Muslim religious leaders disapprove of Reza Khan's reforms?

Nationalism and Conflict in the Middle East

After World War I, the vast Ottoman empire was partitioned into Turkey and several new nations that would make up the modern Arab world. Several Arab lands sat above large oil reserves, giving them global importance in a world that was increasingly dependent on gasoline-powered engines. Instead of granting independence to the Arab states carved out of the Ottoman empire, European powers turned them into mandates under their control.

The Rise of Pan-Arabism Partly in response to foreign influence, Arab nationalism grew after World War I. One form of Arab nationalism was **Pan-Arabism.** This nationalist movement was built on the shared heritage of Arabs who lived in lands from the Arabian Peninsula to North Africa.

Today, this area includes Syria, Jordan, Iraq, Egypt, Algeria, and Morocco. Pan-Arabism emphasized the common history and language of Arabs and recalled the golden age of Arab civilization. The movement sought to free Arabs from foreign domination and unite them in their own state.

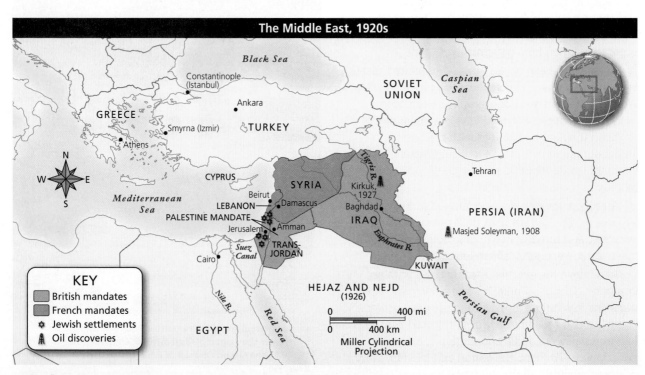

The Middle East, 1920s

KEY
- ☐ British mandates
- ☐ French mandates
- ✿ Jewish settlements
- ⚑ Oil discoveries

>> **Analyze Maps** Population movement, the Treaty of Versailles, and foreign influences changed the Middle East after World War I. How did foreign influences affect the Middle East?

The Pan-Arab movement however, faced obstacles. Arabs generally were not united. They tended to identify with their particular tribe, sect, religion, or region rather than with a single, unified nation-state.

European-Controlled Mandates During World War I, some Arab leaders had helped the Allies against the Ottoman empire. These leaders expected to create their own kingdoms after the war. Even before the revolt, however, France and Britain had secretly agreed that they would take over the Arab lands within the Ottoman empire.

The treaties ending World War I gave German and Ottoman colonies to varied Allied nations in the form of mandates. The mandates were authorized by the League of Nations.

The former Ottoman territories in the Middle East were put under the control of two Allies. France was given mandates in Syria and Lebanon, and Britain received mandates in Palestine and Iraq. Later, Britain gave a large part of the Palestinian Mandate, TransJordan, to an Arab ally, King Abdullah.

Arabs felt betrayed by the West—a feeling that has endured to this day. During the 1920s and 1930s, their anger erupted in frequent protests and revolts against Western imperialism. A major center of turmoil was the British Mandate of Palestine. There, Arab nationalists increasingly clashed with Jewish nationalists, known as Zionists.

Conflicting Promises About Palestine Since Roman times, Jews in the diaspora had dreamed of returning to their ancient homeland of Israel. In 1897, Theodor Herzl (HURT sul) responded to growing anti-Semitism, or prejudice against Jewish people, in Europe by founding the modern Zionist political movement. His goal was to reestablish a Jewish homeland in the region called Palestine.

In tsarist Russia, brutal pogroms prompted thousands of Jews to migrate to Palestine. They joined the small Jewish community that had lived there since biblical times.

During World War I, the Allies made two vague and conflicting sets of promises that greatly impacted Arab and Jewish nationalists. First, in an effort to gain Arab support for the British war effort, Britain promised Arabs their own kingdoms in former Ottoman lands.

Then, in 1917, the British attempted to win Jewish support by issuing the **Balfour Declaration.** The declaration affirmed Britain's support for the idea of establishing "a national home for Jewish people" in the Palestine Mandate.

>> In the early 1920s, the first oil wells were drilled in Persia (now Iran). This photograph shows an oil strike at the oil fields in Masjed Soleyman.

Many Jews took this to mean that Britain was announcing its intention to establish a Jewish homeland, but the Balfour Declaration stopped short of making this promise.

The declaration noted that "nothing shall be done which may prejudice the civil and religious rights of existing non-Jewish communities in Palestine, or the rights and political status enjoyed by Jews in any other country." The conflicting promises made to Arab and Jewish settlers set the stage for conflict between Arab and Jewish nationalists.

A Bitter Struggle Begins From 1919 to 1940, tens of thousands of Arabs and Jews immigrated to the Palestine Mandate. Both the Zionist movement and the effects of anti-Semitism in Europe encouraged Jewish immigration. Despite great hardships, Jewish immigrants set up factories, built new towns, and established farming communities. At the same time, the Arab population almost doubled. Some were immigrants from nearby lands. As a result, the population of the Palestine Mandate included a changing mix of settlers. The Jewish population, which was less than 60,000 in 1919, grew to about 400,000 in 1936, while the Muslim population increased from about 568,000 in 1919 to about 1 million in 1940.

At first, some Arabs welcomed the money and modern technical skills that the newcomers brought with them. But as more Jews moved to Palestine Mandate, tensions between the two groups developed.

Jewish organizations tried to purchase as much land as they could, while many Arabs sought to slow down or stop Jewish immigration. Arabs attacked Jewish communities, hoping to discourage Jewish immigration. To protect themselves, the Jewish settlers established their own military defense force. Competing claims to the land continue to lie at the heart of the Arab-Israeli conflict

☑ **IDENTIFY CAUSE AND EFFECT** Why did the Palestine Mandate become a center of conflict after World War I?

☑ ASSESSMENT

1. **Synthesize** What significance does the phrase "Africa for Africans" have?

2. **Draw Conclusions** How did nationalism contribute to changes in Africa and the Middle East following World War I?

3. **Identify Central Ideas** How did Africans resist colonial rule?

4. **Compare and Contrast** What are the similarities in the way Atatürk and Reza Khan modernized Turkey and Persia and changed their governments?

5. **Connections to Today** How did the mandate system affect the Middle East? How have these effects continued to the present?

The Salt March, shown here, began at Gandhi's ashram in Sabermati. When Gandhi reached the shore, he picked up a handful of salt and claimed he was shaking the British empire's foundation.

India Seeks Self-Rule

Indians had long struggled to end British control. Since 1885, the Indian National Congress party, called the Congress party, had pressed for self-rule within the British empire but had not yet called for full independence.

India's Struggle for Independence Begins

During World War I, more than a million Indians had served overseas. Under pressure from Indian nationalists, the British promised Indians greater self-government in return for their service.

However, when the fighting ended, Britain proposed only a few minor reforms. The reforms did little to change the system of bureaucratic rule. The British continued to have little regard for Indian beliefs and customs. Indian frustrations continued to mount, and many began calling for independence from British rule.

A New Leader Emerges Congress party members were mostly middle-class, Western-educated elite who had little in common with the masses of Indian peasants. Then a new leader named **Mohandas Gandhi** emerged and was able to unite Indians across class lines. Admiring Indians came to call him Mahatma, or "Great Soul."

BOUNCE to Activate Flipped Video

Objectives

Explain the impact of World War I and the Amritsar massacre on Indian nationalism.

Evaluate the ideas of Mohandas Gandhi.

Analyze how Gandhi led resistance to political oppression in India.

Key Terms

Mohandas Gandhi
Amritsar massacre
ahimsa
civil disobedience
untouchable
boycott
Muhammad Ali
  Jinnah

>> **Analyze Images** Because the Jallian wala Bagh in Amritsar had only one entrance, demonstrators could not escape the gunfire. How does this painting help you understand the public's reaction to the massacre?

[🅑 BOUNCE to Activate Chart]

>> In 1913, Muhammad Ali Jinnah joined the Muslim League. Although he and Gandhi disagreed on many things, both believed that cooperation between Muslims and Hindus was necessary for independence from Britain.

Gandhi came from a middle-class Hindu family. At age 19, he went to England to study law. Then, like many Indians, Gandhi went to South Africa. For 20 years, Gandhi fought laws that discriminated against Indians in South Africa. In his struggle against injustice, he began to develop a tactic of nonviolent, resistance. He called it satyagraha, or "soul force."

In 1915, Gandhi returned to India and was hailed as a national hero for his work in Africa. Gandhi joined the Congress party, and began to campaign for the rights of Indian workers. He was not, however, calling for Indian independence. His views changed thanks to a tragic event in 1919.

The Muslim League Other leaders also worked for Indian independence. **Muhammad Ali Jinnah** was one of the most influential leaders of India's large Muslim population. He was a leader of the Muslim League, which was founded in 1906 to protect Muslim interests. Jinnah and other leading Muslims feared that the Congress Party did not represent their interests. The Indian Congress Party, while made up primarily of Hindus, also had Muslim members.

In the early decades of the century, the Congress party and the Muslim League cooperated in working to achieve an independent India. As time passed, however, the two organizations began to diverge.

The Amritsar Massacre In 1919, the British passed the Rowlatt Acts, which allowed British officials to arrest and imprison any Indian citizen suspected of sedition, or urging people to disobey the government. These political prisoners could then be tried without a jury.

Gandhi opposed the act, which also threatened freedom of the press, and helped organize protests. When violence threatened, he called for an end to the protest campaign.

On April 13, 1919, a large but peaceful crowd of protesters, most of them Sikhs, jammed into an enclosed field in Amritsar, a city in northern India. The protest took place during Vaisakhi, the most important Sikh religious holiday, and a religious holiday for Hindus. The British commander, General Reginald Dyer, had banned public meetings, but many in the crowd were unaware of the order. As Indian leaders spoke, Dyer ordered his troops to open fire on the unarmed crowd, killing nearly 400 people and wounding more than 1,100.

The **Amritsar massacre** was a turning point for many Indians, including Gandhi. Up to that point, Gandhi had hoped to win partial self-rule for India. After Amritsar, he was convinced that India had to seek full independence.

Gandhi's Philosophy of Civil Disobedience

In 1921, Gandhi was elected president of the Congress party. He remained the dominant figure in Indian politics for more than twenty years. His words, actions, and ideas inspired Indians of all religious and ethnic backgrounds.

Nonviolent Protest Gandhi was horrified by the violence at Amritsar, but he also condemned Indian acts of violence in response to the massacre. Instead, he preached a philosophy of nonviolent protest that he had first begun to develop during his years in South Africa. His philosophy was based on the ancient Hindu and Jain doctrine of **ahimsa** (uh HIM sah), or nonviolence and reverence for all life. By using the power of love, Gandhi believed, people could convert even the worst wrongdoer to the right course of action. To fight against injustice, he advocated the use of nonviolent resistance. Hindu tradition also informed Gandhi's belief that all Indians regardless of religion had a common spiritual character and common interests.

Gandhi's philosophy reflected Western as well as Indian influences. He admired Christian teachings about love. He believed in the American philosopher Henry David Thoreau's ideas about **civil disobedience,** the refusal to obey unjust laws. Gandhi also embraced Western ideas of democracy and nationalism.

Inspired by both Indian and Western ideas, Gandhi rejected the inequalities of the Indian caste system and fought hard to end the harsh treatment of **untouchables,** the lowest caste of Indian society. He called these outcasts Harijans, or "children of God." Gandhi also urged equal rights for all Indians, women as well as men.

Restoring National Pride Over the next two decades, Gandhi initiated a series of nonviolent actions against British rule. He called for Indians to **boycott,** or refuse to buy, British goods, especially cotton textiles. The move was designed to boost local Indian industries and help restore Indian pride. For centuries, India had produced fine textiles, but cheap British imports had hurt sales.. Gandhi wanted to rebuild such traditional industries.

>> Gandhi taught his ways to people throughout India. Here, he speaks to harijan workers at his ashram, or spiritual retreat, in the village of Sevagram.

🔲 BOUNCE to Activate Gallery

He made the spinning wheel the symbol of the nationalist movement. In a symbolic move, he abandoned Western-style clothing for the *dhoti,* a garment traditionally worn by village Indians.

Through his own example, Gandhi inspired Indians to "get rid of our helplessness." When protests led to violent riots, Gandhi would fast, pray, and call on patriotic Indians to practice self control. His campaigns of civil disobedience attracted wide support, and his nonviolent protests caught the attention of the British government and the world.

✅ **IDENTIFY CENTRAL IDEAS** What force did Gandhi propose using to free India from British colonial rule, and what was the basis for his ideas?

Gandhi Takes a Stand

To mobilize mass support, Gandhi decided to take a stand against the British salt monopoly, which he saw as a symbol of British oppression. Natural salt was available along the shore, and people had traditionally gotten their salt supplies by boiling seawater. But under colonial rule, the British claimed the sole right to produce and sell salt. By taxing those sales, they collected money to maintain their government in India. The tax on salt, a basic human need, imposed another hardship on the Indian people.

The Salt March Early in 1930, Gandhi wrote to the British viceroy in India. He stated his intention to break the hated salt laws and condemned British rule as "a curse."

On March 12, 1930, Gandhi set out with 78 followers on a 240-mile march to the sea. As the tiny band passed through villages, crowds responded to Gandhi's message. By the time they reached the sea, the marchers numbered in the thousands.

On April 6, Gandhi waded into the surf and picked up a lump of sea salt by the edge of the water. He was soon arrested and jailed.

Still, Indians followed his lead. Coastal villagers started collecting salt and evaporating seawater to make it. Indians sold salt on city streets—and went to jail. As Gandhi's campaign gained force, tens of thousands of Indians were imprisoned.

World Opinion Shifts All around the world, newspapers criticized Britain's harsh reaction to the protests. Stories revealed how police brutally clubbed peaceful marchers who tried to occupy a government saltworks. "Not one of the marchers even raised an arm to fend off the blows," wrote an outraged American newspaper. In 1931, 60,000 Indians were arrested for taking part in nonviolent resistance against the salt laws.

The Salt March embarrassed Britain, which prided itself on its democratic traditions. Slowly, Gandhi's campaign forced Britain to hand over some power to Indians. Britain also agreed to meet other demands of the Congress party.

The Future of India In 1939, a new world war exploded. Britain outraged Indian leaders by postponing independence and bringing Indians into the war without consulting them. Angry nationalists launched a campaign of noncooperation and were jailed. Millions of Indians, however, did help Britain during World War II.

When the war ended in 1945, India's independence could no longer be delayed. As it neared, Muslim fears of the Hindu majority increased. Conflict between Hindus and Muslims would trouble the new nation in the years to come.

☑ **ANALYZE INFORMATION** How did the Salt March force Britain to respond to Indian demands?

☑ ASSESSMENT

1. **Identify Cause and Effect** What impact did the Amritsar massacre have on the Indian independence movement?

2. **Draw Conclusions** Why was Gandhi able to unite Indians and shift political thought when earlier attempts had not succeeded?

3. **Identify Cause and Effect** How did Gandhi and the National Congress party work for independence in India?

4. **Analyze Information** What were Gandhi's key ideas? How did Gandhi implement these ideas in his fight against political oppression?

5. **Infer** How might fighting discrimination in South Africa have influenced Gandhi when he returned to India?

6. **Connections to Today** Do you think Gandhi's methods could be used in the struggle against authoritarian governments today? Why or why not?

The Influence of Gandhi

Mohandas Gandhi led a successful, peaceful revolution in India against British rule. In the following excerpt from his book Hind Swaraj *(Indian Home Rule)*, Gandhi explains the ideas behind his nonviolent method of passive resistance in the form of an imaginary conversation between an editor and a reader. Hind Swaraj was first published in 1909 in South Africa, but was banned in India.

Both Gandhi and Martin Luther King, Jr. were influenced by Henry Thoreau's ideas on civil disobedience. In the second primary source, King, who was influenced by Gandhi's stance on passive resistance, refers to Thoreau in his book *The Autobiography of Martin Luther King, Jr.*

As you read, notice the similarities in Gandhi's and King's ideas.

>> Mohandas Gandhi

Primary Source 1

Hind Swaraj: Mohandas Gandhi

Editor: Passive [accepting or allowing] resistance is a method of securing rights by personal suffering; it is the reverse of resistance by arms. When I refuse to do a thing that is repugnant [offensive] to my conscience, I use soul-force. For instance, the government of the day has passed a law which is applicable to me. I do not like it. If by using violence, I force the government to repeal the law, I am employing what may be termed body-force. If I do not obey the law, and accept the penalty for its breach [act of breaking a law], I use soul-force. It involves sacrifice of self.

☑ **COMPARE AND CONTRAST** How are "soul-force" and "body-force" related?

Everybody admits that sacrifice of self is infinitely superior to sacrifice of others. Moreover, if this kind of force is used in a cause that is unjust, only the person using it suffers. He does not make others suffer for his mistakes. Men have before now done many things which were subsequently found to have been wrong. No man can claim that he is absolutely in the right, or that a particular thing is wrong, because he thinks so, but it is wrong for him so long as that is his deliberate judgment. It is therefore meet [proper] that he should not do that which he knows to be wrong, and suffer the consequence whatever it may be. This is the key to the use of soul-force.

☑ **DISTINGUISH AMONG FACT, OPINION, AND REASONED JUDGMENT** Why does Gandhi say that right and wrong are judgments, not facts?

Reader: You would then disregard laws— this is rank [complete and utter] disloyalty.

We have always been considered a law-abiding nation. You seem to be going even beyond the extremists. They say that we must obey the laws that have been passed, but that, if the laws be bad, we must drive out the lawgivers even by force.

Editor: Whether I go beyond them or whether I do not is a matter of no consequence to either of us. We simply want to find out what is right, and to act accordingly. The real meaning of the statement that we are a law-abiding nation is that we are passive resisters. When we do not like certain laws, we do not break the heads of law-givers, but we suffer and do not submit to the laws.

☑ **IDENTIFY CENTRAL IDEAS** According to Gandhi, why is it acceptable to disregard laws?

Primary Source 2

The Autobiography of Martin Luther King, Jr.

During my student days I read Henry David Thoreau's essay *On Civil Disobedience* for the first time. Here, in this courageous New Englander's refusal to pay his taxes and his choice of jail rather than support a war that would spread slavery's territory into Mexico, I made my first contact with the theory of nonviolent resistance. Fascinated by the idea of refusing to cooperate with an evil system, I was so deeply moved that I reread the work several times. I became convinced that noncooperation with evil is as much a moral obligation as is cooperation with good. No other person

has been more eloquent and passionate in getting this idea across than Henry David Thoreau. As a result of his writings and personal witness, we are the heirs of a legacy of creative protest. The teachings of Thoreau came alive in our civil rights movement; indeed, they are more alive than ever before. Whether expressed in a sit-in at lunch counters, a freedom ride into Mississippi, a peaceful protest in Albany, Georgia, a bus boycott in Montgomery, Alabama, these are outgrowths of Thoreau's insistence that evil must be resisted and that no moral man can patiently adjust to injustice.

☑ **DRAW CONCLUSIONS** What does King mean when he says "we are the heirs of a legacy of creative protest"?

☑ ASSESSMENT

1. **Draw Inferences** Why does Gandhi advocate suffering and self-sacrifice?

2. **Analyze Style and Rhetoric** Why do you think Gandhi chooses to structure his book as a conversation between an editor and a reader? How does this help him to get his point across?

3. **Draw Conclusions** Gandhi helped bring about Indian independence from British rule. Why do you think his approach was effective in enacting social and political change?

4. **Explain** How did King and Gandhi unite their roles as religious leaders with their roles as social activists?

GO ONLINE to access primary sources

Mao was introduced to communist ideas while he was working at Peking University as a librarian's assistant. He later became the leader of the Chinese Communist Party.

New Forces in China and Japan

A new Chinese republic took shape after the fall of the Qing dynasty in 1911. Nationalists like Sun Yixian set the goal of "catching up and surpassing the powers, east and west." But that goal would remain a distant dream as China suffered the turmoil of civil war and foreign invasion.

Trouble in the Chinese Republic

Struggles for Power Sun Yixian, the "father of modern China," hoped to rebuild China on the Three Principles of the People—nationalism, democracy, and economic security for everyone. But he made little progress. One problem, he noted, was that the Chinese people felt more loyalty to families and clans than to the nation.

> Therefore, even though we have four hundred million people gathered together in one China, in reality they are just a heap of loose sand. Today we are the poorest and weakest nation in the world and occupy the lowest position in international affairs. Other men are the carving knife and serving dish, we are the fish and the meat.

—Sun Yixian

BOUNCE to Activate Flipped Video

Objectives

Explain the key challenges faced by the Chinese republic in the early 1900s.

Analyze the struggle between nationalists and Communists in China.

Summarize the effects of liberal changes in Japan in the 1920s.

Describe the rise of extreme nationalism and militarism in Japan.

Describe the impact of the Japanese invasion of China.

Key Terms

Twenty-One
 Demands
May Fourth
 Movement
vanguard
Guomindang
Jiang Jieshi
Mao Zedong
Long March
ultranationalist
Manchuria
Hirohito

In 1912, Sun Yixian stepped down as president in favor of Yuan Shikai (yuahn shihky), a powerful general. Sun hoped that Yuan would create a strong central government. Instead, the ambitious general tried to set up a new dynasty. The military, however, did not support Yuan, and opposition divided the nation. When Yuan died in 1916, China plunged into still greater disorder.

In the provinces, local warlords seized power. As rival armies battled for control, the economy collapsed and millions of peasants suffered terrible hardships. Famine and attacks by bandits added to their misery.

Foreign Imperialism During this period of upheaval, foreign powers increased their influence over Chinese affairs. They dominated Chinese port cities and extended their influence inland. During World War I, Japanese officials presented Yuan Shikai with the **Twenty-One Demands,** a list of demands that sought to make China a Japanese protectorate.

With China too weak to resist, Yuan gave in to some of the demands. Then, at the Paris Peace Conference in 1919, the Allies gave Japan control over some former German possessions in China. That news infuriated Chinese Nationalists.

>> Jiang Jieshi led the Guomindang after Sun's death in 1925. He headed the Guomindang government in China from 1928 to 1949.

The May Fourth Movement Seeks Reform In response, student protests erupted in Beijing on May 4, 1919, and later spread to cities across China. "China's territory may be conquered," they declared, "but it cannot be given away!" The students organized boycotts of Japanese goods and businesses.

The protests set off a cultural and intellectual ferment known as the **May Fourth Movement.** Western-educated leaders blamed the imperialists' success on China's own weakness. As in Meiji Japan, Chinese reformers wanted to learn from the West and use that knowledge to end foreign domination. Most reformers rejected Confucian traditions in favor of Western science and ideas such as democracy and nationalism.

Women played a key role in the May Fourth Movement. They campaigned to end traditional practices, such as footbinding and the seclusion of women within the home. Their work helped open doors for women in education and the economy.

Chinese Communism Is Born Some Chinese turned to the revolutionary ideas of Marx and Lenin. The Russian Revolution seemed to offer a model of how a strong, well-organized party could transform a nation.

The Soviet Union trained Chinese students and military officers to become the **vanguard,** or elite leaders, of a communist revolution. By the 1920s, a small group of Chinese Communists had formed their own political party.

☑ **IDENTIFY CAUSE AND EFFECT** How did warlord uprisings and foreign imperialism lead to the May Fourth movement?

Nationalists and Communists

In 1921, Sun Yixian and his **Guomindang** (gwoh meen DAWNG) or Nationalist party, established a government in south China. Sun planned to raise an army to defeat the warlords and unite China. When Western democracies refused to help, Sun accepted aid from the Soviet Union and joined forces with the small group of Chinese Communists to defeat the warlords. However, he still believed that China's future should be based on his Three Principles of the People.

The Nationalists and Jiang Jieshi After Sun's death in 1925, an energetic young army officer, **Jiang Jieshi** (jahng jeh shur), took over the Guomindang. Jiang Jieshi was determined to

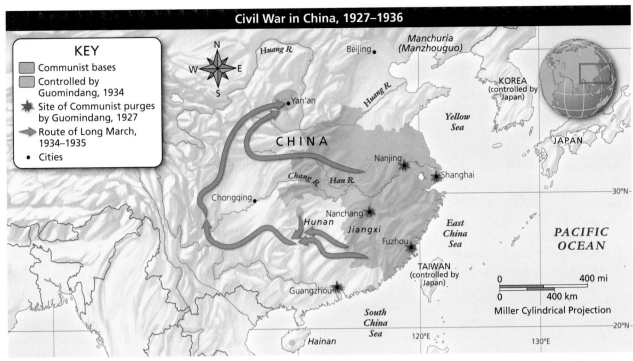

Civil War in China, 1927–1936

KEY
- Communist bases
- Controlled by Guomindang, 1934
- ✳ Site of Communist purges by Guomindang, 1927
- ➡ Route of Long March, 1934–1935
- • Cities

>> **Analyze Maps** The Guomindang and the Communists waged a long and bitter war for control of China. What natural features made the Long March difficult?

BOUNCE to Activate Chart

smash the power of the warlords and reunite China, but he had little interest in either democracy or communism.

In 1926, Jiang Jieshi began the Northern Expedition in order to crush or win over local warlords as he advanced on Beijing. In mid-campaign, Jiang turned on his sometime allies the Chinese Communists, who he saw as a threat to his power. The Communists were winning converts among the small working class in cities like Shanghai.

Early in 1927, on orders from Jiang, Guomindang troops slaughtered Communist Party members and the workers who supported them. In Shanghai and elsewhere, thousands of people were killed. This massacre marked the beginning of a bitter civil war between the Communists and the Guomindang that lasted for 22 years.

Communism and Mao Zedong
Among the Communists who escaped Jiang's attack was a young revolutionary of peasant origins, **Mao Zedong** (mow dzuh doong). Unlike earlier Chinese Communists, Mao believed that the Communists should seek support not among the small urban working class but among the large peasant masses.

Although the Communists were pursued at every turn by Guomindang forces, Mao was optimistic about eventual success. In southeastern China, Mao and the Communists redistributed land to peasants and offered them schooling and health care.

The Long March
Jiang Jieshi, however, was determined to destroy the "Red bandits," as he called the Communists. He led the Guomindang in a series of "extermination campaigns" against them. Mao and about 100,000 of his followers fled the Guomindang in an epic retreat known as the **Long March.** From 1934 to 1935, they trekked more than 6,000 miles, facing daily attacks as they crossed rugged mountains and raging rivers. Mao's forces used guerrilla, or irregular hit-and-run, tactics to fight back. Only about 20,000 of the marchers survived the ordeal.

During the march, the Communists enforced strict discipline. Soldiers were told to treat peasants politely, pay for goods they wanted, and avoid damaging crops. Such behavior made Mao's forces welcome among peasants, many of whom had suffered greatly at the hands of the Guomindang.

For decades, the Long March stood as a symbol of communist heroism and inspired new recruits to follow Mao. At the end of the Long March, the Communists set up a new base in a remote region of northern China. There, Mao rebuilt his forces and plotted new strategies for fighting the Guomindang.

☑ **IDENTIFY SUPPORTING DETAILS** How did the communists manage to survive Jiang's "extermination campaigns"?

China Faces Japanese Imperialism

While Jiang was pursuing the Communists across China, the country faced another danger. In 1931, Japan invaded Manchuria in northeastern China, adding it to the growing Japanese empire. As Japanese aggression increased, some of Jiang's generals pushed him to form a united front with the Communists against Japan.

In 1937, the Japanese struck again, starting what became the Second Sino-Japanese War. Airplanes bombed Chinese cities, and Japanese troops overran eastern China, including Beijing and Guangzhou. Jiang Jieshi and his government retreated to the interior and set up a new capital at Chongqing (chawng CHING).

After a lengthy siege, Japanese troops marched into the city of Nanjing (nahn jing) on December 13. Nanjing was an important cultural center and had been the Guomindang capital before Chongqing.

>> During the Russo-Japanese War in 1904–1905, Japan used Korea as a base for its military operations against Russia. Japanese leaders later annexed Korea.

After the city's surrender, the Japanese killed hundreds of thousands of soldiers and civilians and brutalized still more. The cruelty and destruction became known as the "Rape of Nanjing."

The invasion suspended China's civil war as the Guomindang and Communists formed a temporary, uneasy alliance. Jiang's army battled Japanese troops, while Communists engaged in guerrilla attacks against the invaders. The Soviet Union sent advisors and equipment to help. Great Britain, France, and the United States gave economic aid.

☑ **EXPLAIN** Why did the Japanese invasion help unify the Chinese temporarily?

Conflicting Forces in Japan

The Japanese invasions of China were part of a rising tide of Japanese imperialism. Like China, Japan sought to become a major world power, equal to Western nations. However, Japan lacked the resources needed to fuel its industrial achievements. The small nation looked to the West as an example, attempting to conquer lands to form a huge empire. As you will see, the invasion of China takes on new meaning when viewed from the Japanese perspective.

Unlike China in the 1920s, which was shaken by conflict and economic turmoil, Japan was a powerful, united country with a growing industrial economy. Beneath the surface, however, conflicts brewed that would undermine its moves toward democratic reforms.

Expansion and Economic Growth During World War I, the Japanese economy enjoyed remarkable growth. Its exports to Allied nations soared. Heavy industrial production grew, making Japan a true industrial power. At the same time, it sought to win international recognition as equal to the Western powers.

While Western powers battled in Europe, Japan expanded its influence throughout East Asia. Japan had already annexed Korea as a colony in 1910. During the war, Japan also sought further rights in China with the Twenty-One Demands. After the war, Japan was given some former German possessions in East Asia, including the Shandong province in China.

Liberal Reforms of the 1920s During the 1920s, Japan moved toward more widespread democracy.

Political parties grew stronger. Elected members of the Diet—the Japanese parliament—exercised their power. In 1925, all adult men, regardless of class, won the right to vote. Western ideas about women's rights brought some changes.

Overall, however, the status of Japanese women remained below that of men. They would not win suffrage until 1945.

Despite greater democracy, powerful business leaders, called the zaibatsu (zy baht soo), strongly influenced the government through donations to political parties. They pushed for policies that favored international trade and their own interests.

Japan's aggressive expansion threatened its economic relationship with the Western powers. To improve relations, moderate Japanese politicians decided to slow down foreign expansion. In 1922, Japan signed an agreement with the United States, Britain, Italy, and France to limit the size of its navy. It also agreed to leave Shandong. The government reduced military spending.

Lurking Problems Behind its seeming well-being, Japan faced some grave problems. The economy grew more slowly in the 1920s than at any time since the country had modernized. Rural peasants did not share in the nation's prosperity. In the cities, factory workers earning low wages were attracted to the ideas of Marx and Lenin.

In the cities, members of the younger generation were also in revolt against tradition. They adopted Western fads and fashions. Also, they rejected family authority for the Western ideal of individual freedom, shocking their elders.

During the 1920s, tensions between the government and the military simmered not far below the surface. Conservatives, especially military officers, blasted government corruption, including payoffs by powerful zaibatsu. They also condemned Western influences for undermining basic Japanese values of obedience and respect for authority.

A devastating earthquake, one of the most destructive quakes in history, struck the Tokyo area in 1923. The earthquake and the widespread fires it caused resulted in the deaths of over 100,000 people and damaged more than 650,000 buildings. Almost half of surviving workers lost their jobs because so many businesses were destroyed. With help from the government, the Tokyo area gradually recovered—just as Japan faced a worldwide economic crisis.

☑ **SUMMARIZE** How did democratic participation in Japan grow in the 1920s? How was it limited?

>> Members of the Japanese Woman Suffrage League approach the government with 20,000 signed petitions demanding the right to vote.

>> In 1923, Tokyo suffered from one of the most destructive earthquakes in history, the Great Kanto Earthquake. The quake caused fires and tidal waves and killed more than 100,000 people.

The Ultranationalist Reaction

In 1929, the Great Depression—a global economic slump that began in the United States—rippled across the Pacific, striking Japan with devastating force. Trade suffered as foreign buyers could no longer afford to purchase Japanese silks and other exports. Unemployment in the cities soared, while rural peasants were only a mouthful from starvation.

Increasing Unrest Economic disaster fed the discontent of the leading military officials and extreme nationalists, or **ultranationalists.** They condemned politicians for agreeing to Western demands to stop overseas expansion. Western industrial powers, they pointed out, had long ago grabbed huge empires. By comparison, Japan's empire was tiny.

Japanese nationalists were further outraged by racial policies in the United States, Canada, and Australia that shut out Japanese immigrants. The Japanese took great pride in their industrial achievements. They bitterly resented being treated as second-class citizens in other parts of the world.

As the economic crisis worsened, nationalists demanded renewed expansion. An empire in Asia, they argued, would provide much-needed raw materials as well as an outlet for Japan's rapidly growing population. They set their sights on the northern Chinese province of **Manchuria.** This region was rich in natural resources, and Japanese businesses had already invested heavily there.

The Manchurian Incident In 1931, a group of Japanese army officers provoked an incident that provided an excuse to seize Manchuria. They set explosives and blew up tracks on a Japanese-owned railroad line. Then they claimed that the Chinese had committed the act. Claiming self-defense, the army attacked Chinese forces.

Without consulting their own government, the Japanese military forces conquered all of Manchuria and set up a puppet state there that they called Manzhouguo (mahn joh gwaw). They brought in Puyi, the last Chinese emperor, to head the puppet state.

Politicians in Tokyo objected to the army's highhanded actions, but public opinion sided with the military. When the League of Nations condemned Japanese aggression against China, Japan simply withdrew from the League. The League's member states failed to take military action against Japanese aggression. Japan also nullified its naval disarmament agreements with the Western powers.

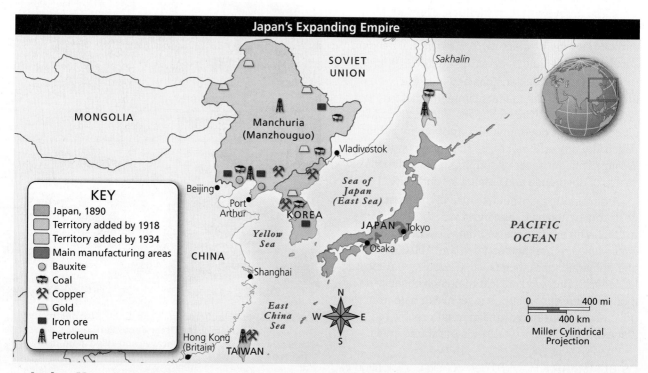

>> **Analyze Maps** Japan expanded its territory in Asia between 1918 and 1934. From the conquered lands, the Japanese acquired natural resources to fuel industry. Where were Japan's main manufacturing areas located?

✅ **IDENTIFY CAUSE AND EFFECT** How did the Great Depression lead to calls for renewed expansion?

Militarists Gain Power

In the early 1930s, ultranationalists were winning support from the people for renewing foreign conquests and taking a tough stand against the Western powers. Members of extreme nationalist societies assassinated a number of politicians and business leaders who opposed expansion. Military leaders plotted to overthrow the government and, in 1936, briefly occupied the center of Tokyo.

Revival of Traditional Values Civilian government survived, but by 1937, the unrest forced the government to accept military domination. To please the ultranationalists, the government cracked down on socialists and suppressed most democratic freedoms. It revived ancient warrior values and built a cult around Emperor **Hirohito,** who had ascended to the throne in 1926. According to Japanese tradition, the emperor was descended from the sun goddess and was himself a living god.

In theory, Hirohito was the nation's supreme authority. In practice, however, he merely approved the policies that his ministries formulated. To spread its nationalist message, the government used schools to teach students absolute obedience to the emperor and service to the state.

Expansion into China Japan took advantage of China's civil war to increase its influence there. By 1937, as you have read, its armies had invaded the Chinese mainland and overran eastern China.

Japan expected to complete its conquest of China within a few years. But in 1939, while the two nations were locked in deadly combat, World War II broke out in Europe. That conflict swiftly spread to Asia, where France and Britain had large empires.

In 1936, Japan had allied with two aggressive European powers, Germany and Italy. These three powers signed the Tripartite Pact in September 1940, cementing the alliance known as the Axis Powers. That alliance, combined with renewed Japanese conquests, would turn World War II into a brutal, wide-ranging conflict waged not only across the continent of Europe but across Asia and the islands of the Pacific as well.

>> Japanese soldiers occupied Beijing in 1937. Japan took control of large parts of China during the Second Sino-Japanese War, from 1937 to 1945.

🅑 BOUNCE to Activate Gallery

✅ **IDENTIFY CAUSE AND EFFECT** How did Japanese militarists rise to power in the 1930s?

☑ ASSESSMENT

1. **Summarize** What political and economic changes occurred in Japan during the 1920s?

2. **Identify Cause and Effect** Why did the new republic of China fall into chaos after 1912?

3. **Integrate Information** Why did the Communists and the Guomindang cooperate during the Northern Expedition in 1926? How did the expedition affect their long-term relationship?

4. **Identify Central Ideas** How did the Japanese invasion affect the civil war in China?

5. **Connections to Today** Judging from the example of Japan, why might a nation turn to military leaders and extreme nationalists during a crisis? Cite details from the text.

17.5

Duke Ellington was a composer, pianist, and bandleader. He referred to his music as "American Music" rather than "jazz." His career spanned the 1920s to the 1970s.

 BOUNCE to Activate Flipped Video

Objectives

Analyze how Western society and culture changed after World War I.

Identify the contributions of modern scientists such as Marie Curie and Albert Einstein.

Summarize the domestic and foreign policy issues that the Western democracies faced after World War I.

Describe how the global depression began and spread.

Explain the responses of Britain, France, and the United States to the Great Depression.

Key Terms

flapper
Miriam Ferguson
Prohibition
Marie Curie
Albert Einstein
psychoanalysis
Harlem Renaissance
abstract art
dada
surrealism
Maginot Line

Kellogg-Briand Pact
disarmament
general strike
overproduction
finance
Federal Reserve
Great Depression
Franklin D. Roosevelt
New Deal

GO ONLINE to access your digital course

The West After World War I

The catastrophe of World War I shattered the sense of optimism that had grown in the West since the Enlightenment. Despair gripped survivors on both sides as they added up the staggering costs of the war. Europeans mourned a generation of young men who had been lost on the battlefields.

Social Change After World War I

Many people talked about a "return to normalcy," to life as it had been before 1914. But rebellious young people rejected the moral values and rules of the Victorian Age and chased after excitement. Gertrude Stein, an American writer living in Paris, called them the "lost generation." Others saw them as immoral pleasure-seekers.

The Roaring Twenties During the 1920s, new technologies helped create a mass culture shared by millions in the world's developed countries. Affordable cars, improved telephones, and new forms of media such as motion pictures and radio brought people around the world closer together than ever before.

In the 1920s, many radios tuned into the new sounds of jazz. In fact, the decade in the West is often called the Jazz Age. African American musicians combined Western harmonies with African rhythms to create jazz. Jazz musicians, like trumpeter Louis Armstrong and pianist Duke Ellington, took simple melodies and improvised endless subtle variations in rhythm and beat.

Throughout the 1920s, the popularity of jazz moved from the United States to Europe. Europeans embraced American popular culture, with its greater freedom and willingness to experiment. The nightclub and jazz were symbols of that freedom. Jazz came to embody the universal themes of creativity and self-expression.

Much of today's popular music has been influenced by jazz. It has transcended the "Roaring Twenties" American culture to become an international musical language.

After the war, rebellious young people, disillusioned by the war, rejected the moral values and rules of the Victorian Age and chased after excitement. During the Jazz Age, this rebellion was exemplified by a new type of liberated young woman called the **flapper.** The first flappers were American, but their European sisters soon adopted the fashion. Flappers rejected old ways in favor of new, exciting freedoms.

> The Flapper awoke from her lethargy (tiredness) . . . bobbed her hair, put on her choicest pair of earrings and a great deal of audacity (boldness) and rouge and went into battle. She flirted because it was fun to flirt and . . . refused to be bored chiefly because she wasn't boring . . . Mothers disapproved of their sons taking the Flapper to dances, to teas, to swim, and most of all to heart.
>
> —Zelda Fitzgerald, flapper and wife of author F. Scott Fitzgerald

Women's Progress Flappers were highly visible, but they were a small minority. Most women saw mixed progress in the postwar period. During the war, women had held a wide range of jobs. Although most women left those jobs when the war ended, their war work helped them win the vote in many Western countries, such as Britain, Germany, the Netherlands, and the United States. A few women were elected to public office, such as Texas governor **Miriam Ferguson** or Lady Nancy Astor, the first woman to serve in the British Parliament.

By the 1920s, labor-saving devices had become common in middle class homes. Washing machines, vacuum cleaners, and canned foods lightened the burden of household chores. Some women then sought work outside the home or did volunteer work to help the less fortunate.

In the new atmosphere of emancipation, women sought higher education and pursued careers in many areas—from sports to the arts. Women golfers, tennis players, swimmers, and pilots set new records.

Women worked as newspaper reporters, published bestselling novels, and won recognition as artists. Most professions, though, were still dominated by men. Women doing the same work as men were paid much less.

Diverse Reactions to the Jazz Age Not everyone approved of the freewheeling lifestyle of the Jazz Age. In 1920, the Eighteenth Amendment to the Constitution of the United States ushered in **Prohibition,** which banned the manufacture and sale of alcoholic beverages. Temperance reformers had long sought the amendment to stop alcohol abuse. It was later repealed in part because it had spurred the growth of organized crime, which supplied illegal alcohol to speakeasies, or illegal bars.

In the United States in the early 1900s, a Christian fundamentalist movement swept rural areas. Fundamentalists support traditional Christian beliefs. Popular fundamentalist preachers traveled around the country holding inspirational revival meetings. Some used the new technology of radio to spread their message.

☑ **SOLVE PROBLEMS** What problem was Prohibition intended to solve? How well did it succeed?

>> Amelia Earhart was an American aviation pioneer and author. She was the first woman to fly solo across the Atlantic Ocean. She was also an avid supporter of women's rights.

Scientific Discoveries

Even before World War I, new ideas and scientific discoveries were challenging long-held ideas about the nature of the world and even of people. Like the war, science helped feed a sense of uncertainty that flowed through Western culture.

Curie Experiments with Radioactivity The ancient Greeks were the first to propose that all matter is composed of tiny, indivisible atoms. Over the centuries, most scientists came to accept this idea. But discoveries made in the early 1900s showed that the atom was more complex than anyone suspected.

The Polish-born French scientist **Marie Curie** and others experimented with an atomic process called radioactivity. They found that the atoms of certain elements, such as radium and uranium, spontaneously release charged particles. As scientists studied radioactivity further, they discovered that it can change atoms of one element into atoms of another. Such findings proved that atoms are not solid and indivisible.

Einstein Proposes the Theory of Relativity In 1905 and 1916, the German-born physicist **Albert Einstein** introduced his theories of relativity. Einstein argued that measurements of space and time are not absolute but are determined by many factors, including the relative position of the observer. Einstein's ideas raised questions about Newtonian science, which compared the universe to a machine operating according to absolute laws.

In the postwar years, many scientists came to accept the theories of relativity. To the general public, however, Einstein's ideas were difficult to understand. They seemed to further reinforce the unsettling sense of a universe whirling beyond the understanding of human reason.

In 1934, building on Curie's and Einstein's theories, Italian physicist Enrico Fermi and other scientists around the world discovered atomic fission, or the splitting of the nuclei of atoms in two. This splitting produces a huge burst of energy. In the 1940s, Fermi (now an American), along with fellow American physicists J. Robert Oppenheimer and Edward Teller, would use this discovery to create the devastating atomic bomb.

Fleming Discovers Penicillin In 1928, the Scottish scientist Alexander Fleming made a different type of scientific discovery. One day, he picked up a discarded laboratory dish that he had used to grow bacteria. The dish had grown some mold, which had killed the bacteria. Fleming called this nontoxic mold "penicillin." Fleming's penicillin was the first antibiotic, or medicine used to kill micro-organisms such as bacteria. Later scientists developed a wide range of antibiotics.

Freud Analyzes the Mind The Austrian physician Sigmund Freud (froyd) also challenged faith in reason. He suggested that the subconscious mind drives much of human behavior. Freud said that learned social values such as morality and reason help people to repress, or check, powerful urges. But an individual feels constant tension between repressed drives and social training. This tension, argued Freud, may cause psychological or physical illness.

Freud pioneered **psychoanalysis,** a method of studying how the mind works and treating mental disorders. Although many of his theories have been discredited, Freud's ideas have had an extraordinary impact far beyond medicine. They strongly influenced the art and literature of the postwar West.

>> Albert Einstein received the 1921 Nobel Prize in Physics and is well known for his mass-energy formula. Einstein fled Germany and became an American citizen in 1940.

IDENTIFY PATTERNS How did scientific discoveries in the 1920s change people's views of the world?

Literature Reflects New Perspectives

In the 1920s, war novels, poetry, plays, and memoirs flowed off the presses. Novels such as *All Quiet on the Western Front* by German author Erich Remarque exposed the grim horrors faced by soldiers in World War I. Other writers heaped scorn on the leaders who took them into war. Their realistic works stripped away any romantic notions about the glories of warfare and reflected a powerful disgust with war that influenced an entire generation.

The Lost Generation To many postwar writers, the war symbolized the moral breakdown of Western civilization. In 1922, the English poet T. S. Eliot published *The Waste Land.* This long poem portrays the modern world as spiritually empty and barren.

In *The Sun Also Rises,* the American novelist Ernest Hemingway shows the rootless wanderings of young people who lack deep convictions. "I did not care what it was all about," says the narrator. "All I wanted to know was how to live in it." In *The Great Gatsby,* American novelist F. Scott Fitzgerald exposed the emptiness of the 1920s world of flappers and parties.

American poet Gertrude Stein considered herself, her writer friends, and young people part of a "lost generation." They had become adults during or right after World War I and were disillusioned by the upheaval of the war and its aftermath.

Literature Explores the Inner Mind As Freud's ideas became popular, many writers began to explore the inner workings of the mind. Some experimented with stream of consciousness. In this technique, a writer appears to present a character's random thoughts and feelings without imposing any logic or order. In the novel *Mrs. Dalloway,* British novelist Virginia Woolf used stream of consciousness to explore the thoughts of people going through the ordinary actions of their everyday lives. In *Finnegans Wake,* the Irish novelist James Joyce explored the inner mind of a hero who remains sound asleep throughout the novel.

>> Austrian neurologist Sigmund Freud founded the field of psychoanalysis. In his later years, Freud used psychoanalysis to interpret religion and culture.

>> F. Scott Fitzerald's 1925 novel *The Great Gatsby* is a portrait of the Jazz Age and Roaring Twenties. It emphasizes the glittering but empty life of parties and excess.

The Harlem Renaissance A more optimistic literary movement arose in the United States during the 1920s. The **Harlem Renaissance** was an African American cultural awakening. It began in Harlem, a neighborhood in New York City that was home to many African Americans. African American writers and artists expressed their pride in their unique culture.

Among its best known figures was the poet and playwright Langston Hughes. In his poem, "The Negro Speaks of Rivers," Hughes reflects on the rivers associated with the African and African-American experience from the Euphrates, Congo, and Nile to the Mississippi. Novelist and anthropologist Zora Neale Hurston studied African American folklore and traditions.

☑ **COMPARE POINTS OF VIEW** How did postwar authors show disillusionment with prewar institutions?

Modern Art and Architecture

In the early 1900s, many Western artists rejected traditional styles. Instead of trying to reproduce the real world, they explored other dimensions of color, line, and shape. Painters like Henri Matisse (ma TEES) utilized bold, wild strokes of color and odd distortions to produce works of strong emotion. He and fellow artists outraged the public and were dubbed *fauves*(fohv), or wild beasts, by critics.

Painters Embrace Revolutionary Trends Before World War I, the Spanish artist Pablo Picasso and the French artist Georges Braque (brak) created a revolutionary new style called cubism. Cubists painted three-dimensional objects as complex patterns of angles and planes. By redefining objects into separate shapes, they offered a new view of reality.

Later, the Russian Vasily Kandinsky and the Swiss Paul Klee moved even further away from representing reality. They created a new style of **abstract art,** composed only of lines, colors, and shapes, sometimes with no recognizable subject matter at all.

During and after the war, the dada movement burst onto the Paris art world. **Dada** was a European art movement that rejected traditional artistic values by producing works that seemed like absurd nonsense. Dada was a revolt against civilization. Paintings and sculptures by Jean Arp and Max Ernst were intended to shock and disturb viewers. Some Dadaists created works made of objects they found abandoned or thrown away.

Cubism and dada both helped to inspire **surrealism,** a movement that attempted to portray the workings of the unconscious mind. Surrealism rejected rational thought, which had produced the horrors of World War I, in favor of irrational or unconscious ideas. The Spanish surrealist Salvador Dali used images of melting clocks and burning giraffes to suggest the chaotic dream state described by Freud.

Architecture Reflects a New World Architects, too, rejected classical traditions and developed new styles to match a new urban, industrialized world. The famous Bauhaus school in Germany influenced architecture by blending science and technology with design. Bauhaus buildings used glass, steel, and concrete but very little ornamentation.

The American architect Frank Lloyd Wright reflected the Bauhaus belief that the function of a building should determine its form. He used materials and forms that fit a building's environment. He believed that "a building should grace its environment rather than disgrace it." One of Wright's most famous designs is Fallingwater, a house in Pennsylvania built on a waterfall. The structure works in harmony with the surrounding environment, as Wright intended.

>> Pablo Picasso, one of the most important artists of the 20th century, co-developed the movement known as Cubism. He painted *Woman Sitting in an Armchair* in 1920.

▶ BOUNCE to Activate Gallery

☑ **IDENTIFY CAUSE AND EFFECT** What effect did World War I have on artistic movements in the 1920s?

Postwar Politics in the West

As nations recovered from the war, people began to feel hope rising out of their disillusionment. But soon, the "lost generation" would face a new crisis that would revive many old problems and spark new conflicts.

In 1919, the three Western democracies—Britain, France, and the United States—appeared powerful. They had ruled the Paris Peace Conference and boosted hopes for democracy among the new nations of Eastern Europe. Beneath the surface, however, postwar Europe faced grave problems. To make matters worse, many members of the younger generation who might have become the next great leaders had been killed in the war.

At first, the most pressing issues were finding jobs for returning veterans and rebuilding war-ravaged lands like France and Belgium. Economic problems fed social unrest and made radical ideas more popular. The Russian Revolution unleashed fears of the spread of communism. Some people saw socialism as the answer to economic hardships. Others embraced nationalist political movements.

Political Parties Clash in Britain In Britain during the 1920s, the Labour party surpassed the Liberal party in strength. The Labour party gained support among workers by promoting a gradual move toward socialism. The Liberal party passed some social legislation, but it traditionally represented middle-class business interests. As the Liberal party faltered, the middle class began to back the Conservative party, joining the upper class, professionals, and farmers. With this support, the Conservative party held power during much of 1920s. After a massive strike of over three million workers in 1926, Conservatives passed legislation limiting the power of workers to strike.

Irish Independence at Last Britain still faced the "Irish question." In 1914, Parliament passed a home-rule bill that was shelved when the war began. Militant Irish nationalists, however, were unwilling to wait any longer. On Easter 1916, a small group launched a revolt against British rule. Although the Easter Rising was quickly suppressed, it stirred wider support for the Irish cause.

>> Fallingwater, a Pennsylvania home designed by architect Frank Lloyd Wright, incorporates nature into its design. It appears to hover over a tranquil waterfall.

>> The major outcomes of the Paris Peace Conference were five peace treaties ending World War I, including the Treaty of Versailles with Germany, and the creation of the League of Nations.

When Parliament again failed to grant home rule in 1919, members of the Irish Republican Army (IRA) began a guerrilla war against British forces and their supporters. In 1922, moderates in Ireland and Britain reached an agreement. Most of Ireland became the independent Irish Free State. The largely Protestant northern counties remained under British rule. The settlement ended the worst violence, but the IRA and others never accepted the division of Ireland. In years to come, Catholics in the north faced discrimination, creating new tensions and conflict.

Peacetime Troubles in France Like Britain, France emerged from World War I both a victor and a loser. Fighting on the Western front had destroyed much of northern France. The French had suffered huge casualties. Survivors felt battered and insecure.

After the war, political divisions and financial scandals continued to plague the Third Republic. Several parties—from conservatives to communists—competed for power. During the postwar years, France was again ruled by a series of coalition governments that created temporary alliances among rival political parties.

Postwar Fears in the United States In contrast, the United States emerged from World War I in good shape.

>> **Analyze Political Cartoons** This political cartoon's original caption was "Communism. A Destructive Worm." What message is the cartoonist conveying in this cartoon?

A late entrant into the war, it had suffered relatively few casualties and little loss of property. However, the United States did experience some domestic unrest. Fear of radicals and the Bolshevik Revolution in Russia set off a "Red Scare" in 1919 and 1920. Police rounded up suspected foreign-born radicals, and a number were expelled from the United States.

The "Red Scare" fed growing demands to limit immigration. Millions of immigrants from southern and eastern Europe had poured into the United States between 1890 and 1914. Some native-born Americans sought to exclude these newcomers, whose cultures differed from those of earlier settlers from northern Europe. In response, Congress passed laws limiting immigration from Europe. Earlier laws had already excluded or limited Chinese and Japanese immigration.

☑ **IDENTIFY CENTRAL ISSUES** What political issues did France face after World War I?

International Relations

In addition to problems at home, the three democracies faced a difficult international situation. The peace settlements that ended World War I caused friction, especially in Germany and among some ethnic groups in Eastern Europe.

Allies Disagree Over Direction France's chief concern after the war was securing its borders against Germany. The French remembered the German invasions of 1870 and 1914. To prevent a third invasion, France built massive fortifications called the **Maginot Line** (ma zhee NOH) along its border with Germany. The Maginot Line offered a sense of security—a false one. The line would be of little use when Germany invaded again in 1940.

In its quest for security, France also strengthened its military and sought alliances with other countries, including the Soviet Union. It insisted on strict enforcement of the Versailles treaty and complete payment of reparations. France's goal was to keep the German economy weak.

Britain was more interested in protecting its overseas empire and rebuilding trade than in punishing Germany. British leaders strongly supported the limits on German naval power. Still, during the postwar period, many British leaders began to think that the Treaty of Versailles had been too harsh on Germany, and they called for easing its terms. They feared that if Germany became too weak, the Soviet Union and France would become too powerful.

Searching for Peace During the 1920s and 1930s, many people worked for peace. Hopes soared in 1925 when representatives from seven European nations signed a series of treaties at Locarno, Switzerland. These treaties settled Germany's disputed borders with France, Belgium, Czechoslovakia, and Poland.

The Locarno treaties became the symbol of a new era of peace. "France and Germany Ban War Forever," trumpeted a *New York Times* headline.

The hopeful "spirit of Locarno" was echoed in the **Kellogg-Briand Pact,** signed in 1928. Almost every independent nation signed this agreement, promising to "renounce war as an instrument of national policy." Although the Kellogg-Briand Pact outlawed war, it provided no way of enforcing the ban.

In the same optimistic spirit, the great powers also pursued **disarmament,** the reduction of armed forces and weapons. The United States, Britain, France, Japan, and other nations signed treaties to reduce the size of their navies. However, they failed to agree on limiting the size of their armies.

The League of Nations Despite grumblings about the Versailles treaty, people around the world put their hope in the League of Nations. From its headquarters in Geneva, Switzerland, the League encouraged cooperation and tried to get members to make a commitment to stop aggression. At first, the League did have some successes. Although the United States never joined, the League grew in the 1920s. In 1926, after signing the Locarno agreements, Germany joined the League. Later, the Soviet Union was also admitted.

Despite its lofty aims, the League of Nations was powerless to stop aggression. In 1931, the League vigorously condemned Japan's invasion of Manchuria, but it had no military means to stop it. Ambitious dictators in Europe noted the League's weakness. They began to rearm and pursue aggressive foreign policies.

☑ **COMPARE POINTS OF VIEW** Why did Britain and France disagree over how to enforce the Treaty of Versailles?

Economics in the Postwar Era

The war affected economies all over the world, hurting some and helping others. Britain and France both owed huge war debts to the United States. Both relied on reparation payments from Germany to pay back their loans. Meanwhile, the crushing

>> **Analyze Political Cartoons** This political cartoon, called "The Doormat," makes a statement about the world's reaction to Japan's rising militarism. Who is the doormat in the cartoon, and why might this be the case?

🅑 BOUNCE to Activate Cartoon

reparations and other conditions hurt Germany's economy.

Britain and France Recover Britain faced serious economic problems in the 1920s. It was deeply in debt, and its factories were out of date. Unemployment was severe. Wages remained low, leading to worker unrest and frequent strikes. In 1926, a **general strike,** or strike by workers in many different industries at the same time, lasted nine days and involved some three million workers.

In comparison, the French economy recovered fairly rapidly. Financial reparations and territories gained from Germany helped. Still, economic swings did occur, adding to an unstable political scene.

Despite these problems, Europe made a shaky recovery during the 1920s. Economies returned to peacetime manufacturing and trade. Veterans gradually found jobs, although unemployment never ceased to be a problem. Middle-class families enjoyed a rising standard of living.

The American Economy Booms In contrast, the United States emerged from the war as the world's leading economic power. In the affluent 1920s, middle-class Americans enjoyed the benefits of capitalism. American loans and investments backed the recovery in Europe. As long as the American economy prospered, the global economy remained stable.

☑ **IDENTIFY CAUSE AND EFFECT** How did World War I and its peace treaties affect the international economy?

The Great Depression

During the 1920s, European nations made a shaky recovery from World War I, helped in part by American loans and investments. Then, at the end of the decade, an economic crisis began in the United States and spread to the rest of the world. This global economic slump, called the **Great Depression,** was the longest, most severe economic downturn to strike the industrialized Western world.

Overproduction and a Drop in Demand Both the American and the world economy had weak points. In the industrial world, a major problem was **overproduction,** meaning that factories and farms produced more goods than were being sold. In other words, supply outpaced demand.

By the 1920s, improved technology and farming methods had led to higher output. When demand for goods slowed, prices fell. Consumers benefited from the lower prices, but farmers, miners, and other suppliers of raw materials did not. Overproduction created a backlog of unsold goods, leading businesses to cut back on output and lay off workers. Unemployed workers had no money to spend on buying goods, which slowed demand further and brought more layoffs. This cycle then had a ripple effect throughout the economy.

Crash Leads to Collapse Meanwhile, a crisis in **finance**—the management of money matters, including the circulation of money, loans, investments, and banking—was brewing. Few saw the danger. Prices on the New York Stock Exchange were at an all-time high. Eager investors acquired stocks through risky methods. To slow the run on the stock market, the **Federal Reserve,** the central banking system of the United States, raised interest rates in 1928 and again in 1929.

In the autumn of 1929, jitters about the economy caused brokers to call in the loans made to investors. When investors were unable to repay, financial panic set in. Stock prices crashed in October, wiping out the fortunes of many investors. The stock market

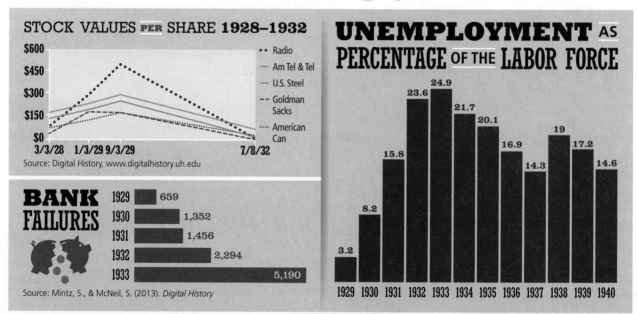

THE GREAT DEPRESSION IN THE UNITED STATES

STOCK VALUES PER SHARE 1928–1932

- •• Radio
- ···· Am Tel & Tel
- — U.S. Steel
- –– Goldman Sacks
- ···· American Can

Source: Digital History, www.digitalhistory.uh.edu

BANK FAILURES

Year	Failures
1929	659
1930	1,352
1931	1,456
1932	2,294
1933	5,190

Source: Mintz, S., & McNeil, S. (2013). *Digital History*

UNEMPLOYMENT AS PERCENTAGE OF THE LABOR FORCE

Year	Percentage
1929	3.2
1930	8.2
1931	15.8
1932	23.6
1933	24.9
1934	21.7
1935	20.1
1936	16.9
1937	14.3
1938	19
1939	17.2
1940	14.6

>> **Analyze Information** In what year did unemployment and bank failures peak in the United States?

crash worsened the economic decline. The Great Depression had begun.

Over the next few years, consumer spending and investment fell, causing still more businesses and factories to close. Millions of people lost their jobs. The cycle spiraled steadily downward. By 1933, between 13 to 15 million Americans were jobless and almost half the banks had closed. The jobless could not afford to buy goods, so more factories had to close, which in turn increased unemployment. People slept on park benches and lined up to eat in soup kitchens.

The Depression Spreads Around the World The economic problems quickly spread around the world. American banks stopped investing or making loans abroad and demanded repayment of foreign loans. Without new investments, European prosperity slowed. Hardest hit were countries, like Britain and Germany, that owed the most to the United States.

In Germany, unemployment rose steeply, leaving one in four workers jobless. Britain was less badly hurt, but its industries and trade were depressed.

Desperate governments tried to protect their economies from foreign competition. The United States imposed the highest tariffs in its history. The policy backfired when other nations retaliated by raising their tariffs. In the end, all countries lost access to the global markets as world trade continued to shrink. The collapse of world trade spread the misery of the Great Depression beyond the industrial world to Latin America, Africa, and Asia.

☑ **GENERATE EXPLANATIONS** What were three root causes of the Great Depression?

Western Democracies React to the Depression

The Great Depression led to changes in government economic policies. For more than a century, Western governments had backed laissez-faire capitalism, the policy that calls for little or no government interference in the economy. During the 1930s, governments in Britain, France, the United States, and elsewhere stepped in to ease the impact of the Great Depression. None of their methods provided a quick fix, but they did alleviate some of the suffering.

International Industrial Production, 1926–1938

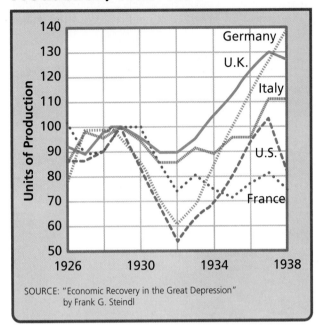

SOURCE: "Economic Recovery in the Great Depression" by Frank G. Steindl

>> **Analyze Information** In which two countries did industrial production decline the most?

Britain and France Search for Solutions In response to the Depression, Britain set up a coalition government made up of leaders from all three of its major political parties. The government provided some unemployment benefits. It kept tariffs low throughout the British empire to boost trade but raised tariffs against the United States and other countries. By the mid-1930s, Britain was slowly recovering from the worst of the Great Depression. Still, unemployment remained high, and the recovery was uneven.

The Great Depression took longer to hurt France than some other countries. However, by the mid-1930s, France was feeling the pinch of decreased production and unemployment. In response, several leftist parties united behind the socialist leader Leon Blum. His Popular Front government tried to solve labor problems and passed some social legislation. But it could not satisfy more radical leftists. Strikes soon brought down Blum's government. Democracy survived, but the country lacked strong leadership able to respond to the clamor for change.

Roosevelt's New Deal Meanwhile, in the United States, President Herbert Hoover firmly believed that the government should not intervene in private business matters. Even so, he did try a variety of limited measures to solve the crisis. Nothing worked.

>> Striking workers walk down a boulevard in Paris in June 1936.

creating the Dust Bowl. The storms destroyed crops, land, and equipment. Thousands of farmers lost their land. Many migrated to the cities of the West Coast in search of work and a new life.

The New Deal failed to end the Great Depression, although it did ease the suffering for many. Still, some critics fiercely condemned FDR's expansion of the role of government. The debate about the size and role of the U.S. federal government continues to this day.

Loss of Faith in Democracy As the Depression dragged on, many people lost faith in the ability of democratic governments to solve the problems of the modern world. Misery and hopelessness created fertile ground for extremists who promised radical solutions. Communists gloated over what they called the failure of capitalism. Right-wing extremists played on themes of intense nationalism, the failure of democracy, the virtues of authoritarian rule, and the need to rearm. By the late 1930s, aggressive rulers once again threatened the peace.

☑ **EXPLAIN** How did the U.S. government react to the Great Depression?

In 1932, Americans elected a new President, **Franklin D. Roosevelt,** or FDR. Roosevelt argued that the government had to take an active role in combating the Great Depression. He introduced the **New Deal,** a massive package of economic and social programs.

Under the New Deal, the federal government took a more active role in managing the economy than ever before. New laws regulated the stock market and protected bank deposits. Government programs created jobs and gave aid to farmers. A new Social Security system provided pensions for the elderly and other benefits.

As the New Deal programs were being put into effect, a natural disaster in 1934 hit several central states. After years of drought and overfarming, huge winds blew across the plains. The winds picked up and carried away the topsoil exposed by erosion,

☑ ASSESSMENT

1. **Identify Central Ideas** What cultural changes did Western society experience after World War I?

2. **Make Generalizations** How did the ideas of Einstein and Curie contribute to a sense of uncertainty?

3. **Synthesize** How did Britain and France emerge from World War I as both victors and losers?

4. **Summarize** What were three causes of the Great Depression?

5. **Connections to Today** How did the Great Depression change government in the United States? Discuss with your classmates the ways in which these changes are still in effect today.

17.6

Mussolini and the National Fascist Party led the March on Rome in October 1922. Fewer than 30,000 men participated in the march, but the king feared a civil war and asked Mussolini to form a cabinet.

Fascism Emerges in Italy

"I hated politics and politicians," said Italo Balbo. Like many Italian veterans of World War I, he had come home to a land of economic chaos and political corruption. Italy's constitutional government, he felt, "had betrayed the hopes of soldiers, reducing Italy to a shameful peace." Disgusted and angry, Balbo rallied behind a fiercely nationalist leader, **Benito Mussolini.** Mussolini's rise to power in the 1920s served as a model for ambitious strongmen elsewhere in Europe.

The Rise of Mussolini

Postwar Discontent When Italy agreed to join the Allies in 1915, France and Britain secretly promised to give Italy certain Austro-Hungarian territories that had large Italian populations. When the Allies won, Italy received some of the promised territories, but others became part of the new Yugoslavia. The broken promises outraged Italian nationalists.

In the postwar years, disorders within Italy multiplied. Inspired in part by the Russian Revolution, peasants seized land, and workers went on strike or seized factories. Their actions frightened landowners and industrialists who had traditionally held power.

Amid the chaos, returning veterans faced unemployment. Trade declined and taxes rose. The government, split into feuding factions, seemed powerless to end the crisis.

Mussolini and the Fascist Party Into this turmoil stepped Benito Mussolini. The son of a socialist blacksmith and a teacher, Mussolini had been a socialist in his youth. During the war, however, he rejected socialism for intense nationalism. In 1919, he

BOUNCE to Activate Flipped Video

Objectives

Describe the rise of Mussolini.

Summarize Mussolini's policies as leader of Italy.

Identify the characteristics of totalitarianism and fascism.

Key Terms

Benito Mussolini
Black Shirt
March on Rome
totalitarian state
fascism

organized veterans and other discontented Italians into the Fascist party. They took the name from the Latin *fasces,* a bundle of sticks wrapped around an ax. In ancient Rome, the fasces symbolized unity and authority.

Mussolini was a fiery and charismatic speaker. He promised to end corruption and replace turmoil with order. He also spoke of reviving Roman greatness, pledging to turn the Mediterranean into a "Roman lake" once again. He held a great deal of power over crowds when he gave his rousing speeches.

> [Only joy at finding such a leader] can explain the enthusiasm [Mussolini] evoked at gathering after gathering, where his mere presence drew the people from all sides to greet him with frenzied acclamations. Even the men who first came out of mere curiosity and with indifference or even hostile feelings gradually felt themselves fired by his personal magnetic influence. . .
>
> —Margherita G. Sarfhatti, *The Life of Benito Mussolini* (tr. Frederic Whyte)

Control by Terror Mussolini organized his supporters into "combat squads." The squads wore black shirts to emulate an earlier nationalist revolt.

>> The fasces, a bundle of sticks wrapped around an ax, was an ancient Roman symbol of unity and authority. Fascists adopted the name and symbol for their party.

These **Black Shirts,** or party militants, rejected the democratic process in favor of violent action. They broke up socialist rallies, smashed leftist presses, and attacked farmers' cooperatives. Fascist gangs used intimidation and terror to oust elected officials in northern Italy. Hundreds were killed as new gangs of Black Shirts sprang up all over Italy. Many Italians accepted these actions because they, too, had lost faith in constitutional government.

In 1922, the Fascists made a bid for power. At a rally in Naples, they announced their intention to go to Rome to demand that the government make changes. In the **March on Rome,** tens of thousands of Fascists swarmed toward the capital. Fearing civil war, King Victor Emmanuel III asked Mussolini to form a government as prime minister. Mussolini entered the city triumphantly on October 30, 1922. Without firing a shot, Mussolini thus obtained a legal appointment from the king to lead Italy.

☑ **DRAW CONCLUSIONS** How did postwar disillusionment contribute to Mussolini's rise?

Mussolini's Totalitarian Rule

At first, Fascists held only a few cabinet posts in the new government. By 1925, though, Mussolini had assumed more power and taken the title Il Duce (eel DOO chay), "The Leader." He suppressed rival parties, muzzled the press, rigged elections, and replaced elected officials with Fascist supporters. In 1929, Mussolini received recognition from Pope Pius XI in return for recognizing Vatican City as an independent state, although the pope continued to disagree with some of Mussolini's goals.

In theory, Italy remained a parliamentary monarchy. In fact, it was a dictatorship upheld by terror. Critics were thrown into prison, forced into exile, or murdered. Secret police and propaganda bolstered the regime.

The State Controls the Economy To spur economic growth and end conflicts between owners and workers, Mussolini brought the economy under state control. However, he preserved capitalism.

Under Mussolini's corporate state, representatives of business, labor, government, and the Fascist party controlled industry, agriculture, and trade. This policy did help business, and production increased. This success came at the expense of workers. They were forbidden to strike, and their wages were kept low.

Loyalty to the State To the Fascists, the individual was unimportant except as a member of the state. Men, women, and children were bombarded with slogans glorifying the state and Mussolini. "Believe! Obey! Fight!" loudspeakers blared and posters proclaimed. Men were urged to be ruthless, selfless warriors fighting for the glory of Italy. Women were pushed out of paying jobs. Instead, Mussolini called on women to "win the battle of motherhood." Those who bore more than 14 children were given a medal by Il Duce himself.

Shaping the young was a major Fascist goal. Fascist youth groups toughened children and taught them to obey strict military discipline. Boys and girls learned about the glories of ancient Rome.

Young Fascists marched in torchlight parades, singing patriotic hymns and chanting, "Mussolini is always right." By the 1930s, a generation of young soldiers stood ready to back Il Duce's drive to expand Italian power.

Building a Totalitarian State Mussolini and the Fascist Party built the first modern **totalitarian state.** In this form of government, a one-party dictatorship regulates every aspect of the lives of its citizens. Fascist Italy served as a model for fascist rule in other European nations. Still, Fascist rule in Italy was never as absolute as those imposed by the communists in the Soviet Union or the Nazis in Germany.

Mussolini's rule was fascist in nature, as was Hitler's. However, totalitarian governments rise under other kinds of ideology as well, such as communism in Stalin's Soviet Union.

All of these totalitarian governments shared common features. They were single-party dictatorships in which the state controlled the economy. The party was led by a dictator, who used police spies and terrorism to control the people and demanded unquestioning obedience. The government controlled the media and enforced strict censorship. It used every means possible to indoctrinate, or mold, its citizens' ideas and thoughts.

☑ **IDENTIFY MAIN IDEAS** How did the Fascist party transform Italy's government and economy?

Characteristics of Fascism

Historians still debate the real nature of Mussolini's fascist ideology. Mussolini coined the term, but fascists had no unifying theory as Marxists did.

>> Mussolini viewed children as the Fascists of the future and took great interest in education and the youth program. Boys were taught to be strong soldiers and girls were taught to be strong, nurturing mothers.

🅑 BOUNCE to Activate Gallery

Today, we generally use the term **fascism** to describe any centralized, authoritarian government that is not communist whose policies glorify the state over the individual and are destructive to basic human rights. In the 1920s and 1930s, though, fascism meant different things in different countries.

Features of Fascism All forms of fascism, however, shared some basic features. They were rooted in extreme nationalism. Fascists glorified action, violence, discipline, and, above all, blind loyalty to the state.

Fascists also pursued aggressive foreign expansion. Echoing the idea of "survival of the fittest," Fascist leaders glorified warfare as a noble struggle for survival. "War alone," declared Mussolini, "brings to its highest tension all human energy and puts the stamp of nobility upon peoples who have the courage to face it."

Fascists were also antidemocratic. They rejected the Enlightenment emphasis on reason and the concepts of equality and liberty. To them, democracy led to corruption and weakness. They claimed democracy put individual or class interests above national goals and destroyed feelings of community.

La DOMENICA DEL CORRIERE

Anno XXXVII - N. 9   3 Marzo 1935 - Anno XIII   Centesimi 30 la copia

Si pubblica a Milano ogni settimana

Supplemento illustrato del "Corriere della Sera"

>> This poster depicts Mussolini working alongside Italian builders. Like much Fascist propaganda, it was designed to convey a sense of purpose and strength.

BOUNCE to Activate Chart

Instead, fascists emphasized emotion and the need for individuals to serve the state.

The Appeal of Fascism Given its restrictions on individual freedom, why did fascism appeal to many Italians? First, it promised a strong, stable government and an end to the political feuding that had paralyzed democracy in Italy. Mussolini projected a sense of power and confidence at a time of disorder and despair. His intense nationalism also revived national pride, which helped further the shift of political thought throughout Italy.

At first, Il Duce received good press outside Italy. Newspapers in Britain, France, and North America applauded the discipline and order of Mussolini's government. "He got the trains running on time," admirers said. Only later, when Mussolini embarked on a course of foreign conquest, did Western democracies protest.

Fascism and Communism Compared Three systems of government competed for influence in postwar Europe. Democracy endured in Britain and France but faced an uphill struggle in hard times. In Italy, fascism offered a different option. As the Great Depression spread, other nations—most notably Germany—looked to fascist leaders. Communism emerged in Russia and won support elsewhere.

Fascists were the sworn enemies of socialists and communists. While communists called for a worldwide revolution of the working class, fascists pursued nationalist goals. Fascists supported a society with defined classes. They found allies among business leaders, wealthy landowners, and the lower middle class. Communists touted a classless society. They won support among both urban and agricultural workers.

Despite basic differences, in practice these two ideologies had much in common. Both flourished during economic hard times by promoting extreme programs of social change. In both communist Russia and fascist Italy, dictators imposed totalitarian governments in order to bring about their revolutions. Both encouraged blind devotion to the state or a charismatic leader. Both used terror to guard their power. In both, a party elite claimed to rule in the name of the national interest.

☑ **COMPARE POINTS OF VIEW** Describe the similarities between fascism and communism.

☑ ASSESSMENT

1. **Identify Cause and Effect** What problems did Italy face after World War I, and how did these problems help Mussolini win power?

2. **Summarize** Describe one of Mussolini's economic or social goals, and explain the actions he took to achieve it.

3. **Compare and Contrast** List two similarities and two differences between fascism and communism.

4. **Explain** Why is control of the media important in a totalitarian state?

5. **Contrast** How did fascist values differ from democratic principles and goals?

6. **Connections to Today** Why is a one-party system a critical part of a totalitarian state? What political parties exist in the U.S. today? What are the advantages and disadvantages of this system?

GO ONLINE to access this biography: Benito Mussolini

17.7

One million Russians attended Lenin's funeral march in Red Square. His death set off a power struggle within the Soviet Union.

The Soviet Union Under Stalin

By 1921, Lenin and the Communists had won the civil war that followed the Russian Revolution. They were then faced with the enormous task of rebuilding Russian society. Millions of Russians had died since the outbreak of World War I, from fighting and from famine, and Russia was in a state of chaos. Lenin's policy of "war communism" outraged the people and brought the Russian economy to the brink of collapse.

Stalin Builds a Command Economy

That year, Lenin introduced his New Economic Policy, which allowed limited capitalism. This brief compromise with capitalism helped the Soviet economy recover and ended the armed resistance to Lenin's government.

Stalin Takes Charge Lenin died in January 1924. Tens of thousands of people lined up in Moscow's historic Red Square to view his body. Lenin's widow, Nadezhda Krupskaya, had wanted to bury him simply next to his mother. But Joseph Stalin wanted to preserve Lenin's body and put it on permanent display. In the end, Lenin's body was displayed in Red Square for more than 65 years. By preserving Lenin's body, Stalin wanted to show that he would carry on the goals of the revolution.

In fact, Stalin moved the Soviet Union in directions Karl Marx had never foreseen. Marx had predicted that under communism the state would eventually wither away. Instead, Stalin turned the Soviet Union into a totalitarian state controlled by a powerful and complex bureaucracy. For almost 30 years, Stalin held more power than any other leader in history.

[BOUNCE to Activate Flipped Video]

Objectives

Explain how Stalin built a command economy in the Soviet Union.

Describe how Stalin used terror to build a totalitarian state.

Analyze Stalin's use of propaganda to control thought and the arts.

Summarize the characteristics of Soviet society under Stalin.

Understand the goals of Soviet foreign policy.

Key Terms

command economy
collective
kulak
Gulag
socialist realism
Osip Mandelstam
Boris Pasternak
russification
atheism
Comintern

Stalin's Five-Year Plans Once in power, Stalin set out to make the Soviet Union a modern industrial power. In the past, said Stalin, Russia had suffered because of its economic backwardness. In 1928, he proposed the first of several "five-year plans" aimed at building heavy industry, improving transportation, and increasing farm output.

To achieve his goals, Stalin brought all economic activity under government control. The government owned all businesses and distributed all resources. The Soviet Union developed a **command economy,** in which government officials made all basic economic decisions. By contrast, in a capitalist system, the free market determines most economic decisions. Privately owned businesses compete to win the consumer's choice. This competition regulates the price and quality of goods.

Stalin's five-year plans set high production goals, especially for heavy industry and transportation. The government pushed workers and managers to meet these goals by giving bonuses to those who succeeded—and by punishing those who did not. Between 1928 and 1939, large factories, hydroelectric power stations, and huge industrial complexes rose across the Soviet Union. Oil, coal, and steel production grew. Mining expanded, and new railroads were built.

Industrial Policy Yields Mixed Results During this time, the West was in the grip of the Great Depression. The Soviet Union had little international trade, so it was insulated from many of the harshest effects of the global economic crisis. Some people in Europe and North American pointed to the industrial growth of the Soviet Union as proof that Stalin's economic policies were successful—ignoring the fact that this success came at a staggering human cost.

Despite impressive progress in some areas, Soviet workers had little to show for their efforts. Some former peasants did become skilled factory workers or managers. Overall, though, the standard of living remained low. Wages were low, workers were forbidden to strike, and consumer goods were scarce. Central planning was often inefficient, causing shortages of some goods and surpluses of others. Many managers, concerned only with meeting production quotas, turned out large quantities of low-quality goods.

During and after the Stalin era, the Soviet Union continued to produce well in heavy industry, such as the manufacture of farm machinery. But its planned economy failed to match the capitalist world in making consumer goods, such as clothing and cars.

Forced Collectivization in Agriculture Causes Misery Stalin also brought agriculture under government control, but at a horrendous cost. The

EFFECTS OF STALIN'S FIVE-YEAR PLANS

UKRAINIAN POPULATION REGISTRATION

(THOUSANDS OF PEOPLE)

DEATHS		BIRTHS
538.1	**1930**	1023
514.7	**1931**	975.3
668.2	**1932**	782
1,850.3	**1933**	471
483.4	**1934**	571.6

Sources: Library of Congress; F. Meslé and J. Vallin, *Mortality and Causes of Death in 20th-Century Ukraine.*

SOVIET INDUSTRY & AGRICULTURE OUTPUT

Output (millions of metric tons)

CORN
WHEAT
STEEL

1928 1929 1930 1931 1932

Source: B.R. Mitchell, European Historical Statistics, 1750–1970

PER CAPITA GDP

☒ SOVIET UNION
■ UNITED STATES

	1928	1929	1930	1931	1932
UNITED STATES	$6,569	$6,899	$6,213	$5,691	$4,908
SOVIET UNION	$1,370	$1,386	$1,448	$1,462	$1,439

Source: The Organisation for Economic Co-operation and Development (OECD). "Historical Statistics of the World Economy: 1–2008 A.D."

>> **Analyze Information** Describe the effect of the Five-Year Plans on steel and corn production.

government wanted farmers to produce more grain to feed workers in the cities. It also hoped to sell grain abroad to earn money.

Under Lenin's New Economic Plan (NEP), peasants had held on to small plots of land. Many had prospered. Stalin saw that system as being inefficient and a threat to state power. Stalin wanted all peasants to farm on either state-owned farms or **collectives,** large farms owned and operated by peasants as a group.

On collectives, the government provided tractors, fertilizers, and better seed, and peasants learned modern farm methods. Peasants were permitted to keep their houses and personal belongings, but all farm animals and implements had to be turned over to the collective. The state set all prices and controlled access to farm supplies.

Many peasants resisted collectivization by killing farm animals, destroying tools, and burning crops. The government responded with brutal force. Stalin targeted **kulaks,** or wealthy farmers.

In 1929, Stalin declared his intention to "liquidate the kulaks as a class." To this end, the government confiscated the kulaks' land and sent them to forced labor camps, where thousands were executed or died from overwork.

Despite the repression, angry peasants continued to resist by growing just enough to feed themselves. In response, the government seized all of their grain for the cities, purposely leaving the peasants to starve. In 1932, this ruthless policy, combined with poor harvests, led to a terrible famine. Later called the Terror Famine, it caused between five and eight million people to die of starvation in the Ukraine alone. Millions more died in other parts of the Soviet Union.

Although collectivization increased Stalin's control of the peasantry, it did not improve farm output. During the 1930s, grain production inched upward, but meat, vegetables, and fruits remained in short supply. Feeding the population would remain a major problem in the Soviet Union.

☑ **EXPLAIN** How did Stalin take control of the Soviet Union's economic life?

Control Through Terror

In addition to tactics like the Terror Famine, Stalin's totalitarian state used secret police, torture, and violent purges to ensure obedience. Stalin tightened his grasp on every aspect of Soviet life, stamping out any signs of dissent even within the Communist elite.

>> This propaganda poster supports one element of Stalin's Five-Year Plan for industry: the creation of an industrial area in Siberia that took advantage of the region's vast coal reserves.

>> The Gulag was the system of Soviet forced-labor camps It housed political prisoners as well as actual criminals and became a symbol of political repression in the Soviet Union.

Terror as a Weapon Stalin ruthlessly used terror as a weapon against his own people. He perpetrated crimes against humanity, carried out politically motivated mass murders, and systematically violated his people's individual rights. Police spies did not hesitate to open private letters or plant listening devices. A vast network of internal spies reported on groups or individuals. Nothing appeared in print without official approval. There was no free press, and no safe method of voicing protest. Grumblers or critics were rounded up and sent to the **Gulag**, a system of brutal labor camps, where many died.

Stalin's Great Purge Even though Stalin's power was absolute, he had obsessive fears that rival party leaders were plotting against him. In 1934, he launched the Great Purge. During this reign of terror, Stalin and his secret police cracked down especially on Old Bolsheviks, or party activists from the early days of the revolution. His net soon widened to target army heroes, industrial managers, writers, and ordinary citizens. They were charged with a wide range of crimes, from counter-revolutionary plots to failure to meet production quotas.

Between 1936 and 1938, Stalin staged a series of spectacular public "show trials" in Moscow. Former

Communist leaders confessed to all kinds of crimes after officials tortured them or threatened their families or friends.

Many of the purged party members were never tried but were sent straight to the Gulag. Secret police files reveal that at least four million people were purged during the Stalin years. Some historians estimate the toll to be much greater.

Impact of the Great Purge The purges increased Stalin's power. The purges destroyed the older generation of revolutionaries, replacing them with younger party members who owed absolute loyalty to Stalin. The program of terror increased Stalin's power by impressing on the Soviet people the dangers of disloyalty.

However, the Soviet Union paid a heavy price. Among the victims of the purges were experts in industry, economics, and engineering, and many of the Soviet Union's most talented writers and thinkers. The purged also included most of the nation's military leaders and about half of its military officers. The loss of so many military leaders would come back to haunt Stalin in 1941, when Germany invaded the Soviet Union.

☑ **IDENTIFY CAUSE AND EFFECT** In what ways did Stalin's terror tactics harm the Soviet Union?

Stalin Builds a Totalitarian State

The use of terror and intimidation was one of the major characteristics of Stalin's totalitarian stage. Like other totalitrarian rulers, Stalin sought to control the hearts and minds of Soviet citizens. He tried to do this by tirelessly distributing propaganda, censoring opposing ideas, imposing Russian culture on minorities, and replacing religion with communist ideology.

Propaganda and the "Cult of Personality"
Stalin tried to boost morale and faith in the communist system by making himself a godlike figure. He used propaganda as a tool to build up a "cult of personality" around himself.

Using modern technology, the party bombarded the public with relentless propaganda. Radios and loudspeakers blared into factories and villages. In movies, theaters, and schools, citizens heard about communist successes and the evils of capitalism.

Billboards and posters urged workers to meet or exceed production quotas. Headlines in the

>> Stalin used propaganda to win the hearts and minds of Soviet citizens. This poster reads, "Thanks to dear Stalin for a happy childhood."

▶ BOUNCE to Activate Gallery

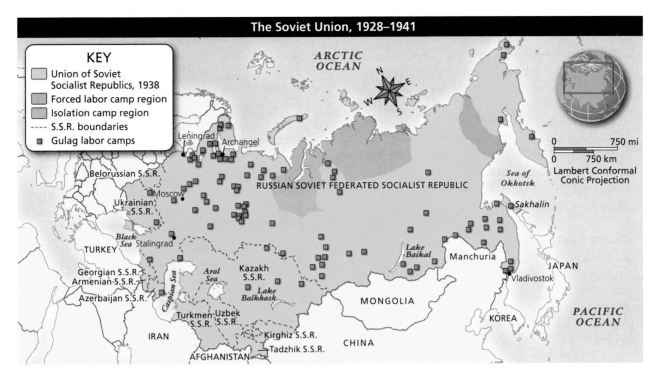

The Soviet Union, 1928–1941

KEY
- ☐ Union of Soviet Socialist Republics, 1938
- ☐ Forced labor camp region
- ☐ Isolation camp region
- ---- S.S.R. boundaries
- ▪ Gulag labor camps

ARCTIC OCEAN

Leningrad
Archangel
Belorussian S.S.R.
RUSSIAN SOVIET FEDERATED SOCIALIST REPUBLIC
Moscow
Ukrainian S.S.R.
Sea of Okhotsk
Sakhalin
Black Sea
Stalingrad
TURKEY
Georgian S.S.R.
Armenian S.S.R.
Azerbaijan S.S.R.
Caspian Sea
Aral Sea
Kazakh S.S.R.
Lake Balkhash
Lake Baikal
Manchuria
JAPAN
Vladivostok
Turkmen S.S.R.
Uzbek S.S.R.
IRAN
Kirghiz S.S.R.
Tadzhik S.S.R.
AFGHANISTAN
MONGOLIA
CHINA
KOREA
PACIFIC OCEAN

0 — 750 mi
0 — 750 km
Lambert Conformal Conic Projection

>> **Analyze Maps** Stalin used terror and labor camps to control the huge, multinational Soviet Union. In which part of the Soviet Union was the heaviest concentration of Gulag labor camps?

Communist party newspaper *Pravda,* or "Truth," linked enemies at home to foreign agents seeking to overthrow the Communist regime.

Censoring the Arts At first, the Bolshevik Revolution had meant greater freedom for Soviet artists and writers. Under Stalin, however, the heavy hand of state control also gripped the arts. The government controlled what books were published, what music was heard, and which works of art were displayed. Stalin required artists and writers to follow a style called **socialist realism.** Its goal was to show Soviet life in a positive light. Artists and writers could criticize the bourgeois past, but their overall message had to promote hope in the socialist future. Popular themes for socialist realist artists were peasants, workers, and heroes of the revolution—and, of course, Stalin.

Artists who ignored socialist realism guidelines could not get materials, work space, or jobs. Writers, artists, and composers also faced government persecution. The Jewish poet **Osip Mandelstam,** for example, was imprisoned, tortured, and exiled for composing a satirical verse about Stalin. Out of fear for his wife's safety, Mandelstam finally submitted to threats and wrote an "Ode to Stalin." **Boris Pasternak,** who would later win fame for his

novel *Doctor Zhivago,* was afraid to publish anything at all during the Stalin years. Rather than write in the favored style of socialist realism, he translated foreign literary works instead.

Despite restrictions, some Soviet writers produced magnificent works whose themes reflected the history and culture of Stalinist Russia. Yevgeny Zamyatin's classic anti-Utopian novel *We* became well known outside of the Soviet Union, but was not published in his home country until 1989. The novel depicts a nightmare future in which people go by numbers, not names, and the "One State" controls people's thoughts.

And Quiet Flows the Don, by Mikhail Sholokhov, passed the censor. The novel tells the story of a man who spends years fighting in World War I, the Russian Revolution, and the civil war. Sholokhov later won the Nobel Prize for literature.

Russification of the Republics Yet another way Stalin controlled the cultural life of the Soviet Union was by promoting a policy of **russification,** or imposing Russian culture on the diverse Soviet empire. During the Soviet era, the U.S.S.R. came to include 15 separate republics. Russia, or the Russian Soviet Federated Socialist Republic, was the largest and dominant republic. The others, such as Uzbek and the Ukraine, had their own languages, historical traditions, and cultures.

At first, Stalin encouraged the autonomy, or independence, of these cultures. However, in the late 1920s, Stalin turned this policy on its head and systematically tried to promote Russian culture. He appointed Russians to high-ranking positions in non-Russian SSRs and required the Russian language to be used in schools and businesses. Many Russian citizens were sent to settle in the other republics, furthering the spread of Russian customs and culture.

Communists Wage War on Religion In accordance with the ideas of Marx, **atheism,** or the belief that there is no god, became the official Soviet state policy. Early on, the Communists targeted the Russian Orthodox Church, which had strongly supported the tsars. The party seized most religious property, converting many churches into offices and museums. Many priests and other religious leaders were killed in the purges or sent to die in prison camps.

Other religions were persecuted as well. At one show trial, 15 Roman Catholic priests were charged with teaching religion to the young, a counter-

revolutionary activity. The state seized Jewish synagogues and banned the use of Hebrew. Islam was also officially discouraged.

The Communists tried to replace religion with their own ideology. Communist ideology had its own "sacred" texts—the writings of Marx and Lenin—and its own shrines, such as the tomb of Lenin. Portraits of Stalin replaced religious icons in Russian homes. However, millions of Soviets continued to worship, in private and sometimes in public, in defiance of government prohibitions.

☑ **IDENTIFY CENTRAL IDEAS** How did Stalin use censorship and propaganda to support his rule?

Soviet Society Under Stalin

The terror and cultural coercion of Stalin's rule made a mockery of the original theories and promises of communism. The lives of most Russians did change. But, while the changes had some benefits, they were often outweighed by continuous shortages and restricted freedoms.

The Soviet Elite Takes Control The Communists destroyed the old social order of landowning nobles at the top and peasants at the bottom. But instead of creating the classless society that Marx had predicted, they created a society where a few elite groups emerged as a new ruling class. At the top of society were members of the Communist party. Only a small fraction of Soviet citizens could join the party. Many who did so were motivated by a desire to get ahead, rather than a belief in communism. The Soviet elite also included industrial managers, military leaders, scientists, and some artists and writers.

The elite enjoyed benefits denied to most people. They lived in the best apartments in the cities and rested at the best vacation homes in the country. They could shop at special stores for scarce consumer goods. On the other hand, Stalin's purges often targeted the elite.

>> To weaken the power of the Russian Orthodox Church, the party seized church property and converted churches into offices and museums. Here, Red Army soldiers carry off religious relics from a church.

▶ BOUNCE to Activate Chart

Limited Benefits Although excluded from party membership, most people did enjoy several new benefits. The party required all children to attend free Communist-built schools. The state supported technical schools and universities as well.

Schools served many important goals. Educated workers were needed to build a modern industrial state. The Communist party also set up programs for students outside school. These programs included sports, cultural activities, and political classes to train teenagers for party membership. However, in addition to important basic skills, schools also taught communist values, such as atheism, the glory of collective farming, and love of Stalin.

The state also provided free medical care, day care for children, inexpensive housing, and public recreation. While these benefits were real, many people still lacked vital necessities. Although the state built massive apartment complexes, housing was scarce. Entire families might be packed into a single room. Bread was plentiful, but meat, fresh fruit, and other foods remained in short supply.

Women Win Greater Equality Long before 1917, women such as Lenin's wife, Nadezhda Krupskaya, worked for the revolution, spreading radical ideas among peasants and workers. In 1905, Alexandra Kollontai noted "how little our party concerned itself with the fate of working class women." After becoming the only high-ranking woman in Lenin's government, she continued her campaign for women's rights.

Under the Communists, women won equality under the law. They gained access to education and a wide range of jobs.

By the 1930s, many Soviet women were working in medicine, engineering, or the sciences. By their labor, women contributed to Soviet economic growth. They worked in factories, in construction, and on collectives. Within the family, their wages were needed because men and women earned the same low salaries.

☑ **GENERATE EXPLANATIONS** How did Communist schools benefit the state and Communist party?

Soviet Foreign Policy

Between 1917 and 1939, the Soviet Union pursued two very different goals in foreign policy. As communists, both Lenin and Stalin wanted to bring about the worldwide revolution that Marx had predicted. But as Soviets, they wanted to guarantee their nation's security by winning the support of other countries. The result was a contradictory and generally unsuccessful foreign policy.

Promoting Communist Revolution In 1919, Lenin formed the Communist International, or **Comintern.** Its purpose was to encourage worldwide revolution. To this end, it aided revolutionary groups around the

>> Soviet ideology stressed gender equality in labor and education. Many Soviet women held jobs and earned advanced degrees.

world and urged colonial peoples to rise up against imperialist powers.

The Comintern's support of revolutionary groups outside the Soviet Union and its loud propaganda against capitalism made Western powers suspicious of the Soviet Union.

In the United States, fear of Bolshevik plots led to the "Red Scare" in the early 1920s. Britain temporarily broke off relations with the Soviet Union when evidence revealed Soviet schemes to turn the 1926 general strike into a revolution.

Seeking Recognition Even while the Comintern supported the global communist struggle, the Soviet Union sought international recognition and trade with capitalist countries, especially the United States and Britain. In 1933, the United States and Soviet Union finally set up diplomatic relations, and the following year, the Soviets joined the League of Nations. However, mistrust still poisoned relations, especially after the Great Purge.

In the early years of Stalin's rule, the Soviet Union remained, for the most part, isolated from the West. By the late 1930s, however, Stalin feared a growing threat from Nazi Germany. In April 1939, he suggested that Russia, France, and Britain form an alliance against Germany. Western suspicions of Soviet intentions made an agreement impossible. Within months, Stalin made an about-face and signed an alliance with Nazi Germany.

☑ **ANALYZE INFORMATION** How did the Soviet Union's foreign policy goals contradict one another?

☑ **ASSESSMENT**

1. **Identify Cause and Effect** What were the goals and results of Stalin's five-year plans?

2. **Contrast** For those not in the elite party, how did life change under Soviet rule?

3. **Summarize** What methods did Stalin use to create a totalitarian state?

4. **Quest Connections** What foreign policy goals did both Lenin and Stalin pursue?

GO ONLINE to access this biography: Joseph Stalin

17.8

The Nazi Party was active between 1920 and 1945. Hitler served as the party's leader starting in 1921. Initially, the Nazis focused on anti-big business and anti-capitalist rhetoric.

The Rise of Nazi Germany

As World War I drew to a close, Germany tottered on the brink of chaos. Under the threat of a socialist revolution, Kaiser William II abdicated. Moderate leaders signed the armistice and later, under protest, the Treaty of Versailles.

The Weimar Republic

In 1919, German leaders drafted a constitution in the city of Weimar (VY mahr). It created a democratic government known as the Weimar Republic. The constitution set up a parliamentary system led by a **chancellor,** or prime minister. It gave women the right to vote and included a bill of rights. However, the Weimar Republic faced numerous problems, including political extremists, extreme inflation, and the Great Depression, all of which led to the Republic's eventual fall.

Political Turmoil The republic faced severe problems from the start. Politically, it was weak because Germany, like France, had many small parties. The chancellor had to form coalitions that easily fell apart.

The government, led by moderates, came under constant fire from both the left and right. Communists demanded radical changes like those Lenin had brought to Russia. Conservatives—including the old Junker nobility, military officers, and wealthy bourgeoisie—attacked the government as too liberal and weak. They longed for another strong leader like Bismarck.

BOUNCE to Activate Flipped Video

Objectives

Summarize the political and economic problems faced by the Weimar Republic.

Analyze Hitler's rise to power.

Describe the political, social, economic, and cultural policies of Nazi Germany.

Explain why Eastern Europe turned to authoritarian rule.

Key Terms

chancellor
Ruhr Valley
hyperinflation
Adolf Hitler
Third Reich
Gestapo
Nuremberg Laws

GO ONLINE to access your digital course

Germans of all classes blamed the Weimar Republic for the hated Versailles treaty, with its war guilt clause and heavy reparations. Bitter, they looked for scapegoats. Many scapegoated Marxists or German Jews for Germany's economic and political problems.

Economic Hardship Economic disaster fed unrest. In 1923, when Germany fell behind in reparations payments, France occupied the coal-rich **Ruhr Valley,** (roor) taking over its iron, coal, and steel industries. German workers in the Ruhr protested using passive resistance and refused to work. To pay the workers, the German government printed huge quantities of paper money.

Inflation soon spiraled out of control, spreading misery and despair. The German mark became almost worthless. An item that cost 100 marks in July 1922 might have cost 944,000 marks by August 1923. Such an extremely rapid and sharp increase in prices is known as **hyperinflation.** Salaries rose by billions of marks, but they still could not keep up with skyrocketing prices. Many middle-class families saw their savings wiped out.

Recovery and Depression With help from the Western powers, the government did bring inflation under control. In 1924, the United States gained British and French approval for a plan to reduce German reparations payments. Under the Dawes

Plan, France withdrew its forces from the Ruhr, and American loans helped the German economy recover.

Germany began to prosper. Then the Great Depression hit, reviving memories of the miseries of 1923. Germans turned to an energetic leader, Adolf Hitler, who promised to solve the economic crisis and restore Germany's former greatness.

Culture in the Weimar Republic Despite political and economic turmoil, culture flourished in the Weimar Republic. The tumultuous times helped to stimulate new cultural movements, such as dadaist art and Bauhaus architecture. Berlin attracted writers and artists from around the world, just as Paris did. The German playwright Bertolt Brecht sharply criticized middle-class values with *The Three-Penny Opera*. The artist George Grosz, through scathing drawings and paintings, blasted the failings of the Weimar Republic.

Most of the art and music produced during the Weimar Republic reflected the culture of that time. However, many believed that this modern culture and the Weimar Republic itself were not in keeping with Germany's illustrious past. They condemned the new culture as immoral and rejected American influences, such as jazz.

☑ **SUPPORT IDEAS WITH EXAMPLES** Describe the problems of the Weimar Republic.

Hitler Leads the Nazi Party

The Great Depression sent the German economy into a downward spiral. As discontent rose, Germans began to listen to the ideas of **Adolf Hitler**, who had operated on the fringe of German politics for a decade.

Early Years Hitler was born in Austria in 1889. When he was 18, he went to Vienna, then the capital of the multinational Hapsburg empire. German Austrians made up just one of many ethnic groups in Vienna. Yet they felt superior to Jews, Serbs, Poles, and other groups. While living in Vienna, Hitler developed the fanatical anti-Semitism, or prejudice against Jewish people, that would later play a major role in his rise to power.

Hitler went to Germany and fought in the German army during World War I. In 1919, he joined a small group of right-wing extremists. Like many ex-soldiers, he despised the Weimar government, which he saw as weak. Within a year, he was the

COME ALONG, GENTS, DINNER'S READY.

>> **Analyze Political Cartoons** The terms of the Treaty of Versailles resulted in Germany losing large amounts of territory as well as its overseas colonies. What do you think the turkey in this cartoon represents?

▶ BOUNCE to Activate Timeline

unquestioned leader of the National Socialist German Workers, or Nazi, party. Like Mussolini, Hitler organized his supporters into fighting squads. Nazi "storm troopers" fought in the streets against their political enemies.

Hitler's Ideological Manifesto In November 1923, Hitler tried to follow Mussolini's example by staging a small-scale coup known as the Beer Hall Putsch in Munich. The coup failed, and Hitler was soon behind bars. While in prison, Hitler wrote *Mein Kampf ("My Struggle")*. It would later become the basic book of Nazi goals and ideology.

Mein Kampf reflected Hitler's obsessions—extreme nationalism, racism, and anti-Semitism. Germans, he said, belonged to a superior "master race" of Aryans, or light-skinned Europeans, whose greatest enemies were the Jews.

Hitler's ideas were rooted in a long tradition of European anti-Semitism, dating back to the persecutions of the Middle Ages. The rise of nationalism in the 1800s caused people to identify Jews as ethnic outsiders. Hitler viewed Jews not as members of a religion but as a separate race. (He defined a Jew as anyone with one Jewish grandparent.) Echoing a familiar right-wing theme, he blamed Germany's defeat in World War I on a conspiracy of Marxists, Jews, corrupt politicians, and business leaders.

In his recipe for revival, Hitler urged Germans everywhere to unite into one great nation. Germany must expand, he said, to gain *Lebensraum* (LAY buns rowm), or living space, for its people. Slavs and other inferior races must bow to Aryan needs. To achieve its greatness, Germany needed a strong leader, or Führer (FYOO rur). Hitler was determined to become that leader.

Hitler Comes to Power After less than a year, Hitler was released from prison. He soon renewed his table-thumping speeches. The Great Depression played into Hitler's hands. As unemployment rose, Nazi membership grew to almost a million. Hitler's program appealed to veterans, workers, the lower middle classes, small-town Germans, and business people alike. He promised to end reparations, create jobs, and defy the Versailles treaty by rearming Germany.

With the government paralyzed by divisions, both Nazis and Communists won more seats in the Reichstag, or lower house of the legislature. Fearing the growth of communist political power, conservative politicians turned to Hitler. Although they despised him, they believed they could control

>> A Nazi propaganda poster from 1934 urges the German people to support their country by purchasing German produce.

him. Thus, with conservative support, Hitler was appointed chancellor in 1933 through legal means under the Weimar constitution.

Within a year, Hitler was dictator of Germany. He and his supporters suspended civil rights, destroyed the Communists, and disbanded other political parties. Germany became a one-party, totalitarian state. Like Stalin in Russia, Hitler purged his own party, brutally executing Nazis he felt were disloyal. Nazis learned that Hitler demanded unquestioning obedience.

Hitler's rise to power raises disturbing questions that we still debate today. Why did Germany turn from democracy to totalitarianism? How could a ruthless, hate-filled dictator gain the enthusiastic support of many Germans?

☑ **CHECK UNDERSTANDING** Describe the ideology of Hitler and the Nazi Party.

The Third Reich

Once in power, Hitler and the Nazis moved to build a new Germany. Like Mussolini, Hitler appealed to nationalism by recalling past glories. Germany's First Reich, or empire, was the medieval Holy Roman Empire, which had lasted more than 800 years. The Second Reich was the empire forged by Bismarck in 1871. Under Hitler's new **Third Reich,** he boasted, the German master race would dominate Europe for a thousand years. His aggressive goals would eventually lead Germany—and the world—into another war.

To combat the Great Depression, Hitler launched large public works programs (as did Britain and the United States). Tens of thousands of people were put to work building highways and housing or replanting forests. Hitler also repudiated, or rejected, the Versailles treaty. He launched a crash program to rearm Germany and schemed to unite Germany and Austria.

Like Mussolini, Hitler preserved capitalism but brought big business and labor under government control. Few objected to this loss of freedom because their standard of living rose. Nazi propaganda highlighted the improvements.

>> The Gestapo was the official secret police agency of Nazi Germany. It was formed in 1933 and was under the administration of Heinrich Himmler by April 1934.

A Totalitarian State Emerges To achieve his goals, Hitler organized an efficient but brutal system of terror, repression, and totalitarian rule. Nazis controlled all areas of German life—from government to religion to education. Elite, black-uniformed troops, called the SS, enforced the Führer's will. His secret police, the **Gestapo** (guh STAH poh), rooted out opposition.

At first, many Germans welcomed Hitler, who took forceful action to ease the effects of the Great Depression and promised to revive German greatness. Any people who criticized Hitler became victims of terror or were cowed into silence in fear for their own safety.

Anti-Semitism Campaign Begins In his fanatical anti-Semitism, Hitler set out to drive Jews from Germany. In 1935, the Nazis passed the **Nuremberg Laws,** which deprived Jews of German citizenship and placed severe restrictions on them. They were prohibited from marrying non-Jews, attending or teaching at German schools or universities, holding government jobs, practicing law or medicine, or publishing books. Nazis beat and robbed Jews and roused mobs to do the same. Many German Jews fled, seeking refuge in other countries, but these countries often closed their doors and limited Jewish immigration.

On November 7, 1938, a young German Jew whose parents had been deported to their native Poland shot and wounded a German diplomat in Paris. Hitler used the incident as an excuse to stage an attack on all Jews. The incident became known as *Kristallnacht* (krih STAHL nahkt), or the "Night of Broken Glass." On the night of November 9 and into the following day, Nazi mobs in Germany, Austria, and Czechoslovakia smashed the windows of Jewish homes and businesses. The experience was terrifying for Jews.

> They broke our windowpanes, and the house became very cold.". . . We were standing there, outside in the cold, still in our night clothes, with only a coat thrown over. . .Then they made everyone lie face down on the ground. . .'Now, they will shoot us,' we thought. We were very afraid."
>
> —Sophie Nussbaum, quoted in *48 Hours of Kristallnacht*

Over 1,000 synagogues were burned and more than 7,000 Jewish businesses destroyed. Many Jewish schools, hospitals and homes were damaged, and many Jews were injured and killed. The Nazis arrested 30,000 Jews and forced them into concentration camps.

Kristallnacht reflected so badly on Germany that it was not repeated. Yet Hitler made the Jewish victims of the attacks pay for the damage. Before long, Hitler and his henchmen were making even more sinister plans for what they called the "Final Solution"—the extermination of all Jews.

Nazi Social Policies Like Italian Fascists and Soviet Communists, the Nazis indoctrinated young people with their ideology. In passionate speeches, the Führer spewed his message of racism.

He urged young Germans to destroy their so-called enemies without mercy. On hikes and in camps, the "Hitler Youth" pledged absolute loyalty to Germany and undertook physical fitness programs to prepare for war. School courses and textbooks were rewritten to reflect Nazi racial views.

Like Mussolini's Fascists, Nazis sought to limit women's roles. Women were dismissed from upper-level jobs and turned away from universities. To raise the birthrate, Nazis offered "pure-blooded Aryan" women rewards for having more children.

Still, Hitler's goal to keep women in the home and out of the workforce applied mainly to the privileged. As German industry expanded, women factory workers were needed.

Purifying German Culture The Nazis used education and the arts as propaganda tools to purge, or purify, German culture. At huge public bonfires, Nazis burned books of which they disapproved. They denounced modern art, saying that it was corrupted by Jewish influences. They condemned jazz because of its African roots. Instead, the Nazis glorified old German myths such as those re-created in the operas of Richard Wagner (VAHG nur).

Hitler despised Christianity as "weak" and "flabby." He sought to replace religion with his racial creed. To control the churches, the Nazis combined all Protestant sects into a single state church. They closed Catholic schools and muzzled the Catholic clergy. Although many clergy either supported the new regime or remained silent, some courageously spoke out against Hitler.

☑ **DESCRIBE** How did the Nazi Party maintain its control of Germany?

Authoritarian Rule in Eastern Europe

Like Germany, most new nations in Eastern Europe slid from democratic to authoritarian rule in the postwar era. In 1919, a dozen countries were carved

>> The Hitler Youth program emphasized activism, physical training, and Nazi ideology, as well as absolute obedience to Hitler and the Nazi Party.

🅑 BOUNCE to Activate Gallery

out of the old Russian, Austro-Hungarian, Ottoman, and German empires. Although they differed from one another in important ways, they faced some common problems. They were small countries whose rural agricultural economies lacked capital to develop industry. Social and economic inequalities separated poor peasants from wealthy landlords. None had much experience with the democratic process.

Further complicating the situation, rivalries left over from World War I hindered economic cooperation between countries. Each country in the region tried to be independent of its neighbors, which hurt all of them. The region was hit hard by the Great Depression.

Ethnic Rivalries Old rivalries between ethnic and religious groups created severe tensions. In Czechoslovakia, Czechs and Slovaks were unwilling partners. More than three million Germans lived in northern Czechoslovakia, and some of them wanted to join Hitler's Nazi Germany.

Serbs dominated the new state of Yugoslavia, but restless Slovenes and Croats living there pressed for independence. In Poland, Hungary, and Romania, conflict flared among various ethnic minorities.

Dictators Replace Democracy Economic problems and ethnic tensions contributed to instability, which in turn helped fascist rulers gain power. In Hungary, military strongman Nicholas Horthy (HAWR tay) overthrew a Communist-led government in 1919. By 1926, the military hero Joseph Pilsudski (peel SOOT skee) had taken control of Poland. Eventually, right-wing dictators emerged in every Eastern European country except Czechoslovakia and Finland.

Like Hitler, these dictators promised order and won the support of the military and wealthy. They also turned to anti-Semitism, using Jewish people as scapegoats for many national problems. Meanwhile, strong, aggressive neighbors eyed these small, weak states of Eastern Europe as tempting targets. Before long, Eastern Europe would fall into the orbit of Hitler's Germany and then of Stalin's Soviet Union.

☑ **IDENTIFY CENTRAL ISSUES** How did World War I impact the growth of authoritarian states in Eastern Europe?

☑ ASSESSMENT

1. **Describe** Describe the weaknesses of the Weimar Republic.

2. **Support Ideas with Examples** How was Hitler able to shift political thought in Germany in order to establish and maintain a totalitarian state?

3. **Identify Cause and Effect** Describe the effects of Eastern Europe's economic problems and ethnic and religious tensions.

4. **Describe** Describe Hitler's fanatical anti-Semitism and how he tried to drive Jewish people from Germany.

5. **Summarize** Why did the Nazi Party glorify old German myths and denounce modern art?

6. **Connections to Today** Discuss the role of propaganda in shaping a totalitarian state. Is propaganda used today? Explain.

Connections to Today

President Rodrigo Duterte of the Philippines met with President Xi Jinping of China in Beijing for talks in August 2019.

Take Action to Learn About Authoritarian Leaders

What political changes occurred that led to the rise of authoritarian states in Turkey, the Philippines, and China?

1. **Choose** one of the following regimes to research:

   - **Turkey:** How did Turkey move from the promise of democracy to a one-party autocracy?

   - **Philippines:** What was the government like before 2016? How did Duterte's election change the regime?

   - **China:** Why is Xi Jinping committed to maintaining a one-party system?

2. **Ask Questions** Generate a list of questions you have about the topic.

3. **Learn** about the topic and the major issues related to the topic. Were there common factors that allowed for the rise of autocratic governments? Take notes as you conduct your research and continue to generate questions as you learn more.

4. **Raise Awareness** Have small groups of students choose one of the regimes. Each group will then present a report to the class.

Topic 17 Quick Study Guide

LESSON SUMMARIES

Use these Lesson Summaries, and the longer versions available online, to review the key ideas for each lesson in this Topic.

Lesson 1: Revolution and Nationalism in Latin America

Revolution swept through Mexico between 1910 and 1920. As the revolution spread, Indian peasants battled to end centuries of oppression and to win land. It was a long and difficult struggle.

Lesson 2: Nationalist Movements in Africa and the Middle East

After World War I, nationalist sentiment contributed to many changes in Africa and the Middle East.

Lesson 3: India Seeks Self Rule

During WWI, as thousands of Indian troops died on distant battlefields, Indian nationalists grew angry that they had no freedom at home. In the 1920s a leader emerged—Mohandas Gandhi. In his struggle against injustice, he adopted the weapon of nonviolent resistance. Eventually, his ideas would inspire many others.

Lesson 4: New Forces in China and Japan

Civil war and foreign invasions plagued the new Chinese republic. Japan, in the 1930s, had a military dominated government that emphasized service to the nation and a policy of imperialistic expansion.

Lesson 5: The West After World War I

In 1919, three western democracies – Great Britain, France, and the United States—appeared powerful. They had ruled the Paris Peace Conference and boosted hopes for democracy among the new nations of Eastern Europe. But postwar all faced difficult political and economic crises. The Great Depression of the 1930s marked a period of global economic collapse.

Lesson 6: Fascism Emerges in Italy

In 1919, Italian nationalists were outraged by the Paris peace treaties. Disorder grew in the country with economic and political upsets. Mussolini rose in the midst of this turmoil. Supporters rallied to his claims to end corruption and restore Italy to its former glory. But his government would become a dictatorship upheld by terror—critics were harshly suppressed.

Lesson 7: The Soviet Union Under Stalin

Stalin turned the Soviet Union into a totalitarian state that regulated every aspect of the lives of its citizens.

Lesson 8: The Rise of Nazi Germany

In 1919, the German republic was entangled in economic and political difficulties. These hardships helped Adolf Hitler rise to power. But under Hitler, the Nazi government would use terror, repression, and one-party rule to establish a totalitarian state.

QUEST! FINDINGS

Prepare for a Discussion Refer to your responses in the Quest Connections to help you prepare arguments for a discussion about Lenin and Stalin to present to the class. Use the rubric and other Quest sources online to guide your work.

GO ONLINE to access lesson summaries

VISUAL REVIEW

Use these graphics to review some of the key terms, people, and ideas from this Topic.

Nationalism Around the World 1910–1939

LOCATION	GOALS	EXPRESSION
Mexico	To reject foreign influence	Nationalizing foreign companies; emphasizing Latin American culture
Africa	To fight for rights under colonial system	Organizing resistance, including protests, boycotts, strikes; founding of associations and political parties
Turkey and Persia	To strengthen countries by modernizing and westernizing	Secularizing daily life; adopting Western ways; building industry
The Middle East	To create a Pan-Arab state	Resisting mandate system; ongoing friction between Jewish and Arab nationalists in the Palestine Mandate
India	To gain independence from British	Protesting British rule using nonviolent methods, under Gandhi's leadership
China	To lessen foreign domination of China	Resisting Japanese encroachment; attempting to strengthen China
Japan	To build an empire	Issuing the Twenty-One demands; invading China multiple times

Effects of World War I on World Events

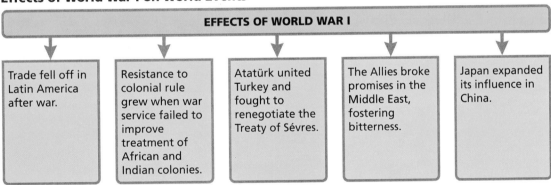

EFFECTS OF WORLD WAR I

Trade fell off in Latin America after war.

Resistance to colonial rule grew when war service failed to improve treatment of African and Indian colonies.

Atatürk united Turkey and fought to renegotiate the Treaty of Sévres.

The Allies broke promises in the Middle East, fostering bitterness.

Japan expanded its influence in China.

Three Totalitarian States: Italy, the Soviet Union, and Germany

COUNTRY	DICTATOR IN POWER	IDEOLOGY	EXAMPLE OF TERROR TACTICS
Italy	Benito Mussolini in power in 1922	Fascist; Fanatic nationalism	Black Shirts suppressed dissent.
Soviet Union	Joseph Stalin in power 1924	Communist	Stalin sends millions to Gulag labor camps.
Germany	Adolf Hitler in power in 1933	Fascist; Racial policies of hatred, aimed particularly at Jews	Nazis began to restrict and terrorize German Jews.

KEY TERMS, PEOPLE, AND IDEAS

1. Why What prompted the push **for economic nationalism** in Latin America after WWI?

2. What postwar issues did most European nations face after WWI?

3. What philosophy did **Gandhi** follow? How did he use this philosophy in his move for an independent India?

4. Once in power, how did Stalin attempt to improve the economy of Russia? What were the results?

5. How did geography determine Japan's goal toward expanding its empire?

6. What change in social attitude did the **flapper** represent in 1920s America?

7. How did postwar disillusionment pave the way for the rise of totalitarian governments?

8. How did **overproduction** become one cause of the **Great Depression**?

9. Why did Hitler pass the **Nuremberg Laws**?

CRITICAL THINKING

10. **Drawing Conclusions** Why did the Palestine Mandate become a center of conflict after World War I?

11. **Synthesize Information** Two literary movements arose in the United States during the 1920s—works by writers who were part of the Lost Generation and works by writers who represented the Harlem Renaissance. What factors after the war shaped these movements?

12. **Explain** What similarities exist in the governing of totalitarian regimes?

13. **Draw Conclusions** How might have the Pan African Congress contributed to the African nationalist movement?

14. **Analyze Information** How did Britain, France, and the United States respond to the Great Depression?

15. **Evaluate Information** How did the Treaty of Versailles lay the seeds for the rise of Hitler in Germany?

16. **Analyze Images** Look at the image below. It is a poster supporting Stalin's Five Year economic plan. What conclusions can you draw about how propaganda is used in this poster?

17. **Writing Activity: Write an Informative Essay** The following excerpt is from the Manifesto of the Second Pan-African Congress. The members wrote it to detail their beliefs. (a) What does it say about the spread of democracy? (b) How would it encourage African pride and nationalism? Use your knowledge of the topic and information in the excerpt to write a short essay.

> The absolute equality of races—physical, political, and social—is the founding stone of world peace and human advancement . . .
>
> That is the vast range of time, one group should in its industrial technique, or social organization, or spiritual vision, lag a few hundred years behind another, or forge fitfully ahead, . . . is proof of the essential richness and variety of human nature . . . The doctrine of racial equality does not interfere with individual liberty, rather it fulfills it . . .
>
> The habit of democracy must be made to encircle the earth. Despite the attempt to prove that its practice is the secret and divine gift of the few, no habit is more natural or more widely spread . . .
> —*Manifesto of the Second Pan-African Congress*

18. **Connections to Today** After World War I, authoritarian and totalitarian states rose in Japan, Italy, Germany, and Russia. During the decade between 2000 and 2010, several democratic regimes collapsed. They were replaced with modern authoritarian governments. Have the causes for the rise of authoritarian regimes changed? Explain.

DOCUMENT-BASED QUESTIONS

In 1930, Mohandas Gandhi organized the Salt March to protest the British salt monopoly. Read the documents below, then answer the questions that follow.

DOCUMENT A

"Wherever possible, civil disobedience of the salt laws should be started. These laws can be violated in three ways. It is an offense to manufacture salt wherever there are facilities for doing so. The possession and sale of contraband salt, which includes natural salt or salt earth, [is] also an offense. The purchasers of such salt will be equally guilty. To carry away the natural salt deposits on the seashore is likewise violation of the law. So is the hawking of such salt. In short, you may choose any one or all of these devices to break the salt monopoly."

—*Gandhi on the Salt March*

DOCUMENT B

"The Salt Satyagraha started with a dramatic long march by Gandhi and a group of picked companions from Sabarmati to the coast at Dandi, 240 miles away, where he proceeded to make salt illegally by boiling sea water. The march was a publicity enterprise of great power as the press followed the party's progress . . . As he journeyed . . ., deliberately challenging established authority, village headmen began to resign in large numbers . . . in April, [India's Viceroy, Lord] Irwin reported to London that in Gujarat 'the personal influence of Gandhi threatens to create a position of real embarrassment to the administration . . . as in some areas he has already achieved a considerable measure of success in undermining the authority of Government.'"

—*Modern India: The Origins of Asian Democracy by Judith M. Brown*

DOCUMENT C

"Suddenly, at a word of command, scores of native policemen rushed upon the advancing marchers and rained blows on their heads with their steel-shod lathis. Not one of the marchers even raised an arm to fend off the blows. They went down like tenpins. . . . The survivors, without breaking ranks, silently and doggedly marched on until struck down."

—*Webb Miller, a British journalist reporting on a march to the salt deposits at Dharsana*

DOCUMENT D

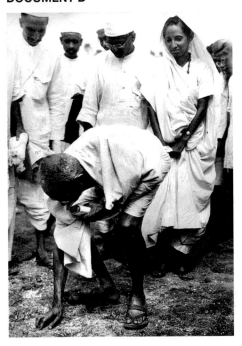

Gandhi picking up salt at the coastal village of Dandi in India, April 6, 1930

19. In Document A, Gandhi was mainly addressing
   A. British authorities.
   B. journalists around the world.
   C. the British people.
   D. the Indian people.

20. In Document B, the historian describes the effect of the Salt March on
   A. the supply of salt.
   B. the authority of the British government.
   C. protesters in other countries.
   D. Gandhi's health.

21. Which words from Document C reflect the attitude of the reporter toward the marchers?
   A. suddenly, command
   B. steel-shod, lathis, ten-pins
   C. fend, blows
   D. silently, doggedly

22. **Writing Tasks** How was the Salt March a turning point in India's struggle for independence? Use what you have learned from these documents and the topic in your response.

World War II
(1930–1945)

ESSENTIAL QUESTION When is war justified?

GO ONLINE to access the eText, videos, Interactive Primary Sources, Biographies, and other online resources.

Allied troops landing at the beach at Normandy, France

PA 3-27

Connections to Today

Have you ever visited a memorial to the victims of the September 11, 2001, terrorist attacks on the United States? Or seen a Memorial Day parade, honoring members of the armed forces who gave their lives? These are ways we remember the heroism or suffering of people in our past.

Since World War II, people in many nations and states have taken special measures to remember victims of Nazi genocide, in particular the six million European Jews murdered in the Holocaust. What can the Holocaust teach us about the dangers of prejudice and hate?

NBC LEARN

Witness an interview with a survivor of the bombing of Britain.

 BOUNCE to Activate My Story Video

869

Topic 18 Overview

In this Topic, you will learn about the events of World War II. Look at the lesson outline and explore the timeline. As you study this Topic, you will complete the Quest Inquiry.

LESSON OUTLINE

18.1 Aggression, Appeasement, and War

18.2 Axis Powers Advance

18.3 The Holocaust

18.4 The Allies Turn the Tide

18.5 Victory for the Allies

Key Events of World War II

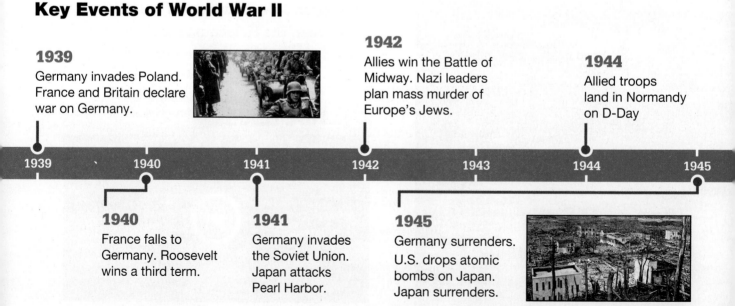

1939
Germany invades Poland. France and Britain declare war on Germany.

1942
Allies win the Battle of Midway. Nazi leaders plan mass murder of Europe's Jews.

1944
Allied troops land in Normandy on D-Day

1939 1940 1941 1942 1943 1944 1945

1940
France falls to Germany. Roosevelt wins a third term.

1941
Germany invades the Soviet Union. Japan attacks Pearl Harbor.

1945
Germany surrenders. U.S. drops atomic bombs on Japan. Japan surrenders.

ⓆUEST! INQUIRY

Create a World War II Tribute

The arrival of war always changes the usual pace of life. Much is sacrificed and rearranged for the national good. In this Quest, you will explore life during World War II and commemorate a special tribute to a person or an event.

STEP ❶
Decide what is needed in a good tribute. Choose the kind of tribute you will create. Brainstorm ideas.

STEP ❷
Choose an event, person, or experience to honor. Outline a draft of the presentation. Consider researching multimedia elements, books, or picture collections.

STEP ❸
Complete the first generation of your tribute. Review, edit, and revise.

STEP ❹
Share your presentation with classmates, family, and community. Reflect on what you learned about World War II. When is war justified? Discuss current issues and wars facing the United States.

GO ONLINE to access complete Quest materials

18.1

Germany rebuilt its military during the 1930s in defiance of the Treaty of Versailles. Here, troops stand at attention during a Nazi rally in Nuremberg, Germany.

BOUNCE to Activate Flipped Video

Objectives

Describe how the Western democracies responded to aggression.

Explain the significance of the Spanish Civil War.

Understand how German aggression led Europe into World War II.

Key Terms

appeasement
pacifism
Neutrality Acts
Axis powers
Francisco Franco
Anschluss
Sudetenland
Winston Churchill
Nazi-Soviet Pact

Aggression, Appeasement, and War

Throughout the 1930s, the rulers of Germany, Italy, and Japan were preparing to build new empires. After the horrors of World War I, the leaders of Britain, France, and the United States tried to avoid conflict through diplomacy. During the 1930s, the two sides tested each other's commitment and will.

A Pattern of Aggression

Challenges to peace followed a pattern. Dictators took aggressive action but met only verbal protests and pleas for peace from the democracies. Mussolini, Hitler, and Japanese militarists viewed that desire for peace as weakness and responded with new acts of aggression. With hindsight, we can see the shortcomings of the policies followed by the democracies. These policies, however, were the product of long and careful deliberation. At the time, many people believed they would prevent war.

Japanese Imperialism Grows One of the earliest tests had been posed by Japan. Japanese military leaders and ultranationalists thought that Japan should have an empire equal to those of the Western powers. In pursuit of this goal, Japan seized the Chinese province of Manchuria in 1931. When the League of Nations condemned the aggression, Japan simply withdrew from the organization.

Japan's easy success strengthened the militarist faction in Japan. In 1937, Japanese armies overran much of eastern China,

GO ONLINE to access your digital course

starting the Second Sino-Japanese War. Once again, Western protests did not stop Japan's acts of imperialism.

Italy Invades Ethiopia In Italy, Mussolini decided to act on his own imperialist ambitions. Italy's defeat by the Ethiopians at the battle of Adowa in 1896 still rankled after almost 40 years. In 1935, Italy invaded Ethiopia, located in northeastern Africa. Although the Ethiopians resisted bravely, their outdated weapons were no match for Mussolini's tanks, machine guns, poison gas, and airplanes.

The Ethiopian king Haile Selassie (HY lee suh LAH see) appealed to the League of Nations for help. The League voted sanctions against Italy for violating international law. League members agreed to stop selling weapons or other war materials to Italy. But the sanctions did not extend to petroleum, which fueled modern warfare. In addition, the League had no power to enforce the sanctions. By early 1936, Italy had conquered Ethiopia.

Hitler Violates the Treaty of Versailles Hitler had also tested the will of the Western democracies, as well as of the League of Nations, and found it weak. First, he built up the German military in defiance of the Treaty of Versailles. Then, in 1936, he sent troops into the "demilitarized" Rhineland bordering France—another treaty violation. Germans hated the Versailles treaty, and Hitler's successful challenge made him more popular at home.

The Western democracies denounced his moves but took no real action. Instead, they adopted a policy of **appeasement,** or giving in to the demands of an aggressor in order to keep the peace.

Reasons for Appeasement The Western policy of appeasement developed for a number of reasons. France was demoralized, suffering from political divisions at home. It could not take on Hitler without British support. The British, however, had no desire to confront the German dictator. Some even thought that Hitler's actions constituted a justifiable response to the terms of the Treaty of Versailles, which they believed had been too harsh on Germany.

In both Britain and France, many saw Hitler and fascism as a defense against a worse evil— the spread of Soviet communism. Additionally, the Great Depression sapped the energies of the Western democracies. Finally, widespread **pacifism,** or opposition to all war, and disgust with the destruction from the previous war pushed many governments to seek peace at any price.

STEPPING STONES TO GLORY.

>> **Analyze Political Cartoons** British cartoonist David Low was known for speaking out against the policy of appeasement. How does this cartoon reflect his message?

🅑 BOUNCE to Activate Cartoon

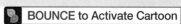

>> Here, Japanese cavalry have successfully occupied the northern section of Manchuria. The freezing weather did not stop Japanese imperialism.

The United States Remains Neutral As war clouds gathered in Europe in the mid-1930s, the United States Congress passed a series of **Neutrality Acts.** One law forbade the sale of arms to any nation at war. Others outlawed loans to warring nations and prohibited Americans from traveling on ships of warring powers. The fundamental goal of American policy, however, was to avoid involvement in a European war, not to prevent such a conflict.

Formation of the Axis Powers Germany, Italy, and Japan were encouraged by the apparent weakness of the western democracies. The three aggressor nations formed what became known as the **Axis powers,** or the Rome-Berlin-Tokyo Axis. The Axis powers agreed to fight Soviet communism. They also agreed not to interfere with one another's plans for territorial expansion. The agreement cleared the way for these anti-democratic, aggressor powers to take even bolder steps.

☑ **RECALL** Describe the early acts of aggression of Germany, Italy, and Japan.

The Spanish Civil War

In 1936, Spain was plunged into civil war. Although the Spanish civil war was a local struggle, it soon drew other European powers into the fighting.

From Monarchy to Republic In the early 1900s, Spain was a monarchy dominated by a landowning upper class. Most Spaniards were poor peasants or urban workers. In 1931, popular unrest against the old order forced the king to leave Spain. A republic was set up with a new, more liberal constitution.

The republican government passed a series of controversial reforms. It took over some Church lands, redistributed some land to peasants, and ended some privileges of the old ruling class. These moves split the country. Communists and others on the left demanded more radical reforms. Conservatives and the military rejected the changes.

In 1936, a conservative general named **Francisco Franco** led a revolt that touched off a bloody civil war. Franco's forces, called Nationalists, rallied conservatives to their side. Supporters of the republic, known as Loyalists, included communists, socialists, and supporters of democracy.

Other Countries Get Involved People from other nations soon jumped in to support both sides. Hitler and Mussolini sent arms and forces to help Franco. The Soviet Union sent soldiers to fight against fascism alongside the Spanish Loyalists. Although the governments of Britain, France, and the United States remained neutral, individuals from those countries, as well as other countries, also fought with the Loyalists. Anti-Nazi Germans and anti-Fascist Italians joined the Loyalist cause as well.

A Bloody War Both sides committed horrible atrocities. The ruinous struggle took more than 500,000 lives.

Acts of Aggression

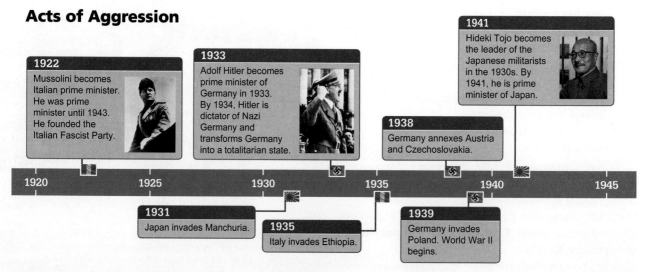

>> Italy, Germany, and Japan formed an alliance and continued their aggressive actions.
Analyze Information Why was it important for these three nations to form an alliance?

One of the worst horrors was a German air raid on Guernica, a small Spanish market town, in April 1937. Germans timed their attack for an afternoon on a market day with thousands of people in town. German planes dropped their load of bombs, and then swooped low to machine-gun anyone who had survived the bombs. Nearly 1,000 innocent civilians were killed.

To Nazi leaders, the attack on Guernica was an experiment to identify what their new planes could do. To the rest of the world, it was a grim warning of the destructive power of modern warfare. Later, commentators viewed the Spanish Civil War as a "dress rehearsal" for World War II because it had allowed new tactics and weapons to be tested, which would soon be used in a new global war.

By 1939, Franco had triumphed. Once in power, he created a fascist dictatorship similar to the dictatorships of Hitler and Mussolini. He rolled back earlier reforms, killed or jailed enemies, and used terror to promote order.

☑ **RECALL** Explain how other countries got involved in the Spanish Civil War.

>> Robert Capa's famous photograph, *The Fallen Soldier*, shows the death of a Loyalist militiaman during the Spanish Civil War. The Loyalists were supported by most urban workers and peasants, along with much of the educated middle class, which preferred a liberal democracy.

German Aggression Continues

In the meantime, Hitler pursued his goal of bringing all German-speaking people into the Third Reich. He also took steps to gain "living space" for Germans in Eastern Europe. Hitler, who believed in the superiority of the German people, thought that Germany had a right to conquer the Slavs to the east. Hitler claimed, "I have the right to remove millions of an inferior race that breeds like vermin."

Hitler also had economic and military reasons for expanding eastward. He wanted access to the natural resources of Eastern Europe, which would help boost production of military equipment. New lands would also provide additional markets for German products.

Germany Annexes Austria From the outset, Nazi propaganda had found fertile ground in Austria. By March, 1938, Hitler was ready to engineer the **Anschluss** (AHN shloos), or union of Austria and Germany.

When Austria's chancellor refused to agree to Hitler's demands, Hitler sent in the German army to "preserve order." To indicate his new role as ruler of Austria, Hitler made a speech from the Hofburg Palace, the former residence of the Hapsburg emperors.

>> On March 15, 1938, Hitler gave a speech at the Hofburg Palace in Vienna announcing annexation of Austria by Nazi Germany.

>> British prime minister Neville Chamberlain believed he had delivered peace to Europeans. After the Munich Pact, he assured a jubilant crowd in London that they could sleep soundly, as he returned from Germany bringing peace with honor.

The Anschluss violated the Versailles treaty and created a brief war scare. Hitler quickly silenced any Austrians who opposed annexation. And since the Western democracies took no action, Hitler easily had his way.

The Czech Crisis Germany turned next to Czechoslovakia. At first, Hitler insisted that the three million Germans in the **Sudetenland** (soo DAY tun land)—a region of western Czechoslovakia—be given autonomy. Czechoslovakia was one of only two remaining democracies in Eastern Europe. (Finland was the other.) Still, Britain and France were not willing to go to war to save it. As British and French leaders searched for a peaceful solution, Hitler increased his demands. The Sudetenland, he said, must be annexed to Germany.

At the Munich Conference in September 1938, British and French leaders again chose appeasement. They caved in to Hitler's demands and then persuaded the Czechs to surrender the Sudetenland without a fight. In exchange, Hitler assured Britain and France that he had no further plans to expand his territory.

The Munich Pact Returning from Munich, British Prime Minister Neville Chamberlain told cheering crowds that he had achieved "peace for our time." He told Parliament that the Munich Pact had "saved Czechoslovakia from destruction and Europe from Armageddon." French leader Edouard Daladier (dah lahd yay) reacted differently to the joyous crowds that greeted him in Paris. "The fools, why are they cheering?" he asked.

British politician **Winston Churchill,** who had long warned of the Nazi threat, judged the diplomats harshly: "They had to choose between war and dishonor. They chose dishonor; they will have war." Churchill vocalized his strong opposition to appeasement and the Munich Pact in a speech he gave in the House of Commons:

"And do not suppose that this is the end. This is only the beginning of the reckoning. This is only the first sip, the first foretaste of a bitter cup which will be proffered to us year by year unless by a supreme recovery of moral health and martial vigour, we arise again and take our stand for freedom as in the olden time."

—Winston Churchill, October 5, 1938

>> German troops ride in a convoy through the streets of Prague during the occupation of Czechoslovakia in March 1939. Czech citizens lined the streets and watched silently in the rain and sleet.

BOUNCE to Activate Timeline

Churchill's warning was largely ignored amid the celebration of the Munich Pact. However, he would very soon play a dominant role in the war he had predicted.

☑ **CHECK UNDERSTANDING** How did Hitler justify taking over Austria and the Sudetenland?

World War II Begins

Just as Churchill predicted, Europe plunged rapidly toward war. In March 1939, Hitler broke his promises and gobbled up the rest of Czechoslovakia. The democracies finally accepted the fact that appeasement had failed. At last, thoroughly alarmed, they promised to protect Poland, most likely the next target of Hitler's expansion.

Nazi-Soviet Pact In August 1939, Hitler stunned the world by announcing a nonaggression pact with his great enemy—Joseph Stalin, the Soviet dictator. Publicly, the **Nazi-Soviet Pact** bound Hitler and Stalin to peaceful relations. Secretly, the two agreed not to fight if the other went to war and to divide up Poland and other parts of Eastern Europe between them.

The pact was based not on friendship or respect but on mutual need. Hitler feared communism as much as Stalin feared fascism. But Hitler wanted a free hand in Poland. Also, he did not want to fight a war with the Western democracies and the Soviet Union at the same time.

For his part, Stalin had sought allies among the Western democracies against the Nazi menace. Mutual suspicions, however, kept them apart. By joining with Hitler, Stalin tried to protect the Soviet Union from the threat of war with Germany and grabbed a chance to gain land in Eastern Europe.

Germany Invades Poland On September 1, 1939, a week after the Nazi-Soviet Pact, German forces invaded Poland. Two days later, Britain and France declared war on Germany. World War II had begun. History had again arrived at one of its great turning points.

The devastation of World War I and the awareness of the destructive power of modern technology made the idea of more fighting unbearable. Unfortunately, the war proved to be even more horrendous than anyone had imagined.

WONDER HOW LONG THE HONEYMOON WILL LAST?

>> The cartoon portrays the two long-time enemies, Hitler and Stalin, uniting in marriage, representing the nonaggression pact they signed. **Analyze Political Cartoons** Why would the cartoonist caption this cartoon "Wonder how long the honeymoon will last?"

☑ **IDENTIFY CENTRAL IDEAS** Why did Britain and France end their policy of appeasement?

☑ ASSESSMENT

1. **Identify Central Issues** Why did the western powers follow a policy of appeasement even though it seemed to encourage more aggression?

2. **Synthesize** Why did Germany and Italy become involved in the Spanish Civil War?

3. **Infer** Why did Churchill believe the Munich Pact was the "beginning of the reckoning"?

4. **Describe** How did the Nazi-Soviet Pact contribute to the start of World War II?

5. **Identify Central Ideas** What reaction did Britain have to Germany's invasion of Poland in 1939?

6. **Connections to Today** Historians and politicians today sometimes refer to the "Lessons of Munich." What do you think this phrase means?

🛜 **GO ONLINE** to access this biography: Winston Churchill

On June 22, 1941, under the code name Operation Barbarossa, Germany invaded the Soviet Union. It was the largest German military operation of World War II. German authorities planned to annihilate the Communist nation.

BOUNCE to Activate Flipped Video

Objectives

Trace the course of German aggression and British resistance in Europe.

Describe the Nazi invasion of the Soviet Union.

Explain how Japanese imperialism and the attack on Pearl Harbor brought the United States into the war.

Key Terms

blitzkrieg
Luftwaffe
Dunkirk
Vichy
Erwin Rommel
Franklin Delano
  Roosevelt
Lend-Lease Act
Atlantic Charter
Hideki Tojo

Axis Powers Advance

World War II lasted from 1939 to 1945. It pitted the Axis powers against the Allies, which eventually included Britain, France, the Soviet Union, China, the United States, and 43 other nations. Unlike World War I, with its defensive trenches, the new global conflict was a war of aggressive movement. In the early years, things went badly for the Allies as Axis forces swept across Europe, North Africa, and Asia.

Axis Domination of Europe

Germany's "Lightning War" The Nazi invasion of Poland revealed the power of Hitler's **blitzkrieg,** or "lightning war." The blitzkrieg used tank and air power technology to strike a devastating blow against the enemy.

First, the **Luftwaffe,** or German air force, bombed airfields, factories, towns, and cities. Screaming dive bombers attacked troops and civilians. Then fast-moving tanks and troop transports pushed their way into the defending Polish army, encircling whole divisions and forcing them to surrender.

As Germany attacked from the west, Stalin's forces invaded from the east, grabbing lands promised to them under the Nazi-Soviet Pact. Within a month, Poland ceased to exist as an independent nation. Because of Poland's location and the speed of the attacks, Britain and France could do nothing beyond declaring war on Germany.

Hitler passed the winter without much further action. Stalin's armies, however, forced the Baltic states of Estonia, Latvia, and Lithuania to host bases for the Soviet military. Soviet forces also seized part of Finland, which put up stiff but unsuccessful resistance.

In April 1940, Hitler launched a blitzkrieg against Norway and Denmark, both of which soon fell. Next, his forces slammed into the Netherlands and Belgium.

The Rescue at Dunkirk During that first winter, the French hunkered down behind the Maginot Line, a border created by the French in the 1930s to protect from German invasion. Britain sent troops to wait with them. Some reporters referred to this quiet time as the "phony war."

In May 1940, German forces surprised the French and British by attacking through the Ardennes Forest in Belgium, an area that was considered invasion proof. Bypassing the Maginot Line, German troops poured into France. Retreating British forces were soon trapped between the Nazi army and the English Channel.

In a desperate gamble, the British sent all available naval vessels, merchant ships, and even fishing and pleasure boats across the channel to pluck stranded troops off the beach of **Dunkirk.** Despite German air attacks, the improvised armada ferried more than 300,000 troops to safety in Britain. This heroic rescue raised British morale.

France Surrenders Meanwhile, German forces were heading south toward Paris. In June, Mussolini had declared war on France and Britain. He sent Italian troops to attack France from the south.

Overrun and demoralized, France surrendered. On June 22, 1940, Hitler forced the French to sign the surrender documents in the same railroad car in which Germany had signed the armistice ending World War I. Following the surrender, Germany occupied northern France. In the south, the Germans set up a "puppet state," with its capital at **Vichy** (VEE shee).

Some French officers escaped to England and set up a government-in-exile. Led by Charles de Gaulle, these "free French" worked to liberate their homeland. Within France, resistance fighters used guerrilla tactics against German forces.

Operation Sea Lion With the fall of France, Britain stood alone in Western Europe. Hitler was sure that the British would sue for peace. But Winston Churchill, who had replaced Neville Chamberlain as prime minister, had other plans. Churchill's defiance gave voice to the determination of the British.

"We shall defend our island, whatever the cost may be, we shall fight on the beaches, we shall fight on the landing grounds, we shall fight in the fields and in the streets, we

German Expansion, 1936–1939

KEY
- Axis Powers
- Areas under Axis control
- Area militarized, violating treaty, 1936

>> Germany advanced aggressively from 1936 to 1939, until its invasion of Poland sparked another world war. **Analyze Maps** How did Germany violate the Treaty of Versailles?

BOUNCE to Activate Map

>> In his first speech in Parliament as prime minister, Winston Churchill vowed, "I have nothing to offer but blood, toil, tears and sweat." He ended with the words, "Come then, let us go forward together with our united strength."

>> The Battle of Britain started in July 1940, but by September, Hitler decided on a new tactic. Hitler believed the British would surrender if he targeted civilians, so he began a daily bombing campaign. London was Hitler's first target.

BOUNCE to Activate Gallery

shall fight in the hills; we shall never surrender."

Winston Churchill, June 4, 1940

Faced with this defiance, Hitler made plans for Operation Sea Lion—the invasion of Britain. In preparation for the invasion, he launched massive air strikes against the island nation. In August 1940, German bombers began a daily bombardment of England's southern coast. In what was known as the Battle of Britain, Britain's Royal Air Force (RAF) valiantly battled the Luftwaffe. Then the Germans changed their tactics. Instead of concentrating on military targets in the south, they began to bomb London and other cities.

England Survives the Blitz German bombers first appeared over London late on September 7, 1940. All through the night, relays of aircraft showered high explosives and firebombs on the sprawling capital. The bombing continued for 57 nights in a row and then sporadically until the next May. These bombing attacks are known as "the Blitz." Much of London was destroyed, and thousands of people lost their lives.

London did not break under the Blitz. Defiantly, Parliament continued to meet. Citizens carried on their daily lives, seeking protection in shelters and then emerging to resume their routines when the all-clear sounded. Even Churchill and the British king and queen chose to support Londoners by joining them in bomb shelters rather than fleeing to the countryside.

German planes continued to bomb London and other cities off and on until May 1941. But contrary to Hitler's hopes, the Luftwaffe could not gain air superiority over Britain, and British morale was not destroyed. In fact, the bombing only made the British more determined to turn back the enemy. Operation Sea Lion was a failure.

Hitler's "New Order" As Nazi forces rampaged across Europe, Hitler expanded his plan to build a "new order" in the occupied lands. Hitler's new order grew out of his racial obsessions. He set up puppet governments in Western European countries that were peopled by light-skinned Europeans, whom Hitler and his followers believed to be an Aryan "master race." The Slavs of Eastern Europe were considered to be an inferior "race." They were shoved aside to provide more "living space" for Germans.

To the Nazis, occupied lands were an economic resource to be plundered and looted. The Nazis systematically stripped conquered nations of their works of art, factories, and other resources. To counter resistance movements that emerged in occupied countries, the Nazis took savage revenge, shooting hostages and torturing prisoners.

War in North Africa and the Balkans Axis armies also pushed into North Africa and the Balkans. In September 1940, Mussolini ordered forces from Italy's North African colony of Libya into Egypt. When the British army repulsed these invaders, Hitler sent one of his most brilliant commanders, General **Erwin Rommel,** to North Africa. The "Desert Fox," as he was called, chalked up a string of successes in 1941 and 1942. He pushed the British back across the desert toward Cairo, Egypt.

In October 1940, Italian forces invaded Greece. They encountered stiff resistance, and in 1941 German troops once again provided reinforcements. Both Greece and Yugoslavia were added to the growing Axis empire. Even after the Axis triumph, however, Greek and Yugoslav guerrillas plagued the occupying forces. Meanwhile, both Bulgaria and Hungary had joined the Axis alliance. By 1941, the Axis powers or their allies controlled most of Europe.

☑ **DESCRIBE** Describe how the Axis powers gained control of most of Europe in 1941.

>> Erwin Rommel led the military operation in Libya. Rommel was sent to North Africa to help the Italian forces fight the British. Rommel was an expert at tank warfare.

Nazis Attack the Soviet Union

After the failure in Britain, Hitler turned his military might to a new target—the Soviet Union. The decision to invade the Soviet Union took pressure off Britain. It also proved to be one of Hitler's costliest mistakes.

In June 1941, Hitler broke the Nazi-Soviet Pact by invading the Soviet Union in Operation Barbarossa, a plan which took its name from the medieval Germanic leader, Frederick Barbarossa. Hitler made his motives clear. He wanted to gain "living space" for Germans and to win control of regions rich in resources. "If I had the Ural Mountains with their incalculable store of treasures in raw materials," he declared, "Siberia with its vast forests, and the Ukraine with its tremendous wheat fields, Germany under National Socialist leadership would swim in plenty." He also wanted to crush communism in Europe and defeat his powerful rival, Stalin.

A Rapid Advance Hitler unleashed a new blitzkrieg in the Soviet Union. About three million German soldiers invaded. The Germans caught Stalin unprepared. His army was still suffering from the purges that had wiped out many of its top officers.

The Soviets lost two and a half million soldiers trying to fend off the invaders. As they were forced back, Soviet troops destroyed factories and farm equipment and burned crops to keep them out of enemy hands. But they could not stop the German war machine. By autumn, the Nazis had smashed deep into the Soviet Union and were poised to take Moscow and Leningrad (present-day St. Petersburg).

Winter Halts the Blitzkrieg There, however, the German advance stalled. Like Napoleon's Grand Army in 1812, Hitler's forces were not prepared for the fury of "General Winter." By early December, temperatures plunged to 0°F (-18°C).

Cold was a killer. German troops had set out in summer and had no warm winter uniforms. Fuel froze in tanks, and much of the Germans' mechanized equipment was useless. Thousands of German soldiers starved or froze to death.

Siege of Leningrad The Soviets, meanwhile, suffered appalling hardships. In September 1941, the two-and-a-half-year siege of Leningrad began. Food was rationed to two pieces of bread a day. Desperate Leningraders ate almost anything. For example, they boiled wallpaper scraped off walls because its paste was said to contain potato flour.

Although more than a million Leningraders died during the siege, the city did not fall to the Germans. Hoping to gain some relief for his exhausted people, Stalin urged Britain to open a second front in Western Europe. Although Churchill could not offer much real help, the two powers did agree to work together.

☑ **IDENTIFY SUPPORTING DETAILS** Why did Hitler nullify the Nazi-Soviet Pact by invading the Soviet Union?

U.S. Involvement in the War

When the war began in 1939, the United States declared its neutrality. Although isolationist feeling remained strong, many Americans, including President **Franklin Delano Roosevelt,** sympathized with those who battled the Axis powers. In time, Roosevelt found ways around the Neutrality Acts to provide aid, including for Britain, as it stood alone against Hitler.

Roosevelt Supports the Allies In March 1941, FDR persuaded Congress to pass the **Lend-Lease Act.** It allowed him to sell or lend war materials to "any country whose defense the President deems vital to the defense of the United States." The United States, said Roosevelt, would not be drawn into the war, but it would become "the arsenal of democracy," supplying arms to those who were fighting for freedom.

To show further support, Roosevelt met secretly with Churchill on a warship in the Atlantic in August 1941. The two leaders issued the **Atlantic Charter,** which set goals for the war—"the final destruction of the Nazi tyranny"—and for the postwar world. They pledged to support "the right of all peoples to choose the form of government under which they will live" and called for a "permanent system of general security."

Growing Tensions with Japan Although Roosevelt viewed Hitler as the greatest menace to world peace, it was tensions with Japan that finally brought the United States into the war. The United States held several possessions in the Pacific, including the Philippines and Hawaii.

When war broke out in Europe in 1939, the Japanese saw a chance to grab European possessions in Southeast Asia. Japanese forces took control across Asia and the Pacific. Japan claimed that its mission was to help Asians escape Western colonial rule. In fact, the real goal was a Japanese empire in Asia. The rich resources of the region, including oil, rubber, and tin, would be of immense value in fighting Japan's war against the Chinese.

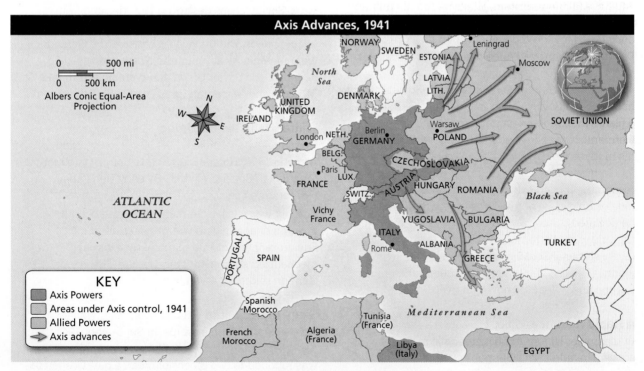

Axis Advances, 1941

KEY
- Axis Powers
- Areas under Axis control, 1941
- Allied Powers
- → Axis advances

>> The Soviet Union joined the Allies after Germany's invasion. **Analyze Maps** How might this new enemy affect Germany's war effort in geographic terms?

In 1940, with Europeans distracted by war, Japan advanced into French Indochina and the Dutch East Indies. In response, the United States banned the sale of war materials, such as iron, steel, and oil, to Japan. Japanese leaders saw this move as a threat to Japan's economy and its Asian sphere of influence.

Japan and the United States held talks to ease the growing tension. But extreme militarists were gaining power in Japan, including General **Hideki Tojo** who became prime minister in 1941. Prior to the war, Tojo had strongly supported the invasion of China and formation of the alliance with Germany and Italy. Tojo and other militarists hoped to seize more lands in Asia and the Pacific and believed the United States was interfering with their plans.

The Attack on Pearl Harbor With talks at a standstill, General Tojo ordered a surprise attack. Early on December 7, 1941, Japanese airplanes bombed the American fleet at Pearl Harbor in Hawaii. The attack took the lives of about 2,400 people and destroyed battleships and aircraft.

The next day, a grim-faced President Roosevelt told the nation that December 7 was "a date which will live in infamy." He asked Congress to declare war on Japan. On December 11, Germany and Italy, as Japan's allies, declared war on the United States.

Japanese Victories in the Pacific In the long run, the Japanese attack on Pearl Harbor would be as serious a mistake as Hitler's invasion of the Soviet Union. But in the months immediately after Pearl Harbor, European and American possessions in the Pacific fell one by one to the Japanese.

The Japanese captured the Philippines and other islands held by the United States. They overran the British colonies of Hong Kong, Burma, and Malaya, advanced deeper into the Dutch East Indies, and completed the takeover of French Indochina. By 1942, the Japanese empire stretched from Southeast Asia to the western Pacific Ocean.

The Japanese invaders treated the Chinese, Filipinos, Malaysians, and other conquered people with great brutality. In China, the Philippines, Malaysia, and elsewhere, they killed and tortured civilians. They seized food crops, destroyed cities and towns, and enslaved local people. Whatever welcome the Japanese had first met as "liberators" soon turned to hatred. In the Philippines, Indochina, and elsewhere, resistance forces waged guerrilla warfare against the Japanese invaders.

☑ **IDENTIFY CENTRAL ISSUES** Why did Japanese leaders view the United States as an enemy?

>> On Sunday morning, December 7, 1941, the U.S. naval base at Pearl Harbor, Hawaii, was jolted awake by a surprise air attack. Japanese planes dropped bombs and torpedoes, stunning Americans.

☑ ASSESSMENT

1. **Integrate Information** How were people of occupied territories treated by the Axis powers?

2. **Describe** Explain why Hitler's blitzkrieg tactics were successful at the beginning of the war.

3. **Synthesize** What was the role of Winston Churchill during World War II?

4. **Describe** Explain the purpose of Hitler's "new order."

5. **Synthesize** What role did Japanese imperialism play in igniting World War II?

6. **Quest Connections** Churchill said of the RAF, "Never in the field of human conflict was so much owed by so many to so few." What do you think he meant by this tribute?

📶 **GO ONLINE** to access these biographies: Franklin D. Roosevelt, Hideki Tojo

Japanese Rule in Asia

In 1940, Japan declared its goal of creating the Greater East Asian Co-Prosperity Sphere, a bloc of East Asian nations free of western influence and dominated by Japan. Three years later, Tokyo hosted the Greater East Asia Conference. Participants included representatives from Japanese-controlled governments in China, Burma, and the Philippines, as well as from India (then a British colony) and independent Thailand.

The first Primary Source below is from a speech given at the conference by the Japanese prime minister, Hideki Tojo. In the second, taken from the autobiography of future Burmese prime minister Thakin Nu, he recalls the day Japanese forces drove the British out of Burma.

As you read, notice the differences in how they present the relationship of Japan to Burma.

>> Japanese troops march through a Burmese village during the occupation.

Speech to the Greater East Asia Conference, 1943, Hideki Tojo

The United States of America and the British Empire have in seeking their own prosperity oppressed other nations and peoples. Especially in East Asia, they indulged in insatiable aggression and exploitation, and sought to satisfy their inordinate ambitions of enslaving the entire region, and finally they came to menace seriously the stability of East Asia. Herein lies the cause of the recent war.

☑ **IDENTIFY CENTRAL IDEAS** According to Tojo, what was the primary cause of World War II?

The countries of Greater East Asia, with a view to contributing to the cause of world peace, undertake to cooperate toward prosecuting the War of Greater East Asia to a successful conclusion, liberating their region from the yoke of British-American domination, and ensuring their self-existence and self-defense, and in constructing a Greater East Asia in accordance with the following principles:

☑ **ANALYZE ARGUMENTS** What does Tojo suggest is Japan's wartime role in relation to the other nations at the Conference?

1. The countries of Greater East Asia through mutual cooperation will ensure the stability of their region and construct an order of common prosperity and well-being based upon justice.
2. The countries of Greater East Asia will ensure the fraternity of nations in their region, by respecting one another's sovereignty and independence and practicing mutual assistance and amity.

☑ **ANALYZE WORD CHOICES** What does Tojo suggest by using words such as *fraternity, sovereignty,* and *independence?*

3. The countries of Greater East Asia by respecting one another's traditions and developing the creative faculties of each race, will enhance the culture and civilization of Greater East Asia.

4. The countries of Greater East Asia will endeavor to accelerate their economic development through close cooperation upon a basis of reciprocity [mutual exchange] and to promote thereby the general prosperity of their region.

5. The countries of Greater East Asia will cultivate friendly relations with all the countries of the world, and work for the abolition of racial discrimination, the promotion of cultural [interchange] and the opening of resources throughout the world, and contribute thereby to the progress of mankind.

☑ **DRAW INFERENCES** What does Tojo suggest will be Japan's role in Asia after the war is over?

Burma Under the Japanese, 1954, Thakin Nu

The whole village and the neighbouring villages, boys and girls, old men and old women, were in a state of great excitement. Some were laden up with bananas and melons and all kinds of fruit ; some had bowls of rice on their heads. Soon three or four monks appeared, and they all formed up into a procession in double file. Two aged dames distributed sprigs of thabyeban (eugenia) to everyone. . . . All were exulting in the thought that Burma would be free, and as the grand old song resounded throughout the countryside, no one could hear it without trembling with emotion.

☑ **DRAW INFERENCES** Based on this description, how do you think these villagers felt about British rule in Burma?

This can readily be understood. The whole air was breathing rumours. 'The Japanese are our great friends.' 'When a Japanese meets a Burman he greets him with our own war cry.' 'The Japanese will die for Burma's freedom.' 'A Burman prince is coming as a leader in the Japanese army. They all firmly believed the messages scattered down from aeroplanes and broadcast on the wireless [radio] that the Japanese were coming to help Burma, and rumour had swollen a handful of hope until it overflowed the basket. Now they were off to welcome their great ally the Japanese, and though it was close on noon under the scorching sun of Mandalay, the poor people were so keen to greet their great ally that they did not even notice the heat.

☑ **SUMMARIZE** What is the general reaction of these villagers to news of the Japanese invasion?

We met them again in the afternoon about four o'clock. They were no longer marching in a procession but limping along in clumps of three or four. Their faces were no longer joyful and exultant as in the morning, and they seemed quite shy of facing the people who had stayed at home. When they came up to us we asked what had happened. One of them replied in a surly tone. 'Don't talk about it. We expected the Japanese commander to be very thankful for our bowls of rice, but all he did was to take his hand out of his trouser pocket and give us a hard slap in the face.

☑ **PREDICT** Based on this excerpt, what do you think Japanese rule in Burma will be like?

☑ ASSESSMENT

1. **Determine Author's Purpose** What do you think was the main purpose of Tojo's speech?

2. **Cite Evidence** What evidence suggests that Nu did not share the general mood of the villagers about the arrival of the Japanese?

3. **Determine Author's Point of View** What do both of these sources suggest about Asian views of western imperialism?

4. **Compare and Contrast** How do these two sources present different perspectives on Japan's role in Southeast Asia?

5. **Develop Empathy** Describe how you think the people of Burma might have felt on hearing Tojo's speech.

GO ONLINE to access primary sources

18.3

The Warsaw Uprising ended on October 2, 1944. The entire civilian population of the Warsaw ghetto was expelled; most were sent to labor and death camps.

BOUNCE to Activate Flipped Video

Objectives

Identify the roots of Nazi persecution of the Jews.

Describe how the Nazis carried out a program of genocide.

Describe the various acts of Jewish resistance.

Summarize the response of the Allies to the Holocaust.

Key Terms

concentration camp
Holocaust
crematorium
Auschwitz

The Holocaust

Hitler came to power in the midst of the Great Depression, promising to end reparations, create jobs, and defy the hated Versailles treaty by rearming Germany. Hitler also played on anti-Semitism, which had existed for centuries in Europe. Hitler saw Jews as a separate, inferior race whom he blamed for Germany's defeat in World War I. He launched a campaign against the Jews, which began with persecution and escalated to mass murder.

The Nazi Campaign Against the Jews

Early Persecution The Nuremberg Laws of 1935 put Nazi racist ideology into practice. They removed citizenship from German Jews and banned marriage between Jews and non-Jews. Before long, the Nazis imposed other restrictions that forced Jews from their jobs and homes and embarked on escalating violence and terror against Jews. Schools and the Hitler Youth Movement taught children that Jews were "polluting" German society and culture.

Anti-Semitic propaganda triggered one of the most violent early attacks on Jews. In November 1938, Nazi-led mobs smashed windows, looted, and destroyed Jewish homes, businesses, and places of worship. This wave of violence in Germany and Austria became known as Kristallnacht, or Night of Broken Glass.

Nazi Concentration Camps After gaining power in 1933, the Nazis began rounding up political opponents and placing them in **concentration camps,** detention centers for civilians who were considered enemies of the state. Before long, they were sending Jews, communists, and others they despised to these camps. By

1934, Hitler had given Heinrich Himmler control of the concentration camps throughout Germany.

During the war, the Nazis built more camps for Jews from Poland and other parts of Eastern Europe, as well as for resistance fighters, Roma (Gypsies), Slavs, and other "racially undesirable elements." The physically and mentally disabled, gay men, and ordinary criminals were also sent to the camps. So were political and religious leaders who spoke out against the Nazis.

During the war, Nazis used people in the camps as forced laborers, who had to produce weapons and other goods for the German war effort. They faced brutal mistreatment, hunger, disease, and execution. Hundreds of thousands of people were murdered.

Brutal Medical Experiments In some camps, Nazi doctors conducted painful and deadly medical experiments on prisoners. They tested dangerous new drugs on prisoners and tried out treatments designed to help Axis forces survive injuries. They also ran experiments to try to prove Nazi racial ideas.

Josef Mengele, a physician at the notorious Auschwitz concentration camp, conducted experiments to see how different ethnic groups responded to contagious diseases such as malaria or yellow fever. Still other experiments were linked to the Nazi goal of sterilizing people they claimed were "inferior races."

Hitler's "Final Solution" As Nazi troops advanced into Eastern Europe, they forced Jews in Poland and elsewhere to live in ghettos, or restricted areas sealed off from the surrounding city. By 1941, however, Hitler and other Nazi leaders had devised what they called the "Final Solution to the Jewish question." Their goal was the extermination of all European Jews. This campaign of genocide eventually became known as the **Holocaust.**

Hitler took steps to carry out his Final Solution. After the Nazi invasion of the Soviet Union in 1941, mobile killing units followed the German army and murdered over a million Jewish men, women, and children in Eastern Europe.

Hitler then had six "death camps" built in Poland. There, the Nazis shipped Jews and others marked for extermination from all over occupied Europe. Nazi engineers designed efficient means of killing millions of men, women, and children.

As the prisoners reached the camps, they were stripped of their clothes and valuables. Their heads were shaved. Guards separated men from women, and children from their parents. The young, elderly, and sick were murdered immediately. Falsely told they were to be disinfected, they were herded into fake "shower rooms" and gassed. Then their bodies were burned in specially designed **crematoriums.** An American soldier later described the machinery of murder he witnessed at the Dachau camp:

Nazi Concentration Camps, 1933–1945

KEY
- Death camp
- Labor camp
- National borders, 1933

>> **Analyze Maps** Where were the death camps located? How did this location reflect the goals of the "Final Solution"?

BOUNCE to Activate Map

Behind the furnaces was the execution chamber, a windowless cell twenty feet square with gas nozzles every few feet across the ceiling. Outside, in addition to a huge mound of charred bone fragments, were the carefully sorted and stacked clothes of the victims–which obviously numbered in the thousands.

—Harold Porter, American soldier

The Nazis worked younger, healthier prisoners to death or used them for their inhumane "medical" experiments. By June 1945, the Nazis had massacred more than six million Jews. Almost as many other "undesirable" people were killed as well.

☑ **SYNTHESIZE** Describe the escalation of Hitler's campaign against the Jews.

>> Anne Frank was one of over a million Jewish children who was murdered by the Nazis or died of disease in the horrifying conditions of the concentration camps. She and her family lived in hiding in Amsterdam for over two years until they were found and sent to concentration camps. Anne's diary remains a key document of the Holocaust.

Jewish Resistance

Jewish people resisted the Nazis even though they knew their efforts could not succeed. In the early 1940s, Jews in the ghettos of Eastern Europe at times took up arms. The largest uprising occurred in the Warsaw ghetto in occupied Poland.

The Warsaw Ghetto Uprising In July 1942, the Nazis began sending Polish Jews from the Warsaw ghetto to the Treblinka death camp and to slave labor camps. As the mass deportations continued, Jewish groups organized an underground resistance movement.

By the spring of 1943, the German plan to liquidate the Warsaw ghetto was clear, and resistance groups planned a full-scale revolt. Armed with smuggled weapons and homemade bombs, the Jews took over the ghetto and prepared to fight to the end.

After holding out for a month, the resistance forces were crushed. The ghetto was in ruins, and thousands were killed in the fighting. Any survivors were sent to death camps or forced labor camps. Although the uprising was doomed, the courage of the resistance inspired uprisings elsewhere

Continuing Resistance A few Jews escaped the Warsaw ghetto and from ghettos elsewhere in Eastern Europe. About 25,000 Jews, many of them teenagers, joined resistance groups waging guerrilla warfare against the Nazis. These fighters were called partisans. Some joined Soviet units or formed their own Jewish units. In Western Europe, Jews were active in the French and Belgian resistance movements.

Jewish resistance took different forms. In addition to armed uprisings and fighting with guerrilla forces, a few Jews challenged Nazi death camps. Uprisings occurred at Treblinka and Sobibor. In October 1944, a group of Jews in **Auschwitz,** the largest Nazi death camp, destroyed one of the gas chambers.

Jews also resisted by hiding or sending their children into hiding. And despite Nazi persecution, they preserved their culture and traditions as best they could.

Hiding Jews In some parts of Europe, friends, neighbors, or even strangers protected Jews. When Mussolini undertook a vicious campaign against Italian Jews, peasants hid Jews in their villages. Denmark and Bulgaria saved almost all their Jewish populations. The Danish resistance movement, assisted by many common citizens, coordinated the flight of over 7,000 Jews to safety in neutral Sweden.

Many individuals who were not Jewish took great risks to save Jewish lives. One of the best-known stories of the Holocaust is about Anne Frank and her tale of silent resistance. Anne and her family hid for just over two years in her father's Amsterdam office building, while eight people from the office worked together to secretly feed and care for the family in hiding. There are many similar stories of courageous citizens who helped to hide and protect Jewish friends, neighbors, and strangers.

Most people, however, closed their eyes to what was happening. Many people collaborated, or cooperated, with the Nazis, actively taking part in killing Jews or informing on Jews in hiding. In France, the Vichy government helped ship thousands of Jews to their deaths. Strict immigration policies in many Western countries as well as conscious efforts to block Jewish immigration prevented many Jews from gaining refuge elsewhere.

☑ INFER Explain why the Jews in the Warsaw Ghetto decided to fight back.

The Allies Respond to the Holocaust

Even before the war started, some people outside Germany expressed concern about the Nazi persecution of the Jews. Still, the response was limited. The United States and other countries could have accepted many more Jewish refugees from Germany and Austria.

The Question of Jewish Refugees In the summer of 1938, delegates from 32 countries met in France to discuss the "refugee problem." During the nine-day meeting, delegates expressed sympathy for the refugees, but most countries, including the United States and Britain, offered excuses for not accepting more refugees. In the midst of the Great Depression, many Americans worried that refugees would take jobs away from them and overburden social welfare programs. Widespread racial prejudices among the Allies, including anti-Semitic attitudes, also played a role in the failure to admit more Jewish refugees.

In 1939, the United States refused asylum to Jewish refugees on board the ship the *St. Louis*. The passengers were forced to return to Germany.

On the eve of World War II, Britain briefly lifted some restrictions and accepted almost 10,000 mostly Jewish children from Nazi Europe. Their parents were not allowed to accompany the children, and many children never saw their parents again.

>> Passengers on the refugee ship *St. Louis* were turned away from Cuba and the U.S. In June 1939, the ship was forced to return to Europe and an uncertain fate.

The Allies Take Limited Action After the war began, the Allies were mostly concerned with military strategy. Throughout 1940 and 1941, Britain was fighting the war against the Nazis alone. Even when reliable reports concerning the murder of the Jews started to surface, the Allies were slow to respond. Despite urgent calls from resistance groups in occupied Europe, the Allies did not undertake any military operations.

By 1942, the Allies knew that Jews were being taken to death camps in Poland, but often kept this information classified. They refused to release early photographs taken of the camps. Over the next two years, both Britain and the United States considered the idea of bombing Auschwitz, but neither country took action, focusing instead on their ultimate war aim to defeat the Nazis. The only way to rescue Jews, argued some U.S. officials, was to win the war as fast as possible.

President Roosevelt began to respond to reports of Jewish genocide in 1944. He established the War Refugee Board, a government agency that worked with the Red Cross to save thousands of Eastern European Jews. Its greatest success was due to the brave actions of Raoul Wallenberg, a Swedish diplomat, in Hungary. Wallenberg issued thousands of Swedish passports to Hungarian Jews, which saved them from being deported to Auschwitz. Overall, the War Refugee Board is credited with saving as many as 200,000 Jews.

The Liberation of the Concentration Camps The Allies only became fully aware of the enormity of the Nazi genocide program toward the end of the war, as Soviet, British, and American troops began liberating the camps. These liberators, hardened by war, were not prepared to see the piles of dead bodies, the warehouses full of human hair and jewelry, the ashes from the crematoriums, or the half-dead, emaciated survivors.

Soviet forces were the first to liberate a major Nazi camp in Majdanek, Poland. The Nazis had been surprised by the rapid Soviet advance and attempted to destroy the evidence of mass murders by demolishing the camp. In the summer of 1944, the Soviets also liberated the Belzec, Sobibor, and Treblinka killing centers. By January 1945, the Soviets had liberated Auschwitz.

American and British forces also liberated many camps in Germany. On April 11, 1945, U.S. forces freed more than 20,000 prisoners at Buchenwald. British forces liberated concentration camps in northern Germany, and in mid-April 1945 freed more than 60,000 prisoners from the Bergen-Belsen concentration camp.

Most of the prisoners they released were in critical condition because of a typhus epidemic. More than 10,000 prisoners died within a few weeks of liberation from the effects of malnutrition.

Impact of the Holocaust By 1945, the Nazis had massacred some six million Jews in the Holocaust, two-thirds of European Jews. Nearly five million other people were killed as well. The scale and savagery of the Holocaust are unequaled in history. The Nazis deliberately set out to destroy the Jews for no reason other than their religious and ethnic heritage. Today, the record of that slaughter is a vivid reminder of the monstrous results of racism and intolerance.

Survivors of the Holocaust often had nowhere to go in Europe. Their homes, villages, and communities had been destroyed. Many ended up in refugee camps in Allied-occupied Germany, waiting to find new homes in other countries. They still faced discrimination, however, and many countries refused to accept them.

As the horrors of the Holocaust were revealed, worldwide support for an independent Jewish homeland increased. On May 14, 1948, Jewish leader David Ben-Gurion proclaimed the establishment

PERSECUTION UNDER THE NAZIS 1933-1945

JEWISH POPULATION IN EUROPE 1933-1950

1933 — **9.5 MILLION**

1950 — **3.5 MILLION**

50,000 MEN WERE CONVICTED OF HOMOSEXUALITY, AND BETWEEN

5,000 AND 15,000 WERE SENT TO CONCENTRATION CAMPS.

Source: Jewish Virtual Library

OTHER VICTIMS OF NAZI PERSECUTION

Death Toll (millions)

- Roma: 220,000 (APPROX.)
- Non-Jewish Poles: 1.9 MILLION
- Soviet POWs: 3.3 MILLION
- Disabled: 200,000 (APPROX.)

Source: United States Holocaust Memorial Museum

>> **Analyze Information** Besides the Jewish population, what was the next-largest group of victims of Nazi persecution? Why do you think that group was targeted?

of the State of Israel in the former British Palestine Mandate, site of the ancient Jewish kingdom of Israel. Many displaced Holocaust survivors immigrated to Israel to make a new start.

The Holocaust had a significant impact on international law. The term "genocide" for an attempt to deliberately destroy a race was created in 1944 to describe the Nazi Final Solution. Four years later, nations signed the Convention on the Prevention and Punishment of the Crime of Genocide which established genocide as a crime that could be prosecuted in international courts.

Today, people in the United States and around the world are working to make sure the Holocaust is not forgotten. Holocaust museums can be found in many states and countries. Some of the concentration camps, such as Auschwitz, have been preserved and stand as authentic memorials to honor those who died and those who survived.

☑ **DRAW CONCLUSIONS** Why were Soviet and American forces finally able to liberate many concentration camp victims?

>> Holocaust museums around the world attract millions of visitors each year. Their goal is to remind the world of the horrors of genocide.

🔳 BOUNCE to Activate Gallery

☑ ASSESSMENT

1. **Synthesize** In what was Hitler's campaign against German Jews rooted?

2. **Compare and Contrast** Describe the difference between Hitler's "Final Solution" and the Nazis' earlier persecution of the Jews.

3. **Recall** In what ways did Jews resist Nazi persecution?

4. **Infer** Why did the Allied Powers refuse admittance to Jewish refugees before Hitler's launch of the "Final Solution"?

5. **Connections to Today** Why are people from around the world working to make sure the Holocaust is not forgotten?

The Diary of a Young Girl: Anne Frank

In 1933, Adolf Hitler was elected Chancellor of Germany. During World War II, his Nazi Party rounded up European Jews, many of whom were transported to death camps. Anne Frank was a young Jewish girl who hid with her family in small concealed rooms in her father's office. Frank kept a diary from June 12, 1942 to August 1, 1944, when her family's hiding place was discovered. She died in a concentration camp in 1945. Frank's father survived and published her diary to share Anne's story with the world.

>> Anne Frank

Primary Source

Saturday, June 20, 1942

. . . My father . . . didn't marry my mother until he was thirty-six and she was twenty-five. My sister Margot was born in Frankfort am Main in Germany in 1926. I was born on June 12, 1929. . . . Because we're Jewish, my father immigrated to Holland in 1933, when he became the Managing Director of the Dutch Opekta Company. . . .

Our lives were not without anxiety, since our relatives in Germany were suffering under Hitler's anti-Jewish laws. After the pogroms [organized killing and other persecution of Jews] in 1938 my two uncles (my mother's brothers) fled Germany, finding safe refuge in North America. . . .

After May 1940 the good times were few and far between: first there was the war, then the capitulation [surrender] and then the arrival of the Germans, which is when the trouble started for the Jews.

☑ **ANALYZE SEQUENCE** List the chronology of events that Anne Frank describes in this passage from June 20. What does this sequence of events suggest about life for European Jews during the 1930s and early 1940s?

Our freedom was severely restricted by a series of anti-Jewish decrees: Jews were required to wear a yellow star; Jews were required to turn in their bicycles; Jews were forbidden to use streetcars; Jews were forbidden to ride in cars, even their own; Jews were required to do their shopping between 3 and 5 p.m.; Jews were required to frequent only Jewish-owned barbershops and beauty parlors; Jews were forbidden to be out on the streets between 8 p.m. and 6 a.m.; Jews were forbidden to go to theaters, movies, or any other forms of entertainment; Jews were forbidden to use swimming pools, tennis courts, hockey fields or any other athletic fields; . . . Jews were forbidden to sit in their gardens or those of their friends after 8 p.m.; Jews were forbidden to visit Christians in their homes; Jews were required to attend Jewish schools, etc. You couldn't do this and you couldn't do that, but life went on. Jacque [Anne's best friend] always said to me, "I don't dare do anything anymore, 'cause I'm afraid it's not allowed." . . .

☑ **DRAW CONCLUSIONS** Choose a decree described in this passage, and explain how it limited Jews' rights and freedoms.

Thursday, November 19, 1942

. . . Countless friends and acquaintances have been taken off to a dreadful fate. Night after night, green and gray military vehicles cruise the streets. They [the Germans] knock on every door, asking whether any Jews live there. If so, the whole family is immediately taken away. If not, they proceed to the next house. It's impossible to escape their clutches unless you go into hiding. They often go around with lists, knocking only on those doors where they know there's a big haul to be made. They frequently offer a bounty, so much per head. It's like the slave hunts of the olden days. I don't mean to make light of this; it's much too tragic for that. In the evenings when it's dark, I often see long lines of good, innocent people accompanied by crying children, walking on and on, ordered about by a handful of men who bully and beat them until they nearly drop. No one is spared. The sick, the elderly, children, babies and pregnant women—all are marched to their death.

We're so fortunate here, away from the turmoil. We wouldn't have to give a moment's thought to all this suffering if it weren't for the fact that we're so worried about those we hold dear, whom we can no longer help. I feel wicked sleeping in a warm bed, while somewhere out there my dearest friends are dropping from exhaustion or being knocked to the ground.

I get frightened myself when I think of close friends who are now at the mercy of the cruelest monsters ever to stalk the earth.

And all because they're Jews. . . .

☑ **SUMMARIZE** As Frank describes in her diary, how has life changed for Jews from June to November 1942?

Wednesday, May 3, 1944

The question is understandable, but up to now no one has come up with a satisfactory answer. Why is England manufacturing bigger and better airplanes and bombs and at the same time churning out new houses for reconstruction? Why are millions spent on the war each day, while not a penny is

available for medical science, artists or the poor? Why do people have to starve when mountains of food are rotting away in other parts of the world? Oh, why are people so crazy? . .

Saturday, July 15, 1944

. . . I still believe, in spite of everything, that people are truly good at heart.

It's utterly impossible for me to build my life on a foundation of chaos, suffering, and death. I see the world being slowly transformed into a wilderness, I hear the approaching thunder that, one day, will destroy us too, I feel the sufferings of millions. And yet, when I look up at the sky, I somehow feel that everything will change for the better, that this cruelty too will end, that peace and tranquility [calm] will return once more. . . . .

☑ **EXPLAIN AN ARGUMENT** Why does Frank describe people as "crazy"? What problems does she observe?

☑ ASSESSMENT

1. **Draw Inferences** What was the purpose of the restrictions the Nazis imposed on Jews? What were the effects of these laws?

2. **Analyze Style and Rhetoric** How would you describe the tone of Frank's diary? How does she relate to her subject matter?

3. **Determine Central Ideas** How does reading Frank's diary differ from reading a secondary source about the Holocaust? What might her diary teach readers today that other sources cannot?

18.4

Women learned new skills in order to participate in the war effort. In some countries, they served in combat and worked in manufacturing. Women also offered day care for children of those who worked or served.

 BOUNCE to Activate Flipped Video

Objectives

Understand how nations committed all of their resources to fighting World War II.

Explain how the Allies began to push back the Axis powers in Europe and the Pacific.

Describe the Normandy landings and the Allied advance toward Germany.

Key Terms

internment
Rosie the Riveter
aircraft carrier
Dwight Eisenhower
Stalingrad
D-Day
Yalta Conference

The Allies Turn the Tide

As 1942 began, the Allies were in trouble. German bombers flew unrelenting raids over Britain, and the German army advanced deep into the Soviet Union. In the Pacific, the Japanese onslaught seemed unstoppable. But helped by extraordinary efforts on the home front and a series of military victories, the tide was about to turn.

A Commitment to Total War

Like the Axis powers they were fighting, the Allies committed themselves to total war. In total war, nations devote all of their resources to the war effort.

Governments Redirect Resources To achieve maximum war production, democratic governments in the United States and Great Britain increased their economic and political power. They directed economic resources into the war effort, ordering factories to stop making cars or refrigerators and to turn out airplanes or tanks instead.

They raised money by holding war bond drives. By buying bonds, citizens lent their government certain sums of money that would be returned with interest later.

Wartime economic policies placed limits on individual economic freedoms. Governments implemented programs to ration, or control, the amount of certain vital goods consumers could buy. Rationed items included rubber, tin, gasoline, and certain food items. Prices and wages were also regulated. In the United States, the war stimulated the economy by creating millions of new jobs. Unemployment, which had remained high during the Great Depression, was almost wiped out.

Limits on Individual Rights Under the pressures of war, even democratic governments limited the rights of citizens. They censored the press and used propaganda to win public support for the war. In the United States and Canada, racial prejudice and concerns about security led to the **internment,** or confinement during wartime, of citizens of Japanese descent. Japanese Americans on the West Coast and Japanese Canadians were forced to move to camps inland, where conditions were very poor.

In Britain, Germans, Austrians, and Italians were subjected to internment, although some of them, including Jewish refugees from Nazi Germany, were released. Some 40 years later, both the United States and Canada provided former internees with reparations, or payment for damages. For most, the compensation came too late.

Women Help Win the War As men joined the military, millions of women around the world replaced them in essential war industry jobs. Women, symbolized by the character **"Rosie the Riveter"** in the United States, built ships and planes and produced munitions.

British and American women served in the armed forces in many auxiliary roles—driving ambulances, delivering airplanes, and decoding messages. In occupied Europe, women fought in the resistance. Marie Fourcade, a French woman, helped downed Allied pilots escape to safety. Soviet women served in combat roles. Soviet pilot Lily Litvak, for example, shot down 12 German planes before she herself was killed.

☑ **IDENTIFY CENTRAL ISSUES** What changes did the Allies make at home to ensure that they had sufficient resources for fighting World War II?

Progress on Three Fronts

During 1942 and 1943, the Allies won several victories that would turn the tide of battle. They fought on three main fronts— in North Africa and Italy, in the Soviet Union, and in the Pacific.

Japan Suffers Setbacks In the Pacific, the Japanese suffered their first serious setback at the Battle of the Coral Sea. The battle lasted for five days in May 1942. For the first time in naval history,

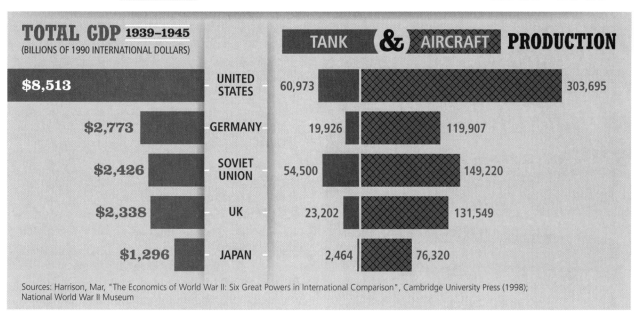

WWII GDP COMPARED TO AIRCRAFT AND TANK PRODUCTION 1939–1945

TOTAL GDP 1939–1945
(BILLIONS OF 1990 INTERNATIONAL DOLLARS)

TANK & AIRCRAFT PRODUCTION

	TOTAL GDP	TANK	AIRCRAFT
UNITED STATES	$8,513	60,973	303,695
GERMANY	$2,773	19,926	119,907
SOVIET UNION	$2,426	54,500	149,220
UK	$2,338	23,202	131,549
JAPAN	$1,296	2,464	76,320

Sources: Harrison, Mar, "The Economics of World War II: Six Great Powers in International Comparison", Cambridge University Press (1998); National World War II Museum

>> The Allies' commitment to all-out war meant a shift in manufacturing from commercial to military goods and equipment. Producing for the war effort also helped keep Americans employed. **Analyze Charts** What generalization can you make about GDP and war production based on the data in the chart?

ships engaged in a battle in which they never even saw each other. Attacks were carried out by planes launched from **aircraft carriers,** or ships that transport aircraft and accommodate the take-off and landing of airplanes. The Allies prevented Japan from seizing several important islands. More importantly, the Americans sank one Japanese aircraft carrier and several cruisers and destroyers.

This Allied victory was followed by an even more impressive win at the Battle of Midway in June 1942, which was also fought entirely from the air. The Americans destroyed four Japanese carriers and more than 250 planes. The battle was a devastating blow to the Japanese. After Midway, Japan was unable to launch any more offensive operations.

The loss was a setback to Japanese prime minister Hideki Tojo. Tojo, who also served as war minister, had been popular during Japan's string of victories. After Midway, he faced increasing opposition at home.

"Big Three" Strategize After the United States entered the war, the Allied leaders met periodically to hammer out their strategy. In 1942, the "Big Three"— Franklin Delano Roosevelt, Winston Churchill, and Joseph Stalin—agreed to focus on finishing the war in Europe before trying to end the war in Asia.

From the outset, the Allies distrusted one another. Churchill and Roosevelt feared that Stalin wanted to dominate Europe. Stalin believed the

West wanted to destroy communism. None of the new Allies wanted to risk a breakdown in their alliance, however. At a conference in Tehran, Iran, in late 1943, Churchill and Roosevelt yielded to Stalin by agreeing to let the borders outlined in the Nazi-Soviet Pact stand, against the wishes of Poland's government-in-exile.

Stalin also wanted Roosevelt and Churchill to open a second front against Germany in Western Europe to relieve the pressure on the Soviet Union. Roosevelt and Churchill replied that they did not yet have the resources. Stalin saw the delay as a deliberate policy to weaken the Soviet Union.

Victory in North Africa In North Africa, British forces led by General Bernard Montgomery fought Rommel. After the fierce Battle of El Alamein in November 1942, the Allies finally halted the Desert Fox's advance. Allied tanks drove the Axis back across Libya into Tunisia.

Later in 1942, American General **Dwight Eisenhower** took command of a joint British and American force in Morocco and Algeria. Advancing on Tunisia from the west, the Allies trapped Rommel's army, which surrendered in May 1943. However, Rommel himself never saw the end of the fighting in North Africa. He had returned to Germany after a final failed offensive in March.

Allied Invasion of Italy With North Africa under their control, the Allies were able to cross the Mediterranean into Italy. In July 1943, a combined British and American army landed first in Sicily and then in southern Italy. They defeated the Italian forces there in about a month.

After the defeats, the Italians overthrew Mussolini, dissolved the Fascist party, and signed an armistice, but fighting did not end. Hitler sent German troops to rescue Mussolini and stiffen the will of Italians fighting in the north.

For the next 18 months, the Allies pushed slowly up the Italian peninsula, suffering heavy losses against strong German resistance. Still, the Italian invasion was a decisive event for the Allies. It weakened Hitler by forcing him to fight on another front. And the German troops failed in their mission to rescue Mussolini.

Turning Point in Stalingrad A major turning point occurred in the Soviet Union. After their lightning advance in 1941, the Germans were stalled outside Moscow and Leningrad. In 1942, Hitler launched a

>> The Tehran conference was the first meeting of the Allied leaders. Roosevelt and Churchill sought to ensure Soviet cooperation with Allied war policies. Stalin agreed, but the American and British leaders had to make concessions to the Soviet dictator.

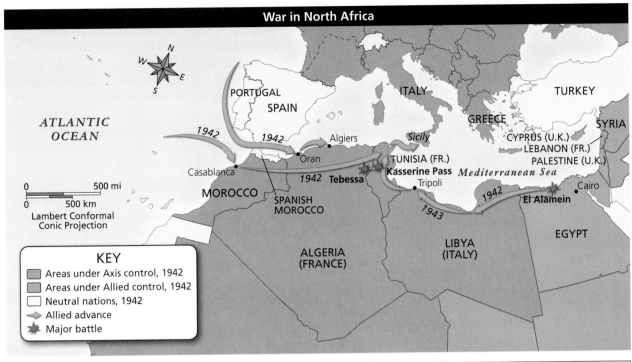

War in North Africa

KEY
- Areas under Axis control, 1942
- Areas under Allied control, 1942
- Neutral nations, 1942
- Allied advance
- Major battle

>> The Allies had tremendous challenges to overcome in order to regain control of western Europe and Africa from the Axis. **Analyze Maps** By what two routes did the Allies meet in Tunisia? What do you think was their reason for meeting at this location?

BOUNCE to Activate 3D Model

new offensive. This time, he aimed for the rich oil fields of the south.

His troops, however, got only as far as **Stalingrad.** The Battle of Stalingrad was one of the costliest of the war. Hitler was determined to capture Stalin's namesake city, and Stalin was equally determined to defend it. The battle began when the Germans surrounded the city.

As winter closed in, a bitter street-by-street, house-by-house struggle raged. A German officer wrote that soldiers fought for two weeks for a single building. Corpses "are strewn in the cellars, on the landings and the staircases," he said. In November, the Soviets encircled their attackers. Trapped, without food or ammunition and with no hope of rescue, the German commander finally surrendered in January 1943.

After the Battle of Stalingrad, the Red Army took the offensive and drove the invaders out of the Soviet Union entirely. Hitler's forces suffered irreplaceable losses of both troops and equipment. By early 1944, Soviet troops were advancing into Eastern Europe.

☑ **DRAW CONCLUSIONS** What was the impact of the Battles of Coral Sea and Midway?

A Second Front in Europe

By 1944, the Western Allies were at last ready to open a second front in Europe by invading France. General Dwight Eisenhower was made the supreme Allied commander. He and other Allied leaders faced the enormous task of planning the operation and assembling troops and supplies.

To prepare the way for the invasion, Allied bombers flew constant missions over Germany. They targeted factories and destroyed aircraft that might be used against the invasion force. They also destroyed many German cities and bombed railroads and bridges in France that could carry German troops and supplies to the front.

The Normandy Landings The Allies chose June 6, 1944—known as **D-Day**—for the invasion of France. Just before midnight on June 5, Allied planes dropped paratroopers behind enemy lines. Then, at dawn, thousands of ships ferried 156,000 Allied troops across the English Channel. The troops fought their way to shore amid underwater mines and raking machine-gun fire, and the casualties mounted as they reached the shore.

It all seemed unreal, a sort of dreaming while awake, men were screaming and dying all around me. . . . I honestly could have walked the full length of the beach without touching the ground, they were that thickly strewn about.

—Melvin B. Farrell, *War Memories*

The Liberation of France Despite heavy losses, the Allied troops clawed their way inland from the beaches of Normandy. In early August, a massive armored division under American General George S. Patton helped the joint British and American forces break through German defenses and advance toward Paris.

Meanwhile, other Allied forces sailed from Italy to land in southern France. In Paris, French resistance forces rose up against the occupying Germans. Under pressure from all sides, the Germans retreated. On August 25, the Allies entered Paris. Within a month, all of France was free.

Advancing Toward Germany After freeing France, Allied forces battled toward Germany. As their armies advanced into Belgium in December 1944, Germany launched a massive counterattack. At the bloody Battle of the Bulge, which lasted more than a month, both sides took terrible losses. The Germans drove the Allies back in several places, but were unable to break through. The battle delayed the Allied advance from the west, but only for six weeks. The Battle of the Bulge was Germany's last major offensive attack.

By this time, Germany was reeling under round-the-clock bombing. For two years, Allied bombers had hammered military bases, factories, railroads, oil depots, and cities. The goal of the bombing was to cripple Germany's industries and destroy the morale of its civilians.

By 1945, Germany could no longer defend itself in the air. In one 10-day period, bombing almost erased the huge industrial city of Hamburg, killing 40,000 civilians and forcing one million to flee their homes. In February 1945, Allied raids on Dresden killed as many as 135,000 people. The attack on Dresden later stirred controversy because the city was not an industrial center and had long been seen as one of Europe's most beautiful cities.

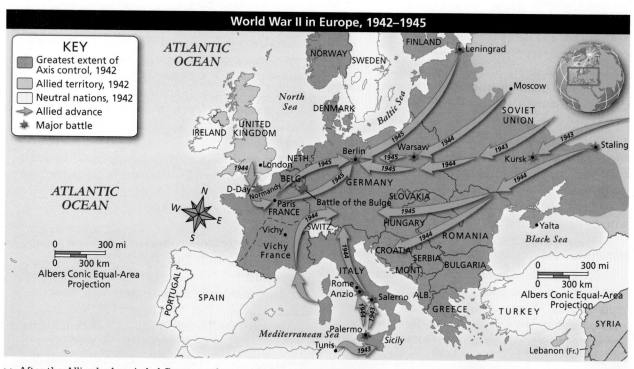

>> After the Allies had encircled Germany, they continued to bomb German industrial and military centers. German defenses were eliminated, and the European war came to an end. **Analyze Maps** From which direction did the Allies come when they launched the D-Day invasion?

BOUNCE to Activate Map

Meanwhile, the Soviet army battled through Germany and advanced on Berlin from the east. Hitler's support within Germany was declining, and he had already survived one assassination attempt by senior officers in the German military. By early 1945, the defeat of Germany seemed inevitable.

The Yalta Conference As the Allies advanced on Germany, the Big Three met in the Soviet city of Yalta. At the **Yalta Conference** in February 1945, Roosevelt, Churchill, and Stalin planned for the final stages of the war and for post-war Europe. The meeting took place in an atmosphere of distrust. Stalin insisted that the Soviet Union needed to maintain control of Eastern Europe to be able to protect itself from future aggression. Churchill and Roosevelt favored self-determination for Eastern Europe, which would give people the right to choose their own form of government. Although Stalin agreed to hold free elections in the newly liberated nations of Eastern Europe, he soon showed he had no intention of upholding that promise.

The three leaders also outlined a plan for postwar Germany. It would be temporarily divided into four zones, to be governed by American, French, British, and Soviet forces.

Although the war in Europe was almost over, the Allies were less certain of the outcome in the Pacific. Roosevelt and Churchill were eager to get the Russians to declare war on Japan. Stalin agreed that the Soviet Union would enter the war against Japan within three months of Germany's surrender. In return, Churchill and Roosevelt promised Stalin that the Soviets would take possession of southern Sakhalin Island, the Kuril Islands, and an occupation zone in Korea.

☑ **EXPLAIN** How did the Allied advance toward Germany limit that country's ability to wage war?

>> The Allies launched a massive invasion on the fortified beaches of Normandy, France. By the end of D-Day, they had a foothold in Nazi-occupied France and had taken a major step toward its liberation.

 BOUNCE to Activate Chart

☑ ASSESSMENT

1. **Draw Conclusions** What actions did democratic governments take during the war that many citizens would probably reject in peace time?

2. **Summarize** Describe the strategy involved in the invasion of Normandy on D-Day.

3. **Identify Cause and Effect** How did the total war effort in the United States affect the nation's economy?

4. **Identify Main Ideas** What was the significance of Hitler's offensive in the southern Soviet Union?

5. **Interpret** What challenges faced the Big Three at the Yalta Conference?

6. **Quest Connections** In 1998, American journalist Tom Brokaw coined the term "the Greatest Generation" to describe those Americans who fought in World War II or helped win it on the home front. List three reasons why you think he used this phrase.

🖥 **GO ONLINE** to access these biographies: Dwight Eisenhower, George S. Patton

The Allied strategy in Europe was to encircle Germany, advancing from the south, west, and east. Here, Soviet and American soldiers meet at the Elbe River in eastern Germany.

 BOUNCE to Activate Flipped Video

Objectives

Understand the reasons for the final defeat of the Nazis.

Describe how the Allies began to push back the Japanese in the Pacific.

Explain how the dropping of the atomic bombs ended the war.

Describe the aftermath of World War II and the founding of the United Nations.

Key Terms

V-E Day
Bataan Death March
"island-hopping"
Douglas MacArthur
kamikaze
Manhattan Project
Harry Truman
Hiroshima
Nagasaki
Nuremberg Trials
United Nations (UN)

Victory for the Allies

By early spring 1945, the war in Europe was nearing its end. That April, the Allies lost a key leader, Franklin Roosevelt. Though he did not live to see the final victory, he knew the defeat of the Nazis was inevitable.

End of the War in Europe

Germany Is Defeated By March 1945, the Allies had crossed the Rhine into western Germany. From the east, Soviet troops closed in on Berlin. In late April, American and Soviet soldiers met and shook hands at the Elbe River. All over Europe, Axis armies began to surrender.

In Italy, guerrillas captured and executed Mussolini. As Soviet troops fought their way into Berlin, Hitler committed suicide in his underground bunker. After just 12 years, Hitler's "thousand-year Reich" was bomb-ravaged and in ruins. On May 7, Germany surrendered.

Officially, the war in Europe ended the next day, May 8, 1945, which was proclaimed **V-E Day** (Victory in Europe).

Reasons for Victory in Europe The Allies were able to defeat the Axis powers in Europe for a number of reasons. By 1942, Germany and its allies had to fight on several fronts simultaneously. Hitler insisted on making major military decisions himself and some proved disastrous, especially the invasion of the Soviet Union. He underestimated the ability of the Soviet Union to fight in defense of their land.

The enormous productive capacity of the United States was another factor. By 1944, the United States was producing twice as much as all of the Axis powers combined. Meanwhile, Allied bombing hindered German production. Oil became so scarce because of bombing that the Luftwaffe was almost grounded by the time of the D-Day invasion.

With victory in Europe achieved, the Allies could focus all their attention on defeating Japan in the Pacific. There, they still faced stiff opposition.

☑ **INFER** Why were the Allies able to defeat the Axis in Europe?

Battles in the Pacific

During the war in the Pacific, the Japanese at first won a string of victories. They also controlled much of China and Southeast Asia. Despite the early Japanese advances, the Allies slowly turned the tide.

Bataan Death March Just hours after Pearl Harbor, the Japanese bombed the Philippines, which the United States had controlled since 1898. By May 1942, the Japanese had gained control of the islands. After the U.S. and Filipino defenders of Bataan surrendered, the Japanese forced their prisoners to

march more than 60 miles in incredible heat with almost no water or food. The cruel **Bataan Death March** resulted in the death of as many as 10,000 prisoners.

One survivor described the ordeal as "a macabre litany of heat, dust, starvation, thirst, flies, filth, stench, murder, torture, corpses, and wholesale brutality that numbs the memory." Many Filipino civilians risked—and sometimes lost—their lives to give food and water to captives on the march.

Americans Take the Offensive After the battle of Midway, the United States took the offensive. That summer, United States Marines landed at Guadalcanal in the Solomon Islands. Victory at Guadalcanal marked the beginning of an **"island-hopping"** campaign. The goal of the campaign was to recapture some Japanese-held islands while bypassing others. Each captured island served as a stepping stone to the next objective. As a result, American forces, led by General **Douglas MacArthur,** gradually moved north towards Japan.

On the captured islands, the Americans built air bases to enable them to carry the war closer to Japan. By 1944, the United States Navy, commanded by Admiral Chester Nimitz, was blockading Japan, and American bombers pounded Japanese cities

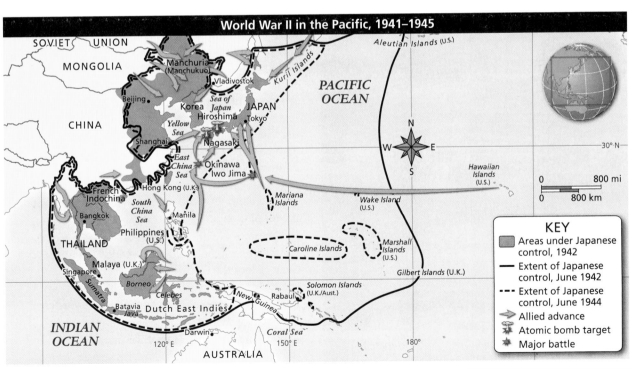

>> After winning the war in Europe, the Allies poured all their resources into victory in the Pacific theater. **Analyze Maps** Based on the map, how would you describe the Allied strategy to defeat Japan?

▶ BOUNCE to Activate Map

>> Kamikaze attacks were a desperate attempt to ward off American advances. Japanese pilots crashed into Allied aircraft carriers and other ships, killing American sailors along with themselves.

>> President Harry S. Truman and U.S. Secretary of State James Byrne examine a map of Europe aboard the U.S.S. *Augusta* on their way to the "big three" conference in Potsdam in the summer of 1945.

and industries. In October 1944, MacArthur began the fight to retake the Philippines. The British, meanwhile, were pushing Japanese forces back into the jungles of Burma and Malaya. Despite such setbacks, the militarists who dominated the Japanese government rejected any suggestions of surrender.

☑ **INFER** Why might a naval blockade prove to be an effective war strategy?

End of the War in the Pacific

With war won in Europe, the Allies poured their resources into defeating Japan. By mid-1945, most of the Japanese navy and air force had been destroyed. Yet the Japanese still had an army of two million men. The road to victory, it appeared, would be long and costly.

Japanese Resistance As American forces closed in on Japan, the Japanese put up fierce resistance. By 1944, young Japanese **kamikaze** (kah muh KAH zee) pilots were undertaking suicide missions, crashing their explosive-laden airplanes into American warships.

The next year, in bloody battles on the islands of Iwo Jima from February to March 1945 and Okinawa from April to July 1945, Japanese forces showed that they would fight to the death rather than surrender. Some American officials estimated that an invasion of Japan would cost a million or more casualties.

A Powerful New Weapon While Allied military leaders planned for invasion, scientists offered another way to end the war. Since the early 1900s, scientists had understood that matter, made up of atoms, could be converted into pure energy. In military terms, this meant that by splitting the atom, scientists could create an explosion far more powerful than any yet known.

During the war, Allied scientists—some of them German and Italian refugees—raced to harness the atom before the Germans could. In July 1945, the top secret **Manhattan Project** successfully tested the first atomic bomb at Alamogordo, New Mexico.

News of this test was brought to the new American president, **Harry Truman.** He realized that the atomic bomb was a terrible new force for destruction. Still, after consulting with his advisors, he decided to use the new weapon against Japan. Truman believed that dropping the atomic bomb would bring the war to a faster end and save American lives.

At the time, Truman was meeting with other Allied leaders in the city of Potsdam, Germany. They issued a warning to Japan to surrender or face "complete destruction" and "utter devastation." When the Japanese ignored the warning, the United States took action.

Dropping of the Atomic Bombs On August 6, 1945, an American plane dropped an atomic bomb over the city of **Hiroshima.** The bomb flattened four square miles and instantly killed more than 70,000 people. In the months that followed, many more would die from radiation sickness, a deadly aftereffect of exposure to radioactive materials.

Truman warned the Japanese that if they did not surrender, they could expect "a rain of ruin from the air, the like of which has never been seen on this Earth." And on August 8, the Soviet Union declared war on Japan and invaded Manchuria. Again, Japanese leaders did not respond. The next day, the United States dropped a second atomic bomb, this time on the city of **Nagasaki.** More than 40,000 people were killed in this second explosion.

Some members of the Japanese cabinet wanted to fight on. Other leaders disagreed. Finally, on August 10, Emperor Hirohito intervened, an action unheard of for a Japanese emperor. He forced his government to surrender. On September 2, 1945, the formal peace treaty was signed on board the American battleship *Missouri,* anchored in Tokyo Bay. After more than five years of fighting, World War II was over.

An Ongoing Controversy Using the atomic bomb against Japan brought a quick end to World War II. It also unleashed terrifying destruction. Ever since, people have debated whether or not the United States should have used the bomb.

Truman later said he made his decision based only on military considerations. He was concerned that Japan would not surrender without an invasion that would cost an enormous loss of lives. After all, the Japanese still had a home army of 2 million.

Critics of Truman's decision argued that Japan was almost defeated at that point and the bomb was not needed. They also claim that by using the atomic bomb, the United States unleashed a dangerous arms race that grew over the next decades. Some critics think that racism may also have played a role in the willingness to bomb Japanese civilians.

Growing differences between the United States and the Soviet Union may also have influenced

>> After Japan failed to accept Allied surrender terms, Truman ordered the atomic bombings of Hiroshima and Nagasaki. The destruction was unlike anything the world had seen.

🅑 BOUNCE to Activate Timeline

Truman's decision. Truman may have hoped the bomb would impress the Soviets with American power. The debate over Truman's decision has continued to the present.

☑ **INTERPRET** What was the purpose of the declaration issued by the Allies at Potsdam?

Aftermath of the War

Even as the Allies celebrated victory, the appalling costs of the war began to emerge. The war had killed as many as 50 million people around the world. In Europe alone, over 30 million people had lost their lives, more than half of them civilians. The Soviet Union suffered the worst casualties, with over 20 million dead.

Europe in Ruins "Give me ten years and you will not be able to recognize Germany," Hitler had predicted in 1933. Indeed, Germany in 1945 was an unrecognizable ruin. Parts of Poland, the Soviet Union, Japan, China, and other countries also lay in ruins. Total war had gutted cities, factories, harbors, bridges, railroads, farms, and homes.

>> Representatives of the four major Allies sat in judgment of Nazi war criminals. It was the first time that war criminals were punished for "crimes against humanity" during war.

>> Prime Minister Tojo did not have the same totalitarian powers as Hitler and Mussolini. Still, he was tried and executed for war crimes committed by Japan during the war.

Over 20 million refugees wandered Europe. Amid the devastation, hunger, disease, and mental illness took their toll for years after the fighting ended. As they had after World War I, the Allies faced difficult decisions about the future.

The Holocaust Is Revealed Numbers alone did not tell the story of the Nazi nightmare in Europe or the Japanese brutality in Asia. During the war, the Allies were aware of the existence of Nazi concentration camps and death camps. But only at war's end did they learn the full extent of the inhumanity of the Holocaust. American General Dwight Eisenhower, who visited the camps, was stunned to come "face to face with indisputable evidence of Nazi brutality and ruthless disregard of every sense of decency."

War Crimes Trials At wartime meetings, the Allies had agreed that Axis leaders should be tried for "crimes against humanity." In Germany, the Allies held the **Nuremberg Trials** in the city where Hitler had staged mass rallies in the 1930s. Nearly 200 Germans and Austrians were tried for war crimes. Most were found guilty. A handful of top Nazis received death sentences. Others were imprisoned.

Similar war crimes trials were held in Italy and Japan. Among those found guilty and executed was Japanese prime minister Tojo. Many of those accused of war crimes were never captured or brought to trial. However, the trials showed that political and military leaders could be held accountable for actions in wartime.

The war crimes trials served another purpose. By exposing the savagery of the Axis regimes, they further discredited the totalitarian and militarist ideologies that had led to the war. Yet disturbing questions remained. Why had ordinary people in Germany, Poland, France, and elsewhere accepted—and even collaborated in—Hitler's "Final Solution"? How could the world prevent dictators from again terrorizing Europe or Asia?

The Allies tried to address those issues when they occupied Germany and Japan. The United States felt that strengthening democracy would ensure tolerance and peace. The Western Allies built new governments in occupied Germany and Japan with democratic constitutions to protect the rights of all citizens. In German schools, for example, Nazi textbooks and courses were replaced with a new curriculum that taught democratic principles. In Japan, the occupying forces under General MacArthur helped Japanese politicians to create a new constitution that gave power to the Japanese people, rather than the emperor and military elite.

Impact of the War on Japan The new constitution was part of a massive postwar transformation in Japan. Gone were the extreme militarists that had set Japan on a course of aggression and empire. Although Emperor Hirohito remained on the throne, he was a figurehead. The Japanese military was largely disbanded. To enforce the constitution and oversee the rebuilding of Japan, the country remained under Allied military occupation until 1952. For the only time in its history, Japan was under the control of a foreign power.

Like Germany, Japan had to deal with the effects of conventional bombing. Allied raids had devastated many major cities. The firebombing of Tokyo alone killed an estimated 100,000 people, left one million homeless, and destroyed some 16 square miles of the city.

But Japan was also the first nation to face the aftereffects of atomic warfare. The casualties did not end with the bombings of Hiroshima and Nagasaki. Many who survived the blasts died afterwards from radiation sickness. The full impact on such conditions as cancer and birth defects, as well as the psychological effects, are still being debated.

☑ **ANALYZE INFORMATION** What were the main goals of the Allies' post-war policies toward the defeated Axis countries?

The United Nations Is Formed

In April 1945, delegates from 50 nations convened in San Francisco to draft a charter for the **United Nations (UN).** They hoped that, unlike the ineffective League of Nations, the UN would be able to keep peace among nations by providing a forum where differences could be resolved peacefully. In the years to follow, the UN would play a greater role in world affairs than its predecessor did.

Structure of the United Nations Under the UN Charter, each of the member nations has one vote in the General Assembly. A much smaller body called the Security Council has greater power. Each of its five permanent members—the United States, the Soviet Union (today Russia), Britain, France, and China—has the right to veto any council decision. The goal was to give these great powers the authority to ensure the peace.

The Security Council has the power to apply economic sanctions or send a peace-keeping military force to try to resolve disputes. Still, differences

>> In 1948, Ralph Bunche served as UN mediator in negotiating a ceasefire between Israel and Egypt. He became the first African American to win the Nobel Peace Prize. **Infer** How did Bunche's work reflect the goals of the United Nations?

between the United States and the Soviet Union often hampered Security Council decisions. Since the fall of the Soviet Union in 1991, more peacekeeping delegations have been approved.

UN Activities Over time, the work of the UN would go far beyond peacekeeping. It has taken on many issues from human rights and economic development to health and education. UN agencies have worked to end diseases such as smallpox and set up vaccination programs around the world. It has set up refugee camps and organized resettlement programs for refugees from war zones. It has worked with national governments to reduce poverty and protect the environment.

From the first, the UN has faced critics. Some have argued that the UN is ineffective in preventing or resolving conflicts. Others claim that UN resolutions interfere with national governments or are biased. Differences have also risen between rich industrial nations and the poorer nations of the world. And some smaller nations have criticized the veto power of the five permanent members of the Security Council.

☑ **CONTRAST** What is the difference between the United Nations General Assembly and the Security Council?

☑ ASSESSMENT

1. **Draw Conclusions** How did wartime production of resources play a role in Hitler's final defeat?

2. **Distinguish** Which military campaign did the victory at Guadalcanal initiate?

3. **Infer** Why did Japanese emperor Hirohito call for Japan to surrender?

4. **Cite Evidence** How costly was World War II in terms of European and Soviet casualties?

5. **Summarize** How were the Nazis' "crimes against humanity" dealt with at the Nuremberg trials?

6. **Quest Connections** Some people argue that the scientists who worked on the Manhattan Project were as important to the Allied victory as the soldiers who fought. Give one reason for and one reason against this viewpoint.

GO ONLINE to access this biography: Chester Nimitz

Charter of the United Nations

Introduction

After World War I, more than 50 countries joined together to form the League of Nations. The League was supposed to prevent future wars by providing a forum for the peaceful settlement of international disputes. The United States never joined the League.

The idea of an international peacekeeping organization was revisited after World War II. In 1944, representatives from the United States, the Soviet Union, China, and the United Kingdom met for several months to work out the framework for the United Nations.

In 1945, representatives of 50 countries met in San Francisco to sign the United Nations charter, bringing the organization into being.

Here are the preamble and first two articles of that charter.

>> The United Nations

Primary Source

We the peoples of the united nations determined

- to save succeeding [later] generations from the scourge of war, which twice in our lifetime has brought untold sorrow to mankind, and
- to reaffirm faith in fundamental human rights, in the dignity and worth of the human person, in the equal rights of men and women and of nations large and small, and
- to establish conditions under which justice and respect for the obligations arising from treaties and other sources of international law can be maintained, and
- to promote social progress and better standards of life in larger freedom,

And for these ends

- to practice tolerance and live together in peace with one another as good neighbours, and
- to unite our strength to maintain international peace and security, and

- to ensure, by the acceptance of principles and the institution of methods, that armed force shall not be used, save in the common interest, and
- to employ international machinery for the promotion of the economic and social advancement of all peoples,

Have resolved to combine our efforts to accomplish these aims

Accordingly, our respective Governments, through representatives assembled in the city of San Francisco, who have exhibited their full powers found to be in good and due form, have agreed to the present Charter of the United Nations and do hereby establish an international organization to be known as the United Nations.

Chapter 1: purposes and principles
Article 1

The Purposes of the United Nations are:

1. To maintain international peace and security, and to that end: to take effective collective measures for the prevention and removal of threats

to the peace, and for the suppression of acts of aggression or other breaches of the peace, and to bring about by peaceful means, and in conformity with the principles of justice and international law, adjustment or settlement of international disputes or situations which might lead to a breach of the peace;

2. To develop friendly relations among nations based on respect for the principle of equal rights and self-determination of peoples, and to take other appropriate measures to strengthen universal peace;

3. To achieve international co-operation in solving international problems of an economic, social, cultural, or humanitarian character, and in promoting and encouraging respect for human rights and for fundamental freedoms for all without distinction as to race, sex, language, or religion; and

4. To be a centre for harmonizing the actions of nations in the attainment of these common ends.

Article 2

The Organization and its Members, in pursuit of the Purposes stated in Article 1, shall act in accordance with the following Principles.

1. The Organization is based on the principle of the sovereign equality of all its Members.

2. All Members, in order to ensure to all of them the rights and benefits resulting from membership, shall fulfill in good faith the obligations assumed by them in accordance with the present Charter.

3. All Members shall settle their international disputes by peaceful means in such a manner that international peace and security, and justice, are not endangered.

4. All Members shall refrain in their international relations from the threat or use of force against the territorial integrity or political independence of any state, or in any other manner inconsistent with the Purposes of the United Nations.

5. All Members shall give the United Nations every assistance in any action it takes in accordance with

the present Charter, and shall refrain from giving assistance to any state against which the United Nations is taking preventive or enforcement action.

6. The Organization shall ensure that states which are not Members of the United Nations act in accordance with these Principles so far as may be necessary for the maintenance of international peace and security.

7. Nothing contained in the present Charter shall authorize the United Nations to intervene in matters which are essentially within the domestic jurisdiction of any state or shall require the Members to submit such matters to settlement under the present Charter; but this principle shall not prejudice the application of enforcement measures under Chapter VII.

☑ **PARAPHRASE** Paraphrase Article 1, Purpose 1.

☑ ASSESSMENT

1. **Cite Evidence** The government of a country is inflicting terrible human rights abuses on members of the opposition party. Based on the excerpt, can the United Nations intervene? Cite the part(s) of the charter that support your opinion.

2. **Explain an Argument** Several years of drought in western Asia have led to widespread famine. The UN arranges to bring convoys of food to starving people. One country, a member of the UN, does not want to let relief workers come inside its borders. Does any part of the charter cited here support or rebut the country's position? Explain your answer.

3. **Draw Conclusions** Has the United Nations been successful in its mission "to save succeeding generations from the scourge of war"? Explain your answer.

GO ONLINE to access primary sources

Connections to Today

Visitors to the United States Holocaust Memorial Museum in Washington, D.C., view photographs of victims of Nazi genocide.

Take Action About Remembering the Holocaust

The Holocaust is one of the most well-documented events in history. Yet there are people today who, due to anti-Jewish prejudice, try to deny that it happened. And every year, fewer survivors remain. As a result, efforts to remember the Holocaust have become increasingly important.

1. **Choose** one of these ways people today work to keep the memory of the Holocaust alive.

   - **Memorials and Museums:** In addition to the United States Holocaust Memorial Museum in Washington, D.C., there are Holocaust memorials in 30 states.

   - **Media:** Movies about the Holocaust include *Schindler's List, The Boy in the Striped Pajamas,* and *Defiance.*

   - **Testimony:** Groups like Stephen Spielberg's Shoah Foundation and Fortunoff Video Archives for Holocaust Testimony record the stories of survivors.

2. **Ask Questions** How do the people or organizations you are researching work to keep the memory of the Holocaust alive? Write a list of questions you would ask them about their work.

3. **Learn** Do research on the subject you have chosen. There are many online resources, including Holocaust memorial museums. (Unfortunately, there are also websites devoted to denying the Holocaust. Your teacher can help you determine reliable online resources.)

4. **Take Action** Write a blog post describing what you learned from your research, how it affected you, and why you think it is important to preserve the memory of the Holocaust.

LESSON SUMMARIES

Use these Lesson Summaries, and the longer versions available online, to review the key ideas for each lesson in this Topic.

Lesson 1: Aggression, Appeasement, and War

Dictators in Germany and Italy, along with militarists in Japan, pursued ambitious goals for empire. Dictators took aggressive action but met only verbal protests and pleas for peace from the democracies.

Lesson 2: Axis Powers Advance

The early years of World War II were marked by Axis victories. Germany invaded Poland and soon country after country gave way to Axis powers. With the fall of France in 1940, Britain stood alone in Western Europe.

Lesson 3: The Holocaust

Before the war, Hitler started his policy of persecuting people he considered "racially inferior," particularly Jews. Eventually, millions of European Jews were sent to death camps and murdered in what became known as the Holocaust. Almost as many other people the Nazis viewed as "undesirable" were killed as well.

Lesson 4: The Allies Turn the Tide

In 1942 and 1943, the tide of the war began to turn as Allied forces won key victories. By 1944, the Allies were ready to open a second front in Europe—with the planned D-Day invasion of France. With France free, focus turned on conquering Germany and defeating Japan.

Lesson 5: Victory for the Allies

After freeing France, Allies closed in on Germany from both the east and west. Germany surrendered. In August 1945, American planes dropped atomic bombs on Hiroshima and Nagasaki. Japan surrendered.

QUEST! FINDINGS

Create Your World War II Tribute Refer to your responses to the Quest Connections to help you prepare your presentation to share with the class. Use the rubric and other Quest resources online to guide your work.

GO ONLINE to access lesson summaries

VISUAL REVIEW

Use these graphics to review some of the key terms, people, and ideas from this Topic.

Key Causes of World War II

- Failure of Word War I peace settlement, Treaty of Versailles
- Global economic depression
- Fascism, militarism, and imperialism in Germany, Italy, and Japan
- Weakness of the League of Nations
- British and French appeasement

Key Political Leaders

Allies
- Franklin Delano Roosevelt, *U.S. president*
- Harry S Truman, *U.S. president*
- Neville Chamberlain, *British prime minister*
- Winston Churchill, *British prime minister*
- Joseph Stalin, *Soviet dictator*
- Charles de Gaulle, *leader of Free French*

Axis Powers
- Adolf Hitler, *German dictator*
- Benito Mussolini, *Italian dictator*
- Hirohito, *Japanese emperor*
- Tojo Hideki, *Japanese prime minister*

Reasons for Allied Victory

Location of Germany—surrounded by enemies
Location of Japan—dependent on imported goods
Poor military decisions by Axis leaders
Huge productive capability of the United States
Better technology developed and used by Allies

Acts of Aggression

1931	Japan invades Manchuria
1935	Italy invades Ethiopia
1938	Germany annexes Austria and Czechoslovakia
1939	Germany invades Poland. World War II begins

KEY TERMS, PEOPLE, AND IDEAS

1. Why did the western democracies adopt a policy of **appeasement** in response to Axis aggression?

2. Did the **Lend Lease Act** violate America's stand of neutrality during the beginning of WWII? Explain.

3. Why were Hitler's **blitzkrieg** tactics successful at the beginning of the war?

4. What were the expectations of Stalin, Roosevelt, and Churchill at their 1943 strategy meeting in Tehran?

5. Why did Allied nations limit individual rights during the war? How were rights limited?

6. Why did Hitler begin a campaign against the Jews? How did it become the **Holocaust?**

7. What was the Bataan Death March?

8. How did the **Nuremberg Trials** change the way the global community felt about human rights?

CRITICAL THINKING

9. **Summarize** List the causes of WWII. Then consider the statement made by some historians that WWII was the continuation of WWI. Do you agree or disagree? Explain your position.

10. **Draw Conclusions** What post-war plans did the Allies have? What decisions were made at the Yalta Conference?

11. **Analyze Maps** Look at the map below. What does it show about the scope of the Normandy invasion? Why did the Allies choose to invade Normandy? What challenges did the Allies face?

12. **Analyze Information** Discuss the German, Italian, and Japanese drives for power in the 1930s. Create a graphic organizer that lists the locations and dates of Axis aggression, the motivating factors, and the results of the campaigns.

13. **Writing Activity: Write an Argument** The excerpt below is from a speech Winston Churchill gave in Parliament about the Munich Pact.

> "And do not suppose that this is the end. This is only the beginning of the reckoning. This is only the first sip, the first foretaste of a bitter cup which will be pre-offered to us year by year unless by a supreme recovery of moral health and martial vigour, we arise again and take our stand for freedom as in the olden time."
> —*Winston Churchill, October 5, 1938*

Write a two-paragraph response to his speech. In the first paragraph, summarize his opinion of the Pact, his reasons, and the action he favors. In the second paragraph, explain whether you would have supported his view. Remember that, at the time, you would not have known what would happen in the next few years.

14. **Connections to Today** (a) In what ways did women support the Allied war effort? Give three examples. (b) How have women's roles in the military changed since World War II? (c) Today, 1940s images of Rosie the Riveter still appear on posters, t-shirts, and elsewhere. Why do you think the character of Rosie has remained such a powerful symbol for many women?

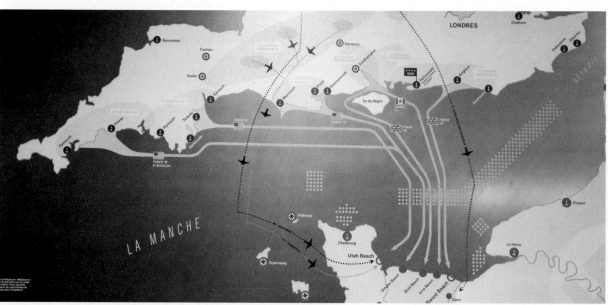

DOCUMENT-BASED QUESTIONS

Perhaps no decision in American history has been more hotly debated than Harry S Truman's decision to drop atomic bombs on Hiroshima and Nagasaki, Japan, in August 1945. Read the documents below, then answer the questions that follow.

DOCUMENT A

"It was believed with deep apprehension that many thousands, probably tens of thousands, of lives of Allied combatants would have been spent in the continuation of our air and sea bombardment and blockade. . . . But the people who would have suffered most, had the war gone on much longer and their country invaded, were the Japanese. One American incendiary air raid on the Tokyo area in March 1945 did more damage and killed and injured more Japanese than the bomb on Hiroshima."

—*The Atomic Bomb and the End of World War II* by Herbert Feis

DOCUMENT B

"Even without the use of the atomic bombs, the war would probably have ended before an American invasion of Kyushu [one of the four main islands of Japan] became necessary. Conditions in Japan were steadily deteriorating . . . The destruction of cities from B-29 raids, diminishing food supplies, [and] decreased public morale fostered enough discontent to worry the emperor and his advisors. . . . Even without the atomic attacks, it seems likely that the emperor at some point would have acted in the same way that he did in the aftermath of Hiroshima to end the war."

—*Prompt and Utter Destruction: Truman and the Use of Atomic Bombs Against Japan* by J. Samuel Walker

DOCUMENT C

In the spring of 1945, the Allies' island-hopping campaign in the Pacific brought them closer to the heart of Japan. When American troops invaded first the island of Iwo Jima, then the island of Okinawa, the Japanese fought fiercely, but unsuccessfully, to keep them from gaining control. They knew that the Allies planned to use the islands as a base for an invasion of Japan itself.

Troops Killed at Iwo Jima and Okinawa, 1945

BATTLE	JAPANESE TROOPS KILLED	AMERICAN TROOPS KILLED
Iwo Jima	21,000	6,800
Okinawa	100,000	12,000

SOURCE: Encyclopedia Britannica

DOCUMENT D

15. Which of the following cities experienced the most damage from the American bombing raids?
    A. Tokyo
    B. Yokohama
    C. Hiroshima
    D. Osaka

16. Which of the following statement BEST summarizes Herbert Feis's explanation for Truman's use of the atomic bomb?
    A. Use of the atomic bombs would cause more destruction.
    B. Use of the atomic bombs would save lives.
    C. Use of the atomic bombs would ensure surrender.
    D. Use of the atomic bombs would make it more difficult for Japan to rebuild its military.

17. J. Samuel Walker's main argument against the use of atomic bombs is that
    A. atomic bombs were more destructive than conventional bombs.
    B. an American invasion would not have been as destructive as the bombs.
    C. the war would have ended anyway.
    D. the Japanese emperor opposed the use of atomic bombs.

18. **Writing Tasks** Which of the historians quoted in Documents A and B do you agree with most strongly? Why? Use your knowledge of World War II and specific evidence from the documents to support your opinion.

GO ONLINE to access more practice

The Cold War Era (1945–1991)

ESSENTIAL QUESTION How Should We Handle Conflict?

Protesters on the Berlin Wall, 1989

Connections to Today

Today, global humanitarian assistance—which includes emergency crisis assistance, poverty assistance, and development assistance—is provided to millions of people living in nearly 81 countries. After World War II, humanitarian aid to millions of survivors in war-torn countries became a huge international effort. The United Nations Relief and Rehabilitation Administration, and the Marshall Plan were instrumental in this effort. In this topic, you will learn about the impact of the Marshall Plan on the recovery of post-war Europe. How effective is humanitarian aid today?

NBC LEARN

Hear a former resident of East Germany describe life behind the iron curtain during the Cold War.

BOUNCE to Activate My Story Video

Topic 19 Overview

In this Topic, you will learn about the events of the Cold War era. Look at the lesson outline and explore the timeline. As you study this Topic, you will complete the Quest team inquiry.

LESSON OUTLINE

19.1 A New Global Conflict

19.2 The Western Democracies and Japan

19.3 Communism in East Asia

19.4 War in Southeast Asia

19.5 The Cold War Ends

Key Events of the Cold War

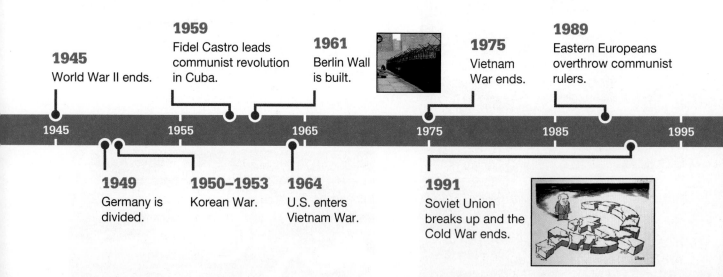

1945
World War II ends.

1959
Fidel Castro leads communist revolution in Cuba.

1961
Berlin Wall is built.

1975
Vietnam War ends.

1989
Eastern Europeans overthrow communist rulers.

1945 · 1955 · 1965 · 1975 · 1985 · 1995

1949
Germany is divided.

1950–1953
Korean War.

1964
U.S. enters Vietnam War.

1991
Soviet Union breaks up and the Cold War ends.

QUEST! INQUIRY

Launching a Seminar

Did the end of the Cold War make the world safer? You are part of an international affairs seminar for a Cold War Studies institute. In this Quest, you will prepare a presentation that addresses that question.

 STEP 1
Review what you already know about the rivalry between the U.S. and the Soviet Union after WWII. Read and evaluate the primary sources. Ask questions.

 STEP 2
In addition to the primary sources, interview one or two people who lived through that era. Gather all your information. Divide the groups into YES or NO groups. Create a preliminary outline of your presentation.

 STEP 3
As you prepare your presentations, use charts, timelines, and maps to support your viewpoint. Review, edit, and revise.

 STEP 4
Consider opposing arguments. Then have the "institute" members vote on a decision. What did you learn from the opposing group? Reflect on the effect of the Cold War on present international affairs.

GO ONLINE to access complete Quest materials

Churchill, Truman, and Stalin shake hands at the Potsdam Conference, held in Germany in July, 1945. Still at war with Japan, the leaders of the wartime alliance hid the growing tensions among them.

BOUNCE to Activate Flipped Video

Objectives

Summarize how the outcome of World War II contributed to the development of the Cold War.

Identify continuing Cold War conflicts in Germany and Eastern Europe.

Explain the growth of the nuclear arms race.

Analyze how the Cold War became a global conflict.

Compare the United States and the Soviet Union in the Cold War.

Key Terms

superpower
Cold War
Truman Doctrine
containment
Marshall Plan
North Atlantic Treaty
   Organization
   (NATO)
Warsaw Pact
détente
Fidel Castro
John F. Kennedy
ideology
Nikita Khrushchev
Leonid Brezhnev

A New Global Conflict

Amid the rubble of war, a new power structure emerged. In Europe, Germany was defeated. France and Britain were exhausted. Two other powers, the United States and the Soviet Union, emerged as superpowers, nations with the economic resources and military might to dominate the globe. The United States abandoned its traditional policy of isolationism to counter what President Truman saw as the communist threat.

Wartime Alliance Breaks Apart

Tensions Grow Among the Allies During the war, the Soviet Union and the nations of the West had cooperated to defeat Nazi Germany. However, differences between the two nations were long apparent before the end of WWII. The relationship had long been a tense one. The United States did not trust Soviet Russia and remained concerned about Joseph Stalin's tyrannical rule of his country. An embargo that the United States imposed against Germany was extended to include Russia.

In turn, the Russians resented the refusal of the United States, during the 1920s, to recognize their government and to accept them as a legitimate part of the international community. They also blamed the late entry of the United States into WWII for the deaths of millions of Russians. By 1945, the wartime alliance was crumbling. Conflicting ideologies and mutual distrust soon led to the conflict known as the Cold War.

The **Cold War** was a state of tension and hostility between nations aligned with the United States on one side, and the Soviet

GO ONLINE to access your digital course

Union on the other side. There was no armed conflict between the United States and the Soviet Union, the major rivals during the Cold War.

At wartime conferences and postwar discussions, the Allies had forged a united front. At the Yalta Conference, Churchill and Roosevelt accepted some of Stalin's demands regarding Eastern Europe. They also agreed to the Allied occupation of Germany and the principle of reparations. Despite these agreements, tensions among the Allies deepened once the war ended, helping to create a divided world during the Cold War.

The Cold War Begins At first, the focus of the Cold War was Eastern Europe. Stalin had two main goals in Eastern Europe. First, he wanted to spread communism into the area. Second, he wanted to create a buffer zone of friendly governments as a defense against Germany, which had invaded Russia during World War I and again in 1941.

As the Red Army pushed German forces out of Eastern Europe, it left behind occupying forces. The Soviet dictator pointed out that the United States was not consulting the Soviet Union about peace terms for Italy or Japan, both of which were defeated and occupied by American and British troops. In the same way, the Soviet Union would determine the fate of the Eastern European lands that it occupied.

Roosevelt and Churchill rejected Stalin's view, making him promise "free elections" in Eastern Europe. Stalin ignored that pledge. Most Eastern European countries had existing Communist parties, many of which had actively resisted the Nazis during the war. Backed by the Red Army, these local Communists in Poland, Czechoslovakia, and elsewhere destroyed rival political parties and even assassinated democratic leaders. By 1948, pro-Soviet communist governments were in place throughout Eastern Europe.

☑ **GENERATE EXPLANATIONS** What postwar issues caused the Western Allies and the Soviet Union to disagree?

Soviet Aggression Grows

Stalin soon showed his aggressive intentions outside of Eastern Europe. In Greece, Stalin backed communist rebels who were fighting to overturn a right-wing monarchy supported by Britain. By 1947, however, Britain could no longer afford to defend Greece. Stalin was also menacing Turkey and the vital shipping lane through the Dardanelles.

The Iron Curtain In 1946, Winston Churchill, former prime minister of Britain, spoke of how the Soviet Union was sealing off the countries in Eastern Europe that its armies had occupied at the end of World War II. He said an "iron curtain has descended across the Continent."

In the West, the "iron curtain" became a symbol of the Cold War fear of communism. It described the division of Europe into an "eastern" and a "western" bloc. In the East were the Soviet-dominated, communist countries of Eastern Europe. In the West were the Western democracies led by the United States.

The Truman Doctrine President Truman saw communism as an evil force threatening countries around the world. To deal with the growing communist threat in Greece and Turkey, he took action. On March 12, 1947, Truman outlined a new policy to Congress. The policy, known as the **Truman Doctrine,** was rooted in the idea of **containment,** limiting communism to the areas already under Soviet control. Stalin, however, saw containment as "encirclement" by the capitalist world that wanted to isolate the Soviet Union.

>> The Red Army entered Berlin in April 1945. The Soviets installed communist governments in East Germany and throughout Eastern Europe in the postwar years.

The Truman Doctrine would guide the United States for decades. It made clear that Americans would resist Soviet expansion in Europe or elsewhere in the world. Truman soon sent military and economic aid and advisers to Greece and Turkey so that they could withstand the communist threat.

Marshall Plan Aids Europe Postwar hunger and poverty made Western European lands fertile ground for communist ideas. To strengthen democratic governments, the United States offered a massive aid package called the **Marshall Plan.** Under it, the United States funneled food and economic assistance to Europe to help countries rebuild. Billions of dollars in American aid helped war-shattered Europe recover rapidly and reduced communist influence there.

President Truman also offered aid to the Soviet Union and its satellites, or dependent states, in Eastern Europe. However, Stalin declined and forbade Eastern European countries to accept American aid. Instead, he promised help from the Soviet Union in its place.

A Divided Germany Defeated Germany became another focus of the growing tensions between the Soviet Union and the United States. The Soviets took reparations for their massive war losses by dismantling and moving factories and other resources from its occupation zone to help rebuild the Soviet Union. Above all, the Soviets feared the danger of a restored Germany.

The Western powers also took some reparations, but they wanted to create a stable, democratic Germany. Therefore, they united their zones of occupation and encouraged Germans to rebuild industries with Marshall Plan aid. The Soviets were furious at this move and strengthened their hold on Eastern Germany.

Germany became a divided nation. In West Germany, the Western democracies let the people write a constitution and regain self-government. In East Germany, the Soviets installed a socialist dictatorship tied to Moscow.

The Berlin Airlift Stalin's resentment at Western moves to rebuild Germany triggered a crisis over Berlin. Even though it lay deep within the Soviet zone, the former German capital was occupied by all four victorious Allies. In June 1948, Stalin tried to force the Western Allies out of Berlin by sealing off every railroad and highway into the Western sectors of the city. The Western powers responded to the blockade by mounting a round-the-clock airlift. For more than a year, cargo planes supplied West Berliners with food and fuel. Their success forced the Soviets to end the blockade. Although the West had won a victory in the Cold War, the crisis deepened the hostility between the two camps.

New Alliances Tensions continued to grow. In 1949, the United States, Canada, and ten other countries formed a new military alliance called the **North Atlantic Treaty Organization (NATO).** Members pledged to help one another if any one of them were attacked.

In 1955, the Soviet Union responded by forming its own military alliance, the **Warsaw Pact.** It included the Soviet Union and seven satellites in Eastern Europe. Unlike NATO, however, the Warsaw Pact was often invoked by the Soviets to keep its satellites in order.

The Propaganda War Both sides participated in a propaganda war. The United States spoke of defending capitalism and democracy against communism and totalitarianism. The Soviet Union claimed the moral high ground in the struggle

>> An airplane brings food and other supplies to Berlin as part of the Berlin Airlift. **Cite Evidence** Based on this image, how much progress has been made in the rebuilding of Berlin? Provide evidence.

NATO and Warsaw Pact, 1977

KEY
- NATO
- Warsaw Pact
- Neutral

>> Though some countries remained neutral, in general, Western European nations were part of NATO, while Eastern European nations joined the Warsaw Pact. **Analyze Maps** Which Warsaw Pact countries bordered NATO nations?

against Western imperialism. Yet, linked to those stands, both sides sought world power.

☑ **IDENTIFY MAIN IDEAS** Why did the United States establish the NATO alliance? What was the Soviet Union's response?

Two Opposing Sides in Europe

As the Cold War deepened, the superpowers—the United States and the Soviet Union—faced off against each other in Europe and around the world. For more than 40 years, the Cold War loomed over Europe. In general, the superpowers avoided direct confrontation. Yet several incidents brought Europe to the brink of war.

The Berlin Wall Berlin was a key focus of Cold War tensions. The city was divided into democratic West Berlin and communist East Berlin. In the 1950s, West Berlin became a showcase for West German prosperity. Unhappy with communism, many low-paid East Germans fled into West Berlin.

To stop the flight, the East German government built a wall in 1961 that separated the two sectors

of the city. When completed, the Berlin Wall was a massive concrete barrier, topped with barbed wire and patrolled by guards. The wall showed that workers, far from enjoying a communist paradise, had to be forcibly kept from fleeing.

Revolts in Eastern Europe During the Cold War, the Soviet Union had more than 30 divisions of troops stationed across the region. Yet, in East Germany, Poland, Hungary, and elsewhere, unrest simmered. In 1953, about 50,000 workers confronted the Soviet army in the streets of the German capital. The uprising spread to other East German cities, but the protesters could not withstand Soviet tanks.

In 1956, economic woes in Poland touched off riots and strikes. To end the turmoil, the Polish government made some reforms, but dissatisfaction with communism remained. That year, Imre Nagy (nahj), a communist reformer and strong nationalist, gained power in Hungary. He ended one-party rule, ejected Soviet troops, and withdrew from the Warsaw Pact. In response, the Soviet Union invaded Hungary and ended the reforms. Nagy was later executed.

In early 1968, Czechoslovakian leader Alexander Dubcek introduced greater freedom of expression and limited democracy. This movement of freedom became known as the "Prague Spring." Soviet leaders feared that democracy would threaten communist power and Soviet domination. Once again, the Soviets responded with force, sending Warsaw Pact troops to oust Dubcek and end the reforms.

☑ **IDENTIFY CAUSE AND EFFECT** How was Europe divided following the end of World War II?

The Nuclear Arms Race

One of the most frightening aspects of the Cold War was the arms race. Each side wanted to be able to withstand an attack by the other. At first, the United States, which had the atomic bomb, was the only nuclear power. By 1949, however, the Soviet Union had also developed an atomic bomb. By 1953, both sides in the Cold War had developed the far more destructive military technology—the hydrogen bomb.

The Balance of Terror The United States and the Soviet Union spent vast sums to develop new, more deadly nuclear and conventional weapons. They invested still more to improve "delivery systems"—

the bombers, missiles, and submarines to launch these terrifying weapons of mass destruction.

Critics of the arms race argued that a nuclear war would destroy both sides. Yet each superpower wanted to be able to deter the other from launching its nuclear weapons.

By the 1960s, the terrifying possibility of nuclear war led to the idea of mutually assured destruction (MAD), which meant that if one side launched a nuclear attack, the other side would retaliate in kind, and both sides would be destroyed. Even though MAD might discourage nuclear war, the fear of such a conflict haunted the world. In the words of Winston Churchill, the balance of power had become a "balance of terror."

Disarmament Talks To reduce the threat of nuclear war, the two sides met at disarmament talks. Although mutual distrust slowed progress, the rival powers did reach some agreements. In 1963, they agreed to the Nuclear Test Ban Treaty, which prohibited the testing of nuclear weapons in the atmosphere.

In 1969, the United States and the Soviet Union began the Strategic Arms Limitation Talks (SALT) to limit the number of nuclear weapons held by each

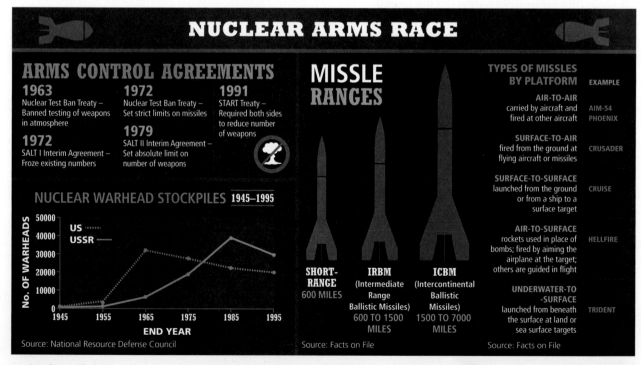

NUCLEAR ARMS RACE

ARMS CONTROL AGREEMENTS

1963
Nuclear Test Ban Treaty – Banned testing of weapons in atmosphere

1972
SALT I Interim Agreement – Froze existing numbers

1972
Nuclear Test Ban Treaty – Set strict limits on missiles

1979
SALT II Interim Agreement – Set absolute limit on number of weapons

1991
START Treaty – Required both sides to reduce number of weapons

NUCLEAR WARHEAD STOCKPILES 1945–1995

US ·······
USSR ——

NO. OF WARHEADS
50000
40000
30000
20000
10000
0

END YEAR
1945   1955   1965   1975   1985   1995

Source: National Resource Defense Council

MISSLE RANGES

SHORT-RANGE
600 MILES

IRBM
(Intermediate Range Ballistic Missiles)
600 TO 1500 MILES

ICBM
(Intercontinental Ballistic Missiles)
1500 TO 7000 MILES

Source: Facts on File

TYPES OF MISSLES BY PLATFORM

	EXAMPLE
AIR-TO-AIR carried by aircraft and fired at other aircraft	AIM-54 PHOENIX
SURFACE-TO-AIR fired from the ground at flying aircraft or missiles	CRUSADER
SURFACE-TO-SURFACE launched from the ground or from a ship to a surface target	CRUISE
AIR-TO-SURFACE rockets used in place of bombs; fired by aiming the airplane at the target; others are guided in flight	HELLFIRE
UNDERWATER-TO-SURFACE launched from beneath the surface at land or sea surface targets	TRIDENT

Source: Facts on File

>> **Analyze Charts** Compare the Nuclear Test Ban Treaty of 1963, the SALT II Treaty of 1972, and the START Treaty of 1991. How did each of the later treaties advance beyond the treaty that came before it?

🔲 BOUNCE to Activate Gallery

side. In 1972 and 1979, both sides signed agreements setting these limits.

In 1991, the United States and Russia negotiated a Strategic Arms Reduction Treaty (START), which has been renewed in recent years. These START agreements led to the removal of a large number of nuclear weapons.

An Era of Détente During the 1970s, American and Soviet leaders promoted an era of **détente** (day TAHNT), or relaxation of tensions. Détente brought new agreements to reduce nuclear stockpiles as both sides turned to diplomacy to resolve issues. The era of détente ended in 1979, when the Soviet Union invaded Afghanistan.

Limiting the Spread of Nuclear Weapons By the late 1960s, Britain, France, and China had developed their own nuclear weapons. By then, many world leaders were eager to stop the spread of nuclear weapons. In 1968, dozens of nations signed the Nuclear Non-Proliferation Treaty (NPT). They agreed not to develop nuclear weapons and cooperate in the peaceful use of nuclear energy.

☑ **INTEGRATE INFORMATION** What factors discouraged the use of nuclear weapons in the Cold War?

The Cold War Around the World

The superpowers waged the Cold War not only in Europe, but also around the world. By the end of World War II, the Soviets were helping communist forces in China, Korea, and elsewhere. The United States took action to respond to the global threat of communism.

Establishing Alliances and Bases To stop the spread of communism, the United States sought regional alliances with friendly powers. In Europe, it backed NATO. In Asia, the United States promoted another regional alliance, the Southeast-Asia Treaty Organization (SEATO). It included the United States, Britain, France, Australia, Pakistan, Thailand, New Zealand, and the Philippines.

The United States also formed military alliances with individual nations, such as Japan and South Korea. Often, these agreements included the right to set up American military bases. As a result, American bases circled the globe from North America to Europe, Asia, and the islands of the Pacific.

>> The United States had many military bases overseas, and its navy played a vital role in maintaining the U.S. presence around the world.

Meanwhile, the Soviet Union formed its own alliances. In addition to the Warsaw Pact in Europe, the Soviet Union formed alliances with newly independent nations in Africa and Asia. However, the Soviet Union had few bases overseas.

Where the Cold War Got Hot Because both superpowers had a global reach, local conflicts in many places played into the Cold War. Often, the United States and its allies supported one side, and the Soviet bloc supported the other. Through such struggles, the superpowers could confront each other indirectly, rather than head to head.

Political shifts around the world added to Cold War tensions. When communist forces won control of mainland China in 1949, the United States feared that a tide of communism would sweep around the world. During this period, European colonies in Africa and Asia battled for independence. Liberation leaders and guerrillas frequently sought help from one or the other Cold War power.

On occasion, the Cold War erupted into "shooting wars," especially in Asia. Both Korea and Vietnam were torn by brutal conflicts in which the United States, the Soviet Union, and China played crucial roles. More commonly, however, the superpowers provided weapons, training, or other aid to opposing forces in Asia, Africa, or Latin America.

The United States and Latin America The United States was especially concerned about the threat of communism in the Western Hemisphere. Seeing reform movements in Latin American countries as communist threats, it backed right-wing, anti-communist dictators and helped topple elected socialist leaders. In 1962, Cuba, a small island nation just 90 miles from Florida, became the chief focus of United States concern.

The Communist Revolution in Cuba In the 1950s, a young lawyer, **Fidel Castro,** organized an armed rebellion against the corrupt dictator who then ruled Cuba. By 1959, Castro had led his tiny guerrilla army to victory and set about transforming the country into a communist state.

During the Cuban Revolution, Castro nationalized, or took over, foreign-owned businesses. He put most land under government control and distributed the rest to peasant farmers. While Castro imposed harsh authoritarian rule, he did at first improve conditions for the poor. But Castro's revolution angered many Cubans, especially from the middle class. Critics were jailed or silenced. Hundreds of thousands of Cubans fled to the United States.

>> The Soviet Union celebrated the anniversary of the Bolshevik Revolution with this military parade in Moscow in 1969.

The United States, alarmed as Castro turned to the Soviet Union for support, attempted to bring down the communist regime next door. In 1961, President **John F. Kennedy** backed a plan by anti-Castro exiles to invade Cuba and lead an uprising against Castro.

The poorly planned plot was a disaster. An invasion force landed at the Bay of Pigs in Cuba, but was quickly crushed. News of the plot helped Castro rally Cuban popular opinion against foreign interference, and the bungled invasion hurt the reputation of the United States.

The Cuban Missile Crisis In 1962, the United States imposed a trade embargo on Cuba. Castro, seeking closer ties with the Soviet Union, let the Soviets build nuclear missile bases in Cuba. The threat of Soviet nuclear bases in its backyard outraged the United States and touched off a dangerous crisis.

In October 1962, President Kennedy imposed a naval blockade on Cuba. Kennedy demanded that the Soviet Union remove its nuclear missiles from Cuba, and for a few tense days, the world faced the risk of nuclear war. Finally, however, Soviet Premier Nikita Khrushchev backed down. He agreed to remove the Soviet missiles, but won a secret pledge from Kennedy to not invade Cuba.

☑ **MAKE GENERALIZATIONS** How did the United States and the Soviet Union confront each other around the world during the Cold War?

The Soviet Union During the Cold War

Victory in World War II brought few rewards to the Soviet people. Stalin continued his ruthless policies. He filled labor camps with "enemies of the state" and seemed ready to launch new purges when he died in 1953.

Soviet Communism In the Soviet Union, the government controlled most aspects of public life. Communists valued obedience, discipline, and economic security. They sought to spread their communist **ideology,** or value systems and beliefs, around the globe.

The Soviet Union also aimed to spread its command economy to other countries. In a command economy, the government makes most economic decisions. A huge bureaucracy, rather than supply and demand, decided what to produce, how much, and for whom. Government planners in Moscow often had little knowledge of local conditions. The government owned most of the property.

Collectivized agriculture remained so unproductive that the Soviet Union often had to import grain to feed its people. Nor could Russia's command economy match the free-market economies of the West in producing consumer goods. Since workers had lifetime job security, they had little incentive, or reason, to produce better-quality goods.

Stalin's Successors After Stalin's death in 1953, **Nikita Khrushchev** (KROOSH chawf) emerged as the new Soviet leader. In 1956, he shocked top Communist Party members when he publicly denounced Stalin's abuse of power. Khrushchev maintained the Communist Party's tight political control, but he closed prison camps and eased censorship. He called for a "peaceful coexistence" with the West.

Khrushchev's successor, **Leonid Brezhnev** (BREZH nef), held power from the mid-1960s until he died in 1982. Under Brezhnev, dissidents, or people who criticized the government, faced arrest and imprisonment.

Dissidents Resist Despite the risk of harsh punishment, some courageous people dared to criticize the government. Andrei Sakharov (SAH kuh rawf), a brilliant physicist, spoke out against human rights abuses. He was exiled to a remote Soviet city.

Another critic, Aleksandr Solzhenitsyn (sohl zhuh NEET sin), wrote a letter to a friend criticizing Stalin. He was sent to a prison camp. Under Khrushchev, he was released and wrote fictional works that drew on his experiences in Soviet prison camps. His writings were banned in the Soviet Union, and in 1974, he was deported to West Germany. Despite the government's actions, Sakharov and Solzhenitsyn inspired others to resist communist repression and demand greater freedom.

☑ **CHECK UNDERSTANDING** How did the Soviet Union handle critics of its policies?

The United States in the Cold War

The Cold War was not just a military rivalry. It was also a competition between two contrasting economic and political value systems. Unlike the communist countries, the democratic, capitalist

>> Americans who feared nuclear war built bomb shelters in their backyards and stocked them with canned goods and other supplies.

countries, led by the United States, gave citizens the freedom to make economic and political choices. These nations valued freedom and prosperity. They held that economic freedom and free market principles helped improve the human condition—especially compared to the command economies of the communist world.

Free Markets While communist countries had command economies, capitalist countries had market economies. In market economies, producers and consumers make economic decisions. Prices are based on supply and demand in a free market. Property is privately owned. Producers compete to offer the best products for the lowest prices. By deciding what to buy, consumers ultimately decide which products are produced. In a free enterprise system, producers who win consumers' business make profits and grow.

The United States economy is basically a market economy. However, the United States and Western Europe have what can be called mixed economies, because their governments have an economic role.

The Cold War at Home Early in the Cold War, fierce anti-communists in the United States warned that Soviet agents were operating everywhere within the country. The House Un-American Activities Committee (HUAC) led a campaign to identify supposed communist sympathizers. In the early 1950s, Senator Joseph McCarthy charged many innocent citizens with harboring communist sympathies. Government probes produced little evidence of subversion. Eventually, the Senate condemned McCarthy's reckless behavior, but not before his charges and the investigations of the HUAC had ruined the careers of thousands of Americans.

The fear of a nuclear war also affected Americans. Some families built fallout shelters, where they could hide in the event of a nuclear bomb. Schools conducted air-raid drills in which children were taught to duck under their desks. Although these measures would not have protected children in a nuclear attack, the drills reflected the widespread fear of nuclear war.

☑ **DISTINGUISH** How did the United States respond to the threat of communism at home and around the world?

☑ ASSESSMENT

1. **Identify Central Ideas** What foreign policy did the United States establish with the Truman Doctrine?

2. **Make Generalizations** What kinds of conflicts resulted from the global confrontation between the two superpowers?

3. **Infer** How did the buildup of nuclear weapons discourage their actual use?

4. **Cite Evidence** List three occasions when the Soviet Union put down revolts in Eastern Europe during the Cold War.

5. **Connections to Today** After the war, the Marshall Plan helped Europe recover from the devastation of World War II. What organizations today offer aid to people around the world?

The Cuban Revolution

In 1959, as Cuban dictator Fulgencia Batista fled Cuba, Fidel Castro and his followers marched triumphantly into Havana. The victory parade lasted eight days. The Revolution was popular. Castro promised a better life for Cubans, and he had won the hearts and minds of the people who lined the streets waiting for his arrival. The following primary sources show two views of the Revolution. The first, *The Manifesto to the Workers and the People in General* (1959), expresses the disillusion of workers who felt the new regime was moving toward a dictatorship rather than the promised democracy. The second, *On the Export of Revolution* (1962), is Castro's explanation of the purpose of the Revolution.

As you read, think about how you may have felt about these events if you had been living during this time. Then answer the questions about these two views on the Cuban Revolution.

>> Castro's victory march into Havana, 1959

Primary Source 1

From the Libertarian Association of Cuba: *The Manifesto to the Workers and the People in General* (1959)

In this historic moment of the nation and the working class, the ALC is obliged to call attention to certain fundamental problems. . . The Revolution that recently freed the people of Cuba from the bloody tyranny of Batista is a people's revolution for liberty and justice, made by the people.

☑ **CITE EVIDENCE** Was there popular support for the Revolution? Explain.

The labor movement of our country was captured by the tyrants, who used it to promote their own sinister purposes. The voices of the rebels and the non-conformists were stilled by the prison officer, the persecutor and the assassin. Unions which dared question the authorities were immediately taken over by the Secretary-General of the Confederation of Cuban Workers (C.T.C.) and/or the Ministry of Labor. Their freely elected representatives were ousted [or even arrested] and replaced by hand-picked faithful servants of the dictatorship, who were imposed upon the membership without the least semblance of democratic procedure. The workers themselves must see to it that such atrocities are never again revived in Cuba. . .

☑ **DESCRIBE** What changes occurred in the labor movement soon after the Revolution that caused concern for the authors of this source?

In the midst of the revolutionary turmoil, we do not expect everything, including the labor organizations, to function normally in so short a time. But it is our duty, and the duty of all the workers, by militant action, to see to it that the democratic procedures, the freedoms, and the rights gained by us with the triumph of the Revolution are respected. . .

We must immediately hold free elections in the unions, where the workers will freely choose their representatives ... It is absolutely necessary that general membership meetings be called immediately to freely discuss and deal with the great and urgent problems. . . It is absolutely necessary that the workers themselves elect, dismiss or reinstate their officials. To permit any other procedure would be to allow the very same dictatorial practices which we fought against under Batista. . .

We, the people who fought a bitter war against the old dictatorship, must now make sure that the Revolution will build a new social order that will guarantee liberty and justice for all, without exception. . . We workers, who felt on our own bodies the blows inflicted by the old tyranny, must now, again, defend our fundamental rights.

☑ **SUMMARIZE** According to the source, how can workers ensure that the true values of the Revolution are carried through?

Primary Source 2

Fidel Castro *On the Export of Revolution* (February, 1962)

To the accusation that Cuba wants to export its revolution, we reply: Revolutions are not exported, they are made by the people. . .

☑ **SUMMARIZE** What do you think the term "export its revolution" means in this source?

What Cuba can give to the people, and has already given, is its example. And what does the Cuban Revolution teach? That revolution is possible, that the people can make it, that in the contemporary world there are no forces capable of halting the liberation movement of the peoples.

☑ **EXPLAIN** Why does Castro praise the Cuban Revolution as being successful?

Our triumph would never have been feasible if the Revolution itself had not been inexorably destined to arise out of existing conditions in our socio-economic reality, a reality which exists to an even greater degree in a good number of Latin American countries. It inevitably occurs that in the nations where the control of the Yankee monopolies is strongest, the exploitation of the oligarchy cruelest, and the situation of the laboring and peasant masses most unbearable, the political power appears most solid. The state of siege becomes habitual.

Every manifestation of discontent by the masses is repressed by force. The democratic path is closed completely. The brutal character of dictatorship, the form of rule adopted by the ruling classes, reveals itself more clearly than ever. It is then that the revolutionary explosion of the peoples becomes inevitable. Although it is true that in those underdeveloped countries of America the working class is generally relatively small, there is a social class which, because of the subhuman conditions in which it lives, constitutes a potential force that, led by the workers and the revolutionary Intellectuals, has a decisive importance in the struggle for national liberation—the peasants. . .

☑ **ANALYZE INFORMATION** According to Castro, what ignites the "revolutionary explosion" of the peasants?

☑ ASSESSMENT

Be sure to cite the specific evidence from the sources as you answer the following questions.

1. **Draw Conclusions** Why would workers be the likeliest group to support the Revolution?

2. **Compare and Contrast** Why might Castro have seen the Revolution as an example for Latin America?

3. **Analyze Information** Based on both sources, what do you think the labor movement in Cuba was like during the Batista era? What changes occurred after the Revolution?

4. **Synthesize** Why do you think the Revolution began to develop into a dictatorship?

5. **Develop Empathy** How likely would it have been for middle-class Cubans to have supported the Revolution? Explain.

GO ONLINE to access primary sources

19.2

New York City was chosen as the headquarters of the new United Nations.

The Western Democracies and Japan

Despite the tensions of the Cold War, the United States enjoyed a period of great prosperity and growth in the postwar decades. Its booming economy became a symbol of the power of capitalism and democratic freedoms in the ongoing propaganda war against communism.

Postwar Prosperity in the United States

In the postwar decades, the American economic system flourished. American businesses expanded into markets around the globe. The dollar was the world's strongest currency. Foreigners flocked to invest in American industry and to buy U.S. government bonds. America's wealth was a model for other democracies and a challenge to the stagnant economies of the communist world.

America in a Central Role During the Cold War, the United States was a global political leader. The headquarters of the League of Nations had been symbolically located in neutral Switzerland. The headquarters of the newly formed United Nations was built in New York City.

The United States also played a leading economic role. America had emerged untouched from the horrendous destruction

 BOUNCE to Activate Flipped Video

Objectives

Analyze the postwar American economy.

Identify developments in American society and government.

Explain how Western Europe rebuilt and moved toward greater unity.

Describe how Japan changed after World War II.

Key Terms

interdependence
recession
segregation
discrimination
Dr. Martin Luther
    King, Jr.
Konrad Adenauer
welfare state
Margaret Thatcher
European Union
gross domestic
    product (GDP)

of the Second World War. Other nations needed American goods and services, and foreign trade helped the United States achieve a long postwar boom. The long postwar peace among democratic nations helped to spread this boom worldwide.

An Economic Boom In 1945, the United States produced 50 percent of the world's manufactured goods. Factories soon shifted from making tanks and bombers to peacetime production. With the Cold War looming, government military spending increased, creating many jobs in defense industries.

During the 1950s and 1960s, the American economy was booming. At home, a growing population demanded homes, cars, refrigerators, and thousands of other products. Overseas, American businesses were investing in Europe's recovery and expanding into new markets. American cultural influences spread, and people around the globe enjoyed American movies, television programs, and music—especially jazz and rock and roll.

America's postwar economic strength impacted social systems in the United States. Although segments of the population were left behind, many Americans grew more affluent and moved from the cities to the suburbs. The movement to

>> In the postwar boom, Americans moved out of the cities and into the suburbs, where they could own a home with a yard. **Connect** What role did the car play in the suburbanization of America?

🔲 BOUNCE to Activate Gallery

communities outside an urban core is known as **suburbanization.** Suburbanites typically lived in single-family houses with lawns and access to good schools. Suburban highways allowed residents to commute to work by car.

During the postwar decades, many Americans also moved to the Sunbelt, or the states in the South and Southwest of the United States. Jobs in these states were becoming more plentiful than in the industrialized North. The warmer climate was an added bonus. The availability of air conditioning and water for irrigation helped make the movement to the Sunbelt possible.

A Wider Role for Government In the postwar decades, the government's role in the economy grew. Under President Truman, Congress created generous benefits that helped veterans attend college or buy homes. Other Truman programs expanded FDR's New Deal, providing greater security for the elderly and poor.

Truman's successor, Dwight Eisenhower, tried to reduce the government's role in the economy. At the same time, he approved government funding to build a vast interstate highway system. This program spurred the growth of the auto, trucking, and related industries. Highways and home building changed the face of the nation. Suburbanization led to the decay of many inner-city neighborhoods.

The United States and the Global Economy In the postwar decades, the United States profited from the growing global economy. But **interdependence**—mutual dependence of countries on goods, resources, and knowledge from other parts of the world—brought problems, too. In the 1970s, a political crisis in the Middle East led to a global oil shortage and soaring oil prices. In the United States, people waited in long lines for costly gasoline, which made Americans aware of how much they relied on imported oil.

The oil crisis and other economic issues brought periods of **recession,** or economic downturn. For the most part, recessions were fairly mild.

Other economic issues, however, such as competition from nations in Asia and elsewhere posed challenges for the United States. During the 1980s, the United States lost manufacturing jobs to Asia and Latin America. Some American corporations even moved their operations overseas to take advantage of lower wages.

Still, the United States remained a rich nation and a magnet for immigrants. These newcomers came largely from Latin America and Asia. By the 1980s, some Americans were calling for stricter laws to halt illegal immigration.

☑ **IDENTIFY MAIN IDEAS** How was the U.S. economy linked to the broader global economy during the Cold War?

The United States Responds to New Challenges

The 1950s seemed a peaceful time within the United States. Yet changes were underway that would reshape American society. Among the most far-reaching was the Civil Rights Movement, which sought to ensure the promise of equal opportunity for all Americans.

The Civil Rights Movement Although African Americans had won freedom nearly a century before, many states, especially in the South, denied them equality. **Segregation,** or forced separation, was legal in education and housing. African Americans also faced **discrimination,** or unequal treatment and barriers, in jobs and voting. The Civil Rights Movement of the 1950s and 1960s renewed earlier efforts to end racial injustice.

In 1954, the Supreme Court issued a landmark ruling in *Brown* v. *Board of Education of Topeka.* It declared that segregated schools were unconstitutional. President Eisenhower and his successors used federal power to uphold the order to desegregate public schools.

Martin Luther King, Jr. By 1956, a gifted preacher, **Dr. Martin Luther King, Jr.,** had emerged as a leader of the Civil Rights Movement. Inspired by Gandhi's campaign of civil disobedience in India, King organized boycotts and led peaceful marches to end segregation in the United States. Many Americans of all races joined the Civil Rights Movement. Their courage in the face of sometimes brutal attacks stirred the nation's conscience.

In 1963, at a huge civil rights rally, King made a stirring speech. "I have a dream," he proclaimed, "that one day this nation will rise up and live out the true meaning of its creed: 'We hold these truths to be self-evident, that all men are created equal.'"

Progress and Problems In time, Congress responded. It outlawed segregation in public accommodations, protected the rights of Black voters, and required equal access to housing

>> Segregated drinking fountains were a common sight in the southern states.

>> People from all over the country came to the March on Washington, held on August 28, 1963. Martin Luther King Jr. was a keynote speaker. **Analyze Information** How do the demands on the signs represent the civil rights movement?

and jobs. Despite these victories, racial prejudice survived, and African Americans faced many economic obstacles. Poverty and unemployment plagued African American communities in urban areas.

Still, the Civil Rights Movement provided wider opportunities. Many African Americans won elected offices or gained top jobs in business and the military.

Other Groups Demand Equality The Civil Rights Movement inspired other groups, such as American Indians and Latinos, to campaign for equality. Women, too, renewed their efforts to gain equal rights. New civil rights laws banned discrimination based on gender as well as race in hiring and promotion. More women won political office, and some made progress into high positions in business.

The Great Society During the 1960s, the government further expanded social programs to help the poor and disadvantaged. President Lyndon Johnson created a program that he called the Great Society. It funded Medicare, which ensured health care for the elderly, job training and low-cost housing for the poor, and support for education. Many Americans came to rely on these programs in the next decades.

The Conservative Response In the 1980s, conservatives challenged costly social programs and the growth of government. President Ronald Reagan called for cutbacks in government spending on social programs. Congress ended some welfare programs, reduced government regulation of the economy, and cut taxes. At the same time, military spending increased.

Government spending and tax cuts greatly increased the national deficit, the gap between what a government spends and what it takes in through taxes and other sources. As the deficit grew, conservatives crusaded for deeper cuts in social and economic programs. Debate raged about how far to cut spending on programs ranging from education and welfare to environmental protection.

☑ **CITE EXAMPLES** Over time, how did the U.S. government expand opportunities for individuals? Give examples.

Rebuilding Western Europe

The impact of—and recovery from—World War II on the political and economic systems of Europe was profound. With Marshall Plan aid from the United States, Western European countries recovered from

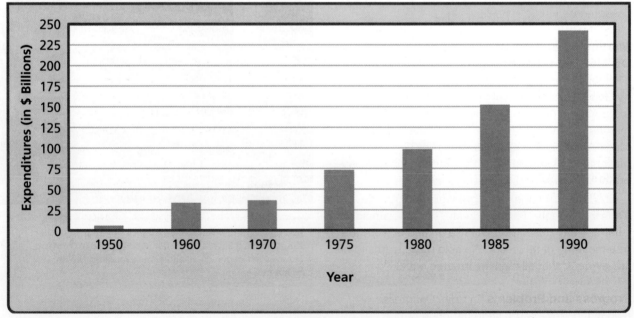

U.S. Military Spending, 1950-1980

>> **Analyze Charts** U.S. military spending increased dramatically during the Cold War years. In which five-year period did military spending increase the most?

EAST AND WEST GERMANY IN 1968 AN ECONOMIC COMPARISON

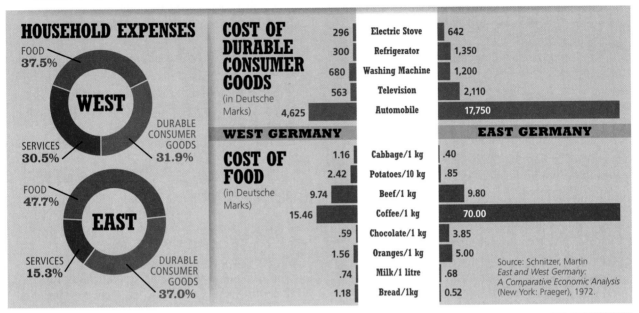

HOUSEHOLD EXPENSES

WEST
- FOOD 37.5%
- DURABLE CONSUMER GOODS 31.9%
- SERVICES 30.5%

EAST
- FOOD 47.7%
- DURABLE CONSUMER GOODS 37.0%
- SERVICES 15.3%

COST OF DURABLE CONSUMER GOODS
(in Deutsche Marks)

WEST GERMANY		EAST GERMANY
296	Electric Stove	642
300	Refrigerator	1,350
680	Washing Machine	1,200
563	Television	2,110
4,625	Automobile	17,750

COST OF FOOD
(in Deutsche Marks)

WEST GERMANY		EAST GERMANY
1.16	Cabbage/1 kg	.40
2.42	Potatoes/10 kg	.85
9.74	Beef/1 kg	9.80
15.46	Coffee/1 kg	70.00
.59	Chocolate/1 kg	3.85
1.56	Oranges/1 kg	5.00
.74	Milk/1 litre	.68
1.18	Bread/1kg	0.52

Source: Schnitzer, Martin *East and West Germany: A Comparative Economic Analysis* (New York: Praeger), 1972.

>> **Analyze Charts** What types of goods were expensive in East Germany in 1968? What types of goods were inexpensive?

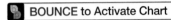
BOUNCE to Activate Chart

World War II. They rebuilt industries, farms, and transportation networks destroyed during the war. In the 1950s, economies in Western Europe boomed. Standards of living rose dramatically, and people began to enjoy comforts unheard of in earlier times.

West Germany's Economic Miracle The early postwar years were a desperate time for Germany. People were starving amid a landscape of destruction. The Cold War left Germany divided. West Germany was a member of the Western alliance. East Germany lay in the Soviet orbit. Over the next decades, differences between the two Germanys widened.

Early on, the United States rushed aid to West Germany in order to strengthen it against the communist tide sweeping Eastern Europe. From 1949 to 1963, a strong-minded chancellor, **Konrad Adenauer** (AD eh now er), led West Germans as they rebuilt cities, factories, and trade.

Despite high taxes to pay for the recovery, West Germany created a booming industrial economy. This "economic miracle" raised European fears of a German revival. But West German leaders worked closely with France and the United States in NATO and other international organizations.

While West Germany remained a capitalist country, some later chancellors belonged to the Socialist party. They expanded the **welfare state.**

Under this political system, a government keeps most features of a capitalist economy but takes much responsibility for the social and economic needs of its people. In the welfare state, a government provides national health care, unemployment insurance, old-age pensions, and support for qualified students to attend college.

Germany Reunites The postwar decades brought no economic miracle to East Germany. Under communist rule, its economy stagnated. The Soviet Union exploited East German workers and industry for its own benefit. Still, unemployment was low, and East German workers had some basic benefits such as health care and free education.

By 1989, communism was declining in the Soviet Union. Without Soviet power to back them, East Germany's communist leaders were forced out of office. The Berlin Wall was torn down, and in 1990, Germany was reunited.

While Germans welcomed unity, the change brought new challenges. Prosperous West Germans had to pay higher taxes to finance the rebuilding of the east. At the same time, East Germans faced a difficult transition to a market economy.

Britain Recovers World War II left Britain physically battered and economically drained. After the war, Britain could no longer afford its overseas colonies, which demanded independence. Britain gave up global leadership to its close ally, the United States.

The war also impacted the British political system. After the war, British voters elected a Labour Party government, which began building a welfare state. The government nationalized industries and expanded social welfare benefits. It built housing for the poor and opened new state-funded universities. A national health service extended free or low-cost medical care to all citizens. To pay for these benefits, taxes rose tremendously.

By 1979, Britain and the rest of Europe faced economic hard times. Britain's Conservative party, led by **Margaret Thatcher,** won power and set out to roll back the welfare state. Thatcher privatized government-run industries, curbed the power of labor unions, reduced the size of the government bureaucracy, and cut back welfare services.

Other Western Nations Achieve Prosperity

Other nations in Western Europe, including France, the Netherlands, and Belgium, rebuilt after the war, helped by Marshall Plan aid. Like Britain, these Europeans powers had to give up their overseas colonial empires. France faced bloody conflicts in Vietnam and Algeria, which it tried to hold on to in the face of nationalist demands for independence.

The Scandinavian countries of Norway, Sweden, and Denmark created extensive socialist welfare programs. By the 1990s, rising costs revived debate about how much people were willing to pay for the welfare state. Yet many peoples saw these social programs as essential to a democratic society.

Postwar Italy faced many challenges, including a multiparty political system that led to frequent changes of government. Corruption and financial scandals shook the government. Despite these problems, Italy made impressive economic gains.

Building the European Union Europe's postwar recovery was helped by economic cooperation. In 1952, six nations—West Germany, the Netherlands, Belgium, Luxembourg, France, and Italy—set up the European Coal and Steel Community. It eased barriers to trade in coal and steel, which spurred economic growth. Later, these nations formed the European Community to expand free trade. Over time, it ended tariffs, or taxes on imports, and allowed workers and capital to move freely across national borders.

In 1993, the European Community was renamed the **European Union** (EU). Since then, it has expanded to include 28 nations, including Britain, Ireland, Denmark, and other European countries. In 2016, Britain voted to leave the EU. They met this goal in 2020. However the exit was not immediate. During the eleven month transition period, negotiations continued.

The EU set up a common currency, the euro, which is used by 17 European nations. The EU became a powerful economic force and promoted regional trade and peace by replacing destructive competition with an amazing degree of cooperation.

☑ **COMPARE** What are some advantages and disadvantages of the welfare state in Europe?

Japan Is Transformed

In 1945, Japan, like Germany, lay in ruins. It had suffered perhaps the most devastating damage of any nation involved in World War II. Tens of thousands of Japanese were homeless and hungry.

Occupation Bring Changes The war had a deep impact on the political system of Japan. Under General Douglas MacArthur, the American military government set two main goals for the occupation of Japan: to destroy militarism and to ensure democratic government. Japan's armed forces were disbanded. War crime trials were held to punish those responsible for wartime atrocities.

>> British miners protest the closure of a government-operated coal mine. Many British industries were once again privatized under Prime Minister Margaret Thatcher.

In 1946, Japan adopted a new constitution, which set up a parliamentary democracy. Although the Japanese emperor lost all political power, he remained the symbolic head of the nation. Japan renounced war and banned any military forces, except for its own defense.

To build Japanese democracy, American occupying forces backed changes to the economic and social systems. They opened the education system to all people and emphasized legal equality for women. A land-reform program bought out large landowners and gave land to tenant farmers, erasing lingering traces of feudalism in Japan. Other reforms protected the rights of workers.

Japan and the Cold War By 1950, Japan was on the road to recovery. At the same time, the Cold War was making the United States eager to end the occupation. As the Cold War erupted into armed conflict in nearby Korea, the United States and Japan signed a peace treaty, and in 1952, the occupation ended.

Japan and the United States had close ties during the Cold War. The American military operated out of bases that they had set up in Japan, while Japan enjoyed the protection of the American "nuclear umbrella." The two nations were trading partners, and in time, competitors for global markets.

The Japanese Economic Miracle Between 1950 and 1975, Japan produced its own economic miracle, even more spectacular than Germany's. It chalked up huge jumps in **gross domestic product (GDP).** GDP is the total value of all goods and services produced by a nation in a particular year.

Japan's success was built on producing goods for export. At first, it manufactured textiles. Later, it shifted to selling steel and machinery. By the 1970s, Japanese cars, cameras, and televisions found eager buyers on the world market. Soon, a wide range of Japanese electronic goods were competing with Western, and especially American, products.

Japan's economic miracle was due in part to its new modern factories built after the war. Because Japan spent little on its military, it could invest more in its economy. It benefited from an educated and skilled workforce and imposed tariffs and regulations that limited imports and helped Japanese manufacturers at home.

By the 1980s, Japan was seen as an economic superpower. Its vast trade network reached around the world and resulted in a trade surplus for Japan. By the 1980s, United States manufacturers were angered by what they saw as unfair competition, and

>> The American occupation of Japan lasted about seven years and resulted in a firm friendship between the former enemies.

>> Japan became an export powerhouse by building cars, electronics, and other products.

the United States pushed Japan to open its economy to more imports. Japan's stunning economic growth ended in the 1990s. However, it continued as a major world economic power.

☑ **IDENTIFY** What factors explain Japan's economic success in the decades after World War II?

☑ **ASSESSMENT**

1. **Compare Points of View** How did Democrats and Republicans differ on the best ways to improve opportunity for Americans?

2. **Compare** During the Cold War, how was economic development in Western Europe similar to, or different from, that of Japan?

3. **Infer** How did Europe benefit economically from greater unity?

4. **Make Generalizations** How was trade important to the economic development of Western Europe, the United States, and Japan during the postwar decades?

5. **Quest Connections** What challenges did American democracy face during the 1950s and 1960s? How did Americans respond to these challenges? What challenges do you think American democracy faces today?

📶 **GO ONLINE** to access this biography: Martin Luther King, Jr.

The support of Chinese peasants helped Mao Zedong (left) and the communists achieve victory in China's civil war.

Communism in East Asia

Civil war raged across China during the late 1940s as Mao Zedong (mow dzuh doong) and his Communist forces fought to overthrow Jiang Jieshi's Nationalists. In 1949, Mao's forces triumphed. The defeated Jiang and his supporters fled to the island of Taiwan. After decades of struggle, China was finally united, with the Chinese Communists in control. They renamed the country the People's Republic of China.

The Chinese Communist Victory

Soon afterward, the Communists conquered Tibet, claiming it was part of China. In 1959, as the Chinese cracked down, Tibet's revered religious leader, the Dalai Lama, was forced to flee to India.

How the Communists Won Mao's victory in China was due to several causes. Mao had won the support of China's huge peasant population. Peasants had long suffered from brutal landlords and crushing taxes. The Communists promised to redistribute land to peasants and end oppression by landlords. Many women backed the Communists, who rejected the old inequalities of Chinese society. Finally, Mao's army outfought Jiang's armies with guerrilla tactics they had perfected fighting the Japanese.

Jiang and the Nationalists who ruled China had failed to end widespread economic hardship. Many Chinese resented corruption in Jiang's government and his reliance on support from Western powers that had long dominated China. Many educated Chinese were drawn to the Communists' vision of a new China free from foreign domination.

BOUNCE to Activate Flipped Video

Objectives

Analyze how Mao Zedong turned China into a communist state.

Describe China's role in the Cold War.

Explain the causes and impact of the Korean War.

Key Terms

Mao Zedong
collectivization
Great Leap Forward
Cultural Revolution
38th parallel
Kim Il Sung
Syngman Rhee
Pusan Perimeter
demilitarized zone

GO ONLINE to access your digital course

Remaking Chinese Life Once in power, the Communists set out to turn China from a backward peasant society into a modern industrial nation. Communist ideology guided the government's efforts to reshape the economy and society that China had inherited from the dynastic period. To build socialism, China nationalized all businesses and tried to increase coal and steel output and develop heavy industry. With help from the Soviet Union, the Chinese built hydroelectric plants, dams, and railroads.

To boost agriculture, Mao at first distributed land to peasants. Before long, the government imposed **collectivization,** or the forced pooling of peasant land and labor to increase productivity.

To increase literacy, reformers simplified Chinese characters, making it easier to learn to read and write. Schools were opened for young and old. The Communists sent health-care workers to remote rural areas. Although many had little training, they did help reduce disease and teach better hygiene.

Under China's new constitution, women won equality under the law. Although Chinese woman made real progress, they did not enjoy full equality. Often paid less than men for the same work, women toiled in fields and factories while still maintaining the home.

>> The government forced collectivization on Chinese farmers in order to increase productivity. During the Great Leap Forward, tractors arrive at a farmer's cooperative.

Communism Takes a Huge Toll Like Lenin in the Soviet Union, Mao Zedong built a one-party, Communist totalitarian state. Communist ideology replaced Confucian beliefs and traditional religions. Buddhists, Christians, and others faced persecution and death. The government attacked crime and corruption. It did away with the old landlord and business classes. In their place, peasant and workers were honored as the builders of the new China.

These revolutionary changes came at an enormous human cost. Communist leaders committed politically motivated mass murder, as hundreds of thousands of landlords, middle class property owners, and others suffered persecution, torture, and death. Many more were sent to forced labor camps, where they died under brutal conditions.

Great Leap Forward Fails From 1958 to 1960, Mao pursued a policy known as the **Great Leap Forward,** which was designed to increase farm and industrial output. To make agriculture more efficient, he created communes. The communes were composed of several villages, thousands of acres of land, and up to 25,000 people.

Rural communes set up "backyard" industries to produce steel and other products. The Great Leap Forward was a disastrous failure. Backyard industries turned out useless goods. The commune system slowed food output. Bad weather added to the problems and led to a terrible famine. Between 1959 and 1961, as many as 55 million Chinese are thought to have starved to death.

The Cultural Revolution In 1966, Mao launched a new program known as the **Cultural Revolution.** Its goal was to purge China of "bourgeois" (non revolutionary) tendencies. He urged young Chinese to experience revolution firsthand, as his generation had.

During the Cultural Revolution, bands of teenaged Red Guards, waving copies of the "Little Red Book," *Quotations From Chairman Mao Tse-tung,* attacked people they considered bourgeois. The accused were publicly humiliated, beaten, and sometimes murdered. Skilled workers and managers were forced out of their jobs and sent to work on rural farms or put into forced labor camps. Schools and factories closed. As the economy stalled and unrest rose, Mao finally had the army restore order.

☑ **COMPARE** What were the main successes and failures of the Chinese Communist Revolution?

China and the Cold War

The Communist victory in China dominated the Cold War in the years after 1949. The United States had supported Jiang Jieshi in the civil war. After Jiang fled to Taiwan, the United States continued to support the Nationalist government there, providing military and economic aid as it faced shelling from the mainland. For decades, the United States refused to recognize the People's Republic of China, or, as many Americans called it, "Red China."

An Uneasy Alliance with the Soviet Union

Despite a treaty of friendship between China and the Soviet Union, the two communist giants were uneasy allies. In fact, Chinese communism differed from Soviet communism. In the 1950s, Stalin sent economic and technical experts to help China modernize. But he and Mao disagreed on many issues, especially on Marxist ideology. A key difference was the role of the peasantry. Mao believed that peasants were the major force behind communist revolution, while Soviets trusted in a "revolutionary elite" of urban intellectuals and workers.

By 1959, border clashes and disputes over ideology led the Soviets to withdraw all aid and advisors from China and end their alliance. Western powers welcomed the split, which eased fears of the global threat posed by communism.

China and the United States

The rift between the United States and China deepened when they supported opposing sides in the Korean War. For years, the United States tried to isolate China, which it saw as an aggressive communist power seeking to expand across Asia.

As the Cold War dragged on, however, the United States reassessed its policy towards China. There were strategic advantages to improving relations with China after its split with the Soviet Union. By "playing the China card," the United States might isolate the Soviets between NATO in the west and a hostile China in the east.

In 1971, China won admission to the United Nations. A year later, American President Richard Nixon visited Mao in Beijing, opening the door to improved relations. Formal diplomatic relations finally came in 1979.

The Nationalists in Taiwan

During the Cold War, Jiang Jieshi (Chiang Kai-shek) exercised authoritarian rule over Taiwan, hoping one day to regain control of China. By the early 1990s, however,

>> Mao Zedong's "Little Red Book" of quotations became required reading for all Chinese. Here, peasants take a break from their work in the fields to read it. **Infer** Why do you think the picture of Mao is displayed?

BOUNCE to Activate Gallery

>> **Analyze Political Cartoons** The Soviet Union and China, both communist, had a tense relationship. In 1978, China rejected a Soviet proposal to improve relations. Who does the bear represent? Who has the upper hand in this cartoon?

Taiwan had made the transition to democratic government.

On the mainland, Mao and his successors saw Taiwan as a breakaway province and insisted that it must someday be reunited with China. Tensions between Taiwan and the mainland continued throughout the Cold War, but in recent years, trade and other links between the two have grown. Although few countries recognized Taiwan, it became an economic powerhouse in Asia and a center of computer technology.

☑ **SUMMARIZE** How did China's relationships with the Soviet Union and the United States change during the Cold War?

The Two Koreas

In 1950, the Cold War erupted into a "shooting war" in Korea, a peninsula on the northeastern edge of Asia. The Korean War pitted UN forces, largely from the Western democracies, against communist North Korea, which was supported by the Soviet Union and China. It was a key event of the Cold War.

A Nation Divided Korea was an independent kingdom until Japan annexed the country in 1910 and imposed a harsh regime. After Japan's defeat in World War II, Soviet and American forces agreed to divide Korea temporarily along the **38th parallel** of latitude. American forces occupied the south, while the Soviets held the north.

During the Cold War, Korea's division—like Germany's—seemed to become permanent. North Korea, ruled by the dictator **Kim Il Sung,** became a communist ally of the Soviet Union.

In South Korea, the United States backed an authoritarian—but noncommunist—leader, **Syngman Rhee.** Each leader wanted to reunite the country—under his own rule.

The Korean War Begins In June 1950, North Korean forces invaded South Korea and soon overran most of the peninsula. Backed by the UN, which condemned the invasion, the United States organized an international force to help South Korea.

UN forces, mostly Americans and South Koreans under the command of General Douglas MacArthur, fell back in the face of the North Korean advance. They took up a defensive line known as the **Pusan Perimeter,** holding their ground against repeated North Korean attacks. MacArthur then landed troops at Inch'on, behind enemy lines, and drove the invaders back across the 38th parallel. He continued to push northward toward the Yalu River on the border of China.

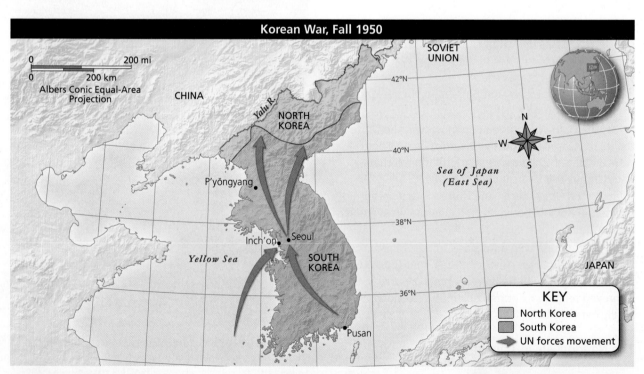

Korean War, Fall 1950

0 — 200 mi
0 — 200 km
Albers Conic Equal-Area Projection

CHINA

Yalu R.

NORTH KOREA

P'yŏngyang

SOVIET UNION

42°N

40°N

Sea of Japan (East Sea)

38°N

Inch'on • Seoul

Yellow Sea

SOUTH KOREA

JAPAN

36°N

Pusan

KEY
- North Korea
- South Korea
- → UN forces movement

>> **Analyze Maps** War broke out in Korea in 1950. Communist North Korea invaded South Korea in an effort to reunite Korea. In the fall of 1950, who controlled most of the Korean Peninsula?

Ⓑ BOUNCE to Activate Map

China Responds MacArthur's success alarmed China, which feared an American invasion. Mao Zedong sent Chinese troops to help the North Koreans. In tough winter fighting, the Chinese and North Koreans pushed the UN forces back across the 38th parallel. The Korean War then turned into a long, deadly stalemate.

Korea Remains Divided Fighting continued until 1953, when both sides signed an armistice to end the fighting. Almost two million North Korean and South Korean troops dug in on either side of the **demilitarized zone (DMZ),** an area with no military forces, near the 38th parallel. American forces, too, remained in South Korea to guarantee the peace. The ceasefire has held for more than 60 years, but no peace treaty has ever been negotiated.

After the war, the two Koreas slowly rebuilt their economies which were destroyed by the fighting and by the Japanese occupation. Korea itself remained a focus of Cold War rivalry. The United States funneled aid to South Korea, while the Soviets helped communist North Korea.

South Korea Prospers For decades, a dictatorial government backed by the military ruled South Korea. By 1987, however, growing prosperity and fierce student protests forced the government to ease controls and hold direct elections. The country also faced new social pressures as more people moved to the cities, undermining traditional rural ways of life.

North Korea Isolates Itself Under Kim Il Sung, North Korea recovered from the war, but by the late 1960s, growth stalled. Kim emphasized self-reliance and kept North Korea isolated from much of the world. When its old partners, the Soviet Union and China, tried out economic reforms in the 1980s, North Korea clung to hardline communism and its command economy in which the government controlled economic decisions.

In North Korea, a barrage of propaganda glorified Kim as the "Great Leader." Kim's successors, his son and grandson, continued to isolate the country and impose ruthless totalitarian control over all aspects of life.

For years, North Koreans lived on the edge of starvation as the country suffered from food shortages, natural disasters, and economic mismanagement. North Korea, meanwhile, poured resources into developing nuclear weapons in spite of international condemnation.

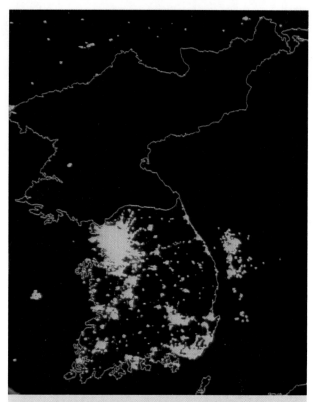

>> South Korea has a modern economy and infrastructure, while North Korea's infrastructure is limited. This 2006 nighttime satellite image shows an eerily dark North Korea and a brightly lit South Korea.

☑ **EXPLAIN** Explain why China became involved in the Korean War.

☑ ASSESSMENT

1. **Contrast** How did Chinese communism differ from Soviet communism?

2. **Infer** How did the United States use the changing relationship between China and the Soviet Union to its own advantage?

3. **Predict** How might Korea be different if UN forces had not stepped in to oppose the North Korean invasion in 1950?

4. **Recall** How did North Korea's economic performance compare with South Korea's?

5. **Connections to Today** One of the effects of the Great Leap Forward was mass famine in China. It remains a global problem. Why do you think organizations today working to eliminate hunger are also teaching new farming methods and better nutrition?

GO ONLINE to access this biography: Mao Zedong

19.4

Vietnam became the focus of Cold War tensions when communist guerrilla fighters fought against French rule. Here, Viet Minh troops enter Hanoi on October 14, 1954.

 BOUNCE to Activate Flipped Video

Objectives

Describe events in Indochina after World War II.

Explain how the United States became involved in the Vietnam War.

Explore the end of the Vietnam War.

Summarize the impact of the war on Vietnam and Cambodia.

Key Terms

Ho Chi Minh
guerilla
Dien Bien Phu
domino theory
Viet Cong
Tet Offensive
Khmer Rouge
Pol Pot

War in Southeast Asia

During World War II, Japan seized much of Southeast Asia from the European colonial powers that ruled the region. After Japan's defeat, local nationalists rejected European efforts to reclaim their colonial empires. Some Southeast Asian nations won freedom without much violence. Others, like Vietnam, faced long wars of liberation.

The Road to War in Southeast Asia

Cold War tensions complicated the drive for freedom. The United States supported independence for colonial people in principle. But the West was anxious to stop the spread of communism. As a result, the United States helped anti-communist leaders win power, even if they had little popular support.

The Long War Begins In mainland Southeast Asia, an agonizing liberation struggle tore apart the region once known as French Indochina. It affected the emerging nations of Vietnam, Cambodia, and Laos. The 30-year conflict was a key event of the Cold War and had two major phases: the battle against the French from 1946 to 1954, and the Cold War conflict that involved the United States and lasted from 1955 to 1975.

In 1946, the French set out to reestablish their authority over Indochina. In Vietnam, the French faced opposition forces led by **Ho Chi Minh** (hoh chee min). Ho, a nationalist and a communist, had waged warfare against Japanese occupying forces using

GO ONLINE to access your digital course

guerrillas, or small groups of loosely organized soldiers making surprise raids.

In 1954, Ho Chi Minh's guerilla forces decisively defeated French troops at the battle of **Dien Bien Phu** (dyen byen foo). The defeat forced France to end its efforts to reclaim Indochina. Cambodia, and Laos meanwhile, had won independence separately.

Vietnam Is Divided By 1954, the struggle in Vietnam had become part of the Cold War. At an international conference that year, Western and communist powers agreed to a temporary division of Vietnam.

Ho and the communists ruled North Vietnam. A fierce anti-communist government, led by Ngo Dinh Diem (ngoh Dinh dee EM) and supported by the United States, ruled South Vietnam.

The agreement called for elections to be held to reunite Vietnam within a year. The elections never took place, however, largely because the Americans and Diem feared the communists might win.

Although prodded by the United States, Diem refused to undertake needed reforms, and his increasingly dictatorial rule and corrupt government alienated many South Vietnamese. By 1959, South Vietnam was facing a growing challenge from both communist guerrillas and rising discontent with Diem.

☑ **IDENTIFY CENTRAL IDEAS** Why did Vietnamese guerrillas fight the French in Indochina?

The United States Enters the War

American officials believed in the domino theory, which held that a communist victory in South Vietnam would cause noncommunist governments across Southeast Asia to fall to communism—like a row of dominoes. To prevent such a disaster, the United States stepped in to shore up the Diem government.

However, there were limits to what American power could achieve in Vietnam. President John F. Kennedy realized that the United States alone could not prop up the unpopular Diem government in South Vietnam. In an interview, he noted:

> I don't think that unless a greater effort is made by the Government to win popular support that the war can be won out there. . . . We can help

them, we can give them equipment, we can send our men out there as advisors, but they have to win it, the people of Vietnam, against the Communists.

—President John F. Kennedy

Diem was overthrown and killed in early November 1963 by South Vietnamese military leaders. After Diem's death, the United States became more deeply involved in Vietnam, working with the ruling generals against the growing threat from communist rebels.

American Involvement In North Vietnam, Ho Chi Minh was determined to reunite the country under communist rule. He helped the **Viet Cong,** the communist rebels trying to defeat South Vietnam's government. At first, the United States sent only supplies and military advisers to South Vietnam. But as the Viet Cong won control of more areas, the United States was dragged into the fighting, turning a local struggle into a major Cold War conflict.

In August 1964, the *Maddox,* an American warship in the Gulf of Tonkin, reported attacks by North Vietnamese torpedo boats in retaliation for

>> U.S. soldiers search for Viet Cong hideouts in the jungle northeast of Saigon.

▶ BOUNCE to Activate Gallery

South Vietnamese commando raids nearby. Without mentioning the commando raids, President Lyndon Johnson used the attacks to win congressional approval for the Gulf of Tonkin Resolution. It authorized the president to take all necessary measures to prevent further aggression.

The United States soon began bombing targets in North Vietnam, although no war was ever declared. When air strikes failed to force Ho to abandon the war, the United States committed more and more troops to the conflict. By 1969, more than 500,000 American troops were serving in Vietnam. Meantime, the Soviet Union and China sent aid—but no troops—to help North Vietnam.

Guerrilla Warfare Like the French before them, American forces faced a guerrilla war. Many rebels in South Vietnam were local peasants who knew the countryside. They often found safe haven among villagers who resented the foreign troops and bombings that destroyed their homes and crops. American forces were hard put to tell whether villagers were rebels or innocent civilians.

Supplies for the guerrillas came from North Vietnam, along a series of trails, known as the Ho Chi Minh Trail. These trails wound through the rainforests of neighboring Laos and Cambodia. In an effort to stop the flow of supplies, the United States sent bombers and ground troops across the border into these nations, widening the war in Southeast Asia.

The Tet Offensive Even with massive American help, South Vietnam could not defeat the Viet Cong and their North Vietnamese allies. In January 1968, communist forces launched the **Tet Offensive,** a series of attacks by the Viet Cong on cities across the south. North Vietnamese forces assaulted an American marine base. The attacks were unexpected because they took place during Tet, the Vietnamese New Year.

During bloody fighting, the communists lost many troops and were unable to hold any cities against the American counterattacks. Still, the Tet Offensive marked a turning point in American public opinion. Up to then, Americans believed that the war was winnable. Tet shook public confidence in the war and its leaders.

☑ **APPLY CONCEPTS** How did the domino theory lead the United States to send troops to Vietnam?

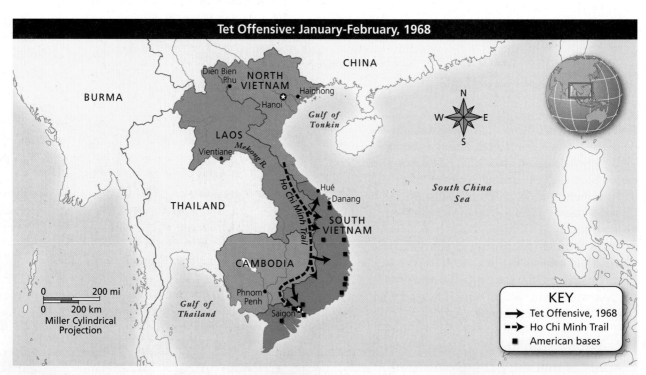

>> **Analyze Maps** The Tet Offensive was a series of attacks by communist guerrillas on South Vietnamese cities. Through which countries did the Ho Chi Minh Trail pass on the way to South Vietnam?

🔵 BOUNCE to Activate Timeline

The Vietnam War Ends

In the United States, the bombing of North Vietnam and increasing American casualties helped inflame anti-war opinion. Growing numbers of American troops were prisoners of war (POWs) or missing in action (MIAs). Many opponents called the Vietnam War a quagmire, or swamp, in which the United States was trapped without the possibility of victory.

American Opposition to the War Grows As the United States committed more troops and poured vast sums into the war, the nation grew increasingly divided. At first, the majority of Americans backed the war effort to stop the spread of communism. By the mid-1960s, a growing number of Americans were calling for an end to the war. They questioned why the United States was sending its troops to fight in a local conflict in Southeast Asia.

By 1967, the anti-war movement was spreading. Television news programs relayed vivid pictures of American casualties and the burning ruins of Vietnamese villages. On college campuses, students rallied against the war, especially as more young men faced the draft, or compulsory military service.

Prominent leaders from all walks of life joined the protests in cities across the nation. Many Americans had mixed feelings. "I want to get out," said one woman, "but I don't want to give up."

A Negotiated Peace Faced with mounting protests at home, President Johnson, who had greatly widened the war, decided not to run for a second term in 1968. His successor, President Richard Nixon, eventually arranged a cease-fire agreement in 1973. Under the agreement, the United States began to withdraw troops from South Vietnam. North Vietnam agreed it would not send any more troops to the south. The accord left South Vietnam to determine its own future.

Vietnam Is Reunited Two years after American troops withdrew, the North Vietnamese captured Saigon, capital of South Vietnam. In 1976, they renamed the city Ho Chi Minh City, in honor of their liberation leader. Hanoi, the capital of North Vietnam, became the capital of the reunited nation.

The communist victors imposed harsh rule on the south. Tens of thousands of Vietnamese fled in small boats. Many of these "boat people" drowned. Survivors ended up in refugee camps in nearby countries. Eventually, some were accepted into the United States or other countries.

Vietnam had to rebuild a land mangled by decades of war. Recovery was slow due partly to

>> People gathered on the Mall in Washington, D.C., on November 15, 1969, to protest the Vietnam War. The Peace Moratorium was estimated to be the largest demonstration in U.S. history.

>> Between the 1973 ceasefire and the final American pullout in 1975, refugees flooded seaports in Vietnam to escape. This Vietnamese navy ship carried more than 7,000 refugees.

>> The Khmer Rouge used children as soldiers in its five-year-long civil war to establish a communist government in Cambodia.

gained ground and overthrew the government in 1975. Led by the brutal dictator **Pol Pot,** the Khmer Rouge unleashed a reign of terror. To destroy all Western influences, they drove people from the cities and forced them to work in the fields. They slaughtered, starved, or worked to death more than one million Cambodians, about a third of the population. The international community failed to readily respond to the genocide.

In 1979, Vietnam invaded and occupied Cambodia, ending the genocide. From 1979 until 1994, no international legal action was taken against the Khmer Rouge for their crimes. Pol Pot and his forces retreated to remote areas. In 1993, UN peacekeepers supervised elections. Despite guerrillas who still terrorized parts of the country, a new government began to rebuild Cambodia. In 1997 at Cambodia's request, the United Nations set up a committee to investigate the crimes. The recommendation was an international tribunal to try Khmer Rouge and other Cambodian leaders for war crimes and crimes against humanity.

☑ **SUMMARIZE** Why did the United States withdraw its troops from Vietnam?

government inefficiency and partly to an American-led boycott of Vietnam. For years, the country was mired in poverty. By the 1990s, however, a new generation of Vietnamese leaders opened the door to investors by introducing free-market reforms. After the Cold War ended, the United States and Vietnam edged toward better relations.

Politically Motivated Mass Murder in Cambodia

During the Vietnam War, fighting spilled over into neighboring Cambodia. The North Vietnamese sent supplies through Cambodia to guerrilla forces in South Vietnam. In 1969, the United States bombed those routes and then briefly invaded Cambodia.

After the Americans left, Cambodian communist guerrillas, the **Khmer Rouge** (kuh MEHR roozh),

☑ ASSESSMENT

1. **Draw Conclusions** Why did the French withdraw from Indochina in the 1950s?

2. **Apply Concepts** How was American involvement in Vietnam an extension of the Truman Doctrine?

3. **Compare Points of View** What different opinions did Americans have about U.S. involvement in the Vietnam War?

4. **Synthesize** Woud you agree that the "dominoes fell" after the Vietnam War? Why or why not?

5. **Summarize** How did the local struggle in Vietnam reflect the larger Cold War conflict?

GO ONLINE to access this biography: Lyndon B. Johnson

Missiles are paraded in Red Square in Moscow. The heavy military commitments of the Soviet Union was one of the factors that led to its decline.

The Cold War Ends

During the Cold War, relations between the Soviet Union and the United States swung back and forth between confrontation and détente. The superpowers confronted each other over issues such as the Berlin Wall, Soviet intervention in Eastern Europe, and Cuba. However, in the 1970s, Soviet leader Leonid Brezhnev pursued détente and disarmament with the United States.

The Soviet Union Declines

Détente came to an abrupt end in 1979, after the Soviet Union invaded Afghanistan to ensure its influence in that neighboring nation. Like the Vietnam War in the United States, the Afghan War drained the Soviet economy and provoked a crisis at home.

The Soviets in Afghanistan The Soviet Union invaded Afghanistan in late 1979 to support an Afghan communist government that had seized power a year earlier. The new government's efforts to introduce social reforms and redistribute land roused bitter resentment among the anti-communist, devoutly Muslim Afghan people. As insurgencies, or uprisings, threatened the government, the Soviet Union stepped in.

For ten years, Soviet forces battled widely scattered groups of **mujahedin** (moo jah heh DEEN), or Muslim guerrilla fighters. Despite 100,000 troops, the Soviets controlled only the cities, not the countryside. When the Soviets turned to bombing rural areas, millions of Afghan refugees fled into neighboring Pakistan. The United States funneled weapons and other military supplies to help the insurgents battle Soviet troops.

By the late 1980s, the Afghan War had become a quagmire for the Soviet Union. It was draining badly needed resources

BOUNCE to Activate Flipped Video

Objectives

Understand why the Soviet Union declined.

Identify the reforms introduced by Mikhail Gorbachev.

Describe the collapse of communism in Eastern Europe and the Soviet Union.

Evaluate how the end of the Cold War affected the remaining communist nations and the United States.

Key Terms

mujahedin
Mikhail Gorbachev
glasnost
perestroika
Lech Walesa
Solidarity
Václav Havel
Nicolae Ceausescu

and costing many casualties. In 1989, the Soviets withdrew from Afghanistan to focus on troubling issues at home.

The Command Economy Stagnates

The Soviet economy faced severe problems. Unlike the economies of Western Europe and the United States, which experienced booms during the Cold War, the communist economies of Eastern Europe and the Soviet Union stagnated. Central economic planning led to inefficiency and waste. In competition with free market economies of the West, the Soviet command economy began to collapse. It could not match the West in production of quality consumer goods. People saw little improvement in their lives and envied their western neighbors.

The arms race put an additional strain on the Soviet economy. By the 1980s, both superpowers were spending massive sums on costly weapons systems. U.S. President Ronald Reagan began a massive military buildup, partly because he believed that the Soviet Union could not afford to spend as much on defense as the United States. When Reagan launched a new round of missile development, it was clear that the Soviet economy could not afford to match it.

>> Gorbachev struggled at home, but the United States welcomed Soviet reforms. President Ronald Reagan and Mikhail Gorbachev shake hands before a summit near Geneva in 1985. In a 1987 speech near the Berlin Wall, Reagan urged Gorbachev to "tear down this wall!"

Gorbachev Tries Reform

In 1985, an energetic new leader, **Mikhail Gorbachev** (GAWR buh chawf), came to power in the Soviet Union. In foreign policy, Gorbachev sought to end Cold War tensions. To ease tensions, Gorbachev renounced the Brezhnev Doctrine, which had asserted the Soviet Union had a right to intervene militarily in any Warsaw Pact nation.

He signed arms control treaties with the United States and eventually pulled Soviet troops out of Afghanistan.

At home, Gorbachev launched a two-pronged effort at reform. First, he called for **glasnost,** or openness. He ended censorship and encouraged people to talk openly about the country's problems.

Second, he urged **perestroika** (pehr uh STROY kuh), or the restructuring of government and the economy. Gorbachev's reforms also included a lessening of restraints on emigration. Natan Sharansky, a Soviet scientist and human rights activist, had been imprisoned for ten years for treason. Long denied permission to emigrate, he was released in exchange for a Soviet spy in 1986 and settled in Israel.

Gorbachev hoped that streamlining government and reducing the size of the bureaucracy would boost efficiency and output. He backed some free-market ideas, including limited private enterprise. But he still wanted to keep the essence of communism.

Corrupt or inefficient officials were dismissed. To produce more and higher-quality goods, factory managers, instead of central planners, were made responsible for decisions. To increase food supplies, farmers were allowed more land on which to grow food to sell on the free market.

☑ **IDENTIFY SUPPORTING DETAILS** What economic problems did the Soviets face in the 1970s and 1980s?

The Soviet Union Collapses

Gorbachev faced a host of problems. His policies brought rapid change that led to economic turmoil. Shortages grew worse, and prices soared. Factories that could not survive without government help closed, throwing thousands out of work. Old-line Communists and bureaucrats whose careers were at stake denounced the reforms. At the same time, other critics demanded even more changes.

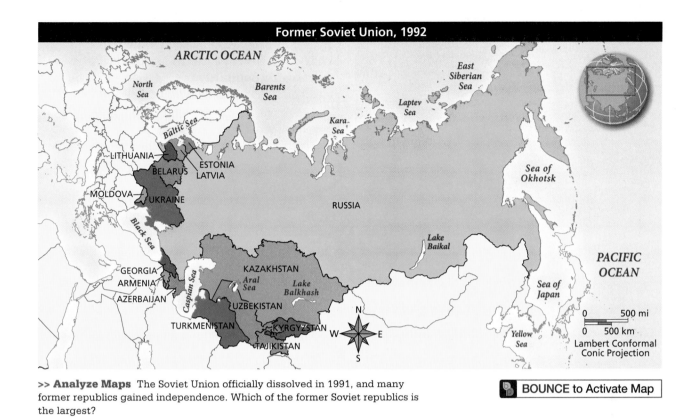

Former Soviet Union, 1992

>> **Analyze Maps** The Soviet Union officially dissolved in 1991, and many former republics gained independence. Which of the former Soviet republics is the largest?

BOUNCE to Activate Map

The Soviet Empire Crumbles Glasnost encouraged unrest in the multinational Soviet empire. The Baltic republics of Estonia, Latvia, and Lithuania, which had been seized by the Soviet Union in 1940, broke away in 1990, declaring independence soon after. In Eastern Europe, countries from Poland to Bulgaria broke out of the Soviet orbit, beginning in 1989. Russia's postwar empire seemed to be collapsing.

In mid-1991, Soviet hardliners tried to overthrow Gorbachev and restore the old order. Their attempted coup failed, but it further weakened Gorbachev. By year's end, as other Soviet republics declared independence, Gorbachev resigned.

End of the Soviet Union In December 1991, the Union of Soviet Socialist Republics was officially dissolved after almost 70 years. Its 15 republics became separate independent nations. Russia, the largest republic, had dominated the Soviet Union.

After the breakup, Russia and its new president, Boris Yeltsin, faced a difficult future. They struggled to build a market economy and prevent violent conflict between pro-democracy and pro-communist groups. Like Russia, the other former Soviet republics like Ukraine and Kazakhstan faced hard times. They wanted to build stable governments and improve their standards of living. But ethnic violence and economic

troubles proved obstacles. Some republics had stores of nuclear weapons, which they agreed to give up in exchange for aid and investment from the West.

☑ **SUMMARIZE** How did Gorbachev's reforms lead to a new map of Europe and Asia?

Eastern Europe Transformed

During the Cold War, Eastern Europe lay in the Soviet orbit. Efforts to resist Soviet domination were met with harsh repression. Despite the Soviet threat, some nations in Eastern Europe slowly made reforms. After Mikhail Gorbachev announced that the Soviet Union would no longer intervene in Eastern Europe, a "democracy movement" swept the region, and the nations of Eastern Europe were remarkably transformed.

Poland Struggles Toward Democracy Poland was the Soviet Union's most troublesome satellite. In 1956, protests had led to some reforms, but dissatisfaction with communism remained strong. The Roman Catholic Church, which often faced persecution, became a rallying symbol for Poles who opposed the communist regime.

>> Lech Walesa traveled to Italy in 1981 to meet Pope John Paul II, the first Polish pope. The pope was a great supporter of the Solidarity movement.

🔊 BOUNCE to Activate Timeline

>> Residents of East and West Berlin walk atop the Berlin Wall in front of the Brandenburg Gate on November 11, 1989. The wall was torn down shortly after.

In 1980, economic hardships ignited strikes of shipyard workers. Led by **Lech Walesa** (lek vah WEN suh), they organized an independent labor union, called **Solidarity.** It soon claimed millions of members, who pressed for political change.

Under pressure from the Soviet Union, the Polish government outlawed Solidarity and arrested its leaders, including Walesa. Still, unrest simmered. Walesa became a national hero and the Polish government eventually released him from prison.

Pressure from the world community further strained Poland's communist government and helped hasten its collapse. Pope John Paul II visited Poland, met with Solidarity leaders, and criticized communist policies. The pope was the former Karol Wojtyla, archbishop of the Polish city of Cracow.

In the late 1980s, Poland—like the Soviet Union—began to introduce radical economic reforms. It legalized Solidarity and in 1989 sponsored the first free elections in 50 years. Lech Walesa was soon elected president of Poland. The new government began a difficult but peaceful transition from socialism to a market economy. It helped mark the start of the collapse of Soviet domination and communism in Eastern Europe.

Revolution and Freedom By 1989, the "democracy movement" in Eastern Europe was sweeping out old governments and ushering in new ones. People took to the streets, demanding reform.

In the 1970s and 1980s, Hungary had quietly introduced some modest economic reforms. Later, in the spirit of glasnost, Hungarians began to criticize their government more openly. Under growing pressure, the communist government allowed other political parties and opened its border with Austria.

That move allowed thousands of East Germans to escape into Hungary, and from there, to the West. Within a few months, Germans tore down the Berlin Wall, a move that would soon lead to the reunification of Germany.

One by one, communist governments fell across Eastern Europe. In Czechoslovakia, **Václav Havel** (VAHTS lahv HAH vul), a dissident writer and human rights activist, was elected president. Most changes came peacefully, but when **Nicolae Ceausescu** (chow SHES koo), Romania's long time dictator, refused to step down, he was overthrown and executed.

For the first time since 1945, Eastern European countries were free to settle their own affairs. They withdrew from the Warsaw Pact and requested that Soviet troops leave. By then, Soviet power itself was crumbling.

Ethnic Tensions in Eastern Europe Centuries of migrations and conquest left most Eastern European nations with ethnically diverse populations. Most countries had a majority population with one or more ethnic minorities that asserted their own identities. Nationalism helped unite some countries such as Poland and Hungary, but it was also a divisive force.

Faced with ethnic tensions, Czechoslovakia peacefully split into two countries, the Czech Republic and Slovakia. In 1991, however, ethnic conflict tore apart the Balkan nation of Yugoslavia.

The Breakup of Yugoslavia During World War II, a skilled guerrilla leader, Josip Tito, had battled Germany occupying forces. Later, Tito set up a communist government in Yugoslavia, but he pursued a path independent of Moscow. He refused to join the Warsaw Pact and claimed to be neutral in the Cold War.

After Tito's death and the fall of communism, a wave of nationalism tore Yugoslavia apart. The country consisted of six republics, including Bosnia-Herzegovina, Croatia, Macedonia, Montenegro, Serbia, and Slovenia. In 1992, Slovenia and Croatia broke away after a bitter conflict with Serbia. That year, another conflict erupted in Bosnia, which declared independence.

Most Bosnians were Muslims, but many Serbs and Croats lived there. Bosnian Serbs rejected independence, and with money and arms from Serbia, they seized much of Bosnia. In a brutal war, Serbs practiced "ethnic cleansing," forcibly removing other ethnic groups from the areas they controlled. Hundreds of thousands of Bosnians became refugees. Others were tortured or killed. Sarajevo, the capital of Bosnia, came under a deadly siege by Bosnian Serb forces.

Restoring Peace Bosnia became a test case for the role of the United States and the Western powers in the post Cold-War world. For three years, the UN tried unsuccessfully to bring about peace. In 1994, as Bosnian Serbs advanced, the United States and its NATO allies began air strikes against Serbian targets in Bosnia.

In 1995, the United States helped broker a peace agreement, known as the Dayton Accords, which ended the war in Bosnia. NATO peacekeepers enforced the agreements in the troubled Balkan region, and the various new nations set out to recover from the brutal ethnic conflict.

☑ **IDENTIFY CAUSE AND EFFECT** How did glasnost in the Soviet Union contribute to the end of communist rule in Eastern Europe?

>> At a 1992 peace demonstration in Sarajevo, the capital of Bosnia, protesters crouch to avoid fire from Serbian snipers on a hotel roof. The Bosnian special forces soldier returns fire.

Communism Declines Around the World

The collapse of communism in the Soviet Union and Eastern Europe affected other communist nations. Cuba, which had long depended on Soviet aid and support, faced severe difficulties. Its economy suffered, too, from sanctions imposed by the United States decades earlier.

In 2006, Raul Castro, brother of the ailing leader, Fidel Castro, took over the Cuban government. He allowed some market reforms and sought investment from countries in Europe, Asia, and Latin America. After nearly half a century of tense relations, Cuba and the United States resumed diplomatic relations in 2015. President Trump, in 2017, imposed some former restrictions. But the U.S. embassy remained open in Havana. Raul Castro stepped down as president in 2018.

Other Communist Nations Adopt Market Reforms China began to introduce limited market reforms, such as allowing some private enterprise and foreign investment, in the early 1980s. The reforms brought increased prosperity for some Chinese. By the early 2000s, China's economy was

>> The role of the United States as the sole remaining superpower means that the U.S. military often responds to problems and conflicts all over the world.

The Post-Cold War World

When the Cold War ended in the early 1990s, as the sole superpower, the United States played a leading role in trying to resolve world conflicts. The United States and its European allies were also eager to help the new nations of Eastern Europe to make the difficult transition to democracy and capitalism. They provided advice and loans, but also required far-reaching economic reforms.

The Move Toward Market Economies In the aftermath of the Cold War, the nations of Eastern Europe—as well as Russia and the former Soviet republics—set out to build stable democratic governments and replace their old command economies with free-market economies. To attract badly needed foreign investment, governments had to push radical economic reforms. They privatized industries and stopped keeping prices for basic goods and services low. They ended many benefits from the old days such as free tuition at universities. At first, the changes brought hardships such as high unemployment, soaring prices, and crime. Consumer goods were more plentiful, but few people could afford them.

A further stumbling block to progress was the global economic recession that started in 2008. Economic hard times brought a rise of anti-foreign sentiment along with anti-Semitic and anti-Roma (Gypsy) hate speech from extremist groups. By 2019, governments in many European countries saw the growth of populist parties that opposed immigration, rejected increasing globalization, and promoted nationalist traditions.

☑ **SUMMARIZE** What steps did former Communist nations take to transition to market economies?

booming, and its many new factories were turning out manufactured goods for a growing global market.

In China, as in Cuba, economic change did not bring political reform. The Chinese Communist party kept its monopoly on power, and the government cracked down on any signs of discontent.

China's government undertook no major political reforms. However, as the global economic crisis that began in 2008 led to factory closings, protests by unemployed workers increased. China's government responded with a $600 billion stimulus package to retrain workers and improve productivity.

Different Paths for Vietnam and North Korea Two other communist nations in Asia, Vietnam and North Korea, took different paths. Vietnam allowed some market reforms and won increased foreign investment. North Korea, however, clung to its old ideology, continuing its strict isolation from the world.

☑ **COMPARE** How did other communist countries react to the collapse of the Soviet bloc?

☑ ASSESSMENT

1. **Draw Conclusions** Why was the Soviet Union unable to keep up with the market economies of the West?

2. **Summarize** How did Gorbachev's reforms lead to the breakup of the Soviet empire?

3. **Identify Cause and Effect** Why were Eastern Europeans able to break free of Soviet domination in the late 1980s?

4. **Infer** How did the collapse of the Soviet Union affect the United States?

5. **Infer** Why might some communist nations have adopted market principles after the fall of the Soviet Union?

GO ONLINE to access these biographies: Mikhail Gorbachev and Lech Walesa

"Tear Down This Wall": Ronald Reagan

On June 12, 1987, President Reagan spoke in West Berlin, near the Berlin Wall, not far from where the Brandenburg Gate stood in the eastern sector. His speech acknowledged the new Soviet leader Mikhail Gorbachev's efforts at reform in the Soviet Union. However, Reagan was not satisfied with Gorbachev's limited measures. He challenged the Soviet leader to show a real commitment to reform by tearing down the Berlin Wall that had stood between East and West Berlin since 1961. This wall symbolized the division between communism and democracy.

The wall came down in 1989. The second primary source is an excerpt from an article, written in 2007, from Time magazine. It revisits Reagan's decisions about the speech before it was given.

>> Ronald Reagan and Mikhail Gorbachev

Primary Source 1

In the 1950s, Khrushchev predicted: "We will bury you." But in the West today, we see a free world that has achieved a level of prosperity and well-being unprecedented [never having happened or existed before] in all human history. In the Communist world, we see failure, technological backwardness, declining standards of health, even want of the most basic kind—too little food. Even today, the Soviet Union still cannot feed itself. After these four decades, then, there stands before the entire world one great and inescapable conclusion: Freedom leads to prosperity. Freedom replaces the ancient hatreds among the nations with comity [courtesy] and peace. Freedom is the victor [winner].

☑ **ANALYZE WORD CHOICES** Reagan characterizes Khrushchev's statement "We [Communism] will bury you" as a prediction and not as a threat. If that is true, what did Khrushchev mean when he said "We will bury you"?

And now the Soviets themselves may, in a limited way, be coming to understand the importance of freedom. We hear much from Moscow about a new policy of reform and openness. Some political prisoners have been released. Certain foreign news broadcasts are no longer being jammed. Some economic enterprises have been permitted to operate with greater freedom from state control.

☑ **DETERMINE MEANING** What does it mean to "jam" a radio or television broadcast?

Are these the beginnings of profound changes in the Soviet state? Or are they token gestures, intended to raise false hopes in the West, or to strengthen the Soviet system without changing it? We welcome change and openness; for we believe that freedom and security go together, that the advance of human liberty can only strengthen the cause of world peace. There is one sign the Soviets can make that would be unmistakable, that would advance dramatically the cause of freedom and peace.

General Secretary Gorbachev, if you seek peace, if you seek prosperity for the Soviet Union and Eastern Europe, if you seek liberalization: Come here to this gate! Mr. Gorbachev, open this gate! Mr. Gorbachev, tear down this wall!

Primary Source 2

Twenty years ago, on the morning of June 12, 1987, Reagan arrived in Berlin, on the occasion of the city's 750th birthday. He was scheduled to speak on the Western side of the Brandenburg Gate, for years the city's symbolic dividing line. His speechwriters had drafted an address intended as much for Soviet leader Mikhail Gorbachev, with whom Reagan was forging a close relationship, as for the 20,000 people who gathered to hear him speak. In the speech, Reagan would call on Gorbachev to tear down the Berlin Wall, but that language was opposed strongly by Reagan's National Security Council and the State Department, who feared it would be used by hard-liners in the Kremlin to discredit Gorbachev.

☑ **DRAW CONCLUSIONS** How do you think West Berliners would have received Reagan's message about the Wall?

When the President's entourage arrived in Berlin, Reagan's team was still arguing over the final wording. State and NSC submitted yet another draft of the speech. But in the limousine ride to the Wall, Reagan told his deputy chief of staff, Kenneth Duberstein, that he intended to issue the fateful challenge to Gorbachev. "It's the right thing to do," he said.

Two decades later, what can we learn from the epochal events that followed–the fall of the Berlin Wall, the reunification of Germany and the collapse of the Soviet Union? "People were afraid of the consequences of what Reagan would say," George Shultz, Reagan's long-serving Secretary of State, told me over lunch in Berlin last week. "But it turns out he [Reagan] was right. Saying something like, 'Mr. Gorbachev, tear down this wall'–that could be perceived as provocative. Things were breaking and were in a lot of flux. But knowing Ronald Reagan as I did, I would have said don't bother. He was going to express his feelings."

☑ ASSESSMENT

1. **Determine Central Ideas** According to the first paragraph of the first passage, why should Gorbachev tear down the Berlin Wall?

2. **Determine Author's Purpose** What was the purpose of Reagan's speech?

3. **Distinguish Among Fact, Opinion, and Reasoned Judgment** When Reagan says, "freedom is the victor," is that a fact, an opinion, or a reasoned judgment? Cite evidence from the speech to support your answer.

4. **Infer** What can you infer from the fact that such a large crowd gathered to hear President Reagan's speech?

5. **Draw Conclusions** Why do you think the President gave his speech at the Brandenburg Gate?

Connections to Today

US marines hand out food to locals after a destructive typhoon.

Take Action to Learn About Humanitarian Aid

Many organizations offer humanitarian aid on the local level. Schools, churches, synagogues, and mosques provide meals and other services for those in need. On a more global level many organizations work to meet the needs of those impacted by poverty, wars, famine, and natural disasters.

1. **Choose** one of the following humanitarian organizations to research:

   - Doctors Without Borders

   - Partners in Health

   - Habitat for Humanity

   As you conduct your research, discuss the history of the organization, its goals, and the services it provides.

2. **Ask Questions** Generate a list of questions you have about the topic.

3. **Learn** about the topic and the major issues related to the topic. What universal goals are followed by all humanitarian organizations? What are the strengths of the organizations? Are there any weaknesses? Take notes as you conduct your research and continue to generate questions as you learn more.

4. **Raise Awareness** Create a digital or print poster highlighting the work of the organization you researched. Share your poster with your class and your community.

Topic 19 Quick Study Guide

LESSON SUMMARIES

Use these Lesson Summaries, and the longer versions available online, to review the key ideas for each lesson in this Topic.

Lesson 1: A New Global Conflict

During the war, the Soviet Union and the nations of the West had cooperated to defeat Nazi Germany. By 1945, the wartime alliance was crumbling. The United States and the Soviet Union became superpowers. They also became tense rivals in a conflict known as the Cold War.

Lesson 2: The Western Democracies and Japan

After World War II, western ideas and technology helped Japan rebuild and become an economic superpower.

Lesson 3: Communism in East Asia

Even though communism in the Soviet Union did not develop as promised, many leaders still favored communism. In China, leaders such as Mao Zedong still believed communism could overturn the old order and yield economic and political success.

Lesson 4: War in Southeast Asia

For decades after the end of WWII, Southeast Asia was shaped by the nationalist drive for independence. The struggle for Vietnam became part of the Cold War.

Lesson 5: The Cold War Ends

In the 1980s, the Soviet economy began to crumble. Efforts at reform failed. After years of Communist rule, the Soviet Union collapsed and was replaced by Russia and other independent republics.

QUEST! FINDINGS

Launching a Seminar Refer to your responses to the Quest Connections to help you start a discussion about the end of the Cold War. Use the rubric and other Quest resources online to guide your work.

VISUAL REVIEW

Use these graphics to review some of the key terms, people, and ideas from this Topic.

Cold War Contrasts

COMMUNIST COUNTRIES	INDUSTRIALIZED DEMOCRACIES
Compete in arms race to maintain "balance of terror."	Compete in arms race to maintain "balance of terror."
Form Warsaw Pact. China follows separate path.	Form NATO and SEATO.
Seek to spread communism.	Seek to contain communism.
Command economies.	Market economies.
Economic stagnation, low standards of living.	Economic "miracles", prosperity with scattered recessions
Repress of dissent, labor camps	Free expression, but fears lead to an episode of McCarthyism
Power is closely held by communist parties.	Democracy is established in Japan, civil rights movement extends democracy in United States.
Lost arms race.	Won arms race.

Cold War Hot Spots

KOREA	VIETNAM
Divided into communist north and noncommunist, U.S.-supported south.	Divided into communist north and noncommunist, U.S.-supported south.
China provided troops to support North Korea.	China and the Soviet Union provided economic and military aid, but not troops, to North Vietnam.
The United States led United Nations troops supporting South Korea.	The United States and some allies provided troops to support South Vietnam.
Warfare mainly involved regular troops.	Viet Cong fighting in the south were mainly guerrillas.
United States troops remained in South Korea after war.	United States troops withdrew before the war ended.
Korean War ended in a stalemate between the two sides and a ceasefire.	Vietnam War ended when North Vietnam defeated South Vietnam and reunited the country.

Steps in the Collapse of the Soviet Empire

- The command economy could not create wealth or raise living standards as quickly as market economies.
- The Soviet Union could not afford the expense of maintaining a "balance of terror" in the arms race.
- East Europeans resisted communism and Soviet control.
- Soviet military failure in Afghanistan led to calls for change.
- Reforms in Russia included glasnost, or freedom of expression, and perestroika, or market reforms.
- East Germans forced their government to open the Berlin Wall.
- Eastern European nations rejected Soviet control and adopted market economies and democracy.
- Glasnost led to drive for independence by Soviet ethnic minorities and the breakup of the Soviet Union.
- Soviet Union was divided into 15 independent nations.
- The Warsaw Pact was dissolved.

Topic 19 Assessment

KEY TERMS, PEOPLE, AND IDEAS

1. How did the Yalta Conference cause a postwar power shift between the United States, Britain, and the Soviet Union?

2. What was the **iron curtain**? Why did Churchill choose that term?

3. What was the state of the economy in post-war United States?

4. Discuss the establishment of organizations such as NATO and the **Warsaw Pact**. What did each organization represent to western and communist nations?

5. Why did Japan experience an economic upturn decades after WWII?

6. What role did **collectivization** have in the communist economy?

7. What were the goals of Mao's economic plan "**The Great Leap Forward**"? Why did it fail?

8. What are proxy wars? Were the Vietnam War and the Korean war proxy wars? Explain.

9. Why did uprisings in Eastern Europe increase during the early years of the Cold War?

CRITICAL THINKING

10. **Explain** How did perestroika and glasnost contribute to the end of communism?

11. **Analyze Information** How did the Truman Doctrine underscore Truman's belief that the key to preventing the fall of nations to communism was to attack the "conditions of misery and want" that led to totalitarianism?

12. **Summarize** How did postwar production push the United States into an economic boom? Why was the economic performance of Eastern Europe and the Soviet Union different?

13. **Synthesize Information** What was the effect of World War II on the status of women in the United States?

14. **Draw Conclusions** Why did the Korean War end in a stalemate?

15. **Summarize** How did a local struggle in Vietnam become a major Cold War conflict?

16. **Analyze Images** The picture below shows residents of Berlin gathering around and on top of the Berlin Wall. (a) what does the gathering of people indicate about the changed feeling in Berlin? (b) The wall was torn down shortly after. How did the fall of the wall represent a change in history?

17. **Writing Activity** The excerpt below is from Robert Kaiser, a reporter for the Washington Post who was stationed in Moscow. He describes what is needed to shop at the stores in Moscow. What does it reveal about the Soviet command system? Could the command system have been another factor in the collapse of communism? Use your knowledge of the topic and what you have learned about the free market economy when writing your response.

> "A good shopper will jump into a queue [line] wherever he or she finds it, taking a place and then asking what is being offered at the other end. The queue is everywhere in Soviet life . . . the queue to buy a private car may be five years long. . . . At the neighborhood bread store, three lines are not uncommon; one to make a selection; another to pay the cashier, a third to exchange the cashier's receipt for the chosen loaf."
> —*Robert G. Kaiser, Russia from the Inside*

18. **Connections to Today** Humanitarian assistance helps people during emergencies. Reports confirm that the need has increased over the last fifty years. Do you think humanitarian aid is effective? Explain your position.

DOCUMENT-BASED QUESTIONS

The United States and the Soviet Union confronted each other in the Cold War—a global conflict that included a nuclear arms race. Read the documents below, then answer the questions that follow.

DOCUMENT A

"Seeing that their government had reasserted control over its own frontiers, the East Germans were heartened by the solidification and fortification of their state. . . .I know there are people who claim that the East Germans are imprisoned in paradise and that the gates of the Socialist paradise are guarded by armed troops. I'm aware that a defect exists, but I believe it's a necessary and only temporary defect."
—*Khrushchev Remembers by Nikita Khrushchev*

DOCUMENT B

". . . I hope the Prime Minister has understood all the implications of what I said," Nixon went on, with an oblique [indirect] reference to Berlin. "What I mean is that the moment we place either one of these powerful nations, through an ultimatum, in a position where it has no choice but to accept dictation or fight, then you are playing with the most destructive force in the world."

Khrushchev: (flushed, wagging a finger near Nixon's face): We too are giants. If you want to threaten, we will answer threat with threat.

Nixon: We never engage in threats.

Khrushchev: You wanted indirectly to threaten me. But we have means at our disposal that can have very bad consequences.

Nixon: We have too.
—*Time, August 3, 1959*

DOCUMENT C

The wall that kept East Germans from crossing into West Germany.

DOCUMENT D

Divided Germany and Berlin, 1949–1990

KEY
West Germany and West Berlin
East Germany and East Berlin

19. The author's purpose in Document A was to
   A. explain East German discipline.
   B. offer a balanced perspective on the Cold War.
   C. argue for a fortified barrier between East and West Germany.
   D. explain the role of the Soviet Union in East Germany.

20. The tone of the exchange in Document B is
   A. friendly and joking
   B. tense and hostile
   C. cautious
   D. businesslike

21. Document D shows that
   A. West Berlin was located inside West Germany.
   B. the border between East and West Germany passes through Berlin.
   C. East Germany surrounded West Gemany.
   D. two East German borders separated West Berlin from West Germany.

22. Writing Activity How was the Cold War fought? Use what you have read in the topic, along with these documents, to write a response.

GO ONLINE to access more practice

Developing Nations Emerge
(1945–Present)

ESSENTIAL QUESTION What should governments do?

GO ONLINE for immersive experiences designed to help you explore some of the experiences of Africans between 1945 and 1985 through rich primary sources. Also access the eText, videos, Biographies, and other online resources.

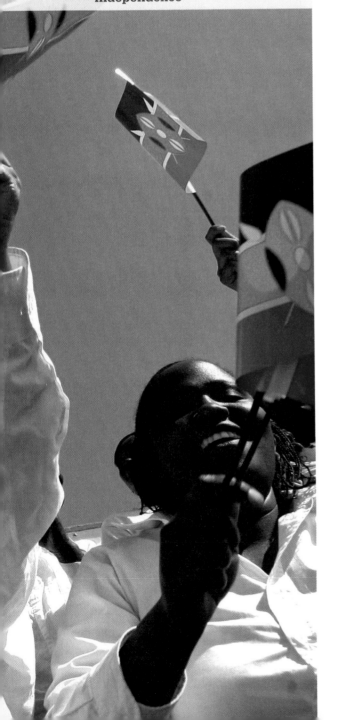

Women in Kenya celebrating the anniversary of winning independence

Connections to Today

Natural resources often have an enormous impact on new countries or in developing regions. They can spur rapid economic development, but they can also lead to conflict or environmental damage. In this Topic, you'll learn about how resources have affected developing nations around the world. How does the presence or lack of resources affect areas of the world today?

NBC LEARN

Learn about Aung San Suu Kyi's efforts to bring democracy to Myanmar.

BOUNCE to Activate My Story Video

In this Topic, you will learn about the events that occurred as nations emerged and developed after World War II. Look at the lesson outline and explore the timeline. As you study this Topic, you will complete the Quest inquiry.

LESSON OUTLINE

20.1 New Nations in South Asia and Southeast Asia

20.2 Rapid Development in China and India

20.3 African Nations Win Independence

20.4 Challenges for African Nations

20.5 The Modern Middle East Takes Shape

20.6 Conflicts in the Middle East

20.7 Latin American Nations Move Towards Democracy

Key Events as New Nations Emerge

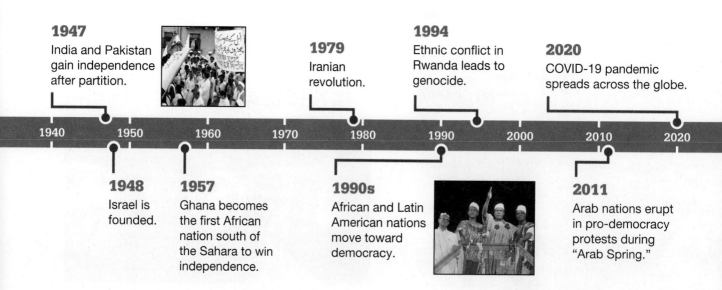

1947
India and Pakistan gain independence after partition.

1979
Iranian revolution.

1994
Ethnic conflict in Rwanda leads to genocide.

2020
COVID-19 pandemic spreads across the globe.

1948
Israel is founded.

1957
Ghana becomes the first African nation south of the Sahara to win independence.

1990s
African and Latin American nations move toward democracy.

2011
Arab nations erupt in pro-democracy protests during "Arab Spring."

1940 1950 1960 1970 1980 1990 2000 2010 2020

ⓠUEST! INQUIRY

Present a Position Paper

Is genocide a preventable crime? You are part of the global conversation about this topic at the United Nations. Review the outcome of the Genocide Convention at the United Nations in 1948. In this Quest, you will research and explore this issue.

 STEP 1

First, research the laws and action plans which are in place to prevent genocide. Are these actions effective? Discuss with your team. Prepare a list of questions you might want to address as you continue.

 STEP 2

Review the primary sources. Discuss the various viewpoints. Begin a draft outline of your position paper.

 STEP 3

Review, edit, and revise your paper. Your team is ready to address the General Assembly of the United Nations on the issue of genocide. What were the viewpoints of other teams?

 STEP 4

Reflect on what you have learned. Consider this quote: The Genocide Convention said "never again" to genocide. But it has become "again" and "again." Discuss the issue.

GO ONLINE to access complete Quest materials

20.1

Indians celebrated independence from Britain during this parade in Mumbai on August 15, 1947.

 BOUNCE to Activate Flipped Video

Objectives

Explain how independence led to the partition of India.

Describe the national development of India, Pakistan, and Bangladesh.

Define the role of South Asia in the Cold War.

Explain the impact of independence on the nations of Southeast Asia.

Key Terms

partition	Suharto
Sikh	East Timor
Kashmir	Ferdinand Marcos
Jawaharlal Nehru	Benigno Aquino
dalits	Corazon Aquino
Indira Gandhi	
Punjab	
Golden Temple	
Bangladesh	
nonalignment	
autocratic	
Aung San Suu Kyi	
Sukarno	

New Nations in South Asia and Southeast Asia

At the same time that the Cold War was unfolding, a global independence movement was reshaping the world. The European colonial powers, especially Britain and France, had been weakened by World War II. Their military and financial resources were exhausted, and so was their will to hold on to their colonial empires. While nationalists in the colonies were ready to fight for their freedom, many war-weary Europeans had no desire for further conflict.

Independence and Partition in South Asia

Among the first new nations to win independence were the former British colonies of South Asia, or the Indian subcontinent. Nationalists in British-ruled India had demanded self-rule since the late 1800s. As independence neared, however, a long-simmering issue surfaced. What would happen to the Muslim minority in a Hindu-dominated India?

The Formation of India and Pakistan Like Mohandas Gandhi, most of the leaders and members of the Congress Party were Hindus. However, the party wanted a unified India that would include both Muslims and Hindus.

The Muslim League, led by Muhammad Ali Jinnah, had a different view of liberation. Although they had cooperated with the Congress Party in the drive for independence, they feared discrimination against the Muslim minority in a unified India. Therefore, the Muslim League demanded the creation of a separate nation, called Pakistan, that would include the parts of British India where Muslims formed a majority.

After World War II, the British government decided that it could no longer afford to resist Indian demands for independence. As independence approached, violence between Hindus and Muslims worsened, pushing Britain to accept the idea of **partition,** or dividing the subcontinent into two nations. In 1947, British officials hastily drew borders to create a mostly Hindu India, and a Pakistan made up of two widely separated areas that had Muslim majorities. In August 1947, the two nations celebrated their independence.

Partition Leads to Violence Drawing fair borders for the two new nations was impossible because Hindus and Muslims lived side by side in many areas. As soon as the new borders became known, a mass migration began. On the Pakistani side of the borders, millions of Hindus and **Sikhs** (seeks) members of a South Asian religious minority, packed their belongings and fled to the new India. At the same time, millions of Muslims fled from India into newly created Pakistan. An estimated 10 million people left their homes, most of them on foot.

Muslims fleeing along the crowded roads into Pakistan were slaughtered by Hindus and Sikhs. Muslims massacred Hindu and Sikh neighbors. Around one million people died in these massacres. Others died of starvation and exposure on the road.

Horrified at the partition and the violence, Gandhi turned once more to satyagraha, or nonviolent resistance to evil. On January 30, 1948, he was shot and killed by a Hindu extremist. Prime Minister Nehru told a stricken nation, "The light has gone out of our lives and there is darkness everywhere." Gandhi's death discredited extremists and helped end the worst violence. Still, Hindu-Muslim tensions remained.

The Battle for Kashmir Since independence, India and Pakistan have fought a series of wars over **Kashmir,** a state in the Himalayas. In 1947, Kashmir's Hindu ruler tried to join India. However, Kashmir's Muslim majority wanted to be part of Pakistan. The two new countries quickly went to war over the state. India held on to more than half of Kashmir, but tensions led to additional wars with Pakistan as well as with Kashmiri separatists. Today, Kashmir remains a flashpoint in the tense relations between India and Pakistan.

A Nuclear Arms Race In the 1970s, first India and then Pakistan developed nuclear weapons programs. By 1998, both nations had successfully tested nuclear weapons. The emergence of these two nuclear powers alarmed neighbors in South Asia and the world, in part because of the ongoing hostility between India and Pakistan. Another concern was the danger that extremists in either country might get access to nuclear technology or even nuclear weapons.

Terror in Sri Lanka The island of Ceylon won freedom from Britain in 1948. Later, it took the name Sri (sree) Lanka. In the 1970s, ethnic tensions sparked a long, brutal guerrilla war in Sri Lanka.

Most Sri Lankans are Buddhists who speak Sinhalese. A large Tamil-speaking Hindu minority living in the north and east charged the government with discrimination. When efforts to win equality failed, Tamil rebels waged war to set up a separate nation. For three decades, terrorism and brutality fed the deadly conflict between government forces and Tamil rebels. In 2009, the government regained control of Tamil-held towns and restored peace. Ten years later, suicide bombers belonging to a radical Islamist group targeted Christian churches and hotels, shocking the island nation and the world.

>> Indian refugees crowd onto trains after India and Pakistan are separated into two independent states. Muslims fled to Pakistan and Hindus fled to India in one of the largest transfers of population in history.

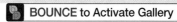 BOUNCE to Activate Gallery

>> Indira Gandhi served as India's prime minister for almost 15 years, though not consecutively. She lost her election in 1977 due to unpopular policies, but won back the seat in 1980.

>> Jawaharlal Nehru meets with Indian citizens of Pashtun ethnicity. Pashtuns are ethnic Afghans and are predominantly Muslim.

☑ **IDENTIFY MAIN IDEAS** Why is Kashmir a source of conflict between India and Pakistan?

Challenges to Modern India

Upon achieving independence, India built on the legacy of British rule to form a parliamentary democracy. Although India is today the world's largest democracy, it has faced many challenges. Ethnic and religious tensions threatened its unity. Its people speak over 100 languages and many dialects. Hundreds of millions of Indians lived in desperate poverty. Despite unrest and diversity, India has emerged as a major world power.

Strong Prime Ministers Set Goals During its early decades, India benefited from strong leadership. The Congress Party, which had spearheaded the independence movement, worked to turn India into a modern nation. From 1947 to 1964, **Jawaharlal Nehru** (juh WAH huhr lahl NAY roo), leader of the Congress Party, was India's prime minister. He worked to build a modern, secular state dedicated to promoting economic growth and social justice. Under Nehru, food output rose, but so did India's population. The government encouraged family planning to reduce the birthrate, but with limited success.

Although India's 1947 constitution banned discrimination against people in the lowest castes, discrimination based on caste continued. Nehru's government set aside jobs and places in universities for **dalits,** and other lower-caste Indians. Still, higher-caste Hindus generally got better schooling and jobs.

Later, Nehru's daughter, **Indira Gandhi,** served as prime minister for most of the years between 1966 and 1984. She had a global influence and challenged traditional discrimination against women.

Religious Conflicts Persist India was a land of many religions. A majority of Indians were Hindu, but millions were Muslim, Sikh, Christian, or Buddhist. At times, religious divisions led to violence.

Some Sikhs wanted greater autonomy for **Punjab,** a prosperous, largely Sikh state in northern India. Sikh dissidents engaged in protests, most of them nonviolent, against government policies. These protests were organized from the **Golden Temple,** the most prominent Sikh house of worship. Indira Gandhi planned an attack to remove Sikh dissidents hiding in the Golden Temple.

Under Chinese control

AFGHANISTAN

Pakistani Kashmir

Indian Kashmir

PAKISTAN

Indus R.

BHUTAN

NEPAL

Ganges R.

INDIA

Arabian Sea

BANGLADESH

Bay of Bengal

0 400 mi
0 400 km
Miller Cylindrical Projection

INDIAN OCEAN

SRI LANKA

>> **Analyze Maps** This map shows South Asia today. West Pakistan is now called Pakistan. East Pakistan is now called Bangladesh. Ceylon is now called Sri Lanka. What geographic reason made it difficult for Pakistan to retain control of Bangladesh?

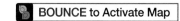

BOUNCE to Activate Map

As news of this planned attack leaked, Sikh activists fortified the Golden Temple with arms and weapons. Indian troops attacked the temple in 1984. Over a thousand Sikhs were killed and many religious artifacts were destroyed. Soon after, Gandhi was assassinated by two of her Sikh bodyguards. In the state-sponsored anti-Sikh riots that followed, thousands more Sikhs were killed.

In the 1980s, the Hindu nationalist party, Bharatiya Janata Party (BJP), began to challenge the secular, or nonreligious, Congress Party. The BJP accused Indira Gandhi of overstepping her authority and favoring minority religions at the expense of Hinduism. They wanted a government based on Hindu traditions. Religious minority groups accused the party of stoking violence.

☑ **SUMMARIZE** How did the Indian government try to improve conditions for lower castes?

Pakistan and Bangladesh Separate

When Pakistan gained independence in 1947, it was a divided country. West Pakistan and East Pakistan were located on either side of India, separated by a

thousand miles. India made trade and travel between the two Pakistans difficult.

Bangladesh Declares Independence Although most East and West Pakistanis were Muslims, their languages and cultures differed. Bengalis in the east outnumbered Punjabis in the west, but Punjabis dominated the government. The government concentrated most economic development programs in West Pakistan, while East Pakistan remained deep in poverty. Many Bengalis resented governmental neglect of East Pakistan.

In 1971, Bengalis in East Pakistan declared independence. They named their country **Bangladesh,** or "Bengali nation." Pakistan's military ruler ordered the army to crush the rebellion. Millions of Bengalis fled into India. India responded by attacking and defeating the Pakistani army in Bangladesh. Pakistan was then compelled to recognize the new country.

Pakistan's Unstable Government After independence, Pakistan struggled to build a stable government. Power shifted back and forth between elected civilian leaders and military rulers. Tensions among the country's diverse ethnic groups posed problems. The fiercely independent people in the

>> Afghan children, refugees in Pakistan, are transported by truck. Since the 1970s, millions of Afghan refugees have fled into Pakistan.

>> A woman walks through flooded streets in Dhaka, the capital of Bangladesh.

northwestern "tribal areas" were left largely on their own and resisted government control.

The activities of Islamic fundamentalists created tension. The fundamentalists wanted a government that followed strict Islamic principles, while other Pakistanis wanted greater separation between religion and state.

Militants in Pakistan In 2008, after nine years in power, General Pervez Musharraf allowed elections. Before the election, Islamic extremists assassinated one of the candidates, Benazir Bhutto, a popular former prime minister. Pakistan's new civilian government faced tough challenges. Still, when new elections were held in 2013, it marked the first time in Pakistani history that power passed from one elected government to another.

Meanwhile, support for Islamic fundamentalist groups based in Pakistan grew, especially in the northwest. In November 2008, Islamic militants from Pakistan launched terror attacks on hotels and tourists in Mumbai, India, fueling tensions between the hostile neighbors.

Islamic traditions were strong in the rugged border area between Pakistan and Afghanistan. When the Soviet Union invaded Afghanistan in 1979, one million Afghan refugees fled into Pakistan. There, many joined Islamic fundamentalist groups to battle the invaders.

After Russia withdrew from Afghanistan, the Taliban, an extreme Islamist group, seized power with the support of Pakistan. The Taliban backed Al Qaeda, which launched terrorist attacks on the United States in 2001. When U.S. forces invaded Afghanistan and overthrew the Taliban, its supporters fled into Pakistan.

By then, Pakistan had withdrawn its open support of the Taliban. Still, Taliban fighters and other Islamic extremists set up strongholds in northwestern Pakistan. The Pakistani government waged on and off again war against the militants and reluctantly accepted U.S. aid. Many Pakistanis, however, were outraged by American drone—or pilotless aircraft—attacks on suspected terrorists within its borders. Although the attacks were aimed at militants, they sometimes caused civilian casualties.

Bangladesh Struggles Bangladesh ranks among the world's poorest, most crowded countries. Its population, more than half as large as that of the United States, lives in an area the size of Alabama. The large population is crowded on the low-lying Ganges Delta, just a few feet above sea level. Bangladesh has suffered repeatedly from devastating tropical storms and floods. Explosive population growth has strained resources further. More than 50 million people live below the poverty level.

During its early years, Bangladesh was ruled by authoritarian military governments that controlled the economy. In the 1990s, the nation moved from military to democratic rule. The new civilian government encouraged foreign investment. Foreign companies took advantage of cheap labor costs to make clothes in Bangladesh. However, human rights group protested the widespread use of child labor and and dangerous working conditions that have led to the deaths of many workers.

One hopeful program for combating poverty came from the Grameen Bank, founded by Bangladeshi economist Muhammad Yunus. It gave tiny loans, or "microcredit," to poor people so they could open small businesses. Many of the beneficiaries were poor village women who used the funds to buy dairy cows or set up small crafts businesses. Although microcredit helped only a few, it offered a model to poor nations around the world. In 2006, Yunus was awarded the Nobel Peace Prize for his efforts. Since then, many organizations have begun to offer microcredit to millions of the world's poorest families. Such loans helped people create their own jobs, earn enough to educate their children, and gain respect within their communities.

☑ **SUMMARIZE** How does geography pose challenges for Bangladesh?

South Asia in the Cold War

India and Pakistan were among the first of more than 90 new nations to emerge after World War II. By the 1930s, nationalist movements had taken root in European colonies across Africa, Asia, and the Middle East. After India and Pakistan gained independence, nationalist leaders in other regions demanded the same for their countries.

India, Pakistan, and other new nations condemned colonialism. They also rejected Cold War expansion and the divisions between the West and the Soviet Union. In response, they sought **nonalignment,** or political and diplomatic independence from the Cold War superpowers. In 1955, India and Pakistan helped organize a conference of newly independent nations in Bandung, Indonesia, which marked the birth of the nonaligned movement.

>> In 1983, the Nonaligned Movement held a summit in India. Ugandan president Dr. Apolo Milton Obote and Indian president Zail Singh (front) gathered with other leaders of developing nations.

The nonaligned movement had its first formal meeting in 1961 in Yugoslavia. India was a leader of the nonaligned movement, which came to include more than 100 nations, mainly in Asia, Africa, and Latin America. Because they rejected both the Western allies, or the First World, and the Soviet alliance, or the Second World, the Nonaligned Movement was seen as the voice of a "Third World" of countries.

☑ **IDENTIFY MAIN IDEAS** What important global role did India and Pakistan play after independence?

Independent Nations in Southeast Asia

Southeast Asia includes part of the Asian mainland and thousands of islands that stretch from the Indian Ocean to the South China Sea. In 1939, most of the region was under colonial rule by European nations or the United States. During World War II, Japan seized the region. After the war, nationalist groups demanded independence and resisted reoccupation by European nations.

Mainland Southeast Asia is a region of contrasts. Thailand and Malaysia have mostly prospered as market economies, although they have been affected by global financial crises. However, nearby Myanmar has suffered under a brutal **autocratic,** or repressive, government with unlimited power.

Malaysia Prospers British colonies on the Malay Peninsula and the island of Borneo gained independence in the 1950s and joined to form the nation of Malaysia. The oil-rich monarchy of Brunei, on Borneo, and the prosperous city-state of Singapore gained independence as separate nations.

Malaysia has a diverse population. Malays make up about 60 percent of the people, but the country is home to many people of Chinese and Indian descent. In general the communities exist in harmony but with little interaction among them.

Ethnic Chinese have long dominated business and grown into a wealthy business class. They helped Malaysia develop profitable industries such as rubber, timber, and electronics. Since the 1970s, the government, however, has taken steps to make sure Malays have access to education and business opportunity. As a result, Malaysia has a more equal distribution of wealth than most countries in the region.

Suffering and Oppression in Myanmar Burma won independence from Britain in 1948 and took the name Myanmar in 1989. From 1962 until 2011, a repressive military government held absolute power, suppressed dissent, and isolated the country from the rest of the world. It stood accused of widespread human rights abuses such using forced labor—even child labor—for its own purposes.

Under mounting pressure, the military held elections in 1990. When an opposition party won the election, the military rejected the results. It put the opposition leader, **Aung San Suu Kyi,** (awn sahn soo chee) under house arrest, and jailed, killed, or exiled many opponents. In 1991, Suu Kyi won the Nobel Peace Prize for her "nonviolent struggle for democracy and human rights." The military continued to stifle demands for new elections and crushed peaceful demonstrations by Buddhist monks. Under widespread pressure, it finally allowed elections, and a civilian government took over in 2011. It introduced some reforms although the military still held much power.

Since 2011, a civilian government has passed some reforms. Though the new president, Thein Sein, continued the practice of appointing military figures to national office, he worked on substantial reforms, including releasing many political prisoners and enacting laws to protect human rights and freedom of information. Under this government, Aung San Suu Kyi regained political office.

The Rohingya Crisis Myanmar is home to many ethnic and religious groups. The Burmese majority has dominated the country. In 2017, the government cracked down on the Rohingya, a Muslim minority ethnic group. It allowed Buddhist mobs to slaughter Rohingya families and torch their villages. International groups labeled the attacks as ethnic cleansing. Almost 700,000 Rohingya fled to nearby Bangladesh. Thousands perished. Myanmar and Bangladesh negotiated a plan to repatriate— or return home—thousands of Rohingya, but the refugees rejected resettlement.

As head of government in her role as State Counselor in Myanmar, Aung San Suu Kyi has drawn international criticism for her failure to protect the Rohingya people. She is seen as the head of a regime that allows genocide and remains repressive.

☑ **COMPARE** How did Malaysia's approach to ethnic diversity differ from Myanmar's?

Populous Indonesia Faces Challenges

After the Japanese were defeated in World War II, the Netherlands attempted to regain their colony in the Dutch East Indies. Nationalists resisted. In 1949, after an armed struggle, the Dutch East Indies won independence as the nation of Indonesia.

>> Hundreds of Rohingya people crossed Bangladesh's border after fleeing Myanmar.

Geography and diversity posed an obstacle to unity in Indonesia and have in some cases led to conflict. Indonesia includes more than 13,000 islands, many very small but some as large as European nations. Javanese make up almost half of the population, but there are hundreds of other ethnic groups. About 90 percent of Indonesians are Muslims, but the population includes substantial Christian, Buddhist, and Hindu minorities.

Search for Stability Upon achieving independence, Indonesia formed a parliamentary government under its first president, **Sukarno.** But Sukarno shifted from democracy to authoritarian rule. In 1967, an army general, **Suharto,** seized power and ruled for the next 31 years.

Under these authoritarian rulers, Indonesia suppressed ethnic and other dissent. In the mid 1960s, the government crushed what it claimed was a communist uprising and massacred thousands of Chinese whose ancestors had settled in Indonesia.

In 1998, riots forced Suharto from power. Since then, elected governments have worked to build democracy, strengthen the economy, and fight corruption. In recent years, it has attracted much foreign investment capital, which has helped it develop an expanding economy.

The Independence Movement in East Timor In 1975, Indonesia seized **East Timor,** which had been a Portuguese colony for centuries. Many of the largely Catholic East Timorese wanted independence. For more than 25 years, they pushed their struggle. The Indonesian government responded by imprisoning leaders, burning towns, and slaughtering civilians.

Helped by UN peacekeepers, East Timor finally won independence in 2002. This very poor new nation struggled to meet its people's need for jobs and decent living standards.

Ethnic Conflicts and Natural Disasters Inspired by East Timor's success in breaking away, several other regions have demanded independence from Indonesia. Rebels in Papua, on the island of New Guinea, sought independence, as did Muslim separatists in Aceh (AH chay) in the northwest.

Islamist extremism has challenged Indonesia's long tradition of religious tolerance. Terrorist groups in Indonesia have targeted foreigners and non-Muslims. In the some parts of the country, fighting between Muslims and Christians has killed thousands.

>> Ferdinand Marcos and his wife, Imelda, meet with the press at their palace. The pair was accused of embezzling government money to fund their lavish lifestyle.

Natural disasters have added to Indonesia's troubles. In 2004, a tsunami (tsoo NAH mee), or giant wave, devastated the coast of Aceh and killed more than 100,000 people. The tsunami also ravaged Thailand, Sri Lanka, and other lands around the Indian Ocean. Following the disaster, rebels in Aceh and the Indonesian government signed a peace accord. Helped by international aid donors, they worked together to rebuild Aceh.

☑ **IDENTIFY MAIN IDEAS** How has diversity posed challenges to Indonesia?

Struggle for Democracy in the Philippines

Like Indonesia, the Philippines include thousands of islands with diverse ethnic and religious groups. Catholics make up the majority of the population, but many Filipino Muslims live in the south. After centuries as a Spanish colony and nearly 50 years of American rule, the Philippines gained independence in 1946. American influence remained strong through military and economic aid.

>> Filipino soldiers perform a counter-terrorism drill in the southern Philippines.

Clashes with Rebels For decades, various rebel groups have waged guerrilla wars in various parts the Philippines. Some rebels were communists. In a 2012 peace deal, they agreed to work toward peace, despite serious mistrust. Other groups, such as the Moros, wanted a separate Muslim state within the largely Catholic country. After 40 years of fighting, Moro rebels accepted a peace deal, which promised to allow greater Muslim rights in the southern Philippines. Other rebels belonged to a radical Islamist group with links to international terrorist groups such as Al Qaeda and ISIS. They have launched deadly attacks, including on Christian churches.

Duterte's War on Drugs In 2016, Rodrigo Duterte was elected president on the promise to crush the growing illegal drug trade. He launched a bloody war on drugs, allowing death squads to kill suspected drug dealers and drug users without trials. More than 12,000, mostly poor Filipinos, have been killed.

Duterte also moved away from the country's longtime ally, the United States, and sought closer ties with China and Russia. While he welcomed Chinese investment, he rejected China's aggressive moves in taking over tiny islands in the South China Sea.

☑ **IDENTIFY CAUSE AND EFFECT** Why has the Philippines had trouble preserving its democracy?

☑ ASSESSMENT

1. **Identify Cause and Effect** Why did the partition of British India cause a refugee crisis?

2. **Summarize** Why did Bangladesh separate from Pakistan?

3. **Draw Conclusions** How did a policy of nonalignment influence the relations of India and Pakistan with the Cold War superpowers?

4. **Compare** Which country in Southeast Asia has faced the challenge of a diverse population most effectively? Explain your answer.

5. **Quest Connections** How have ethnic and religious differences contributed to conflict in the region?

Marcos Becomes a Dictator Although the Filipino constitution set up a democratic government, a wealthy elite controlled politics and the economy. The peasant majority was poor. For years, the government battled Huks (hooks), local communists with strong peasant support. **Ferdinand Marcos,** was elected president in 1965. Marcos had promised reform, but instead became a dictaor. He cracked down on basic freedoms and forced opponents into exile. He even had **Benigno Aquino** (beh NEE nyoh ah KEE noh), a popular rival, murdered.

A Demand for Democracy When Marcos finally held elections in 1986, voters chose **Corazon Aquino** (kawr ah SOHN), the widow of the slain Benigno. Marcos tried to overturn the results, but massive protests forced him to resign in what was called the "people power" revolution. Under Aquino and her successors, this fragile democracy survived, despite many political scandals. Economic growth was limited, and poverty remained widespread.

20.2

Shanghai is China's main industrial center. A population of more than 16 million makes it China's largest city. Increased business has led to growth, but also to problems.

Rapid Development in China and India

China and India dominate much of Asia. Together, they are home to about two-fifths of the world's population. China is a major industrial nation. Although India's economy is smaller, it has grown rapidly in recent years and is a leading Asian and global power. Both China and India have followed their own paths toward development.

Reform and Repression in China

A New Approach to the Chinese Economy Mao Zedong, the architect of China's communist revolution, died in 1976. After his death, more moderate leaders took control of China. By 1981, **Deng Xiaoping** (dung show ping), had adopted a new approach to China's economy. Deng was a practical reformer, more interested in improving economic output than in political purity.

Deng's program, the Four Modernizations, emphasized agriculture, industry, science, and defense. The plan allowed some features of a market economy, such as some private ownership of property. Communes, or collectively owned farms, were dismantled, and peasant families were allotted plots of land to farm in what was called the "responsibility system." Farmers did not own the land, and the government took a share of their crops. However, farmers could sell any surplus produce and keep the profits.

Entrepreneurs were allowed to set up businesses. Managers of state-run factories were given more freedom, but they had to make their plants more efficient. Deng also welcomed foreign capital and technology. Investors from Japan, Hong Kong, Taiwan, and Western nations invested heavily in China.

BOUNCE to Activate Flipped Video

Objectives

Describe how China has moved toward a market economy without allowing democratic reform.

Identify continuing challenges that China faces.

Explain how India has built its economy.

Summarize social reforms in modern India.

Key Terms

Deng Xiaoping
Tiananmen Square
one-child policy
Green Revolution
Kolkata
Mumbai
Mother Teresa
dalit

GO ONLINE to access your digital course

Economic reforms brought growth. In coastal cities, foreign investment created an economic boom. Some people enjoyed a higher standard of living. They bought refrigerators, televisions, and cars. On the other hand, crime and corruption increased and a growing gap developed between poor rural farmers and wealthy city dwellers.

Protest in Tiananmen Square Economic reforms and increased contact with the West led some to demand greater political freedom. In the late 1980s, students, workers, and others created a democracy movement similar to those sweeping across Eastern Europe. However, Deng and other Chinese Communist leaders were determined to preserve the communist political system.

In 1989, a political crisis erupted as thousands of protesters, many of them students, occupied **Tiananmen (*TYEN* ahn mun) Square,** a huge public plaza in Beijing. Protester waved banners calling for democracy. The government ordered the protesters to disperse. When they refused, the government sent in troops and tanks. Thousands of demonstrators were killed or wounded in the Tiananmen Square Massacre. Many protesters across China were imprisoned and tortured. The

crackdown showed that the communist government was determined to keep its monopoly on power.

✅ **DRAW CONCLUSIONS** What unintended consequences did the Chinese government's reforms during the 1980s have on the Chinese population?

Growth and Challenges

Economic reforms helped China emerge as a global economic superpower. Its economy today is the second largest in the world, after the United States. Economic growth lifted millions of Chinese people out of poverty, but this growth also brought many challenges to the country.

Rapid Industrialization In China, as elsewhere, industrialization led to rapid urbanization. Boom times brought millions of rural workers into Chinese cities. They worked for low wages in manufacturing and other jobs. Their needs strained local resources for housing, education, and other services.

Economic growth led to increasing environmental issues such as air and water pollution. In many cities, air quality is so poor that parents sometimes keep their children indoors. Coal burning and emissions from automobiles are major sources of pollution. Although China has taken steps to fight pollution, economic growth takes priority over the environment.

The 2009 global financial crisis hurt China, as it hurt other industrialized nations, but its economy was one of the first to recover. By 2011, China's economy had passed Japan's to become the second-largest in the world. In 2020, a coronavirus, or respiratory disease, disrupted economic growth, as manufacturing slowed and people lost their jobs. The economic upheaval caused China's economy to shrink for the first time since 1976.

Human Rights Abuses For decades, human rights campaigners both inside China and outside have criticized the government for limiting freedom and jailing critics as well as torturing and executing large numbers of prisoners. Activists protested abuses such as lack of free speech and the use of prison labor to produce goods for export. The Chinese government has rejected calls from other countries to end abuses, claiming that outsiders have no right to impose "Western-style" ideas of human rights on China.

>> The day after the massacre in Tiananmen Square, a lone protestor stepped in front of a line of tanks. The "Tank Man" became a worldwide symbol of individuals standing against government oppression.

🅑 BOUNCE to Activate Gallery

A global human rights campaign has focused on Tibet, a region occupied by China in 1950. The government claims that Tibet has been part of China for centuries. China has cracked down hard on Tibetan Buddhists, who have accused China of suppressing their culture and religion. They also resent China's policy of moving Han Chinese migrants into Tibet, which they see as another effort to undermine their traditions.

In November 2013, the Chinese government took more tentative steps toward reform. It announced new policies on some of China's most notorious human rights issues, such as an end to labor camps, which had long been used to punish political dissidents. However, many critics argued that no real political reforms were announced. The government still holds a tight rein on individual rights and freedoms.

In recent years, China has arrested and imprisoned an estimated 1 million Uighurs, an ethnic and religious minority living in northwestern China. Many were sent to "reeducation camps," where they were forced to work in factories and abandon their cultural traditions. China claimed Muslim Uighurs were extremists who wanted to break away from China.

In 2019, China faced massive protests in Hong Kong, a bustling financial center and city once ruled by Britain. Hong Kong has its own legal system, and residents enjoy more freedoms than people elsewhere in China. When China tried to impose new controls, protesters flooded the streets, demanding democratic reforms.

China's One-Child Policy With more than 1.4 billion people, China has the world's largest population. To slow population growth, in the 1980s, the government imposed a **one-child policy,** which limited urban families to a single child and allowed rural families two children. The government enforced this harsh policy with steep fines and other penalties. Children born in violation of the policy often could not get an education or other services because they did not have identity cards.

Although the one-child policy was widely condemned, it did slow population growth. Finally, in 2016, faced with an aging population and shrinking workforce, China ended the policy, allowing families to have a second child.

☑ **IDENTIFY CAUSE AND EFFECT** What developments caused China to abandon the one-child policy?

>> China imposed a strict one-child policy in the 1980s. This mural encourages parents to be satisfied with a single child.

India Builds a Modern Economy

Like China, India is a huge country with a large, diverse population. India continues to face widespread poverty. After gaining independence in 1947, India set up a democratic government and planned to develop a modern economy.

The Green Revolution Beginning in the 1950s, India and much of the developing world benefited from the **Green Revolution**, when scientists applied new technology to increase food production. They introduced new high-yield seeds that yielded more food per acre than older crops. The Green Revolution had limits, however. It succeeded only in areas with regular moisture. Also, it required chemical fertilizers and pesticides, as well as irrigation systems, which only wealthy farmers could afford.

Developing a Market Economy After independence, India, like many developing countries, followed a mixed model of development, using features of both socialism and capitalism. By the late 1980s, however, India had begun to introduce more market reforms. It privatized some industries and made foreign investment easier. Before long, it emerged as one of the world's fastest-growing economies. Today, India has the third largest economy in Asia, after China and Japan.

India, like all nations, has faced economic swings. In recent years, India's strong growth has slowed. However, it has a well-educated population in the field of information technology and provides a variety of technological services to the world. Many Western companies lower their costs by outsourcing work to Indian companies because skilled Indian workers earn less than their counterparts in the West.

Obstacles to Progress Despite many successes, India faces major economic hurdles. Among them are population and poverty, unemployment, the rural-urban divide, and the need for agricultural development. India, like China, experienced rapid population growth, which hurt efforts to improve standards of living. As food output rose, so did demand. More than one-third of Indians lived in poverty, unable to meet basic needs for food, clothing, and shelter. Although India's economy was expanding, it could not provide enough jobs for everyone, leading to high unemployment.

>> As India's economy grows, so does demand for cars. India is now the world's sixth-largest carmaker. Traffic in the narrow streets of crowded cities is a growing problem, as is air pollution.

BOUNCE to Activate Gallery

As India modernized, tens of millions of people left villages to live in cities, and the gap between rural and urban dwellers grew. Still, an estimated 70 percent of Indians lived in villages. Rural poverty remained high, despite government programs to provide education and jobs. Farming communities still lacked roads, electricity, and other services. Many farm workers still used traditional farming methods and owed much of their output to absentee landowners.

The government has worked to introduce modern farming methods and technology. It has also tried to make Indian farmers less dependent on the seasonal monsoon rainfall. Building irrigation systems is a costly, but ongoing, process.

India faces challenges from climate changes. Rising sea levels, changing weather patterns, and increased cyclone activity affect economic growth and hurt efforts to reduce poverty.

Rapid Population Growth With 1.3 billion people, India has the world's second largest population after China. The Indian government supported family planning but did not adopt the harsh policies used in China.

Although India's growth rate is slowing, its population is predicted to surpass China's by 2030. While middle class families have fewer children than in the past, poor families, especially in rural areas, still see children as an economic resource to work the land and care for parents in old age.

In overcrowded cities like **Kolkata** (or Calcutta) and **Mumbai** (or Bombay), millions live in poverty without jobs, adequate food, or health care. The government, aid groups, and others have tried to help the urban poor. In Kolkata, **Mother Teresa,** a Roman Catholic nun, founded the Missionaries of Charity. This group provides food and medical care to thousands. Many organizations pursue similar goals. Still, millions remain in desperate need in both urban and rural areas.

☑ **IDENTIFY CAUSE AND EFFECT** How did market reforms affect India's economy in the 1990s?

Social Reform in India

Unlike China, where the government cracks down on dissent, India has a democratic system that allows people to demand reforms. Since independence, activists in India have pressed for many social reforms, such as ending caste discrimination and child labor, as well as increasing access to education.

Dalits Education, economic growth, and urbanization continue to undermine India's traditional caste system. In India's competitive economy, new classes are emerging based on individual success and wealth. Some older castes are losing their privileged positions while successful entrepreneurs from any caste have gained status. Cities allow for greater social mobility, or the ability of individuals or groups to move up in society.

India's constitution banned discrimination against **dalits,** or people of the lowest caste. Although conditions for dalits have improved in parts of India, discrimination has continued. Especially in poor, rural areas, dalits who seek equal rights have been attacked by those who want to maintain the old social order. Higher caste Indians still generally receive better education and jobs.

Improving Women's Lives India's constitution granted equal rights to women. In the cities, girls from well-to-do families were educated. Women entered many professions. Girls from poor families, however, received little or no education. Although women in rural areas worked the land or contributed to household industries, few received wages. Across India, women organized self-help groups to start small businesses and improve their lives.

Women's rights groups have strongly protested inequality and violence against women in India. Young women and men have demanded an end to discrimination based on gender. They are battling deeply-rooted cultural traditions that gave men authority over women.

Human Rights Issues Despite India's success as a global economic power, it has faced criticism for human rights abuses, especially against women and dalits. Efforts to end the worst cases of child labor have had limited effect. Both children and adults sometimes end up in debt bondage—where a person works off his or her debt.

Violence has flared against minority groups such as Muslims and Christians. India's ruling party, the Bharatiya Janata Party (BJP) had its roots in Hindu supremacy. In recent years, Hindu extremists have set out to terrorize other religious groups. Some BJP leaders publicly supported such attacks.

In 2019, India passed a controversial law that made it easier for migrants from three neighboring countries to gain citizenship, but the law specifically excluded Muslims. The law reflected Hindu nationalist goals, but it sparked widespread protests. Critics claimed it violated India's constitution that guarantees equality for all.

>> This rural woman used a small loan from an Indian bank to buy a sewing machine that she can use to generate income and improve her life.

In another controversial move, India's Hindu nationalist prime minister, Narendra Modi, ended 70 years of autonomy for the Muslim-majority state of Kashmir. Modi's action reflects India's efforts to exert more control over the disputed region.

☑ **EXPLAIN** How did the Indian government try to improve the status of dalits?

☑ ASSESSMENT

1. **Describe** How did China move toward economic reform without allowing for political reform?

2. **Identify Central Issues** What challenges does the Chinese government continue to face?

3. **Express Problems Clearly** What social reforms has the Indian government made over the last few decades, and why?

4. **Identify Cause and Effect** How does a rapidly expanding population affect life in India?

5. **Connections to Today** How have China and India used resources to build their economies?

20.3

⬚ **GO ONLINE** to **Project Imagine: Experience African Independence Movements** for first-person perspectives on several independence struggles, including the one in Ghana.

 BOUNCE to Activate Flipped Video

Objectives

Summarize how African nations won independence.

Analyze the issues facing new African nations and the different paths they took.

Identify examples of and summarize the reasons for ethnic conflict and genocide in African nations.

Key Terms

savanna
Kwame Nkrumah
Jomo Kenyatta
coup d'état
Mobutu Sese Seko
Islamist
Katanga
Biafra
Hutus
Tutsis
Darfur

African Nations Win Independence

In 1945, four European powers—Britain, France, Belgium, and Portugal—controlled almost all of Africa. Only Egypt, Ethiopia, Liberia and white-ruled South Africa were independent nations.

The New Nations of Africa

World War II sparked a rising tide of nationalism in Africa. Japanese victories in Asia shattered the West's reputation as an unbeatable force. African troops who had fought for the Allies were unwilling to accept discrimination when they returned home. Nationalists also won support among workers who had migrated to the cities to work in war industries.

After the war, most European nations struggled to find the resources and will needed to fight to hold onto colonies. Faced with nationalist demands, Britain and France introduced political reforms that they thought would gradually lead to independence. But they soon discovered that they could not control the pace of change. Starting in the late 1950s, they lost direct control of most of their colonies. In countries with large settler populations, however, independence was thwarted for years.

In the new nations, crowds celebrated their freedom, while bands played new national anthems. However, even as independence celebrations took place, African nations faced tough challenges.

A Geographically Diverse Continent Africa is the world's second-largest continent. It has the world's largest desert—the Sahara—in the north and the smaller Kalahari Desert in the south, as well as fertile coastal strips in North and South Africa. **Savannas,** or grasslands with scattered trees, make up much of the interior. Tropical rain forests cover central Africa's Congo Basin and coastal West Africa.

Africa's population has long been concentrated in the most fertile areas, such as the highlands of East Africa. Like people in other parts of the world, however, millions of Africans are migrating to cities. About 40 percent of Africans live in fast-growing cities.

Africa has rich deposits of minerals such as gold ore, copper ore, and diamonds. However, these resources are distributed unevenly across the continent. Some African nations produce valuable cash crops, including coffee and cacao. Some regions also have large oil reserves. European powers had established colonies in Africa to tap into these natural resources.

Nationalism Leads to Freedom Most nationalist leaders were Western educated. Many were powerful speakers whose words inspired supporters. **Kwame Nkrumah**(KWAH may un KROO muh) in Gold Coast, **Jomo Kenyatta** in Kenya, and Léopold Senghor (sahn GAWR) in Senegal were skilled organizers.

Nationalist leaders organized political parties. In the cities, parties published newspapers, held mass rallies, and mobilized popular support for independence. Colonial powers imprisoned many nationalists, including Nkrumah and Kenyatta. But demonstrations, strikes, and boycotts eventually forced European rulers to negotiate timetables for freedom.

Most African nations won independence through largely peaceful efforts. However, colonies with large numbers of white settlers, such as Algeria and Kenya, were unwilling to grant Africans their freedom. Africans in these colonies were forced to go to war against the colonial powers. Later, you will examine five of these nations in detail.

☑ **IDENTIFY CAUSE AND EFFECT** How did World War II affect African independence efforts?

A Variety of New Governments

More than 50 new nations were born in Africa during the great liberation. Throughout the continent, Africans had great hopes for the future. After 70 years of colonial rule, Africans were again in control of their destinies. The new nations took different paths to modernization. Some made progress despite huge obstacles. Many others were plunged into crisis by civil war, military rule, or corrupt dictators. In recent decades, a number of African nations have taken steps toward democracy.

Old Boundaries, New Problems In Africa, as in other regions such as Eastern Europe, the question of where to draw national borders created challenges. European colonial powers had drawn boundaries around their colonies without regard to the many rival ethnic groups living there. Most newly independent African nations included a patchwork of peoples with different languages, religions, and traditions.

Within these new nations, people often felt their first loyalty was to their own ethnic group, not to a distant national government. As a result, ongoing conflict between rival ethnic groups has plagued many African nations.

>> Some mining operations in Africa employ the most modern technology and machinery, but in poorer nations, older methods are still used. Here, men mine diamonds by hand in Sierra Leone.

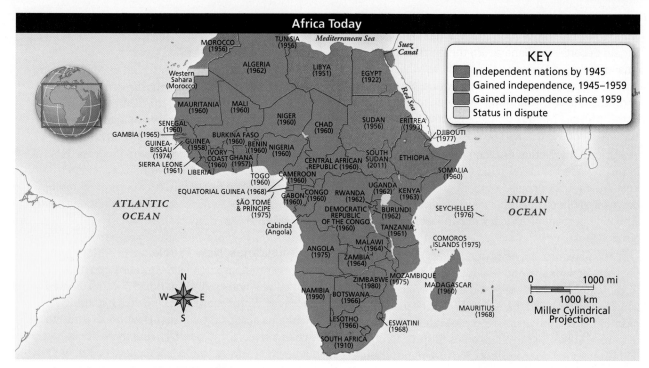

Africa Today

KEY
- Independent nations by 1945
- Gained independence, 1945–1959
- Gained independence since 1959
- Status in dispute

MOROCCO (1956)
TUNISIA (1956)
Mediterranean Sea
Suez Canal
Western Sahara (Morocco)
ALGERIA (1962)
LIBYA (1951)
EGYPT (1922)
Red Sea
MAURITANIA (1960)
MALI (1960)
NIGER (1960)
CHAD (1960)
SUDAN (1956)
ERITREA (1993)
DJIBOUTI (1977)
SENEGAL (1960)
GAMBIA (1965)
GUINEA-BISSAU (1974)
GUINEA (1958)
BURKINA FASO (1960)
BENIN (1960)
NIGERIA (1960)
IVORY COAST (1960)
GHANA (1957)
CENTRAL AFRICAN REPUBLIC (1960)
SOUTH SUDAN (2011)
ETHIOPIA
SIERRA LEONE (1961)
LIBERIA
TOGO (1960)
CAMEROON (1960)
SOMALIA (1960)
EQUATORIAL GUINEA (1968)
SÃO TOMÉ & PRÍNCIPE (1975)
GABON (1960)
CONGO (1960)
RWANDA (1962)
UGANDA (1962)
KENYA (1963)
DEMOCRATIC REPUBLIC OF THE CONGO (1960)
BURUNDI (1962)
SEYCHELLES (1976)
ATLANTIC OCEAN
Cabinda (Angola)
TANZANIA (1961)
COMOROS ISLANDS (1975)
INDIAN OCEAN
ANGOLA (1975)
MALAWI (1964)
ZAMBIA (1964)
ZIMBABWE (1980)
MOZAMBIQUE (1975)
MADAGASCAR (1960)
MAURITIUS (1968)
NAMIBIA (1990)
BOTSWANA (1966)
LESOTHO (1966)
ESWATINI (1968)
SOUTH AFRICA (1910)

N W E S

0   1000 mi
0   1000 km
Miller Cylindrical Projection

>> Over the course of many years, African nations gained their independence from European powers. **Analyze Maps** What do the dates on this map tell you about when nations gained independence?

BOUNCE to Activate Map

The Rise of Dictators After independence, the new African nations set up governments modeled on those of the departing colonial rulers. But parliamentary systems did not work in Africa as they had in Europe, where they had evolved over centuries. Creating unified nations with stable governments proved to be a hard goal to reach.

Many leaders of the new nations were heroes of the liberation struggle. Some chose to build one-party states. They argued that multiparty systems encouraged disunity, which was often true. Many of these one-party governments became repressive, and some liberation leaders became dictators. Dictators often used their positions to enrich themselves and their supporters at the expense of the nation.

In many nations, unsuccessful policies or corrupt governments led to civil unrest. This in turn, led to military coups (kooz). A coup, or **coup d'état** (koo day TAH), is the forcible overthrow of a government. Some coup leaders became brutal tyrants. Others tried to end corruption and improve conditions. Military leaders usually promised to restore civilian rule. But in many cases, they only surrendered power when they were toppled by another coup.

Democracies Emerge By the 1990s, many African nations were moving away from strongman rule. Africans organized and demanded democratic elections. In some countries, independent newspapers came out, with their editors risking arrest for their publications. Religious leaders spoke out for greater freedom. Outside pressures also played a role. Western governments and lenders, such as the World Bank, demanded political reforms before granting loans needed for economic development.

In response, some governments allowed opposition parties to emerge and lifted censorship. In nations such as Nigeria and Benin, multiparty elections were held, unseating long-ruling leaders.

Outside Influences on African Nations Even after African nations won independence, colonial powers and foreign companies often retained control of businesses and resources in these former colonies. Many new nations remained dependent on their former colonial rulers for aid, trade, and investment.

The new nations were also buffeted by the Cold War. Both the United States and the Soviet Union competed for military and strategic advantage through alliances with several African countries. The United States, for example, backed

Mobutu Sese Seko, (seh-say say-koh) the dictator of Zaire (now called the Democratic Republic of Congo). It wanted to counter Soviet influence in nearby Angola. During the 1970s, the United States backed Somalia, while the Soviet Union supported neighboring Ethiopia. Both African countries were important because they controlled access to the Red Sea, a vital world shipping route.

☑ **INFER** Why did one-party rule often lead to repression and tyranny?

Case Studies: Five African Nations

Making accurate generalizations about Africa is difficult. Every nation is different. Some nations have rich resources to help finance progress. Others are poor in resources. Each has its own set of problems and its own history. To gain a better understanding of the process of nation-building in Africa, we will examine the histories of five important nations.

Ghana In 1957, Ghana was the first African nation south of the Sahara to win independence. Britain had called this colony Gold Coast, for its rich mineral resources. Under independence leader Kwame Nkrumah, it took the name Ghana, after the ancient West African kingdom.

As president, Nkrumah supported socialism and government ownership of major industries. He backed the building of a huge dam to provide electric power, but the project left Ghana with massive debts. Nkrumah's government became increasingly corrupt and dictatorial. In 1966, Nkrumah was toppled by the first of several military coups.

In the 1980s, Jerry Rawlings, a military officer, took power in a coup. He strengthened the economy and moved Ghana toward democracy. In 1992, Rawlings allowed multiparty elections and was chosen president. Other elections followed. Although the economy suffered from falling prices for its main exports of cocoa and gold, Ghana made progress toward improving life for its people. The recent discovery of offshore oil raised hopes for more economic growth.

Kenya While Ghana made a peaceful transition to freedom, Kenya faced an armed struggle. Under colonial rule, white settlers carved out plantations on lands once occupied by the Kikuyu (kee KOO yoo), Kenya's largest ethnic group. White Kenyans then passed laws to ensure their domination over the Black majority. Nationalist leader and Kikuyu

spokesman Jomo Kenyatta called for nonviolent resistance to end oppressive laws.

In the 1950s, some Black Kenyans turned to guerrilla warfare, attacking and killing white settlers. The British called them Mau Mau. Claiming that he was a secret leader of the Mau Mau, the British imprisoned Kenyatta. The British used internment, torture, and executions to try to defeat the rebels. Thousands were killed. In 1963, the British finally withdrew, and Kenyatta became the first president of an independent Kenya.

Kenyatta and his successor dominated the country for decades. They limited freedom of expression and suppressed other parties. Unrest and international pressure forced Kenya to restore multiparty rule in the 1990s.

Since then, Kenya has faced many challenges from high unemployment to periodic droughts. Corruption and disputed elections have sparked violence and ethnic unrest. With its many national parks and game reserves, tourism is a major industry in Kenya, so any conflict hurts this vital source of income. Kenya has faced a growing number of extremist attacks by the Islamist extremist group, Al Shabab, based in neighboring Somalia.

Algeria Like Kenya, French-ruled Algeria had a large population of European settlers who saw the

>> In this image, British troops search a village in Kenya seeking people who participated in the Mau Mau Rebellion.

>> Patrice Lumumba was newly independent Congo's first prime minister. Here, Lumumba waves to a crowd after receiving a 41–2 vote of confidence from the Congolese senate in September 1960.

BOUNCE to Activate Gallery

country as their homeland. France, too, had come to see Algeria as part of their country. From 1954 to 1962, a long, costly war of liberation raged in Algeria.

Algerian nationalists set up the National Liberation Front, which used guerrilla warfare to win freedom. France, which had just lost Vietnam, was unwilling to retreat from Algeria. As the war dragged, both sides suffered huge casualties. Finally, French public opinion turned against the war, and Algeria won independence.

After independence, Algeria suffered periods of military rule and internal conflict. During the 1990s, a civil war erupted between the military and Islamists after the government rejected an election won by an Islamist party. **Islamists** are people who want a government based on Islamic law and beliefs. The fighting left an estimated 150,000 people dead. The violence slowed after 1999, but tensions remained. Algeria has also been rocked by suicide bombings by Islamist militants

Algeria's economy has seen some improvements. It first adopted a socialist model of development, but since the 1980s, has moved toward a market economy. Its oil and gas resources have helped the country economically. Still, like many

developing countries it faces the problems of high unemployment, widespread poverty, and corruption.

Democratic Republic of Congo The Democratic Republic of Congo (or Congo), once ruled by Belgium, covers about a million square miles of central Africa. It has rich resources, including vast tropic rainforests, plantations, and great mineral wealth, especially copper and diamonds.

Belgium was eager to keep control of Congo's resources, such as the copper and diamonds of the **Katanga** province. Fearing a struggle like the French war in Algeria, Belgium suddenly rushed Congo to independence in 1960. But the new nation had no preparation for self-government and no sense of unity. More than 100 political parties sprang up, representing diverse regional and ethnic groups.

Katanga rebelled against Congo shortly after independence. The country's first prime minister, Patrice Lumumba, appealed for Soviet help. This led the United States to back Lumumba's rival, Colonel Joseph Mobutu, later known as Mobutu Sese Seko. Mobutu captured Lumumba, who was soon executed. The United Nations ended the Katanga rebellion in 1963.

For 32 years, Mobutu imposed a harsh, corrupt dictatorship on Congo. Mobutu survived in power in part because his strong anti-communism won favor in the West during the Cold War. Rebels finally forced Mobutu from power in 1997. A brutal civil war erupted among rival leaders and led to the deaths of more than 6 million people.

After a fragile peace was restored in 2006, Congo held its first free elections in 41 years. Joseph Kabila held power for the next 12 years despite charges of corruption and ongoing unrest. A large UN force tried to keep the peace in eastern Congo, but violence, especially against women, continued.

Nigeria Located in West Africa, Nigeria has the continent's largest population. Its people belong to more than 250 ethnic groups, speak many languages, and practice different religions. The dominant groups are the mainly Christian Ibo (EE boh) and Yoruba (YOH roo buh) in the south, and the Muslim Hausa (HOW suh) in the north.

After gaining independence from Britain in 1960, Nigeria experienced frequent military coups. Military leaders ruled with an iron hand but failed to improve Nigeria's government or its economy. Since 1999, Nigeria has had elected civilian governments.

Ethnic and religious divisions have threatened to tear Nigeria apart. In 1966, the Ibo people in the oil-rich south rebelled and set up the independent Republic of **Biafra.** A brutal civil war led to famine and a huge death toll. After three years, Nigeria crushed the rebels and reunited the country. More recently, Islamists in the north have imposed Sharia law in several areas, causing many Christians to flee. A radical Islamist group, Boko Haram, has launched terrorist attacks throughout the country.

Nigeria has rich oil resources, which has brought benefits as well as disadvantages. When oil prices are high, the country reaps great profits that can be invested in development. But falling oil prices have caused problems and cutbacks in spending. Also oil wealth has contributed to corruption. In the oil-producing Niger Delta region, local people were bitter about the environmental damage caused by oil drilling and the huge profits going to foreign oil companies. Armed groups have attacked pipelines and held foreign oil workers for ransom.

☑ **IDENTIFY CENTRAL ISSUES** How did the conflicts in Katanga and Biafra reflect the challenges that new African nations faced after independence?

The Wars of Southern Africa

Colonies in southern Africa were among the last to win independence. Unlike the peaceful transition to independence in much of Africa, the road to freedom in southern Africa was marked by long, violent struggles.

Zimbabwe During the colonial period, many whites had settled in British-ruled Southern Rhodesia. Whites made up only five percent of Rhodesia's population but owned half the land and controlled the government. White Rhodesians rejected any move to give up power to the Black majority. When Britain supported demands for majority rule, whites led by Ian Smith declared independence in 1965.

Guerrilla forces took up arms to win majority rule. They finally succeeded in 1980. Rhodesia became the independent nation of Zimbabwe. Liberation leader Robert Mugabe was elected president.

Although popular at first, Mugabe grew increasingly dictatorial. He cracked down on opponents, ended basic freedoms, and ruined the economy. In 2017, he was finally forced to step down.

Angola and Mozambique Portugal clung fiercely to its profitable colonies of Angola and Mozambique. To achieve independence, nationalist groups had to wage a long guerrilla war. In 1975, Portugal finally agreed to withdraw.

Brutal civil wars, largely supported by foreign powers, soon developed in both countries. White-ruled South Africa feared the rise of strong, Black-dominated governments on its borders. As a result, they funded rebel groups in both Mozambique and Angola. The Cold War also fueled tensions. In Angola, the Soviet Union financed Cuban troops who supported the left-wing government, while the United States backed insurgent anti-communist forces.

The fighting continued until 1992 in Mozambique and until 2002 in Angola. After decades of war, both countries struggled to rebuild. In 2019, Cyclone Idai devastated Mozambique, destroying half its crops and causing widespread damage.

☑ **DRAW CONCLUSIONS** Why did fighting continue after Angola achieved independence?

Ethnic Conflict and Genocide

After independence, ethnic conflicts plagued some African nations. The causes were complex. Often one group held political and economic power at the expense of other groups. Weak or unstable governments were unable to build national unity. Regional and cultural differences also fed rivalries

>> By the year 2009, when this photo was taken, Robert Mugabe was being forced to share power, but Zimbabwe still faced terrible inflation, food shortages, and disease epidemics.

>> The Kigali Memorial Centre in Kigali, Rwanda, displays photographs of people killed in the genocide. **Analyze Image** How could these photographs affect a person's understanding of the genocide?

>> Children celebrate with a Republic of South Sudan flag cake during Sudanese independence celebrations in 2011.

that on occasion led to tragic violence. At times, ambitious leaders took advantage of rivalries to increase their own power.

Rwanda and Burundi Power struggles between rival groups led to a deadly genocide in Rwanda, a small central African nation. The country is home to two main groups, the majority **Hutus** and the minority **Tutsis.** Though often considered separate ethnic groups, they speak the same language, share the same culture, and follow the same Catholic religion. In colonial times, the Belgian government had favored Tutsis over the Hutus. After independence, the majority Hutu came into power and violence against Tutsis increased. Over the next 30 years, many Tutsis fled to neighboring countries.

In early 1994, a suspicious plane crash killed the presidents of Rwanda and neighboring Burundi. The crash triggered a coordinated attack on Tutsis. Urged on by extremist Hutu officials, civilians turned on their Tutsi neighbors. At least 800,000 Tutsis and moderate Hutus were brutally slaughtered within a few months. Even as the death toll rose, the world community was slow to act to stop the genocide. By July, a Tutsi-led army had invaded from Burundi, ended the slaughter, and set up a unity government.

Rwandan leaders tried to heal the horrors of the genocide. Almost two million people were tried in traditional community courts where the goal was to achieve truth and reconciliation. The hearings resulted in some convictions, but many of those who took part in the killings remained in their communities. The main leaders of the genocide, however, faced trials in an international court.

Burundi faced similar tensions between Hutus and Tutsis. Violence erupted, but did not lead to genocide as in Rwanda. In 2005, voters approved a new constitution that guaranteed both groups participation in the government and military.

Rebellion and Civil War in Sudan The large, geographically diverse country of Sudan has faced decades of conflict. After independence, the Arab Muslim north dominated the non-Muslim, non-Arab south. A long civil war pitted the north against the south, killing more than a million and a half people.

The Sudanese government and rebels in the south finally agreed to a peace accord. In 2011, the people of South Sudan voted to secede and set up their own independent nation. Relations between the two countries remain strained over disputed borders and the sharing of oil revenues, which both countries desperately need. Within South Sudan itself, tensions threatened civil war as rival groups jockeyed for power.

Another conflict raged in **Darfur,** in the western region of Sudan. There, the rebels were non-Arab Muslims who fought against the Arab-dominated Sudanese government. The government launched a campaign of genocide, encouraging Arab militias to destroy the villages and slaughter the Black Sudanese residents. An estimated 300,000 people were killed and more than two million fled their homes.

The United States and other countries sent humanitarian aid to refugees in Darfur. The UN sent peacekeepers to prevent further violence but with little success. The International Criminal Court (ICC) charged Sudan's president, Omar al-Bashir, with crimes against humanity and genocide. However, the ICC is not recognized in Sudan, and no arrest was ever made. In 2010, al-Bashir won reelection, though many believe those elections were not fair or free. The conflict in Darfur has lessened but not ended. The situation is complex with many warring groups and no easy solution.

☑ **DESCRIBE** Why was there conflict between northern and southern Sudan?

☑ ASSESSMENT

1. **Analyze Information** Where did struggles for independence in Africa turn violent and why?

2. **Compare and Contrast** What were the issues facing the Democratic Republic of Congo and Kenya as they achieved independence and what paths did those countries take?

3. **Synthesize** Why did many new nations in Africa have difficulty building democratic governments?

4. **Compare** How was the conflict in Darfur similar to the conflict in Rwanda?

5. **Quest Connections** How did the ethnic conflict in Rwanda become a genocide?

African Independence

In the mid-1900s, Africans seeking to end colonial rule had to decide how best to work for independence. In some places, they led violent uprisings; in others, they used nonviolent protest to try to achieve their goals. Here, you will compare two sources on this push for independence. The first, written by Kwame Nkrumah of the British-controlled Gold Coast (now Ghana), argues that peaceful protest is the best way to weaken imperialism and strengthen self-government movements. The second, written by philosopher Frantz Fanon, a native of the French colony Martinique, strongly criticizes Africans who cooperate in any way with the French colonial government.

As you read, look for contrasts in their viewpoints on the independence movements.

>> Women celebrate the anniversary of the founding of the CPP. The CPP spearheaded the Positive Action campaign, leading Ghana to independence after years of nonviolent protest.

Primary Source 1

What I Mean by Positive Action, Kwame Nkrumah

There are two ways to achieve Self-government: either by armed revolution and violent overthrow of the existing regime, or by constitutional and legitimate non-violent methods. In other words, either by armed might or by moral pressure. We believe that we can achieve Self-government even now by constitutional means without resort to any violence.

☑ **DETERMINE CENTRAL IDEAS** What is Nkrumah's preferred way to achieve self-government?

… From our knowledge of the history of man, from our knowledge of colonial liberation movements, Freedom or Self-government has never been handed over to any colonial country on a silver platter. . . . Hence the decision by the Convention People's Party to adopt a program of non-violent Positive Action to attain Self-government for the people of this country and their chiefs. . . .

By Positive Action we mean the adoption of all legitimate and constitutional means by which we can cripple the forces of imperialism in this country. The Weapons of Positive Action are:
1) Legitimate political agitation:
2) Newspaper and educational campaigns and
3) as a last resort, the constitutional application of strikes, boycotts, and non-co-operation based on the principle of absolute non-violence.

☑ **SUMMARIZE** What is positive action, according to the author?

Primary Source 2

"Letter to the Youth of Africa," Frantz Fanon

In the fine hours of French imperialism, it could be a kind of honor for a colonized person to be a part of the French government. . . .

In the past ten years, however, it has become truly intolerable and unacceptable for Africans to hold a post in the government that dominates them.

Every colonized person who today accepts a governmental post must know clearly that he will sooner or later be called upon to sponsor a policy of repression, of massacres, of collective murders in one of the regions of "the French Empire."

. . . this is a case of treason, of complicity, and of incitation to murder.

☑ **ANALYZE ARGUMENTS** Why does Fanon say that Africans who work for the French government are complicit in murder?

Youth of Africa, of Madagascar, of the West Indies, the soldiers of your respective countries drafted by force into the French army have enthusiastically rallied to the ranks of the National Liberation Army. Today, side by side with the Algerian patriots, they carry on a heroic struggle against the common enemy. . . .

The time has come for all colonials to participate in the routing of the French colonialists.

Wherever you may be, you must know that the moment has come for all of us to unite our efforts and deal the death blow to French imperialism.

Youth of Africa! Youth of Madagascar! Youth of the West Indies! We must, all of us together, dig the grave in which colonialism will finally be entombed!

☑ **ANALYZE WORD CHOICES** Why do you think the author explicitly addresses the "youth of Africa" rather than all Africans?

☑ ASSESSMENT

Be sure to cite specific evidence from the sources as you answer the following questions.

1. **Analyze Style** What is the tone of Nkrumah's call for self-government?

2. **Analyze Word Choices** Why does Fanon use the word *treason*?

3. **Compare and Contrast** How do the sources present different perspectives on African independence movements?

4. **Draw Conclusions** Fanon's piece was written nearly a decade after Nkrumah's, years during which Africans increasingly struggled to win their independence. Do you think this difference in time might have influenced Fanon's perspective? Why or why not?

5. **Assess an Argument** Do you think Fanon's argument was correct? Why or why not?

20.4

 GO ONLINE to Project Imagine: Explore Life After Independence to learn more about the region following independence, including the struggle against apartheid in South Africa.

Black South Africans protest for equal rights and an end to apartheid in Johannesburg in 1952.

BOUNCE to Activate Flipped Video

Objectives

Summarize the struggle for equality in South Africa and identify how Nelson Mandela led resistance efforts.

Describe how African nations developed their economies.

Understand the challenges African nations face.

Key Terms

apartheid
African National
  Congress (ANC)
Sharpeville
Nelson Mandela
Desmond Tutu
F.W. de Klerk
socialism
desertification
urbanization
endangered species
Wangari Maathai
sustainable
  development

Challenges for African Nations

In the 1950s and 1960s, almost all African nations won independence. In South Africa, the struggle for freedom was different. South Africa had achieved self-rule from Britain in 1910. Self-rule, however, was limited to white South Africans. Whites made up less than 15 percent of the population but controlled the government and the economy. The Black majority was denied all political and economic rights in their own land. The white-minority government passed racial laws that severely restricted the Black majority.

The Struggle for Equality in South Africa

Apartheid Is Established In 1948, the government expanded the existing system of racial segregation, and created the policy known as **apartheid,** or the separation of the races. Under apartheid, all South Africans were registered by race: Black, White, Colored (people of mixed ancestry), Asian. Supporters of apartheid claimed it would allow each race to develop its own culture. In fact, the policy was designed to preserve white control over South Africa.

Under apartheid, Blacks were treated like foreigners in their own land. By the early 1900s whites had seized rights to 87 percent of all land, including all of South Africa's huge mineral wealth. Whites held almost all the top jobs and prevented Blacks from being promoted to better positions. Although Black workers were needed to make mines, factories, and other industries profitable, they were paid less than whites for the same job.

Laws restricted where Black people could live and banned marriages between the races. Among the most hated were the Pass Laws enacted in 1952, which required all Black people to carry pass books at all times, wherever they went. Black schools received less funding than white schools. Low wages and inferior schooling condemned most Black people to poverty.

Resistance Against Apartheid Resistance to white rule began almost as soon as white rule itself was established. The **African National Congress (ANC)** emerged as the main party opposed to apartheid and led the struggle for majority rule. As the government passed ever-harsher laws, the ANC organized larger and larger marches, boycotts, and strikes.

In 1960, police gunned down 69 men, women, and children during a peaceful protest in **Sharpeville,** a Black township. The government then outlawed the ANC and cracked down on other groups that opposed apartheid. The Sharpeville massacre was a turning point in the struggle against apartheid, leading some ANC activists to shift from nonviolent protest to armed struggle.

Some leaders, like **Nelson Mandela,** went underground. As an ANC leader, Mandela had first mobilized young South Africans to peacefully resist apartheid laws. As government oppression grew, Mandela joined ANC militants. Mandela was arrested, tried, and, in 1964, condemned to life in prison for treason. He stated at his trial: "I have cherished the ideal of a democratic and free society in which all persons live together in harmony and with equal opportunities. It is an ideal which I hope to live for and to achieve. But if needs be, it is an ideal for which I am prepared to die." Even in prison, he remained a powerful symbol of the struggle for freedom and resistance against political oppression.

In 1976, as a shocked world looked on, government forces killed almost 600 people in protests that started in the township of Soweto. International pressure against the regime grew. In the 1980s, demands for an end to apartheid and for Mandela's release began to have an effect. Many countries imposed economic sanctions on South Africa, including the United States, which began to impose sanctions in 1986. In 1984, Black South African bishop **Desmond Tutu** won the Nobel Peace Prize for his nonviolent opposition to apartheid.

Majority Rule Is Established Massive protests across South Africa and mounting international pressure led to change. In a surprise move in 1990, the newly chosen South African president **F. W. de Klerk** lifted the ban on the ANC and freed Mandela and other political prisoners. In 1993, Mandela and

de Klerk jointly won the Nobel Peace Prize for their efforts in ending apartheid.

Finally in 1994, South Africans of every race were allowed to vote for the first time. Voters chose Nelson Mandela as president in South Africa's first non-racial election. Mandela worked to heal the country's wounds. "Let us build together," he declared. He welcomed old foes into his government, including whites who had supported apartheid. Through his powerful example, he helped shift the political climate in South Africa.

Since 1994, South Africa has faced huge challenges. With majority rule, Black South Africans expected a better life. Although South Africa was a rich, industrial country, it had limited resources to spend on housing, education, and other programs. The income and education gap between Black and white people remained large. Poverty and unemployment were high among Black South Africans. The AIDS epidemic hit South Africa severely.

Today, South Africa has one of Africa's most developed economies. Yet in recent years, the country has suffered from corruption scandals as political and business leaders have enriched themselves through government contracts. This corruption has hurt economic growth and shaken faith in government.

>> More than 5,000 people attended the funerals of some of the people killed at Sharpeville. **Analyze Visuals** How does this image convey the impact of the Sharpeville massacre?

🅑 BOUNCE to Activate Timeline

>> Many industries flourish throughout Africa. In Nigeria, for example, the oil industry is dominant. These men are working on an oil rig in Nigeria's River State.

☑ **SUMMARIZE** What factors finally brought about the end of apartheid?

African Nations Face Economic Choices

African economies are diverse. Each country has a different mix of economic resources. A few have rich farmland. Others have cash crops that the world wants, such as cotton, cocoa, tea, and coffee. Some countries have great mineral resources, such as diamonds or oil. After achieving independence, each African nation had to make choices as to how to best develop their resources.

Economic Models After independence, many African nations were attracted to **socialism,** an economic system in which major economic decisions are made by the government rather than by individuals, companies, and the market. They hoped to industrialize rapidly and looked to the models of the Soviet Union and China, which had made impressive gains in a short period. Some developed their own form of "African socialism," based on traditions of consensus and shared responsibility.

These early models of development did not succeed. By the 1980s, most African nations moved toward market reforms, which international lenders required before making badly needed loans.

Cash Crops or Food Crops? For decades, African governments and multinational corporations worked to boost production of cash crops for export, such as coffee, cocoa, rubber, and cotton. However, the drive to develop cash crops for badly needed income hurt many countries. Land used to grow cash crops could not be used to produce food. Faced with growing populations, some countries had to buy costly imported food. To prevent unrest among the urban poor, many governments then kept food prices artificially low, which was costly.

Today, the demand for both cash crops and food crops remains high. Governments want to produce enough food for their people and have encouraged small farmers to adopt new practices to increase food output. At same time, they focus on competing in global markets for cash crops.

Economic Growth In the past ten years, economic activity across Africa has increased with some nations experiencing strong economic gains. Progress is due to many causes, including the end of some long running local conflicts. Among the fastest growing economies are Ethiopia, Rwanda, Ghana, and Côte d'Ivoire. Government policies to diversify their economies and promote middle class growth have helped drive more growth.

Trade has also stimulated economic growth. African nations have expanded trade and other economic ties with industrial giants such as China and India. Many African nations have turned to China for investments in infrastructure, or underlying transportation and other systems.

While economic growth is solid, it remains uneven. Some countries have suffered setbacks due to price swings for export crops and commodities. Other countries struggle with huge debt, high unemployment, political instability, and corruption. Natural disasters, such as Cyclone Idai, which devastated Mozambique, also hurt economic growth.

About a third of African countries have made progress toward reducing poverty and inequality. To promote further growth, many nations today focus on education and skills development, especially in poor and rural areas. The continent's human capital is one of its major resources.

Cooperation Furthers Development African nations have benefited from regional and international cooperation. In 1963, African nations set up the Organization of African Unity, which later became the 55-nation African Union (AU). Among its chief goals are encouraging cooperation, promoting economic growth, and seeking peaceful settlements of disputes. Through the African Development Bank, it channels investment capital from foreign sources into development programs.

The UN has also promoted development. It has worked with individual countries and regional organizations like the AU to support democratic government, promote economic growth, and protect the environment. UN programs have introduced drought resistant farming methods to Ethiopia and other regions of limited rainfall. Elsewhere, they have helped poor women open small businesses, which helps families out of poverty.

☑ **GENERATE EXPLANATIONS** Why did some African governments promote cash crops? What problems did this create?

Ongoing Challenges

Impact of Urbanization Like developing countries worldwide, African nations experienced rapid **urbanization** as millions of people moved from rural areas to cities. Today some 40 percent of Africans live in urban areas, compared to 28 percent in 1980. As in other developing regions, people hoped to escape rural poverty and better their lives in cities with greater access to jobs and education. The growth of megacities strained resources, however, leaving many newcomers without jobs, housing, or access to schools and medical care.

City life affected family life. While respect for elders and ancestors remain important values, modernization has created strains between traditional and modern family life. In cities—and even some rural areas—smaller households have replaced the larger extended family. Although better health care led to a population boom across Africa, the recent trend has been toward families having fewer children.

Environmental Concerns In Africa, as elsewhere, development and urbanization have contributed to environmental issues. Some nations, especially in the Congo Basin region, have vast forests. But

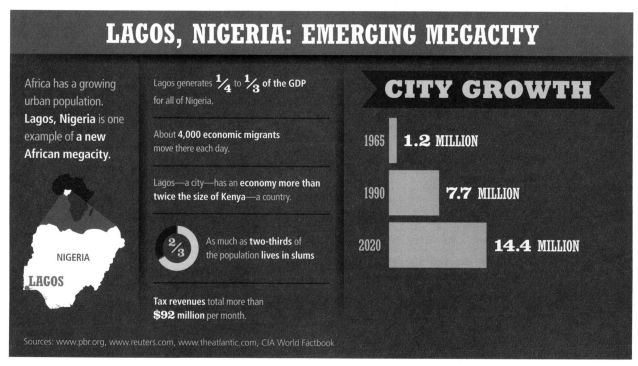

LAGOS, NIGERIA: EMERGING MEGACITY

Africa has a growing urban population. **Lagos, Nigeria** is one example of **a new African megacity**.

NIGERIA

LAGOS

Lagos generates $\frac{1}{4}$ to $\frac{1}{3}$ of the GDP for all of Nigeria.

About **4,000 economic migrants** move there each day.

Lagos—a city—has an **economy more than twice the size of Kenya**—a country.

$\frac{2}{3}$ As much as **two-thirds** of the population **lives in slums**

Tax revenues total more than **$92 million** per month.

CITY GROWTH

1965	1.2 MILLION
1990	7.7 MILLION
2020	14.4 MILLION

Sources: www.pbr.org, www.reuters.com, www.theatlantic.com, CIA World Factbook

>> Lagos, Nigeria, is growing rapidly and is one of the biggest cities in Africa. **Analyze Data** What does the data shown here tell you about the benefits and drawbacks of rapid urban growth?

>> Wangari Maathai of Kenya won the Nobel Peace Prize in 2004 for her work in promoting sustainable development.

>> Drought is a problem in many areas of Africa. This woman in Kenya digs for water at the bottom of a dry riverbed.

BOUNCE to Activate Gallery

millions of acres of forest are cleared each year. Deforestation, or the clearing of forests for wood and farming, has led to soil erosion and other harmful effects.

Deforestation endangers many species of plants and animals. Other animal habitats face destruction through human encroachment and development. The possible loss of these **endangered species** poses a threat to the tourism industries of some countries.

Oil and mining industries create great profits for their owners but also cause widespread pollution. Water pollution is another serious threat, caused by urban and industrial wastes as well as fertilizers, pesticides, and other products used in large scale farming.

Growing awareness of environmental issues has led to national and community efforts to bring change. In Kenya, **Wangari Maathai** challenged government inaction by starting the Green Belt Movement.

Her aim was to restore forest land while opening up opportunities for women in jobs such as planting, marketing, and forestry. Maathai and many other environmentalists want to promote **sustainable development** that meets the needs of the present without compromising the ability of future generations to meet their own needs.

Drought and Desertification Droughts are common in parts of Africa. The Sahel, a semi-desert region south of the Sahara, has suffered frequent droughts, which have led to **desertification,** or the change of habitable land into desert.

In the Sahel, overgrazing, farming, and deforestation has led to destruction of plant life and loss of topsoil. During droughts, herds have died off, crops withered, and many people have faced famine. International relief efforts have eased the famines, but wars that rage in several countries in the Sahel added to the suffering.

Today, an ambitious project called the Great Green Wall is underway to reverse desertification in some 20 African countries by reforesting the Sahel.

A wall of trees is set to reach from Senegal in the west to Djibouti in the east. Senegal has planted more than 12 million, mostly acacia, trees. The trees can survive in a dry climate and protect the soil from erosion. Acacia trees also produce gum arabic, a substance used in some medicines and other products, which can be exported for profit.

Higher temperatures and shifts in weather patterns cause floods or droughts, which have negative impacts on African nations. In some regions, these changes have reduced the amount of land that can be farmed. They also affect the outbreak and distribution of infectious diseases such as malaria.

AIDS and Other Diseases Today, as in the past, malaria remains a major health threat, especially among children. Efforts to combat malaria, such as providing mosquito netting, have slowed death rates. Still, the World Health Organization estimates that a child in Africa dies of malaria every 30 seconds.

By the 1990s, many African nations were reeling from the deadly effects of AIDS (Acquired Immune Deficiency Syndrome). The disease is caused by HIV, a virus that damages the body's ability to fight infections. In South Africa and Botswana, up to one third of adults were infected with HIV. More than 11 million children in Africa have been orphaned by the AIDS epidemic.

The loss of many skilled and productive workers hurt the economies of some African countries. A global effort to combat AIDS led to the development of drugs to treat people infected with HIV. African nations set up treatment programs and worked hard to stop the spread of AIDS.

A few African countries have slowed the spread of HIV/AIDS. Countries have worked to make antiretroviral drugs available to more people. These drugs can slow the progress of the virus and let people infected with HIV/AIDS live relatively normal lives.

Conflict and Terrorism Some African nations have endured decades of violence due to local conflicts and terrorism. In South Sudan, the Central African Republic, the Democratic Republic of Congo, and elsewhere, local strongmen, or warlords, gained power. Warlords use their own private militias, or armies, and take advantage of weak governments to impose brutal rule over a region.

Some warlords consider themselves freedom fighters and battle their rivals in complicated local ethnic or religious conflicts. To fund their militias, they often work alongside criminal groups. They also kidnap children to train as child soldiers in their militias. Conflicts between warlords and governments pose a major obstacle to development.

In recent years, terrorist groups, many linked to the Islamist terrorist organizations ISIS or Al Qaeda, have had a devastating impact in many countries, especially in the Sahel region. In Nigeria and nearby countries, the radical Islamist group Boko Haram began by opposing non-Islamic education, but by 2015 had turned to terrorism. Boko Haram terrorists have attacked villagers, kidnapped girls from schools, and sent suicide bombers into cities. To the east in Somalia, Al Shabab has attacked the government and targeted civilians locally and in neighboring Kenya. Both Boko Haram and Al Shabab want to establish a fundamentalist state based on Sharia, or Islamic law. African nations, along with the UN, the United States, and other governments, have worked to develop counterterrorism strategies to deal with these threats.

☑ **IDENTIFY CAUSE AND EFFECT** Why has the AIDS epidemic so profoundly affected the economies of Africa?

☑ ASSESSMENT

1. **Summarize** How did Nelson Mandela help shift political thought in South Africa?

2. **Describe** Describe the apartheid regime and the struggle for equality in South Africa.

3. **Infer** Why did some African leaders believe that "African socialism" would work better than a European model? What problems arose?

4. **Identify Central Issues** What do you think is the greatest challenge facing developing African countries today? Give reasons for your answer.

5. **Make Predictions** What effect will urbanization have on Africa? Will it be positive or negative?

6. **Connections to Today** How has the use of natural resources shaped modern Africa?

Change in South Africa

Nelson Mandela delivered this speech after having been elected president in South Africa's first multiracial election in 1994. Knowing that the injustices of apartheid would be hard to overcome, Mandela asked the people to work together for peace and justice.

F.W. de Klerk, shown here with Mandela, served as President of South Africa from 1989 to 1994. He worked with Mandela to dismantle the country's system of apartheid. The second primary source is an excerpt from his 1990 speech to Parliament calling for a non-racist South Africa.

As you read, compare their viewpoints on South Africa's future.

>> Nelson Mandela and F.W. de Klerk

Primary Source 1

"Glory and Hope," Nelson Mandela

Today, all of us do, by our presence here, and by our celebrations . . . confer [give] glory and hope to newborn liberty.

Out of the experience of an extraordinary human disaster that lasted too long must be born a society of which all humanity will be proud.

Our daily deeds as ordinary South Africans must produce an actual South African reality that will reinforce humanity's belief in justice, strengthen its confidence in the nobility of the human soul and sustain all our hopes for a glorious life for all. . . .

☑ **DETERMINE MEANING** What does Mandela mean by "an actual South African reality"?

The time for the healing of the wounds has come. . . .

The time to build is upon us.

We have, at last, achieved our political emancipation [freedom from bondage or control by others]. We pledge ourselves to liberate all our people from the continuing bondage [slavery] of poverty, deprivation [lack of materials necessary for survival], suffering, gender and other discrimination. . . .

We have triumphed in the effort to implant [insert] hope in the breasts of the millions of our people. We enter into a covenant [binding agreement] that we shall build the society in which all South Africans, both black and white, will be able to walk tall, without any fear in their hearts, assured of their inalienable right to human dignity—a rainbow nation at peace with itself and the world. . . .

☑ **SUMMARIZE** What freedoms does Mandela call for in this passage?

We understand it still that there is no easy road to freedom.

We know it well that none of us acting alone can achieve success.

We must therefore act together as a united people, for national reconciliation [a settling of differences that results in harmony], for nation building, for the birth of a new world.

Let there be justice for all. Let there be peace for all. Let there be work, bread, water, and salt for all. . . . The sun shall never set on so glorious a human achievement!

☑ **PARAPHRASE** In one or two sentences, write in your own words how Mandela concludes his speech.

Primary Source 2

Speech to Parliament, F.W. de Klerk

The Government accepts the principle of the recognition and protection of the fundamental individual rights which form the constitutional basis of most Western democracies. We acknowledge, too, that the most practical way of protecting those rights is vested in a declaration of rights justiciable (subject to a court trial) by an independent judiciary. However, it is clear that a system for the protection of the rights of individuals, minorities and national entities has to form a well-rounded and balanced whole. South Africa has its own national composition and our constitutional dispensation has to take this into account. The formal recognition of individual rights does not mean that the problems of a heterogeneous population will simply disappear. Any new constitution which disregards this reality will be inappropriate and even harmful. Naturally, the protection of collective, minority and national rights may not bring about an imbalance in respect of individual rights. It is neither the Government's policy nor its intention that any group—in whichever way it may be defined—shall be favoured above or in relation to any of the others.

☑ **ANALYZE INFORMATION** Why does de Klerk warn against an easy compromise of individual rights in South Africa?

☑ ASSESSMENT

1. **Explain an Argument** When apartheid ended, there was a danger of a backlash by Black South Africans against whites who supported apartheid. How does Mandela's speech respond to that danger?

2. **Explain** Reread the beginning of de Klerk's speech. Why do you think he feels the need to state this?

3. **Compare and Contrast** How would you describe the tone of Mandela's speech? How does this tone reflect Mandela's view of his country and its future, and how is it similar to or different than de Klerk's speech?

4. **Determine Author's Purpose** Why do you think Mandela talks about building a new world, not just a new South Africa?

5. **Describe** The day de Klerk made the speech excerpted here was also the day he announced the release of Mandela from prison after 27 years. Describe what the reaction might have been not only in South Africa but around the world.

20.5

These Iraqi women wear the modified hijab covering their hair. Hijab is required by law in Iran and Saudi Arabia, but it has been freely adopted by many Muslim women worldwide as a sign of their faith.

 BOUNCE to Activate Flipped Video

Objectives

Analyze the development of modern nations in the Middle East.

Describe the founding of Israel and the impact of the Arab rejection of Israel.

Understand how oil has affected nations of the Middle East.

Examine the impact of Islam on government, law, and the lives of women.

Define the "Arab Spring."

Key Terms

kibbutz
Golda Meir
Suez Canal
Gamal Abdel Nasser
Anwar Sadat
Ruhollah Khomeini
theocracy
secular
hijab

The Modern Middle East Takes Shape

The Middle East, as we use the term in this lesson, is the region stretching from Egypt in the west to Iran in the east and from Turkey in the north to the Arabian Peninsula in the south. Although the majority of people in the region today are Muslims, there are also Christian communities and the mostly Jewish nation of Israel.

The Challenges of Diversity

As a world crossroads since ancient times, the Middle East is home to many ethnic groups. Arabs are a majority in some countries, such as Egypt, Saudi Arabia, and Syria. In other countries, the majority populations are non-Arab Muslims, such as the Turks of Turkey and the Persians of Iran.

Mandates Gain Independence At the end of World War I, the Treaty of Versailles and other agreements parceled out many of the lands once dominated by the defeated Central Powers. Britain and France were given mandates over large parts of the Middle East.

Under the mandate system in the Middle East, territories taken from the defeated Ottoman empire were administered, or run, by Europeans. Britain, for example, controlled the Palestine mandate and three provinces of the old Ottoman empire that were joined together into modern-day Iraq. The stated goal of the mandate system was to move the mandates gradually toward independence.

From the outset, Arabs resisted the mandates. In British-ruled Palestine, tensions also grew between Arab and Jewish residents. In the Balfour Declaration, Britain had supported a Jewish national home in part of the Palestine mandate, while Arabs in the region demanded self-rule. During the 1930s, independence movements and nationalist calls for an end to European control grew. Following World War II, the former mandates became the independent countries of Iraq, Syria, and Jordan. The Palestine mandate was partitioned into Arab areas and Israel.

Religious and Ethnic Divisions The borders of the new nations were artificially drawn and lumped together diverse ethnic and religious communities. Some ethnic minorities demanded self-rule, or even independence.

Different religious sects, or groups loyal to their own set of beliefs, further divided the new nations. Many countries were home to both Shiite and Sunni Muslims, along with Alawites, Druze, different Christian sects, and Jews. In Iraq and Bahrain, for example, the Shiite majority was ruled by the Sunni minority. Sectarian violence, or conflict based on religious loyalties, posed challenges to unity. Many nations like Syria and Lebanon had diverse groups, including Muslim and Christian Arabs, Assyrians, Greeks, Armenians, and Kurds.

Kurdish Nationalism The Kurds are an ethnic group with their own language and culture. They form important minorities in Turkey, Iran, Syria and Iraq. Kurdish nationalists have long called for an independent homeland. In Turkey, Kurdish rebels resisted government efforts to suppress their culture. In Iraq, a Kurdish uprising in 1991 was brutally suppressed. Today, Kurds in Iraq have much autonomy, but many Kurds still want their own state.

☑ **EXPRESS PROBLEMS CLEARLY** What is the main cause of ethnic and sectarian violence in the Middle East?

The Founding of Israel

As early as the 1880s, Jews had begun actively organizing and advocating for the re-establishment of a home in their ancient homeland. The horrors of the Holocaust created strong worldwide support for a Jewish state. Many Jews, including Holocaust survivors, migrated to the Palestine Mandate after World War II.

In 1947, the UN drew up a plan to divide, or partition, the Palestine mandate between the Arabs and Jews. The plan called for the division of Palestine into an Arab and a Jewish state. The UN

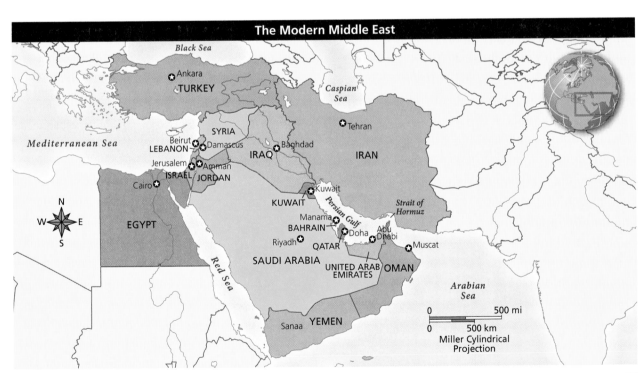

The Modern Middle East

>> **Analyze Maps** This map shows the countries of the modern Middle East. Saudi Arabia, Kuwait, and Iran are three of the world's largest oil-producing countries. Why might control of the Strait of Hormuz be important?

BOUNCE to Activate Map

>> Israeli flags fly in New York City to celebrate the birth of Israel, which became an independent state on May 14, 1948. **Explain** Why was an Arab state not established as well?

📱 BOUNCE to Activate Gallery

>> Palestinian women and children flee to Arab-held territories in June 1948. Refugee camps were set up to accept those who could not find shelter. **Recall** How long did some Palestinian refugees live in the refugee camps?

General Assembly voted to adopt the plan. While the Jews accepted partition, Arabs rejected the partition plan. They argued that Palestine was one of the lands that had been promised to them by the British in return for Arab support in World War I.

Arabs and Israelis in Conflict In 1948, when Britain withdrew from the Palestine mandate, Jews proclaimed the independent State of Israel. Neighboring Arab nations launched the first of several wars against Israel, but were defeated.

As a result of these wars, Israel gained control of more territory. After the 1948 war, Jordan took control of the West Bank and East Jerusalem, while Egypt took the Gaza Strip. Today, Palestinian Arabs do not have an independent state, but a series of negotiations over the years has resulted in peace treaties between Israel and Egypt and the creation of an autonomous Palestinian authority within Israeli-controlled territories.

The 1948 Arab-Israeli war created a huge refugee problem. Hundreds of thousands of Palestinian Arabs fled their homes in Israeli territory. The UN housed them in temporary camps in nearby countries, where they remained for decades. At the same time, hundreds of thousands of Jewish refugees expelled from Arab lands fled to Israel.

The Growth of Israel After the 1948 war, Israel developed rapidly. A skilled workforce set up businesses. Kibbutzim produced crops for export. A **kibbutz** (kih BOOTS) is a collective farm.

In 1950, Israel passed a law called the right of return, granting every Jew the right to live in Israel and become an Israeli citizen. This was a response to the Holocaust when countries closed their doors to Jews fleeing the Nazis. This law established Israel as a safe haven for the Jewish people. Jews from around the world migrated to Israel. They joined native Israelis who had struggled to win independence.

An early leader was **Golda Meir,** who had emigrated from Russia to the United States as a child. In the 1920s, she moved to a kibbutz in Palestine and later joined the Jewish independence movement. In 1969, she became Israel's first woman prime minister.

☑ **INFER** Why did people around the world support a Jewish homeland in Palestine?

New Nations in the Middle East

After independence, Middle Eastern nations set out to build strong modern economies. Only a handful of nations in the region had rich oil reserves. Most Middle Eastern nations were poor, and each faced its own set of challenges.

In some countries, nationalist military leaders seized power. They wanted to promote economic growth and end foreign influence, but they were also authoritarian rulers who suppressed critics, often brutally. Some countries, such as Jordan and Saudi Arabia, had hereditary monarchs. Only Israel and Turkey had lasting multiparty systems.

Egypt's Leadership in the Arab World Egypt is the most populous nation in the Arab world. Since most of Egypt is desert, its population is crammed into the narrow Nile River valley.

Egypt controls the **Suez Canal,** the vital waterway that provides the shortest sea route between Europe and Asia. Egypt also shares a border with Israel.

In 1952, **Gamal Abdel Nasser** seized power in Egypt. Determined to modernize Egypt and end Western domination, Nasser soon nationalized the Suez Canal, ending British and French control. Nasser's Arab nationalism made him popular in the Arab world. He led two unsuccessful wars against Israel. Egypt relied on Soviet aid during the Cold War.

In 1979, Nasser's successor, **Anwar Sadat,** reduced ties with the Soviet Union and sought aid from the United States. He also became the first Arab leader to make peace with Israel. In exchange for peace, Israel returned the Sinai Peninsula to Egypt. Sadat was assassinated by Islamist extremists in 1981. Hosni Mubarak took over and cracked down hard on extremists, jailing even moderate critics.

The Arab Spring and Its Impact In 2011, popular unrest swept across the Middle East, launching pro-democracy movements, known as the Arab Spring. Frustration with corrupt and dictatorial governments, along with high unemployment, fed demands for change. The Arab Spring, which started in Tunisia, spread to Egypt and other nations. During the Arab Spring, massive street protests forced Egypt's Hosni Mubarak to step down after 30 years in office.

The "Arab Spring" took different paths in different nations. Some governments suppressed the protests. Other countries, such as Egypt, held elections. Egyptians went to the polls with great hopes in

>> This photograph shows members of the royal family of Saudi Arabia, one of the most oil-rich nations on Earth. Most power remains with the king and royal family, but tribal sheikhs also have influence. **Recall** Which other Middle Eastern state has a hereditary monarchy? Which two states have multiparty systems?

>> Gamal Abdel Nasser (left) led Egypt from 1952 until 1970. Here, he and the president of Syria celebrate the union of their countries to form the United Arab Republic in 1958. This Pan-Arab experiment lasted only three years. **Hypothesize** Why is Egypt such an important country in the Middle East?

>> Women played an important role in the Arab Spring movement. This massive demonstration took place in Cairo on July 8, 2011. **Hypothesize** What motivated women to participate in the Arab Spring movement?

2012. An Islamist leader, Mohammed Morsi, was elected president. Soon afterwards, he was ousted by the military, which helped Abdel Fatah al Sisi win election as president. Sisi returned Egypt to authoritarian rule, jailing critics and limiting many freedoms. He faced challenges from Islamist attacks and weak economic growth.

Elsewhere in the Middle East, the hopes of the Arab Spring were dashed. Many countries faced ongoing conflict with Islamist extremists. In the oil rich states on the Persian Gulf, rulers squashed dissent.

In Syria, pro-democracy protests of the Arab Spring triggered a devastating civil war. Syrian president Bashar al-Assad battled various rebel groups determined to overthrow his regime. World powers, including the United States and Russia, became involved after Assad used chemical weapons on Syrian rebel groups. After ISIS won control of parts of Syria, the United States helped Syrian Kurdish forces defeat ISIS fighters. With aid from Iran and Russia, Assad gradually regained control. More than 400,000 Syrians were killed in the seven-year conflict while many more were made homeless by the fighting.

An Islamic Revolution in Iran Because of its vast oil fields, Iran was a focus of Cold War rivalries. Its ruler, Shah Mohammad Reza Pahlavi, favored the West but faced nationalist critics at home, led by Mohammad Mosaddeq (MAW sah dek). After Mosaddeq was elected prime minister in 1951, he nationalized the foreign-owned oil industry. The shah, with U.S. help, ousted Mosaddeq and retuned the oil industry to Western control. This move outraged many Iranians.

Although the shah modernized industry, redistributed land to peasants, and gave new rights to women, opposition to his rule grew, especially among the Islamic clergy. In response, the government brutally silenced critics.

The shah's foes rallied behind Ayatollah **Ruhollah Khomeini** (ROO hoh lah koh MAY nee). The Ayatollah, a religious leader, condemned Western influences and accused the shah of violating Islamic law. In 1979, massive protests drove the shah from power. Khomeini and his supporters proclaimed the Islamic Republic of Iran.

The new government was a **theocracy,** or government by religious leaders. The Iranian Revolution introduced strict Islamic law. Like the shah, the new leaders silenced critics. In 1979, Islamists seized the American embassy in the capital and held 52 hostages for more than a year.

>> Ayatollah Khomeini was Iran's ultimate political and religious authority for 10 years after the Iranian Revolution. Khomeini, who died in 1989, is still revered in Iran. This mural is in Tehran.

The new Islamic republic soon faced a long, bloody war with its neighbor Iraq, and tense relations with the West. The United States accused Iran of backing terrorists. Along with its allies, the United States imposed harsh economic sanctions to keep Iran from developing nuclear weapons. Years of sanctions hurt Iran's economy. In 2015, Iranian president, Hassan Rouhani, signed an international agreement to limit its nuclear activities in exchange for the lifting of sanctions. In 2018, U.S. President Trump withdrew from the Iran nuclear deal.

Hopes rose for an easing of tensions between Iran and the West. At home, however, Rouhani faced an economy hurt by years of economic sanctions and deep political divisions between hardliners and reformists.

Modern Turkey Once the heart of the Ottoman empire, Turkey became a republic in the 1920s under Ataturk. It has the third-largest population in the Middle East after Egypt and Iran. Although it is a Muslim country, most of its people are Turks, not Arabs. Turkey commands a strategic location, straddling Europe and Asia, and has served as a link between Europe and the Middle East. Turkey applied to join the European Union, but some EU members demanded that it make economic and other reforms. Turkey also sought closer ties with its Middle Eastern neighbors.

Although the military intervened in the past, today Turkey is a multiparty democracy with a market economy. Turkey was long run by secularists who followed Ataturk's ideas. More recently, an Islamic government has come to power. Its leader, Recep Tayyip Erdogan, has moved aggressively to consolidate authority, especially after a failed coup attempt in 2016. His government has cracked down on critics, jailing journalists and other opponents.

☑ **CATEGORIZE** What types of governments are most common in the Middle East?

The Importance of Oil in the Middle East

Parts of the Middle East have huge oil resources, giving the region global importance. A handful of oil-producing nations prospered. They included Saudi Arabia, Iran, Iraq, Kuwait, and several small states along the Persian Gulf. The oil-producing nations also border vital shipping lanes that carry oil from the region to the world. Even though these oil-rich countries provide aid to their neighbors, most Middle Eastern nations lack oil and have struggled economically.

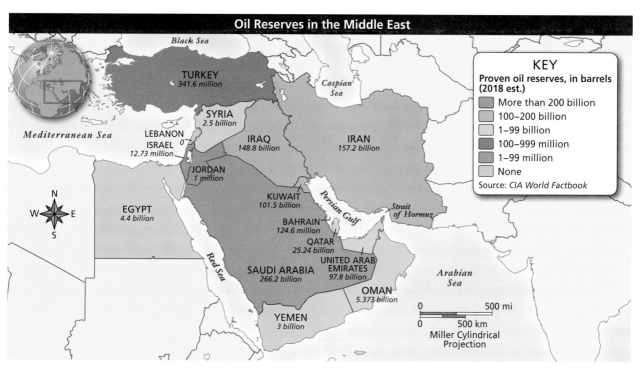

Oil Reserves in the Middle East

KEY
Proven oil reserves, in barrels (2018 est.)
- More than 200 billion
- 100–200 billion
- 1–99 billion
- 100–999 million
- 1–99 million
- None

Source: *CIA World Factbook*

TURKEY 341.6 million
SYRIA 2.5 billion
LEBANON
ISRAEL 12.73 million
IRAQ 148.8 billion
IRAN 157.2 billion
JORDAN 1 million
EGYPT 4.4 billion
KUWAIT 101.5 billion
BAHRAIN 124.6 million
QATAR 25.24 billion
UNITED ARAB EMIRATES 97.8 billion
SAUDI ARABIA 266.2 billion
OMAN 5.373 billion
YEMEN 3 billion

0   500 mi
0   500 km
Miller Cylindrical Projection

>> **Analyze Maps** This map shows the known oil reserves of Middle Eastern countries. On what body of water do the nations with the largest oil reserves lie?

>> Men worship at the Sheikh Zayed Mosque in Abu Dhabi, capital of the United Arab Emirates. The mosque is large enough to accommodate more than 40,000 worshipers.

OPEC In 1960, the oil-producing nations of the Middle East, along with Venezuela, set up the Organization of Petroleum Exporting Countries (OPEC). OPEC wanted to end the power of Western oil companies and set its own oil production quotas and prices.

In 1973, Middle Eastern members of OPEC used oil as a political weapon. They stopped oil shipments to the United States and other countries that had supported Israel in the Yom Kippur War. This oil embargo triggered a global recession and led other countries to try to develop other sources of oil. Since then, OPEC has focused on setting production quotas and has added new members.

Saudi Arabia Saudi Arabia has one of the world's largest oil reserves. It exports vast amounts of oil to the West. In return, it has received military aid from the United States. Its ruling family is committed to Wahhabism, a strict sect within Sunni Islam. Oil wealth allowed Saudi Arabia to modernize its infrastructure, such as transportation and communication systems. At the same time, the government has suppressed opposition.

☑ **INFER** How can OPEC influence global events?

Islam and the Modern World

After independence, some Middle Eastern countries adopted Western-style secular governments. Leaders in Egypt and Syria, for example, saw secular government as a means to modernization. In time, however, many secular leaders became authoritarian rulers. At the same time, Western cultural influences, introduced during the age of imperialism, spread. In cities, people bought goods imported from the West. They wore Western fashions and watched American television shows and movies.

Islamic Revival Some Muslims claimed that Western culture and capitalism were undermining Islamic society. They called for a return to Sharia, or Islamic law based on the Quran, and to traditional customs and values. These conservative reformers, known as Islamists or Islamic fundamentalists, blamed social and economic ill on the West. Only a renewed commitment to Islam, they declared, could improve conditions for Muslims around the world.

Many Muslims welcomed the Islamic movement as a way to cope with rapid social and economic changes. Moderate Islamists wanted to work toward

>> Egyptian supporters of the Muslim Brotherhood, an Islamist organization, celebrate the election of Muhammed Morsi. Morsi, who won the first election held in Egypt after the "Arab Spring," was overthrown by the military in 2013.

democratic reforms within Islam. Radical Islamists, or fundamentalist extremists, however, advocated violence to achieve their goal.

Radical Islam Radical Islamic fundamentalist groups in Egypt, Saudi Arabia, and elsewhere sought to overthrow governments that they saw as too closely allied to the West. They also targeted Israel, which had defeated Arabs in several wars, and the United States. Although many governments cracked down on radical Islamic fundamentalists, these groups survived. In 1979, Islamic fundamentalists welcomed Iran's revolution. Iran became the first modern nation to topple a secular government and replace it with a government based on Sharia.

Islam and the Lives of Women Conditions for women vary greatly across the Muslim Middle East. In most countries, women won equality before the law, but women still faced legal and social hurdles, especially to jobs. Over time, however, educated women entered professions such as law and medicine.

In Turkey, Egypt, and Syria, many urban women had given up wearing the **hijab,** or traditional Muslim headscarf, or loose, ankle-length garments meant to conceal. With the Islamic revival, many educated women returned to the hijab as a symbol of their faith. In religiously conservative countries like Saudi Arabia and Iran, women must follow local Islamic traditions, such as wearing the hijab.

Women stood on the front lines of the "Arab Spring" to demand democratic reforms and equal opportunity. "I grew up in a world where we believed we could not do anything," noted a young woman and online activist in Jordan. "Generations believed we could do nothing, and now, in a matter of weeks, we know that we can."

Some women's rights advocates pointed out that their goals were not based on Western values but on the traditions of early Islam that improved the status of women. Women's rights movements faced serious challenges, however. While access to education has improved for women, girls are often less likely to attend school than boys because of the tradition that girls do not need a formal education for their expected roles as wives and mothers. Although governments recognized the productive value of women in the workforce, local cultural restrictions often kept women from holding jobs outside the home.

☑ **IDENTIFY CAUSE AND EFFECT** Why do Islamists oppose secular government and culture in the Muslim world?

☑ ASSESSMENT

1. **Identify** What are two events that have powerfully influenced the development of the modern nations of the Middle East?

2. **Express Problems Clearly** How do religious and ethnic differences affect the Middle East?

3. **Identify Cause and Effect** What effect did the Arab rejection of the State of Israel have on today's Palestinians?

4. **Cite Evidence** What influence has Islam had on the government of Iran since the overthrow of the shah?

5. **Connections to Today** What are some ways oil wealth has affected the nations of the Middle East?

Afro-Asian Solidarity, Anwar Sadat

Anwar Sadat was an Egyptian military officer who worked to end British control of Egypt and helped overthrow the Egyptian monarchy in 1952. He later became president of Egypt.

In 1957, delegates from African and Asian nations and territories gathered in Cairo, Egypt, for the Afro-Asian Peoples' Solidarity Conference. There, they worked to encourage cooperation against foreign imperialism and sought to ensure that Africa and Asia would be free of nuclear weapons. In the speech excerpted below, Sadat urges African and Asian people to work together.

>> Anwar Sadat addressing Parliament in Cairo, Egypt, shortly after being sworn in as president in 1970.

Primary Source

More than two years ago twenty nine governments of independent states convened together at the Bandung Conference to declare to the world at large that the tide of history has changed its course, and that Asia and Africa, which hitherto have been common playground, where trespassers went by unheeded or a forest in which foreign beasts of prey roamed at leisure, have now become free world powers, majestic and serene, with a decisive role in shaping the future of the whole family of Nations. . . .

☑ **ANALYZE STYLE AND RHETORIC** How does Sadat describe the relationship between foreign nations and Africa and Asia?

Today this people's Conference of ours meets, partly in honour of the spirit of Bandung and as a reminder of the principles and ideals it stands for, and partly to push it a step forward. . . . No doubt each country has its own particular problems for which she is more competent than anyone else to gauge the nature of the difficulties they represent; but at the same time, there is not a shadow of a doubt also that it is within the power of each of us to extend a helping hand to his brother in time of need, in an endeavour to assist in solving his problems. . . . Consequently, our particular national problems, and the problems common to us all, must of necessity go along, side by side. . . .

We cannot live peacefully in a world threatened by the shadow of war. We can no longer enjoy the products of our hands and the fruits of our labour in a world where plunder prevails and flourishes. We can no longer build and reconstruct in a world which manufactures weapons for destruction and devastation. We can no longer raise the standard of living of our peoples and stamp out diseases and epidemics in a world where nations vie with each other for the production of lethal weapons of massacre and annihilation.

☑ **DETERMINE CENTRAL IDEAS** What is the main idea in this passage?

GO ONLINE to access primary sources

Gone forever is the era where the future of war and peace was decided upon in a few European capitals, because today we happen to be strong enough to make the decision ourselves in that respect. …
Only think of the colossal number of our people, our natural resources, the vastness of the area covered by our respective countries, and our strategic positions. You will surely come to the conclusion that the outbreak of war is impossible so long as we insist on peace … Here in Egypt we, for instance, believe in the principle of neutrality and non-alignment. Many of our friends in Asia and Africa share this belief. We are confident that by adopting this attitude, we eliminate the shadow of war and limit the area of conflict between the two belligerent blocks, thus creating a vast region for Peace. . . .

☑ **DRAW CONCLUSIONS** What is Sadat's belief about the role of Africa and Asia in the Cold War?

In the name of Egypt, I address a message to the world at large, for the preservation of Peace, and the abolition of war; for the removal of world tension, and the cessation of the cold war of nerves. We have seen war at Port Said. We have been hit by it, and faced its ravages and woes. But a World War, once it breaks out with its nuclear weapons and hydrogen bombs, will unquestionably annihilate mankind and destroy forever our existing civilization. As a

section of humanity, which has been treacherously attacked by imperialistic States, we demand that atomic experiments should be abolished, and that manufacture and use of nuclear weapons should be prohibited. We further press for disarmament in the interests of World Peace. The People of Egypt who are sparing no effort for the establishment of universal justice, equity, liberty and peace, welcome you as messengers of justice, equity, liberty and peace.

☑ **IDENTIFY SUPPORTING DETAILS** How does Sadat use Egypt's own experiences to urge peace?

☑ ASSESSMENT

1. **Explain** Why does Sadat recommend neutrality and non-alignment?

2. **Determine the Author's Point of View** How does Sadat connect the Cold War to Africa and Asia's experiences under imperialism?

3. **Predict** How do you think people attending the conference reacted to Sadat's speech?

4. **Summarize** What is the main idea of the source?

20.6

The Iran-Iraq War lasted eight years and took an enormous toll on both countries. These Iraqi soldiers were photographed near Basra, Iraq, in 1984.

 BOUNCE to Activate Flipped Video

Objectives

Explain the ongoing Israeli-Palestinian conflict and the obstacles to peace.

Explain the causes and effects of conflicts in Lebanon and Syria.

Understand why Iraq became a battleground.

Key Terms

Yasir Arafat
intifada
Yitzhak Rabin
Jerusalem
militia
Saddam Hussein
no-fly zone
weapon of mass
   destruction (WMD)
insurgent

Conflicts in the Middle East

Modern Israel was established in 1948 under the United Nations Partition Plan. Although the UN plan offered Palestinians territory for their own state, Arab leaders rejected the plan because they viewed it as illegal and unfair. Instead, they called for the destruction of Israel.

Israel and Palestine

In 1948, five Arab nations invaded the newly independent Israel and were defeated. Israel and its Arab neighbors fought three more wars, in 1956, 1967, and 1973. In these wars, Israel fought for its existence, and in the process of turning back attacking Arab forces gained more land. Between and since these wars, Israel has faced many terrorist attacks within its borders, and ongoing rocket attacks from Gaza and Lebanon. The United States and other nations worked to find a solution to the long-standing conflict.

The West Bank, Gaza, and the Golan Heights In the Six Day War of 1967, in response to ongoing hostility by its Arab neighbors, Israel took control of the West Bank and East Jerusalem from Jordan along with the Gaza Strip and Sinai Peninsula from Egypt. Israel also took the Golan Heights from Syria.

Angered by their loss in the Six Day War, Arab countries held a summit at Khartoum several months later and issued the "Three No's": no recognition of Israel, no negotiations with Israel, and no peace with Israel. In 1973, these Arab nations attacked Israel on

Yom Kippur, the holiest day of the Jewish calendar. In the Yom Kippur War, Arabs failed to regain the lands that they had lost to Israel in 1967. Arabs referred to these lands as the "occupied territories." Later, Israel annexed East Jerusalem and the Golan Heights. Israel then allowed Jewish settlers to build homes in some of these territories, which increased bitterness among the Palestinians.

The PLO and Intifada The number of Palestinians in refugee camps grew in the decades after 1948. The majority of these camps were overcrowded, and lacked adequate services such as roads and sewers. Unable to return to Israel, the refugees were also not granted rights in the countries that hosted them. Such conditions fed growing anger. Many Palestinians came to support the Palestinian Liberation Organization (PLO), which led the struggle against Israel.

Led by **Yasir Arafat,** the PLO called for the destruction of Israel and waged guerrilla war against Israelis at home and abroad. The PLO gained world attention with airplane hijackings and the killing of Israeli athletes at the 1972 Olympic Games.

In 1987, Palestinians in the West Bank and Gaza started to resist Israel with **intifadas,** or uprisings. Young Palestinians demanded an end to Israeli control and hurled rocks at or fired on Israeli soldiers.

Suicide bombers blew up buses, stores, and clubs in Israel. Israel responded by sealing off and raiding Palestinian towns and targeting terrorist leaders. The violence killed many civilians on both sides.

☑ **IDENTIFY CENTRAL IDEAS** How did Arab nations respond to the creation of Israel?

The Difficult Road to Peace

During the Cold War, efforts to solve the Arab-Israeli conflict had little success, despite ongoing attempts by the UN, the United States, and other nations. However, as you have read, Egyptian leader Anwar Sadat did take a courageous first step by agreeing to peace talks, the first Arab leader to do so. Israel and Egypt signed a peace accord in 1979 in which Israel returned the Sinai Peninsula to Egypt

The collapse of the Soviet Union led to renewed peace talks. Without Soviet aid, some Arab governments accepted the need to negotiate with Israel. In 1994, Jordan and Israel signed a peace agreement. Talks between Syria and Israel stalled over issues such as the future of the Golan Heights. Israel had taken control of the heights, which Syria had long used to fire on its neighbors.

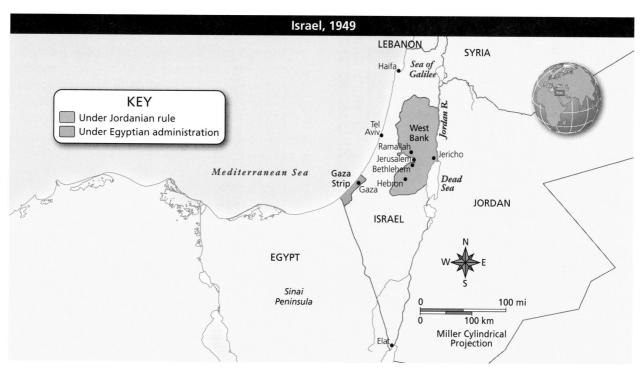

>> **Analyze Maps** This map shows the boundaries of the State of Israel in 1949. How does the map illustrate one challenge to achieving Mideast peace?

▶ BOUNCE to Activate Map

>> In 1977, Egyptian president Anwar Sadat became the first Arab leader to visit and recognize Israel. Here, he exchanges gifts with former Israeli prime minister Golda Meir.

The Oslo Accords In 1993, Yasir Arafat and Israeli Prime Minister **Yitzhak Rabin**(rah BEEN) signed the Oslo Accords. This plan gave Palestinians in Gaza and the West Bank limited self-rule. It also set up a Palestinian Authority to govern the area. The PLO recognized Israel's right to exist and pledged to stop terrorist attacks on Israel. Arafat led the Palestinian Authority until his death in 2004.

Violence Continues Although Arafat's successor, Mahmoud Abbas (ah BAHS), pledged to stop Palestinian attacks on Israel, violence continued. Fierce divisions split the Palestinian Authority between Fatah, the party of Arafat and his successors, and Hamas, a radical Islamist group. Hamas was funded by Iran and rejected Israel's right to exist. It was ready to use violence to achieve its aims.

In 2007, Hamas seized control of Gaza. Israel then imposed a blockade on Gaza, controlling access to the region in order to stop weapons from reaching Hamas. From Gaza, Hamas launched frequent rocket attacks on Israel. The Israeli military responded with air strikes and several invasions.

During a 50-day war in 2014, Hamas again launched attacks against Israel. In response, Israel targeted Hamas rocket launching sites. The war caused huge damage and many civilian deaths in Gaza. Israel, too, suffered losses. Although a ceasefire was arranged, difficult issues remained. Palestinians demanded an end to the Israeli blockade, which limited their access to food, water, electricity, and other basic necessities. Israelis wanted Hamas to disarm and end its rocket attacks.

Obstacles to Peace Decades of conflict and mistrust have made peace hard to achieve. One obstacle to peace concerns the Palestinian refugees who fled or were forced off their lands in earlier wars. They and their descendants want the "right of return," or the right to resettle on their land in Israel proper. Israelis oppose this demand, which could overwhelm the only Jewish state with large numbers of Palestinians. Israelis view this demand as an attempt to destroy Israel.

A second obstacle is **Jerusalem,** a city sacred to Jews, Christians, and Muslims. Jordan controlled East Jerusalem and the Old City from 1948 to 1967 and did not allow Jewish access to holy sites. Israel gained control in 1967 and later added it to the capital of Israel, reuniting the city of Jerusalem. Muslims and Christians control their holy sites within the city. In 2017, U.S. President Trump recognized Jerusalem as the capital of Israel. Palestinians, and many in the international community, however, continued to see East Jerusalem as the capital of a future Palestinian state.

A third stumbling block is the issue of Jewish settlements in East Jerusalem and the West Bank, areas claimed by Palestinians. Israel voluntarily withdrew all of its settlements in the Sinai and in Gaza but has not withdrawn from the West Bank and East Jerusalem. Disagreements about final borders affect negotiations over the future of the West Bank.

Another issue is security. Israel fears that if extremists gained control over a Palestinian state, they could attack Israel as Hamas has done since Israel withdrew from Gaza. Israel therefore wants to limit the military capacity of any Palestinian state and control security in the area. Palestinians argue that security will improve when Palestinians have their own state.

Over time, the Israeli-Palestinian conflict has fueled the anger of fundamentalist, radical Islamist groups such as Hamas in Gaza and Hezbollah in Lebanon. These radical groups reject Israel's right to exist. They condemn its ally, the United States, along with any Arab government involved in the peace process. Ongoing violence and threats from these groups increase Israel's security concerns and impede the peace process.

Another important issue is how to allocate and protect water resources. The distribution of water resources impacts negotiations between Israel and the Palestinians concerning the control of the water supply, water consumption, and the costs of investments in water management. The rights to water resources are also major issues between countries in the region.

A Two-State Solution For years, peace talks have revolved around the idea of a two-state solution, with peaceful coexistence between Israel and a stable, democratic Palestinian state. However, attempts to achieve a peace settlement on these grounds have not succeeded.

In 2020, Israel signed peace agreements with two Arab nations, the United Arab Emirates and Bahrain. Like Israel, these countries oppose Iran's goals in the region. The agreements raised hopes for a new peace agreement between Israel and the Palestinians.

☑ **INTEGRATE INFORMATION** Why is Jerusalem so important to both Israelis and Palestinians?

Conflict in Lebanon and Syria

Internal divisions and the ongoing Israeli-Palestinian conflict impacted neighboring Lebanon and Syria. Both nations gained independence in the 1940s. Both are home to diverse religious and ethnic groups.

The Lebanese Civil War Historically, Lebanon was a thriving center of commerce. After gaining independence from France in 1943, its government depended on a delicate balance among diverse Arab Christian sects, such as the Maronites, Sunni and Shiite Muslims, and Druze, people with a religion related to Islam. Palestinian immigration after the 1948 and 1967 wars increased the Muslim population. By the 1970s, Muslims outnumbered Christians. In 1971, PLO fighters were expelled from Jordan after attempting to overthrow its government. The enlarged PLO presence in Lebanon and the intensification of fighting on the Israeli-Lebanese border added to the internal unrest in Lebanon.

Tensions among the diverse groups erupted into civil war that lasted from 1975 to 1990. Christian and Muslim **militias,** or armed groups of citizen soldiers, battled each other. Syria invaded Lebanon and Syrian troops remained for 29 years. Israel briefly invaded Lebanon to stop cross-border attacks first by PLO guerrillas and later by Hezbollah fighters, the militant group backed by Iran and Syria.

Sectarian divisions remained even after a fragile peace was restored. By 2012, the civil war in neighboring Syria threatened renewed violence among rival militias in Lebanon. In addition, a huge number of refugees fled the civil war in Syria, straining Lebanon's resources.

The Syrian Civil War Syria's diverse population includes Armenians, Assyrians, Christians, Druze, Kurds, Alawite Shiites, and Arab Sunnis. For decades, Hafez al-Assad and later his son, Bashir al-Assad, ruled the country and its diverse population with an iron hand. The Assads opposed peace with Israel and supported militant groups such as Hezbollah and Hamas.

During the "Arab Spring," the Syrian government met pro-democracy protests with brutal force, plunging the country into civil war. Rebel groups were deeply divided between moderates and extremist groups. Hezbollah and Iran supported the Assad regime. Western countries, however, hesitated to support the rebels, fearful that weapons could fall into the hands of radical groups. After Assad

>> A woman is helped by the military after a bombing in Beirut, Lebanon, in 1986. **Analyze Visuals** What does this image tell you about the way that the Lebanese civil war was fought?

🅑 BOUNCE to Activate Timeline

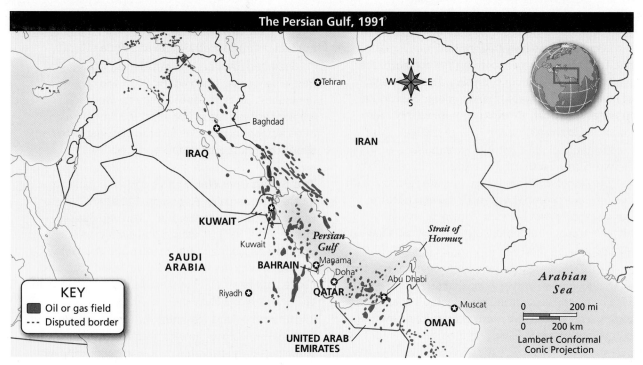

The Persian Gulf, 1991

KEY
- ▮ Oil or gas field
- --- Disputed border

Lambert Conformal Conic Projection

>> **Analyze Maps** The Persian Gulf region has seen numerous wars in recent years. What information on this map suggests one reason why this region is so important to the nations of the industrialized world?

was accused of using chemical weapons, global condemnation forced Syria to agree to give up its chemical arms stockpiles.

As the death toll mounted, millions more Syrians were displaced by the fighting. Refugees flooded into nearby countries and raised fears that the Syrian civil war could destabilize the region. International efforts to negotiate peace were complicated by disunity among rebel groups and Assad's continued grip on power.

☑ **RECALL** What is Hezbollah, and why is it signficant?

Warfare in Iraq

The modern nation of Iraq was carved out of the Ottoman empire after World War I. Its population included Sunni and Shiite Arabs, as well as Kurds who lived in the north. Although Shiites were the majority population, Sunnis controlled the government. Kurds distrusted the government and wanted self-rule.

Divisions among these groups fed tensions in Iraq. During the Cold War, the United States and the Soviet Union competed for influence in Iraq, which had vast oil resources and was strategically located on the Persian Gulf.

The Iran-Iraq War In 1980, Iraq's neighbor Iran was engulfed in its Islamic Revolution. Iraqi dictator, **Saddam Hussein,** took advantage of the turmoil to seize a disputed border region. His action sparked the long, costly Iran-Iraq War. After both sides attacked foreign oil tankers in the Persian Gulf, the United States sent naval forces to protect shipping lanes. The war ended in a stalemate in 1988, but with huge human and economic costs for both Iran and Iraq.

During the war, Saddam Hussein brutally suppressed a Kurdish revolt, using chemical weapons on civilians. His actions sparked international outrage and charges of genocide.

The 1991 Gulf War In 1990, Iraq invaded its oil-rich neighbor, Kuwait. Saddam Hussein wanted Kuwait's vast oil fields and greater access to the Persian Gulf. The United States saw the invasion as a threat to its ally, Saudi Arabia, and to the vital oil resources of the region.

In 1991, a U.S.-led coalition of international forces under the UN banner drove Saddam's forces out of Kuwait. Despite this defeat, Saddam remained in power. He brutally crushed revolts by Shiite Iraqis and Kurds. To protect the Shiites and Kurds, the UN set up **no-fly zones,** or areas where Iraqi aircraft were banned.

The Iraq War The 2001 terrorist attacks on the U.S. led to new moves against Saddam Hussein. The United States organized a new international coalition to remove Saddam from power. The U.S. claimed that the Iraqi dictator supported terrorists. The country also charged that Iraq was stockpiling **weapons of mass destruction (WMDs),** or nuclear, biological, and chemical weapons. In 2003, coalition forces quickly toppled Saddam. However, no weapons of mass destruction were ever found.

Saddam Hussein was later tried for war crimes by an elected Iraqi government. He was executed in 2006.

Iraq Continues to Struggle After Saddam's overthrow, Iraq became a bloody battleground as rival factions fought for power. **Insurgents,** or rebels, from Shiite and Sunni groups targeted civilians and government workers along with coalition forces. The death toll grew to over 162,000 Iraqis. The United States sent more troops in a "surge" to end the fighting.

The United States worked to convince moderate Sunnis, who had prospered under Saddam, to back the newly elected Iraqi government. It also tried to improve Iraqi security forces. In 2011, the last American troops withdrew, leaving a Shiite-led government in control.

Iraq still faced steep hurdles. Car bombings, suicide attacks, and assassinations continued to plague the country. The main political parties, representing Shiites, Sunnis, and Kurds, were often deadlocked over key issues.

The ongoing violence hurt efforts to rebuild Iraq's once-prosperous economy. Although Iraq has the world's third-largest oil reserves, decades of conflict had left much of the country, and its oil fields, in ruins. In addition, corruption and sabotage slowed oil exports.

During the fighting, millions of Iraqis fled the country. Many more were displaced within Iraq. Some refugees returned, but others were unwilling to risk moving back until security and stability were assured.

The Rise of ISIS Tensions between Sunnis and Shiites burst into fierce fighting in 2014. An Al Qaeda breakaway group, known as the Islamic State of Iraq and Syria (ISIS), seized control of parts of northern and eastern Iraq. They won support from some Sunnis who felt oppressed by the Shiite-led government in Baghdad. ISIS militants were also involved in Syria's civil war. They called for an Islamic state to be set up in the region of Syria, Jordan, Iraq, and Lebanon.

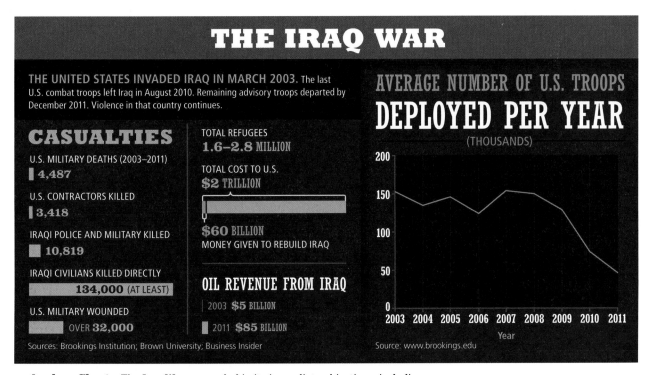

THE IRAQ WAR

THE UNITED STATES INVADED IRAQ IN MARCH 2003. The last U.S. combat troops left Iraq in August 2010. Remaining advisory troops departed by December 2011. Violence in that country continues.

CASUALTIES

U.S. MILITARY DEATHS (2003–2011)
4,487

U.S. CONTRACTORS KILLED
3,418

IRAQI POLICE AND MILITARY KILLED
10,819

IRAQI CIVILIANS KILLED DIRECTLY
134,000 (AT LEAST)

U.S. MILITARY WOUNDED
OVER **32,000**

TOTAL REFUGEES
1.6–2.8 MILLION

TOTAL COST TO U.S.
$2 TRILLION

$60 BILLION
MONEY GIVEN TO REBUILD IRAQ

OIL REVENUE FROM IRAQ

2003 **$5** BILLION

2011 **$85** BILLION

Sources: Brookings Institution; Brown University; Business Insider

AVERAGE NUMBER OF U.S. TROOPS
DEPLOYED PER YEAR
(THOUSANDS)

Source: www.brookings.edu

>> **Analyze Charts** The Iraq War succeeded in its immediate objectives, including deposing Saddam Hussein, but the costs were high. How does the information shown here support this generalization?

ISIS militants were known for their brutality in the areas they controlled. They targeted Shiite Muslims, Armenian Christians, and others groups. They also publicly executed several hostages, including American journalists.

The United States launched air strikes to protect various Iraqi minority groups from ISIS atrocities and to destroy weapons and equipment ISIS fighters had seized from the Iraqi army. A new government came to power in Baghdad, hoping to ease tensions with Sunnis and regain control of lost territories.

☑ **DRAW CONCLUSIONS** Why did Sunni control of government in Iraq create tension in that country?

☑ ASSESSMENT

1. **Identify Central Issues** How did the Israeli-Palestinian conflict begin?

2. **Identify Cause and Effect** How did the Israeli-Palestinian conflict affect Lebanon and why?

3. **Draw Conclusions** How has the growth of radical Islamic fundamentalism affected conflicts in the Middle East?

4. **Cite Evidence** Why did the removal of Saddam Hussein's regime fail to bring peace to Iraq? Use details from the text in your answer.

5. **Quest Connections** Why has peace between Israel and the Palestinians been so difficult to achieve? Include issues from both perspectives.

20.7

Flags of the member nations decorate the hall of the Organization of American States headquarters in Washington, D.C. Representatives discuss how to improve the lives of their citizens.

Latin American Nations Move Toward Democracy

Latin America comprises Mexico, Central America, the Caribbean, and South America. It includes 33 independent nations, ranging from small islands, such as Grenada, to giant Brazil. It is a diverse region in which each country has its own history and traditions. Despite differences, Latin American nations faced political, economic, and social challenges similar to those of other developing nations—poverty, illiteracy, political instability, and authoritarian governments..

Challenges to Development

From the 1950s to the 1980s, economic development failed to change deep-rooted inequalities in many Latin American countries. Due to inequality and poor policies, most countries saw little improvement in living standards.

Promoting Industry and Agriculture In Latin America, as in other developing regions, nations often relied heavily on a single cash crop or commodity. If harvests failed or if world demand for that commodity fell, their economies were hard hit.

To reduce dependence on imported goods, many Latin American governments in the 1950s and 1960s adopted a policy of **import substitution,** or manufacturing goods locally to replace expensive imported goods. Results were mixed. Many new industries did not produce efficiently and needed government or foreign capital to survive.

BOUNCE to Activate Flipped Video

Objectives

Analyze how Latin American nations have grappled with poverty.

Describe the struggles of Latin American nations to build democratic governments.

Explain the struggle between repression and freedom in Argentina.

Key Terms

import substitution
agribusiness
liberation theology
indigenous
Sandinista
contra
Organization of
  American States
  (OAS)
Juan Perón
Mothers of the Plaza
  de Mayo
Oscar Romero

In time, Latin American governments moved from import substitution to promoting exports. They developed a variety of cash crops and encouraged mining and other industries that produced goods for export. Some worked with multinational corporations willing to invest in new projects.

In many Latin American countries, governments backed the growth of **agribusinesses,** giant commercial farms owned by multinational corporations. Agribusinesses produce export crops that help boost national incomes. However, the clearing of tropical forests to use as farmland has caused widespread damage. Deforestation has taken a toll on plant and animal habitats, polluted water supplies, and contributed to soil erosion, especially in Brazil, Argentina, and Bolivia.

The Income Gap A major challenge facing Latin American nations is the uneven distribution of wealth, or income gap, between rich and poor. The income gap is evident in both urban and rural areas. In cities, comfortable residential neighborhoods stand in marked contrast to shantytowns, or urban slums. There, squatters have built makeshift housing and live in dangerous conditions.

In recent decades, efforts to reduce income inequality have had some impact, but progress has been limited. Today, Latin America remains the most unequal region in the world. A tiny class of super rich controls the majority of the region's wealth. Such extreme inequality is a barrier to economic development and a cause of unrest.

Population and Migration Like other parts of the developing world, Latin America experienced a population boom from the 1950s to 1990s. Growing populations strained national resources and contributed to poverty.

Rural poverty, economic hardships, violence, and other conditions have fueled migration both within countries and across Latin America. For example, earthquakes and other disasters led many people to leave Haiti. Political turmoil and economic crises have pushed more than 3 million refugees to leave Venezuela.

One pattern of migration has seen people move from rural areas to cities. As elsewhere around the world, poor farm workers flocked to cities. Some have found steady jobs, but many more survive by working odd jobs. Today, 80 percent of Latin America's population live in urban areas, many in shantytowns on the edges of cities. As migration to cities grows, it increases the need for jobs, housing, and other services.

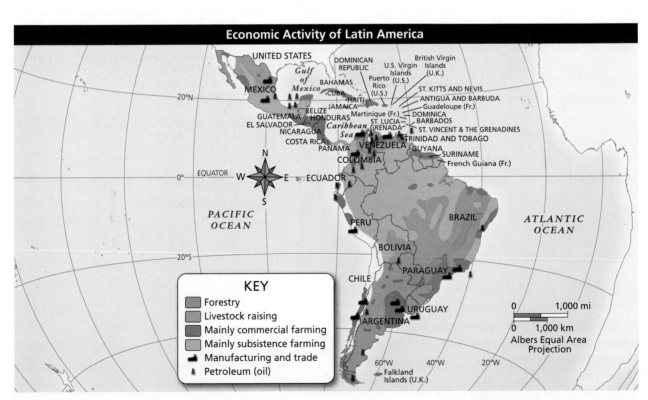

Economic Activity of Latin America

KEY
- Forestry
- Livestock raising
- Mainly commercial farming
- Mainly subsistence farming
- Manufacturing and trade
- Petroleum (oil)

>> **Analyze Maps** Much of the land in Latin America is devoted to farming. Which type of farming is most widespread?

BOUNCE to Activate Map

Religion in Latin America Since colonial times, the Catholic Church has played a major role in Latin America. Until recently, almost 90 percent of people were Catholic, but that percentage has been declining. Despite this change, Catholic traditions remain strong across the region, and Catholics are in the majority in most countries. In the past, the Catholic Church often allied itself with governments backed by the wealthy class.

During the 1960s and 1970s, however, many priests, nuns, and church workers pushed for social justice reforms and an end to poverty. This movement, known as **liberation theology**, urged the church to become a force for change. In 2013, people across Latin America celebrated the selection of Argentina's Jorge Bergoglio as Pope Francis.

Today, many evangelical Protestant groups have thriving congregations in Latin America. Other world religions also have a presence throughout the region, although a growing number of people identify as non-religious.

☑ **DRAW CONCLUSIONS** What problems did the gap between the rich and the poor cause in Latin America?

>> Thousands of Catholics crowd into St. Peter's Square in Rome to see and hear Pope Francis on Easter Day 2013. Pope Francis, who is from Argentina, is the first pope from the Americas.

Dictators and Civil Wars

Most Latin American countries had constitutions that set up representative governments. Building true democracy, however, was difficult to achieve when traditional elites held power. From the 1950s onward, many groups pressed for reforms. They included liberals, socialists, urban workers, peasant farmers, and Catholic priests and nuns. Although they differed over how to achieve social and economic justice, all wanted to improve conditions for the poor.

Conservative forces resisted change, especially the military, wealthy landowners, and many in the middle class. Conflict between conservatives and reformers contributed to political instability in many nations.

Military Rule In the 1960s and 1970s, as social unrest increased, military leaders seized power in Argentina, Brazil, and Chile. They imposed harsh, autocratic regimes, outlawed political parties, censored the press, and closed universities. They also imprisoned and executed thousands. "Death squads" linked to military rule murdered many more.

Writers, such as Pablo Neruda of Chile and Gabriel García Márquez of Colombia, went into exile after speaking out against repressive governments or social inequality.

>> This March 1982 photograph shows police detaining people who were protesting the dictatorship in Argentina. Many protesters were jailed, and thousands who disagreed with the government were killed.

>> Archbishop Oscar Romero of El Salvador became widely known for defending the poor and oppressed. His sharp criticism of the government gained him a large following, but also many enemies.

Revolutions Break Out

In Latin America, as elsewhere, leftists wanted to build socialist societies, which they believed would end inequalities. Some leftists joined guerrilla movements to battle repressive governments. After building a communist state in Cuba, Fidel Castro supported leftist guerrillas throughout Latin America. Many young people were impressed by Castro's revolution and joined the call for radical change.

Cold war fears about the Cuban revolution and the spread of Marxism complicated efforts for reform. While many groups urged peaceful change, conservatives saw any call for reform as a communist threat. At the same time, the United States backed military leaders and conservative groups that were strongly anti-communist.

Civil War in Central America

For decades, Central American nations were torn by civil wars. In 1954, the United States helped the Guatemalan military overthrow an elected, leftist government. Leftists and others fought the military regime, which responded savagely.

The military targeted Guatemala's **indigenous,** or native, people, slaughtering tens of thousands in a campaign that sparked accusations of genocide. Fighting ended in 1996, after the government signed a peace accord and held elections. Although Guatemala has seen economic growth in recent years, its people face widespread poverty, violence, and corruption.

In El Salvador, too, reformers and leftist revolutionaries challenged the landowning and military elite. During a vicious 12-year civil war, right-wing death squads slaughtered student and labor leaders, church workers, and anyone else thought to sympathize with leftists. One reformer, Archbishop **Oscar Romero,** was assassinated in 1980 while celebrating mass. In 1992, both sides finally agreed to a UN-brokered peace. Today, however, El Salvador still suffers from brutal violence, poverty, and inequality, which have pushed many people to migrate to the United States and elsewhere.

In 1979, the **Sandinistas,** socialist rebels in Nicaragua, toppled the Somoza family, which had ruled since 1936. The Sandinistas introduced land reform and other socialist measures. Fearing that Nicaragua could become "another Cuba," U.S. President Ronald Reagan financed the **contras,** guerrillas who fought the Sandinistas. Fighting raged until 1990, when a peace settlement brought multiparty elections.

Movement Toward Democracy

By the 1990s, international pressure and activists within each country pushed military governments to restore civilian rule. Argentina, Brazil, Chile, and other countries held elections. In some countries, such as Brazil, Venezuela, and Bolivia, leftist leaders won office. Since then, many Latin American countries have experienced the peaceful transition of power from one elected government to another.

Venezuela in Crisis

Venezuela, the most urbanized country in Latin America, has oil and other resources, yet millions of people live in poverty. Hugo Chavez, elected president in 1998, implemented a socialist program. His government took over many companies and poured oil riches into social programs to help the poor. By 2013, his successor, Nicolas Maduro, faced falling oil prices and a growing political and economic crisis. After a disputed election, Maduro cracked down on critics and brought the country to near collapse. As you have read, millions of Venezuelans fled the country.

Mexico Develops and Struggles Unlike many Latin American nations, Mexico escaped military rule, but still faced many struggles for reform. Between 1930 and 2000, a single political party–the Institutional Revolutionary Party (PRI)–won every election and controlled the government. It claimed to represent all groups in Mexican society from workers and peasants to business and industrial interests as well as the military. In 2000, Vicente Fox became the first candidate from an opposition party to be elected president. Fox and later presidents faced tough challenges, including rural poverty, crime, corruption, and growing drug related violence. For decades, Mexico waged a war on drugs, which failed to reduce the violence.

Despite ongoing problems with inequality and crime, Mexico has in fact made strides in recent decades. Its GDP per capita has risen dramatically since the 1990s, although poverty remains a persistent problem.

☑ **IDENTIFY CAUSE AND EFFECT** What social and political conditions led to civil wars in many Latin American countries?

Latin America and the United States

A complex network of ties links Latin American nations and the United States. Since the late 1800s, the United States has been a looming presence in the Western Hemisphere. It has intervened in local conflicts and taken other steps to ensure its influence in the region.

Today, Latin America and the United States remain closely linked. The **Organization of American States (OAS),** was formed in 1948 to promote democracy, economic cooperation, and peace in the Americas. Although the United States often used its power to dominate the OAS, Latin American members have at times pursued an independent line. The United States is economically linked to Mexico through the North American Free Trade Agreement (NAFTA), recently updated into the United States Mexico Canada Agreement (USMCA).

Despite these links, the United States and Latin American nations view each other very differently. The United States sees itself as the defender of democracy and capitalism in the region.

While many people in Latin America admire the wealth of the United States, they often resent what they see as its political, economic, and cultural

domination. Latin Americans were surprised when U.S. President Donald Trump ordered tariffs on some imports from Brazil and Argentina. In response, they looked for new trade alliances with countries across Latin America and with China.

U.S. Intervention During the Cold War, the United States helped train and equip the military in many Latin American countries and often backed anti-communist dictators. It also returned to a policy of intervention, usually sending its military to stop what it saw as the threat of communism. In 1954, it helped overthrow Guatemala's leftist government. In 1965, the U.S. sent troops to the Dominican Republic when unrest raised fears the island nation could become a "second Cuba." In 1973, the United States secretly backed a military coup in Chile against democratically elected socialist president, Salvador Allende (ah YEN day), putting military dictator Augusto Pinochet (pee noh SHAY) in power.

On other occasions, the United States stepped in for different reasons. In 1989, it sent forces to Panama to bring its drug-smuggling president Manuel Noriega to justice. In 1994, a UN force led by the United States landed in Haiti to restore its elected leader after a military coup. Since then, the United States has provided much aid to Haiti after it

>> American soldiers joined UN forces to keep the peace after the coup in Haiti. Peacekeepers also did practical work, such as building, supplying food, and spreading cement to repair roads.

>> American soldiers entered Panama to arrest military dictator Manuel Noriega, a major drug dealer. The United States wanted to put an end to the drug trade in the country.

>> Juan Perón, shown here with his wife, Eva, made some improvements in Argentina. However, as his government became more repressive and corrupt, he relied increasingly on military force to hold on to power.

was devastated by a strong earthquake and struck by hurricanes.

The War on Drugs As illegal drug use increased in the United States and around the world in the 1970s, criminal gangs in Latin America began producing and smuggling ever-larger quantities of cocaine and other drugs for export. In the 1980s, the U.S. government declared a "war on drugs" and set out to halt the flow of illegal drugs into the country from Colombia, Peru, Bolivia, and elsewhere. It funneled military and financial aid to Latin American governments to destroy drug crops and crush the drug cartels, or criminal gangs that ran the drug trade.

Latin American governments cooperated with U.S. anti-drug efforts. After all, drug lords were bribing government officials and hiring assassins to kill judges, journalists, and others who spoke out against them. But the 50-year war on drugs largely failed to stop the flow of illegal substances while organized crime groups continued to flourish.

Migration Immigration from Latin America to the United States increased rapidly after the 1970s. Decades of civil wars, weak and corrupt governments along with growing violence from urban gangs and drug traffickers led many refugees, especially from Central America, to flee their homelands. Many entered the country legally and eventually became citizens. A large number, however, were undocumented immigrants. The earnings they sent home helped to raise the standard of living for their families in Latin America.

Pressure rose within the United States to halt illegal immigration. The United States tightened security along its border with Mexico, building walls and increasing patrols. President Barack Obama stepped up deportations, or the removal of undocumented immigrants. Under President Trump, the crackdown on deportations increased. Hostility toward immigrants from Latin America also rose within the United States.

Despite the risk of deportation, large numbers of immigrants from Central America continued to seek asylum, or protection from torture or serious harm in their homelands. While many refugees were fleeing dangerous situations in their homelands, others were economic migrants seeking a better life.

Under U.S. pressure, Mexico and other Central American countries took steps to stop the flow of migrants. Many asylum seekers who crossed the U.S. border were later deported. Some were tortured and killed after being sent back to their homelands.

☑ **DRAW CONCLUSIONS** Why do people in Latin America have mixed opinions of the United States?

The Long Road to Democracy in Argentina

Argentina is among the most prosperous countries in Latin America. During much of the last century, it enjoyed a robust economy based on exports of beef and grain. But it also experienced political and economic upheavals.

The Military Takes Control From 1946 to 1955, nationalist president Juan Perón enjoyed great support from workers. He increased the government's economic role, boosted wages, and backed labor unions. Perón was helped greatly by his glamorous wife, Eva Perón, who used her influence to help the poor. While Perón wooed the urban poor, his authoritarian government stifled opposition.

When Perón's policies led to an economic crisis, he was ousted in a 1955 military coup. The military was in and out of power for more than two decades. To combat leftist guerrillas, the military waged a "dirty war," torturing and murdering people it claimed were enemies of the state. As many as 20,000 people simply "disappeared." The Dirty War lasted from 1976 to 1983.

In 1977, a group of mothers whose children had disappeared began to meet each week in the Plaza de Mayo in Buenos Aires. They demanded to know what had happened to their missing sons and daughters. The nonviolent protests of the **Mothers of the Plaza de Mayo,** drew worldwide attention.

In 1982, the military hoped to mask economic troubles by seizing the British-ruled Falkland Islands. In the brief but decisive war, the British retook the islands.

Restoration of Democracy Defeat in the Falklands War undermined the military, and it was forced to hold free elections. In 1983, Argentina gained a democratically elected government. Despite economic setbacks and corruption scandals, democracy has survived in Argentina.

Argentina has a history of economic boom-and-bust cycles. It is rich in natural resources, but a cycle of financial crises have devastated the economy and worsened poverty. Argentine voters have alternated between pro-business and populist governments, and these swings have led to policy reversals and economic uncertainty. In 2020, a newly elected populist government set out to get the economy back on track to sustained growth.

>> The Mothers of the Plaza de Mayo gathered weekly in Argentina's capital, carrying photos of their "disappeared" children, who had been kidnapped and probably killed by the government.

🅱 BOUNCE to Activate Gallery

☑ **EXPLAIN** Why did the military restore democratic rule in Argentina?

☑ ASSESSMENT

1. **Describe** What changes did Latin American nations make to economic policy to try to cope with poverty and economic hardship?

2. **Identify Cause and Effect** Why did Latin American nations find it difficult to establish democratic governments?

3. **Identify Central Ideas** How have repeated U.S. interventions in Latin America affected Latin American attitudes toward the United States?

4. **Sequence Events** Describe the changes Argentina's government went through after the 1930s. List significant events in the order in which they occurred.

5. **Quest Connections** Why do you think many of the repressive dictatorships in Latin America were led by the military?

Connections to Today

Resource extraction, such as this open-pit coal mine in Liaoning, China, can have a significant effect on the environment.

Take Action About Resource Usage

The presence—or lack—of different natural resources can have an enormous impact on a country or region. How should these places use resources?

1. **Choose** one of the following natural resources:

   - oil, natural gas, coal, diamonds and other gemstones, copper ore, rare earth elements, fresh water, or fertile farmland

2. **Ask Questions** What are some of the things you want to know about the resource and its extraction and use? Write a list of questions you want to answer or ideas you want to learn more about.

3. **Learn** Research how the extraction or use of that resource—or the lack of it—has affected a region or country covered in this topic.

4. **Develop Your Recommendations** Create a list of recommendations for how the place you studied should handle the chosen resource in the future. Should the extraction or use of that resource be encouraged or limited in some way? If the resource is in short supply, what could be done to increase its availability? Are there ways in which international organizations can or should take any actions?

Use the texts, quizzes, interactivities, Quest Inquiries, Flipped Videos, and other resources from this Topic to prepare for the Topic Test.

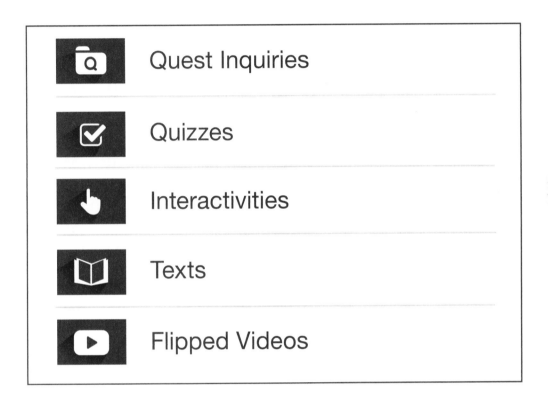

Quest Inquiries

Quizzes

Interactivities

Texts

Flipped Videos

While online you can also check the progress you've made learning the topic and course content by viewing your grades, test scores, and assignment status.

Topic 20 Quick Study Guide

LESSON SUMMARIES
Use these Lesson Summaries, and the longer versions available online, to review the key ideas for each lesson in this Topic.

Lesson 1: New Nations in South Asia and Southeast Asia

At independence, British India was partitioned into Hindu-majority Pakistan and Muslim-majority India.

Lesson 2: Rapid Development in China and India

Both China and India are large countries with huge populations. By the mid-1990s, China was a major industrial power with a rapidly growing economy, but the nation still faced many challenges. India is the world's largest democratic nation. It too still faces major economic issues.

Lesson 3: African Nations Win Independence

During the 1950s and 1960s, dozens of new nations emerged in Africa. As celebration erupted across the continent, people faced many challenges.

Lesson 4: Challenges for African Nations

In 1945, four European powers—Britain, France, Belgium, and Portugal—controlled almost all of the African continent. After World War II, a rising tide of nationalism spread through European colonies. This spirit would lead many African nations to seek and declare independence. In South Africa, this meant ending the bonds of apartheid.

Lesson 5: The Modern Middle East Takes Shape

In the Arab world, as in South Asia and in Africa, nationalists sought to free themselves from the legacy of imperialism. Aside from nationalism, the other forces shaping the modern Middle East were diversity and the availability of resources such as oil and water.

Lesson 6: Conflicts in the Middle East

For new nations in the Middle East, religious, ethnic, and cultural diversity bought concerns and challenges. The major sources of conflict have come from issues between Arab nations and Israel. Major civil wars have engulfed Lebanon, Syria, and Iraq. Revolution has led to conflict in Iran.

Lesson 7: Latin American Nations Move Toward Democracy

Latin America's development is influenced by geography, culture, social patterns, and political and economic conditions. Similar to other growing countries, inequality and the growing population continue to contribute to poverty.

GO ONLINE to access lesson summaries

VISUAL REVIEW

Use these graphics to review some of the key terms, people, and ideas from this Topic.

Common Themes in New Nations

- Borders drawn by European colonial powers left nations with diverse religious and ethnic groups.
- Ethnic and religious diversity has brought conflict.
- Military coups, one-party systems, and dictatorships kept some countries from achieving democracy.
- Citizens and foreign leaders have forced former dictatorships to hold elections and transition to democracy.
- Natural resources such as oil have been a source of wealth for some nations but have fueled conflicts in others.
- During the Cold War, the United States and Soviet Union competed for influence, particularly in regions with natural resources such as oil, or locations near strategic waterways.

Leaders of New Nations

- Jawaharlal Nehru, *first prime minister of India*
- Indira Gandhi, *first female prime minister of India*
- Aung San Suu Kyi, *leader of Myanmar democracy movement*
- Sukarno, *founder and first president of Indonesia*
- Suharto, *military dictator of Indonesia*
- Corazon Aquino, *democratic president of the Philippines*
- Kwame Nkrumah, *founder and first president of Ghana*
- David Ben-Gurion, *first prime minister of Israel*
- Gamal Abdel Nasser, *an Arab nationalist and president of Egypt*
- Mohammad Reza Pahlavi, *shah of Iran*
- Ruhollah Khomeini, *leader of the religious government of Iran*

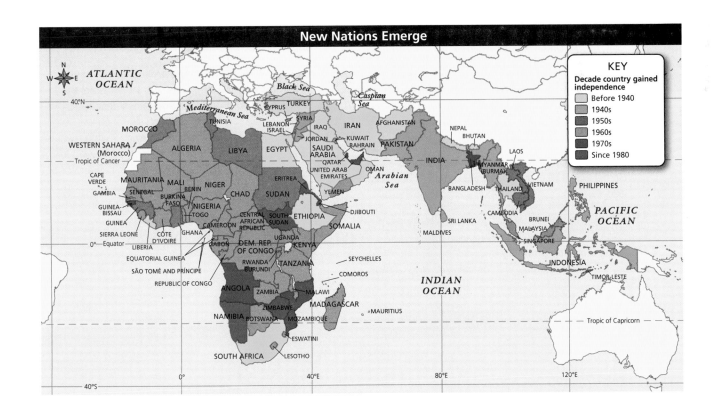

New Nations Emerge

KEY
Decade country gained independence
- Before 1940
- 1940s
- 1950s
- 1960s
- 1970s
- Since 1980

KEY TERMS, PEOPLE, AND IDEAS

1. Why did the **partition** of British India cause a refugee crisis?

2. How did the **African National Congress** work to help end apartheid in South Africa?

3. Compare the nations of Southeast Asia in the progress they have made toward individual freedom and democracy.

4. What factors led to the support of a Jewish homeland after WWII? How did this initiate the ongoing conflict between the Israelis and the Arabs?

5. What sparked the conflict between the **Hutus** and the **Tutsis**?

6. Why did more nationalist movements rise after World War II?

7. Why did Nasser seize control of the **Suez Canal**? Was the strategy successful? Explain.

8. How did **Deng Xiaoping** plan to change China's economy?

9. Describe one cause of each of the following: (a) the civil war in Lebanon (b) the Iran-Iraq war (c) the Persian Gulf War.

CRITICAL THINKING

10. **Synthesize Information** How has religion influenced the recent history of the Middle East?

11. **Analyze Information** How did the Cold War affect (a) the Middle East (b) Africa?

12. **Summarize** How have the natural resources of the Middle East affected its recent history?

13. **Analyze Information** Discuss the effectiveness of Gamal Abdel Nasser and Indira Gandhi as nationalist leaders.

14. **Compare** How was the conflict in Darfur similar to the one in Rwanda?

15. **Draw Conclusions** Why has the Arab Spring sometimes been referred to as the Arab Awakening? Explain.

16. **Compose Arguments** In many African nations that gained independence after World War II, dictators seized power and established one-party political systems. These leaders claimed that multiparty systems encouraged disunity. Do you agree? Take a stand. Were the leaders' concerns genuine? What appeal might this argument have for citizens of a newly independent nation?

17. **Writing Activity: Write an Informative Essay** The following excerpt is from Prime Minister Nehru's speech before the Indian Assembly when they met to celebrate independence. Describe Nehru's hope for the nation. How does he indicate that this moment has been long fought for? Use your knowledge of the Topic and what you have learned about India's struggle for independence to write a short informative essay.

> "Long years ago we made an [appointment] with destiny, and now the time comes when we shall redeem our pledge, not wholly or in full measure, but very substantially. At the stroke of the midnight hour, when the world sleeps, India will awake to life and freedom. A moment comes, which comes but rarely in history, when we step out from the old to the new, when an age ends and when the soul of a nation long suppressed finds utterance."
> —*Jawaharlal Nehru, "Tryst With Destiny" speech*

18. **Connections to Today** Developing countries face economic challenges as they industrialize and urbanize. Choose one of the countries described in this Topic. How has that nation's economic development and use of its resources created challenges for its people? Consider the following in your answer: poverty; the gap between rich and poor; lack of resources for healthcare, education, and food; and human rights.

DOCUMENT-BASED QUESTIONS

Kashmir has been claimed by both India and Pakistan and has been a battleground between the two countries. Read the documents below, then answer the questions that follow.

DOCUMENT A

"Mr. Jinnah and his colleagues in the Muslim League, the creators of Pakistan, had always considered that the Vale of Kashmir at least would form part of the new Islamic State . . . When in 1933 Choudhri Rahmat Ali coined the word Pakistan as a suitable name for the State, he intended the letter K in 'Pak' to stand for Kashmir. The geographical and historical links between the Panjab and the Vale of Kashmir were so close that it was inevitable that the two regions should find themselves combined in the thoughts of the protagonists of a separate Islamic State."

—From Crisis in Kashmir, 1947–1966 by Alastair Lamb

DOCUMENT B

LETS MAKE KASHMIR A PARADISE ONCE AGAIN

DOCUMENT C

Religions of Kashmir, 1941

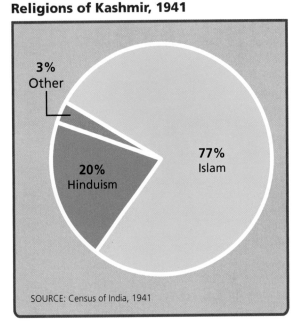

3% Other

20% Hinduism

77% Islam

SOURCE: Census of India, 1941

19. According to Document A, Kashmir and Pakistan share
    A. the same heroes and poets.
    B. a similar history and geography.
    C. the same language and literature.
    D. similar architecture and art.

20. What argument does the sign in Document B support?
    A. Citizens of Kashmir want to live peacefully.
    B. India will never let go of Kashmir.
    C. Kashmir is more beautiful than other parts of India.
    D. Indians are tired of dealing with Kashmir and its problems.

21. According to Document C, Kashmir's populations
    A. is evenly balanced among its different religions.
    B. is about one-half Hindu and "Other".
    C. only has two religion affiliations.
    D. is more than three-quarters Muslim.

22. **Writing Tasks** Why has Kashmir continued to be a volatile spot for so long? What are the main causes of the conflict there? Use information from these documents along with information from the Topic to write your response.

The World Today
(1990–Present)

ESSENTIAL QUESTION What are the benefits and risks of interdependence?

An artist's version of our interconnected world

Connections to Today

In much of the world today, people are living longer, healthier lives than ever before thanks to scientific advancements and the spread of modern healthcare. New communication technologies and improved education are improving people's quality of life as well.

In this Topic you'll read how economic and social advancements have spread in recent years. What risks and opportunities exist for these kinds of improvements in the future?

NBC LEARN

Learn how young people created a technology-based organization to deal with world issues.

BOUNCE to Activate My Story Video

Topic 21 Overview

In this Topic, you will learn about issues and events in the world today. Look at the lesson outline and explore the timeline. As you study this Topic, you will complete the Quest Inquiry.

LESSON OUTLINE

21.1 The Developing World

21.2 The More Developed World

21.3 Globalization and Trade

21.4 Social and Environmental Issues

21.5 International Security

21.6 Advances in Science and Technology

Key Events of the World Since 1990

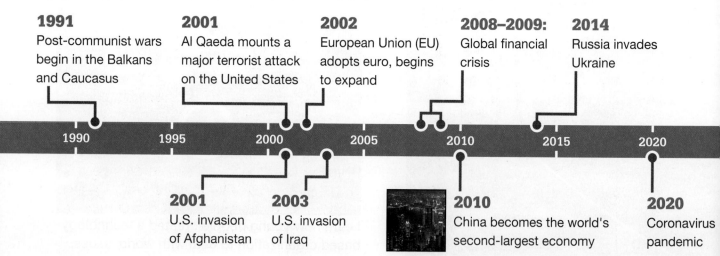

1991
Post-communist wars begin in the Balkans and Caucasus

2001
Al Qaeda mounts a major terrorist attack on the United States

2002
European Union (EU) adopts euro, begins to expand

2008–2009:
Global financial crisis

2014
Russia invades Ukraine

1990   1995   2000   2005   2010   2015   2020

2001
U.S. invasion of Afghanistan

2003
U.S. invasion of Iraq

2010
China becomes the world's second-largest economy

2020
Coronavirus pandemic

QUEST!

Comparing Developed and Developing Countries

What are the differences between developed and developing countries? In this Quest, you will research this question and then write an essay in response.

STEP 1

Before starting your research, review what you know about developing and developed countries. Prepare a list of characteristics.

STEP 2

Study the primary sources. Compare the sources and analyze the information they present.

STEP 3

Draw conclusions supported by evidence from the sources, then write a draft of your essay presenting those conclusions and the evidence supporting them. Read, review, and revise.

STEP 4

Share your essay with your classmates. Reflect on the problems still facing developing countries today. What challenges face developed countries?

Poverty and rapidly increasing populations often lead to growing slums in urban areas, like these in Brazil. Brazil's slums, or *favelas*, often have serious problems with crime, gangs, and drugs.

 BOUNCE to Activate Flipped Video

Objectives

Understand how people in the developing world have tried to build strong economies.

Describe obstacles to development in the global South.

Explain how development is changing patterns of life in the developing world.

Key Terms

development
literacy
developing world
command economy
mixed economy
globalization
fundamentalist
shantytown

The Developing World

The new Asian and African countries that won independence in the mid-1900s, along with the countries in Latin America, focused on modernization and **development**. Development is the process of building stable governments, improving agriculture and industry, and raising standards of living. Development involves such goals as building stronger economies and increasing **literacy,** or the ability to read and write.

Working Toward Development

The developing nations emerged during the Cold War, when the world was split between the communist East and the capitalist West. Today, an economic gulf divides the world into two spheres—the relatively rich nations of the global North and the relatively poor nations of the global South.

The Global South The nations working toward development in Africa, Asia, and Latin America are known collectively as the **developing world.** The developing world is sometimes called the global South because most of these nations are located in the zone between the tropics of Cancer and Capricorn. The global South holds 75 percent of the world's people and much of its natural resources.

Some nations have enjoyed strong growth, especially the industrial nations of East Asia and the oil-exporting nations of the Middle East. Overall, though, the global South remains generally poor and underdeveloped. Unlike the fully developed countries of the global North, many newer countries have not had enough time to build up their capital, resources, or industries.

Uneven Development Developing countries include a wide range of different economies. The World Bank divides developing countries into three groups by income per person, which is a measure of average living standards.

In low-income countries—including Haiti, Afghanistan, and Mozambique—many people live on less than $2 per day and struggle to pay for food and shelter. In lower-middle-income countries, such as El Salvador, Egypt, or India, many people are poor, but a modest middle class can afford decent housing, a healthy diet, and some means of transportation. In upper-middle-income countries, such as Mexico, Russia, or China, some poverty exists, but there is also a large industrial or commercial sector, and it is not unusual for families to own a car and other modern conveniences.

Economic Choices Leaders in the developing world had ambitious economic goals. They wanted to boost farm output, develop natural resources, set up industries, and build roads, airports, and power plants.

At first, some leaders set up **command economies,** in which the government made most economic decisions and owned most industries. However, command economies were often inefficient and inflexible. In many countries, they failed to raise standards of living.

In addition, many developing countries fell into heavy debt. Developing countries needed vast amounts of money to finance development. Most borrowed from foreign lenders. When prices for their exports were high, they were able to pay interest on their debt. But when prices fell, they could not pay their debts.

Since the 1980s, most developing countries have made market reforms meant to improve economic growth. These reforms have boosted competition and private enterprise. Today, many developing countries have **mixed economies,** with some government controls and some free market forces at work.

Some countries with strong institutions, such as China or Malaysia, were able to develop industries that exported much of what they produced. Those export earnings allowed those countries to grow rapidly and improve living standards. In the late 1900s, some countries, such as South Korea, were able to transform themselves from developing to developed countries.

Many developing countries have welcomed foreign investment. Investors put money into businesses that produced profits for them and

SELECTED DEVELOPED & DEVELOPING COUNTRIES

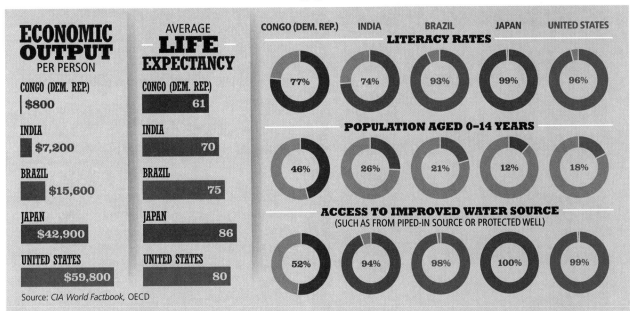

ECONOMIC OUTPUT PER PERSON

CONGO (DEM. REP.) $800

INDIA $7,200

BRAZIL $15,600

JAPAN $42,900

UNITED STATES $59,800

AVERAGE LIFE EXPECTANCY

CONGO (DEM. REP.) 61

INDIA 70

BRAZIL 75

JAPAN 86

UNITED STATES 80

Source: *CIA World Factbook,* OECD

	CONGO (DEM. REP.)	INDIA	BRAZIL	JAPAN	UNITED STATES
LITERACY RATES	77%	74%	93%	99%	96%
POPULATION AGED 0–14 YEARS	46%	26%	21%	12%	18%
ACCESS TO IMPROVED WATER SOURCE (SUCH AS FROM PIPED-IN SOURCE OR PROTECTED WELL)	52%	94%	98%	100%	99%

>> This chart compares developed and developing countries on a number of measures. **Analyze Charts** What generalization can you make about the age distribution in developed and developing countries, based on the data in this chart?

BOUNCE to Activate Map

consumer goods for the industrialized world. Some critics have argued that these economic decisions benefited foreign investors more than the developing country's economy. By 2019, China had become a major investor, lending huge amounts for development projects and greatly increasing its global influence.

Economic and political upheavals led to increased migration to more developed countries. Migrants sought better jobs, education, and living standards. Despite efforts to limit immigration, the influx continued.

Impact of Globalization Beginning in the 1990s, there was a dramatic increase in **globalization,** or economic and social connections across borders. Globalization involved increased movements of people, ideas, and money across borders and the development of production processes with multiple steps taking place in different countries.

The global South benefited from increased trade and investment. New technologies helped spread literacy and raise living standards. Computers, the internet, and cell phones improved communications. Some developing countries gained jobs through outsourcing, or arranging for work to be done in countries with lower labor costs. As these countries

exported more, incomes and living standards often rose.

While outsourcing brought jobs, though, workers in the developing world were poorly paid and often faced dangerous working conditions. Industrial growth also greatly increased pollution.

Globalization spread Western culture, overwhelming local cultures and traditions. In the long run, globalization greatly increased inequality of wealth and income, or the gap between rich and poor people within countries.

Globalization, along with climate change and political unrest in developing countries, led to increased migration. Migrants left their homelands in search of better jobs, education, and living standards.

Meanwhile, globalization sparked a backlash in the global North. During the 2010s, opposition to migration from less developed countries grew. Some in the global North also opposed outsourcing of jobs to the global South as a threat to workers in developed countries.

☑ **DESCRIBE** How did leaders of developing countries first try to modernize their economies?

Challenges to Development

While some developing countries have modernized, progress has been slower in others. The reasons have varied, but many countries shared similar problems. In parts of Africa, Asia, and Latin America, geography has posed an obstacle to progress. Some African countries are tiny and have few natural resources. Difficult climates, uncertain rainfall, lack of good farmland, and disease have added to the problems of some countries.

Rising Populations Better medical care and greater food supplies have reduced death rates and led to rapid population growth. Each year, the populations of countries like Nigeria, Egypt, and India increase by millions. All these people need food, housing, education, jobs, and medical care. Meeting the needs of so many puts a huge burden on developing countries.

Many developing countries have tried to slow population growth, but few countries, except China, have tried to force people to limit family size. In many farming societies, children are valued as a source of labor and a support for parents in old age. Religious traditions also encourage large families.

>> Western companies that want to reduce labor costs find a large, available workforce in developing countries. In this factory in India, women create computer parts for a growing electronics industry.

Poverty Alongside population growth, a major obstacle to economic development is poverty. A poor country cannot develop because it does not have the income to invest in industries, agriculture, education, and other basic services, such as safe water and sanitation. People face food insecurity, lacking enough affordable, nutritious food. With populations that are often hungry and unhealthy, countries find it difficult to attract investment that would bring economic growth.

Economic Dependence The economic patterns established during the age of imperialism changed little after developing countries won independence. Most new nations remained economically dependent on their former colonial rulers. They sold agricultural products and raw materials to the industrial world. In turn, they relied on the West for manufactured goods, technology, and investment. In recent years, lower labor costs have led Western companies to manufacture goods in the global South.

Some developing nations produce only a single export crop or commodity, such as sugar or cocoa. Their economies depend on global demand for the cash crop or commodity. If demand weakens and prices drop, their economies suffer.

Violence and Conflict Civil wars and other conflicts have devastated some countries in Latin America, the Middle East, Southeast Asia, and Africa. Wars have created millions of refugees living in camps. The loss of their labor and the devastation caused by fighting has further hurt war-torn countries. When violence threatens investments, it is difficult for economies to grow.

Corrupt Governments Dictators spent huge sums on weapons and warfare. Many enriched themselves instead of funding government services or economic development. Poverty persisted as a result. In some countries, there is a culture of bribery. Corruption adds to the cost of doing business and discourages investment.

☑ **SUMMARIZE** How did corruption affect economic progress in the developing world?

>> In Kolkata, India, a young boy works along with adults in a factory that produces gold jewelry. Many of the hundreds of goldsmiths in Kolkata employ children, who work 14 to 18 hours a day.

🅑 BOUNCE to Activate Gallery

Development Brings Social Change

In recent decades, hundreds of millions of people in the developing world have migrated from rural villages to urban centers. Urbanization has transformed the lives of people in the developing world just as it did in Europe and North America during the Industrial Revolution.

New Opportunities for Women Women worked actively in independence movements. After independence, new constitutions granted equality to women, at least on paper. Although women still have less access to education than men, the gap has narrowed. Women are joining the work force in growing numbers and contributing their skills to their nations' wealth. In countries such as India, Argentina, and Liberia, women have served as heads of state. Still, women continued to shoulder a heavy burden of work both inside the home and in the workplace.

Child Labor In traditional economies, children worked alongside parents, farming or herding to meet the family's needs. As modernization and urbanization have changed traditional life, families often move to cities and take whatever jobs they can. Because these jobs pay such low wages, poor families need their children to work in order for the family to survive. Children are sent to work in factories, mines, or workshops.

Worldwide, more than 160 million children between the ages of 5 and 14 work up to 12 hours or more a day. Some young children are chained to looms or other machines. Many children are forced to work full time as farm laborers.

International pressure has led to efforts to reduce child labor. Reformers have called for safer work environments and basic education for child workers. Although many countries have laws about child labor, these laws are often ignored.

Religious Fundamentalism Despite revolutionary changes brought by urbanization, many traditions remain strong. The major world religions and their offshoots still shape modern societies. Since the 1980s, religious revivals have swept many regions. Christian, Muslim, Buddhist, and Hindu reformers have offered their own solutions to the problems of today's world. Some have been called **fundamentalists,** because they stress what they see as the fundamental, or basic, values of their religion. Many seek political power to oppose changes that undermine their valued religious traditions.

Rapid Growth of Cities Across the developing world, people have flooded into cities to find jobs and escape rural poverty. Cities offer not only economic opportunities but also attractions such as entertainment, stores, and sports.

With no money and few jobs, many newcomers cannot afford to ride buses or go to movies. Instead, most settle in **shantytowns,** crowded, poorly built neighborhoods on the edges of cities. These neighborhoods often suffer from crime and unsanitary conditions. They lack basic services such as running water, electricity, or sewer systems. Today, tens of millions of people struggle to survive in these conditions.

In cities, the traditional extended family of rural villages gives way to the nuclear family. As urban children attend school and become literate, they often reject their parents' ways. Without the support of the village and extended family, older beliefs and values are undermined by urban values such as material wealth, education, and job status. People who move from villages to cities frequently suffer a sense of overwhelming stress and isolation.

☑ **EXPLAIN** In what ways have women's lives changed due to economic development in the developing world?

☑ ASSESSMENT

1. **Express Ideas Clearly** Describe how economic policy in developing countries has changed in the years since independence.

2. **Summarize** What are the main obstacles to economic and political progress in developing countries?

3. **Recall** What are four ways that development has changed life in the developing world?

4. **Contrast** Describe the differences between the global South and the global North.

5. **Quest Connections** Which problem facing developing countries today do you think is most serious? Explain.

Hong Kong has long been a major trading center of East Asia, thanks to its splendid harbor. Since 1997, when it was returned to China, it has emerged as a financial gateway to a new, modernized China.

The More Developed World

The relatively wealthy countries of North America, Europe, Australia, and New Zealand—together with Japan and some of its neighbors—make up the developed world. These countries have changed since the end of the Cold War. Most of Europe has joined the European Union. Meanwhile, China became a major rival to the United States. Tensions between these rivals and a backlash against globalization shook the global economy by 2020.

A New Europe

The collapse of communism ended decades of division between communist Eastern Europe and democratic Western Europe. Conditions were favorable for the spread of democracy. Trade, business, travel, and communications across the continent became easier. At the same time, many European nations had to deal with issues such as large-scale immigration from the developing world, growing discrimination against foreigners, and rising unemployment.

A Reunited Germany In 1990, after 45 years of division, East Germany and West Germany were reunited. Germans welcomed reunification, even though it brought many challenges. Prosperous West Germans had to pay higher taxes to finance the rebuilding of the east. At the same time, East Germans faced a difficult transition to a market economy. Despite a continued gap between the east and west decades after reunification, Germany remained an economic giant and a key European leader.

🅑 BOUNCE to Activate Flipped Video

Objectives

Examine social, political, and economic trends in Europe since the Cold War.

Analyze Russia's evolving role in the world since the end of the Soviet Union.

Describe the challenges facing the United States in the 21st century.

Summarize economic developments in Asia.

Key Terms

European Union (EU)
euro
multiethnic
ethnic cleansing
Northern Ireland
Good Friday
  Agreement
default
oligarch
Vladimir Putin
autocracy
surplus
deficit
polarization
Pacific Rim

GO ONLINE to access your digital course

Reunification brought social problems. A few right-wing extremists revived Nazi ideology. Seeing the answer to economic challenges in racism and hatred, these neo-Nazis viciously attacked foreign workers. Most Germans condemned such actions.

Changes in NATO With the collapse of communism, the Warsaw Pact dissolved. Many democratic nations of Eastern and Central Europe joined NATO, including Poland, Hungary, and the Czech Republic. Today, NATO includes 28 member nations. Russia disliked NATO's expansion, but agreed to a NATO-Russia Council to consult on issues of common interest.

In the post Cold War world, NATO redefined its goals. It helped UN peacekeeping and humanitarian missions. As threats from global terrorism grew, NATO worked to track and uncover terrorist groups and improved preparedness and response to attacks. After the 2001 terrorist attacks on the United States, NATO forces joined the U.S. against the Taliban in Afghanistan. The Taliban had given shelter to the Al Qaeda terrorists who planned the attack.

Growth of the European Union The end of the Cold War also changed trade relations in Europe. In 1993, the European Economic Community became the **European Union (EU),** a bloc of European nations that work together to promote a freer flow of capital, labor, services, and goods. Members also cooperate on security matters. In 2004, the EU added 10 new members mostly from Central and Southeastern Europe.

In 2002, the **euro** became the common currency for most of Western Europe. Today, the expanded EU has the world's largest economy and competes with economic superpowers like the United States and Japan. Some European leaders supported even greater economic and political unity for the region. However, many ordinary citizens felt greater loyalty to their own nations than to the EU.

The EU Confronts Crises The 2009 global economic crisis shook the EU as some member nations came close to bankruptcy. They had borrowed heavily to pay for expensive government programs. As the economic crisis worsened, countries such as Spain and Greece were unable to pay their debts. The EU provided financial bailouts, or loans, and required severe cuts in spending. Even as the debt crisis eased, it left a legacy of shaken confidence.

In 2016, the British chose to leave the EU in a move known as Brexit, or British exit. That vote set off complex negotiations between Britain and the EU over the terms of Britain's departure in 2020 and future trade, travel, and border rules. Negotiating a

European Union, 2020

>> This map shows the European Union in 2020. **Analyze Maps** Which EU members border the Black Sea?

BOUNCE to Activate Map

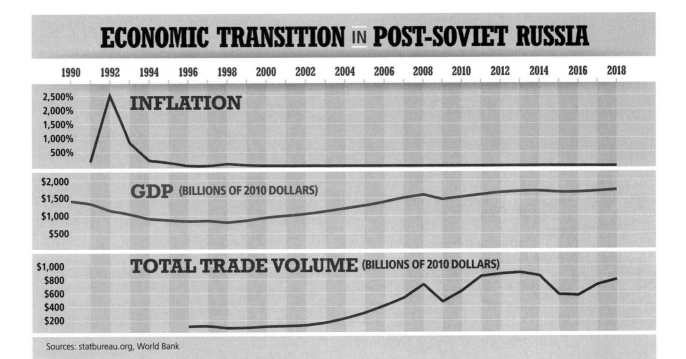

ECONOMIC TRANSITION IN POST-SOVIET RUSSIA

| 1990 | 1992 | 1994 | 1996 | 1998 | 2000 | 2002 | 2004 | 2006 | 2008 | 2010 | 2012 | 2014 | 2016 | 2018 |

INFLATION

2,500%
2,000%
1,500%
1,000%
500%

GDP (BILLIONS OF 2010 DOLLARS)

$2,000
$1,500
$1,000
$500

TOTAL TRADE VOLUME (BILLIONS OF 2010 DOLLARS)

$1,000
$800
$600
$400
$200

Sources: statbureau.org, World Bank

>> **Analyze Graphs** After the fall of the Soviet Union, Russia's economy took time to adapt to a free market economy. In what year did inflation start to drop in Russia?

deal outlining Britain's future relationship with the EU proved to be extremely difficult.

Wars in the Balkans Yugoslavia was a **multiethnic** country, made up of many ethnic groups. After communist rule collapsed in 1992, the country broke apart. Ethnic rivalries led to fighting in which all sides committed atrocities. In Bosnia, civil war erupted in 1992 between Bosnian Serbs and Bosniaks. Serbia sent arms to Bosnian Serbs, fueling the violence. Bosnian Serbs conducted a vicious campaign of **ethnic cleansing,** killing or forcibly removing people of an unwanted ethnic group. An estimated 80,000 Muslim Bosniaks were killed, some in mass executions. Ethnic cleansing is often seen as a form of genocide.

The United States and its NATO allies intervened militarily and forced the warring parties into peace talks. In 1995, rival groups signed the Dayton Accords to end the fighting. A new conflict flared in 1998 when Kosovo, with a mostly Muslim Albanian population, declared independence from Serbia. International mediation led Serbia to withdraw in 1999.

Challenges Facing Northern Ireland When the Republic of Ireland won independence from the United Kingdom in 1922, **Northern Ireland,** which

then had a Protestant majority, voted to remain part of the United Kingdom. Catholics, then a large minority, largely wanted to join the rest of Ireland. In the late 1960s, many Catholics demanded equal rights and unification with Ireland. Protestants wanted to remain part of the United Kingdom. Tensions turned to violence, as extremists on both sides carried out bombings, kidnappings, and murders. Northern Ireland's land border became a focal point for violence.

Finally, a peace accord, known as the **Good Friday Agreement,** was signed in 1998. It created a new power-sharing government. Border checkpoints between Northern Ireland and the Republic disappeared.

New issues emerged as Britain withdrew from the EU while Ireland remained an EU member and followed EU rules. The need to regulate trade into and out of the EU threatened to restore border checkpoints and revive tensions.

☑ **CITE EVIDENCE** What challenges did Germany face after reunification?

Russia and Its Neighbors

As communism collapsed, the Soviet Union, like Yugoslavia, broke up into many independent republics. By far the largest was the Russian Federation, or Russia. Some new republics had tense relations with their neighbors, sparking regional conflicts. Other tensions erupted among ethnic minorities. Although Russia at first struggled economically, it soon began to reassert power, straining relations with the United States.

Russia Moves to Autocracy After the Soviet Union collapsed, Russian president Boris Yeltsin shifted to a market economy. Economic reforms, especially the privatization of many state-run industries and collective farms, brought severe hardships to many Russians. Unemployment and prices soared. A financial crisis wiped out the savings of millions. In 1998, Russia **defaulted,** or failed to make payments, on much of its foreign debt. A few Russians however, grew rich by buying up old Soviet industries at bargain prices. They formed a new class of **oligarchs,** or rich and powerful business leaders.

>> Russian president Vladimir Putin and American president Barack Obama confer at the G20 Summit in Mexico in June 2012. The United States and Russia are powerful forces in the United Nations and other international organizations.

Since 2000, **Vladimir Putin** has dominated Russia. Over time, Putin has tightened his grip on power, moving Russia away from democratic practices toward **autocracy,** a government dominated by a strong leader. While many Russians support their leader, Putin has faced criticism for corruption and trampling on civil liberties.

Putin managed to rebuild the economy based on the export of Russia's vast natural resources. Rising prices for oil and gas boosted the country's earnings. Those who benefited most from Russia's growth, though, were those connected to the country's oligarchs and ruling elite. Many ordinary Russians continued to face hardship.

Wars in the Caucasus The Caucasus region lies between the Black and Caspian seas and is home to many ethnic groups. It includes Russian-ruled Chechnya and several independent former Soviet republics. In 1994, Chechen separatists tried to break away from Russian rule, sparking ten years of horrendous fighting. Muslim Chechen rebels won support from Islamic extremists around the world. Russia crushed the revolt with great brutality, but soon faced terrorist attacks on civilian targets, including a theater and a school.

The former Soviet republics of Azerbaijan and Armenia also experienced ethnic conflict over the disputed border area of Nagorno-Karabakh in the Caucasus. While this area is claimed by Azerbaijan, most of its residents are Armenians. Fierce fighting ended in 1994 but resumed in 2020.

Meanwhile, Russia backed two breakaway provinces of the independent Republic of Georgia, triggering brief wars. Russian forces occupied the breakaway provinces, which proclaimed independence, Today, however, few countries recognize their claims.

☑ **CHECK UNDERSTANDING** What troubles did Russia face after the collapse of the Soviet Union?

The United States Faces New Challenges

United States has the world's largest economy, valued in market terms. The country has weathered economic swings, deepening political divisions, and shocking terrorist attacks. In global affairs, the U.S. has sought to maintain its strong position and to negotiate trade agreements that benefit its economy.

Recession and Recovery An economic boom in the 1990s left the U.S. federal government with a budget **surplus,** or money left over after expenditures. By the early 2000s, slower growth, military spending, and tax cuts fed a growing budget deficit. When a government spends more than it gets in revenue, the difference is a **deficit**.

During the 1990s, the United States relaxed financial regulations. After a recession in the early 2000s, the country's monetary authority—the Federal Reserve System—lowered interest rates. The result was an explosion in risky lending. Debt levels soared, and the prices of homes and other assets rose to unsustainable levels. In 2007, growing numbers of Americans were unable to repay their mortgage loans. Financial institutions around the world holding those loans began to face difficulties. In 2008, the resulting financial crisis set off a global recession. Millions of Americans lost their jobs as businesses cut back or closed. America had not had an economic crisis so severe since the Great Depression of the 1930s.

President Barack Obama, the country's first African American President, responded with an economic stimulus package. Although recovery was slow, unemployment began to decline, and the economy gradually recovered. Under President Donald Trump, job growth continued, and the unemployment rate fell to its lowest level in almost 50 years. While a tax cut boosted growth, it produced larger budget deficits.

Political Divisions Deepen Beginning in the 1990s, a gap between mostly Republican conservatives and mostly Democratic liberals grew and intensified in the United States, leading to **polarization,** or a concentration of people in distinct camps at opposite extremes of a spectrum. Polarization had an impact on government, the media, and American society in general. Americans embraced sharply different views about issues, including gun rights, the environment, and other controversial subjects.

The growing divide affected Congress, which saw less bipartisanship, or cooperation between Republicans and Democrats to compromise on pressing issues. Without compromise, the government failed to solve urgent problems. Disagreements over budgets led to government shutdowns more than once, when Congress could not agree on how to fund the government. In national elections, the map was divided into red states, where Republican candidates mostly won, and blue states, where Democratic candidates usually won.

>> Trade with Canada and Mexico is vital to the U.S. economy. Here, trucks are lined up waiting to cross the U.S.–Mexican border.

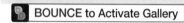

BOUNCE to Activate Gallery

>> In late 2018, Republicans and Democrats failed to agree on a federal budget. This led to a 35-day partial government shutdown, which these workers are protesting.

The 2020 elections took place in this polarized context, with each side predicting devastating consequences if the other won. The victory of the Democratic candidate, Joe Biden, left the country bitterly divided.

When it became clear that Biden had won enough states' votes in the Electoral College to secure the presidency, President Trump refused to concede, announced he had won, and mounted a series of legal challenges claiming electoral fraud. The courts found that the legal challenges lacked evidence and dismissed nearly all of the cases. Trump and many of his followers continued to claim victory and voter fraud.

On January 6, 2021, the day that members of both houses of Congress gathered in the Capitol building in Washington, D.C., to certify the electoral votes, Trump urged his followers to march to the Capitol to fight to overturn the results of the election, which they did. Trump's followers violently broke into the Capitol building in an attempted coup to stop the legislators from carrying out their constitutional duties. After the mob was cleared from the building, the legislators returned later that evening and certified the electoral votes. Over 100 Republicans in the House and a handful in the Senate voted to reject the electoral votes from Arizona and Pennsylvania.

In response to this blatant attack on the U.S. government, members of the U.S. House of Representatives voted to impeach President Trump for incitement of insurrection. The House had already impeached Trump 13 months earlier for abuse of power and obstruction of Congress. Within this environment of deep political division and continued threats of violence from Trump's supporters, Joe Biden was sworn in as President on January 20, 2021.

New Calls for Social Justice During the 2000s, one effect of an increase in the use of mobile devices and social media was the spread of images of police violence, sometimes deadly, against Black Americans. The deaths of Black Americans outraged many Americans and led to a growing awareness of systemic racism that permeated the broader society.

In 2013, a new social and political movement called Black Lives Matter formed to protest violence against Black Americans. The movement called for an end to systemic racism and white supremacy.

In 2020, bystanders captured video footage of a white Minneapolis police officer killing George Floyd, an unarmed Black American accused of using a counterfeit $20 bill. Floyd's brutal killing horrified many Americans, and protests broke out in cities across the country.

While many Americans sympathized with the Black Lives Matter movement, others were critical. Critics blamed the movement for incidences of violence or looting at protests. Others charged that the movement was anti-police, especially after some in the movement called for local governments to cut or eliminate funding for the police.

The United States and Its Neighbors Trade between the United States and its two North American neighbors is worth trillions of dollars annually. In 1994, the United States, Mexico, and Canada signed **NAFTA,** or the North American Free Trade Agreement. It reduced barriers to trade among the three nations. Although the agreement provided benefits to many in all three countries, some workers in the United States lost their jobs as industries moved to Mexico.

These job losses and the decline of many former industrial regions sparked opposition to free trade in the United States. President Trump won election in 2016 in part by promising to revise trade agreements. In 2018, President Trump negotiated a new agreement called the United States–Mexico–Canada Agreement, (USMCA). It updated NAFTA with stronger protections for U.S. patents, limits on Canada's protection of its dairy industry, and new labor and environmental policies.

Facing a New Rival In recent decades, trade between the United States and China has expanded greatly as China's economy and industrial production have grown. However, tensions developed over various issues, including a growing U.S. trade deficit. A U.S. trade deficit means that the United States imports more goods from a country such as China than it exports there. The United States also accused China of stealing technology. During the 2016 election campaign, Donald Trump accused China of acting unfairly and hurting the United States. After his election, President Trump imposed tariffs, or taxes, on Chinese imports, sparking a trade war

Major U.S. Trade Partners

RANK	COUNTRY	TOTAL TRADE, 2018*	RANK	COUNTRY	TOTAL TRADE, 2018*
1	Mexico	615	14	Brazil	74
2	Canada	612	15	Ireland	71
3	China	559	16	Switzerland	62
4	Japan	218	17	Singapore	58
5	Germany	188	18	Belgium	55
6	South Korea	134	19	Malaysia	54
7	United Kingdom	132	20	Thailand	47
8	France	95	21	Australia	37
9	India	92	22	Hong Kong	36
10	Taiwan	85	23	Israel	34
11	Netherlands	81	24	Spain	32
12	Italy	81	25	Colombia	29
13	Vietnam	78	*Billions of U.S. dollars		

>> Trade between the United States and the rest of the world is worth trillions of dollars each year. **Analyze Charts** What might explain the positions of Mexico and Canada in this chart?

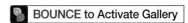
BOUNCE to Activate Gallery

between the two economic giants. To ease tensions, the two countries entered talks. In 2020, a partial trade agreement between the United States and China led to a truce in their conflict.

☑ **IDENTIFY CAUSE AND EFFECT** What process made it difficult for Congress to pass new laws?

The Asian Pacific Region

The countries of East Asia, Southeast Asia, and South Asia are all part of the Asian Pacific region. It includes more than 45 countries linked by busy trade routes and a vibrant regional economy. Some nations, such as Laos and Cambodia, have relatively poor developing economies. Others are middle-income countries, such as India, Thailand, and the Philippines. Several have rich developed economies including Japan, Singapore, Australia, and New Zealand.

The Asian Pacific region is part of an even larger region, called the **Pacific Rim,** which includes all countries bordering the Pacific Ocean from Australia and Asia to North and South America. The Pacific Ocean first became a highway for world trade in the 1500s. By the 1990s, the volume of trade across the Pacific was greater than that across the Atlantic, and the expansion continued into the 2000s.

The Asian Tigers Among the powerhouses of the Asian Pacific Rim were Taiwan, Hong Kong, Singapore, and South Korea. Because of their economic successes, they were nicknamed the "Asian tigers" or "four tigers."

Although the Asian tigers differed in important ways, all had modernized and industrialized by the 1980s. All four were influenced to some degree by China, and Confucian traditions of loyalty, hard work, and consensus. Each stressed education as a way to increase worker productivity.

The Asian tigers first focused on light industries, such as textiles. As their economies grew, they shifted to higher-priced exports, such as electronics. Their stunning growth was due in part to low wages, long hours, and other worker sacrifices.

Japan Loses Ground For decades, Japan dominated the Asian Pacific region. In the 1990s, however, Japan suffered a long economic downturn, and economic growth was slower than in other developed countries in the 2000s. A low birth rate and an aging population caused Japan's population to shrink. In 2011, an earthquake and tsunami killed thousands of people and caused a serious nuclear accident in northern Japan. The country's decision to scale back nuclear power increased its dependence on energy imports.

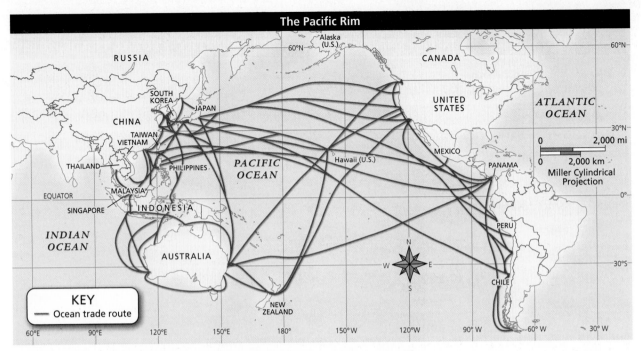

The Pacific Rim

>> The countries of the Pacific Rim have geographic, cultural, and economic ties. The region is a major center of ocean trade routes. **Analyze Maps** According to the map, with which East Asian countries does the United States trade?

Despite setbacks, Japan remained the world's third largest economy after the United States and China. It continued to play a major role both in the Asian Pacific region and in the global economy.

China and Its Neighbors China's emergence as an economic superpower brought both benefits and challenges to its neighbors in the Asian Pacific region. Chinese demand for minerals and agricultural products boosted the economies of Australia and New Zealand. Other countries, such as South Korea and Vietnam, benefited from increased trade with their giant neighbor. China also provided loans and investments to developing countries across the region. In exchange, it gained access to natural resources, fisheries, and new markets for its products.

At the same time, China's neighbors were alarmed by its military expansion and growing economic dominance. At least ten countries had overlapping claims to islands in the East China Sea and South China Sea, where China built military outposts. China continued to claim that Taiwan was part of China and to oppose that country's independence.

As the United States and China faced off over trade tensions and China's military expansion, Asian Pacific nations faced a difficult balancing act. Some

nations, such the Philippines, had close military and economic ties to the United States. Most had close economic ties with China. They welcomed the benefits of trade with China but shrank from its military moves in the Pacific.

☑ **SUMMARIZE** How did China's growth affect the region?

☑ ASSESSMENT

1. **Summarize** How has Europe changed since the end of the Cold War?

2. **Make Generalizations** What challenges did Russia face after the fall of the Soviet Union?

3. **Identify Cause and Effect** What effects did increased foreign trade have on the United States?

4. **Summarize** How have developments in Asia changed the global economy?

5. **Connections to Today** Identify at least three challenges developed countries have to overcome to continue to improve the quality of life of their residents.

This textile plant in India represents one of the many industries that have migrated from European and North American countries to the developing world.

Globalization and Trade

Global trade has existed since ancient times, but it was limited. New seafaring technologies and the European age of exploration set off increasing trade and contacts around the world. This set the stage for modern globalization. Globalization is the process by which nations' economies, politics, cultures, and societies become closely linked with those of other nations around the world. For economists, globalization is the growth of international investment and trade, which reduces the ability of individual nations to control their own economies. Globalization increased dramatically in the late 1900s and early 2000s.

Global Interdependence

Several events in the 1980s and 1990s are closely linked to the rise of globalization. First, economic reforms in China led to increased foreign investment and trade. Second, many developing countries made reforms that opened them to trade and investment. Third, the collapse of communism in the Soviet Union and Eastern Europe reconnected these economies to global markets. Finally, new information technologies accelerated the exchange of information and made the world more connected.

Working in the Global Economy Rich and poor nations have become increasingly interdependent. **Interdependence** is the dependence of countries on one another for goods, resources, knowledge, and labor from other parts of the world. Developed countries control much of the world's capital, trade, and technology. At the same time, they depend on the developing world for many resources and, increasingly, for labor.

 BOUNCE to Activate Flipped Video

Objectives

Explain how investment and trade have tied global economies to one another.

Describe how international organizations and treaties promote economic ties.

Analyze the costs and benefits of globalization.

Key Terms

interdependence
outsourcing
multinational
  corporation
World Trade
  Organization
  (WTO)
protectionism
bloc
sustainability

GO ONLINE to access your digital course

As the global economy grew, many companies in developed countries began to outsource jobs to the developing world. **Outsourcing** is the practice of sending work to outside enterprises in order to save money or increase efficiency. Many companies in the developed world outsourced technological jobs to India, China, and the Philippines.

Growth of Multinational Corporations Over the past 50 years, multinational corporations have expanded their power over the global economy. **Multinational corporations** have offices and investments in many countries and sell their goods and services worldwide.

These corporations have invested heavily in the developing world. They have built factories and provided much-needed jobs to people in developing countries. Critics, however, have accused multinationals of taking large profits out of developing countries, causing environmental damage, and paying low wages.

Global Economic Crises Due to financial interdependence, an economic crisis in one country or region can have a global impact.

During the 1990s, the United States relaxed financial regulations, allowing financial institutions to make high-risk loans. Many Americans borrowed too much. Banks around the world bought American debt, because they wanted to collect interest payments on it.

In 2007, many homeowners began defaulting on mortgages. Banks around the world became unwilling to loan money. Businesses that needed money had to lay off workers. Nearly every country in the world felt the impact of the U.S. debt crisis, although the severity varied from one country to another. Some European countries, such as Spain, Ireland, and Greece, experienced soaring unemployment and social unrest. Developing countries also felt the impact as prices for their goods fell and international aid decreased.

Wealthy nations, like the United States, shored up their economies and helped banks and other troubled industries survive the crisis. After 2010, a slow but fragile recovery began.

Global links mean that the world remains vulnerable to economic crises. Another crisis in China or Europe, for example, could have a global impact, because businesses in many countries count on trade or investment from China or Europe.

Changing Oil Prices Energy resources play a huge role in the global economy. All nations, for example, need oil for transportation and to manufacture products ranging from plastics to fertilizers. Any

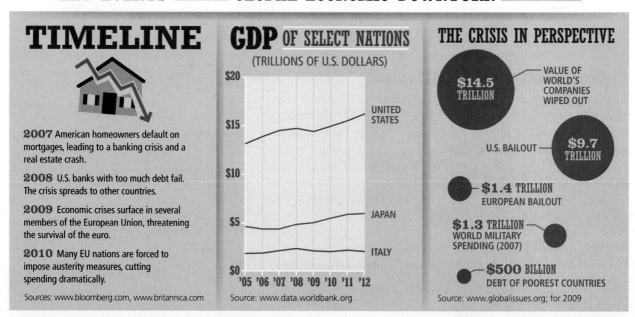

KEY EVENTS OF THE **GLOBAL ECONOMIC DOWNTURN** 2005–2012

TIMELINE

2007 American homeowners default on mortgages, leading to a banking crisis and a real estate crash.

2008 U.S. banks with too much debt fail. The crisis spreads to other countries.

2009 Economic crises surface in several members of the European Union, threatening the survival of the euro.

2010 Many EU nations are forced to impose austerity measures, cutting spending dramatically.

Sources: www.bloomberg.com, www.britannica.com

GDP OF SELECT NATIONS (TRILLIONS OF U.S. DOLLARS)

UNITED STATES
JAPAN
ITALY

'05 '06 '07 '08 '09 '10 '11 '12

Source: www.data.worldbank.org

THE CRISIS IN PERSPECTIVE

$14.5 TRILLION — VALUE OF WORLD'S COMPANIES WIPED OUT

U.S. BAILOUT — $9.7 TRILLION

$1.4 TRILLION EUROPEAN BAILOUT

$1.3 TRILLION WORLD MILITARY SPENDING (2007)

$500 BILLION DEBT OF POOREST COUNTRIES

Source: www.globalissues.org; for 2009

>> **Analyze Charts** Which year of the downturn was the low point for the U.S. GDP? For Japan? For Italy? Based on information in the infographic, what is a likely reason why Italy's low point was different from that of the U.S. and Japan?

BOUNCE to Activate Gallery

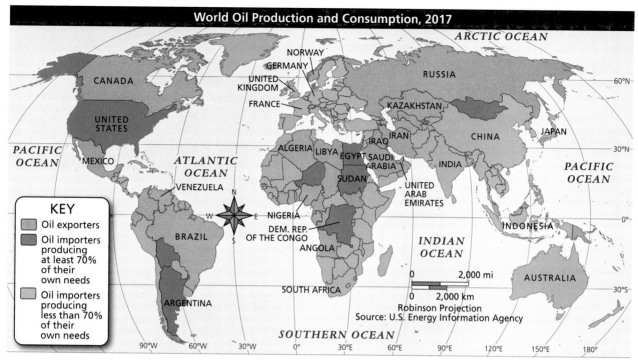

World Oil Production and Consumption, 2017

KEY
- Oil exporters
- Oil importers producing at least 70% of their own needs
- Oil importers producing less than 70% of their own needs

0 2,000 mi
0 2,000 km
Robinson Projection
Source: U.S. Energy Information Agency

>> This map shows net consumption or production of oil by various countries.
Analyze Maps Name at least three countries that produce more oil than they use.

change in the global oil supply can have a huge impact worldwide.

Whenever oil prices have risen sharply, people have faced economic uncertainties. In 2008, oil prices shot up, partly because the growing economies in China, India, and elsewhere led to increased demand. A year later, as the global economic crisis slowed demand, prices fell. This sudden, rapid change in oil prices has led to renewed calls to develop alternative energy sources. Still, the world has remained largely dependent on oil.

☑ **IDENTIFY CAUSE AND EFFECT** How do changes in the supply of oil affect economies around the world?

Global Organizations and Trade Agreements

Many international organizations and treaties connect people and nations around the world. These organizations have various goals, such as promoting peace and security, supporting development, and promoting free trade.

International Organizations The United Nations is the world's largest international organization. Its membership has grown from 50 nations in 1945

to 193 today. The UN grew rapidly as nations won independence from colonial rule. It expanded again after the former Soviet republics joined.

As the UN expanded, its global role grew. The UN and its many agencies have provided economic and humanitarian aid to developing nations. It has sent peacekeepers to dozens of trouble spots, including Cambodia, Congo, and the Balkans. The UN deals with social development, human rights, and international law.

Various other organizations deal with economic issues. The World Bank, for example, offers loans and technical advice to developing countries. The International Monetary Fund (IMF) promotes international monetary cooperation and helps developing countries solve economic problems. It also lends to countries in crisis.

Thousands of organizations not linked to governments also provide aid. These non-governmental organizations (NGOs) are voluntary, non-profit groups. They address issues such as human rights, disaster relief, the environment, and medical care. The International Red Cross is an example of an NGO.

Treaties and Global Trade Governments have signed international treaties to help regulate world trade. In 1947, 23 nations signed the General

Agreement on Tariffs and Trade (GATT) to expand world trade and reduce tariffs, or taxes on imported goods. GATT later evolved into the **World Trade Organization (WTO),** which included 164 nations as of 2013.

The WTO seeks to resolve trade disputes. The WTO opposes **protectionism,** or the use of tariffs and other restrictions to protect a country's home industries against international competition. President Trump, however, refused to appoint members to the WTO's dispute-resolution board. When board members' terms expired in 2019, the WTO was no longer able to resolve trade disputes.

Since the 2008 global economic crisis, a major world economic forum is the Group of Twenty (G20). It includes 19 leading industrial nations plus the EU. G20 leaders meet yearly to discuss ways to strengthen the global economy. They have focused on promoting job growth and free trade.

Regional Trade Blocs Many nations have formed regional **blocs,** or groups, to boost trade and meet common needs. Regional trade groups perform an important function by lowering trade barriers and encouraging the free exchange of goods and services. Among the largest is the EU (European Union). APEC (Asian-Pacific Economic Cooperation)

was formed to further trade among Pacific Rim nations. OPEC, representing oil-producing countries, regulates the production of oil to stabilize the market.

In 1994, NAFTA (the North American Free Trade Agreement) eased restrictions and promoted trade between the United States, Canada, and Mexico. President Trump argued that NAFTA needed to be replaced with an agreement better protecting U.S. interests. Negotiators signed a new agreement, the USMCA (United States–Mexico–Canada Agreement), in 2018, and the three member countries had ratified the agreement by 2020.

☑ **SUMMARIZE** How do trade blocs benefit nations?

Challenges to Globalization

Instant communications, modern transportation networks, and increasing economic ties continue to push globalization, which has affected every aspect of life. In recent years, though, critics have challenged or even tried to roll back the effects of globalization.

Benefits of Globalization Competition and the use of low-wage workers in the developing world has allowed multinational corporations to offer goods and services at low prices. People in the industrial world, especially, have benefited from lower prices and a variety of goods. Many developing countries have used increased wealth from global trade to build needed transportation, raise standards of living, and provide better services.

The mass migration of people in developing countries from rural areas to cities has transformed lives. In cities, people often have better access to education and health care. The movement of people worldwide, along with modern communication, has furthered the exchange of goods and ideas and contributed to a rich blending of cultures.

Criticisms Critics argue that the costs of globalization outweigh the benefits. Some claim it has offered great profits to companies but few benefits to the poor. These critics argue that multinational corporations seek to maximize profits at the expense of worker safety and the environment. They describe globalization as a way for the powerful capitalist economies of the Western world to profit from the weaker nations of the developing world.

>> Officials of the African Union meet with European representatives in Addis Ababa, Ethiopia, in 2013. The AU is one of many regional organizations that engages in peacekeeping, emergency relief, and other operations.

Members of the anti-globalization movement reject the emphasis on competition and profit in favor of social responsibility and justice. Many target the World Bank and the IMF because, in exchange for aid, these organizations require developing nations to make tough reforms and cut costly social programs. Such changes result in hardships for a population and few opportunities for economic growth. Others condemn Western cultural dominance.

Environmentalists have also criticized globalization. They claim that industries eager for profits encourage too-rapid development, endangering **sustainability,** or development that balances people's needs today with the need to preserve the environment for future generations.

Challenges to Globalization In the 2010s, some countries started to challenge what they saw as harmful impacts of globalization on their countries. Some developed countries restricted immigration. The EU set new rules and imposed fines and taxes on multinational Internet firms.

In 2016, Donald Trump won election as U.S President promising to penalize other countries for what he saw as unfair trade practices. During the late 2010s, President Trump imposed tariffs meant to protect U.S. producers. Critics argued that those tariffs might hurt American consumers and businesses by raising prices.

☑ **EXPLAIN** Why have some people criticized globalization?

☑ ASSESSMENT

1. **Compare and Contrast** How does globalization affect economies around the world?

2. **Compare** In what ways are developed and developing countries affected differently by economic interdependence? Explain.

3. **Make Generalizations** How do international organizations work to expand trade?

4. **Compare Points of View** Describe one of the criticisms against multinational corporations.

5. **Connections to Today** How has globalization both improved and set back the quality of life of people in the world today? Cite examples from the text.

>> The Pantip Plaza shopping center in Bangkok, Thailand, offers a dizzying array of electronics from around the world. Globalization has greatly enabled the quicker and easier worldwide movement of consumer and other goods.

 BOUNCE to Activate Gallery

>> Some people believe that globalization negatively affects society. The World Trade Organization has sometimes met with stormy opposition to its role in increasing globalization.

21.4

A homeless child in Katmandu, Nepal, sleeps on the sidewalk. Nearly half of the world's people live in relative poverty.

🅱 BOUNCE to Activate Flipped Video

Objectives

Explain the impact of poverty, disasters, and disease on nations around the world.

Describe global efforts to protect human rights.

Evaluate the environmental challenges facing the world.

Key Terms

tsunami
epidemic
pandemic
famine
refugee
acid rain
indigenous people
deforestation
erosion
global warming

Social and Environmental Issues

Globalization has spread new technologies, ideas, and greater prosperity to many nations and people. At the same time, the world faces enduring problems, such as poverty, hunger, and disease. These problems have global dimensions that often require global solutions.

Global Challenges

The world's people face ongoing challenges from natural disasters, poverty, and disease.

Natural Disasters Natural disasters range from earthquakes, floods, and avalanches to droughts, fires, hurricanes, and volcanic eruptions. They strike all over the world, causing death, destruction, and unsanitary conditions that often lead to disease. Although such events may strike anywhere, they often hit developing countries especially hard due to poor building construction.

In 2005, Hurricane Katrina struck the coastal regions of Louisiana and Mississippi. A 30-foot storm surge and high winds caused a devastating flood in New Orleans and killed more than 1,800 people. Hurricanes Irma and Maria in 2017 pounded the Caribbean region, causing terrible destruction on many islands and on the U.S. territory of Puerto Rico.

🖥 **GO ONLINE** to access your digital course

In 2011, a huge underwater earthquake in the Pacific Ocean triggered a **tsunami** (tsoo NAH mee), or tidal wave. It swept along the coast of Japan, flooding towns, killing around 16,000 people, and leaving many more homeless. The tsunami flooded a nuclear power plant, causing several meltdowns that contaminated the area with radioactive waste and forced 150,000 people to evacuate.

A local disaster can disrupt the economy of a country and even have a ripple effect on the global economy. When a typhoon destroyed Myanmar's rice-producing region, the country faced a threat of famine. One benefit of globalization is that news of natural disasters spreads instantly and triggers a quick aid response.

Worldwide Poverty Another great challenge facing the world is the gap between rich and poor. The gap is huge and growing. It exists within rich nations as well as within poor nations. The gap also exists between rich and poor countries.

Nearly half of the world's population, more than 3 billion people, live on less than $5.50 a day. About 750 million adults cannot read or write. Globally, the poor lack access to healthcare and education. They face hunger and malnutrition and are susceptible to disease. They have little voice in government and face other obstacles that make it hard to escape poverty.

Global poverty is a complex issue with many causes. In the developing world, political upheavals, civil war, corruption, and poor planning hurt efforts to reduce poverty. Rapid population growth has made it harder for countries to provide basic services.

Poverty in the developing world is also due in part to dependence on rich nations. Developing countries compete to offer access to cheap resources and labor. Poverty has increased as a result of market reforms required by IMF and the World Bank. In order to get new loans, developing countries have had to reduce spending, especially on health, education and development.

The World Bank and other organizations realize that erasing poverty is essential to global security. They call on poor nations to limit population growth. They encourage rich nations to forgive the debt of poor nations, making more funds available for education, healthcare, and other services.

Although some progress has been made toward reducing poverty, it has been uneven. India, China, and other newly industrialized nations have enjoyed great economic growth, and have fewer people overall living in poverty.

Hunger and Famine For tens of millions of people, hunger is a daily threat. Overall, the world produces enough food to feed the entire population, but food is unevenly distributed. Governments and international

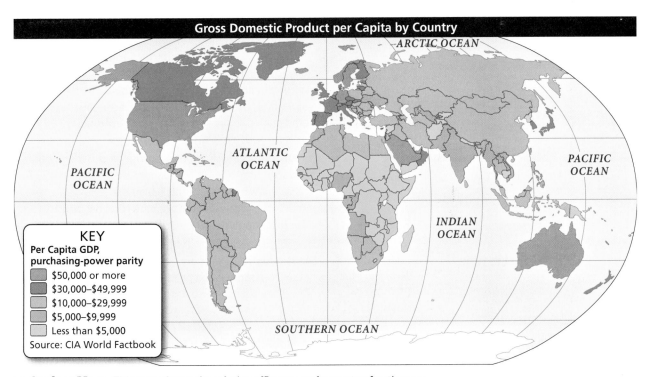

Gross Domestic Product per Capita by Country

KEY
Per Capita GDP, purchasing-power parity
- $50,000 or more
- $30,000–$49,999
- $10,000–$29,999
- $5,000–$9,999
- Less than $5,000
Source: CIA World Factbook

>> **Analyze Maps** This map shows the relative affluence and poverty of nations as determined by the gross domestic product (GDP) per capita. What areas of the world are the most affluent?

organizations have tried to find ways to improve farming and food distribution and to address the underlying causes of poverty and hunger.

In countries racked by conflict or struck by natural disasters, hunger often escalates into famine. A **famine** occurs when large numbers of people in a region or country face death by starvation.

In 2011 and 2012, civil war in Somalia worsened the effects of a severe drought, leading to widespread famine. Each side in the conflict tried to keep food from reaching the other. More than 100,000 died as a result of the famine, hundreds of thousands more were severely malnourished, and nearly a million people fled to neighboring countries as refugees. Since 2015 an ongoing civil war in Yemen has led to famine. More than 85,000 children under the age of 5 are thought to have died from starvation.

People Search for a Better Life Globalization has led to the vast movement of people around the world. Millions of migrants, both legal and illegal, head to Europe, Asia, and North America. In recent years, more than 2 million people have crossed the Mediterranean Sea from the Middle East and North Africa into Europe. Thousands have drowned when overloaded ships have sunk during the passage. Today, many migrants live in temporary camps set up in Italy, Greece, Spain, and elsewhere in Europe.

>> Malaria, transmitted by the mosquito, is common in regions close to the Equator. Netting draped over bedding can help prevent this dangerous disease.

Although some people migrate to find jobs or reunite with families, millions more are **refugees,** people who are forced to move because of poverty, war, persecution, natural disasters, or other crises.

Many migrants find jobs and create better lives in their new countries. But they sometimes face hostility and discrimination. While many industrial countries have offered safety to people fleeing persecution, they have tried to limit the flood of economic migrants, people seeking jobs or better lives. Many people in the developed world resent these economic migrants, claiming they take jobs and services from natural-born citizens.

As migration has grown, so has the smuggling of people across borders. Many illegal immigrants pay smugglers large sums to help them reach their destinations. The UN estimates that human smuggling is a multi-billion dollar global industry.

Global Diseases With millions of people on the move daily, diseases spread rapidly. Globalization, however, has also allowed health experts around the world to quickly identify outbreaks of disease. The International Health Regulations, first written in 1969 and revised in 2005, represented an agreement among 196 countries to work together. The regulations aim for all countries to be able to detect, assess, report, and respond to health crises.

A problem that is prevalent worldwide is obesity. The World Health Organization has worked to raise awareness about this growing epidemic. Obesity can lead to strokes, heart disease, and diabetes.

Other diseases, including avian flu (bird flu), mad cow disease, West Nile virus, swine flu (H1N1), and influenza have raised concerns about the global spread of disease. When a disease spreads rapidly across a wide area, it is called an **epidemic**.

The HIV/AIDS epidemic was first reported in 1981 and soon spread around the world. It has taken a staggering human and economic toll, especially in southern Africa and Southeast Asia. The treatment and prevention of AIDS became a global priority. Despite progress, HIV/AIDS continues to spread.

World health officials remained concerned that new, unknown, and possibly very dangerous diseases might emerge and spread around the world. Diseases that are widespread in a country or around the world are known as **pandemics.**

A New Coronavirus Wreaks Havoc Late in 2019, scientists in China detected a new virus that was infecting people in the city of Wuhan. The virus spread rapidly and became a serious health crisis. The World Health Organization (WHO) named the viral disease *COVID-19,* an abbreviation for *coronavirus disease 2019.* Coronaviruses are a family of viruses, some of which cause the common cold.

COVID-19, however, was far more deadly than the common cold. In January 2020, hundreds died of the disease in China, and the virus spread around the world. In March, the WHO declared the disease a global pandemic. During 2020, the disease killed more than 1 million people worldwide. While the virus was most deadly for older people and people with underlying medical conditions, it also killed healthy young people and children.

Governments reacted sharply. China's government severely limited travel. It required people to stay home or wear face masks in public. Many other countries imposed strict lockdowns, requiring people to stay in their homes except for essential errands. Some countries chose to close their borders. Health experts worldwide called on people to wear face masks and to "social-distance," or stay at least 6 feet (2 meters) apart, to limit the spread of the virus.

These restrictions slowed the spread of the virus, but they also disrupted lives and economies. In many countries, schools and businesses closed. People canceled their travel plans. Government restrictions and fears of infection hurt businesses involving close contact—such as airlines, restaurants, gyms, and professional sports. As a result, economies around the world shrank.

As the pandemic wore on, doctors and scientists developed treatments that could save the lives of infected people. Researchers also worked to develop vaccines that might prevent infection. Vaccination and improved treatments seemed likely to make the virus less deadly during the early 2020s as economies around the world gradually recovered.

☑ **CONTRAST** Explain both the negative and positive effects of globalization on the spread of disease.

Human Rights

In 1948, UN members approved the Universal Declaration of Human Rights. It stated that every person is entitled to basic rights, including "life, liberty and security of person." It called for freedom from slavery, torture, or discrimination along with "freedom of thought, conscience and religion." It further recognized the right to work, to receive an education, and to maintain an adequate standard of living.

During the Cold War, 35 nations from the Western world and the Soviet bloc signed the Helsinki Accords that guaranteed such basic rights as freedom of speech, religion, and the press as well as

>> To avoid spreading COVID-19, people around the world wore face masks and avoided close contact and indoor gatherings. These Mexican students are taking a university-entrance exam outdoors.

>> Members of Iraq's Yazidi minority suffered serious human rights violations at the hands of the ISIS terrorist group. These Yazidis were forced from their homes and are living in a refugee camp.

>> Two Hmong women work in a field in Laos. Globally, around one out of four women who work outside the home work in agriculture.

🅑 BOUNCE to Activate Gallery

>> In recent decades, women have built careers in a growing number of fields. This scientist is working in a biological laboratory.

the rights to a fair trial, to earn a living, and to live in safety. Despite such agreements, human rights abuses occur daily around the world. They range from arbitrary arrest to torture and slavery.

World Community Confronts Abuses
Organizations around the world work to protect human rights and end abuses. They include governments and international organizations like the UN. In 2014, for example, several nations joined the United States in part to stop human rights abuses by ISIS, a terrorist group centered in Syria.

Citizen groups often take the lead in highlighting abuses. NGOs monitor the actions of governments and pressure them to defend human rights. Human rights groups report on violations such as attacks on migrant workers or unsafe working conditions in factories. They have reported on attacks against indigenous people, Chinese abuses against Tibetan Buddhists, and discrimination against Roma people in some Eastern European countries. North Korea has the world's worst human rights record.

The Struggle for Women's Rights The UN Charter supported "equal rights for men and women." A global women's movement has addressed conditions for women worldwide.

By 1950, women had won the right to vote in most western nations, as well as in Japan, China, Brazil, and other countries. At independence, most African nations guaranteed women the right to vote. Women have headed elected governments in such nations as Argentina, Brazil, Britain, Germany, Israel, India, Liberia, Pakistan, and the Philippines.

Still, a UN report noted that while women represent half of the world's people, "they perform nearly two thirds of all working hours, receive only one tenth of the world's income, and own less than one percent of world property." Women in many countries are subject to violence.

The UN and other groups have condemned violence and discrimination against women. A UN-backed Treaty for the Rights of Women has been ratified by 187 nations. The treaty was designed to ensure gender equality worldwide. The United States has not ratified the treaty. Some groups in the U.S. say the treaty can bring more harm than good to women.

Changing Roles for Women In developed nations, a growing number of women work outside their homes. Some have high-profile jobs as business owners and executives, scientists, and technicians. Yet women often receive less pay than men doing the same work, and many must balance demanding jobs with parenting and housework. Many women work outside the home because families need two incomes to provide the necessities of life.

In the developing world, women often work as subsistence farmers and craftworkers or in domestic service and small-scale manufacturing. In rural areas, especially in Africa, as men migrate to cities to work, women do the farm work in addition to household tasks. In other regions, such as Southeast Asia, young women help support the family or pay for their brothers' education. In some places, cultural traditions confine women to the home or segregate men and women in the workplace. Still, the education gap in the developing world has narrowed. Women from the middle and elite classes have entered the workforce in growing numbers.

The Rights and Protection of Children Human rights groups have drawn attention to the plight of children worldwide. In 1989, UN members approved the Convention on the Rights of the Child, a treaty that outlines basic rights for children, such as the right to life, liberty, education, and healthcare. Providing and protecting these rights has proved difficult. Human rights groups, however, continue to press for change.

Today, almost half the world's children—about 1 billion children—suffer the effects of poverty. Some suffer from HIV/AIDS and have little or no access to treatment. Children have been recruited into armed conflicts, where they are forced to serve as soldiers or even enslaved. Some are abandoned on the street or suffer various other forms of violence. Abuses like these not only damage children but also hurt a country's future development.

In developing countries, tens of millions of children between the ages of 5 and 14 do not attend school. Instead, they work full time. Often, these child laborers work long hours in dangerous, unhealthy conditions for little pay. Many are physically abused by their employers and live in conditions of near slavery. Still, their families need the income the children earn. In some cases, children must work to pay off a family's debt. Human rights groups, the UN, and developed nations have tried to end such practices.

Threats to Indigenous Peoples **Indigenous peoples** are generally those considered to be the descendants of the earliest inhabitants of a region. They include such ethnic and cultural groups as Native Americans, the Aborigines of Australia, and the Maoris of New Zealand. Indigenous peoples in

>> Decades of armed conflict in Colombia have forced some 41,000 indigenous people from their ancestral lands. Here, displaced families struggle to survive in makeshift huts.

many areas face discrimination and other abuses. Often, their lands have been forcibly taken.

In South America, developers have pushed into once-isolated areas, threatening the ways of life of indigenous peoples. Many Indians have died of diseases carried by the newcomers. During Guatemala's long civil war, the government targeted indigenous Mayan villagers, killing tens of thousands. The UN has worked to set standards to protect the rights of indigenous peoples.

Confronting Racism Growing calls for social justice following the killing of George Floyd in the United States inspired people throughout the world to confront racism in their own countries. Demonstrations were held against racial discrimination to express solidarity with American protesters. Many European countries, for example, were confronting their history both as colonizers and as countries whose merchants had traded enslaved people. Today, people from these former colonies live in European countries where they have faced discrimination because of their race.

In Britain, demonstrators tore down a statue of an enslaver and called for the removal of statues of historical figures seen as racist. Activists in countries such as Iran, Thailand, and Kenya used murals of George Floyd along with his words "I can't breathe," to draw parallels to the violence in their own countries and to pursue their own struggle for social justice.

☑ **CATEGORIZE** What common characteristics are found in countries that deny human rights to women?

Development and the Environment

Since earliest times, people have taken what they needed from the environment. In the past, damage was limited because populations were small and technology was simple. Industrialization and the world population explosion have increased threats to the environment.

Development improves lives and strengthens economies—but at a price. One of the great challenges for the future is how to achieve necessary development without causing permanent damage to the environment.

>> Fire boats battle an explosion on the offshore oil rig Deepwater Horizon in 2010. The disaster in the Gulf of Mexico, off the coast of Louisiana, caused the worst oil spill in U.S. history.

Threats to the Environment Modern technologies can harm the environment. Strip mining provides ores for industry but destroys land. Chemical pesticides and fertilizers increase food output but harm the soil and water and may cause cancer. Oil spills kill marine life.

Gases from power plants and factories produce **acid rain,** in which toxic chemicals in the air fall back to Earth as rain, snow, or hail. Acid rain has damaged forests, lakes, and farmland, especially in Europe and North America.

Accidents and industrial disasters have killed people and hurt the environment. In 2010, the Deepwater Horizon oil rig exploded in the Gulf of Mexico off of Louisiana, killing 11 oil workers and injuring 17. The explosion caused the largest marine oil spill in history, poisoning large areas of the Gulf of Mexico. In 2015, an explosion of industrial chemicals in Tianjin, China, killed 173 people.

In many parts of the world, there are severe shortages of clean water. Water shortages exist in heavily populated regions, such as the northern plains of China or some of India's biggest cities. In places such as Syria and Yemen, water shortages have contributed to deadly conflicts, in part over control of this precious resource.

Impact of Development on the Environment As you have read, desertification is a major problem, especially in the Sahel region of Africa. Another threat—especially in Africa, Latin America, and Asia—is **deforestation,** or the cutting of trees without replacing them. In many developing countries, forests are resources that provide needed jobs and increased wealth. People cut trees for firewood or shelter, or to sell in markets abroad. Some burn down forests to make way for farms and cattle ranches, or for industry.

However, once forests are cleared, rains wash nutrients from the soil, destroying its fertility. Deforestation also causes **erosion,** or the wearing away of land, which encourages flooding.

Rain forests like those of the Amazon basin play a key role in absorbing poisonous carbon dioxide from the air and releasing essential oxygen. They are also home to millions of animal and plant species, many of which have become extinct because of deforestation.

Rich nations are the greatest consumers of the world's resources and produce much of the world's pollution. However, they have also led the campaign to protect the environment. They have passed laws to control pollution and ensure conservation in their own countries. In 1992, the UN sponsored the first "earth summit," at which world leaders discussed how to clean up and preserve the planet. Although governments agreed to limit damage, they disagreed over who was responsible and how to pay for any clean up.

The summit raised other hotly debated issues. Should economic development take priority over protecting the environment? Are people, especially in rich nations, willing to do with less in order to preserve the environment? How can emerging nations afford costly safeguards for the environment?

The Threat of Climate Change Another environmental challenge is climate change, including global warming. **Global warming** refers to the increase in Earth's average surface temperature over time. Scientists have recorded rising temperatures over the past century and a greater rise since 1975. Warming has accelerated still further since 2000. The warming trend is changing precipitation patterns, raising ocean temperatures and sea levels, and causing glaciers to melt.

Based on data, climate scientists agree that today's climate change is the result of rising levels of carbon dioxide and other gases released into the atmosphere by human activity, primarily burning of fossil fuels, such as coal, natural gas, oil, and gasoline. These fuels produce "greenhouse gases," such as carbon dioxide, which trap heat in Earth's atmosphere. Climate scientists predict that catastrophic damage could result if businesses and consumers continue to emit greenhouse gases at present levels.

Some American politicians and a few scientists, however, reject the shared consensus of climate scientists. They argue that climate change is due to natural fluctuations in Earth's climate. Others argue that sharp reductions in fossil fuel use would harm the economy.

In 2016, almost 200 countries signed the Paris Agreement to reduce greenhouse gas emissions to try to prevent catastrophic climate change. This agreement raised the question: Does economic development have to conflict with protecting the environment?

U.S. President Trump felt that the economic cost of complying with this treaty was too great. In 2017, he announced that the United States would withdraw from the Paris Agreement, effective in 2020. That

>> A soy plantation in the Amazon rain forest in Brazil shows how acres of forest are cleared for agricultural purposes.

BOUNCE to Activate Map

same year, though, President-Elect Joe Biden said that the United States would rejoin the agreement.

☑ **IDENTIFY SUPPORTING DETAILS** Describe how a regional environmental problem can affect other parts of the world.

☑ ASSESSMENT

1. **Infer** Why might the elimination of poverty be considered essential to global security and peace?

2. **Identify Patterns** What are some of the causes of migration? What characteristics might a migrant look for in a new country?

3. **Identify Central Ideas** How are the human rights of children around the world violated?

4. **Compare and Contrast** Give three examples of how development can conflict with the preservation of a clean and safe environment.

5. **Connections to Today** What social and environmental issues in the world today threaten people's quality of life? Cite four examples from the text.

Universal Declaration of Human Rights

Introduction

The General Assembly of the United Nations adopted this declaration on December 10, 1948. The document sets forth the basic liberties and freedoms to which all people are entitled.

As chairperson of the UN Commission on Human Rights, Eleanor Roosevelt not only helped to draft the document, she also worked to ensure its acceptance. The second primary source is from her speech in Paris on human rights.

>> Eleanor Roosevelt with a copy of the declaration.

Primary Source 1

Article 1 All human beings are born free and equal in dignity [worthiness] and rights. They are endowed with reason and conscience and should act toward one another in a spirit of brotherhood.

Article 2 Everyone is entitled to all the rights and freedoms set forth in this Declaration, without distinction [difference] of any kind, such as race, colour, sex, language, religion, political or other opinion, national or social origin, property, birth or other status. . . .

Article 3 Everyone has the right to life, liberty and security of person.

Article 4 No one shall be held in slavery or servitude. . . .

Article 5 No one shall be subjected [forced to undergo] to torture or to cruel, inhuman or degrading [humiliating] treatment or punishment.

Article 9 No one shall be subjected to arbitrary arrest, detention or exile.

☑ **PARAPHRASE** Restate Article 2 in your own words.

Article 13 Everyone has the right to freedom of movement. . . .

Article 18 Everyone has the right to freedom of thought, conscience and religion. . . .

Article 19 Everyone has the right to freedom of opinion and expression. . . .

Article 20 Everyone has the right to freedom of peaceful assembly and association. . . .

Article 23 Everyone has the right to work, to free choice of employment, to just and favourable conditions of work and to protection against unemployment. . . .

Article 25 Everyone has the right to a standard of living adequate [satisfactory] for the health and well-being of himself and of his family, including food, clothing, housing and medical care and necessary social services, and the right to security in the event of unemployment, sickness, disability, widowhood, old age or other lack of livelihood in circumstances beyond his control.

Article 26 Everyone has the right to education. Education shall be free, at least in the elementary and fundamental stages. . . .

☑ **DETERMINE MEANING** What is meant by the phrase "standard of living" in Article 25? Based on this excerpt, what does it mean for a standard of living to be adequate?

Primary Source 2

People who continue to be denied the respect to which they are entitled as human beings will not acquiesce forever in such denial.

The Charter of the United Nations is a guiding beacon along the way to the achievement of human rights and fundamental freedoms throughout the world. The immediate test is not only to the extent to which human rights and freedoms have already been achieved, but the direction in which the world is moving. Is there a faithful compliance with the objectives of the Charter if some countries continue to curtail human rights and freedoms instead of to promote the universal respect for an observance of human rights and freedoms for all as called for by the Charter?

The place to discuss the issue of human rights is in the forum of the United Nations. The United Nations has been set up as the common meeting ground for nations, where we can consider together our mutual problems and take advantage of our differences in experience. It is inherent in our firm attachment to democracy and freedom that we stand always ready to use the fundamental democratic procedures of honest discussion and negotiation. It is now as always our hope that despite the wide differences in approach we face in the world today, we can with mutual good faith in the principles of the United Nations Charter, arrive at a common basis of understanding.

☑ **EXPLAIN** Why did Eleanor Roosevelt feel the United Nations was the best organization to address human rights?

☑ ASSESSMENT

1. **Analyze Interactions** How do you think the U.S. Bill of Rights might have influenced this declaration?

2. **Determine Author's Purpose** Why do you think the members of the United Nations wrote this declaration, and what did they hope it would accomplish?

3. **Determine Central Ideas** Based on this passage, how would you define the term "human rights"?

4. **Draw Conclusions** Why did Eleanor Roosevelt call the Declaration of Human Rights the "international Magna Carta for all mankind"?

21.5

These Houthi rebel soldiers in Yemen in 2018 were supported by Iran in a deadly civil war against a government backed by Saudi Arabia.

 BOUNCE to Activate Flipped Video

Objectives

Explain how nuclear, biological, and chemical weapons threaten international security.

Analyze the risks of aggression by China, Russia, and states such as Iran and North Korea.

Describe U.S. military operations in the 2000s.

Explain concerns over cybersecurity.

Key Terms

proliferate
terrorism
al Qaeda
Afghanistan
Taliban
ISIS
cyberwarfare
cybersecurity

International Security

At the end of the Cold War, the United States was the world's leading military power, with a global network of military operations. Together with other nations, the United States confronted new challenges in the 2000s, including the spread of nuclear weapons, the rise of China, terrorism, and the risks of cyberwarfare and climate insecurity.

The Threat of Deadly Weapons

During the Cold War, the United States and the Soviet Union built huge arsenals of nuclear weapons. When the Cold War ended, the question remained about what would happen to these deadly weapons. There was also a desire to limit the development of new weapons and to limit the spread of nuclear weapons to additional countries.

The Nuclear Nonproliferation Treaty In 1968, the United States, the Soviet Union, and 60 other nations signed the Nuclear Nonproliferation Treaty (NPT). The treaty aimed to ensure that nuclear weapons did not **proliferate,** or rapidly spread. The treaty sought to limit nuclear weapons to the five countries that already had them—the United States, the Soviet Union, China, France, and Britain. Since then, 190 nations have agreed not to develop or possess nuclear weapons.

Three nations did not sign the NPT: India, Israel, and Pakistan. All three have secretly developed nuclear weapons. North Korea withdrew from the treaty and later tested nuclear weapons.

Western powers accuse Iran of working to develop nuclear weapons. Iran claims its nuclear program is to produce nuclear

GO ONLINE to access your digital course

power as an energy source only. The UN imposed economic sanctions on Iran to stop its uranium enrichment program, a step toward building nuclear weapons. The sanctions severely hurt the Iranian economy and led Iran to accept a nuclear deal in 2015 with the United States, Russia, and major European powers. It agreed to limit its nuclear program to peaceful uses, with strict outside monitoring. In 2018, however, the United States withdrew from the agreement.

Nuclear Arms Control The United States and Russia control most of the world's nuclear weapons. After the breakup of the Soviet Union, Russia secured control of all former Soviet nuclear weapons.

During the 1950s and 1960s, the Soviet Union and United States engaged in an arms race, with each trying to produce more nuclear weapons than the other. To end this dangerous process, beginning in the 1970s, they negotiated treaties to limit their weapon stockpiles. One of these was the Intermediate-Range Nuclear Forces (INF) Treaty, which banned medium-range nuclear missiles. In 2011, the United States and Russia ratified a new overall nuclear arms control treaty, known as New START.

In the 2010s, Russia and the United States accused each other of violating the INF Treaty. In 2019, they abandoned the treaty, raising concerns that more medium-range nuclear missiles would go into use. Russia and the United States also accused each other of violating the New START Treaty, which was due to expire in 2021. A failure to renew that treaty could increase the risk of nuclear war.

Another concern was that nuclear weapons might fall into the hands of terrorists. Securing all nuclear weapons and materials worldwide remains a top priority.

Weapons of Mass Destruction Weapons of mass destruction (WMDs) include nuclear, biological, and chemical weapons. Nuclear weapons include the atomic bomb. Biological weapons refer mainly to germs that can be released into the air or into water supplies. Chemical weapons are toxins, such as nerve gas and mustard gas. The United States and other nations have worked to keep WMDs from falling into the hands of hostile states or terrorists.

☑ **SUMMARIZE** How has the risk from deadly weapons changed in recent years?

>> Iranian leaders claim that the Iranian nuclear program is for generating power. At an event marking the anniversary of the Islamic revolution, a man carries a sign supporting Iran's nuclear program.

>> Investigators must wear protective gear in order to shield them from possible biological or chemical weapons.

Terrorism and the U.S. Response

During the 2000s, the world experienced a dramatic increase in attacks of terrorism. **Terrorism** is the use of violence, especially against civilians, by groups of extremists to achieve political goals. Deaths from terrorism reached a peak in the mid-2010s and then began to decline. The countries at greatest risk from terrorism were in Asia and Africa, but terrorist attacks also occurred in the United States and other western countries. Following terrorist attacks, the United States took military action in Afghanistan and Iraq.

Al Qaeda and the September 11 Attacks When much of the Islamic world was under Western colonial rule in the 1900s, some Islamic thinkers advocated government according to certain principles of Islam. This idea is known as Islamism. Many followers of Islam want democracy and oppose Islamism. By the late 1900s, though, small Islamist groups sought to impose their vision of Islamic government violently, including through terrorism. **Al Qaeda** was one such Islamist terrorist group. Its leader was Osama bin Laden.

On September 11, 2001, Al Qaeda hijacked four passenger jets and crashed two of them into the World Trade Center in New York City and one into the Pentagon in northern Virginia. A fourth plane, aimed at the White House, crashed into a Pennsylvania field after passengers threatened the hijackers. Nearly 3,000 people died in the attacks. These attacks shocked and angered many Americans.

War in Afghanistan The United States determined to find and punish those behind the 2001 attacks. Osama bin Laden was based in Afghanistan. The government of Afghanistan, an extremist Islamist group called the **Taliban**, refused U.S. demands to surrender the terrorists. The United States then formed a coalition of forces, including NATO allies, to invade Afghanistan. In 2002, this coalition overthrew the Taliban.

The Taliban, however, found refuge in remote rural areas and in neighboring Pakistan. They continued to fight U.S. and allied forces for many years. By the late 2010s, the War in Afghanistan had become the longest war in U.S. history. In 2011, though, the United States achieved an important goal when it located Osama bin Laden in Pakistan and killed him.

President Donald Trump negotiated an agreement with the Taliban in 2020 for a withdrawal of U.S. troops from Afghanistan. The region's future remained uncertain.

Fighting ISIS in Iraq and Syria You have learned that, during the early 2000s, the United States was engaged in a war in Iraq. By 2011, the United States had withdrawn all combat forces from Iraq. When a power-sharing agreement among Iraq's religious and ethnic groups collapsed, the country's Sunni Arab minority felt abandoned.

Some Sunni Arabs backed **ISIS**, or Islamic State in Iraq and Syria, an Islamist terrorist organization. Many Sunnis were opposed to this extremist group. By 2014, though, ISIS had won control of large parts of both Iraq and Syria. ISIS ruled ruthlessly and brutally, targeting Christians and other minority groups as well as other Muslims. ISIS fighters executed foreign journalists and aid workers. With U.S. help, local forces finally recovered the lost territory, ending ISIS control in most areas by 2019.

Cells of experienced ISIS fighters remained in remote areas of Iraq and Syria, from which they launched terrorist attacks. ISIS inspired terrorist groups elsewhere, especially in parts of Africa.

Homegrown Terrorism in the West While Islamist terrorism in the early 2000s alarmed the United States and led it to take military action overseas,

>> U.S. troops often faced difficult combat conditions in Afghanistan.

▶ BOUNCE to Activate Map

another source of terrorism proved just as deadly. So-called homegrown, or domestic, terrorists launched brutal attacks, often motivated by racism, anti-Semitism, or other forms of hatred. Such attacks occurred not only in the United States, but also in many European countries, Canada, Australia, and New Zealand.

In the United States, there was at least one domestic terrorist attack every year between 2015 and 2019. In one such attack in 2019, an attacker motivated by hatred toward Hispanic Americans killed 22 people and injured 24 others.

Because domestic terrorists often prepared for their attacks secretly, preventing this form of terrorism proved very difficult. Police monitored extremist websites and online forums to identify domestic terrorists and stop them before they killed.

☑ **IDENTIFY CAUSE AND EFFECT** What factors led to the rise of ISIS?

Aggressive Governments

Although the United States was the world's most powerful nation, during the 2000s several other nations threatened world peace through aggressive actions. Among these aggressive states were Russia and China, both of which possess nuclear weapons. Aggressive action by Russia and China raised the risk of conflict with the United States, which could lead to a world war involving nuclear-armed nations.

Russian Aggression in the Caucasus After the Soviet Union broke apart in 1991, Russia gained independence as the world's largest country in area. Russia retained control of the Soviet nuclear-weapon arsenal. Partly for this reason, Russia's aggressive actions caused concern in other countries.

During the 1990s, Russia supported separatist regions in the Republic of Georgia whose leaders declared independence from that country. Few countries recognized the independence of these Georgian regions. Russia sent troops to prevent Georgia from regaining control of the regions.

In 2008, forces in one of the regions—South Ossetia—bombed villages in Georgia outside of South Ossetia. When Georgia sent troops to respond to these attacks, Russia invaded Georgia. At the same time, criminals believed to be from Russia attacked computers and servers in Georgia. Electronic attacks on networked systems and equipment are known as **cyberwarfare**. Russia agreed to a ceasefire and eventually withdrew its

>> In 2014, according to investigators, a Russian missile shot down a passenger plane over Ukraine, killing everyone aboard. Ukrainians created this memorial to the victims of the attack.

troops. Russia had shown, however, that it was prepared to attack beyond its borders.

Russian Aggression in Ukraine and Beyond In Ukraine, another former Soviet country, protestors and lawmakers forced the country's pro-Russian president out of office in 2014. A new, pro-European government took charge.

Less than a week later, Russia invaded and seized the Ukrainian region of Crimea. Russia then declared Crimea part of Russia. Most nations condemned Crimea's seizure by Russia. Russia also sent troops and weapons to support separatists in eastern Ukraine. With Russian help, these separatists seized Ukraine's most important industrial region. Deadly combat between separatists and Ukrainian forces continued for several years. Separatists or their Russian backers even shot down a civilian airplane, killing everyone on board. Ceasefires reduced fighting, but the region's fate remained uncertain. Leaders of other countries condemned Russia's actions in eastern Ukraine.

In response to Russian aggression, Europe and the United States imposed economic sanctions on Russia. The sanctions hurt Russia's economy but failed to force Russia out of Ukraine.

>> Demonstrators protest China's violations of the human rights of its Uighur minority.

In 2015, Russia sent troops and weapons to support Syria's dictator Bashar al-Assad in a civil war. Assad had committed war crimes and used WMDs against his own people in this war. Russia's support for the brutal dictator drew international condemnation.

Russia has used cyberwarfare to target elections in democracies, including the United States. Such interference threatens democracies by undermining faith in their elections.

Chinese Threats to Peace As you have learned, China has added to global tensions by claiming most of the South China Sea. The area has rich oil and natural gas resources and is a busy seaway with ships from around the world. China built military outposts on tiny islands in the sea. This outraged its neighbors, including the Philippines and Vietnam. They, too, had claims in the region. U.S. naval maneuvers to protect freedom for shipping and to support China's neighbors created a flashpoint for U.S.–China relations.

China also claims Taiwan—which has had an independent government since 1949—as a Chinese province. China has threatened to use force, if necessary, to bring Taiwan under Chinese control. The United States has promised military support for Taiwan. Any Chinese attack on Taiwan would risk a deadly clash between China and the United States.

China also treated its own people harshly. It committed human-rights abuses against its mostly Muslim Uighur minority. China arbitrarily detained more than a million Uighurs in the late 2010s in internment camps and subjected them to forced labor. In 2019, protesters demanded democracy in Hong Kong, a territory under Chinese rule. China's government refused to grant greater democratic rights in Hong Kong.

Aggressive Regional Powers Besides China and Russia, two regional powers—Iran and North Korea—drew strong concern in the early 2000s because of their nuclear programs.

In the early 2000s, Iran began a program that could lead to a nuclear weapon. This alarmed countries in the region, such as Israel and Saudi Arabia. The Persian Gulf, bordering Iran and Saudi Arabia, supplies much of the world's oil and gas. Any disruption to that supply would threaten the global economy. The United States and other nations therefore sought to limit Iran's nuclear program. In 2019, Iranian naval vessels attacked ships in the Strait of Hormuz, which connects the Persian Gulf to the rest of the world.

North Korea threatened world peace with nuclear weapons and long-range missiles capable of carrying nuclear warheads. Wanting North Korea to halt its nuclear program, the UN and the United States imposed harsh economic sanctions during the early 2000s. North Korea dodged the sanctions while developing new weapons systems.

☑ **DRAW INFERENCES** What do Russia, China, North Korea, and Iran have in common that made their aggressive actions a cause for concern?

New Risks Emerge

During the 2000s, the world confronted new risks in several areas. Criminals and hostile state actors used information technology to threaten people's safety and well-being. Climate change was another emerging risk. Along with political violence, it spurred disorderly migration, or movements of people.

Threats to Cybersecurity A growing threat to global security today are cyberattacks, electronic attacks on information systems and services that depend on them. These attacks have fueled the need for greater **cybersecurity**, ways to protect computers, networks, and data against unauthorized use. The United States and other nations have invested heavily in cybersecurity.

Despite these efforts, the cost of cybercrime has risen to hundreds of billions of dollars annually. Through ransomware, for example, hackers kidnap the databases of individuals, businesses, or governments, and force victims to pay ransom before releasing vital information.

Through another threat, cyberwarfare, governments sponsor cyberattacks. Through cyberwarfare, a smaller, weaker country can attack a stronger military rival. The United States has accused countries such as Russia, Iran, China, and North Korea of cyberattacks. These could disrupt essential infrastructure, such as electrical or water supply systems.

In response to Russian cyberattacks on elections in Europe and the United States, governments have taken steps to protect against online propaganda or interference with election equipment.

Environmental Risks In the 2000s, global climate change posed an increasing risk to peace and security. It threatened the security of millions of people through damage and loss of life from storms, droughts, and excessive temperatures. Warmer temperatures caused seawater to expand and glaciers to melt, raising sea levels worldwide. As this process accelerated, sea-level rise threatened to flood coastal regions where hundreds of millions of people lived. A number of island countries in the Pacific Ocean faced the risk of becoming uninhabitable.

As a result of sea-level rise, drought, and other climate-related disasters, the world faced the additional risk of large numbers of climate refugees forced to seek new homes. Large refugee flows could further damage global stability.

Migration Global migration grew rapidly in the 2000s as millions of people moved from developing nations to the developed world. Many migrants were refugees, forced to escape wars and other threats. Some were economic migrants, who left their homelands to escape poverty or seek a better life. Refugees fled violence in countries such as Syria, Afghanistan, Libya, Honduras, and Venezuela. Large flows of migrants into developed countries sparked a backlash in Europe and elsewhere and contributed to the rise of anti-immigrant parties and politicians.

To slow migration, governments in Europe, the United States, and Australia took a hard line on immigration and closed busy migration routes. Migrants often found new, more dangerous ways to reach these countries. Thousands died along the

>> Rising sea levels due to climate change threatened many places along the world's seacoasts, such as the Italian city of Venice.

routes. Efforts to slow migration had limited results in part because wars and poverty in the developing world kept driving people to flee.

☑ **IDENTIFY CAUSE AND EFFECT** How are environmental risks and migration linked?

☑ ASSESSMENT

1. **Check Understanding** How do nuclear, biological, and chemical weapons threaten international security?

2. **Analyze Sequence** How did the United States respond to the attacks that took place on September 11, 2001?

3. **Summarize** How did aggressive actions by Russia and China threaten peace?

4. **Draw Inferences** How might cyberwarfare pose a serious military threat?

5. **Connections to Today** How does the quality of life for people in the world today depend on addressing global security threats?

An Italian astronaut takes photographs aboard the International Space Station in 2013. Astronauts conduct scientific research aboard the station.

BOUNCE to Activate Flipped Video

Objectives

Describe the exploration of space and the innovations that have resulted.

Analyze the development and impact of computer technology and telecommunications.

Summarize key advancements in medicine and biotechnology.

Key Terms

artificial satellite
International Space
   Station (ISS)
Internet
biotechnology
laser
genetics
genetic engineering

Advances in Science and Technology

Since the mid-1900s, scientific research and technological development have transformed life for much of the world. Masses of new inventions, the computer revolution, and advances in the medicine and biology have had enormous impact. Among the most dramatic advances was the exploration of space.

Space Exploration

By the mid-1900s, there were few places on Earth that people had not begun to explore. Space was seen as the "final frontier"—an unknown world filled with opportunity. Within a few short decades, people had developed the transportation technology to explore space and gained knowledge about this new frontier.

The Space Race Rockets are projectiles or vehicles propelled by the ejection of burning gasses from the rear of the rocket. In the early 1900s, pioneers in rocketry like the American physicist Robert Goddard probed the potential of liquid-fueled rockets.

Goddard believed that a rocket could carry people to the moon. At first people met his ideas with disbelief, but German scientists took an interest in Goddard's work. During World War II German scientists, led by Wernher von Braun, developed Germany's V-2 rockets that flew across the English Channel to rain down on London. Von Braun later became a leader in the U.S. space program.

During the Cold War, the United States and the Soviet Union competed to see which superpower would take the lead in space exploration. This "space race" began in 1957, when the Soviet Union launched into orbit *Sputnik*, the first **artificial satellite,** or man-made object that orbits a larger body in space. Four years later, the Soviets sent the first person, Yuri Gagarin, into space.

The United States soon surpassed the Soviets. In 1969, the United States Apollo program landed the first people on the moon. Both superpowers also explored the military uses of space and sent spy satellites to orbit Earth.

Today, the United States and Russia still have the largest space programs and have even cooperated in joint space ventures. Several other countries have also developed space programs, including China, Pakistan, Japan, France, Britain, India, and both North Korea and South Korea.

Science in Space In the decades since *Sputnik* and *Apollo*, nations have launched rockets to other planets and beyond. Robotic space vehicles have penetrated the mists of Venus and the rings of Saturn, landed on Mars, and circled the moons of Jupiter. Space missions have pursued a variety of goals. Some take scientific measurements, release permanent satellites or telescopes, or gather information about the composition and formation of the universe itself. On manned space missions, astronauts conduct medical or biological experiments.

Increasingly, nations have worked together to explore space. Russia, the United States, Canada, Japan, and several European countries developed the **International Space Station (ISS).** Construction on the ISS began in 1998 and was completed in 2010.

The ISS has served as a space laboratory, allowing scientists to observe space, conduct research, and develop new space-related technologies. China has its own space station, and plans are underway for other joint stations. Future plans include setting up a colony on Mars as well as searching for signs of life in other galaxies.

In the 21st century, space travel and exploration is no longer the business of only governments. Several private companies now launch rockets into space. One California company founded in 2002 has the goal of enabling people to live on other planets.

Space technology has benefited life on earth. Dozens of new products, developed for use in space, are today used on Earth. They include liquid-cooled garments, hang gliders, metalized plastics for use in construction and other areas, foam cushions used in helmets and for medical needs, a blood pump that can be used as a temporary heart, and a lightweight breathing system for firefighters.

Artificial Satellites Thousands of artificial satellites orbit Earth every day. They are used in one of three ways: communications, observation, and navigation. They have both military and non-military uses

Communications satellites, for example, relay information that can be used for television, telephone, and high-speed data transmission. Maintaining stationary orbits over specific points on Earth's surface, communications satellites can transmit phone messages or television pictures anywhere on Earth. Linked to cell phones or computers, they allow people, separated by thousands of miles, to communicate instantly.

Observation satellites provide data to scientists, weather forecasters, and military planners. A satellite can receive transmissions from underwater detectors and track the size and strength of tsunamis. Navigation satellites, or global positioning satellites (GPS), beam precise locations to ships, ground vehicles, airplanes, and even hand-held devices.

☑ **INTERPRET** What is the International Space Station and what is its significance?

>> NASA, the U.S. space agency, landed this rover, or robot—named Curiosity—on Mars in 2012. It continued to explore the planet and transmit data to Earth for several years.

🔷 BOUNCE to Activate Timeline

The Digital Revolution

The invention of the computer in the 1900s caused an information revolution. Few aspects of modern life remain untouched by computers. Computers help to run businesses and power plants. They help scientists conduct advanced research. When computers are connected to satellites, they make global communications possible. The development of the computer technology has given rise to the phrase "Information Age."

The Birth of Computers A computer is a device for making mathematical calculations and for storing, processing, and rapidly manipulating data. A smart phone is a small computer. There are also lightning-fast supercomputers that can fill a large room. Computers have made it possible to handle vast amounts of data in a relatively short time. When computers are linked up in a vast network, they allow people to communicate instantaneously over long distances.

Many people contributed to the development of the computer. The first electronic computers were built in the 1940s. They were giant, slow machines, with thousands of vacuum tubes. After the invention of the silicon chip in 1958, the computer

>> Machines like this one, an early "computing machine" for codebreaking used during World War II, marked the start of an information revolution that transformed the world.

was gradually reduced in size. Personal computers became widely available in the 1970s. By installing basic programs, individual users could perform complex and difficult tasks quickly and easily.

Over the next few decades, personal computers replaced typewriters and account books in homes and businesses worldwide. During the 2000s, hand-held computers such as smart phones became the main computing device for many people. At the same time, computer technology spread into many different fields. Computerized robots operate in factories. Computers remotely control satellites and probes in space, and students use them in school classrooms. Researchers developed computer models to predict disasters or understand environmental changes. In today's world, computers are everywhere, providing essential information and controlling critical services.

The Internet Like the computer, the Internet has no single inventor. In the 1970s, the U.S. government along with several American universities led efforts to link computer systems together via cables and satellites. In 1989, British computer scientist Tim Berners-Lee proposed a system of linked documents that could be reached through a computer network. His proposal quickly developed into the World Wide Web, or Internet. Using the **Internet,** a person can instantly communicate with other users around the world and access vast storehouses of information.

By 2000, the Internet had grown to a gigantic network, linking individuals, governments, and businesses around the world. E-commerce, or buying and selling on the Internet, contributed to economic growth. The Internet affected people in both the industrial and the developing world. It connected people anywhere with access to a computer to a world of ideas and information. In 2018, it was estimated that more than half of the world's 7.5 billion people used the Internet on a regular basis.

☑ **SUMMARIZE** What impact have personal computers had on people's lives?

Breakthroughs in Medicine and Biotechnology

Science and technology have revolutionized our understanding of all forms of life and changed the face of our planet. Every year, new developments in medicine improve treatments for diseases. In recent

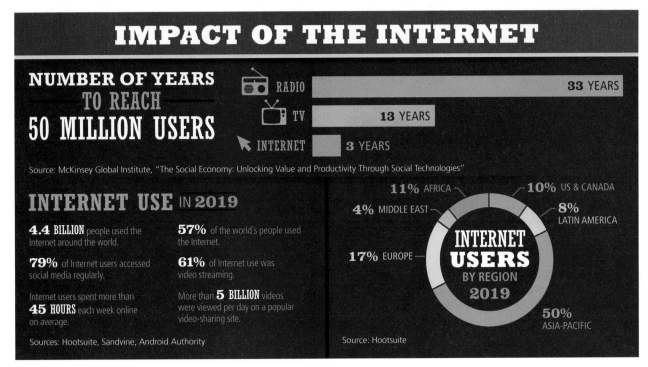

IMPACT OF THE INTERNET

NUMBER OF YEARS TO REACH 50 MILLION USERS

RADIO — 33 YEARS
TV — 13 YEARS
INTERNET — 3 YEARS

Source: McKinsey Global Institute, "The Social Economy: Unlocking Value and Productivity Through Social Technologies"

INTERNET USE IN 2019

4.4 BILLION people used the Internet around the world.

79% of Internet users accessed social media regularly.

Internet users spent more than **45 HOURS** each week online on average.

57% of the world's people used the Internet.

61% of Internet use was video streaming.

More than **5 BILLION** videos were viewed per day on a popular video-sharing site.

Sources: Hootsuite, Sandvine, Android Authority

INTERNET USERS BY REGION 2019

- 11% AFRICA
- 10% US & CANADA
- 4% MIDDLE EAST
- 8% LATIN AMERICA
- 17% EUROPE
- 50% ASIA-PACIFIC

Source: Hootsuite

>> **Analyze Graphs** More than 4 billion people around the world use the Internet. Which region of the world has the largest number of Internet users?

decades, scientists and engineers have made great advances in **biotechnology,** or the application of biological research to technology.

Medical Advances Researchers have found treatments for a number of diseases. In 1952, Jonas Salk developed the first vaccine to prevent polio, a highly infectious disease that causes paralysis. The use of polio vaccines has almost wiped out the disease worldwide. Vaccines has completely eradicated smallpox, once a deadly and much feared disease. Medical researchers continue to develop vaccines to protect against many other diseases.

Breakthroughs in surgery also transformed the field of medicine. In the 1970s, surgeons learned to transplant organs, including the human heart, to save lives. Today, lung, kidney, and other transplants are common procedures in the developed world.

New technologies such as lasers have made surgery safer and more precise. **Lasers** are high-energy light beams that surgeons use to cut or repair tissues and organs. Scientists have developed a range of treatments for many types of cancers. Doctors, engineers, and other scientists have worked together on breakthroughs in diagnosing and treating diseases. Computers have also helped researchers do more and communicate with each other.

The Rise of Biotechnology and Genetic Engineering The field of biotechnology has exploded in recent years. Biotechnology is not new. Humans have used biotechnology for thousands of years to produce better plants or breed animals with certain characteristics. Today's biotechnology, however, uses micro-organisms such as bacteria, yeasts, and enzymes to carry out certain industrial of manufacturing processes. For example, biotechnology has produced synthetic drugs or vaccines. New techniques use bacteria to treat waste or clean up toxic spills.

Biotechnology is closely linked to **genetics,** the study of genes and heredity. Starting in the 1950s, genetic researchers, spearheaded by John Watson, Francis Crick, and Rosalind Franklin, showed the importance of DNA, the material that carries all the genetic information for living organisms. DNA research has revolutionized medicine, agriculture, forensics—crime-solving—and many other fields. In medicine, it has helped researchers understand genetic diseases and find treatments for them.

In recent decades, scientists have made great advances in **genetic engineering** or the manipulation of genetic material to produce specific results. Scientists have created new strains of fruits and vegetables that can resist disease or thrive in less favorable conditions such as cold or dry climates.

a successful vaccine could be distributed to the world's nearly 8 billion people, and whether a vaccine would be effective for an extended period of time.

☑ **SUMMARIZE** How has biotechnology improved medicine?

Standards of Living Rise

Science and technology have changed the way we live. Like older inventions—such as the wheel, printing press, or steam engine—the inventions of the last century have improved lives and helped societies advance. Overall, standards of living have risen worldwide.

Technology and information sharing will continue to be tools to solve global problems and build a better future. But to use these tools properly, we must continue to understand and learn from the past.

☑ **MAKE GENERALIZATIONS** How have scientific advances affected people's standard of living?

☑ ASSESSMENT

1. **Generate Explanations** How have advances in biotechnology and genetic engineering been built on past discoveries?

2. **Synthesize** Why did the United States and the Soviet Union compete against each other to achieve dominance in the space race?

3. **Identify Cause and Effect** What impact has the computer revolution had on globalization?

4. **Summarize** Biotechnology has provided many benefits, but many people worry about its long-term effects. Explain why this is so.

5. **Connections to Today** How have science and technology improved people's quality of life in recent years?

>> **Analyze Political Cartoons** Below the tomato plant in this cartoon lies a double helix, which is the structural arrangement of a DNA molecule. These molecules contain the genetic information in living cells. What is the cartoonist trying to portray in this cartoon?

🔲 BOUNCE to Activate Timeline

Biotechnology and genetic engineering have brought benefits, but also sparked debate. Some people believe that genetically modified foods are unnatural and possibly dangerous. The possibility of cloning genetically identical animals, including human beings, has raised ethical questions about the role of science in creating and changing life.

Tackling COVID-19 Beginning in 2020, doctors and medical scientists made great efforts to develop treatments and vaccines to bring the COVID-19 pandemic under control. By late 2020, they had made progress in both areas.

Meanwhile, in late 2020, more than 100 teams were working to produce a safe and effective vaccine. Medical experts were hopeful that one or more of these would provide some protection against the virus. They were less certain, though, how quickly

Connections to Today

After being banned from schools until 2002, girls in Afghanistan like these gained the right to an education.

Take Action on Future Improvements to People's Quality of Life

In recent years, many people around the world have moved out of poverty and lived healthier, more productive lives. However, the world today faces a number of challenges if we want people's quality of life to continue to improve.

1. **Choose** Select one of the following challenges that needs to be addressed:

   - **Gender equality:** What progress is being made in removing obstacles faced by women and girls in education and work?

   - **Climate change:** What progress is being made to minimize harmful impacts of climate change on people and the environment?

   - **Economic freedom:** What progress is being made toward free markets and removing government barriers to economic activity?

2. **Ask Questions** What are some of the things you want to learn about these future challenges? Write a list of questions.

3. **Learn** Research the topic you have chosen, collecting specific examples from reliable sources. Look for recent data.

4. **Raise Awareness** Create a poster or website illustrating actions that people or groups are taking to address the challenge you researched. Share your poster or website with classmates or a wider audience in your community. Be sure to include information for your audience about where they can go to learn more.

LESSON SUMMARIES

Use these Lesson Summaries, and the longer versions available online, to review the key ideas for each lesson in this Topic.

Lesson 1: The Developing World

An economic gulf divides the world into two spheres—the global North, which is the developed world, and the global South, which is the developing world. In order to develop, countries need to deal with rising populations, poverty, economic dependence, violence, and corruption. Development brings deep change to societies.

Lesson 2: The More Developed World

The European Union and NATO expanded after the Cold War, but Europe faced economic crises. After the breakup of the Soviet Union, Russia was the most powerful country in that region; it moved toward autocracy. The United States dealt with recession, political division, redefining its relationship with neighbors, and the challenge of China's rise. China's rise also posed challenges in the Asia-Pacific region.

Lesson 3: Globalization and Trade

CANTAO

The developed countries of the global North and the developing countries of the global South have become increasingly interdependent. As a result, crises can affect the entire global economy. Several international organizations promote global ties. Globalization has costs as well as benefits.

Lesson 4: Social and Environmental Issues

Along with globalization come the continuing problems of poverty, hunger, and diseases, which usually affect populations in developing countries. Many countries face the challenge of defending and expanding human rights. Environmental issues confront both developed and developing countries. Among these issues is climate change.

Lesson 5: International Security

Nuclear weapons and other weapons of mass destruction threatened peace and security. After a deadly terrorist attack in 2001, the United States and other countries mounted military responses. Aggression by Russia, China, Iran, and North Korea threatened global security. New security risks included cyberwarfare, environmental crises, and uncontrolled migration.

Lesson 6: Advances in Science and Technology

Advances in science and technology have included space exploration; the development of computers, the internet, and mobile devices; biotechnology; and other medical advances. Standards of living have risen worldwide as a result.

VISUAL REVIEW

Use these graphics to review some of the key terms, people, and ideas from this Topic.

DEVELOPING COUNTRIES	DEVELOPED COUNTRIES
Have a relatively low standard of living	Have a relatively high standard of living
Range from extremely poor countries to middle-income countries	High-income countries
Need greater investment in education, healthcare, business, and infrastructure to become developed	Have strong systems of education, healthcare, business, and infrastructure
Struggle with poverty, corruption, conflict, and other barriers to development	While poverty exists and some challenges remain, have widespread prosperity, rule of law, and stability
Located in Latin America, eastern Europe, Africa, and Asia (except Japan and the "Asian tigers")	Include the United States, Canada, western and central Europe, Japan, the "Asian tigers," Australia, and New Zealand

Key Components of Globalization

- Interdependence: dependence of countries on goods, resources, knowledge, and labor from other parts of the world
- Advances in communications and transportation
- Rise of huge multinational corporations
- Far-reaching effects of financial crisis, shortages of natural resources, and debt
- Rise of global economy with many global organizations and treaties

Major Challenges to Society Today

- Global poverty, disasters, and disease
- Ensuring human rights for all, including women, children, and indigenous peoples
- Threat of nuclear weapons, other deadly weapons, and warfare between nations
- Terrorism
- Environmental problems including pollution, deforestation, and desertification
- Threat of catastrophic climate change

Influential Technology From the Twentieth Century

TECHNOLOGY	DESCRIPTION	USES
Artificial satellite	Man-made object that orbits a larger body	Space exploration, spying and other military purposes; scientific research; navigation; communications
Computer	Device for storing, processing, and rapidly manipulating data	Creating and preserving data; making businesses and homes run more efficiently; controlling satellites and factories
Internet	Network of world computer systems linked by cables and satellites	Instant communication with users around world; instant data retrieval; means of commerce
Biotechnology	Application of biological research to industry	Vaccinations and medicines; industrial

Topic 21 Assessment

KEY TERMS, PEOPLE, AND IDEAS

1. Why do many countries seek **development**?

2. What kind of government is an **autocracy**?

3. How does **protectionism** affect trade?

4. How might a person become a **refugee**?

5. What effects might **cyberwarfare** have on a target country?

6. What benefits have come from **biotechnology**?

7. What is biotechnology? Why is there a debate about the effects of biotechnology?

8. Discuss the benefits and costs of global interdependence.

9. What are the social and environmental effects of deforestation?

CRITICAL THINKING

10. **Recognize Cause and Effect** What impact has the growth of the internet had on globalization?

11. **Summarize** How was the war in Afghanistan related to the 2001 terrorist attacks in the United States?

12. **Compare and Contrast** What are the key differences between developing and developed countries?

13. **Analyze information** How has the rise of regional trade blocs such as the European Union affected world economies?

14. **Summarize** What are the main challenges today in the effort to promote human rights?

15. **Recognize Cause and Effect** Some critics of globalization cite threats to cultural traditions and higher unemployment as harmful consequences. Discuss why they feel these effects might occur. Those supporting the effects of globalization cite the economic benefits. Discuss these benefits.

16. **Using Primary Sources** The quote below comes from a policy paper on climate and the economy issued by an NGO. (a) What challenges does it identify? (b) What response to those challenges does it suggest? Explain.

> "We live in a moment of great opportunity. The next 15 years will be critical, as the global economy undergoes a deep structural transformation that will determine the future of the world's climate system.
>
> It will not be 'business as usual.' The global economy will grow by more than half, a billion more people will come to live in cities, and rapid technological advance will continue to change businesses and lives.
>
> Low-carbon and climate-resilient growth is possible.... What is needed is strong political leadership...
>
> [C]ountries across the world can reduce the risks of climate change and achieve high-quality, resilient, and inclusive economic growth."
>
> —From The New Climate Economy, *Better Growth, Better Climate,* 2014

17. **Writing Activity: Write an Argument** Consider the economic, political, and environmental challenges facing the world today. Which of these challenges do you think is most serious? Cite evidence from the text to support your argument. Based on that evidence, explain what policies you think would be the best response to that challenge.

18. **Connections to Today** Consider how science and technology have improved lives in recent years. What new benefits might science and technology bring to people's lives in the near future?

DOCUMENT-BASED QUESTIONS

For many scientists, politicians, and citizens, energy consumption is a troubling issue. Intense debate surrounds the question of which alternate energy sources we should use. Read the documents below, then answer the questions that follow.

DOCUMENT A

U.S. Energy Consumption by Source, 2018

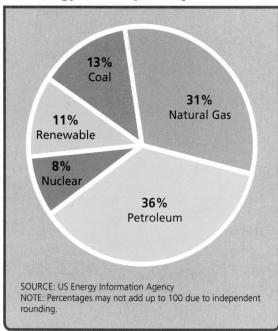

13%
Coal

31%
Natural Gas

11%
Renewable

8%
Nuclear

36%
Petroleum

SOURCE: US Energy Information Agency
NOTE: Percentages may not add up to 100 due to independent rounding.

DOCUMENT B

"As we approach the end of the twentieth century there is no single thing we can do that will have as large an impact on the people of the world during the new century than the development of solar power satellites. They will bring prosperity, an opportunity for the poor nations of the earth to achieve true freedom from want, healing of our environment, and open the vast new frontier of space to all of us.

… With the develoment of solar power satellites we will tap directly into the power of the sun and save the world from impending chaos. There will be hope for the future as we enter the twenty-first century."

—*Sun Power by Ralph Nansen*

DOCUMENT C

"Renewables are not without their drawbacks. Solar and wind farms cannot generate much electricity on cloudy or still days. As intermittent energy sources, they require vast systems to store the energy they produce, or must rely on the rest of the electrical system for backup. And despite federal subsidies to spur technological innovation, renewable sources have not become economical enough to seriously challenge fossil fuels in an open market."

—*CQ Researcher, November 7, 1997*

19. Which document is supported by the actual U.S. energy consumption data shown in Document A?
   A. Document B
   B. Document C
   C. both Documents B and C
   D. neither Document B nor C

20. Which statement best describes the viewpoint of the author of Document B?
   A. Biomass generators are a better alternative to fossil fuel than solar powered satellites.
   B. Solar powered satellites are the most promising alternative to fossil fuel.
   C. Solar powered satellites are not realistic or cost effective as an alternative to fossil fuel.
   D. More research must be carried out to determine whether solar powered satellites are a realistic alternative to fossil fuel.

21. According to Document C, all are drawbacks of renewables except which of the following?
   A. They are intermittent energy sources.
   B. They are not cost-efficient.
   C. They rely on traditional electricity sources.
   D. They are worse for the environment.

22. **Writing Tasks** What does our energy future look like? Make some predictions for the next 50 years. Use information from these documents along with information from the Topic to support your predictions.

Stock Connection Blue/Alamy

Constitution Quick Study Guide

Amendments

1st Amendment:	**Freedom of Religion, Speech, Press, Assembly, and Petition**
2nd Amendment:	**Right to Keep, Bear Arms**
3rd Amendment:	**Lodging Troops in Private Homes**
4th Amendment:	**Search, Seizures, Proper Warrants**
5th Amendment:	**Criminal Proceedings, Due Process, Eminent Domain**
6th Amendment:	**Criminal Proceedings**
7th Amendment:	**Jury Trials in Civil Cases**
8th Amendment:	**Bail; Cruel, Unusual Punishment**
9th Amendment:	**Unenumerated Rights**
10th Amendment:	**Powers Reserved to the States**
11th Amendment:	**Suits Against the States**
12th Amendment:	**Election of President and Vice President**
13th Amendment:	**Slavery and Involuntary Servitude**
Section 1.	Slavery and Involuntary Servitude Prohibited
Section 2.	Power of Congress
14th Amendment:	**Rights of Citizens**
Section 1.	Citizenship; Privileges and Immunities; Due Process; Equal Protection
Section 2.	Apportionment of Representation
Section 3.	Disqualification of Officers
Section 4.	Public Debt
Section 5.	Powers of Congress
15th Amendment:	**Right to Vote—Race, Color, Servitude**
Section 1.	Suffrage Not to Be Abridged
Section 2.	Power of Congress
16th Amendment:	**Income Tax**
17th Amendment:	**Popular Election of Senators**
Section 1.	Popular Election of Senators
Section 2.	Senate Vacancies
Section 3.	Inapplicable to Senators Previously Chosen
18th Amendment:	**Prohibition of Intoxicating Liquors**
Section 1.	Intoxicating Liquors Prohibited
Section 2.	Concurrent Power to Enforce
Section 3.	Time Limit on Ratification
19th Amendment:	**Equal Suffrage—Sex**
Section 1.	Suffrage Not to Be Abridged
Section 2.	Power of Congress
20th Amendment:	**Commencement of Terms; Sessions of Congress; Death or Disqualification of President-Elect**
Section 1.	Terms of President, Vice President, members of Congress
Section 2.	Sessions of Congress
Section 3.	Death or Disqualification of President-Elect
Section 4.	Congress to Provide for Certain Successors
Section 5.	Effective Date
Section 6.	Time Limit on Ratification
21st Amendment:	**Repeal of 18th Amendment**
Section 1.	Repeal of Prohibition
Section 2.	Transportation, Importation of Intoxicating Liquors
Section 3.	Time Limit on Ratification
22nd Amendment:	**Presidential Tenure**
Section 1.	Restriction on Number of Terms
Section 2.	Time Limit on Ratification
23rd Amendment:	**Inclusion of District of Columbia in Presidential Election Systems**
Section 1.	Presidential Electors for District
Section 2.	Power of Congress
24th Amendment:	**Right to Vote in Federal Elections—Tax Payment**
Section 1.	Suffrage Not to Be Abridged
Section 2.	Power of Congress
25th Amendment:	**Presidential Succession; Vice Presidential Vacancy; Presidential Inability**
Section 1.	Presidential Succession
Section 2.	Vice Presidential Vacancy
Section 3.	Presidential Inability
26th Amendment:	**Right to Vote—Age**
Section 1.	Suffrage Not to Be Abridged
Section 2.	Power of Congress
27th Amendment:	**Congressional Pay**

The Preamble states the broad purposes the Constitution is intended to serve—to establish a government that provides for greater cooperation among the States, ensures justice and peace, provides for defense against foreign enemies, promotes the general well-being of the people, and secures liberty now and in the future. The phrase We the People emphasizes the twin concepts of popular sovereignty and of representative government.

Legislative Department

Section 1. Legislative power; Congress

Congress, the nation's lawmaking body, is bicameral in form; that is, it is composed of two houses: the Senate and the House of Representatives. The Framers of the Constitution purposely separated the lawmaking power from the power to enforce the laws (Article II, the Executive Branch) and the power to interpret them (Article III, the Judicial Branch). This system of separation of powers is supplemented by a system of checks and balances; that is, in several provisions the Constitution gives to each of the three branches various powers with which it may restrain the actions of the other two branches.

Section 2. House of Representatives

▶ **Clause 1. Election** Electors means voters. Members of the House of Representatives are elected every two years. Each State must permit the same persons to vote for United States representatives as it permits to vote for the members of the larger house of its own legislature. The 17th Amendment (1913) extends this requirement to the qualification of voters for United States senators.

▶ **Clause 2. Qualifications** A member of the House of Representatives must be at least 25 years old, an American citizen for seven years, and a resident of the State he or she represents. In addition, political custom requires that a representative also reside in the district from which he or she is elected.

▶ **Clause 3. Apportionment** The number of representatives each State is entitled to is based on its population, which is counted every 10 years in the census. Congress reapportions the seats among the States after each census. In the Reapportionment Act of 1929, Congress fixed the permanent size of the House at 435 members with each State having at least one representative. Today there is one House seat for approximately every 700,000 persons in the population.

The words "three-fifths of all other persons" referred to slaves and reflected the Three-Fifths Compromise reached by the Framers at Philadelphia in 1787; the phrase was made obsolete, was in effect repealed, by the 13th Amendment in 1865.

---

* The gray words indicate portions of the Constitution altered by subsequent amendments to the document.

▶ **Clause 4. Vacancies** The executive authority refers to the governor of a State. If a member leaves office or dies before the expiration of his or her term, the governor is to call a special election to fill the vacancy.

United States Constitution

PREAMBLE

We the People of the United States, in Order to form a more perfect Union, establish Justice, insure domestic Tranquility, provide for the common defence, promote the general Welfare, and secure the Blessings of Liberty to ourselves and our Posterity, do ordain and establish this Constitution for the United States of America.

Article I.

Section 1.

All legislative Powers herein granted shall be vested in a Congress of the United States, which shall consist of a Senate and House of Representatives.

Section 2.

▶ 1. The House of Representatives shall be composed of Members chosen every second Year by the People of the several States, and the Electors in each State shall have the Qualifications requisite for Electors of the most numerous Branch of the State Legislature.

▶ 2. No Person shall be a Representative who shall not have attained to the age of twenty-five Years, and been seven Years a Citizen of the United States, and who shall not, when elected, be an Inhabitant of that State in which he shall be chosen.

▶ 3. Representatives and direct Taxes* shall be apportioned among the several States which may be included within this Union, according to their respective Numbers, which shall be determined by adding to the whole Number of free Persons, including those bound to Service for a Term of Years and excluding Indians not taxed, three fifths of all other Persons. The actual Enumeration shall be made within three Years after the first Meeting of the Congress of the United States, and within every subsequent term of ten Years, in such Manner as they shall by Law direct. The Number of Representatives shall not exceed one for every thirty Thousand, but each State shall have at Least one Representative; and, until such enumeration shall be made, the State of New Hampshire shall be entitled to choose three, Massachusetts eight, Rhode Island and Providence Plantations one, Connecticut five, New York six, New Jersey four, Pennsylvania eight, Delaware one, Maryland six, Virginia ten, North Carolina five, South Carolina five, and Georgia three.

▶ 4. When vacancies happen in the Representation from any State, the Executive Authority thereof shall issue Writs of Election to fill such Vacancies.

5. The House of Representatives shall choose their Speaker and other Officers; and shall have the sole Power of Impeachment.

Section 3.

▶ 1. The Senate of the United States shall be composed of two Senators from each State chosen by the Legislature thereof for six Years; and each Senator shall have one Vote.

▶ 2. Immediately after they shall be assembled in Consequences of the first Election, they shall be divided, as equally as may be, into three Classes. The Seats of the Senators of the first Class shall be vacated at the Expiration of the second Year; of the second Class, at the Expiration of the fourth Year; and of the third Class, at the Expiration of the sixth Year; so that one-third may be chosen every second Year; and if Vacancies happen by Resignation, or otherwise, during the Recess of the Legislature of any State, the Executive thereof may make temporary Appointments until the next Meeting of the Legislature, which shall then fill such Vacancies.

▶ 3. No Person shall be a Senator who shall not have attained to the Age of thirty Years, and been nine Years a Citizen of the United States, and who shall not, when elected, be an Inhabitant of that State for which he shall be chosen.

▶ 4. The Vice President of the United States shall be President of the Senate but shall have no Vote, unless they be equally divided.

▶ 5. The Senate shall choose their other Officers, and also a President pro tempore, in the Absence of the Vice President, or when he shall exercise the Office of President of the United States.

▶ 6. The Senate shall have the sole Power to try all Impeachments. When sitting for that Purpose, they shall be on Oath or Affirmation. When the President of the United States is tried, the Chief Justice shall preside: And no Person shall be convicted without the Concurrence of two thirds of the Members present.

▶ 7. Judgment in Cases of Impeachment shall not extend further than to removal from Office, and disqualification to hold and enjoy any Office of honor, Trust, or Profit under the United States: but the Party convicted shall nevertheless be liable and subject to Indictment, Trial, Judgment and Punishment, according to Law.

▶ **Clause 5.** **Officers; impeachment** The House elects a Speaker, customarily chosen from the majority party in the House. Impeachment means accusation. The House has the exclusive power to impeach, or accuse, civil officers; the Senate (Article I, Section 3, Clause 6) has the exclusive power to try those impeached by the House.

Section 3. Senate

▶ **Clause 1.** **Composition, election, term** Each State has two senators. Each serves for six years and has one vote. Originally, senators were not elected directly by the people, but by each State's legislature. The 17th Amendment, added in 1913, provides for the popular election of senators.

▶ **Clause 2.** **Classification** The senators elected in 1788 were divided into three groups so that the Senate could become a "continuing body." One-third of the Senate's seats are up for election every two years.

The 17th Amendment provides that a Senate vacancy is to be filled at a special election called by the governor; State law may also permit the governor to appoint a successor to serve until that election is held.

▶ **Clause 3.** **Qualifications** A senator must be at least 30 years old, a citizen for at least nine years, and must live in the State from which elected.

▶ **Clause 4.** **Presiding officer** The Vice President presides over the Senate, but may vote only to break a tie.

▶ **Clause 5.** **Other officers** The Senate chooses its own officers, including a president pro tempore to preside when the Vice President is not there.

▶ **Clause 6.** **Impeachment trials** The Senate conducts the trials of those officials impeached by the House. The Vice President presides unless the President is on trial, in which case the Chief Justice of the United States does so. A conviction requires the votes of two-thirds of the senators present.

No President has ever been convicted. In 1868 the House voted eleven articles of impeachment against President Andrew Johnson, but the Senate fell one vote short of convicting him. In 1974 President Richard M. Nixon resigned the presidency in the face of almost certain impeachment by the House. The House brought two articles of impeachment against President Bill Clinton in late 1998. Neither charge was supported by even a simple majority vote in the Senate, on February 12, 1999.

▶ **Clause 7.** **Penalty on conviction** The punishment of an official convicted in an impeachment case has always been removal from office. The Senate can also bar a convicted person from ever holding any federal office, but it is not required to do so. A convicted person can also be tried and punished in a regular court for any crime involved in the impeachment case.

Section 4. Elections and Meetings

▶ **Clause 1.** **Election In 1842** Congress required that representatives be elected from districts within each State with more than one seat in the House. The districts in each State are drawn by that State's legislature. Seven States now have only one seat in the House: Alaska, Delaware, Montana, North Dakota, South Dakota, Vermont, and Wyoming. The 1842 law also directed that representatives be elected in each State on the same day: the Tuesday after the first Monday in November of every even-numbered year. In 1914 Congress also set that same date for the election of senators.

▶ **Clause 2.** **Sessions Congress** must meet at least once a year. The 20th Amendment (1933) changed the opening date to January 3.

Section 5. Legislative Proceedings

▶ **Clause 1.** **Admission of members; quorum** In 1969 the Supreme Court held that the House cannot exclude any member-elect who satisfies the qualifications set out in Article I, Section 2, Clause 2.

A majority in the House (218 members) or Senate (51) constitutes a quorum. In practice, both houses often proceed with less than a quorum present. However, any member may raise a point of order (demand a "quorum call"). If a roll call then reveals less than a majority of the members present, that chamber must either adjourn or the sergeant at arms must be ordered to round up absent members.

▶ **Clause 2.** **Rules** Each house has adopted detailed rules to guide its proceedings. Each house may discipline members for unacceptable conduct; expulsion requires a two-thirds vote.

▶ **Clause 3.** **Record** Each house must keep and publish a record of its meetings. The Congressional Record is published for every day that either house of Congress is in session, and provides a written record of all that is said and done on the floor of each house each session.

▶ **Clause 4.** **Adjournment** Once in session, neither house may suspend (recess) its work for more than three days without the approval of the other house. Both houses must always meet in the same location.

Section 4.

▶ 1. The Times, Places and Manner of holding Elections for Senators and Representatives, shall be prescribed in each State by the Legislature thereof; but the Congress may at any time by law make or alter such Regulations, except as to the Places of choosing Senators.

▶ 2. The Congress shall assemble at least once in every Year, and such Meeting shall be on the first Monday in December, unless they shall by Law appoint a different Day.

Section 5.

▶ 1. Each House shall be the Judge of the Elections, Returns and Qualifications of its own Members, and a Majority of each shall constitute a Quorum to do Business; but a smaller Number may adjourn from day to day, and may be authorized to compel the Attendance of absent Members, in such Manner, and under such Penalties, as each House may provide.

▶ 2. Each House may determine the Rules of its Proceedings, punish its Members for disorderly Behavior, and, with the Concurrence of two thirds, expel a Member.

▶ 3. Each House shall keep a Journal of its Proceedings, and from time to time publish the same, excepting such Parts as may in their Judgment require Secrecy; and the Yeas and Nays of the Members of either House on any question shall, at the Desire of one fifth of those Present, be entered on the Journal.

▶ 4. Neither House, during the Session of Congress, shall, without the Consent of the other, adjourn for more than three days, nor to any other Place than that in which the two Houses shall be sitting.

Section 6.

▶ 1. The Senators and Representatives shall receive a Compensation for their Services, to be ascertained by Law, and paid out of the Treasury of the United States. They shall in all Cases, except Treason, Felony, and Breach of the Peace, be privileged from Arrest during their Attendance at the Session of their respective Houses, and in going to and returning from the same; and for any Speech or Debate in either House, they shall not be questioned in any other Place.

▶ 2. No Senator or Representative shall, during the Time for which he was elected, be appointed to any civil Office under the Authority of the United States, which shall have been created, or the Emoluments whereof shall have been increased during such time; and no Person holding any Office under the United States, shall be a Member of either House during his Continuance in Office.

Section 7.

▶ 1. All Bills for raising Revenue shall originate in the House of Representatives; but the Senate may propose or concur with amendments as on other Bills.

▶ 2. Every Bill which shall have passed the House of Representatives and the Senate, shall, before it become a law, be presented to the President of the United States: If he approve, he shall sign it, but if not he shall return it, with his Objections to that House in which it shall have originated, who shall enter the Objections at large on their Journal, and proceed to reconsider it. If after such Reconsideration two thirds of the House shall agree to pass the Bill, it shall be sent, together with the Objections, to the other House, by which it shall likewise be reconsidered, and if approved by two thirds of that House, it shall become a Law. But in all such Cases the Votes of both Houses shall be determined by Yeas and Nays, and the Names of the Persons voting for and against the Bill shall be entered on the Journal of each House respectively. If any Bill shall not be returned by the President within ten Days (Sunday excepted) after it shall have been presented to him, the Same shall be a law, in like Manner as if he had signed it, unless the Congress by their Adjournment, prevent its Return, in which Case it shall not be a Law.

▶ 3. Every Order, Resolution, or Vote to which the Concurrence of the Senate and House of Representatives may be necessary (except on a question of adjournment) shall be presented to the President of the United States; and before the Same shall take Effect, shall be approved by him, or, being disapproved by him, shall be repassed by two thirds of the Senate and House of Representatives, according to the Rules and Limitations prescribed in the Case of a Bill.

Section 6. Compensation, Immunities, and Disabilities of Members

▶ **Clause 1.** **Salaries; immunities** Each house sets its members' salaries, paid by the United States; the 27th Amendment (1992) modified this pay-setting power. This provision establishes "legislative immunity." The purpose of this immunity is to allow members to speak and debate freely in Congress itself. Treason is strictly defined in Article III, Section 3. A felony is any serious crime. A breach of the peace is any indictable offense less than treason or a felony; this exemption from arrest is of little real importance today.

▶ **Clause 2.** **Restrictions on office holding** No sitting member of either house may be appointed to an office in the executive or in the judicial branch if that position was created or its salary was increased during that member's current elected term. The second part of this clause—forbidding any person serving in either the executive or the judicial branch from also serving in Congress—reinforces the principle of separation of powers.

Section 7. Revenue Bills, President's Veto

▶ **Clause 1.** **Revenue bills** All bills that raise money must originate in the House. However, the Senate has the power to amend any revenue bill sent to it from the lower house.

▶ **Clause 2.** **Enactment of laws; veto** Once both houses have passed a bill, it must be sent to the President. The President may (1) sign the bill, thus making it law; (2) veto the bill, whereupon it must be returned to the house in which it originated; or (3) allow the bill to become law without signature, by not acting upon it within 10 days of its receipt from Congress, not counting Sundays. The President has a fourth option at the end of a congressional session: If he does not act on a measure within 10 days, and Congress adjourns during that period, the bill dies; the "pocket veto" has been applied to it. A presidential veto may be overridden by a two-thirds vote in each house.

▶ **Clause 3.** **Other measures** This clause refers to joint resolutions, measures Congress often passes to deal with unusual, temporary, or ceremonial matters. A joint resolution passed by Congress and signed by the President has the force of law, just as a bill does. As a matter of custom, a joint resolution proposing an amendment to the Constitution is not submitted to the President for signature or veto. Concurrent and simple resolutions do not have the force of law and, therefore, are not submitted to the President.

Section 8. Powers of Congress

▶ **Clause 1.** The 18 separate clauses in this section set out 27 of the many expressed powers the Constitution grants to Congress. In this clause Congress is given the power to levy and provide for the collection of various kinds of taxes, in order to finance the operations of the government. All federal taxes must be levied at the same rates throughout the country.

▶ **Clause 2.** Congress has power to borrow money to help finance the government. Federal borrowing is most often done through the sale of bonds on which interest is paid. The Constitution does not limit the amount the government may borrow.

▶ **Clause 3.** This clause, the Commerce Clause, gives Congress the power to regulate both foreign and interstate trade. Much of what Congress does, it does on the basis of its commerce power.

▶ **Clause 4.** Congress has the exclusive power to determine how aliens may become citizens of the United States. Congress may also pass laws relating to bankruptcy.

▶ **Clause 5.** has the power to establish and require the use of uniform gauges of time, distance, weight, volume, area, and the like.

▶ **Clause 6.** Congress has the power to make it a federal crime to falsify the coins, paper money, bonds, stamps, and the like of the United States.

▶ **Clause 7.** Congress has the power to provide for and regulate the transportation and delivery of mail; "post offices" are those buildings and other places where mail is deposited for dispatch; "post roads" include all routes over or upon which mail is carried.

▶ **Clause 8.** Congress has the power to provide for copyrights and patents. A copyright gives an author or composer the exclusive right to control the reproduction, publication, and sale of literary, musical, or other creative work. A patent gives a person the exclusive right to control the manufacture or sale of his or her invention.

▶ **Clause 9.** Congress has the power to create the lower federal courts, all of the several federal courts that function beneath the Supreme Court.

▶ **Clause 10.** Congress has the power to prohibit, as a federal crime: (1) certain acts committed outside the territorial jurisdiction of the United States, and (2) the commission within the United States of any wrong against any nation with which we are at peace.

Section 8.

The Congress shall have Power

▶ 1. To lay and collect Taxes, Duties, Imposts and Excises to pay the Debts and provide for the common Defence and general Welfare of the United States; but all Duties, Imposts and Excises, shall be uniform throughout the United States;

▶ 2. To borrow Money on the credit of the United States;

▶ 3. To regulate Commerce with foreign Nations, and among the several States, and with the Indian Tribes;

▶ 4. To establish an uniform Rule of Naturalization, and uniform Laws on the subject of Bankruptcies throughout the United States;

▶ 5. To coin Money, regulate the Value thereof, and of foreign Coin, and fix the Standard of Weights and Measures;

▶ 6. To provide for the Punishment of counterfeiting the Securities and current Coin of the United States;

▶ 7. To establish Post Offices and post Roads;

▶ 8. To promote the Progress of Science and useful Arts, by securing, for limited Times to Authors and Inventors the exclusive Right to their respective Writings and Discoveries;

▶ 9. To constitute Tribunals inferior to the supreme Court;

▶ 10. To define and punish Piracies and Felonies committed on the high Seas, and Offences against the Law of nations;

11. To declare War, grant Letters of Marque and Reprisal, and make Rules concerning Captures on Land and Water;

12. To raise and support Armies; but no Appropriation of Money to that Use shall be for a longer Term than two Years;
13. To provide and maintain a Navy;

14. To make Rules for the Government and Regulation of the land and naval Forces;

15. To provide for calling forth the Militia to execute the Laws of the Union, suppress Insurrections and repel Invasions;
16. To provide for organizing, arming, and disciplining the Militia, and for governing such Part of them as may be employed in the Service of the United States, reserving to the States respectively the Appointment of the Officers, and the Authority of training the Militia according to the discipline prescribed by Congress;

17. To exercise exclusive Legislation in all Cases whatsoever, over such District (not exceeding ten Miles square) as may, by Cession of Particular States, and the Acceptance of Congress, become the Seat of the Government of the United States, and to exercise like Authority over all Places purchased by the Consent of the Legislature of the State in which the Same shall be, for the Erection of Forts, Magazines, Arsenals, Dockyards and other needful Buildings;—And
18. To make all Laws which shall be necessary and proper for carrying into Execution the foregoing Powers and all other Powers vested by this Constitution in the Government of the United States, or in any Department or Officer thereof.

Section 9.
1. The Migration or Importation of such Persons as any of the States now existing shall think proper to admit, shall not be prohibited by the Congress prior to the Year one thousand eight hundred and eight, but a Tax or duty may be imposed on such Importation, not exceeding ten dollars for each Person.

▶ **Clause 11.** Only Congress can declare war. However, the President, as commander in chief of the armed forces (Article II, Section 2, Clause 1), can make war without such a formal declaration. Letters of marque and reprisal are commissions authorizing private persons to outfit vessels (privateers) to capture and destroy enemy ships in time of war; they were forbidden in international law by the Declaration of Paris of 1856, and the United States has honored the ban since the Civil War.

▶ **Clauses 12 and 13.** Congress has the power to provide for and maintain the nation's armed forces. It established the air force as an independent element of the armed forces in 1947, an exercise of its inherent powers in foreign relations and national defense. The two-year limit on spending for the army insures civilian control of the military.

▶ **Clause 14.** Today these rules are set out in three principle statutes: the Uniform Code of Military Justice, passed by Congress in 1950, and the Military Justice Acts of 1958 and 1983.

▶ **Clauses 15 and 16.** In the National Defense Act of 1916, Congress made each State's militia (volunteer army) a part of the National Guard. Today, Congress and the States cooperate in its maintenance. Ordinarily, each State's National Guard is under the command of that State's governor; but Congress has given the President the power to call any or all of those units into federal service when necessary.

▶ **Clause 17.** In 1791 Congress accepted land grants from Maryland and Virginia and established the District of Columbia for the nation's capital. Assuming Virginia's grant would never be needed, Congress returned it in 1846. Today, the elected government of the District's 69 square miles operates under the authority of Congress. Congress also has the power to acquire other lands from the States for various federal purposes.

▶ **Clause 18.** This is the Necessary and Proper Clause, also often called the Elastic Clause. It is the constitutional basis for the many and far-reaching implied powers of the Federal Government.

Section 9. Powers Denied to Congress
▶ **Clause 1.** The phrase "such persons" referred to slaves. This provision was part of the Commerce Compromise, one of the bargains struck in the writing of the Constitution. Congress outlawed the slave trade in 1808.

► **Clause 2.** A writ of habeas corpus, the "great writ of liberty," is a court order directing a sheriff, warden, or other public officer, or a private person, who is detaining another to "produce the body" of the one being held in order that the legality of the detention may be determined by the court.

► **Clause 3.** A bill of attainder is a legislative act that inflicts punishment without a judicial trial. See Article I, Section 10, and Article III, Section 3, Clause 2. An ex post facto law is any criminal law that operates retroactively to the disadvantage of the accused. See Article I, Section 10.

► **Clause 4.** A capitation tax is literally a "head tax," a tax levied on each person in the population. A direct tax is one paid directly to the government by the taxpayer—for example, an income or a property tax; an indirect tax is one paid to another private party who then pays it to the government—for example, a sales tax. This provision was modified by the 16th Amendment (1913), giving Congress the power to levy "taxes on incomes, from whatever source derived."

► **Clause 5.** This provision was a part of the Commerce Compromise made by the Framers in 1787. Congress has the power to tax imported goods, however.

► **Clause 6.** All ports within the United States must be treated alike by Congress as it exercises its taxing and commerce powers. Congress cannot tax goods sent by water from one State to another, nor may it give the ports of one State any legal advantage over those of another.

► **Clause 7.** This clause gives Congress its vastly important "power of the purse," a major check on presidential power. Federal money can be spent only in those amounts and for those purposes expressly authorized by an act of Congress. All federal income and spending must be accounted for, regularly and publicly.

► **Clause 8.** This provision, preventing the establishment of a nobility, reflects the principle that "all men are created equal." It was also intended to discourage foreign attempts to bribe or otherwise corrupt officers of the government.

Section 10. Powers Denied to the States

► **Clause 1.** The States are not sovereign governments and so cannot make agreements or otherwise negotiate with foreign states; the power to conduct foreign relations is an exclusive power of the National Government. The power to coin money is also an exclusive power of the National Government. Several powers forbidden to the National Government are here also forbidden to the States.

► **Clause 2.** This provision relates to foreign, not interstate, commerce. Only Congress, not the States, can tax imports; and the States are, like Congress, forbidden the power to tax exports.

► 2. The Privilege of the Writ of Habeas Corpus shall not be suspended, unless when in Cases of Rebellion or Invasion the public safety may require it.

► 3. No Bill of Attainder or ex post facto Law shall be passed.

► 4. No Capitation, or other direct, Tax shall be laid, unless in Proportion to the Census of Enumeration hereinbefore directed to be taken.

► 5. No Tax or Duty shall be laid on Articles exported from any State.

► 6. No Preference shall be given by any Regulation of Commerce or Revenue to the Ports of one State over those of another: nor shall Vessels bound to, or from, one State, be obliged to enter, clear or pay Duties in another.

► 7. No Money shall be drawn from the Treasury, but in Consequence of Appropriations made by Law; and a regular Statement and Account of the Receipts and Expenditures of all public Money shall be published from time to time.

► 8. No Title of Nobility shall be granted by the United States: And no Person holding any Office of Profit or Trust under them, shall, without the Consent of the Congress, accept of any present, Emolument, Office, or Title, of any kind whatever, from any King, Prince, or foreign State.

Section 10.

► 1. No State shall enter into any Treaty, Alliance, or Confederation; grant Letters of Marque and Reprisal; coin Money; emit Bills of Credit; make any Thing but gold and silver Coin a Tender in Payment of Debts; pass any Bill of Attainder, ex post facto Law, or Law impairing the Obligation of Contracts, or grant any Title of Nobility.

► 2. No State shall, without the Consent of the Congress, lay any Imposts or Duties on Imports or Exports, except what may be absolutely necessary for executing its inspection Laws; and the net Produce of all Duties and Imposts, laid by any State on Imports or Exports, shall be for the Use of the Treasury of the United States; and all such Laws shall be subject to the Revision and Control of the Congress.

▶ 3. No State shall, without the Consent of Congress, lay any Duty of Tonnage, keep Troops, or Ships of War in time of Peace, enter into any Agreement or Compact with another State, or with a foreign Power, or engage in War, unless actually invaded, or in such imminent Danger as will not admit of delay.

Article II

Section 1.

▶ 1. The executive Power shall be vested in a President of the United States of America. He shall hold his Office during the Term of four Years, and, together with the Vice President, chosen for the same Term, be elected as follows:

▶ 2. Each State shall appoint, in such Manner as the Legislature thereof may direct, a Number of Electors, equal to the whole Number of Senators and Representatives to which the State may be entitled in the Congress: but no Senator or Representative, or Person holding an Office of Trust or Profit, under the United States, shall be appointed an Elector.

▶ 3. The Electors shall meet in their respective States, and vote by Ballot for two Persons, of whom one at least shall not be an Inhabitant of the same State with themselves. And they shall make a List of all the Persons voted for, and of the Number of Votes for each; which List they shall sign and certify, and transmit sealed to the Seat of the Government of the United States, directed to the President of the Senate. The President of the Senate shall, in the Presence of the Senate and House of Representatives, open all the Certificates, and the Votes shall then be counted. The Person having the greatest Number of Votes shall be the President, if such Number be a majority of the whole Number of Electors appointed; and if there be more than one who have such Majority, and have an equal Number of Votes, then, the House of Representatives shall immediately choose by Ballot one of them for President; and if no Person have a Majority, then from the five highest on the List the said House shall in like Manner choose the President. But in choosing the President, the Votes shall be taken by States, the Representatives from each State having one Vote; a quorum for this Purpose shall consist of a Member or Members from two thirds of the States, and a Majority of all the States shall be necessary to a Choice. In every Case, after the Choice of the President, the Person having the greatest Number of Votes of the Electors shall be the Vice President. But if there should remain two or more who have equal Votes, the Senate shall choose from them by Ballot the Vice President.

Clause 3. A duty of tonnage is a tax laid on ships according to their cargo capacity. Each State has a constitutional right to provide for and maintain a militia; but no State may keep a standing army or navy. The several restrictions here prevent the States from assuming powers that the Constitution elsewhere grants to the National Government.

Executive Department

Section 1. President and Vice President

▶ **Clause 1. Executive power, term** This clause gives to the President the very broad "executive power," the power to enforce the laws and otherwise administer the public policies of the United States. It also sets the length of the presidential (and vice-presidential) term of office; see the 22nd Amendment (1951), which places a limit on presidential (but not vice-presidential) tenure.

▶ **Clause 2. Electoral college** This clause establishes the "electoral college," although the Constitution does not use that term. It is a body of presidential electors chosen in each State, and it selects the President and Vice President every four years. The number of electors chosen in each State equals the number of senators and representatives that State has in Congress.

▶ **Clause 3. Election of President and Vice President** This clause was replaced by the 12th Amendment in 1804.

Clause 4. Date Congress has set the date for the choosing of electors as the Tuesday after the first Monday in November every fourth year, and for the casting of electoral votes as the Monday after the second Wednesday in December of that year.

Clause 5. Qualifications The President must have been born a citizen of the United States, be at least 35 years old, and have been a resident of the United States for at least 14 years.

Clause 6. Vacancy This clause was modified by the 25th Amendment (1967), which provides expressly for the succession of the Vice President, for the filling of a vacancy in the Vice Presidency, and for the determination of presidential inability.

Clause 7. Compensation The President now receives a salary of $400,000 and a taxable expense account of $50,000 a year. Those amounts cannot be changed during a presidential term; thus, Congress cannot use the President's compensation as a bargaining tool to influence executive decisions. The phrase "any other emolument" means, in effect, any valuable gift; it does not mean that the President cannot be provided with such benefits of office as the White House, extensive staff assistance, and much else.

Clause 8. Oath of office The Chief Justice of the United States regularly administers this oath or affirmation, but any judicial officer may do so. Thus, Calvin Coolidge was sworn into office in 1923 by his father, a justice of the peace in Vermont.

Section 2. President's Powers and Duties

Clause 1. Military, civil powers The President, a civilian, heads the nation's armed forces, a key element in the Constitution's insistence on civilian control of the military. The President's power to "require the opinion, in writing" provides the constitutional basis for the Cabinet. The President's power to grant reprieves and pardons, the power of clemency, extends only to federal cases.

▶4. The Congress may determine the Time of choosing the Electors, and the Day on which they shall give their Votes; which Day shall be the same throughout the United States.

▶5. No Person except a natural born Citizen, or a Citizen of the United States, at the time of the Adoption of this Constitution, shall be eligible to the Office of President; neither shall any person be eligible to that Office who shall not have attained to the Age of thirty-five Years, and been fourteen Years a Resident within the United States.

▶6. In Case of the Removal of the President from Office, or of his Death, Resignation, or Inability to discharge the Powers and Duties of the said Office, the Same shall devolve on the Vice President, and the Congress may by Law provide for the Case of Removal, Death, Resignation or Inability, both of the President and Vice President, declaring what Officer shall then act as President, and such Officer shall act accordingly, until the Disability be removed, or a President shall be elected.

▶7. The President shall, at stated Times, receive for his Services, a Compensation, which shall neither be increased nor diminished during the Period for which he shall have been elected, and he shall not receive within that Period any other Emolument from the United States, or any of them.

▶8. Before he enter on the Execution of his Office, he shall take the following Oath or Affirmation:
"I do solemnly swear (or affirm) that I will faithfully execute the Office of President of the United States, and will to the best of my Ability, preserve, protect and defend the Constitution of the United States."

Section 2.

▶1. The President shall be Commander in Chief of the Army and Navy of the United States, and of the Militia of the several States, when called into the actual Service of the United States; he may require the Opinion, in writing, of the principal Officer in each of the executive Departments, upon any Subject relating to the Duties of their respective Offices, and he shall have Power to Grant Reprieves and Pardons for Offences against the United States, except in Cases of Impeachment.

2. He shall have Power, by and with the Advice and Consent of the Senate, to make Treaties, provided two thirds of the Senators present concur; and he shall nominate, and by and with the Advice and Consent of the Senate, shall appoint Ambassadors, other public Ministers and Consuls, Judges of the supreme Court, and all other Officers of the United States, whose Appointments are not herein otherwise provided for, and which shall be established by Law: but the Congress may by Law vest the Appointment of such inferior Officers, as they think proper, in the President alone, in the Courts of Law, or in the Heads of Departments.

3. The President shall have Power to fill up all Vacancies that may happen during the Recess of the Senate, by granting Commissions which shall expire at the End of their next Session.

Section 3.

He shall from time to time give to the Congress Information of the State of the Union, and recommend to their Consideration such Measures as he shall judge necessary and expedient; he may, on extraordinary Occasions, convene both Houses, or either of them, and in Case of Disagreement between them, with Respect to the Time of Adjournment, he may adjourn them to such Time as he shall think proper; he shall receive Ambassadors and other public Ministers; he shall take Care that the Laws be faithfully executed, and shall Commission all the Officers of the United States.

Section 4.

The President, Vice President and all Civil Officers of the United States, shall be removed from Office on Impeachment for and Conviction of, Treason, Bribery, or other high Crimes and Misdemeanors.

Article III
Section 1.

The judicial Power of the United States, shall be vested in one supreme Court, and in such inferior Courts as the Congress may from time to time ordain and establish. The Judges, both of the supreme and inferior Courts, shall hold their Offices during good Behaviour, and shall, at stated Times, receive for their Services, a Compensation, which shall not be diminished during their Continuance in Office.

▶ **Clause 2. Treaties, appointments** The President has the sole power to make treaties; to become effective, a treaty must be approved by a two-thirds vote in the Senate. In practice, the President can also make executive agreements with foreign governments; these pacts, which are frequently made and usually deal with routine matters, do not require Senate consent. The President appoints the principal officers of the executive branch and all federal judges; the "inferior officers" are those who hold lesser posts.

▶ **Clause 3. Recess appointments** When the Senate is not in session, appointments that require Senate consent can be made by the President on a temporary basis, as "recess appointments." Recess appointments are valid only to the end of the congressional term in which they are made.

Section 3. President's Powers and Duties

The President delivers a State of the Union Message to Congress soon after that body convenes each year. That message is delivered to the nation's lawmakers and, importantly, to the American people, as well. It is shortly followed by the proposed federal budget and an economic report; and the President may send special messages to Congress at any time. In all of these communications, Congress is urged to take those actions the Chief Executive finds to be in the national interest. The President also has the power: to call special sessions of Congress; to adjourn Congress if its two houses cannot agree for that purpose; to receive the diplomatic representatives of other governments; to insure the proper execution of all federal laws; and to empower federal officers to hold their posts and perform their duties.

Section 4. Impeachment

The Constitution outlines the impeachment process in Article I, Section 2, Clause 5 and in Section 3, Clauses 6 and 7.

Judicial Department
Section 1. Judicial Power, Courts, Terms of Office

The judicial power conferred here is the power of federal courts to hear and decide cases, disputes between the government and individuals and between private persons (parties). The Constitution creates only the Supreme Court of the United States; it gives to Congress the power to establish other, lower federal courts (Article I, Section 8, Clause 9) and to fix the size of the Supreme Court. The words "during good Behaviour" mean, in effect, for life.

Section 2. Jurisdiction

▶ **Clause 1. Cases to be heard** This clause sets out the jurisdiction of the federal courts; that is, it identifies those cases that may be tried in those courts. The federal courts can hear and decide—have jurisdiction over—a case depending on either the subject matter or the parties involved in that case. The jurisdiction of the federal courts in cases involving States was substantially restricted by the 11th Amendment in 1795.

▶ **Clause 2. Supreme Court jurisdiction** Original jurisdiction refers to the power of a court to hear a case in the first instance, not on appeal from a lower court. Appellate jurisdiction refers to a court's power to hear a case on appeal from a lower court, from the court in which the case was originally tried. This clause gives the Supreme Court both original and appellate jurisdiction. However, nearly all of the cases the High Court hears are brought to it on appeal from the lower federal courts and the highest State courts.

▶ **Clause 3. Jury trial in criminal cases** A person accused of a federal crime is guaranteed the right to trial by jury in a federal court in the State where the crime was committed; see the 5th and 6th amendments. The right to trial by jury in serious criminal cases in the State courts is guaranteed by the 6th and 14th amendments.

Section 3. Treason

▶ **Clause 1. Definition** Treason is the only crime defined in the Constitution. The Framers intended the very specific definition here to prevent the loose use of the charge of treason—for example, against persons who criticize the government. Treason can be committed only in time of war and only by a citizen or a resident alien.

▶ **Clause 2. Punishment** Congress has provided that the punishment that a federal court may impose on a convicted traitor may range from a minimum of five years in prison and/or a $10,000 fine to a maximum of death; no person convicted of treason has ever been executed by the United States. No legal punishment can be imposed on the family or descendants of a convicted traitor. Congress has also made it a crime for any person (in either peace or wartime) to commit espionage or sabotage, to attempt to overthrow the government by force, or to conspire to do any of these things.

Section 2.

▶ 1. The judicial Power shall extend to all Cases, in Law and Equity, arising under this Constitution, the Laws of the United States, and Treaties made, or which shall be made, under their Authority;— to all Cases affecting Ambassadors, other public ministers, and Consuls;— to all Cases of Admiralty and maritime Jurisdiction;— to Controversies to which the United States shall be a Party;— to Controversies between two or more States;— between a State and Citizens of another State;— between Citizens of different States;— between Citizens of the same State claiming Lands under Grants of different States, and between a State, or the Citizens thereof, and foreign States, Citizens, or Subjects.

▶ 2. In all Cases affecting Ambassadors, other public Ministers and Consuls, and those in which a State shall be a Party, the supreme Court shall have original Jurisdiction. In all the other Cases before mentioned, the supreme Court shall have appellate Jurisdiction, both as to Law and Fact, with such Exceptions, and under such Regulations as the Congress shall make.

▶ 3. The trial of all Crimes, except in Cases of Impeachment, shall be by Jury; and such Trial shall be held in the State where the said Crimes shall have been committed; but when not committed within any State, the Trial shall be at such Place or Places as the Congress may by Law have directed.

Section 3.

▶ 1. Treason against the United States shall consist only in levying War against them, or in adhering to their Enemies, giving them Aid and Comfort. No Person shall be convicted of Treason unless on the Testimony of two Witnesses to the same overt Act, or on Confession in open Court.

▶ 2. The Congress shall have Power to declare the Punishment of Treason, but no Attainder of Treason shall work Corruption of Blood, or Forfeiture except during the Life of the Person attainted.

Article IV

Section 1.

Full Faith and Credit shall be given in each State to the public Acts, Records, and judicial Proceedings of every other State. And the Congress may by general Laws prescribe the Manner in which such Acts, Records and Proceedings shall be proved, and the Effect thereof.

Section 2.

▶ 1. The Citizens of each State shall be entitled to all Privileges and Immunities of Citizens in the several States.

▶ 2. A Person charged in any State with Treason, Felony, or other Crime, who shall flee from justice, and be found in another State, shall on Demand of the executive Authority of the State from which he fled, be delivered up, to be removed to the State having Jurisdiction of the Crime.

▶ 3. No Person held to Service or Labor in one State, under the Laws thereof, escaping into another, shall, in Consequence of any Law or Regulation therein, be discharged from Service or Labor, but shall be delivered up on Claim of the Party to whom such Service or Labor may be due.

Section 3.

▶ 1. New States may be admitted by the Congress into this Union; but no new State shall be formed or erected within the Jurisdiction of any other State; nor any State be formed by the Junction of two or more States, or Parts of States, without the Consent of the Legislatures of the States concerned as well as of the Congress.

▶ 2. The Congress shall have Power to dispose of and make all needful Rules and Regulations respecting the Territory or other Property belonging to the United States; and nothing in this Constitution shall be so construed as to Prejudice any Claims of the United States, or of any particular State.

Section 4.

The United States shall guarantee to every State in this Union a Republican Form of Government, and shall protect each of them against Invasion; and on Application of the Legislature, or of the Executive (when the Legislature cannot be convened) against domestic Violence.

Relations Among States

Section 1. Full Faith and Credit

Each State must recognize the validity of the laws, public records, and court decisions of every other State.

Section 2. Privileges and Immunities of Citizens

▶ **Clause 1.** **Residents of other States** In effect, this clause means that no State may discriminate against the residents of other States; that is, a State's laws cannot draw unreasonable distinctions between its own residents and those of any of the other States. See Section 1 of the 14th Amendment.

▶ **Clause 2.** **Extradition** The process of returning a fugitive to another State is known as "interstate rendition" or, more commonly, "extradition." Usually, that process works routinely; some extradition requests are contested however—especially in cases with racial or political overtones. A governor may refuse to extradite a fugitive; but the federal courts can compel an unwilling governor to obey this constitutional command.

▶ **Clause 3.** **African Americans seeking freedom from enslavement** This clause was nullified by the 13th Amendment, which abolished slavery in 1865.

Section 3. New States; Territories

▶ **Clause 1.** **New States** Only Congress can admit new States to the Union. A new State may not be created by taking territory from an existing State without the consent of that State's legislature. Congress has admitted 37 States since the original 13 formed the Union. Five States—Vermont, Kentucky, Tennessee, Maine, and West Virginia— were created from parts of existing States. Texas was an independent republic before admission. California was admitted after being ceded to the United States by Mexico. Each of the other 30 States entered the Union only after a period of time as an organized territory of the United States.

▶ **Clause 2.** **Territory, property** Congress has the power to make laws concerning the territories, other public lands, and all other property of the United States.

Section 4. Protection Afforded to States by the Nation

The Constitution does not define "a republican form of government," but the phrase is generally understood to mean a representative government. The Federal Government must also defend each State against attacks from outside its border and, at the request of a State's legislature or its governor, aid its efforts to put down internal disorders.

Provisions for Amendment

This section provides for the methods by which formal changes can be made in the Constitution. An amendment may be proposed in one of two ways: by a two-thirds vote in each house of Congress, or by a national convention called by Congress at the request of two-thirds of the State legislatures. A proposed amendment may be ratified in one of two ways: by three-fourths of the State legislatures, or by three-fourths of the States in conventions called for that purpose. Congress has the power to determine the method by which a proposed amendment may be ratified. The amendment process cannot be used to deny any State its equal representation in the United States Senate. To this point, 27 amendments have been adopted. To date, all of the amendments except the 21st Amendment were proposed by Congress and ratified by the State legislatures. Only the 21st Amendment was ratified by the convention method.

National Debts, Supremacy of National Law, Oath

Section 1. Validity of Debts

Congress had borrowed large sums of money during the Revolution and later during the Critical Period of the 1780s. This provision, a pledge that the new government would honor those debts, did much to create confidence in that government.

Section 2. Supremacy of National Law

This section sets out the Supremacy Clause, a specific declaration of the supremacy of federal law over any and all forms of State law. No State, including its local governments, may make or enforce any law that conflicts with any provision in the Constitution, an act of Congress, a treaty, or an order, rule, or regulation properly issued by the President or his subordinates in the executive branch.

Section 3. Oaths of Office

This provision reinforces the Supremacy Clause; all public officers, at every level in the United States, owe their first allegiance to the Constitution of the United States. No religious qualification can be imposed as a condition for holding any public office.

Ratification of Constitution

The proposed Constitution was signed by George Washington and 37 of his fellow Framers on September 17, 1787. (George Read of Delaware signed for himself and also for his absent colleague, John Dickinson.)

Article V

The Congress, whenever two thirds of both Houses shall deem it necessary, shall propose Amendments to this Constitution, or, on the Application of the Legislatures of two thirds of the several States, shall call a Convention for proposing Amendments, which, in either Case, shall be valid to all Intents and Purposes, as Part of this Constitution, when ratified by the Legislatures of three fourths of the several States, or by Conventions in three fourths thereof, as the one or the other Mode of Ratification may be proposed by the Congress; Provided that no Amendment which may be made prior to the Year One thousand eight hundred and eight shall in any Manner affect the first and fourth Clauses in the Ninth section of the first Article; and that no State, without its Consent, shall be deprived of its equal Suffrage in the Senate.

Article VI

Section 1.

All Debts contracted and Engagements entered into, before the Adoption of this Constitution, shall be as valid against the United States under this Constitution, as under the Confederation.

Section 2.

This Constitution, and the Laws of the United States which shall be made in Pursuance thereof; and all Treaties made, or which shall be made, under the Authority of the United States, shall be the supreme Law of the Land; and the Judges in every State shall be bound thereby, anything in the constitution or Laws of any State to the Contrary notwithstanding.

Section 3.

The Senators and Representatives before mentioned, and the Members of the several State legislatures, and all executive and judicial Officers, both of the United States and of the several States, shall be bound by Oath or Affirmation, to support this Constitution; but no religious Test shall ever be required as a Qualification to any Office or public Trust under the United States.

Article VII

The ratification of the Conventions of nine States, shall be sufficient for the Establishment of this Constitution between the States so ratifying the same.

Done in Convention by the Unanimous Consent of the States present the Seventeenth Day of September in the Year of our Lord one thousand seven hundred and Eighty-seven and of the Independence of the United States of America the twelfth. In witness whereof We have hereunto subscribed our Names.

Attest:
William Jackson,
Secretary
George Washington,
President and Deputy
from Virginia

New Hampshire
John Langdon
Nicholas Gilman

Massachusetts
Nathaniel Gorham
Rufus King

Connecticut
William Samuel Johnson
Roger Sherman

New York
Alexander Hamilton

New Jersey
William Livingston
David Brearley
William Paterson
Jonathan Dayton

Pennsylvania
Benjamin Franklin
Thomas Mifflin
Robert Morris
George Clymer
Thomas Fitzsimons
Jared Ingersoll
James Wilson
Gouverneur Morris

Delaware
George Read
Gunning Bedford, Jr.
John Dickinson
Richard Bassett
Jacob Broom

Maryland
James McHenry
Daniel of St. Thomas
Jenifer
Daniel Carroll

Virginia
John Blair
James Madison, Jr.

North Carolina
William Blount
Richard Dobbs Spaight
Hugh Williamson

South Carolina
John Rutledge
Charles Cotesworth
Pinckney
Charles Pinckney
Pierce Butler

Georgia
William Few
Abraham Baldwin

The first 10 amendments, the Bill of Rights, were each proposed by Congress on September 25, 1789, and ratified by the necessary three-fourths of the States on December 15, 1791. These amendments were originally intended to restrict the National Government—not the States. However, the Supreme Court has several times held that most of their provisions also apply to the States, through the 14th Amendment's Due Process Clause.

1st Amendment. Freedom of Religion, Speech, Press, Assembly, and Petition

The 1st Amendment sets out five basic liberties: The guarantee of freedom of religion is both a protection of religious thought and practice and a command of separation of church and state. The guarantees of freedom of speech and press assure to all persons a right to speak, publish, and otherwise express their views. The guarantees of the rights of assembly and petition protect the right to join with others in public meetings, political parties, interest groups, and other associations to discuss public affairs and influence public policy. None of these rights is guaranteed in absolute terms, however; like all other civil rights guarantees, each of them may be exercised only with regard to the rights of all other persons.

2nd Amendment. Bearing Arms

The right of the people to keep and bear arms was insured by the 2nd Amendment.

3rd Amendment. Quartering of Troops

This amendment was intended to prevent what had been common British practice in the colonial period; see the Declaration of Independence. This provision is of virtually no importance today.

4th Amendment. Searches and Seizures

The basic rule laid down by the 4th Amendment is this: Police officers have no general right to search for or seize evidence or seize (arrest) persons. Except in particular circumstances, they must have a proper warrant (a court order) obtained with probable cause (on reasonable grounds). This guarantee is reinforced by the exclusionary rule, developed by the Supreme Court: Evidence gained as the result of an unlawful search or seizure cannot be used at the court trial of the person from whom it was seized.

5th Amendment. Criminal Proceedings; Due Process; Eminent Domain

A person can be tried for a serious federal crime only if he or she has been indicted (charged, accused of that crime) by a grand jury. No one may be subjected to double jeopardy—that is, tried twice for the same crime. All persons are protected against self-incrimination; no person can be legally compelled to answer any question in any governmental proceeding if that answer could lead to that person's prosecution. The 5th Amendment's Due Process Clause prohibits unfair, arbitrary actions by the Federal Government; a like prohibition is set out against the States in the 14th Amendment. Government may take private property for a legitimate public purpose; but when it exercises that power of eminent domain, it must pay a fair price for the property seized.

1st Amendment

Congress shall make no law respecting an establishment of religion, or prohibiting the free exercise thereof, or abridging the freedom of speech, or of the press; or the right of the people peaceably to assemble, and to petition the Government for a redress of grievances.

2nd Amendment

A well-regulated Militia being necessary to the security of a free State, the right of the people to keep and bear Arms, shall not be infringed.

3rd Amendment.

No Soldier shall, in time of peace be quartered in any house, without the consent of the Owner, nor, in time of war, but in a manner to be prescribed by law.

4th Amendment.

The right of the people to be secure in their persons, houses, papers, and effects, against unreasonable searches and seizures, shall not be violated, and no Warrants shall issue, but upon probable cause, supported by Oath or affirmation, and particularly describing the place to be searched, and the persons or things to be seized.

5th Amendment.

No person shall be held to answer for a capital, or otherwise infamous crime, unless on a presentment or indictment of a Grand Jury, except in cases arising in the land or naval forces, or in the Militia, when in actual service in time of War, or public danger; nor shall any person be subject for the same offence to be twice put in jeopardy of life or limb; nor shall be compelled in any criminal case to be a witness against himself, nor be deprived of life, liberty, or property, without due process of law; nor shall private property be taken for public use, without just compensation.

6th Amendment

In all criminal prosecutions, the accused shall enjoy the right to a speedy and public trial, by an impartial jury of the State and district wherein the crime shall have been committed, which district shall have been previously ascertained by law, and to be informed of the nature and cause of the accusation; to be confronted with the witnesses against him; to have compulsory process for obtaining witnesses in his favor, and to have the Assistance of Counsel for his defence.

7th Amendment

In Suits at common law, where the value in controversy shall exceed twenty dollars, the right of trial by jury shall be preserved, and no fact tried by a jury, shall be otherwise re-examined in any Court of the United States, than according to the rules of the common law.

8th Amendment

Excessive bail shall not be required, nor excessive fines imposed, nor cruel and unusual punishment inflicted.

9th Amendment

The enumeration in the Constitution, of certain rights, shall not be construed to deny or disparage others retained by the people.

10th Amendment

The powers not delegated to the United States by the Constitution, nor prohibited by it to the States, are reserved to the States respectively, or to the people.

6th Amendment. Criminal Proceedings

A person accused of crime has the right to be tried in court without undue delay and by an impartial jury; see Article III, Section 2, Clause 3. The defendant must be informed of the charge upon which he or she is to be tried, has the right to cross-examine hostile witnesses, and has the right to require the testimony of favorable witnesses. The defendant also has the right to be represented by an attorney at every stage in the criminal process.

7th Amendment. Civil Trials

This amendment applies only to civil cases heard in federal courts. A civil case does not involve criminal matters; it is a dispute between private parties or between the government and a private party. The right to trial by jury is guaranteed in any civil case in a federal court if the amount of money involved in that case exceeds $20 (most cases today involve a much larger sum); that right may be waived (relinquished, put aside) if both parties agree to a bench trial (a trial by a judge, without a jury).

8th Amendment. Punishment for Crimes

Bail is the sum of money that a person accused of crime may be required to post (deposit with the court) as a guarantee that he or she will appear in court at the proper time. The amount of bail required and/or a fine imposed as punishment must bear a reasonable relationship to the seriousness of the crime involved in the case. The prohibition of cruel and unusual punishment forbids any punishment judged to be too harsh, too severe for the crime for which it is imposed.

9th Amendment. Unenumerated Rights

The fact that the Constitution sets out many civil rights guarantees, expressly provides for many protections against government, does not mean that there are not other rights also held by the people.

10th Amendment. Powers Reserved to the States

This amendment identifies the area of power that may be exercised by the States. All of those powers the Constitution does not grant to the National Government, and at the same time does not forbid to the States, belong to each of the States, or to the people of each State.

11th Amendment. Suits Against States

Proposed by Congress March 4, 1794; ratified February 7, 1795, but official announcement of the ratification was delayed until January 8, 1798. This amendment repealed part of Article III, Section 2, Clause 1. No State may be sued in a federal court by a resident of another State or of a foreign country; the Supreme Court has long held that this provision also means that a State cannot be sued in a federal court by a foreign country or, more importantly, even by one of its own residents.

12th Amendment. Election of President and Vice President

Proposed by Congress December 9, 1803; ratified June 15, 1804. This amendment replaced Article II, Section 1, Clause 3. Originally, each elector cast two ballots, each for a different person for President. The person with the largest number of electoral votes, provided that number was a majority of the electors, was to become President; the person with the second highest number was to become Vice President. This arrangement produced an electoral vote tie between Thomas Jefferson and Aaron Burr in 1800; the House finally chose Jefferson as President in 1801. The 12th Amendment separated the balloting for President and Vice President; each elector now casts one ballot for someone as President and a second ballot for another person as Vice President. Note that the 20th Amendment changed the date set here (March 4) to January 20, and that the 23rd Amendment (1961) provides for electors from the District of Columbia. This amendment also provides that the Vice President must meet the same qualifications as those set out for the President in Article II, Section 1, Clause 5.

13th Amendment. Slavery and Involuntary Servitude

Proposed by Congress January 31, 1865; ratified December 6, 1865. This amendment forbids slavery in the United States and in any area under its control. It also forbids other forms of forced labor, except punishments for crime; but some forms of compulsory service are not prohibited—for example, service on juries or in the armed forces. Section 2 gives to Congress the power to carry out the provisions of Section 1 of this amendment.

11th Amendment

The Judicial power of the United States shall not be construed to extend to any suit in law or equity, commenced or prosecuted against one of the United States by Citizens of another State, or by Citizens or Subjects of any Foreign State.

12th Amendment

The Electors shall meet in their respective States and vote by ballot for President and Vice President, one of whom, at least, shall not be an inhabitant of the same State with themselves; they shall name in their ballots the person voted for as President, and in distinct ballots the person voted for as Vice President, and they shall make distinct lists of all persons voted for as President, and of all persons voted for as Vice President, and of the number of votes for each, which lists they shall sign and certify, and transmit sealed to the seat of the government of the United States, directed to the President of the Senate;— The President of the Senate shall, in the presence of the Senate and the House of Representatives, open all the certificates and the votes shall then be counted;— the person having the greatest Number of votes for President shall be the President, if such number be a majority of the whole number of Electors appointed; and if no person have such a majority, then, from the persons having the highest numbers not exceeding three on the list of those voted for as President, the House of Representatives shall choose immediately, by ballot, the President. But in choosing the President, the votes shall be taken by States, the representation from each State having one vote; a quorum for this purpose shall consist of a member or members from two thirds of the States, and a majority of all the States shall be necessary to a choice. And if the House of Representatives shall not choose a President whenever the right of choice shall devolve upon them, before the fourth day of March next following, then the Vice President shall act as President, as in case of death or other constitutional disability of the President. The person having the greatest number of votes as Vice President, shall be the Vice President, if such number be a majority of the whole number of Electors appointed, and if no person have a majority, then from the two highest numbers on the list, the Senate shall choose the Vice President; a quorum for the purpose shall consist of two thirds of the whole number of Senators, a majority of the whole number shall be necessary to a choice. But no person constitutionally ineligible to the office of President shall be eligible to that of Vice-President of the United States.

13th Amendment

Section 1. Neither slavery nor involuntary servitude, except as a punishment for crime whereof the party shall have been duly convicted, shall exist within the United States, or any place subject to their jurisdiction.

Section 2. Congress shall have power to enforce this article by appropriate legislation.

14th Amendment

Section 1. All persons born or naturalized in the United States and subject to the jurisdiction thereof, are citizens of the United States and of the State wherein they reside. No State shall make or enforce any law which shall abridge the privileges or immunities of citizens of the United States; nor shall any State deprive any person of life, liberty, or property, without due process of law; nor deny to any person within its jurisdiction the equal protection of the laws.

Section 2. Representatives shall be apportioned among the several States according to their respective numbers, counting the whole number of persons in each State, excluding Indians not taxed. But when the right to vote at any election for the choice of electors for President and Vice President of the United States, Representatives in Congress, the Executive and Judicial officers of a State, or the members of the Legislature thereof, is denied to any of the male inhabitants of such State, being twenty-one years of age and citizens of the United States, or in any way abridged, except for participation in rebellion, or other crime, the basis of representation therein shall be reduced in the proportion which the number of such male citizens shall bear to the whole number of male citizens twenty-one years of age in such State.

Section 3. No person shall be a Senator or Representative in Congress, or elector of President and Vice President, or hold any office, civil or military, under the United States, or under any State, who, having previously taken an oath, as a member of Congress, or as an officer of the United States, or as a member of any State legislature, or as an executive or judicial officer of any State, to support the Constitution of the United States, shall have engaged in insurrection or rebellion against the same, or given aid or comfort to the enemies thereof. But Congress may, by a vote of two thirds of each House, remove such disability.

Section 4. The validity of the public debt of the United States, authorized by law, including debts incurred for payment of pensions and bounties for services in suppressing insurrection or rebellion, shall not be questioned. But neither the United States nor any State shall assume or pay any debt or obligation incurred in aid of insurrection or rebellion against the United States, or any claim for the loss or emancipation of any slave; but all such debts, obligations and claims shall be held illegal and void.

Section 5. The Congress shall have power to enforce, by appropriate legislation, the provisions of this article.

14th Amendment. Rights of Citizens

Proposed by Congress June 13, 1866; ratified July 9, 1868. Section 1 defines citizenship. It provides for the acquisition of United States citizenship by birth or by naturalization. Citizenship at birth is determined according to the principle of jus soli—"the law of the soil," where born; naturalization is the legal process by which one acquires a new citizenship at some time after birth. Under certain circumstances, citizenship can also be gained at birth abroad, according to the principle of jus sanguinis—"the law of the blood," to whom born. This section also contains two major civil rights provisions: the Due Process Clause forbids a State (and its local governments) to act in any unfair or arbitrary way; the Equal Protection Clause forbids a State (and its local governments) to discriminate against, draw unreasonable distinctions between, persons.

Most of the rights set out against the National Government in the first eight amendments have been extended against the States (and their local governments) through Supreme Court decisions involving the 14th Amendment's Due Process Clause.

The first sentence here replaced Article I, Section 2, Clause 3, the Three-Fifths Compromise provision. Essentially, all persons in the United States are counted in each decennial census, the basis for the distribution of House seats. The balance of this section has never been enforced and is generally thought to be obsolete.

This section limited the President's power to pardon those persons who had led the Confederacy during the Civil War. Congress finally removed this disability in 1898.

Section 4 also dealt with matters directly related to the Civil War. It reaffirmed the public debt of the United States; but it invalidated, prohibited payment of, any debt contracted by the Confederate States and also prohibited any compensation of former slave owners.

15th Amendment. Right to Vote— Race, Color, Servitude

Proposed by Congress February 26, 1869; ratified February 3, 1870. The phrase "previous condition of servitude" refers to slavery. Note that this amendment does not guarantee the right to vote to African Americans, or to anyone else. Instead, it forbids the States from discriminating against any person on the grounds of his "race, color, or previous condition of servitude" in the setting of suffrage qualifications.

16th Amendment. Income Tax

Proposed by Congress July 12, 1909; ratified February 3, 1913. This amendment modified two provisions in Article I, Section 2, Clause 3, and Section 9, Clause 4. It gives to Congress the power to levy an income tax, a direct tax, without regard to the populations of any of the States.

17th Amendment. Popular Election of Senators

Proposed by Congress May 13, 1912; ratified April 8, 1913. This amendment repealed those portions of Article I, Section 3, Clauses 1 and 2 relating to the election of senators. Senators are now elected by the voters in each State. If a vacancy occurs, the governor of the State involved must call an election to fill the seat; the governor may appoint a senator to serve until the next election, if the State's legislature has authorized that step.

18th Amendment. Prohibition of Intoxicating Liquors

Proposed by Congress December 18, 1917; ratified January 16, 1919. This amendment outlawed the making, selling, transporting, importing, or exporting of alcoholic beverages in the United States. It was repealed in its entirety by the 21st Amendment in 1933.

19th Amendment. Equal Suffrage—Sex

Proposed by Congress June 4, 1919; ratified August 18, 1920. No person can be denied the right to vote in any election in the United States on account of his or her sex.

15th Amendment

Section 1. The right of citizens of the United States to vote shall not be denied or abridged by the United States or by any State on account of race, color, or previous condition of servitude.

Section 2. The Congress shall have power to enforce this article by appropriate legislation.

16th Amendment

The Congress shall have power to lay and collect taxes on incomes, from whatever source derived, without apportionment among the several States, and without regard to any census or enumeration.

17th Amendment

The Senate of the United States shall be composed of two Senators from each State, elected by the people thereof, for six years; and each Senator shall have one vote. The electors in each State shall have the qualifications requisite for electors of the most numerous branch of the State legislatures.

When vacancies happen in the representation of any State in the Senate, the executive authority of such State shall issue writs of election to fill such vacancies: Provided, That the legislature of any State may empower the executive thereof to make temporary appointments until the people fill the vacancies by election as the legislature may direct.

This amendment shall not be so construed as to affect the election or term of any Senator chosen before it becomes valid as part of the Constitution.

18th Amendment.

Section 1. After one year from the ratification of this article the manufacture, sale, or transportation of intoxicating liquors within, the importation thereof into, or the exportation thereof from the United States and all territory subject to the jurisdiction thereof for beverage purposes is hereby prohibited.

Section 2. The Congress and the several States shall have concurrent power to enforce this article by appropriate legislation.

Section 3. This article shall be inoperative unless it shall have been ratified as an amendment to the Constitution by the legislatures of the several States, as provided in the Constitution, within seven years of the date of the submission hereof to the States by Congress.

19th Amendment

The right of citizens of the United States to vote shall not be denied or abridged by the United States or by any State on account of sex.

Congress shall have power to enforce this article by appropriate legislation.

20th Amendment

Section 1. The terms of the President and Vice President shall end at noon on the 20th day of January, and the terms of Senators and Representatives at noon on the 3d day of January, of the years in which such terms would have ended if this article had not been ratified; and the terms of their successors shall then begin.

Section 2. The Congress shall assemble at least once in every year, and such meeting shall begin at noon on the 3d day of January, unless they shall by law appoint a different day.

Section 3. If, at the time fixed for the beginning of the term of the President, the President elect shall have died, the Vice President elect shall become President. If a President shall not have been chosen before the time fixed for the beginning of his term, or if the President-elect shall have failed to qualify, then the Vice President elect shall act as President until a President shall have qualified; and the Congress may by law provide for the case wherein neither a President elect nor a Vice President elect shall have qualified, declaring who shall then act as President, or the manner in which one who is to act shall be selected, and such person shall act accordingly until a President or Vice President shall have qualified.

Section 4. The Congress may by law provide for the case of the death of any of the persons from whom the House of Representatives may choose a President whenever the right of choice shall have devolved upon them, and for the case of the death of any of the persons from whom the Senate may choose a Vice President whenever the right of choice shall have devolved upon them.

Section 5. Sections 1 and 2 shall take effect on the 15th day of October following the ratification of this article.

Section 6. This article shall be inoperative unless it shall have been ratified as an amendment to the Constitution by the legislatures of three fourths of the several States within seven years from the date of its submission.

21st Amendment

Section 1. The eighteenth article of amendment to the Constitution of the United States is hereby repealed.

Section 2. The transportation or importation into any State, Territory, or possession of the United States for delivery or use therein of intoxicating liquors, in violation of the laws thereof, is hereby prohibited.

Section 3. This article shall be inoperative unless it shall have been ratified as an amendment to the Constitution by conventions in the several States, as provided in the Constitution, within seven years from the date of the submission hereof to the States by the Congress.

20th Amendment. Commencement of Terms; Sessions of Congress; Death or Disqualification of President-Elect

Proposed by Congress March 2, 1932; ratified January 23, 1933. The provisions of Sections 1 and 2 relating to Congress modified Article I, Section 4, Clause 2, and those provisions relating to the President, the 12th Amendment. The date on which the President and Vice President now take office was moved from March 4 to January 20. Similarly, the members of Congress now begin their terms on January 3. The 20th Amendment is sometimes called the "Lame Duck Amendment" because it shortened the period of time a member of Congress who was defeated for reelection (a "lame duck") remains in office.

This section deals with certain possibilities that were not covered by the presidential selection provisions of either Article II or the 12th Amendment. To this point, none of these situations has occurred. Note that there is neither a President-elect nor a Vice President-elect until the electoral votes have been counted by Congress, or, if the electoral college cannot decide the matter, the House has chosen a President or the Senate has chosen a Vice President.

Congress has not in fact ever passed such a law. See Section 2 of the 25th Amendment, regarding a vacancy in the vice presidency; that provision could some day have an impact here.

Section 5 set the date on which this amendment came into force.

Section 6 placed a time limit on the ratification process; note that a similar provision was written into the 18th, 21st, and 22nd amendments.

21st Amendment. Repeal of 18th Amendment

Proposed by Congress February 20, 1933; ratified December 5, 1933. This amendment repealed all of the 18th Amendment. Section 2 modifies the scope of the Federal Government's commerce power set out in Article I, Section 8, Clause 3; it gives to each State the power to regulate the transportation or importation and the distribution or use of intoxicating liquors in ways that would be unconstitutional in the case of any other commodity. The 21st Amendment is the only amendment Congress has thus far submitted to the States for ratification by conventions.

22nd Amendment. Presidential Tenure

Proposed by Congress March 21, 1947; ratified February 27, 1951. This amendment modified Article II, Section I, Clause 1. It stipulates that no President may serve more than two elected terms. But a President who has succeeded to the office beyond the midpoint in a term to which another President was originally elected may serve for more than eight years. In any case, however, a President may not serve more than 10 years. Prior to Franklin Roosevelt, who was elected to four terms, no President had served more than two full terms in office.

23rd Amendment. Presidential Electors for the District of Columbia

Proposed by Congress June 16, 1960; ratified March 29, 1961. This amendment modified Article II, Section I, Clause 2 and the 12th Amendment. It included the voters of the District of Columbia in the presidential electorate; and provides that the District is to have the same number of electors as the least populous State—three electors—but no more than that number.

24th Amendment. Right to Vote in Federal Elections—Tax Payment

Proposed by Congress August 27, 1962; ratified January 23, 1964. This amendment outlawed the payment of any tax as a condition for taking part in the nomination or election of any federal officeholder.

25th Amendment. Presidential Succession, Vice Presidential Vacancy, Presidential Inability

Proposed by Congress July 6, 1965; ratified February 10, 1967. Section 1 revised the imprecise provision on presidential succession in Article II, Section 1, Clause 6. It affirmed the precedent set by Vice President John Tyler, who became President on the death of William Henry Harrison in 1841. Section 2 provides for the filling of a vacancy in the office of Vice President. The office had been vacant on 16 occasions and remained unfilled for the rest of each term involved. When Spiro Agnew resigned the office in 1973, President Nixon selected Gerald Ford per this provision; and, when President Nixon resigned in 1974, Gerald Ford became President and chose Nelson Rockefeller as Vice President.

22nd Amendment

Section 1. No person shall be elected to the office of the President more than twice, and no person who has held the office of President, or acted as President, for more than two years of a term to which some other person was elected President shall be elected to the office of the President more than once. But this Article shall not apply to any person holding the office of President, when this Article was proposed by the Congress, and shall not prevent any person who may be holding the office of President, or acting as President, during the term within which this Article becomes operative from holding the office of President or acting as President during the remainder of such term.

Section 2. This article shall be inoperative unless it shall have been ratified as an amendment to the Constitution by the legislatures of three fourths of the several states within seven years from the date of its submission to the States by the Congress.

23rd Amendment.

Section 1. The District constituting the seat of Government of the United States shall appoint in such manner as the Congress may direct:

A number of electors of President and Vice President equal to the whole number of Senators and Representatives in Congress to which the District would be entitled if it were a State, but in no event more than the least populous State; they shall be in addition to those appointed by the States, they shall be considered, for the purposes of the election of President and Vice President, to be electors appointed by a State; and they shall meet in the District and perform such duties as provided by the twelfth article of amendment.

24th Amendment.

Section 1. The right of citizens of the United States to vote in any primary or other election for President or Vice President, for electors for President or Vice President, or for Senator or Representative in Congress, shall not be denied or abridged by the United States or any State by reason of failure to pay any poll tax or other tax.

Section 2. The Congress shall have power to enforce this article by appropriate legislation.

25th Amendment.

Section 1. In case of the removal of the President from office or of his death or resignation, the Vice President shall become President.

Section 2. Whenever there is a vacancy in the office of the Vice President, the President shall nominate a Vice President who shall take office upon confirmation by a majority vote of both Houses of Congress.

Section 3. Whenever the President transmits to the President pro tempore of the Senate and the Speaker of the House of Representatives his written declaration that he is unable to discharge the powers and duties of his office, and until he transmits to them a written declaration to the contrary, such powers and duties shall be discharged by the Vice President as Acting President.

Section 4. Whenever the Vice President and a majority of either the principal officers of the executive departments or of such other body as Congress may by law provide, transmit to the President pro tempore of the Senate and the Speaker of the House of Representatives their written declaration that the President is unable to discharge the powers and duties of his office, the Vice President shall immediately assume the powers and duties of the office as Acting President.

Thereafter, when the President transmits to the President pro tempore of the Senate and the Speaker of the House of Representatives his written declaration that no inability exists, he shall resume the powers and duties of his office unless the Vice President and a majority of either the principal officers of the executive department or of such other body as Congress may by law provide, transmit within four days to the President pro tempore of the Senate and the Speaker of the House of Representatives their written declaration that the President is unable to discharge the powers and duties of his office. Thereupon Congress shall decide the issue, assembling within forty-eight hours for that purpose if not in session. If the Congress, within twenty-one days after receipt of the latter written declaration, or, if Congress is not in session, within twenty-one days after Congress is required to assemble, determines by two-thirds vote of both Houses that the President is unable to discharge the powers and duties of his office, the Vice President shall continue to discharge the same as Acting President; otherwise, the President shall resume the powers and duties of his office.

This section created a procedure for determining if a President is so incapacitated that he cannot perform the powers and duties of his office.

Section 4 deals with the circumstance in which a President will not be able to determine the fact of incapacity. To this point, Congress has not established the "such other body" referred to here. This section contains the only typographical error in the Constitution; in its second paragraph, the word "department" should in fact read "departments."

26th Amendment.

Section 1. The right of citizens of the United States, who are eighteen years of age or older, to vote shall not be denied or abridged by the United States or by any State on account of age.

Section 2. The Congress shall have the power to enforce this article by appropriate legislation.

27th Amendment.

No law varying the compensation for the services of the Senators and Representatives, shall take effect, until an election of Representatives shall have intervened.

26th Amendment. Right to Vote—Age

Proposed by Congress March 23, 1971; ratified July 1, 1971. This amendment provides that the minimum age for voting in any election in the United States cannot be more than 18 years. (A State may set a minimum voting age of less than 18, however.)

27th Amendment. Congressional Pay

Proposed by Congress September 25, 1789; ratified May 7, 1992. This amendment modified Article I, Section 6, Clause 1. It limits Congress's power to fix the salaries of its members—by delaying the effectiveness of any increase in that pay until after the next regular congressional election.

Use the texts, quizzes, interactivities, Quest Inquiries, Flipped Videos, and other resources from this Topic to prepare for the Topic Test.

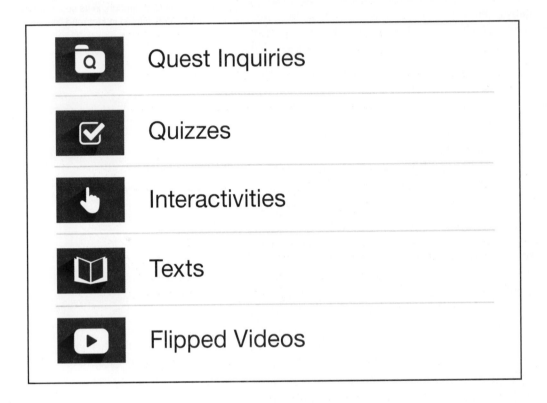

	Quest Inquiries
	Quizzes
	Interactivities
	Texts
	Flipped Videos

While online you can also check the progress you've made learning the topic and course content by viewing your grades, test scores, and assignment status.

Sequence

Sequence means "order," and placing things in the correct order is very important. What would happen if you tried to put toppings on a pizza before you put down the dough for the crust? When studying history, you need to analyze the information by sequencing significant events, individuals, and time periods in order to understand them. Practice this skill by using the reading below. Which words indicate sequence?

> **The Persian Empire** Before modern times, Iran was called Persia. Ancient Persia was influenced by Mesopotamian civilization, in modern-day Iraq. Around 550 B.C., the Persian king Cyrus the Great conquered the Babylonian empire, in Mesopotamia, and many other lands. He created the Persian empire.
>
> Cyrus and the rulers who followed him spread Persian control from modern Pakistan and Afghanistan in the east to modern Turkey, Cyprus, and Egypt in the west. This empire lasted about two hundred years. A Persian ruler was called the King of Kings, or the Great King.

[**1.**] Identify the topic and the main events that relate to the topic. Quickly skim titles and headings to determine the topic of the passage. As you read the passage, write a list of significant events, individuals, or time periods related to the topic.

[**2.**] Note any dates and time words such as "before" and "after" that indicate the chronological order of events. Look through your list of events, individuals, or time periods and write down the date for each. This will give you information to apply absolute chronology by sequencing the events, individuals, or time periods. Remember that some events may have taken place over a number of months or years. Is your date the time when the event started or ended? Make sure to note enough details that you can remember the importance of the information. If no date is given, look for words such as "before" or "after" that can tell you where to place this event, time period, or individual compared to others on your list. This will allow you to apply relative chronology by sequencing the events, individuals, or time periods.

[**3.**] Determine the time range of the events. Place the events in chronological order on a timeline. Look for the earliest and latest events, individuals, or time periods on your list. The span of time between the first and last entries gives you the time range. To apply absolute chronology, sequence the entries by writing the date of the first event on the left side of a piece of paper and the date of the last event on the right side. Draw a line connecting the two events. This will be your timeline. Once you have drawn your timeline, put the events in order by date along the line. Label their dates. To apply relative chronology, sequence the significant individuals, events, or time periods on an undated timeline, in the order that they happened. You now have a clear image of the important events related to this topic. You can organize and interpret information from visuals by analyzing the information and applying absolute or relative chronology to the events. This will help you understand the topic better when you can see how events caused or led to other events. You will also be able to analyze information by developing connections between historical events over time.

Categorize

When you analyze information by categorizing, you create a system that helps you sort items into categories, or groups with shared characteristics, so that you can understand the information. Categorizing helps you see what groups of items have in common. What categories are shown on the chart below? Name at least one challenge you would list under each category. Then create your own chart following the steps below.

Foreign Policy Challenge	Economic Challenge

[1.] Identify similarities and differences among items you need to understand. You need to pay careful attention and sometimes do research to find the similarities and differences among the facts, topics, or objects that you need to understand. Scientists find groups, or categories, of related animals by analyzing the details of the animals' bodies. For example, insects with similar wings, legs, and mouthparts probably belong in the same category. Gather similar information about all the things you need to understand. For example, if you know the location of one thing, try to find the locations of all the things you are studying. If you have different types of information about your topics, you will not be able to group them easily.

[2.] Create a system to group items with common characteristics. Once you have gathered similar kinds of information on the items you need to understand, look for items that share characteristics or features. Create categories based on a feature shared by all of the facts, topics, or objects you need to understand. For example, if you have gathered information on the population and political systems of several countries, you could categorize them by the size of their population or their type of political system.

[**3.**] Identify similarities and differences in the topics, and draw conclusions about them. Look through your notes and analyze the ways in which your topics are similar and different. Usually, topics have both similarities and differences. Try to find patterns in these similarities and differences. For example, all the similarities between two countries might be related to climate, and all the differences might be related to economics. Draw conclusions based on these patterns. In this example, you might conclude that a country's economy does not depend on its climate. Identifying similarities and differences by comparing and contrasting two topics lets you draw conclusions that help you analyze both topics as well as other topics like them.

Identify Main Ideas and Details

You can analyze information in a selection by finding the main idea. A main idea is the most important point in a selection. Identifying the main idea will help you remember details, such as names, dates, and events, which should support the main idea. Practice this skill by reading the paragraph on this page. Find the main idea of this paragraph and the supporting details.

> During his first hundred days in office, which became known as the Hundred Days, Roosevelt proposed and Congress passed 15 major bills. These measures had three goals: relief, recovery, and reform. Roosevelt wanted to provide relief from the immediate hardships of the depression and achieve a long-term economic recovery. He also instituted reforms to prevent future depressions.

[**1.**] Scan titles, headings, and visuals before reading to see what the selection is about. Often, important ideas are included in titles, headings, and other special text. Special text may be primary sources, words that are highlighted, or ideas listed with bullet points. Also, take a look at visuals and captions. By analyzing these parts of the text, you should quickly get a sense of the main idea of the article.

[**2.**] Read the selection and then identify the main point of the selection, the point that the rest of the selection supports: this is the main idea. Read through the selection to identify the main idea. Sometimes, the main idea will be the first or second sentence of one of the first few paragraphs. Sometimes, it will be the last sentence of the first paragraph. Other times, no single sentence will tell you the main idea. You will have to come up with your own sentence answering the question, "What is the main point of this selection?"

[**3.**] Find details or statements within the selection that support or build on the main idea. Once you have identified the main idea, look for details that support the main idea. Many or most of the details should be related to the main idea. If you find that many of the details are not related to what you think is the main idea, you may not have identified the main idea correctly. Identify the main idea that the details in the selection support. Analyze the information in the text by finding the main idea and supporting details.

Summarize

When you analyze information by summarizing, you restate the main points of a passage in your own words. Using your own words helps you understand the information. Summarizing will help you understand a text and prepare for tests or assignments based on the text. Practice this skill by follow the steps to summarize the excerpt below.

> One of the most terrifying aspects of the Cold War was the arms race that began right after World War II. At first, the United States was the only nuclear power. By 1949, however, the Soviet Union had also developed nuclear weapons.
>
> Critics argued that a nuclear war would destroy both sides. Yet each superpower wanted to be able to deter the other from launching its nuclear weapons. Both sides engaged in a race to match each other's new weapons. The result was a "balance of terror." Mutually assured destruction—in which each side knew that the other side would itself be destroyed if it launched its weapons—discouraged nuclear war. Still, people around the world lived in constant fear of nuclear doom.

[**1.**] Identify and write down the main point of each paragraph in your own words. You may identify the main idea right at the beginning of each paragraph. In other cases, you will have to figure out the main idea. As you read each paragraph, ask yourself, "What is the point this paragraph makes?" The point the paragraph makes is the main idea. Write this idea down in your own words.

[**2.**] Use these main points to write a general statement of the overall main idea of the passage in your own words. Once you have written down the main idea for each paragraph, write down the main idea of the passage. Write the main idea in your own words. If you have trouble identifying the main idea of the passage, review the titles and headings in the passage. Often, titles and headings relate to the main idea. Also, the writer may state the main idea in the first paragraph of the passage. The main idea of a passage should answer the question, "What is the point this passage makes?"

[**3.**] Use this general statement as a topic sentence for your summary. Then, write a paragraph tying together the main points of the passage. Leave out unimportant details. Analyze the information in the passage by summarizing. Use the main idea of the passage as a topic sentence for your summary paragraph. Use the main ideas that you identified for each paragraph of the passage to write sentences supporting the main idea of the passage. Leave out details that are not needed to understand the main idea of the passage. Your summary should be in your own words, and it should be much shorter than the original passage. Once your summary is written, review it to make sure that it contains all the main points of the passage. If any are missing, revise your summary to include them. If the summary includes unimportant details, remove them.

Generalize

One good way to analyze materials about a particular subject is to make generalizations and predictions. What are the patterns and connections that link the different materials? What can you say about the different materials that is true of all them? Practice this skill by reading the following statements. What generalization can you make about how new thought and inventions change the economy and society?

- Beginning in the 1500s, profound changes took place in the sciences. These new understandings about the physical world became part of what is now called the Scientific Revolution. These startling discoveries radically changed the way Europeans viewed the physical world.

- The Industrial Revolution brought radical change to people's lives. Before industrialization, people lived in villages and farmed. The economy was based on farming and craftwork. By the late 1800s, the economy had shifted. Manufacturing by machine in factories and urbanization became commonplace.

- The invention of the computer in the twentieth century caused an unprecedented information revolution. It has helped spur development of the modern global economy and society. Few, if any, aspects of modern life remain untouched by computers.

[**1.**] Make a list. Listing all of the specific details and facts about a subject will help you find patterns and connections.

[**2.**] Generate a statement. From your list of facts and specific details, decide what most of the items listed have in common. Analyze your information by making generalizations and predictions.

[**3.**] Ensure your generalization is logical and well supported by facts. Generalizations can be valid or invalid. A generalization that is not logical or supported by facts is invalid.

Make Predictions

You can analyze information by making generalizations and predictions. Predictions are educated guesses about the future, based on clues you find in written material and information you already have. When you analyze information by making generalizations and predictions, you are thinking critically about the material you read. Practice this skill by analyzing the passage below and predicting the impact this epidemic might have on society and the economy.

> In the mid 1300s, a disease moved throughout Europe and North Africa. The bubonic plague, or Black Death, spread quickly. Boils erupted all over the body—a sign that the plague would likely claim more victims because the disease spread through contact. The plague brought terror and bewilderment, as people had no way to stop the disease. Entire villages were wiped out. It ravaged Europe: one in three people died.

[1.] Review the content. Read your material carefully and research any terms or concepts that are new to you. It's important to understand the material before analyzing the information to make a prediction.

[2.] Look for clues. Gathering evidence is an important part of making predictions. Look for important words, statements, and evidence that seem to support the writer's point of view. Ask questions about what you are reading, including who, what, where, when, why, and how. Look for and analyze clues to help you generalize and predict.

[3.] Consider what you already know. Use related prior knowledge and/or connect to your own experiences to help you make an informed prediction. If you have experience with the subject matter, you have a much better chance of making an accurate prediction.

[4.] Generate a list of predictions. After studying the content, list the clues you've found. Then use these clues, plus your prior knowledge, to form your predictions. List as many possible outcomes as you can based on clues in the material and the questions you have considered.

Draw Inferences

What is the author trying to tell you? To make a determination about the author's message, you analyze information by drawing inferences and conclusions. You consider details and descriptions included in the text, compare and contrast the text to prior knowledge you have about the subject, and then form a conclusion about the author's intent. Practice this skill by analyzing the primary source report below to infer the feelings of the crew towards Magellan.

> . . . Talking began amongst the crews about the old eternal hatred between the Portuguese and the Spaniards, and about Magellan's being a Portuguese. He, they said, could do nothing more glorious for his own country than to cast away this fleet, with so many men. Nor was it credible [believable] that he should wish to discover the Moluccas [a group of spice islands]. . . . Nor even had their course begun to turn towards those happy Moluccas, but rather to distant snow and ice, and to perpetual storms.
>
> Magellan, very much enraged by these sayings, punished the men, but rather more harshly than was proper for a foreigner, especially when commanding in a distant country.
> –Maximillianus Transylvanus, report to King Charles I of Spain

[1.] Study the image or text. Consider all of the details and descriptions included. What is the author trying to tell you? Look for context clues that hint at the topic and subject matter.

[2.] Make a connection. Use related prior knowledge to connect to the text or image. Analyze information by asking questions such as who, what, where, when, and how. Look for cause-and-effect relationships; compare and contrast. This strategy will help you think beyond the available surface details to understand what the author is suggesting or implying.

[**3.**] Form a conclusion. When you draw an inference, you combine your own ideas with evidence and details you found within the text or image to form a new conclusion. This action leads you to a new understanding of the material.

Draw Conclusions

When you analyze information by drawing inferences and conclusions, you connect the ideas in a text with what you already know in order to understand a topic better. Using this skill, you can "fill in the blanks" to see the implications or larger meaning of the information in a text. Practice this skill by reading the excerpt of text below. What conclusions can you draw based on the information in the passage?

> Indian merchants and Hindu priests filtered into Southeast Asia, slowly spreading their culture. Later, Buddhist monks and scholars introduced Theravada beliefs. Following the path of trade and religion came the influence of writing, law, government, art, architecture, and farming.
>
> In time, local Indian families exercised considerable power in Southeast Asia. Also, people from Southeast Asia visited India as pilgrims or students. As these contacts increased, Indian beliefs and ideas won widespread acceptance. Indian influence reached its peak between 500 and 1000.
>
> Long after Hinduism and Buddhism took root in Southeast Asia, Indians carried a third religion, Islam, into the region. By the 1200s, Muslims ruled northern India. From there, traders spread Islamic beliefs and Muslim culture throughout the islands of Indonesia and as far east as the Philippines. Today, Indonesia has the largest Muslim population of any nation in the world.

[**1.**] Identify the topic, main idea, and supporting details. Before reading, look at the titles and headings within a reading. This should give you a good idea of the topic, or the general subject, of a text. After reading, identify the main idea. The main idea falls within the topic and answers the question, "What is the main point of this text?" Find the details that the author presents to support the main idea.

[**2.**] Use what you know to make a judgment about the information. Think about what you know about this topic or a similar topic. For example, you may read that the English settlers of Jamestown suffered from starvation because many of them were not farmers and did not know how to grow food. Analyzing the information about their situation and what you know about people, you could draw the conclusion that these settlers must have had little idea, or the wrong idea, about the conditions that they would find in America.

[3.] Check and adjust your judgment until you can draw a well-supported conclusion. Look for details within the reading that support your judgment. Reading a little further, you find that these settlers thought that they would become rich after discovering gold or silver, or through trading with Native Americans for furs. You can use this information to support your conclusion that the settlers were mistaken about the conditions that they would find in America. By analyzing the information further, you might infer that the settlers had inaccurate information about America. To support your conclusions, you could look for reliable sources on what these settlers knew before they left England.

Interpret Sources

Outlines and reports are good sources of information. In order to interpret these sources, though, you'll need to identify the type of document you're reading, identify the main idea, organize the details of information, and evaluate the source for point of view and bias. Practice this skill by finding a newspaper or online report on a recent meeting between the President or Secretary of State and a foreign leader. What steps will you take to interpret this report?

[1.] Identify the type of document. Is the document a primary or secondary source? Determine when, where, and why it was written.

[2.] Examine the source to identify the main idea. After identifying the main idea, identify details or sections of text that support the main idea. If the source is an outline or report, identify the topic and subtopics; review the supporting details under each subtopic. Organize the information from the outline or report and think about how it connects back to the overall topic listed at the top of the outline or report.

[3.] Evaluate the source for point of view and bias. Primary sources often have a strong point of view or bias; it is important to analyze primary sources critically to determine their validity. Evaluating each source will help you interpret the information they contain.

Create Databases

Databases are organized collections of information which can be analyzed and interpreted. You decide on a topic, organize data, use a spreadsheet, and then pose questions which will help you to analyze and interpret your data. Practice this skill by creating a database of population statistics for five countries in the Middle East. Show information for each country for each decade from 1910 to 2010, then compare the statistics. What conclusions can you draw from your data?

[1.] Decide on a topic. Identify the information that you will convert into a table. This information may come from various sources, including textbooks, reference works, and Internet sites.

[**2.**] Organize the data. Study the information and decide what to include in your table. Only include data that is pertinent and available. Based on the data you choose, organize your information. Identify how many columns there will be and what the column headings will be. Decide the order in which you are going to list the data in the rows.

[**3.**] Use a spreadsheet. A spreadsheet is a computer software tool that allows you to organize data so that it can be analyzed. Spreadsheets allow you to make calculations as well as input data. Use a spreadsheet to help you create summaries of your data. For instance, you can compute the sum, average, minimum, and maximum values of the data. Use the graphing features of your spreadsheet program to show the data visually.

[**4.**] Analyze the data. Once all of your data is entered and you have made any calculations you need, you are ready to pose questions to analyze and interpret your data. Organize the information from the database and use it to form conclusions. Be sure to draw conclusions that can be supported by the data available.

Analyze Data and Models

Data and models can provide useful information about geographic distributions and patterns. To make sense of that information, though, you need to pose and answer questions about data and models. What does the data say? What does it mean? What patterns can you find? Practice this skill as you study the data below.

SELECTED DEVELOPED & DEVELOPING COUNTRIES

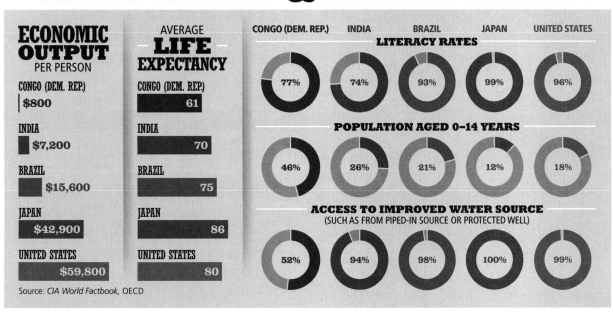

ECONOMIC OUTPUT PER PERSON

CONGO (DEM. REP.) $800
INDIA $7,200
BRAZIL $15,600
JAPAN $42,900
UNITED STATES $59,800

AVERAGE LIFE EXPECTANCY

CONGO (DEM. REP.) 61
INDIA 70
BRAZIL 75
JAPAN 86
UNITED STATES 80

	CONGO (DEM. REP.)	INDIA	BRAZIL	JAPAN	UNITED STATES
LITERACY RATES	77%	74%	93%	99%	96%
POPULATION AGED 0–14 YEARS	46%	26%	21%	12%	18%
ACCESS TO IMPROVED WATER SOURCE (SUCH AS FROM PIPED-IN SOURCE OR PROTECTED WELL)	52%	94%	98%	100%	99%

Source: *CIA World Factbook*, OECD

[1.] Read the title to learn the geographic distributions represented by the data set, graph, or model.

[2.] Read the data given. When reviewing a graph, read the labels and the key to help you comprehend the data provided. Pose and answer questions to further understand the material. For example, you might ask "Who could use this data?" or "How could this data be used?" or even "Why is this data presented in this particular format?" Thinking critically about the data presented will help you make predictions and comprehend the data.

[3.] Study the numbers, lines, and/or colors to find out what the graphs or data represent. Next, find similarities and differences between multiple models of the same data. Do any additional research to find out more about why the information in the models differs.

[4.] Interpret the graph, data set, or model. Look for interesting geographic distributions and patterns in the data. Look at changes over time or compare information from different categories. Draw conclusions.

Read Charts, Graphs, and Tables

If you pose and answer questions about charts, graphs, or tables you find in books or online, you can find out all sorts of information, such as how many calories are in your favorite foods or what the value of a used car is. Analyzing and interpreting the information you find in thematic charts, graphs, and tables can help you make decisions in your life. Practice this skill as you study the infographic below.

EFFECTS OF THE **PRINTING PRESS**

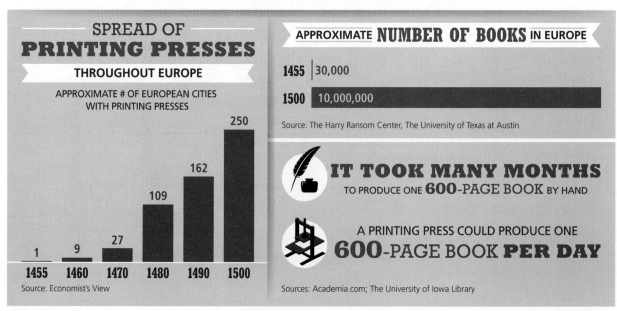

SPREAD OF
PRINTING PRESSES
THROUGHOUT EUROPE

APPROXIMATE # OF EUROPEAN CITIES
WITH PRINTING PRESSES

Year	Cities
1455	1
1460	9
1470	27
1480	109
1490	162
1500	250

Source: Economist's View

APPROXIMATE **NUMBER OF BOOKS** IN EUROPE

Year	Books
1455	30,000
1500	10,000,000

Source: The Harry Ransom Center, The University of Texas at Austin

IT TOOK MANY MONTHS TO PRODUCE ONE **600**-PAGE BOOK BY HAND

A PRINTING PRESS COULD PRODUCE ONE **600**-PAGE BOOK **PER DAY**

Sources: Academia.com; The University of Iowa Library

[**1.**] Identify the title and labels of a chart, graph, or table, and read the key, if there is one, to understand the information presented. The title often tells you the topic of the chart, graph, or table, or the type of information you will find. Make sure you understand how the graph shows information. A key or legend often appears in a small box near the edge of the graph or chart. The key will tell you the meaning of lines, colors, or symbols used on the chart or graph. Notice also the column and row headings, and use your reading skills to figure out the meanings of any words you don't know.

[**2.**] Determine consistencies and inconsistencies, to see whether there is a trend in a graph, chart, or table. Organize information from visuals such as charts and graphs and decide whether or not there is a trend or pattern in the information that you see. Evaluate the data and determine whether the trend is consistent, or steady. Remember that there could be some inconsistencies, or exceptions to the pattern. Try not to miss the overall pattern because of a couple of exceptions.

[**3.**] Draw conclusions about the data in a chart, graph, or table. Once you understand the information, try to analyze and interpret the information and draw conclusions. If you see a pattern, does the pattern help you to understand the topic or predict future events?

[**4.**] Create a chart or graph to make the data more understandable or to view the data in a different way. Does the data in the chart or graph help you answer questions you have about the topic or see any causes or effects? For example, you could use your mathematical skills to create circle graphs or bar graphs that visually organize the data in a different way that allows you to interpret the data differently.

[**5.**] Use the data or information in charts and graphs to understand an issue or make decisions. Use your social studies skills to make inferences, draw conclusions, and take a stand on the issue.

Create Charts and Maps

Thematic charts, graphs, and maps are visual tools for representing information. When you create a thematic chart, graph, or map you will start by selecting the type of data you want to represent. Then you will find appropriate data to include, organize your data, and then create symbols and a key to help others understand your chart, graph, or map. Practice this skill by creating a map of Asia showing which countries have a democratic government. Use computer software to generate the map, color the democratic countries, and create the key.

[**1.**] To create a chart or map, first select a region or set of data. Use a map to represent data pertaining to a specific region or location; use a chart to represent trends reflected in a set of data.

[2.] Research and find the data you would like to present in the chart or map. Your choice of data will be based on the theme you wish to explore. For example, a chart or map that explores the theme of changing demographics in Texas might include data about the location of different ethnic groups in Texas in the nineteenth, twentieth, and twenty-first centuries.

[3.] Organize the data according to the specific format of your chart or map.

[4.] Create symbols, a key (as needed), and a title. Create symbols to represent each piece of data you would like to highlight. Keep each symbol simple and easy to understand. After you have created the symbols, place them in a key. Add a title to your map or chart that summarizes the information presented. Your symbols and key will make it easier for others to interpret your charts and maps.

Analyze Political Cartoons

Political cartoons are visual commentaries about events or people. As you learn to analyze political cartoons, you will learn to identify bias in cartoons and interpret their meaning. You can start by carefully examining the cartoon and considering its possible meanings. Then you can draw conclusions based on your analysis. Practice this skill as you study the political cartoon below.

[**1.**] Fully examine the cartoon. Identify any symbols in the cartoon, read the text and title, and identify the main character or characters. Analyze the cartoon to identify bias and determine what each image or symbol represents. Conduct research if you need more information to decipher the cartoon.

[**2.**] Consider the meaning. Think about how the cartoonist uses the images and symbols in the cartoon to express his or her opinion about a subject. Try to interpret the artist's purpose in creating the image.

[**3.**] Draw conclusions. Use what you have gleaned from the image itself, plus any prior knowledge or research, to analyze, interpret, and form a conclusion about the artist's intentions.

Read Physical Maps

What mountain range is closest to where you live? What major rivers are closest to you? To find out, you would look at a physical map. You can use appropriate reading skills to interpret social studies information such as that found on different kinds of maps. Physical maps show physical features, such as elevation, mountains, valleys, oceans, rivers, deserts, and plains. Practice this skill as you study the map below.

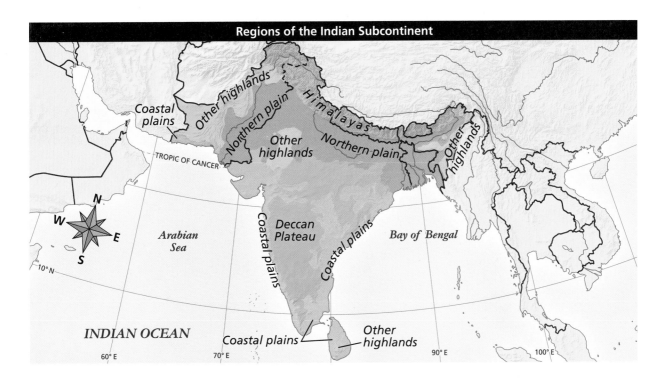

[**1.**] Identify the title and region shown on a map. A map's title can help you to identify the region covered by the map. The title may also tell you the type of information you will find on the map. If the map has no title, you can identify the region by reading the labels on the map.

[2.] Use the map key to interpret symbols and colors on a map. A key or legend often appears in a small box near the edge of the map. The legend will tell you the meaning of colors, symbols, or other patterns on the map. On a physical map, colors from the key often show elevation, or height above sea level, on the map.

[3.] Identify physical features, such as mountains, valleys, oceans, and rivers. Using labels on the map and colors and symbols from the key, identify the physical features on the map. The information in the key allows you to interpret the information from visuals such as a map. Rivers, oceans, lakes, and other bodies of water are usually colored blue. Colors from the key may indicate higher and lower elevation, or there may be shading on the map that shows mountains.

[4.] Draw conclusions about the region based on natural resources and physical features. Once you understand all the symbols and colors on the map, try to interpret the information from the map. Is it very mountainous or mostly flat? Does it have a coastline? Does the region have lots of lakes and rivers that suggest a good water supply? Pose and answer questions about geographic distributions and patterns shown on the map. Physical maps can give you an idea of lifestyle and economic activities of people in the region.

Read Political Maps

What is the capital of your state? What countries border China? To find out, you could look at a political map. Political maps are colorful maps that show borders, or lines dividing states or countries. They also show capitals and sometimes major cities. Practice reading political maps by studying the map below.

Former Soviet Union, 1992

[**1.**] Identify the title of the political map and the region shown. A map's title can help you identify the region covered by the map. The title may also tell you the type of information you will find on the map. If the map has no title, you can identify the region by reading the labels on the map.

[**2.**] Use the map key to interpret symbols and colors on the map. A key or legend often appears in a small box near the edge of the map. The key will help you interpret information from visuals, including maps, by telling you the meaning of colors, symbols, or other patterns on the visual.

[**3.**] Identify boundaries between nations or states. Evaluate government data, such as borders, using the map. It is often easy to see borders, because each state or country will be a different color. If you cannot find the borders, check the key to find the lines used to mark borders on the map.

[**4.**] Locate capital cities. Look at the key to see how capital cities are shown on the map. They are often marked with a special symbol, such as a star.

[**5.**] Draw conclusions about the region based on the map. Once you understand all the symbols and colors on the map, use appropriate reading and mathematical skills to interpret social studies information, such as that shown on the map, in order to draw conclusions about the region. For example, are some countries very large with many cities? These countries are likely to be powerful and influential.

Read Special-Purpose Maps

Some maps show specific kinds of information. These special-purpose maps may show features such as climate zones, ancient trade routes, economic and government data, geographic patterns, or population. Locating and interpreting information from visuals, including special-purpose maps, is an important research skill. Practice this skill as you study this map.

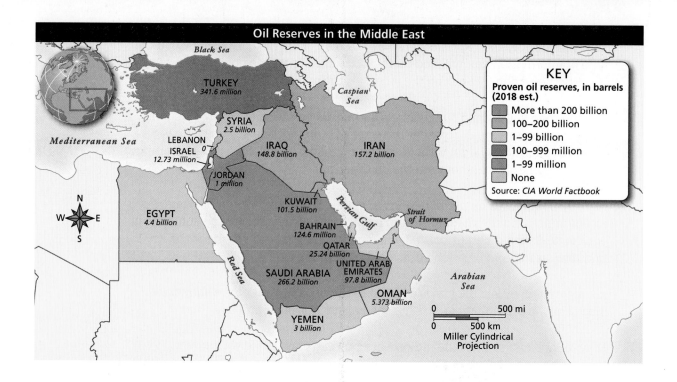

Oil Reserves in the Middle East

KEY
Proven oil reserves, in barrels (2018 est.)
- More than 200 billion
- 100–200 billion
- 1–99 billion
- 100–999 million
- 1–99 million
- None

Source: *CIA World Factbook*

TURKEY 341.6 million
SYRIA 2.5 billion
LEBANON
ISRAEL 12.73 million
JORDAN 1 million
IRAQ 148.8 billion
IRAN 157.2 billion
KUWAIT 101.5 billion
BAHRAIN 124.6 million
QATAR 25.24 billion
UNITED ARAB EMIRATES 97.8 billion
EGYPT 4.4 billion
SAUDI ARABIA 266.2 billion
OMAN 5.373 billion
YEMEN 3 billion

Black Sea
Caspian Sea
Mediterranean Sea
Persian Gulf
Strait of Hormuz
Red Sea
Arabian Sea

0   500 mi
0   500 km
Miller Cylindrical Projection

[**1.**] Identify the title and determine the purpose of a map. A map's title can help you identify the region covered by the map. The title may also tell you the purpose of the map. If the map has no title, see what information the map shows to determine its purpose.

[**2.**] Use the map key to make sense of symbols and colors on a map. A key or legend often appears in a small box near the edge of the map. The key will tell you the meaning of colors, symbols, or other patterns on the map. Special-purpose maps use these colors and symbols to present information.

[**3.**] Draw conclusions about the region shown on a map. Once you understand all the symbols and colors on the map, you can use appropriate skills, including reading and mathematical skills, to analyze and interpret social studies information such as maps. You can pose and answer questions about geographic patterns and distributions that are shown on maps. For example, a precipitation or climate map will show you which areas get lots of rainfall and which are very dry. You can evaluate government and economic data using maps. For example, a population map will show you which regions have lots of people and which have small, scattered populations. A historical map will show you the locations of ancient empires or trade routes. Thematic maps focus on a single theme or topic about a region. For example, you can interpret information from a thematic map representing various aspects of Texas during the nineteenth or twentieth century by studying the Great Military Map, which shows forts established in Texas during the nineteenth century, or by studying a map covering Texas during the Great Depression and World War II. By mapping this kind of detailed information, special-purpose maps can help you understand a region's history or geography.

Use Parts of a Map

If you understand how to organize and interpret information from visuals, including maps, you will be able to find the information you are looking for. Understanding how to use the parts of a map will help you find locations of specific places and estimate distances between different places. Practice this skill as you study the map below.

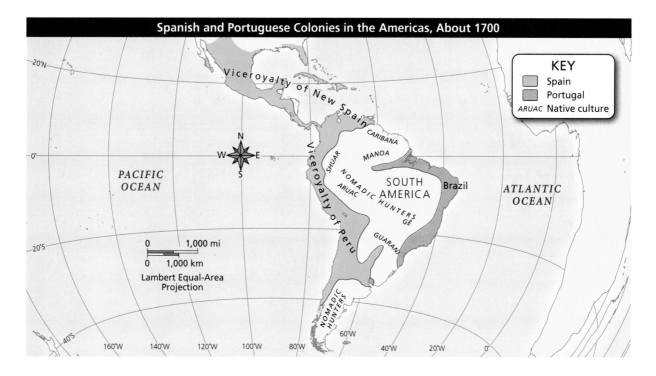

[**1.**] Identify the title and region of a map. Use appropriate reading skills to interpret social studies information such as map labels. A map's title can help you to identify the region covered by the map. The title may also tell you the type of information you will find on the map. If the map has no title, you can identify the region by reading the labels on the map.

[**2.**] Use the compass rose to determine direction. Although on most maps north is at the top of the map, you should always double check the compass rose. Often, on the compass rose, the first letter of each direction represents that direction. For example, "N" represents the direction "north." Some compass roses are as simple as an arrow pointing north.

[**3.**] Use the scale to estimate the distance between places. Use appropriate mathematical skills to interpret social studies information such as a map scale. The scale on a map shows how a measurement on the map compares to the distance on the ground. For example, if one inch on the map represents a mile, the number of inches between two places on the map is the distance in miles.

[4.] Use the key or legend on a map to find information about colors or symbols on a map. A key or legend often appears in a small box near the edge of the map. The legend will tell you the meaning of colors, symbols, or other patterns on the map.

[5.] Use the latitude and longitude grid to determine absolute locations. An absolute location is an exact description of a location on Earth's surface based on latitude and longitude. You can use the latitude and longitude lines on a map to find the absolute location of a place.

Analyze Primary and Secondary Sources

Primary sources are firsthand accounts of events. By contrast, secondary sources are secondhand accounts of events. Both sources are useful, but it is important to differentiate between valid primary and secondary sources. In this lesson, you'll learn how to locate and use primary and secondary sources to acquire information about the treatment of Native Americans. Practice this skill by analyzing the quotation and the image. Using the steps below, distinguish between the primary and the secondary source.

> "They [the Spanish] have set out to line their pockets with gold. . . . The Spaniards have shown not the slightest consideration for these people, treating them (and I speak from first-hand experience, having been there from the outset) not as brute animals—indeed, I would to God they had done and had shown them the consideration they afford their animals—so much as piles of dung in the middle of the road."
> –Bartolomé de Las Casas, 1542

[**1.**] Determine who created the source as well as when and why it was created. Determine whether it is a primary or secondary source. Identify the author of the document. Next, look for the date the document was written or the date when the document was first published. Most primary sources are written close to the date of the events described. Secondary sources are often written well after the events described. Firsthand observers or participants in an event create primary sources. People who did not witness an event create secondary sources. Primary sources record an event. Secondary sources analyze or draw conclusions about events. Secondary sources rely on both primary and secondary sources. Good research requires you to analyze and evaluate the validity of information, arguments, and counterarguments from a primary or secondary source for frame of reference.

[**2.**] Identify the main idea and supporting details, and determine whether they are facts or opinions. Read the text carefully and ask yourself, "What point is this text making?" This point is the main idea. Then reread the text and list details that support this main idea. Decide whether these details are facts or opinions. If the details are facts, it should be possible to confirm them in other sources. If the author uses emotional language that shows feelings, the supporting details are probably opinions. Carefully analyze and evaluate the validity of information, arguments, and counterarguments from primary and secondary sources for point of view.

[**3.**] Decide whether the source's information is biased or if it is accurate and credible. Check statements in the text against reliable sources, such as encyclopedias or books written by experts on the topic. If reliable sources agree with the text, it is probably fairly accurate. If most of the text seems to be opinions rather than facts, it is not an accurate source of information. Still, these opinions can teach you about the author's world. A writer who observed an exciting or scary event may use emotional language to describe the event, but the source may still be a reliable account. An important part of research is analyzing and evaluating the validity of the information, arguments, and counterarguments from primary and secondary sources for bias or propaganda.

Compare Viewpoints

When people disagree about a topic, they have different viewpoints. Knowing how to analyze and evaluate the validity of information, arguments, and counterarguments from both primary and secondary sources for point of view can help you to learn more about a topic. Practice this skill by reading the following quotes and comparing the viewpoints.

> "Dictatorship...involves costs which the American people will never pay: The cost of having our children brought up, not as free and dignified human beings, but as pawns...
> –Franklin Roosevelt, State of the Union Address, January 4, 1939

> "The [Nazi Party] has laid down the directive...we must insist that all organs of education...have to [fulfill] their duty towards the community...
> –Adolf Hitler, Speech delivered in German Reichstag on January 30, 1937

[1.] Identify the authors of texts presenting different points of view and identify each author's frame of reference. Frame of reference is a term that describes the experiences, values, and ideas that influence a person's opinions and actions. It can also be referred to as *point of view*. First, identify the group or individual that wrote each text. Determine if the source is primary or secondary. As you read, take note of any information about the author's experiences or background. Also, look for any signs of what the author thinks is important. These types of statements can help you analyze and evaluate the validity of information, arguments, and counterarguments from both primary and secondary sources for point of view.

[2.] Recognize any similarities and differences between the authors' frames of reference and identify the opinion of each author. Pay attention to any similarities and differences between the two authors' experiences, values, and ideas. Read carefully to identify the opinion of each author. In an article about a rock band, an author who played guitar in a band for ten years argues that Band A is the best band today because of its great guitarist. In a second article, another author who sang for many years argues that Band B is the best because of its lead singer. Notice how authors' arguments and counterarguments are shaped by their frame of reference, or point of view.

[3.] Draw conclusions about similarities and differences between authors' points of view. With some information about the point of view of each author, you can understand why they have different opinions. This helps you to analyze and evaluate the validity of the information, arguments, and counterarguments. In the example of the two authors writing about rock bands, each author stresses his or her own areas of expertise. You might decide to listen to the band recommended by the singer if you share an interest in vocals. If you are more interested in instrumentals, you might choose the band recommended by the guitarist.

Identify Bias

Being able to analyze and evaluate the validity of information, arguments, and counterarguments for bias helps you to determine whether primary or secondary sources you find online, in books, or in the media are reliable. When you are able to identify bias in written, oral, and visual material, you can see when someone is presenting only one side of an issue or basing an argument on emotion instead of facts. Use the Internet to locate an English-language newspaper in a foreign country. Practice identifying bias as you read an editorial or a political cartoon.

[1.] Identify the author of a source and the author's purpose. First, identify the author of the source. The author may be a group or an organization rather than a single person. The author may state his or her purpose very clearly in the source. If not, the type of source may give you an idea of the purpose. For example, the writer of an encyclopedia aims to summarize information about a subject. The author of a political Web site may want you to vote for a candidate.

[2.] Identify the main idea, and check whether the main idea is supported with facts or opinions. Read the document carefully and ask yourself, "What is the main point of this selection?" Your answer to this question is the main idea. Reread the document and list details that support this main idea. Decide whether these details are facts or opinions. To find out whether they are facts, check whether other reliable sources include the same information. If your source uses statements that shows feelings, those statements are probably opinions.

[3.] Look for the use of emotional language or one-sided opinions. Look for words that can show opinions such as "good" and "bad." Be aware of statements that make you feel angry, scared, or excited. Also, watch out for statements that only express one side of an issue. These are all signs of bias.

[4.] Draw conclusions about the author's bias, if any. Is the author using mostly emotional language with few facts to support his or her ideas? Are there insults or other very negative language in the source? If so, the source is probably biased. Similarly, if you notice that the author is presenting only one side of an issue, the source is probably not reliable. It is important to analyze and evaluate the information, arguments, and counterarguments in both primary and secondary sources for bias.

Evaluate Existing Arguments

When you evaluate existing arguments, you must evaluate and analyze the point of view and biases of your sources and their authors. Who is the author and what is he or she trying to accomplish? How valid are the arguments in your primary and secondary sources? If you master these skills, you will be able to analyze and interpret social studies information such as speeches. Practice this skill as you read and evaluate the excerpt below.

> There are two main ways in which those who have traveled to this part of the world pretending to be Christians have uprooted these pitiful peoples and wiped them from the face of the earth. First, they have waged war on them: unjust, cruel, bloody and tyrannical [using power unjustly] war. Second, they have murdered anyone and everyone who has shown the slightest sign of resistance. . . .
>
> The reason the [Spanish] have murdered on such a vast scale and killed anyone and everyone in their way is purely and simply greed. They have set out to line their pockets with gold. . . . The Spaniards have shown not the slightest consideration for these people, treating them (and I speak from first-hand experience, having been there from the outset) not as brute animals—indeed, I would to God they had done and had shown them the consideration they afford their animals—so much as piles of dung in the middle of the road. They have had as little concern for their souls as for their bodies. . . .
>
> —Bartolomé de Las Casas, *The Destruction of the Indies*, 1542

[1.] Identify the claim or thesis. What is the author or source claiming? The claim or thesis is usually found in the introduction and/or conclusion of a written or spoken argument.

[2.] Identify the reasons (claims to truth or facts) the author offers in support of his or her claim. What evidence does the author or source provide to support their claims? Make a list of the evidence provided to support each claim.

[3.] Evaluate the argument. Analyze and evaluate the validity of the evidence presented to support each claim. Use the appropriate skills to analyze and interpret social studies information, such as speeches. Research each claim to be sure that the author's statements are accurate. Carefully check for evidence of bias or propaganda. Be sure you understand the author's point of view and his or her frame of reference. Finally, check to be sure that the author's conclusions follow logically from the evidence presented. If the evidence is accurate, the author is free from bias, and conclusions follow logically from the evidence, the claims are probably valid.

Consider and Counter Opposing Arguments

Before you can effectively counter opposing arguments, you'll need to analyze possible counterarguments for frame of reference, bias, point of view, and propaganda. You'll plan your response ahead of time, collecting research and data. Then, you'll make a point of acknowledging the opposing view before presenting your counterarguments. To practice this skill, suppose you are preparing for a debate about whether the United States should take a more active role in promoting human rights in other parts of the world. Choose a side of the debate to support. What arguments will you use to support your side of the debate? What counterarguments will you anticipate the other side using? Why is it useful to anticipate the other side's arguments?

[1.] Fully understand your argument and the potential counter points. Do research as needed to find out more about other opposing views. Analyze and evaluate the validity of possible counterarguments from primary and secondary sources for frame of reference, bias, point of view, and propaganda.

[2.] Make predictions and outline a response to several of the opposing views. Continue researching as needed. Researching, analyzing, and evaluating the validity of opposing arguments will help you support and strengthen your own. Opposing arguments can consist of any reasons, conclusions, or claims that oppose yours. Outline your response to each opposing reason, conclusion, or claim.

[3.] To counter an opposing argument, first acknowledge the opposing view. This strategy shows that you have heard the opposing argument and are responding accordingly. Consider using statements such as "I understand your point, but you should also consider the following..." You can also respond by refuting facts, logic, etc. Be sure to respond to each opposing argument. Ignoring or dismissing a counterargument shows that your response is weak and unsupported.

Participate in a Discussion or Debate

When you participate in a discussion or debate, your goal is to explain, analyze, and defend a point of view–often related to a current political or economic issue. To be a successful debater, you'll do your research, present your position, and defend your point of view in a courteous manner. Use the steps below to prepare for a discussion on this question: Do you think the United States should act as a "global policeman?" Why or why not?

[**1.**] Research. Before participating in a discussion or debate, do research to gain knowledge of your subject so that you may be an informed and prepared participant. Take notes as needed to help you prepare. Jot down main points and any questions you may have. As you research, decide where you might stand on the issue. Be sure to gather research and sources that will allow you to explain, analyze, and defend your point of view.

[**2.**] Present your position. After you have organized your thoughts and decided where you stand, explain and defend your point of view. Be sure to stay focused on the topic and your line of argument. Ask questions that challenge the accuracy, logic, or relevance of opposing views.

[**3.**] During the discussion or debate, be patient and courteous. Listen attentively, be respectful and supportive of peers, and speak only when instructed to do so by the moderator. Be sure to allow others to express their views; do not monopolize the debate or discussion. Speak clearly and slowly.

Give an Effective Presentation

When you create a written, visual, and oral presentation, you teach, convince, or share information with an audience. Effective presentations use both words and visuals to engage audiences. Delivery is also important. For example, you can use the way you move, speak, and look at the audience to keep people interested. Use the steps below to prepare and deliver a presentation on the Silk Road.

[**1.**] Identify the purpose of your presentation and your audience. Think about the purpose of your written, visual, and oral presentation. If this is a research report, you will need facts and data to support your points. If you are trying to persuade your audience, look for powerful photos. Keep your audience in mind. Consider their interests and present your topic in a way that will engage them.

[**2.**] Write the text and find visual aids for your presentation. Look online and in books and magazines for information and images for your presentation. Organize the information and write it up carefully so that it is easy for your audience to understand. Diagrams can show complicated information in a clear way. Visuals also get people interested in the presentation. So choose large, colorful images that people in the back of the audience will be able to see.

[3.] Practice and work to improve your presentation. Keep practicing your oral presentation until you know the material well. Then, practice some more, focusing on improving your delivery.

[4.] Use body language, tone of voice, and eye contact to deliver an effective presentation. Answer questions if the audience has them. At the beginning of your oral presentation, take a breath, smile, and stand up tall. Speak more loudly and more clearly than you would in normal conversation. Also, try not to rush through the presentation. Glance at your notes but speak naturally, rather than reading. Look at people in the audience. If people are confused, pause to clarify. Finally, leave time for people in the audience to ask questions.

Write an Essay

There are four steps to writing an essay. You'll start by selecting a topic and research sources, then you'll write an outline and develop a thesis or point of view. After drafting your essay, you'll carefully proofread it to be sure you've used standard grammar, spelling, sentence structure, and punctuation. Finally, you'll revise and polish your work. To practice this skill, select a topic that interests you about the early history of Africa and develop a thesis. Then explain to a partner the steps you will take to write your essay.

[1.] Choose your topic and research sources. Check which types of sources you will need. Gather different types of reliable sources that support the argument you will be making.

[2.] Write an outline and generate a thesis. First write your topic at the top of the page then list all the points or arguments you want to make about the topic; also list the facts and examples that support these points. Your thesis statement will inform the reader of the point you are making and what question you will be answering about the topic. When writing your thesis, be as specific as possible and address one main idea.

[3.] Draft your essay. After finishing your research and outline, begin writing the body of your essay; start with the introduction then write a paragraph for each of your supporting points, followed by a conclusion. As you write, do your best to use standard grammar, spelling, sentence structure, and punctuation. Be sure any terminology is used correctly.

[4.] Revise. An important part of the writing process involves checking for areas in which information should be added, removed, or rewritten. Try to imagine that this paper belongs to someone else. Does the paper have a clear thesis? Do all of the ideas relate back to the thesis? Read your paper out loud and listen for awkward pauses and unclear ideas. Lastly, check for mistakes in standard grammar, spelling, sentence structure, punctuation, and usage.

Avoid Plagiarism

When you don't attribute ideas and information to source materials and authors, you are plagiarizing. Plagiarizing–claiming others' ideas and information as your own–is considered unethical. You can avoid plagiarizing by carefully noting down which authors and sources you'll be using, citing those authors and sources in your paper, and listing them in a bibliography. To practice this skill, suppose you have been assigned to write a research paper on the development of river valley civilizations. Name three types of sources you might use to help you gather information. Explain how you will avoid plagiarism when you use these sources.

[**1.**] Keep a careful log of your notes. As you read sources to gain background information on your topic, keep track of ideas and information and the sources and authors they come from. Write down the name of each source next to your notes from that particular source so you can remember to cite it later on. Create a separate section in your notes where you keep your own thoughts and ideas so you know which ideas are your own. Using someone else's words or paraphrasing their ideas does not make them yours.

[**2**] Cite sources in your paper. You must identify the source materials and authors you use to support your ideas. Whenever you use statistics, facts, direct quotations, or paraphrases of others' views, you need to attribute them to your source. Cite your sources within the body of your paper. Check your assignment to find out how they should be formatted.

[**3.**] List your sources in a bibliography at the end of your paper. List your source materials and authors cited in alphabetical order by author, using accepted formats. As you work, be sure to check your list of sources from your notes so that none are left out of the bibliography.

Solve Problems

Problem solving is a skill that you use every day. It is a process that requires an open mind, clear thinking, and action. Consider the fact that many of natural resources are in high demand around the world, and that some may be in danger of being depleted. Consider one source of power, such as natural gas, oil, or electricity, and use the steps below to solve the problem of conserving energy.

[**1.**] Understand the problem. Before trying to solve a problem, make sure that you gather as much information as possible in order to identify the problem. What are the causes and effects of the problem? Who is involved? You will want to make sure that you understand different perspectives on the problem. Try not to jump to conclusions or make assumptions. You might end up misunderstanding the problem.

[2.] Consider possible solutions and choose the best one. Once you have identified the problem and gathered some information, list and consider a number of possible options. Right away, one solution might seem like the right one, but try to think of other solutions. Be sure to consider carefully the advantages and disadvantages of each option. It can help to take notes listing benefits and drawbacks. Look for the solution whose benefits outweigh its drawbacks. After considering each option, choose the solution you think is best.

[3.] Make and implement a plan. Choose and implement a solution. Make a detailed, step-by-step plan to implement the solution that you choose. Write your plan down and assign yourself a deadline for each step. That will help you to stay on track toward completing your plan. Try to think of any problems that might come up and what you will do to address those problems. Of course, there are many things that you cannot predict. Stay flexible. Evaluate the effectiveness of the solution and adjust your plan as necessary.

Make Decisions

Everyone makes decisions. The trick is to learn how to make good decisions. How can you make good decisions? First, identify a situation that requires a decision and gather information. Then, identify possible options and predict the consequences of each option. Finally, choose the best option and take action to implement a decision. You know there are many issues in the world that affect children who are just like you. Some children face hunger, poverty, lack of schools or medical facilities, poor water supplies, or other challenges. What could you do to help? Practice this skill by following these steps to decide which issue you can best support and how you can help.

[1.] Determine the options between which you must decide. In some cases, like ordering from a menu at a restaurant, your options may be clear. In other cases, you will need to identify a situation that requires a decision, gather information, and identify the options that are available to you. Spend some time thinking about the situation and brainstorm a number of options. If necessary, do a little research to find more options. Make a list of options that you might choose.

[2.] Review the costs and benefits of each option. Carefully predict the consequences of each option. You may want to make a cost-benefit list for each option. To do this, write down the option and then draw two columns underneath it. One column will be the "pro" or benefit list. The other column will be the "con" or cost list. Note the pros and cons for each of your options. Try not to rush through this process. For a very important decision, you may even want to show your list to someone you trust. This person can help you think of costs and benefits that you had not considered.

[3.] Determine the best option and act on it. Look through your cost-benefit lists. Note any especially serious costs. If an option has the possibility of an extremely negative consequence, you might want to cross it off your list right away. Look closely at the options with the most benefits and the fewest costs, and choose the one that you think is best. Once you have made a choice, take action to implement a decision. If necessary, make a detailed plan with clear steps. Set a deadline to complete the steps to keep yourself moving toward your goal.

Being an Informed Citizen

Informed citizens understand the responsibilities, duties, and obligations of citizenship. They are well informed about civic affairs, involved with their communities, and politically active. When it comes to issues they personally care about, they take a stand and reach out to others.

[1.] Learn the issues. A great way to begin to understand the responsibilities of citizenship is to first find topics of interest to you. Next, become well informed about civic affairs in your town, city, or country. Read newspapers, magazines, and articles you find online about events happening in your area or around the world. Analyze the information you read to come to your own conclusions. Radio programs, podcasts, and social media are also great ways to keep up with current events and interact with others about issues.

[2.] Get involved. Attend community events to speak with others who know the issues. Become well informed about how policies are made and changed. Find out who to speak to if you would like to take part in civic affairs and policy creation. There are government websites that can help direct you to the right person. These websites will also provide his or her contact details.

[3.] Take a stand and reach out. Write, call, or meet with your elected officials to become a better informed, more responsible citizen. Do research about candidates who are running for office to be an informed voter. Start your own blog or website to explore issues, interact with others, and be part of the community or national dialogue.

Political Participation

Political participation starts with an understanding of the responsibilities, duties and obligations of citizenship, such as serving the public good. When you understand your role as a political participant, you can get involved through volunteering for a political campaign, running for office, or interacting with others in person or online.

[1.] Volunteer for a political campaign. Political campaigns offer a wide variety of opportunities to help you become involved in the political process and become a responsible citizen by serving the public good. As a political campaign volunteer you may have the opportunity to attend events, make calls to voters, and explore your community while getting to know how other voters think about the responsibilities, duties, and obligations of citizenship.

[2.] Run for office in your school or community. A good way to become involved in your school or community is to run for office. Student council or community positions offer a great opportunity for you to become familiar with the campaign and election process.

[3.] Reach out to others. Start or join an interest group. Interest groups enable people to work together on common goals related to the political process. Write a letter or email to a public official. By contacting an elected official from your area, you can either support or oppose laws or policies. You can also ask for help or support regarding certain issues.

[4.] Interact online. Social networking sites and blogs offer a great way for people of all ages to interact and write about political issues. As you connect with others, you'll become more confident in your role as a citizen working for the public good.

Voting

Voting is not only a right. It is also one of the primary responsibilities, duties, and obligations of citizenship. Before you can legally vote, however, you must understand the voter registration process and the criteria for voting in elections. You should also understand the issues and know where different candidates stand on those issues.

[1.] Check eligibility and residency requirements. In order to vote in the United States, you must be a United States citizen who is 18 years or older, and you must be a resident of the place where you plan to vote.

[2.] Register to vote. You cannot vote until you understand the voter registration process. You can register at city or town election offices, or when you get a driver's license. You can also register by mail or online. You may also have the option of registering at the polls on Election Day, but this does not apply in all states. Make sure to find out what you need to do to register in your state, as well as the deadline for registering. You may have the option of declaring a political party when registering.

[3.] Learn the issues. As the election approaches, research the candidates and issues in order to be an informed voter. Watch televised debates, if there are any. You can also review the candidates' websites. By doing these things and thinking critically about what you learn, you will be prepared to exercise your responsibility, duty and obligation as a United States citizen.

[4.] Vote. Make sure to arrive at the correct polling place on Election Day to cast your ballot. Research to find out when the polls will be open. Advance voting, absentee voting, and voting by mail are also options in certain states for those who qualify.

Serving on a Jury

As an American, you need to understand the duties, obligations and responsibilities of citizenship; among these is the expectation that you may be required to serve on a jury. You will receive a written notice when you are summoned to jury duty and you'll receive instruction on the special duties and obligations of a juror. You'll follow the American code of justice which assumes that a person is innocent until proven guilty, and you'll follow instructions about keeping trial information confidential.

[1.] Wait to receive notification. If you are summoned to serve as a juror, you will be first notified by mail. If you are chosen to move on to the jury selection phase, lawyers from both sides will ask you questions as they select the final jury members. It is an honor to serve as a juror, as it is a responsibility offered only to American citizens.

[2.] Follow the law and remain impartial. Your job is to determine whether or not someone broke the law. You may also be asked to sit on the jury for civil cases (as opposed to criminal cases); these cases involve lawsuits filed against individuals or businesses for any perceived wrong doing (such as broken contracts, trespassing, discrimination, etc.). Be sure to follow the law as it is explained to you, regardless of whether you approve of the law or not. Your decision about the trial should not be influenced by any personal bias or views you may have.

[3.] Remember that the defendant is presumed innocent. In a criminal trial, the defendant must be proven guilty "beyond a reasonable doubt" for the verdict to be guilty. If the trial team fails to prove the defendant to be guilty beyond a reasonable doubt, the jury verdict must be "not guilty."

[4.] During the trial, respect the court's right to privacy. As a juror, you have specific duties, obligations, and responsibilities under the law. Do not permit anyone to talk about the case with you or in your presence, except with the court's permission. Avoid media coverage once the trial has begun so as to prevent bias. Keep an open mind and do not form or state any opinions about the case until you have heard all of the evidence, the closing arguments from the lawyers, and the judge's instructions on the applicable law.

Paying Taxes

Paying taxes is one of the responsibilities of citizenship. How do you go about figuring out how much you've already paid in taxes and how much you still owe? It's your duty and obligation to find out, by determining how much has been deducted from your pay and filing your tax return.

[1.] Find out how taxes are deducted from your pay. In the United States, payroll taxes are imposed on employers and employees, and they are collected and paid by the employers. Check your pay stub to find out how much money was deducted for taxes. Be sure to also save the W-2 tax form your employer sends to you. You will need this form later on when filing your tax paperwork. Also save any interest income statements. All this information will help you fulfill your obligation as an American taxpayer.

[2.] Check the sales taxes in your state. All but five states impose sales and use taxes on retail sale, lease, and rental of many goods, as well as some services. Sales tax is calculated as the purchase price times the appropriate tax rate. Tax rates vary widely from less than one percent to over ten percent. Sales tax is collected by the seller at the time of sale.

[3.] File your tax return. Filing your tax return is more than an obligation: it's also a duty and responsibility of citizenship. You may receive tax forms in the mail, or pick them up at the local Post Office or library. Fill the forms in and then mail or electronically send completed tax forms and any necessary payments to the Internal Revenue Service (IRS) and your state's department of revenue. The IRS provides free resources to help people prepare and electronically file their tax returns; go to IRS.gov to learn more. Note: certain things such as charitable donations and business expenses are tax deductible.

The United States: Political

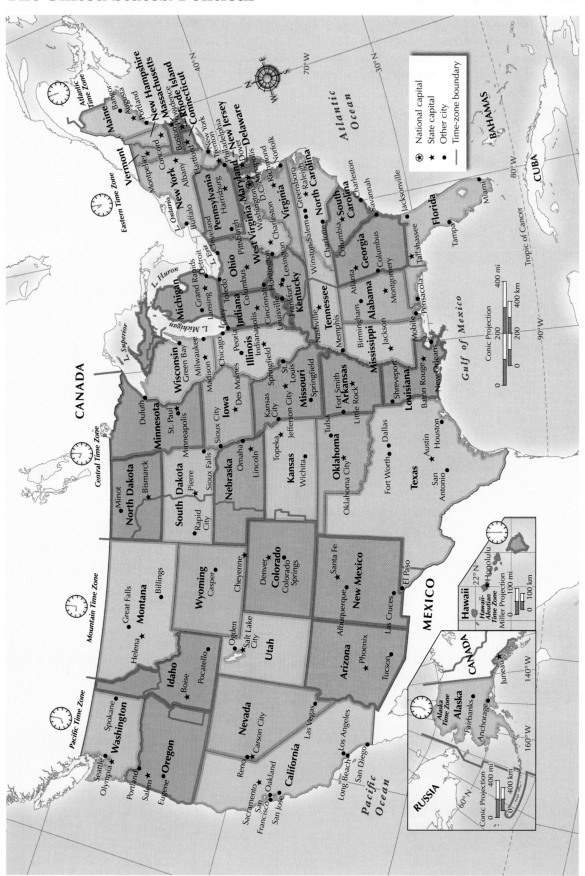

The United States: Physical

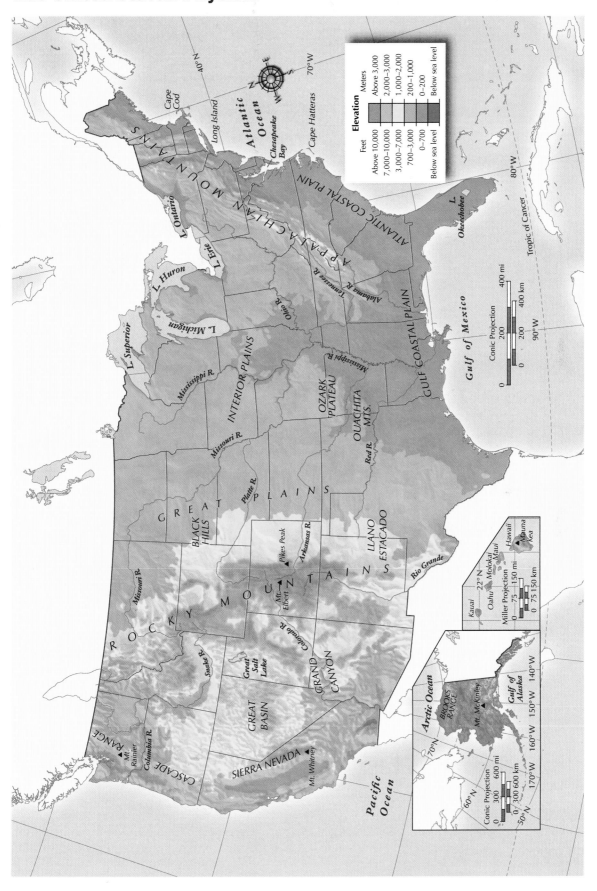

Elevation

Feet	Meters
Above 10,000	Above 3,000
7,000–10,000	2,000–3,000
3,000–7,000	1,000–2,000
700–3,000	200–1,000
0–700	0–200
Below sea level	Below sea level

Atlantic Ocean

Cape Cod

Long Island

Chesapeake Bay

Cape Hatteras

ATLANTIC COASTAL PLAIN

APPALACHIAN MOUNTAINS

L. Ontario

L. Erie

L. Huron

L. Superior

L. Michigan

Tennessee R.

Alabama R.

Ohio R.

Mississippi R.

INTERIOR PLAINS

Missouri R.

Mississippi R.

OZARK PLATEAU

OUACHITA MTS.

GULF COASTAL PLAIN

Gulf of Mexico

L. Okeechobee

Tropic of Cancer

Red R.

GREAT PLAINS

BLACK HILLS

Platte R.

Pikes Peak

Arkansas R.

LLANO ESTACADO

Rio Grande

Missouri R.

ROCKY MOUNTAINS

Mt. Elbert

GRAND CANYON

Colorado R.

Great Salt Lake

Snake R.

GREAT BASIN

SIERRA NEVADA

Mt. Whitney

CASCADE RANGE

Mt. Rainier

Columbia R.

Pacific Ocean

Conic Projection

0   200   400 mi

0   200   400 km

Hawaii

Kauai   Oahu   Molokai   Maui   Mauna Kea

22°N

Miller Projection

0   75   150 mi

0   75   150 km

Arctic Ocean

BROOKS RANGE

Mt. McKinley

Gulf of Alaska

70°N

60°N

50°N

170°W   160°W   150°W   140°W

Conic Projection

0   300   600 mi

0   300   600 km

40°N

70°W

80°W

90°W

The World: Political

Alaska (United States)
CANADA
NORTH AMERICA
Toronto •
Chicago •
• New York
UNITED STATES
⊛ Washington, D.C.
Los Angeles •
Atlantic Ocean
• Houston
Hawaii (United States)
Tropic of Cancer
MEXICO
see inset below
⊛ Mexico City
Pacific Ocean
Equator
0°
KIRIBATI
Galápagos Islands (Ecuador)
COLOMBIA
⊛ Bogotá
SURINAME
French Guiana (France)
ECUADOR
American Samoa (United States)
PERU
BRAZIL
SOUTH AMERICA
SAMOA
BOLIVIA
French Polynesia (France)
Tropic of Capricorn
Rio de Janeiro
TONGA
Pitcairn Islands (U.K.)
PARAGUAY
São Paulo •
CHILE
ARGENTINA
URUGUAY
⊛ Buenos Aires

⊛ Capital
• Other city

Southern Ocean
Antarctic Circle

Inset map

Gulf of Mexico
UNITED STATES
B A H A M A S
Tropic of Cancer
CUBA
Turks and Caicos Islands (U.K.)
U.S. Virgin Islands (U.S.)
British Virgin Islands (U.K.)
Anguilla (U.K.)
St. Martin (St. Maarten) (France & Neth. Antilles)
ANTIGUA AND BARBUDA
MEXICO
Cayman Islands (U.K.)
HAITI
Puerto Rico (U.S.)
ST. KITTS AND NEVIS
Montserrat (U.K.)
Guadeloupe (France)
DOMINICA
BELIZE
JAMAICA
DOMINICAN REPUBLIC
GUATEMALA
Martinique (France)
ST. LUCIA
BARBADOS
HONDURAS
Caribbean Sea
ST. VINCENT AND THE GRENADINES
EL SALVADOR
GRENADA
Conic Projection
0   200   400 mi
0   200   400 km
Aruba (Neth.)
Netherlands Antilles (Neth.)
TRINIDAD AND TOBAGO
NICARAGUA
⊛ Caracas
COSTA RICA
Lake Maracaibo
VENEZUELA
PANAMA
COLOMBIA
Pacific Ocean
SOUTH AMERICA
GUYANA

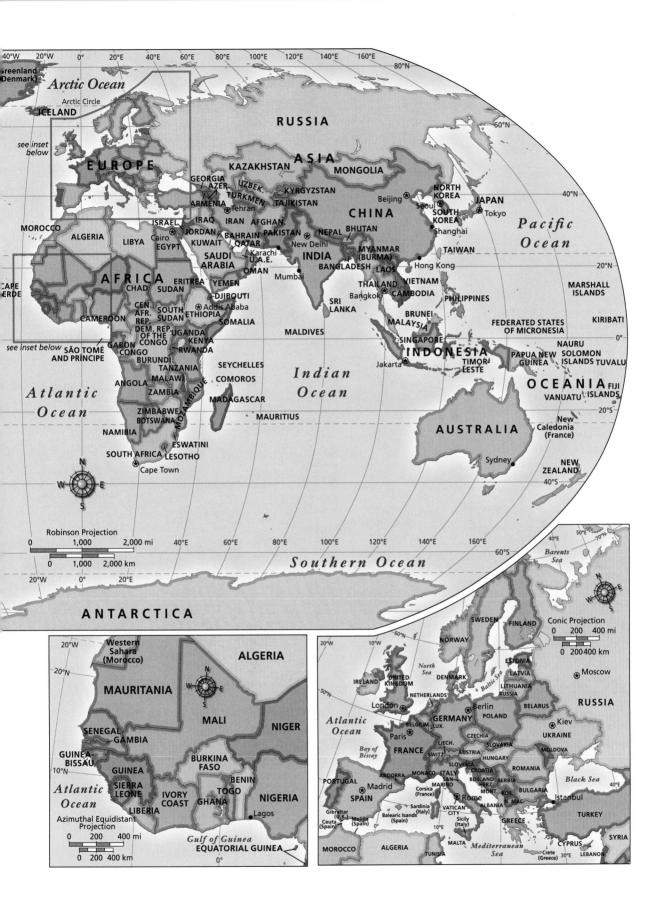

20°W 0° 20°E 40°E 60°E 80°E 100°E 120°E 140°E 160°E 80°N

Greenland (Denmark)

Arctic Ocean

Arctic Circle

ICELAND

RUSSIA

60°N

see inset below

EUROPE

ASIA

KAZAKHSTAN

MONGOLIA

GEORGIA
AZER.
ARMENIA
UZBEK.
TURKMEN.
KYRGYZSTAN
TAJIKISTAN

40°N

NORTH KOREA
SOUTH KOREA
JAPAN

Beijing
Seoul
Tokyo

Pacific Ocean

Tehran

CHINA

IRAQ
IRAN
AFGHAN.
NEPAL
BHUTAN

Shanghai

MOROCCO

ISRAEL
JORDAN
KUWAIT
BAHRAIN
QATAR
PAKISTAN

New Delhi

TAIWAN

ALGERIA
LIBYA
Cairo
EGYPT
U.A.E.
OMAN
Karachi
INDIA
MYANMAR (BURMA)

Hong Kong

20°N

CAPE VERDE

SAUDI ARABIA
YEMEN
Mumbai
BANGLADESH
LAOS

MARSHALL ISLANDS

AFRICA
CHAD
SUDAN
ERITREA
DJIBOUTI
Addis Ababa
SRI LANKA
THAILAND
VIETNAM

Bangkok
CAMBODIA

PHILIPPINES

KIRIBATI

CAMEROON
CEN. AFR. REP.
SOUTH SUDAN
ETHIOPIA
SOMALIA

BRUNEI
MALAYSIA

FEDERATED STATES OF MICRONESIA

0°

DEM. REP. OF THE CONGO
UGANDA
KENYA
MALDIVES

SINGAPORE
NAURU

GABON
CONGO
RWANDA
BURUNDI
SEYCHELLES

INDONESIA
Jakarta
PAPUA NEW GUINEA
TIMOR-LESTE
SOLOMON ISLANDS TUVALU

see inset below
SÃO TOMÉ AND PRÍNCIPE
TANZANIA

Atlantic Ocean

ANGOLA
MALAWI
ZAMBIA
COMOROS

Indian Ocean

OCEANIA FIJI
VANUATU ISLANDS

MADAGASCAR
MOZAMBIQUE
ZIMBABWE
BOTSWANA
MAURITIUS

20°S

NAMIBIA

AUSTRALIA

New Caledonia (France)

N
W E
S

ESWATINI
SOUTH AFRICA
LESOTHO
Cape Town

Sydney

NEW ZEALAND

40°S

Robinson Projection

0 1,000 2,000 mi

0 1,000 2,000 km

40°E 60°E 80°E 100°E 120°E 140°E 160°E

60°S

Southern Ocean

20°W 0° 20°E

ANTARCTICA

Inset (West Africa):

20°W

Western Sahara (Morocco)

ALGERIA

20°N

MAURITANIA

N
W E
S

SENEGAL
GAMBIA

MALI

NIGER

GUINEA-BISSAU

10°N

GUINEA

BURKINA FASO

SIERRA LEONE
IVORY COAST
GHANA
TOGO
BENIN

NIGERIA

Atlantic Ocean

LIBERIA

Lagos

Azimuthal Equidistant Projection

0 200 400 mi

0 200 400 km

Gulf of Guinea
EQUATORIAL GUINEA

0°

Inset (Europe):

20°W 10°E

60°N

SWEDEN
FINLAND

NORWAY

Barents Sea

40°E 50°E 70°N

Conic Projection

0 200 400 mi

0 200 400 km

North Sea
DENMARK
ESTONIA
LATVIA

Moscow

IRELAND
UNITED KINGDOM
NETHERLANDS
Baltic Sea
LITHUANIA
RUSSIA

RUSSIA

50°N

London
Berlin
BELARUS

Atlantic Ocean

BELGIUM
LUX.
GERMANY
POLAND

Paris
Kiev

Bay of Biscay

FRANCE
LIECH.
SWITZ.
CZECHIA
SLOVAKIA

UKRAINE
MOLDOVA

AUSTRIA
HUNGARY
SLOVENIA
ROMANIA

PORTUGAL
ANDORRA
MONACO
ITALY
CROATIA
BOS. AND HERZ.
SERBIA

Black Sea

40°E

SAN MARINO
MONT.
KOS.
BULGARIA

Madrid
SPAIN
Corsica (France)
VATICAN CITY
Rome
ALBANIA
N. MAC.
Istanbul

Gibraltar (U.K.)
Ceuta (Spain)
Melilla (Spain)
Balearic Isands (Spain)
Sardinia (Italy)
Sicily (Italy)
GREECE
TURKEY

MOROCCO
ALGERIA
MALTA
Mediterranean Sea
Crete (Greece)
30°E
CYPRUS
LEBANON
SYRIA
TUNISIA

Africa: Political

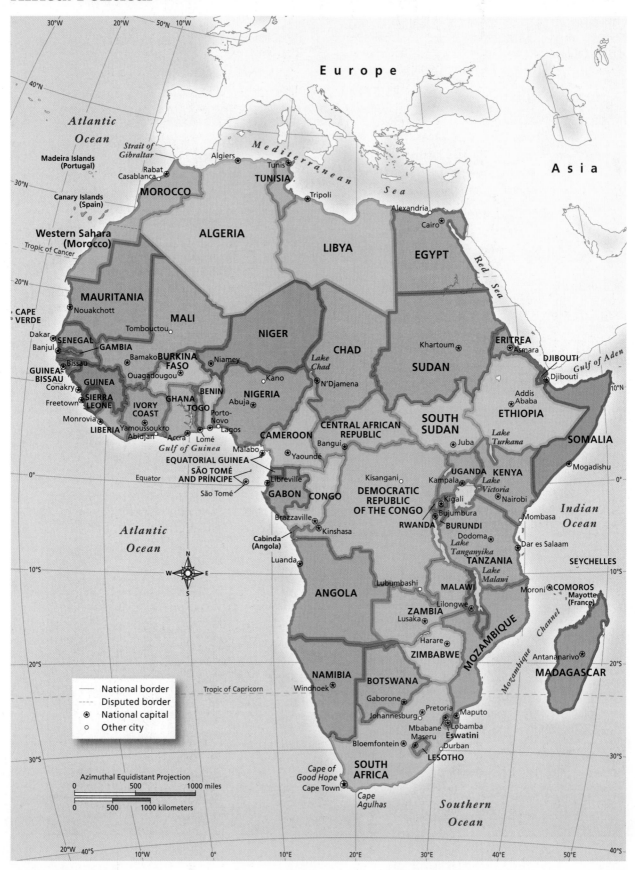

National border
Disputed border
⊛ National capital
○ Other city

Azimuthal Equidistant Projection

0   500   1000 miles

0   500   1000 kilometers

Africa: Physical

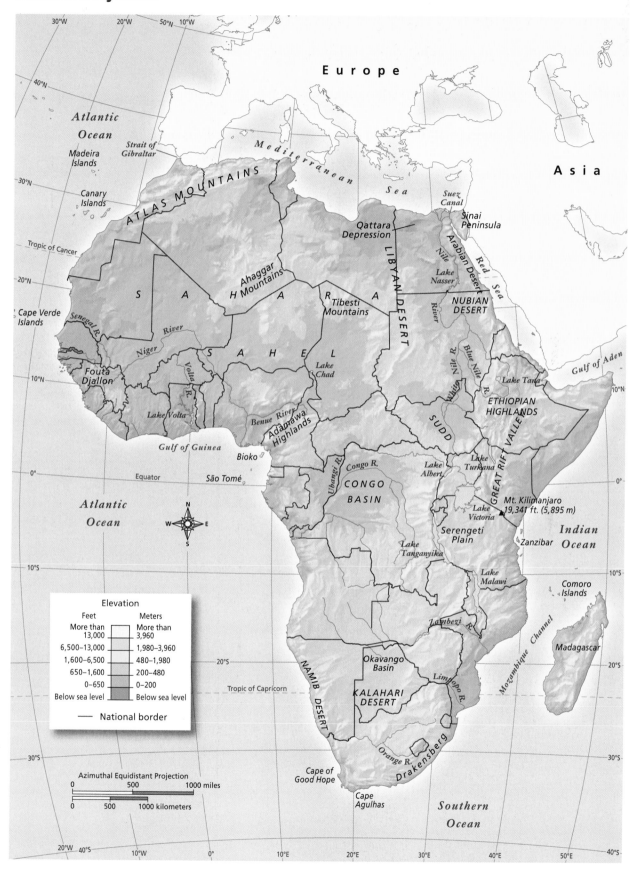

Europe

Asia

Atlantic
Ocean

Madeira
Islands

Strait of
Gibraltar

Mediterranean

Sea

Suez
Canal

Sinai
Peninsula

Canary
Islands

ATLAS MOUNTAINS

Tropic of Cancer

Qattara
Depression

LIBYAN DESERT

Arabian Desert

Nile

Cape Verde
Islands

Senegal R.

S   A

Ahaggar
H Mountains

Lake
Nasser

Red Sea

River

NUBIAN
DESERT

A

R   A

River

River

Niger

Tibesti
Mountains

Fouta
Djallon

Volta R.

S   A   H   E   L

Lake
Chad

White Nile R.

Blue Nile R.

Lake Tana

Gulf of Aden

ETHIOPIAN
HIGHLANDS

Lake Volta

Benue River

SUDD

Gulf of Guinea

Adamawa
Highlands

GREAT RIFT VALLEY

Bioko

São Tomé

Ubangi R.

Congo R.

Lake
Albert

Lake
Turkana

Equator

CONGO
BASIN

Lake
Victoria

Mt. Kilimanjaro
19,341 ft. (5,895 m)

Atlantic

Ocean

Serengeti
Plain

Zanzibar

Indian
Ocean

N

W   E

S

Lake
Tanganyika

Lake
Malawi

Comoro
Islands

Zambezi R.

Mozambique Channel

Madagascar

Elevation

Feet	Meters
More than 13,000	More than 3,960
6,500–13,000	1,980–3,960
1,600–6,500	480–1,980
650–1,600	200–480
0–650	0–200
Below sea level	Below sea level

— National border

Okavango
Basin

NAMIB DESERT

KALAHARI
DESERT

Limpopo R.

Tropic of Capricorn

Azimuthal Equidistant Projection

0   500   1000 miles

0   500   1000 kilometers

Orange R.

Cape of
Good Hope

Drakensberg

Cape
Agulhas

Southern

Ocean

Asia: Political

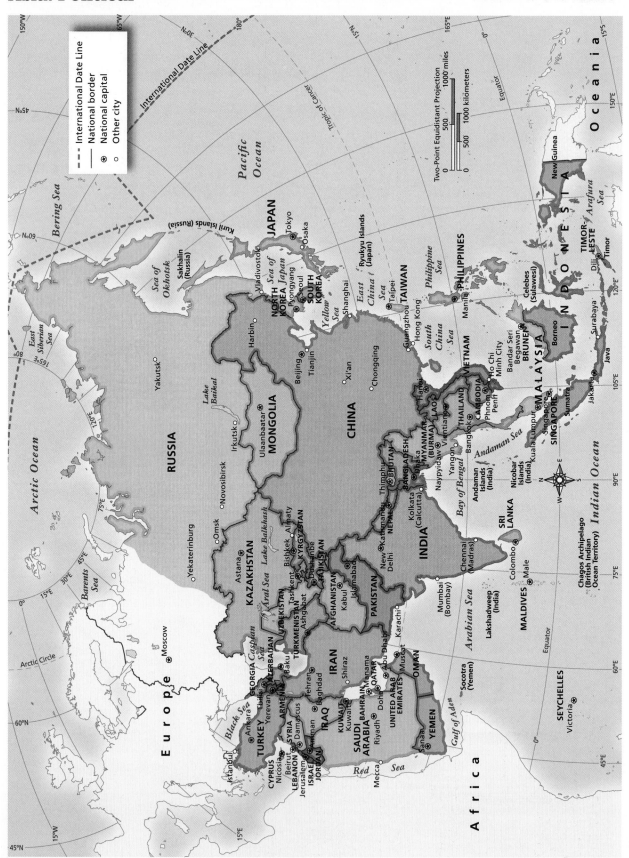

Asia: Physical

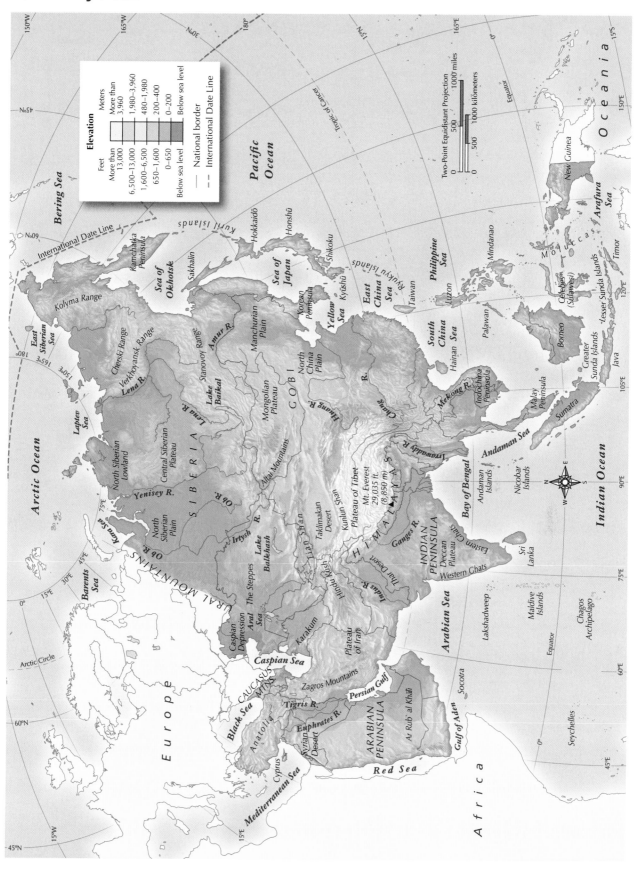

Elevation

Feet	Meters
More than 13,000	More than 3,960
6,500–13,000	1,980–3,960
1,600–6,500	480–1,980
650–1,600	200–400
0–650	0–200
Below sea level	Below sea level

— National border
-- International Date Line

Two-Point Equidistant Projection

1000 miles
1000 kilometers

Arctic Ocean

Bering Sea

Pacific Ocean

Oceania

New Guinea

Arafura Sea

Moluccas

Timor

Lesser Sunda Islands

Celebes (Sulawesi)

Mindanao

Philippine Sea

Luzon

Palawan

Borneo

Greater Sunda Islands

Java

Sumatra

Malay Peninsula

Indochina Peninsula

Indian Ocean

Andaman Sea

Bay of Bengal

Andaman Islands

Nicobar Islands

Sri Lanka

Eastern Ghats

Western Ghats

Deccan Plateau

INDIAN PENINSULA

Ganges R.

Maldive Islands

Chagos Archipelago

Lakshadweep

Arabian Sea

Seychelles

Socotra

Gulf of Aden

Red Sea

Africa

ARABIAN PENINSULA

Ar Rub' al Khāli

Persian Gulf

Zagros Mountains

Plateau of Iran

Tigris R.

Euphrates R.

Syrian Desert

Anatolia

Cyprus

Mediterranean Sea

Black Sea

CAUCASUS MTNS.

Caspian Sea

Caspian Depression

Aral Sea

The Steppes

Karakum

URAL MOUNTAINS

Europe

Barents Sea

Kara Sea

Arctic Circle

North Siberian Plain

North Siberian Lowland

Yenisey R.

Ob R.

Irtysh

Lake Balkhash

Laptev Sea

SIBERIA

Central Siberian Plateau

Lena R.

East Siberian Sea

Chersky Range

Verkhoyansk Range

Kolyma Range

Stanovoy Range

Lake Baikal

Amur R.

Sea of Okhotsk

Kamchatka Peninsula

Kuril Islands

Sakhalin

Hokkaido

Honshū

Sea of Japan

Shikoku

Kyūshū

Korean Peninsula

Manchurian Plain

Mongolian Plateau

GOBI

Altai Mountains

North China Plain

Huang R.

Yellow Sea

East China Sea

Ryukyu Islands

Taiwan

South China Sea

Hainan

Chang R.

Mekong R.

Irrawaddy R.

Taklimakan Desert

Tian Shan

Kunlun Shan

Plateau of Tibet

Mt. Everest 29,035 ft. (8,850 m)

HIMALAYAS

Thar Desert

Indus R.

Hindu Kush

International Date Line

Atlas **1139**

Europe: Political

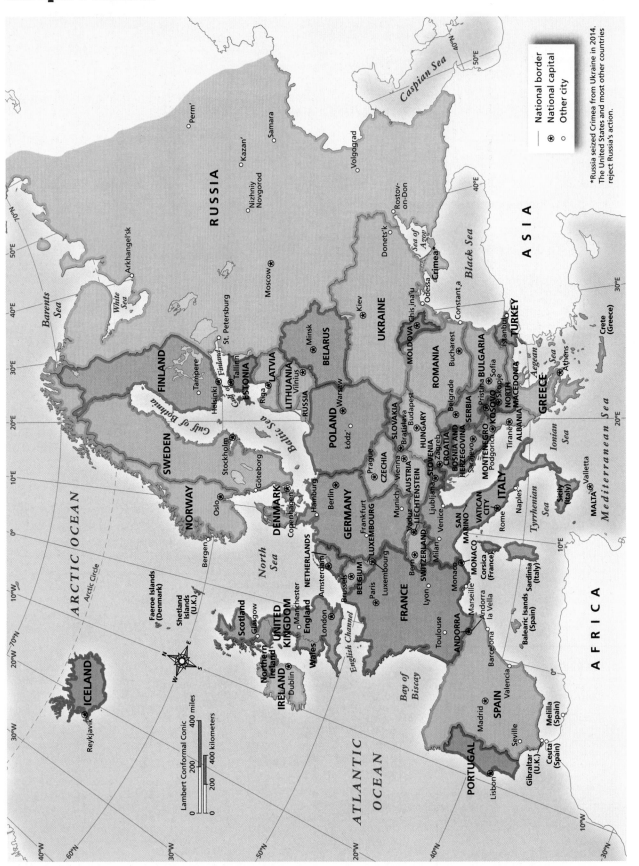

National border
⊛ National capital
○ Other city

*Russia seized Crimea from Ukraine in 2014. The United States and most other countries reject Russia's action.

ARCTIC OCEAN

Arctic Circle

Barents Sea

White Sea

RUSSIA

Perm'

Kazan'

Samara

Nizhniy Novgorod

Volgograd

Arkhangel'sk

Caspian Sea

FINLAND

Tampere

Helsinki

Gulf of Bothnia

St. Petersburg

Moscow ⊛

Rostov-on-Don

ASIA

Sea of Azov

Donets'k

Crimea*

Black Sea

SWEDEN

NORWAY

Stockholm ⊛

Göteborg

Oslo ⊛

Bergen

Baltic Sea

Gulf of Finland

Tallinn ⊛

ESTONIA

Riga ⊛

LATVIA

LITHUANIA

Vilnius ⊛

RUSSIA

Minsk ⊛

BELARUS

Kiev ⊛

UKRAINE

Chişinău ⊛

MOLDOVA

Odessa

Constanţa

Bucharest ⊛

ROMANIA

Istanbul

TURKEY

BULGARIA

Sofia ⊛

NORTH MACEDONIA

Skopje ⊛

Pristina ⊛ KOSOVO

Tiranë ⊛

ALBANIA

GREECE

Athens ⊛

Aegean Sea

Crete (Greece)

Ionian Sea

North Sea

DENMARK

Copenhagen ⊛

Hamburg

Berlin ⊛

GERMANY

POLAND

Warsaw ⊛

Łódź

Prague ⊛

CZECHIA

Vienna ⊛

SLOVAKIA

Bratislava

Budapest ⊛

HUNGARY

AUSTRIA

SLOVENIA

Ljubljana ⊛

Zagreb ⊛

CROATIA

BOSNIA AND HERZEGOVINA

Sarajevo ⊛

SERBIA

Belgrade ⊛

MONTENEGRO

Podgorica ⊛

NETHERLANDS

Amsterdam ⊛

BELGIUM

Brussels ⊛

LUXEMBOURG

Luxembourg ⊛

Frankfurt

Munich

Vaduz ⊛ LIECHTENSTEIN

SWITZERLAND

Bern ⊛

Milan

Venice

SAN MARINO

VATICAN CITY

Rome ⊛

ITALY

MONACO

Monaco ⊛

Naples

Tyrrhenian Sea

Sicily (Italy)

MALTA

Valletta ⊛

Mediterranean Sea

Sardinia (Italy)

Corsica (France)

UNITED KINGDOM

Scotland

Glasgow

Northern Ireland

England

Wales

Manchester

London ⊛

IRELAND

Dublin ⊛

English Channel

FRANCE

Paris ⊛

Lyon

Marseille

Toulouse

Bordeaux

Bay of Biscay

ANDORRA

Andorra la Vella ⊛

Barcelona

Balearic Islands (Spain)

SPAIN

Madrid ⊛

Valencia

Seville

PORTUGAL

Lisbon ⊛

Gibraltar (U.K.)

Ceuta (Spain)

Melilla (Spain)

AFRICA

ATLANTIC OCEAN

ICELAND

Reykjavik ⊛

Faeroe Islands (Denmark)

Shetland Islands (U.K.)

N
S
E
W

Lambert Conformal Conic

0   200   400 miles

0   200   400 kilometers

Europe: Physical

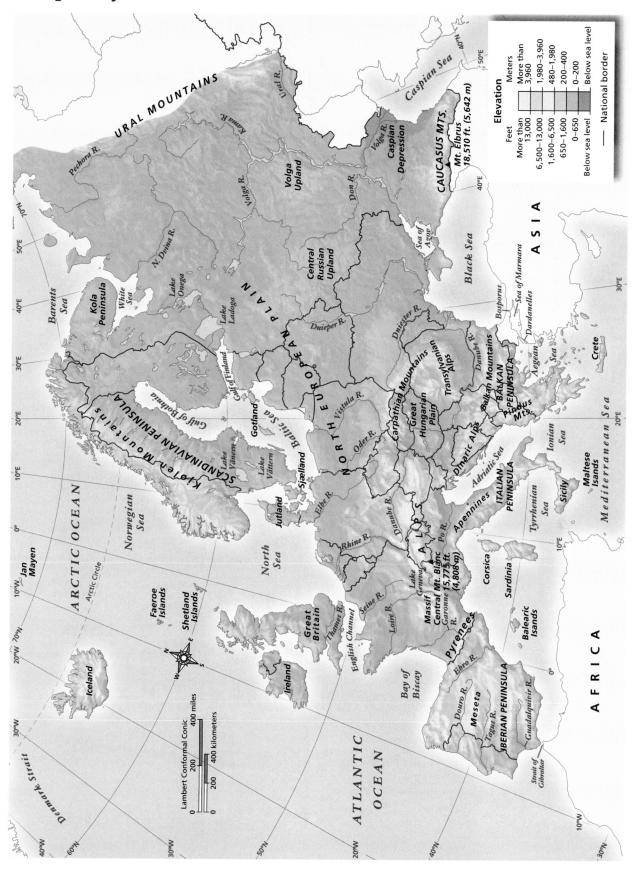

North and South America: Political

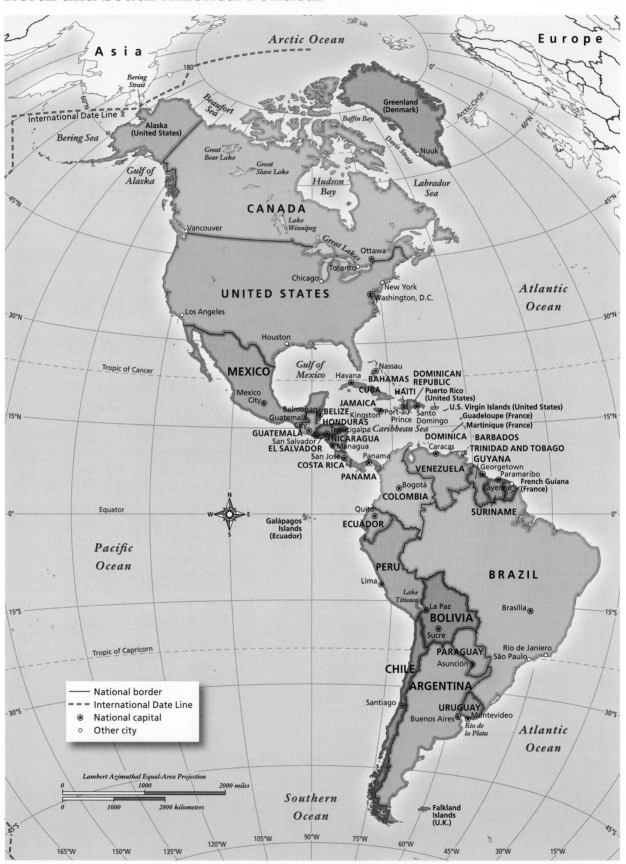

- —— National border
- --- International Date Line
- ⊛ National capital
- ○ Other city

Lambert Azimuthal Equal-Area Projection

North and South America: Physical

Elevation

Feet	Meters
More than 13,000	More than 3,960
6,500–13,000	1,980–3,960
1,600–6,500	480–1,980
650–1,600	200–400
0–650	0–200
Below sea level	Below sea level

—— National border
- - - International Date Line

Lambert Azimuthal Equal-Area Projection

0   1000   2000 miles

0   1000   2000 kilometers

Australia, New Zealand, and Oceania: Political-Physical

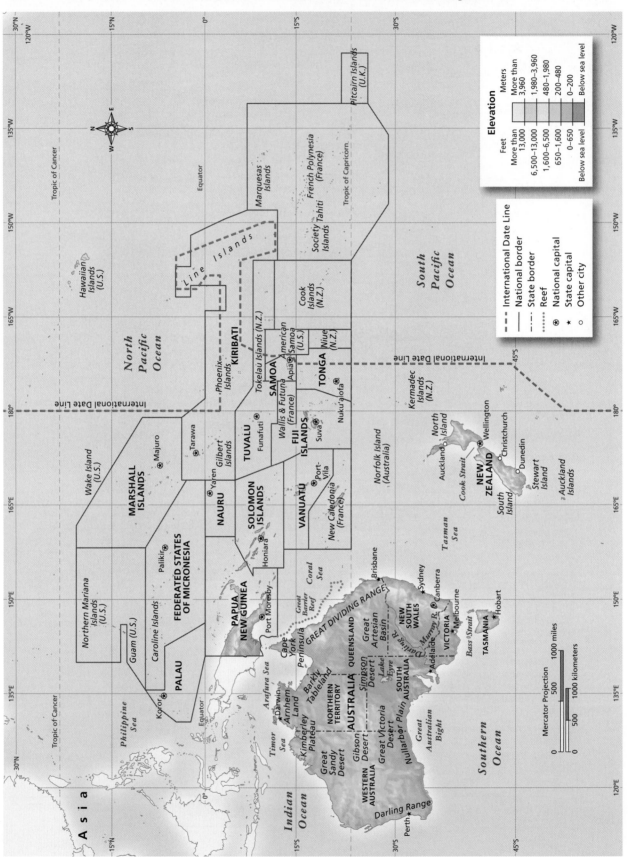

Elevation

Feet	Meters
More than 13,000	More than 3,960
6,500–13,000	1,980–3,960
1,600–6,500	480–1,980
650–1,600	200–480
0–650	0–200
Below sea level	Below sea level

- - - International Date Line
——— National border
——— State border
········· Reef
⊛ National capital
★ State capital
○ Other city

The Arctic: Physical

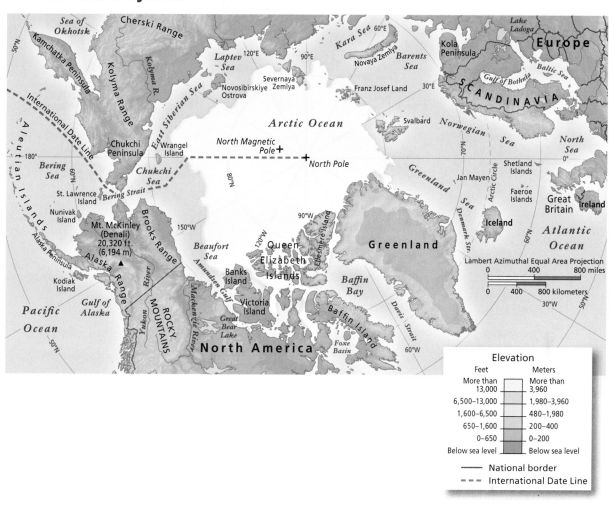

Elevation

Feet	Meters
More than 13,000	More than 3,960
6,500–13,000	1,980–3,960
1,600–6,500	480–1,980
650–1,600	200–400
0–650	0–200
Below sea level	Below sea level

—— National border
- - - International Date Line

Antarctica: Physical

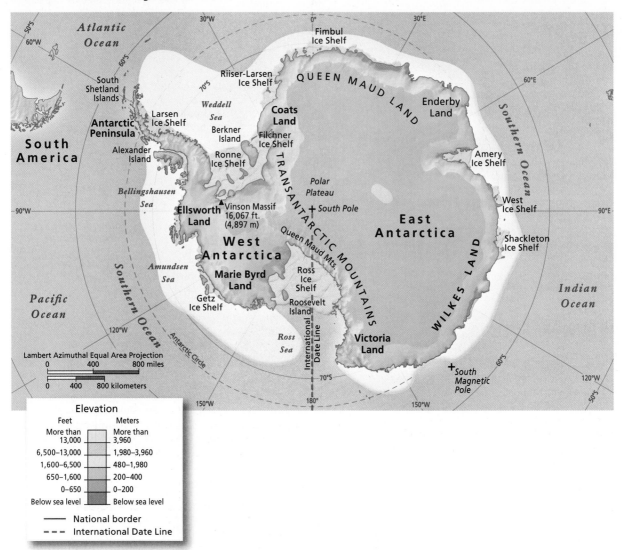

Elevation

Feet	Meters
More than 13,000	More than 3,960
6,500–13,000	1,980–3,960
1,600–6,500	480–1,980
650–1,600	200–400
0–650	0–200
Below sea level	Below sea level

——— National border

- - - International Date Line

A

abacus a device used for counting and calculating by sliding small balls or beads along rods or in grooves

Abbas the Great, Shah Abbas the Great (1571–1629) was the shah of the Safavid dynasty from 1588 until his death. He drove Ottoman and Uzbek troops from Persia and sponsored a golden age of Persian arts and achievement.

Abbasid dynasty that ruled in Baghdad from 750 to 1258

abdicate give up or step down from power

abolition the campaign against slavery and the slave trade

Abraham According to Jewish tradition, Abraham is the ancestor of the Jewish people. From the city of Ur and the son of an idol merchant, Abraham made a special covenant with God. Abraham led his descendants to Canaan, which Jews consider their Promised Land.

absentee landlord one who owns a large estate but does not live there

absolute monarchy a form of government in which a ruler has complete authority over the government and lives of the people he or she governs

absolutism the belief of complete and unrestricted power in government

abstract art style of art composed of lines, colors, and shapes, sometimes with no recognizable subject matter at all

Abu Bakr Abu Bakr (573–634) was Muhammad's father-in-law and the first Muslim caliph, or leader, following Muhammad's death. An early convert to Islam, Abu Bakr advised Muhammad and traveled on the hijra with the prophet. He helped unite the Muslim people through his role as successor to Muhammad. Under his rule, the Muslim empire expanded.

acculturation the blending of two or more cultures

acid rain a form of pollution in which toxic chemicals in the air come back to Earth in the form of rain, snow, or hail

acropolis highest and most fortified point within a Greek city-state

acupuncture medical treatment, originated in ancient China, in which needles are inserted into the skin at specific points to relieve pain or treat various illnesses

Adenauer, Konrad Konrad Adenauer (1876–1967) served as the first chancellor of West Germany, from 1949 to 1963. He led West Germany during its recovery and reconstruction after World War II. His accomplishments included West Germany's entry into NATO and the founding of the European Economic Community.

adobe a mixture of clay and plant fibers that becomes hard as it dries in the sun and that can be used for building

Adulis strategic trading port of the kingdom of Axum

Afghanistan an Islamic country in Central Asia; invaded by the Soviet Union in 1979; later home to the radical Islamist Taliban and the terrorist group al Qaeda

Afonso I (born around 1460–died 1542), was the ruler of Kongo, a historical kingdom in west-central Africa, in the early 16th century. Afonso encouraged trade with Portugal, promoted European culture in his kingdom, and adopted Christianity as the state religion and as his own religion.

African National Congress (ANC) the main organization that opposed apartheid and pushed for majority rule in South Africa; later a political party

agribusiness giant commercial farm, often owned by a multinational corporation

ahimsa Hindu belief in nonviolence and reverence for all life

aircraft carrier ship that accommodates the taking off and landing of airplanes, and transports aircraft

Akbar Akbar (1542–1605) is considered by most to be the greatest of the Mughal emperors of India. He extended the empire over most of India, and maintained an efficient centralized government through policies that won the loyalty of non-Muslim subjects. His greatness was also built on his support of scholars, artists, and musicians, who made his court a center of culture.

Akhenaton Akhenaton was king of Egypt for 17 years. He abandoned traditional Egyptian polytheism and established a new cult dedicated to the Aton, the sun's disk. His attempt to start a new religion died with him in 1336 B.C.

al Qaeda a fundamentalist terrorist organization founded and led by Saudi Arabian Osama bin Laden until his death in 2011

al-Khwarizmi al-Khwarizmi (c. 780–c. 850) was a Muslim mathematician who developed groundbreaking concepts related to the study of algebra and introduced the term *algebra,* or *al-jabr.* Through his writings, he introduced Europeans to the study of this branch of mathematics. Working in the field of geography as well, al-Khwarizmi also supervised the production of one of the earliest maps of the world.

Albuquerque, Afonso de Afonso de Albuquerque (1453–1515) was a Portuguese admiral who helped found Portugal's trade empire in the East. He captured and built strategic forts at Goa, Calicut, Malacca, and Hormoz; reconstructed other forts; set up shipbuilding and other Portuguese industries in India; and built churches.

Alexander II Alexander II (1818–1881), son of emperor Nicholas I, became tsar in 1855. Alexander II assumed power in the middle of the Crimean War, which revealed Russia's backwardness. He instituted broad modernizing reforms, including emancipating the serfs in 1861. However, growing internal rebellion and increased revolutionary activity in Poland led Alexander to enact repressive measures. He was assassinated in 1881.

Alexander the Great Alexander the Great (356 B.C.–324 B.C.), Philip II's son and Aristotle's pupil, at age 20 became heir to Philip's territories. He conquered the Persian empire, founding new cities as his armies won victories in Asia Minor, Palestine, and Egypt, and then captured Babylon. Continuing eastward into India, his tired troops refused to go farther. Returned to Babylon, Alexander, age 32, died from a sudden fever.

Alexandria Alexandria, founded in 332 B.C. by Alexander the Great, became one of the greatest cities of the Mediterranean world. Located in Egypt on the sea lanes between Europe and Asia, Alexandria became known for its size, great markets, huge Pharos lighthouse, and the Museum, a learning center with a famous library.

Alighieri, Dante Dante Alighieri (1265–1321) was a philosopher, writer, and poet who was deeply involved in Italian politics, including the battles between the popes and monarchs of his time. He held political offices at different times throughout his life. Although he wrote many poems and other works, he is known best for *Divine Comedy.*

alliance formal agreement between two or more nations or powers to cooperate and come to one another's defense

alphabet writing system in which each symbol represents a single basic sound

Alsace and Lorraine region of northern Europe on the border between France and Germany, which was ceded to Germany after the Franco-Prussian War

Amon-Re Amon-Re was considered the king of the gods. He was present in the mythology and culture of the Egyptian people from their beginning.

Amritsar massacre an incident in 1919 in which British troops fired on an unarmed crowd of Indian protestors in the northern Indian town of Amritsar

anarchist a person who wants to abolish all government

ancien régime old order system of government in pre-revolutionary France

anesthetic drug that prevents pain during surgery

animism the belief that spirits and forces live within animals, objects, or dreams

annex add a territory to an existing state or country

Anschluss union of Austria and Germany

anthropology the study of the origins and development of people and their societies

anti-Semitism prejudice against Jews

apartheid a policy of rigid racial segregation in the Republic of South Africa

apostle leader or teacher of a new faith or movement

appeasement policy of giving in to an aggressor's demands in order to keep the peace

apprentice a young person learning a trade from a master

aqueduct in ancient Rome, underground or bridge-like stone structure that carried water from the hills into the city

Aquinas, Thomas Thomas Aquinas (1225–1274) was a philosopher, theologian, and monk who helped bridge the gap between medieval faith and the philosophy of reason promoted by Greek philosophy. He also explained the idea of natural law, that there are universal laws based on reason that are independent of laws passed by government.

Aquino, Benigno Benigno Aquino, Jr., (1932–1983) was the opposition leader during Ferdinand Marcos's dictatorship of the Philippines. His career in politics included terms as a provincial governor and senator, but when he planned to run for president in 1973, Marcos threw him in jail. Aquino spent eight years on death row but was then released to the U.S. to receive heart surgery. In 1983, Aquino returned to the Philippines and was assassinated at the Manila Airport. The military conspiracy against the popular politician led to support for his wife, Corazon Aquino, who proceeded to defeat Marcos in a presidential election.

Aquino, Corazon Corazon Aquino (1933–2009) was president of the Philippines, restoring democracy after Ferdinand Marcos's reign. Educated in the U.S., Aquino married politician Benigno Aquino and focused on raising their children. She accompanied her husband during his exile in the U.S., and when he was executed upon his return to the Philippines, people rallied behind her. She won in a presidential election against Marcos and soon after reestablished congress and appointed a team to write a new constitution. Though Aquino restored freedom to the Philippines, many of her policies were unpopular, and she lost the presidency to her defense secretary in 1992.

Arafat, Yasir Yasir Arafat (1929–2004) fought for Palestinian independence most of his life. He was a founder of Al-Fatah, a group that resisted Israel, and also of the Palestinian Liberation Organization (PLO). In 1969, he became chairman of the PLO. In the early 1990s, he reached a peace agreement with Israel. In 1994, together with Shimon Peres

and Yitzhak Rabin, he won the Nobel Peace Prize. He then became the president of the newly created Palestinian Authority.

archaeology the study of people and cultures through material remains

Archimedes Archimedes (c. 287 B.C.–c. 212 B.C.), a famous Hellenistic mathematician and inventor from Syracuse, a Greek colony (now in Italy), is known for understanding the principle of levers, discovering the relation between the surface and volume of a sphere, and inventing the Archimedes screw, a device for raising water.

archipelago chain of islands

aristocracy government headed by a privileged minority or upper class

Aristotle Aristotle (384 B.C.–322 B.C.), a student of Plato, was a philosopher, writer about many branches of knowledge, founder of the Lyceum, and tutor of Alexander the Great.

armada fleet of ships

armistice agreement to end fighting in a war

artifact an object made by human beings

artificial satellite manmade object that orbits a larger body in space

artisan a skilled craftsperson

Asante kingdom kingdom that emerged in the 1700s in present-day Ghana and was active in the trade in enslaved people

Asia Minor a peninsula in western Asia between the Black Sea and the Mediterranean Sea

Ashoka Ashoka, who died about 238 B.C., was the last major Mauryan emperor in India. A committed Buddhist, he helped to spread Buddhism throughout India. His rule was characterized by fairness, compassion, and the principles of right life, which he had inscribed on stone pillars erected throughout the empire.

assassination murder of a public figure, usually for political reasons

assembly line a production method that breaks down a complex job into a series of smaller tasks

assimilate absorb or adopt another culture

Atatürk Atatürk (1881–1938) is the name that Mustafa Kemal gave himself when he ordered all Turkish people to take on surnames. In 1920, he led Turkish nationalists in the fight against Greek forces trying to enforce the Treaty of Sèvres, establishing the borders of the modern Republic of Turkey. Once in power, he passed many reforms to modernize, Westernize, and secularize Turkey.

atheism belief that there is no god

Athens city-state in ancient Greece that evolved from a monarchy to a limited direct democracy and became famous for its great cultural achievements

Atlantic Charter agreement in which Franklin Roosevelt and Winston Churchill set goals for the defeat of Nazi Germany and for the postwar world

atman in Hindu belief, a person's essential self

atrocity horrible act committed against innocent people

Augustine Augustine (A.D. 364–A.D. 430) was a Christian scholar whose written works had long-lasting effects on the Christian religion. He studied in Roman Africa and went on to become a bishop.

Augustus (63 B.C.–14 A.D.) was the first Roman emperor of the newly established Roman empire. Augustus's rule began a long-lasting period of peace and wealth known as the *Pax Romana*.

Auschwitz a group of three German concentration camps and extermination camps in southern Poland, built and operated during the Third Reich

autocracy system of government in which an individual or a small group of individuals rules with unlimited power

autocrat ruler who has complete authority

autocratic having unlimited power

autonomy self-rule

Axis powers group of countries led by Germany, Italy, and Japan that fought the Allies in World War II

Axum trading center and powerful ancient kingdom in northern present-day Ethiopia

ayllu in the Inca empire, a close-knit village

B

Babur Babur (1483–1530) was the founder of the Mughal Dynasty in India. He came from Turkish and Mongol heritages, a descendent of the great Mongol leader, Genghis Khan. His name is the Arabic word for "tiger," but he was as accomplished a poet as he was a warrior. His wise rule helped launch a powerful Muslim dynasty that had a permanent influence on northern India.

Bacon, Francis Francis Bacon (1561–1626) was a distinguished English philosopher, statesman, and lawyer. A man of many talents, he promoted rational thought. Bacon was held in high regard by philosophers and scientists in Europe as well as England.

Baghdad capital city of present-day Iraq; capital of the Muslim empire during Islam's golden age

balance of power distribution of military and economic power that prevents any one nation from becoming too strong

balance of trade difference between how much a country imports and how much it exports

Balfour Declaration statement issued by the British government in 1917 supporting the idea of a homeland for Jews in the Palestine Mandate

Balkan Peninsula triangular arm of land that juts from southeastern Europe into the Mediterranean

Bangladesh nation east of India that was formerly part of Pakistan

Bantu root language of West Africa on which some early African migration patterns are based

Barbarossa, Frederick Frederick Barbarossa (c. 1123–1190) was a German king who became Holy Roman Emperor in 1152. He fought hard against growing papal authority and led six expeditions into Italy in an attempt to increase his royal holdings. He died while on the Third Crusade.

baroque ornate style of art and architecture popular in the 1600s and 1700s

barter economy economic system in which one set of goods or services is exchanged for another

Bastille fortress in Paris used as a prison; French Revolution began when Parisians stormed it in 1789

Bataan Death March during World War II, the forced march of Filipino and American prisoners of war under brutal conditions by the Japanese military

battle of Tours battle in 732 in which the Christian Franks led by Charles Martel defeated the Muslim armies and stopped the Muslim advance into Europe

Bedouin a desert-dwelling Arab nomad

Beethoven, Ludwig van Ludwig van Beethoven (1770–1827) was a German composer trained in piano and violin by his father Johannes. At the age of 12, he published his first work and began playing viola in the symphony orchestra in Bonn, Germany. In 1792, he went to Vienna and began studying with Haydn. Beethoven remained in Vienna, where he wrote most of his symphonies, concertos, sonatas, and string quartets. Although he began to lose his hearing 1798, he continued to compose music he could hear only in his mind.

Benedictine Rule rules drawn up in 530 by Benedict, a monk, regulating monastic life. The Rule emphasizes obedience, poverty, and chastity and divides the day into periods of worship, work, and study

Bentham, Jeremy Jeremy Bentham (1748–1832) was a British philosopher and economist who advocated for utilitarianism, the belief that right and wrong can be measured by the greatest happiness of the greatest number of people. Bentham was trained in the law but did not become a practicing lawyer. Instead, he focused on legal reforms. Not content to simply suggest new laws, he also detailed plans for how to implement his proposals. His ideas were influential during his lifetime, and some of his reforms were enacted.

Bessemer, Henry Henry Bessemer (1813–1879) was a British inventor and engineer. His greatest invention was the Bessemer Converter, which could create high-quality steel quickly and inexpensively. In 1956 he patented his process for making steel. His process was essential to advances in transportation, construction, and defense. Today, steel is still made by a method based on the Bessemer process.

Biafra region of southeastern Nigeria that launched a failed bid for independence from Nigeria in 1966, resulting in a bloody war

biotechnology the application of biological research to industry, engineering, and technology

bishop high-ranking Church official with authority over a local area, or diocese

Bismarck, Otto von Otto von Bismarck (1815–1898) worked briefly as a civil servant before his career in government. He served as a diplomat to the German Federation, and he became chancellor of the German Empire in 1871, a position he held for 19 years.

Black Death an epidemic of the bubonic plague that ravaged Europe in the 1300s

Black Shirt any member of the militant combat squads of Italian Fascists set up under Mussolini

blitzkrieg lightning war

bloc a group of nations acting together in support of one another

Boer War (1899–1902) a war in which Great Britain defeated the Boers of South Africa

Boers Dutch farmers who settled in Cape Town, Africa, and eventually migrated inland

Bolívar, Simón Simón Bolívar (1783–1830) was a South American soldier and leader who was instrumental in the revolutions against Spain. He was born into wealth and educated in Spain. After France invaded Spain, he became involved in the resistance movement and played a key role in the Latin American fight for independence. He died in 1830 from tuberculosis.

Bonaparte, Napoleon Napoleon Bonaparte (1769–1821) was a huge figure in European history. He was a military genius who was elected consul for life. He later crowned himself France's emperor. His legal, educational, and militaristic reforms impacted French society for generations.

bourgeoisie the middle class

Boxer Uprising anti-foreign movement in China from 1898–1900

boyar landowning noble in Russia under the tsars

boycott refuse to buy

Boyle, Robert Robert Boyle (1627–1691) was one of the leading minds of the late 1600s. An English-Irish philosopher and writer, Boyle focused on chemistry, physics, and natural history. His work with pressurized air led to the development of Boyle's Law, which describes the relationship between pressure and the volume of gas. Boyle was one of the founders of the Royal Society of London.

Brahe, Tycho Tycho Brahe (1546–1601) was a Danish astronomer who produced the most accurate measurements and locations of the stars before the use of the telescope. His observation that a new star had appeared in an existing constellation challenged the belief that the stars were fixed and forever unchanging.

Brahman in the belief system established in Vedic India, a single spiritual power that resides in all things

Brezhnev, Leonid Leonid Brezhnev (1906–1982) led the Soviet Union from 1964, when he organized the removal of Nikita Khrushchev, until his death in 1982. He presided over the Soviet Union's last arms build-up and the economic stagnation that encouraged the reforms of Mikhail Gorbachev.

bureaucracy system of government through departments and subdivisions administered by officials who follow set rules

bushido code of conduct for samurai during the feudal period in Japan

Byron, Lord Lord Byron (1788–1824) was a member of the House of Lords, a political and social satirist, and one of the most memorable, fashionable, and captivating Romantic poets. He became the model for the Romantic hero and the embodiment of the movement. Byron believed in liberty, which he often focused on in both his works and deeds. Although Byron died before he completed his poem *Don Juan,* it is considered to be his masterpiece and one of England's great long poems.

C

cabinet parliamentary advisors to the king who originally met in a small room, or cabinet

Cabot, John John Cabot (c. 1450–c. 1499) had his early roots in Venice, Italy, working in a mercantile firm. He became a navigator and explorer who, during 1497–1498, claimed parts of Canada for Britain.

Caesar, Julius (c. 100 B.C.–44 B.C.) was a Roman general, master of political maneuvers, and a reformist. He advocated for the re-organization of Rome's government. In 47 B.C., he became dictator, and three years later was assassinated.

cahiers notebooks used in pre-revolutionary France to record grievances

Cahokia in Illinois, the largest earthwork of the Mississippian culture, c. A.D. 700

calculus a branch of mathematics in which calculations are made using special symbolic notations, developed by Isaac Newton

caliph successor to Muhammad as political and religious leader of the Muslims

calligraphy the art of producing beautiful handwriting

Calvin, John John Calvin (1509–1564) was a French theologian and lawyer. Influenced by the humanist philosophy of Erasmus, Calvin became involved with the Protestant movement while a student at the University of Paris. He later moved to Geneva, Switzerland, where he set up a theocracy and wrote *Institutes of the Christian Religion.* Calvin's interpretation of Christian doctrine is called Calvinism.

canon law body of laws of a church

canonize recognize a person as a saint

Cape Town the first permanent European settlement in Africa, established by the Dutch in 1652

capital money or wealth used to invest in business or enterprise

capital offense crime punishable by death

capitalism economic system in which the means of production are privately owned and operated for profit

Cárdenas, Lázaro Lázaro Cárdenas (1895–1970) joined the revolutionary forces when he was 18 and later became a general in the Mexican army. After the revolution, he served as governor of Michoacán and then as president of the PNR. In 1934, he was elected president of Mexico. During his presidency, Cárdenas worked to establish the social and economic reforms the revolutionaries had fought for, including the redistribution of land, the organization of confederations for both workers and peasants, and the nationalization of foreign-owned industries.

Carranza, Venustiano Venustiano Carranza (1859–1920) served as a leader in the Mexican Revolution in support of political, rather than social, reform. He was elected the first president after the revolution, and though he signed the Constitution of 1917, he did little to implement promised reforms. This reluctance led to social unrest and economic difficulties. When a rebellion began in April 1920, Carranza fled the capital and eventually went into hiding in the mountains. He was betrayed and murdered in May.

cartel a group of companies that join together to control the production and price of a product

Cartier, Jacques Jacques Cartier (1491–1557) is credited with naming Canada. He is also recognized for his limited exploration of the St. Lawrence River, stopped short by severe weather and hostile Iroquois Indians.

cartographer a person who makes maps

caste in traditional Indian society, an unchangeable social group into which a person is born

Castiglione, Baldassare Castiglione (1478–1529) was an Italian courtier, diplomat, and writer. His handbook, *The Book of the Courtier,* was widely read for its advice on the manners, skills, learning, and virtues that court members should display. He described an ideal courtier as well-mannered, well-educated, and multitalented.

Castro, Fidel Fidel Castro (b. 1926) served as leader of Cuba beginning in 1959, when he led the Cuban Revolution and installed a communist regime. During the Cold War, Castro's Cuba was allied with the Soviet Union and, therefore, at odds with the United States. His policies remained socialist after the fall of the Soviet Union. When his health began to fail in 2006, his brother, Raul, took over as the Cuban leader.

Çatalhöyük one of the world's first villages, established in modern-day Turkey around 7000 B.C.

cataract waterfall

Catherine the Great Catherine the Great (1729–1796) was the German-born empress of Russia (1762–1796) who led her country in becoming part of the political and cultural life of Europe.

caudillo military dictator in Latin America

Cavour, Camillo Camillo Cavour (1810–1861) was the second son of a noble family. After a brief career in the military, he decided that politics was his true strength. His ability to manipulate political situations to further the cause of Italian unification made him a valuable leader.

Ceausescu, Nicolae Nicolae Ceausescu (1918–1989) led the communist government in Romania from 1965 until his death in 1989. His regime was noted for its massive corruption, crippling economic conditions, and unchecked secret police. He was executed, along with his wife, Elena, after the coup that ended communist rule in Romania.

celadon porcelain made in Korea with an unusual blue-green glaze

censorship restriction on access to ideas and information

census population count

Cervantes, Miguel de Miguel de Cervantes (1547–1616), a Spanish novelist, playwright, and poet, was the most important figure in Spanish literature. His novel Don Quixote is his most well-known work.

Champlain, Samuel de Samuel de Champlain (1567–1635) was a French navigator and explorer who established the colony of Quebec in 1608. He became known as the "Father of New France" and was honored by the court of King Henry IV.

chancellor the highest official of a monarch, prime minister

characters written symbols in writing systems such as that of the Chinese

Charlemagne Charlemagne (747–814), (or "Charles the Great") king of the Franks, the Lombards, and emperor of the Romans, began as a warrior king seeking to conquer territory and distribute plunder in the Frankish tradition. But he also strove to unite and govern an increasingly diverse collection of conquered peoples as well as cope with threats from new invaders. He conducted a long series of successful military campaigns, made efforts to spread Christianity and implement religious reform, sought to make more effective inherited political institutions and procedures, and supported cultural renewal through a revival of learning.

Charles I Charles I (1600–1649) was the second Stuart king of England, Scotland, and Wales. His belief in the divine right of kings brought him into constant conflict with Parliament. This conflict eventually led to the English Civil War and Charles's defeat and execution for treason.

Charles V Charles V (1500–1558) was the Holy Roman emperor during the time of Martin Luther's reformation efforts. His immense empire included large areas of Europe. A staunch Catholic, he rejected Luther's doctrines. The Protestant upheaval, along with political pressures, led Charles to voluntarily give up his throne. He divided the empire between his son and his brother. Charles entered a Catholic monastery where he remained until his death.

charter in the Middle Ages, a written document that set out the rights and privileges of a town

Chaucer, Geoffrey Geoffrey Chaucer (1343–1400) was the first important poet of his time to write in English. At various times during his life he worked as a copywriter, member of Parliament, and justice of the peace. His keen observations of many different types of people was reflected in his famous work, *Canterbury Tales*.

Chavín a culture that thrived in the Andean region from about 900 to 200 B.C.

Chechnya a republic within Russia, where rebels have fought for independence

checks and balances system in which each branch of a government has the power to monitor and limit the actions of the other two

Cheka early Soviet secret police force

chinampa in the Aztec empire, an artificial island used to cultivate crops and made of mud piled atop reed mats that were anchored to the lake bed with willow trees

chivalry code of conduct for knights during the Middle Ages

Choson dynasty Korean dynasty that ruled from 1392 to 1910, the longest-lived of Korea's three dynasties

Christian Bible the sacred writings of the Christian religion

Churchill, Winston Winston Churchill (1874–1965) was born to British aristocracy and became prime minister of the British empire in 1940. Early on, he proclaimed the threats posed by Nazi Germany. His determination persuaded the country to defend itself against an encroaching enemy.

circumnavigate to travel completely around the world

citizen a native or resident of a town or city

city-state a political unit that includes a city and its surrounding lands and villages

civil disobedience the refusal to obey unjust laws

civil law branch of law that deals with private rights and matters

civil servants government officials

civil war a war fought between groups of people in the same nation

civilization an advanced stage of human society marked by a well-organized government and high levels of culture, science, and industry.

clan group of families with a common ancestor

clergy the body of people who conduct Christian services

Clovis Clovis (466–511) is known as the political and religious founder of the kingdom of the Franks. He ruled much of Gaul from the late fifth century until 511. His kingdom, which expanded south and west from what is present-day Belgium and northeastern France, was the most powerful in Gaul. He was also the most important ally of the Byzantine emperor Anastasius I. Born a pagan, Clovis corresponded with the powerful bishops of Gaul and, in 496 or perhaps later, became famous as one of the first Germanic kings to convert to Christianity.

coalition temporary alliance of various political parties

codify to arrange or set down in writing

Colbert, Jean-Baptiste Jean-Baptiste Colbert (1619–1683) served under King Louis XIV of France as controller general of finance (from 1665) and secretary of state for the navy (from 1668). He carried out economic programs that helped make France the strongest power in Europe.

Cold War state of tension and hostility between nations aligned with the United States on one side and the Soviet Union on the other that rarely led to direct armed conflict

collective large farm owned and operated by peasants as a group

collective security system in which a group of nations acts as one to preserve the peace of all

collectivization the forced joining together of workers and property into collectives, such as rural collectives that absorb peasants and their land

colony territory settled and ruled by people from another land

colossus giant

Columbian Exchange the global exchange of goods, ideas, plants and animals, and disease that began with Columbus's journey to the Americas

Columbus, Christopher Christopher Columbus (1451–1506) was an Italian explorer and navigator who went on Mediterranean and Africa expeditions, thought up a plan to sail west to reach India and China, and found support from the Spanish monarchs Ferdinand and Isabella. In 1492, he sailed west from Spain and reached the Caribbean Islands, which he mistakenly thought were the Indies of Asia. He made other voyages, but strained relations with the Spanish royal officials led to his arrest and dismissal as governor of the settlements on the island of Hispaniola.

comedy in ancient Greece, play that mocked people or social customs

Comintern Communist International, international association of communist parties led by the Soviet Union for the purpose of encouraging worldwide communist revolution

command economy system in which government officials make all basic economic decisions

Commercial Revolution A period of European economic expansion, colonialism, and mercantilism which lasted from about the 1500s until the early 1700s. It included the growth of capitalism, banking, and investing.

commissar Communist party official assigned to the army to teach party principles and ensure party loyalty during the Russian Revolution

commodity valuable product

common law a legal system based on custom and court rulings

communism form of socialism advocated by Karl Marx; According to Marx, class struggle was inevitable and would lead to the creation of a classless society in which all wealth and property would be owned by the community as a whole.

compact an agreement among people

compromise an agreement in which each side makes concessions; an acceptable middle ground

concentration camp detention center for civilians considered enemies of the state

Concert of Europe loose peacekeeping organization whose goal was to preserve the agreements set up by the Congress of Vienna

concession special economic right given to foreign companies or individuals

confederation unification

Confucius (551 B.C.–479 B.C.) is China's most famous philosopher. His teachings about the importance of education and public service influenced many eastern Asian civilizations. His ancestors, members of the aristocracy, were poor by the time of Confucius's birth. By the age of 15, Confucius was dedicated to the life of a scholar. Although his ideas about the proper way to live guided millions of people, Confucius's own life was simple and reflected a deep humility.

Congress of Vienna assembly of European leaders that met after the Napoleonic era to piece Europe back together; met from September 1814 to June 1815

conquistador "conqueror" in Spanish; a leader in the Spanish conquests of America, Mexico, and Peru in the sixteenth century

conscription "the draft," which required all young men to be ready for military or other service

consensus widespread agreement among all members of a group

Constantine Constantine (c. A.D. 280– A.D. 337) was the first Roman Emperor to become a Christian. During his reign, he prevented the persecution of Christians and helped to strengthen the early church.

Constantinople the capital of the eastern Roman empire; capital of the Byzantine and Ottoman empires, now called Istanbul

constitutional government government whose power is defined and limited by law

consul an official from the patrician class who supervised the government and commanded the armies

containment the U.S. strategy of limiting communism to the areas already under Soviet control

Continental System blockade designed by Napoleon to hurt Britain economically by closing European ports to British goods; ultimately unsuccessful

contra guerrilla who fought the Sandinistas in Nicaragua

contraband during wartime, military supplies and raw materials needed to make military supplies that may legally be confiscated by any belligerent

convoy group of merchant ships protected by warships

Copernicus, Nicolaus Nicolaus Copernicus (1473–1543) was a Polish astronomer who concluded that the sun is the center of the universe around which Earth and the other planets revolve. This contradicted the religious and scientific belief that Earth was the center of the universe. Although he did not suffer immediate challenges from the Church, his most important work did not appear in print until after his death.

corporation a business owned by many investors who buy shares of stock and risk only the amount of their investment

Cortés, Hernán Hernán Cortés (c. 1485–1547) was a Spanish landowner in Cuba and conquistador who in 1518 led an expedition to Mexico. Allied with some Native American groups, he conquered the Aztec empire, including its capital Tenochititlán in 1521. The Holy Roman Emperor Charles V in 1522 appointed him governor of New Spain, but Cortés was eventually removed from power and retired to Spain in 1540.

Council of Trent a group of Catholic leaders that met between 1545 and 1563 to respond to Protestant challenges and direct the future of the Catholic Church

coup d'état the forcible overthrow of a government

Courbet, Gustave Gustave Courbet (1819–1877) was a leading French painter in the Realist movement. While he more painted traditional subjects, such as seascapes, portraits, and landscapes, he also focused on representing daily life by painting the rural middle class and bohemian culture, as well as social issues by depicting the harsh lives of the poor.

covenant a binding agreement; specifically, in the Jewish tradition, the binding agreement God made with Abraham

Cranmer, Thomas Thomas Cranmer (1489–1556) was a Catholic theologian who strongly supported reform. When Henry VIII broke with the Roman Catholic Church, Cranmer became England's first Protestant archbishop of Canterbury. He distributed English language Bibles to parish churches and, later, developed the *Book of Common Prayer*. Cranmer also acted as an adviser to both Henry VIII and his son, Edward VI.

crematorium a place used to burn corpses

creole in Spanish colonial America, an American-born descendant of Spanish settlers

Crimean War war fought mainly on the Crimean Peninsula between the Russians and the British, French, and Turks from 1853–1856

criminal law branch of law that deals with offenses against others

Cromwell, Oliver Oliver Cromwell (1599–1658) was an English soldier and gentleman who led the forces against Charles I of England during the English Civil War. He made himself Lord Protector of England in 1653, leading the country as a republic until his death.

Crusades a series of wars from the 1000s through 1200s in which European Christians tried to win control of the Holy Land from Muslims

cult of domesticity idealization of women and the home

cultural diffusion the spread of ideas, customs, and technologies from one people to another

cultural nationalism pride in the culture of one's country

Cultural Revolution a Chinese Communist program in the late 1960s to purge China of nonrevolutionary tendencies that caused economic and social damage

culture the way of life of a society, which is handed down from one generation to the next by learning and experience

cuneiform in the ancient Middle East, a system of writing that used wedge-shaped marks

Curie, Marie Marie Curie (1867–1934) was born in Warsaw to Polish schoolteachers. She later moved to Paris, where she gained a formal education and met her husband Pierre Curie. The Curies conducted groundbreaking work on radioactivity, revolutionizing the fields of physics and chemistry. The first woman to win a Nobel Prize, Marie Curie also worked tirelessly to promote practical and medicinal applications of her work. She died in 1934, most likely from her many years of exposure to radioactive materials.

Cuzco capital city of the Inca empire

cybersecurity ways to protect computers, networks, and data against unauthorized use

cyberwarfare a series of government-sponsored attacks on networked computer systems that could disrupt critical infrastructure in a target country

Cyrillic relating to the Slavic alphabet derived from the Greek and traditionally attributed to St. Cyril; in modified form still used in modern Slavic languages

D

D-Day code name for June 6, 1944, the day that Allied forces invaded France during WWII

dada artistic movement in which artists rejected tradition and produced works that often shocked their viewers

Daguerre, Louis Louis Daguerre (1787–1851) was a French painter and physicist who invented photography. Before Daguerre invented the camera, he was a printmaker and painter. For years he had been experimenting with ways to capture detailed, photographic images. Finally, in 1839, he showed his process to the Académie des Sciences and the Académie des Beaux-Arts. He astounded everyone, and his invention revolutionized both the arts and the sciences.

dalit outcast or member of India's lowest caste

Dalton, John John Dalton (1766–1844) was an English teacher, lecturer, meteorologist, physicist, and chemist. His interest in the atmosphere led to his development of the Atomic Theory in 1803. His theory stated that atoms have mass, that elements are made up of atoms, and that chemical reactions could be explained by the combination and separation of atoms. Although parts of his theory have now been proved wrong, it remains the foundation of modern chemistry and physical science.

Dardanelles vital strait connecting the Black Sea and the Mediterranean Sea in present-day Turkey

Darfur a region in western Sudan where ethnic conflict threatened to lead to genocide

Darwin, Charles Charles Darwin (1809–1882) was an English naturalist who developed the theory of evolution through the process of natural selection. In 1831, he set sail on a five-year voyage around the world. While in the Galápagos Islands, Darwin observed that the four species of finches on the islands had different beaks and eating habits. He theorized that isolation, time, and adapting to local conditions, leads to new species. His observation and the samples he collected helped him develop his theory of evolution.

David As described in the Books of Samuel, 1 Kings, and 1 Chronicles, David was from the tribe of Judah and began his life as a shepherd in Bethlehem. Eventually, David became king of a united Israel. Jews and Christians also believe he edited the Book of Psalms.

Deák, Ferenc Ferenc Deák (1803–1876), also known as the Sage of the Country, was a Hungarian politician, reformer, and thinker. He is most famous for developing the concept of the Dual Monarchy and guiding that compromise to its final adoption.

decimal system system of numbers based on 10

decipher to figure out the meaning of

default fail to make payments

deficit gap between what a government spends and what it takes in through taxes and other sources

deficit spending situation in which the government spends more money than it takes in

deforestation the destruction of forest land

Delhi the third-largest city in India, capital of medieval India

delta triangular area of marshland formed by deposits of silt at the mouth of some rivers

demilitarized zone a thin band of territory across the Korean peninsula separating North Korean forces from South Korean forces; established by the armistice of 1953

democracy government in which the people hold ruling power

Deng Xiaoping Deng Xiaoping (1904–1997) was born in Sichuan province in China. As a young man, he studied in France and the Soviet Union. He became involved in the communist movement while in France. After the Communists took over China, he served in several high positions in the government, eventually becoming the most powerful policy maker in the nation. His policies are responsible for much of China's economic growth after the failures of the Cultural Revolution.

depopulation reduction in the number of people in an area

Descartes, René René Descartes (1596–1650) was a French philosopher, mathematician, and scientist. Descartes was one of the first to abandon traditional methods of thought based on Aristotle's teachings. Instead, he promoted a new science based on observation and experiments. For this, he has been called the father of modern philosophy.

desertification process by which fertile or semi-desert land becomes desert

détente the relaxation of Cold War tensions during the 1970s

developing world nations working toward development in Africa, Asia, and Latin America

development the process of building stable governments, improving agriculture and industry, and raising the standard of living

dharma in Hindu belief, the religious and moral duties of an individual

Diaspora the spreading of the Jews beyond their historic homeland

Díaz, Porfirio Porfirio Díaz (1830–1915) served as president of Mexico twice: 1877–1880 and 1884–1911. Díaz consolidated power in the central government and put wealth in the hands of a few by bringing in foreign investors to build infrastructure and dig mines. Because the wealth was not evenly distributed, discontent spread. By 1910, the economy was in a sharp decline, and workers and peasants were living in poverty or debt. In 1911, Díaz resigned and went into exile.

Dickens, Charles Charles Dickens (1812–1870) was an English author who began his writing career as a freelance reporter. In 1836, he began publishing installments of his first novel, *The Pickwick Papers,* which launched his career as a novelist. Dickens created some of literature's most famous and vivid characters. As a realist, Dickens was dedicated to depicting real life. He hoped to bring about reform, so his novels often focused on the problems of the poor to expose social ills.

dictator ruler who has complete control over a government

Dien Bien Phu small town and former French army base in northern Vietnam; site of the battle that ended in a Vietnamese victory, the French withdrawal from Vietnam, and the securing of North Vietnam's independence

diet assembly or legislature

Diocletian (A.D. 245–A.D. 311) was a Roman general who became emperor. To make the government more effective, he divided the large empire into East and West and appointed a co-emperor.

direct democracy system of government in which citizens participate directly in the day-to-day affairs of government rather than through elected representatives

disarmament reduction of armed forces and weapons

discrimination unequal treatment or barriers

Disraeli, Benjamin Benjamin Disraeli (1804–1881) was a leading Conservative politician and spent seven years as prime minister. Along with other political leaders, Disraeli worked to expand suffrage and slowly transformed the British Parliament during the 1800s into a more democratic institution. His spearheading of the Second Reform Act of 1867, allowed more men to vote, including members of the working class. Disraeli also focused on other social reforms, including public health laws and recognition of workers' unions.

dissent ideas that oppose those of the government

dissenter Protestant whose views and opinions differed from those of the Church of England

divine right idea that a ruler's authority came directly from God

domesticate to tame animals and adapt crops so they are best suited to use by humans

dominion self-governing nation

domino theory the belief that a communist victory in South Vietnam would cause noncommunist governments across Southeast Asia to fall to communism, like a row of dominoes

dowry in some societies, payment a bride's family makes to the bridegroom and his family; payment a woman brings to a marriage

Dreyfus Affair a political scandal that caused deep divisions in France; it centered on the 1894 wrongful conviction for treason of Alfred Dreyfus, a Jewish officer in the French army.

Dual Monarchy the monarchy of Austria-Hungary

due process of law the requirement that the government act fairly and in accordance with established rules in all that it does

Duma elected national legislature in Russia

Dunkirk port in France from which 300,000 Allied troops were evacuated when their retreat by land was cut off by the German advance in 1940

Dürer, Albrecht Albrecht Dürer (1471–1528) was born in Nuremberg, Germany. A painter, draftsman, and writer, his greatest artistic impact was in engraving. He traveled to Italy, studied the Italian masters, and helped spread Renaissance ideas to northern Europe. Many of his famous works, such as *The Apocalypse,* and *Adam and Eve,* had religious themes.

Dutch East India Company a trading company established with full sovereign powers by the Netherlands in 1602 to protect and expand its trade in Asia

dynamo a machine used to generate electricity

dynastic cycle rise and fall of Chinese dynasties according to the Mandate of Heaven

dynasty ruling family

E

earthwork an embankment or other construction made of earth

East Timor a former Portuguese colony, seized by Indonesia, that gained independence in 2002

economic nationalism an emphasis on domestic control and protection of the economy

Edict of Nantes law issued by French king Henry IV in 1598 giving more religious freedom to French Protestants

Edison, Thomas Thomas Edison (1847–1931) applied for his first patent while working as a telegraph operator for Western Union. Although this first invention was a flop, Edison did not give up and went on to become one of the world's most prolific inventors. Throughout his life he patented 1,093 inventions and improvements in several industries, including telecommunications, electric power, mining, sound recording, automotive, military defense, and motion pictures.

Eightfold Path as taught by the Buddha, the path one must follow to achieve nirvana

Einstein, Albert Albert Einstein (1879–1955) was born into a middle-class Jewish family in Germany. He published his theories of relativity in 1905 and 1916, winning the Nobel Prize for Physics in 1921. These ideas challenged long-held beliefs regarding the nature of the universe. As German Nazis came to power, Einstein emigrated with his family to the United States in 1932 and became a citizen in 1940. During World War II, his work was used in the creation of the atomic bomb. As nuclear technology spread, Einstein advocated for international controls and limitations. He is widely considered the most influential physicist of the 20th century.

Eisenhower, Dwight Dwight Eisenhower (1890–1969) grew up poor and came from a hard-working family. During World War II, he was the American general who commanded the Allied forces in western Europe. "Ike" later served as the 34th president of the United States, from 1953–1961.

Eleanor of Acquitaine Eleanor of Aquitaine (1122–1204), was an heiress to the dukedom of Aquitaine. At age 15, she married the French royal heir, Louis VI, and became queen of France. Intelligent and energetic, she strongly influenced her husband and went with him on the Second Crusade. Her second marriage was to Henry Plantagenet, who became Henry II of England in 1154. While caring for five sons and three daughters, she actively helped administer England, managed her own domains—making the court at Poitiers a model of courtly life—and remained politically active into her 80s.

elector one of seven German princes who would choose the Holy Roman emperor

electorate body of people allowed to vote

elite upper class

Elizabeth Elizabeth Tudor (1533–1603) became Queen Elizabeth I of England upon the death of Queen Mary. Shifting politics made her early years quite hazardous. Elizabeth used her experiences to become a shrewd and powerful monarch. Under her reign, England became an important European power. England prospered both economically, and culturally. Her balanced handling of the English religious conflicts earned her the nickname Good Queen Bess.

emancipation granting of freedom to serfs or enslaved people

emigration movement away from one's homeland

émigré a person who flee his or her country for political reasons

empire a group of states or territories controlled by one ruler

enclosure the process of taking over and consolidating land formerly shared by peasant farmers

encomienda the right, granted by Spanish monarchs to conquistadors, to demand labor or tribute from Native Americans in a particular area

endangered species species threatened with extinction

engineering application of science and mathematics to develop useful structures and machines

English Bill of Rights series of acts passed in 1689 by the English Parliament that limited the rights of the monarchy and ensured the superiority of Parliament

engraving art form in which an artist etches a design on a metal plate with acid and then uses the plate to make multiple prints

enlightened despot absolute ruler who used his or her power to bring about political and social change

entente nonbinding agreement to follow common policies

enterprise business organization in such areas as shipping, mining, railroads, or factories

entrepreneur person who assumes financial risk in the hope of making a profit

Epic of Gilgamesh, The Mesopotamian narrative poem that was first recited in Sumer

epidemic outbreak of a rapidly spreading disease

Equiano, Olaudah (1745–1797) Olaudah Equiano was captured in West Africa when he was a boy of 11, sold into slavery, and transported to the Americas. Later, he found paying work and earned enough money to buy his freedom. In 1789, he wrote his autobiography, *The Interesting Narrative of the Life of Olaudah Equiano.* He died in London in 1797.

Erasmus Erasmus (c. 1466–1536) was a Dutch priest, writer, and scholar who promoted humanism. He wrote texts on various subjects and produced a new Greek edition of the Christian Bible. He also called for a translation of the Bible into the vernacular, or everyday language, to help spread learning, ideas, and education. He also wanted to reform Church corruption.

erosion the wearing away of land

estates social classes

Estates-General legislative body made up of the representatives of the three estates in pre-revolutionary France

ethics moral standards of behavior

Ethiopia ancient Greek term for Axumite kingdom; present-day country in East Africa

ethnic cleansing the killing or forcible removal of people of different ethnicities from an area by aggressors so that only the ethnic group of the aggressors remains

ethnic group large group of people who share the same language and cultural heritage

Etruscans a people who inhabited early Italy

euro common currency used by most member nations of the European Union

European Union (EU) an international organization made up of over two dozen European nations and dedicated to establishing free trade among its members, with a common currency and common policies and laws

excommunication exclusion from the Roman Catholic Church as a penalty for refusing to obey Church law

expansionism policy of increasing the amount of territory a government holds

extraterritoriality right of foreigners to be protected by the laws of their own nation

F

faction a group or clique within a larger group that has different ideas and opinions than the rest of the group

famine a severe shortage of food in which large numbers of people starve

Faraday, Michael Michael Faraday (1791–1867) was a British chemist and physicist who made significant contributions to the field of electricity. Some of his most important discoveries include electricity generation and transmission, the electric motor, and the chemical benzene. His discoveries have shaped the modern world.

fascism any centralized, authoritarian government system that is not communist, whose policies glorify the state over the individual and are destructive to basic human rights

federal republic government in which power is divided between the national, or federal, government and the states

Federal Reserve central banking system of the United States, which regulates banks

Ferdinand and Isabella Ferdinand III (1452–1516) and Isabella I (1451–1504) were the king of Aragon and the queen of Castile. Their marriage joined the two countries to become the country of Spain. Their military efforts were responsible for the final success of the Reconquista.

Ferguson, Miriam Miriam Ferguson (1875–1961), known to many as "Ma" Ferguson, was elected the first female governor of Texas in 1924. She ran when her husband, the politically disgraced Governor James E. Ferguson, was unable to secure a place on the ballot. Mrs. Ferguson was the first woman elected for the office in the United States but second to serve as governor because Wyoming's Nellie T. Ross was inaugurated upon the death of her husband. Mrs. Ferguson was reelected in 1932 for a second term.

Fertile Crescent region of the Middle East in which civilizations first arose

feudal contract exchange of pledges between lords and vassals

feudalism loosely organized system of government in which local lords governed their own lands but owed military service and other support to a greater lord

fief in medieval Europe, an estate granted by a lord to a vassal in exchange for service and loyalty

filial piety respect for parents

finance the management of money matters including the circulation of money, loans, investment, and banking

Firdawsi Firdawsi (c. 940–1020) was a Muslim poet most famous for the *Shah Namah,* or *Book of Kings,* which he wrote in Persian using Arabic script. Firdawsi wrote at a time when Persia, or Iran, was fairly free from the control of the Muslim empire and local leaders encouraged a flowering of Persian culture. The famed poet centered his writing on the stories of royalty and heroes, and many of the themes he introduced are still relevant today.

First Sino-Japanese War conflict between China and Japan in 1894–1895 over control of Korea

Flanders a region that included parts of present-day northern France, Belgium, and the Netherlands; was an important industrial and financial center of northern Europe during the Middle Ages and Renaissance

flapper in the United States and Europe in the 1920s, a rebellious young woman

Florence a city in the Tuscany region of northern Italy that was the center of the Italian Renaissance

flying buttresses stone supports on the outside of a building that allowed builders to construct higher, thinner walls that contained large stained-glass windows.

Four Noble Truths as taught by the Buddha, the four basic beliefs that form the foundation of Buddhism

Fourteen Points list of terms for resolving WWI and future wars outlined by American President Woodrow Wilson in January 1918

Francis Joseph Francis Joseph (1830–1916) became emperor of Austria in 1848 after the abdication of Ferdinand I. After the creation of the Dual Monarchy in 1867, he also became king of Hungary. In 1879, Francis Joseph formed an alliance with Germany, which was led by the Prussians. His handling of relations with Serbia after the assassination of Archduke Francis Ferdinand, in 1914 was one of the catalysts for World War I.

Franco, Francisco Francisco Franco (1892–1975) was a Spanish military leader who came to power during the Spanish Civil War. He was dictator of Spain from 1939 to 1973, when he left his position as premier. He continued to be head of state until his death in 1975.

Franklin, Benjamin Benjamin Franklin (1706–1790) was a man of many talents. Born in 1706, Franklin was an author, inventor, and a statesman who helped persuade France to enter the Revolutionary War on the side of the Americans. He was actively involved in framing the Declaration of Independence.

Franks a Germanic tribe that conquered present-day France and neighboring lands in the 400s

Frederick II Frederick II (1712–1786) succeeded his father, Frederick William I, to serve as king of Prussia (1740–1786).

Frederick William I Frederick William I (1688–1740) was the second Prussian king who helped transform his country into a prosperous state.

free enterprise system An economic system, also known as capitalism, in which private businesses are able to compete with each other with little control by government. Products, prices, and services are driven by free market laws of supply and demand rather than government regulations.

free market market regulated by the natural laws of supply and demand

free trade trade between countries without quotas, tariffs, or other restrictions

French and Indian War war between Britain and France in the Americas that happened from 1754 to 1763; it was part of a global war called the Seven Years' War

French Indochina Western name for the colonial holdings of France on mainland Southeast Asia; present-day Vietnam, Laos, and Cambodia

fresco colorful painting completed on wet plaster

friar a medieval European monk who traveled from place to place preaching to the poor

fundamentalist religious leader who calls for a return to what he or she sees as the fundamental, or basic, values of his or her faith

G

Galileo Galileo Galilei (1564–1642) was an Italian astronomer and mathematician whose discoveries using a telescope supported the heliocentric universe theories of Copernicus. His discoveries challenged established scientific and religious thinking. Galileo was an important contributor to the development of the scientific method used by modern scientists.

Gama, Vasco da Vasco da Gama (c. 1460–1524) was a Portuguese explorer and navigator who in 1498 was the first person to directly reach India by sailing around Africa. He returned to India in 1502, fought Arab Muslim ships along the way, and established trading posts along the East African coast. After serving as an advisor to Portugal's king for 20 years, he returned to India in 1524 with the title of viceroy, but fell ill and died soon after arriving.

Gandhi, Indira Indira Gandhi (1917–1984) was a four-term prime minister of India. The daughter of Jawaharlal Nehru, Gandhi entered politics as part of the Congress Party, soon becoming its leader. After her father's death, she was elected India's prime minister. Gandhi stayed in power until 1977, when some of her authoritarian policies led to her popular defeat. In 1980, however, she was reelected to a fourth term as prime minister. After she ordered a military attack on a Sikh holy site, the Golden Temple, Gandhi was assassinated by her Sikh bodyguards.

Gandhi, Mohandas Mohandas Gandhi (1869–1948) was a mediocre student who went through a period of rebellion during his early teens. He married at age 13 and later was sent to England to attend law school. In 1891, Gandhi accepted a position in South Africa. Although he planned to be there only one year, he stayed until 1914, fighting for Indian rights. In 1919, Gandhi became active in the Indian independence movement and remained dedicated to the cause until his death. He was assassinated in 1948—just a few months after India won its independence.

Garibaldi, Giuseppe Giuseppe Garibaldi (1807–1882) was a nationalist soldier and military leader who effectively used guerilla tactics to win military victories throughout southern Italy. In his earlier years he was a member of Mazzini's Young Italy, where he began his involvement in the cause of Italian unity.

Garvey, Marcus Marcus Garvey (1887–1940) founded the Universal Negro Improvement and Conservation Association and African Communities League (UNIA) in Jamaica in 1914, with the goal of building a Black-governed nation. Finding little support, Garvey moved to the United States and established the UNIA in Harlem. Garvey taught his followers about the African culture and preached the need for Blacks to form a strong, independent economy. His adamant belief in separation of the races brought many enemies, and he was deported in 1927.

Gautama, Siddhartha Siddhartha Gautama (circa 563 B.C.– 483 B.C.) was born a prince in India. Encounters with human suffering led him to leave his royal life to seek out the cause of suffering and sorrow. He sought answers from scholars and meditated until he developed a spiritual explanation for life. He became known as the "Buddha," and began teaching his beliefs to others. He taught the Four Noble Truths and encouraged the faithful to follow the Eightfold Path.

general strike strike by workers in many different industries at the same time

genetic engineering manipulation of living organism's chemical code in order to produce specific results

genetics a branch of biology dealing with heredity and variations among plants and animals

Geneva Swiss city-state that became a Calvinist theocracy in the 1500s; today a major city in Switzerland

Genghis Khan Genghis Khan (1162–1227) rose from poverty to unite the warring Mongol tribes. He imposed discipline, exacted loyalty, and then proceeded to build an army that conquered the vast areas of Central Asia and China and became the Mongol empire. He was known for both his fierceness and his generosity. The Mongol empire lasted long after his death during a military campaign. His descendants added to the empire until it became the largest empire in the world prior to the British empire.

genocide deliberate and systematic killing of people who belong to a particular racial, ethnic, or cultural group.

gentry wealthy, landowning class

George III George III (1738–1820) was the longest reigning monarch in British history, ruling at a time when Britain and France struggled to dominate Europe; he shared the blame for the loss of Britain's American colonies.

germ theory the theory that infectious diseases are caused by certain microbes

Gestapo secret police in Nazi Germany

Ghana early West African trading kingdom located in parts of present-day Mauritania and Mali

ghetto separate section of a city where members of a minority group are forced to live

Gladstone, William William Gladstone (1809–1898) Gladstone served as prime minister four separate times and was a leader of the Whigs, and later, the Liberal Party. He extended suffrage to farmworkers and most other men during the 1880s, most notably with the Representation of the People Act in 1884. Gladstone also strongly supported Irish home rule. Along with his chief rival, Benjamin Disraeli, Gladstone helped transform the British government into a parliamentary democracy.

glasnost "openness" in Russian; a Soviet policy of greater freedom of expression introduced by Mikhail Gorbachev in the late 1980s

global warming the increase in Earth's average surface temperature over time

globalization the process by which national economies, politics, cultures, and societies become closely linked with those of other nations around the world

Goa a coastal city seized in 1510 that became the commercial and military base of Portugal's India trade

golden age period of great cultural achievement

Golden Bull of 1222 charter that strictly limited royal power in Hungary

Golden Temple the most prominent Sikh house of worship

Good Friday Agreement an agreement to end the conflict in Northern Ireland signed in 1998 by Protestants and Catholics

Good Neighbor Policy policy in which American President Franklin Roosevelt promised that the United States would interfere less in Latin American affairs

Gorbachev, Mikhail Mikhail Gorbachev (b. 1931) was the leader of the Soviet Union from 1985 to 1991. He was responsible for introducing the reforms (glasnost and perestroika) that brought about the break up of the Soviet Union and the end of Soviet domination of Eastern Europe. He was driven from office by his popular rival, democratic advocate Boris Yeltsin, in 1991.

Gothic style type of European architecture that developed in the Middle Ages, characterized by flying buttresses, ribbed vaulting, thin walls, and high roofs

Gouges, Olympe de Olympe de Gouges (1745?–1793), author of the Declaration of the Rights of Women, railed against the treatment of women in France, addressing her concerns directly to Marie Antoinette.

Gracchus, Gaius (c. 154 B.C.–121 B.C.) was the brother of Tiberius and a plebeian political reformist who sought to limit senatorial power. He advanced checks and balances to minimize financial influence. Like his brother, he was murdered by thugs hired by the Roman Senate.

gravity force that pulls objects in Earth's sphere to the center of Earth

Great Depression a painful time of global economic collapse, starting in 1929 and lasting until about 1939

Great Leap Forward a Chinese Communist program from 1958 to 1960 to boost farm and industrial output that failed miserably

Great Schism the official split between the Roman Catholic and Byzantine churches that occurred in 1054; another event was the Great Western Schism, a period when rival popes fought for exclusive power and divided the Roman Catholic Church from 1378–1417

Great Zimbabwe powerful East African medieval trading center and city-state located in south-eastern present-day Zimbabwe

Greco, El El Greco (1541–1614) was a master of Spanish painting who also worked as a sculptor and architect during Spain's Golden Age.

Green Revolution the improved seeds, pesticides, mechanical equipment, and farming methods introduced in the developing world beginning in the 1950s

Gregory VII Gregory VII (c. 1025–1085) achieved success in his battle with the Holy Roman Emperor Henry IV on the matter of lay investiture. He greatly expanded papal power by claiming his supremacy over secular rulers.

griot professional storyteller in early West Africa

gross domestic product (GDP) the total value of all goods and services produced in a nation within a particular year

Guang Xu Guang Xu (1871–1908) was the ninth emperor of the Qing dynasty. When previous emperor Tongzhi died, his mother Ci Xi named Guang, her nephew, as new emperor. Ci Xi dominated his reign, influencing the government and making him ineffectual. During the Hundred Days of Reform, Guang attempted progressive reforms, angering conservatives. Ci Xi had Guang imprisoned. He died under suspicious circumstances.

Guangzhou coastal city in southeastern China, also known as Canton, where, during the Ming dynasty, the Dutch, English, and other Europeans could trade with Chinese merchants under the supervision of imperial officials, only during each year's trading season and only at Canton

guerrilla a soldier in a loosely organized force making surprise raids

guerrilla warfare fighting carried on through hit-and-run raids

guild in the Middle Ages, an association of merchants or artisans who cooperated to uphold standards of their trade and to protect their economic interests

guillotine device used during the Reign of Terror to execute thousands by beheading

Gulag in the Soviet Union, a system of forced labor camps in which millions of criminals and political prisoners were held under Stalin

Guomindang Nationalist party; active in China 1912 to 1949

Gutenberg, Johannes Gutenberg (c. 1400–1468) was born in Germany. He became a goldsmith, printer, and publisher. His pioneering invention of a printing press with moveable type changed the world. Around 1455, Gutenberg printed the first complete edition of the Christian Bible using his press.

H

habeas corpus principle that a person cannot be held in prison without first being charged with a specific crime

hacienda a large plantation

Hadrian (A.D. 76–A.D. 138) was a Roman Emperor from A.D. 117 to A.D. 138. Considered one of the "Five Good Emperors," he codified Roman law and traveled extensively, uniting the empire.

hajj one of the Five Pillars of Islam, the pilgrimage that all Muslims are expected to make at least once in their lifetime

Hammurabi (1792 B.C.–1750 B.C.) Hammurabi became the first king of the Babylonian empire. He inherited the power from his father, who extended Babylon's control across Mesopotamia. Hammurabi is known for writing the first code of law in recorded history.

hangul alphabet that uses symbols to represent the sounds of spoken Korean

Hapsburg empire Central European empire that lasted from the 1400s to the 1900s and at its height included the lands of the Holy Roman Empire and the Netherlands

Harappa large ancient city of the Indus civilization, located in present-day Pakistan

Harlem Renaissance an African American cultural movement in the 1920s and 1930s, centered in Harlem

Hatshepsut (Died 1458 B.C.) Queen Hatshepsut served for 20 years alongside her husband, Thutmose II, but after his death took the role of pharaoh and served as regent to Thutmose III. She is known for building temples and monuments and generally making Egypt flourish.

Havel, Václav Václav Havel (1936–2011) was a Czech playwright and human rights activist who became president of Czechoslovakia in 1989, after the Velvet Revolution. Because of his persecution during the later stages of communist rule in Czechoslovakia, Havel became a worldwide symbol of communist repression. After the division of Czechoslovakia, he served as the first president of the Czech Republic.

hejab headscarves and loose-fitting, ankle-length garments meant to conceal the body; traditionally worn by many Muslim women

heliocentric based on the belief that the sun is the center of the universe

Henry IV Henry IV (1050–1106) was a German king who became Holy Roman Emperor in 1084. His efforts to increase the power of the monarchy led him into conflict with Pope Gregory VIII over lay investiture. Gregory excommunicated Henry but later reinstated him in the church after Henry did penance.

Henry VIII Henry VIII (1491–1547) was the second Tudor king of England. Well-educated and athletic, he was initially a favorite of the English people. He lost much of that popularity with his constant involvement in wars. Henry's desire for a male heir was the catalyst for his eventual break with the Roman Catholic Church and the formation of the Church of England.

Henry, Prince Prince Henry (1394–1460) was a Portuguese prince and patron of explorers who helped his father capture the Moroccan city of Ceuta, became its governor, and sponsored voyages to the Madeira Islands and the West African coast. He raised money for expeditions and established a base for explorers in Sagres, later adding an arsenal, an observatory, and a school for studying geography. His support of cartography, advances in navigation, and exploration provided a foundation for Portugal's rise to international dominance and acquisition of its colonial empire in the sixteenth century.

heresy religious belief that is contrary to the official teachings of a church

Herodotus Herodotus (c. 484 B.C.–c. 425 B.C.), often called the "Father of History," traveled widely throughout the ancient Mediterranean world, collecting information for his chronicles of past events, including the Persian wars. In his writings, he noted bias and conflicting accounts in his sources.

Hidalgo, Father Miguel Father Miguel Hidalgo (1753–1811) was a Catholic priest in Mexico. He led Indians and mestizos in a revolution against the Spanish until he was captured and killed in 1811.

hierarchy system of ranking groups

hieroglyphics system of writing in which pictures called hieroglyphs represent objects, concepts, or sounds

hijra Muhammad's journey from Mecca to Medina in 622

Hippocrates Hippocrates (c. 460 B.C.–c. 375 B.C.), a Greek physician traditionally regarded as the father of medicine, who studied the causes of illnesses, seeking their cures. Many ancient medical writings are attributed to him, although he probably wrote few of them. He is honored for his Hippocratic oath that sets ethical standards for medical practice.

Hirohito Hirohito (1901–1989) became emperor in 1926 when his father died. Many believed he was a living god, descended from the sun goddess. Japanese military ultranationalists built a cult around the emperor, reviving ancient warrior values and suppressing most democratic freedoms. Although Hirohito was invested with supreme authority theoretically, he did little more than approve the policies presented by his ministers. He was more interested in marine biology, authoring several books on the subject. Hirohito was the longest reigning monarch in Japanese history, serving as emperor for an astonishing 63 years until his death in 1989.

Hiroshima city in Japan where the first atomic bomb was dropped in August 1945

historian a person who studies how people lived in the past

Hitler, Adolf Adolf Hitler (1889–1945) was chancellor of Germany from 1933 to 1945 and dictator of Nazi Germany from 1934 to 1945. After Hitler was appointed chancellor, he immediately transformed the Weimar Republic into the Third Reich. He wanted to establish a "New Order" and create more "living space" for what he believed was the superior Aryan race. Hitler aggressively invaded neighboring nations. which led to World War II. As Germany faced defeat in 1945, Hitler committed suicide to avoid capture by the Soviets.

Ho Chi Minh Ho Chi Minh (1890–1969) was born Nguyen That Thanh. He founded the Indochinese Communist Party and was the leader of the armed independence movement in Vietnam. Ho proclaimed Vietnam's independence in 1945 and became the leader of North Vietnam when the country was divided in 1954. He was the leader of North Vietnam until his death in 1969, and refused to negotiate an end to the war.

Hobbes, Thomas Thomas Hobbes (1588–1679) was an influential English political philosopher, best known for his work *Leviathan*. In it, Hobbes strongly advocated that only a powerful government was capable of protecting society. He believed that people entered into a social contract with their government to avoid the inevitable chaos and lawlessness of life in "the state of nature." Hobbes's political philosophy was foundational for later thinkers of the Enlightenment, including Locke, Rousseau, and Kant.

Holocaust the systematic genocide of about six million European Jews by the Nazis in World War II

Holy Land Jerusalem and other places where Christians believe Jesus had lived and preached

Holy Roman Empire empire of west central Europe from 962 to 1806, comprising present-day Germany and neighboring lands

home rule local self-government

Homer (c. 750 B.C.), according to tradition the author of the epic poems, the *Illiad* and the *Odyssey,* is thought to have traveled from village to village singing about heroic deeds of warriors during the Trojan War

homogeneous society society that has common culture and language

Huari a culture that thrived in the Andean region from about A.D. 600 to 1000

Hugo, Victor Victor Hugo (1802–1885) was a leading literary, intellectual, and political figure in France. His works were not only extremely popular—most notably *Notre Dame de Paris* and *Les Misérables* —but also highly influential and respected. Hugo believed in the cause of the common people and saw in them both strength and potential. He sought to portray both their virtues and their plights in his works. Although Hugo did not live in poverty, he associated with the lower class, and, according to his wishes, he had a pauper's funeral and grave

Huguenots French Protestants of the 1500s and 1600s

humanism an intellectual movement at the heart of the Renaissance that focused on education and the classics

humanities study of subjects such as grammar, rhetoric, poetry, and history that were taught in ancient Greece and Rome

Huns a nomadic people of central Asia

Hutus an ethnic group that forms the majority in Rwanda and Burundi

hyperinflation an extremely rapid and sharp rise in prices that causes money to lose value

hypothesis an unproved theory accepted for the purposes of explaining certain facts or to provide a basis for further investigation.

I

Ibn Khaldun Ibn Khaldun (1332–1406) was an Arab thinker who helped establish the principles of many branches of knowledge including history and economics. He is perhaps best known for the development of standards for studying and writing about history, which he explained in his landmark book, the *Muqaddimah.* He also introduced or refined many economic concepts relating to labor, profits, supply and demand, use of resources, production, and supply and demand.

Ibn Rushd Ibn Rushd (1128–1198), also known as Averroes, was a philosopher and scientist who lived in Córdoba and influenced European thought. As a philosopher, he placed a variety of subject matter under the scrutiny of reason and analysis and argued that humans were partially but not completely controlled by fate. In the field of science, Ibn Rushd contributed to the study of diseases.

Ibn Sina Ibn Sina (980–1037), also known as Avicenna, was a Persian physician who wrote the *Canon on Medicine,* which focused on past medical practices throughout the known world as well as his own procedures. This work features descriptions of anatomy, symptoms of diseases, and medicines and cures. Ibn Sina wrote on a variety of other topics as well, including philosophy, mathematics, and astronomy.

icon holy image of Christ, the Virgin Mary, or a saint venerated in the Eastern Orthodox Church

ideology system of thought and belief

Ignatius of Loyola Ignatius of Loyola (1491–1556) went from an early career as a Spanish nobleman soldier to become a theologian and an influential participant in the Catholic Reformation. While recovering from leg surgery, Ignatius read a book on the lives of the saints and decided that serving God was holy chivalry. From that time until his death, Ignatius studied, preached, and did missionary work as founder of the Society of Jesus, an order of religious men who came to be known as Jesuits.

illumination the artistic decoration of books and manuscripts

immunity resistance, such as the power to keep from being affected by a disease

imperialism domination by one country of the political, economic, or cultural life of another country or region

import substitution manufacturing goods locally to replace imports

impressionism school of painting of the late 1800s and early 1900s that tried to capture fleeting visual impressions

indemnity payment for losses in war

indigenous original or native inhabitants of a country or region

indigenous people term generally used to describe a group descended from the earliest inhabitants of a region

Indra in ancient India, the god of war

indulgence in the Roman Catholic Church, pardon for sins committed during a person's lifetime

Industrial Revolution period beginning in the 1700s in which production shifted from simple hand tools to complex machinery and sources of energy shifted from human or animal power to steam and electricity

inflation economic cycle that involves a rapid rise in prices linked to a sharp increase in the amount of money available

Innocent III, Pope Pope Innocent III (c. 1160–1216) was only 37 years old when he became pope and quickly extended the authority of the papacy over Rome and in Italy. When King John of England appointed the archbishop of Canterbury without Innocent's approval, the pope excommunicated John.

Inquisition A Church court set up to try people accused of heresy

insurgent rebel

intendant official appointed by French king Louis XIV to govern the provinces, collect taxes, and recruit soldiers

interchangeable parts identical components that can be used in place of one another in manufacturing

interdependence mutual dependence of countries on goods, resources, labor, and knowledge from other parts of the world

interdict in the Roman Catholic Church, excommunication of an entire region, town, or kingdom

International Space Station (ISS) an artificial structure built and maintained by a coalition of nations with the purpose of research

Internet a huge international computer network linking millions of users around the world

internment confinement during wartime

Inti the Inca sun god

intifada Palestinian Arab uprising against the Israeli occupation

Iroquois League political alliance of five Iroquois groups, known as the Five Nations, in the late 1500s

Isfahan capital of Safavid empire during the 1600s; located in present-day Iran

Islamic State in Iraq and Syria (ISIS) an Islamist terrorist organization

Isis Isis is the Egyptian god worshiped as the ideal mother and wife. She is known as the protector of the dead and goddess of children. She is usually portrayed as a woman, wearing a throne-shaped headdress.

Islamist a person who wants government policies to be based on the teachings of Islam

island-hopping during World War II, Allied strategy of recapturing some Japanese-held islands while bypassing others

Istanbul capital of the Ottoman empire, formerly called Constantinople when it was the center of the eastern Roman empire and also capital of the Byzantine empire

Ivan the Great Ivan the Great (1462–1505) was one of the most powerful Russian rulers. He consolidated his power by winning the voluntary allegiance of Russian princes and preventing further Mongol invasions.

Ivan the Terrible Ivan the Terrible (1530–1584) was the grandson of Ivan the Great. He continued to centralize power in his own hands, developing a brutal secret group that terrorized members of the hereditary nobility, or boyars. His eventual insanity contributed to his name "the Terrible."

J

Jacobin a member of a radical political club during the French Revolution

Jahan, Nur Nur Jahan (1577–1645) was a Persian widow with a small child who became the powerful wife of the Mughal emperor Jahangir. Her administrative, political, economic, and cultural skills so impressed Jahangir that she had virtual control over the empire until his death in 1627. Since women were not allowed to interact face to face with men in court, Nur Jahan relied on trusted men to act for her.

Jahan, Shah Shah Jahan (1592–1666) was the third son of the Mughal emperor Jahangir. With support from court nobles, he won succession to become emperor upon Jahangir's death. An effective and tolerant ruler, Shah Jahan was also an enthusiastic builder, involving himself in every detail of the building process. When his beloved wife Mumtaz Mahal died, he built the famous mausoleum called the Taj Mahal in her honor.

James I James I (1566–1625) was a king of Scotland who also became king of England and Ireland. He deeply believed in the divine right of kings to rule over all their subjects without interference from anyone. His views were in sharp contrast to Parliament, leading to constant conflict. He was also the author of the King James version of the Bible.

janizary a member of the elite forces of the Ottoman army

jati in India, an occupational group, part of the caste system

Jefferson, Thomas Thomas Jefferson (1743–1826) is known mainly as the primary author of the Declaration of Independence. Jefferson also served as minister to France and later as the third president of the United States.

Jericho the world's first village, established in the modern-day West Bank between 10,000 and 9000 B.C.

Jerusalem capital of the Jewish state of Judea in ancient times and capital of the modern state of Israel; city sacred to Jews, Muslims, and Christians

Jesus Jesus (c. 4 B.C.–A.D. 30) was the founder of Christianity. He is considered by most Christians to be the Son of God. Raised in a Jewish family, he began preaching a message of salvation and eternal life. He was put to death under Roman law. According to the Gospels, he rose from the dead. He is worshipped as a savior today by Christians around the world.

Jiang Jieshi Jiang Jieshi (1887–1975), also known as Chiang Kai-shek, was born to a merchant family in eastern China. Along with Sun Yixian, he formed the Nationalist Party, or Guomindang, and following Sun's death in 1925, Jiang took over control. After years of battling, Jiang joined forces with the Communists against the Japanese invaders. Jiang also led the Chinese military to assist the Allies in defeating Japan in World War II. Eventually, the Communists wrestled back control and Jiang fled to the island of Taiwan, which he ruled until his death in 1975.

Jinnah, Muhammad Ali Muhammad Ali Jinnah (1876–1948) was an Indian Muslim politician and leader of the Muslim League, which was founded in 1906 to protect Muslim interests in India. The League worked closely with the Indian Congress Party early on but later diverged from the Congress when Jinnah and other Muslims began to lobby for their own state. Jinnah helped found Pakistan in 1947 and was its first governor-general.

Johanson, Donald Born in 1942, anthropologist Donald Johanson found one of the most important early humans in history, a skeleton of a woman he called "Lucy." After studying her bones, Johanson concluded that Lucy walked upright and was about 4 feet tall.

John, King King John (c. 1166–1216) was a son of King Henry II. He seized control of the English throne when his brother, King Richard the Lionheart, was captured while on crusade. Conflicts with the English nobles led to John's forced signature to Magna Carta in 1215, which limited the power of the English kings.

joint family family organization in which several generations share a common dwelling

Joseph II Joseph II (1741–1790) ruled as Holy Roman Emperor in Austria and is considered the most radical of the enlightened despots. He continued many of the modernizing governmental reforms introduced by his mother, Maria Theresa, with the goal of equal treatment for all his subjects. He abolished serfdom and encouraged freedom of the press. Most notably, Joseph supported religious equality for Protestants and even Jews. He is also remembered for traveling among his subjects in disguise to learn about the everyday problems of the peasantry.

journeyman a salaried worker employed by a guild master

Juárez, Benito Benito Juárez (1806–1872) was a Mexican lawyer and politician. Coming from a Zapotec Indian heritage and peasant family background, he supported reforms to help oppressed people in Mexico. He helped start the La Reforma movement and became president of Mexico in 1861. He died while in office, but his reforms helped unite Mexico and bring mestizos into politics.

jury group of people with authority to make a decision in a legal case

Justinian Justinian (483–565) was born of peasant stock and adopted by his uncle Justin (emperor from 518). As the Byzantine emperor from 527 to 565, Justinian continued war with Persia and sought to win back former western Roman provinces from barbarian invaders. After riots and a major fire in 532, he rebuilt much of Constantinople in glorious style. He also instituted reforms to stop imperial corruption and promote justice for his subjects. His most influential achievement is Justinian's Code, a collection, organization, and revision of Roman laws.

Justinian's Code collection of Roman laws organized by the Byzantine emperor Justinian and later serving as a model for the Catholic Church and medieval monarchs

K

Kaaba the most sacred temple of Islam, located at Mecca

kaiser emperor of Germany

kamikaze Japanese pilot who undertook a suicide mission

kana in the Japanese writing system, phonetic symbols representing syllables

Karl Marx Karl Marx (1818–1883) was a German political thinker whose ideas became the foundation for communism. Marx trained as a lawyer and later studied philosophy, with plans to enter the academic world. His radical ideas, however, left him with few prospects, so he turned to writing. His most famous work was the *Communist Manifesto,* which criticized capitalism and predicted that alienated workers would rise up to overthrow the bourgeoisie. In the 1860s, Marx was an influential member of the International Working Men's Association.

karma in Hindu belief, all the actions that determine a person's fate in the next life

Kashmir a former princely state in the Himalayas claimed by both India and Pakistan, which have fought wars over its control

Katanga a province of the Democratic Republic of the Congo with rich copper and diamond deposits that tried to gain independence from Congo in 1960

Kellogg-Briand Pact an international agreement, signed by almost every nation in 1928, to stop using war as a method of national policy

Kennedy, John F. John F. Kennedy (1917–1963) was president of the United States from 1961 to 1963. A decorated naval commander in World War II, he was elected president at the age of 42. He was president during the communist revolution in Cuba and the Cuban Missile Crisis, and he increased U.S. involvement in Vietnam. On the domestic front, Kennedy's administration began the federal effort to enforce civil rights in the South. He was assassinated on November 22, 1963, by Lee Harvey Oswald.

Kenyatta, Jomo (1894–1978) was a nationalist and leader in the fight for Kenyan independence from Britain. In 1963, he became the country's first prime minister, and in 1964, the country's first president. He was president until his death.

Kepler, Johannes Johannes Kepler (1571–1630) was a German astronomer whose discoveries expanded on Copernicus's heliocentric universe. Kepler's research showed that the planets move in a particular orbit around the sun. His achievements included a correct description of how vision occurs, as well as how a telescope uses light.

Khan, Reza Reza Khan (1878–1944) joined the Iranian military at a young age. After leading the 1921 coup, Khan became the minister of war and then prime minister. Four years later, he was elected as shah and continued to radically reform both the government and nation. At the start of World War II, the Soviet Union and Britain occupied Iran. Khan abdicated, and his son became shah. The British exiled Khan to Mauritius and then Johannesburg, where he died.

Khayyám, Omar Omar Khayyám (1048–1131) is best known today as a poet who crafted many rubáiyáts, or quatrains. In his day, he was praised for his expertise in many areas. As a mathematician, he contributed to the development of algebra. As a astronomer, he carefully studied the sky to help improve the Muslim calendar. The Persian scholar also examined issues related to law, philosophy, and history.

Khmer Rouge a political movement and a force of Cambodian communist guerrillas that gained power in Cambodia in 1975

Khomeini, Ruhollah Ruhollah Khomeini (1902–1989) was a Shiite Muslim cleric (Ayatollah) who led the 1979 Islamic Revolution in Iran, which overthrew the Shah (Mohammed Reza). He was Iran's highest religious and political leader until his death 10 years later.

Khrushchev, Nikita Nikita Khrushchev (1894–1971) served in the Red Army during World War II as a lieutenant general and afterwards was a Communist Party official in Ukraine. He became part of the central party leadership in 1947 and rose to prominence after Stalin's death in 1953. As leader of the Soviet Union from 1955 to 1964, he introduced domestic reforms that made life in the Soviet Union less harsh, but he crushed rebellions in Eastern Europe. He was the Soviet leader during the Cuban Missile Crisis.

kibbutz a collective farm in Israel

Kiev capital of medieval Russia and of present-day Ukraine

Kim Il Sung Kim Il Sung (1912–1994) led the Democratic People's Republic of Korea (North Korea) from 1949 until his death in 1994. Supported by the Soviet Union during the Cold War, Kim established a totalitarian state with massive military budgets and virtually no political freedoms. In 1993, he declared that North Korea would withdraw from the Nuclear Nonproliferation Treaty.

King, Jr., Dr. Martin Luther Dr. Martin Luther King, Jr. (1929–1968), was an American minister and civil rights leader. He gained national prominence with his leadership of the Montgomery, Alabama, bus boycott in 1955. King helped organize the massive March on Washington in 1963, where he gave his famous "I Have a Dream" speech. He was assassinated on April 14, 1968.

kiva large underground chamber that the Anasazi used for religious ceremonies and political meetings

Klerk, F.W. de F.W. de Klerk (1936–) was a National Party member and the last president of South Africa under apartheid. With Nelson Mandela, he negotiated the transition of power from the white minority to majority rule, for which he and Mandela won the Nobel Peace Prize in 1993.

knight a European noble who served as a mounted warrior

Knossos city in ancient Crete, the principle center of Minoan civilization that dominated the Aegean between about 1600 B.C. and 1400 B.C. Excavations beginning in 1900 discovered a palace and surrounding buildings of a sophisticated culture.

Koch, Robert Robert Koch (1843–1910) was a German physician who was one of the founders of bacteriology, or the study of bacteria. Koch discovered the bacteria responsible for tuberculosis and cholera and determined the cycle of the anthrax disease. Koch also improved methods for studying bacteria, including cultivating pure cultures and staining bacteria to make them more visible and identifiable. In 1905 he was awarded the Nobel Prize for Physiology or Medicine.

Kolkata a large city in India, also known as Calcutta

Koryo dynasty Korean dynasty that ruled from 935 to 1392

Kossuth, Louis Louis Kossuth (1802–1894) was a Hungarian lawyer, journalist, politician and ruler of Hungary during the revolution of 1848–89.

Kublai Khan Kublai Khan (1215–1294) was the grandson of Genghis Khan and founded the Yuan dynasty, conquered the Song dynasty in the south to complete Mongol control of China, and proved a strong and intelligent ruler of the vast empire. Guided by Confucian Chinese advisors, he undertook reforms in his territories and politically reunited China, but also engaged in a series of costly and fruitless wars with neighboring kingdoms. He generally left Chinese life unchanged and, although religious, was known for his acceptance of various religious practices and for granting economic privileges to favored sects.

kulak wealthy peasant in the Soviet Union in the late 1930s

Kulturkampf Bismarck's "battle for civilization," intended to make Catholics put loyalty to the state above their allegiance to the Church

L

L'Ouverture, Toussaint Toussaint L'Ouverture (1743–1803) was born in Haiti as the son of an educated enslaved person. He led an army of enslaved people, who he trained in guerrilla warfare, in a revolt against the French colonists. He was captured in 1802 by French forces and died in prison a year later.

La Reforma an era of liberal reform in Mexico from 1855 to 1876

labor union organization of workers who bargain for better pay and working conditions

Lafayette, Marquis de Marquis de Lafayette (1757–1834), a French noble, fought alongside the Americans in the Revolutionary War. Upon his return to France, Lafayette led the call for reform and in 1789 presented a draft of the Declaration of the Rights of Man to the National Assembly. He was hated by some for his moderate stance, and fled to Austria, but later returned.

laissez faire policy allowing business to operate with little or no government interference

Lalibela Ruler of Ethiopia who came to power in the 1200s. He built eleven Christian churches carved from ground level into the solid rock of the mountains below.

land reform break-up of large agricultural holdings for redistribution among peasants

Laozi Laozi means "Master Lao" or "Old Master" in the Chinese language. An old man when Confucius was a young scholar, Laozi was born in a small village in ancient China. He was appointed a historian in one of the Zhou dynasty courts. Laozi developed a philosophy of inner calm, purity of mind, and living in harmony with nature that is called Dao, or the way of the universe. His book, *The Way of Life,* had enormous influence on Chinese life.

Las Casas, Bartolomé de Bartolomé de Las Casas (c. 1474–July 17, 1566) was a Dominican priest and historian famed as an early advocate for human rights in the Americas. Knowing the evils suffered by Native Americans under the encomienda system, his vivid reports of abuses helped the passage of laws prohibiting enslavement and abuse in 1542. He spent the rest of his life fighting for the rights of peoples in the Americas.

laser a high-energy light beam that can be used for many purposes, including surgery, engineering, and scientific research

latifundia huge estates bought up by newly wealthy Roman citizens

Lawrence, T. E. Thomas Edward Lawrence, (1888–1935), also known as Lawrence of Arabia, was a British archaeologist, writer, and expert on Arabia who helped lead an Arab rebellion and guerilla war against the Ottoman Turks during World War I. In 1926, he published a memoir of his activities in those years, *The Seven Pillars of Wisdom.*

lay investiture appointment of bishops by anyone who is not a member of the clergy

Leakey, Louis (1903–1972) As an archaeologist, Louis Leakey, and his wife, Mary, searched for the remains of early humans in East Africa, finding many tools and bones that increased our understanding of early humans.

Leakey, Mary (1913–1996) Born in London, England, Mary Leakey traveled throughout Europe visiting numerous prehistoric sites, which increased her interest in archaeology and geology. She married Louis Leakey in 1936, and they spent 30 years digging for early humans in East Africa. Mary Leakey eventually found many remains that have increased our understanding of early hominids.

legion basic unit of the ancient Roman army, made up of about 5,000 soldiers

legislature lawmaking body

legitimacy principle by which monarchies that had been unseated by the French Revolution or Napoleon were restored

Lend-Lease Act act passed by the U.S. Congress in 1941 that allowed the president (FDR) to sell or lend war supplies to any country whose defense was considered vital to the United States

Lenin, V. I. V. I. Lenin (1870–1924) was a Russian communist revolutionary who led the Bolsheviks to victory in the Russian October Revolution. He served as the premier of the Soviet Union from 1922 until his death in 1924. He adapted the ideas of Karl Marx to create a type of communism known as Marxism-Leninism.

Leonard da Vinci Leonardo da Vinci (1452–1519) was an Italian artist considered the ideal Renaissance man due to his varied talents. His interests included botany, anatomy, optics, music, architecture, and engineering. His sketches for flying machines and undersea boats resembled the later inventions of airplanes and submarines. Leonardo's paintings, such as the *Mona Lisa* and *The Last Supper,* remain famous today.

Leopold II Leopold II (1835–1909) was the king of Belgium who led the first Western efforts to develop and control the Congo basin. He ruled personally over the Congo Free State, which became part of Belgium in 1908.

levée morning ritual during which nobles would wait upon French king Louis XIV

libel knowing publication of false and damaging statements

liberation theology movement within the Catholic Church that urged the church to become a force for reform, social justice, and put an end to poverty

Liliuokalani Liliuokalani, born Lydia Kamakaeha (1838–1917), was the last Hawaiian sovereign before the islands were annexed by the United States in 1898. A princess during her brother's reign, Liliuokalani played an active role in Hawaii's government, improving education and meeting with foreign dignitaries. After her brother's death, she inherited the throne, becoming the first queen of Hawaii. In 1893, American planters, led by Sanford Dole, overthrew her.

limited monarchy government in which a constitution or legislative body limits the monarch's powers

Line of Demarcation line set by the Treaty of Tordesillas dividing the non-European world into two zones, one controlled by Spain and the other by Portugal

lineage a group claiming a common ancestor

Lister, Joseph Joseph Lister (1827–1912) was a Scottish surgeon who furthered medical knowledge by recognizing that the lack of cleanliness in hospitals directly correlated to deaths after surgeries. By studying the works of other scientists, he became convinced that microorganisms in the air entered the body through open wounds and caused infections that often led to death after surgery. He began using carbolic acid to clean patient wounds. He also began using an antiseptic liquid to treat dressings and later developed techniques to clean surgical instruments and keep wounds clean during surgery. He is known as the "Father of Antiseptic Surgery."

literacy the ability to read and write

literacy rate percentage of people who can read and write

Liverpool industrial city in northern Britain that was part of the first major railway line; it went from Liverpool to Manchester

Livingstone, David David Livingstone (1813–1873) was a Scottish missionary and explorer who influenced Western attitudes toward Africa.

Locke, John John Locke (1632–1704) grew up during the tumultuous era of the English Civil Wars. A prolific writer on political philosophy, Locke's works strongly influenced the U.S. Constitution and the development of American government. Locke proposed that people are born with certain natural rights that cannot be taken away, including life, liberty, and property. His radical ideas on government's responsibility to the people were fundamental to the leaders of the American Revolution.

loess fine windblown yellow soil

logic rational thinking

Long March epic march in which a group of Chinese Communists retreated from Guomindang forces by marching over 6,000 miles

longbow six-foot-long bow that could rapidly fire arrows with enough force to pierce most armor

Louis IX Louis IX (1214–1270) was King of France from 1226 to 1270. He was one of the most popular kings of France. He led the Seventh Crusade to the Holy Land and was canonized as a saint in recognition of his faith and services to the Church.

Louis Philippe Louis Philippe (1773–1850) was king of France from 1830 to 1848. He was known as the Citizen King because the people put him on the throne. He ultimately lost power because he did not support the working classes.

Louis XIV Louis XIV (1638–1715) served as king of France (1643–1715) and is considered the symbol of absolute monarchy.

Louis XVI Louis XVI (1754–1793) was king of pre-revolutionary France. He failed to support his ministers, who tried to reform France's finances and social institutions. Although he agreed in 1789 to summon the Estates-General, he resisted demands for reform by the National Assembly. He was later branded a traitor and executed in 1793.

Louisiana Purchase territory purchased by Thomas Jefferson from France in 1803

Luftwaffe German air force

Lusitania British liner torpedoed by a German submarine in May 1915

Luther, Martin Martin Luther (1483–1546) was a German monk and theologian who was the catalyst of the Protestant Reformation. Trained to become a lawyer, he changed his path, joined a strict order of Roman Catholic monks, and studied theology. Seeking to reform abuses within the Church, Luther challenged Church teachings with his 95 Theses. This led to his excommunication and the development of Lutheranism, the first of several Protestant sects.

M

Maathai, Wangari Wangari Maathai (1940–2011) was the founder of the Green Belt Movement as well as a human rights, AIDs prevention, and women's rights activist. She was elected to Kenya's national assembly in 2002 and won the Nobel Peace Prize in 2004.

Macao region of southeastern China made up of a peninsula and two islands; the Ming dynasty allowed the Portuguese to set up a trading post here

MacArthur, Douglas Douglas MacArthur (1880–1964) led the Allied assaults in the Southwest Pacific. He also commanded troops in World War I and the Korean War. He became a general and army chief of staff during the Depression.

Macartney, Lord Lord Macartney (1737–1806) Born to a Scots-Irish family in Ireland, Lord Macartney served as a member of the British Parliament, chief secretary for Ireland, and governor of several British colonies. King George III sent him on an unsuccessful mission to persuade Emperor Qianlong of China to allow British traders into northern port cities. He later became governor of the colony at the Cape of Good Hope.

Machiavelli, Niccoló Machiavelli (1469–1527) was born in Florence. He was a Renaissance political philosopher, statesman, and writer. His most famous work was a guide for rulers on how to gain and keep power. *The Prince* was realistic about political power. Machiavelli argued that the end justified the means in politics. The term "Machiavellian" is still used today to describe deceitful politics.

Madison, James James Madison (1751–1836) was a renowned U.S. statesman and fourth president of the United States. He is often called the "father of the Constitution" for the major role he played at the Constitutional Convention of 1789, which framed the federal Constitution.

Magellan, Ferdinand Ferdinand Magellan (1480–1521) was a Portuguese navigator and explorer who as a young man went on Portuguese expeditions to India and Africa, and later won Spanish support for his September 1519 expedition to sail west to reach the Moluccas. Beginning with five ships and a crew of 270, the long voyage through unknown waters encountered rough weather, scurvy, starvation, and eventual mutiny. Magellan was killed in 1521 during a battle in the present-day Philippines, and only one of his ships, carrying spices and 18 of the original crew, circumnavigated the world and at last returned to Spain in September 1522.

Maginot Line massive fortifications built by the French along their border with Germany in the 1930s to protect against invasion

Magna Carta The Great Charter approved by King John of England in 1215; it limited royal power and established certain rights of English freemen

Magyars an ethnic group centered in present-day Hungary

Mahdi a Muslim savior of the faith according to some Muslim beliefs

maize corn

Malacca city located on the Malay Peninsula near the strategic Straits of Malacca

Mali medieval West African trading empire located in present-day Mali

Malinche Malinche (c. 1501–1550) was a young Indian woman, called Doña Marina by the Spanish, who spoke Maya and Aztec languages, learned Spanish, and served as Cortés's translator and advisor during his conquest of Mexico. Malinche converted to Christianity, later married one of Cortés's soldiers, and visited Spain, where she enjoyed a friendly reception at the Spanish court.

Malindi existing East African coastal city and hub of international trade, attacked in the 1400s by Portuguese explorers to expel the Arabs who control East African trade routes, and then take over those routes for themselves

Malthus, Thomas Thomas Malthus (1766–1834) was a British economist. He was born in Surrey to a wealthy family. After being educated at home, he attended college in Cambridge, where he earned a master's degree. His most well-known work is *An Essay on the Principle of Population*. In it, he argued that population increases would eventually use up the food supply, leading to poverty. He was a professor of history and political economy until his death.

Manchester industrial city in northern Britain that was part of the first major railway line; it went from Manchester to Liverpool

Manchuria historic province in northeastern China; rich in natural resources

Manchus people originally from Manchuria, north of China, who conquered the Ming dynasty and ruled China as the Qing dynasty from the mid-1600s to the early 1900s

mandate after World War I, a territory administered by a Western power

Mandela, Nelson Nelson Mandela (1918–2013) was a leader of the African National Congress and a freedom fighter during South Africa's apartheid era. He was jailed for 27 years and became the lightening rod for protests calling for an end to apartheid. He was freed from jail in 1990 and became South Africa's first Black president in 1994, a post he held for only one term. Together with F.W. de Klerk he won the Nobel Peace Prize in 1993.

Mandelstam, Osip Osip Mandelstam (1891–1938?) grew up in St. Petersburg, Russia, in a Jewish household. Although Mandelstam is remembered as one of the foremost Russian poets of the 20th century, most of his work went unpublished during his lifetime. The Communists sent him into exile for a second time in 1938, and his wife, Nadezhda Khazina, received his last communication some months afterwards. He was never heard from again, but through the tireless efforts of his wife, the majority of Mandelstam's work was saved for future generations.

Manhattan Project code name for the project to build the first atomic bomb during WWII

Manifest Destiny American idea that the United States should stretch across the entire North American continent

manor during the Middle Ages in Europe, a lord's estate that included one or more villages and the surrounding lands

manor system also called manorial system; economic system during the Middle Ages in Europe that was built around large estates called manors, which included one or more villages and the surrounding lands

Mansa Musa Mansa Musa (died c. 1337) was a devoted Islamic ruler of Mali who came to the throne in 1312 and expanded Mali's borders to the Atlantic Ocean. He was one of the richest men of his era. His famous journey to Mecca was lavish and awakened the world to the riches of Mali.

Mao Zedong Mao Zedong (1893–1976) was born in central China to a peasant family. He helped form the Chinese Communist Party in 1921. After Jiang Jieshi launched "extermination campaigns" against the Communists, Mao led his army on the epic Long March. Mao briefly joined with the Guomindang to suppress Japanese aggression, but the partnership did not last after World War II ended. The People's Republic of China was established in 1949. Mao initiated drastic reforms, some of which had disastrous consequences. Mao's use of terror and intolerance of opposition became internationally notorious.

Maori the indigenous people of New Zealand

March on Rome planned march of thousands of Fascist supporters to take control of Rome; in response Mussolini was given the legal right to control Italy

Marconi, Guglielmo Guglielmo Marconi (1874–1937) was an Italian inventor who received the first patent for a wireless telegraphy system. In 1900, Marconi proved that wireless waves were not affected by Earth's shape when he transmitted a wireless signal across the Atlantic ocean for a distance of 2,100 miles. He continued to study waves, which resulted in a beam system for long distance communication, the first microwave radio, and the principles of radar. He received many honors and awards, including the Nobel Prize in Physics.

Marcos, Ferdinand Ferdinand Marcos (1917–1989) was the authoritarian leader of the Philippines from 1966–1986. Formerly a lawyer, Marcos won democratic presidential elections in the Philippines in 1965 and 1969. His reign became increasingly marked by corruption and human-rights incidents. In 1972, he declared martial law and persecuted his opponents. When exiled politician and Marcos critic Benigno Aquino, Jr., was assassinated, the majority of Filipinos threw their support behind his widow, Corazon, in the 1986 presidential election. After a contested loss, Marcos and his wife fled to exile in Hawaii.

Maria Theresa Maria Theresa (1717–1780) was the archduchess of Austria and queen of Hungary and Bohemia (1740–1780), wife and empress of the Holy Roman emperor Francis I (1745–1765) and mother of the Holy Roman emperor Joseph II (1765–1790).

Marie Antoinette Marie Antoinette's (1755–1793) frivolous ways, conduct, and various scandals helped discredit the monarchy. She told her husband, Louis XVI, to resist reform demands by the National Assembly. Like Louis, she was branded a traitor and executed.

Marseilles French port city; troops marched to a patriotic song as they left the city, the song eventually became the French national anthem

Marshall Plan massive aid package offered by the U.S. to Europe to help countries rebuild after World War II

Martel, Charles Charles Martel (688–741) served as mayor of the palace (the person who ruled in the name of the king) for the eastern part of the Frankish kingdom from 715 until 741. The illegitimate son of the former mayor, Martel seized power, eventually reunited, and then ruled the entire kingdom of the Franks. Since 711, Muslims had raided Frankish lands, and in 732 they reached Bordeaux. Called to help at the battle of Tours that year, Charles's cavalry halted this last great Muslim advance into Europe.

martyr a person who suffers or dies because of his or her beliefs

Mary Tudor Mary Tudor (1516–1558) was the first queen to rule England in her own right. The daughter of Henry VIII and his first wife, Catherine of Aragon, Mary was a staunch Catholic who failed to turn back the tide of the Protestant Reformation in England. Her vigorous persecution of Protestants earned her the nickname "Bloody Mary."

matrilineal kinship ties that are passed on through the mother's side of the family

Maurya, Chandragupta Chandragupta Maurya, who reigned from about 321 B.C. to 297 B.C., was the first Mauryan emperor. The son of a Mauryan chief, his family was left in poverty when his father died. After overcoming many challenges, Chandragupta learned military tactics and eventually formed a force strong enough to conquer most of India.

May Fourth Movement cultural movement in China that sought to reform China and make it stronger

means of production farms, factories, railways, and other large businesses that produce and distribute goods

Mecca a city in western Saudi Arabia; birthplace of Muhammad, viewed by Muslims as the prophet of Islam, and the most holy city for Islamic people

medieval referring to the Middle Ages in Europe or the period of history between ancient and modern times

Medina a city in western Saudi Arabia; a city where Muhammad preached

Meiji Restoration in Japan, the reign of emperor Meiji from 1868 to 1912 that was marked by rapid industrialization

Meir, Golda Golda Meir (1898–1978) was a founder and the first female prime minister of Israel (1969–1974). She was a founding member of the Israel Labour Party and had been foreign minister (1956–1966).

Menelik II Menelik II (1844–1913) was the emperor of Ethiopia who expanded his empire, modernized his country, and defeated the Italian invasion in 1896.

mercantilism policy by which a nation sought to export more than it imported in order to build its supply of gold and silver

mercenaries soldiers serving in a foreign army for pay

mercenary soldier serving in a foreign country for pay

Meroë capital of the ancient kingdom of Nubia

Mesa Verde the largest complex of Anasazi cliff-dwellings in the North American Southwest, built between A.D. 1150 and A.D. 1300

Mesoamerica region of North America, including Mexico and Central America, in which civilizations with common cultural features developed before Europeans entered the continent

Mesopotamia region within the Fertile Crescent that lies between the Tigris and Euphrates rivers.

messiah savior sent by God

mestizo in Spanish colonial America, a person of Native American and European descent

métis people of mixed Native American and French Canadian descent

Michelangelo Michelangelo Buonarroti (1475–1564) was an Italian painter also known for his sculpture, engineering, architecture, and poems. His famous marble statue, *David,* shows the influence of ancient Greek traditions on Renaissance artists. Michelangelo painted biblically themed ceiling murals for the Sistine Chapel in Rome. As an architect, he designed the dome of St. Peter's Cathedral in Rome, later a model for the U.S. Capitol in Washington D.C.

middle class a group of people, including merchants, traders, and artisans, whose rank was between nobles and peasants

Middle Passage the leg of the triangular trade route on which slaves were transported from Africa to the Americas

militarism glorification of the military

militia armed group of citizen soldiers

Milosevic, Slobodan Slobodan Milosevic (1941–2006) was a Serbian Socialist party leader, whose Serbian nationalist policies contributed to the breakup of the former Yugoslavia. He died in The Hague, Netherlands, while on trial at the UN's International Criminal Tribunal for the Former Yugoslavia (ICTY) for his role in the genocide in the Balkans.

minaret slender tower of a mosque, from which Muslims are called to prayer

Ming dynasty Chinese dynasty in which Chinese rule was restored; held power from 1368 to 1644

missionary someone sent to do religious work in a territory or foreign country

mixed economy economic system involving a mix of government ownership or control and private ownership with market forces

mobilize prepare military forces for war

Mobutu Sese Seko (1930–1997) was born Joseph-Desire Mobutu. He changed his name after he took control of Congo in 1965 in a military coup. He also renamed the country Zaire. Mobutu ruled Zaire as a dictator until he was overthrown by Laurent Kabila in 1997. He died of cancer a short time later.

Moche a culture that thrived in the Andean region from about 400 B.C. to A.D. 600

Moctezuma Moctezuma (Moctezuma II, 1466–c. June 30, 1520) was the last Aztec emperor, who mistakenly thought that the conquistador Cortés might be the god-king Quetzalcoatl. He was defeated by Cortés and forced to sign over his land and treasure. He was taken prisoner and killed as the Aztecs attempted to drive the Spanish from Tenochtitlán.

Mohenjo-Daro ancient city of the Indus civilization, located in present-day Pakistan

moksha in Hindu belief, the ultimate goal of existence, which is to achieve union with Brahman

Moluccas an island chain in present-day Indonesia, which Europeans in the 1400s called the Spice Islands because it was the chief source of spices

Mombasa established East African coastal city and hub of international trade, attacked in the 1400s by Portuguese explorers to expel the Arabs who controlled East African trade routes, so they could take over those routes for themselves

monarchy government in which a king or queen exercises central power

Monet, Claude Claude Monet (1840–1926) was one of the leading figures in the French Impressionist movement. Much like the Romantics, the Impressionists found inspiration in the outdoors and rejected traditional European artistic conventions. Monet sought to create an accurate depiction of nature through his use of color, tones, texture, and brush strokes. He often painted the same object or scene at different times of day to see how light and shadow changed its appearance. Two of his most famous series are the grain stacks and water lily pond.

money economy economic system in which goods or services are paid for through the exchange of a token of an agreed value

Mongkut Mongkut (1804–1868) was king of Siam (modern-day Thailand) from 1851–1868. Mongkut lived as a Buddhist monk while his older brother held the throne. Upon his brother's death, Mongkut's many influential friends helped him become king. The learned king was fond of Western philosophies and worked to modernize his kingdom. His educated children were able to further his progress after his death.

monopoly complete control of a product or business by one person or a group

monotheistic believing in one god

Monroe Doctrine American policy of discouraging European intervention in the Western Hemisphere

monsoon seasonal wind that regularly blows from a certain direction for part of the year

Montesquieu Baron de Montesquieu (1689–1755) was born Charles Louis de Secondat into a family of wealth and inherited the title Baron de Montesquieu from his uncle. Like many other reformers, he did not let his privileged status keep him from becoming a voice for democracy. His first book, titled *Persian Letters,* ridiculed the French government and social classes. In his work published in 1748, *The Spirit of the Laws,* he advanced the idea of separation of powers—a foundation of modern American democracy.

More, Sir Thomas Thomas More (1478–1535) was born in London. He became a lawyer, scholar, writer, and member of British parliament during the reign of Henry VIII. He wrote *Utopia,* describing an ideal society. The word *utopian* came to mean idealistic or visionary. In 1521, he was knighted.

Morelos, Father José Father José Morelos (1765–1815) was a Catholic priest who took command of the revolutionary movement after Father Miguel Hidalgo's death. He led the movement throughout southern Mexico, and in 1813, he called the Congress of Chilpancingo to form a government. In 1815 he was captured and executed as a traitor.

mosaic picture made of chips of colored stone or glass

Moses As described in the Hebrew Bible, Moses was a Jewish religious leader who led the Israelites out of Egyptian slavery back to Canaan. Jews believe that during the journey, or Exodus, God presented Moses with a set of religious and ethical laws for the Jewish people known as the Ten Commandments.

mosque Muslim house of worship

Mothers of the Plaza de Mayo a movement of women who protested weekly in a central plaza in the capital of Argentina against the disappearance or killing of relatives

Mughal Muslim dynasty that ruled much of present-day India from 1526 to 1857

Mughal empire Muslim empire that ruled most of northern India from the mid-1500s to the mid-1700s; also known as the Mogul empire

Muhammad Muhammad (c. 570–632) introduced the religion of Islam to southwestern Asia. According to Muslim belief, Muhammad heard the voice of the angel Gabriel instructing him to serve as a messenger for God. Muhammad spent the rest of his life spreading Islam. Muslims today honor Muhammad as God's final prophet.

Muhammad Ahmad Muhammad Ahmad (1844–1885) assumed the title and role of Mahdi in 1881, believing he was appointed by God to purify the Muslim religion and restore its greatness. Through his campaigns, he created a vast Islamic state in the Sudan region.

Muhammad al-Razi Muhammad al-Razi (865–925) was a renowned Muslim physician who pioneered the study of many diseases. In addition to a well-received book on measles and smallpox, he also wrote texts about the history of medicine and ways to advance the field. Al-Razi held the position of chief physician, first in the city of Rayy and then in Baghdad. Also a philosopher, al-Razi analyzed the works of Plato while presenting his own ideas.

Muhammad Ali Muhammad Ali (1769–1849) was the son of a military commander who died when Muhammad Ali was a young boy. He was appointed governor of Egypt by the Ottomans and seized power during the chaos of the civil war following Napoleon's invasion. Often called the "founder of modern Egypt," Muhammad Ali set in motion a number of economic, political, administrative, and military reforms. His reforms were intended to secure Egyptian independence and place Egypt on the road to becoming a major Middle Eastern power.

mujahedin Muslim religious warriors

multiethnic made up of several ethnic groups

multinational corporation company with branches in many countries

Mumbai a large city in India, also known as Bombay

mummification the preservation of dead bodies by embalming and wrapping them in cloth

Mussolini, Benito Benito Mussolini (1883–1945) was born into a poor household in Italy. His father was a blacksmith and his mother a schoolteacher. Although Mussolini grew up in a socialist home and strongly advocated socialist policies as a young man, he formed the Fascist party in Italy after returning from fighting in World War I. Using terror and fear tactics together with the Black Shirts, Mussolini created and ruled Italy as a totalitarian state. After Italy invaded Ethiopia in 1935, Mussolini and Hitler made an alliance and, with Japan, fought against the Allies in World War II.

mutiny revolt, especially of soldiers or sailors against their officers

Mutsuhito Mutsuhito (1852–1912) was declared emperor Meiji in 1868 following the death of his father, the emperor Kōmei. Emperor Meiji embodied a blend of Western and Japanese ideals, seeking out foreign examples as models for his country. He initiated major political, economic, and cultural reforms that led to an era of rapid modernization.

mutual-aid society self-help group to aid sick or injured workers

mystic person who devotes his or her life to seeking direct communication with the divine

N

Nagasaki Japanese city; on an island in its harbor, the Tokugawa shoguns in the 1600s permitted one or two Dutch ships to trade with Japan each year

Nanak, Guru Guru Nanak (1469–c. 1539) was the founder of Sikhism. According to Sikh beliefs, Nanak entered a trance while swimming and experienced a spiritual revelation. He preached a message of equality and opportunity, and of one God for all humanity. His teachings, and those of his successors, shaped the core beliefs of Sikhism.

Napoleon III Napoleon III (1808–1873) was the nephew of Napoleon Bonaparte. He was president of the Second Republic (1850–1852), then emperor of the Second Empire of France (1852–1870). Napoleon III built France's economic and political power, but his foreign policies were unsuccessful. He was deposed in 1870 after France's defeat in the Franco-Prussian War.

Napoleonic Code body of French civil laws introduced in 1804; served as a model for many nations' civil codes

Napoleonic Wars a series of wars from 1804 to 1805 that pitted Napoleon's French empire against the major powers of Europe

Nasser, Gamal Abdel Gamal Abdel Nasser (1918–1970) was the president of Egypt (1956–1970). He nationalized the Suez Canal, was a leader of the Pan Arab movement, and allied Egypt with the Soviet Union during the Cold War. He led his country to war with Israel in 1956 and 1967.

Nationalism a strong feeling of pride and devotion to one's country

nationalization takeover of property or resources by the government

natural law unchanging principle, discovered through reason, that governs human conduct

natural rights rights that belongs to all humans from birth, such as life, liberty, and property

Nazca a culture that thrived in the Andean region from about 200 B.C. to A.D. 600

Nazi-Soviet Pact agreement between Germany and the Soviet Union in 1939 in which the two nations promised not to fight each other and to divide up land in Eastern Europe

Nebuchadnezzar (634 B.C.–562 B.C.) Nebuchadnezzar was king of the Babylonian empire from 605 B.C. to 562 B.C. He led several military campaigns, which expanded the empire to Aramea, Judah, and other cities. He rebuilt the city of Babylon and is credited with the construction of the famous Hanging Gardens.

Necker, Jacques Jacques Necker (1732–1804) was director of the French treasury before the revolution, Necker attempted to reform the country's finances, although he also tried to finance France's participation in the American Revolution through heavy borrowing, while trying to conceal the country's huge deficit. Later, his calls for reform were thwarted by Louis XVI.

négritude movement movement in which writers and artists of African descent expressed pride in their African heritage

Nehanda Nehanda (c. 1840–1898) was a spiritual leader of the Shona people in southern Africa and the inspiration for a revolt against the British South Africa Company's colonization of the territory that is now Zimbabwe. She was eventually captured and executed by the British.

Nehru, Jawaharlal Jawaharlal Nehru (1889–1964) was the first prime minister of independent India. Educated in England, Nehru returned to India to practice law. He joined the Indian National Congress, an independence movement led by Mohandas Gandhi. Named Gandhi's successor, Nehru led the Congress until India achieved independence from Great Britain. As prime minister, Nehru focused on industrialization, socialist economic policies, and neutrality in the Cold War.

Neolithic Period the final era of prehistory, which began about 9000. B.C.; also called the New Stone Age

Neolithic Revolution the period of time during which the introduction of agriculture led people to transition from nomadic to settled life

neutrality policy of supporting neither side in a war

Neutrality Acts a series of acts passed by the U.S. Congress from 1935 to 1939 that aimed to keep the U.S. from becoming involved in WWII

New Deal a massive package of economic and social programs established by Franklin Delano Roosevelt to help Americans during the Great Depression

New France French possessions in present-day Canada from the 1500s to 1763

New Stone Age the final era of prehistory, which began about 9000 B.C.; also called the Neolithic Period

Newton, Isaac Isaac Newton (1642–1727) was one of the most important figures of the Scientific Revolution. An English mathematician and physicist, Newton's three laws of motion form the basic principles of modern physics and led to the formulation of the universal law of gravity. His 1687 book, *Mathematical Principles of Natural Philosophy,* is considered one of the most important works in the history of modern science.

Nightingale, Florence Florence Nightingale (1820–1910) was a nurse in the British military hospital in Crimea. When she arrived at the hospital in 1854, she was shocked by the state of the hospital and the rate at which the men were dying. She fought to have the barracks cleared, latrines dug, laundry washed, and the sick cared for. Six months after her arrival, the death rate dropped from 60 percent to 2 percent. When she returned to Britain, she pressured the government to reform hospitals to improve sanitation and care.

nirvana in Buddhist belief, union with the universe and release from the cycle of rebirth

Nkrumah, Kwame (1909–1972) fought to make Ghana (then Gold Coast) independent from Britain. He then became the first president of independent Ghana, which he led from 1957 until he was forced from office during a military coup. He spent the rest of his life in Guinea.

no-fly zone in Iraq, area where the United States and its allies banned flights by Iraqi aircraft after the 1991 Gulf War

Nobel, Alfred Alfred Nobel (1833–1896) was a Swedish chemist, inventor, engineer, business man, and author. Although dynamite is his most well-known invention, he holds 355 patents. In 1895, Nobel bequeathed most of his fortune to create the Nobel Prize in order to honor men and women for important achievements in physics, chemistry, medicine, literature, and peace.

nomad person who moves from place to place in search of food

nonalignment political and diplomatic independence from both Cold War powers

North Atlantic Treaty Organization (NATO) a military alliance between several North Atlantic states to safeguard them from the presumed threat of the Soviet Union's communist bloc; countries from other regions later joined the alliance

Northern Ireland the northeastern portion of the island of Ireland, a part of the United Kingdom that has had a long religious conflict

Nubia ancient kingdom of northeastern Africa, also called Kush

nuclear family family unit consisting of parents and children

Nuremberg Laws laws approved by the Nazi Party in 1935, depriving Jews of German citizenship and taking some rights away from them

Nuremberg Trials series of war crimes trials held in Germany after WWII

O

Old Stone Age the era of prehistory that lasted from 2 million B.C. to about 9000 B.C.

Olduvai Gorge Located in eastern Africa, the gorge is made up of numerous sedimentary layers of ash and lava deposited over millions of years. It has provided archaeologists with a geological yardstick for measuring the age of early stone tools and hominid bones excavated at the site.

oligarch member of an oligarchy; typically a wealthy person with political power

oligarchy government in which ruling power belongs to a few people

Olmec the earliest American civilization, located along the Gulf Coast of Mexico from about 1200 B.C. to 400 B.C.

one-child policy a Chinese government policy limiting urban families to a single child

Open Door Policy American approach to China around 1900, favoring open trade relations between China and other nations

Opium War war between Great Britain and China over restrictions to foreign trade

oracle bone in Shang China, animal bone or turtle shell used by priests to predict the future

Organization of American States (OAS) a group formed in 1948 to promote democracy, economic cooperation, and human rights in the Americas

Osiris Osiris is the Egyptian god identified as the god of the afterlife. He is often depicted as a green-skinned man with a pharaoh's beard, partially mummy-wrapped at the legs wearing a crown with ostrich feathers, holding a symbolic crook.

ostracism practice used in ancient Greece to banish or send away a public figure who threatened democracy

Ottoman a member of a Turkish-speaking nomadic people who migrated from Central Asia into northwestern Asia Minor

outpost a distant military station or a remote settlement

outsourcing the practice of sending work to outside enterprises in order to save money or increase efficiency

overproduction condition in which production of goods exceeds the demand for them

Owen, Robert Robert Owen (1771–1858) set up a model community in New Lanark, Scotland based on Utopianism. At New Lanark, Owen established revolutionary changes by limiting the age for children workers and providing a school for all children. In 1824, he invested in an experimental community in America called New Harmony. He became a leader in the labor movement in England and continued his involvement in the movement until his death.

Oyo empire Yoruba people formed this state in present-day southwestern Nigeria in the 1600s. This empire used wealth from trade, including slave trading, to maintain a trained army and to eventually conquer the neighboring Dahomey kingdom. The Yoruba people then traded with European merchants from Dahomey's ports.

P

Pachacuti Inca Yupanqui Pachacuti Inca Yupanqui (1438–1471) was a skilled warrior growing up. He expanded the Inca empire to what is now Peru and Ecuador. His capital was Cuzco, and he is credited with developing its city plan.

Pacific Rim vast region of nations, including countries in Southeast Asia, East Asia, and the Americas, that border the Pacific Ocean

pacifism opposition to all war

paddy rice field

pagoda multi-storied Buddhist temple with eaves that curve up at the corners

Paleolithic Period the era of prehistory that lasted from at least 2 million B.C. to about 9000 B.C.; also called the Old Stone Age

Pan-Africanism movement which began in the 1920s that emphasized the unity and strength of Africans and people of African descent around the world

Pan-Arabism movement in which Arabs sought to unite all Arabs into one state

Panama Canal manmade waterway connecting the Atlantic and Pacific oceans

pandemic spread of a disease across a large area, country, continent, or the entire world

papal supremacy the claim of medieval popes that they had authority over all secular rulers

papyrus plant used to make a paper-like writing material in ancient Egypt

Parliament the legislature of England, and later of Great Britain

parliamentary democracy a form of government in which the executive leaders (usually a prime minister and cabinet) are chosen by and responsible to the legislature (parliament), are also members of it

Parthenon the chief temple of the Greek goddess Athena on the Acropolis in Athens, Greece

partition a division into pieces

partnership a group of merchants who joined together to finance a large-scale venture that would have been too costly for any individual trader

pasha provincial ruler in the Ottoman empire

Pasternak, Boris Boris Pasternak (1890–1960) grew up in an well-educated Jewish family. His father was an artist and professor, while his mother was an accomplished concert pianist. Pasternak is best remembered for his epic novel *Doctor Zhivago,* which helped him to win the Nobel Prize for Literature in 1958. The accolades and publicity from the West only created problems for Pasternak at home in the Soviet Union. He was expelled from the Union of Soviet Writers and died in poverty. Pasternak's literary masterpiece remained banned in the Soviet Union until the mid-1980s.

Pasteur, Louis Louis Pasteur (1822–1895) was a French chemist and one of the founders of microbiology. Pasteur developed the germ theory of disease and identified the causes of many diseases, including rabies, anthrax, small pox, and chicken cholera. By discovering the causes of these diseases, Pasteur determined that they could be prevented by vaccines. He helped develop several vaccines, including the rabies vaccine. He also invented the process of pasteurization for wine, beer, milk, and vinegar.

paternalistic the system of governing a country as a father would a child

patriarch in the Roman and Byzantine empires, the highest church official in a major city

patriarchal relating to a society in which men hold the greatest legal and moral authority

patrician a member of the land-holding upper class

patrilineal kinship ties that are passed on through the father's side of the family

patron a person who provides financial support for the arts

Paul Paul (C. 4 B.C.–A.D. 64) was an early opponent of Christianity who, after having a vision, was converted to the teachings of Jesus. He became a missionary to spread the teachings of Jesus.

Peace of Westphalia series of treaties that ended the Thirty Years' War

Pedro, Dom Dom Pedro (1825–1891) was the second and final emperor of Brazil. Pedro II turned Portugese-speaking Brazil into an emerging power. He created political stability and sought to protect freedom of speech and civil rights. Dom Pedro's government was a parliamentary monarchy. Under his leadership, Brazil experienced significant economic growth. His reign ended in 1889 after a military coup took control of the government and forced him into exile in Europe.

penal colony place where people convicted of crimes are sent

peninsular in Spanish colonial America, a person born in Spain

peon a worker forced to labor for a landlord to pay off a debt that is impossible to pay off in his or her lifetime, which is incurred by food, tool, or seeds the landlord has advanced to him or her

peonage system by which workers owe labor to pay their debts

perestroika a Soviet policy of democratic and free-market reforms introduced by Mikhail Gorbachev in the late 1980s

Pericles (495 B.C.–429 B.C.) was an Athenian statesman in the 400s B.C. who led Athens during its golden age of cultural achievement under democratic government

Perón, Juan Juan Perón (1895–1974) was first elected president of Argentina in 1946. He ruled with the help of his wife, Eva, who was popular with Argentinians. Perón established an authoritarian government and instituted broad reforms, but his government was plagued with corruption. He was overthrown in a coup in 1955. His supporters, known as Peronists, continued to fight for control of the government, and Perón returned to power in the 1970s. His third wife, Isabel, became president upon her husband's death in 1974. She was overthrown by the military in 1976.

Perry, Matthew Matthew Perry (1794–1858) was a successful officer in the U.S. Navy. He led a naval expedition to Japan in an effort to establish diplomatic and trade relations after centuries of Japanese isolation. The overwhelming military presence opened the way for U.S. trading privileges in Japan, with other Western powers soon to follow.

perspective artistic technique used to give paintings and drawings a three-dimensional effect

Peter the Great Peter the Great (1672–1725), tsar of Russia, reigned jointly with his half-brother Ivan V (1682–1696) and alone (1696–1725). He was proclaimed emperor in 1721. He was one of Russia's greatest statesmen, organizers, and reformers.

Petrarch Francesco Petrarch (1304–1374) lived in Florence and was an early Renaissance humanist, poet, and scholar. He assembled a library of Greek and Roman manuscripts gathered from monasteries and churches, helping to preserve these classic works for future generations.

phalanx in ancient Greece, a massive tactical formation of heavily armed foot soldiers

pharaoh title of the rulers of ancient Egypt

Philip II Philip II (359 B.C.–336 B.C.), restored internal peace to Macedonia, built an effective army, and then formed alliances with many Greek city-states or conquered them. After defeating the united forces of Athens and Thebes at Chaeronea, all of Greece came under his control. Assassination ended his aim to conquer Persia.

Philippines a country in southeastern Asia made up of several thousand islands; seized by the Spanish in the 1500s; became an important link in Spain's overseas trading empire as the destination of silver fleets sent from the Americas

philosophe French for "philosopher"; French thinker who desired reform in society during the Enlightenment

philosopher someone who seeks to understand and explain life; a person who studies philosophy

philosophy system of ideas

Piankhi Piankhi was king of Kush from around 750 to 719 B.C. He was known for his military prowess throughout North Africa. A very conservative ruler, Piankhi sought to strengthen some of Egypt's declining institutions.

pictograph a simple drawing that looks like the object it represents

Pilgrim English Protestants who rejected the Church of England

Pisan, Christine de Christine de Pisan (c. 1364–1430) was the daughter of a physician and astronomer in the French court. Highly educated, de Pisan spoke several languages. After being widowed at 25, she began to write poetry and then comment on social issues.

Pizarro, Francisco Francisco Pizarro (c. 1476–June 26, 1541) was born into a very poor Spanish family and in 1513 joined Balboa's expedition to discover the "South Sea." In 1532, he arrived in Peru with his brothers, deposed the Incan ruler Atahualpa, conquered Peru, founded Lima in 1535, and was later assassinated by Spanish rivals.

plantation large estate run by an overseer and worked by laborers who live there

plateau raised area of level land

Plato Plato (437 B.C.–347 B.C.), a student of Socrates, was an Athenian thinker, writer of philosophical dialogues, and founder of the Academy in Athens.

plebeian a members of the class that included farmers, merchants, artisans, and traders

plebiscite a ballot in which voters have a direct say on an issue

pogrom violent attack on a Jewish community

Pol Pot Pol Pot (1925–1998) was the leader of the Khmer Rouge, a communist guerrilla army that took over Cambodia in 1975. Under his rule, roughly two million of his nation's people died from murder, starvation, and disease. In 1979, Pol Pot was driven from power. He was captured in 1997, tried, and sentenced to life imprisonment. He died of natural causes while under house arrest.

polarization in a political context, a concentration of people in distinct camps at opposite extremes of the political spectrum

polis city-state in ancient Greece

Polo, Marco Marco Polo (c. 1254–1324) was a traveler, merchant, and adventurer from Venice who journeyed from Europe to Asia in 1271–95, spending 17 years serving the Mongol emperor Kublai Khan. Polo dictated the account of his travels, *The Travels of Marco Polo* (originally iii *Il Milione* in Italian), to a fellow prisoner while imprisoned during a war with Genoa. His book proved a great success, but few readers believed it was true. Evidence outside his book that he journeyed so far to the east has not been found; however, during the centuries since his death, others have confirmed the accuracy of most of what he described.

polytheistic believing in many gods

pope head of the Roman Catholic Church; in ancient Rome, bishop of Rome who claimed authority over all other bishops

popular sovereignty limited government based on the separation of powers and a system of checks and balances

potlatch among Native American groups of the Northwest Coast, ceremonial gift-giving by people of high rank and wealth

predestination Calvinist belief that God long ago determined who would gain salvation

prehistory the period of time before writing was invented

premier prime minister

price revolution period in European history when inflation rose rapidly

prime minister the chief executive of a parliamentary government

privateer Dutch, English, and French pirates who preyed on treasure ships from the Americas in the 1500s, operating with the approval of European governments

Prohibition a ban on the manufacture and sale of alcohol in the United States from 1920 to 1933

proletariat working class

proliferate to multiply rapidly

propaganda spreading of ideas to promote a cause or to damage an opposing cause

prophet spiritual leader who interprets God's will

protectionism the use of tariffs and other restrictions to protect a country's home industries against competition

protectorate country with its own government but under the control of an outside power

Prussia area of eastern and central Europe which came under Polish and German rule in the Middle Ages and from 1701 was ruled by the German Hohenzollern dynasty

psychoanalysis a method of studying how the mind works and treating mental disorders

Ptolemy Ptolemy (A.D. 100–A.D. 170) was a Roman astronomer, mathematician, and geographer who incorrectly theorized that Earth is the center of the universe. He lived in Alexandria, Egypt, where he studied the planets and stars and developed a system to explain their movements.

pueblo Native American village of the North American Southwest

Pueblo Bonito the largest Anasazi pueblo, built in New Mexico in the A.D. 900s

Punjab state in northwestern India with a largely Sikh population

purdah isolation of women in separate quarters

Puritan member of an English Protestant group who wanted to "purify" the Church of England by making it more simple and more morally strict

Pusan Perimeter a defensive line around the city of Pusan, in the southeast corner of Korea, held by South Korean and United Nations forces in 1950 during the Korean War; marks the farthest advance of North Korean forces

Putin, Vladimir Vladimir Putin (b. 1952) served as president of Russia (1999–2008, 2012–). He began his career with the Soviet KGB (Committee for State Security) and also served as Russia's prime minister (1999, 2008–2012).

putting-out system system developed in the 18th century in which tasks were distributed to individuals who completed the work in their own homes; also known as cottage industry

Pythagoras Pythagoras (570 B.C.–c. 490 B.C.), a Greek philosopher and mathematician who studied the meaning of numbers and their relationships. He formulated principles that influenced the thinking of Plato and Aristotle, and also established an academy in Croton (now in Italy). Today he is best known for deriving the Pythagorean Theorem, a formula to calculate the relationship between the sides of a right triangle.

Q

Qajar a member of the dynasty that ruled present-day Iran from the late 1700s until 1925

Qianlong Qianlong (1711–1799) was a Chinese emperor who expanded the size of China's empire to include Tibet and much of central Asia, creating a multiethnic state that included Han Chinese, Mongols, Tibetans, and Manchus. Qianlong saw himself as a "Universal Monarch" both within and beyond the Chinese empire. He patronized the arts, commissioned great literary works, and formed China's national palace museum with art collections that remain important today.

Qing dynasty established by the Manchus in the mid-1600s that lasted until the early 1900s; China's last dynasty

quipu knotted strings used by Inca officials for record-keeping

Quran the holy book of Islam

R

Rabin, Yitzhak Yitzhak Rabin (1922–1995) was born in Jerusalem and served as an important military leader both before and after the creation of Israel. He served as prime minister twice, from 1974 to 1977 and from 1992 to 1995. In the 1990s, he reached a peace agreement with the PLO, for which he shared the Nobel Peace Prize with Shimon Peres and Yasir Arafat. Rabin was assassinated in 1995 by a Jewish extremist.

racism belief that one racial group is superior to another

radical one who favors extreme changes

rajah in ancient India, the elected warrior chief of an Aryan tribe

Ramses II (1292 B.C.–1190 B.C.) Ramses II is known for his building programs and for the wars he waged with the Hittites and Libyans. He reigned for more than 66 years and is known for the construction of Egypt's most famous monuments and architecture.

Raphael Raphael (1483–1520) was a Renaissance painter who blended Christian and classical styles. His famous paintings include one of the Madonna, the mother of Jesus, and *School of Athens,* showing an imaginary gathering of great thinkers, scientists, and artists including Michelangelo, Leonardo, and himself.

realism 19th-century artistic movement whose aim was to represent the world as it is

Realpolitik realistic politics based on the needs of the state

recession period of reduced economic activity

Reconquista During the 1400s, the campaign by European Christians to drive the Muslims from present-day Spain

refugee a person who flees from home or country to seek refuge elsewhere, often because of political upheaval or famine

regionalism loyalty to a local area

Reich German empire

Reign of Terror time period during the French Revolution from September 1793 to July 1794 when people in France were arrested for not supporting the revolution and many were executed

reincarnation in Hindu belief, the rebirth of the soul in another bodily form

reparation payment for war damage or damage caused by imprisonment

repeal cancel

republic system of government in which officials are chosen by the people

revenue money taken in through taxes

Rhee, Syngman Syngman Rhee (1875–1965) was president of the Republic of Korea (South Korea) from its founding in 1949 until 1960. He was elected to four terms of office, but accusations of election fraud in 1960 led to student-led protests and demands for his resignation from the National Assembly and the U.S. government. He resigned and went into exile in Hawaii.

rhetoric art of skillful speaking

Ricci, Matteo Matteo Ricci (1552–1610) was an Italian scholar and Jesuit priest who traveled to China. In 1589, Ricci began to teach Chinese scholars European mathematical ideas. Later he lived in Nanjing, where he worked on mathematics, astronomy, and geography. He became famous in China for his knowledge of astronomy, writing books in Chinese, and his talents as a painter.

Richelieu, Cardinal Cardinal Richelieu (1585–1642) considered one of the greatest politicians in history, he played an important role in France's history while serving as chief minister to Louis XIII.

Robespierre, Maximilien Maximilien Robespierre (1758–1794) was a French revolutionary elected to the Estates-General in 1789. He later became an important member of the Jacobin club and a member of the Committee of Public Safety. As a member of the Committee he began the Reign of Terror. He was later arrested and executed by the revolution's leaders.

rococo personal, elegant style of art and architecture made popular during the mid-1700s that featured designs with the shapes of leaves, shells, and flowers

romanticism 19th-century artistic movement that appealed to emotion rather than reason

Romero, Oscar Oscar Romero (1917–1980) was a Roman Catholic archbishop in El Salvador who became an outspoken critic of human rights abuses in his country and an advocate for the poor. He frequently came into conflict with the Salvadoran government for his criticism of the regime, and he was assassinated in 1980 while performing mass in a hospital chapel, most likely by Salvadoran death squads.

Rommel, Erwin Erwin Rommel (1891–1944) was a career military officer and one of Hitler's most successful generals. He took his own life after a failed attempt to assassinate Hitler.

Roosevelt, Franklin Delano Franklin D. Roosevelt (1882–1945) was the longest serving American president, elected to the office four times. Roosevelt was born into a wealthy family in New York and was a distant cousin of the early president Theodore Roosevelt. Elected in 1932, his first term as president focused on lifting America out of the Great Depression. He successfully passed legislation, crafting a massive package of economic and social programs, called the New Deal. During his third term, Roosevelt inspired many through his strong leadership during the Japanese attack on Pearl Harbor and America's subsequent entry into World War II. He was elected to a fourth term in 1944, but his health deteriorated as the war came to an end. Roosevelt died in April 1945.

Rosetta Stone stone monument that includes the same passage carved in hieroglyphics, demotic script, and Greek and that was used to decipher the meanings of many hieroglyphs

Rosie the Riveter popular name for women who worked in war industries during WWII

rotten borough rural town in England that sent members to Parliament despite having few or no voters

Rousseau, Jean-Jacques Jean-Jacques Rousseau (1712–1778) was a Swiss-born philosopher and writer whose works inspired leaders of the French Revolution. He revolutionized thought in politics and ethics, had an impact on how parents educated their children, and even influenced people's taste in music and in other arts.

Roy, Ram Mohun Ram Mohun Roy (1772–1833) was a founder of Hindu College in Calcutta, which provided an English-style education to Indians. While Roy wanted to reform some parts of traditional Indian and Hindu culture, he also revived India's pride in its culture. He is considered the founder of Indian nationalism.

Ruhr Valley coal-rich industrial region of Germany

russification Stalin's policy of imposing Russian culture on the Soviet Union

Russo-Japanese War conflict between Russia and Japan in 1904–1905 over control of Korea and Manchuria

S

Sabbath a holy day for rest and worship

sacrament sacred ritual of the Roman Catholic Church

Sadat, Anwar Anwar Sadat (1918–1981) was president of Egypt (1970–1981). He signed a peace treaty with Israel, the Camp David Accords, which was brokered by the U.S. He was assassinated by Muslim extremists in 1981.

Saddam Hussein Saddam Hussein (1937–2006) was a member of the Ba'ath Party and spent several years in prison when the Ba'athists were not in power. In 1968, he participated in a coup where the Ba'athists took over the government, and by 1979 he had total control of the government. Hussein was the dictator of Iraq until the 2003 Iraq War. In 2006, he was convicted in an Iraqi court of crimes against humanity and executed shortly afterward.

Safavid Shiite Muslim dynasty that ruled much of present-day Iran from the 1500s into the 1700s

Sahara largest desert in the world, covering almost all of North Africa

St. Francis of Assisi St. Francis of Assisi (1181?–1226) came from a wealthy family and had been a fun-loving and worldly young man. He gave up his wealth to "walk in the footsteps" of Jesus. The first Franciscan friars were his followers, and together they lived a life of service to the poor and sick. Francis regarded all nature as the mirror of God, and called animals his brothers and sisters. Famous stories tell of him preaching to the birds and convincing a wolf to stop attacking townspeople, if they, in turn, would feed the wolf. The Church made him a saint in 1228.

St. Petersburg a port city in northwestern Russia founded in 1703 by Peter the Great

salon informal social gathering at which writers, artists, *philosophes,* and others exchanged ideas

samurai member of the warrior class in Japanese feudal society

San Martín, José de José de San Martín (1778–1850) was born in Argentina and educated in Spain. He helped lead the revolutions against Spanish rule in Argentina, Chile, and Peru. He became protector of Peru after its liberation from Spain but resigned in 1822 after conflict with Simón Bolívar. He lived in exile in Europe after his resignation.

Sandinista a socialist political movement and party that held power in Nicaragua during the 1980s

sans-culottes members of the working class who made the French Revolution more radical; called such because men wore long trousers instead of the fancy knee breeches that the upper class wore

Sapa Inca the title of the Inca emperor

Sargon The exact dates of King Sargon's birth and death are unknown, but according to Sumerian historians, he reigned from 2334 B.C. to 2279 B.C. He is known for creating the first empire in Mesopotamia.

sati custom that called for a widow to join her husband in death by throwing herself on his funeral pyre

satirize make fun of

savanna grassy plain with irregular patterns of rainfall

schism a split or divide

scholasticism in medieval Europe, the school of thought that used logic and reason to support Christian belief

scientific method careful, step-by-step process used to confirm findings and to prove or disprove a hypothesis

scribe in ancient civilizations, a person specially trained to read, write, and keep records

secede withdraw

secret ballot votes cast without announcing them publicly

sect a subgroup of a major religious group

secular having to do with worldly, rather than religious, matters; nonreligious

segregation forced separation by race, sex, religion, or ethnicity

Sejong, King King Sejong (1397–1450), Korea's most celebrated ruler and known as the Great, in 1443 he replaced the complex Chinese system of writing with hangul. His numerous cultural and intellectual accomplishments have led historians to call his reign the Korean Golden Age.

selective borrowing adopting or adapting some cultural traits but discarding others

self-determination right of people to choose their own form of government

sepoy Indian soldier who served in an army set up by the French or English trading companies

Septimius Severus Septimius Severus was born around A.D. 145 in what is today Tripoli. Before his death in 211, he was the emperor who converted the Roman government into a military monarchy. His reign set the stage for other Roman rulers.

serf in medieval Europe, a peasant bound to the lord's land

shah king

Shaka Shaka (1787–1828) was a Zulu chief and founder of southern Africa's Zulu empire.

Shakespeare William Shakespeare (1564–1616), born in England, became a famous poet and playwright during the reign of Queen Elizabeth I. Between 1590 and 1613, he wrote 37 plays that are still performed around the world. He invented words and phrases still used today. Like other Renaissance writers, he took a humanist approach to his characters.

shantytown slum of flimsy shacks

Sharia body of Islamic law that includes interpretation of the Quran and applies Islamic principles to everyday life

Sharpeville a Black township in South Africa where the government killed anti-apartheid demonstrators in 1960

Shi Huangdi (about 259 B.C.–210 B.C.) was originally named Zhao Zheng. He was the son of the king of the Qin territory. At age 13, Zhao became the king of Qin. He proclaimed himself Shi Huangdi, or "First Emperor." Using spies, loyal generals, and bribery, he removed the leaders of six other surrounding states to create a unified China under his authoritarian rule. However, the unified China he created was too dependent on Shi Huangdi. The Qin dynasty collapsed four years after his death.

Shiite a member of one of the two major Muslim sects; believe that the descendants of Muhammad's daughter and son-in-law, Ali, are the true Muslim leaders

Shikibu, Murasaki Muraski Shikibu (c. 973–c. 1014 or 1025) was a lady-in-waiting in the Heian Court. Historians credit her with writing the world's first full-length novel, *The Tale of Genji,* written between A.D. 1000 and 1008.

Shinto principal religion in Japan that emphasizes the worship of nature

shrine altar, chapel, or other sacred place

Sikh member of an Indian religious minority

Sikhism monotheistic religion founded in the late 1400s by Guru Nanak in the Punjab region of India

Silla dynasty Korean dynasty that ruled from 668 to 935

Sino-Japanese War war between China and Japan in which Japan gained Taiwan

smelt melt in order to get the pure matter away from its waste matter

Smith, Adam Adam Smith (1723–1790) was a Scottish economist most remembered for his masterpiece, *An Inquiry into the Nature and Causes of the Wealth of Nations.* His argument for free markets with minimal government interference has helped shape productive economies around the world for more than 200 years. He has been called the father of modern economics and remains one of the most influential economic philosophers in history.

social contract an agreement by which people gave up their freedom to a powerful government in order to avoid chaos

social democracy political ideology in which there is a gradual transition from capitalism into socialism instead of a sudden, violent overthrow of the system

social gospel movement of the 1800s that urged Christians to do social service

social mobility the ability to move in social class

social welfare programs provided by the state for the benefit of its citizens

socialism system in which the people as a whole rather than private individuals own all property and operate all businesses

socialist realism artistic style whose goal was to promote socialism by showing Soviet life in a positive light

Socrates Socrates (469 B.C.–399 B.C.) was an Athenian stonemason and philosopher who sought truth by questioning, as described in dialogues written by Plato.

Solidarity a Polish labor union and democracy movement

Solomon In Jewish tradition, Solomon was the son of David, known for building the Temple in Jerusalem. He was also famous for his wisdom. After his death, the Kingdom of Israel was divided into two parts.

Song dynasty Chinese dynasty from 960 to 1279

Songhai medieval West African kingdom located in present-day Mali, Niger, and Nigeria

sovereign having full, independent power

soviet council of workers and soldiers set up by Russian revolutionaries in 1917

Spanish-American War conflict between the United States and Spain in 1898 over Cuban independence

Sparta city-state in ancient Greece settled by the Dorians and built as a military state

sphere of influence area in which an outside power claims exclusive investment or trading privileges

stalemate deadlock in which neither side is able to defeat the other

Stalin, Joseph Joseph Stalin (1879–1953) (real name: Iosif Vissarionovich Dzhugashvili) adopted the name Stalin, meaning "man of steel," after he joined the Bolshevik underground. He was the sole ruler of the Soviet Union for 33 years. Stalin stood his ground against Hitler and refused to leave Moscow. He eventually forced the Germans into retreat.

Stalingrad now Volgograd, a city in SW Russia that was the site of a fierce battle during WWII

Stamp Act law passed in 1765 by the British Parliament that imposed taxes on items such as newspapers and pamphlets in the American colonies; repealed in 1766

standard of living the level of material goods and services available to people in a society

Stanley, Henry Henry Stanley (1841–1904) was a British explorer of central Africa, famous for the rescue of Dr. David Livingstone and discoveries in the region of the Congo River.

Stanton, Elizabeth Cady Elizabeth Cady Stanton (1815–1902) was an author, lecturer, and activist who played a major role in the women's right movement. She drafted speeches and many of the movement's important documents, including the women's "Declaration of Rights." Stanton helped plan and lead the 1848 Seneca Falls Convention. Later in life, she began to focus more on social reforms, including child care, divorce laws, and temperance. Stanton died 18 years before women were granted the right to vote.

stela in the ancient world, a tall, commemorative monument that was often decorated

steppe sparse, dry, treeless grassland

stipend a fixed salary given to public office holders

stock shares in a company

Stolypin, Peter Peter Stolypin (1862–1911) was a Russian statesman under Tsar Nicholas II. He served as minister of the interior and president of the Council of Ministers. Although he instituted agricultural reforms that improved the lives of the peasantry, he made enemies on both sides of the political spectrum. He was assassinated in 1911.

strait narrow water passage

stupa large domelike Buddhist shrine

subcontinent large landmass that juts out from a continent

suburbanization the movement to build up areas outside of central cities

Sudetenland a region of western Czechoslovakia

Suez Canal a canal in Egypt linking the Red Sea and the Indian Ocean to the Mediterranean Sea, which also links Europe to ports in Asia and East Africa

suffrage right to vote

Sufi Muslim mystic who seeks communion with God through meditation, fasting, and other rituals

Suharto Suharto (1921–2008) was a highly ranked Indonesian military official who became the country's second president. Suharto fought against the Dutch in Indonesia's independence movement and achieved a distinguished rank in the new country's government. When Sukarno, the country's first president, started to institute communist policies, the anti-communist military rebelled. Suharto led purges against communists and a violent coup against Sukarno. Taking power in 1967, he worked to modernize and stabilize the country.

Sukarno Sukarno (1901–1970) was a freedom fighter and Indonesia's first president. Involved in the independence movement against the Dutch, Sukarno spent some time jailed or exiled. During World War II, Japan invaded the Indies, and Sukarno cooperated with the new regime. The collapse of Japan at the end of the war enabled Indonesia's independence, despite Dutch attempts to regain power. As the new country's president, Sukarno dismantled the parliamentary government and instituted communist policies. A violent coup led by General Suharto deposed Sukarno in 1967.

Suleiman Suleiman (1494–1566) was a sultan of the Ottoman Empire who ruled from 1520 to 1566. During this time he brought bureaucracy and stability to the empire and advanced the arts, law, and architecture. His military campaigns greatly expanded the scope of the empire.

sultan Muslim ruler

Sumer site of the world's first civilization, located in southeastern Mesopotamia

Sun Yixian Sun Yixian (1866–1925), also known as Sun Yat-sen, was the son of poor farmers in a small village. He left a career in medicine to revolt against the Qing government. After a failed uprising, Sun was forced into exile in Japan. In 1911, delegates elected Sun as provisional president of the newly established Republic of China. In 1921, Sun established a Nationalist government in South China and allied with the communists to defeat the warlords.

Sundiata Sundiata was a West African ruler who was responsible for laying the groundwork for Mali to be a rich and powerful kingdom. He died in 1255.

Sunni a member of one of the largest Muslim sects; believe that inspiration came from the example of Muhammad as recorded by his early followers

superpower a nation stronger than other powerful nations

surplus an amount that is more than needed; excess

surrealism artistic movement that attempts to portray the workings of the unconscious mind

Suryavarman II, King Suryavarman II was a famous king of Cambodia, who died in 1150 A.D. He built the world's largest religious structure at Angkor Wat and conquered much of what is now Thailand and Vietnam. He made the capital, Angkor, into one of the great cities of the world at that time.

sustainability development that balances people's needs today with the need to preserve the environment for future generations

sustainable development development that meets the needs of the present without compromising the ability of future generations to meet their own needs

Suu Kyi, Aung San Aung San Suu Kyi (1945–) is a human rights leader and Nobel Peace Prize recipient from Myanmar. The daughter of the leader of independent Burma and an ambassador to India, Suu Kyi was inspired to fight for peace and freedom against the military oppressors who had ruled Burma since 1962. She helped to found the independence movement the National League for Democracy, which won a democratic election in 1990 but was silenced by the military. In 2010, Suu Kyi was released from house arrest and won a seat in the legislature. She continues to lead the opposition to the authoritarian rulers and is expected to run for the country's presidency.

Swahili an East African culture that emerged about A.D. 1000; also a Bantu-based language, blending Arabic words and written in Arabic script.

T

Taíno Native American group encountered by Columbus when he first arrived in the West Indies

Taiping Rebellion peasant revolt in China

Taj Mahal a tomb built by Shah Jahan for his wife

Taliban Islamist fundamentalist faction that ruled Afghanistan for nearly ten years until ousted from power by the United States in 2002

Tang dynasty Chinese dynasty from 618 to 907

Tang Taizong Tang Taizong (598–649) was an accomplished general, government reformer, historian, Confucian scholar, and artist. These qualities and skills helped him to become China's most admired emperor.

tariff tax on imported goods

technology the skills and tools people use to meet their basic needs

Tehran capital of the Qajar dynasty and present-day Iran

temperance movement campaign to limit or ban the use of alcoholic beverages

tenant farmer someone who would pay rent to a lord to farm part of the lord's land

tenement multistory building divided into crowded apartments

Tennis Court Oath famous oath made by on a tennis court by the Third Estate in pre-revolutionary France

Tenochtitlán capital city of the Aztec empire, on which modern-day Mexico City was built

Teotihuacán city that dominated the Valley of Mexico from about A.D. 200 to A.D. 750 and that influenced the culture of later Mesoamerican peoples

Teresa, Mother Mother Teresa (baptized 1910, died 1997) was the Romanian-born founder of the Order of the Missionaries of Charity, a Roman Catholic group of women dedicated to helping the poor, especially those in India. She won the Nobel Peace Prize in 1979 and was also honored for her work by the Indian government. She was beatified, or named a blessed one, by the Roman Catholic Church in 2003 for her lifetime of commitment to those in need.

Teresa of Avila, St. Teresa of Avila, St. (1515–1582) gained renown as the author of several books on spiritual matters. She was a key influence during the Catholic Reformation. As a Carmelite nun, she dedicated herself to a simple religious life built on quiet reflection. Teresa dedicated most of her life to the reform of the Carmelite order, founding many convents throughout Spain.

terrorism deliberate use of random violence, especially against civilians, to achieve political goals

Tet Offensive a massive and bloody offensive by communist guerrillas against South Vietnamese and American forces on Tet, the Vietnamese New Year, 1968; helped turn American public opinion against military involvement in Vietnam

Thatcher, Margaret Margaret Thatcher (1925–2013) was Britain's first female prime minister, serving from 1979 to 1990. Thatcher was a conservative and an avowed opponent of socialism, seeing it as anti-British because it eroded self-reliance. Under Thatcher, the British government sold nationalized industries to private firms. Thatcher also led the country during the Falklands War (1982) with Argentina.

theocracy government run by religious leaders

Theodora Theodora (497–548) was the wife of the emperor Justinian and was his most trusted advisor. Known for her powerful intelligence and shrewd political insight, Theodora exerted decisive influence in Byzantine political affairs. She is mentioned by name in almost every law passed during Justinian's reign. Theodora used her position and power to advance her interests, including pioneering efforts for women's rights. She supported strong laws to end the traffic in young women and revised divorce laws in favor of more benefits to women.

Third Reich official name of the Nazi party for its regime in Germany; held power from 1933 to 1945

38th parallel an imaginary line marking 38 degrees of latitude, particularly the line across the Korean Peninsula, dividing Soviet forces to the north and American forces to the south after WWII

Thutmose III (1504 B.C.–1426 B.C.) Thutmose III shared power with his aunt Queen Hatshepsut before becoming pharaoh. He battled to regain Egyptian rule of Syria and Palestine and created Egypt's largest dynasty.

Tiahuanaco a culture that thrived in the Andean region from about A.D. 200 to 1000

Tiananmen Square a huge public plaza at the center of China's capital, Beijing

Tiberius (c. 163 B.C.–133 B.C.) was a Roman plebeian who became a tribune and lobbied for government reform. He was killed in 133 B.C. by gangs hired by Roman senators.

Tojo, Hideki Hideki Tojo (1884–1948) was born in Tokyo and was a career military man. He was a general of the Imperial Japanese Army and the 40th prime minister of Japan during most of World War II, from 1941 to 1945. He was directly responsible for the attack on Pearl Harbor, and was arrested and sentenced to death for Japanese war crimes.

Tokugawa shoguns, descended from Tokugawa Ieyasu (1542–1616) who were supreme military leaders; ruled Japan from 1603 through 1869; reunified Japan and reestablished order following a century of civil war and disturbance

Tokyo capital of Japan

Torah the most sacred text of the Hebrew Bible, includes the first five books

total war channeling of a nation's entire resources into a war effort

totalitarian state government in which a one-party dictatorship regulates every aspect of citizens' lives

Touré, Samori Samori Touré (c. 1830–1900) was a Muslim military leader who founded a powerful West African kingdom in the Niger River region and fought against French forces.

tournament a mock battle in which knights would compete against one another to display their fighting skills

trade deficit situation in which a country imports more than it exports

trade surplus situation in which a country exports more than it imports

traditional economy undeveloped economic systems that rely on custom and tradition

tragedy in ancient Greece, a play about human suffering often ending in disaster

Treaty of Paris treaty of 1763 that ended the Seven Years' War and resulted in British dominance of the Americas

Treaty of Tordesillas treaty signed between Spain and Portugal in 1494, which divided the non-European world between them

triangular trade colonial trade routes among Europe and its colonies, the West Indies, and Africa in which goods were exchanged for enslaved people

tribune an official elected by the plebeians to protect their interests

tributary state independent state that has to acknowledge the supremacy of another state and pay tribute to its ruler

tribute payment that conquered peoples may be forced to pay their conquerors

Trojan War military conflict around 1250 B.C. between Mycenae and Troy, a rich trading city in present-day Turkey, described in Homer's epic poems, the *Illiad* and the *Odyssey*

troubadour a wandering poet or singer of medieval Europe

Truman Doctrine United States policy, established in 1947, of trying to contain the spread of communism

Truman, Harry Harry Truman (1884–1972) was the vice president of the United States when Roosevelt died and became the 33rd president upon his death. After being in office for only a few months, Truman made the decision to drop atomic bombs on Japan.

Truth, Sojourner Sojourner Truth (1797–1883) was one of the most well-known African American women during the 19th century. She was born into slavery, and when she gained her freedom in 1826, she changed her name to Sojourner Truth. In 1843, she began travelling the country to spread the truth about injustice and to preach for human rights. Truth was an important figure in several movements— including the women's rights movement, temperance, racial equality, and prison reform—and she was not afraid to petition the government for reform.

tsunami a very large wave caused by an earthquake or very strong wind

turnpike private road built by entrepreneurs who charged a toll to travelers to use it

Tutsis the main ethnic minority group in Rwanda and Burundi

Tutu, Desmond Desmond Tutu (1931–) is an archbishop of the Anglican church and was a leader in the fight against apartheid in South Africa. In 1984 he won the Nobel Peace Prize for his efforts.

Tutu, Osei Osei Tutu was born around 1660 and died in the early 1700s. He was a founder and first ruler of the Asante empire in present-day Ghana. He started as the chief of the small state of Kumasi. But he realized that small separate Asante kingdoms needed to unite in order to protect themselves from powerful Denkyera neighbors.

Twenty-One Demands list of demands given to China by Japan in 1915 that would have made China a protectorate of Japan

tyrant in ancient Greece, ruler who gained power by force

U

U-boat German submarine

ultimatum final set of demands

ultranationalist extreme nationalist

Umayyad Sunni dynasty of caliphs that ruled from 661 to 750

United Nations (UN) an international organization formed in 1945 at the end of World War II. Since then, its global role has expanded to include economic and social development, human rights, humanitarian aid, and international law.

universal manhood suffrage right of all adult men to vote

untouchable in India, a member of the lowest caste

Urban II, Pope Pope Urban II (1042–1099) was the leader of the Roman Catholic church at the time the Seljuk Turks were threatening the Byzantine empire. He convened the Council of Clermont, where he launched the First Crusade to win the Holy Land from the Muslims.

urban renewal the process of fixing up the poor areas of a city

urbanization movement of people from rural area to cities

Usman dan Fodio Usman dan Fodio (1754–1817) was a Fulani revolutionary leader, mystic, and philosopher. He led a revolt (1804–1808) to create a new Muslim state, the Fulani empire, in what is now northern Nigeria.

usury the practice of lending money at interest

utilitarianism idea that the goal of society should be to bring about the greatest happiness for the greatest number of people

utopian idealistic or visionary, usually used to describe a perfect society

V

V-E Day Victory in Europe Day, May 8, 1945, the day the Allies won WWII in Europe

Valley of Mexico valley in Mexico in which the numerous Mesoamerican civilizations, including the Aztecs, arose

van Gogh, Vincent Vincent van Gogh (1853–1890) was an artist for only ten years, yet he produced more than 2,000 drawings, sketches, and paintings. Early on, the Impressionists greatly influenced his style. Van Gogh later moved to Arles, France. While there he had a breakdown and committed himself to an asylum. During this time, he began to use more vibrant colors, wide brushstrokes, movement in form and line, and thick layers of paint. He was released in May 1890 and died two months later.

vanguard group of elite leaders

varna in the Vedic society of ancient India, a personality type that determined a person's occupation; later a category in India's caste system

vassal in medieval Europe, a lord who was granted land in exchange for service and loyalty to a greater lord

Vedas a collection of prayers, hymns, and other religious teachings developed in ancient India beginning around 1500 B.C.

veneration special regard

vernacular everyday language of ordinary people

Versailles royal French residence and seat of government established by King Louis XIV

veto block a government action

viceroy representative of the king of Spain who ruled colonies in his name

Vichy city in central France where a puppet state governed unoccupied France and the French colonies

Victoria, Queen Queen Victoria (1819–1901) reigned from 1837 until 1901, the longest reign in British history. She symbolized British life during the period now known as the Victorian age. Queen Victoria set a tone of moral respectability and strict social manners. A trend-setter for the growing middle class, she introduced customs such as displaying a Christmas tree (a German practice) and wearing a white wedding gown.

Viet Cong communist rebels in South Vietnam who sought to overthrow South Vietnam's government; received assistance from North Vietnam

Vikings Scandinavian peoples whose sailors raided Europe from the 700s through the 1100s

Virgil Virgil (70 B.C–19 B.C.) was a Roman poet who wrote the *Aeneid* in 30 B.C. He studied mathematics and other subjects in Rome and Naples and was inspired by Greek poets

vizier chief minister who supervised the business of government in ancient Egypt

Voltaire Voltaire (1694–1778) was born François-Marie Arouet, but was known as Voltaire. He was an impassioned poet, historian, essayist, and philosopher who wrote with cutting sarcasm and sharp wit. Voltaire was sent to the Bastille prison twice due to his criticism of French authorities and was eventually banned from Paris. When he was able to return to France, he wrote about political and religious freedom. Voltaire spent his life fighting what he considered to be the enemies of freedom, such as ignorance, superstition, and intolerance.

W

Walesa, Lech Lech Walesa (b. 1943) helped found and direct the Polish independent trade union, Solidarity, at the Lenin Shipyards in Gdansk, where he was an electrician. After the Polish government crackdown on Solidarity in 1981, he was imprisoned for nearly a year. Walesa was awarded the Nobel Peace Prize in 1983. After the fall of the communist regime in Poland, Walesa was elected president of Poland, serving from 1990 to 1995.

War of the Austrian Succession series of wars in which various European nations competed for power in Central Europe after the death of Hapsburg emperor Charles VI

warlords local military rulers

warm-water port port that is free of ice year round

Warsaw Pact mutual-defense alliance between the Soviet Union and seven satellites in Eastern Europe set up in 1955

Washington, George George Washington (1732–1799) was a wealthy Virginia planter before becoming the commander of American forces during the Revolutionary War and first president of the United States. He owned a vast estate named Mount Vernon. Using his skill as a politician, negotiator, and general, Washington was able to keep the American cause of liberty alive during and after the revolution.

Watt, James James Watt (1736–1819) of Scotland invented the steam engine. James Watt first developed an interest in building models and measuring instruments in the workshop of his father, who built houses and ships. Watt apprenticed with a maker of mathematical instruments. In 1765, Watt worked on his steam engine. It had a separate condenser that helped keep steam from escaping. Later in life, he worked as a land surveyor and then returned to inventing and perfecting machines, until his retirement in 1800.

weapon of mass destruction (WMD) nuclear, biological, or chemical weapon

welfare state a country with a market economy but with increased government responsibility for the social and economic needs of its people

westernization adoption of western ideas, technology, and culture

Whitney, Eli Eli Whitney (1765–1825) showed mechanical and engineering skill at a young age. After he graduated from Yale College, he headed south where plantation owners learned of his mechanical skill and asked for his help. The cost of the labor to process cotton was too high. In response, Whitney invented the cotton gin, which revolutionized the textile industry and helped the South's economy. Unfortunately, Whitney did not profit from his invention. He left the South in debt but continued to design new inventions until his death.

William II William II (1859–1941) was the last German emperor and king of Prussia. He ruled the German empire and the kingdom of Prussia from 1888 to 1918. He led Germany into World War I. An ineffective military leader, he lost the support of his army and fled to exile in the Netherlands in November 1918.

William the Conqueror William the Conqueror (1028–1087) became the Duke of Normandy at age 7 and was knighted at age 15. He pressured King Edward of England to name him heir to the throne. Upon Edward's death, William invaded England and won the throne after the Battle of Hastings in 1066.

Wittenberg a city in northern Germany, where Luther drew up his 95 Theses

women's suffrage right of women to vote

Wordsworth, William William Wordsworth (1770–1850) was instrumental in launching Romanticism and wrote some of Western literature's most influential poems. While touring Europe, he encountered the French Revolution, which sparked in him an interest in the plight of the "common man." His sympathy for people and recognition of societal ills—particularly in urban areas—served as an inspiration for his work and his strong focus on emotion. It also inspired his view of the poet's role in society and his political ideals.

World Trade Organization (WTO) international organization set up to facilitate global trade

Wright, Orville and Wilbur Orville (1871–1948) and Wilbur (1867–1912) Wright were bicycle mechanics who used their knowledge of science and their experience in mechanics to create the first flying machine. After nearly 1,000 flights in gliders and testing in wind tunnels, the brothers built a powered plane. On December 17, 1903, the brothers tested their machine at Kitty Hawk, North Carolina. The first flight lasted 12 seconds; the longest flight that day lasted 59 seconds.

Wudi (156 B.C.–87 B.C.) was given the name Liu Che at birth. As the eleventh son of the Han emperor Jingdi, he would not have been destined to rule. However, the influence of his relatives changed this and he became emperor in 141 B.C. Determined to expand his dynasty's rule, he succeeded, though it came at a high cost to his soldiers and people. Liu Che made Confucianism the state religion. He was given the title Wudi (Martial Emperor) upon his death.

Y

Yaa Asantewaa Yaa Asantewaa (c. 1850–c. 1920) was the queen mother of the Edweso tribe of the Asante, who led a revolt against British rule starting in 1900.

Yalta Conference meeting between Churchill, Roosevelt, and Stalin in February 1945 where the three leaders made agreements regarding the end of World War II

Yathrib final destination of Muhammad's hijra and the home of the first community of Muslims; later renamed Medina; located in the northwest of present-day Saudi Arabia

Yorktown, Virginia location where the British army surrendered in the American Revolution

Yuan dynasty Chinese dynasty ruled by the Mongols from 1279 to 1368; best-known ruler was Kublai Khan

Z

zaibatsu since the late 1800s, powerful banking and industrial families in Japan

Zapata, Emiliano Emiliano Zapata (1879–1919) grew up a peasant. In 1897, he began a long struggle against the hacienda system to regain peasant land. After Francisco Madero lost the election to Porfirio Díaz, Zapata joined the revolution and fought for social reform. Zapata built up a strong following and played an essential role in ousting Victoriano Huerta in 1914. After Venustiano Carranza was elected president, he turned on Zapata. Zapata's revolutionaries went to war with the moderates who supported Carranza. In 1919, Carranza's army ambushed and killed Zapata.

zemstvo local elected assembly set up in Russia under Alexander II

Zen the practice of meditation; a school of Buddhism in Japan

zeppelin large gas-filled balloon

Zheng He Zheng He (c. 1371–1433) was an admiral in the Ming Chinese navy and diplomat who made his first voyage in 1405 to Vietnam, India, and Africa to both explore and trade. His huge fleet of hundred of junks (Chinese ships) and thousands of sailors carried silk, porcelain, and lacquerware to trade for pearls, spices, ivory, and timber. Zheng He made seven voyages in all, exploring, trading successfully, and thereby motivating Chinese merchants to establish trade centers in Southeast Asia and India.

ziggurat in ancient Mesopotamia, a large, stepped platform thought to have been topped by a temple dedicated to a city-state's chief god or goddess

Zionism a movement devoted to rebuilding a Jewish state in the ancient homeland

Zoroaster (about 628 B.C.–551 B.C.) Zoroaster was an Iranian religious reformer and founder of Zoroastrianism. He emphasized individual freedom to choose right or wrong and individual responsibility for one's actions. Zoroaster's ideas influenced the early development of philosophy.

A

abacus > ábaco Artefacto que sirve para contar y calcular al deslizar pequeñas bolas o cuentas a lo largo de varillas o muescas.

Abbas the Great, Shah > Abbas el Grande, sah Abbas el Grande (1571–1629) fue el sah de la dinastía Safávida desde 1588 hasta su muerte. Expulsó a las tropas otomanas y uzbekas de Persia y patrocinó una era de oro de las artes y los logros persas.

Abbasid > Abasí Dinastía que gobernó Bagdad de 750 a 1258.

abdicate > abdicar Renunciar a un puesto de poder.

abolition > abolición Campaña contra la esclavitud y contra el tráfico de esclavos.

Abraham > Abraham Según la tradición judía, Abraham es el ancestro del pueblo judío. Hijo de un mercader de ídolos de la ciudad de Ur, Abraham hizo una alianza especial con Dios. Llevó a sus descendientes a Canaán, que los judíos consideran su Tierra Prometida.

absentee landlord > dueño ausente Dueño de una gran propiedad que no vive en ella.

absolute monarchy > monarquía absoluta Forma de gobierno en la cual el gobernante tiene autoridad completa sobre el gobierno y las vidas de las personas a las que dirige.

absolutism > absolutismo Creencia de un poder total y sin restricciones en el gobierno.

abstract art > abstracto Estilo de arte compuesto de líneas, colores y formas, que a veces no tiene un tema reconocible.

Abu Bakr > Bakr, Abu Abu Bakr (573–634) fue el suegro de Mahoma y el primer califa musulmán, o líder, después de la muerte de Mahoma. Convertido al islam, Abu Bakr aconsejó a Mahoma e hizo un viaje llamado hégira con el profeta. En su papel de sucesor de Mahoma, ayudó a unir al pueblo musulmán. Bajo su gobierno, el imperio musulmán se expandió.

acculturation > aculturación Mezcla de dos o más culturas.

acid rain > lluvia ácida Forma de contaminación en la que los productos químicos tóxicos que se encuentran en el aire vuelven a la tierra en la lluvia, nieve o granizo.

acropolis > acrópolis El punto más alto y fortificado de una ciudad-estado griega.

acupuncture > acupuntura Tratamiento médico, originado en la antigua China, en el cual se insertan agujas en puntos específicos de la piel para aliviar el dolor o tratar diferentes enfermedades.

Adenauer, Konrad > Adenauer, Konrad Konrad Adenauer (1876–1967) fue el primer canciller de Alemania Occidental, de 1949 a 1963. Gobernó Alemania Occidental durante su recuperación y reconstrucción después de la Segunda Guerra Mundial. Sus logros incluyeron la entrada de Alemania Occidental en la OTAN y la fundación de la Comunidad Económica Europea.

adobe > adobe Mezcla de arcilla y fibras vegetales que se endurece cuando se seca al sol y que se usa para la construcción.

Adulis > Adulis Puerto comercial estratégico del reino de Aksum.

Afghanistan > Afganistán País islámico en Asia central; invadido por la Unión Soviética en 1979; más tarde hogar de los radicales islamistas talibán y de los terroristas de al-Qaeda.

Afonso I > Afonso I Afonso I (nacido alrededor de 1460– muerto en 1542) fue gobernador de Kongo, un reino histórico de África centro-occidental, a principios del siglo XVI. Afonso fomentó el comercio con Portugal, promovió la cultura europea en su reino y adoptó el cristianismo como su religión y la del estado.

African National Congress (ANC) > Congreso Nacional Africano (CNA) Principal organización que se oponía al apartheid y abogaba por un gobierno de mayoría en Sudáfrica; más tarde se convirtió en un partido político.

agribusiness > agroindustria Inmensa granja comercial generalmente administrada por una corporación multinacional.

ahimsa > ahimsa Creencia hindú en la no violencia y el respeto a todas las formas de vida.

aircraft carrier > portaaviones Buque dotado de las instalaciones necesarias para el transporte, despegue y aterrizaje de aparatos de aviación.

Akbar > Akbar Akbar (1542–1605) es considerado por la mayoría como el más grande de los emperadores mogoles de India. Amplió su imperio por la mayor parte de India, y mantuvo un gobierno eficiente a través de políticas que se ganaron la lealtad de los súbditos no musulmanes. Su grandeza creció también por su apoyo a eruditos, artistas y músicos que hicieron de su corte un centro de cultura.

Akhenaton > Aknatón Aknatón fue rey de Egipto durante 17 años. Abandonó el tradicional politeísmo egipcio y estableció un nuevo culto dedicado a Atón, el disco del sol. Su intento de comenzar una nueva religión murió con él en 1336 a. C.

al Qaeda > al-Qaeda Grupo terrorista establecido y dirigido por el saudita Osama bin Laden hasta su muerte en 2011.

al-Khwarizmi > al-Khwarizmi al-Khwarizmi (alrededor del año 780–alrededor del año 850) fue un matemático musulmán que desarrolló conceptos básicos relacionados con el estudio del álgebra e introdujo el término *álgebra*, o *al-jabr*. Por medio de sus escritos, introdujo a los europeos al estudio de esta rama de las matemáticas. Al trabajar en el campo de la geografía, al-Khwarizmi también supervisó la producción de uno de los primeros mapas del mundo.

Albuquerque, Afonso de > Albuquerque, Afonso de Afonso de Albuquerque (1453–1515) fue un almirante portugués que ayudó a fundar el imperio comercial de Portugal en el este. Capturó y construyó fuertes estratégicos en Goa, Calicut, Malaca y Hormoz; reconstruyó otros fuertes; estableció la construcción de barcos y otras industrias portuguesas en India y construyó iglesias.

Alexander II > Alejandro II Alejandro II (1818–1881), hijo del emperador Nicolás I, llegó a ser zar en 1855. Alejandro II asumió el poder en medio de la Guerra de Crimea, la cual reveló el retraso de Rusia. Instituyó amplias reformas de modernización, incluyendo la emancipación de los siervos en 1861. Sin embargo, las crecientes rebeliones internas y el aumento de la actividad revolucionaria en Polonia llevó a Alejandro a tomar medidas represivas. Fue asesinado en 1881.

Alexander the Great > Alejandro Magno Alejandro Magno (356 a. C.–324 a. C.), hijo de Filipo II y alumno de Aristóteles, se convirtió a los 20 años en el heredero de los territorios de su padre. Conquistó el imperio Persa, fundando nuevas ciudades a medida que sus ejércitos lograban victorias en Asia Menor, Palestina y Egipto, y luego tomó Babilonia. Continuó hacia el este de India, pero sus tropas cansadas se negaron a seguir adelante. De regreso en Babilonia, Alejandro, murió de una fiebre repentina a los 32 años de edad.

Alexandria > Alejandría Alejandría, fundada en el año 332 a. C. por Alejandro Magno, se convirtió en una de las mayores ciudades del mundo mediterráneo. Ubicada en Egipto en las rutas marítimas entre Europa y Asia, Alejandría fue conocida por su tamaño, grandes mercados, el enorme faro de la isla de Faro y el Museo, un centro de enseñanza con una famosa biblioteca.

Alighieri, Dante > Alighieri, Dante Dante Alighieri (1265–1321) fue un filósofo, escritor y poeta que participó activamente en la política italiana, incluyendo las batallas entre los papas y los monarcas de su época. Ocupó varios cargos en diferentes momentos de su vida. Aunque escribió muchos poemas y otras obras, es más conocido por *La Divina Comedia*.

alliance > alianza Acuerdo formal de cooperación y defensa mutua entre dos o más naciones o potencias.

alphabet > alfabeto Sistema de escritura en el que cada símbolo representa un sonido básico único.

Alsace and Lorraine > Alsacia-Lorena Región del norte de Europa en la frontera entre Francia y Alemania que fue cedida a Alemania después de la Guerra Franco-Prusiana.

Amon-Re > Amón (Ra) Amón (Ra) era considerado el rey de los dioses. Estuvo presente en la mitología y cultura del pueblo egipcio desde sus comienzos.

Amritsar massacre > masacre de Amritsar Incidente ocurrido en 1919 en el que tropas británicas abrieron fuego contra una multitud de manifestantes indios desarmados en la ciudad de Amritsar, al norte de India.

anarchist > anarquista Persona que quiere abolir toda forma de gobierno.

ancien régime > ancien regime Antiguo sistema de gobierno en la Francia prerrevolucionaria.

anesthetic > anestesia Fármaco que suprime el dolor durante la cirugía.

animism > animismo Creencia de que el mundo estaba lleno de espíritus y fuerzas que podían residir en los animales, objetos o sueños.

annex > anexar Agregar un territorio a un estado o país existente.

Anschluss > Anschluss Unión de Alemania y Austria en 1933.

anthropology > antropología Campo de estudio relacionado con los orígenes y el desarrollo de las personas y sus sociedades.

anti-Semitism > antisemitismo Prejuicio contra los judíos.

apartheid > apartheid Política de estricta separación racial en la República de Sudáfrica.

apostle > apóstol Líder o maestro de una nueva fe o movimiento.

appeasement > apaciguamiento Política de otorgar concesiones para mantener la paz.

apprentice > aprendiz Persona joven que aprende un oficio de un maestro.

aqueduct > acueducto En la antigua Roma, estructura de piedra parecida a un puente que llevaba agua desde las colinas hasta la ciudad

Aquinas, Thomas > Aquino, Tomás de Tomás de Aquino (1225–1274) fue un filósofo, teólogo y monje que ayudó a cerrar la brecha entre la fe medieval y la filosofía de la razón que promovía la filosofía griega. También explicó la idea de la ley natural, es decir que hay leyes universales basadas en la razón, y que son independientes de las leyes que aprueben los gobiernos.

Aquino, Benigno > Aquino, Benigno Benigno Aquino, Jr., (1932–1983) fue el líder de la oposición durante la dictadura de Ferdinand Marcos en Filipinas. Su carrera en la política incluyó periodos como gobernador provincial y senador, pero cuando planeaba postularse para presidente en 1973, Marcos lo encarceló. Aquino pasó ocho años en el corredor de la muerte pero fue liberado para ser operado en los Estados Unidos de una cirugía de corazón. En 1983, Aquino regresó a Filipinas y fue asesinado en el aeropuerto de Manila. La conspiración militar contra el popular político llevó el apoyo a su esposa, Corazón Aquino, quien continuó hasta derrotar a Marcos en una elección presidencial.

Aquino, Corazon > Aquino, Corazón Corazón Aquino (1933–2009) fue presidenta de Filipinas, restaurando la democracia después del gobierno de Ferdinand Marcos. Educada en los Estados Unidos, Aquino se casó con el político Benigno Aquino y se centró en la crianza de sus hijos. Acompañó a su esposo durante el exilio en los Estados Unidos y cuando él fue ejecutado en su regreso a Filipinas, la gente se unió apoyándola. Ganó una elección presidencial en contra de Marcos y poco después reestableció el congreso y nombró a un equipo para escribir una nueva constitución. Aunque Aquino restauró la libertad en Filipinas, muchas de sus políticas fueron impopulares y perdió la presidencia ante su secretario de defensa en 1992.

Arafat, Yasir > Arafat, Yasir Yasir Arafat (1929–2004) luchó por la independencia palestina la mayor parte de su vida. Fue el fundador de Al-Fatah, un grupo que resistía a Israel, y también de la Organización para la Liberación de Palestina (OLP). En 1969 fue nombrado presidente de la OLP. A principios de la década de 1990, llegó a un acuerdo de paz con Israel. En 1994, junto con Shimon Peres y Yitzhak Rabin, ganó el Premio Nobel de la Paz. Luego fue el presidente de la recién creada Autoridad Palestina.

archaeology > arqueología Estudio de los pueblos y culturas pasados mediante sus restos materiales

Archimedes > Arquímedes Arquímedes (c. 287 a. C.–212 a. C.), un famoso matemático e inventor helenístico de Siracusa, una colonia griega (ahora en Italia), es conocido por entender el principio de las palancas, descubriendo la relación entre la superficie y el volumen de una esfera, e inventar el tornillo de Arquímedes, un aparato para elevar agua.

archipelago > archipiélago Cadena de islas.

aristocracy > aristocracia Gobierno encabezado por una minoría provilegiada o de clase alta.

Aristotle > Aristóteles Aristóteles (384 a. C.–322 a. C.), alumno de Platón, fue un filósofo y escritor sobre muchas ramas del conocimiento, fundador del Liceo y tutor de Alejandro Magno.

armada > armada Flota de barcos.

armistice > armisticio Acuerdo para dejar de luchar en una guerra.

artifact > artefacto Objeto fabricado por los seres humanos.

artificial satellite > satélite artificial Objeto artificial que gira en el espacio alrededor de un cuerpo más grande.

artisan > artesano Trabajador cualificado que hace objetos a mano.

Asante kingdom > reino Asante Reino que surgió en el siglo XVIII en el actual territorio de Ghana y participó activamente en el comercio de personas esclavizadas.

Asantewaa, Yaa > Asantewaa, Yaa Yaa Asantewaa (c. 1850–c. 1920) fue la reina madre de la tribu edweso de los asante y lideró una rebelión en contra del gobierno británico que comenzó en 1900.

Asia Minor > Asia Menor Península en Asia occidental entre el mar Negro y el mar Mediterráneo.

Asoka > Asoka Asoka, que murió aproximadamente en 238 a. C., fue el último gran emperador Maurya de India. Budista comprometido, ayudó a difundir el budismo a través de India. Su gobierno se caracterizó por la justicia, la compasión y los principios de la vida recta que él había inscrito en pilares de piedra que mandó erigir por todo el imperio.

assassination > magnicidio Asesinato de una figura pública, generalmente por razones políticas.

assembly line > línea de montaje Método de producción que distribuye un trabajo complejo en una serie de pequeñas tareas.

assimilate > asimilar Absorber o adoptar otra cultura.

Atatürk > Atatürk Atatürk (1881–1938) es el nombre que Mustafa Kemal se dio a sí mismo cuando ordenó a todo el pueblo turco que adoptara apellidos. En 1920 lideró a los nacionalistas turcos en la lucha contra del ejército griego, que trataba de hacer cumplir el Tratado de Sèvres, el establecer las fronteras de la moderna República de Turquía. Una vez en el poder, aprobó muchas reformas para modernizar, occidentalizar y secularizar Turquía.

atheism > ateísmo Creencia de que no existe dios.

Athens > Atenas Ciudad-estado de la antigua Grecia que evolucionó de una monarquía a una democracia directa limitada y se hizo famosa por sus grandes logros culturales.

Atlantic Charter > Carta del Atlántico Acuerdo en el que Franklin Roosevelt y Winston Churchill fijaron los objetivos para la derrota de la Alemania nazi y para el mundo de la posguerra.

atman > atman En la creencia hindú, naturaleza de una persona.

atrocity > atrocidad Acto brutal cometido en contra de inocentes.

Augustine > Agustín Agustín (364 d. C.–430 d. C.) fue un erudito cristiano cuyas obras escritas tuvieron efectos duraderos en la religón cristiana. Estudió en la África romana y llegó a ser obispo.

Augustus > Augusto Augusto (63 a. C.–14 d. C.) fue el primer emperador romano del recién establecido Imperio Romano. El gobierno de Augusto comenzó un largo periodo de paz y riqueza conocido como la Pax Romana.

Auschwitz > Auschwitz Grupo de tres campos de concentración y campos de exterminio alemanes al sur de Polonia, construidos y operados durante el Tercer Reich.

autocrat > autócrata Gobernante que tiene poder ilimitado.

autocracy > autocracia Sistema de gobierno en el que un individuo o un pequeño grupo de individuos gobierna con poder ilimitado.

autocratic > autocrático Que tiene poder ilimitado.

autonomy > autonomía Autogobierno

Axis powers > Potencias del Eje Grupo de países liderado por Alemania, Italia y Japón que luchó contra los Aliados en la Segunda Guerra Mundial.

Axum > Aksum Centro de comercio y poderoso reino antiguo del norte situado en lo que actualmente es Etiopía.

ayllu > ayllu En el Imperio Inca, una aldea que se mantenía estrechamente unida.

B

Babur > Babur Babur (1483–1530) fue el fundador de la dinastía Mogol en India. Tenía herencia turca y mongola, descendiente del gran líder mongol, Genghis Khan. Su nombre es la palabra árabe para "tigre", pero era tan buen poeta como guerrero. Su sabio gobierno ayudó a lanzar una poderosa dinastía musulmana que tuvo una influencia permanente en el norte de India.

Bacon, Francis > Bacon, Francis Francis Bacon (1561–1626) fue un distinguido filósofo, estadista y abogado inglés. Hombre de muchos talentos, promovió el pensamiento racional. Bacon fue muy reconocido por filósofos y científicos de Europa, así como de Inglaterra.

Baghdad > Bagdad Capital del actual Iraq; capital del Imperio Musulmán durante la época dorada del islam.

balance of power > equilibrio de poder Distribución del poder militar y económico que evita que una nación se vuelva demasiado fuerte.

balance of trade > balanza comercial Diferencia entre lo que importa y exporta un país.

Balfour Declaration > Declaración Balfour Declaración hecha por el gobierno británico en 1917 en la que apoyaba la constitución de un estado judío en Palestina.

Balkan Peninsula > península de los Balcanes Extensión triangular de tierra que sobresale del sureste de Europa hasta el Mediterráneo.

Bangladesh > Bangladesh País al este de India que antiguamente formaba parte de Pakistán.

Bantu > bantú Lengua madre de África occidental en la que están basados algunos patrones migratorios africanos.

Barbarossa, Frederick > Barbarroja, Federico Federico Barbarroja (c. 1123–1190) fue un rey alemán que llegó a ser emperador del Sacro Imperio Romano en 1152. Luchó contra la creciente autoridad papal y dirigió seis expediciones a Italia en un intento de aumentar sus territorios. Murió en la Tercera Cruzada.

baroque > barroco Estilo artístico y arquitectónico elaborado que se dio en los siglos XVII y XVIII.

barter economy > economía de trueque Sistema económico en el que un conjunto de bienes o servicios se intercambia por otro.

Bastille > Bastilla Fortificación en París usada como prisión; la Revolución Francesa empezó cuando los parisinos la asaltaron en 1789.

Bataan Death March > marcha de la muerte de Bataan Durante la Segunda Guerra Mundial, la marcha forzada de prisioneros de guerra estadounidenses y filipinos bajo condiciones brutales impuestas por los militares japoneses.

battle of Tours > Batalla de Tours Batalla en 732 en la que los francos cristianos liderados por Charles Martel derrotaron al ejército musulmán y detuvieron el avance árabe en Europa.

Bedouin > beduino Nómada árabe que vive en el desierto.

Beethoven, Ludwig van > Beethoven, Ludwig van Ludwig van Beethoven (1770–1827) fue un compositor alemán que aprendió a tocar el piano y el violín con su padre Johannes. A la edad de 12 años, publicó su primera obra y comenzó a tocar la viola en la orquesta sinfónica de Bonn, Alemania. En 1792, fue a Viena y comenzó a estudiar con Haydn. Beethoven permaneció en Viena, donde escribió la mayoría de sus sinfonías, conciertos, sonatas y cuartetos de cuerda. Aunque comenzó a perder el oído en 1798, siguió componiendo la música que él podía oír en su mente.

Benedictine Rule > regla benedictina En el año 530, reglas establecidas por Benedicto, un monje, para regular la vida monástica. La regla enfatiza la obediencia, pobreza y castidad, y divide el día en períodos de adoración, trabajo y estudio.

Bentham, Jeremy > Bentham, Jeremy Jeremy Bentham (1748–1832) fue un filósofo y economista británico que defendía el utilitarismo, la creencia de que se podía medir el bien y el mal por la máxima felicidad del mayor número de personas. Bentham estudió leyes pero no ejerció como abogado. En lugar de eso, se centró en las reformas legales. No contento con simplemente sugerir nuevas leyes, también detalló planes sobre cómo implementar sus propuestas. Sus ideas influyeron durante su vida y algunas de sus reformas fueron aprobadas.

Bessemer, Henry > Bessemer, Henry Henry Bessemer (1813–1879) fue un inventor e ingeniero británico. Su mayor invento fue el convertidor Bessemer, que podía crear acero de alta calidad rápidamente y de forma económica. En 1956 patentó su proceso para fabricar acero. Su proceso fue esencial para lograr avances en el transporte, la construcción y la defensa. Hoy en día, el acero todavía se fabrica siguiendo un método basado en el proceso Bessemer.

Biafra > Biafra Región del sureste de Nigeria que lanzó un fallido intento de independizarse de Nigeria en 1966, y por el que se desató una cruenta guerra.

biotechnology > biotecnología Aplicación de la investigación biotecnológica en la industria, ingeniería y tecnología.

bishop > obispo Funcionario de alto rango de la Iglesia con autoridad sobre una zona local, o diócesis.

Bismarck, Otto von > Bismarck, Otto von Otto von Bismarck (1815–1898) trabajó brevemente como funcionario civil antes de hacer carrera en el gobierno. Fue diplomático de la Federación Alemana y llegó a ser canciller del Imperio Alemán en 1871, un cargo que ocupó durante 19 años.

Black Death > Muerte Negra Epidemia de la peste bubónica que arrasó Europa en el siglo XIV.

Black Shirt > Camisa Negra Cualquier miembro de las escuadras militares de combate de los fascistas italianos que estableció Mussolini.

blitzkrieg > blitzkrieg Guerra relámpago.

bloc > bloque Grupo de naciones que actúan conjuntamente en apoyo mutuo.

Boer War > guerra de los bóers (1899–1902) guerra en la que Gran Bretaña venció a los Bóers de Sudáfrica.

Boers > bóers Neerlandeses establecidos en Ciudad del Cabo, África, que con el tiempo emigraron hacia el interior.

Bolívar, Simón > Bolívar, Simón Simón Bolívar (1783–1830) fue un soldado y líder sudamericano que fue esencial en las revoluciones en contra de España. Nació en el seno de una familia acaudalada y culta en España. Después de que Francia invadiera España, participó en el movimiento de resistencia y desempeñó un papel clave en la lucha latinoamericana por la independencia. Murió de tuberculosis en 1830.

Bonaparte, Napoleon > Bonaparte, Napoleón Napoleón Bonaparte (1769–1821) fue una figura importante en la historia europea. Fue un genio militar que fue electo cónsul de por vida. Más tarde se coronó él mismo emperador de Francia. Sus reformas legales, educativas y militares impactaron la sociedad francesa por generaciones.

bourgeoisie > burguesía Clase media.

Boxer Uprising > Rebelión de los bóxers Movimiento en contra de los extranjeros ocurrido en China de 1898 a 1900.

boyar > boyardo En la época de los zares, noble terrateniente ruso.

boycott > boicot Negarse a comprar.

Boyle, Robert > Boyle, Robert Robert Boyle (1627–1691) fue una de las mentes destacadas de finales del siglo XVII. Fue un filósofo y escritor inglés-irlandés que se centró en la química, física e historia natural. Su trabajo con el aire presurizado llevó al desarrollo de la ley de Boyle, que describe la relación entre la presión y el volumen del gas. Boyle fue uno de los fundadores de la Real Sociedad de Londres.

Brahe, Tycho > Brahe, Tycho Tycho Brahe (1546–1601) fue un astrónomo danés que produjo las medidas y ubicaciones más precisas de las estrellas antes de usar el telescopio. Su observación de que una nueva estrella había aparecido en una constelación existente desafió la creencia de que las estrellas estaban fijas y eran inmutables.

Brahman > brahmán En el sistema de creencias establecido en la India aria, el único poder espiritual que reside en todas las cosas.

Brezhnev, Leonid > Brezhnev, Leonid Leonid Brezhnev (1906–1982) gobernó la Unión Soviética desde 1964, cuando organizó la destitución de Nikita Khrushchev, hasta su muerte en 1982. Presidió la última acumulación de armas de la Unión Soviética y el estancamiento económico que fomentó las reformas de Mijaíl Gorbachov.

bureaucracy > burocracia Sistema de gobierno mediante departamentos y subdivisiones administrados por funcionarios que siguen un conjunto de reglas.

bushido > bushido Código de conducta de los samuráis durante el periodo feudal japonés.

Byron, Lord > Byron, Lord Lord Byron (1788–1824) fue miembro de la Cámara de los Lores, satírico político y social y uno de los poetas románticos más sobresalientes, novedosos y cautivadores. Llegó a ser el modelo del héroe romántico y la personificación del movimiento. Byron creía en la libertad, que él a menudo reflejaba en sus obras y hazañas. Aunque Byron murió antes de haber terminado su poema *Don Juan,* este es considerado su obra maestra y uno de los grandes poemas de Inglaterra.

C

cabinet > gabinete Consejeros parlamentarios del rey que originalmente se reunían en un pequeño cuarto o gabinete.

Cabot, John > Caboto, Juan Juan Caboto (alrededor de 1450–alrededor de 1499) tuvo sus primeras raíces en Venecia, Italia, trabajando en una empresa mercantil. Llegó a ser un navegante y explorador, que durante los años 1497 y 1498, reclamó partes de Canadá para Gran Bretaña.

Caesar, Julius > César, Julio Julio César (alrededor del año 100 a. C.–44 a. C.) fue un general romano, maestro de las maniobras políticas y un reformista. Defendió la reorganización del gobierno de Roma. En el año 47 a. C. se nombró dictador, y tres años más tarde fue asesinado.

cahiers > memorándum Cuaderno usado durante la Francia prerrevolucionaria para anotar los agravios.

Cahokia > Cahokia En Illinois, el mayor terraplén de la cultura de los misisipianos, construido alrededor del año 700 d. C.

calculus > cálculo Rama de las matemáticas en la que los cálculos se hacen con notaciones simbólicas especiales; fue desarrollado por Isaac Newton.

caliph > califa Sucesor de Mahoma como líder religioso y político de los musulmanes.

calligraphy > caligrafía Arte de producir una bella escritura a mano.

Calvin, John > Calvino, Juan Juan Calvino (1509–1564) fue un abogado y teólogo francés. Influenciado por la filosofía humanista de Erasmo, Calvino llegó a participar en el movimiento protestante mientras estudiaba en la Universidad de París. Más tarde se trasladó a Ginebra, Suiza, donde estableció una teocracia y escribió *Institutos de la Religión Cristiana.* La interpretación de Calvino de la doctrina cristiana se llama calvinismo.

canon law > ley canónica Serie de leyes de una iglesia.

canonize > canonizar Reconocer a una persona como un santo.

Cape Town > Ciudad del Cabo El primer asentamiento permanente europeo en África, establecido por los neerlandeses en 1652.

capital > capital Dinero o bienes que se usan para invertir en negocios o empresas.

capital offense > delito capital Crimen que puede castigarse con la muerte.

capitalism > capitalismo Sistema económico en el que los medios de producción son propiedad privada y se administran para obtener beneficios.

Cárdenas, Lázaro > Cárdenas, Lázaro Lázaro Cárdenas (1895–1970) se unió a las fuerzas revolucionarias cuando tenía 18 años y más tarde llegó a ser general del ejército mexicano. Después de la revolución, fue gobernador de Michoacán y luego presidente del PNR. En 1934, fue electo presidente de México. Durante su presidencia, Cárdenas trabajó para establecer las reformas sociales y económicas por las que habían luchado los revolucionarios, entre ellas la redistribución de la tierra, la organización de las confederaciones para trabajadores y campesinos, y la nacionalización de las industrias propiedad de extranjeros.

Carranza, Venustiano > Carranza, Venustiano Venustiano Carranza (1859–1920) fue un líder de la Revolución Mexicana en apoyo de una reforma política, más que social. Fue electo el primer presidente después de la revolución, y aunque firmó la Constitución de 1917, hizo poco para implementar las reformas prometidas. Esa renuencia llevó a disturbios sociales y dificultades económicas. Cuando en abril de 1920 comenzó una rebelión, Carranza huyó de la capital y finalmente se fue a esconder a las montañas. Fue traicionado y asesinado en mayo.

cartel > cartel Asociación de grandes corporaciones formada para controlar la producción y el precio del producto.

Cartier, Jacques > Cartier, Jacques Jacques Cartier (1491–1557) recibe el crédito de haber dado nombre a Canadá. También es reconocido por su exploración limitada del río San Lorenzo, detenida al poco tiempo por las severas condiciones del clima y la hostilidad de los indígenas iroqueses.

cartographer > cartógrafo Persona que hace mapas.

caste > casta Grupo social en la sociedad tradicional de India en el que una persona nace y del que no se puede cambiar.

Castiglione, Baldassare > Castiglione, Baldassare Castiglione (1478–1529) fue un cortesano, diplomático y escritor italiano. Su manual, *El Cortesano,* fue muy leído por sus consejos sobre buenos modales, habilidades, aprendizaje y virtudes que los miembros de la corte debían mostrar. Describía al cortesano ideal como bien educado, de buenas costumbres y con muchos talentos.

Castro, Fidel > Castro, Fidel Fidel Castro (n. 1926) fue líder de Cuba desde 1959, cuando dirigió la Revolución Cubana e instaló un régimen comunista. Durante la Guerra Fría, la Cuba de Castro se alió con la Unión Soviética y, por consiguiente, en desacuerdo con los Estados Unidos. Sus políticas siguieron siendo socialistas después de la caída de la Unión Soviética. Cuando su salud comenzó a fallar en 2006, su hermano, Raúl, quedó a cargo como el líder cubano.

Çatalhüyük > Çatalhüyük Una de las primera aldeas del mundo, establecida en la Turquía actual alrededor del año 7000 a. C.

cataract > catarata Cascada; caída de agua.

Catherine the Great > Catalina la Grande Catalina la Grande (1729–1796) fue una emperatriz de Rusia nacida en Alemania (1762–1796) que llevó a su país a formar parte de la vida cultural y política de Europa.

caudillo > caudillo Dictador militar en América Latina.

Cavour, Camillo > Cavour, Camillo Camillo Cavour (1810–1861) fue el segundo hijo de una familia noble. Después de una breve carrera en el ejército, decidió que la política era su verdadera fortaleza. Su capacidad para manipular situaciones políticas con el fin de impulsar la causa de la unificación italiana hizo de él un valioso líder.

Ceausescu, Nicolae > Ceausescu, Nicolae Nicolae Ceausescu (1918–1989) dirigió el gobierno comunista en Rumania desde 1965 hasta su muerte en 1989. Su régimen fue notorio por su corrupción masiva, devastadoras condiciones económicas y una policía secreta desenfrenada. Fue ejecutado, junto con su esposa, Elena, después del golpe de estado que terminó con el gobierno comunista en Rumania.

celadon > celadon Porcelana hecha en Corea con brillo azulverdoso poco común.

censorship > censura Restricción en el acceso a ideas o información.

census > censo Conteo de población.

Cervantes, Miguel de > Cervantes, Miguel de Miguel de Cervantes (1547–1616), novelista, dramaturgo y poeta español, fue la figura más importante de la literatura española. Su novela Don Quijote es su obra más conocida.

Champlain, Samuel de > Champlain, Samuel de Samuel de Champlain (1567–1635) fue un navegante y explorador francés que estableció la colonia de Quebec en 1608. Se le conoció como el "Padre de la Nueva Francia" y fue honrado en la corte del rey Enrique IV.

chancellor > canciller Oficial con mayor rango dentro de una monarquía; primer ministro.

characters > caracteres Símbolos escritos de algunos sistemas de escritura como la de los chinos.

Charlemagne > Carlomagno Carlomagno (747–814), (o "Carlos el Grande") rey de los francos, los lombardos y emperador de los romanos, comenzó como un rey guerrero que buscaba conquistar territorios y distribuir el botín siguiendo la tradición de los francos. Pero también luchó por unir y gobernar una creciente diversidad de pueblos conquistados, además de tratar con las amenazas de nuevos invasores. Dirigió una larga serie de campañas militares exitosas, realizó esfuerzos para difundir el cristianismo e implementar una reforma reliigiosa, buscó hacer más eficaces las instituciones y los procedimientos políticos, y apoyó la renovación cultural mediante un resurgimiento de la enseñanza.

Charles I > Carlos I Carlos I (1600–1649) fue el segundo rey Estuardo de Inglaterra, Escocia y Gales. Su creencia en el derecho divino de los reyes lo puso en un conflicto continuo con el Parlamento. Finalmente este conflicto llevó a la Guerra Civil inglesa, a la derrota de Carlos y a su ejecución por traición.

Charles V > Carlos V Carlos V (1500–1558) fue emperador del Sacro Imperio Romano durante la época de la reforma de Martín Lutero. Su inmenso imperio incluía grandes zonas de Europa. Como católico devoto, rechazó las doctrinas de Lutero. La revuelta protestante, junto con las presiones políticas, llevó a Carlos a dejar voluntariamente el trono. Dividió el imperio entre su hijo y su hermano y entró a un monasterio católico donde permaneció hasta su muerte.

charter > cédula En la Edad Media, documento escrito que establecía los derechos y privilegios de un pueblo.

Chaucer, Geoffrey > Chaucer, Geoffrey Geoffrey Chaucer (1343–1400) fue el primer poeta importante de su tiempo que escribió en inglés. En diversos momentos trabajó como redactor, miembro del Parlamento y juez de paz. Sus agudas observaciones de muchos tipos diferentes de personas se reflejaron en su famosa obra, *Cuentos de Canterbury.*

Chavín > chavín Cultura que tuvo su apogeo en la región andina, aproximadamente desde el año 900 a. C. al año 200 a. C.

Chechnya > Chechenia República dentro del territorio ruso en la que grupos rebeldes lucharon por su independencia.

checks and balances > controles y equilibrios Sistema en el que cada poder del estado tiene la facultad para monitorear y limitar las acciones de los otros dos.

Cheka > Cheka Una de las primeras fuerzas policiales secretas soviéticas.

chinampa > chinampa En el Imperio Azteca, una isla artificial que se usaba para cultivar las cosechas y estaba fabricada de lodo apilado encima de bases de juncos que estaban anclados al lecho del lago con sauces.

chivalry > Código de Caballería Durante la Edad Media, código de conducta para los caballeros.

Choson dynasty > dinastía Choson Dinastía coreana que gobernó de 1392 a 1910; la que más perduró de las tres dinastías coreanas.

Christian Bible > Biblia cristiana Escrituras sagradas de la religión cristiana.

Churchill, Winston > Churchill, Winston Winston Churchill (1874–1965) nació en la aristocracia inglesa y fue primer ministro del Imperio Británico en 1940. Desde el principio avisó de la amenaza que suponía la Alemania nazi. Su determinación convenció al país de defenderse a sí mismo contra el enemigo invasor.

circumnavigate > circunnavegar Viajar alrededor del mundo.

citizen > ciudadano Nativo o residente de un pueblo o ciudad.

city-state > ciudad-estado Unidad política que incluía una ciudad y las tierras y aldeas que la rodean.

civil disobedience > desobediencia civil Práctica de renuencia pacífica a obedecer las leyes injustas.

civil law > derecho civil Rama del derecho acerca de los derechos y los asuntos privados.

civil servants > siervos civiles Funcionarios del gobierno.

civil war > guerra civil Guerra en la que luchan dos grupos de personas de una misma nación.

civilization > civilización Orden social complejo y sumamente organizado.

clan > clan Grupo de familias con un ancestro común.

clergy > clero Aquellos que dirigen los servicios religiosos cristianos.

Clovis > Clodoveo Clodoveo (466–511) es conocido como el fundador político y religioso del reino de los francos. Gobernó gran parte de la Galia desde finales del siglo V hasta el año 511. Su reino, que se expandió al sur y al oeste de lo que hoy en día es Bélgica y el noreste de Francia, fue el más poderoso de la Galia. También fue el aliado más importante del emperador bizantino Anastasio I. Nacido pagano, Clodoveo correspondió con los poderosos obispos de la Galia y, en el año 496 o quizá más tarde, se hizo famoso como uno de los primeros reyes germanos en convertirse al cristianismo.

coalition > coalición Alianza temporal de varios partidos políticos.

codify > codificar Organizar o dejar por escrito.

Colbert, Jean-Baptiste > Colbert, Jean Baptiste Jean Baptiste Colbert (1619–1683) fue, bajo el rey Luis XIV de Francia, controlador general de finanzas (desde 1665) y secretario de estado para la armada (desde 1668). Llevó a cabo programas que ayudaron a hacer de Francia la potencia más fuerte de Europa.

Cold War > Guerra Fría Después de la Segunda Guerra Mundial, largo periodo de intensa rivalidad y hostilidad entre las naciones alineadas con los Estados Unidos, por un lado, y la Union Soviética, por el otro, que rara vez llevó a un conflicto armado directo.

collective > granja colectiva Granja grande que pertenece a campesinos que la administran en grupo.

collective security > seguridad colectiva Sistema por el que un grupo de naciones actúa como una para preservar la paz común.

collectivization > colectivización Unión forzada de trabajadores y propiedad en colectivos, como colectivos rurales que absorben a campesinos y sus tierras.

colony > colonia Territorio ocupado y gobernado por personas de otro territorio.

colossus > coloso Gigante

Columbian Exchange > intercambio colombino Intercambio global de bienes, ideas, plantas, animales y enfermedades entre Europa, Africa y las Americas posterior al primer viaje trasatlántico de Colón en 1492.

Columbus, Christopher > Colón, Cristóbal Cristóbal Colón (1451–1506) fue un explorador y navegante italiano que realizó expediciones por el Mediterráneo y África, estableció un plan para navegar por el oeste hasta llegar a India y China, y contó con el apoyo de los reyes de España, Fernando e Isabel. En 1492, navegó hacia el oeste desde España y llegó a las islas del Caribe, las cuales creyó equivocadamente como las Indias de Asia. Hizo otros viajes, pero las tensas relaciones con los oficiales reales españoles lo llevaron a su arresto y dimisión como gobernador de los asentamientos de la isla de La Española.

comedy > comedia En la antigua Grecia, obra de teatro humorística que se burló de las personas o de las costumbres sociales.

Comintern > Comintern Internacional Comunista, asociación internacional de partidos comunistas liderada por la Unión Soviética con el propósito de extender por el mundo una revolución comunista.

command economy > economía dirigida Sistema en el que los funcionarios del gobierno toman todas las decisiones económicas básicas.

Commercial Revolution > Revolución Comercial Un periodo de expansión económica, colonialismo y mercantilismo en Europa que duró desde el siglo XVI hasta principios del siglo XVIII. Incluye el crecimiento del capitalismo, la banca y las inversiones.

commissar > comisario Funcionario del partido comunista asignado al ejército para enseñar los principios del partido y asegurar la lealtad al mismo durante la Revolución Rusa.

commodity > bien de consumo Producto valioso.

common law > derecho consuetudinario Sistema legal basado en la costumbre y en las sentencias de los tribunales.

communism > comunismo Forma de socialismo defendida por Karl Marx; según Marx, la lucha de clases era inevitable y llevaría a la creación de una sociedad sin clases en la que toda la riqueza y la propiedad pertenecería a la comunidad como un todo.

compact > pacto Acuerdo entre personas.

compromise > compromiso Acuerdo en el que cada parte hace concesiones; un término medio aceptable.

concentration camp > campos de concentración Campos usados por los nazis para encarcelar a miembros "indeseables" de la sociedad.

Concert of Europe > Concierto de Europa Organización de conservación de la paz cuyo objetivo era preservar los acuerdos establecidos por el Congreso de Viena.

concession > concesión Derechos económicos especiales que se dan a un poder extranjero.

confederation > confederación Unificación

Confucius > Confucio Confucio (551 a. C.–479 a. C.) es el filósofo más famoso de China. Sus enseñanzas sobre la importancia de la educación y el servicio público influyeron en muchas civilizaciones asiáticas. Sus ancestros, miembros de la aristocracia, eran pobres cuando Confucio nació. A la edad de 15 años, se dedicó a la vida de erudito. Aunque sus ideas sobre el camino apropiado para vivir guiaron a millones de personas, su vida fue sencilla y reflejaba una profunda humildad.

Congress of Vienna > Congreso de Viena Asamblea de líderes europeos que se reunió después de la era napoleónica para reconstruir Europa; se realizó de septiembre de 1814 a junio de 1815.

conquistador > conquistador Líder en las conquistas españolas de America, México y Perú, en el siglo XVI.

conscription > conscripción Llamado a filas que exigía que todos los hombres jóvenes estuvieran listos para el servicio militar u otro servicio.

consensus > consenso Acuerdo general entre todos los miembros de un grupo.

Constantine > Constantino Constantino (alrededor del año 280 d. C.–alrededor del año 337 d. C.) fue el primer emperador romano en hacerse cristiano. Durante su reinado, impidió la persecución de los cristianos y ayudó a fortalecer la iglesia de los primeros tiempos.

Constantinople > Constantinopla Capital del Imperio Romano Oriental; capital de los imperios bizantino y otomano, en la actualidad llamada Estambul.

constitutional government > gobierno constitucional Gobierno cuyo poder está definido y limitado por las leyes.

consul > cónsul Funcionario de la clase de los patricios que supervisaba el gobierno y comandaba los ejércitos.

containment > política de contención Estrategia de los Estados Unidos para mantener el comunismo dentro de las áreas que ya estaban dentro del control soviético.

Continental System > sistema continental Bloqueo diseñado por Napoleón para dañar a Gran Bretaña económicamente al cerrar los puertos europeos a los productos británicos; con el tiempo no tuvo éxito.

contra > contras Grupo guerrillero que luchó contra los sandinistas en Nicaragua.

contraband > contrabando Durante el tiempo de guerra, provisiones militares y materias primas necesarios para fabricar artículos militares, y que pueden ser confiscados legalmente por cualquiera de las partes beligerantes.

convoy > convoy Grupo de buques mercantes que navegan juntos bajo la protección de buques de guerra.

Copernicus, Nicolaus > Copérnico, Nicolás Nicolás Copérnico (1473–1543) fue un astrónomo polaco que concluyó que el Sol es el centro del universo alrededor del cual giraban la Tierra y los otros planetas. Esto contradecía la creencia religiosa y científica de que la Tierra era el centro del universo. Aunque no sufrió retos inmediatos de la Iglesia, su trabajo más importante no fue publicado hasta después de su muerte.

corporation > corporación Empresa de varios inversionistas que comparten acciones y riesgos con base en lo que invirtió cada uno de sus miembros.

Cortés, Hernán > Cortés, Hernán Hernán Cortés (alrededor de 1485–1547) fue un terrateniente de Cuba y conquistador que en 1518 lideró una expedición a México. Aliado con algunos grupos indígenas americanos, conquistó el Imperio Azteca, incluyendo su capital, Tenochtitlán, en 1521. En 1522, el emperador del Sacro Imperio Romano, Carlos V, lo nombró gobernador de la Nueva España, pero Cortés fue finalmente retirado del poder y enviado a España en 1540.

Council of Trent > Concilio de Trento Grupo de líderes católicos que se reunió entre 1545 y 1563 para responder a los retos protestantes y dirigir el futuro de la Iglesia católica.

coup d'état > golpe de estado Derrocamiento obligado de un gobierno.

Courbet, Gustave > Courbet, Gustave Gustave Courbet (1819–1877) fue un destacado pintor francés del movimiento realista. Aunque pintaba temas más tradicionales como vistas del mar, retratos y paisajes, también se centró en representar la vida diaria al pintar la clase media rural y la cultura bohemia, así como temas sociales al representar la difícil vida de los pobres.

covenant > alianza Acuerdo vinculante; específicamente, en la tradición judía, el acuerdo vinculante que Dios hizo con Abraham.

Cranmer, Thomas > Cranmer, Thomas Thomas Cranmer (1489–1556) fue un teólogo católico que apoyó fuertemente la reforma. Cuando Enrique VIII rompió con la Iglesia católica, Cranmer se convirtió en el primer arzobispo protestante de Canterbury, Inglaterra. Distribuyó biblias escritas en inglés a las parroquias y, más tarde, desarrolló el *Book of Common Prayer*. Cranmer fue consejero de Enrique VIII y de su hijo, Eduardo VI.

crematorium > crematorio Lugar donde se queman los cadáveres.

creole > criollo En las colonias españolas de América, descendiente de colonos españoles nacido en América.

Crimean War > Guerra de Crimea Guerra librada principalmente en la península de Crimea entre los rusos y los británicos, franceses y turcos entre 1853 y 1856.

criminal law > derecho penal Rama del derecho que trata de los delitos contra los demás.

Cromwell, Oliver > Cromwell, Oliver Oliver Cromwell (1599–1658) fue un soldado y caballero inglés que dirigió los ejércitos en contra de Carlos I de Inglaterra durante la Guerra Civil inglesa. Se nombró a sí mismo Lord Protector de Inglaterra en 1653, gobernando el país como una república hasta su muerte.

Crusades > Cruzadas Serie de guerras entre el siglo XI y el siglo XIII en las que los cristianos europeos intentaron ganar el control sobre los musulmanes de la Tierra Santa.

cult of domesticity > culto a lo doméstico Idealización de las mujeres y del hogar.

cultural diffusion > difusión cultural Expansión de las ideas, costumbres y tecnologías de un pueblo a otro.

cultural nationalism > nacionalismo cultural Orgullo por la cultura del país propio.

Cultural Revolution > Revolución Cultural Programa de la China comunista a finales de la década de 1960 que pretendía eliminar de China todas las tendencias no revolucionarias y que causó daños económicos y sociales.

culture > cultura Forma de vida de una sociedad, que pasa de una generación a la siguiente por el aprendizaje y la experiencia.

cuneiform > cuneiforme En el antiguo Oriente Medio, sistema de escritura cuyos caracteres tenían forma de cuña.

Curie, Marie > Curie, Marie Marie Curie (1867–1934) nació en Varsovia en una familia de maestros polacos. Más tarde se trasladó a París, donde obtuvo educación formal y conoció a su esposo Pierre Curie. Los Curie fueron pioneros en los estudios sobre la radioactividad, revolucionando los campos de la física y la química. Fue la primera mujer en ganar un Premio Nobel. Marie Curie trabajó incansablemete para promover las aplicaciones prácticas y médicas de su trabajo. Murió en 1934, probablemente a causa de sus muchos años de exposición a materiales radioactivos.

Cuzco > Cuzco Capital del imperio Inca.

cybersecurity > seguridad cibernética Formas de proteger computadoras, redes y datos contra el uso no autorizado.

cyberwarfare > guerra cibernética Serie de ataques patrocinados por el gobierno contra sistemas informáticos en red que podrían interrumpir la infraestructura crítica en un país determinado.

Cyrillic > cirílico relativo al alfabeto eslavo derivado del griego y atribuido por tradición a San Cirilo; en forma modificada todavía se utiliza en lenguas eslavas modernas.

D

D-Day > Día D Nombre clave para el 6 de junio de 1944, el día en que los Aliados desembarcaron en las playas de Normandía, Francia, durante la Segunda Guerra Mundial.

da Vinci, Leonardo > da Vinci, Leonardo Leonardo da Vinci (1452–1519) fue un artista italiano considerado el hombre ideal del Renacimiento debido a su variedad de talentos. Sus intereses incluían la botánica, anatomía, óptica, música, arquitectura e ingeniería. Sus bocetos de máquinas voladoras y de botes submarinos recuerdan los inventos posteriores de aviones y submarinos. Las pinturas de Leonardo, como la iii Mona Lisa y iii La última cena, siguen siendo famosas hoy en día.

dada > dadaísmo Movimiento artístico en el que los artistas rechazaban la tradición y producían obras que a menudo sorprendían a su público.

Daguerre, Louis > Daguerre, Louis Louis Daguerre (1787–1851) fue un pintor y físico francés que inventó la fotografía. Antes de que inventara la cámara, fue grabador y pintor. Durante años había estado experimentando con formas de captar imágenes fotográficas detalladas. Finalmente, en 1839, mostró su proceso a la Académie des Sciences y la Académie des Beaux-Arts. Sorprendió a todo el mundo y su invento revolucionó las artes y las ciencias.

dalit > dalit Marginado; miembro de la casta más baja de India

Dalton, John > Dalton, John John Dalton (1766–1844) fue un profesor, conferencista, meteorólogo, físico y químico inglés. Su interés en la atmósfera le llevó al desarrollo de su teoría atómica en 1803. Su teoría establecía que los átomos tienen masa, que los elementos están formados de átomos y que las reacciones químicas podían explicarse por la combinación y separación de los átomos. Aunque ahora se ha comprobado que partes de su teoría están equivocadas, sigue siendo la base de la química y la física modernas.

Dardanelles > Dardanelos Estrecho de vital importancia que conecta el mar Negro y el mar Mediterráneo en la actual Turquía.

Darfur > Darfur Región occidental de Sudán donde un conflicto étnico amenazó con provocar un genocidio.

Darwin, Charles > Darwin, Charles Charles Darwin (1809–1882) fue un naturalista inglés que desarrolló la teoría de la evolución mediante el proceso de la selección natural. En 1831, se embarcó en un viaje de cinco años alrededor del mundo. Mientras estaba en las islas Galápagos, Darwin observó que cuatro especies de pinzones de las islas tenían diferentes picos y hábitos de alimentación. Promulgó la teoría de que el aislamiento, el tiempo y la adaptación a las condiciones locales lleva a nuevas especies. Su observación y las muestras que recolectó le ayudaron a desarrollar su teoría de la evolución.

David > David Como se describe en los Libros de Samuel, 1 Reyes y 1 Crónicas, David pertenecía a la tribu de Judá y comenzó su vida como pastor en Belén. Finalmente, David se convirtió en el rey de un Israel unido. Los judíos y cristianos creen también que editó el Libro de los Salmos.

Deák, Ferenc > Deák, Ferenc Ferenc Deák (1803–1876), también conocido como el Sabio del País, fue un político, reformador y pensador húngaro. Es conocido por desarrollar el concepto de la monarquía dual y guiar ese compromiso hasta su adopción final.

decimal system > sistema decimal Sistema numérico basado en el 10.

decipher > descifrar Averiguar el significado de algo.

default > cese de pagos Imposibilidad de realizar pagos.

deficit > déficit Diferencia entre los gastos de un gobierno y las recaudaciones por impuestos y otras fuentes de ingresos.

deficit spending > déficit de gastos Práctica de las naciones que gastan más de lo que reciben por ingresos.

deforestation > deforestación Destrucción de tierras forestales.

Delhi > Delhi Tercera ciudad más grande de India; capital de la India medieval.

delta > delta Zona triangular pantanosa que se forma por depósitos de cieno en la desembocadura de algunos ríos.

demilitarized zone > zona desmilitarizada Estrecha franja de tierra que cruza la península de Corea y que separa las fuerzas de Corea del Norte y las fuerzas de Corea del Sur; establecida por el armisticio de 1953.

democracy > democracia Forma de gobierno en el que la soberanía reside en el pueblo.

Deng Xiaoping > Deng Xiaoping Deng Xiaoping (1904–1997) nació en la provincia de Sichuan en China. De joven, estudió en Francia y en la Unión Soviética. Se involucró con el movimiento comunista mientras estaba en Francia. Después de que los comunistas tomaran el poder en China, ocupó diversos cargos en el gobierno, llegando a ser finalmente el político más poderoso de la nación. Sus políticas son responsables de gran parte del crecimiento económico de China después de los fracasos de la Revolución Cultural.

depopulation > despoblación Reducción del número de la población en una zona.

Descartes, René > Descartes, René René Descartes (1596–1650) fue un filósofo, matemático y científico francés. Descartes fue uno de los primeros en abandonar los medios tradicionales de pensamiento basado en las enseñanzas de Aristóteles. En su lugar, promovió una nueva ciencia basada en la observación y los experimentos. Por eso, se le ha llamado el padre de la filosofía moderna.

desertification > desertización Proceso por el que la tierra fértil o semifértil se convierte en desierto.

détente > distensión Relajamiento de las tensiones de la Guerra Fría en los años 70.

developing world > mundo en desarrollo Naciones de África, Asia y América Latina que trabajan para lograr el desarrollo.

development > desarrollo Proceso de establecer gobiernos estables, mejorar la agricultura, la industria y las condiciones de vida.

dharma > dharma Según la creencia hindú, deberes personales religiosos y morales.

Diaspora > diáspora Diseminación de los judíos más allá de su patria histórica.

Díaz, Porfirio > Díaz, Porfirio Porfirio Díaz (1830–1915) fue presidente de México dos veces: 1877–1880 y 1884–1911. Díaz consolidó el poder en el gobierno central y puso la riqueza en manos de unos pocos al llevar inversores extranjeros para construir infraestructuras y explotar las minas. Como la riqueza no estaba repartida equitativamente, el descontento se generalizó. Para 1910, la economía iba en grave declive, y los trabajadores y campesinos vivían en la pobreza o sumidos en deudas. En 1911, Díaz renunció y salió al exilio.

Dickens, Charles > Dickens, Charles Charles Dickens (1812–1870) fue un escritor inglés que comenzó su carrera como reportero independiente. En 1836, comenzó a publicar capítulos de su primera novela, *The Pickwick Papers,* que impulsó su carrera como novelista. Dickens creó algunos de los personajes más famosos y vívidos de la literatura. Como realista, Dickens se dedicó a representar la vida real. Esperaba llevar a cabo una reforma, así que sus novelas a menudo se enfocaban en los problemas de los pobres para exponer desgracias sociales.

dictator > dictador Gobernante que tiene control total sobre un gobierno.

Dien Bien Phu > Dienbienphu Pequeño pueblo y antigua base del ejército francés en el norte de Vietnam; lugar de la batalla que terminó con la victoria vietnamita, la expulsión de los franceses de Vietnam y la obtención de la independencia de Vietnam del Norte.

Diet > dieta Asamblea o cuerpo legislativo.

diet > dieta Asamblea o cuerpo legislativo.

Diocletian > Diocleciano Diocleciano (245 d. C.–311 d. C.) fue un general romano que llegó a ser emperador. Para hacer el gobierno más eficaz, dividió el gran imperio en Oriente y Occidente y nombró un coemperador.

direct democracy > democracia directa Sistema de gobierno en el que los ciudadanos participan directamente, en lugar de hacerlo a través de representantes, en los asuntos diarios del gobierno.

disarmament > desarme Reducción del ejército y del armamento.

discrimination > discriminación Tratamiento desigual o barreras.

Disraeli, Benjamin > Disraeli, Benjamin Benjamin Disraeli (1804–1881) fue un político conservador destacado y primer ministro durante siete años. Junto con otros líderes políticos, Disraeli trabajó para expandir el sufragio y transformó lentamente el Parlamento Británico durante el siglo XIX para convertirlo en una institución más democrática. Su vehemente defensa de la Ley de la Segunda Reforma de 1867, permitió que más hombres votaran, entre ellos los miembros de la clase trabajadora. Disraeli también se enfocó en otras reformas sociales, incluyendo leyes de salud pública y el reconocimiento de los sindicatos de los trabajadores.

dissent > disensión Ideas que se oponen a las del gobierno.

dissenter > disidente Protestante cuyos puntos de vista y opiniones diferían de los de la Iglesia de Inglaterra.

divine right > derecho divino Creencia de que la autoridad de un gobernante proviene directamente de Dios.

domesticate > domesticar Amansar animales y adaptar cosechas para que sean más adecuados para el uso de los seres humanos.

dominion > dominio Nación que se gobierna a sí misma.

domino theory > efecto dominó Creencia de que una victoria comunista en Vietnam del Sur podría causar que los gobiernos no comunistas del sureste de Asia cayeran bajo dominio del comunismo, como una fila de fichas de dominó.

dowry > dote En algunas sociedades, pago de la familia de la novia al novio y a su familia; pago que una mujer proporciona a su matrimonio.

Dreyfus Affair > Caso Dreyfus Escándalo político que causó divisiones profundas en Francia entre los realistas, liberales y republicanos; basado en la injusta condena en 1894 de Alfred Dreyfus, un oficial judío del ejército francés.

Dual Monarchy > monarquía dual Monarquía de Austria-Hungría

due process of law > garantías procesales debidas Requisito para que el gobierno actúe justamente y en concordancia con las normas establecidas en todo lo que hace.

Duma > Duma En Rusia, asamblea legislativa nacional electa.

Dunkirk > Dunkirk Puerto de Francia desde donde fueron evacuadas 300,000 tropas aliadas en 1940 al ser bloqueada su retirada terrestre por el avance del ejército alemán.

Dürer, Albrecht > Durero, Alberto Alberto Durero (1471–1528) nació en Nuremberg, Alemania. Fue pintor, dibujante y escritor; su mayor impacto artístico fue en el grabado. Viajó a Italia, estudió con los maestros italianos y ayudó a difundir las ideas del Renacimiento al norte de Europa. Muchas de sus obras famosas, como *El Apocalipsis* y *Adán y Eva,* eran de temas religiosos.

Dutch East India Company > Compañía Neerlandesa de las Indias Orientales Compañía de comercio con poder soberano y absoluto establecida por los Países Bajos en 1602 para proteger y aumentar su comercio con Asia.

dynamo > dínamo Máquina que se usa para generar electricidad.

dynastic cycle > ciclo dínastico Florecimiento y caída de las dinastías chinas de acuerdo con el Mandato del Cielo.

dynasty > dinastía Familia gobernante.

E

earthwork > bancal Muros de contención u otro tipo de construcciones hechos de tierra.

East Timor > Timor Oriental Antigua colonia portuguesa, ocupada por Indonesia, que obtuvo su independencia en 2002.

economic nationalism > nacionalismo económico Énfasis en el control nacional y en la protección de la economía.

Edict of Nantes > Edicto de Nantes Ley promulgada por el rey francés Enrique IV en 1598 en la que se concedía mayor libertad religiosa a los protestantes franceses.

Edison, Thomas > Edison, Thomas Alva Thomas Alva Edison (1847–1931) solicitó su primera patente mientras trabajaba como operador de telégrafos para la Western Union. Aunque su primer invento fue un fracaso, Edison no abandonó el esfuerzo, y continuó hasta convertirse en uno de los inventores más prolíficos del mundo. Durante su vida patentó 1,093 inventos y mejoras en varias industrias, entre ellas de telecomunicaciones, energía eléctrica, minería, registro de sonidos, automotriz, defensa militar y películas de cine.

Eightfold Path > Óctuple Sendero Según las enseñanzas de Buda, el camino que uno debe seguir para lograr el nirvana.

Einstein, Albert > Einstein, Albert Albert Einstein (1879–1955) nació en Alemania, en el seno de una familia judía de clase media. Publicó sus teorías de la relatividad en 1905 y 1916, ganando el Premio Nobel de Física en 1921. Estas ideas cambiaron las creencias sostenidas por mucho tiempo respecto a la naturaleza del universo. Cuando los nazis llegaron al poder en Alemania, Einstein emigró a los Estados Unidos en 1932 y se nacionalizó en 1940. Durante la Segunda Guerra Mundial, se usó su trabajo en la creación de la bomba atómica. A medida que la tecnología nuclear se expandía, Einstein estuvo a favor de controles y limitaciones internacionales. Es ampliamente considerado como el físico más influyente del siglo XX.

Eisenhower, Dwight > Eisenhower, Dwight Dwight Eisenhower (1890–1969) creció en una familia pobre muy trabajadora. Durante la Segunda Guerra Mundial, fue el general estadounidense que comandó las fuerzas aliadas en Europa occidental. Más tarde, "Ike" fue el 34º Presidente de los Estados Unidos, de 1953 a 1961.

Eleanor of Acquitaine > Aquitania, Leonor de Leonor de Aquitania (1122–1204) fue una heredera al ducado de Aquitania. A la edad de 15 años, se casó con el heredero al trono francés, Luis VI, y fue reina de Francia. Inteligente y tenaz, influyó fuertemente en su esposo y fue con él a la Segunda Cruzada. Su segundo matrimonio fue con Henry Plantagenet, quien se convirtió en Enrique II de Inglaterra en 1154. Mientras cuidaba de cinco hijos y tres hijas, ayudó activamente a administrar Inglaterra, gestionó sus propios dominios —haciendo de la corte en Poitiers un modelo de vida cortesana— y permaneció políticamente activa ya cumplidos los 80 años.

elector > elector Uno de los siete príncipes germanos que elegían al emperador del Sacro Imperio Romano.

electorate > electorado Conjunto de personas a quienes se permite votar.

elite > élite Clase alta.

Elizabeth > Isabel I Isabel Tudor (1533–1603) llegó a ser la reina Isabel I de Inglaterra después de la muerte de la reina María. Los cambios políticos hicieron que su infancia fuera bastante peligrosa. Isabel usó sus experiencias para convertirse en una monarca poderosa y astuta. Bajo su reinado, Inglaterra se convirtió en una potencia europea importante. Inglaterra prosperó, tanto económica como culturalmente. Su equilibrado manejo de los conflictos religiosos ingleses le ganaron el apodo de la Buena Reina Isabel.

emancipation > emancipación Otorgamiento de libertad a siervos o personas esclavizadas.

emigration > emigración Trasladarse de su propio país a otro.

émigré > exiliado Persona que deja su país por razones políticas.

empire > imperio Grupo de estados o territorios controlados por un gobernante.

enclosure > cercamiento Proceso de apropiarse y consolidar una tierra que anteriormente compartían campesinos.

encomienda > encomienda Derecho que los monarcas españoles otorgaban a los conquistadores para exigir tributos o trabajo a los indígenas americanos en una zona determinada.

endangered species > especie en vías de extinción Especie amenazada de extinción, es decir, de desaparición.

engineering > ingeniería Aplicación de la ciencia y las matemáticas para desarrollar estructuras y máquinas.

English Bill of Rights > Declaración de Derechos inglesa Serie de leyes aprobadas por el parlamento inglés en 1689 que limitaba los derechos de la monarquía y establecía la primacía del Parlamento.

engraving > grabado Forma de arte en la que un artista graba un diseño en una placa de metal y después la usa para producir múltiples impresiones.

enlightened despot > déspota ilustrado Gobernante absoluto que usaba su poder para precipitar cambios políticos y sociales.

entente > entente Acuerdo no vinculante de seguir normas comunes.

enterprise > empresa Entidad empresarial en áreas como transportes, minería, ferrocarriles o fábricas.

entrepreneur > empresario Persona que asume riesgos financieros con la esperanza de obtener beneficios.

Epic of Gilgamesh, The > Epopeya de Gilgamesh Poema narrativo de Mesopotamia que se contó por primera vez en Sumeria.

epidemic > epidemia Brote de una enfermedad que se extiende rápidamente.

Equiano, Olaudah > Equiano, Olaudah Olaudah Equiano (1745–1797) fue capturado en África occidental cuando era un niño de 11 años, vendido como esclavo y enviado a las Américas. Más tarde, encontró un trabajo pagado y ganó dinero suficiente para comprar su libertad. En 1789, escribió su autobiografía, *Interesante relato de la vida de Olaudah Equiano*. Murió en Londres en 1797.

Erasmus > Erasmo Erasmo (c. 1466–1536) fue un sacerdote, escritor y erudito holandés que promovió el humanismo. Escribió textos sobre varios temas y produjo una nueva edición griega de la Biblia cristiana. También pidió la traducción de la Biblia a un lenguaje vernáculo, o cotidiano, para ayudar a difundir las enseñanzas, las ideas y la educación. También quería reformar la corrupción de la Iglesia.

erosion > erosión El desgaste paulatino de la tierra.

estates > estado Clase social.

Estates-General > Estados Generales Cuerpo legislativo formado por representantes de los tres estados en la Francia prerevolucionaria.

ethics > ética Estándares morales de comportamiento.

Ethiopia > Etiopía Antiguo término griego para el reino de Axumite; también es un país actual del este de África.

ethnic cleansing > limpieza étnica La matanza o expulsión forzosa de personas de diferentes grupos étnicos de una zona, llevadas a cabo por agresores para que su grupo étnico tenga permanencia exclusiva.

ethnic group > grupo étnico Grupo grande de personas que comparten el mismo idioma y herencia cultural.

Etruscans > etruscos Pueblo que habitó en la Italia antigua.

euro > euro Moneda común usada por la mayoría de las naciones que pertenecen a la Unión Europea.

European Union (EU) > Unión Europea (UE) Organización internacional formada por más de dos docenas de naciones europeas y dedicada a establecer el libre comercio entre las naciones miembros, con una moneda común y leyes y políticas comunes.

excommunication > excomunión Exclusión de la Iglesia católica romana como castigo por negarse a obedecer la ley de la Iglesia.

expansionism > expansionismo Política de aumentar el territorio que posee un gobierno.

extraterritoriality > extraterritorialidad Derecho de los extranjeros a que las leyes de su propia nación los protejan.

F

faction > facción Un grupo o camarilla dentro de un grupo más grande que tiene diferentes ideas y opiniones que el resto del grupo.

famine > hambruna Escasez severa de alimentos por la que perece gran número de personas.

Faraday, Michael > Faraday, Michael Michael Faraday (1791–1867) fue un químico y físico británico que hizo contribuciones importantes en el campo de la electricidad. Algunos de sus descubrimientos más importantes incluyen la generación y transmisión de electricidad, el motor eléctrico y el benceno químico. Sus descubrimientos han dado forma al mundo moderno.

fascism > fascismo Cualquier sistema de gobierno autoritario centralizado no comunista, cuya política glorifica al estado por encima del individuo y que destruye los derechos humanos fundamentales.

federal republic > república federal Gobierno en el que el poder se divide entre el gobierno nacional o federal y los estados.

Federal Reserve > Reserva Federal Sistema central de banca de los Estados Unidos, el cual regula los bancos.

Ferdinand and Isabella > Fernando e Isabel Fernando III (1452–1516) e Isabel I (1451–1504) fueron el rey de Aragón y la reina de Castilla. Su matrimonio unió los dos países para convertirse en la nación de España. Sus campañas militares fueron responsables del éxito final de la Reconquista.

Ferguson, Miriam > Ferguson, Miriam Miriam "Ma" Ferguson (1875–1961), conocida por muchos como "Ma" Ferguson, fue electa la primera gobernadora de Texas en 1924. Se postuló cuando su esposo, el políticamente deshonrado gobernador James E. Ferguson, fue incapaz de asegurar un lugar en la votación. La Sra. Ferguson fue la primera mujer electa para el cargo en los Estados Unidos pero la segunda en ser gobernadora porque Nellie T. Ross de Wyoming fue investida después de la muerte de su esposo. La Sra. Ferguson fue reelecta en 1932 para un segundo periodo.

Fertile Crescent > Creciente Fértil Región de Oriente Medio en la cual surgieron las primeras civilizaciones.

feudal contract > contrato feudal Intercambio de garantías entre los señores y los vasallos.

feudalism > feudalismo Sistema de gobierno poco organizado en el que los señores gobernaban sus propias tierras, pero debían servicio militar y otras formas de apoyo a un superior.

fief > feudo En la Europa medieval, estado que un señor otorga a un vasallo a cambio de sus servicios y lealtad.

filial piety > amor filial Respeto hacia los padres.

finance > finanzas Gestión de los asuntos monetarios incluyendo la circulación de dinero, préstamos, inversiones y banca.

Firdawsi > Firdusi Firdusi (c. 940–1020) fue un poeta musulmán famoso por el *Shah Namah*, o *Libro de los Reyes*, que escribió en persa usando grafía árabe. Firdusi escribió en una época en la que Persia, o Irán, era bastante libre del control del Imperio Musulmán y los líderes locales fomentaban un florecimiento de la cultura persa. El afamado poeta centró sus escritos en historias de realeza y héroes, y muchos de los temas que introdujo siguen siendo relevantes hoy en día.

First Sino-Japanese War > Primera guerra sino-japonesa Conflicto entre China y Japón de 1894 a 1895 por el control de Corea.

Flanders > Flandes Región que incluye partes de los actuales norte de Francia, Bélgica y Países Bajos; fue un importante centro industrial y financiero del norte de Europa durante la Edad Media y el Renacimiento.

flapper > flapper En los Estados Unidos y Europa, mujer joven de la década de 1920 que desafiaba las reglas tradicionales de conducta y atuendo.

Florence > Florencia Ciudad de la región de Toscana en el norte de Italia que fue el centro del Renacimiento italiano.

flying buttresses > contrafuertes flotantes Soportes de piedra en la parte exterior de un edificio que permitía a los constructores construir paredes más finas y más altas que contenían ventanas con vidrieras.

Four Noble Truths > Cuatro Nobles Verdades Según las enseñanzas de Buda, las cuatro creencias básicas que forman la base del budismo.

Fourteen Points > Los Catorce Puntos Lista de condiciones planteada por el presidente estadounidense Woodrow Wilson en enero de 1918 para resolver la Primera Guerra Mundial y guerras futuras.

Francis Joseph > Francisco José Francisco José (1830–1916) fue emperador de Austria en 1848 después de la abdicación de Fernando I. Después de la creación de la monarquía dual en 1867, también fue rey de Hungría. En 1879, Francisco José formó una alianza con Alemania, que fue dirigida por los prusianos. Su manejo de las relaciones con Serbia después del asesinato del archiduque Francisco Fernando en 1914 fue uno de los catalizadores de la Primera Guerra Mundial.

Franco, Francisco > Franco, Francisco Francisco Franco (1892–1975) fue un líder militar español que llegó al poder durante la Guerra Civil española. Fue dictador de España de 1939 a 1973, cuando dejó su cargo como jefe de gobierno. Siguió siendo jefe del estado hasta su muerte en 1975.

Franklin, Benjamin > Franklin, Benjamin Benjamin Franklin (1706–1790) fue un hombre de muchos talentos. Nacido en 1706, Franklin fue un autor, inventor y estadista que ayudó a convencer a Francia de que entrara a la Guerra de Independencia del lado de los estadounidenses. Participó activamente en la redacción de la Declaración de Independencia.

Franks > francos Tribu germánica que conquistó la actual Francia y las tierras colindantes en el siglo V.

Frederick II > Federico II Federico II (1712–1786) heredó de su padre, Federico Guillermo I, el trono como rey de Prusia (1740–1786).

Frederick William I > Federico Guillermo I Federico Guillermo I (1688–1740) fue el segundo rey prusiano; ayudó a transformar su país en un estado próspero.

free enterprise system > sistema de libre empresa Sistema económico, también conocido como capitalismo, en el que las empresas privadas son capaces de competir entre sí con poco control del gobierno. Productos, precios y servicios son impulsados por las leyes del libre mercado de la oferta y la demanda en lugar de las regulaciones del mercado.

free market > libre mercado Mercado regulado por las leyes naturales de la oferta y la demanda.

free trade > libre comercio Comercio entre países, sin cuotas, tasas u otras restricciones.

French and Indian War > Guerra contra la Alianza Franco- Indígena Guerra entre Gran Bretaña y Francia en las Américas, que ocurrió de 1754 a 1763; fue parte de una guerra global que se conoció como la Guerra de los Siete Años.

French Indochina > Indochina francesa Nombre occidental para las colonias de Francia en el sureste asiático continental. Actualmente es Vietnam, Laos y Camboya.

fresco > fresco Pinturas de acuarela sobre yeso húmedo.

friar > fraile Monje de la Europa medieval que viajaba de un lugar a otro predicando a los pobres.

fundamentalist > fundamentalista Líder religioso que aboga por el retorno de los que considera que son los valores fundamentales, o básicos, de sus creencias.

G

Galileo > Galileo Galileo Galilei (1564–1642) fue un astrónomo y matemático italiano cuyos descubrimientos con el telescopio apoyaron las teorías heliocéntricas del universo de Copérnico. Sus descubrimientos desafiaron el pensamiento religioso y científico establecido. Galileo contribuyó de manera importante al desarrollo del método científico usado por los científicos modernos.

Gama, Vasco da > Gama, Vasco da Vasco da Gama (c. 1460–1524) fue un explorador y navegante portugués que en 1498 fue la primera persona en llegar directamente a India navegando alrededor de África. Regresó a India en 1502, luchó contra barcos árabes musulmanes en el camino y estableció puestos de comercio a lo largo de la costa de África oriental. Después de servir al rey de Portugal durante 20 años, regresó a India en 1524 con el título de virrey, pero enfermó y murió poco después de llegar.

Gandhi, Indira > Gandhi, Indira Indira Gandhi (1917–1984) fue primer ministro de India durante cuatro periodos. Hija de Jawaharlal Nehru, Gandhi entró en la política como parte del Partido del Congreso, convirtiéndose pronto en su líder. Después de la muerte de su padre, fue electa primera ministra de India. Gandhi permaneció en el poder hasta 1977, cuando algunas de sus políticas autoritarias llevaron a su derrota popular. Sin embargo, en 1980, fue reelecta para un cuarto periodo como primera ministra. Después de que ordenara un ataque militar al Templo Dorado, un lugar sagrado para los sijs, Gandhi fue asesinada por sus guardaespaldas sijs.

Gandhi, Mohandas > Gandhi, Mohandas Mohandas Gandhi (1869–1948) fue un estudiante mediocre que pasó por un periodo de rebelión durante su adolescencia. Se casó a los 13 años y más tarde fue enviado a Inglaterra a la escuela de leyes. En 1891, Gandhi aceptó un cargo en Sudáfrica. Aunque planeaba estar solo un año, permaneció hasta 1914, luchando por los derechos de los indios. En 1919, Gandhi comenzó a ser activo en el movimiento de independencia de India y se dedicó a la causa hasta su muerte. Fue asesinado en 1948, solo unos cuantos meses después de que India ganara su independencia.

Garibaldi, Giuseppe > Garibaldi, Giuseppe Giuseppe Garibaldi (1807–1882) fue un soldado nacionalista y líder militar que usó eficazmente tácticas de guerrilla para obtener victorias militares por el sur de Italia. En su juventud fue miembro de la Joven Italia de Mazzini, donde comenzó a involucrarse con la causa de la unidad italiana.

Garvey, Marcus > Garvey, Marcus Marcus Garvey (1887–1940) fundó la Asociación Universal para el Progreso de la Raza Negra y la Liga de Comunidades Africanas (UNIA) en Jamaica en 1914, con la intención de construir una nación gobernada por negros. Al descubrir que tenía poco apoyo, Garvey se trasladó a los Estados Unidos y estableció la UNIA en Harlem. Garvey enseñaba a sus seguidores sobre la cultura africana y predicaba la necesidad de que los negros formaran una economía fuerte e independiente. Su creencia firme en la separación de las razas le trajo muchos enemigos y fue deportado en 1927.

Gautama, Siddhartha > Gautama, Siddhartha Siddhartha Gautama (alrededor del año 563 a. C.–483 a. C.) nació siendo un príncipe de India. Su encuentro con el sufrimiento humano le llevó a dejar su vida de realeza para buscar la causa del sufrimiento y la pena. Buscó respuestas de los eruditos y meditó hasta que desarrolló una explicación espiritual de la vida. Llegó a ser conocido como "Buda" y comenzó a enseñar sus creencias a los demás. Enseñó las Cuatro Nobles Verdades y fomentó la fe de seguir el Óctuple Sendero.

general strike > huelga general Huelga de trabajadores de muchas industrias diferentes al mismo tiempo.

genetic engineering > ingeniería genética Alteración del código genético que portan todas las formas de vida con el fin de producir resultados específicos.

genetics > genética Rama de la biología que trata sobre la herencia y las variaciones entre sí de los animales y las plantas.

Geneva > Ginebra Ciudad-estado suiza que se convirtió en una teocracia calvinista en el siglo XVI; en la actualidad es una de las principales ciudades de Suiza.

Genghis Khan > Gengis Kan Gengis Kan (1162–1227) surgió de la pobreza para unir a las guerreras tribus mongolas. Impuso disciplina, exigió lealtad y luego procedió a formar un ejército que conquistó las amplias áreas de Asia central y China y que se convirtieron en el Imperio Mongol. Fue conocido por su ferocidad y su generosidad. El Imperio Mongol duró largo tiempo después de que él muriera durante una campaña militar. Sus descendientes aumentaron el imperio hasta que llegó a ser el imperio más grande del mundo antes del Imperio Británico.

genocide > genocidio Intento deliberado de destruir la totalidad de un grupo religioso o étnico.

gentry > clase alta Clase adinerada, terrateniente.

George III > Jorge III Jorge III (1738–1820) fue el monarca reinante que más tiempo estuvo en el trono en la historia británica; gobernó en una época en la que Gran Bretaña y Francia luchaban por dominar Europa; compartió la culpa por la pérdida de las colonias americanas de Gran Bretaña.

germ theory > teoría de los gérmenes Teoría de que las enfermedades infecciosas son causadas por ciertos microbios.

Gestapo > Gestapo Policía secreta de la Alemania nazi.

Ghana > Ghana Antiguo reino comerciante de África occidental ubicado en partes de las actuales Mauritania y Malí.

ghetto > gueto Área separada de una ciudad donde se obliga a vivir a los miembros de una minoría.

Gladstone, William > Gladstone, William William Gladstone (1809–1898) fue primer ministro cuatro veces por separado, líder de los Whigs y más tarde del Partido Liberal. Amplió el sufragio a los campesinos y a la mayoría de los demás hombres durante la década de 1880, muy especialmente con la Ley de Representación del Pueblo de 1884. Gladstone también fue un firme defensor de la autonomía gubernamental irlandesa. Junto con su principal rival, Benjamin Disraeli, Gladstone ayudó a transformar el gobierno británico en una democracia parlamentaria.

glasnost > glásnost Término ruso para "nueva apertura", una política en la Unión Soviética en la década de 1980 para garantizar mayor libertad de expresión.

global warming > calentamiento global Aumento de la temperatura de la superficie terrestre a través del tiempo.

globalization > globalización Proceso por el cual las economías nacionales, la política, las culturas y las sociedades se relacionan con las de otras naciones en todo el mundo.

Goa > Goa Ciudad costera tomada en 1510 que se convirtió en la base comercial y militar de la India de Portugal.

golden age > época dorada Periodo de grandes logros culturales.

Golden Bull of 1222 > Bula de Oro de 1222 Carta constitucional que limitaba rigurosamente el poder de la realeza en Hungría.

Golden Temple > Templo Dorado Santuario de mayor peso sagrado en la religión sij.

Good Friday Agreement > Acuerdo del Viernes Santo Acuerdo firmado por protestantes y católicos en 1998 para poner fin al conflicto en Irlanda del Norte.

Good Neighbor Policy > Política del Buen Vecino Política con la que el presidente estadounidense Franklin Roosevelt prometió que los Estados Unidos interferirían menos en los asuntos de America Latina.

Gorbachev, Mikhail > Gorbachov, Mijaíl Mikhail Gorbachev (n. 1931) fue el líder de la Unión Soviética de 1985 a 1991. Fue responsable de introducir las reformas (glasnost y perestroika) que llevaron a la división de la Unión Soviética y al fin del dominio soviético en Europa Oriental. Fue relevado del cargo por su rival popular, el defensor democrático, Boris Yeltsin, en 1991.

Gothic style > estilo gótico Tipo de arquitectura europea que se desarrolló en la Edad Media, caracterizada por contrafuertes flotantes, bóvedas estriadas, paredes finas y techos altos.

Gouges, Olympe de > Gouges, Olympe de Olympe de Gouges (1745?–1793), autora de la Declaración de los Derechos de la Mujer, clamó contra el trato que recibían las mujeres en Francia, abordando sus asuntos directamente con María Antonieta.

Gracchus, Gaius > Graco, Cayo Cayo Graco (alrededor del año 154 a. C.–121 a. C.) fue hermano de Tiberio y un reformista político plebeyo que buscó limitar el poder del Senado. Propuso un equilibrio de poderes para minimizar la influencia financiera. Al igual que su hermano, fue asesinado por matones contratados por el Senado Romano.

gravity > gravedad Fuerza que atrae los objetos dentro de la esfera terrestre al centro de la Tierra.

Great Depression > Gran Depresión Periodo difícil de colapso económico global entre 1929 y 1939.

Great Leap Forward > Gran Salto Adelante Programa de la China comunista de 1958 a 1960 para aumentar la producción agrícola e industrial, el cual fracasó estrepitosamente.

Great Schism > Gran Cisma División oficial entre las iglesias católica romana y bizantina ocurrida en 1054; otro caso fue el Gran Cisma occidental, un periodo en el cual los papas rivales lucharon por el poder exclusivo y en el que se dividió la Iglesia católica romana desde 1378 hasta 1417.

Great Zimbabwe > Gran Zimbabue Poderoso centro de comercio medieval de África oriental y ciudad estado ubicada en el sureste del actual Zimbabue.

Greco, El > Greco, El El Greco (1541–1614) fue un maestro de la pintura española que también trabajó como escultor y arquitecto durante el Siglo de Oro de España.

Green Revolution > Revolución verde La introducción, en los países en vías de desarrollo durante la década de 1950, de semillas, pesticidas, equipo mecánico y métodos de agricultura mejorados.

Gregory VII > Gregorio VII Gregorio VII (alrededor de 1025–1085) logró el éxito en su batalla contra el emperador del Sacro Imperio Romano Enrique IV por la cuestión de la investidura. Expandió mucho el poder papal al reclamar su supremacía sobre los gobernantes seculares.

griot > griot Antiguo narrador profesional de historias en África occidental.

gross domestic product (GDP) > producto interno bruto (PIB) Valor total de todos los productos y servicios producidos en una nación en un determinado año.

Guang Xu > Guang Xu Guang Xu (1871–1908) fue el noveno emperador de la dinastía Qing. Cuando murió el emperador anterior Tongzhi, su madre Ci Xi nombró a Guang, su sobrino, como nuevo emperador. Ci Xi dominó su reino, influyendo en el gobierno y haciéndole inútil. Durante los Cien Días de Reforma, Guang intentó reformas progresistas, enojando a los conservadores. Ci Xi encarceló a Guang. Murió en circunstancias sospechosas.

Guangzhou > Guangzhou Ciudad costera del sureste de China, también conocida como Cantón, donde, durante la dinastía Ming, los neerlandeses, británicos y otros europeos, podían comerciar con mercaderes chinos bajo la supervisión de funcionarios imperiales, sólo durante la temporada comercial de cada año y sólo en Canton.

guerrilla > guerrilla Pequeños grupos de soldados pertenecientes a una fuerza poco organizada que despliega ataques por sorpresa.

guerrilla warfare > guerra de guerrillas Método de combate no tradicional.

guild > gremio En la Edad Media, asociación de mercaderes o artesanos que cooperaban para mantener los valores de sus oficios y para proteger sus intereses económicos.

guillotine > guillotina Aparato usado durante el Terror para decapitar a miles de personas.

Gulag > *Gulag* En la Unión Soviética, un sistema de campos de trabajo forzado donde millones de criminales y prisioneros políticos fueron detenidos durante el gobierno de Stalin.

Guomindang > Guomindang Partido nacionalista, activo en China entre 1912 y 1949.

Gutenberg, Johannes > Gutenberg, Johannes Gutenberg (c. 1400–1468) nació en Alemania. Fue herrero, impresor y editor. Su invento vanguardista de una imprenta con tipos movibles cambió el mundo. Alrededor de 1455, Gutenberg imprimió la primera edición completa de la Biblia cristiana usando su prensa.

H

habeas corpus > hábeas corpus Garantía constitucional que evita arrestos y encarcelamientos injustos o sin cargos específicos.

hacienda > hacienda Plantación grande.

Hadrian > Adriano Adriano (76 d. C.–138 d. C.) fue emperador romano desde el año 117 d. C. hasta el año 138 d. C. Considerado uno de los "Cinco emperadores buenos", codificó la ley romana y viajó mucho, uniendo al imperio.

hajj > *hajj* Uno de los Cinco Pilares del islam, la peregrinación a La Meca que se espera hagan todos los musulmanes por lo menos una vez en la vida.

Hammurabi > Hammurabi Hammurabi (1792 a. C.–1750 a. C.) fue el primer rey del Imperio Babilónico. Heredó el poder de su padre, quien extendió el control de Babilonia por Mesopotamia. Hammurabi es conocido por escribir el primer código de leyes de la historia escrita.

hangul > hangul Alfabeto que usa símbolos para representar gráficamente los sonidos del idioma coreano.

Hapsburg empire > Imperio Habsburgo Imperio centroeuropeo que duró desde el siglo XV hasta el siglo XX, y que en su plenitud abarcó los territorios del Sacro Imperio Romano y los Países Bajos.

Harappa > Harappa Antigua gran ciudad de la civilización del Indo, ubicada en el presente Pakistán.

Harlem Renaissance > Renacimiento de Harlem Movimiento cultural afroamericano durante las décadas de 1920 y 1930, centrado en Harlem.

Hatshepsut > Hatshepsut (Murió en 1458 a. C.) La reina Hatshepsut sirvió durante 20 años junto con su esposo, Tutmosis II, pero después de la muerte de éste tomó la función de faraona y actuó como regente de Tutmosis III. Es conocida por haber construido templos y monumentos y, en general, por una época de prosperidad en Egipto.

Havel, Václav > Havel, Václav Václav Havel (1936–2011) fue un dramaturgo checo y activista de los derechos humanos que llegó a ser presidente de Checoslovaquia en 1989, después de la Revolución de Terciopelo. Debido a que fue perseguido durante las últimas etapas del gobierno comunista en Checoslovaquia, Havel llegó a ser un símbolo mundial de represión comunista. Después de la división de Checoslovaquia, fue el primer presidente de la República Checa.

hejab > hejab Velos, pañuelos y prendas de vestir amplias y hasta los tobillos cuya finalidad es ocultar el cuerpo; lo visten por lo general las mujeres musulmanas.

heliocentric > heliocéntrico Sistema basado en la creencia de que el Sol es el centro del universo.

Henry IV > Enrique IV Enrique IV (1050–1106) fue un rey alemán que llegó a ser emperador del Sacro Imperio Romano en 1084. Sus esfuerzos para aumentar el poder de la monarquía le llevaron a entrar en conflicto con el papa Gregorio VIII sobre la investidura. Gregorio excomulgó a Enrique pero más tarde lo readmitió en la iglesia después de que Enrique hiciera penitencia.

Henry VIII > Enrique VIII Enrique VIII (1491–1547) fue el segundo rey Tudor de Inglaterra. Bien educado y atlético, al principio fue un favorito del pueblo inglés. Perdió gran parte de su popularidad debido a su constante participación en guerras. El deseo de Enrique de tener un heredero varón fue el catalizador de su ruptura final con la Iglesia Católica Romana y la formación de la Iglesia de Inglaterra.

Henry, Prince > Enrique el Navegante, príncipe El príncipe Enrique (1394–1460) fue un príncipe portugués y patrón de exploradores que ayudó a su padre a capturar la ciudad marroquí de Ceuta; fue gobernador y patrocinó viajes a las islas Madeira y la costa de África occidental. Reunió dinero para las expediciones y estableció una base de exploradores en Sagres, añadiendo más tarde un arsenal, un observatorio y una escuela para estudiar geografía. Su apoyo a la cartografía, avances en la navegación y la exploración proporcionó una base para el surgimiento del dominio internacional de Portugal y la adquisición de su imperio colonial en el siglo XVI.

heresy > herejía Creencia religiosa en contra de las enseñanzas oficiales de una Iglesia.

Herodotus > Herodoto Herodoto (484 a. C.–425 a. C.), a menudo llamado el "Padre de la Historia", hizo numerosos viajes por todo el mundo mediterráneo, recopilando información para sus crónicas de eventos pasados, entre ellos las guerras persas. En sus escritos, observó prejuicios y relatos opuestos a sus fuentes.

Hidalgo, Father Miguel > Hidalgo, padre Miguel El padre Miguel Hidalgo (1753–1811) fue un sacerdote católico de México. Dirigió a indígenas y mestizos en una revolución en contra de los españoles hasta que fue capturado y asesinado en 1811.

hierarchy > jerarquía Sistema que clasifica a las personas de una sociedad.

hieroglyphics > jeroglíficos Sistema de escritura en el que dibujos llamados jeroglifos representan objetos, conceptos o sonidos.

hijra > hégira Viaje de Mahoma desde La Meca hacia Medina en el año 622.

Hippocrates > Hipócrates Hipócrates (c. 460 a. C.–375 a. C.) fue un médico griego considerado tradicionalmente como el padre de la medicina; estudió las causas de las enfermedades y buscó sus curas. Se le atribuyen muchos escritos médicos antiguos, aunque probablemente escribió pocos de ellos. Es honrado por su juramento hipocrático que fija los estándares éticos para la práctica médica.

Hirohito > Hirohito Hirohito (1901–1989) fue emperador en 1926 cuando murió su padre. Muchos creían que era un dios vivo, descendiente de la diosa del sol. Los ultranacionalistas militares japoneses construyeron un culto alrededor del emperador, reviviendo antiguos valores guerreros y suprimiendo la mayoría de las libertades democráticas. Aunque Hirohito fue investido teóricamente con la autoridad suprema, no hizo más que aprobar las políticas que le presentaban sus ministros. Estaba más interesado en la biología marina y escribió varios libros sobre el tema. Hirohito fue el monarca que más tiempo reinó en la historia de Japón, siendo emperador durante la increíble cantidad de 63 años, hasta su muerte en 1989.

Hiroshima > Hiroshima Ciudad de Japón donde fue lanzada la primera bomba atómica en agosto de 1945.

historian > historiador Persona que estudia cómo vivía la gente en el pasado.

Hitler, Adolf > Hitler, Adolf Adolf Hitler (1889–1945) fue canciller de Alemania de 1933 a 1945 y dictador de la Alemania nazi de 1934 a 1945. Después de ser nombrado canciller, transformó inmediatamente la República de Weimar en el Tercer Reich. Quería establecer un "Nuevo Orden" y crear más "espacio para vivir" para la raza aria, la cual creía que era superior. Hitler invadió agresivamente las naciones vecinas, lo que llevó a la Segunda Guerra Mundial. Cuando Alemania se enfrentó a la derrota en 1945, Hitler se suicidó para evitar que lo capturaran los soviéticos.

Ho Chi Minh > Ho Chi Minh Ho Chi Minh (1890–1969); su nombre fue Nguyen That Thanh. Fundó el Partido Comunista Indochino y fue el líder del movimiento armado de independencia en Vietnam. Ho proclamó la independencia de Vietnam en 1945 y se convirtió en el líder de Vietnam del Norte cuando el país quedó dividido en 1954. Fue el líder de Vietnam del Norte hasta su muerte en 1969 y se negó a negociar el fin de la guerra.

Hobbes, Thomas > Hobbes, Thomas Thomas Hobbes (1588–1679) fue un influyente filósofo político inglés, mejor conocido por su obra *Leviathan*. En ella, Hobbes defiende fuertemente que solo un gobierno poderoso es capaz de proteger a la sociedad. Creía que las personas entraban en un contrato social con su gobierno para evitar el caos inevitable y la anarquía de la vida en el "estado natural". La filosofía política de Hobbes fue fundamental para los pensadores posteriores de la Ilustración, incluyendo a Locke, Rousseau y Kant.

Holocaust > Holocausto Genocidio sistemático de aproximadamente seis millones de judíos europeos por parte de los nazis.

Holy Land > Tierra Santa Jerusalén y otros lugares donde los cristianos creen que Jesús vivió y predicó.

Holy Roman Empire > Sacro Imperio Romano Imperio de la Europa central occidental desde 962 a 1806, que comprendía la actual Alemania y las tierras aledañas.

home rule > autogobierno Autogobierno local.

Homer > Homero Homero (c. 750 a. C.) según la tradición es el autor de poemas épicos, la *Ilíada* y la *Odisea;* se cree que viajó de aldea en aldea cantando sobre las hazañas heroicas de los guerreros de la Guerra de Troya.

homogeneous society > sociedad homogénea Sociedad que tiene un lenguaje y una cultura en común.

Huari > huari Cultura que tuvo su apogeo en la región andina, aproximadamente desde el año 600 d. C. al año 1000 d. C.

Hugo, Victor > Hugo, Víctor Víctor Hugo (1802–1885) fue una destacada figura literaria, intelectual y política de Francia. Sus obras no solo fueron extremadamente populares, siendo las más notables *Nuestra Señora de París* y *Los miserables,* sino que también fueron muy influyentes y respetadas. Hugo creía en la causa de la gente común y veía en ella fuerza y potencial. Trató de representar en sus obras tanto sus virtudes como sus preocupaciones. Aunque Victor Hugo no vivió en la pobreza, se asociaba con la clase baja y, según sus deseos, tuvo un funeral y una tumba pobres.

Huguenots > hugonotes Protestantes franceses de los siglos XVI y XVII.

humanism > humanismo Movimiento intelectual durante el auge del Renacimiento que se centraba en la educación y los clásicos.

humanities > humanidades Estudio de asignaturas como la gramática, la retórica, poesía e historia que se enseñaban en las antiguas Grecia y Roma.

Huns > hunos Pueblo nómada del centro de Asia.

Hutus > hutus Grupo mayoritario de Ruanda y Burundi.

hyperinflation > hiperinflación Aumento rápido y brusco de los precios que hace que el dinero pierda su valor.

hypothesis > hipótesis Teoría sin probar, aceptada con el propósito de explicar determinados hechos o de proveer una base para investigaciones posteriores.

I

Ibn Khaldun > Abenjaldún Abenjaldún (1332–1406) fue un pensador árabe que ayudó a establecer los principios de muchas ramas del conocimiento, entre ellas la historia y la economía. Quizá sea más conocido por el desarrollo de estándares para estudiar y escribir sobre historia, mismos que explicó en su obra maestra, el *Muqaddimah.* También introdujo o refinó muchos conceptos económicos relacionados con el trabajo, las ganancias, la oferta y la demanda, el uso de los recursos y la producción.

Ibn Rushd > Ibn Rushd Ibn Rushd (1128–1198), también llamado Averroes, fue un filósofo y científico que vivió en Córdoba e influyó en el pensamiento europeo. Como filósofo, puso una variedad de temas bajo el escrutinio de la razón y el análisis y argumentó que los seres humanos estaban parcial, pero no completamente, controlados por el destino. En el campo de la ciencia, Ibn Rushd contribuyó al estudio de las enfermedades.

Ibn Sina > Ibn Sina Ibn Sina (980–1037), también llamado Avicena, fue un médico persa que escribió el *Canon de Medicina,* que se enfocaba en prácticas médicas antiguas de todo el mundo conocido así como en sus propios procedimientos. Esta obra presenta descripciones de anatomía, síntomas de enfermedades, medicinas y curas. Ibn Sina también escribió sobre una variedad de otros temas, entre ellos filosofía, matemáticas y astronomía.

icon > ícono Imagen sagrada de Cristo, la Virgen María o de un santo venerado por la Iglesia ortodoxa oriental.

ideology > ideología Sistema de pensamiento y creencias.

Ignatius of Loyola > Ignacio de Loyola Ignacio de Loyola (1491–1556) pasó de una temprana carrera de soldado noble español a teólogo y participante influyente en la Reforma Católica. Mientras se recuperaba de una herida en una pierna, Ignacio leyó un libro sobre la vida de los santos y decidió que servir a Dios era una hidalguía santa. Desde ese momento hasta su muerte, Ignacio estudió, rezó y realizó trabajo misionero como fundador de la Sociedad de Jesús, una orden de hombres religiosos que fue conocida como los jesuitas.

illumination > iluminación Decoración artística de libros y manuscritos.

immunity > inmunidad Resistencia, como la facultad de evitar ser afectado por una enfermedad.

imperialism > imperialismo Dominio político, militar y económico de naciones poderosas sobre territorios más débiles.

import substitution > sustitución de importaciones Producción local de bienes para reemplazar su importación.

impressionism > impresionismo Escuela de pintura de finales del siglo XIX y principios del siglo XX que trataba de captar impresiones visuales fugaces.

indemnity > indemnización Compensación como pago por pérdidas de guerra.

indigenous > Indígena Originario o nativo de un país o región.

indigenous peoples > pueblos indígenas Término generalmente usado para describir a los descendientes de los primeros habitantes de una región.

Indra > Indra En la antigua India, dios de la guerra, la deidad principal.

indulgence > indulgencia Perdón por los pecados cometidos en vida concedido por la Iglesia católica romana.

Industrial Revolution > Revolución Industrial Periodo que comienza en el siglo XVIII en el cual la producción pasó de utilizar sencillas herramientas manuales a máquinas complejas, y las fuentes de energía cambiaron de usar energía humana y animal a vapor y, más tarde, electricidad.

inflation > inflación Ciclo económico caracterizado por una rápida subida de los precios ligada a un aumento rápido del dinero disponible.

Innocent III, Pope > Inocencio III, papa El papa Inocencio III (c. 1160–1216) tenía solo 37 años cuando fue nombrado papa y rápidamente extendió la autoridad del papado sobre Roma e Italia. Cuando el rey Juan de Inglaterra nombró al arzobispo de Canterbury sin la aprobación de Inocencio, el Papa le excomulgó.

Inquisition > Inquisición Tribunal de la Iglesia establecido para juzgar a la gente acusada de herejía.

insurgent > insurgente Rebelde

intendant > intendente Funcionario nombrado por el rey francés Luis XVI para gobernar las provincias, recaudar impuestos y reclutar soldados.

interchangeable parts > repuestos intercambiables Componentes idénticos que pueden usarse unos en lugar de otros en el proceso de producción.

interdependence > interdependencia Dependencia mutua de los países con los de otras partes del mundo en cuanto a productos, recursos, mano de obra y conocimientos.

interdict > interdicto En la Iglesia católica romana, excomunión de una región, pueblo o reino.

International Space Station (ISS) > Estación Espacial Internacional Estructura artificial construida y mantenida por una coalición de naciones con el fin de llevar a cabo investigaciones.

Internet > Internet Inmensa red internacional de computadoras que une a millones de usuarios en todo el mundo.

internment > campo de internamiento Confinamiento durante tiempos de guerra.

Inti > Inti Dios sol inca.

intifada > intifada Levantamiento de árabes palestinos en contra de Israel.

Iroquois League > Liga Iroquesa Alianza política de cinco grupos iroqueses, conocida como las Cinco Naciones, de finales del siglo XVI.

Isfahan > Isfahan Capital del Imperio Safávida durante el siglo XVII, situada en el actual Irán.

Isis > Isis Isis es la diosa egipcia adorada como la madre y esposa ideal. Es conocida como la protectora de los muertos y diosa de los niños. Por lo general se la representa como una mujer que viste un tocado en forma de trono.

Islamic State in Iraq and Syria (ISIS) > Estado Islámico de Irak y Siria (ISIS) Por sus siglas en inglés) organización terrorista islamista.

Islamist > islamista Persona que desea que las políticas del gobierno tengan su fundamento en las enseñanzas del islam.

island-hopping > salto entre islas Estrategia durante la Segunda Guerra Mundial que involucraba apoderarse de islas selectas que mantenía Japón en el Pacífico a la vez que se evitaban otras.

Istanbul > Estambul Nombre usado comunmente para referirse a la capital del Imperio Otomano, la ciudad también se conoció como Constantinopla (lo cual comenzó cuando era el centro del Imperio Romano oriental) y Bizancio (cuando fue la capital del Imperio Bizantino).

Ivan the Great > Iván el Grande Iván el Grande (1462–1505) fue uno de los gobernantes rusos más poderosos. Consolidó su poder al ganar la lealtad voluntaria de los príncipes rusos e impedir más invasiones mongolas.

Ivan the Terrible > Iván el Terrible Iván el Terrible (1530–1584) fue el nieto de Iván el Grande. Siguió centralizando el poder en sus manos, desarrollando un grupo secreto brutal que atrerrorizaba a los miembros de la nobleza hereditaria, o boyardos. Su locura contribuyó a su nombre "el Terrible".

J

Jacobin > jacobino Miembro de un club político radical durante la Revolución Francesa.

Jahan, Nur > Jahan, Nur Nur Jahan (1577–1645) fue una viuda persa con un hijo pequeño. Jahan se convirtió en la poderosa esposa del emperador mogol Jahangir. Sus habilidades administrativas, políticas, económicas y culturales impresionaron tanto a Jahangir que ella tuvo prácticamente el control sobre el imperio hasta su muerte en 1627. Dado que no se permitía a las mujeres interactuar cara a cara con los hombres en la corte, Nur Jahan dependía de que hombres confiables actuaran en su nombre.

Jahan, Shah > Jahan, sah El sah Jahan (1592–1666) fue el tercer hijo del emperador mogol, Jahangir. Con el apoyo de los nobles de la corte, ganó la sucesión y se convirtió en emperador tras la muerte de Jahangir. Gobernante tolerante y eficaz, el sah Jahan fue también un constructor entusiasta, participando personalmente en cada detalle del proceso de construcción. Cuado su amada esposa Mumtaz Mahal murió, construyó en su honor el famoso mausoleo llamado Taj Mahal.

James I > Jacobo I Jacobo I (1566–1625) fue rey de Escocia que también llegó a ser rey de Inglaterra e Irlanda. Creía profundamente en el derecho divino de los reyes a gobernar sobre todos sus súbditos sin interferencia de nadie. Sus puntos de vista discrepaban con los del Parlamento, lo que llevó a conflictos constantes. También fue el autor de la versión de la Biblia del rey Jacobo.

janizary > jenízaro Miembro de la élite del ejército otomano.

jati > jati En India, grupo ocupacional, parte del sistema de castas.

Jefferson, Thomas > Jefferson, Thomas Thomas Jefferson (1743–1826) es conocido principalmente como el autor principal de la Declaración de Independencia. También sirvió como ministro ante Francia y más tarde como el tercer Presidente de los Estados Unidos.

Jericho > Jericó La primera aldea del mundo, establecida en la actual Cisjordania entre los años 10,000 y 9000 a. C.

Jerusalem > Jerusalén Capital del estado judío de Judea en la antigüedad, y capital del actual estado de Israel; ciudad sagrada para los judíos, musulmanes y cristianos.

Jesus > Jesús (c. 4 a. C.–30 d. C.) Fue el fundador del cristianismo. Es considerado por la mayoría de los cristianos como el hijo de Dios. Criado en una familia judía, comenzó a predicar un mensaje de salvación y vida eterna. Fue condenado a muerte bajo la ley romana. Según los evangelios, resucitó de entre los muertos. En la actualidad, es venerado como un salvador por los cristianos de todo el mundo.

Jiang Jieshi > Chiang Kai-chek Chiang Kai-chek (1887–1975) nació en el seno de una familia comerciante en el este de China. Junto con Sun Yixian, formó el Partido Nacionalista, o Guomindang; después de la muerte de Sun en 1925, Chiang tomó el control. Después de años de batallas, Chiang unió fuerzas con los comunistas en contra de los invasores japoneses. Chiang también lideró el ejército chino para ayudar a los Aliados a derrotar a Japón en la Segunda Guerra Mundial. Finalmente, los comunistas volvieron a luchar para recuperar el control y Chiang huyó a la isla de Taiwán, la cual gobernó hasta su muerte en 1975.

Jinnah, Muhammad Ali > Jinnah, Muhammad Ali Muhammad Ali Jinnah (1876–1948) fue un político indio musulmán y líder de la Liga Musulmana, que fue fundada en 1906 para proteger los intereses musulmanes en India. Al prinicpio la Liga trabajó de cerca con el Partido del Congreso Indio pero más tarde se separó del Congreso cuando Jinnah y otros musulmanes comenzaron a cabildear a favor de su propio estado. Jinnah ayudó a fundar Pakistán en 1947 y fue su primer gobernador general.

Johanson, Donald > Johanson, Donald Nacido en 1942, el antropólogo Donald Johanson encontró los restos más importantes de uno de los primeros seres humanos de la historia, el esqueleto de una mujer a la que él llamó "Lucy". Después de estudiar sus huesos, Johanson concluyó que Lucy caminaba erguida y que medía aproximadamente 4 pies de altura.

John, King > Juan, rey El rey Juan (alrededor de 1166–1216) fue hijo del rey Enrique II. Se hizo del control del trono de Inglaterra cuando su hermano, el rey Ricardo Corazón de León, fue capturado mientras estaba en una cruzada. Los conflictos con los nobles ingleses hicieron que se viera obligado a firmar la Carta Magna en 1215, que limitaba el poder de los reyes ingleses.

joint family > familia extensa Organización familiar en la cual conviven diferentes generaciones en una misma vivienda.

Joseph II > José II José II (1741–1790) gobernó como emperador del Sacro Imperio Romano en Austria y es considerado el más radical de los déspotas ilustrados. Siguió muchas de las reformas de modernización gubernamental introducidas por su madre, María Teresa, con el objetivo de alcanzar el mismo trato para todos sus súbditos. Abolió la servidumbre y fomentó la libertad de prensa. Lo más destacado es que José apoyó la igualdad religiosa para los protestantes e incluso los judíos. También es recordado por viajar entre sus súbditos disfrazado para conocer los problemas cotidianos de los campesinos.

journeyman > oficial trabajor Empleado asalariado por el maestro del gremio.

Juárez, Benito > Juárez, Benito Benito Juárez (1806–1872) fue un abogado y político mexicano. Proveniente de una familia de herencia indígena zapoteca y campesina, apoyó las reformas para ayudar a los oprimidos de México. Ayudó a comenzar el movimiento de la Reforma y fue nombrado presidente de México en 1861. Murió en el cargo, pero sus reformas ayudaron a unir a México y a introducir a los mestizos en la política.

jury > jurado Grupo de ciudadanos con autoridad para emitir un veredicto final en un tribunal.

Justinian > Justiniano Justiniano (483–565) nació de linaje campesino y fue adoptado por su tío Justino (emperador desde 518). Como emperador bizantino de 527 a 565, Justiniano siguió la guerra contra Persia y buscó recuperar las provincias romanas occidentales de los invasores bárbaros. Después de disturbios y de un importante incendio en el año 532, reconstruyó gran parte de Constantinopla con un estilo majestuoso. También instituyó reformas para detener la corrupción imperial y promover la justicia para sus súbditos. Su logro más influyente es el Código Justiniano, una recopilación, organización y revisión de las leyes romanas.

Justinian's Code > Código de Justiniano Recopilación de leyes romanas organizada por el emperador bizantino Justiniano y que luego sirvió como modelo para la iglesia católica y los monarcas medievales.

K

Kaaba > Kaaba El templo más sagrado del islam, ubicado en La Meca.

kaiser > káiser Emperador de Alemania.

kamikaze > kamikaze Piloto japonés que tomaba misiones suicidas.

kana > kana En el sistema japonés de escritura, símbolos fonéticos que representan sílabas.

Karl Marx > Marx, Karl Karl Marx (1818–1883) fue un pensador político alemán cuyas ideas llegaron a ser la base del comunismo. Marx estudió para abogado y más tarde estudió filosofía, con planes para entrar en el mundo académico. Sin embargo, sus ideas radicales le dejaron con pocas posibilidades, así que se dedicó a escribir. Su obra más famosa fue el *Manifiesto Comunista,* el cual criticaba el capitalismo y predecía que los trabajadores alineados se levantarían para derrotar a la burguesía. En la década de 1860, Marx fue un miembro influyente de la Asociación Internacional de Hombres Trabajadores.

karma > karma Según la creencia hindú, todas las acciones que afectan el destino de una persona en la próxima vida.

Kashmir > Cachemira Antiguo estado principesco de los Himalayas, reclamado tanto por India como Pakistán, y por cuyo control han librado varias guerras.

Katanga > Katanga Provincia de la República Democrática del Congo con ricos depósitos de cobre y diamantes, que intentó independizarse del Congo en 1960.

Kellogg-Briand Pact > Pacto de Kellogg-Briand Acuerdo internacional firmado por casi todas las naciones en 1928 para erradicar el uso de la guerra como un método de política nacional.

Kennedy, John F. > Kennedy, John F. John F. Kennedy (1917–1963) fue presidente de los Estados Unidos de 1961 a 1963. Comandante naval condecorado en la Segunda Guerra Mudial, fue electo presidente a los 42 años de edad. Fue presidente durante la revolución comunista en Cuba y la crisis de los misiles de Cuba y aumentó la participación de los Estados Unidos en Vietnam. En el frente doméstico, la administración de Kennedy comenzó el esfuerzo federal por hacer cumplir los derechos civiles en el Sur. Fue asesinado el 22 de noviembre de 1963 por Lee Harvey Oswald.

Kenyatta, Jomo > Kenyatta, Jomo Jomo Kenyatta (1894–1978) fue un nacionalista y líder de la lucha de independencia keniana de Gran Bretaña. En 1963, se convirtió en el primer ministro del país, y en 1964, en el primer presidente del país, cargo que ocupó hasta su muerte.

Kepler, Johannes > Kepler, Johannes Johannes Kepler (1571–1630) fue un astrónomo alemán cuyos descubrimientos ampliaron la idea del universo heliocéntrico descrita por Copérnico. La investigación de Kepler mostró que los planetas se mueven en una órbita particular alrededor del Sol. Sus logros incluyeron una descripción correcta de cómo ocurre la visión, así como la forma en que un telescopio usa la luz.

Khan, Reza > Khan, Reza Reza Khan (1878–1944) se unió de joven al ejército iraní. Después de liderar el golpe de estado de 1921, Khan fue ministro de guerra y luego primer ministro. Cuatro años más tarde, fue electo sah y siguió reformando radicalmente el gobierno y la nación. A principios de la Segunda Guerra Mudial, la Unión Soviética y Gran Bretaña ocuparon Irán. Khan abdicó y su hijo fue designado sah. Los ingleses exiliaron a Khan a Mauricio y luego a Johannesburgo, donde murió.

Khayyám, Omar > Khayyám, Omar Omar Khayyám (1048–1131) es más conocido hoy en día como un poeta que creó muchos rubáiyáts, o cuartetos. En sus días, fue elogiado por su experiencia en muchas áreas. Como matemático, contribuyó al desarrollo del álgebra. Como astrónomo, estudió cuidadosamente el cielo para ayudar a mejorar el calendario musulmán. El erudito persa también examinó los temas relacionados con la ley, la fillosofía y la historia.

Khmer Rouge > Jemeres Rojos Movimiento político y fuerza guerrillera comunista de Camboya que llegó al poder en ese país en 1975.

Khomeini, Ruhollah > Jomeini, Ruhollah Ruhollah Jomeini (1902–1989) fue un clérigo musulmán chiíta (ayatolá) que lideró en 1979 la Revolución Islámica en Irán, la cual derrocó al sah (Mohammed Reza). Fue el mayor líder político y religioso hasta su muerte 10 años más tarde.

Khrushchev, Nikita > Jruschov, Níkita Níkita Jruschov (1894–1971) sirvió en el Ejército Rojo durante la Segunda Guerra Mundial como teniente general y después fue funcionario del Partido Comunista oficial de Ucrania. Llegó a formar parte del liderazgo del partido central en 1947 y se destacó después de la muerte de Stalin en 1953. Como líder de la Unión Soviética de 1955 a 1964, introdujo reformas domésticas que hicieron menos difícil la vida en la Unión Soviética, pero aplastó las rebeliones en Europa oriental. Fue el líder soviético durante la crisis de los misiles de Cuba.

kibbutz > kibbutz En Israel, granja comunitaria.

Kiev > Kiev Capital de la Rusia medieval y de la actual Ucrania.

Kim Il Sung > Kim Il Sung Kim Il Sung (1912–1994) gobernó la República Popular Democrática de Corea (Corea del Norte) desde 1949 hasta su muerte en 1994. Apoyado por la Unión Soviética durante la Guerra Fría, Kim estableció un estado totalitario con presupuestos enormes para el ejército y prácticamente ninguna libertad política. En 1993, declaró que Corea del Norte se retiraría del Tratado de No Proliferación Nuclear.

King, Jr., Dr. Martin Luther > King, Jr., Dr. Martin Luther Dr. Martin Luther King, Jr. (1929–1968) fue un ministro y líder de los derechos civiles estadounidense. Se destacó a nivel nacional con su liderazgo al boicot al autobús de Montgomery, Alabama, en 1955. King ayudó a organizar la marcha masiva a Washington en 1963, donde dio su famoso discurso "Yo tengo un sueño". Fue asesinado el 14 de abril de 1968.

kiva > kiva Gran habitación subterránea que los anasazi usaban para ceremonias religiosas y reuniones políticas.

Klerk, F.W. de > Klerk, F.W. de F.W. de Klerk (1936–) fue miembro del Partido Nacional y el último presidente de Sudáfrica bajo el apartheid. Junto con Nelson Mandela, negoció la transición del poder de la minoría blanca al gobierno de la mayoría, por lo cual él y Mandela ganaron el Premio Nobel de la Paz en 1993.

knight > caballero Noble europeo que servía como guerrero montado.

Knossos > Cnosos Antigua ciudad de la isla de Creta, centro principal de la civilización minoica que dominó el mar Egeo aproximadamente entre los años 1600 a. C. y 1400 a. C. Las excavaciones que comenzaron en 1900 descubrieron un palacio y edificios aledaños de una cultura sofisticada.

Koch, Robert > Koch, Robert Robert Koch (1843–1910) fue un médico alemán y uno de los fundadores de la bacteriología, o el estudio de las bacterias. Koch descubrió las bacterias responsables de la tuberculosis y el cólera y determinó el ciclo de la enfermedad del ántrax. También mejoró métodos para estudiar las bacterias, entre ellos el cultivo de cepas puras y el teñido de las bacterias para hacerlas más visibles e identificables. En 1905 recibió el Premio Nobel de Fisiología o Medicina.

Kolkata > Calcuta Ciudad grande de India.

Koryo dynasty > dinastía Koryo Dinastía coreana que gobernó desde 935 a 1392.

Kossuth, Louis > Kossuth, Louis Louis Kossuth (1802–1894) fue un abogado, periodista, político y gobernante húngaro durante la revolución de 1848–89.

Kublai Khan > Kublai Khan Kublai Khan (1215–1294) fue nieto de Gengis Kan y fundó la dinastía Yuan, conquistó la dinastía Song del sur para completar el control absoluto de los mongoles en China, y demostró ser un gobernante fuerte e inteligente del vasto imperio. Guiado por consejeros chinos confucionistas, llevó a cabo reformas en sus territorios y reunificó políticamente a China, pero también participó en una serie de costosas e infructuosas guerras con los reinos vecinos. Por lo general, no cambió la vida china y, aunque religioso, fue conocido por aceptar diversas prácticas religiosas y por otorgar privilegios económicos a las sectas preferidas.

kulak > kulak Campesino adinerado de la Unión Soviética a finales de la década de 1930.

Kulturkampf > Kulturkampf "Batalla por la civilización" de Bismarck, cuyo objetivo era que los católicos pusieran la lealtad al estado por encima de la lealtad a la Iglesia.

L

L'Ouverture, Toussaint > L'Ouverture, Toussaint (1743-1803) Nació en Haiti, hijo de una persona en condición de esclavitud pero con educación. Dirigió un ejército de personas esclavizadas, que entrenó en la guerra de guerrillas, en una revuelta en contra de los colonos franceses. El ejército francés lo capturó en 1802 y murió en prisión un año después.

La Reforma > La Reforma Era de reforma liberal en México de 1855 a 1876.

labor union > sindicato Organización de trabajadores que negocian por mejores pagas y condiciones de trabajo.

Lafayette, Marquis de > Lafayette, marqués de El marqués de Lafayette (1757–1834), un noble francés, luchó en las Américas en la Guerra de Independencia. Tras su regreso a Francia, Lafayette dirigió la petición de reforma en 1789 y presentó un boceto de la Declaración de los Derechos del Hombre a la Asamblea Nacional. Odiado por algunos debido a su actitud moderada, huyó a Austria, pero regresó después.

laissez faire > *laissez faire* Política que permite a los negocios y empresas operar con poca o ninguna interferencia del gobierno.

Lalibela > Lalibela Gobernante de Etiopía que llegó al poder en el siglo XIII. Construyó once iglesias cristianas excavadas desde el nivel del suelo en la roca sólida de las montañas.

land reform > reforma agraria División de grandes propiedades dedicadas a la agricultura para distribuirlas entre los campesinos.

Laozi > Laozi (o Lao Tsé) Laozi significa "Maestro Lao" o "Viejo Maestro" en el idioma chino. Ya un hombre anciano cuando Confucio era un joven erudito, Laozi nació en una pequeña aldea en la antigua China. Fue nombrado historiador en una de las cortes de la dinastía Zhou. Laozi desarrolló una fiolosofía de calma interna, pureza de mente y vida en armonía con la naturaleza que se llama Dao (o Tao), o el camino del universo. Su libro, *El camino de la vida,* tuvo una enorme influencia en la vida china.

Las Casas, Bartolomé de > Las Casas, Bartolomé de Bartolomé de Las Casas (c. 1474–17 de julio de 1566) fue un sacerdote e historiador dominico, famoso por ser uno de los primeros defensores de los derechos humanos en las Américas. Al conocer los males que sufrían los indígenas americanos bajo el sistema de encomiendas, sus vívidos informes sobre los abusos ayudaron en 1542 a la aprobación de leyes que prohibieron la esclavitud y el maltrato. Pasó el resto de su vida luchando por los derechos de los pueblos de las Américas.

laser > láser Haz luminoso de alta energía que puede ser usado para muchos fines, entre ellos la cirugía, la ingeniería y la investigación científica.

latifundia > latifundio Grandes propiedades adquiridas por los ciudadanos romanos que se habían vuelto ricos recientemente.

Lawrence, T. E. > Lawrence, T.E. Thomas Edward Lawrence, (1888–1935), también conocido como Lawrence de Arabia, fue un arqueólogo inglés, escritor y experto en Arabia que ayudó a dirigir una rebelión árabe y una guerrilla en contra de los turcos otomanos durante la Primera Guerra Mundial. En 1926, publicó una memoria de sus actividades en esos años, *Los siete pilares de la sabiduría.*

lay investiture > investidura Nombramiento de obispos por cualquiera que no sea miembro del clero.

Leakey, Louis > Leakey, Louis (1903–1972) Como arqueólogo, Louis Leakey y su esposa, Mary, buscaron los restos de los primeros seres humanos en el este de África, encontrando muchas herramientas y huesos que aumentaron nuestros conocimientos sobre los primeros seres humanos.

Leakey, Mary > Leakey, Mary (1913–1996) Nacida en Londres, Inglaterra, Mary Leakey viajó por Europa visitando numerosos sitios prehistóricos, lo cual aumentó su interés por la arqueología y la geología. En 1936, se casó con Louis Leakey y pasaron 30 años cavando en busca de los primeros seres humanos en el este de África. Finalmente Mary Leakey encontró muchos restos que han aumentado nuestros conocimientos sobre los primeros homínidos.

legion > legión Unidad militar básica del ejército romano que incluía aproximadamente 5,000 soldados.

legislature > cuerpo legislativo Organismo que hace o establece leyes.

legitimacy > legitimidad Principio por el que las monarquías que habían sido derrocadas por la Revolución Francesa o por Napoleón fueron restituidas.

Lend-Lease Act > Ley de Préstamo y Arriendo Decreto aprobado por el Congreso de los Estados Unidos en 1941 que permitió al presidente (FDR) vender o arrendar materiales de guerra a cualquier país cuya defensa fuese considerada de vital importancia para los Estados Unidos.

Lenin, V. I. > Lenin, V.I. V. I. Lenin (1870–1924) fue un revolucionario comunista ruso que llevó a los bolcheviques a la victoria en la Revolución de Octubre rusa. Fue jefe de gobierno de la Unión Soviética de 1922 hasta su muerte en 1924. Adaptó las ideas de Karl Marx para crear un tipo de comunismo conocido como marxismo-leninismo.

Leopold II > Leopoldo II Leopoldo II (1835–1909) fue el rey de Bélgica que lideró los primeros esfuerzos de Occidente para desarrollar y controlar la cuenca del Congo. Gobernó personalmente sobre el Estado Libre del Congo, el cual llegó a formar parte de Bélgica en 1908.

levée > recepción matutina Ritual de la mañana en el que los nobles esperaban al rey Luis XIV.

libel > difamación Publicación de declaraciones falsas y perjudiciales.

liberation theology > teología de la liberación Movimiento dentro de la Iglesia católica que urgía a la iglesia a liderar un llamamiento a favor de la reforma, la justicia social y el fin de la pobreza.

Liliuokalani > Liliuokalani Liliuokalani, nacida Lydia Kamakaeha (1838–1917), fue la última soberana hawaiana antes de que se anexaran las islas a los Estados Unidos en 1898. Durante el reinado de su hermano, la princesa Liliuokalani desempeñó un papel activo en el gobierno de Hawái, mejorando la educación y recibiendo a dignatarios extranjeros. Después de la muerte de su hermano, heredó el trono y se convirtió en la primera reina de Hawái. En 1893, plantadores estadounidenses, liderados por Sanford Dole, la derrocaron.

limited monarchy > monarquía limitada Gobierno en el que la constitución o el cuerpo legislativo limitan los poderes de la monarquía.

Line of Demarcation > Línea de demarcación Línea establecida por el Tratado de Tordesillas que dividía el mundo fuera de Europa en dos zonas: una controlada por España y otra por Portugal.

lineage > linaje Grupo que reivindica un antepasado en común.

Lister, Joseph > Lister, Joseph Joseph Lister (1827–1912) fue un cirujano escocés que amplió el conocimiento médico al reconocer que la falta de limpieza en los hospitales estaba directamente relacionada con las muertes ocurridas después de las cirugías. Al estudiar las obras de otros científicos, se convenció de que los microorganismos del aire entraban en el cuerpo por las heridas abiertas y provocaban infecciones que a menudo llevaban a la muerte después de la cirugía. Comenzó a usar ácido carbólico para limpiar las heridas de los pacientes. También empezó a usar un líquido antiséptico para tratar los vendajes y más tarde desarrolló técnicas para limpiar los instrumentos quirúrgicos y mantener las heridas limpias durante las cirugías. Es conocido como el "padre de la cirugía antiséptica".

literacy > alfabetismo Conocimiento básico de la lectura y la escritura.

literacy rate > tasa de alfabetización Porcentaje de personas que pueden leer y escribir.

Liverpool > Liverpool Ciudad industrial y uno de los puertos más grandes de Inglaterra que fue parte de la línea principal de ferrocarril; unió Liverpool con Manchester en 1830.

Livingstone, David > Livingstone, David David Livingstone (1813–1873) fue un misionero y explorador escocés que influyó en las posturas occidentales hacia África.

Locke, John > Locke, John John Locke (1632–1704) creció durante la tumultuosa época de las Guerras Civiles inglesas. Prolífico escritor sobre filosofía política, las obras de Locke influyeron fuertemente en la Constitución de los Estados Unidos y el desarrollo del gobierno estadounidense. Locke proponía que las personas nacían con ciertos derechos naturales que no podían serles arrebatados, entre ellos la vida, la libertad y la propiedad. Sus ideas radicales sobre la responsabilidad del gobierno para con el pueblo fueron fundamentales para los líderes de la Guerra de Independencia.

loess > loes Fina arena amarilla que transporta el viento.

logic > lógica Pensamiento racional.

Long March > Larga Marcha Marcha épica en la que un grupo de comunistas chinos marcharon en retirada de las fuerzas del Guomindang por más de 6,000 millas.

longbow > arco largo Arco de seis pies de largo que podía disparar rápidamente flechas con suficiente fuerza como para agujerear una armadura.

Louis IX > Luis IX Luis IX (1214–1270) fue rey de Francia de 1226 a 1270. Fue uno de los reyes más populares de Francia. Dirigió la Séptima Cruzada a Tierra Santa y fue canonizado como santo en reconocimiento a su fe y servicios a la Iglesia.

Louis Philippe > Luis Felipe Luis Felipe (1773–1850) fue rey de Francia de 1830 a 1848. Fue conocido como el "rey ciudadano" porque el pueblo le puso en el trono. Finalmente perdió el poder porque no apoyó a las clases trabajadoras.

Louis XIV > Luis XIV Luis XIV (1638–1715) fue rey de Francia (1643–1715) y es considerado el símbolo de la monarquía absoluta.

Louis XVI > Luis XVI Louis XVI (1754–1793) fue rey de la Francia prerrevolucionaria. No logró apoyar a sus ministros, quienes trataron de reformar las finanzas y las instituciones sociales de Francia. En 1789, aunque estuvo de acuerdo en convocar los Estados Generales, se resistió a las demandas de reforma de la Asamblea Nacional. Más tarde fue acusado de traidor y ejecutado en 1793.

Louisiana Purchase > Compra de Luisiana Territorio comprado por Thomas Jefferson a Francia en 1803.

Luftwaffe > Luftwaffe Fuerza aérea alemana.

Lusitania > Lusitania Trasatlántico británico hundido por un submarino alemán en mayo de 1915.

Luther, Martin > Lutero, Martín Martín Lutero (1483–1546) fue un monje y teólogo alemán que fue el catalizador de la Reforma Protestante. Formado como abogado, se unió a una orden estricta de monjes católicos romanos y estudió teología. Buscando reformar los abusos dentro de la Iglesia, Lutero desafió las enseñanzas de la Iglesia con sus 95 tesis. Esto se llevó a la excomunión y al desarrollo del luteranismo, la primera de varias sectas protestantes.

M

Maathai, Wangari > Maathai, Wangari Wangari Maathai (1940–2011) fue la fundadora del Movimiento del Cinturón Verde así como una activista de los derechos humanos, prevención del SIDA y derechos de las mujeres. Fue electa para la Asamblea Nacional de Kenya en 2002 y ganó el Premio Nobel de la Paz en 2004.

Macao > Macao Región al sudeste de China formada por una península y dos islas; la dinastía Ming permitió a los portugueses instalar un puesto comercial aquí.

MacArthur, Douglas > MacArthur, Douglas Douglas MacArthur (1880–1964) dirigió los ataques aliados en el sureste del Pacífico. También comandó las tropas en la Primera Guerra Mundial y en la Guerra de Corea. Fue general y jefe del ejército durante la Depresión.

Macartney, Lord > Macartney, Lord Lord Macartney (1737–1806) nacido en una familia escocesa-irlandesa en Irlanda, fue miembro del Parlamento británico, secretario en jefe de Irlanda y gobernador de varias colonias británicas. El rey Jorge III le envió a una misión que no tuvo éxito para convencer al emperador Qianlong de China para que permitiera a los comerciantes británicos operar en las ciudades portuarias del norte. Más tarde fue gobernador de la colonia del Cabo de Buena Esperanza.

Machiavelli, Niccoló > Maquiavelo, Nicolás Maquiavelo (1469–1527) nació en Florencia. Fue un filósofo político, estadista y escritor. Su obra más famosa fue una guía para los gobernantes sobre cómo ganar y mantener el poder. *El príncipe* era realista sobre el poder político. Maquiavelo argumentaba que en la política el fin justifica los medios. El término "maquiavélico" todavía se usa actualmente para describir políticas engañosas.

Madison, James > Madison, James James Madison (1751–1836) fue un renombrado estadista estadounidense y cuarto Presidente de los Estados Unidos. A menudo se le llama el "padre de la Constitución" por el papel destacado que desempeñó en la Convención Constitucional de 1789, que dio el marco de la Constitución federal.

Magellan, Ferdinand > Magallanes, Fernando de Fernando de Magallanes (1480–1521) fue un navegante y explorador portugués que de joven fue en expediciones portuguesas a India y África, y más tarde obtuvo el apoyo de España para su expedición de septiembre de 1519 de navegar hacia el oeste para llegar a las Molucas. Comenzó con cinco barcos y una tripulación de 270 hombres; en la larga travesía por aguas desconocidas se enfrentó a aguas revueltas, el escorbuto, hambre y a un motín. Magallanes fue asesinado en 1521 durante una batalla en lo que hoy es Filipinas, y solo uno de sus barcos, llevando especias y 18 hombres de la tripulación original, circunnavegó el globo y regresó por fin a España en septiembre de 1522.

Maginot Line > Línea Maginot Grandes fortificaciones construidas por los franceses a lo largo de su frontera con Alemania en la década de 1930 para protegerse contra invasiones.

Magna Carta > Carta Magna Carta constitucional aprobada por el rey Juan de Inglaterra en 1215; limitó el poder del rey y estableció ciertos derechos a los ciudadanos ingleses.

Magyars > magiares Grupo étnico establecido en la actual Hungría.

Mahdi > Mahdi Salvador musulmán de la fe.

maize > mais Maíz.

Malacca > estrecho de Malaca Uno de los primeros centros de comercio de especias; tomado por los portugueses en 1511.

Mali > Malí Imperio comercial medieval de África occidental ubicado en el actual Malí.

Malinche > Malinche Malinche (alrededor de 1501–1550) fue una joven indígena, llamada Doña Marina por los españoles, que hablaba maya y azteca, aprendió español y fue la intérprete y consejera de Cortés durante su conquista de México. Malinche se convirtió al cristianismo y se casó después con uno de los soldados de Cortés; visitó España donde disfrutó de una cálida recepción en la corte española.

Malindi > Malindi Pueblo costero de África oriental y eje del comercio internacional; fue atacado en el siglo XV por los exploradores portugueses para expulsar a los árabes que controlaban las rutas comerciales de África oriental, y luego tomar ellos mismos el control de esas rutas.

Malthus, Thomas > Malthus, Thomas Thomas Malthus (1766–1834) fue un economista británico. Nació en Surrey en una familia acomodada. Después de recibir su educación en casa, asistió a la universidad en Cambridge, donde obtuvo un título de maestro. Su obra más conocida es *Ensayo sobre el principio de la población.* En ella, argumentaba que el aumento de la población finalmente agotaría el suministro de alimentos, llevando a la pobreza. Fue catedrático de historia y economía política hasta su muerte.

Manchester > Manchester Ciudad industrial del norte de Inglaterra que fue parte de la primera línea de ferrocaril importante que unía Manchester con Liverpool.

Manchuria > Manchuria Provincia histórica en el noreste de China rica en recursos naturales.

Manchus > manchú Personas originalmente de Manchuria, al norte de China, que derrotaron a la dinastía Ming y gobernaron como la dinastía Chin desde mediados del siglo XVII hasta priinicipios del siglo XX.

mandate > mandato Territorio administrado por un poder occidental después de la Primera Guerra Mundial.

Mandela, Nelson > Mandela, Nelson Nelson Mandela (1918–2013) fue un líder del Congreso Nacional Africano y un luchador de la libertad durante la época del apartheid en Sudáfrica. Fue encarcelado durante 27 años y se convirtió en la antorcha de las manifestaciones que pedían el fin del apartheid. Fue liberado en 1990 y en 1994 se convirtió en el primer presidente negro de Sudáfrica, un cargo que ocupó durante solo un periodo. En 1993 ganó el Premio Nobel de la Paz junto con F.W. de Klerk.

Mandelstam, Osip > Osip, Mandelstam Osip Mandelstam (1891–1938?) creció en San Petersburgo, Rusia, en un hogar judío. Aunque es recordado como uno de los principales poetas rusos del siglo XX, la mayor parte de su trabajo quedó sin publicar durante su vida. Los comunistas le enviaron al exilio una seguda vez en 1938, y su esposa, Nadezhda Khazina, recibió su última comunicación unos meses más tarde. Nunca se volvió a saber de él, pero gracias a los incansables esfuerzos de su esposa, la mayor parte de la obra de Mandelstam fue salvada para las generaciones futuras.

Manhattan Project > Proyecto Manhattan Nombre en clave del proyecto para la fabricación de la primera bomba atómica durante la Segunda Guerra Mundial.

Manifest Destiny > Destino Manifiesto Idea estadounidense que establecía que los Estados Unidos debían expandirse a través de todo el norte del continente americano.

manor > feudo En la Europa medieval, estado de un señor que incluye una o más villas y las tierras aledañas.

manor system > feudo También llamado sistema feudal; sistema económico durante la Edad Media en Europa que se construía alrededor de grandes estados llamados feudos que incluían uno o más pueblos y sus terrenos adyacentes.

Mansa Musa > Mansa Musa Mansa Musa (murió alrededor del año 1337) fue un devoto gobernante islámico que llegó al trono en 1312 y expandió las fronteras de Malí hasta el océano Atlántico. Fue uno de los hombres más ricos de su época. Su famoso viaje a la Meca fue espléndido y dio a conocer al mundo las riquezas de Malí.

Mao Zedong > Mao Zedong Mao Zedong (1893–1976) nació en el centro de China en una familia campesina. Ayudó a formar el Partido Comunista Chino en 1921. Después de que Chiang Kai-chek lanzara sus "campañas de exterminación" en contra de los comunistas, Mao llevó su ejército a la épica Larga Marcha. Mao se unió brevemente con el Guomindang para suprimir la agresión japonesa, pero su asociación no duró después de que terminara la Segunda Guerra Mundial. La República Popular de China se estableció en 1949. Mao inició reformas drásticas, algunas de las cuales tuvieron consecuencias desastrosas. El uso del terror de Mao y la intolerancia a la oposición fueron notorios a nivel internacional.

Maori > maoríes Pueblo indígena de Nueva Zelanda.

March on Rome > marcha hacia Roma Marcha planeada por miles de simpatizantes fascistas sobre Roma para tomar su control; en respuesta a ella a Mussolini se le concedió el derecho legal del control de Italia.

Marconi, Guglielmo > Marconi, Guglielmo Guglielmo Marconi (1874–1937) fue un inventor italiano que recibió la primera patente de un sistema de telégrafos sin cable. En 1900, Marconi demostró que las ondas transmitidas sin cables no se veían afectadas por la forma de la Tierra cuando transmitió una señal inalámbrica por el océano Atlántico a una distancia de 2,100 millas. Siguió estudiando las ondas, lo cual resultó en un sistema de rayos para la comunicación de larga distancia, el primer radio de microondas y los principios del radar. Recibió muchos honores y premios, entre ellos el Premio Nobel de Física.

Marcos, Ferdinand > Marcos, Ferdinand Ferdinand Marcos (1917–1989) fue el líder autoritario de Filipinas de 1966 a 1986. Anteriormente abogado, Marcos ganó las elecciones presidenciales democráticas en Filipinas en 1965 y 1969. Su gobierno estaba cada vez más marcado por la corrupción y los incidentes de derechos humanos. En 1972, declaró la ley marcial y persiguió a sus opositores. Cuando Benigno Aquino, Jr., un político exiliado y crítico de Marcos fue asesinado, la mayoría de los filipinos apoyaron a su viuda, Corazón, en la elección presidencial de 1986. Después de perder, Marcos y su esposa se exiliaron en Hawái.

Maria Theresa > María Teresa María Teresa (1717–1780) fue archiduquesa de Austria y reina de Hungría y Bohemia (1740–1780), emperatriz y esposa del emperador del Sacro Imperio Romano Francisco I (1745–1765) y madre del emperador del Sacro Imperio Romano José II (1765–1790).

Marie Antoinette > María Antonieta Los modales, la conducta y los diversos escándalos de María Antonieta (1755–1793) ayudaron al descrédito de la monarquía. Dijo a su esposo, Luis XVI, que se resistiera a las demandas de la Asamblea Nacional. Al igual que Luis, fue acusada de traición y ejecutada.

Marseilles > Marsella Ciudad portuaria francesa; las tropas que marcharon al ritmo de una canción patriótica mientras abandonaban esta ciudad inspiraron que la canción posteriormente llegara a ser el himno nacional francés.

Marshall Plan > Plan Marshall Cuantioso paquete de ayuda que ofrecieron los Estados Unidos a los países de Europa occidental después de la Segunda Guerra Mundial.

Martel, Charles > Martel, Carlos Carlos Martel (688–741) sirvió como mayordomo de palacio (la persona que gobernaba en nombre del rey) para la zona oriental del reino franco desde el año 715 hasta el año 741. Hijo ilegítimo del mayordomo principal, Martel se fortaleció con el poder, y finalmente reunificó y gobernó todo el reino de los francos. Desde el año 711, los musulmanes saquearon las tierras francas y en el año 732 llegaron a Burdeos. Requerida para ayudar en la batalla de Tours ese año, la caballería de Carlos detuvo este gran avance musulmán en Europa.

martyr > mártir Persona que sufre o muere por sus creencias.

matrilineal > matrilineal Organización familiar en la que los lazos de parentesco se siguen a través de la madre.

Maurya, Chandragupta > Maurya, Chandragupta Chandragupta Maurya, que reinó aproximadamente desde el año 321 a. C. al año 297 a. C., fue el primer emperador maurya. Era hijo de un jefe maurya, y su familia quedó en la pobreza cuado su padre murió. Después de superar muchos retos, Chandragupta aprendió tácticas militares y finalmente formó un ejército lo suficientemente fuerte como para conquistar la mayor parte de India.

May Fourth Movement > Movimiento del Cuatro de Mayo Movimiento cultural en China que se centró en reformar China para fortalecerla.

means of production > medios de producción Granjas, fábricas, ferrocarriles y otros grandes negocios que producen y distribuyen mercancías.

Mecca > Meca Ciudad en el oeste de Arabia Saudita; lugar de nacimiento del profeta Mahoma, visto por los musulmanes como el profeta, y ciudad sagrada para los creyentes islámicos.

medieval > medieval Se refiere a la Edad Media en Europa, es decir, el período de la historia entre la edad antigua y la edad moderna.

Medina > Medina Ciudad en el oeste de Arabia Saudita; ciudad donde predicó Mahoma.

Meiji Restoration > restauración Meiji En Japón, reino del emperador Meiji desde 1868 a 1912 que fue marcado por la rápida modernización e industrialización.

Meir, Golda > Meir, Golda Golda Meir (1898–1978) fue fundadora y la primera mujer que ocupó el cargo de primer ministro de Israel (1969–1974). Fue miembro fundador del Partido Laborista de Israel y también fue ministra de asuntos exteriores (1956–1966).

Menelik II > Menelik II Menelik II (1844–1913) fue el emperador de Eitopía que expandió su imperio, modernizó su país y derrotó la invasión italiana de 1896.

mercantilism > mercantilismo Política por la que una nación trataba de exportar más de lo que importaba para aumentar sus reservas de oro y plata.

mercenaries > mercenarios Soldado que sirve en un ejército extranjero a cambio de dinero.

mercenary > mercenario Soldado que sirve en un ejército extranjero a cambio de dinero.

Meroë > Meroe Capital del antiguo reino de Nubia.

Mesa Verde > Mesa Verde El mayor complejo de viviendas anasazi construidas en acantilados en el sudeste de los Estados Unidos, entre alrededor de 1150 d. C. y 1300 d. C.

Mesoamerica > Mesoamérica Región de América del Norte, que incluye a México y América Central, en la cual se desarrollaron, antes de la llegada de los europeos al continente, civilizaciones con características en común.

Mesopotamia > Mesopotamia Región del Creciente Fértil que se encuentra entre los ríos Tigris y Éufrates.

messiah > mesías Rey ungido enviado por Dios.

mestizo > mestizo En las colonias españolas de América, descendiente de indígenas americanos y europeos.

métis > métis Pueblo de descendientes con mezcla de indígenas americanos y franceses canadienses.

Michelangelo > Miguel Ángel Miguel Ángel Buonarroti (1475–1564) fue un pintor italiano también conocido por sus esculturas, obras de ingeniería, arquitectura y poemas. Su famosa estatua de mármol, *David,* muestra la infuencia de las antiguas tradiciones griegas en los artistas del Renacimiento. Miguel Ángel pintó temas bíblicos en los murales del techo de la Capilla Sixtina en Roma. Como arquitecto diseñó el domo de la catedral de San Pedro en Roma, que después sería el modelo para el Capitolio de los Estados Unidos en Washington D. C.

middle class > clase media Grupo de personas, incluyendo mercaderes, comerciantes y artesanos, cuyo rango estaba entre los nobles y los campesinos.

Middle Passage > Travesía Intermedia El tramo de la ruta del comercio triangular en la cual los esclavos eran transportados desde África a las Américas.

militarism > militarismo Glorificación de lo militar.

militia > milicia Cuerpo organizado de voluntarios armados.

Milosevic, Slobodan > Milosevic, Slobodan Slobodan Milosevic (1941–2006) fue un líder del Partido Socialista serbio, cuyas políticas nacionalistas contribuyeron a la ruptura de la antigua Yugoslavia. Murió en La Haya, Países Bajos, mietras estaba en juicio en el Tribunal Criminal Internacional de la ONU para la Antigua Yugoslavia (ICTY) por su papel en el genocidio de los Balcanes.

minaret > minarete Torre esbelta de una mezquita desde la que se convoca a los musulmanes a la oración.

Ming dynasty > dinastía Ming Dinastía china en la que se restauró el gobierno chino; se mantuvo en el poder desde 1368 hasta 1644.

missionaries > misioneros Personas enviadas a hacer trabajo religioso en un territorio o país.

missionary > misionero Persona enviada para hacer trabajos religiosos en un territorio u otro país.

mixed economy > economía mixta Sistema económico que involucra una combinación de propiedad o control del gobierno y propiedad privada con las fuerzas del mercado.

mobilize > mobilizar Preparar las fuerzas militares para la guerra.

Mobutu Sese Seko > Mobutu Sese Seko Mobutu Sese Seko (1930–1997) recibió al nacer el nombre de Joseph Desire Mobutu. Cambió su nombre después de hacerse con el control de Congo en 1965 en un golpe de estado militar. También renombró al país como Zaire. Mobutu gobernó Zaire como dictador hasta que fue derrocado por Laurent Kabila en 1997. Murió de cáncer poco después.

Moche > moche Cultura que tuvo su apogeo en la región andina, desde alrededor de 400 a. C. a 600 d. C.

Moctezuma > Moctezuma Moctezuma (Moctezuma II, 1466–alrededor del 30 de junio de 1520) fue el último emperador azteca, que por error confudió al conquistador Cortés con el rey dios Quetzalcoatl. Fue derrotado por Cortés y obligado a renunciar a su tierra y sus tesoros. Fue hecho prisionero y asesinado cuando los aztecas trataron de expulsar a los españoles de Tenochtitlán.

Mohenjo-Daro > Mohenjo-Daro Antigua ciudad de la civilización del Indo, ubicada en el actual Pakistán.

moksha > moksha En la creencia hindú, objetivo final de la existencia, que es alcanzar la unión con el brahmán.

Moluccas > Molucas Grupo de islas en el este de la actual Indonesia, la cual fue llamada por los europeos la isla de las Especias en el s. XV por ser la fuente principal de especias.

Mombasa > Mombasa Ciudad costera establecida al este de África y centro del comercio internacional; fue atacada en el s. XV por exploradores portugueses para expulsar a los árabes que controlaban las rutas comerciales del este de África, con el fin de obtener el control de esas rutas.

monarchy > monarquía Gobierno en el que el poder reside en el rey o la reina.

Monet, Claude > Monet, Claude Claude Monet (1840–1926) fue una de las figuras más destacadas del movimiento impresionista francés. De forma muy similar a los románticos, los impresionistas se inspiraban en el exterior y rechazaban las tradiciones convencionales artísticas de Europa. Monet trató de crear una representación precisa de la naturaleza mediante su uso del color, los tonos, la textura y las pinceladas. A menudo pintaba el mismo objeto o escena en diferentes momentos del día para ver cómo la luz y la sombra cambiaban su apariencia. Dos de sus series más famosas son montones de grano y nenúfares.

money economy > economía monetaria Sistema económico en el que los bienes y servicios se pagan mediante el intercambio de una ficha que tiene un valor acordado.

Mongkut > Mongkut Mongkut (1804–1868) fue rey de Siam (hoy Tailandia) de 1851 a 1868. Mongkut vivió como un monje budista mientras su hermano mayor ocupaba el trono. Después de la muerte de su hermano, los muchos amigos influyentes de Mongkut le ayudaron a ser rey. El rey instruido era aficionado a las filosofías occidentales y trabajó para modernizar su reino. Después de su muerte, sus hijos, también instruidos, pudieron continuar sus avances.

monopoly > monopolio Control total de un producto o negocio por una persona o grupo.

monotheistic > monoteísta Que cree en un solo dios.

Monroe Doctrine > Doctrina Monroe Política estadounidense para desalentar la intervención europea en el hemisferio Occidental.

monsoon > monzón Viento estacional que sopla regularmente desde una dirección determinada durante parte del año.

Montesquieu > Montesquieu El barón de Montesquieu (1689–1755) nació como Charles Louis de Secondat en una famiia acaudalada y heredera del título de barón de Montesquieu de su tío. Al igual que muchos otros reformadores, no dejó que su estatus privilegiado le impidiera ser una voz de la democracia. Su primer libro, titulado *Cartas persas,* ridiculizaba al gobierno francés y las clases sociales. En su obra publicada en 1748, *El espíritu de las leyes,* avanzó la idea de la separación de poderes, la base de la democracia estadounidense moderna.

More, Sir Thomas > Moro, Tomás, sir Tomás Moro (1478–1535) nació en Londres. Fue abogado, erudito, escritor y miembro del parlamento británico durante el reinado de Enrique VIII. Escribió *Utopía,* que describía una sociedad ideal. La palabra *utópico* llegó a significar idealista o visionario. En 1521, fue nombrado caballero.

Morelos, Father José > Morelos, padre José El padre José Morelos (1765–1815) fue un sacerdote católico que tomó el mando del movimiento revolucionario después de la muerte del padre Miguel Hidalgo. Dirigió el movimiento por el sur de México y en 1813 llamó al Congreso de Chilpancingo a formar un gobierno. En 1815 fue capturado y ejecutado como traidor.

mosaic > mosaico Dibujos hechos de teselas de piedra o cristal coloreado.

Moses > Moisés Según lo describe la Biblia hebrea, Moisés fue un líder religioso judío que sacó a los israelitas de la esclavitud egipcia de regreso a Canaán. Los judíos creen que durante el viaje, o Éxodo, Dios presentó a Moisés un conjunto de leyes éticas y religiosas que el pueblo judío conoce como los Diez Mandamientos.

mosque > mezquita Templo musulmán.

Mothers of the Plaza de Mayo > Madres de la Plaza de Mayo Movimiento de mujeres que se reunía semanalmente en una céntrica plaza de la capital de Argentina para protestar por la desaparición o asesinato de sus familiares.

Mughal > Mogol Dinastía musulmana que gobernó gran parte de la India actual de 1526 a 1857.

Mughal empire > Imperio Mogol Imperio musulmán que gobernó la mayor parte del norte de India desde mediados del siglo XVI hasta mediados del siglo XVIII; también se conoce como Imperio Mogol.

Muhammad > Mahoma Mahoma (alrededor de 570–632) introdujo la religión del islam al suroeste de Asia. Según la creencia musulmana, Mahoma oyó la voz del ángel Gabriel instruyéndole a servir como mensajero de Dios. Mahoma pasó el resto de su vida difundiendo el islam. Actuamente, los musulmanes honran a Mahoma como el profeta final de Dios.

Muhammad Ahmad > Muhammad Ahmad Muhammad Ahmad (1844–1885) asumió el título y el papel de Mahdi en 1881, creyendo que había sido designado por Dios para purificar la religión musulmana y restaurar su grandeza. Mediante sus campañas, creó un vasto estado islámico en la región de Sudán.

Muhammad al-Razi > Muhammad al-Razi Muhammad al-Razi (865–925) fue un renombrado médico musulmán, pionero en el estudio de muchas enfermedades. Además de haber escrito un libro que tuvo buena acogida sobre el sarampión y la viruela, también escribió textos sobre la historia de la medicina y formas de avanzar en el campo. Al-Razi ocupó el cargo de médico jefe, primero en la ciudad de Rayy y luego en Bagdad. También fue filósofo y analizó las obras de Platón mientras presentaba sus propias ideas.

Muhammad Ali > Muhammad Ali Muhammad Ali (1769–1849) fue el hijo de un comandante militar que murió cuando él era un niño. Fue nombrado gobernador de Egipto por los otomanos y se apoderó del poder durante el caos de la guerra civil que siguió a la invasión de Napoléon. A menudo llamado "el padre del Egipto moderno", Muhammad Ali puso en marcha una serie de reformas económicas, políticas, administrativas y militares. Sus reformas trataron de asegurar la independencia de Egipto y colocar a Egipto en el camino para ser una potencia de Oriente Medio.

mujahedin > muyahidín Guerrero religioso musulmán.

multiethnic > multiétnico Formado por diferentes grupos étnicos.

multinational corporation > corporación multinacional Empresas que producen y venden sus productos y servicios en todo el mundo.

Mumbai > Bombay Ciudad grande de India.

mummification > momificación Preservación de los cadáveres al embalsamarlos y envolverlos en tela.

Mussolini, Benito > Mussolini, Benito Benito Mussolini (1883–1945) nació en una familia pobre en Italia. Su padre era herrero y su madre, maestra. Aunque Mussolini creció en un hogar socialista y de joven defendía fuertemente las politicas socialistas, formó un partido fascista en Italia cuando regresó de luchar en la Primera Guerra Mundial. Usando el terror y las tácticas de miedo junto con los Camisas Negras, Mussolini creó y gobernó Italia como un estado totalitario. Después de que Italia invadiera Etiopía en 1935, Mussolini y Hitler firmaron una alianza y, con Japón, lucharon en contra de los Aliados en la Segunda Guerra Mundial.

mutiny > motín Revuelta, especialmente de soldados o marineros contra sus oficiales.

Mutsuhito > Mutsuhito Mutsuhito (1852–1912) fue declarado emperador Meiji en 1868 después de la muerte de su padre, el emperador Kōmei. El emperador Meiji personificaba una mezcla de ideales occidentales y japoneses, tratando de encontrar ejemplos extranjeros como modelos para su país. Inició reformas políticas, económicas y culturales importantes que llevaron a una época de rápida modernización.

mutual-aid society > sociedades de ayuda mutua Grupos de apoyo establecidos para ayudar a los trabajadores enfermos o heridos en accidentes laborales.

mystic > místico Persona que dedica su vida a buscar la comunión directa con las fuerzas divinas.

N

Nagasaki > Nagasaki Ciudad japonesa; en una isla y su puerto, los sogún Tokugawa permitieron que uno o dos barcos neerlandeses comerciaran con Japón cada año en el s. XVII.

Nanak, Guru > Nanak, Guru (1469–c. 1539) Fue el fundador del sijismo. Según las creencias sijs, Nanak entró en trance mientras nadaba y experimentó una revelación espiritual. Predicó un mensaje de igualdad y oportunidad, y de un solo Dios para toda la humanidad. Sus enseñanzas y las de sus sucesores dieron forma a las creencias fundamentales del sijismo.

Napoleon III > Napoleón III Napoleón III (1808–1873) fue sobrino de Napoleón Bonaparte, presidente de la Segunda República (1850–1852) y luego emperador del Segundo Imperio de Francia (1852–1870). Napoleón III construyó el poder económico y político de Francia, pero sus políticas extranjeras no tuvieron éxito. Fue depuesto en 1870 después de la derrota de Francia en la Guerra Franco-Prusiana.

Napoleonic Code > Código Napoleónico Cuerpo de las leyes civiles francesas presentadas en 1804, que sirvieron como modelo para los códigos civiles de muchos países.

Napoleonic Wars > Guerras Napoleónicas Serie de guerras libradas de 1804 a 1805 que enfrentaron al Imperio Francés de Napoléon contra las principales potencias de Europa.

Nasser, Gamal Abdel > Nasser, Gamal Abdel Gamal Abdel Nasser (1918–1970) fue presidente de Egipto (1956–1970). Nacionalizó el canal de Suez, fue líder del movimiento panárabe y se alió con la Unión Soviética durante la Guerra Fría. Dirigió a su país a la guerra contra Israel en 1956 y 1967.

Nationalism > nacionalismo Fuerte sentimiento de orgullo y devoción hacia el país propio.

nationalization > nacionalización Apropiación de propiedades o recursos por parte del gobierno.

natural law > ley natural Principio inmutable, descubierto por la razón, que rige la conducta humana.

natural rights > derechos naturales Derecho que pertenece a todos los humanos desde el nacimiento, como la vida, la libertad y la propiedad.

Nazca > Nazca Cultura que tuvo su apogeo en la región andina desde alrededor de 200 a. C. a 600 d. C.

Nazi-Soviet Pact > Pacto nazi-soviético Acuerdo en 1939 entre Alemania y la Unión Soviética mediante el cual las dos naciones prometen no atacarse mutuamente y dividirse entre sí el territorio de Europa del Este.

Nebuchadnezzar > Nabucodonosor (634 a. C.–562 a. C.) Nabucodonosor fue rey del Imperio Babilónico desde el año 605 a. C. al año 562 a. C. Dirigió muchas campañas que expandieron el imperio a Aramea, Judá y otras ciudades. Reconstruyó la ciudad de Babilonia y se le acredita la construcción de los famosos Jardines Colgantes.

Necker, Jacques > Necker, Jacques Jacques Necker (1732–1804) fue director de la tesorería francesa antes de la revolución. Necker intentó reformar las finanzas del país, aunque también intentó financiar la participación de Francia en la Guerra de Independencia mediante préstamos sólidos, a la vez que intentaba ocultar el enorme déficit del país. Más tarde, sus llamadas por la reforma fueron frustradas por Luis XVI.

négritude movement > movimiento de la negritud Movimiento en el que escritores y artistas descendientes de africanos expresaban su orgullo por su herencia africana.

Nehanda > Nehanda Nehanda (alrededor de 1840–1898) fue una líder espiritual del pueblo Shona al sur de África y la inspiración de una revuelta en contra de la colonización de la Compañía Inglesa de Sudáfrica del territorio que ahora es Zimbabue. Finalmente fue capturada y ejecutada por los británicos.

Nehru, Jawaharlal > Nehru, Jawaharlal Jawaharlal Nehru (1889–1964) fue el primer ministro de la India independiente. Educado en Inglaterra, Nehru regresó a India para practicar la abogacía. Se unió al Congreso Nacional Indio, un movimiento de independencia liderado por Mohandas Gandhi. Nombrado sucesor de Gandhi, Nehru lideró el Congreso hasta que India logró la independencia de Gran Bretaña. Como primer ministro, Nehru se enfocó en la industrialización, las políticas económicas socialistas y la neutralidad en la Guerra Fría.

Neolithic Period > periodo neolítico Era final de la prehistoria que empezó hacia el 9000 a. C; también llamado Nueva Edad de Piedra.

Neolithic Revolution > revolución neolítica Periodo durante el cual el comienzo de la agricultura llevó a la gente a la transición de la vida nómada a la vida sedentaria.

neutrality > neutral Política que no apoya a ninguna de las partes en una guerra.

Neutrality Acts > Leyes de Neutralidad Serie de decretos aprobados por el Congreso de los Estados Unidos de 1935 a 1939 con el fin de evitar la implicación del país en la Segunda Guerra Mundial.

New Deal > Nuevo Trato Paquete de programas económicos y sociales establecidos por Franklin D. Roosevelt para ayudar a los estadounidenses durante la Gran Depresión.

New France > Nueva Francia Posesiones francesas en el actual Canadá del siglo XVI a 1763.

New Stone Age > Nueva Edad de Piedra Era final de la prehistoria que empezó aproximadamente hacia el 9000 a. C. ; también llamado periodo neolítico.

Newton, Isaac > Newton, Isaac Isaac Newton (1642–1727) fue una de las figuras más importantes de la Revolución Científica. Matemático y físico inglés, las tres leyes del movimiento de Newton forman los principios básicos de la física moderna y llevaron a la formulación de la ley universal de la gravedad. Su libro de 1687, *Principios Matemáticos de la Filosofía Natural,* es considerado una de las obras más importantes de la historia de la ciencia moderna.

Nightingale, Florence > Nightingale, Florence Florence Nightingale (1820–1910) fue enfermera en el hospital militar británico en Crimea. Cuando llegó al hospital en 1854, quedó conmocionada por el estado del hospital y la velocidad con la que los hombres morían. Luchó para que tuvieran las barracas limpias, cavaran letrinas, la ropa estuviera lavada y los enfermos cuidados. Seis meses después de su llegada, la tasa de mortalidad bajó de 60 por ciento a 2 por ciento. Cuando regresó a Gran Bretaña, presionó al gobierno para que reformara los hospitales y mejoraran la higiene y los cuidados.

nirvana > nirvana Según la creencia budista, unión con el universo y liberación del ciclo de muerte y renacimiento.

Nkrumah, Kwame > Nkrumah, Kwame Kwamw Nkrumah (1909–1972) luchó por la independencia de Ghana (entonces Costa de Oro) de Gran Bretaña. Luego se convirtió en el primer presidente de la Ghana independiente, a la cual lideró desde 1957 hasta que se vio obligado a dejar el cargo durante un golpe militar. Pasó el resto de su vida en Guinea.

no-fly zone > zona de exclusión aérea En Iraq, área en la que los Estados Unidos y sus aliados prohibieron los vuelos de la aviación iraquí después de la guerra del Golfo, en 1991.

Nobel, Alfred > Nobel, Alfred Alfred Nobel (1833–1896) fue un químico, inventor, ingeniero, hombre de negocios y escritor sueco. Aunque la dinamita es su invento más conocido, registró 355 patentes. En 1895, Nobel legó la mayor parte de su fortuna para crear el Premio Nobel con el fin de honrar a los hombres y las mujeres que tuvieran logros importantes en física, química, medicina, literatura y paz.

nomad > nómada Persona que se traslada de un lugar a otro en busca de alimentos.

nonalignment > sin alineación Independencia política y diplomática de ambas potencias de la Guerra Fría.

North Atlantic Treaty Organization (NATO) > Organización del Tratado del Atlántico Norte (OTAN) Alianza militar entre varios estados del Atlántico Norte para salvaguardarlos de la presunta amenaza del bloque comunista de la Unión Soviética; países de otras regiones más tarde se unieron a la alianza.

Northern Ireland > Irlanda del Norte Parte norte de la isla de Irlanda y territorio del Reino Unido, que ha sufrido un conflicto religioso durante mucho tiempo.

Nubia > Nubia Antiguo reino del noreste africano, también llamado Kush.

nuclear family > núcleo familiar Hogar ideal o típico con un padre, una madre y niños.

Nuremberg Laws > Leyes de Nuremberg Leyes aprobadas por el Partido Nazi en 1935 que negaban la ciudadanía alemana a los judíos y los privaban de otros derechos.

Nuremberg Trials > juicios de Nuremberg Serie de juicios de crímenes de guerra llevados a cabo en Alemania después de la Segunda Guerra Mundial.

O

Old Stone Age > Antigua Edad de Piedra Era de la prehistoria que duró desde aproximadamente dos millones de años a. C. hasta el 9000 a. C.

Olduvai Gorge > garganta de Olduvai Ubicado en el este de África, el desfiladero está formado por numerosas capas sedimentarias de ceniza y lava depositadas durante millones de años. Ha proporcionado a los arqueólogos un criterio para medir la edad de las primeras herramientas de piedra y de huesos de homínidos excavados en el lugar.

oligarch > oligarca Miembro de una oligarquía; típicamente, una persona rica con poder político.

oligarchy > oligarquía Gobierno en el que el poder está en manos de unas pocas personas.

Olmec > olmeca La primera civilización americana, ubicada a lo largo de la costa del Golfo de México, desde alrededor de 1200 a. C. a 400 a. C.

one-child policy > política de hijo único Política del gobierno chino que limita a las familias urbanas a tener únicamente un hijo.

Open Door Policy > Política de puertas abiertas Acercamiento estadounidense a China alrededor de 1900, que favorecía el libre comercio entre China y otras naciones.

Opium War > Guerra del opio Guerra librada entre Gran Bretaña y China por las restricciones sobre el comercio exterior.

oracle bone > huesos oraculares En la China Shang, los sacerdotes usaban huesos de animales o caparazones de tortugas para predecir el futuro.

Organization of American States (OAS) > Organización de los Estados Americanos (OEA) Grupo formado en 1948 con el fin de promover la democracia, la cooperación económica y los derechos humanos en las Américas.

Osiris > Osiris Osiris es el dios egipcio identificado como el dios de la vida después de la muerte. A menudo es representado como un hombre de piel verde con barba de faraón y con las piernas parcialmente envueltas en vendas; lleva una corona de plumas de avestruz y un báculo simbólico.

ostracism > ostracismo Práctica de la antigua Grecia de prohibir o apartar a una figura pública que amenazara la democracia.

Ottoman > otomano Miembro de un pueblo nómada de habla turca que emigró de Asia Central al noroeste de Asia Menor.

outpost > fuerte fronterizo Estación militar distante o asentamiento lejano.

outsourcing > subcontratación Práctica empresarial de enviar trabajo a compañías de países en vías de desarrollo con el fin de ahorrar dinero o aumentar el rendimiento.

overproduction > superproducción Condición en la que la producción de mercancías excede la demanda.

Owen, Robert > Owen, Robert Robert Owen (1771–1858) estableció un modelo de comunidad en Nueva Lanark, Escocia, basada en el utopismo. Allí, Owen estableció cambios revolucionarios al limitar la edad de los niños trabajadores y dar escuela a todos los niños. En 1824, invirtió en una comunidad experimental en los Estados Unidos llamada Nueva Armonía. Llegó a ser un líder en el movimiento sindicalista de Inglaterra y siguió participando en el movimiento hasta su muerte.

Oyo empire > Imperio Oyo Los Yoruba crearon este imperio en el siglo XVII en la actual Nigeria. Este imperio utilizó la riqueza del comercio, incluido el comercio de esclavos, para mantener un ejército entrenado y conquistar finalmente el reino vecino Dahomey. El pueblo Yoruba negociaba con los comerciantes europeos de los puertos de Dahomey.

P

Pachacuti Inca Yupanqui > Pachacuti Inca Yupanqui Pachacuti Inca Yupanqui (1438–1471) fue de joven un hábil guerrero. Expandió el Imperio Inca a lo que hoy en día es Perú y Ecuador. Su capital fue Cuzco y recibe el crédito de haber desarrollado el plan de su ciudad.

Pacific Rim > Cuenca del Pacífico Vasta región de naciones, que incluye los países del sureste y este asiático y de las Américas, que limitan con el océano Pacífico.

pacifism > pacifismo Oposición a las guerras.

paddy > arrozal Campo de arroz.

pagoda > pagoda Templo budista de varios pisos con aleros que se curvan en las esquinas.

Paleolithic Period > periodo paleolítico Era de la prehistoria que duró desde aproximadamente dos millones de años a. C. hasta el 9000 a. C.; también llamado la Antigua Edad de Piedra.

Pan-Africanism > panafricanismo Movimiento que empezó en la década de 1920 que se centraba en la unidad y fuerza de los africanos y personas con ascendencia africana en todo el mundo.

Pan-Arabism > panarabismo Movimiento en el que los árabes pretendían unir a todos los árabes en un sólo estado.

Panama Canal > Canal de Panamá Vía fluvial artificial que une los océanos Atlántico y Pacífico.

pandemic > pandemia Propagación de una enfermedad a una gran área, país, continente o al mundo entero.

papal supremacy > supremacía papal Demanda de los papas medievales de que ellos tenían autoridad sobre todos los gobernantes laicos.

papyrus > papiro Planta que se usaba en el antiguo Egipto para hacer un material para escribir parecido al papel.

Parliament > Parlamento Asamblea legislativa de Inglaterra, y más tarde de Gran Bretaña.

parliamentary democracy > democracia parlamentaria Forma de gobierno en la que la dirección ejecutiva (normalmente un primer ministro y el gabinete) es elegida por la asamblea legislativa (parlamento) y controlada por la misma, además de formar parte de ella.

Parthenon > Partenón Templo principal de la diosa griega Atenea, situado en la Acrópolis de Atenas, Grecia.

partition > partición División en partes.

partnership > sociedad Grupo de mercaderes que se unen para financiar una empresa más grande que hubiera sido demasiado costosa para un solo comerciante.

pasha > bajá Gobernante provincial del Imperio Otomano.

Pasternak, Boris > Pasternak, Boris Boris Pasternak (1890–1960) creció en una familia judía bien educada. Su padre era artista y profesor, mientras que su madre era una destacada concertista de piano. Pasternak es muy conocido por su novela épica *Doctor Zhivago,* que le ayudó a ganar el Premio Nobel de Literatura en 1958. Los premios y la publicidad que recibió del occidente solo le crearon problemas en la Unión Soviética. Fue expulsado de la asociación de Escritores de la Unión Soviética y murió en la pobreza. La obra maestra literaria de Pasternak estuvo prohibida en la Unión Soviética hasta mediados de la década de 1980.

Pasteur, Louis > Pasteur, Louis Louis Pasteur (1822–1895) fue un químico francés y uno de los fundadores de la microbiología. Pasteur desarrolló la teoría de los gérmenes de las enfermedades e identificó las causas de muchas enfermedades, entre ellas, la rabia, el ántrax, la varicela y el cólera. Al descubrir las causas de estas enfermedades, Pasteur determinó que podían prevenirse con vacunas. Ayudó a desarrollar varias vacunas, incluyendo la vacuna contra la rabia. También inventó el proceso de pasteurización para el vino, la cerveza, la leche y el vinagre.

paternalistic > paternalista Sistema de gobernar un país como un padre lo hace con su hijo.

patriarch > patriarca En los imperios Romano y Bizantino, el funcionario de rango más alto en la iglesia de una ciudad importante.

patriarchal > patriarcal Relativo a una sociedad en la que los hombres ostentan la máxima autoridad legal y moral.

patrician > patricio Miembro de la clase alta terrateniente.

patrilineal > patrilineal Organización familiar en la que los lazos de parentesco se siguen a través del padre.

patron > mecenas Persona que proporciona apoyo financiero a las artes.

Paul > san Pablo San Pablo (alrededor del año 4 a. C.–64 d. C.) fue un opositor al cristianismo, quien después de tener una visión, se convirtió a las enseñanzas de Jesús. Se hizo misionero para difundir las enseñanzas de Jesús.

Peace of Westphalia > Paz de Westfalia Serie de tratados por los que se puso fin a la Guerra de los Treinta Años.

Pedro, Dom > Pedro, Dom Dom Pedro (1825–1891) fue el segundo y último emperador de Brasil. Pedro II convirtió al Brasil de habla portuguesa en una potencia emergente. Creó estabilidad política y buscó proteger la libertad de expresión y los derechos civiles. El gobierno de Dom Pedro fue una monarquía parlamentaria. Bajo su liderazgo, Brasil experimentó un importante crecimiento económico. Su reinado terminó en 1889 después de que un golpe militar tomara el control del gobierno y le obligara a exiliarse en Europa.

penal colony > colonia penal Lugar al que se manda a los condenados por crímenes.

peninsular > peninsular En las colonias españolas de América, persona nacida en España.

peon > peón Trabajador forzado a trabajar para un terrateniente con el fin de pagar una deuda que es imposible de saldar durante su vida, en la cual incurrió por alimento, herramientas o semillas que el terrateniente le adelantó.

peonage > peonaje Sistema en el que los trabajadores deben trabajar como pago por sus deudas.

perestroika > perestroika Política soviética de reformas democráticas y de libre mercado que introdujo Mikhail Gorbachev a finales de la década de 1980.

Pericles > Pericles Pericles (495 a. C.–429 a. C.) fue un estadista ateniense del siglo V a. C. que lideró Atenas durante la época dorada de logros culturales bajo un gobierno.

Perón, Juan > Perón, Juan Juan Perón (1895–1974) fue electo por primera vez presidente de Argentina en 1946. Gobernó con la ayuda de su esposa, Eva, quien fue popular entre los argentinos. Perón estableció un gobierno autoritario e instituyó amplias reformas, pero su gobierno estaba plagado de corrupción. Fue destituido en un golpe de estado en 1955. Sus partidarios, llamados peronistas, siguieron luchando por el control del gobierno, y Perón regresó al poder en la década de 1970. Su tercera esposa, Isabel, llegó a ser presidenta después de la muerte de su esposo en 1974. Fue derrocada por los militares en 1976.

Perry, Matthew > Perry, Matthew Matthew Perry (1794–1858) fue un exitoso oficial de la Marina de los Estados Unidos. Dirigió una expedición naval a Japón en un intento de establecer relaciones diplomáticas y comerciales después de siglos de aislamiento japonés. La abrumadora presencia militar abrió el camino entre los Estados Unidos y Japón, que otras potencias occidentales se apresuraron a seguir.

perspective > perspectiva Técnica artística usada para lograr el efecto de tercera dimensión en dibujos y pinturas.

Peter the Great > Pedro el Grande Pedro el Grande (1672–1725), zar de Rusia, reinó junto con su medio hermano Iván V (1682–1696) y luego solo (1696–1725). Fue proclamado emperador en 1721. Fue uno de los mayores estadistas, organizadores y reformadores de Rusia.

Petrarch > Petrarca Francesco Petrarca (1304–1374) vivió en Florencia y fue uno de los primeros humanistas, poetas y eruditos del Renacimiento. Recopiló una biblioteca de manuscritos griegos y romanos reunidos de monasterios e iglesias, lo que ayudó a conservar estas obras clásicas para las generaciones futuras.

phalanx > falange En la antigua Grecia, sólida formación táctica de soldados de infantería pesada.

pharaoh > faraón Título de los gobernantes del antiguo Egipto.

Philip II > Filipo II Filipo II (359 a. C.–336 a. C.) restauró la paz en Macedonia, construyó un ejército eficaz y luego formó alianzas con muchas ciudades-estado griegas o las conquistó. Después de derrotar a los ejércitos unidos de Atenas y Tebas en Queronea, toda Grecia quedó bajo su control. Su asesinato terminó con el objetivo de conquistar Persia.

Philippines > Filipinas País al sureste de Asia formado por varios miles de islas. Invadido por los españoles en el s. XVI, llegó a ser un importante vínculo comercial internacional al que llegaron flotas con cargas de plata proveniente de las Américas.

philosophe > *philosophe* Palabra francesa que significa "filósofo"; pensador francés que abogaba por reformas en la sociedad durante la Ilustración.

philosopher > filósofo Alguien que busca entender y explicar la vida; persona que estudia filosofía.

philosophy > filosofía Sistema de ideas.

Piankhi > Piye Piye fue rey de Kush desde alrededor del año 750 al año 719 a. C. Fue conocido por su destreza militar en todo el norte de África. Gobernante muy conservador, Piye buscó fortalecer algunas de las instituciones egipcias en declive.

pictograph > pictografía Dibujo sencillo que se parece al objeto que representa.

Pilgrim > peregrinos Protestantes ingleses que rechazaron la Iglesia de Inglaterra.

Pisan, Christine de > Pisan, Christine de Christine de Pisan (c. 1364–1430) fue la hija de un médico y astrónomo de la corte francesa. Altamente educada, de Pisan hablaba varios idiomas. Después de enviudar a los 25 años de edad, comenzó a escribir poesía y luego a comentar cuestiones sociales.

Pizarro, Francisco > Pizarro, Francisco Francisco Pizarro (alrededor de 1476–26 de junio de 1541) nació en el seno de una familia española muy pobre y en 1513 se unió a la expedición de Balboa para descubrir el "mar del Sur". En 1532, llegó a Perú con sus hermanos, depuso al gobernador inca Atahualpa, conquistó Perú, fundó Lima en 1535 y más tarde fue asesinado por rivales españoles.

plantation > plantación Gran propiedad administrada por un dueño o capataz y cultivada por trabajadores que viven en ella.

plateau > meseta Área elevada del terreno llano.

Plato > Platón Platón (437 a. C.–347 a. C.), alumno de Sócrates, fue un pensador ateniense, escritor de diálogos filosóficos y fundador de la Academia en Atenas.

plebeian > plebeyo Granjeros, mercaderes y artesanos que conformaban la mayor parte de la población.

plebiscite > plebiscito Votación en la que los votantes expresan su opinión sobre un tema en particular.

pogrom > pogromo Ataque violento a una comunidad judía.

polarization > polarización En un contexto político, una concentración de personas en distintos bandos en extremos opuestos del espectro político.

Pol Pot > Pol Pot Pol Pot (1925–1998) fue el líder de los Jemeres Rojos, una guerrilla comunista que tomó el control de Camboya en 1975. Bajo su gobierno, casi 2 millones de personas de su nación murieron asesinadas o murieron de hambre y enfermedades. En 1979, Pol Pot fue retirado del poder. Fue capturado en 1997, juzgado y sentenciado a prisión de por vida. Murió por causas naturales mientras estaba en arresto domiciliario.

polis > polis Ciudad-estado de la antigua Grecia.

Polo, Marco > Polo, Marco Marco Polo (alrededor de 1254–1324) fue un viajero, mercader y aventurero de Venecia que hizo la travesía de Europa a Asia en 1271–95, pasando 17 años al servicio de emperador mongol Kublai Khan. Polo dictó el relato de sus viajes, *Los viajes de Marco Polo* (originalmente *Il Milione* en italiano), a un compañero de prisión mientras estuvo encarcelado durante la guerra con Génova. Su libro demostró ser un gran éxito, pero pocos lectores creyeron que era verdad. Aparte de su libro, no se ha encontrado evidencia de que viajara tan lejos hacia el este; sin embargo, durante siglos después de su muerte, otros han confirmado la precisión de la mayor parte de lo que describió.

polytheistic > politeísta Creencia en muchos dioses.

pope > papa Cabeza de la Iglesia católica romana; en la antigua Roma, obispo de Roma que afirmaba tener la autoridad sobre los otros obispos.

popular sovereignty > soberanía popular Gobierno limitado basado en la separación de poderes y un sistema de controles y equilibrios.

potlatch > potlatch Entre los grupos de indígenas americanos de la costa noroeste, ceremonias en las que personas de alto rango y riquezas ofrecían regalos.

predestination > predestinación Creencia calvinista de que Dios decidió hace mucho tiempo quién conseguiría la salvación.

prehistory > prehistoria Largo periodo antes de que el ser humano inventara la escritura.

premier > premier Primer ministro.

price revolution > revolución de los precios Periodo en la historia europea en el que la inflación aumentó rápidamente.

prime minister > primer ministro Jefe del ejecutivo de un gobierno parlamentario.

privateer > corsario Piratas neerlandeses, ingleses y franceses que apresaban los barcos que llevaban los tesoros desde las Américas en el siglo XVI y que operaban con la aprobación de los gobiernos europeos.

Prohibition > Ley Seca Prohibición total de la venta y consumo de alcohol en los Estados Unidos, de 1920 a 1923.

proletariat > proletariado Clase trabajadora.

proliferate > proliferar Multiplicarse rápidamente.

propaganda > propaganda Divulgación de ideas para promover cierta causa o para perjudicar una causa opuesta.

prophet > profeta Líder espiritual a quien se le atribuye la interpretación de la voluntad de Dios.

protectionism > proteccionismo Uso de aranceles y otras medidas restrictivas para proteger a las empresas de un país frente a la competencia.

protectorate > protectorado País con su propio gobierno pero que está bajo el control de una potencia exterior.

Prussia > Prusia Zona de Europa oriental y central, que estuvo bajo el dominio polaco y alemán en la Edad Media y desde 1701 fue gobernada por la dinastía alemana Hohenzollern.

psychoanalysis > psicoanálisis Método que estudia el funcionamiento de la mente y trata los trastornos mentales.

Ptolemy > Ptolomeo Ptolomeo (100 d. C.–170 d. C.) fue un astrónomo, matemático y geógrafo romano que expuso erróneamente la teoría de que la Tierra era el centro del Universo. Vivió en Alejandría, Egipto, donde estudió los planetas y desarrolló un sistema para explicar sus movimientos.

pueblo > pueblos Aldeas de los indígenas norteamericanos del Suroeste de América del Norte.

Pueblo Bonito > Pueblo Bonito El mayor poblado anasazi, construido en Nuevo México en el siglo X.

Punjab > Punjab Estado del noroeste de India de población mayoritariamente sij.

purdah > purdah Aislamiento de las mujeres en recintos separados.

Puritan > puritanos Miembros de un grupo de protestantes ingleses que querían "purificar" la Iglesia de Inglaterra, haciéndola más sencilla y moralmente más estricta.

Pusan Perimeter > Perímetro de Pusan Línea defensiva alrededor de la ciudad de Pusan, en el sudeste de Corea, custodiada por Corea del Sur y las fuerzas de las Naciones Unidas en 1950 durante la Guerra de Corea; marca el mayor avance de las fuerzas de Corea del Norte.

Putin, Vladimir > Putin, Vladimir Vladimir Putin (b. 1952) fue presidente de Rusia (1999–2008, 2012–). Comenzó su carrera con la KGB soviética (Comité para la Seguridad del Estado) y también fue primer ministro de Rusia (1999, 2008–2012).

putting-out system > sistema de trabajo a domicilio Sistema desarrollado en el siglo XVIII en el que las tareas se distribuían a individuos que completaban el trabajo en sus hogares; tambien se conoce como industria familiar.

Pythagoras > Pitágoras Pitágoras (570 a. C.–490 a. C.) fue un filósofo y matemático griego que estudió el significado de los números y sus relaciones. Formuló principios que influyeron en el pensamiento de Aristóteles y Platón, y también estableció una academia en Croton (hoy en día en Italia). Actualmente es más conocido por derivar el teorema de Pitágoras, una fórmula para calcular la relación entre los lados de un triángulo rectángulo.

Q

Qajar > Qajar Miembro de la dinastía que gobernó la zona del actual Irán desde fines del siglo XVIII hasta 1925.

Qianlong > Qianlong Qianlong (1711–1799) fue un emperador chino que amplió el tamaño del imperio de China para incluir Tíbet y gran parte de Asia central, creando un estado multiétnico que incluía chinos Han, tibetanos y manchús. Qianlong se veía a sí mismo como un "monarca universal", tanto dentro como fuera del Imperio Chino. Patrocinó las artes, comisionó grandes obras literarias y formó un museo palacio nacional de China con colecciones de arte que siguen siendo importantes hoy en día.

Qing > Chin Dinastía establecida por los manchús a mediados del siglo XVII que duró hasta principios del siglo XX; fue la última dinastía china.

quipu > quipu Cuerdas con nudos que usaban los funcionarios incas para guardar sus registros.

Quran > Corán El libro sagrado del islam.

R

Rabin, Yitzhak > Rabin, Yitzhak Yitzhak Rabin (1922–1995) nació en Jerusalén y fue un importante líder militar antes y después de la creación de Israel. Fue dos veces presidente, de 1974 a 1977 y de 1992 a 1995. En la década de 1990, llegó a un acuerdo de paz con la OLP, por lo que compartió el Premio Nobel de la Paz con Shimon Peres y Yasir Arafat. Rabin fue asesinado en 1995 por un extremista judío.

racism > racismo Creencia de que un grupo racial es superior a otro.

radical > radical Persona que quiere hacer cambios extremos.

rajah > rajah Jefe guerrero electo de una tribu aria en la antigua India.

Ramses II > Ramsés II Ramsés II (1292 a. C.– 1190 a. C.) es conocido por sus programas de construcción y por las guerras que declaró a los hititas y los libios. Reinó por más de 66 años y es conocido por la construcción de los monumentos y la arquitectura más famosos de Egipto.

Raphael > Rafael Rafael (1483–1520) fue un pintor renacentista que fusionó los estilos clásico y cristiano. Sus famosas pinturas incluyen una de la Madonna, la madre de Jesús, y *Escuela de Atenas,* que muestra una reunión imaginaria de grandes pensadores, científicos y artistas, entre ellos Miguel Ángel, Leonardo y él mismo.

realism > realismo Movimiento artístico del siglo XIX cuyo objetivo era representar el mundo tal como es.

Realpolitik > realpolitik Política realista basada en necesidades concretas del estado.

recession > recesión Contracción económica prolongada.

Reconquista > Reconquista Durante el siglo XV, campaña por parte de cristianos europeos para expulsar a los musulmanes de la actual España.

refugee > refugiado Persona que abandona su hogar o país en busca de refugio en otro lugar, a menudo como consecuencia de inestabilidad política o hambruna.

regionalism > regionalismo Lealtad a un área local.

Reich > Reich Imperio alemán.

Reign of Terror > el Terror Periodo durante la Revolución Francesa de septiembre de 1793 a julio de 1794, en el que la gente en Francia era arrestada por no apoyar la revolución y mucha fue ejecutada.

reincarnation > reencarnación Según la creencia hindú, renacimiento del alma en otra forma corporal.

reparation > reparación Pago de los daños causados por la guerra.

repeal > derogar Cancelar

republic > república Sistema de gobierno en el cual los funcionarios son elegidos por el pueblo.

revenue > renta Dinero que se recauda por impuestos.

Rhee, Syngman > Rhee, Syngman Syngman Rhee (1875–1965) fue presidente de la República de Corea (Corea del Sur) desde su fundación en 1949 hasta 1960. Fue electo para cuatro periodos en el cargo, pero las acusaciones de fraude electoral en 1960 llevaron a manifestaciones estudiantiles y demandas de renuncia por parte de la Asamblea Nacional y el gobierno de los Estados Unidos. Renunció y se fue al exilio en Hawái.

rhetoric > retórica Arte de hablar con habilidad.

Ricci, Matteo > Ricci, Matteo Matteo Ricci (1552–1610) fue un erudito italiano y sacerdote jesuita que viajó a China. En 1589, Ricci comenzó a enseñar a los eruditos chinos ideas matemáticas europeas. Más tarde vivió en Nanjing, donde trabajó en matemáticas, astronomía y geografía. Se hizo famoso en China por sus conocimientos de astronomía, escrituras en chino y su talento como pintor.

Richelieu, Cardinal > Richelieu, cardenal El cardenal Richelieu (1585–1642) es considerado uno de los más grandes políticos de la historia; desempeñó un papel importante en la historia de Francia como primer ministro de Luis XIII.

Robespierre, Maximilien > Robespierre, Maximilien Maximilien Robespierre (1758–1794) fue un revolucionario francés electo para los Estados Generales en 1789. Más tarde llegó a ser un miembro importante del club jacobino y miembro del Comité de Seguridad Pública. Como miembro del comité comenzó su reinado de terror. Más tarde fue arrestado y ejecutado por los líderes de la revolución.

rococo > rococó Estilo de arte y arquitectura elegante y personal que se hizo popular a mediados del siglo XVIII y que incluía diseños con formas de hojas, conchas y flores.

romanticism > romanticismo Movimiento artístico del siglo XIX que apelaba a la emoción más que a la razón.

Romero, Oscar > Romero, Óscar Óscar Romero (1917–1980), un arzobispo católico romano de El Salvador, fue un crítico franco de los abusos de los derechos humanos en su país y defensor de los pobres. Con frecuencia, entraba en conflicto con el gobierno salvadoreño por su crítica del régimen. Fue asesinado en 1980 mientras daba misa en la capilla de un hospital, probablemente por escuadras de la muerte salvadoreñas.

Rommel, Erwin > Rommel, Erwin Erwin Rommel (1891–1944) fue un militar de carrera y uno de los generales más exitosos de Hitler. Se suicidó después de un intento fallido de asesinar a Hitler.

Roosevelt, Franklin Delano > Roosevelt, Franklin Delano Franklin D. Roosevelt (1882–1945) fue el presidente estadounidense que más tiempo ocupó el cargo, ya que fue elegido cuatro veces. Roosevelt nació en una familia acomodada de Nueva York y era primo lejano del presidente Theodore Roosevelt. Elegido en 1932, su primer periodo como presidente se centró en sacar a los Estados Unidos de la Gran Depresión. Pasó con éxito leyes, creando un paquete masivo de programas económicos y sociales, llamado el Nuevo Trato. Durante su tercer periodo, Roosevelt inspiró a muchos a través de su fuerte liderazgo durante el ataque japonés a Pearl Harbor y la consiguiente entrada de los Estados Unidos en la Segunda Guerra Mundial. Fue elegido para un cuarto periodo en 1944, pero su salud se deterioró conforme se acercaba el final de la guerra. Roosevelt murió en abril de 1945.

Rosetta Stone > piedra de Rosetta Piedra arquitectónica que incluye el mismo pasaje con caracteres jeroglíficos, demóticos y en escritura griega que se usó para descifrar el significado de muchos jeroglíficos.

Rosie the Riveter > Rosita la Remachadora Nombre popularmente dado a las mujeres que trabajaban en las fábricas de armamento durante la Segunda Guerra Mundial.

rotten borough > "distrito podrido" En Inglaterra, ciudad rural que enviaba miembros al parlamento a pesar de no tener o tener pocos votantes.

Rousseau, Jean-Jacques > Rousseau, Jean-Jacques Jean-Jacques Rousseau (1712–1778) fue un filósofo y escritor nacido en Suiza cuyos trabajos inspiraron a líderes de la Revolución Francesa. Su pensamiento revolucionario en política y ética tuvo un impacto en cómo los padres educaban a sus hijos e incluso influyó en el gusto de las personas por la música y por otras artes.

Roy, Ram Mohun > Roy, Ram Mohun Ram Mohun Roy (1772–1833) fue fundador del Colegio Hindú de Calcuta, que daba educación al estilo inglés a los indios. Aunque Roy quería reformar algunas partes de la cultura tradicional india e hindú, también revivió el orgullo de India por su cultura. Es considerado el fundador del nacionalismo indio.

Ruhr Valley > Valle del Ruhr Región industrial alemana rica en carbón.

russification > rusificación Política de Stalin para imponer la cultura rusa a la Unión Soviética.

Russo-Japanese War > Guerra ruso-japonesa Guerra entre Japón y Rusia durante 1904–1905 por el control de Corea y Manchuria.

S

Sabbath > sabbat Día sagrado para descansar y rendir culto.

sacrament > sacramento Ritual sagrado de la Iglesia católica romana.

Sadat, Anwar > Sadat, Anwar Anwar Sadat (1918–1981) fue presidente de Egipto (1970–1981). Firmó un tratado de paz con Israel, los Acuerdos de Camp David, moderado por los Estados Unidos. En 1981 fue asesinado por extremistas musulmanes.

Saddam Hussein > Saddam Hussein Saddam Hussein (1937–2006) fue miembro del Partido Baas y pasó siete años en prisión cuando los baasistas no estaban en el poder. En 1968, participó en un golpe de estado en el que los baasistas se apoderaron del gobierno, y para 1979 él tenía el control total del gobierno. Hussein fue el dictador de Iraq hasta la Guerra de Iraq de 2003. En 2006, fue condenado en un tribunal iraquí por crímenes contra la humanidad y poco después fue ejecutado.

Safavid > safávida Imperio musulmán chiíta que gobernó la mayor parte del actual Irán desde el siglo XVI hasta el siglo XVIII.

Sahara > Sahara Desierto más grande del mundo que cubre casi todo el norte de África.

St. Francis of Assisi > san Francisco de Asís San Francisco de Asís (1181?–1226) provenía de una familia acaudalada y fue un joven cosmopolita. Abandonó su riqueza para "caminar tras las huellas de Jesús". Los primeros frailes franciscanos fueron sus seguidores, y juntos llevaron una vida de servicio a los pobres y enfermos. Francisco consideraba a toda la naturaleza como un reflejo de Dios, y llamaba a los animales sus hermanos y hermanas. Relatos famosos cuentan que él predicaba a las aves y convencía al lobo de que dejara de atacar a los aldeanos si ellos, a cambio, daban de comer al lobo. La Iglesia lo nombró santo en 1228.

St. Petersburg > San Petersburgo Capital portuaria del noroeste de Rusia fundada en 1703 por Pedro el Grande.

St. Teresa of Avila > santa Teresa de Jesús Santa Teresa de Jesús (1515–1582) obtuvo fama como autora de varios libros sobre temas espirituales. Fue una influencia clave durante la Reforma Católica. Como monja carmelita, se dedicó a la sencilla vida religiosa basada en la tranquila reflexión. Teresa dedicó gran parte de su vida a la reforma de la orden de las carmelitas, fundando muchos conventos por toda España.

salon > salón Reuniones sociales informales en las que escritores, artistas, *philosophes* y otros intercambiaban ideas.

samurai > samurái Miembro de la clase guerrera en la sociedad japonesa feudal.

San Martín, José de > San Martín, José de José de San Martín (1778–1850) nació en Argentina y fue educado en España. Ayudó a liderar las revoluciones en contra del gobierno español en Argentina, Chile y Perú. Se convirtió en protector de Perú después de su liberación de España pero renunció en 1822 después de un conflicto con Simón Bolívar. Vivió en el exilio en Europa después de su renuncia.

Sandinista > sandinista Partido y movimiento político socialista que gobernó Nicaragua durante la década de 1980.

sans-culottes > sans culottes Miembros de la clase obrera que hicieron la Revolución Francesa más radical; llamados así porque los hombres llevaban pantalones largos en vez de los pantalones ajustados a la rodilla, como los que llevaba la clase alta.

Sapa Inca > Sapa Inca Título del emperador inca.

Sargon > Sargón Las fechas exactas del nacimiento y muerte de Sargón no se conocen, pero según los historiadores sumerios, reinó desde el año 2334 a. C. hasta el año 2279 a. C. Es conocido por crear el primer imperio de Mesopotamia.

sati > sati Costumbre que requería que la esposa se uniera a su marido en la muerte arrojándose a su pira funeraria.

satirize > satirizar Hacer burla de algo o alguien.

savanna > sabana Planicie con pastizales cuyo régimen de lluvias es irregular.

schism > cisma División o ruptura.

scholasticism > escolástica En la Edad Media europea, escuela de pensamiento que usaba la lógica y el razonamiento para apoyar las creencias cristianas.

scientific method > método científico Proceso cuidadoso y de varios pasos que se usa para confirmar descubrimientos y para aprobar o desaprobar una hipótesis.

scribe > escriba En las civilizaciones antiguas, persona especialmente educada para leer, escribir y mantener registros.

secede > separarse Retirarse.

secret ballot > voto secreto Votos que se dan sin hacerlos públicos.

sect > secta Subgrupo de un grupo religioso importante.

secular > laico Que tiene que ver más con asuntos mundanos que religiosos; no religioso.

segregation > segregación Separación forzada por razón de raza, sexo, religión o etnia.

Sejong, King > Sejong, rey El rey Sejong (1397–1450), el gobernante más famoso de Corea y conocido como el Grande, reemplazó en 1433 el complejo sistema chino de escritura con el hangul. Sus numerosos logros culturales e intelectuales han llevado a los historiadores a llamar a su reinado la Edad de Oro de Corea.

selective borrowing > préstamo selectivo Adoptar o adaptar algunos rasgos culturales y descartar otros.

self-determination > autodeterminación Derecho de los pueblos a elegir su propia forma de gobierno.

sepoy > cipayo Soldado indio que sirvió en un ejército establecido por las compañías de comercio francesas o inglesas.

Septimius Severus > Septimio Severo Septimio Severo nació alrededor del año 145 d. C. en lo que hoy es Trípoli. Antes de morir en el año 211, fue el emperador que convirtió el gobierno romano en una monarquía militar. Su reinado fijó la organización para otros gobernantes romanos.

serf > siervo En la Europa medieval, campesino vinculado a las tierras del señor.

shah > sah Rey.

Shaka > Shaka Shaka (1787–1828) fue un jefe zulú y fundador del Imperio Zulú de África.

Shakespeare > Shakespeare William Shakespeare (1564–1616), nacido en Inglaterra, fue un famoso poeta y dramaturgo durante el reinado de Isabel I. Entre 1590 y 1613 escribió 37 obras de teatro que todavía se representan en todo el mundo. Inventó palabras y frases que todavía se usan en la actualidad. Al igual que otros autores del Renacimiento, adoptó un enfoque humanista en sus personajes.

shantytown > barrio de chabolas Barrios muy pobres de casuchas endebles.

Sharia > sharia Ley canónica del islam que incluye la interpretación del Corán y que aplica los principios islámicos a la vida diaria.

Sharpeville > Sharpeville Municipio sudafricano habitado por personas de raza negra donde el gobierno mató a decenas de manifestantes antiapartheid en 1960.

Shi Huangdi > Shi Huang Shi Huang (alrededor del año 259 a. C.–210 a. C.) se llamaba originalmente Zhao Zheng. Fue hijo del rey del territorio Quin. A los 13 años de edad, Zheng fue el rey de Qin. Se proclamó a sí mismo Shi Huang, o "Primer Emperador". Con espías, generales leales y sobornos, retiró a los otros seis líderes de los estados de alrededor para crear una China unificada bajo su gobierno autoritario. Sin embargo, la China unificada que él creó era demasiado dependiente de Shi Huang. La dinastía Qin colapsó cuatro años después de su muerte.

Shiite > chiíta Miembro de una de las dos sectas musulmanas principales; creyente de que los descendientes de la hija y el yerno de Mahoma, Alí, son los verdaderos líderes musulmanes.

Shikibu, Murasaki > Shikibu, Murasaki Murasaki Shikibu (alrededor de 973–alrededor de 1014 o 1025) fue dama de compañía en la corte Heian. Los historiadores le otorgan el crédito de haber escrito la primera novela larga del mundo, *La historia de Genji*, escrita entre los años 1000 y 1008 d. C.

Shinto > sintoísmo Principal religión de Japón que enfatiza la adoración a la naturaleza.

shrine > santuario Altar, capilla u otro lugar sagrado.

Sikh > sij Miembro de una minoría religiosa de India.

Sikhism > sijismo Religión monoteísta fundada a finales del siglo XV por Gurú Nanak en la región Punjab de India.

Silla dynasty > dinastía Silla Dinastía coreana que gobernó de 668 a 935.

Sino-Japanese War > Primera guerra sino-japonesa Guerra entre China y Japón en la cual Japón adquirió Taiwán.

smelt > refinar Fundir mineral para separar el mineral puro de las impurezas.

Smith, Adam > Smith, Adam Adam Smith (1723–1790) fue un economista escocés recordado por su obra maestra, *An Inquiry into the Nature and Causes of the Wealth of Nations*. Su argumento a favor del libre mercado con interferencias mínimas del gobierno ha ayudado a determinar las economías productivas en todo el mundo durante más de 200 años. Se le ha llamado el padre de la economía moderna y sigue siendo uno de los filósofos de la economía más influyentes de la historia.

social contract > contrato social Acuerdo mediante el cual el pueblo cede sus libertades a un gobierno poderoso para evitar el caos.

social democracy > democracia social Ideología política en la que hay una transición gradual del capitalismo al socialismo en vez de un derrocamiento violento y repentino del sistema.

social gospel > evangelio social Movimiento del siglo XIX que urgía a los cristianos a que hicieran servicios sociales.

social mobility > movilidad social Capacidad de cambiar de clase social.

social welfare > bienestar social Programas ofrecidos por el estado para el beneficio de sus ciudadanos.

socialism > socialismo Sistema en el que el pueblo como un todo, en vez de los individuos, es dueño de todas la propiedades y controla todos los negocios.

socialist realism > realismo socialista Estilo artístico cuyo objetivo era promover el socialismo mostrando la vida en la Unión Soviética desde un perspectiva positiva.

Socrates > Sócrates Sócrates (469 a. C.–399 a. C.) fue un cantero y filósofo ateniense que buscaba la verdad mediante el cuestionamiento, como lo describen los diálogos escritos por Platón.

Solidarity > Solidaridad Sindicato laboral y movimiento democrático polaco.

Solomon > Salomón En la tradición judía, Salomón fue el hijo de David, conocido por la construcción del Templo de Jerusalén. También fue famoso por su sabiduría. Después de su muerte, el reino de Israel se dividió en dos partes.

Song dynasty > dinastía Song Dinastía china que gobernó de 960 a 1279.

Songhai > Songay Reino medieval de África occidental ubicado en el presente Malí, Níger y Nigeria.

sovereign > soberanía Tener poder total e independiente.

soviet > sóviet Consejo de trabajadores y soldados establecido por los revolucionarios rusos en 1917.

Spanish-American War > Guerra Hispano-Estadounidense Conflicto entre los Estados Unidos y España en 1898 por la independencia de Cuba.

Sparta > Esparta Antigua ciudad-estado en Grecia establecida por los dorios y construida como un estado militar.

sphere of influence > esfera de influencia Área sobre la que un poder exterior se reserva privilegios comerciales o la exclusividad de realizar inversiones.

stalemate > estancamiento Punto muerto en una confrontación, en el que ninguna de las partes puede vencer a la otra.

Stalin, Joseph > Stalin, Joseph Joseph Stalin (1879–1953) (nombre real: Iosif Vissarionovich Dzhugashvili) adoptó el nombre Stalin, que significa "hombre de acero", después de unirse a los bolcheviques clandestinos. Fue el único gobernante de la Unión Soviética durante 33 años. Stalin se mantuvo firme en contra de Hitler y se negó a dejar Moscú. Finalmente obligó a los alemanes a retirarse.

Stalingrad > Stalingrado Actualmente Volgogrado; ciudad del suroeste de Rusia donde se libró una encarnizada batalla durante la Segunda Guerra Mundial.

Stamp Act > Ley del Timbre Ley promulgada en 1765 por el Parlamento Británico, la cual imponía gravámenes a artículos como diarios y panfletos en las colonias americanas; revocada en 1766.

standard of living > estándar de vida Nivel de bienes materiales y de servicios disponibles en una sociedad.

Stanley, Henry > Stanley, Henry Henry Stanley (1841–1904) fue un explorador británico de África central, famoso por el rescate del Dr. David Livingstone y sus descubrimientos en la región del río Congo.

Stanton, Elizabeth Cady > Stanton, Elizabeth Cady Elizabeth Cady Stanton (1815–1902) fue una escritora, conferencista y activista que desempeñó un papel importante en el movimiento de los derechos de la mujer. Esbozó discursos y muchos de los documentos importantes del movimiento, incluyendo la "Declaración de derechos" de las mujeres. Stanton ayudó a planear y dirigió la Convención de Seneca Falls de 1848. Más adelante, comenzó a enfocarse más en las reformas sociales, incluyendo el cuidado infantil, las leyes de divorcio y la templanza. Stanton murió 18 años antes de que las mujeres obtuviera el derecho al voto.

stela > estela En el mundo antiguo, altos monumentos conmemorativos que a menudo estaban decorados.

steppe > estepa Tierra de pastos secos.

stipend > estipendio Salario fijo de los funcionarios públicos.

stock > acciones Títulos o valores de una compañía.

Stolypin, Peter > Stolypin, Peter Peter Stolypin (1862–1911) fue un estadista ruso bajo el zar Nicolás II. Fue ministro del interior y presidente del Consejo de Ministros. Aunque instituyó reformas agrícolas que mejoraron la vida de los campesinos, hizo enemigos a ambos lados del espectro político. Fue asesinado en 1911.

strait > estrecho Vía marítima angosta.

stupa > stupa Gran altar budista en forma de cúpula.

subcontinent > subcontinente Gran masa continental que sobresale de un continente.

suburbanization > suburbanización Proceso de construcción en áreas fuera del centro de la ciudad.

Sudetenland > Sudetes Región occidental de la antigua Checoslovaquia.

Suez Canal > canal de Suez Canal de Egipto que une el mar Rojo y el océano Índico con el mar Mediterráneo, que a la vez une Europa con puertos en Asia y África oriental.

suffrage > sufragio Derecho al voto.

Sufi > sufí Místico musulmán que busca la comunión con Dios mediante la meditación, el ayuno y otros rituales.

Suharto > Suharto Suharto (1921–2008) fue un oficial militar indonesio de alto rango que se convirtió en el segundo presidente del país. Suharto luchó contra los neerlandeses en el movimiento de independenca de Indonesia y logró un rango distinguido en el gobierno del nuevo país. Cuando Sukarno, el primer presidente del país, comenzó a instituir políticas comunistas, el ejército anticomunista se rebeló. Suharto llevó a cabo purgas en contra de los comunistas y un violento golpe de estado en contra de Sukarno. Habiendo tomado el poder en 1967, trabajó para modernizar y estabilizar el país.

Sukarno > Sukarno Sukarno (1901–1970) fue un luchador de la libertad y primer presidente de Indonesia. Participó en el movimiento de independencia en contra de los neerlandeses, y pasó algún tiempo encarcelado o exiliado. Durante la Segunda Guerra Mundial, Japón invadió las Indias y Sukarno cooperó con el nuevo régimen. El colapso de Japón al final de la guerra permitió la independencia de Indonesia, a pesar de los intentos neerlandeses de recuperar el poder. Como el nuevo presidente de Indonesia, Sukarno desmanteló el gobierno parlamentario e instituyó políticas comunistas. Un violento golpe de estado liderado por el general Suharto depuso a Sukarno en 1967.

Suleiman > Solimán Solimán (1494–1566) fue un sultán del Imperio Otomano que gobernó de 1520 a 1566. Durante este tiempo llevó burocracia y estabilidad al imperio y fomentó las artes, las leyes y la arquitectura. Sus campañas militares ampliaron mucho el alcance del imperio.

sultan > sultán Gobernante musulmán.

Sumer > Sumeria Lugar de la primera civilización del mundo, ubicada en el sureste de Mesopotamia.

Sun Yixian > Sun Yixian (también llamado Sun Yat-Sen) Sun Yixian (1866–1925) fue hijo de unos campesinos pobres de una pequeña aldea. Dejó la carrera de medicina para participar en una revuelta en contra del gobierno Qing. Después de un levantamiento fallido, Sun se vio obligado a exiliarse en Japón. En 1911, los delegados eligieron a Sun como presidente provisional de la recién establecida República de China. En 1921, Sun estableció un gobierno nacionalista en el sur de China y se alió con los comunistas para derrotar a los señores de la guerra.

Sundiata > Sundiata Sundiata fue un gobernante de África occidental que fue el responsable de poner las bases para que Malí se convirtiera en un reino rico y poderoso. Murió en 1255.

Sunni > suní Miembro de una de las dos sectas musulmanas principales; los sunitas creen que la inspiración proviene del ejemplo de Mahoma según fue registrada por sus primeros seguidores.

superpower > superpotencia Una nación más fuerte que otras naciones poderosas.

surplus > superávit Cantidad que rebasa lo necesario; exceso.

surrealism > surrealismo Movimiento artístico que trata de mostrar el funcionamiento del inconsciente.

Suryavarman II, King > Suryavarman II, rey Suryavarman II fue un famoso rey de Camboya, que murió en 115 d. C. Construyó la estructura religiosa más grande del mundo en Angkor Wat y conquistó gran parte de lo que ahora es Tailandia y Vietnam. Hizo de la capital, Angkor, una de las grandes ciudades del mundo de esa época.

sustainability > sostenibilidad Desarrollo que equilibra las necesidades actuales de las personas con la necesidad de conservar el medio ambiente para las generaciones futuras.

sustainable development > desarrollo sostenible Desarrollo que cubre las necesidades del presente sin perjudicar la capacidad de las generaciones futuras de cubrir sus necesidades.

Suu Kyi, Aung San > Suu Kyi, Aung San Aung San Suu Kyi (1945–) es una líder de los derechos humanos de Myanmar y Premio Nobel de la Paz. Hija del líder de la Birmania independiente y embajador en India, Suu Kyi estaba motivada para luchar por la paz y la libertad en contra de los opresores militares que habían gobernado Birmania desde 1962. Ayudó a fundar el movimiento de independencia de la Liga Nacional por la Democracia, la cual ganó la elección democrática en 1990 pero fue callada por los militares. En 2010, Suu Kyi fue liberada de su arresto domiciliario y obtuvo un escaño en la Cámara de Diputados. Sigue liderando la oposición a los gobernantes autoritarios y se espera que se postule para la presidencia del país.

Swahili > suajili Cultura del este de África que emergió alrededor del año 1000 d. C.; también un idioma basado en el bantú, que mezcla palabras árabes y usa la escritura árabe.

T

Taíno > taínos Grupo indígena americano que encontró Colón cuando llegó por primera vez a las Indias Occidentales.

Taiping Rebellion > Rebelión Taiping Revuelta campesina en China.

Taj Mahal > Taj Mahal Tumba construida por Sah Jahan para su esposa.

Taliban > talibán Facción fundamentalista islámica que controló la mayor parte de Afganistán durante diez años hasta que los Estados Unidos la removió del poder en 2002.

Tang dynasty > dinastía Tang Dinastía china que gobernó de 618 a 907.

Tang Taizong > Tang Taizong Tang Taizong (598–649) fue un consumado general, reformador del gobierno, historiador, erudito de la sabiduría de Confucio y artista. Estas cualidades y habilidades le ayudaron a ser el emperador más admirado de China.

tariff > arancel Impuesto a mercancías importadas.

technology > tecnología Habilidades y herramientas que las personas usan para satisfacer sus necesidades básicas.

Tehran > Teherán Capital de la dinastía Qajar y del actual Irán.

temperance movement > movimiento por la templanza Movimiento encausado a eliminar el abuso del alcohol y los problemas que éste genera.

tenant farmer > granjero arrendatario Alguien que paga renta a un señor para cultivar parte de la tierra del señor.

tenement > vecindad Edificios de varios pisos divididos en apartamentos para alojar a tantos residentes como sea posible.

Tennis Court Oath > Juramento del juego de pelota Famoso juramento hecho en una cancha de frontón por los miembros del Tercer Estado en la Francia prerrevolucionaria.

Tenochtitlán > Tenochtitlán Capital del Imperio Azteca sobre la cual se construyó la actual Ciudad de México.

Teotihuacán > Teotihuacán Ciudad que dominó el valle de México desde alrededor del año 200 d. C. hasta el año 750 d. C.; influyó en la cultura de los pueblos mesoamericanos posteriores.

Teresa, Mother > Teresa, Madre La Madre Teresa (bautizada en 1910, murió en 1997) fue la fundadora de origen rumano de la Orden de las Misioneras de la Caridad, un grupo católico romano dedicado a ayudar a los pobres, especialmente a los de India. Ganó el Premio Nobel de la Paz en 1979, y también fue honrada por su trabajo por el gobierno indio. Fue beatificada, o nombrada bendita, por la Iglesia católica romana en 2003 por toda una vida comprometida con aquellos que sufren necesidades.

terrorism > terrorismo Uso deliberado de la violencia indiscriminada, especialmente en contra de civiles, para lograr fines políticos.

Tet Offensive > ofensiva del Tet Ofensiva masiva y sangrienta de las guerrillas comunistas contra las fuerzas estadounidenses y las de Vietnam del Sur durante el Tet, el año nuevo vietnamita, en 1968. Influyó a que la opinión pública estadounidense se opusiera a la intervención militar en Vietnam.

Thatcher, Margaret > Thatcher, Margaret Margaret Thatcher (1925–2013) fue la primera mujer en ocupar el cargo de primera ministra en Gran Bretaña, de 1979 a 1990. Thatcher era conservadora y una firme opositora al socialismo, al que consideraba como antibritánico porque erosionaba la autoconfianza. Bajo Thatcher, el gobierno británico vendió las industrias nacionalizadas a empresas privadas. Thatcher también lideró al país durante la Guerra de las Malvinas (1982) contra Argentina.

theocracy > teocracia Gobierno administrado por líderes religiosos.

Theodora > Teodora Teodora (497–548) fue la esposa del emperador Justiniano y su más leal consejera. Conocida por su poderosa inteligencia y astuta perspectiva política, Teodora ejerció una influencia decisiva en los asuntos políticos bizantinos. Su nombre se menciona en casi todas las leyes aprobadas durante el reinado de Justiniano. Ella usó su posición y poder para sus intereses, entre ellos ser una pionera en los esfuerzos a favor de los derechos de las mujeres. Respaldó sólidas leyes para terminar el tráfico de mujeres jóvenes y revisó las leyes de divorcio a favor de más beneficios para las mujeres.

Third Reich > Tercer Reich Nombre oficial del partido nazi durante su mandato en Alemania; mantuvo el poder de 1933 a 1945.

38th parallel > paralelo 38 Línea imaginaria que marca los 38 grados de latitud, en particular la línea que cruza la península coreana, que dividía las fuerzas soviéticas al norte y las fuerzas estadounidenses al sur, después de la Segunda Guerra Mundial.

Thutmose III > Tutmosis III (1504 a. C.–1426 a. C.) Tutmosis III compartió el poder con su tía la reina Hatshepsut antes de ser faraón. Luchó contra Siria y Palestina para recuperar el gobierno egipcio y creó la mayor dinastía de Egipto.

Tiahuanaco > Tiahuanaco Cultura preincaica que tuvo su apogeo en la región andina desde alrededor de 200 d. C. a 1000 d. C.

Tiananmen Square > Plaza de Tiananmen Inmensa plaza pública en el centro de Beijing, la capital de China.

Tiberius > Tiberio Tiberio (alrededor de 163 a. C.–133 a. C.) fue un plebeyo romano que llegó a ser tribuno y cabildeó para lograr una reforma del gobierno. Fue asesinado en el año 133 a. C. por matones contratados por los senadores romanos.

Tojo, Hideki > Tōjō, Hideki Hideki Tōjō (1884–1948) nació en Tokio y fue militar de carrera. Fue general del ejército del Imperio Japonés y el 40º primer ministro de Japón durante la mayor parte de la Segunda Guerra Mundial, de 1941 a 1945. Fue directamente responsable del ataque a Pearl Harbor, y fue arrestado y sentenciado a muerte acusado de crímenes de guerra japoneses.

Tokugawa > Tokugawa Los sogún, descendientes de Tokugawa Ieyasu (1542–1616), eran líderes militares supremos; gobernaron Japón de 1603 a 1869; reunificaron Japón y establecieron el orden después de un siglo de guerra civil y disturbios.

Tokyo > Tokio Capital de Japón.

Torah > Tora El texto más sagrado de la Biblia hebrea que incluye sus cinco primeros libros.

total war > guerra total Tipo de guerra en la que todos los objetivos son atacados, incluidos los civiles y las líneas de suministro.

totalitarian state > estado totalitario Gobierno en el que una dictadura de partido único regula todos los aspectos de la vida de los ciudadanos.

Touré, Samori > Touré, Samori Samori Touré (c. 1830–1900) fue un líder militar musulmán que fundó un poderoso reino en África occidental, en la región del río Nilo y luchó contra el ejército francés.

tournament > torneo Batalla simulada en la que los caballeros competían entre ellos para lucir sus destrezas de lucha.

trade deficit > déficit comercial Situación en la que un país importa más de lo que exporta.

trade surplus > superávit comercial Situación en la cual las exportaciones de bienes y servicios de un país son más altas que las importaciones.

traditional economy > economía tradicional Sistema económico que depende del hábito, la costumbre o los rituales y tiende a no cambiar con el tiempo.

tragedy > tragedia En la antigua Grecia, obra de teatro sobre el sufrimiento humano que termina, por lo general, en un desastre.

Treaty of Paris > Tratado de París Tratado de paz de 1763 que finalizó la Guerra de los Siete Años y culminó con el dominio británico de las Americas.

Treaty of Tordesillas > Tratado de Tordesillas Tratado firmado por España y Portugal en 1494 por el que se dividían entre ellos el mundo fuera de Europa.

triangular trade > comercio triangular Rutas comerciales que existían entre Europa y sus colonias en las Indias Occidentales y África, usadas para el intercambio de mercancías y personas esclavizadas.

tribune > tribuno Funcionario elegido por los plebeyos para proteger sus intereses.

tributary state > estado tributario Estado independiente que debe reconocer la supremacía de otro estado y pagar tributo a su gobernante.

tribute > tributo Pago que los conquistadores podían obligar a pagar a los pueblos conquistados.

Trojan War > Guerra de Troya Conflicto militar que surgió alrededor del año 1250 a. C. entre Micenas y Troya, una rica ciudad comercial en lo que hoy es Turquía; descrito en los poemas épicos de Homero, la *Ilíada* y la *Odisea*.

troubadour > trovador Poeta o cantante itinerante de la Europa medieval.

Truman Doctrine > Doctrina Truman Promesa del presidente Truman de ayudar a las naciones en lucha contra los movimientos comunistas.

Truman, Harry > Truman, Harry Harry Truman (1884–1972) era vicepresidente de los Estados Unidos cuando Roosevelt murió y se convirtió en el 33º Presidente después de la muerte de Roosevelt. Después de estar en el cargo durante solo unos cuantos meses, Truman tomó la decisión de lanzar las bombas atómicas sobre Japón.

Truth, Sojourner > Truth, Sojourner Sojourner Truth (1797–1883) Fue una de las mujeres afroamericanas más conocidas del siglo XIX. Nació en condición de esclava y cuando obtuvo su libertad en 1826, cambió su nombre a Sojourner Truth. En 1843, comenzó a viajar por el país para difundir la verdad sobre la injusticia y abogar por los derechos humanos. Truth fue una figura importante en varios movimientos —entre ellos el movimiento de los derechos de las mujeres, la templanza, la igualdad racial y la reforma de las prisiones— y no temía pedir reformas al gobierno.

tsunami > tsunami Ola enorme y destructiva causada por un terremoto o vientos muy fuertes.

Tudor, Mary > Tudor, María María Tudor (1516–1558) fue la primera reina en gobernar Inglaterra por derecho propio. Hija de Enrique VIII y de su primera esposa, Catalina de Aragón, María fue una devota católica que no logró acabar con la oleada de la Reforma Protestante en Inglaterra. Su activa persecución contra los protestantes le valieron el apodo de "María la Sanguinaria".

turnpike > camino de peaje Camino construido por una compañía privada que cobra una cuota por su uso.

Tutsis > tutsis Principal grupo étnico minoritario de Ruanda y Burundi.

Tutu, Desmond > Tutu, Desmond Desmond Tutu (1931–) es un arzobispo de la Iglesia Anglicana y fue líder de la lucha en contra del apartheid en Sudáfrica. En 1984 ganó el Premio Nobel de la Paz por sus esfuerzos.

Tutu, Osei > Tutu, Osei Osei Tutu nació alrededor de 1660 y murió a principios del siglo XVIII. Fue fundador y primer gobernante del Imperio Asante en lo que hoy en día es Ghana. Comenzó como el jefe del pequeño estado de Kumasi, pero se dio cuenta de que los pequños reinos asantes independientes tenían que unirse para protegerse de los poderosos vecinos Denkiera.

Twenty-One Demands > Veintiuna Exigencias Lista de exigencias dadas por Japón a China en 1915 por las que, si hubiera estado de acuerdo, China se habría convertido en un protectorado de Japón.

tyrant > tirano En la antigua Grecia, gobernante que obtenía el poder por la fuerza.

U

U-boat > U boot Submarino alemán.

ultimatum > ultimátum Serie final de exigencias.

ultranationalist > ultranacionalista Nacionalista extremo.

Umayyad > omeyas Miembros de la dinastía sunita de califas que gobernó de 661 a 750.

United Nations (UN) > Organización de las) Naciones Unidas (ONU) Organización internacional fundada en 1945 al final de la Segunda Guerra Mundial. Desde entonces, su rol global ha crecido e incluye economía y desarrollo social, derechos humanos, ayuda humanitaria y derecho internacional.

universal manhood suffrage > sufragio universal masculino Derecho de todos los hombres adultos a votar.

untouchable > intocable Marginados o miembros de la casta más baja de India.

Urban II, Pope > Urbano II, papa El papa Urbano II (1042–1099) fue el líder de la Iglesia católica romana en la época en la que los turcos selyúcidas amenazaban el Imperio Bizantino. Convocó el Concilio de Clermont, donde lanzó la Primera Cruzada para liberar Tierra Santa a los musulmanes.

urban renewal > renovación urbana Programas gubernamentales para el desarrollo de las áreas urbanas.

urbanization > urbanización Movimiento de personas de las áreas rurales a las ciudades.

Usman dan Fodio > Usman dan Fodio Usman dan Fodio (1754–1817) fue un líder revolucionario, místico y filósofo fulani. Lideró una revuelta (1804–1808) para crear un nuevo estado musulmán, el Imperio Fulani, en lo que ahora es el norte de Nigeria.

usury > usura Práctica de prestar dinero a interés.

utilitarianism > utilitarismo Idea de que el objetivo de la sociedad debería ser lograr la mayor felicidad para el mayor número de personas.

utopian > utópico Idealista o visionario; normalmente se usa para describir una sociedad perfecta.

V

V-E Day > Día V-E Día de la Victoria en Europa, el 8 de mayo de 1945, fecha en que los Aliados vencieron en Europa durante la Segunda Guerra Mundial.

Valley of Mexico > valle de México Valle en México en el cual se desarrollaron numerosas civilizaciones mesoamericanas, incluyendo los aztecas.

van Gogh, Vincent > van Gogh, Vincent Vincent van Gogh (1853–1890) fue un artista durante solo diez años, pero produjo más de 2,000 dibujos, bocetos y pinturas. Desde el principio, los impresionistas influyeron mucho en su estilo. Más tarde se trasladó a Arles, Francia. Mientras estaba allí tuvo un colapso nervioso y él mismo pidió que le internaran en un hospital psiquiátrico. Durante este tiempo, comenzó a usar colores más llamativos, pinceladas amplias, movimiento en formas y líneas y gruesas capas de pintura. Fue dado de alta en mayo de 1890 y murió dos meses más tarde.

vanguard > vanguardia Grupo de líderes de la élite.

varna > varna En la sociedad védica de la antigua India, un tipo de personalidad que determinaba la ocupación de una persona; luego una categoría en el sistema de castas de la India.

vassal > vasallo Durante la Edad Media, señor a quien se le cedía un terreno a cambio de servicio y lealtad al señor más importante.

Vedas > Vedas Conjunto de oraciones, himnos y otras enseñanzas religiosas desarrolladas en la antigua India a partir de alrededor del siglo XVI a. C.

veneration > veneración Consideración especial.

vernacular > vernáculo Lenguaje diario de la gente común.

Versailles > Versalles Residencia de la realeza francesa y sede de gobierno establecidos por el rey Luis XIV.

veto > veto Bloqueo a la acción de un gobierno.

viceroy > virrey Representante del rey de España que gobernaba las colonias en su nombre.

Vichy > Vichy Ciudad en el centro de Francia desde donde un gobierno títere dirigió la Francia no ocupada y las colonias francesas.

Victoria, Queen > Victoria, reina La reina Victoria (1819–1901) reinó de 1837 a 1901, el reinado más largo de la historia de Inglaterra. Simbolizó la vida inglesa durante el periodo conocido como la época victoriana. Fijó un tono de respetabilidad moral y estrictos modales sociales. Iniciadora de las tendencias entre la creciente clase media, introdujo costumbres como poner el árbol de Navidad (una costumbre alemana) y llevar un vestido de boda blanco.

Viet Cong > Vietcong Rebeldes comunistas sudvietnamitas que hicieron guerra de guerrillas que buscó derrocar al gobierno de Vietnam del Sur; recibió ayuda de Vietnam del Norte.

Vikings > vikingo Pueblo escandinavo cuyos marineros asaltaron Europa durante los siglos VIII al XII.

Virgil > Virgilio Virgilio (70 a. C.–19 a. C.) fue un poeta romano que escribió la *Eneida* en el año 30 a. C. Estudió matemáticas y otros temas en Roma y Nápoles y se inspiró en los poetas griegos.

vizier > visir Primer ministro que supervisaba los asuntos de gobierno en el antiguo Egipto.

Voltaire > Voltaire Voltaire (1694–1778) al nacer recibió el nombre de François-Marie Arouet, pero fue conocido como Voltaire. Fue un apasionado poeta, historiador, ensayista y filósofo que escribió con mordaz sarcasmo y aguda inteligencia. Voltaire fue enviado a la prisión de La Bastilla dos veces debido a sus críticas a las autoridades francesas y finalmente fue expulsado de París. Cuando pudo regresar a Francia, escribió sobre libertad política y religiosa. Voltaire pasó su vida luchando contra aquellos que consideraba enemigos de la libertad, como la ignorancia, la superstición y la intolerancia.

W

Walesa, Lech > Walesa, Lech Lech Walesa (n. 1943) ayudó a fundar y dirigir el sindicato independiente polaco, Solidaridad, en el Astillero Lenin en Gdansk, donde era electricista. Después de las enérgicas medidas que el gobierno polaco tomó sobre Solidaridad en 1981, fue encarcelado durante casi un año. Walesa fue premiado con el Premio Nobel de la Paz en 1983. Después de la caída del régimen comunista en Polonia, Walesa fue electo presidente de Polonia desde 1990 hasta 1995.

War of the Austrian Succession > Guerra de Sucesión Austriaca Serie de guerras en las que diversos países europeos lucharon por la hegemonía en Centroeuropa después de la muerte de Carlos IV, emperador Habsburgo.

warlords > señores de la guerra Gobernantes militares locales.

warm-water port > puerto de aguas templadas Puerto en el que sus aguas nunca se congelan a lo largo del año.

Warsaw Pact > Pacto de Varsovia Alianza de mutua defensa establecida en 1955 entre la Unión Soviética y siete estados satélite en Europa del Este

Washington, George > Washington, George George Washington (1732–1799) fue un acaudalado hacendado de Virginia antes de ser el comandante del ejército americano durante la Guerra de Independencia y primer Presidente de los Estados Unidos. Poseía una gran propiedad llamada Mount Vernon. Usando sus habilidades como político, negociador y general, Washington pudo mantener viva la causa americana de la libertad durante y después de la guerra.

Watt, James > Watt, James James Watt (1736–1819) de Escocia inventó la máquina de vapor. Desarrolló primero un interés por construir modelos y medir instrumentos en el taller de su padre, que construía casas y barcos. Watt fue aprendiz con un fabricante de instrumentos matemáticos. En 1765, trabajó en su máquina de vapor. Tenía un condensador independiente que ayudaba a impedir que se escapara el vapor. Más tarde, trabajó como topógrafo y luego volvió a inventar y perfeccionar máquinas, hasta su retiro en 1800.

weapon of mass destruction (WMD) > arma de destrucción masiva Arma nuclear, biológica o química.

welfare state > estado de bienestar Un país con una economía de mercado, pero con una mayor responsabilidad del gobierno hacia las necesidades sociales y económicas de su pueblo.

westernization > occidentalización Adopción de ideas, tecnología y cultura occidentales.

Whitney, Eli > Whitney, Eli Eli Whitney (1765–1825) mostró tener habilidades mecánicas y de ingeniería desde temprana edad. Después de graduarse de la Universidad de Yale, se dirigió hacia el sur donde los propietarios de plantaciones supieron de su habilidad mecánica y le pidieron ayuda. El costo de la mano de obra para procesar el algodón era demasiado alto. En respuesta, Whitney inventó la desmotadora, que revolucionó la industria textil y ayudó a la economía del Sur. Lamentablemente, Whitney no sacó beneficios de su invento. Dejó el Sur lleno de deudas pero siguió diseñando inventos hasta su muerte.

William II > Guillermo II Guillermo II (1859–1941) fue el último emperador alemán y rey de Prusia. Gobernó el Imperio Alemán y el reino de Prusia de 1888 a 1918. Llevó a Alemania a la Primera Guerra Mundial. Fue un líder militar ineficaz y perdió el apoyo de su ejército; en noviembre de 1918 huyó al exilio en los Países Bajos.

William the Conqueror > Guillermo el Conquistador Guillermo el Conquistador (1028–1087) fue duque de Normandía a los 7 años de edad y nombrado caballero a los 15. Presionó al rey Eduardo de Inglaterra para que lo nombrara heredero del trono. Después de la muerte de Eduardo, Guillermo invadió Inglaterra y ganó el trono después de la batalla de Hastings en 1066.

Wittenberg > Wittenberg Ciudad al norte de Alemania donde Lutero redactó sus 95 tesis.

women's suffrage > sufragio femenino Derecho de las mujeres a votar.

Wordsworth, William > Wordsworth, William William Wordsworth (1770–1850) fue decisivo en el surgimiento del Romanticismo y escribió algunos de los poemas más influyentes de la literatura occidental. Mientras viajaba por Europa, se encontró con la Revolución Francesa, que despertó en él un interés en las preocupaciones del "hombre común". Su simpatía por la gente y el reconocimiento de las desgracias sociales, particularmente en las zonas urbanas, le sirvieron de inspiración para su obra y su fuerte enfoque en las emociones. También inspiró su punto de vista del papel del poeta en la sociedad y sus ideales políticos.

World Trade Organization (WTO) > Organización Mundial del Comercio (OMC) Organización internacional formada para estimular el comercio mundial.

Wright, Orville and Wilbur > Wright, Orville y Wilbur Orville (1871–1948) y Wilbur (1867–1912) Wright fueron mecánicos de bicicletas que usaron sus conocimientos de ciencia y su experiencia como mecánicos para crear la primera máquina voladora. Después de casi 1,000 vuelos en planeadores y pruebas en túneles de viento, los hermanos construyeron un avión a motor. El 17 de diciembre de 1903, los hermanos probaron su máquina en Kitty Hawk, Carolina del Norte. El primer vuelo duró 12 segundos; ese día el vuelo más largo duró 59 segundos.

Wudi > Wudi Wudi (156 a. C.–87 a. C.) recibió al nacer el nombre de Liu Che. Fue el onceavo hijo de Jingdi, el emperador Han y, por tanto, no hubiera estado destinado a gobernar. Sin embargo, la influencia de sus parientes cambió esto y fue nombrado emperador en el año 141 a. C. Determinado a ampliar el gobierno de su dinastía, tuvo éxito, aunque a un gran costo de soldados y gente. Liu Che hizo de la doctrina de Confucio la religión de estado. Después de su muerte recibió el título de Wudi (Emperador Marcial).

Y

Yalta Conference > Conferencia de Yalta Reunión entre Roosevelt, Churchill y Stalin realizada en febrero de 1945 en la que los tres líderes llegaron a acuerdos para finalizar la Segunda Guerra Mundial.

Yathrib > Yathrib Destino final de la hégira de Mahoma y hogar de la primera comunidad de musulmanes; posteriormente rebautizada como Medina; ubicada en el noroeste de la actual Arabia Saudita.

Yorktown, Virginia > Yorktown, Virginia Lugar donde el ejército británico se rindió en la Guerra de Independencia.

Yuan dynasty > dinastía Yuan Dinastía china gobernada por los mongoles de 1279 a 1368; su gobernante más conocido fue Kublai Khan.

Z

zaibatsu > zaibatsu Familias japonesas de banqueros e industriales poderosos desde finales del siglo XIX.

Zapata, Emiliano > Zapata, Emiliano Emiliano Zapata (1879–1919) creció como campesino. En 1897 comenzó una larga lucha contra el sistema de haciendas para recuperar la tierra a los campesinos. Después de que Francisco Madero perdiera las elecciones frente a Porfirio Díaz, Zapata se unió a la revolución y luchó a favor de la reforma social. Zapata formó un fuerte grupo de seguidores y desempeñó un papel esencial en la derrota de Victoriano Huerta en 1914. Después de que Venustiano Carranza fuera electo presidente, este se volvió contra Zapata. Los revolucionarios de Zapata fueron a la guerra con los moderados que apoyaban a Carranza. En 1919, el ejército de Carranza emboscó y mató a Zapata.

zemstvo > zemstvos Asamblea local electa que se estableció en Rusia en la época de Alejandro II.

Zen > zen Práctica de meditación; escuela del budismo en Japón.

zeppelin > zepelín Dirigible, globo grande lleno de gas.

Zheng He > Cheng Ho Cheng Ho (c. 1371–1433) fue un diplomático y almirante de la Marina china de los Ming que hizo su primer viaje en 1405 a Vietnam, India y África para explorar y comerciar. Su enorme flota de cientos de juncos (barcos chinos) y miles de marineros llevaron seda, porcelana y artesanías lacadas para intercambiar por perlas, especias, marfil y madera. Cheng Ho hizo en total siete viajes, explorando y comercializando con éxito y, por tanto, motivando a los mercaderes chinos a establecer centros de comercio en el sureste de Asia e India.

ziggurat > zigurat Templo piramidal de la antigua Mesopotamia dedicado al dios o diosa principal de una ciudad-estado.

Zionism > sionismo Movimiento dedicado a la reconstrucción del estado judío en Palestina.

Zoroaster > Zaratustra Zaratustra (alrededor del año 628 a. C.–551 a. C.) Zaratustra fue un reformador religioso iraní y fundador del zaratustrismo. Enfatizó la libertad individual para elegir lo correcto de lo incorrecto y la responsabilidad individual de las acciones de cada uno. Las ideas de Zaratustra influyeron en los primeros tiempos de la filosofía.

Akkadians, cuneiform of, 36
"Aladdin and His Magic Lamp", 323
Alamo, 751
Alaska, 124
al-Assad, Bashir, 1009, 1062
al-Assad, Hafez, 1009
Alawites, 997
Al-Bakri, 343q
Al-Bashir, Omar, 985
Albert, prince, 675
Albigensian Crusades, 267, 272
Albuquerque, Afonso de, 466, 466p
Alchemy, 103
Alcuin of York, 238
Alexander I, 582
Alexander II, 695, 695p
Alexander III, 696
Alexander the Great, 180–184, 181m
Alexandra, tsarina, 793, 794
Alexandra Kollontai, 855
Alexandria, Egypt, 182, 221
Alexiad **(Comnena)**, 281
Alexius I, 259, 281
Algeria, 718, 896, 934, 979, 981–982
Alhambra, 316
Ali, Muhammad, 726
"Ali Baba and the Forty Thieves",
 323
Alighieri, Dante, 278–279
al-Khwarizmi, 324
Allah, 305
Allende, Salvador, 1017
alliances, 167, 477
Allies, World War II. *see also* Britain;
 Union of Soviet Socialist Republics
 (USSR); United States of America
 aircraft and tank production of, 895,
  895c
 China, 878
 disagreements of, 899
 Europe, victory in, 900–901
 France liberated, 898
 Germany, invasion of, 898–899
 Holocaust revealed to, 904
 Normandy landings, 897–898
 in North Africa, 896, 897m
 in the Pacific, 895–896, 901m–902
 Pacific, victory in, 902–903
 Potsdam Conference, 902, 902p, 903,
  918, 918p
 resources for, 894–895
 response to the Holocaust, 889–891
 Soviet Union, 878
 in Stalingrad, 896–897
 tensions in, 896, 918
 three fronts of, 895–897
 U.S. supporting, 878, 882
 war crimes trials, 904–905
 Yalta Conference, 899, 919
All Quiet on the Western Front
 (Remarque), 837
Almoravids, 338

alpaca, 135
alphabet, development of
 Arabic, 817
 Chinese, 104
 Etruscan and early Roman, 195
 Greek, 45t, 160
 Korean, 391, 392–393
 Latin, 45t, 817
 Minoan, 154
 Modern English, 45t
 Nubian, 333
 Phoenician, 44–45t, 69, 69c
 Russian, 528
 Slavic, 288
Al Qaeda, 968, 972, 1036, 1060
al-Razi, Muhammad, 324–325, 361q
Alsace and Lorraine, 682, 770, 789
Al Shabab, 981
Aluminum, 626
Alvaro II, 353, 353p
Amado, Gilbert, 760q
Amaterasu, 395
Amazon river, 125
American Civil War, 632, 688, 688p
American Federation of Labor, 689
American-Mexican War, 686
American Revolution
 Declaration of Independence, 554
 France, alliance with, 555
 French Revolution, compared to,
  576–577
 impact of, 557
 military strengths and weaknesses,
  555
 tensions leading to, 554–555
 Treaty of Paris, 555
Americas
 British territories, 552–553m
 colonies in, 553–555
 Columbian Exchange, 499–500, 500t
 early civilizations of, 15
 European conquests of, 475–483
 imperialism in, 750–755
 Incan Empire, 135–139
 Mesoamerica, civilizations of,
  124–132
 North America (*see* North America)
 settlements/colonies, 507t
 Spanish America, 481–482
 timeline of, 122, 122c
Amina, 341
Amon-Re, 58–59, 60
Amrit, 369
Amritsar Massacre, 822–823
Anabaptists, 440–441
Anada temple, 405
Analects, 105–106
anarchists, 672
anatomy, 448–449
Anawrahta, King, 404, 404p, 405
ancestor worship, 100–101
Ancestral Puebloans, 141

ancien régime, 560
Ancient Greece (1700 B. C.–331 B. C.)
 achievements of, 187, 187c
 Alexander the Great, 180–184, 181m
 alphabet of, 160
 architecture and art, 174–175,
  182–183
 Athens (city-state), 162–164, 163,
  163c, 166–169
 citizen of, 160
 city-states, 159–169, 187, 187c
 culture unifying, 164–165, 182
 Dorians, 156–158, 158c
 Empire of Alexander the Great,
  181m
 foreigners, view of, 165
 geography of, 159–160
 governments of, 160, 160c
 Historians, 176
 languages of, 164–165
 literature, 175–176
 math and astronomy in, 183
 Minoans, 154–155, 158, 158c, 187,
  187c
 Mycenaean civilization, 155–156,
  158, 158c, 187, 187c
 myths and beliefs, 165
 Olympic games, 165
 Persian wars, 166–167m, 183m
 Philosophers of, 172–174, 182–183
 Sparta (city-state), 161–162, 169
 Thebes, 169
 timeline of, 152, 152c
Andean region
 early civilizations of, 135–136
 Incan Empire, 136–139
Anderson, Arthur J.O., 133–134
Andes mountains, 125, 135–136
anesthetic, 597, 597p, 619
Angkor Wat, 406, 406p
Anglo-Saxons
 in Britain, 264–267
 Christian conversion of, 245, 264
Angola, 981, 983
animism, 10
Annalin, 761q
Annam, 406
annex, 580, 664
Anschluss, 875–876
Anthony, Mark, 204
Anthony, Susan B., 626, 639, 639c
anthrax vaccines, 618
anthropology, 5, 25t
anti-globalization movement, 1047,
 1047p
Antigon **(Sophocles)**, 164
Antioch, 221
anti-Semitism
 in Austria, 858
 in Europe, 819
 in France, 684–685
 in Germany, 859, 860–861, 886–888

in Mayan culture, 129
in New Babylon, 42
in Roman Empire, 214
in Song dynasty, 375
in Sumerian civilization, 36
in Timbuktu, 340, 340c
Atacama, 125
Atahualpa, 478, 478p
Atatürk, 816, 817, 817p, 818, 1001
atheism, 844, 855
Athena, 165, 168, 168p, 174
Athens (city-state)
Acropolis, 162, 162p
Age of Pericles, 167–169, 170
Delian League, 169
democracy in, 162–164
fall to Macedonia, 180
The Funeral Oration of Pericles
(431BCE), 170–171
Peloponnesian War, 169
Persian wars, 166–167m
phalanx used by, 161
playwrights of, 175–176
Atlantic Charter, 882
Atlantic slave trade, 494–496, 495,
495c
atman, 84
atomic bomb, 836, 902–903, 913m,
913q, 922c, 922–923
atomic fission, 836
atomic theory, 627
Aton, Egyptian god, 60
atrocities, defined, 783
Attica, 162
Attila (the Hun), 208
Augustine, Bishop, 222, 222p, 245,
247, 334
Augustus, 204–205, 213
Aurangzeb, 371
Aurelius, Marcus, 205, 212
Auschwitz, 887, 889, 890
Australia
developed economy of, 1041
imperialism in, 747–748, 749
industrialization in, 603
Pacific Ring of Fire, 395
during Paleolithic Period, 10
as penal colony, 677
in SEATO, 923
Australian ballot, 748
Australopithecus afarenis, 7, 7c
Austria
annexation by Germany, 874, 874c,
875–876, 875p
Catholic Church in, 647
challenges for, 691–692
Denmark, war with, 664
diverse population of, 648
in the Enlightenment, 549
expansion, 525
France, 582
independence of, 789
nationalism, 701, 701c

revolts in, 653
Serbia and, 771, 789
Seven Years' War, 531
Austria-Hungary, 692, 710, 768,
770–771, 777
Austrian Hapsburg empire, 662. *see
also* Hapsburgs
Austro-Prussian war, 664, 671
authoritarian rule, 805, 861–862, 863
autocracy, 1038
autocratic, 234, 527, 970
automobiles, 617
autonomy, 649
Avars, 292
Averroës, 277
avian flu (bird flu), 1050
Avicenna (Sina, Ibn), 324–325
Avignon, 268, 284
Axis powers
development of, 833, 874
European domination by, 878–883
German expansion (1936–1939),
879m
Axum, 333, 344–345m
Ayatollah, 1000
ayllu, 137
Ayurveda, 92, 92p
Azerbaijan, 1038
Aztecs, 15, 125m, 130c, 130–132,
138–139, 148m, 476–478
Aztec temple, 131, 131p

B

Babur, 370
Babylon
Alexander the Great conquering, 181
cuneiform of, 36, 36c
Hammurabi's code, 39c, 39–40
Hanging Gardens, 41
innovations of, 69, 69c
Judah conquered by, 49
laws of, 39c, 39–40
Nebuchadnezzar, 41–42
New Babylonian Empire, 41–42
religion in, 40
slavery laws in, 39
women in, 39
**Babylonian Captivity of the
Church**, 284
Bach, Johann Sebastian, 548, 548p
Bacon, Francis, 447–448
Baghdad, 315–316, 315p, 317, 323
Bahrain, 997
**Bakr al-Wangariai, Mohammad
abu**, 340, 340c
balance of power, 522
balance of terror, 922
balance of trade, 733
Balbo, Italo, 845
Balboa, Vasco Núñez de, 464
Balfour Declaration, 819, 997
Balkan Peninsula, 291

Balkans
in Middle Ages, 291–294, 292, 292c
nationalism, 701, 701c
revolts in, 648–649
wars, 693–694, 771, 1037
in World War I, 693–694
in World War II, 878, 881
ball courts, 126
Baltic Sea, 292
Baltic states, 789
Bang Chiang, 404
Bangkok, 1047, 1047p
Bangladesh, 76, 967m, 968–969
Banister, John, 449, 449p
banks
in Arab empire, 320
origins of, 256
Bantu migrations, 332–333
Ban Zhao, 112
baptism, in early Christianity, 220
barbarians (*barbaroi*), 165
***barbaroi* (barbarians)**, 165
Barbarossa, Frederick, 270–271, 881
baroque, 547
barter economy, 43
Bastille, 564–565
Bataan Death March, 901
batteries, 616
Battle of Britain, 880, 880p
Battle of El Alamein, 896
Battle of Hastings, 264
Battle of Midway, 896
Battle of Myeongnyang, 471, 471p
Battle of Sekigahara, 399, 399p
Battle of Stalingrad, 897
Battle of the Bulge, 898
Battle of the Coral Sea, 895–896
Battle of the Pyramids, 723, 723p
Battle of Tours, 236, 236p, 314
Battuta, Ibn, 342q, 347–348, 348q
Batu, 289
Bauhaus, 838
Bayeaux Tapestry, 280, 280p
Bay of Pigs, 924
Becket, Thomas, 265, 279, 279p
Bedouins, 304, 314
Beer Hall Putsch, 859
Beethoven, Ludwig van, 630, 639,
639c
Beijing, 382, 384
Belgian Congo, 718
Belgium
in Africa, 717–718, 978, 982, 984
independence of, 650–651
Industrial Revolution, 602
post-World War II, 934
in World War I, 772, 772p
in World War II, 879, 898
Belisarius, 233
Bell, Alexander Graham, 617, 639,
639c
Belzec, 890
Benedictine Rule, 247

Sikhism, 369
  in Song dynasty, 377–378
  in Spanish America, 482
  in Tang dynasty, 377–378
cuneiform, 35–36, 36, 36c, 41
Curie, Marie, 836
Curiosity rover, 1065, 1065p
Cuzco, 136, 137
cybersecurity, 1062–1063
cyberwarfare, 1061
Cyril and Methodius, 288
Cyrillic, 288
Czechoslovakia, 789, 874, 874c,
  876–877, 876p, 919, 921–922, 950, 951
Czech Republic, 292, 951, 1036
Czechs, 692

D

Dachau, 887–888
d'Ache, Caren, 703q
dada, 838
Da Gama, Vasco, 460, 460p
Daguerre, Louis, 632, 632p
Daimler, Gottlieb, 617, 639, 639c
daimyo, 398, 399–400
Daladier, Edouard, 876
Dali, Salvador, 838
Dalits, 85, 966, 977
Dalton, John, 627, 639, 639c
Damascus, 312, 313
Daniel, Annie, 623
Danube river, 292
Daoism, 102–103
Darby, Abraham, 598–599
Dardanelles, 181, 725, 778, 919
Darfur, 985
Darius I, 42–43, 166, 166p
Darius III, 181
Dark Ages, 236
Darwin, Charles, 628, 628p, 639, 639c
David, King of Israel, 48
Davies, Emily, 627
Dawes Plan, 858
Dayton Accords, 951, 1037
D-Day, 897, 899, 899p
Dead Sea Scrolls, 50
Deák, Ferenc, 692
death camps, 887
death squads, 1016
Deborah, Israeli judge, 49
debt crisis, 1036, 1044
debt slavery, 162
Deccan Kingdom, 91
Deccan plateau, 77, 370
decimal system, 92
decipher, 61
Declaration of Independence (U.S.),
  554, 557, 589t
Declaration of Pilnitz, 571–572
Declaration of the Rights of Man,
  566, 566p

**Declaration of the Rights of
  Woman and the Female Citizen**,
  566
Deepwater Horizon, 1053, 1053p,
  1054
default, 1038
Defenestration of Prague, 524
deficit, 1038
deficit spending, 562, 562c
Defoe, Daniel, 283, 548
deforestation, 730, 991–992, 1054
Degas, Edgar, 633, 639, 639c
De Gaulle, Charles, 879
De Gouges, Olympe, 566, 569–570
Dekanawidah, 143
de Klerk, F.W., 989, 995
Delacroix, Eugène, 631, 631p
De Lesseps, Ferdinand, 726
Delhi, 371
Delhi, India, 729, 729p
Delhi Sultanate, 366–369
Delian League, 167, 169
Delos, 167
delta, 55
demilitarized zone (DMZ), 941
democracy
  in Africa, 980
  in Age of Pericles, 167–168
  in Argentina, 1018, 1018p, 1019
  in Athens, 162–164
  British Parliament, 674, 675–676
  in Eastern Europe, 861–862, 949
  the Enlightenment, 589, 589c
  fascists' view of, 847
  in Japan, 830–831
  in Latin America, 1013–1015,
    1016–1017
  loss of faith in, 844
  parliamentary democracy, 676
  in the Philippines, 971–972
  roots of, 489t
  social democracy, 612
  timeline, 644
  in US, 687
Democracy in America, 644
Democratic Republic of Congo, 981,
  982
Deng Xiaoping, 973
Denmark
  in European Union (EU), 934
  post–World War II, 934
  Prussia, war with, 664
  Vikings, 239
  during World War II, 888
De Pisan, Christine, 277q
depopulation, 524
Descartes, René, 447–448
desegregation, 931
Desert Fox, 881, 881p, 896
desertification, 332, 992–993, 1054
De Sigma, Boncomagno, 276
Despots, enlightened, 548–549

De Staël, Germaine, 545
détente, 923
developed countries, 612, 835
developing countries, 982, 1030,
  1031c, 1031–1032, 1044, 1053–1054
developing world, 1030
development of countries
  challenges to, 991–993, 1032–1033
  in China, 973–975
  cooperation, 991
  defined, 1030
  the environment impacted by,
    991–992, 1053–1055
  in India, 975–977
  social change, 1033–1034
  sustainable development, 992
  urbanization, 991, 991c
  working toward, 1030–1032
De Vivar, Rodrigo Díaz (El Cid), 278
dharma, 84
The Diary of a Young Girl, 892
Dias, Bartholomeu, 349
Diasopra, 50, 50m
Díaz, Porfirio, 752, 808
Dibble, Charles E., 133–134
Dickens, Charles, 631, 639, 639c, 641q
dictators
  in Africa, 980
  caudillos, 751
  in early Rome Republic, 196, 225, 225c
  in Eastern Europe, 861–862
  in Latin America, 1015–1016
  Napoleon III, 681
Diderot, Denis, 544–545, 550
Dien Bien Phu, 943
diet (assembly), 294, 434, 434p, 740
Digital Revolution, 1066
dikes, 597
Diocletian, 207
Dionysus, 175
direct democracy, 167
direct rule, 711
dirty war, 1019
disarmament, 841, 922c, 922–923
Discourse on Methods, 448
discrimination, 931
diseases
  Black Death (bubonic plague),
    282–283
  in concentration camps, 890
  global, 1050
  government regulation of, 993, 1050
  influenza (Spanish Flu 1918), 787
  during the Middle Passage, 494
  Native Americans dying of, 476, 477
  polio, 1067
  prevention, 598, 618–619, 621, 905,
    938, 1066–1068
  in slums, 606, 620
  typhus epidemic, 890
Disraeli, Benjamin, 673q–674,
  675–676, 678, 726

Acknowledgments

[Photography]

Front Matter:

v: Letter from Harold Porter. Courtesy of Dwight D. Eisenhower Library and Museum; Pictorial Press Ltd/Alamy Stock Photo, Goodluz/Shutterstock; **vii:** Fuse/Getty Images; **xT:** Mebla Photo Agency/Alamy Stock Photo; **xB:** Larry Lilac/Alamy Stock Photo; **xiT:** Ke Wang/Shutterstock; **xiB:** Afterdan/Fotolia; **xiiT:** Drimi/Fotolia; **xiiB:** Archive Timothy McCarthy/Art Resource, NY; **xiiiT:** S.Borisov/Shutterstock; **xiiiB:** Tupungato/Shutterstock; **xivT:** JorgHackemann/Shutterstock; **xivB:** Dennis Hallinan/Alamy; **xv:** The Map House of London/Exactostock-1491/Superstock; **xviT:** Scala/Art Resource, NY; **xviB:** World History Archive/Alamy; **xvii:** Stuart Forster/Alamy; **xviiiT:** Derek Bayes/Lebrecht Music & Arts/Lebrecht Music & Arts/Corbis; **xviiiB:** Susan Law Cain/Shutterstock; **xixT:** Chronicle/Alamy; **xixB:** Bettmann/Corbis; **xxT:** Robert Maass/Corbis; **xxB:** Daniel Irungu/EPA/Newscom; **xxi:** Massimo_g/Fotolia

Topic 1:

001: Mebla Photo Agency/Alamy Stock Photo; **002L:** © Look and Learn/The Bridgeman Art Library; **002C:** SuperStock/Alamy Stock Photo; **002R:** Lordprice Collection/Alamy Stock Photo; **003:** Nik Wheeler/Alamy Stock Photo; **004:** Kenneth Garrett/National Geographic/Getty Images; **005:** Sunpix People/Alamy Stock Photo; **006:** Sabena Jane Blackbird/Alamy Stock Photo; **009:** © Look and Learn/The Bridgeman Art Library; **010:** National Geographic Image Collection/Alamy Stock Photo; **011T:** Fmajor/iStock Unreleased/Getty Images; **011B:** Chris Howes/Wild Places Photography/Alamy stock photo; **014:** Egyptian/Getty Images; **016:** Robert Harding World Imagery/Corbis; **018:** Julian Money-Kyrle/Alamy Stock Photo; **019:** Matej Kastelic/Shutterstock; **020:** Universal Art Archive/Alamy Stock Photo; **022:** Industryview/Alamy Stock Photo; **024:** Joerg Boethling/Alamy Stock Photo; **026:** Joerg Boethling/Alamy Stock Photo; **027:** Peter Brown/KRT/Newscom

Topic 2:

028: Larry Lilac/Alamy Stock Photo; **030T:** Adam Eastland Art + Architecture/Alamy Stock Photo; **030BL:** Zuma Press, Inc./Alamy Stock Photo; **030BR:** Eddie Gerald/Alamy Stock Photo; **031:** Granger Historical Picture Archve/Alamy Stock Photo; **032:** Mary Evans Picture Library/Alamy Stock Photo; **034:** Zuma Press, Inc./Alamy Stock Photo; **037:** Heritage Image Partnership Ltd/Alamy stock photo; **038:** Dea/M. Carrieri/De Agostini/Getty Images; **040T:** Interfoto/Alamy Stock Photo; **040B:** Interfoto/Alamy Stock Photo; **043T:** Universal Images Group/DeAgostini/Alamy Stock Photo; **043B:** Adam Eastland Art + Architecture/Alamy Stock Photo; **046:** ArtPix/Alamy stock photo; **048T:** Jozefsedmak/Alamy Stock Photo; **048B:** Eddie Gerald/Alamy Stock Photo; **052:** World History Archive/Alamy Stock Photo; **054:** Heritage Image Partnership Ltd/Alamy Stock Photo; **058T:** World History Archive/Alamy Stock Photo; **058B:** SuperStock/Alamy Stock Photo; **059T:** Dudarev Mikhail/Fotolia; **059B:** Roger Wood/Corbis; **060:** Larry Lilac/Alamy Stock Photo; **061:** 300dpi/Shutterstock; **063:** Pius Lee/Shutterstock; **064:** Guildhall Library & Art Gallery/Heritage Images/Hulton Archive/Getty Images; **066:** Jacek Dudzinski/Alamy Stock Photo; **071:** World History Archive/Alamy Stock Photo

Topic 3:

072: Ke Wang/Shutterstock; **074T:** Dea/A DagliOrti/Age Fotostock; **074B:** V&A Images, London/Art Resource, NY; **075:** Lapas77/Fotolia; **076:** Dea/A. DagliOrti/Age Fotostock; **078:** Anonymous/AP Images; **079:** Dea Picture Library/De Agostini Editore/Age Fotostock; **081:** Dinodia Photos/Alamy Stock Photo; **083:** Visvamitra visits Vasishtha's hermitage, Kulu, Punjab Hills, 1700 (w/c & gold on paper), Indian School, (18th century)/University of East Anglia, Norfolk, UK/Robert and Lisa Sainsbury Collection/The Bridgeman Art Library; **084:** PitchayaThammasamisorn/Alamy Stock Photo; **085:** DeAgostini/Dea/M. Seemuller/Getty Images; **086:** Ivan Nesterov/Alamy Stock Photo; **089:** Borromeo/Art Resource, NY; **090T:** Album/Alamy Stock Photo; **090B:** Ephotocorp/Alamy Stock Photo; **092:** The Stapleton Collection/The Bridgeman Art Library; **093:** Dinodia/The Image Works; **094:** SCPhotos/Alamy Stock Photo; **095:** Historic Collection/Alamy Stock Photo; **097:** The Metropolitan Museum of Art. Image source/Art Resource, NY; **098:** V&A Images, London/Art Resource, NY; **100:** SSPL/

The Image Works; **101:** BnF, Dist. RMN-Grand Palais/Art Resource, NY; **102:** DoctorKan/Shutterstock; **103T:** Heritage Image Partnership Ltd/Alamy Stock Photo; **103B:** Ms 202 fol.10 Weaving, from a book on the silk industry (gouache on paper), Chinese School, (19th century) BibliothequeMunicipale, Poitiers, France/Giraudon/The Bridgeman Art Library; **104:** LCM NW/Alamy Stock Photo; **105:** Keren Su/China Span/Alamy Stock Photo; **107:** Hung Chung Chih/Shutterstock; **108T:** Erich Lessing/Art Resource, NY; **108B:** Building the Great Wall of China (gouache on paper), McBride, Angus (1931-2007)/Private Collection/Look and Learn/The Bridgeman Art Library; **109T:** Lapas77/Fotolia; **109B:** Snark/Art Resource, NY; **111T:** A Confucian Classroom (Sodang) (colour print), Hong-Do, Kim (18th century)/National Museum, Seoul, Korea/The Bridgeman Art Library; **111B:** Asian Art & Archaeology, Inc/Corbis; **112:** SSPL/The Image Works; **113T:** Danita Delimont/Alamy Stock Photo; **113B:** Dorling Kindersley ltd/Alamy Stock Photo; **114:** FEMA/Alamy Stock Photo; **116:** Dea/A DagliOrti/Age Fotostock; **118:** Yang Liu/Corbis

Topic 4:

120: Afterdan/Fotolia; **122TL:** Zbiq/Shutterstock; **122TR:** Lordprice Collection/Alamy Stock Photo; **122B:** Jess Kraft/Shutterstock; **123:** Kelsey Green/Shutterstock; **124:** Dea Picture Library/Art Resource, NY; **126T:** Zbiq/Shutterstock; **126B:** Danita Delimont/Alamy Stock Photo; **128T:** Jess Kraft/Shutterstock; **128B:** Richard Maschmeyer/Robert Harding Picture Library/SuperStock; **131T:** Akg-Images/The Image Works; **131B:** Gianni DagliOrti/The Art Archive/Art Resource, NY; **132:** De Agostini Picture Library/Getty Images; **133:** De Agostini Picture Library/Getty Images; **135:** Mark Green/Alamy Stock Photo; **136:** Lordprice Collection/Alamy Stock Photo; **137:** Kelsey Green/Shutterstock; **140:** Robert Shantz/Alamy Stock Photo; **142T:** Ira Block/National Geographic/SuperStock; **142B:** Richard A. Cooke/Corbis; **145:** JPL-Caltech/ESA/Harvard-Smithsonian CfA/NASA; **146:** Jess Kraft/Shutterstock; **149:** World History Archive/Alamy Stock Photo

Topic 5:

150: Drimi/Fotolia; **152TL:** Leonid Serebrennikov/Alamy Stock Photo; **152TR:** Prisma Archivo/Alamy Stock Photo; **152B:** Marble bust of Solon (640-ca 561 BC), Athenian law-maker and poet, Roman copy of greek original from 4th century BC/De Agostini Picture Library/L. Pedicini/The Bridgeman Art Library; **153:** Alinari/Art Resource, NY; **154:** Hervé Lewandowski/©RMN-Grand Palais/Art Resource, NY; **155:** Leonid Serebrennikov/Alamy Stock Photo; **157:** De Agostini Picture L/Age Fotostock; **159:** Universal History Archive/Getty Images; **160G:** Hervé Lewandowski/©RMN-Grand Palais/Art Resource, NY; **160M:** Universal History Archive/Getty Images; **160Q:** Album/Alamy Stock Photo; **160U:** Gezmen/Alamy Stock Photo; **161:** Ancient Art & Architecture Collection Ltd/Alamy Stock Photo; **162T:** Lescourret, Jean-Pierre/SuperStock/Alamy Stock Photo; **162B:** Marble bust of Solon (640-ca 561 BC), Athenian law-maker and poet, Roman copy of greek original from 4th century BC/De Agostini Picture Library/L. Pedicini/The Bridgeman Art Library; **164T:** Bpk, Berlin/Art Resource, NY; **164B:** Votive relief depicting a family sacrificing a bull to Asclepius, the god of health and his daughter, Hygieia, Greek, 5th century BC (marble), ./Louvre, Paris, France/The Bridgeman Art Library; **165:** Steve Vidler/SuperStock; **166:** EmmePi Images/Alamy Stock Photo; **168T:** Erich Lessing/Art Resource, NY; **168B:** Scala/Art Resource, NY; **169:** Bpk, Berlin/Art Resource, NY; **170:** Leemage/Universal Images Group Editorial/Getty Images; **172:** Album/Alamy Stock Photo; **174T:** Alinari/Art Resource, NY; **174B:** Vidler/Age Fotostock; **175T:** Antikensammlung, Kassel, Germany/© Museumslandschaft Hessen Kassel/Ute Brunzel/The Bridgeman Art Library; **175B:** Erich Lessing/Art Resource, NY; **176:** Nimatallah/Art Resource, NY; **178:** Classic Image/Alamy Stock Photo; **180:** Gezmen/Alamy Stock Photo; **182:** Album/Art Resource, NY; **183T:** De Agostini Picture Library/G. Costa/The Bridgeman Art Library; **183B:** World History Archive/Alamy Stock Photo; **185:** SOPA Images Limited/Alamy Stock Photo; **186:** Vidler/Age Fotostock; **189:** Scala/Art Resource, NY

Topic 6:

190: Fazon/Fotolia; **192T:** Archive Timothy McCarthy/Art Resource, NY; **192BL:** H. Motte/Mansell/The Life Picture Collection/Getty Images; **192BR:** Erin Babnik/Alamy Stock Photo; **193:** RMN-Grand Palais/Art

Resource, NY; **197:** Album/Art Resource, NY; **199:** Azoor Photo Collection/ Alamy Stock Photo; **201:** RMN-Grand Palais/Art Resource, NY; **202:** H. Motte/Mansell/The Life Picture Collection/Getty Images; **203T:** RMN-Grand Palais/Art Resource, NY; **203B:** Caesar Dictating his Commentaries (oil on canvas), Palagi, Pelagio (1775-1860)/Palazzo del Quirinale, Rome, Italy/The Bridgeman Art Library; **204TL:** Erin Babnik/Alamy Stock Photo; **204TC:** Alinari/Art Resource, NY; **204TR:** Images Etc Ltd/Getty Images; **204BL:** Peter Horree/Alamy Stock Photo; **204BC:** Portrait bust of Marcus Aurelius (AD 121-80) (marble), Roman, (2nd century AD)/Private Collection/ Photo Boltin Picture Library/The Bridgeman Art Library; **204BR:** Archive Timothy McCarthy/Art Resource, NY; **209T:** Erich Lessing/Art Resource, NY; **209B:** North Wind Picture Archives/Alamy Stock Photo; **211:** Adam Eastland Art + Architecture/Alamy Stock Photo; **212T:** MCLA Collection/ Alamy Stock Photo; **212B:** Horatius Cocles, from the Sala dell'Udienza, 1496-1500(fresco), Perugia, Pietro(c.1445-1523)/Collegio del Cambio, Perugia, Italy/Giraudon/The Bridgeman Art Library; **213:** Erich Lessing/ Art Resource, NY; **214T:** Alan Williams/Dorling Kindersley Ltd; **214B:** Erich Lessing/Art Resource, NY; **215:** Ivy Close Images/Alamy Stock Photo; **216:** Martin Froyda/Shutterstock; **217:** Alfredo DagliOrti/The Art Archive/Art Resource, NY; **218:** Hemis/Alamy Stock Photo; **220T:** Scala/Art Resource, NY; **220B:** Richard Goodrich/Alamy Stock Photo; **222:** Gianni DagliOrti/ The Art Archive/Art Resource, NY; **223:** Pixel Power/Alamy Stock Photo; **224:** Konstantin Kulikov/Fotolia; **227T:** Artokoloro Quint Lox Limited/Alamy Stock Photo; **227B:** Mountainpix/Shutterstock

Topic 7:

228: S.Borisov/Shutterstock; **230T:** North Wind Picture Archives/Alamy Stock Photo; **230B:** Corbis; **231:** North Wind Picture Archives/Alamy Stock Photo; **232:** Chronicle/Alamy Stock Photo; **236:** North Wind Picture Archives/Alamy Stock Photo; **239:** Pantheon/SuperStock; **240:** Private Collection/Index/The Bridgeman Art Library; **241:** Stefano Bianchetti/ Corbis; **242:** Everett Collection Inc/Alamy Stock Photo; **245:** North Wind Picture Archives/Alamy Stock Photo; **246:** Gianni DagliOrti/Corbis; **248:** Stefano Bianchetti/Corbis; **250:** Florilegius/Alamy Stock Photo; **253:** North Wind Picture Archives/The Image Works; **256T:** Bettmann/Corbis; **256B:** The Bridgeman Art Library; **257T:** The Bridgeman Art Library; **257B:** North Wind Picture Archives/Alamy Stock Photo; **258:** French School/ Getty Images; **260:** Mary Evans Picture Library/The Image Works; **262:** 19th era 2/Alamy Stock Photo; **263:** UniversalImagesGroup/Getty Images; **264:** GL Archive/Alamy Stock Photo; **265T:** The Art Gallery Collection/ Alamy Stock Photo; **265B:** 19th era/Alamy Stock Photo; **266:** Dea Picture Library/Contributor/Getty Images; **268:** British Library Board/Robana/Art Resource, NY; **270T:** Ivy Close Images/Alamy Stock Photo; **270B:** World History Archive/Alamy Stock Photo; **273:** Image Asset Management Ltd./ Alamy Stock Photo; **275:** De Agostini Picture Library/Getty Images; **277:** Peter Anderson/Dorling Kindersley Ltd; **278:** Tarker/Corbis; **279T:** Mary Evans Picture Library/Alamy Stock Photo; **279B:** Ben Ramos/Alamy Stock Photo; **280T:** S.Borisov/Shutterstock; **280B:** Topham/The Image Works; **281:** Dmitry Kalinovsky/Shutterstock; **282:** Corbis; **283:** Prisma Archivo/ Alamy Stock Photo; **284T:** Chronicle/Alamy Stock Photo; **284B:** Georgios Kollidas/Shutterstock; **287:** Erich Lessing/Art Resource, NY; **288T:** Ivan Vdovin/Alamy Stock Photo; **288B:** Vasilius/Shutterstock; **289:** Interfoto/ Alamy Stock Photo; **295:** Roy Johnson/DBimages/Alamy Stock Photo; **296:** Dea Picture Library/Contributor/Getty Images; **298:** North Wind Picture Archives/Alamy Stock Photo; **299:** Erica Guilane-Nachez/Fotolia

Topic 8:

300: Tupungato/Shutterstock; **302T:** Age Fotostock/SuperStock; **302B:** Bnf, Dist. RMN-Grand Palais/Art Resource, NY; **303:** North Wind Picture Archives/Alamy Stock Photo; **304:** Universal Images Group/Art Resource, NY; **305T:** Historical image collection by Bildagentur-online/Alamy Stock Photo; **305B:** EPA european pressphoto agency b.v./Alamy Stock Photo; **306T:** MidoSemsem/Shutterstock; **306B:** GFC Collection/Alamy Stock Photo; **307T:** Roland and Sabrina Michaud/Akg Images; **307B:** Robert Harding Picture Library Ltd/Alamy Stock Photo; **309:** MidoSemsem/ Shutterstock; **311:** Index/The Bridgeman Art Library; **312T:** Robert Harding World Imagery/Alamy Stock Photo; **312B:** Atif Saeed/Alamy Stock Photo; **314:** Album/Oronoz/Album/SuperStock; **315T:** The Trustees of the British Museum/Art Resource, NY; **315B:** Age Fotostock/SuperStock; **316:** Sheila Terry/Science Source; **319:** Werner Forman/TopFoto/The Image Works;

321T: Persis Alan King/Alamy Stock Photo; **321B:** Ton Koene/Alamy Stock Photo; **322T:** World Religions Photo Library/Alamy Stock Photo; **322B:** The Art Archive/Alamy Stock Photo; **323:** Prisma Archivo/Alamy Stock Photo; **324:** Science Source; **326:** Historimages Collection/Yolanda Perera Sánchez/ Alamy Stock Photo; **327:** Interfoto/Alamy Stock Photo; **328T:** Bora/Alamy Stock Photo; **328B:** Chronicle/Alamy Stock Photo; **330:** Prisma Archivo/ Alamy Stock Photo; **331:** Photo Mere Travel 3/Alamy Stock Photo; **332:** John Warburton Lee/SuperStock; **333:** Jon Bower- art and museums/Alamy Stock Photo; **336:** Akg Images; **338:** Bnf, Dist. RMN-Grand Palais/Art Resource, NY; **341:** Heritage Image Partnership Ltd/Alamy Stock Photo; **344:** Stefan Auth/imagebroker/Alamy Stock Photo; **347T:** Gavin Hellier/Robert Harding Picture Library Ltd/Alamy Stock Photo; **347B:** John Warburton Lee/ SuperStock; **349:** Robert Holmes/Corbis; **351:** Robert Harding Picture Library Ltd/Alamy Stock Photo; **352T:** Ceremonial wine bowl/Werner Forman Archive/The Bridgeman Art Library; **352B:** Imagebroker/Alamy Stock Photo; **353:** The Art Archive/Alamy Stock Photo; **354:** Age Fotostock/ Alamy Stock Photo; **356:** Eric Lafforgue/Alamy Stock Photo; **358:** Bnf, Dist. RMN-Grand Palais/Art Resource, NY; **361:** World History Archive/Alamy Stock Photo

Topic 9:

362: JorgHackemann/Shutterstock; **364T:** Qiu Ying/Bridgeman Art Library/ Getty Images; **364B:** Culver Pictures, Inc./SuperStock; **365:** GL Archive/ Alamy Stock Photo; **366:** Mughal School/Getty Images; **368T:** Dinodia/ The Image Works/Art Resource, NY; **368B:** Jon Bower Oxford/Alamy Stock Photo; **369:** Dinodia Photos/Alamy Stock Photo; **370:** Peter Cook/ Dorling Kindersley Ltd; **372I:** David Lyons/Alamy Stock Photo; **372M:** Werner Forman/Art Resource, NY; **372O:** The Art Gallery Collection/ Alamy Stock Photo; **372:** David Lyons/Alamy Stock Photo; **373T:** Image Asset Management Ltd./Alamy Stock Photo; **373B:** Art Archive, The/ SuperStock; **374T:** Carlos Amarillo/Shutterstock; **374B:** Werner Forman/ Art Resource, NY; **375:** The Art Gallery Collection/Alamy Stock Photo; **376:** Werner Forman/Art Resource, NY; **379:** The Picture Art Collection/Alamy Stock Photo; **381:** Art Resource, NY; **383T:** North Wind Picture Archives/ Alamy Stock Photo; **383B:** Ancient Art & Architecture Collection Ltd/ Alamy Stock Photo; **384T:** GL Archive/Alamy Stock Photo; **384B:** © The Granger Collection Ltd.; **385T:** Kharbine-Tapabor/The Art Archive/Art Resource, NY; **385B:** Heritage Image Partnership Ltd/Alamy Stock Photo; **388:** Travel Pictures/Alamy Stock Photo; **390:** Rick Browne/Science Source; **392:** Take Photo/Shutterstock; **394:** Peter Horree/Alamy Stock Photo; **396:** SeanPavonePhoto/Fotolia; **397T:** Japanese School, (17th century)/Detroit Institute of Arts, USA/The Bridgeman Art Library; **397B:** Doug Steley A/ Alamy Stock Photo; **398:** Werner Forman/Art Resource, NY; **399T:** Nichiren summoning the divine Shinpu wind to destroy the Mongol-Chinese fleet attacking Japan in 13th century (engraving), Kuniyoshi, Utagawa (1798-1861)/Private Collection/Ancient Art and Architecture Collection Ltd./ The Bridgeman Art Library; **399B:** Culver Pictures, Inc./SuperStock; **400T:** Japanese School, (17th century)/Brooklyn Museum of Art, New York, USA/ Gift of W. W. Hoffman/The Bridgeman Art Library; **400B:** Pietro Scozzari/ Getty Images; **401T:** Ashmolean Museum, University of Oxford, UK/ Purchased with the aid of the National Art Collections Fund/and the Victoria and Albert Fund/The Bridgeman Art Library; **401B:** Heritage Image Partnership Ltd/Alamy Stock Photo; **402:** Chris Willson/Alamy Stock Photo; **403:** Cristiano Burmester/Alamy Stock Photo; **404:** Ivan Trizlic/Fotolia; **406:** Olga Lipatova/Shutterstock; **407:** Wolfgang Kaehler/SuperStock; **408:** Steve Edreff/Shutterstock; **410:** Travel Pictures/Alamy Stock Photo; **413:** DeAgostini/Dea Picture Library/Getty Images

Topic 10:

414: Dennis Hallinan/Alamy Stock Photo; **416L:** Ernie Janes/Alamy Stock Photo; **416R:** NTPL/E. Witty/The Image Works; **417:** Interfoto/ Alamy Stock Photo; **418:** Iberfoto/Superstock; **419T:** Private Collection/ Look and Learn/The Bridgeman Art Library; **419B:** Georgios Kollidas/ Alamy Stock Photo; **421T:** SuperStock; **421C:** World Photos/Alamy Stock Photo; **421B:** Dorling kindersley Ltd; **422T:** SuperStock/Alamy Stock Photo; **422B:** Cosmin-Constantin Sava/Alamy Stock Photo; **423T:** Interfoto/ Alamy Stock Photo; **423B:** World History Archive/Alamy Stock Photo; **424G:** Iberfoto/SuperStock; **424O:** Classicpaintings/Alamy Stock Photo; **424:** The Print Collector/Alamy Stock Photo; **425:** FLHC 7/Alamy Stock Photo; **427:** Classicpaintings/Alamy Stock Photo; **428T:** SuperStock/

SuperStock; **428B:** Album/quintlox/Album/SuperStock; **429T:** Photos 12/ Alamy Stock Photo; **429B:** GL Archive/Alamy Stock Photo; **431:** North Wind Picture Archives/Alamy Stock Photo; **432:** Akg Images; **433:** Akg Images/The Image Works; **434:** North Wind Picture Archives/Alamy Stock Photo; **435T:** Bpk, Berlin/Art Resource, NY; **435B:** Prisma Archivo/Alamy Stock Photo; **438:** Interfoto/Alamy Stock Photo; **440:** NTPL/E. Witty/The Image Works; **441:** Tom Taylor/Alamy Stock Photo; **442T:** Visual & Written/ SuperStock; **442B:** World History Archive/Alamy Stock Photo; **443T:** Gianni DagliOrti/The Art Archive/Alamy Stock Photo; **443B:** Album/Prisma/ Album/SuperStock; **445:** 2d Alan King/Alamy Stock Photo; **446:** Image Asset Management Ltd./SuperStock; **447:** Huens, Jean-Leon (1921-82)/ National Geographic Creative/The Bridgeman Art Library; **449T:** Glasgow University Library, Scotland/The Bridgeman Art Library; **449B:** Everett Collection Historical/Alamy Stock Photo; **450:** North Wind Picture Archives/ Alamy Stock Photo; **451:** Ververidis Vasilis/Shutterstock; **452:** North Wind Picture Archives/Alamy Stock Photo; **454:** Cosmin-Constantin Sava/Alamy Stock Photo

Topic 11:

456: The Map House of London/Exactostock-1491/SuperStock; **458L:** Album/Art Resource, NY; **458R:** ClassicStock/Alamy Stock Photo; **459:** North Wind Picture Archives/Alamy Stock Photo; **460:** Mary Evans Picture Library/Alamy Stock Photo; **462:** Historic Map Works LLC and Osher Map Library/Getty Images; **465:** Pictorial Press Ltd/Alamy Stock Photo; **466:** Universal Images Group/SuperStock; **467:** North Wind Picture Archives/Alamy Stock Photo; **468T:** The Trustees of the British Museum/ Art Resource, NY; **468B:** Heritage Image Partnership Ltd/Alamy Stock Photo; **469T:** Dea/G. DagliOrti/De Agostini Picture Library/Getty Images; **469B:** By permission of the Governors of Stonyhurst College/Weld Charles (fl.1850)/The Bridgeman Art Library; **471T:** World History Archive/Alamy Stock Photo; **471B:** Fine Art Images/SuperStock; **472:** RMN-Grand Palais/ Art Resource, NY; **473:** Art Collection/Alamy Stock Photo; **475:** Album/ Art Resource, NY; **476T:** Album/Art Resource, NY; **476B:** North Wind Picture Archives/Alamy Stock Photo; **478T:** Bpk, Berlin/Art Resource, NY; **478B:** North Wind Picture Archives/Alamy Stock Photo; **481:** Scala/Art Resource, NY; **482:** Age Fotostock/Alamy Stock Photo; **484:** North Wind Picture Archives/Alamy Stock Photo; **486:** De Agostini/SuperStock; **491:** ClassicStock/Alamy Stock Photo; **492T:** Mary Evans Picture Library/Alamy Stock Photo; **492B:** Mary Evans Picture Library/Alamy Stock Photo; **494:** 2d Alan King/Alamy Stock Photo; **497:** Portrait of an African, c.1757-60 (oil on canvas), Ramsay, Allan (1713-84) (attr. to)/Royal Albert Memorial Museum, Exeter, Devon, UK/The Bridgeman Art Library; **499:** Theodore de Bry/The Bridgeman Art Library/Getty Images; **502T:** Universal History Archive/ UIG/Getty Images; **502B:** De Agostini Picture Library/Getty Images; **503:** O'Shea Gallery, London, UK/Morden, Robert (fl.1682-1703)/The Bridgeman Art Library; **504:** Stephen Chung/Alamy Live News/Alamy Stock Photo; **506:** North Wind Picture Archives/Alamy Stock Photo; **509T:** Design Pics/ Newscom; **509B:** Dea/G. DagoliOrti/De Agostini/Getty Images

Topic 12:

510: Scala/Art Resource, NY; **512T:** Erich Lessing/Art Resource, NY; **512B:** Collection/Active Museum/Le Pictorium/Alamy Stock Photo; **513:** Rich Koele/Shutterstock; **514:** Erich Lessing/Art Resource, NY; **515:** Reich, Jacques/Copyright by Lea Brothers & Company/Library of Congress; **516T:** Paul M.R. Maeyaert/Akg Images; **516B:** Akg Images; **518:** Peter Horree/ Alamy Stock Photo; **519T:** Akg Images; **519B:** Gianni DagliOrti/The Art Archive/Art Resource, NY; **521T:** Forget Patrick/Sagaphoto.com/Alamy Stock Photo; **521B:** Jose Ignacio Soto/Shutterstock; **522:** North Wind Picture Archives/Alamy Stock Photo; **523:** De Agostini/Getty Images; **525:** De Agostini Pict.Lib./M. Seemuller/Akg Images; **526:** Dea/G. DagliOrti/ De Agostini/Getty Images; **527T:** Sovfoto/Universal Images Group/Getty Images; **527B:** Image Asset Management Ltd./SuperStock; **528T:** The Art Gallery Collection/Alamy Stock Photo; **528B:** Akg Images; **529T:** State Central Navy Museum, St. Petersburg/The Bridgeman Art Library; **529B:** Akg Images; **531:** Akg Images; **532:** Akg Images; **533T:** Glasshouse Images/Alamy Stock Photo; **533B:** Lebrecht Music and Arts Photo Library/ Alamy Stock Photo; **534:** Copley, John Singleton (1738-1815)/Boston Public Library, Boston, Massachusetts, USA/The Bridgeman Art Library; **535T:** Ernest Crofts/The Bridgeman Art Library/Getty Images; **535B:** Akg

Images; **537:** Universal History Archive/Getty Images/Universal Images Group/Getty Images; **539:** Balthasar Nebot/Getty Images; **540:** The Print Collector/Alamy Stock Photo; **542:** National Geographic Image Collection/ Alamy Stock Photo; **543:** Stefano Bianchetti/Corbis; **545:** Tate, London/Art Resource, NY; **546:** North Wind Picture Archives/Alamy Stock Photo; **547:** SuperStock/SuperStock; **548:** Pictorial Press Ltd/Alamy Stock Photo; **549:** Fine Art Images/Age Fotostock; **550:** Peter Horree/Alamy Stock Photo; **552:** North Wind Picture Archives/Alamy Stock Photo; **554:** Akg Images; **555:** Everett Collection Inc/Alamy Stock Photo; **556T:** UniversalImagesGroup/ UniversalHistoryArchive/Getty Images; **556B:** Rich Koele/Shutterstock; **558:** Lebrecht Music and Arts Photo Library/Alamy Stock Photo; **560:** Mary Evans Picture Library/Alamy Stock Photo; **561T:** RMN-Grand Palais/ Art Resource, NY; **561B:** Thomas Naudet/Getty Images; **563:** Stefano Bianchetti/Corbis; **564:** Collection/Active Museum/Le Pictorium/Alamy Stock Photo; **565:** Hulton Archive/Getty Images; **566T:** The Gallery Collection/Corbis; **566B:** Akg Images; **568:** Akg Images; **569:** The Gallery Collection/Corbis; **571:** Mary Evans Picture Library/Age Fotostock; **573:** The Art Gallery Collection/Alamy Stock Photo; **574:** Classic Vision/Age Fotostock/SuperStock; **576:** Nick Hanna/Alamy Stock Photo; **578:** Laurent Lecat/Akg Images; **579:** The Print Collector/Alamy Stock Photo; **581T:** The Gallery Collection/Corbis; **581B:** SuperStock/Alamy Stock Photo; **582T:** Prisma Archivo/Alamy Stock Photo; **582B:** The Print Collector/Alamy Stock Photo; **583:** Mary Evans Picture Library/Alamy Stock Photo; **586:** The Asahi Shimbun/Getty Images; **588:** Collection/Active Museum/Le Pictorium/ Alamy Stock Photo; **590:** The Art Gallery Collection/Alamy Stock Photo; **591:** Pictorial Press Ltd/Alamy Stock Photo

Topic 13:

592: World History Archive/Alamy Stock Photo; **594T:** North Wind Picture Archives/Alamy Stock Photo; **594B:** Colport/Alamy Stock Photo; **595:** Album/Art Resource, NY; **596:** DeAgostini/Getty Images; **597:** Prisma Archivo/Alamy Stock Photo; **598:** North Wind Picture Archives/Alamy Stock Photo; **601T:** Doughty, C.L. (1913-85)/Private Collection/Look and Learn/The Bridgeman Art Library; **601B:** ClassicStock.com/SuperStock; **602G:** DeAgostini/Getty Images; **602M:** Classic Image/Alamy Stock Photo; **602Q:** Louis Haghe/Joseph Nash/David Roberts/Album/British Library/ Alamy Stock Photo; **602U:** Everett Collection/Everett Collection Historical/ Alamy Stock Photo; **603:** Glasshouse Images/Alamy Stock Photo; **604:** Classic Image/Alamy Stock Photo; **606:** Niday Picture Library/Alamy Stock Photo; **607:** Corbis; **608:** Everett Collection Inc/Alamy Stock Photo; **609:** GL Archive/Alamy Stock Photo; **610T:** The Print Collector/Alamy Stock Photo; **610B:** North Wind/North Wind Picture Archives; **611:** Austrian Archives/ Corbis; **613:** Corbis; **615:** Louis Haghe/Joseph Nash/David Roberts/The British Library Collections; **616:** Pictorial Press Ltd/Alamy Stock Photo; **617:** Akg-Images/NASA/Newscom; **618:** The Art Archive/Alamy Stock Photo; **620:** Akg-Images/The Image Works; **621:** Keystone-France/Gamma- Keystone/Getty Images; **622:** Akg-Images/The Image Works; **624:** Everett Collection/Everett Collection Historical/Alamy Stock Photo; **625:** OoteBoe 1/Alamy Stock Photo; **626:** Archive Pics/Alamy Stock Photo; **627:** Science and Society/SuperStock; **628:** The Print Collector/Alamy Stock Photo; **629T:** Underwood & Underwood/Corbis; **629B:** The Art Gallery Collection/Alamy Stock Photo; **630:** V&A Images/Alamy Stock Photo; **631T:** Peter Horree/ Alamy Stock Photo; **631B:** Akg Images; **632T:** Michael Freeman/Alamy Stock Photo; **632B:** ArtPix/Alamy Stock Photo; **633:** Album/Art Resource, NY; **634:** Chronicle/Alamy Stock Photo; **636:** PBNJ Productions/Getty Images; **638:** Archive Pics/Alamy Stock Photo; **641:** North Wind Picture Archives/Alamy Stock Photo

Topic 14:

642: Stuart Forster/Alamy Stock Photo; **644L:** Interfoto/Alamy Stock Photo; **644R:** Snark/Art Resource, NY; **645:** 19th era/Alamy Stock Photo; **646:** World History Archive/Alamy Stock Photo; **647B:** Album/Prisma/Album/ SuperStock; **649:** Gianni DagliOrti/The Art Archive/Alamy Stock Photo; **650:** French School, (19th century)/Musee de la Ville de Paris, Musee Carnavalet, Paris, France/The Bridgeman Art Library; **652:** Chronicle of World History/Alamy Stock Photo; **655:** Album/Oronoz/Album/SuperStock; **657T:** Mary Evans Picture Library/The Image Works; **657B:** Private Collection/Look and Learn/Embleton, Ron (1930-88)/The Bridgeman Art Library; **658:** Gianni DagliOrti/The Art Archive/Art Resource, NY;

660: The Picture Art Collection/Alamy Stock Photo; 662: SuperStock; 664: Niday Picture Library/Alamy Stock Photo; 665: Interfoto/Alamy Stock Photo; 666T: Interfoto/Alamy Stock Photo; 666B: World History Archive/Alamy Stock Photo; 667T: Akg Images; 667B: ©S.M./SZ Photo/The Image Works; 668: Interfoto/Alamy Stock Photo; 669: Interfoto/Alamy Stock Photo; 670T: Interfoto/Alamy Stock Photo; 670B: De Agostini Picture Lib./A. De Gregorio/Akg Images; 671: The Cartoon Collector/Print Collector/Getty Images; 672: Marka/Touring club italiano/Alamy Stock Photo; 673: Lebrecht Music & Arts/Alamy Stock Photo; 674: English School, (19th century)/London Metropolitan Archives, City of London/The Bridgeman Art Library; 675T: GL Archive/Alamy Stock Photo; 675B: Scala/White Images/Art Resource, NY; 676: North Wind Picture Archives/Alamy Stock Photo; 677T: World History Archive/Alamy Stock Photo; 677B: North Wind Picture Archives/Alamy Stock Photo; 678: Everett Collection Historical/Alamy Stock Photo; 679: 19th era/Alamy Stock Photo; 681: Tarker/Corbis; 682: Hulton Archive/Getty Images; 683T: Akg Images; 683B: Interfoto/Alamy Stock Photo; 685: Musee National de l'Education, Rouen, France/Archives Charmet/French Photographer, (20th century)/The Bridgeman Art Library; 686: Library of Congress; 688T: Glasshouse Images/Alamy Stock Photo; 688B: Collection of the New-York Historical Society, USA/Kurz and Allison (fl.1880-98)/The Bridgeman Art Library; 691: Niday Picture Library/Alamy Stock Photo; 692: World History Archive/Alamy Stock Photo; 694: DeAgostini/SuperStock; 695: Pantheon/SuperStock; 696T: HIP/Art Resource, NY; 696B: Akg-Images/The Image Works; 697T: Snark/Art Resource, NY; 697B: Russian Photographer, (20th century)/Private Collection/Calmann & King Ltd/The Bridgeman Art Library; 698: Pictorial Press Ltd/Alamy Stock Photo; 699: Badal Chandra Sarker/Alamy Stock Photo; 700: Album/Oronoz/Album/SuperStock; 702: Mary Evans Picture Library/Alamy Stock Photo; 703: CaranD'Ache, Emmanuel Poire/The Bridgeman Art Library

Topic 15:

704: Derek Bayes/Lebrecht Music & Arts/Lebrecht Music & Arts/Corbis; 706L: Glasshouse Images/Alamy Stock Photo; 706R: Everett Collection Inc/Alamy Stock Photo; 707: Hulton Collection/Getty Images; 708: RMN-Grand Palais/Art Resource, NY; 709: Universal History Archive/UIG/Isaac Holden & Sons' Alston, Bradford, United Kingdom/The Bridgeman Art Library; 710: PhotoQuest/Getty Images; 711: Private Collection/Schuler, Jules Theophile (1821-78) (after)/The Bridgeman Art Library; 712: Bibliotheque des Arts Decoratifs, Paris, France/Archives Charmet/The Bridgeman Art Library; 713: RMN-Grand Palais/Art Resource, NY; 714: Dea Picture Library/Getty Images; 715T: Classic Image/Alamy Stock Photo; 715B: BojanBrecelj/Corbis; 716: English School, (19th century)/Private Collection/The Bridgeman Art Library; 718: Universal Images Group/SuperStock; 719: Prisma Archivo/Alamy Stock Photo; 720: Popperfoto/Getty Images; 721: Niday Picture Library/Alamy Stock Photo; 723: The Art Gallery Collection/Alamy Stock Photo; 725: Thomas Nast/CartoonStock; 726: English Photographer, (19th century)/Private Collection/The Bridgeman Art Library; 727: Hulton Archive/Getty Images; 728: The Print Collector/Alamy Stock Photo; 729T: Pictorial Press Ltd/Alamy Stock Photo; 729B: British Library/Robana/Hulton Fine Art Collection/Getty Images; 730: British Library, London, UK/Haig, Axel (1835-1921)/The Bridgeman Art Library; 732: Hulton-Deutsch Collection/Corbis; 733: De Agostini Picture Library/The Bridgeman Art Library; 734: Niday Picture Library/Alamy Stock Photo; 736T: Everett Collection Historical/Alamy Stock Photo; 736B: Snark/Art Resource, NY; 737: Everett Collection Inc/Alamy Stock Photo; 738: Popperfoto/Getty Images; 739: Glasshouse Images/Alamy Stock Photo; 740: ToyoharaChikanobu; 742T: Rykoff Collection/Corbis; 742B: Apic/Hulton Archive/Getty Images; 743: Michelle Gilders/Alamy Stock Photo; 744: The Castle of Batavia, as Seen from Kali Besar West, c.1656 (oil on canvas), Beeckman, Andries (fl.1651)/Rijksmuseum, Amsterdam, The Netherlands/The Bridgeman Art Library; 746: Private Collection/Photo © Christie's Images/Naval Battle, (oil on canvas), Tyler, James Gale (1855-1931)/The Bridgeman Art Library; 747: Akg-Images/Newscom; 748: Lindsey Talbert/Alamy Stock Photo; 749: Alinari Archives/Getty Images; 750: Interim Archives/Getty Images; 751: Dea/G. DagliOrti/Getty Images; 752: World History Archive/Alamy Stock Photo; 754: Bettmann/Corbis; 755T: H.N. Rudd/Historical/Corbis; 755B: Settler's Log House, 1856 (oil on canvas), Krieghoff, Cornelius (1815-72)/Art Gallery of Ontario, Toronto, Canada/The Bridgeman Art Library; 758: Renaud Rebardy/Alamy Stock Photo; 760:

Universal History Archive/UIG/Isaac Holden & Sons' Alston, Bradford, United Kingdom/The Bridgeman Art Library; 762: Hulton Archive/Getty Images

Topic 16:

764: Susan Law Cain/Shutterstock; 766T: Bettmann/Corbis; 766B: TopFoto/The Image Works; 767: Comando Supremo, Italian Army/National Geographic Society/Corbis; 768: Keystone-France/Gamma-Keystone/Getty Images; 769T: DIZ Muenchen GmbH, Sueddeutsche Zeitung Photo/Alamy Stock Photo; 769B: Mary Evans Picture Library/Alamy Stock Photo; 771: Bettmann/Corbis; 772T: S&M/ANSA/UIG/Getty Images; 772B: General Photographic Agency/Getty Images; 774G: Keystone-France/Gamma-Keystone/Getty Images; 774K: Chronicle/Alamy Stock Photo; 774Q: TopFoto/The Image Works; 774: Chronicle/Alamy Stock Photo; 776T: Hulton-Deutsch Collection/Corbis; 776B: Hulton-Deutsch Collection/Corbis; 777: Comando Supremo, Italian Army/National Geographic Society/Corbis; 779: Akg Images/Alamy Stock Photo; 780: Colin Waters/Alamy Stock Photo; 782: TopFoto/The Image Works; 783T: Akg Images/The Image Works; 783B: Pictorial Press Ltd/Alamy Stock Photo; 784: Photos 12/Alamy Stock Photo; 785T: Akg-images/Alamy Stock Photo; 785B: Robert Hunt Library/Mary Evans/The Image Works; 788: WW/Alamy Stock Photo; 790: Bettmann/Corbis; 791: Woodrow Wilson Clenching Fist During Speech/Corbis; 793: Hulton Archive/Getty Images; 794: Fine Art Images/Heritage Images/The Image Works; 795: World History Archive/Alamy Stock Photo; 796: Fine Art Images/Age Fotostock; 798: Everett Collection Historical/Alamy Stock Photo; 799: Imaginechina Limited/Alamy Stock Photo; 800: Akg Images/The Image Works

Topic 17:

804: Chronicle/Alamy Stock Photo; 806T: Ria Novosti/Alamy Stock Photo; 806B: Interfoto/Alamy Stock Photo; 807: Heritage Image Partnership Ltd/Alamy Stock Photo; 808: Corbis; 809T: Historic Collection/Alamy Stock Photo; 809B: Agencia el Universal/El Universal de Mexico/Newscom; 811T: Daniel Leclair/X00162/Reuters/Corbis; 811B: AP Images; 813: Emiliano Rodriguez/Alamy Stock Photo; 814: FPG/Staff/Archive Photos/Getty Images; 815: Savvas Learning Company, LLC. 816T: Sophie Bassouls/Sygma/Corbis; 816B: Scherl/Süddeutsche Zeitung Photo/Alamy Stock Photo; 817T: DIZ Muenchen GmbH, Sueddeutsche Zeitung Photo/Alamy Stock Photo; 817B: Bettmann/Corbis; 819: Hulton-Deutsch Collection/Corbis; 821: Dinodia/Age Fotostock; 822T: Yvan Travert/Akg Images; 822B: GandhiServe/Archiv Peter Rhe/Akg Images; 823: Dinodia/Age Fotostock; 825: Dinodia/Age Fotostock; 827: Hulton Archive/Getty Images; 828: Age Fotostock/Alamy Stock Photo; 830: Pictorial Press Ltd/Alamy Stock Photo; 831T: Underwood & Underwood/Underwood & Underwood/Corbis; 831B: Sotk2011/Alamy Stock Photo; 833: Interfoto/Alamy Stock Photo; 834: Bettmann/Corbis; 835: DIZ Muenchen GmbH, Sueddeutsche Zeitung Photo/Alamy Stock Photo; 836: Keystone Pictures USA/Alamy Stock Photo; 837T: Everett Collection Historical/Alamy Stock Photo; 837B: Dennis Van Tine/LFI/Photoshot/Newscom; 838: Painting/Alamy Stock Photo; 839T: Mark Burnett/Alamy Stock Photo; 839B: Hulton Archive/Stringer/Getty Images; 840: Bettmann/Corbis; 841: Private Collection/Peter Newark Military Pictures/The Bridgeman Art Library; 844: Interfoto/Alamy Stock Photo; 845: Hulton-Deutsch Collection/Corbis; 846: Leemage/UIG/Getty Images; 847: Hulton-Deutsch Collection/Corbis; 848: Stefano Bianchetti/Corbis; 849: Hulton-Deutsch Collection/Corbis; 851T: Fine Art Images/Heritage Images/The Image Works; 851B: Akg Images; 852: Heritage Image Partnership Ltd/Alamy Stock Photo; 854: Heritage Image Partnership Ltd/Alamy Stock Photo; 855: Planet News Archive/SSPL/Getty Images; 857: Mary Evans Picture Library/Alamy Stock Photo; 858: SSPL/The Image Works; 859: Ullstein Bild/Akg Images; 860: SZ Photo/Scherl/The Image Works; 861: Interfoto/Alamy Stock Photo; 863: XieHuanchi/Xinhua/Alamy Stock Photo; 864: Corbis; 866: Fine Art Images/Heritage Images/The Image Works; 867: Akg Images/Archiv Peter Rhe/Newscom

Topic 18:

868: Bettmann/Corbis; 870T: AP Images; 870B: Roger Viollet/Getty Images; 871: AP Images; 872: FPG/Getty Images; 873T: David Low/British Cartoon Archive, University of Kent/Solo Syndication; 873B: Bettmann/Corbis; 874L: Bettmann/Corbis; 874C: AP Images; 874R: Everett Collection;

875T: Robert Capa/International Center of Photography/Magnum Photos; 875B: AP Images; 876T: Interfoto/Akg Images; 876B: AP Images; 877: De Agostini Picture Library/The Bridgeman Art Library; 878: IBL Collections/Mary Evans/Everett Collection; 880T: The National Archives/SSPL/Getty Images; 880B: Everett Collection; 881: Berliner Verlag/Archiv/picture-alliance/dpa/AP Images; 883: Interfoto/Alamy Stock Photo; 884: Keystone/Hulton Archive/Getty Images; 886: US National Archives/Alamy Stock Photo; 888: Anne Frank Fonds Basel/Getty Images; 889: Akg Images; 891: Jim Hollander/epa/Corbis; 892: Anne Frank Fonds Basel/Getty Images; 894: Hulton-Deutsch Collection/Corbis; 896: AP Images; 899: Lightroom Photos/Alamy Stock Photo; 900: AP Images; 902T: Interfoto/Alamy Stock Photo; 902B: Bettmann/Corbis; 903: Roger Viollet/Getty Images; 904T: Corbis; 904B: Pictorial Press Ltd/Alamy Stock Photo; 905: David Lees/Corbis Historical/Getty Images; 907: Natalia Bratslavsky/Shutterstock; 909: Randy Duchaine/Alamy Stock Photo; 910: IBL Collections/Mary Evans/Everett Collection; 912: Ashley Cooper Pics/Alamy Stock Photo

Topic 19:

914: Robert Maass/Corbis; 916T: Thomas Hoepker/Magnum Photos; 916B: Prints & Photographs Division, drawing by Edmund S. Valtman, [LC-DIG-ppmsc-07958]; 917: Sovfoto/UIG/Getty Images; 918: AP Images; 919: Hulton-Deutsch Collection/Corbis; 920: Walter Sanders/Life Magazine/The Life Picture Collection/Getty Images; 923: MPI/Stringer/Getty Images; 924: Sovfoto/UIG/Getty Images; 925: Universal Images Group Limited/Education Images/Alamy Stock Photo; 927: Everett Collection/Historical Collection/Shutterstock; 929: Bert Morgan/Getty Images; 930: Bettmann/Corbis; 931T: Elliott Erwitt/Magnum Photos; 931B: AP Images; 934: AP Images; 935T: John Florea/The Life Picture Collection/Getty Images; 935B: Jerry Cooke/Corbis; 937: Keystone/Getty Images; 938: Keystone-France/Gamma-Keystone/Getty Images; 939T: AFP/Getty Images; 939B: Edmund S. Valtman/Library of Congress; 941: Jason Reed/Reuters/Corbis; 942: AP Images; 943: Horst Faas/AP Images; 945T: JP Laffont/Sygma/Corbis; 945B: AFP/Getty Images; 946: Bettmann/Corbis; 947: Sovfoto/UIG/Getty Images; 948: Scott Stewart/AP Images; 950T: Fabian Cevallos/Sygma/Corbis; 950B: AP Images; 951: Mike Persson/AFP/Getty Images; 952: Brennan Linsley/AP Images; 953: Scott Stewart/AP Images; 955: US Marines Photo/Alamy Stock Photo; 956: TM and Copyright 20th Century Fox Film Corp. All rights reserved/Everett Collection; 958: AP Images; 959: William Saar/Alamy Stock Photo

Topic 20:

960: Daniel Irungu/EPA/Newscom; 962T: Dinodia Photos/Alamy Stock Photo; 962B: Bettmann/Corbis; 963: Stuart Forster/Alamy Stock Photo; 964: Dinodia Photos/Alamy Stock Photo; 965: Bettmann/Corbis; 966T: Ria Novosti/Alamy Stock Photo; 966B: Interfoto/Alamy Stock Photo; 968T: David Edwards/National Geographic Society/Corbis; 968B: Mike Goldwater/Alamy Stock Photo; 969: AP Images; 970O: Mark Kauffman/The Life Picture Collection/Getty Images; 970U: Popperfoto/Getty Images; 970: Mamunur Rashid/Alamy Stock Photo; 971: Bettmann/Corbis; 972: Stringer/Reuters/Corbis; 973: Raga Jose Fuste/Prisma by DukasPresseagentur GmbH/Alamy Stock Photo; 974: Reuters/Corbis; 975: Jeremy sutton-hibbert/Alamy Stock Photo; 976: Madeleine Jettre/Dbimages/Alamy Stock Photo; 977: Sam Panthaky/AFP/Getty Images; 978: Mark Kauffman/The Life Picture Collection/Getty Images; 979: Tommy Trenchard/Alamy Stock Photo; 981: Bettmann/Corbis; 982: Bettmann/Corbis; 983: Gallo Images/Alamy Stock Photo; 984T: Stuart Forster/Alamy Stock Photo; 984B: Eddie Gerald/Alamy Stock Photo; 986: Baileys African History Archive/African Pictures/The Image Works; 988: Popperfoto/Getty Images; 989: Baileys Archive/africanpictures/The Image Works; 990: Hutchison Archive/Eye Ubiquitous/Alamy Stock Photo; 992T: Micheline Pelletier/Corbis; 992B: Thelma Sanders/Eye Ubiquitous/Alamy Stock Photo; 994: Greg Marinovich/Africa Media Online/The Image Works; 996: Dbimages/Alamy Stock Photo; 998T: Bettmann/Corbis; 998B: Bettmann/Corbis; 999T: Art Directors & TRIP/Alamy Stock Photo; 999B: Bettmann/Corbis; 1000T: Claudia Wiens/Alamy Stock Photo; 1000B: Stefano PolitiMarkovina/Alamy Stock Photo; 1002T: AVI Pictures/Alamy Stock Photo; 1002B: Claudia Wiens/Alamy Stock Photo; 1004: Rolls Press/Popperfoto/Getty Images; 1006: Peter Jordan/Alamy Stock Photo; 1008: AFP/Getty Images; 1009: Bernard Bisson/Sygma/Corbis; 1013: Epa europeanpressphoto agency b.v./Alamy Stock

Photo; 1015T: Stephen Bisgrove/Alamy Stock Photo; 1015B: Horacio Villalobos/Corbis; 1016: Alain Keler/Sygma/Corbis; 1017: Peter Turnley/Corbis; 1018T: Les Stone/The Image Works; 1018B: Bettmann/Corbis; 1019: Micheline Pelletier/Sygma/Corbis; 1020: Imaginechina-Tuchong/Alamy Stock Photo; 1022: Dinodia Photos/Alamy Stock Photo; 1025: Farooq Khan/EPA/Newscom

Topic 21:

1026: Massimo_g/Fotolia; 1028: Leeyiutung/Fotolia; 1029: Thakala/Fotolia; 1030: Thakala/Fotolia; 1032: Dinodia Photos/Alamy Stock Photo; 1033: National Geographic Image Collection/Alamy Stock Photo; 1035: Leeyiutung/Fotolia; 1038: Epaeuropeanpressphoto agency b.v./Alamy Stock Photo; 1039T: Donna Burton/CBP Sourced/Alamy Stock Photo; 1039B: Jim West/Alamy Stock Photo; 1043: Dinodia Photos/Alamy Stock Photo; 1046: Dereje Belachew/Alamy Stock Photo; 1047T: Greg Balfour Evans/Alamy Stock Photo; 1047B: David Hoffman Photo Library/Alamy Stock Photo; 1048: Werli Francois/Alamy Stock Photo; 1050: Irene Abdou/Alamy Stock Photo; 1051T: Edgard Garrido/Reuters/Alamy Stock Photo; 1051B: Eddie Gerald/Alamy Stock Photo; 1052T: Joerg Boethling/Alamy Stock Photo; 1052B: Anyaivanova/Shutterstock; 1053: Imagebroker/SuperStock; 1054: US Coast Guard Photo/Alamy Stock Photo; 1055: BrazilPhotos.com/Alamy Stock Photo; 1056: FPG/Getty Images; 1058: Ricky Simms/Majority World CIC/Alamy Stock Photo; 1059T: Caren Firouz/Reuters/Corbis; 1059B: Rafael Ben-Ari/Fotolia; 1060: Gorodenkoff/Shutterstock; 1061: SergiiKharchenko/NurPhoto/ZUMA Wire/Alamy Stock Photo; 1062: Zuma Press, Inc./Alamy Stock Photo; 1063: Ihor Serdyukov/Shutterstock; 1064: NASA Photo/Alamy Stock Photo; 1065: NASA/Getty Images; 1066: Pictorial Press Ltd/Alamy Stock Photo; 1068: DieKleinert/Alamy Stock Photo; 1069: Xinhua/Alamy Stock Photo; 1070: DeAgostini/SuperStock

End Matter:

1074: Stock Connection Blue/Alamy Stock Photo; 1112: Bill Schorr/Cagle Cartoons, Inc; 1118: World History Archive/Alamy Stock Photo

[Text Acknowledgements]
Topic 1:

The Legend of Yu the Great, from the Shujing, Sima Qian. The Chinese Classics, Volume III, Part I, James Legge (1865); Quote from "The Quest for Human Origins" with Donald C. Johanson Ph.D., Berkeley, California, January 25, 1991, Academy of Achievement.; Excerpt from "Hobbit-Like Human Ancestor Found in Asia" by Hillary Mayell. National Geographic, October 27,2004. Reprinted with permission.; Quote from: *A Stranger from Flores* by Chris Stringer, Nature, October 27, 2004.; Quote from "Dwarf Human Ancestors Lived on Pacific Island" by Guy Gugliotta. Published by Washington Post, October 28,2004.

Topic 2:

Excerpt from *The Code of Hammurabi* translated by L.W. King, 1915; *Book of Exodus 21-22*. Reprinted from the Tanakh: The Holy Scriptures by permission of the University of Nebraska Press. Copyright 1985 by the Jewish Publication Society, Philadelphia.; Excerpt from *Records of the Past*, 2nd series, Vol. III, ed. by A. H. Sayce. Published by Samuel Bagster and Sons, Limited [1890]; "Scripture quotation taken from the New American Standard Bible® (NASB),Copyright © 1960, 1962, 1963, 1968, 1971, 1972, 1973,1975, 1977, 1995 by The Lockman Foundation. Used by permission. www.Lockman.org"; Quote from: Oliver J. Thatcher, ed., The Library of Original Sources, (Milwaukee: University Research Extension Co., 1907), Vol. I: The Ancient World.; Prentice Hall

Topic 3:

Arthashatra or Science of Politics translated by R. Shamasastry. Published by G.T.A. Press, 1908.; Excerpt from *The Analects of Confucius*.; Excerpt: From Sources of Chinese Tradition, compiled by Wm. Theodore de Bary and Irene Bloom, 2nd ed., vol. 1 (New York: Columbia University Press, 1999), 208-210. © 1999 Columbia University Press. Reprinted with permission of Columbia University Press; Quote from *The Edicts of King Ashoka*. English rendering by Ven. S. Dhammika. Published by Buddhist Publication

Society, 1993.; Excerpt from: *The Analects of Confucius* translated by Prof. Robert. Eno, PhD. Copyright © 2003, 2012, 2015 Robert Eno.; Excerpt from Lao Tzu, Tao Te Ching: A New English Version, by Ursula K. Le Guin. Copyright ©1997 by Ursula K. Le Guin. Reprinted by arrangement with The Permissions Company, Inc., on behalf of Shambhala Publications Inc., Boulder, Colorado, www.shambhala.com.; Quote from: China: A New History by John King Fairbank and Merle Goldman. Published by Harvard University Press, 2006.

Topic 4:

Excerpt from: *Florentine Codex General: History of the Things of New Spain* by Bernardino de Sahagún, translated by Arthur J.O. Anderson and Charles E. Dibble. Published by The School of American Research and University of Utah.; Quote from *The Constitution of the Iroquois Nations: The Great Binging Law*, Gayanashagowa by Gerald Murphy.; Quote from: *General History of the Things of New Spain* by Fray Bernardino de Sahagún; Quote from: *Daily Life of the Aztecs* by Jacques Soustelle; Quote from: *The Aztecs* by Brian M. Fagan

Topic 5:

Quote from *Politics* by Aristotle, Book IV, Translated by Benjamin Jowett.; Quote from *Republic* by Plato in Greek Philosphy Thales to Aristotle, edited by Reginald E. Allen, 1966.; Excerpt from *Histories by Polybius*. McMillan and Co, 1889.

Topic 6:

Excerpt from: Lefkowitz, Mary R., and Maureen B. Fant, eds. *Women's Life in Greece and Rome: A Source Book in Translation. Second Edition.* © 1982, 1992 Mary F. Lefkowitz and Maureen B. Fant. Reprinted with permission of Johns Hopkins University Press.; *Women's Life in Greece and* Rome by Mary Lefkowitz and Maureen B. Fant © Mary Lefkowitz and Maureen B. Fant, published by Johns Hopkins Press, 1982. Bristol Classical Press, an imprint of Bloomsbury Publishing Plc. Reprinted with permission.; Quote from *The Pararell Lives: The Life of Tiberius Gracchus* by Plutarch.; 237: Quote from Historian Bryan Ward-Perkins.; Quote from Historian Peter Brown.

Topic 8:

Quote from *Al-Qur'an: Guidance for Mankind* (1997) by M. Farooq-e-Azam Malik. Copyright The Institute of Islamic Knowledge. Reprinted with permission.; Quote from Ibn Sina (Avicenna) (973-1037):On Medicine, c. 1020 CE Charles F. Horne, ed., The Sacred Books and Early Literature of the East, (New York: Parke, Austin, & Lipscomb, 1917), Vol. VI: Medieval Arabia. The text has been modernized by Prof. Arkenberg.; Quote from *Treatise on Smallpox* by Muhammad al-Razi. The Air of History (Part IV): Great Muslim Physicians Al Rhazes, Rachel Hajar, M.D.; Quote from *A Trio of Exemplars of Medieval Islamic Medicine* Al-Razi, Avicenna and Ibn Al-Nafis by Ritu Lakhtakia. Copyright © Sultan Qaboos University Medical Journal, November 2014.

Topic 9:

Poem: *Song of P'eng-ya*, by Du Fu, The Selected Poems of Du Fu. Translated by Burton Watson. Copyright © 2002 Columbia University Press. Reprinted with permission of Columbia University Press; Excerpt From *Sourcebook of Korean Civilization*, edited by Peter H. Lee, Vol. 1 (New York: Columbia University Press, 1993), 517-518. © 1993 Columbia University Press. Reproduced with the permission of the publisher. All rights reserved.; Excerpt From *Sourcebook of Korean Civilization*, edited by Peter H. Lee, Vol. 1 (New York: Columbia University Press, 1993), 517-518. © 1993 Columbia University Press. Reproduced with the permission of the publisher. All rights reserved.; Quote from: *Essays in Idleness* by Yoshida Kenko.; Quote from: Chieng Tuan-li, *A Schedule for Learning*.; Quote from Akbar the Great, Letter to King Philip II of Spain, 1582.; Quote from —Father Christoval de Vega of the Jesuits, Letter of December 2, 1593. Arnulf Camps, Studies in Asian Mission History, 1956-1998, Brill, 2000; Quote from John F. Richards, The New Cambridge History of India: The Mughal Empire, Cambridge University Press, 1995.

Topic 10:

Excerpt from Pico della Mirandola's *Oration on the Dignity of Man*. Translated from the Latin by Richard Hooker.; Excerpt from: *The Twelve Articles of the German Peasantry*, 1525.; Excerpt from Martin Luther (Documents of Modern History) E.G. Rupp & Benjamin Drewery. Published by Edward Arnold, 1970. An imprint of Hodder & Stoughton.

Topic 11:

Excerpt from: *Annals and Memoirs of the Court* of Peking by E. Backhouse and J. O. P. Bland. (Boston: Houghton Mifflin, 1914)

Topic 13:

Excerpt from *Report From the Committee on Employment of Boys in Sweeping of Chimneys*, 1817.; Excerpt from *The Philosophy of Manufactures* by Andrew Ure, 1835.;

Topic 14:

Excerpt from "Letter From Jamaica", in Selected Writings of Bolivar, Lewis Bertrand (New York: The Colonial Press, 1951)

Topic 15:

Excerpt from: An Open Letter to His Serene Majesty Leopold II by Colonel, The Honorable Geo. W. Williams of the United States of America (1890).

Topic 16:

Letter from Captain Peter Strasser. War by Gwynne Dyer. Copyright © 2017 by Gwynne Dyer. Reprinted with permission.; Account of an air raid on London by boys of Princeton Street Elementary School, September 1915.

Topic 18:

Excerpt from Speech by Prime Minister General Hideki Tojo to The Assembly of Greater East-Asiatic Nations. Tokyo, Japan, November 5, 1943.; Excerpt from *Burma Under the Japanese, Pictures and Portraits* by Thakin Nu. Published by St. Martins Press, 1954.

Topic 20:

Excerpt from "What I Mean by Positive Action," by Kwame Nkrumah, 1949.; 997: "Letter to the Youth of Africa," Toward the African Revolution by Franz Fanon, translated by Haakan Chevalier, 1964.; Excerpt from Anwar el Sadat: *Afro-Asian Solidarity and the World Mission of the Peoples of Africa and Asia*, 1957.

Topic 21:

Quote from *Better Growth*, Better Climate. The New Climate Economy.